GUIDE TO

THE HOUSE

OF

COMMONS

2015

THE TIMES

GUIDE TO

THE HOUSE

OF

COMMONS

2015

TIMES BOOKS

LONDON

First published in 2015 by Times Books

An imprint of HarperCollins Publishers
Westerhill Road
Bishopbriggs
Glasgow G64 2QT
www.harpercollins.co.uk

A catalogue record for this book is available from the
British Library

ISBN 978-0-00-812631-5

10 9 8 7 6 5 4 3 2 1

Printed and bound in Great Britain by
Clays Ltd., St Ives plc.

Editor: Ian Brunskill
Deputy Editor: Matthew Lyons
Assistant Editor: Ed Frankl

Design: Esa Matinvesi, Stephen Petch
Sub-editors: Dave Hollander, Catherine Lockwood

Research: Aubrey Allegretti, Harriet Exley,
Gemma Goodman, Steve Penfold, Emily Riddell

Special thanks and acknowledgements to: Ian Amis,
Sam Coates, Matt Dathan, Tim Hames, Greg Hurst,
Dennis Kavanagh, Peter Riddell, Anthony Wells

Thanks to: At The Times, Nic Andrews,
Tim Arbabzadah. Matt Brown, Rebecca Callanan,
Jessica Carsen, Margaret Clark and the Times picture
desk, Magnus Cohen, Hannah Fletcher, Helen Glancy,
Jeremy Griffin, Robert Hands, Olivia Leigh,
Robbie Millen, Peter Robertson, Mike Smith,
Matt Swift and the Times graphics team,
Craig Tregurtha, Emma Tucker, Pauline Watson,
Liesl Wickins, Rose Wild, Danny Wilkins,
John Witherow. At HarperCollins, Jethro Lennox,
Caroline Maddison, Karen Midgeley, Kevin Robbins,
Sarah Woods

Contents

General election 2015

FIVE-YEAR CAMPAIGN, LAST-MINUTE SHOCK

by Francis Elliott

The 2015 general election campaign began, as is traditional, with an unnecessary drive from Downing Street to Buckingham Palace. The prime minister's request to his monarch to dissolve parliament was more than ever a piece of constitutional set dressing: the date of the poll had been known for years and the dissolution had, in fact, already happened.

The Fixed-term Parliaments Act 2011 might have robbed David Cameron of the weapon of surprise but it had allowed him to prepare the ground on which he wished to fight and to prepare his battle-plan with precision. At the turn of the year political and economic cycles appeared to be aligning with particularly strong employment growth, the best indicator of a sustained recovery. The International Monetary Fund, once a critic of the coalition's austerity policies, led a chorus of praise as Britain's growth outperformed all other G7 countries in 2014. Stubbornly slow growth in wages and productivity, however, limited the political dividends for the coalition government. The Labour party was still able, just, to claim that households were worse off at the time of George Osborne's last budget in 2015 than they had been in 2010. Labour's case was that more aggressive state intervention was needed to correct markets disfigured by the global financial crash.

The fine balance in the economic argument was reflected in opinion polls that suggested that the election was to be the closest in a generation. Mr Cameron put his economic record, along with his leadership, at the heart of the Conservative campaign when he returned from his symbolic trip up the Mall. "In 38 days' time you face a stark choice. The next prime minister walking through that door will be me or Ed Miliband," he said from a lectern outside the entrance to No 10. "You can choose an economy that grows, that creates jobs, that generates the money to ensure a properly funded and improving NHS, a government that will cut taxes for 30 million hardworking people and a country that is safe and secure. Or you can choose the economic chaos of Ed Miliband's Britain."

In the event it was to be Mr Cameron who passed back through that famous front door, but in large part as a consequence of a subject he did not mention once during his opening three-minute, 40-second address: Scotland. In the five and a half weeks that passed from March 30 to May 7 Scotland, and in particular its first minister, Nicola Sturgeon, the SNP leader, grew from election sideshow to one of its defining issues.

When Mr Miliband formally launched Labour's campaign he did so in the Olympic Park, close to a venue that Mr Cameron had used the previous year to make a passionate defence of the virtues of the Union. The Labour leader chose not to invoke the spirit of Team GB in his opening address. Instead he pledged to limit the profits made by private providers of NHS services: a totemic policy on Labour's strongest area. He did so buoyed by a better-than-expected performance in the election's first television contest, in which both rivals for No 10 were interviewed by Jeremy Paxman and a studio audience but did not appear together on stage. The broadcast, hosted by Sky and Channel 4, was one of three television events that emerged from tortuous negotiations after Downing Street rejected an initial proposal for a series of head-to-head debates between the leaders as had happened, for the first time in the UK, in 2010. Mr Cameron, well aware that those three-way debates with Gordon Brown had allowed Nick Clegg to steal from him the mantle of the 'change' candidate, was determined to avoid the same mistake. The compromise Downing Street eventually negotiated with the broadcasters was to profoundly shape the election and help to determine its outcome.

In the immediate aftermath of the Paxman encounter it seemed that Mr Cameron had blundered because he was judged to have come off second best to a man the Tories wanted to present as unelectable. The prime minister, who appeared unusually nervous, struggled with questions about food banks and whether he could live on a zero-hour contract while his rival provided one of the election's most memorable soundbites. Asked if he was tough, Mr Miliband cited resisting pressure from Barack Obama to vote against missile strikes on Syria in 2013. "Am I tough enough? Hell yes I'm tough enough," he said.

Evidence of Mr Miliband's rapidly improving personal ratings seemed to bear out warnings that the Tories had blundered by setting voters' expectations of him so low. The second television contest on April 2, however, brought the arrival on the election's main stage of Ms Sturgeon. She had replaced Alex Salmond as SNP leader and Scotland's first minister after the 'No' vote in the independence referendum. After the drama of a result closer than many had predicted, most voters south of the border had stopped paying attention to Scotland as soon as the Union was secured. In Downing Street, however, Conservative strategists had noted that Labour's vulnerability to an energised nationalist movement had been exposed. A slew of polls either side of New Year showing the SNP on course for a dramatic upset coincided with the final set of negotiations over the television debate. No 10's non-negotiable condition was that it should include the leaders of the Scots and Welsh nationalist parties as well as the Greens. It meant that the Labour leader would face three opponents to the left of him. Mr Cameron, meanwhile, had only to face Nigel Farage, the Ukip leader, to his right. The platform given to anti-austerity parties undermined Mr Miliband's efforts to frame the choice between Labour's "moderate" cuts to public spending and the Conservatives' "extreme" cuts.

More significantly still, it introduced Ms Sturgeon to a UK audience. After instant online polls showing that the SNP leader had performed best in the April 2 debate, Labour candidates reported that her offer of a "progressive alternative" to "blind austerity" was being welcomed on the doorsteps of former supporters on both sides of the border. Fears that the SNP could make significant gains against Labour, growing all year, increased markedly. Tory claims that Mr Miliband, needing SNP support to govern, would be dragged to the left gained substance, meanwhile.

Six days later, however, the Tories overreached as they tried to conflate voters' doubts about Mr Miliband's character with those of the SNP and the party's opposition to a renewal of Britian's independent nuclear deterrent. In an article in *The Times*, Michael Fallon drew a parallel between his decision to stand against his brother, David Miliband, for the Labour leadership and his alleged willingness to "trade" Trident for SNP support. "Ed Miliband stabbed his own brother in the back to become Labour leader. Now he is willing to stab the United Kingdom in the back to become prime minister." The Labour leader accused Mr Cameron of ordering the attack and so demeaning himself and his office. Senior Tories, already worried about the absence of a breakthrough in the opinion polls, privately expressed unease at a campaign deemed too negative and failing to connect.

In fact, both rivals for No 10 had structured their campaigns to minimise risk. Labour and the Conservatives favoured staged rallies attended by vetted audiences and aimed squarely at providing "clips" for a travelling corps of tightly controlled broadcasters. The imagery was unsubtle: Mr Miliband favoured a lectern; Mr Cameron was seen in front of a Union Jack.

On April 13 Mr Miliband launched Labour's manifesto with a promise to introduce the so-called Budget Responsibility Lock: every Labour budget would cut the deficit for the following year and would be audited by the Office for Budget Responsibility to ensure that it did so. The introduction to the deliberately austere-looking document emphasised that each spending commitment had been fully costed. In a nod to accusations that the SNP would force a minority Labour administration to abandon spending curbs, Mr Miliband said that no government led by him would compromise on spending restraint. The new "lock" topped a list of five pledges under the slogan, "A better plan. A better future." In addition to a strong economic foundation, they were: higher living standards for working families; an NHS with time to care; controls on immigration; and a country where the next generation can do better than the last.

Mr Cameron switched to a more positive tone as the Conservatives' manifesto launch on April 14 approached. In a speech previewing the manifesto's theme, he said he was offering the "Conservative dream" of a good life and hard work rewarded. There were three main "doorstep offers" in the prospectus for "security at every stage of life". The first was a repeat of the 2010 pledge to cut inheritance tax so that couples could pass on homes worth up to £1 million without penalty, a measure that was later ditched as part of the power-sharing deal with the Liberal Democrats. The second policy, much trailed, was confirmation that a new Conservative administration would extend to housing association tenants the right to buy the properties they rented. Thirdly, parents of three- and four-year-olds wishing to work were offered an increase in free childcare from 15 hours to 30 hours a week.

On April 15 Nick Clegg launched the Liberal Democrat manifesto, which set out the party's five policy priorities: balancing the national budget in a fair way; guaranteeing education funding "from cradle to college"; an increase to £12,500 in the income tax personal allowance; an £8 billion rise in NHS funding; and five green laws to protect the environment. Mr Clegg said that he would fight "tooth and nail" for the policies but avoided making any of them a non-negotiable condition of power-sharing as he tried to maximise his chances of remaining in government with either Mr Cameron or Mr Miliband in No 10.

The likely electoral consequences of coalition had already been made clear the previous May when the party lost all but one of its 12 MEPs and 307 council seats. Mr Clegg, while conceding that his party would lose some of the 57 seats it had taken in 2010, continued to insist throughout the campaign that the Lib Dems would defy predictions of heavy losses. The party's established reputation for defending its holds through diligent local campaigning lent some credence to his claims, despite the evidence of the previous year's drubbing.

The victors of that poll, Ukip, were finding it hard to regain the momentum that had powered the insurgent political force to 26 per cent of the popular vote in the European Parliament polls. Two further by-election wins in Clacton and then Rochester in the autumn, caused by the defections of Douglas Carswell and Mark Reckless respectively, had appeared to put Ukip on course for a breakthrough at the general election. Nigel Farage, the leader, stood for the seat of South Thanet, one of about five constituencies the party believed it could win comfortably. By the time of its manifesto launch on April 15, however, it was clear that Ukip was struggling under the strain of a full-scale campaign. A media focus on whether Mr Farage would win his seat and the Ukip leader's efforts to gain attention were stoking internal tensions. The Ukip leader's decision during the television debate to cite foreign HIV patients being treated by the NHS came to symbolise so-called "shock and awful" tactics that divided the party. They were an effort to raise the salience of immigration in voters' minds: the issue on which Ukip scored most strongly. Statistics released in February showed that not only had Mr Cameron failed to make good a pledge to reduce the net number of migrants arriving in the UK each year to below 100,000, but the numbers were even higher than when he took power. By the time of the short campaign, however, the issue was falling down the list of voters' top concerns.

At the same time, the rise of the SNP was adding potency to the Tories' long-planned "squeeze" message to Ukip supporters. Now it was "Vote Farage, get Miliband, propped up by Sturgeon", a message that resonated more strongly as the campaign wore on. In her manifesto launch on April 20, the SNP leader pitched to former Labour supporters in Scotland with the offer of an alliance with Mr Miliband at Westminster. The prospectus matched Labour's more popular policies, such as the so-called mansion tax, a levy on property worth more than £2 million, and the banker's bonus tax, as well as its promise to abolish zero-hour contracts, but it also positioned the nationalists to the left of Mr Miliband on health spending and on the abolition of Trident.

More controversial policies, such as the demand that Holyrood take full control over tax and spending decisions, were given less prominence as part of an effort by the SNP to reassure voters that they would not treat the general election result as a mandate to reopen the independence question. "To everyone who, like me, wants this election to herald the real and positive change that will make life better for ordinary people across these islands, I hold out a hand of friendship," she said. The decision on how to respond to the overture had divided Labour's leadership for months. Ed Balls, the shadow chancellor, was among those calling for an outright rejection of any cooperation with the Scottish nationalists at Westminster from the outset. Jim Murphy, Labour's leader in Scotland, and Douglas Alexander, the party's UK election coordinator, both of whom were defending seats from strong SNP challenges, countered that to do so would only drive more Labour support to the nationalists. Mr Miliband initially sided with Mr Murphy and Mr Alexander and calibrated his response to the SNP in a way that left the door ajar to an informal alliance. As the short campaign went on he was repeatedly forced to toughen his position, however, as the damage in England outweighed any benefit in Scotland.

Having initially said that there would only be no SNP ministers in a Labour-led government, he was first forced to rule out any other looser pact and finally that he would rather stay out of No 10 than do a deal with the nationalists. The last formulation came in the last television contest, exactly a week before polling day. Mr Cameron, then Mr Miliband and finally Mr Clegg fielded questions from a studio audience in a special edition of BBC1's *Question Time* programme. Although the Tory leader endured some tough questioning over his refusal to spell out the detail of £12 billion of planned welfare cuts, Mr Miliband suffered the most bruising night as he struggled to lay to rest the ghosts of Labour's past.

Asked if he agreed that Gordon Brown's administration had overspent in the years before the global financial crash, the Labour leader said: "No, I don't. I know you may not agree with that, but let me just say very clearly, there are schools that have been rebuilt in our country, there are hospitals that have been rebuilt, there were SureStart centres that were built that wouldn't have happened." The hostile audience reaction to that answer dominated the subsequent media coverage. Figures like Alan Johnson, the Labour former home secretary, identified the question and answer as a defining moment in the campaign. At points during his leadership Mr Miliband had been urged by senior Labour figures to issue a mea culpa for past overspending but had rejected the idea. Better to own the future, his aides had said, than disown the past.

As the consequences of that decision started to weigh down on Mr Miliband the Labour leader unveiled what was to be seen as a totem of his failure. Faced with a disbelieving public the Conservative and Labour leaders reached for measures to overcome scepticism. Mr Cameron was mocked for promising to enshrine in law a commitment not to raise VAT, income tax or national insurance contributions. Mr Miliband's solution was to carve into an 8½ft tablet of Portland stone Labour's election pledges. Unveiling the monument, dubbed the Edstone, in a Hastings car park, he said that the "simple reason" was that he expected to be held to account on all six of Labour's pledges (the last, acquired after the manifesto, was "homes to buy, action on rents").

In the last 48 hours of electioneering Mr Clegg, en route to John O'Groats, claimed that the Lib Dems would be the "surprise story" of the result (a prediction that turned out to be truer than he would have wished). Mr Cameron ended a 36-hour marathon with a rally in Carlisle and Mr Miliband closed his campaign in Leeds.

As Mr Cameron waited for the exit poll in his constituency home in Dean, Oxfordshire, he was confident that the Conservatives would be the largest party but was far from sure of being able to govern alone. His unexpected triumph, described to party workers on May 8 as the Tories' "sweetest victory", allowed him to ditch planned coalition negotiations and plan instead for a majority government.

Francis Elliott is political editor of The Times

WHERE IT ALL WENT WRONG FOR THE POLLS

by Peter Kellner

The result of the general election was a shock to most commentators and politicians. The biggest single reason for this was that the opinion polls pointed clearly to a hung parliament, and a close contest between Labour and the Conservatives to be the largest. A few individual polls during the campaign recorded Conservative leads of 4 to 6 points, but these were outliers. On the eve of the election, all 11 polls indicated a neck-and-neck race, with leads ranging from 2 points for Labour to 1 point for the Conservatives. In the event, the Conservative lead in the popular vote was just under 7 percentage points.

Final opinion poll figures

	YouGov	TNS	BMG	Panel-base	Ashcroft	Survation	Populus	Com-Res	Mori	ICM	Result
Con	34	33	34	31	33	31	33	35	36	34	38
Lab	34	32	34	33	33	31	33	34	35	35	31
Lib Dem	10	8	10	8	10	10	10	9	8	9	8
Ukip	12	14	12	16	11	16	14	12	11	11	13
Green	4	6	4	5	6	5	5	4	5	4	4
Other	6	6	6	7	8	7	6	6	5	7	6
Avg error	2.0	1.5	2.0	2.3	2.5	2.3	1.8	1.3	1.7	2.0	

This was not the first British election in which the outcome was not what the polls indicated. In 1970 and 1992 most polls wrongly pointed to a Labour victory. In October 1974, 1987 and 1997, most polls overstated Labour's support and understated that for the Conservatives. Not every election, however, has conformed to this pattern. In February 1974, the Conservatives seemed to be heading for re-election but, in a close contest, Labour emerged (just) as the largest party. And in 2005 and 2010, YouGov, like most polling companies, accurately predicted the size of the swing from Labour to Conservative.

Even in 2015, the polls were right on a number of things: the SNP landslide in Scotland, Ukip's surge, the collapse in votes for the Liberal Democrats and the significant swing to Labour in London. Nevertheless, on the biggest issue of all, the likely outcome of the battle between Labour and Conservatives, the published polls were all wrong. Had a single poll erred by three points each on Labour and Conservative support, this might be an innocent consequence of random sampling error, but when 11 surveys make the same error, we face a systematic problem not random error. We need to find out what went wrong.

Four sets of theories have been advanced. It is possible that each has some merit, although we should beware of overinterpreting the error. If there is more than one reason for the errors, each was probably quite small and, therefore, hard to detect with certainty.

1 There was an intrinsic Labour bias in the people reached by the polling companies. A variety of sources have suggested such an error: that the demographic measures used to ensure balanced samples are too crude; that Conservatives are less willing to answer pollsters' questions; and that polling samples contain too high a proportion of politically interested voters and too small a proportion of less interested voters. This, it is argued, led, indirectly, to Labour voters being overrepresented and Conservatives being underrepresented. BBC *Newsnight's* Evan Davis proposed this theory when he interviewed me a few days after the election. ICM's Martin Boon has also suggested that sampling methods that worked well in previous elections did not do so this time.

2 Voters told pollsters the truth but, on the day, did something else. Again, this theory has more than one component. We could have been deceived either by "reluctant Tories" who did not like the Conservatives but, in the privacy of the polling booth, decided not to risk a change of government (I believe this played a part); or by "lazy Labour" supporters who said they would vote but, in the end, were slightly more likely to stay at home (a view advanced by Ben Page of Ipsos Mori). There might be an element of truth in both suggestions, which boil down to a gap, in a small minority of voters, between attitude (dislike of the Tories) and action (reluctance to vote Labour).

3 Late swing. This is a variant of No 2, but this time reflecting a last-minute change of attitude. Survation's Damian Lyons Lowe said after the election that he had conducted a late survey on the day before the election that included interviews that evening. This found a 6-point Conservative lead. He had, however, decided not to publish it because he feared that it was wrong.

4 Another variant on No 2 was offered by Labour's pollster, James Morris. He said that his private surveys showed the Tories consistently ahead in the months before the election. He said this was because he warmed up respondents with a series of questions about what issues concerned them most, and which party was best able to handle them, and only then asked people for their voting intention. This, he said, put people into a more considered frame of mind when deciding which party to support and therefore made it more like the act of voting itself.

Each of these theories is plausible, but each presents problems. If the samples were systematically biased, then it seems odd that different companies using different methods — some polling by telephone, some employing online panels — had the same errors. And if this error was systematic, then its intermittent nature must be explained: why it appears in some elections but not others.

If we are dealing with a difference between attitudes and actions, then testing this is difficult, but the exit poll commissioned by broadcasters provides indirect support for some version of 2, 3 and 4. This survey questioned 22,000 people as they left 140 polling stations. It asked people to complete a replica ballot paper and place it in a replica ballot box. This meant that the exit poll was confined to actual voters (so excluded any of the pollsters' "lazy Labour" respondents) and repeated the experience of voting just seconds after people had done the real thing (so removing any problem of late swing or difference between attitude and action). The poll's prediction, broadcast at 10pm on election day, came closer than any pre-election survey to what happened, saying that the Conservatives would win 316 seats (compared with the 331 they actually won), Labour 239 (compared with 232), SNP 58 (compared with 56), Liberal Democrats 10 (compared with 8).

Other evidence, however, casts doubt on the late swing theory. ICM, YouGov and Ipsos Mori all surveyed voters on the Wednesday evening and/or election day itself. None found any sign of a last-minute shift to the Conservatives. As for James Morris's theory regarding the structure of questionnaires, his post-election analysis surprised a number of senior party figures who had access to his findings and were astonished as well as appalled when Labour ended up losing so many seats. This does not make the theory wrong (and some Conservatives briefed reporters that their polls also showed the Tories ahead, and for similar reasons), but without those surveys being placed in the public domain, it is hard to verify.

Nevertheless, one indication that it might contain some truth comes from research that YouGov carried out for the British Election Study, run by a consortium of academic political scientists. This asked about the dominant issues, the party leaders and the likely performance of each party in government, and only then sought voting intention. Over the campaign, the BES data generated figures for Conservative support that was on average 1.8 points higher than YouGov's daily polls for *The Sun* and *Sunday Times*. The gap widened in the final days of the campaign. Together, the responses of the 1,947 people surveyed in the final two days of the campaign produced a 6-point lead, with the Conservatives on 37.5 per cent and Labour on 31.4 per cent: almost exactly the election result. We cannot, however, be certain whether this was because our BES surveys tested voting intention the right way; whether it was luck, with a sampling deviation on those two days offsetting another problem; or a mixture of the two.

In due course, a definitive analysis may become available of what caused the polls to tell the wrong story. YouGov and the other big polling companies came together immediately after the election, through their trade body, the British Polling Council, to commission an independent investigation by Patrick Sturgis, professor of research methodology and director of the ESRC National Centre for Research Methods. It is unlikely to find one overriding explanation.

Meanwhile, it is worth bearing in mind that those who supply and report statistics should apply a little more caution when interpreting data. By definition, polls contain the views of those who agree to be interviewed, whether face-to-face, by telephone or as part of an online panel. The most perfect sample design can be rendered inaccurate when, for example, response rates to telephone polls drop below 20 per cent. None of us can be sure that the man or woman who joins an online panel or stays on the line when a polling company rings, is like the person with identical demographic characteristics and past-vote behaviour who evades the pollsters' attention. One way and another, we are all in the business of extrapolating from the voters we can reach to those we cannot. Perhaps the real mystery is not why we are sometimes three or four points adrift in our figures for party support, but how, given all the things that can go wrong, we are so often within one or two points of the result.

Disraeli's old cliché about lies, damned lies and statistics will doubtless encourage some people to dismiss all polling and economic data out of hand. Perhaps we all need to adopt a more nuanced view. Surveys that dip into public attitudes and behaviour, whether done swiftly by pollsters or more slowly by the best government statisticians, are able to provide important insights. They are neither infallible nor completely useless. We should read them with care. And we who provide such data should always look out for ways to avoid repeating past errors, and admit that we are always liable to be tripped up by new ones.

Peter Kellner is president of YouGov

HOW RECORD BOOKS
WERE REWRITTEN

by Colin Rallings and Michael Thrasher

On May 7, 2015 David Cameron became the first prime minister for more than 100 years to lead his party to victory after a full term in office by securing more votes and seats than at the previous election. The Conservatives were not alone in rewriting the record books. Labour now has its fewest MPs since 1987 and a performance in Scotland that was worse than at any time since it began seriously competing there in 1918.

The Liberal Democrats, with vote share and seats in single figures, declined to their 1970 position. Ukip, on the other hand, polled four times as many votes as in 2010 and in England outscored the Liberal Democrats and all the other smaller parties put together. Polling half of all the votes cast across Scotland, the SNP became the first party to achieve that distinction since the Conservatives in 1955. Rising from 6 to 56 seats out of 59 is among the most rapid advances by any party in a western democratic election. Despite finishing in sixth position in the UK vote, the party has the third largest bloc of MPs in the new parliament.

Yet beneath the historic headlines some change was more modest. The Conservatives increased their number of seats by 24 to 330 and their vote share rose by less than 1 percentage point. Labour suffered a net loss of 26 seats, but polled three quarters of a million more votes than in 2010. The conventional swing was just 0.4 percentage points from Conservative to Labour: the lowest at any general election since the Second World War.

In a real sense the drama of the election is captured in the table below. The first column shows the winning party with each row identifying the party that finished in the runner-up position. The Liberal Democrats not only lost 49 of their 57 seats, but are now second in just 63 (compared with 243 second-place finishes in 2010) and in fourth place (usually behind Ukip) in 338 constituencies. Ukip may have won only a single seat, but they lurk in second place in 120 constituencies, 44 of them Labour-held. The SNP are second in all three seats they failed to win, with Labour their major challengers, albeit usually a long way behind.

THE BATTLE FOR VOTES

Across the UK nearly 30.7 million votes were cast from a total eligible electorate of 46.4 million. A million more votes were cast than in 2010 with turnout increasing by a single percentage point to 66.1 per cent.

The Conservative share of the UK vote was 36.8 per cent and that for Labour 30.4 per cent, a combined two-party vote of 67.2 per cent. With the Liberal Democrats slumping to fourth place, the combined vote for the three traditional Britain-wide parties was 75.1 per cent, the lowest in electoral history. Even more starkly, fewer than half the electorate voted for one of these parties and only 24.4 per cent of electors positively endorsed the now majority Conservative government.

Ukip (12.6 per cent) supplanted the Liberal Democrats (7.9 per cent) in third place with the SNP polling a greater share of the total votes from Scotland alone

(4.7 per cent) than the Greens did across the UK (3.8 per cent). In Northern Ireland the Democratic Unionists and Sinn Fein swapped places in the pecking order, with the former coming out on top this time. The analysis that follows concentrates on the situation in Great Britain with Northern Ireland discussed separately alongside country-specific analyses for the other nations of the UK.

Distribution of first and second places

	C	Lab	LD	Ukip	Green	PC	SNP	DUP	SDLP	SF	UUP	Ind/Oth	Total 1st
C		207	46	75			1					1	330
Lab	168		9	44	4	5	1					1	232
LD	4	2				1	1						8
Ukip	1												1
Green		1											1
Speaker				1									1
PC	1	2											3
SNP	7	41	8										56
Ind								1					1
DUP										2	4	2	8
SDLP								1	2				3
SF								1			2	1	4
UUP								1	1				2
Total 2nd	181	253	63	120	4	6	3	4	0	5	6	4	650

In Britain, Conservative candidates won 37.7 per cent of the popular vote, an increase of just 0.8 points. The Conservatives now have an overall majority of 12 but their victory is modest by historic standards. Their vote share was fully 5 per cent less, and their total vote nearly 3 million fewer, than John Major's achievement in 1992. Some regions contributed more to the Conservatives' success than others. Both the east Midlands and the southwest saw a positive swing from Labour to the Conservatives; in London, the northwest and Yorkshire the pendulum swang in the opposite direction.

A crucial factor for the party was the performance by the "class of 2010", those Conservative MPs first elected five years ago. These incumbents increased support by an average of more than 4 percentage points and thwarted Labour's ambition sufficiently so that it won just 3 of its top 20 Conservative target seats.

Labour finished second overall in votes and seats, but losses to the SNP outnumbered gains from the Conservatives and Liberal Democrats. Its share of votes (31.2 per cent) was its third worst in more than 80 years and its number of seats (232) only narrowly exceeds the total won with Neil Kinnock as leader in 1987 (229). It did do comparatively well in seats characterised by larger-than-average proportions of students, non-white residents and those living in deprived conditions, but significantly failed to make headway in more affluent constituencies.

Although the slaughter in Scotland symbolised Labour's defeat there were also seat losses in the east Midlands and in Wales too. Crucially, the party could make no net gains in either the southeast or the southwest. Labour's "southern discomfort", first identified in the days before new Labour, is back with a vengeance. The map indicates that below a line running from the Severn to the Wash there are just 12 Labour seats out of 181 outside London; Tony Blair won 59 seats in this territory in 1997.

The depths plumbed by the Liberal Democrats surprised many. The party's vote share of 8.1 per cent, a double-digit decline, was its lowest since the 1970 general election when its forerunner the Liberal party returned just six MPs. It now has eight, one in each of Scotland, Wales and London, with a further five scattered across the rest of England. The party suffered grievously in seats where there had seemed some hope of defying destruction. The former southwest heartland simply turned its back as the party's vote collapsed by 20 percentage points and all 15 seats across the region were lost. To a degree the "personal" vote for Liberal Democrat incumbents did materialise. In those seats that the party held and where the incumbent had stood down, its vote share declined by 21.2 per cent; in those where the MP stood for re-election, the decline was 14.5 per cent. Better, certainly, but hardly enough to hold back the tide.

The nationalist parties in Scotland and Wales experienced somewhat contrasting fortunes. The SNP swept aside everything in their path with former Labour and Liberal Democrat supporters switching precipitately and directly to them. The Conservatives retained their single seat and came up just short of the SNP in another. Ukip and the Greens made no impression in Scotland. In Wales, on the other hand, the Plaid Cymru vote was little changed despite the publicity boost received from party leader Leanne Wood's appearance in two UK-wide television debates. It did hold its three seats, but slipped back to fourth in votes, having failed to match the Ukip surge.

Ukip's near 3.9 million votes, a striking jump from little more than 900,000 in 2010, yielded a single seat. It retained its by-election gain in Clacton, but failed to repeat its success in Rochester & Strood. Its support was more evenly spread than that of any other party and this cost it further reward under first past the post. The party topped 30 per cent of the vote in just eight constituencies, but lost its deposit in only 32 seats in England and Wales, all but four of them in London.

The Greens, like Ukip, were a more significant presence than five years ago. They fielded 568 candidates (up from 331), polled well over 750,000 more votes, and improved their share from 1 per cent to 3.8 per cent. They too, however, won only one seat: Brighton Pavilion, which the former leader Caroline Lucas first captured in 2010. Their vote share rose by more than 10 points there and in five other seats, but they came close to winning nowhere else and are in second place in just four constituencies.

Excluding the Speaker, the more than 600 independent and small party candidates polled fewer than 300,000 votes in total and all but 14 of them lost their deposit. The independent Sylvia Hermon retained North Down, but Respect's George Galloway lost Bradford West, gained from Labour in a 2012 by-election upset. The health campaigner Richard Taylor failed in his attempt to recover his Wyre Forest seat, held from 2001 to 2010. The most successful individual candidate was Claire Wright, who polled more than 13,000 votes (24 per cent of the total) in Devon East. The only 'small' party to contest more than 100 constituencies was the Trade Unionist and Socialist Coalition (Tusc). Its best performing candidate, the former Labour MP Dave Nellist in Coventry North West, scored 3.9 per cent but most of his colleagues struggled to breach 1 per cent. The British National Party, which had stood more than 300 candidates in 2010, managed just 8 this time and a paltry total of fewer than 2,000 votes.

ENGLAND

A large majority (83.6 per cent) of the UK electorate is registered to vote in England, which has 533 constituencies, 82 per cent of the total. More than 25.5 million votes were cast from an eligible electorate of just short of 39 million. A total of 3,209 candidates contested the English constituencies, an average of six candidates for each constituency.

The Conservative vote share exceeded 40 per cent for the first time since 1992 and the party made a net gain of 21 seats. They gained 6 from and lost 10 to Labour, lost 1 to Ukip, and took 26 from the Liberal Democrats. Winning seats from the Liberal Democrats, though perhaps not quite on that scale, had been expected, but it was stemming the losses to Labour that proved crucial in delivering an overall majority. The contribution of MPs newly embedded in their constituencies was important, as was Labour's failure to reverse its 2010 defeats across the south.

Labour's vote in England rose by 3.6 points with a swing from the Conservatives of 1.1 points. The party's problems become clear, however, from the pattern of voting across English regions since Tony Blair's second landslide victory in 2001. Only in (mainly inner) London and, to a lesser extent, the northwest does Labour show real signs of electoral recovery. Even where the swing back to the Conservatives over the past decade has been modest, as in the northeast and Yorkshire and the Humber, it has been the smaller parties, Ukip especially, that have taken up the slack.

Patterns of voting in the marginal seats were crucial. In only 17 of 56 seats in England where the Conservative majority over Labour was less than 10 points was there a swing towards the challenger and ten of those were in London and the northwest alone. Four of Labour's ten gains were in London (where there was a 3.5-point swing from the Conservatives); elsewhere in the south it picked up only Hove. The Conservatives conversely took two further seats in the south — Southampton Itchen and Plymouth Moor View — as well as four others, including notably Ed Balls's Leeds suburban seat of Morley and Outwood. In each of these cases it appears that they were net beneficiaries from the fallout from the collapse of the Liberal Democrats and the rise of Ukip. Contrary to pre-election expectations, previous Liberal Democrat voters by no means wholly deserted to Labour and other left-of-centre alternatives, nor was Ukip's support simply a function of wooing ex-Conservatives.

On the other hand, there was a swing to Labour in 39 of the 54 marginal seats it was defending against the Conservatives. It appears that the two parties become ever more entrenched in their respective heartlands at both regional and constituency level.

Five years ago the Liberal Democrats increased their vote share in every region; now they are down by 10 percentage points or more on their 2010 performance across the board. They were brushed aside regardless of the local electoral circumstances: David Laws lost Yeovil on a swing of more than 15 points (it now has a Conservative MP for the first time since Paddy Ashdown won there in 1983); in Bristol West Stephen Williams was relegated behind Labour and the Greens, having lost more than half his 2010 vote. Voters scarcely appeared to discriminate whether their local MP was closely associated with the coalition or not, although the former Defence Minister Sir Nick Harvey lost twice as much support in Devon North as the bedroom tax rebel Andrew George did in St Ives.

England was Ukip's happiest hunting ground. The party contested every seat and averaged more than 14 per cent in share of the vote. In the constituencies, mostly in the eastern half of the country, that were identified before the election as containing the mix of elderly, white, and poorly educated electors thought to be receptive to the party's message, support was often above 20 per cent. The brutal truth, however, is that only once were they within a thousand votes of electing another MP: in Conservative Thurrock, where they finished third. Although it has its second places Ukip is usually a long way behind the winner (a swing of 8 points would yield it a mere dozen more seats) and will need a much more targeted campaign in 2020 to overcome the electoral system.

Nigel Farage's personal failure to win Thanet South encapsulated the Ukip problem. From virtually a standing start it struggled to win enough converts to threaten the incumbent party. In other target areas, such as Conservative-held Great Yarmouth and Labour's Great Grimsby, Ukip again finished a disappointing third. It was clear that not everyone was prepared to vote Ukip just to depose their MP. As with the Liberal Democrats before it, building from the bottom up is really the only way forward.

SCOTLAND

The contrast between the Scots election results in 2010 and this year could not be greater. Then, not a single seat changed hands and no party saw a rise or fall in vote share of more than 4 percentage points. This time only nine constituencies remained in the same hands (six of them SNP-held), Labour lost a third of a million of its 2010 vote, and Liberal Democrat support collapsed by more than half. The flow of votes was all one way, with even Ukip seeing nothing like the rise experienced in England and Wales.

The conventional wisdom about the SNP's rapid rise is borne out. Quite simply, most Yes voters from the September 2014 referendum migrated towards the SNP; No voters largely stuck by their traditional parties, thereby splitting the opposition. A degree of unionist tactical voting was evident in some constituencies: it probably enabled Ian Murray to hang on to Labour's sole Scottish seat in Edinburgh South, but was insufficient to come close to saving either the Labour leader Jim Murphy in East Renfrewshire or the Liberal Democrat minister Jo Swinson in East Dunbartonshire.

The smallest increases in nationalist support tended to be in those areas where SNP MPs were already incumbent; the largest in Yes-voting former Labour citadels in west central Scotland. Labour's safest seat, Glasgow North East, fell on a 39-point swing with the SNP's share also rising by more than 40 percentage points in two other Glasgow seats. Similar rises are evident in another half dozen cases, notably in the Kirkcaldy and Cowdenbeath seat vacated by the former prime minister Gordon Brown. Unsurprisingly, there is a strong correlation between the rise in SNP support and levels of deprivation as the nationalists exploited their campaign brand as the anti-austerity party.

WALES

A record 278 candidates stood for the 40 seats in Wales: nearly seven per constituency. If the election in Scotland was an event apart, that in Wales more closely resembled England's.

In fact, there was even a small swing to the Conservatives, who gained three seats: two from Labour (on swings of more than 3 percentage points in both Gower and Vale of Clwyd) and one from the Liberal Democrats. The Conservatives' share of the vote (27.2 per cent) is, however, the lowest ever in Wales for a party with a UK majority. Labour gained Cardiff Central from the

Liberal Democrats, but was one down overall. The Liberal Democrat vote fell back from 20.1 per cent in 2010 to just 6.5 per cent and the party lost 31 deposits; it finished in fifth place, more than 5 percentage points behind Plaid.

Labour continues to benefit in Wales from the operation of the electoral system, winning 63 per cent of the seats (25) with just 37 per cent of votes. The Conservatives now have their largest number of seats in Wales since 1983 (11) and have recovered much better than in Scotland from their zero return in 1997 and 2001. Not only did they gain seats, but their retention of the highly marginal Cardiff North reflected similar results in more affluent parts of England.

More than five times as many people voted Ukip in Wales as in 2010 (and they may well have cost Labour its century-long hold on Gower), but the party's vote was even flatter than in England, nowhere exceeding 20 per cent.

NORTHERN IRELAND

The electoral battle in Northern Ireland was dominated by a different set of parties from the rest of the UK. The 18 contests attracted a record 138 candidates, but turnout stubbornly remained below 60 per cent, as it had done in 2010.

The Democratic Unionists (DUP) polled the most votes and seats (8), with Sinn Fein fewer than 8,000 votes behind but down from five to four seats. A limited pact between the DUP and the revived Ulster Unionists (UUP) helped the former to win Belfast East back from the Alliance and protected the party's Westminster leader Nigel Dodds in Belfast North. In Sinn Fein's Fermanagh and South Tyrone seat, captured by just four votes in 2010, it was the UUP's turn to benefit from collaboration among the unionist parties. No such cooperation was evident in Antrim South, however, as the UUP gained its second seat from its principal rival. The Social Democratic and Labour party (SDLP) lost vote share for the fourth election running, but retained its three seats.

The former UUP MP Sylvia Hermon once again won North Down as an independent, but other smaller groups did not fare well. The Northern Ireland branch of the UK Conservative party contested 16 seats as "Conservatives", but polled just 1.3 per cent of the vote overall. Ukip fared little better, and the Greens even worse. Together, the three parties lost 24 deposits from 31 candidacies.

TURNOUT

The registered electorate for the 2015 general election was 46.4 million, the largest ever. This was an increase of more than 800,000, or 1.8 per cent, on 2010. Electorate numbers fluctuated in the run-up to the election after the phasing in of the new individual electoral registration system and the removal of some names. The initial count, published by the Office for National Statistics based on December 2014 figures, had shown a UK electorate of just 45.3 million. More than a million names were subsequently added to that list after formal and informal campaigns in the weeks before the registration deadline of April 20.

Across the UK turnout, at 66.1 per cent, was a single percentage point higher than in 2010. Nearly 30.7 million votes were cast: short of the record 33.6 million at the 1992 general election. The pattern of turnout was heavily influenced by Scotland. In England, Wales and Northern Ireland turnout was only marginally greater than five years ago; in Scotland it was more than eight points higher at 71.1 per cent. Yet even this figure fell short of the 84.6 per cent voting at the September 2014 independence referendum and was lower than at all but four of the eighteen general elections held since 1945.

Across the UK a total of 181 constituencies had turnouts in excess of 70 per cent (139 in 2010); just one, Stoke-on-Trent Central, fell below 50 per cent (six in 2010). The highest in England was in Bath (77.5 per cent); that in Wales was in Cardiff North (76.1 per cent).

By contrast, in Scotland, turnout exceeded 70 per cent in 39 of the 59 seats with East Dunbartonshire and East Renfrewshire each topping 80 per cent. Only in two of the seven Glasgow constituencies did turnout slip below 60 per cent.

Six of Northern Ireland's constituencies had turnouts above 60 per cent. The highest was in the ultra-marginal Fermanagh and South Tyrone (72.6 per cent); the lowest in Londonderry East (51.9 per cent).

Turnout has long been correlated with a constituency's socioeconomic character and its political marginality. This election was no exception. Turnout in England and Wales was slightly higher in marginal as opposed to safe seats and increased a little more in those cases too. It also rose by half a percentage point in seats gained by the Conservatives in 2010 and now defended by first-time incumbent MPs. On the other hand, turnout remained considerably lower than average in seats won by Labour last time.

Part of the explanation for this difference is social as much as it is political. Indices of constituency-level deprivation, such as the proportion unemployed, the proportion in poor health and the proportion of single parents with dependent children, are strongly negatively correlated with turnout. The more affluent the area, the greater the proportion of elderly residents and/or the more marginal the seat, the higher is turnout likely to be.

CANDIDATES

The number of candidates contesting the election was 3,971, a slight reduction on the 4,150 that stood in 2010 and an average of 6.1 per constituency.

Thirteen individuals stood in Uxbridge and Ruislip South where Boris Johnson was elected; there were 12 in David Cameron's Witney seat; and Nigel Farage was one of 11 candidates in Thanet South. At the other extreme, only two opponents took on John Bercow, the Commons Speaker, in Buckingham, and there were just four candidates in ten constituencies in England and four in Scotland.

The Conservatives, Labour and the Liberal Democrats contested every seat in Great Britain except that of the Speaker. The Conservatives' sister party in Northern Ireland also fielded 16 candidates. Ukip had a candidate in every seat in England and Wales, but did not fight 18 in Scotland nor 8 in Northern Ireland. The Greens fought 573 seats across the UK compared with 335 in 2010.

A total of 468 MPs were re-elected and five more former members — "re-treads" — returned after a period of absence. They comprised three Labour MPs defeated in 2010, together with Mr Johnson and the SNP's Alex Salmond.

A total of 1,570 candidates lost their deposit by failing to poll 5 per cent or more of the valid vote in their constituency. This is 40 per cent of the total number of candidates; in 2010, 46 per cent suffered this forfeit. Among the major parties Labour lost just 3 deposits and the Conservatives 18 (including 15 in Northern Ireland); the Liberal Democrats 341 (none were forfeited in 2010); Ukip 79; and the Greens 442. Some 137 candidates polled fewer than 100 votes; the smallest being 12 garnered by an independent in Witney and 14 by another independent in Uxbridge and Ruislip South.

A record proportion of women candidates contested the election: 26.1 per cent, compared with 21.1 per cent in 2010. The Conservatives (26.1 per cent), Labour (34.1 per cent), the Liberal Democrats (26.3 per cent), and the Greens

(37.5 per cent) all fielded more women than last time. Ukip's proportion, however, shrank from 14.7 per cent to 12.5 per cent. In Scotland 35.6 per cent of SNP candidates were women, as were 25 per cent of Plaid Cymru's in Wales.

There are also more women MPs than ever before with 191 elected, comprising 29.4 per cent of the House of Commons. In 2010 the corresponding figures were 142 and 21.8 per cent. Labour has the most women: 99 were elected, now comprising 42.7 per cent of the parliamentary party. The number of Conservative women MPs rose from 49 to 68. There are 20 SNP women, and one each for Plaid Cymru, the Greens, and the SDLP together with Syliva Hermon, the independent from Down North. The Liberal Democrats have none.

It is more difficult precisely to record the number of candidates drawn from ethnic minorities. Among major parties a little under 10 per cent of Conservative, Labour and Liberal Democrat candidates were from a black, Asian or other minority ethnic group. The figures for Ukip and the Greens were approximately 6 per cent and 4 per cent respectively. Of these, 41 minority ethnic candidates were elected this year compared with the previous record of 26 in 2010. These included 17 Conservatives, 23 Labour, and one SNP.

PROSPECTS FOR 2020

A consequence of Labour's implosion in Scotland, and of the way in which the fall of the Liberal Democrats and the rise of Ukip played out in England and Wales, was to reverse the disadvantage suffered by the Conservatives (relative to Labour) from the operation of the voting system. While turnout and overall elector numbers still remain lower in Labour constituencies, it took about 6,000 fewer votes to elect each Conservative MP than Labour MP. In short, the Conservative vote was more effectively distributed than that of its main rival.

This matters greatly because this election sets the benchmark for the next. Labour is not only almost 100 seats behind the Conservatives, there are now just 44 constituencies (27 in the south or midlands) where it is within 10 percentage points of them — the "marginals" — compared with 60 after the 2010 contest. Simply to overtake the Conservatives as the largest party in a hung parliament Labour needs a swing of 5.2 points, the pivotal seat being Stevenage; to win an overall majority its target is a daunting 9.5-point swing (equivalent to a Labour lead in the popular vote of 12.5 percentage points) up to and including Shipley, where Philip Davies was re-elected with a near 10,000 majority. Labour's challenge becomes greater still if the party fails to recover in Scotland.

A reprise of boundary changes scuppered in the last parliament by a dispute with the Liberal Democrats over House of Lords reform should also serve to strengthen the Conservative position. Evening out the size of electorates is likely to hurt Labour and benefit the Conservatives by anything up to 20 seats. The 2020 election will be fought against the background of an effective Conservative majority of nearer 50 and with Labour needing a swing of probably more than 10 percentage points. A turnaround of that scale has eluded all parties in recent times with the singular exception of Tony Blair's Labour party in 1997.

Colin Rallings and Michael Thrasher are professors of politics and directors of the Elections Centre at Plymouth University

Concise summary results by country

	VOTES	VOTES%	% CHANGE	CANDIDATES	ELECTED	LOST DEP
ENGLAND						
C	10,449,004	40.9	1.4	532	318	1
Lab	8,087,684	31.6	3.6	532	206	0
LD	2,098,404	8.2	-16.0	532	6	263
Ukip	3,611,367	14.1	10.7	533	1	32
Green	1,073,242	4.2	3.2	502	1	379
Others	251,513	1.0	-2.7	578	1	567
Total Vote	25,571,214			3,209	533	1,242
Electorate	38,811,712					
Turnout	65.9%					
SCOTLAND						
C	434,097	14.9	-1.8	59	1	2
Lab	707,147	24.3	-17.7	59	1	3
LD	219,675	7.5	-11.3	59	1	47
SNP	1,454,436	50.0	30.0	59	56	0
Ukip	47,078	1.6	0.9	41	0	41
Green	39,205	1.3	0.7	31	0	28
Others	8,827	0.3	-0.8	38	0	37
Total Vote	2,910,465			346	59	158
Electorate	4,094,784					
Turnout	71.1%					
WALES						
C	407,813	27.2	1.1	40	11	0
Lab	552,473	36.9	0.6	40	25	0
LD	97,783	6.5	-13.6	40	1	31
PC	181,704	12.1	0.9	40	3	8
Ukip	204,330	13.6	11.2	40	0	0
Green	38,344	2.6	2.1	35	0	32
Others	15,616	1.0	-2.4	43	0	42
Total Vote	1,498,063			278	40	113
Electorate	2,282,297					
Turnout	65.6%					

	VOTES	VOTES%	% CHANGE	CANDIDATES	ELECTED	LOST DEP
NORTHERN IRELAND						
DUP	184,260	25.7	0.7	16	8	0
SF	176,232	24.5	-1.0	18	4	4
UUP	114,935	16.0	0.8	15	2	2
SDLP	99,809	13.9	-2.6	18	3	3
APNI	61,556	8.6	2.2	18	0	8
Ukip	18,324	2.6	2.6	10	0	6
TUV	16,538	2.3	-1.6	7	0	3
C	9,055	1.3	1.3	16	0	15
Green	6,822	1.0	0.4	5	0	3
Others	30,572	4.3	-2.8	15	1	13
Total Vote	718,103			138	18	57
Electorate	1,236,683					
Turnout	58.1%					
GREAT BRITAIN						
C	11,290,914	37.7	0.8	631	330	3
Lab	9,347,304	31.2	1.5	631	232	3
LD	2,415,862	8.1	-15.5	631	8	341
Ukip	3,862,775	12.9	9.7	614	1	73
SNP	1,454,436	4.9	3.2	59	56	0
Green	1,150,791	3.8	2.9	568	1	439
PC	181,704	0.6	0.0	40	3	8
Others	275,956	0.9	-2.6	659	1	646
Total Vote	29,979,742			3,833	632	1,513
Electorate	45,188,793					
Turnout	66.3%					
UNITED KINGDOM						
Con	11,299,969	36.8	0.8	647	330	18
Lab	9,347,304	30.4	1.5	631	232	3
LD	2,415,862	7.9	-15.2	631	8	341
Ukip	3,881,099	12.6	9.5	624	1	79
SNP	1,454,436	4.7	3.1	59	56	0
Green	1,157,613	3.8	2.8	573	1	442
DUP	184,260	0.6	0.0	16	8	0
PC	181,704	0.6	0.0	40	3	8
SF	176,232	0.6	0.0	18	4	4
UUP	114,935	0.4	0.0	15	2	2
SDLP	99,809	0.3	0.0	18	3	3
APNI	61,556	0.2	0.1	18	0	8
TUV	16,538	0.1	0.0	7	0	3
Others	306,528	1.0	-2.6	674	2	659
Total Vote	30,697,845			3,971	650	1,570
Electorate	46,425,476					
Turnout	66.1%					

Voting in the English regions

	C	LAB	LD	UKIP	OTHERS	TOTAL
EAST MIDLANDS						
votes	969,379	705,767	124,039	351,777	79,440	2,230,402
votes %	43.5	31.6	5.6	15.8	3.6	
2010 votes %	41.2	29.8	20.8	3.3	5.0	
change	2.3	1.9	-15.3	12.5	-1.4	
seats	32	14	0	0	0	46
2010 seats	31	15	0	0	0	46
electorate						3,350,769
turnout %						66.6
2010 turnout %						66.8
change						-0.2
EASTERN						
votes	1,445,946	649,320	243,191	478,517	131,648	2,948,622
votes %	49.0	22.0	8.2	16.2	4.5	
2010 votes %	47.1	19.6	24.1	4.3	4.9	
change	1.9	2.4	-15.8	12.0	-0.5	
seats	52	4	1	1	0	58
2010 seats	52	2	4	0	0	58
electorate						4,364,656
turnout %						67.6
2010 turnout %						67.6
change						-0.1
LONDON						
votes	1,233,386	1,545,080	272,544	286,981	198,274	3,536,265
votes %	34.9	43.7	7.7	8.1	5.6	
2010 votes %	34.5	36.6	22.1	1.7	5.0	
change	0.3	7.1	-14.4	6.4	0.6	
seats	27	45	1	0	0	73
2010 seats	28	38	7	0	0	73
electorate						5,401,616
turnout %						65.5
2010 turnout %						64.5
change						1.0
NORTH EAST						
votes	300,883	557,100	77,095	198,823	54,252	1,188,153
votes %	25.3	46.9	6.5	16.7	4.6	
2010 votes %	23.7	43.6	23.6	2.7	6.4	
change	1.6	3.3	-17.1	14.0	-1.9	
seats	3	26	0	0	0	29
2010 seats	2	25	2	0	0	29
electorate						1,941,841
turnout %						61.2
2010 turnout %						61.1
change						0.1

	C	LAB	LD	UKIP	OTHERS	TOTAL
NORTH WEST						
votes	1,050,124	1,502,047	219,998	459,071	132,815	3,364,055
votes %	31.2	44.6	6.5	13.6	3.9	
2010 votes %	31.7	39.4	21.6	3.2	4.1	
change	-0.5	5.2	-15.1	10.5	-0.1	
seats	22	51	2	0	0	75
2010 seats	22	47	6	0	0	75
electorate						5,240,724
turnout %						64.2
2010 turnout %						62.3
change						1.9
SOUTH EAST						
votes	2,234,360	804,774	413,586	646,959	294,682	4,394,361
votes %	50.8	18.3	9.4	14.7	6.7	
2010 votes %	49.3	16.2	26.2	4.1	4.1	
change	1.5	2.1	-16.8	10.6	2.6	
seats	78	4	0	0	2	84
2010 seats	74	4	4	0	2	84
electorate						6,419,548
turnout %						68.5
2010 turnout %						68.2
change						0.3
SOUTH WEST						
votes	1,319,994	501,684	428,873	384,546	201,143	2,836,240
votes %	46.5	17.7	15.1	13.6	7.1	
2010 votes %	42.8	15.4	34.7	4.5	2.6	
change	3.7	2.3	-19.6	9.1	4.5	
seats	51	4	0	0	0	55
2010 seats	36	4	15	0	0	55
electorate						4,076,494
turnout %						69.6
2010 turnout %						69.0
change						0.6
WEST MIDLANDS						
votes	1,098,110	865,075	145,009	412,770	107,975	2,628,939
votes %	41.8	32.9	5.5	15.7	4.1	
2010 votes %	39.5	30.6	20.5	4.0	5.4	
change	2.2	2.3	-14.9	11.7	-1.3	
seats	34	25	0	0	0	59
2010 seats	33	24	2	0	0	59
electorate						4,140,587
turnout %						63.5
2010 turnout %						64.7
change						-1.2

	C	LAB	LD	UKIP	OTHERS	TOTAL
YORKSHIRE AND THE HUMBER						
votes	796,822	956,837	174,069	391,923	124,526	2,444,177
votes %	32.6	39.1	7.1	16.0	5.1	
2010 votes %	32.8	34.4	22.9	2.8	7.0	
change	-0.2	4.8	-15.8	13.2	-1.9	
seats	19	33	2	0	0	54
2010 seats	19	32	3	0	0	54
electorate						3,875,477
turnout %						63.1
2010 turnout %						62.9
change						0.2

Three-way marginal seats

CONSTITUENCY	1ST	% MAJ 1ST OVER 2ND	2ND	% MAJ 1ST OVER 3RD	3RD
Thurrock	C	1.1	Lab	2.0	Ukip
Belfast South	SDLP	2.3	DUP	7.3	APNI
Upper Bann	DUP	4.8	UUP	8.1	SF
Ynys Mon	Lab	0.7	PC	10.0	C
Southport	LD	3.0	C	11.8	Lab
Mansfield	Lab	11.3	C	14.3	Ukip
Thanet South	C	5.7	Ukip	14.4	Lab
Hartlepool	Lab	7.7	Ukip	14.7	C
Great Grimsby	Lab	13.5	C	14.8	Ukip
Stoke-On-Trent North	Lab	12.5	C	15.2	Ukip
Portsmouth South	C	12.5	LD	15.3	Lab
Plymouth Moor View	C	2.4	Lab	16.1	Ukip
Dumfries & Galloway	SNP	11.5	C	16.7	Lab
Stoke-On-Trent Central	Lab	16.7	Ukip	16.8	C
Bristol West	Lab	8.8	Green	16.8	LD
Newry & Armagh	SF	8.4	UUP	17.0	SDLP
Walsall North	Lab	5.3	C	17.0	Ukip
Dagenham & Rainham	Lab	11.6	Ukip	17.0	C
Carmarthen East & Dinefwr	PC	14.2	Lab	17.3	C
Dudley North	Lab	11.0	C	17.8	Ukip
Berwickshire, Roxburgh & Selkirk	SNP	0.6	C	17.9	LD
Stoke-On-Trent South	Lab	6.5	C	18.0	Ukip
Leeds North West	LD	6.7	Lab	18.1	C
Basildon South & Thurrock East	C	16.9	Ukip	18.2	Lab
Renfrewshire East	SNP	6.6	Lab	18.6	C
Aberdeen South	SNP	14.9	Lab	18.8	C
Brighton Pavilion	Green	14.6	Lab	19.1	C
Penistone & Stocksbridge	Lab	14.3	C	19.1	Ukip
Bradford South	Lab	17.2	C	19.3	Ukip
Ashfield	Lab	18.6	C	19.6	Ukip
Antrim South	UUP	2.6	DUP	19.8	SF
Great Yarmouth	C	13.8	Lab	19.8	Ukip
Carshalton & Wallington	LD	3.2	C	20.0	Lab

Seats that changed hands 2010–15

CONSERVATIVE GAINS

From Labour
Bolton West
Derby North
Gower
Morley & Outwood
Plymouth Moor View
Southampton Itchen
Telford
Vale Of Clwyd

From Liberal Democrats
Bath
Berwick-Upon-Tweed
Brecon & Radnorshire
Cheadle
Cheltenham
Chippenham
Colchester
Cornwall North
Devon North
Dorset Mid & Poole North
Eastbourne
Eastleigh
Hazel Grove
Kingston & Surbiton
Lewes
Portsmouth South
Solihull
Somerton & Frome
St Austell & Newquay
St Ives
Sutton & Cheam
Taunton Deane
Thornbury & Yate
Torbay
Twickenham
Wells
Yeovil

LABOUR GAINS

From Conservative
Brentford & Isleworth
Chester, City Of
Dewsbury
Ealing Central & Acton
Enfield North
Hove
Ilford North
Lancaster & Fleetwood
Wirral West
Wolverhampton South West

From Liberal Democrats
Bermondsey & Old Southwark
Birmingham Yardley
Bradford East
Brent Central
Bristol West
Burnley
Cambridge
Cardiff Central
Hornsey & Wood Green
Manchester Withington
Norwich South
Redcar

UKIP GAINS

From Conservative
Clacton

SCOTTISH NATIONAL GAINS

From Labour
Aberdeen North
Aberdeen South
Airdrie & Shotts
Ayr, Carrick & Cumnock
Ayrshire Central
Ayrshire North & Arran
Coatbridge, Chryston & Bellshill
Cumbernauld, Kilsyth
    & Kirkintilloch East
Dumfries & Galloway
Dunbartonshire West
Dundee West
Dunfermline & Fife West
East Kilbride, Strathaven
    & Lesmahagow
East Lothian
Edinburgh East
Edinburgh North & Leith
Edinburgh South West
Falkirk
Glasgow Central
Glasgow East
Glasgow North
Glasgow North East
Glasgow North West
Glasgow South
Glasgow South West
Glenrothes
Inverclyde
Kilmarnock & Loudoun
Kirkcaldy & Cowdenbeath
Lanark & Hamilton East
Linlithgow & Falkirk East
Livingston
Midlothian
Motherwell & Wishaw
Ochil & Perthshire South
Paisley & Renfrewshire North
Paisley & Renfrewshire South
Renfrewshire East
Rutherglen & Hamilton West
Stirling

From Liberal Democrats
Aberdeenshire West & Kincardine
Argyll & Bute
Berwickshire, Roxburgh & Selkirk
Caithness, Sutherland
    & Easter Ross
Dunbartonshire East
Edinburgh West
Fife North East
Gordon
Inverness, Nairn, Badenoch
    & Strathspey
Ross, Skye & Lochaber

DEMOCRATIC UNIONIST GAINS

From Alliance
Belfast East

ULSTER UNIONIST GAINS

From DUP
Antrim South

From Sinn Fein
Fermanagh & South Tyrone

Seats in rank order of percentage turnout

CONSTITUENCY	MAJ	1ST		CONSTITUENCY	MAJ	1ST
1 Dunbartonshire East	81.9	SNP		611 Houghton & Sunderland South	56.3	Lab
2 Renfrewshire East	81.1	SNP		612 Easington	56.1	Lab
3 Stirling	77.5	SNP		613 Down North	56.0	Ind
4 Bath	77.5	C		614 Lagan Valley	55.9	DUP
5 Twickenham	77.3	C		615 Slough	55.9	Lab
6 Ross, Skye & Lochaber	77.2	SNP		616 Preston	55.8	Lab
7 Richmond Park	76.5	C		617 Doncaster North	55.7	Lab
8 Edinburgh West	76.5	SNP		618 Barnsley East	55.7	Lab
9 Paisley & Renfrewshire North	76.2	SNP		619 Wolverhampton North East	55.7	Lab
10 Dumfriesshire, Clydesdale & Tweeddale	76.1	C		620 Normanton, Pontefract & Castleford	55.6	Lab
11 Cardiff North	76.1	C		621 Wolverhampton South East	55.6	Lab
12 Wirral West	75.6	Lab		622 Hull North	55.5	Lab
13 Stroud	75.5	C		623 Glasgow Central	55.4	SNP
14 Paisley & Renfrewshire South	75.4	SNP		624 Coventry North East	55.3	Lab
15 Argyll & Bute	75.3	SNP		625 Antrim North	55.2	DUP
16 Sheffield Hallam	75.3	LD		626 Leeds Central	55.1	Lab
17 Rushcliffe	75.3	C		627 Walsall North	55.0	Lab
18 Dumfries & Galloway	75.2	SNP		628 Sheffield Brightside & Hillsborough	54.8	Lab
19 Inverclyde	75.2	SNP		629 Washington & Sunderland West	54.6	Lab
20 Aberdeenshire West & Kincardine	75.2	SNP		630 Ilford South	54.6	Lab
21 St Albans	75.1	C		631 Leicester West	54.6	Lab
22 Devon Central	74.9	C		632 Birmingham Hodge Hill	54.5	Lab
23 Edinburgh South	74.9	Lab		633 Antrim South	54.2	UUP
24 Perth & Perthshire North	74.8	SNP		634 Hull West & Hessle	53.9	Lab
25 Ochil & Perthshire South	74.8	SNP		635 Nottingham North	53.6	Lab
26 Kenilworth & Southam	74.8	C		636 Hull East	53.6	Lab
27 Chippenham	74.6	C		637 West Bromwich West	53.4	Lab
28 Winchester	74.6	C		638 Antrim East	53.3	DUP
29 Derbyshire Dales	74.6	C		639 Birmingham Erdington	53.3	Lab
30 Inverness, Nairn, Badenoch & Strathspey	74.6	SNP		640 Stoke-On-Trent North	53.2	Lab
31 Wiltshire North	74.5	C		641 Merthyr Tydfil & Rhymney	53.0	Lab
32 Broxtowe	74.4	C		642 Newcastle Upon Tyne East	52.9	Lab
33 Westmorland & Lonsdale	74.3	LD		643 Middlesbrough	52.9	Lab
34 East Lothian	74.2	SNP		644 Foyle	52.8	SDLP
35 Berwickshire, Roxburgh & Selkirk	74.2	SNP		645 Strangford	52.8	DUP
36 Mole Valley	74.2	C		646 Birmingham Ladywood	52.7	Lab
37 Surrey South West	74.1	C		647 Manchester Central	52.7	Lab
38 Hitchin & Harpenden	74.0	C		648 Londonderry East	51.9	DUP
39 Dunbartonshire West	73.9	SNP		649 Blackley & Broughton	51.6	Lab
40 Brecon & Radnorshire	73.8	C		650 Stoke-On-Trent Central	49.9	Lab

Top and bottom 40 constituencies only

Vote share change since 2010 by party

CONSTITUENCY	% CHANGE	1ST	CONSTITUENCY	% CHANGE	1ST
Conservative			**Labour**		
1 Bromsgrove	10.2	C	1 Birmingham Hall Green	26.9	Lab
2 Hampstead & Kilburn	9.6	Lab	2 Brent Central	20.9	Lab
3 Yeovil	9.6	C	3 Sheffield Hallam	19.7	LD
4 Hexham	9.5	C	4 Poplar & Limehouse	18.6	Lab
5 Brent Central	9.2	Lab	5 Bethnal Green & Bow	18.3	Lab
6 Durham, City Of	9.0	Lab	6 Birmingham Ladywood	18.0	Lab
7 Watford	8.5	C	7 Walthamstow	17.0	Lab
8 Somerset North East	8.5	C	8 Manchester Gorton	17.0	Lab
9 Richmond Park	8.5	C	9 Hornsey & Wood Green	16.9	Lab
10 Somerton & Frome	8.5	C	10 Birmingham Hodge Hill	16.4	Lab
11 Wyre Forest	8.4	C	11 Liverpool Wavertree	16.2	Lab
12 Pendle	8.3	C	12 Leyton & Wanstead	15.0	Lab
13 Northampton North	8.3	C	13 Ilford South	14.6	Lab
14 Brigg & Goole	8.2	C	14 Leicester South	14.2	Lab
15 Pudsey	8.0	C	15 Bradford East	13.8	Lab
16 Loughborough	7.9	C	16 Bermondsey & Old Southwark	13.8	Lab
17 Kingswood	7.9	C	17 Sheffield Central	13.7	Lab
18 Warrington South	7.9	C	18 Hull North	13.6	Lab
19 Stockton South	7.8	C	19 Ealing Southall	13.5	Lab
20 Hazel Grove	7.8	C	20 Manchester Withington	13.3	Lab
612 Hartlepool	-7.2	Lab	612 Paisley & Renfrewshire North	-21.3	SNP
613 Aldridge-Brownhills	-7.3	C	613 Ayrshire Central	-21.3	SNP
614 Hornsey & Wood Green	-7.4	Lab	614 Dunbartonshire East	-21.8	SNP
615 Inverness, Nairn, Badenoch & Strathspey	-7.4	SNP	615 Glasgow South	-22.0	SNP
616 Southport	-7.9	LD	616 Kilmarnock & Loudoun	-22.2	SNP
617 Leeds North West	-7.9	LD	617 Glasgow North West	-23.2	SNP
618 Heywood & Middleton	-8.1	Lab	618 East Kilbride, Strathaven & Lesmahagow	-23.2	SNP
619 Ealing Southall	-8.1	Lab	619 Airdrie & Shotts	-24.0	SNP
620 Renfrewshire East	-8.4	SNP	620 Dundee West	-24.8	SNP
621 Wallasey	-8.7	Lab	621 Rutherglen & Hamilton West	-25.6	SNP
622 Argyll & Bute	-9.1	SNP	622 Inverclyde	-25.6	SNP
623 Thanet South	-9.9	C	623 Cumbernauld, Kilsyth & Kirkintilloch East	-27.2	SNP
624 Cambridge	-9.9	Lab	624 Glasgow East	-29.2	SNP
625 Sheffield Hallam	-9.9	LD	625 Motherwell & Wishaw	-29.2	SNP
626 Dagenham & Rainham	-10.0	Lab	626 Glasgow South West	-29.7	SNP
627 Edinburgh West	-10.9	SNP	627 Dunbartonshire West	-30.0	SNP
628 Richmond (Yorks)	-11.4	C	628 Kirkcaldy & Cowdenbeath	-31.2	SNP
629 Bradford East	-15.5	Lab	629 Glenrothes	-31.7	SNP
630 Bradford West	-15.9	Lab	630 Coatbridge, Chryston & Bellshill	-32.7	SNP
631 Clacton	-16.4	Ukip	631 Glasgow North East	-34.7	SNP

Top and bottom 20 constituencies only

CONSTITUENCY	% CHANGE	1ST	CONSTITUENCY	% CHANGE	1ST
Liberal Democrat			**Scottish National**		
1 Dunbartonshire East	-2.4	SNP	1 Glasgow North East	43.9	SNP
2 Edinburgh West	-2.8	SNP	2 Glasgow North	41.2	SNP
3 Gordon	-3.3	SNP	3 Glasgow South West	40.8	SNP
4 Argyll & Bute	-3.7	SNP	4 Coatbridge, Chryston & Bellshill	39.8	SNP
5 Bradford East	-4.2	Lab	5 Dunfermline & Fife West	39.6	SNP
6 Glasgow East	-4.3	SNP	6 Glasgow North West	39.3	SNP
7 Cambridge	-4.3	Lab	7 Dunbartonshire West	38.9	SNP
8 Na H-Eileanan An Iar	-4.6	SNP	8 Motherwell & Wishaw	38.4	SNP
9 Ynys Mon	-5.4	Lab	9 Glenrothes	38.1	SNP
10 Glenrothes	-5.8	SNP	10 Kirkcaldy & Cowdenbeath	37.9	SNP
11 Kilmarnock & Loudoun	-5.9	SNP	11 Inverclyde	37.6	SNP
12 Banff & Buchan	-6.2	SNP	12 Rutherglen & Hamilton West	36.5	SNP
13 Burnley	-6.2	Lab	13 Cumbernauld, Kilsyth &	36.1	SNP
14 Caithness, Sutherland & Easter Ross	-6.3	SNP	Kirkintilloch East		
15 Dunbartonshire West	-6.5	SNP	14 Glasgow Central	35.0	SNP
16 Airdrie & Shotts	-6.6	SNP	15 Glasgow South	34.7	SNP
17 Copeland	-6.7	Lab	16 Aberdeen North	34.2	SNP
18 Hayes & Harlington	-6.8	Lab	17 Ayrshire Central	34.1	SNP
19 Barking	-6.9	Lab	18 Dundee West	33.1	SNP
20 Glasgow North East	-6.9	SNP	19 Ross, Skye & Lochaber	33.0	SNP
			20 Paisley & Renfrewshire South	32.9	SNP
612 Streatham	-26.8	Lab			
613 Salisbury	-26.9	C	40 Falkirk	27.5	SNP
614 Merthyr Tydfil & Rhymney	-26.9	Lab	41 Berwickshire, Roxburgh & Selkirk	27.4	SNP
615 Bath	-26.9	C	42 Orkney & Shetland	27.2	LD
616 Devon West & Torridge	-27.1	C	43 Ayrshire North & Arran	27.2	SNP
617 Taunton Deane	-27.7	C	44 Caithness, Sutherland & Easter Ross	27.1	SNP
618 Somerton & Frome	-28.1	C	45 Fife North East	26.7	SNP
619 Worcestershire West	-28.1	C	46 Linlithgow & Falkirk East	26.6	SNP
620 Liverpool Wavertree	-28.2	Lab	47 East Lothian	26.5	SNP
621 Hull North	-28.3	Lab	48 Edinburgh South	26.1	Lab
622 Manchester Gorton	-28.4	Lab	49 Aberdeenshire West & Kincardine	25.9	SNP
623 Glasgow North	-28.6	SNP	50 Edinburgh West	25.8	SNP
624 Weston-Super-Mare	-28.8	C	51 Gordon	25.5	SNP
625 Bristol West	-29.2	Lab	52 Argyll & Bute	25.3	SNP
626 Edinburgh North & Leith	-29.3	SNP	53 Dundee East	21.9	SNP
627 Edinburgh South	-30.3	Lab	54 Banff & Buchan	19.0	SNP
628 Hereford & Herefordshire South	-30.5	C	55 Ochil & Perthshire South	18.4	SNP
629 Dunfermline & Fife West	-31.1	SNP	56 Angus	14.7	SNP
630 Sheffield Central	-31.2	Lab	57 Perth & Perthshire North	10.9	SNP
631 Brent Central	-35.8	Lab	58 Moray	9.8	SNP
			59 Na H-Eileanan An Iar	8.7	SNP

CONSTITUENCY	% CHANGE	1ST	CONSTITUENCY	% CHANGE	1ST
Plaid Cyrmu			**Democratic Unionist**		
1 Rhondda	8.9	Lab	1 Belfast East	16.5	DUP
2 Arfon	8.0	PC	2 Londonderry East	7.6	DUP
3 Cardiff West	6.9	Lab	3 Belfast North	7.0	DUP
4 Blaenau Gwent	4.9	Lab	4 Foyle	0.5	SDLP
5 Aberavon	4.5	Lab	5 Belfast West	0.3	SF
6 Merthyr Tydfil & Rhymney	4.4	Lab	6 Down South	-0.4	SDLP
7 Ynys Mon	4.3	Lab	7 Ulster Mid	-1.0	SF
8 Pontypridd	4.2	Lab	8 Upper Bann	-1.2	DUP
9 Swansea East	3.7	Lab	9 Belfast South	-1.5	SDLP
10 Cardiff South & Penarth	3.2	Lab	10 Strangford	-1.5	DUP
11 Carmarthen East & Dinefwr	2.8	PC	11 Lagan Valley	-1.9	DUP
12 Swansea West	2.4	Lab	12 Tyrone West	-2.3	SF
13 Brecon & Radnorshire	1.9	C	13 Antrim North	-3.2	DUP
14 Clwyd South	1.7	Lab	14 Antrim South	-3.8	UUP
15 Cardiff Central	1.5	Lab	15 Antrim East	-9.7	DUP
16 Wrexham	1.5	Lab			
17 Newport East	1.4	Lab			
18 Vale Of Clwyd	1.2	C	**Alliance**		
19 Monmouth	1.2	C	1 Belfast East	5.6	DUP
20 Cardiff North	1.2	C	2 Strangford	5.1	DUP
21 Newport West	1.2	Lab	3 Antrim East	3.9	DUP
22 Bridgend	1.1	Lab	4 Down North	3.0	Ind
23 Gower	0.5	C	5 Lagan Valley	2.5	DUP
24 Ogmore	0.5	Lab	6 Down South	2.5	SDLP
25 Torfaen	0.4	Lab	7 Antrim North	2.4	DUP
26 Vale Of Glamorgan	0.1	C	8 Belfast North	2.4	DUP
27 Alyn & Deeside	0.0	Lab	9 Belfast South	2.3	SDLP
28 Carmarthen West & Pembrokeshire South	0.0	C	10 Antrim South	2.1	UUP
			11 Londonderry East	2.1	DUP
29 Delyn	-0.2	Lab	12 Foyle	1.7	SDLP
30 Ceredigion	-0.6	LD	13 Ulster Mid	0.9	SF
31 Neath	-1.8	Lab	14 Upper Bann	0.8	DUP
32 Caerphilly	-2.1	Lab	15 Newry & Armagh	0.5	SF
33 Islwyn	-2.3	Lab	16 Fermanagh & South Tyrone	0.4	UUP
34 Preseli Pembrokeshire	-3.0	C	17 Belfast West	-0.1	SF
35 Montgomeryshire	-3.1	C	18 Tyrone West	-0.1	SF
36 Clwyd West	-3.2	C			
37 Cynon Valley	-3.5	Lab			
38 Dwyfor Meirionnydd	-3.5	PC			
39 Aberconwy	-6.1	C			
40 Llanelli	-7.0	Lab			

CONSTITUENCY	% CHANGE	1ST
SDLP		
1 Foyle	3.2	SDLP
2 Tyrone West	2.7	SF
3 Lagan Valley	1.3	DUP
4 Newry & Armagh	0.7	SF
5 Strangford	0.2	DUP
6 Antrim South	-0.5	UUP
7 Belfast East	-0.7	DUP
8 Down North	-1.0	Ind
9 Antrim East	-1.7	DUP
10 Antrim North	-1.8	DUP
11 Ulster Mid	-1.9	SF
12 Fermanagh & South Tyrone	-2.3	UUP
13 Londonderry East	-3.2	DUP
14 Upper Bann	-3.8	DUP
15 Belfast North	-4.1	DUP
16 Down South	-6.1	SDLP
17 Belfast West	-6.5	SF
18 Belfast South	-16.5	SDLP

CONSTITUENCY	% CHANGE	1ST
Ulster Unionist (vs. UCUNF, 2010)		
1 Newry & Armagh	13.6	SF
2 Ulster Mid	4.4	SF
3 Antrim South	2.3	UUP
4 Upper Bann	2.2	DUP
5 Down South	2.0	SDLP
6 Tyrone West	1.7	SF
7 Antrim North	1.1	DUP
8 Foyle	0.1	SDLP
9 Belfast West	0.0	SF
10 Londonderry East	-2.4	DUP
11 Antrim East	-4.8	DUP
12 Lagan Valley	-5.9	DUP
13 Belfast South	-8.2	SDLP
14 Strangford	-13.5	DUP

CONSTITUENCY	% CHANGE	1ST
Sinn Fein		
1 Londonderry East	0.5	DUP
2 Antrim East	0.1	DUP
3 Down North	0.0	Ind
4 Belfast North	-0.1	DUP
5 Antrim North	-0.1	DUP
6 Fermanagh & South Tyrone	-0.1	UUP
7 Upper Bann	-0.2	DUP
8 Down South	-0.2	SDLP
9 Belfast East	-0.3	DUP
10 Foyle	-0.4	SDLP
11 Newry & Armagh	-0.9	SF
12 Strangford	-1.0	DUP
13 Antrim South	-1.0	UUP
14 Lagan Valley	-1.1	DUP
15 Ulster Mid	-3.3	SF
16 Tyrone West	-4.9	SF
17 Belfast West	-16.8	SF

Seats in rank order of % majority

CONSTITUENCY	% MAJ	MAJ	2ND	CONSTITUENCY	% MAJ	MAJ	2ND
Conservative seats				**Conservative seats**			
1 Gower	0.1	27	Lab	45 Blackpool North & Cleveleys	8.5	3,340	Lab
2 Derby North	0.1	41	Lab	46 Pudsey	8.8	4,501	Lab
3 Croydon Central	0.3	165	Lab	47 Sherwood	9.2	4,647	Lab
4 Vale Of Clwyd	0.7	237	Lab	48 Amber Valley	9.2	4,205	Lab
5 Bury North	0.8	378	Lab	49 Yeovil	9.3	5,313	LD
6 Morley & Outwood	0.9	422	Lab	50 Hastings & Rye	9.4	4,796	Lab
7 Thurrock	1.1	536	Lab	51 Colne Valley	9.5	5,378	Lab
8 Plymouth Sutton & Devonport	1.1	523	Lab	52 Bristol North West	9.5	4,944	Lab
				53 High Peak	9.6	4,894	Lab
9 Eastbourne	1.4	733	LD	54 Harrow East	9.7	4,757	Lab
10 Brighton Kemptown	1.5	690	Lab	55 Stockton South	9.7	5,046	Lab
11 Dumfriesshire, Clydesdale & Tweeddale	1.5	798	SNP	56 Northampton South	9.8	3,793	Lab
				57 Boston & Skegness	10.0	4,336	Ukip
12 Bolton West	1.6	801	Lab	58 Norwich North	10.2	4,463	Lab
13 Weaver Vale	1.7	806	Lab	59 Stevenage	10.4	4,955	Lab
14 Telford	1.8	730	Lab	60 Enfield Southgate	10.4	4,753	Lab
15 Lewes	2.1	1,083	LD	61 Cannock Chase	10.5	4,923	Lab
16 Bedford	2.4	1,097	Lab	62 Morecambe & Lunesdale	10.6	4,590	Lab
17 Plymouth Moor View	2.4	1,026	Lab	63 Nuneaton	10.7	4,882	Lab
18 Thornbury & Yate	3.1	1,495	LD	64 Finchley & Golders Green	11.2	5,662	Lab
19 Lincoln	3.1	1,443	Lab	65 Dudley South	11.2	4,270	Lab
20 Twickenham	3.3	2,017	LD	66 South Ribble	11.4	5,945	Lab
21 Peterborough	4.1	1,925	Lab	67 Worcester	11.4	5,646	Lab
22 Cardiff North	4.2	2,137	Lab	68 Colchester	11.5	5,575	LD
23 Corby	4.3	2,412	Lab	69 Rossendale & Darwen	11.5	5,654	Lab
24 Waveney	4.6	2,408	Lab	70 Swindon South	11.7	5,785	Lab
25 Warrington South	4.6	2,750	Lab	71 Cheltenham	12.1	6,516	LD
26 Kingston & Surbiton	4.8	2,834	LD	72 Cheadle	12.2	6,453	LD
27 St Ives	5.1	2,469	LD	73 Berwick-Upon-Tweed	12.2	4,914	LD
28 Southampton Itchen	5.2	2,316	Lab	74 Preseli Pembrokeshire	12.3	4,969	Lab
29 Thanet South	5.7	2,812	Ukip	75 Pendle	12.3	5,453	Lab
30 Keighley	6.2	3,053	Lab	76 Portsmouth South	12.5	5,241	LD
31 Warwickshire North	6.3	2,973	Lab	77 Dover	12.5	6,294	Lab
32 Carlisle	6.5	2,774	Lab	78 Brecon & Radnorshire	12.7	5,102	LD
33 Torbay	6.8	3,286	LD	79 Reading East	12.9	6,520	Lab
34 Halesowen & Rowley Regis	7.0	3,082	Lab	80 Scarborough & Whitby	13.0	6,200	Lab
35 Crewe & Nantwich	7.3	3,620	Lab	81 Warwick & Leamington	13.1	6,606	Lab
36 Erewash	7.4	3,584	Lab	82 Devon North	13.3	6,936	LD
37 Hendon	7.5	3,724	Lab	83 Aberconwy	13.3	3,999	Lab
38 Ipswich	7.7	3,733	Lab	84 Wells	13.3	7,585	LD
39 Sutton & Cheam	7.9	3,921	LD	85 Vale Of Glamorgan	13.4	6,880	Lab
40 Stroud	8.0	4,866	Lab	86 Crawley	13.4	6,526	Lab
41 Broxtowe	8.0	4,287	Lab	87 Rochester & Strood	13.6	7,133	Ukip
42 Bath	8.1	3,833	LD	88 Cornwall North	13.7	6,621	LD
43 Northampton North	8.2	3,245	Lab	89 Reading West	13.7	6,650	Lab
44 Calder Valley	8.3	4,427	Lab	90 Gloucester	13.8	7,251	Lab

CONSTITUENCY	% MAJ	MAJ	2ND	CONSTITUENCY	% MAJ	MAJ	2ND
Conservative seats				**Conservative seats**			
91 Great Yarmouth	13.8	6,154	Lab	137 Burton	22.8	11,252	Lab
92 Chipping Barnet	14.4	7,656	Lab	138 Monmouth	23.1	10,982	Lab
93 Stourbridge	14.5	6,694	Lab	139 Beverley & Holderness	23.2	12,203	Lab
94 Elmet & Rothwell	14.7	8,490	Lab	140 Portsmouth North	23.2	10,537	Lab
95 Milton Keynes South	14.7	8,672	Lab	141 Thanet North	23.3	10,948	Ukip
96 Carmarthen West &	15.0	6,054	Lab	142 St Albans	23.4	12,732	Lab
Pembrokeshire South				143 Newton Abbot	23.4	11,288	LD
97 Hazel Grove	15.2	6,552	LD	144 Dartford	23.6	12,345	Lab
98 Camborne & Redruth	15.3	7,004	Lab	145 Solihull	23.6	12,902	LD
99 Battersea	15.6	7,938	Lab	146 Wrekin, The	23.6	10,743	Lab
100 Montgomeryshire	15.8	5,325	LD	147 Hornchurch & Upminster	23.7	13,074	Ukip
101 Redditch	16.0	7,054	Lab	148 Putney	23.8	10,180	Lab
102 St Austell & Newquay	16.2	8,173	LD	149 Uxbridge & Ruislip South	23.9	10,695	Lab
103 Eastleigh	16.5	9,147	LD	150 Staffordshire Moorlands	23.9	10,174	Lab
104 Gravesham	16.7	8,370	Lab	151 Tamworth	24.0	11,302	Lab
105 Oxford West & Abingdon	16.7	9,582	LD	152 Welwyn Hatfield	24.2	12,153	Lab
106 Basildon South &	16.9	7,691	Ukip	153 York Outer	24.4	13,129	Lab
Thurrock East				154 Sittingbourne & Sheppey	24.6	12,168	Ukip
107 Milton Keynes North	16.9	9,753	Lab	155 Dorset South	24.7	11,994	Lab
108 Watford	17.4	9,794	Lab	156 Somerset North East	24.9	12,749	Lab
109 Cleethorpes	17.5	7,893	Lab	157 Rushcliffe	25.1	13,829	Lab
110 Loughborough	17.7	9,183	Lab	158 Folkestone & Hythe	25.1	13,797	Ukip
111 Shrewsbury & Atcham	17.7	9,565	Lab	159 Selby & Ainsty	25.7	13,557	Lab
112 Clwyd West	17.7	6,730	Lab	160 Brigg & Goole	25.8	11,176	Lab
113 Chippenham	18.2	10,076	LD	161 Wyre Forest	26.0	12,871	Lab
114 Canterbury	18.3	9,798	Lab	162 Ribble Valley	26.0	13,606	Lab
115 Kingswood	18.7	9,006	Lab	163 Wimbledon	26.1	12,619	Lab
116 Stafford	18.8	9,177	Lab	164 Altrincham & Sale West	26.3	13,290	Lab
117 Harlow	18.9	8,350	Lab	165 Chatham & Aylesford	26.6	11,455	Lab
118 Shipley	19.0	9,624	Lab	166 Kettering	26.7	12,590	Lab
119 Chingford &	19.1	8,386	Lab	167 Cities Of London &	26.7	9,671	Lab
Woodford Green				Westminster			
120 Isle Of Wight	19.5	13,703	Ukip	168 Taunton Deane	26.8	15,491	LD
121 Castle Point	19.7	8,934	Ukip	169 Derbyshire Mid	26.8	12,774	Lab
122 Filton & Bradley Stoke	20.0	9,838	Lab	170 Bridgwater & Somerset West	26.8	14,583	Ukip
123 Bosworth	20.5	10,988	LD	171 Truro & Falmouth	27.2	14,000	LD
124 Basingstoke	20.8	11,063	Lab	172 Eddisbury	27.4	12,974	Lab
125 Bexleyheath & Crayford	21.0	9,192	Lab	173 Norfolk South West	27.7	13,861	Ukip
126 Rugby	21.1	10,345	Lab	174 Hexham	27.8	12,031	Lab
127 Kensington	21.1	7,361	Lab	175 Romford	28.2	13,859	Ukip
128 Maidstone & The Weald	21.4	10,709	LD	176 Cambridgeshire South East	28.3	16,837	LD
129 Rochford & Southend East	21.7	9,476	Lab	177 Wyre & Preston North	28.4	14,151	Lab
130 Leicestershire North West	22.1	11,373	Lab	178 Dorset West	28.6	16,130	LD
131 Forest Of Dean	22.2	10,987	Lab	179 Spelthorne	28.8	14,152	Ukip
132 Gillingham & Rainham	22.4	10,530	Lab	180 Wycombe	28.9	14,856	Lab
133 Devon East	22.4	12,261	Ind	181 Basildon & Billericay	29.0	12,482	Lab
134 Swindon North	22.6	11,786	Lab	182 Hemel Hempstead	29.1	14,420	Lab
135 Derbyshire South	22.6	11,471	Lab	183 Norfolk North West	29.4	13,948	Lab
136 Dorset Mid & Poole North	22.6	10,530	LD	184 Bognor Regis & Littlehampton	29.6	13,944	Ukip

CONSTITUENCY	% MAJ	MAJ	2ND	CONSTITUENCY	% MAJ	MAJ	2ND
Conservative seats				**Conservative seats**			
185 Derbyshire Dales	29.7	14,044	Lab	234 Braintree	35.0	17,610	Ukip
186 Aldridge-Brownhills	29.7	11,723	Lab	235 Wiltshire South West	35.2	18,168	Ukip
187 Croydon South	29.7	17,140	Lab	236 Newark	35.3	18,474	Lab
188 Weston-Super-Mare	29.7	15,609	Lab	237 Grantham & Stamford	35.3	18,989	Ukip
189 Bournemouth West	29.7	12,410	Ukip	238 Lichfield	35.3	18,189	Lab
190 Louth & Horncastle	29.8	14,977	Ukip	239 Meriden	35.7	18,795	Lab
191 Macclesfield	29.9	14,811	Lab	240 Hereford & Herefordshire S.	35.7	16,890	Ukip
192 Yorkshire East	29.9	14,933	Lab	241 Gosport	35.9	17,098	Ukip
193 Worthing East & Shoreham	30.0	14,949	Lab	242 Norfolk South	35.9	20,493	Lab
194 Fylde	30.4	13,224	Lab	243 Bury St Edmunds	35.9	21,301	Lab
195 Suffolk West	30.4	14,984	Ukip	244 Richmond (Yorks)	36.2	19,550	Ukip
196 Winchester	30.6	16,914	LD	245 Hitchin & Harpenden	36.2	20,055	Lab
197 Harrogate & Knaresborough	30.7	16,371	LD	246 Broxbourne	36.3	16,723	Ukip
198 Bromley & Chislehurst	30.8	13,564	Lab	247 Faversham & Kent Mid	36.4	16,652	Ukip
199 Aylesbury	31.0	17,158	Ukip	248 Bexhill & Battle	36.4	20,075	Ukip
200 Havant	31.1	13,920	Ukip	249 Epping Forest	36.4	17,978	Ukip
201 Leicestershire South	31.2	16,824	Lab	250 Hertfordshire North East	36.5	19,080	Lab
202 Harwich & Essex North	31.3	15,174	Lab	251 Romsey & Southampton N.	36.6	17,712	LD
203 Gainsborough	31.4	15,449	Lab	252 Christchurch	36.7	18,224	Ukip
204 Shropshire North	31.4	16,494	Lab	253 Hertsmere	36.9	18,461	Lab
205 Southend West	31.5	14,021	Lab	254 Thirsk & Malton	37.2	19,456	Lab
206 Bromsgrove	31.6	16,529	Lab	255 Suffolk Central &	37.2	20,144	Lab
207 Banbury	31.7	18,395	Lab	Ipswich North			
208 Broadland	31.7	16,838	Lab	256 Wantage	37.3	21,749	Lab
209 Aldershot	32.3	14,901	Lab	257 Harborough	37.4	19,632	Lab
210 Sutton Coldfield	32.3	16,417	Lab	258 Tiverton & Honiton	37.5	20,173	Ukip
211 Rayleigh & Wickford	32.4	17,230	Ukip	259 S. Holland & The Deepings	37.7	18,567	Ukip
212 Charnwood	32.4	16,931	Lab	260 Beckenham	37.8	18,471	Lab
213 Cambridgeshire North West	32.4	19,795	Ukip	261 Cotswolds, The	37.9	21,477	LD
214 Wellingborough	32.5	16,397	Ukip	262 Skipton & Ripon	38.1	20,761	Lab
215 Devon West & Torridge	32.5	18,403	Ukip	263 Hertford & Stortford	38.2	21,509	Lab
216 Cambridgeshire North East	32.6	16,874	Ukip	264 New Forest East	38.8	19,162	Ukip
217 Bournemouth East	32.6	14,612	Lab	265 Totnes	38.8	18,285	Ukip
218 Congleton	32.9	16,773	Lab	266 Bracknell	38.9	20,650	Lab
219 Norfolk Mid	33.1	17,276	Ukip	267 Sleaford & North Hykeham	38.9	24,115	Lab
220 Worthing West	33.2	16,855	Ukip	268 Richmond Park	38.9	23,015	LD
221 Haltemprice & Howden	33.2	16,195	Lab	269 Sevenoaks	39.0	19,561	Ukip
222 Poole	33.3	15,789	Ukip	270 Devon Central	39.1	21,265	Ukip
223 Cambridgeshire South	33.5	20,594	Lab	271 Somerset North	39.2	23,099	Lab
224 Somerton & Frome	33.6	20,268	LD	272 Worcestershire Mid	39.3	20,532	Ukip
225 Ashford	33.6	19,296	Ukip	273 Ludlow	39.4	18,929	Ukip
226 Cornwall South East	33.7	16,995	LD	274 Ruislip, Northwood & Pinner	39.5	20,224	Lab
227 Suffolk South	33.8	17,545	Lab	275 Dorset North	39.6	21,118	Ukip
228 Old Bexley & Sidcup	33.8	15,803	Lab	276 Tewkesbury	39.7	21,972	Lab
229 Suffolk Coastal	33.9	18,842	Lab	277 Rutland & Melton	39.8	21,705	Ukip
230 Chelmsford	33.9	18,250	Lab	278 Chelsea & Fulham	39.8	16,022	Lab
231 Stone	34.6	16,250	Lab	279 Devon South West	39.9	20,109	Lab
232 Huntingdon	34.7	19,404	Lab	280 Woking	40.0	20,810	Lab
233 Bedfordshire South West	34.7	17,813	Lab	281 Daventry	40.1	21,059	Lab

CONSTITUENCY	% MAJ	MAJ	2ND	CONSTITUENCY	% MAJ	MAJ	2ND
Conservative seats				**Labour seats**			
282 Bedfordshire Mid	40.2	23,327	Lab	1 Chester, City Of	0.2	93	C
283 Tatton	40.3	18,241	Lab	2 Ealing Central & Acton	0.5	274	C
284 Salisbury	40.3	20,421	Lab	3 Ynys Mon	0.7	229	PC
285 Wealden	40.3	22,967	Ukip	4 Brentford & Isleworth	0.8	465	C
286 Surrey East	40.4	22,658	Ukip	5 Halifax	1.0	428	C
287 Hertfordshire South West	40.6	23,263	Lab	6 Wirral West	1.0	417	C
288 Fareham	40.7	22,262	Ukip	7 Cambridge	1.2	599	LD
289 Orpington	40.7	19,979	Ukip	8 Ilford North	1.2	589	C
290 Staffordshire South	41.1	20,371	Lab	9 Newcastle-Under-Lyme	1.5	650	C
291 Witham	41.5	19,554	Ukip	10 Barrow & Furness	1.8	795	C
292 Guildford	41.6	22,448	LD	11 Wolverhampton South West	2.0	801	C
293 Wiltshire North	41.6	21,046	LD	12 Hampstead & Kilburn	2.1	1,138	C
294 Herefordshire North	41.6	19,996	Ukip	13 Enfield North	2.4	1,086	C
295 Worcestershire West	41.7	22,578	Ukip	14 Hove	2.4	1,236	C
296 Brentwood & Ongar	42.0	21,810	Ukip	15 Dewsbury	2.7	1,451	C
297 Sussex Mid	42.2	24,286	Lab	16 Lancaster & Fleetwood	3.0	1,265	C
298 Devizes	42.3	20,751	Lab	17 Derbyshire North East	3.9	1,883	C
299 Chichester	42.7	24,413	Ukip	18 Harrow West	4.7	2,208	C
300 Epsom & Ewell	42.8	24,443	Lab	19 Bridgend	4.9	1,927	C
301 Witney	43.0	25,155	Lab	20 Middlesbrough South & Cleveland East	5.0	2,268	C
302 Kenilworth & Southam	43.0	21,002	Lab	21 Westminster North	5.0	1,977	C
303 Wokingham	43.2	24,197	Lab	22 Walsall North	5.3	1,937	C
304 Horsham	43.3	24,658	Ukip	23 Tooting	5.3	2,842	C
305 Hampshire North West	43.4	23,943	Ukip	24 Edinburgh South	5.4	2,637	SNP
306 Northamptonshire South	43.4	26,416	Lab	25 Wrexham	5.6	1,831	C
307 Saffron Walden	43.4	24,991	Ukip	26 Birmingham Northfield	5.9	2,509	C
308 New Forest West	43.5	20,604	Ukip	27 Wakefield	6.1	2,613	C
309 Reigate	43.5	22,334	Ukip	28 Gedling	6.2	2,986	C
310 Bedfordshire North East	43.7	25,644	Lab	29 Eltham	6.2	2,693	C
311 Runnymede & Weybridge	44.2	22,134	Lab	30 Copeland	6.5	2,564	C
312 Tonbridge & Malling	44.2	23,734	Ukip	31 Stoke-On-Trent South	6.5	2,539	C
313 Stratford-On-Avon	44.5	22,876	Ukip	32 Birmingham Edgbaston	6.6	2,706	C
314 Tunbridge Wells	44.5	22,874	Lab	33 Clwyd South	6.9	2,402	C
315 Penrith & The Border	45.3	19,894	Lab	34 Coventry South	7.3	3,188	C
316 Chesham & Amersham	45.4	23,920	Ukip	35 Hartlepool	7.7	3,024	Ukip
317 Surrey Heath	45.6	24,804	Ukip	36 Darlington	7.7	3,158	C
318 Maldon	45.9	22,070	Ukip	37 Delyn	7.8	2,930	C
319 Henley	45.9	25,375	Lab	38 Blackpool South	8.0	2,585	C
320 Newbury	46.0	26,368	LD	39 Alyn & Deeside	8.1	3,343	C
321 Mole Valley	46.2	25,453	LD	40 Burnley	8.2	3,244	LD
322 Meon Valley	46.2	23,913	Ukip	41 Scunthorpe	8.5	3,134	C
323 Arundel & South Downs	46.3	26,177	Ukip	42 Bristol East	8.6	3,980	C
324 Hampshire East	48.7	25,147	Ukip	43 Newport West	8.7	3,510	C
325 Beaconsfield	49.5	26,311	Ukip	44 Southampton Test	8.7	3,810	C
326 Surrey South West	50.0	28,556	Ukip	45 Bermondsey & Old Southwark	8.7	4,489	LD
327 Windsor	50.0	25,083	Lab	46 Chorley	8.8	4,530	C
328 Esher & Walton	50.2	28,616	Lab	47 Bristol West	8.8	5,673	Green
329 Maidenhead	54.0	29,059	Lab				
330 Hampshire North East	55.4	29,916	LD				

CONSTITUENCY	% MAJ	MAJ	2ND	CONSTITUENCY	% MAJ	MAJ	2ND
Labour seats				**Labour seats**			
48 Bishop Auckland	8.9	3,508	C	97 Warrington North	19.6	8,923	C
49 Coventry North West	10.0	4,509	C	98 Swansea West	20.0	7,036	C
50 Bolton North East	10.1	4,377	C	99 Brent North	20.7	10,834	C
51 Hyndburn	10.3	4,400	C	100 Leicester West	20.9	7,203	C
52 Bury South	10.4	4,922	C	101 Don Valley	20.9	8,885	C
53 Heywood & Middleton	10.9	5,299	Ukip	102 Stockton North	21.1	8,367	C
54 Wirral South	11.0	4,599	C	103 Torfaen	21.5	8,169	C
55 Dudley North	11.0	4,181	C	104 Derby South	21.6	8,828	C
56 Mansfield	11.3	5,315	C	105 West Bromwich West	22.1	7,742	Ukip
57 Dagenham & Rainham	11.6	4,980	Ukip	106 Luton North	22.3	9,504	C
58 Batley & Spen	12.0	6,057	C	107 Rotherham	22.3	8,446	Ukip
59 Workington	12.2	4,686	C	108 Erith & Thamesmead	22.4	9,525	C
60 Stoke-On-Trent North	12.5	4,836	C	109 Newcastle Upon Tyne North	22.6	10,153	C
61 Cardiff Central	12.9	4,981	LD	110 Feltham & Heston	23.2	11,463	C
62 Exeter	13.3	7,183	C	111 Durham North West	23.5	10,056	C
63 Newport East	13.4	4,705	C	112 Rhondda	23.6	7,455	PC
64 Ellesmere Port & Neston	13.4	6,275	C	113 Pontypridd	23.7	8,985	C
65 Great Grimsby	13.5	4,540	C	114 Blyth Valley	24.0	9,229	Ukip
66 Oldham East & Saddleworth	13.5	6,002	C	115 Sefton Central	24.2	11,846	C
67 Luton South	13.5	5,711	C	116 Wythenshawe & Sale East	24.4	10,569	C
68 Hammersmith	13.6	6,518	C	117 Doncaster Central	25.0	10,093	Ukip
69 Bristol South	14.0	7,128	C	118 Caerphilly	25.0	10,073	Ukip
70 York Central	14.1	6,716	C	119 Durham, City Of	25.0	11,439	C
71 Worsley & Eccles South	14.1	5,946	C	120 Stretford & Urmston	25.2	11,685	C
72 Penistone & Stocksbridge	14.3	6,723	C	121 West Bromwich East	25.3	9,470	C
73 Walsall South	14.4	6,007	C	122 Stockport	25.4	10,061	C
74 Birmingham Erdington	14.8	5,129	C	123 Redcar	25.4	10,388	LD
75 Leeds North East	15.0	7,250	C	124 Ealing North	25.4	12,326	C
76 Slough	15.2	7,336	C	125 Greenwich & Woolwich	25.6	11,946	C
77 Tynemouth	15.4	8,240	C	126 Neath	25.7	9,548	PC
78 Cardiff West	15.5	6,789	C	127 Lewisham West & Penge	26.4	12,714	C
79 Rother Valley	15.5	7,297	Ukip	128 Vauxhall	26.5	12,708	C
80 Norwich South	15.8	7,654	C	129 Sunderland Central	26.8	11,179	C
81 Nottingham South	16.0	6,936	C	130 Bolsover	26.8	11,778	C
82 Cardiff South & Penarth	16.0	7,453	C	131 Bolton South East	26.8	10,928	Ukip
83 Birmingham Yardley	16.0	6,595	LD	132 Denton & Reddish	27.2	10,511	C
84 Wolverhampton North East	16.2	5,495	C	133 Rochdale	27.4	12,442	Ukip
85 Stalybridge & Hyde	16.3	6,686	C	134 Ashton Under Lyne	27.6	10,756	C
86 Stoke-On-Trent Central	16.7	5,179	Ukip	135 Streatham	27.9	13,934	C
87 Lancashire West	16.8	8,360	C	136 Leeds West	27.9	10,727	C
88 Bradford East	17.1	7,084	LD	137 Wansbeck	28.2	10,881	C
89 Bradford South	17.2	6,450	C	138 Bradford West	28.3	11,420	Respect
90 Sedgefield	17.7	6,843	C	139 Hemsworth	28.5	12,078	C
91 Bassetlaw	17.9	8,843	C	140 Islington South & Finsbury	28.7	12,708	C
92 Huddersfield	18.1	7,345	C	141 Salford & Eccles	29.0	12,541	C
93 Llanelli	18.4	7,095	PC	142 Blackburn	29.0	12,760	C
94 Ashfield	18.6	8,820	C	143 Coventry North East	29.1	12,274	C
95 Birmingham Selly Oak	18.6	8,447	C	144 South Shields	29.3	10,614	Ukip
96 Hornsey & Wood Green	19.1	11,058	LD	145 Hull West & Hessle	29.3	9,333	Ukip

CONSTITUENCY	% MAJ	MAJ	2ND
Labour seats			
146 Hull East	29.4	10,319	Ukip
147 Makerfield	29.4	13,155	Ukip
148 Islwyn	29.4	10,404	Ukip
149 Sheffield South East	29.5	12,311	Ukip
150 Manchester Withington	29.8	14,873	LD
151 Doncaster North	29.8	11,780	Ukip
152 Chesterfield	29.8	13,598	C
153 Oxford East	30.1	15,280	C
154 Sheffield Heeley	30.8	12,954	Ukip
155 Cynon Valley	30.9	9,406	PC
156 Wolverhampton South East	31.0	10,778	C
157 Holborn & St Pancras	31.0	17,048	C
158 Leigh	31.2	14,096	C
159 Barnsley East	31.2	12,034	Ukip
160 Dulwich & West Norwood	31.4	16,122	C
161 Wigan	31.4	14,236	C
162 Blaydon	31.7	14,227	Ukip
163 Newcastle Upon Tyne East	31.9	12,494	C
164 Wentworth & Dearne	32.0	13,838	Ukip
165 Leeds East	32.8	12,533	C
166 Aberavon	33.1	10,445	Ukip
167 Poplar & Limehouse	33.2	16,924	C
168 Lewisham East	33.4	14,333	C
169 Nottingham North	33.6	11,860	C
170 Normanton, Pontefract & Castleford	33.6	15,428	Ukip
171 Houghton & Sunderland S.	33.6	12,938	Ukip
172 Nottingham East	33.8	11,894	C
173 Durham North	34.0	13,644	C
174 Barnsley Central	34.0	12,435	Ukip
175 Oldham West & Royton	34.2	14,738	Ukip
176 Sheffield Brightside & Hillsborough	34.5	13,807	Ukip
177 Hayes & Harlington	34.8	15,700	C
178 Merthyr Tydfil & Rhymney	35.2	11,513	Ukip
179 Washington & Sunderland W.	35.3	13,157	Ukip
180 Barking	35.5	15,272	Ukip
181 Swansea East	35.8	12,028	Ukip
182 Birmingham Perry Barr	35.9	14,828	C
183 Jarrow	36.0	13,881	Ukip
184 Preston	36.1	12,067	C
185 Newcastle Upon Tyne Central	36.1	12,673	C
186 Hull North	36.5	12,899	Ukip
187 Leyton & Wanstead	36.7	14,919	C
188 Tyneside North	36.7	17,194	C
189 Ogmore	37.0	13,043	C
190 Edmonton	37.3	15,419	C
191 St Helens North	37.4	17,291	C

CONSTITUENCY	% MAJ	MAJ	2ND
Labour seats			
192 Mitcham & Morden	37.5	16,922	C
193 Leeds Central	37.7	16,967	C
194 Wallasey	37.7	16,348	C
195 Ilford South	38.1	19,777	C
196 Middlesbrough	38.1	12,477	Ukip
197 Leicester East	38.2	18,352	C
198 Leicester South	38.8	17,845	C
199 Warley	38.9	14,702	C
200 Gateshead	39.0	14,784	Ukip
201 Sheffield Central	39.2	17,309	Green
202 Croydon North	39.9	21,364	C
203 Blaenau Gwent	40.1	12,703	Ukip
204 Brent Central	41.8	19,649	C
205 Birmingham Hall Green	42.1	19,818	C
206 Easington	42.3	14,641	Ukip
207 Islington North	43.0	21,194	C
208 Ealing Southall	43.3	18,760	C
209 St Helens South & Whiston	43.9	21,243	C
210 Halton	45.1	20,285	C
211 Lewisham Deptford	45.4	21,516	C
212 Blackley & Broughton	45.5	16,874	Ukip
213 Bethnal Green & Bow	45.9	24,317	C
214 Manchester Central	47.7	21,639	C
215 Hackney North & Stoke Newington	48.1	24,008	C
216 Camberwell & Peckham	50.1	25,824	C
217 Hackney South & Shoreditch	50.9	24,243	C
218 Birkenhead	52.8	20,652	C
219 West Ham	53.0	27,986	C
220 Liverpool Riverside	55.3	24,463	Green
221 Tottenham	55.4	23,564	C
222 Garston & Halewood	55.4	27,146	C
223 Walthamstow	55.5	23,195	C
224 Birmingham Hodge Hill	56.9	23,362	C
225 Manchester Gorton	57.3	24,079	Green
226 Liverpool Wavertree	59.3	24,303	C
227 Birmingham Ladywood	60.9	21,868	C
228 Bootle	63.6	28,704	Ukip
229 East Ham	65.5	34,252	C
230 Liverpool West Derby	66.7	27,367	Ukip
231 Knowsley	68.3	34,655	Ukip
232 Liverpool Walton	72.3	27,777	Ukip
Liberal Democrat seats			
1 Southport	3.0	1,322	C
2 Carshalton & Wallington	3.2	1,510	C
3 Orkney & Shetland	3.6	817	SNP
4 Sheffield Hallam	4.2	2,353	Lab

CONSTITUENCY	% MAJ	MAJ	2ND
Liberal Democrat seats			
5 Leeds North West	6.7	2,907	Lab
6 Norfolk North	8.2	4,043	C
7 Ceredigion	8.2	3,067	PC
8 Westmorland & Lonsdale	18.3	8,949	C
Scottish National seats			
1 Berwickshire, Roxburgh & Selkirk	0.6	328	C
2 Dunbartonshire East	3.9	2,167	LD
3 Edinburgh West	5.9	3,210	LD
4 Renfrewshire East	6.6	3,718	Lab
5 Fife North East	9.6	4,344	LD
6 Edinburgh North & Leith	9.6	5,597	Lab
7 Caithness, Sutherland & Easter Ross	11.2	3,844	LD
8 Dumfries & Galloway	11.5	6,514	C
9 East Lothian	11.5	6,803	Lab
10 Ross, Skye & Lochaber	12.3	5,124	LD
11 Paisley & Renfrewshire S.	12.3	5,684	Lab
12 Aberdeenshire West & Kincardine	12.7	7,033	C
13 Aberdeen South	14.9	7,230	Lab
14 Gordon	14.9	8,687	LD
15 Edinburgh South West	15.8	8,135	Lab
16 Argyll & Bute	16.3	8,473	LD
17 Rutherglen & Hamilton West	17.3	9,975	Lab
18 Ochil & Perthshire South	17.6	10,168	Lab
19 Perth & Perthshire North	17.8	9,641	C
20 Paisley & Renfrewshire N.	18.0	9,076	Lab
21 Lanark & Hamilton East	18.3	10,100	Lab
22 Moray	18.4	9,065	C
23 Dunfermline & Fife West	18.5	10,352	Lab
24 Inverness, Nairn, Badenoch & Strathspey	18.8	10,809	LD
25 Kirkcaldy & Cowdenbeath	18.9	9,974	Lab
26 Edinburgh East	19.3	9,106	Lab
27 Glasgow Central	19.5	7,662	Lab
28 Airdrie & Shotts	19.8	8,779	Lab
29 Stirling	20.1	10,480	Lab
30 Midlothian	20.4	9,859	Lab
31 Linlithgow & Falkirk East	21.0	12,934	Lab
32 Ayr, Carrick & Cumnock	21.6	11,265	Lab
33 Coatbridge, Chryston & Bellshill	22.7	11,501	Lab
34 Glasgow North West	23.6	10,364	Lab
35 Glasgow South West	24.3	9,950	Lab
36 Glasgow North East	24.4	9,222	Lab
37 Glasgow East	24.5	10,387	Lab

CONSTITUENCY	% MAJ	MAJ	2ND
Scottish National seats			
38 Motherwell & Wishaw	24.7	11,898	Lab
39 Inverclyde	24.8	11,063	Lab
40 Glasgow South	25.2	12,269	Lab
41 Glasgow North	25.2	9,295	Lab
42 Ayrshire North & Arran	25.2	13,573	Lab
43 Angus	25.2	11,230	C
44 Kilmarnock & Loudoun	25.3	13,638	Lab
45 Na H-Eileanan An Iar	25.7	4,102	Lab
46 Ayrshire Central	26.8	13,589	Lab
47 East Kilbride, Strathaven & Lesmahagow	27.3	16,527	Lab
48 Dunbartonshire West	27.7	14,171	Lab
49 Glenrothes	29.2	13,897	Lab
50 Livingston	29.3	16,843	Lab
51 Cumbernauld, Kilsyth & Kirkintilloch East	29.9	14,752	Lab
52 Aberdeen North	30.5	13,396	Lab
53 Banff & Buchan	31.4	14,339	C
54 Falkirk	32.6	19,701	Lab
55 Dundee West	38.2	17,092	Lab
56 Dundee East	39.8	19,162	Lab
Plaid Cymru seats			
1 Arfon	13.7	3,668	Lab
2 Carmarthen East & Dinefwr	14.2	5,599	Lab
3 Dwyfor Meirionnydd	18.2	5,261	C
Speaker			
1 Buckingham	42.7	22,942	Ukip
Green seat			
1 Brighton Pavilion	14.6	7,967	Lab
Ukip seat			
1 Clacton	7.8	3,437	C
Independent seat			
1 Down North	25.6	9,202	DUP
Sinn Fein seats			
1 Newry & Armagh	8.4	4,176	UUP
2 Tyrone West	26.0	10,060	DUP
3 Ulster Mid	33.3	13,617	UUP

CONSTITUENCY	% MAJ	MAJ	2ND	CONSTITUENCY	% MAJ	MAJ	2ND
Sinn Fein seats				**SDLP seats**			
4 Belfast West	35.0	12,365	PBP	1 Belfast South	2.3	906	DUP
				2 Down South	13.8	5,891	SF
				3 Foyle	16.3	6,046	SF
Democratic Unionist seats							
1 Upper Bann	4.8	2,264	UUP	**Ulster Unionist seats**			
2 Belfast East	6.5	2,597	APNI	1 Fermanagh & South Tyrone	1.0	530	SF
3 Belfast North	13.1	5,326	SF	2 Antrim South	2.6	949	DUP
4 Antrim East	17.3	5,795	UUP				
5 Londonderry East	22.5	7,804	SF				
6 Antrim North	27.6	11,546	TUV				
7 Strangford	30.0	10,185	UUP				
8 Lagan Valley	32.7	13,000	UUP				

Defeated MPs

ALLIANCE
Long, Naomi Belfast East

CONSERVATIVE
Bray, Angie Ealing Central
& Acton
de Bois, Nick Enfield North
MacLeod, Mary Brentford &
Isleworth
McVey, Esther Wirral West
Mosley, Stephen City Of Chester
Ollerenshaw, Eric Lancaster &
Fleetwood
Reevell, Simon Dewsbury
Scott, Lee Ilford North
Uppal, Paul Wolverhampton
South West

DEMOCRATIC UNIONIST PARTY
McCrea, William South Antrim

INDEPENDENT
Hancock, Mike Portsmouth South

LABOUR
Alexander, Douglas Paisley &
Renfrewshire South
Bain, William Glasgow
North East
Balls, Ed Morley & Outwood
Banks, Gordon Ochil & South
Perthshire
Begg, Anne Aberdeen South
Brown, Russell Dumfries &
Galloway
Clark, Katy Ayrshire North
& Arran
Clarke, Tom Coatbridge, Chryston
& Bellshill
Connarty, Michael Linlithgow &
East Falkirk
Curran, Margaret Glasgow East
Davidson, Ian Glasgow
South West
Docherty, Thomas Dunfermline
& West Fife
Donohoe, Brian Central Ayrshire
Doyle, Gemma Dunbartonshire
West
Gilmore, Sheila Edinburgh East

Greatrex, Tom Rutherglen &
Hamilton West
Harris, Tom Glasgow South
Hilling, Julie Bolton West
Hood, Jim Lanark &
Hamilton East
Jamieson, Cathy Kilmarnock
& Loudoun
Lazarowicz, Mark Edinburgh
North & Leith
McCann, Michael East Kilbride,
Strathaven & Lesmahagow
McClymont, Gregg Cumbernauld,
Kilsyth & Kirkintilloch East
McKechin, Ann Glasgow North
McKenzie, Iain Inverclyde
Morrice, Graeme Livingston
Murphy, Jim East Renfrewshire
Nash, Pamela Airdrie & Shotts
O'Donnell, Fiona East Lothian
Osborne, Sandra Ayr, Carrick
& Cumnock
Robertson, John Glasgow
North West
Roy, Frank Motherwell
& Wishaw
Ruane, Chris Vale Of Clwyd
Sarwar, Anas Glasgow Central
Sawford, Andy Corby
Seabeck, Alison Plymouth,
Moor View
Sheridan, Jim Paisley &
Renfrewshire North
Williamson, Chris Derby North
Wright, David Telford

LIBERAL DEMOCRAT
Alexander, Danny Inverness,
Nairn, Badenoch & Strathspey
Baker, Norman Lewes
Birtwistle, Gordon Burnley
Burstow, Paul Sutton & Cheam
Burt, Lorely Solihull
Cable, Vincent Twickenham
Crockart, Mike Edinburgh West
Davey, Edward Kingston &
Surbiton
Featherstone, Lynne Hornsey &
Wood Green
George, Andrew St Ives

Gilbert, Stephen St Austell &
Newquay
Hames, Duncan Chippenham
Harvey, Nick North Devon
Hemming, John Birmingham,
Yardley
Horwood, Martin Cheltenham
Hughes, Simon Bermondsey &
Old Southwark
Hunter, Mark Cheadle
Huppert, Julian Cambridge
Kennedy, Charles Ross, Skye
& Lochaber
Laws, David Yeovil
Leech, John Manchester,
Withington
Lloyd, Stephen Eastbourne
Moore, Michael Berwickshire,
Roxburgh & Selkirk
Munt, Tessa Wells
Reid, Alan Argyll & Bute
Rogerson, Dan North Cornwall
Russell, Bob Colchester
Sanders, Adrian Torbay
Smith, Robert West Aberdeenshire
& Kincardine
Swinson, Jo East Dunbartonshire
Thornton, Mike Eastleigh
Thurso, John Caithness,
Sutherland & Easter Ross
Ward, David Bradford East
Webb, Steve Thornbury & Yate
Williams, Roger Brecon &
Radnorshire
Williams, Stephen Bristol West
Willott, Jenny Cardiff Central
Wright, Simon Norwich South

RESPECT
Galloway, George Bradford West

SINN FEIN
Gildernew, Michelle Fermanagh
& South Tyrone

UK INDEPENDENCE PARTY
Reckless, Mark Rochester
& Strood

MPs who stood down before the election

By-elections 2010-15

Rochester and Strood

Held on November 20, 2014. Caused by defection to Ukip of the Conservative MP Mark Reckless

	Electorate	Turnout %	Change from 2010 %
	40,065	50.6	
Mark Reckless Ukip	16,867	42.1	–
Kelly Tolhurst C	13,947	34.8	-14.4
Naushabah Khan Lab	6,713	16.8	-11.7
Clive Gregory Green	1,692	4.2	2.7
Geoff Juby LD	349	0.9	-15.5
Hairy Knorm Davidson Loony	151	0.4	–
Majority	**2,920**		

Clacton

Held on October 9, 2014. Caused by defection to Ukip of the Conservative MP Douglas Carswell

	Electorate	Turnout %	Change from 2010 %
	35,338	51.0	
Douglas Carswell Ukip	21,113	59.7	–
Giles Watling C	8,709	24.6	-28.4
Tim Young Lab	3,957	11.2	-13.8
Chris Southall Green	688	1.9	0.7
Andrew Graham LD	483	1.3	-11.6
Bruce Sizer Ind	205	0.6	–
Alan Hope Loony	127	0.4	–
Majority	**12,404**		

Heywood and Middleton

Held on October 9, 2014. Caused by the death of the Labour MP Jim Dobbin

	Electorate	Turnout %	Change from 2010 %
	28,472	36.0	
Liz McInnes Lab	11,633	40.9	0.8
John Bickley Ukip	11,016	38.7	36.1
Iain Gartside C	3,496	12.3	-14.9
Anthony Smith LD	1,457	5.1	-17.6
Abi Jackson Green	870	3.1	–
Majority	**617**		

Newark

Held on June 5, 2014. Caused by the resignation of the MP Patrick Mercer (Independent, previously Conservative)

	Electorate	Turnout %	Change from 2010 %
	38,707	52.8	
Robert Jenrick C	17,431	45.0	-8.9
Roger Helmer Ukip	10,028	25.9	22.1
Michael Payne Lab	6,842	17.7	-4.7
Paul Baggaley Ind	1,891	4.9	–
David Kirwan Green	1,057	2.7	–
David Watts LD	1,004	2.6	-17.4
Nick The Flying Brick Loony	168	0.4	–
Andy Hayes Ind	117	0.3	–
Majority	**7,403**		

Wythenshawe and Sale East

Held on February 13, 2014. Caused by the death of the Labour MP Paul Goggins

	Electorate	Turnout %	Change from 2010 %
	23,961	28.2	
Mike Kane Lab	13,261	55.3	11.2
John Bickley Ukip	4,301	18.0	14.5
Rev Daniel Critchlow C	3,479	14.5	-11
Mary di Mauro LD	1,176	4.9	-17.4
Nigel Woodcock Green	748	3.1	–
Eddy O'Sullivan BNP	708	3.0	-0.9
Cpt Chaplington-Smythe Loony	288	1.2	–
Majority	**8,960**		

South Shields

Held on May 2, 2013. Caused by resignation of the Labour MP David Miliband

	Electorate	Turnout %	Change from 2010 %
	24,736	39.3	
Emma Lewell-Buck Lab	12,493	0.5	-1.6
Richard Elvin Ukip	5,988	24.2	–
Karen Allen C	2,857	11.5	-10.1
Ahmed Khan Ind	1,331	5.4	–
Phil Brown ISP	750	3.0	–
Dorothy MacBeth Brookes BNP	711	2.9	-3.6
Hugh Annand LD	352	1.4	-12.8
Alan Howling Laud Hope Loony	197	0.8	–
Majority	**6,505**		

Mid Ulster

Held on March 7, 2013. Caused by the resignation of the Sinn Fein MP Martin McGuiness

	Electorate	Turnout %	Change from 2010 %
	37,208	55.7	
Francie Molloy SF	17,462	46.9	-5.1
Nigel Lutton Ind	12,781	34.4	–
Patsy McGlone SDLP	6,478	17.4	3.1
Eric Bullick Alliance	487	1.3	0.3
Majority	**4,681**		

Eastleigh

Held on February 28, 2013. Caused by resignation of the Liberal Democrat MP Chris Huhne

	Electorate	Turnout %	Change from 2010 %
	41,616	52.8	
Mike Thornton Lib Dem	13,342	32.0	-14.4
Diane James Ukip	11,571	27.8	24.2
Maria Hutchings Con	10,559	25.4	-13.9
John O'Farrell Lab	4,088	9.8	0.2
Danny Stupple Ind	768	1.9	–
Iain Maclennan NHA	392	0.9	–
Ray Hall BB&C	235	0.6	–
Kevin Milburn Ch P	163	0.4	–
Howling Laud Hope Loony	136	0.3	–
Jim Duggan Peace	128	0.3	–
Majority	**1,771**		

Croydon North

Held on November 29, 2012. Caused by the death of the Labour MP Malcolm Wicks

	Electorate	Turnout %	Change from 2010 %
	24,568	26.4	
Steve Reed Lab	15,898	64.7	8.7
Andy Stranack C	4,137	16.8	-7.3
Winston McKenzie Ukip	1,400	5.7	4.0
Marisha Ray LD	860	3.5	-10.5
Shasha Islam Khan Green	855	3.5	1.5
Lee Jasper Respect	707	2.9	2.4
Stephen Hammond CPA	192	0.8	–
Richard Edmonds NF	161	0.7	–
Ben Stevenson Communist	119	0.5	0.2
John Cartwright Loony	110	0.5	–
Majority	**11,761**		

Middlesbrough

Held on November 29, 2012. Caused by the death of the Labour MP Sir Stuart Bell

	Electorate	Turnout %	Change from 2010 %
	16,866	25.9	
Andy McDonald Lab	10,201	60.5	14.6
Richard Elvin Ukip	1,990	11.8	8.1
George Selmer LD	1,672	9.9	-10.0
Ben Houchen Con	1,063	6.3	-12.5
Imdad Hussain Peace	1,060	6.3	–
Peter Foreman BNP	328	1.9	-3.9
John Malcolm TUSC	277	1.6	–
Mark Heslehurst ND	275	1.6	–
Majority	**8,211**		

Rotherham

Held on November 29, 2012. Caused by the resignation of the Labour MP Denis MacShane after inquiry into expenses

	Electorate	Turnout %	Change from 2010 %
	21,430	33.6	
Sarah Champion Lab	9,966	46.3	1.6
Jane Collins Ukip	4,648	21.8	15.9
Marlene Guest BNP	1,804	8.5	-2.0
Yvonne Ridley Respect	1,778	8.3	–
Simon Wilson C	1,157	5.4	-11.3
David Wildgoose Eng Dem	703	3.3	–
Simon Copley Ind	582	2.7	-3.6
Michael Beckett LD	451	2.1	-13.9
Ralph Dyson TUSC	261	1.2	–
Majority	5,318		

Corby

Held on November 15, 2012. Caused by the resignation of Conservative MP Louise Mensch

	Electorate	Turnout %	Change from 2010 %
	35,665	44.7	
Andy Sawford Lab	17,267	48.4	9.7
Christine Emmett C	9,476	26.6	-15.6
Margot Parker Ukip	5,108	14.3	–
Jill Hope LD	1,770	5.0	-9.5
Gordon Riddell BNP	614	1.7	-2.9
David Wickham Eng Dem	432	1.2	–
Jonathan Hornett Green	378	1.1	–
Ian Gillman Ind	212	0.6	–
Peter Reynolds Cannabis	137	0.4	–
Majority	7,791		

Cardiff South and Penarth

Held on November 15, 2012. Caused by the resignation of the Labour MP Alun Michael to stand as police and crime commissioner

	Electorate	Turnout %	Change from 2010 %
	19,436	25.7	
Stephen Doughty Lab	9,193	47.3	8.4
Craig Williams C	3,859	19.9	-8.4
Bablin Molik LD	2,103	10.8	-11.4
Luke Nicholas PC	1,854	9.5	5.4
Simon Zeigler Ukip	1,179	6.1	3.5
Anthony Slaughter Green	800	4.1	2.9
Andrew Jordan Soc Lab	235	1.2	–
Robert Griffiths Comm Lge	213	1.1	0.7

Manchester Central

Held on November 15, 2012. Caused by the resignation of Tony Lloyd (Lab) to stand as police and crime commissioner

	Electorate	Turnout %	Change from 2010 %
	16,648	18.2	
Lucy Powell Lab	11,507	69.1	16.4
Marc Ramsbottom Lib Dem	1,571	9.4	-17.2
Matthew Sephton C	754	4.5	-7.3
Chris Cassidy Ukip	749	4.5	3.0
Tom Dylan Green	652	3.9	1.6
Eddy O'Sullivan BNP	492	3.0	-1.1
Loz Kaye Pirate	308	1.9	–
Alex Davidson TUSC	220	1.3	–
Catherine Higgins Respect	182	1.1	–
Majority	9,936		

Bradford West

Held on March 29, 2012. Caused by the resignation for health reasons of the Labour MP Marsha Singh

	Electorate	Turnout %	Change from 2010 %
	32,814	50.8	
George Galloway Respect	18,341	55.9	52.8
Imran Hussain Lab	8,201	25.0	-20.4
Jackie Whiteley C	2,746	8.4	-22.8
Jeanette Sunderland LD	1,505	4.6	-7.1
Sonja McNally Ukip	1,085	3.3	1.3
Dawud Islam Green	481	1.5	-0.9
Neil Craig D Nat	344	1.1	–
Howling Laud Hope Loony	111	0.3	–
Majority	10,140		

Feltham and Heston

Held on December 15, 2011. Caused by the death of the Labour MP Alan Keen

	Electorate	Turnout %	Change from 2010 %
	23,224	28.8	
Seema Malhotra Lab	12,639	54.4	10.8
Mark Bowen C	6,436	27.7	-6.3
Roger Crouch LD	1,364	5.9	-7.8
Andrew Charalambous Ukip	1,276	5.5	3.5
Dave Furness BNP	540	2.3	-1.2
Daniel Goldsmith Green	426	1.8	0.7
Roger Cooper Eng Dem	322	1.4	–
George Hallam LPBP	128	0.6	–
Majority	6,203		

Inverclyde

Held on June 30, 2011. Caused by the death of the Labour MP David Cairns

	Electorate	Turnout %	Change from 2010 %
	28,097	45.5	
Iain McKenzie Lab	15,118	53.8	-2.2
Anne McLaughlin SNP	9,280	33.0	15.5
David Wilson C	2,784	9.9	-2.1
Sophie Bridger LD	627	2.2	-11.1
Mitch Sorbie Ukip	288	1.0	-0.2
Majority	5,838		

Belfast West

Held on June 9, 2011. Caused by to the resignation of Gerry Adams (Sinn Fein) to stand for election in Ireland

	Electorate	Turnout %	Change from 2010 %
	22,951	37.5	
Paul Maskey SF	16,211	70.6	-0.5
Alex Attwood SDLP	3,088	13.5	-2.9
Gerry Carroll PBP	1,751	7.6	–
Brian Kingston DUP	1,393	6.1	-1.5
Bill Manwaring UUP	386	1.7	-1.4
Aaron McIntyre Alliance	122	0.5	-1.4
Majority	13,123		

Leicester South

Held on May 5, 2011. Caused by the resignation of the Labour MP Sir Peter Soulsby to stand for Mayor of Leicester

	Electorate	Turnout %	Change from 2010 %
	34,180	34.2	
Jonathon Ashworth Lab	19,771	57.8	12.2
Zuffar Haq LD	7,693	22.5	-4.4
Jane Hunt C	5,169	15.1	-6.3
Abhijit Pandya Ukip	994	2.9	1.4
Howling Laud Hope Loony	553	1.6	–
Majority	12,078		

Barnsley Central

Held on March 3, 2011. Caused by the resignation of the Labour MP Eric Illsley after his conviction relating to parliamentary expenses

	Electorate	Turnout %	Change from 2010 %
	24,219	36.5	
Dan Jarvis Lab	14,724	60.8	13.5
Jane Collins Ukip	2,953	12.2	7.5
James Hockney C	1,999	8.3	-9.0
Enis Dalton BNP	1,463	6.0	-2.9
Tony Devoy Ind	1,266	5.2	4.6
Dominic Carman LD	1,012	4.2	-13.1
Kevin Riddiough Eng Dem	544	2.2	–
Howling Laud Hope Loony	198	0.8	–
Majority	11,771		

Oldham East and Saddleworth

Held on January 13, 2011. Caused by the courts declaring the 2010 general election result invalid

	Electorate	Turnout %	Change from 2010 %
	34,930	48.0	
Debbie Abrahams Lab	14,718	42.1	10.2
Elwyn Watkins LD	11,160	31.9	0.3
Kashif Ali C	4,481	12.8	-13.6
Paul Nuttall Ukip	2,029	5.8	1.9
Derek Adams BNP	1,560	4.5	-1.2
Peter Allen Green	530	1.5	–
Nick Delves Loony	145	0.4	–
Stephen Morris Eng Dem	144	0.4	–
Majority	3,558		

• Results omit candidates who polled fewer than 100 votes

• Key to abbreviations is on page 72

The new parliament

AN INSIDER'S GUIDE TO PARLIAMENT

by Robert Rogers

We elected 182 new MPs on May 7, 2015. What have been their first impressions of Westminster, and how will they set about doing their new jobs? Some are familiar with the Westminster village, and already have their plans laid; others have found their new workplace a disorientating cross between Gormenghast and Hogwarts. Some were very surprised to find themselves able to write the magic letters "MP" after their names, and not go back to their old jobs the week after polling day; and many will have taken a pay cut to pursue a political career.

On arrival in London SW1, all had a total-immersion induction course run by the House of Commons Service (about 2,000 impartial officials who support every aspect of the work of the House and its members; servants of the legislature and not the executive, and so not civil servants). They have been allocated a member of House staff as their "buddy"; a guide to the geography and services: people who, if they do not know the answer themselves, will certainly know someone who does.

All have been frustrated by not walking straight into their new offices, instead having to wait upon the allocation of rooms by the accommodation whips of the parties. They have been given an @parliament.uk email address, and have begun to tackle the mountains of snail mail as well: congratulations on electoral success; strident calls for interest and support from a bewildering range of outside organisations, and indeed from all-party groups within the House; and the first of a stream of constituency cases, by turns enthralling, emotional, challenging and, in some cases, tiresome.

And of course they will have become very familiar with Ipsa, the Independent Parliamentary Standards Authority. Ipsa was established by the Parliamentary Standards Act 2009 after the expenses scandal, an event that was a disaster for parliament, even though the seeds had been sown under Margaret Thatcher's second administration, when the government lost its nerve over increasing MPs' pay, but contrived to hint that a generous expenses scheme would make up the difference. MPs' pay has been controversial ever since it was introduced in 1911 (at £400 a year), particularly because MPs could in effect set their own salaries. The expenses scandal was the catalyst for a move from a system of self-regulation to regulation by an independent body. Ipsa started by paying salaries and determining the level of expenses, and in 2011 was given the responsibility of determining MPs' pay as well.

In the financial year 2015/16, MPs in London are able to claim a maximum of £147,000 for employing staff, and of £26,050 for office costs. New MPs elected on May 7 get a start-up allowance of £6,000, and an interest-free start-up loan of £4,000 for a year. Living costs have been sharply restricted compared with the pre-Ipsa scheme, and MPs may claim between £10,400 and £20,600 for rent for accommodation (depending on where it is) and a maximum of £5,090 for living in London (again, eligibility varies depending on personal circumstances).

Ipsa reviewed MPs' pay in 2013, unsurprisingly concluding "Quite simply, there is never a good time to determine MPs' pay" but recommending a package, including a one-off pay rise of 10.3 per cent to £74,000 a year, reducing pension entitlements and tightening expenses, which it intended would not increase the cost to the taxpayer. Ipsa consulted on the proposals after the election and they were due to come into effect in September 2015. Many MPs have said that they will not take the pay rise, but it will be statutorily required to be paid, and even if they give the difference away, they will still have to pay tax on it.

The new MPs have started to recruit their staff: assumed, for the purposes of allowances, to be three per MP, but with part-timers and unpaid staff often substantially increasing this number (in the 2010 parliament there were about 3,000 MPs' staff). They are still trying to decide which staff to have with them at Westminster, helping with their daily parliamentary life but filling their offices, and which to have in the constituency, helping with casework, maintaining their local profile, and building up political credit with the next election in mind.

They have made possibly the most important contacts of their Westminster life: the party whips. The whips are famously the Westminster enforcers, with their black books and their range of nameless punishments, and indeed party discipline is their key role. They want to ensure that, whether in government or opposition, their flock vote in the right division lobby. But they also act as channels of communication between the backbencher and the party leadership, both explaining party intentions and policy, and feeding back opinions, hesitations and doubts. No one expects the opinions of every MP to mirror party policy exactly. Events and policies change, and there will always be an element of compromise on individual issues even if the political centre of gravity remains unchanged.

When, as in the 2015 parliament, the government has only a slim majority, the government whips have a balancing act to perform. A government with a small majority is like a boat low in the water. On one hand, people may be reluctant to stand up (rebel) because of the risk of capsizing; on the other hand the threat of people doing exactly that may mean that they have to be bought off with concessions.

Now that there is enough accommodation for every MP, and the chairs and members of select committees are elected, there is much less patronage in the hands of the whips. Although their power should not be underestimated, they have to exercise persuasion as much as give orders, and when MPs get into difficulty (whether personal or, for example, with a huge constituency caseload of emotionally draining problems) they need to be good personnel managers as well. The new MP will have an area whip who doubles as the whip responsible for a particular policy area, and both the whip and the MP will have each other's numbers on speed-dial.

The MP's weekly agenda is set principally by The Whip, a document private to each party, which sets out the business of the week, when votes are expected, and when the MP should be there to support the party. The number of underlinings indicates importance; so a "three-line whip" is one that MPs ignore at their peril.

Perhaps the worst crime in a whip's eyes is voting against the party line, or abstaining, without notice; expression of doubts beforehand at least offers the opportunity of persuasion or compromise. And the MP will need to use the power of rebellion sparingly; it can be a poor career move, and it does not take long for an MP to become a full member of "the awkward squad" and be treated accordingly. On the other hand, significant rebellions can be highly influential, and the constraints of party discipline are looser than they were: the 2010 parliament was the most rebellious against the party line, on both sides of the House, since the Second World War.

The new MP has also been consulting the All-Party Whip, a sort of Westminster noticeboard, which advertises everything from meetings of all-party and country groups to forthcoming memorial services. And getting from place to place will be a continuing challenge: the parliamentary estate is more than 200,000 sq m in 14 buildings housing more than 5,000 people, a total that more than doubles during the working day.

WHAT TO DO?

Faced with this complex and often confusing environment, how does the MP decide what to do? Attlee's advice to new MPs was "specialise, and stay out of the bars", a long sentence for him. But Westminster has long ceased to be fuelled by alcohol; for many of its inhabitants, salads and mineral water have replaced boozy lunches. And the choice of possible specialisations is daunting.   If the MP's party is in government, then Disraeli's "greasy pole" to ministerial office may be attractive. The MP will need to cultivate a reputation for knowledge in a chosen policy field, and become known to the whips and the leadership for energy and effectiveness. The same applies on the other side of the House. Although here the rewards are less — no red dispatch boxes, ministerial cars or additional salaries — today's opposition may be the next government.

Perhaps the new MP is not optimistic about the chances of office, although by the end of the last parliament a significant number of "newbies" who had entered parliament for the first time in 2010 had become ministers (some had even become ministers or whips, had been found wanting and then been returned to the back benches).

If ministerial life does not beckon, the choices will include championing causes, often those that dominated the MP's life before parliament: perhaps supporting women's refuges, encouraging apprenticeships, simplifying the tax system, increasing bio-diversity; the list is endless.

A key area will be select committee work. There has been an effort to make select committees a realistic alternative to ministerial office, only partly successful, as the allure of office is still powerful. But, as we shall see later, select committees have their own attraction and influence. The members of most select committees are elected by their parties; and in 2010 a large number of new MPs voted for each other, thus ensuring a disproportionately high representation on many committees. The chairs are elected by the House as a whole, and in the last parliament two MPs new to the House in 2010 were elected to chair two important departmental select committees: health and defence. So the new MP can set his or her sights high.

Then there is constituency work. Over the past 30 years this has been the biggest change in the character of Westminster. In that time the demands of the constituency have steadily increased, and the number of MPs' own staff has increased in step.

The constituency is of course an MP's power-base: the constituency party will decide whether the MP will be its candidate next time, and the electors will decide whether the MP will be returned to parliament. That is a given; but the expectations of an MP's time and influence are now very much greater. The postbag has reduced (halving over the past ten years) but electronic communication has much more than made up for this, with many MPs getting 500 emails a day.

Many constituents do not understand that the MP has no executive power, but has to be a facilitator and an advocate. The MP must be careful not to tread on the toes of local councillors (especially those of a different party) and is always warned by colleagues not to get involved with planning matters. But whether the issue affects the constituency as a whole or a single individual, a determined MP can achieve a lot. MPs are generally very effective advocates for the interests of their constituencies, whether for manufacturing or service industries, farming, fishing, tourism, or on issues that affect their constituents as a whole, such as pollution, commuting, crime or bypasses.

Individual constituency cases arrive in different ways (a lot arise out of the "surgeries" that the new MP is now getting used to holding in different parts of his or her "patch"). The first step is often to define exactly what the problem is; then can follow a letter to the responsible minister, perhaps taking a delegation to see the minister and senior officials; putting down an early day motion (an EDM) to call attention to the issue or the problem, and enlisting the help of the local or national media. The MP may seek one of the half-hour "adjournment debates" at the end of the day's Commons business, or some of the time allocated by the backbench business committee.

Constituency cases can be very taxing: personal tragedies, or difficult asylum cases, are hard to deal with, and backing the individual against unresponsive bureaucracies can be frustrating; but most MPs regard constituency work as the most rewarding and fulfilling part of their job. It is often thoughtlessly said that MPs (especially those who have come to the House through a political apprenticeship) have no experience of "real life". The contents of many constituency surgeries would provide some critics with enough "real life" to last a lifetime; and often the MP is the last resort of the homeless and the hopeless: the people that society has let down.

NO JOB DESCRIPTION

Everyone has a job description, surely? MPs do not, and it is probably a good thing. Every constituency is different, and the range of things that an MP chooses to do can discharge his or her parliamentary duty just as fully as a colleague whose life as an MP may be very different. And an MP may be an outstanding parliamentarian in every way, always attentive to constituents' needs, yet be sacked at the next election because the tide of opinion is in favour of another party.

One of the first things a new MP must learn is time management. A conscientious Member of Parliament could easily spend 24 hours of every day on parliamentary work, and an MP must quickly master prioritisation, delegation and the effective use of staff. Not all do; and they are often the ones who end up on the wrong side of the tension between activity and achievement. It is easy to be seen here, there and everywhere, and to become a "rent-a-quote" MP, but it is often more difficult and less glamorous to make a real difference.

HOW DOES THE HOUSE WORK?

Just as MPs have no job description, parliament has no mission statement. Every politics A-level student knows what it is supposed to do (legislate, authorise taxation, grant supply to the government of the day, represent constituents, call the government to account and act as a focus of the nation's attention in times of crisis, mourning and celebration). But, as we have no written constitution, nowhere are these functions formally prescribed.

Parliament is always said to be "sovereign" but it does not govern the country (although in Gladstone's words it "calls to account those who do"). It sits comfortably with the role of the Queen as head of state, but it does not control the way that the executive exercises patronage through honours and appointments, controls the structure of government and appoints and dismisses ministers. This "sovereignty" is really legislative supremacy, which is not constrained by a constitution, but only by practical circumstances. So legislation must be consistent with the Human Rights Act, with UK membership of the European Union, and with devolution to the various parts of the UK, but the Westminster parliament could unmake those arrangements, however politically awkward or administratively difficult that might be.

At the same time, though, legislative supremacy limits the powers of parliament, because one parliament cannot bind its successors, and no parliament can entrench an Act to prevent a successor parliament simply repealing it.

THE SIZE OF THE HOUSE

The House of Commons has always been large. In the 1400s it had 250 members and by 1673 there were 513 MPs. The addition of Scotland and then Ireland brought the number to 658, and it reached its peak at 707 in 1918, with reductions to 615 (Irish independence) in 1922 and successively to 659, 646 (reduction post-Scottish devolution), and then to 650 in 2010 (533 MPs in England, 59 in Scotland, 40 in Wales and 18 in Northern Ireland). Even for more than 64 million people, this is a large House. It means that there is a lot of competition for parliamentary opportunities: asking questions, speaking in debates, and so on. It produces big governments: in the last parliament there were 121 ministers, of whom 94 sat in the Commons. Adding the more than 50 parliamentary private secretaries (senior ministers' aides) this produces a "payroll vote" of about 150 (the cast-iron votes that the government of the day can always rely on).

The advantage of a big House — and it will still be a big House even if, as the Conservative government has promised, proposals to reduce it to 600 MPs are carried through — is that constituencies are fairly small. On average, there is one MP for every 98,600 people, or every 71,000 people entitled to vote. In turn this means that an individual MP's focus on the interests of a constituency can be very sharp, because Westminster constituencies (unlike those of the European Parliament) each have a clear local character.

PARLIAMENTARY TIMETABLES

A parliament is the period from the day of first meeting of the new parliament (in 2015, 18 May) to the date of the dissolution of parliament (see the Fixed-term Parliaments Act below). A session is the period from one state opening until the session is ended by prorogation, typically just less than a year later. Prorogation clears the decks; any Bill not passed by then falls, and a few days later a new Queen's Speech at the next state opening outlines the government's plans for the new session.

An adjournment is any time when the House is not sitting; the periodic adjournments (or recesses) follow the holiday seasons: Whitsun (one or two weeks) the summer (six or seven weeks, followed by the September sitting and then a three-week conference recess). The House is normally adjourned for two weeks at Christmas, a week in February (the "constituency recess") and two weeks at Easter, with prorogation following in April or early May. The House can be recalled at any time if the government requests it; in the last parliament, the House was recalled in July 2011 (public confidence in the media and the police after the phone-hacking affair), August 2011 (public disorder), April 2013 (death of Margaret Thatcher) and August 2013 (possible military action in Syria).

The House sits at 2.30pm on Mondays, 11.30am on Tuesdays and Wednesdays, and 9.30am on Thursdays and Fridays. Each sitting starts with four minutes of prayers, and then (except on Fridays) question time for an hour. Then come any urgent questions granted by the Speaker, which force a minister to come to the dispatch box to answer for half an hour or more; and statements by ministers, on a range of government policies or actions, or reporting events to parliament. The main business of the day follows, which may be the second reading (or subsequent stage) of a Bill, or an opposition day debate, of which there are 20 in a session, when the opposition (or, on three days, the minor parties) choose the ground on which to attack the government.

The "moment of interruption" is the time at which the scheduled business of the day normally finishes (although some items, such as financial business or a statutory instrument, can be taken for longer), and is at 10pm on Mondays, 7pm on Tuesdays and Wednesdays, 5pm on Thursdays and 2.30pm on Fridays. Then follows the half-hour adjournment debate in which a topic (which may range from something of international importance down to a constituency case) is raised by an individual backbencher and replied to by a minister in a largely empty chamber. The House then adjourns.

The House of Commons takes many of its decisions without a vote, either because the matter is not contentious, or because it is not sufficiently important; but when there is disagreement between the two sides of the House, or dissent on the part of a group of MPs or even a single individual, there is a vote or division. The occupant of the chair puts the question, the division bells ring and MPs file through the "Aye" and "No" lobbies, where their names are taken by the division clerks and they are counted by two tellers per lobby, one from each side of the issue. MPs have eight minutes to get to the voting lobbies, and the whole process takes about 15 minutes. This may seem excessive, but divisions have a sociological role that is nothing to do with voting. An MP may get the chance to raise an issue privately with a minister, or perhaps garner support for a cause, an amendment, or an EDM, and these few minutes chatting, catching up with some colleagues and buttonholing others are valued by MPs.

TIME IN THE HOUSE

The House of Commons normally sits on about 150 days in a calendar year, about the same as the House of Lords and much more than most parliaments. Since the late 19th and early 20th century, the control of most parliamentary time has been in the hands of the government, and this is still largely true. Debating time not owned by the government consists of the 20 opposition days a session, three days on the financial estimates, initiated by select committees, and 13 Fridays on private member's bills, together with the half-hour adjournment debate each sitting day. In 2010 the backbench business committee was established. It is chaired by a backbencher, and is allocated 27 days' debating time in the House, which it apportions on the basis of applications made by backbench MPs. The backbench business committee has taken some time out of the ownership of the government; but in common with opposition days, estimates days and private member's bill days, it is the government that decides when time is to be allocated.

Since 1999, debates have also been held "in Westminster Hall" — in fact in the large committee room at the north end of the ancient hall. These take place on Mondays, Tuesdays and Wednesdays and are initiated by backbenchers or select committees. The backbench business committee also has eight days allocated here. This parallel chamber, in which there cannot be votes, provides about 400 hours of debating time in a session, compared with 1,200 hours of sitting time in the House itself.

Over the past ten years the amount of time spent on business initiated by the government has fallen from 60 per cent of the total to about 35 per cent, while time spent on business initiated by backbenchers has risen from 10 per cent to about 25 per cent. The main categories of business are government bills, which occupy about 25 per cent of total time, backbench business (13 per cent), oral questions (11 per cent), opposition days (10 per cent) and government statements (7 per cent).

PROCEDURE

The House of Commons is a highly procedural House, although much less so than it used to be. Some form of procedure is needed to regulate any deliberative body, the more so where, as in parliament, there is contention. Commons procedure derives from the Standing Orders (a 200-page booklet), rulings from the chair over the years, which are recorded and distilled in Erskine May, the authoritative textbook of parliamentary procedure, and a small number of acts of parliament (for example setting out how royal assent to bills is to be signified, and the process for oaths and affirmations). Procedure also comes from the practice of the House. For example, there is no formal rule that says that bills have to be read three times before being passed; they just always have been.

Commons procedure owes its complexity to having to deal with often fierce political contention, and to the range of complicated issues with which parliament deals. Good procedural rules should be consistent, so that the same things are dealt with in the same way; certain, so that their operation is known and accepted; and above all clear, so that they themselves do not become the source of contention. MPs know the myriad rules of the House much less well than many of them used to but advice is always on hand from the clerks of the House in the public bill office, the table office and the journal office, as well as at the table of the House itself.

PRIVILEGE

The practical operation of privilege can be very complicated, but it has two key elements, and both allow parliament and its members to perform their duties without outside threat or interference. The first is freedom of speech, underpinned by Article 9 of the Bill of Rights 1688 but with much older origins. This means that no MP can be sued or prosecuted for anything said in proceedings in parliament, which includes debates, questions, EDMs, and select committee inquiries (in which witnesses are similarly protected). The second element is exclusive cognisance, which is the freedom of each House to regulate its own affairs, and in practice means that what is done in, say, passing bills, cannot be investigated or adjudicated upon by the courts or any other body.

"Privilege" is an unfortunate word, implying as it does some special personal treatment. Unlike MPs in many European countries, members of the House of Commons do not have a personal immunity simply because they are Members of Parliament; they have only those protections that are necessary for them to do their jobs: perhaps to speak out against unacceptable behaviour of rich, powerful (and litigious) individuals, or to attack financial or bureaucratic mismanagement, without the fear of lawsuits or prosecution. Privilege has to be used with responsibility, of course; but it is essential to the role of the House of Commons and its members.

SELECT COMMITTEES

If one of the tasks of the House of Commons is to hold the government of the day to account in detail, then select committees provide the firepower. They also have a high reputation outside the Westminster village, and their work makes a refreshing change from the collision of party policies across the floor of the chamber.

Select committee members are almost always backbench MPs and the committees, which involve a majority of those backbenchers (about 300 in a typical session), are just beginning to provide a career alternative to ministerial or shadow office.

House of Commons select committees have been around for a long time. In the 16th and 17th centuries, they were often set up quickly to deal with some issue too detailed for the House itself to handle. In the Journals of the House of that era we find the work of select committees on the Prayer Book and on Mary Queen of Scots, as well as regular committees on the Subsidy (the money to be voted to the Crown) and the Grand Committee for Evils, among many others. The classic 19th-century committee was the highly influential select committee on the Army before Sebastopol, which exposed high-level incompetence and whose appointment led to the fall of Lord Aberdeen's government. The select committee system had a serious setback with the committees on the Jameson raid and on the Marconi scandal in the early 20th century because they divided on bitter party lines. The post-Second World War era saw a gradual increase in confidence but a haphazard coverage of government activity.

The modern select committee system was established in 1979 when Norman St John-Stevas, as Leader of the House (and in a moment of Margaret Thatcher's inattention), took up a procedure committee proposal for select committees linked to government departments, examining their administration, policy and expenditure. This is the basis of the current departmental committee system, which accounts for the majority of select committee activity in the Commons: 19 select committees each shadow a government department and its executive agencies, and the associated regulators and inspectors. If government departments change (as often with a change of government) then the select committee structure changes to match.

The work of a typical departmental select committee is a good vehicle for explaining how most select committees operate. Their task is set out in their orders of reference agreed by the House, which are usually in pretty general terms, giving a lot of flexibility. The departmental select committees, for example, are given the job of examining "the expenditure, administration and policy" of their government department and its associated agencies.

Select committees have the power "to send for persons, papers and records", which has more moral than legal force: the threat of political embarrassment is often the best way to get a recalcitrant witness to attend and answer questions. It has been suggested that this power should be enshrined in statute, but the idea was sensibly rejected by the joint committee on parliamentary privilege in 2013 on the grounds that any problems were rare and that the involvement of the courts would change the character of select committee proceedings, with witnesses coming "lawyered-up" to evidence sessions.

The chairs of most select committees have since 2010 been elected by the House as a whole. They may serve for no longer than two parliaments, or for eight years, whichever is the longer. The chairs of a busy select committee can spend three or more working days a week on committee business and since 2003 most have been paid £14,728 a year in addition to their pay as MPs.

The election of committee chairs has been a positive step, and has widened opportunities. The installation in the last parliament of Rory Stewart and Sarah Wollaston, new to parliament at the 2010 general election, to chair two heavyweight committees — defence and health respectively — would never have happened under the previous whip-controlled system.

As always in the House of Commons, though, the law of unintended consequences has been at work, and one less welcome effect of the election of chairs is that the House, and not the committee, is now the chair's power-base, and on two or three select committees this has had an unwelcome effect on committee cohesion.

Members of a select committee are in the same party proportions, or as close as possible, as the House, and the members of most select committees are elected by their parties. The quorum is three or a quarter of the total number of members, whichever is the larger, with fractions counted as one. Active membership of a busy select committee can take up a lot of an MP's scarce time, perhaps two days a week or more.

The staff of a select committee are drawn from the House of Commons Service, and so are politically impartial. A departmental select committee will usually have a staff of about six, led by the clerk of the committee. They will usually be supplemented by specialist advisers: people from outside the House, often of great distinction in their field.

A committee's initial programme of work will be agreed at the start of a parliament, and adapted and updated as events unfold. There is no one template for a select committee inquiry; they may last for a year, or be a quick inquiry into some burning current issue. Committees may hold evidence sessions without producing a report, and this is a good way to get progress reports from public bodies and regulators in their field. Committees' reports should be responded to by the government within two months of publication.

Departmental select committees are expected to carry out "core tasks" to structure and focus their work: in their subject areas, to examine strategic issues, policy and performance, expenditure, draft bills, bills and delegated legislation (although this does not replace the formal legislative processes), to scrutinise European issues, public appointments and the effectiveness of acts of parliament. They are also expected to contribute to the wider work of the House, and play an active role in parliament's public engagement and outreach.

The classic way to gather evidence is to hold oral evidence sessions at

Westminster (usually on the basis of papers submitted by the witnesses), in addition to gathering written evidence; but committees are increasingly innovative, getting away from the predictable "usual suspects" witnesses, holding seminars and using social media to extend the reach of an inquiry.

Most select committees treat their witnesses with courtesy, and get more out of them as a result ("more flies are caught with honey than with vinegar"). In the last parliament, there was an increasing tendency on the part of (very few) select committees to harangue and insult witnesses. It may be that some witnesses richly deserve criticism — and such exchanges certainly produce headlines — but select committees derive their authority from basing their conclusions on the evidence they take. Considered criticism in an agreed report is much harder to shrug off than insults across a committee table.

There is a more serious point. The possibility of a formal right of reply for people criticised in parliamentary proceedings has been on the table for some time. If a committee is a "tribunal" for the purposes of the European Convention on Human Rights, and it damages reputations without due process, such behaviour will add to pressure for such a change.

Most select committees travel, both in the UK and abroad; and although travel attracts media attention (especially if it is to sunny climes) it is an unrivalled way to find out how other governments and countries tackle a particular issue.

Engaging with a select committee is straightforward. You can find out about current and forthcoming inquiries on each committee's pages on the parliament.uk website, and you can also see most of the evidence that has been submitted, as well as any previous reports the committee has made on the subject. If you want to submit something in writing, this should be done online in Word format. You can ask to give oral evidence, but it may be difficult for the committee to accommodate this in a crowded inquiry timetable. Written or oral, your evidence will be more persuasive the more constructive and innovative it is.

Other Commons select committees fall into three categories: the "cross-cutting" committees, which are not confined to a single government department. In this category are the environmental audit committee; the liaison committee, consisting of all select committee chairs, which among other things takes evidence from the prime minister; the public accounts committee, which draws on the work of the National Audit Office; the public administration committee; and the European scrutiny committee, which scrutinises European issues and especially proposals for European legislation, publishes weekly reports identifying issues of importance, and can recommend debates on the more contentious proposals. Also in this category is the joint committee on the national security strategy (with an equal membership from the House of Lords).

The second category comprises committees who carry out legislative-type work: the joint committees of both Houses on consolidation bills (which simplify the law without changing its substance); on human rights; on regulatory reform; and on statutory instruments.

"Internal" committees are concerned with the way that the House and its members work, and comprise the backbench business committee and committees on procedure, selection (mainly selecting MPs to serve on legislative committees), privileges, standards (of MPs' behaviour), finance and services, and administration (these two last are part of the House administration).

Furthermore, the House may set up ad hoc committees at any time, either Commons-only or, by agreement with the Lords, joint committees (like the banking commission in 2012). So there is no shortage of choice should our new MPs want to go on to a select committee, and there is a great deal of activity. There are 1,300 select committee meetings a year, of which about 900 are public evidence hearings, and committees publish more than 300 reports each year.

So how effective are select committees? There is no point in totting up recommendations accepted by the government and others; that makes no distinction between soft recommendations that are already halfway to being implemented, and tough recommendations that the government is not going to accept, but which may change opinion more widely, and may form the basis for a policy of the next government.

Select committees can go where the parties may fear to tread, not being willing to risk being associated with a "courageous" and possibly unpopular proposal. And committees can provide an authoritative platform for the examination and debate of complex issues, especially where the smoke of controversy has obscured the facts.

So far as the government is concerned, successful select committees provide a climate of accountability, in which ministers and their civil servants cannot be sure when the spotlight of an inquiry will swing their way; as Robin Cook used to say: "Good scrutiny makes for good government."

Select committees are a Westminster success story, at a very reasonable price of less than £20 million a year in total. They play well with the public, who like to see MPs working across political boundaries and achieving consensus (and a tough unanimous report is all the harder for the government to ignore). They encourage MPs to leave their preconceptions and party views at the door of the committee room, and instead to form opinions based firmly on the evidence they hear. And perhaps as valuable as anything else they do, select committees provide access to the political process. Anyone can put ideas to them, and good ideas are often taken up, no matter who has suggested them.

LEGISLATION

Select committees may be popular, but the way Westminster legislates has few admirers. There are various reasons for this: there is too much legislation; it is often not thoroughly thought out; and there is too little parliamentary time to consider it properly. The remark attributed to Bismarck comes to mind: "Laws are like sausages; you don't want to see them being made."

Let us start with some definitions: bills that end up as acts of parliament, or statutes, are primary legislation. Bills are of three sorts. The majority are public bills, which change the law of the land. They apply to everyone (some may apply specifically to Scotland, Wales or Northern Ireland, but less so now after extensive devolution). Most public bills are government bills, of which there are 30 or more passed each session. Private members' bills are public bills, but are promoted by backbenchers, and should not be confused with private bills, which have a local or personal effect. They may be used to give, say, a local authority power to do something (build a livestock market, perhaps, or take over common land) which would otherwise not be legal.

Bills that implement major matters of public policy, but which also affect local and personal interests in different ways, are hybrid bills, like that to build the HS2 railway. Each of these categories is dealt with in a different way, but the bulk of legislation is in the form of public bills, and it is simplest to concentrate on these before looking at secondary legislation.

PRIMARY LEGISLATION

Government bills can have a variety of origins: they may fulfil manifesto commitments, implement changes in policy, give effect to international commitments, or respond to events. The parliamentary business and legislation committee of the Cabinet (PBL) is the gatekeeper for which bills come forward, when, and which bills will start in the Commons and which in the Lords, to make the best use of the time available. Once drafting instructions (what the bill is to achieve, and how) are agreed within government (often involving the devolved administrations), it is the task of parliamentary counsel, a group of specialist drafters, to turn the proposals into effective legal terms (and to ensure that they fit with what is already on the statute book). There will normally be a consultation process, but this tends to involve only "the usual suspects" outside government, and to be fairly short.

The first parliamentary appearance of a bill is when it is introduced, a formality without debate. The second reading will usually take place after two weekends have passed. This is the debate on the principle of a bill, usually for most of a sitting (about five or six hours). The bill is then sent to committee. The default setting is a relatively small public bill committee, but "constitutional" and some other major bills will go to a committee of the whole House, in which any MP can participate. Bills may also be sent to a select committee, which is rare (although of course any select committee can express views on a bill within its subject area).

A public bill committee, normally of 16 to 30 MPs, begins examination of the bill (if it has started in the Commons) by taking evidence on it in "select committee mode" and then debating the provisions of the bill and amendments proposed to it. These amendments are selected and grouped by the chair and clerk of the committee. The idea is that interdependent amendments, and those on a theme, will be debated together no matter where they apply to the bill, thus making the best use of the committee's time. This is often described as "line-by-line" scrutiny, but it is much more about using amendments as vehicles for attacking the proposals in the bill.

At the end of the committee stage, the bill has a report stage on the floor of the House, typically for most of a day's sitting. This is often a rerun of committee arguments, but in the larger forum of the chamber, and under greater pressure of time. This is followed by a relatively brief debate on third reading. The bill is then passed and taken to the Lords, where broadly the same processes are followed.

A contentious feature of legislation in the Commons is the programming of bills. The government proposes a schedule allocating time in committee, and time on report and third reading. This is decided without debate and is not in practice amendable. The original idea of programming was sensible: to ensure that the parts of a bill received debating time commensurate with their importance, rather than the whole process being "front-loaded" as the opposition sought simply to delay a bill they disliked. In practice, however, programming is a useful tool for the government's business managers and its purpose may be defeated if the opposition's ploy is to demonstrate that parts of a bill have not been debated at all in the Commons.

The conventional wisdom is that it is the Lords who have to put matters right, using their expertise and experience to scrutinise the details of a bill, especially the bits that the Commons failed to examine. This conjures up a picture of the Commons' homework coming back from the Lords covered in red ink; but of course it is not quite like that.

The House of Lords undoubtedly does an effective job of examining legislation, but one advantage of Westminster's bicameral system is that it allows a government more easily to have second thoughts, and to make amendments in the second House to reflect undertakings or commitments given in the first. Academic research on 12 bills in the last two parliaments found that, of the 498 amendments made in the Lords, 88 per cent were government amendments. Of these, 65 per cent had their origins with Lords committees or members. But a total of 2,384 amendments had been tabled to these bills in the Lords, and so nearly 2,000 of these were not made.

Any Lords amendments to a Commons bill go back to the Commons, where they are considered under the timetable, often for only an hour, and any disagreements go back to the Lords. This "ping-pong" continues until a compromise is reached, or the Lords back down (as they will normally do if the elected House insists), and the bill goes for royal assent. If agreement cannot be reached on a bill (so-called "double insistence") the bill falls. If the Lords will not pass a bill, it can be presented for royal assent under the Parliament Acts without the agreement of the Lords, after a delay of (in practice) 13 months; but this procedure has been used only four times in the past 65 years.

How could the legislative process be improved? The biggest potential improvement is always in the hands of the government: legislate less, and give parliament more time. But governments (and senior ministers) are always in a hurry — to make their mark, to try to keep ahead of the game, to implement policy in statute — and so it is governments, and not parliament, who must take the blame for the quality of legislation being enacted.

The tools at parliament's disposal are limited, and spending more time on legislation would take time from other functions. Some of the possibilities are assessed below.

Private member's bills are public bills, but of a special type. They come to the House in four main ways: the ballot bills are introduced in the fifth week of a session following a sort of legislative raffle into which almost all backbenchers put their names. Presentation bills may be introduced on any day and ten-minute rule bills are introduced, if the House gives leave, after a ten-minute speech by the proposer (which may be opposed). Private peers' bills come from the Lords in the same way as other bills. Thirteen days are allotted for consideration of private member's bills: seven days for second readings, and six for remaining stages (in which the bills are arranged on the order paper with the most advanced stage (Lords amendments) first. Because no private member's bill may be introduced until the ballot bills have been presented, it follows that they have the best of the slim chances of success.

It is unlikely that any private member's bill will be passed unless it has at least the tacit support of the government. Some "handout" bills are government bills in all but name, and a backbencher who takes one up will have the attractive prospect of the support of a department's civil servants in drafting speeches, advising on amendments and so on.

Presentation and ten-minute rule bills are really ways of bringing a legislative proposal to public attention. Occasionally, with a fair wind, one may make progress, but this is rare. The success rate of private member's bills is about half a dozen a year (but this includes "handout" bills). The way in which a private member's bill can be talked out, or fall victim to a range of procedural tactics, has led to much frustration.

SECONDARY LEGISLATION OR STATUTORY INSTRUMENTS

The original idea of secondary legislation (sometimes called delegated or subordinate legislation, and including "orders", "rules", "schemes", "orders in council" and "codes of practice" — the Highway Code is actually a piece of delegated legislation) was to set out matters of detail, or things that might change, without needing further primary legislation.

That was fairly uncontroversial, but over the years ministers of all parties in government have found secondary legislation very convenient. Not only can details (sometimes surprisingly contentious details) be put in a type of legislation that is less well scrutinised than primary legislation but, when the pressure is on to finalise bills before introduction, details can be finalised later, and second thoughts accommodated.

Statutory instruments can be made only if the powers to do so (which are usually given to ministers) are in an act of parliament ("the parent act"). There are five levels of parliamentary control: the lowest is "no need to inform or consult parliament"; then "lay before parliament, but no decision required"; next are "negative instruments", laid before parliament and brought into force unless either House resolves that the instrument be annulled; then "affirmative instruments", laid before parliament in draft and cannot be made unless approved by both Houses. The most demanding process is the super-affirmative procedure, for which both Houses have special committees, which can require instruments to be amended and then relaid.

In the Commons, affirmative instruments are usually referred to a debating committee, which (often only after very brief consideration) reports them to the House, and the decision to approve is then taken without debate. Negative instruments can also be "sent upstairs" to committee, usually at the request of the opposition.

The main problem (not just for parliament, but also for people who may be affected) is the sheer volume of secondary legislation, which runs at about 3,000 instruments and 11,000 or more printed pages a year. A lot of this is ephemeral, but sifting and scrutinising what is not is a substantial task. The House of Lords, with its delegated powers and regulatory reform committee (which looks in particular at the powers proposed in each bill to make secondary legislation after the bill has been passed) and the secondary legislation scrutiny committee (which sifts instruments of political importance) does this better than the Commons; but nevertheless the tide of statutory instruments is more than parliament can cope with effectively.

PARLIAMENTARY QUESTIONS

Questions were once the jewel in the crown of the House of Commons, but have changed character completely over the past 40 years or so. The threat "I shall put down a question in the House" was once a daunting one, but no longer. Questions in the hands of determined MPs can still, however, be an effective weapon.

Questions are asked primarily of the government, although some other bodies (primarily the House of Commons Commission, the body that oversees the administration of the House, the Electoral Commission, the Church Commissioners and the Public Accounts Commission, which oversees the National Audit Office) answer MPs' questions via a nominated backbencher.

Questions must, in essence, seek information or press for action. The other rules for questions include: they must be within the responsibilities of ministers (so not asking about the cost of opposition policies, nor asking about detailed decisions of devolved administrations or of local authorities, or about the operation of the courts or operational policing); they should not offer information ("is the minister aware ...?"); not seek confirmation of press reports or rumours; not repeat a question fully answered in the previous three months; and not ask about matters *sub judice* (before the courts). MPs table questions online or in the table office, a small office behind the Speaker's chair, where the table office clerks enforce the rules for questions but, more important, help an MP to get questions into order, and to frame them in a way that is most likely to produce results.

Oral questions occupy the first hour of every day's business after prayers, except on a Friday, and government departments answer according to a rota that the government itself draws up, but which brings each department to the head of the queue every five weeks, often sharing the question hour with one or more smaller departments. An MP must table an oral question before 12.30pm three days before a department is due to answer; all the questions then go into a random computer shuffle, but only the first 25 (for a full hour's question time) are printed.

When an MP is called to ask a question, he or she says only the number on the order paper, the minister answers and the MP, followed by other backbenchers and often the shadow minister, ask supplementary questions. It is always said that the most effective supplementary is "Why?" or "When?" or "How much?" because ministers get no time to refer to their extensive briefing folders. But oral questions have become in recent years more an exchange of assertions than an interrogative process, and this change was hastened a few years ago by the ending of the rule against reading or quoting during question time.

On most days, the final 15 minutes of question time is given over to topical questions; a backbencher asks the secretary of state to make a statement on his or her departmental responsibilities, which usually elicits the department's good news for the past month, and then the backbencher asks a supplementary and is followed by other backbenchers. No questions are printed on the order paper, and the ministers on the government front bench must decide almost instantaneously which one of them is going to answer.

Question time can be pretty formulaic but when a minister is badly briefed, or is trying to defend the indefensible, the theatrical brutality of the Commons can take over, and it is a most effective way of asserting parliamentary control over the executive. As Macaulay said more than two centuries ago, "a more terrible audience there is not in the world".

The most high-profile event of the parliamentary week is prime minister's questions (PMQs), which takes place at 12.30pm every Wednesday. Fifteen MPs' names are drawn in the shuffle, and it is a coveted prime-time parliamentary opportunity. The leader of the opposition has a ration of six supplementaries, which he can take in a block or two lots of three, and the focus of PMQs is the duel between him and the prime minister, a duel that has become more bitter and personal over the past decade. Opinions about PMQs are divided. There are those who revel in the jolt of parliamentary adrenaline produced by the fiery atmosphere in the chamber, and there are those who are repelled by the noise and the atmosphere, which is sometimes that of an unruly junior common room. As suggested below, some change will almost certainly come about in the new parliament.

In each session, about 4,000 questions are answered orally in the chamber;

but as many as 50,000 written questions will be asked and answered. MPs may ask ordinary written questions, which are put down formally for two days ahead but which the government is expected to answer within two weeks; or they may table named-day questions for a minimum of three days ahead, but which are expected to be answered on the day specified. There is a limit of five named-day questions per MP per day. From September 2014 the written question process went entirely online, and questions and answers are now paperless.

If oral questions are a way of challenging the government in the more theatrical surroundings of the chamber, written questions can be a more systematic process of eliciting information and exposing the government to criticism (by opposition MPs, but also by its own backbenchers). The rules are the same, although a minister can refuse to answer if the estimated cost of doing so (known as the advisory cost limit) would be disproportionate (at the moment £850).

In the right hands written questions can be very effective, although there is a justified suspicion that a great many written questions are tabled (especially using the e-tabling system) by MPs' staffers with very little involvement by the MP. One way of making this more difficult, and requiring the personal involvement of the elected member, would be to make e-tabling credentials much stronger, but MPs have so far been unwilling to do this, perhaps because they find the present arrangements convenient.

LOOKING AHEAD: THE PROSPECTS FOR THE 2015 PARLIAMENT

In the run-up to the 2010 general election, the Commons clerks, taking counsel from the opinion polls, were thinking about scenarios for a minority government (some had experienced three such periods in the House: 1974, 1978-79 and 1996-97). In the event the Coalition Agreement produced a conventional majoritarian government with comfortable control of the House, not without problems, of course, but the problems were more political than parliamentary. There were some oddities: the prime minister made a statement to the House responding to the report by Lord Justice Leveson on phone-hacking and press regulation, and answered questions from MPs; this was immediately followed by his deputy making a dissenting statement on the same subject, and also answering questions (but even this was not unprecedented).

The landscape of the 2015 parliament is very different, with single-party government, albeit with a small majority. There is an element of continuity, in that some of the most senior ministerial roles are unchanged. At the same time there are greater opportunities for Conservative backbenchers, in that ministerial posts do not have to be shared with a coalition partner.

Our MPs newly elected in May 2015 will find that their votes, if not their views, are eagerly courted. They will be keen to get their maiden speeches over and done with, and to settle down to the business of being professional Members of Parliament. They will need to strike a balance between what they themselves want to do and what they are expected to do for their parties.

The private member's bill ballot and elections to select committees are important milestones in their early weeks, and they will have joined more all-party groups than they later think wise or sustainable.

The House of Commons will be changing around them. The last parliament introduced new rules for the election of the deputy speakers, and of members and chairs of select committees; responsibility for MPs' pay and allowances was transferred away from parliament to the Independent Parliamentary Standards

Authority; the backbench business committee was established, taking time away from the government and giving new debating opportunities to MPs. Sitting times changed: on Tuesdays from 2.30pm to 11.30am, and on Thursdays from 10.30am to 9.30am. Debates on e-petitions started in Westminster Hall on Mondays. The Fixed-term Parliaments Act introduced significant constitutional change.

THE LIKELY CHANGES IN THE 2015 PARLIAMENT

Restoration and renewal One of the biggest issues in the foreground is the one that almost everyone has very successfully managed to ignore for much too long: the condition of the Palace of Westminster. The Palace was completed in the middle of the 19th century, and almost nothing has been done to it since (apart from replacing the Commons chamber destroyed in 1941). The problem is that there has never been a right time to give the Palace the overhaul it has needed; it would have been too expensive, too embarrassing, too disruptive, "too soon after the War" (which gives you an idea of how chronic the problem is).

As technology has advanced, new services have been put higgledy-piggledy over the old, and the basement now contains miles and miles of pipes and wires, carrying water, air-conditioning, high-pressure steam, sewage, electricity, communications, IT and so on. Many of the wires and pipes are unidentifiable. At the same time, the outer stonework is crumbling and the roofs are leaking.

The report of a consortium led by Deloitte Real Estate will be published soon after the general election. It will assess three options: first, "super-aggressive maintenance" in other words, trying to deal with the problems while the building is in use, which might mean years of parliament meeting in a building site; secondly, a "Cox and Box" decant to other premises, of first one House and then the other. The difficulty with this is that there is a lot of (properly contained) asbestos in the building, and a half-and-half decant (and installation of new services by halves) might not be practical.

The third option is the most radical: to decant the whole of parliament for five or six years. There is a lot of emotional opposition to this but if, say, the main sewer collapses, parliament will be decanting within days, never mind the 2020 parliament. Given the truth of Churchill's remark that "we shape our buildings, and afterwards our buildings shape us", will a full decant, and adaptation to different physical surroundings, make a difference to the way the Commons operates? A lot of people think it might, and that MPs in 2025 might be more comfortable with a hemicycle chamber rather than one with two opposing sides.

The key issue may seem simple, but it is not: the two Houses are independent and one cannot tell the other what to do, but clearly they must agree on which option to take.

The Fixed-term Parliaments Act 2011 For as long as the office of prime minister has been recognised, the PM has been able to ask the Sovereign for a dissolution of parliament and so a general election, usually at a time of political advantage for the PM's own party, although this has not always been successful, as Edward Heath found to his cost in February 1974.

The formation of the Conservative/Liberal Democrat coalition in May 2010 changed all that. A key element of the Coalition Agreement was to have a fixed five-year term for each parliament, with polling day in the general election being the first Thursday in May every five years. This reassured the Lib Dems as the junior partners that the prime minister would not be able to end the coalition simply by seeking a dissolution, and it was also said to have been necessary to give the financial markets confidence.

There are two humane killers in the act: if a motion for "an early general election" (that is, before the five years are up) is agreed by at least two thirds of the House of Commons, including vacant seats; or if a motion of no confidence is passed (by a simple majority) and no motion of confidence (either in the original government or an alternative) is passed within 14 days.

The act has come in for a lot of criticism. First, why set a five-year term? The average length of parliament from 1945 to 2010 was three years and ten months. Five years was said by the government to be an incentive to sustainable long-term decision making; but this was unsurprisingly interpreted as a way of keeping the coalition in power for that period.

Moreover, although there are two ways in which a general election can take place before the five years are up, the act does not deal with the situation where the government is defeated on a major matter of public policy, perhaps on the Queen's Speech, the Finance Bill or the estimates. Lashed to the mast of the Fixed-term Parliaments Act, presumably in those circumstances the government has to limp on until things get worse, losing both its credibility and its authority to govern.

The act has serious flaws, and its days may well be numbered. It is now not needed as the glue in a coalition, and a prime minister with a small majority may be attracted by a return to the situation where he is able to seek a dissolution of parliament at a time of his choosing.

Will parliamentary questions stay the same? There will be increasing pressure to "do something" about prime minister's questions. It represents a great opportunity for the Commons: the chance to question the nation's chief executive for half an hour every sitting week, but more and more people dislike the gladiatorial combat and see it as a wasted opportunity. A constructive move would be to have, say, every other PMQs in a committee room, where backbenchers drawn by lot, just as in the House, would have the opportunity to question the PM in calmer and more courteous surroundings.

The success of topical questions, in effect questions without notice, may encourage turning all question times into questions without notice, while allowing MPs to table a substantive question should they prefer to do so.

The size of the House of Commons Before the 2010 election all three major parties committed themselves to reducing the cost of politics after the expenses scandal of 2009. The Conservative/Lib Dem coalition undertook to reduce the size of the House of Commons from 650 to 600. As far as reducing the cost of politics was concerned, a reduction in the size of the Commons of less than 8 per cent was seen as marginal, indeed illogical in view of the increase in the size of the House of Lords. In the event, the coalition partners fell out over reform of the Lords, and one of the casualties was the formal boundary review that would have made the change but was abandoned in January 2013.

The Conservative election victory now makes it likely that this modest reduction in the size of the House, accompanied by a redrawing of constituency boundaries, will take place.

Recall of MPs: a tougher line? The Recall of MPs Act 2015 provided that if an MP were sentenced to a prison term or were suspended from the House for at least 21 days, a "recall petition" could be triggered; if at least 10 per cent of electors in the MP's constituency were to sign the petition, the seat would be declared vacant and a by-election would take place. There may be pressure to make the conditions tougher, for example vacating a seat if an MP changes allegiance to the party other than that for which he or she was elected, and reducing the 21-day suspension trigger, but change is unlikely.

Digital by default There will be a step-change in the use of new technology by parliament. Business will routinely be done using mobile devices; the quantity of printing material (and the expense) will fall dramatically. Engagement and interaction with parliament will be e-enabled to a much greater degree. Online voting, although a Holy Grail for some, will probably not make progress in this parliament.

Setting the agenda There will be renewed pressure to set up a House business committee to set the Commons agenda. This was promised in the Coalition Agreement to be established "by the third year of the [2010] parliament" but there was little progress towards agreement. Part of the difficulty has been that expectations of a House business committee vary considerably. Would it be "the usual channels" (the business managers) meeting in public, or meeting in private and formally reporting their proposals? Or would it be the full-fat option of a voteable agenda put to the House each week by a committee with a substantial backbench membership?

Can the legislative process be improved? It is probably a forlorn hope to expect governments to legislate less, and at a slower pace, but in the absence of a more measured approach to legislation, there are other options. Draft bills offer real improvements. Ministers have less political capital tied up in a draft bill, and are more amenable to making changes. And a select or joint committee is the ideal body to scrutinise a draft bill, being able to draw on expert opinion and the views of those who will actually be affected by the proposed legislation. The first session, however, is not an ideal time to expect greater use of draft bills, as scarce drafting resources are tied up with the "real" legislative programme, which a new government wants to get on with.

It is sometimes suggested that there should be "framework bills", which set out the main elements of proposed legislation, leaving the details to be settled by delegated legislation, but given how poor scrutiny of delegated legislation is already, this is not attractive. A modest improvement would be purposive clauses, setting out in plain language what each part of a bill was intended to achieve. Another change that would be easy to achieve would be the routine use of "Keeling schedules", which set out how a statute would look when amended as proposed by a bill. At the moment one has to work this out using two or more texts in parallel.

There is, moreover, no reason why the essence of a legislative proposal could not be considered separately from the detailed bill to give it effect. In the 19th century, the House would routinely debate motions to bring in bills, a procedure that survives to this day in the ten-minute rule procedure.

English votes for English laws Harold Macmillan once said "The English, you know, have their virtues: they are a patient people, and loyal, and allow themselves to be governed by the Scots." The success of the SNP in the 2015 general election has cast Macmillan's light-hearted remark in an altogether more serious context.

Before the election, the parties were in competition to deliver on "the vow" of more powers to the people of Scotland, in part to soften the blow to the nationalists of having lost the referendum. At the same time there was an expectation of further devolution (reflected in the manifestos of all three main parties) and of "English votes for English laws" (EVEL), reflected in the Conservative and Lib Dem manifestos; Labour and the Lib Dems proposed tackling the issues through a constitutional convention, accompanied by significant devolution to English cities and counties (Labour) and to local areas (Lib Dems).

If there is to be a separate procedure for EVEL bills (and if the votes of English MPs are to be decisive rather than simply advisory), the process has to start long before a bill gets anywhere near Westminster. In order to apply an EVEL procedure, a Bill needs to be certified as applying only to England. But it is in practice very difficult to separate Wales from the process. So do you store up the Welsh provisions relating to English-only legislation and have a Wales (Miscellaneous Provisions) Bill once a session? If not, then EVEL has already become EWVEWL (English and Welsh votes for English and Welsh laws). And how do you cope with an amendment passed in committee (or in the House of Lords) that turns a certified England-only bill into a UK-wide bill? And how do you deal with Lords amendments to English- (and Welsh-) only bills? In seeking to answer "the West Lothian Question" Sir William McKay's Commission on the consequences of devolution for the House of Commons evidently foresaw problems of this sort, which may be why they went for a type of "legislative consent motion". But if EVEL (or EWVEWL) is to be full strength, the process will be a lot more complicated than many expect.

CONCLUSION

Whatever is in store for the 2015 parliament, and — whether or not the Fixed-term Parliaments Act is repealed — however long it lasts, it will be fascinating both from a political and a constitutional point of view, both in terms of the UK's place in Europe, the extraordinary advance of the SNP and the possibility of greater devolution to the countries and regions of the UK. It is to be hoped that the value of what parliament does (at much less than a tenth of 1 per cent of total government spending) will become better known and understood. It is more important than ever that citizens of the United Kingdom feel ownership of their democratic institutions. Whatever else they do, our new MPs need to foster that sense of ownership.

Robert Rogers, former Clerk of the House of Commons, now sits as the crossbench peer Lord Lisvane in the House of Lords

Her Majesty's Government

THE CABINET

Prime Minister, First Lord of the Treasury and Minister for the Civil Service[16]	David Cameron
Chancellor of the Exchequer and First Secretary of State[4]	George Osborne
Leader of the House of Lords and Lord Privy Seal[8]	Baroness Stowell of Beeston
Secretary of State for the Home Department[15]	Theresa May
Secretary of State for Foreign and Commonwealth Affairs[11]	Philip Hammond
Lord Chancellor and Secretary of State for Justice[14]	Michael Gove
Secretary of State for Defence[12]	Michael Fallon
Secretary of State for Work and Pensions[6]	Iain Duncan Smith
Secretary of State for Health[1]	Jeremy Hunt
Lord President of the Council and Leader of the House of Commons[19]	Chris Grayling
Secretary of State for International Development[5]	Justine Greening
Secretary of State for Education and Minister for Women and Equalities[00]	Nicky Morgan
Secretary of State for Transport[2]	Patrick McLoughlin
Secretary of State for Business, Innovation and Skills and President of the Board of Trade[18]	Sajid Javid
Secretary of State for Northern Ireland[17]	Theresa Villiers
Secretary of State for Environment, Food and Rural Affairs[13]	Elizabeth Truss
Secretary of State for Communities and Local Government[7]	Greg Clark
Secretary of State for Wales[9]	Stephen Crabb
Chancellor of the Duchy of Lancaster[10]	Oliver Letwin
Secretary of State for Culture, Media and Sport[3]	John Whittingdale
Secretary of State for Scotland[21]	David Mundell
Secretary of State for Energy and Climate Change[20]	Amber Rudd

ALSO ATTENDING CABINET

Chief Whip (Parliamentary Secretary to the Treasury)	Mark Harper
Minister of State for Employment	Priti Patel
Minister for the Cabinet Office and Paymaster General	Matthew Hancock
Greg Hands Chief Secretary to the Treasury Attorney-General	Jeremy Wright
Minister without portfolio	Robert Halfon
Minister of State at the Foreign and Commonwealth Office	Baroness Anelay of St Johns
Minister for Small Business, Industry and Enterprise	Anna Soubry

THE CABINET TABLE, JUNE 2015

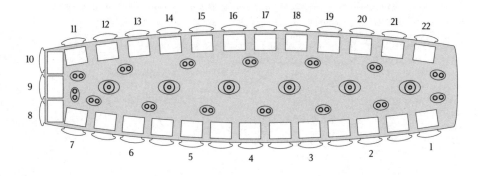

DEPARTMENTAL MINISTERS AND WHIPS

HM TREASURY
Chancellor of the Exchequer
and First Secretary of State
George Osborne
Chief Secretary to the Treasury
Greg Hands
Financial Secretary
David Gauke
Exchequer Secretary
Damian Hinds
Economic Secretary
Harriett Baldwin
Commercial Secretary
Jim O'Neill

HOME OFFICE
Secretary of State for the Home
Department
Theresa May
Minister of State (jointly with the
Ministry of Justice)
Mike Penning
Minister of State
John Hayes
Minister of State
James Brokenshire
Minister of State
Lord Bates
Parliamentary Under Secretary
of State
Karen Bradley
Parliamentary Under Secretary of
State (jointly with the Department
for Transport)
Lord Ahmad of Wimbledon

FOREIGN AND COMMONWEALTH
OFFICE
Secretary of State for Foreign and
Commonwealth Affairs
Philip Hammond
Minister of State
David Lidington
Minister of State
Hugo Swire
Minister of State (Trade and
Investment) (jointly with the
Department for Business,
Innovation and Skills)
Francis Maude

Minister of State
Baroness Anelay of St Johns
Parliamentary Under Secretary
of State
James Duddridge
Parliamentary Under Secretary
of State
Tobias Ellwood

MINISTRY OF JUSTICE
Lord Chancellor, and Secretary of
State for Justice
Michael Gove
Minister of State (jointly with the
Home Office)
Mike Penning
Minister of State
Lord Faulks
Parliamentary Under Secretary
of State
Shailesh Vara
Parliamentary Under Secretary of
State (and an Assistant Whip)
Andrew Selous
Parliamentary Under Secretary
of State
Dominic Raab
Parliamentary Under Secretary of
State (jointly with the Department
for Education)
Caroline Dinenage

MINISTRY OF DEFENCE
Secretary of State for Defence
Michael Fallon
Minister of State
Penny Mordaunt
Minister of State
Philip Dunne
Minister of State (and Deputy
Leader of the House of Lords)
Earl Howe
Parliamentary Under Secretary
of State
Julian Brazier
Parliamentary Under Secretary
of State
Mark Lancaster

DEPARTMENT FOR WORK AND
PENSIONS
Secretary of State for Work and
Pensions
Iain Duncan Smith
Minister of State
Priti Patel
Minister of State
Lord Freud
Minister of State
Ros Altmann
Parliamentary Under Secretary
of State
Justin Tomlinson

DEPARTMENT OF HEALTH
Secretary of State for Health
Jeremy Hunt
Minister of State
Alistair Burt
Parliamentary Under Secretary
of State
Jane Ellison
Parliamentary Under Secretary of
State (jointly with the Department
for Business, Innovation and Skills)
George Freeman
Parliamentary Under Secretary
of State
Ben Gummer
Parliamentary Under Secretary
of State
David Prior

OFFICE OF THE LEADER OF THE
HOUSE OF COMMONS
Lord President of the Council, and
Leader of the House of Commons
Chris Grayling
Parliamentary Secretary (Deputy
Leader of the House of Commons)
Thérèse Coffey

DEPARTMENT FOR
INTERNATIONAL DEVELOPMENT
Secretary of State for International
Development
Justine Greening
Minister of State
Grant Shapps

Minister of State
Desmond Swayne
Parliamentary Under Secretary
of State
Baroness Verma

DEPARTMENT FOR EDUCATION
Secretary of State for Education,
and Minister for Women and
Equalities
Nicky Morgan
Minister of State (jointly with
the Department for Business,
Innovation and Skills)
Nick Boles
Minister of State
Nick Gibb
Minister of State
Edward Timpson
Parliamentary Under Secretary
of State
Lord Nash
Parliamentary Under Secretary
of State
Sam Gyimah
Parliamentary Under Secretary of
State (jointly with the Ministry of
Justice)
Caroline Dinenage

**OFFICE OF THE LEADER OF THE
HOUSE OF LORDS**
Leader of the House of Lords and
Lord Privy Seal
Baroness Stowell of Beeston
Deputy Leader of the House of
Lords (and Minister of State at the
Ministry of Defence)
Earl Howe

DEPARTMENT FOR TRANSPORT
Secretary of State for Transport
Patrick McLoughlin
Parliamentary Under Secretary
of State
Robert Goodwill
Parliamentary Under Secretary
of State
Claire Perry
Parliamentary Under Secretary
of State
Andrew Jones

Parliamentary Under Secretary
of State (jointly with the Home
Office)
Lord Ahmad of Wimbledon

**DEPARTMENT FOR BUSINESS,
INNOVATION AND SKILLS**
Secretary of State for Business,
Innovation and Skills and President
of the Board of Trade
Sajid Javid
Minister of State (Trade and
Investment) (jointly with the
Foreign and Commonwealth
Office)
Francis Maude
Minister of State
Anna Soubry
Minister of State (jointly with the
Department for Education)
Nick Boles
Minister of State (jointly with the
Department for Culture, Media
and Sport)
Ed Vaizey
Minister of State
Jo Johnson
Parliamentary Under Secretary of
State (jointly with the Department
of Health)
George Freeman
Parliamentary Under Secretary of
State (jointly with the Department
for Culture, Media and Sport)
Baroness Neville-Rolfe

NORTHERN IRELAND OFFICE
Secretary of State for Northern
Ireland
Theresa Villiers Parliamentary
Under Secretary of State
Ben Wallace

**DEPARTMENT FOR
ENVIRONMENT, FOOD
AND RURAL AFFAIRS**
Secretary of State for Environment,
Food and Rural Affairs
Elizabeth Truss
Minister of State
George Eustice

Parliamentary Under Secretary
of State
Rory Stewart

**DEPARTMENT FOR COMMUNITIES
AND LOCAL GOVERNMENT**
Secretary of State for Communities
and Local Government
Greg Clark
Minister of State
Brandon Lewis
Minister of State
Mark Francois
Parliamentary Under Secretary
of State
James Wharton
Parliamentary Under Secretary
of State
Marcus Jones
Parliamentary Under Secretary
of State
Baroness Williams of Trafford

WALES OFFICE
Secretary of State for Wales
Stephen Crabb
Parliamentary Under Secretary of
State (and Government Whip)
Alun Cairns
Parliamentary Under Secretary of
State (jointly with the Department
for Energy and Climate Change
and Lord in Waiting)
Lord Bourne of Aberystwyth

CABINET OFFICE
Chancellor of the Duchy of
Lancaster (in overall charge of the
Cabinet Office)
Oliver Letwin
Minister for the Cabinet Office and
Paymaster General
Matt Hancock
Parliamentary Secretary
Rob Wilson
Parliamentary Secretary (and
Government Whip)
John Penrose
Parliamentary Secretary
George Bridges

**DEPARTMENT FOR CULTURE,
MEDIA AND SPORT**
Secretary of State for Culture,
Media and Sport
John Whittingdale
Minister of State (jointly with
the Department for Business,
Innovation and Skills)
Ed Vaizey
Parliamentary Under Secretary of
State (jointly with the Department
for Business, Innovation and Skills)
Baroness Neville-Rolfe
Parliamentary Under Secretary
of State
Tracey Crouch
Parliamentary Under Secretary
of State
Baroness Shields

SCOTLAND OFFICE
Secretary of State for Scotland
David Mundell
Parliamentary Under Secretary
of State
Andrew Dunlop

**DEPARTMENT OF ENERGY AND
CLIMATE CHANGE**
Secretary of State for Energy and
Climate Change
Amber Rudd
Minister of State
Andrea Leadsom
Parliamentary Under Secretary of
State (jointly with the Wales Office
and Lord in Waiting)
Lord Bourne of Aberystwyth

Minister without portfolio
(Minister of State)
Robert Halfon

LAW OFFICERS
Attorney General
Jeremy Wright
Solicitor General
Robert Buckland
Advocate General for Scotland
Richard Keen

WHIPS – HOUSE OF COMMONS
Parliamentary Secretary to the
Treasury (Chief Whip)
Mark Harper
Treasurer of HM Household
(Deputy Chief Whip)
Anne Milton
Comptroller of HM Household
(Government Whip)
Gavin Barwell
Vice Chamberlain of HM
Household (Government Whip)
Kris Hopkins
Junior Lords of the Treasury
Government Whip (Lord
Commissioner of HM Treasury)
David Evennett
Government Whip (Lord
Commissioner of HM Treasury and
a Parliamentary Secretary at the
Cabinet Office)
John Penrose
Government Whip (Lord
Commissioner of HM Treasury and
a Parliamentary Under Secretary of
State at the Wales Office)
Alun Cairns
Government Whip (Lord
Commissioner of HM Treasury)
Mel Stride
Government Whip (Lord
Commissioner of HM Treasury)
George Hollingbery
Government Whip (Lord
Commissioner of HM Treasury)
Charlie Elphicke

ASSISTANT WHIPS
Assistant Government Whips
**Margot James, Julian Smith,
Guy Opperman, Sarah Newton,
Stephen Barclay, Simon Kirby,
Jackie Doyle-Price**
Assistant Government Whip (and a
Parliamentary Under Secretary of
State at the Ministry of Justice)
Andrew Selous

WHIPS – HOUSE OF LORDS
Captain of the Honourable Corps
of Gentlemen at Arms (Lords Chief
Whip)
Lord Taylor of Holbeach
Captain of The Queen's Bodyguard
of the Yeomen of the Guard
(Deputy Chief Whip)
Lord Gardiner of Kimble

Baronesses and Lords in Waiting
**Lord Ashton of Hyde, Baroness
Chisholm of Owlpen, Baroness
Evans of Bowes Park, Earl of
Courtown, Viscount Younger of
Leckie**

Lord in Waiting (and a
Parliamentary Under Secretary of
State at the Wales Office and at
the Department for Energy and
Climate Change)
Lord Bourne of Aberystwyth

General election 2015:
results by constituency

ABBREVIATIONS OF PARTIES WITH MPS AFTER THE GENERAL ELECTION IN 2015
C Conservative; **Lab** Labour; **Lab Co-op** Labour and Co-operative; **LD** Liberal Democrat;
PC Plaid Cymru; **SNP** Scottish National Party; **Green** Green; **Ukip** UK Independence Party;
DUP Democratic Unionist Party; **UUP** Ulster Unionist Party; **SDLP** Social Democratic and
Labour Party; **SF** Sinn Fein; **Alliance** Alliance; **Speaker** The Speaker

MINOR PARTIES

30-50 The 30-50 Coalition; **Above** Above and Beyond Party; **Active** Dem Movement for Active Democracy; **AD** Apolitical Democrats; **AP** All People's Party; **APNI** Alliance Party of Northern Ireland; **Atom** Children of the Atom; **AWP** Animal Welfare Party; **Beer BS** Beer, Baccy and Scratchings; **Birthday** The Birthday Party; **BNP** British National Party; **Bournemouth** Bournemouth Independent Alliance; **Bristol** Independents for Bristol; **Brit Dem** British Democrats; **Brit Ind** British Independents; **Campaign** Campaign Party; **Ch M** Christian Movement for Great Britain; **Ch P** Christian Party; **Change** Alter Change - Politics Only Different; **Christian** Christian; **Class War** Class War; **Comm** Communist Party; **Comm Lge** Communist League; **Comm Brit** Communist Party of Britain; **Communist** Communist; **Community** Communities United Party; **Consensus** Consensus; **CPA** Christian Peoples Alliance; **Croydon** Putting Croydon First!; **CSA** Cannabis is Safer than Alcohol; **CSP** Common Sense Party; **Dem Ref** Democratic Reform Party; **Digital** Digital Democracy; **DP** The Democratic Party; **Eccentric** The Eccentric Party of Great Britain; **Elmo** Vote Elmo; **Eng Dem** English Democrats; **EP** Europeans Party; **FPT** Free Public Transport Party; **Green Soc** Alliance for Green Socialism; **Guildford** Guildford Greenbelt Group; **Hoi** Hoi Polloi; **Hospital** Your Vote Could Save Our Hospital; **Humanity** Humanity; **IASI** Independents Against Social Injustice; **IE** Independence from Europe; **Ind CHC** Independent Community and Health Concern; **Ind** Independent; **IPAP** Independent Political Alliance Party; **ISWSL** Independent Save Withybush Save Lives; **IZB** Islam Zinda Baad Platform; **JACP** Justice and Anti-Corruption Party; **Lib GB** Liberty GB; **Lib** Liberal; **Lincs** Ind Lincolnshire Independents; **Loony** Monster Raving Loony Party; **LP** Land Party; **LU** Left Unity; **Magna Carta** Magna Carta Party; **Mainstream** Mainstream; **Manston** Manston Airport Independent Party; **Meb Ker** Mebyon Kernow; **Nat Lib** National Liberal Party; **ND** No description; **NE Party** The North East Party; **New IC** New Independent Centralists; **NF** National Front; **NHAP** National Health Action Party; **Northern** Northern Party; **Patria** Patria; **PBP** People Before Profit; **Peace** The Peace Party; **PF** People First; **Pilgrim** The Pilgrim Party; **Pirate** Pirate Party UK; **Plural** The Pluralist Party; **Poole** Poole People; **PP UK** Population Party UK; **PPP** The Principles of Politics Party; **PSP** Patriotic Socialist Party; **Real** Keep it Real; **Realist** The Realists' Party; **Reality** We Are The Reality Party; **Rep Soc** Republican Socialist; **Respect** Respect the Unity Coalition; **Restore** Restore the Family; **RFAC** Red Flag Anti-Corruption; **Rochdale** Rochdale First Party; **Roman** The Roman Party. Ave!; **RTP** Removing the Politicians; **S New** Something New; **Scottish CP** Scottish Communist Party; **SCP** Scottish Christian Party; **SEP** Socialist Equality Party; **Soc Dem** Social Democratic Party; **Soc Lab** Socialist Labour Party; **Song** World Peace Through Song; **Southport** The Southport Party; **SPGB** Socialist Party of Great Britain; **SSP** Scottish Socialist Party; **TEP** The Evolution Party; **Thanet** Party for a United Thanet; **TSPP** The Sustainable Population Party; **TUSC** Trade Unionist and Socialist Coalition; **TUV** Traditional Unionist Voice; **U Party** U Party; **Ubuntu** Ubuntu Party; **UKPDP** The UK Progressive Democracy Party; **Uttlesford** Residents for Uttlesford; **Vapers** Vapers in Power; **VAT** Reduce VAT In Sport; **Wessex Reg** Wessex Regionalist; **Whig** Whig Party; **Wigan** Wigan Independents; **Worth** The New Society of Worth; **WP** Workers' Party; **WRP** Workers' Revolutionary Party; **WVPTFP** War Veteran's Pro-Traditional Family Party; **Yorks** Yorkshire First; **Young** Young People's Party UK; **Zeb** Al-Zebabist Nation of Ooog

Abbreviations of additional parties that stood in by-elections 2010-15:
Oldham East & Saddleworth by-election 2011: **Ind English** Independent English Delegate; Nat Dem National Democrat. Belfast West by-election 2011: **People** People Before Profit Alliance. Feltham & Heston by-election 2011: **London People** London People Before Profit. Bradford West by-election 2012: **D Nats** Democratic Nationalists. Corby, Manchester Central and Cardiff South & Penarth by-elections 2012: **Cannabis** Cannabis Law Reform; **Dem 2015** Democracy 2015; **Elvis** Elvis Loves Pets Party; **Loony** Monster Raving Loony William Hill Party; **People's Dem** People's Democratic Party; **Pirate** Pirate Party; **Respect** Respect; **TUSC** Trade Unionists and Socialists Against Cuts; **UPP** United People's Party. Croydon North by-election 2012: **Nine eleven** nine eleven was an inside job. Eastleigh by-election 2013: **Beer** Beer, Baccy and Crumpet Party; **Elvis** Elvis Loves Pets. South Shields by-election 2013: **Ind Soc** Independent Socialist Party. Newark by-election 2014: **Stop Banks** Stop Commercial Banks Owning Britain's Money. Rochester & Strood by-election 2014: **Britain 1st** Britain First

Aberavon

LABOUR HOLD

STEPHEN KINNOCK
BORN Jan 1, 1970
MP 2015-

Son of Labour leader Neil Kinnock and husband of Danish prime minister Helle Thorning-Schmidt. Card-carrying Labour member from age 15. MD of Xynto, energy efficiency consultancy. Previously research assistant at European Parliament before becoming head of British Council in Sierra Leone. Later joined World Economic Forum as director of operations in Europe and Central Asia. Married, two daughters. Ed: Drayton Manor HS; Queens' Coll, Cambridge (BA modern languages); Coll of Europe.

CHALLENGERS
Peter Bush (Ukip) Chief executive of New Swansea Bay community organisation. Previously worked in senior hospitality and NHS positions. Married, two children. Fellow, Institute of Travel and Tourism. Member, Chartered Management Institute. **Edward Yi He** (C) Chinese-born former engineer at Tata Steel in Port Talbot. Previously treasurer of IET and trustee for cancer charity. Ed: Birmingham (BEng); Swansea (MRes, materials engineering). **Duncan Higgitt** (PC) Press & political officer for Bethan Jenkins AM. Journalist and former soldier. **Helen Ceri Clarke** (LD) Caseworker for Peter Black AM. Cllr, Coedffranc community C. Contested Aberavon Welsh Assembly election 2011.

CONSTITUENCY PROFILE
Industrial seat in South Wales, consisting largely of the town of Port Talbot, but also the Afan Valley and the huge Tata steelworks to the south of the town, the oil refinery and Baglan Bay power station. Represented by Labour since 1922, most famously by Ramsay MacDonald during his first term as prime minister. Also contested by Captain Beany, a perennial fringe candidate since 1992.

	Electorate	Turnout %	Change from 2010 %
	49,821	63.3	
S Kinnock Lab	15,416	48.9	-3.0
P Bush Ukip	4,971	15.8	+14.2
E Yi He C	3,742	11.9	-2.4
D Higgitt PC	3,663	11.6	+4.5
H C Clarke LD	1,397	4.4	-11.8
C Beany Ind	1,137	3.6	+0.6
J Tier Green	711	2.3	
A Jordan Soc Lab	352	1.1	
O Herbert TUSC	134	0.4	

Change from 2010

25%

0%

-25%

Lab   Ukip   C   PC   LD

Aberconwy

CONSERVATIVE HOLD

GUTO BEBB
BORN Oct 9, 1968
MP 2010-

Former Plaid Cymru activist and Caernarfon party chairman, the grandson of Ambrose Bebb, Plaid Cymru's co-founder. Native Welsh speaker. Defected to the Tories owing to Eurosceptic views – member, Business for Sterling in Wales, Open Europe. Select cttees: Welsh affairs 2010-; members' expenses 2011-; public accounts 2012-. Contested Conwy 2005, Ogmore 2002; Conwy 2003 Welsh Ass election. Conservative Friends of Israel. Business development director, Innovas Wales. Ran bookshop with wife. Married, two daughters, three sons. Ed: Ysgol Syr Hugh Owen; University of Wales, Aberystwyth (BA history).

CHALLENGERS
Mary Wimbury (Lab) Senior policy adviser to Care Forum Wales. Ran UKMT charity promoting maths education in secondary schools. Previously led BBC's campaign for key sporting events to remain free-to-air. Married, three children. Ed: Oxford (BSc maths; president, OUSU); UCL (MSc public policy). **Dafydd Meurig** (PC) Founder and director: Ogwen Partnership social enterprise; Gwasg Gee Welsh language book publisher. Cllr, Gwynedd C 2012-, planning & transport cabinet member. Previously sound engineer at BBC. Four children. Ed: Ysgol Dyffryn Ogwen. **Andrew Haigh** (Ukip) Assistant to Nathan Gill MEP. MD of commerical marine phytoplankton company.

CONSTITUENCY PROFILE
Features the coastal towns of Conwy and Llandudno and the inland rural Welsh-speaking areas of the Conwy valley. Tory for 27 years, Labour won in 1997 from third place. The removal of Labour-voting Bangor in 2010 made the seat a prime target for the Tories, and they won it back in 2010.

	Electorate	Turnout %	Change from 2010 %
	45,540	66.2	
G Bebb C	12,513	41.5	+5.7
M Wimbury Lab	8,514	28.2	+3.8
D Meurig PC	3,536	11.7	-6.1
A Haigh Ukip	3,467	11.5	+9.4
V Babu LD	1,391	4.6	-14.7
P Haig Green	727	2.4	

Change from 2010

25%

0%

-25%

C   Lab   PC   Ukip   LD

Aberdeen North

SNP GAIN

KIRSTY BLACKMAN
BORN Mar 20, 1986
MP 2015-

SNP spokeswoman, House of Lords 2015-. Parly asst to Mark McDonald MSP, previouly Brian Adam MSP and Nigel Don MSP. Cllr, Aberdeen CC 2007-, SNP Group convenor. Former council spokeswoman for education and convener of authority's licensing committee. Married, two sons. Ed: Robert Gordon's Coll.

CHALLENGERS
Richard Baker (Lab Co-op) Seasoned politician described as "more a tax-and-spend Brownite" than a "third-way Blairite". MSP for Scotland NE 2003- elected as youngest MSP. Former shadow cabinet secretary for justice, later finance in Scottish Parliament. NUS Scotland president 1998-2000. Unite, Co-operative Party. Previously press officer for Help the Aged. Married to Claire

Brennan-Baker MSP. Ed: St Bees Sch, Cumbria; Aberdeen (MA English). **Sanjoy Sen** (C) Engineer in North Sea oil. Fellow, Institution of Chemical Engineers. Ed: Sheffield (BEng chemical engineering); Durham (MBA); Aberdeen (LLM oil & gas law). **Euan Davidson** (LD) Support worker for adults with learning disabilities. Politics & sociology student, University of Aberdeen. Caseworker for Alison McInnes MSP. President, Liberal Youth Scotland.

CONSTITUENCY PROFILE
Contains most of the historic centre of Aberdeen, including the university and the harbour, which serves much of the North Sea oil industry. More urban than the old pre-2005 Aberdeen North, having lost suburban areas like Danestone, Dyce and Bridge of Don. Held by Labour from 1935-2015, although the Scottish Parliamentary seat of Aberdeen North, which does not include Central Aberdeen, has been SNP since 2003.

	Electorate	Turnout %	from 2010 % Change
	67,745	64.9	
K Blackman SNP	24,793	56.4	+34.2
R Baker Lab Co-op	11,397	25.9	-18.5
S Sen C	5,304	12.1	-0.3
E Davidson LD	2,050	4.7	-13.9
T Rutherford TUSC	206	0.5	
C Willett NF	186	0.4	

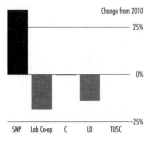

Change from 2010

Aberdeen South

SNP GAIN

CALLUM McCAIG
BORN Jan 6, 1985
MP 2015-

SNP group leader, energy & climate change 2015-. Cllr, Aberdeen CC 2007-, leader 2011-12. Parly asst to Kevin Stewart MSP, formerly to Maureen Watt MSP. Interests: travel, football, Spanish language. Ed: University of Edinburgh (MA politics).

CHALLENGERS
Dame Anne Begg (Lab) MP 1997-2015. Prominent disabled member. Ran Speakers' committee on representation. Chairwoman, work & pensions select cttee 2010-15. Select cttees: liaison 2010-15; W&P 2001-2015; chairmen's panel 2001-10; Scottish affairs 1997-2001. Member: Lab party NEC 1998-99; PLP Lab party policy forum; Educational Inst of Scotland; Gen Teaching Council for Scotland. Disabled Scot of the Year 1988. English teacher. Ed: Brechin HS; Aberdeen (MA

history & politics); Aberdeen Coll of Education. **Ross Thomson** (C) Cllr, Aberdeen CC 2012 -. Volunteer at Aberdeen arts centre. Contested Gordon 2010. Contested Scots parl: Aberdeen Donside by-election 2013; Coatbridge & Chryston 2007. Civil partnership. Ed: Aberdeen (MA politics & international relations). **Denis Rixson** (LD) Bookshop owner and Highland history author. Former schoolteacher for 34 years and secretary of community council. Divorced, two children. Ed: Lincoln Coll, Oxford (BA PPE); Moray House Teacher Training Coll.

CONSTITUENCY PROFILE
Consists of the southern part of Aberdeen city centre, including postwar estates in Torry, Kincorth and Nigg, and more rural areas to the west of the city, with middle-class suburbs Peterculter and Cults. Won by Labour in the 1997 election, having had the distinction of being the only seat that Labour lost in 1992. They lost it again in 2015.

	Electorate	Turnout %	from 2010 % Change
	68,056	71.3	
C McCaig SNP	20,221	41.7	+29.8
A Begg Lab	12,991	26.8	-9.8
R Thomson C	11,087	22.8	+2.1
D Rixson LD	2,252	4.6	-23.8
D Yeats Green	964	2.0	+1.0
S Skinner Ukip	897	1.9	
C Gray Ind	139	0.3	

Change from 2010

Aberdeenshire West & Kincardine

SNP GAIN

STUART DONALDSON
BORN Sep 5, 1991
MP: 2015-

Assistant to Christian Allard MSP. Planned to enter tourism trade but entered politics after Allard's election to late Brian Adam MSP's Aberdeen Donside seat. 23-year-old at election, second youngest MP (after Mhairi Black) and third youngest since 1971 (Charles Kennedy was 23 when elected in 1983). Campaign coordinator for Yes Scotland in Aberdeenshire and member of party's national council. Son of public health minister Maureen Watt MSP, grandson of Hamish Watt MP. Ed: Banchory Academy; University of Glasgow

CHALLENGERS
Alexander Burnett (C) Director, Bancon Group construction company. Entrepreneur and development worker in Azerbaijan, establishing holiday resort and work in agricultural sector.

Former rugby player, now coach for Deeside RFC. Married, three children. Ed: Newcastle (LLB law). **Sir Robert Smith** (LD) MP 1997-2015. Baronet whose grandfather and cousin were Tory MPs in NE Scotland. Had Parkinson's disease diagnosed in 2013. Select cttees include: ECC 2009-15; consolidation bills 2010-15. Lib Dem: whip 2008-10, deputy 2001-06; deputy leader of HoC 2007-10; spokesman, BIS, energy, Scotland 2005-06. Cllr, Aberdeenshire CC 1995-97. Family estate manager. Married, three daughters. Ed: Merchant Taylor's Sch; Aberdeen (BSc maths).

CONSTITUENCY PROFILE
Affluent rural seat, home to Aberdeen commuter towns such as Stonehaven and Inverbervie, countryside villages, and Balmoral. A former area of Tory strength in Scotland, the seat went to Lib Dems in 1997. All seats covering this area in the Scottish Parliament were won by the SNP in 2011.

	Electorate	Turnout %	Change from 2010 %
	73,445	75.2	
S Donaldson SNP	22,949	41.6	+25.9
A Burnett C	15,916	28.8	-1.4
R Smith LD	11,812	21.4	-17.0
B Black Lab	2,487	4.5	-9.1
D Lansdell Ukip	1,006	1.8	+0.9
R Openshaw Green	885	1.6	
G Reid Ind	141	0.3	

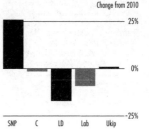

Change from 2010

Airdrie & Shotts

SNP GAIN

NEIL GRAY
BORN Mar 16, 1986
MP 2015-

Office manager for MSP social justice secretary Alex Neil. Previously party press and research assistant. Former journalist on local newspapers and at BBC. Keen athlete. Married, one daughter. Ed: University of Stirling (BA politics & journalism).

CHALLENGERS
Pamela Nash (Lab) MP 2010-15, baby of the House. Local candidate who overcame personal tragedy of death of her mother and stepfather at 17 years old. PPS to: Jim Murphy 2013-15, Margaret Curran 2011-12, Vernon Coaker 2011-13; Shaun Woodward, A. Select cttees: Scottish affairs 2012-15; science & technology 2010-15. Chairwoman, APPG on HIV & Aids. Won all-female shortlist selection in 2010 prompting resignation of local party chairman. Parliamentary

researcher to John Reid. Worked for Boots chemists. Lasallion Developing World project. Young Fabians. MSYP 2007-09. Ed: St Margaret's Sch, Airdrie; University of Glasgow (MA politics). **Eric Holford** (C) Independent financial adviser, set up own firm nine years ago. Married, two children. Ed: Sir Roger Manswood Sch. **Matthew Williams** (Ukip) Studies computing. Part time in security. **John Love** (LD) War historian. Cllr, North Lanarkshire 2007-12.

CONSTITUENCY PROFILE
A solid working-class constituency east of Glasgow, bisected by the M8. Suffered the effects of the decline of industries, has high proportion of social housing. Religion remains a factor in local politics: the 1994 by-election in predecessor seat Monklands East following the death of the Labour leader John Smith was dominated by accusations of sectarian bias by the overwhelmingly Roman Catholic Labour group on Monklands Council.

	Electorate	Turnout %	Change from 2010 %
	66,715	66.4	
N Gray SNP	23,887	53.9	+30.4
P Nash Lab	15,108	34.1	-24.0
E Holford C	3,389	7.7	-1.1
M Williams Ukip	1,088	2.5	
J Love LD	678	1.5	-6.6
D Beaumont Ind	136	0.3	-1.2

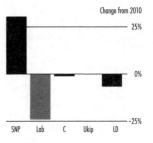

Change from 2010

Aldershot

CONSERVATIVE HOLD

GERALD HOWARTH
BORN Sep 12, 1947
MP 1997-; 1983-92

Diminutive, combative diehard Thatcherite, council member of the Freedom Association, founder member of No Turning Back Group. A champion of defence spending and outspoken on curbing immigration. Parly under-sec, defence 2010-12. Shadow defence minister 2002-10. PPS to Margaret Thatcher 1991-92. MP Cannock & Burntwood 1983-92. Qualified pilot, commissioned into RAFVR. International banker, Bank of America. Loan arranger, Standard Chartered Bank. Married, one daughter, two sons. Ed: Bloxham Sch, Banbury; University of Southampton (BA English).

CHALLENGERS
Gary Puffett (Lab) Workplace rep for Unite. Firefighter for 26 years, before becoming fire safety adviser. Left school at 16 to work

in a factory, returned to education in 2011. Married, two children. Ed: Leicester (LLM employment law). **Bill Walker** (Ukip) Left school at 15 to become a junior leader in the army. Was embroiled in a scandal about posting racist material on the internet. Married twice, five children. Ed: Open University (BSc open degree). **Alan Hilliar** (LD) Business consultant. Contested: Surrey Heath 2010; Chichester 2005. Cllr, Guildford BC 1985-95. Performs musical theatre. Married, two children. Ed: Farnborough Coll

CONSTITUENCY PROFILE
Reliably Conservative, returning Tory MPs since its creation in 1918. Firmly associated with the military, the seat contains Aldershot Barracks, Farnborough Airfield and headquarters of QinetiQ defence contractor privatised in 2006. 2011 census showed the area had the highest proportion of Buddhists of any part of the UK, explained by the number of former Gurkhas settling in the town.

	Electorate	Turnout %	Change from 2010 %
	72,434	63.8	
G Howarth C	23,369	50.6	+3.9
G Puffett Lab	8,468	18.3	+6.2
B Walker Ukip	8,253	17.9	+13.4
A Hilliar LD	4,076	8.8	-25.6
C Hewitt Green	2,025	4.4	

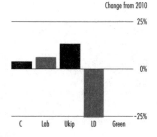

Change from 2010

C   Lab   Ukip   LD   Green

Aldridge-Brownhills

CONSERVATIVE HOLD

WENDY MORTON
BORN Nov 9, 1967
MP 2015-

Runs small manufacturing and electronics business. Previously in diplomatic service. Contested Tynemouth 2010, Newcastle Central 2005. Farmer's daughter. Lobbied for William Hague's "Keep the Pound" campaign. Cllr, Richmondshire DC 2001-06, resigned over accusations of bullying. Former chairman, Richmond Conservatives. Vice-chairman, Conservative party for social action. Strong believer in EU referendum. Married. Ed: Wensleydale Comprehensive Sch; Open University (MBA).

CHALLENGERS
John Fisher (Lab) IT consultant. Cllr, Redditch BC 2012-. IT system implementation project manager. Previously manufacturing consultant. Ed: The Leys HS; Warwick (MA engineering

business management). **Anthony Thompson** (Ukip) Runs software and consultancy business. Former teacher, Dutch wife, three children. Ed: Winchester Coll; Royal Holloway, London. **Ian Garrett** (LD) Head teacher of St Francis of Assisi Comprehensive Sch, Aldridge. Cllr, Sandwell MBC 1994-2002. Contested: West Bromwich East 2010, 2005, 2001; Birmingham Erdington 1997. Married, three daughters. Ed: St Catherine's Coll, Oxford (BA history).

CONSTITUENCY PROFILE
Covers the eastern part of the Walsall MBC on northern edge of West Midlands conurbation. Generally Tory-voting suburbia, but with areas of deprivation and Labour hold some council seats. Brownhills retains strong links with other ex-mining towns across the border in Staffordshire. The anomalous name of the seat is a hangover from the Aldridge-Brownhills local government district, abolished in 1974.

	Electorate	Turnout %	Change from 2010 %
	60,215	65.6	
W Morton C	20,558	52.1	-7.3
J Fisher Lab	8,835	22.4	+2.6
A Thompson Ukip	7,751	19.6	
I Garrett LD	1,330	3.4	-14.3
M Curzey Green	826	2.1	-0.1
M Beech Loony	197	0.5	

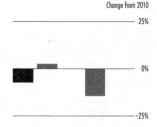

Change from 2010

Altrincham & Sale West

CONSERVATIVE HOLD

GRAHAM BRADY
BORN May 20, 1967
MP 1997-

Genial rightwinger, with a resemblance to Prince Andrew. Resigned from David Cameron's front bench in row over grammar schools and has exploited martyrdom. Key figure in dealing with potential unrest among Tory MPs about coalition, as chairman of 1922 Committee 2010-. Shadow minister: Europe 2004-07; schools 2001-03. PPS to Michael Howard 2003-04; Michael Ancram 1999-2000. Opposition whip 2000. PR career: Waterfront Partnership, Shandwick and Centre for Policy Studies. Married, one daughter, one son. Ed: Altrincham GS; Durham University (LLB law).

CHALLENGERS
James Wright (Lab) Works for a northwest-based housing association. Equal pay for women campaigner. Former county

swimming champion. Married, one daughter. Ed: UCLan (BA politics). **Jane Brophy** (LD) Sub-regional programme manager, NHS. Cllr, Trafford C 1994-. Contested Altrincham & Sale West 2010. Previously vice-chairman of Green Liberal Democrats. Campaign manager for PPC in 2005. School governor. Married, three children. Ed: Chorlton HS; Leeds (BSc biochemistry). **Chris Frost** (Ukip). Works in retail. Served in the British Army, 1997-2006.

CONSTITUENCY PROFILE
The safest Conservative seat in Greater Manchester and from 2001 to 2010 the only one. Along with its predecessor, Altrincham & Sale, it has been Tory since its creation in 1945. Contains some of the wealthiest of Manchester's suburbs, such as Hale and Bowden, with a grammar school system and a significant Jewish community. The western half of the seat is largely rural, made up of small, affluent villages and farms.

	Electorate	Turnout %	Change from 2010 %
	72,004	70.2	
G Brady C	26,771	53.0	+4.1
J Wright Lab	13,481	26.7	+4.3
J Brophy LD	4,235	8.4	-17.1
C Frost Ukip	4,047	8.0	+4.9
N Robertson-Brown Green	1,983	3.9	

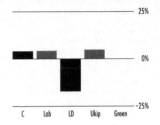

Change from 2010

C Lab LD Ukip Green

Alyn & Deeside

LABOUR HOLD

MARK TAMI
BORN Oct 31, 1962
MP 2001-

Amiable. Labour pairing whip 2011-15. Opposition whip 2010-11. Select cttees: administration 2012-; selection 2010-; Speaker's advisory on works of art 2010-11; Crossrail Bill 2007; human rights 2007; cttee tax law rewrite bills 2005-07; NI affairs 2001-05. Assistantt government whip 2007-10. Chairman, APPG on stem cell transplantation. PPS to: Dawn Primarolo 2005-06, resigned over refusal by Tony Blair to name a date to stand down. Member, AEEU Amicus, TUC general council. AEEU research & communications head; policy head. Norwich City fan. Married, two sons. Ed: Enfield GS; Swansea University (BA history).

CHALLENGERS
Laura Knightly (C) Recruitment consultant in North Wales.

Previously worked for manufacturing and financial multinationals in London. Father, William Knightly, a former Welsh Conservative Conwy Cllr. Ed: Sheffield (BA French, German & Spanish). **Blair Smillie** (Ukip). Great grandson of Labour co-founder, Robert Smillie. Owns a flooring business. **Tudor Jones** (LD) Retired geography teacher and humanities head at St David's HS. Community Cllr. Board member for social enterprise scheme Flintshire Care and Repair. Ed: Bangor; Open University.

CONSTITUENCY PROFILE
A reliable Labour seat, situated on the English border (half the population is born outside Wales), held by the party since its creation in 1983 although not always by large margins. Geographically one of the smallest Welsh constituencies. An industrial area, with Connah's Quay power station, Tata steel, Toyota and BAE Systems factories in the seat.

	Electorate	Turnout %	Change from 2010 %
	62,016	66.6	
M Tami Lab	16,540	40.0	+0.5
L Knightly C	13,197	31.9	-0.3
B Smillie Ukip	7,260	17.6	+15.1
T Jones LD	1,733	4.2	-14.1
J Hurst PC	1,608	3.9	+0.0
A Ibbotson Green	976	2.4	

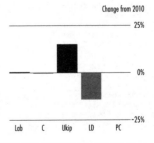

Change from 2010

Lab C Ukip LD PC

Amber Valley

CONSERVATIVE HOLD

NIGEL MILLS
BORN April 21, 1964
MP 2010-

Select cttees: work and pensions 2012-15; NI affairs 2011-15; administration 2010-15. Endured two recounts before being awarded the seat in 2010 with a majority of 536, which he increased to 4,205 in 2015. Cllr; Amber Valley BC 2004-11; Heanor & Loscoe TC 2007-11. Accountant (advising businesses on international tax issues): Deloitte; PwC. Member, Institute of Chartered Accountants. Married. Ed: Loughborough GS, Newcastle University (BA Classics).

CHALLENGERS
Kevin Gillott (Lab) Solicitor. Cllr, Derbyshire CC 1997-, deputy leader Labour group 2013-14. Cabinet member, children and young people. Married. Ed: Henry Fanshaw Comp Sch. **Stuart Bent** (Ukip) Bus driver. Former TV engineer and lecturer in media production. Partner, three step-children. **Kate Smith** (LD) Gift shop asst, National Tramway Museum. Cllr, Crish PC 2003-08. Contested Amber Valley 2005, 01. Married, two sons. Ed: New Hall, Cambridge, (BA modern languages). **John Devine** (Green). Retired. Worked at the Environment Agency and a former nurse. Ex-armed forces. Ed: University of Central Lancashire (BA environmental management).

CONSTITUENCY PROFILE
The eastern part of Derbyshire, north of the city of Derby itself. The former coal-mining towns, including (Alfreton to Oakerthorpe) here all tend to vote Labour, but the more Conservative rural sections of the seat balance this out, to an extent, making the seat a marginal. It was won by the Tories on its creation in 1983, fell to Labour in their 1997 landslide and was won back by the Tories in 2010. Coal mining has been replaced by light industry.

	Electorate	Turnout %	from 2010 Change %
	70,226	65.1	
N Mills C	20,106	44.0	+5.4
K Gillott Lab	15,901	34.8	-2.7
S Bent Ukip	7,263	15.9	+13.9
K Smith LD	1,360	3.0	-11.5
J Devine Green	1,087	2.4	

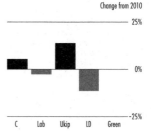

Change from 2010

C Lab Ukip LD Green

Angus

SNP HOLD

MICHAEL WEIR
BORN Mar 24, 1957
MP 2001-

SNP chief whip 2015-. Shad SNP spokesman: business 2010-15; energy and climate change 2010-15; environment, food & rural affairs 2007-10; trade & industry 2004-10; energy 2005-10; work & pensions 2005-07; environment 2004; health 2004. Select cttees: chairmen's panel 2005-; energy and climate change 2009-2010; business and enterprise 2008-09; business, enterprise and regulatory reform 2007-2008; trade & industry 2005-07; Scottish affairs 2001-05. Cllr, Angus DC 1984-88. Contested Aberdeen South 1987. Solicitor. Law Soc of Scotland. Married, two daughters. Ed: Arbroath HS; Aberdeen (LLB law).

CHALLENGERS
Derek Wann (C) Businessman with background in construction. Former general manager, Discovery Roofing, Qatar. Married, four children. Ed: Aberdeen GS. **Gerard McMahon** (Lab) Political asst to Catherine Stihler MEP. GMB. Ed: University of Glasgow (BSc biochemistry). **Calum Walker** (Ukip) Masters student in finance, University of Dundee. Ed: Abertay University (BA business studies & finance). **Sanjay Samani** (LD) IT project manager, small-business owner. Contested Angus 2010. Ed: Loughborough GS; Jesus Coll, Cambridge (BSc computer science).

CONSTITUENCY PROFILE
Angus was once a Conservative seat but with the party's relentless decline in Scotland it has been held by the SNP since 1987. The constituency stretches from sparsely populated hill-farming areas in the Angus Glens towards more built-up areas to the north of Dundee. Employment is mainly in agriculture and forestry but there is also a pharmaceutical industry at Montrose. The other main towns are Forfar, Brechin and Arbroath.

	Electorate	Turnout %	from 2010 Change %
	65,792	67.6	
M Weir SNP	24,130	54.2	+14.7
D Wann C	12,900	29.0	-1.9
G McMahon Lab	3,919	8.8	-8.4
C Walker Ukip	1,355	3.1	+1.5
S Samani LD	1,216	2.7	-8.0
D Mumford Green	965	2.2	

Change from 2010

SNP C Lab Ukip LD

Antrim East

DUP HOLD

SAMMY WILSON
BORN Apr 4, 1953
MP 2005-

Good-humoured finance minister in NI Executive. Shadow DUP Westminster spokesman: Treasury 2009-; education 2003-12; communities 2005-09. Select cttees: transport 2008-09; NI affairs 2005-08. MLA: Antrim East 2003-; Belfast East 1998-2003. Minister in Stormont: finance and personnel 2009-13; environment 2008-09. Member, NI policing board. Cllr, East Belfast CC 1981-2010, lord mayor 2000-01, 1986-87. Contested: Antrim E 2001; Strangford 1992. Former press officer for DUP. Former teacher. Ed: Methodist Coll; Queen's University Belfast (BA economics & politics); Stranmillis Coll (DipEd).

CHALLENGERS
Roy Beggs Jr (UUP) MLA, Antrim East 1998-, deputy speaker 2011-. UUP spokesman, health 2012-14.

Contested Antrim E (Westminster) 2001, 2005. Married, three children. Ed: Queen's (BEng industrial engineering). **Stewart Dickson** (Alliance) MLA, Antrim East 2011-. Alliance chief whip. Member, select cttees: enterprise, trade & investment 2014-; justice 2011-; social development 2013-; business 2011-. Vice-chairman, NI diabetes cttee. Married. **Noel Jordan** (Ukip) Bricklayer, former firefighter. Cllr, Mid & East Antrim BC 2014. Vice-chairman, Ukip NI.

CONSTITUENCY PROFILE
The fourth most Protestant constituency in Northern Ireland, Antrim East is strongly unionist, with the Roman Catholic population concentrated in its southern and northern extremities. A sliver of the coast, it starts in Belfast commuter belt, runs south through dormitory towns and ends in the Antrim Glens. A UUP safe seat under Roy Beggs Sr from 1983 to 2005, when he was defeated by the DUP's Sammy Wilson..

	Electorate	Turnout %	from 2010 %	Change
	62,810	53.3		
S Wilson DUP	12,103	36.1	-9.7	
R Beggs UUP	6,308	18.8		
S Dickson Alliance	5,021	15.0	+3.9	
N Jordan Ukip	3,660	10.9		
O McMullan SF	2,314	6.9	+0.1	
R Wilson TUV	1,903	5.7	-0.3	
M A McKillop SDLP	1,639	4.9	-1.7	
A Wilson C	549	1.6	-22.0	

Change from 2010

25%

0%

-25%

DUP   UUP   Alliance   Ukip   SF

Antrim North

DUP HOLD

IAN PAISLEY JR
BORN Dec 12, 1966
MP 2010-

Nicknamed "Baby Doc" after his father "Papa Doc", the DUP founder who stood down in 2010. DUP Westminster spokesman: work & pensions 2010-; environment, food and rural affairs 2010-. Select cttees: NI affairs 2010-; governance 2014-15. MLA, Antrim North 1998-2010. Member, NI policing board. Member, NI forum for political dialogue 1996-98. Married, two daughters, two sons. Ed: Methodist Coll; Queen's University Belfast (BA history; MA Irish politics)

CHALLENGERS
Timothy Gaston (TUV) Fire, health and safety officer. Surprise pick in TUV's strongest seat ahead of leader Jim Allister. Cllr, Mid & East Antrim BC 2014-. **Daithí McKay** (SF) MLA, North Antrim 2007-. Former bank employee.

SF spokesman: economy 2012-; education 2011-12; environment 2007-11. Select cttees: finance & personnel (chairman); public accounts. Ed: St Louis Grammar School. **Robin Swann** (UUP) MLA, 2011-; chairman, employment & learning cttee 2013-. UUP chief whip 2012-. Chairman, North Antrim Assoc UUP 2010-. Married, one daughter, one son. Ed: Open University (BSc, cert professional management). **Declan O'Loan** (SDLP) MLA 2007-2011. Cllr, Mid & East Antrim 2014-. Maths teacher. Ed: Imperial Coll London (BSc mathematics); Fitzwilliam Coll, Cambridge (PGCE).

CONSTITUENCY PROFILE
A relatively prosperous area that includes the Giant's Causeway and Bushmills distillery. Strong history as a unionist seat. The late Rev Ian Paisley was elected in 1970 and held the seat for 40 years until 2010, when he was replaced by his son. The town of Ballymena is a manufacturing centre.

	Electorate	Turnout %	from 2010 %	Change
	75,874	55.2		
I Paisley DUP	18,107	43.2	-3.2	
T Gaston TUV	6,561	15.7	-1.1	
D McKay SF	5,143	12.3	-0.2	
R Swann UUP	5,054	12.1		
D O'Loan SDLP	2,925	7.0	-1.8	
J Dunlop Alliance	2,351	5.6	+2.4	
R Hill Ukip	1,341	3.2		
C Freeman C	368	0.9	-10.1	
T Palmer Ind	57	0.1		

Change from 2010

25%

0%

-25%

DUP   TUV   SF   UUP   SDLP

Antrim South

UUP GAIN

DANNY KINAHAN
BORN Apr 14, 1958
MP 2015-

MLA, South Antrim 2009-, promised to step down from NI Assembly if elected to Westminster. NI Assembly cttees: vice-chairman, education 2012-; chairman, audit 2011-. Cllr, Antrim BC 2005-10. UUP membership officer 2007-09. High Sheriff of Antrim 1996-97. Fine art and antiques consultant; former Ireland representative, Christie's International. Former officer in British Army. Cousin of singer Chris de Burgh. Married, four children. Ed: Stowe Sch; University of Edinburgh (BComm business studies); RMA Sandhurst.

CHALLENGERS
William McCrea (DUP) MP, Antrim S 2005-15, 2000-01; Ulster Mid 1986-97, 1983-85. Shadow DUP leader, HoC 2010-15. Shadow DUP spokesman: justice 2010-15; home affairs 2010-15; communities

2009-10; environment 2005-10. Select cttees: panel of chairmen 2006-15; HoL reform 2011-12; public accounts 2010-11. MLA, Ulster Mid 1998-2010. Member, NI Assembly 1982-86. Cllr, Magherafelt DC 1973-2010. Former civil servant. Married, five children. Ed: Theological Coll of Free Presbyterian Church of Ulster. **Declan Kearney** (SF) NI SF chairman. Former County Antrim organiser. Background in community and economic development. **Neil Kelly** (Alliance) Cllr, Antrim and Newtownabbey BC 2010-. Ed: St Louis GS, Ballymena; Muckamore Abbey Hospital (learning disability nurse training).

CONSTITUENCY PROFILE
Soldily unionist and held by the UUP until 2000, but it is now a marginal between the UUP and the DUP. Covers the suburban fringes of north Belfast and the rural areas beyond it, including Antrim and Crumlin. Good communications make it home to many Belfast commuters.

	Electorate	Turnout %	Change from 2010 %
	67,423	54.2	
D Kinahan UUP	11,942	32.7	
W McCrea DUP	10,993	30.1	-3.8
D Kearney SF	4,699	12.9	-1.0
N Kelly Alliance	3,576	9.8	+2.1
R Lynch SDLP	2,990	8.2	-0.5
R Cairns TUV	1,908	5.2	-0.2
A Dunlop C	415	1.1	-29.3

Change from 2010

UUP DUP SF Alliance SDLP

Arfon

PLAID CYMRU HOLD

HYWEL WILLIAMS
BORN May 14, 1953
MP 2001-

Lyrical Welshman. Shadow PC spokesman: defence, int devt, FCO 2015-; cab office 2010-2013.; defence, transport 2007-09; Treasury 2006-07; education 2005; CMS 2005-06; int devt 2004-; work & pensions, health 2001-15; disability 2001-05. MP, Caernarfon 2001-10. Select cttees: Welsh affairs 2004-10, 2014; science & technology 2012-14; Speaker's advisory on works of art 2010; panel of chairs 2005. Former social worker; social work and policy lecturer; consultant. Author. Divorced, three daughters. Ed: Glan y Môr Sch; University of Wales: Cardiff (BSc psychology); Bangor (CQSW social work).

CHALLENGERS
Alun Pugh (Lab) AM, Clwyd West 1999-2007. Min: culture, Welsh language and sport. Former

columnist, *Daily Post*, North Wales. Contested Arfon 2010. Former dir, Snowdonia Society. Ed: Tonypandy GS; Polytechnic of Wales (BA business finance); University Coll, Cardiff (PgDip computer science). **Anwen Barry** (C) Customer service asst, Wilko. Former guest house owner. Voluntary dir, Harlech & Ardudwy Leisure. Ed: Llandrillo Technical Coll (hotel catering and managment). **Simon Wall** (Ukip) Training consultant, Parry Williams Partnership. Ed: Bishop Grosseteste Coll (BSc education); Nottingham Trent (PGCE LLS).

CONSTITUENCY PROFILE
A safe Plaid Cymru seat that faces Anglesey across the Menai Strait. With just over 40,000 voters it is the smallest mainland constituency by electorate, half the size of the largest seats, such as Manchester Central. Stretches into Snowdonia National Park in the south. The main settlements are Bangor and Caernarfon.

	Electorate	Turnout %	Change from 2010 %
	40,492	66.3	
H Williams PC	11,790	43.9	+8.0
A Pugh Lab	8,122	30.3	-0.1
A Barry C	3,521	13.1	-3.8
S Wall Ukip	2,277	8.5	+5.9
M Shultan LD	718	2.7	-11.4
K Jones Soc Lab	409	1.5	

Change from 2010

PC Lab C Ukip LD

Argyll & Bute

SNP GAIN

BRENDAN O'HARA
BORN Apr 27, 1963
MP 2015-

Swept to victory in a seat where the SNP could manage only fourth place in 2010. Independent TV producer, including *Comedy Connections* and *Movie Connections* (BBCl); *The Football Years* (STV); *Road To Referendum* (STV) was nominated for Bafta Scotland. Contested: Glasgow Central 1992; Springburn 1987. Married, two daughters. Ed: St. Andrew's, Carntyne; Strathclyde University (MA economic history & modern history).

CHALLENGERS
Alan Reid (LD) MP, Argyll & Bute 2001-15. Opposition LD whip 2010, 2002-05. Shad LD min: Scotland 2007-10; NI 2006-10; trade & industry 2005-06. LD spokes, Scotland 2004-05. Select cttees: Scottish affairs 2010-15; broadcasting 2001-05. Scottish LD

vice-convener. Formerly: computer project manager; teacher. Ed: Strathclyde (BSc maths); Jordanhill Coll (teacher training); Bell Coll (computer data processing) **Alastair Redman** (C) Village postmaster. Vice-chairman, Islay CC. Occasional contributor to BBC Radio 2's *Jeremy Vine* show. Dir, recycling charity, Re-Jig. Ed: Islay HS. **Mary Galbraith** (Lab) Business consultant. Contested: East Dunbartonshire 2010; Highlands 1999, Argyll & B 2007 Scottish elections. Ed: Glasgow (MA political economy & German).

CONSTITUENCY PROFILE
A seat that covers a swathe of sparsely populated countryside and includes many islands, such as Mull, Tiree and Iona. Faslane, the Trident submarine base, sits within the seat and the industries include tourism, forestry, fishing and wind farms. Having been a fairly secure Lib Dem seat, the SNP now has a bigger majority than the Lib Dems had in the previous four elections.

		Electorate	Turnout %	Change from 2010 %
		68,875	75.3	
B O'Hara	SNP	22,959	44.3	+25.3
A Reid	LD	14,486	27.9	-3.7
A Redman	C	7,733	14.9	-9.1
M Galbraith	Lab	5,394	10.4	-12.3
C Santos	Ukip	1,311	2.5	

Change from 2010

SNP LD C Lab Ukip

Arundel & South Downs

CONSERVATIVE HOLD

NICK HERBERT
BORN Apr 7, 1963
MP 2005-

Diffident intellectual and former think-tank director. Missed out on secretarial brief in coalition government, and resigned from govt after disagreeing with 2012 reshuffle. Min for policing 2010-12. Shadow SoS: environment, food and rural affairs 2009-10; justice 2007-09. Shad min, home affairs 2005-07. Member, home affairs select cttee 2005-06. Contested Berwick-upon-Tweed 1997. Co-founder & dir, Reform 2002-05. Chief executive, Business for Sterling 1998-2000. Civil partnership. Ed: Haileybury Sch; Magdalene Coll, Cambridge (BA law & land economy).

CHALLENGERS
Peter Grace (Ukip). Service delivery manager, BAE Systems. Treasurer, Arundel & S Downs Ukip 2014-. Married, two sons.

Ed: Open University, (BA English literature). **Christopher Wellbelove** (Lab). Digital brand manager, BT Group. Cllr, Lambeth BC 2006-, deputy cabinet member: young people 2013-14, customer service 2010-13, housing 2010-12. Mayor 2009-2010. Dir, Walcot Foundation 2008-2014. Ed: Queensmead HS, South Ruislip. **Shweta Kapadia** (LD) Reflexologist and former architect. Cllr, Elmbridge BC 2000-. Trustee, R C Sherriff Trust. Former member, Arts Council England, South East.

CONSTITUENCY PROFILE
A sprawling constituency taking in much of rural West Sussex. It is made up of picturesque villages with no industry of note. The coastal towns of Bognor, Worthing and Hove have been carved out into their own constituencies. Arundel itself, and the castle of the same name, is the historic seat of the Dukes of Norfolk. A very safe Conservative seat, with Lib Dems previously a comfortable second.

		Electorate	Turnout %	Change from 2010 %
		77,272	73.1	
N Herbert	C	34,331	60.8	+3.0
P Grace	Ukip	8,154	14.4	+8.8
C Wellbelove	Lab	6,324	11.2	+2.6
S Kapadia	LD	4,062	7.2	-20.8
I Thurston	Green	3,606	6.4	

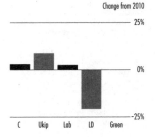

Change from 2010

C Ukip Lab LD Green

Ashfield

LABOUR HOLD

GLORIA DE PIERO
BORN Dec 21, 1972
MP 2010-

Involved in 2015 "Woman to Woman" campaign. As deputy campaign strategist, rode around UK on infamous bright pink bus aiming to rally women into backing Ed Miliband. Shadow min: women & equalities 2013-; home affairs 2011-13; CMS 2010-11. Strategy board member, Progress. Former: political correspondent, *GMTV*; BBC researcher. Chairwoman, Labour students 1996-97. Married. Ed: Bradford & Ilkley Coll; University of Westminster (BA social science); Birkbeck, London (MSc social & political theory).

CHALLENGERS
Helen Harrison (C) Self-employed physiotherapist. Previously worked in NHS city hospitals and GP practices. Ed: Our Lady & Pope John Sch; Liverpool (BSc physiotherapy). **Simon Ashcroft**

(Ukip) Sales and marketing consultant. Previously worked for Nottingham Forest FC and Mansfield Brewery. Married, two children. **Philip Smith** (LD) Runs florists, previously banking IT analyst for 15 years. Magistrate. Cllr, Mansfield DC, deputy executive mayor 2003-07, cabinet member 2002-11. Married, two children.

CONSTITUENCY PROFILE
Ashfield, a former mining constituency in west Nottinghamshire, has a history as a safe Labour area despite being briefly Conservative in the 1970s and becoming a marginal at the height of Tory popularity in the 1980s. The closure of the mines brought economic difficulties but the area is now becoming absorbed into part of Nottingham's commuter belt. In 2015 the Liberal Democrats lost all the gains they made in 2010; most notable, however, was Ukip's rise, up from sixth in 2010 (933 votes) to third in 2015 (10,150 votes).

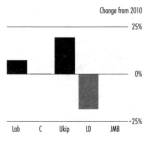

	Electorate	Turnout %	Change from 2010 %
	77,126	61.5	
G De Piero Lab	19,448	41.0	+7.3
H Harrison C	10,628	22.4	+0.2
S Ashcroft Ukip	10,150	21.4	+19.5
P Smith LD	7,030	14.8	-18.5
M Buchanan JMB	153	0.3	

Change from 2010

Lab / C / Ukip / LD / JMB

Ashford

CONSERVATIVE HOLD

DAMIAN GREEN
BORN: Jan 17, 1956
MP 1997-

Disappointed expectations that he would lead modern pro-European faction. Minister: policing, criminal justice & victims 2012-2014; immigration 2010-2012. Shad min, immigration 2005-10. Shad SoS: transport 2003-04; education 2001-03. Defeated David Cameron for Ashford selection, 1997. Financial journalist: Channel 5, BBC, *The Times*. Select cttees: Treasury; home affairs. Special adviser, John Major's policy unit. Married, two daughters. Ed: Reading Sch; Balliol Coll, Oxford (PPE, president OUSU).

CHALLENGERS
Gerald O'Brien (Ukip) Company secretary, Logitag UK. Chairman, Ukip Sevenoaks branch 2014-. Lay member, Church of England synod. Former: dir, Crosslinks, international Christian charity;

int business devt manager, BT. Married, four children. Ed: Dulwich Coll; Bristol (BSc chemistry); Anglian Regional Management Centre (PgDip management studies DMS). **Brendan Chilton** (Lab). Cllr, Ashford BC 2009-. Campaign dir, Labour for a Referendum. Ed: Norton Knatchbull Sch. **Debbie Enever** (LD) Senior regulatory affairs manager, Financial Ombudsman Service. Previously worked for Lib Dem policy unit. Ed: King's Coll, Cambridge (BA history); City, London (Dip law)

CONSTITUENCY PROFILE
Ashford is a large and growing Kent town, and part of the high speed link to the Chanel tunnel thanks to Ashford International station. The constituency includes Tenterton and surrounding villages. A solid Conservative seat held since the 1930s, most famously by the cabinet minister and former *Daily Telegraph* editor Bill Deedes, from 1950 until 1974.

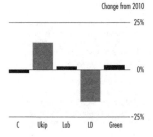

	Electorate	Turnout %	Change from 2010 %
	85,189	67.4	
D Green C	30,094	52.5	-1.7
G O'Brien Ukip	10,798	18.8	+14.3
B Chilton Lab	10,580	18.4	+1.8
D Enever LD	3,433	6.0	-16.8
M Rossi Green	2,467	4.3	+2.5

Change from 2010

C / Ukip / Lab / LD / Green

Ashton-under-Lyne

LABOUR HOLD

ANGELA RAYNER
BORN Mar 28, 1980
MP 2015-

Trade union official, Unison; north west regional convenor; previously branch secretary, Stockport council; national young members' officer. Former member, Labour's nationl policy forum. Selected to replace David Heyes who retired. Political career shaped by her childhood on Bridge Hall estate, Stockport. Had her eldest son when she was 16. Former care assistant for elderly. Member: Labour women's network; Fawcett society; Fabian society. Married, three children, two have disabilities. Ed: Avondale HS.

CHALLENGERS
Tracy Sutton (C) Account manager, Portcullis Public Affairs. Chairwoman, Lewisham Deptford Conservatives 2013-. Parly aide, HoC, 2011-2014. Former teacher. Ed: Birmingham (BA German studies, European literature, philosophy); Goldsmiths, London (PGCE); Gloucestershire (PGCE, professional studies). **Maurice Jackson** (Ukip) Semi-retired, self-employed electrician. Former Labour party member. Two children. Ed: Ashton GS. **Charlotte Hughes** (Green) Blogger and weekly columnist, *Morning Star*. Active local campaigner on austerity and environmental issues. **Carly Hicks** (LD) GDL student, BPP Manchester. Senior parly advisor, Chris Davies MEP 2012-14. Ed: Durham (BA modern European languages and history); King's Coll, London (MA European studies); Sciences Po, Paris (MA affaires européennes).

CONSTITUENCY PROFILE
Ashton, to the East of Manchester, is a safe Labour seat, held continuously since 1931. The town of Ashton was dominated by the textile industry and, since its decline, has suffered high unemployment. Manufacturing is still important and employment in retail is growing.

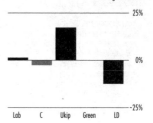

	Electorate	Turnout %	Change from 2010 %
	67,714	57.5	
A Rayner Lab	19,366	49.8	+1.4
T Sutton C	8,610	22.1	-2.6
M Jackson Ukip	8,468	21.8	+17.4
C Hughes Green	1,531	3.9	
C Hicks LD	943	2.4	-12.4

Change from 2010

25%

0%

-25%

Lab   C   Ukip   Green   LD

Aylesbury

CONSERVATIVE HOLD

DAVID LIDINGTON
BORN Jun 30, 1956
MP 1992-

Twice victorious *University Challenge* captain, once with Sidney Sussex Coll, once as a "champion of champions". Min for Europe 2010-. Shadow: min, foreign affairs 2007-10; SoS, NI 2003-07; min, farming and environment 2002; SoS, environment, food and rural affairs 2002-03. Opp spokes, home affairs 1999-01. PPS to Michael Howard as home sec 1994-97. Worked for BP, Rio Tinto Zinc, then special adviser to Douglas Hurd. Contested Vauxhall 1987. Married, four sons. Ed: Haberdashers' Aske's Sch; Sidney Sussex Coll, Cambridge (BA history, PhD).

CHALLENGERS
Chris Adams (Ukip) Cllr, Buckinghamshire CC 2013-; Aylesbury Vale DC 2011-; Aylesbury TC 2011-. Political adviser to Nigel Farage. Contested: Aylesbury 2010, 2005; Henley by-election 2008. Worked in the music industry. Ran family gym for 29 years. **Will Cass** (Lab) Business development manager. Member, Lab Strategy cttee 2014-. Committee member, Labour party strategy board. Ed: University of Westminster (BA politics & sociology); Open University (MBA). **Steven Lambert** (LD) Former project manager, Post Office. Cllr: Buckinghamshire CC 2013; Aylesbury Vale DC 2007-. Ed: Open University, (BSc social sciences).

CONSTITUENCY PROFILE
The seat, once the pocket borough of the Rothschild family, has been Tory since 1924. Aylesbury has at times leaned towards the Liberal Democrats, but the semi-rural commuter towns and villages to the south give the seat a substantial Conservative majority. In 2015 Ukip took second place, after campaigning on the issue of HS2, with 20 per cent tripling their vote share.

	Electorate	Turnout %	Change from 2010 %
	80,611	68.8	
D Lidington C	28,083	50.7	-1.5
C Adams Ukip	10,925	19.7	+12.9
W Cass Lab	8,391	15.1	+2.6
S Lambert LD	5,885	10.6	-17.8
D Lyons Green	2,135	3.9	

Change from 2010

25%

0%

-25%

C   Ukip   Lab   LD   Green

Ayr, Carrick & Cumnock

SNP GAIN

CORRI WILSON
BORN Apr 11, 1965
MP 2015-

Runs own event management company having previously worked in voluntary sector and been a civil servant. Overturned Labour's 2010 majority of 9,900 to win the seat by 11,265 votes. Cllr, South Ayrshire C 2012-. Dir: Septembayr (Ayrshire festival); Ayr Renaissance; Ayrshire Housing. Former member, local NHS partnership forum. Two children. Ed: Ayr Academy; University of the West of Scotland (BSc psychology).

CHALLENGERS
Sandra Osborne (Lab) MP, Ayr, Carrick & Cumnock 2005-15; Ayr 1997-2005. Select cttees included: foreign affairs 2013-15, 2005-10; european scrutiny 2004-10, 2011-2013; panel of chairs 2011-15; defence 2010-2013. PPS to: Helen Liddell 2002-03; George Foulkes 2001-02. Cllr: Kyle & Carrick DC

1990-95; S Ayrshire C 1995-97. Previously community worker. Member, Unite. Married, two daughters. Ed: Camphill Senior; Strathclyde (Dip community ed, MSc equality & discrimination). **Lee Lyons** (C) Owner of artist management firm, Total Music. Partner. Ed: Park Mains HS, Erskine. **Joseph Adam-Smith** (Ukip) Former civil servant. Ed: Netherthorpe GS, Staveley; UWS (BA media). **Richard Brodie** (LD) Former teacher. Cllr, Dumfries & Galloway, 2008-. Contested Scotland Euro elections 2014. Ed: Bathgate Academy; University of Edinburgh.

CONSTITUENCY PROFILE
Created for the 2005 general election, and is a compilation of parts of Ayr, Carrick, Cumnock and Doon Valley. It is a mix of council estates, former mining villages around Cumnock to the east and affluent middle-class areas. Strongly Labour supporting until the SNP triumph in 2015.

	Electorate	Turnout %	Change from 2010 %
	72,985	71.5	
C Wilson SNP	25,492	48.8	+30.8
S Osborne Lab	14,227	27.3	-19.9
L Lyons C	10,355	19.8	-5.7
J Adam-Smith Ukip	1,280	2.5	
R Brodie LD	855	1.6	-7.7

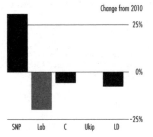

Change from 2010

SNP   Lab   C   Ukip   LD

Ayrshire Central

SNP GAIN

PHILIPPA WHITFORD
BORN Dec 24, 1958
MP 2015-

SNP group leader, health 2015-. Consultant breast surgeon, Crosshouse Hospital, Kilmarnock, until start of election campaign. Led development of Scottish breast-cancer care standards. Active within the Woman for Independence campaign; key advocate during the Yes campaign. Left Labour in protest at its Iraq war policies, and joined SNP 2011. Medical volunteer at UN hospital, Gaza 1991-92. Feminist blogger. YouTube video of her warning of NHS privatisation if Scotland remained part of the Union went viral. Married, one son. Ed: University of Glasgow (medicine).

CHALLENGERS
Brian Donohoe (Lab) MP, Ayrshire Central 2005-15; Cunninghame South 1992-2005. PPS to Lord Adonis 2008-10. Select cttees

included: admin 2005-10; transport 1993-05; transport, local govt, regions 2001-02. Member, TGWU. Former Nalgo district officer. Former: shipyard apprentice; draughtsman, ICI. Married, two sons. Ed: Irvine Royal Academy; Kilmarnock Tech Coll (nat cert engineering). **Marc Hope** (C) Director, rights marketing at the Sports Consultancy. Cllr, Wandsworth BC 2002-2010. Dir, British Athletics Supporters club. Married, three children. Ed: Drumley House Schoool, Ayr; Stowe; Essex (BA English & European literature). **Gordon Bain** (LD) Web designer and developer. Ed: James Watt Coll (software engineering).

CONSTITUENCY PROFILE
A diverse seat that includes working class areas such as Irvine and more affluent towns such as Troon. Despite various boundary changes it had been firmly Labour since the 1950s but made a massive swing to the SNP in 2015.

	Electorate	Turnout %	Change from 2010 %
	69,982	72.6	
P Whitford SNP	26,999	53.2	+34.1
B Donohoe Lab	13,410	26.4	-21.3
M Hope C	8,803	17.3	-3.0
G Bain LD	917	1.8	-10.1
V Tudhope Green	645	1.3	

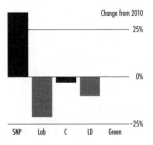

Change from 2010

SNP   Lab   C   LD   Green

Ayrshire North & Arran

SNP GAIN

PATRICIA GIBSON
BORN May 12, 1968
MP 2015-

Former English teacher. Cllr, Glasgow CC 2007-12. SNP spokeswoman, education 2007-11. Pollock constituency sec 2005-07. Contested Ayrshire North & Arran, 2010 moving the SNP from third to second place, before sweeping into parliament in 2015. Married to SNP MSP Ken Gibson. Ed: St Gerard's Secondary Sch; University of Glasgow (BA MA politics & english); Open University (modular courses, child development; approaches to literature).

CHALLENGERS
Katy Clark (Lab) MP, Ayrshire North & Arran. Select cttees include: BIS 2010-15; environment audit 2010-15; arms export controls 2010-15; panel of chairs 2010-15; Scottish affairs 2005-10. Member, Socialist Campaign Group. Contested

Galloway & Upper Nithsdale 2001. Secretary, Trade Union Group of MPs. Head of membership legal services, Unison. TGWU, GMB. Former solicitor. Ed: Kyle Academy, Ayr; Aberdeen (LLB law); Edinburgh (Dip legal practice). **Jamie Greene** (C) Sales director, SeaChange, a multi-screen software specialist. Ed: St Stephens HS, Port Glasgow; Glasgow (MA French, Spanish and education/ linguistic studies). **Sharon McGonigal** (Ukip) Chairwoman, Ukip Ayrshire & Arran. Mother of three. Ed: University of Paisley.

CONSTITUENCY PROFILE
Stretches along a strip of west coast mainland. Used to be a safe Conservative seat, held by the party 1911-87, but boundary changes brought in more industrial areas to the south turning the seat into Labour territory. The equivalent seat in the Scottish parliament has been SNP since 2005, foreshadowing the party's 2015 win.

	Electorate	Turnout %	Change from 2010 %
	75,772	71.1	
P Gibson SNP	28,641	53.2	+27.2
K Clark Lab	15,068	28.0	-19.4
J Greene C	7,968	14.8	-0.9
S McGonigal Ukip	1,296	2.4	
R Kirkwood LD	896	1.7	-8.4

Change from 2010

Banbury

CONSERVATIVE HOLD

VICTORIA PRENTIS
BORN Mar 24, 1971
MP 2015-

Civil service lawyer who defended government in key cases such as the 7/7 inquiry. Director, anti-HS2 group Transport Sense. Founder and former chairwoman, Benefactors' board of the Oxford Hospital's Trust. Fundraising trustee, NorPIP (Northampton Parent Infant Partnership). Father, Tim Boswell (Lord Boswell of Aynho) served as MP for Daventry, 1987-2010. Married, two daughters. Ed: London (BA English literature); Downing Coll, Cambridge (LLM).

CHALLENGERS
Sean Woodcock (Lab) Neighbourhood officer, for housing association. Cllr, Cherwell DC 2012-, leader Lab group 2013-. Member: Unison; Co-operative party. Ed: University of Reading (BA history); University of Birmingham (MA reformation

& early modern studies). **Dickie Bird** (Ukip) Former head porter at Oriel Coll, Oxford, resigned to run for parliament. Formerly, Royal Green Jackets for 23 years. **John Howson** (LD) CEO, Oxford Teacher Services. Former teacher and university lecturer. Cllr, Oxfordshire CC 2013-. Vice-president: Magistrates' Association for England and Wales; Lib Dem Education Association. Contested Reading East 2005. Ed: LSE (BA economics and governance of education).

CONSTITUENCY PROFILE
Set in North Oxfordshire. A solidly Conservative seat in the northeast of Oxfordshire, held by the party since 1922. The main centres are Banbury and the fast growing commuter town, Bicester. The seat's position on the M40 and the rail line to Marylebone make it a popular and affluent commuter area for both London and Birmingham, but it retains an agricultural economy.

	Electorate	Turnout %	Change from 2010 %
	86,420	67.1	
V Prentis C	30,749	53.0	+0.2
S Woodcock Lab	12,354	21.3	+2.1
D Bird Ukip	8,050	13.9	+8.9
J Howson LD	3,440	5.9	-14.5
I Middleton Green	2,686	4.6	+2.9
R Edwards NHAP	729	1.3	

Change from 2010

Banff & Buchan

SNP HOLD

EILIDH WHITEFORD
BORN April 24, 1969
MP 2010-

Long-term SNP activist, worked for Alex Salmond, MEPs Allan Macartney, Ian Hudghton, and Irene McGugan MSP. Shadow SNP Westminster group leader, social justice & welfare. Labelled Danny Alexander as hypocrite in 2015 after he launched attack on Conservative coalition partners. Shad SNP spokes: agriculture & fisheries 2010-15; women 2010-15; int devt 2010-15; W&P 2010-15. Select cttees: Scottish affairs 2010-. Scottish campaigns manager, Make Poverty History for Oxfam. Co-ordinator, Scottish Carers' Alliance. Lecturer, Scottish Literature at Glasgow University and Newbattle Abbey Coll. Fed of Student Nats (nat organiser, president). Ed: Banff Academy; Glasgow (MA English & Scottish literature); Guelph, Ontario (MA English lang & lit); Glasgow (PhD Scottish literature).

CHALLENGERS
Alex Johnstone (C) MSP, NE Scotland 1999-. Conservative spokes, communities & housing 2014-. Previously Scottish Conservatives chief whip & business manager. Dairy farmer before election to parliament. Married, two children. Ed: Mackie Academy. **Sumon Hoque** (Lab) Suspended as candidate for drink driving charge 2015, still on ballot paper. Works for independent TV company. Ed: Aberdeen University. **David Evans** (LD) Administrator, NHS Aberdeen Royal Infirmary. Cllr, South Lakeland DC 2010-. Ed: Ellon Academy; Aberdeen (LLB law).

CONSTITUENCY PROFILE
Banff and Buchan is most associated with Alex Salmond, its MP for 23 years until 2010. An SNP stronghold, but Conservatives challenged in 2010, although in 2015 the SNP received twice as many votes as the Tories. Home to the St Fergus gas terminal, with fishing and farming other key industries.

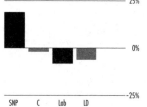

	Electorate	Turnout %	Change from 2010 %
	68,609	66.5	
E Whiteford SNP	27,487	60.2	+19.0
A Johnstone C	13,148	28.8	-2.0
S Hoque Lab	2,647	5.8	-8.2
D Evans LD	2,347	5.1	-6.2

Change from 2010

SNP   C   Lab   LD

Barking

LABOUR HOLD

MARGARET HODGE
BORN Sep 8, 1944
MP 1994-

Hard-edged chairwoman of the public accounts select cttee 2010-15 who put tax avoidance at the top of the political agenda. Some in Treasury trying to attract foreign investment will be happy to see her gone. Her own tax affairs came in for scrutiny in 2012. Also chairwoman, liaison cttee 2010-15. Shad min: culture & tourism 2010. Min: CMS, 2009-10; 2007-08; t&i 2006-07; w&p 2005-06; education & skills 2001-05. Parly under-sec, education & employment 1998-2001. Pulled out of race for London mayor February 2015 and said would support fellow London MP David Lammy. Cllr, Islington 1973-94, leader 1982-92). TGWU. Price Waterhouse consultant. Teacher. Market researcher. Divorced, one daughter, one son. Remarried, widowed, two daughters. Ed: Oxford HS; LSE (BSc economics).

CHALLENGERS
Roger Gravett (Ukip). Site manager, Lordship Lane Primary Sch. Chairman Ukip Enfield and Haringey branch. **Mina Rahman** (C) Social housing manager, Tower Hamlets Community Housing. Chairwoman, Conservative Friends Bangladesh (Redbridge). Vice-chairwoman, Ilford South Conservative Association. **Rev Tony Rablen** (Green). Vicar and NHS mental health chaplain. Ed: Durham (BA economics); Nottingham (BA theology).

CONSTITUENCY PROFILE
Barking is a safe Labour seat, held by the party since its creation in 1945. Formerly one of the BNP's strongest seats in the country and the far-right party came third in 2005 election. In 2010 it was contested by the BNP leader Nick Griffin but Conservatives retained second place. It carried into a strong Ukip performance in the 2015 election, with a seven-fold increase in its number of votes.

	Electorate	Turnout %	Change from 2010 %
	74,004	58.1	
M Hodge Lab	24,826	57.7	+3.4
R Gravett Ukip	9,554	22.2	+19.3
M Rahman C	7,019	16.3	-1.5
T Rablen Green	879	2.0	+1.3
P Wilcock LD	562	1.3	-6.9
J Mambuliya TUSC	183	0.4	

Change from 2010

Lab   Ukip   C   Green   LD

Barnsley Central

LABOUR HOLD

DAN JARVIS
BORN Nov 30, 1972
MP 2011-

A Labour leadership front-runner in 2015, ruled himself out to put his family first. Shad min: justice 2013-2015; CMS 2011-2013. Select cttees: BIS 2011. Launched Proud of Barnsley campaign. Took over from Eric Illsley, after the latter was jailed for expenses fraud. Former army officer, Parachute Regiment. First person since Second World War to resign commission to contest the by-election. Vice-president, Kexborough Cricket Club. Honorary patron, Barnsley Youth Choir. Completed 2015 London Marathon. Widowed, remarried, three children. Ed: Rushcliffe CS; Aberystwyth University (international politics and strategic studies); RMA Sandhurst.

CHALLENGERS
Lee Hunter (Ukip) CNC Waterjet profiler, ThyssenKrupp. Cllr,

Rotherham MBC 2014-. Ed: Dearne Valley Business Sch. **Kay Carter** (C) Former contributor, *The Sunday Times*. Mother of two daughters. **Michael Short** (Green) Trade union officer and business liason, Unison. Former Labour member, defected to Green party 2014. Ed: Barnsley Coll; Huddersfield University. **John Ridgway** (LD) Chairman, Valleys Broadband. Cllr, Kirklees DC 2008-, 1996-2004, chairman 1997-2004, mayor 2012-13.

CONSTITUENCY PROFILE
Ultra-safe Labour seat, along with its predecessor, Barnsley, it has been held by Labour since 1935, often with truly daunting majorities. Barnsley is a town with deep industrial heritage, and at the start of the Eighties, a fifth of Barnsley's workforce were in mining and pit closures hit the town hard. Eric Illsley was suspended in 2010 for three charges of false accounting to which he pleaded guilty.

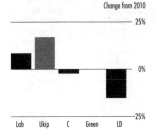

	Electorate	Turnout %	Change from 2010 %
	64,534	56.7	
D Jarvis Lab	20,376	55.7	+8.5
L Hunter Ukip	7,941	21.7	+17.1
K Carter C	5,485	15.0	-2.3
M Short Green	938	2.6	
J Ridgway LD	770	2.1	-15.2
D Gibson TUSC	573	1.6	
I Sutton Eng Dem	477	1.3	

Change from 2010

Barnsley East

LABOUR HOLD

MICHAEL DUGHER
BORN Apr 26, 1975
MP 2010-

Special adviser from union background. Grew up in working-class pit village of Edlington. Chief political spokesman for Gordon Brown, adviser to Geoff Hoon and John Spellar. Embroiled in a Twitter row with Jeremy Clarkson 2015. Shad SoS transport 2014-. Shadow min: Cab Office 2013-14; without portfolio (Cabinet Office), 2011-13; defence 2010-11. Member, select cttee: public administration 2010-12. Political interests: economy, defence. Contested Skipton & Ripon 2001. Unite, Unison, Fabian Society. Labour First, Labour Friends of Israel. Was UK dir of gov't relations, EDS & head of policy, AEEU. Researcher and speechwriter for Frank Dobson. Chairman of Labour Students. Guitar player. Married, two daughters. Ed: McAuley RC Sch, Doncaster; University of Nottingham (BA politics).

CHALLENGERS
Robert Swiffen (Ukip) Miner. Left school at 14. Worked at Houghton Main colliery for almost 27 years. Married, two daughters. **Katharine Harborne** (C) Businesswoman and chartered environmentalist. Cllr, Richmond-upon-Thames BC 2010-14. Ed: University of Reading (BSc horticultural botany); Natal (MSc epidemiology, microbiology and plant pathology). **Ruth Coleman-Taylor** (LD) Self-employed, Todmorden. Cllr, North Wiltshire DC 1991-07. Contested Leeds West 2010. Ed: University of York (BA social sciences); University of Manchester (Post-grad general studies, statistics); The Open University (BA creative writing, global politics, environment).

CONSTITUENCY PROFILE
Very safe Labour seat, represented by the party since before the Second World War. BNP won 3,000 votes in 2010, and Ukip gained five times their 2010 numbers this election.

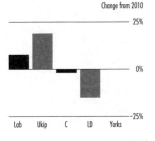

	Electorate	Turnout %	Change from 2010 %
	69,135	55.7	
M Dugher Lab	21,079	54.7	+7.7
R Swiffen Ukip	9,045	23.5	+19.0
K Harborne C	5,622	14.6	-1.9
R Coleman-Taylor LD	1,217	3.2	-15.0
T Devoy Yorks	647	1.7	
K Riddiough Eng Dem	440	1.1	
R Dyson TUSC	364	1.0	
B Marsden Vapers	103	0.3	

Change from 2010

Barrow & Furness

LABOUR CO-OPERATIVE HOLD

JOHN WOODCOCK
BORN Oct 14, 1978
MP 2010-

Political spokesman for Gordon Brown as prime minister, but never very comfortable with the art of political spin. On the Progress wing of the party. Recently apologised after being reported to the Standards Commissioner for breaking the rules on the use of pre-paid House of Commons envelopes. Worked as special adviser to John Hutton. Shad min: transport, 2010-2013. Mem, select cttees: defence 2010, 2013-15. Sheffield-born. Former journalist, *North West Evening Mail*. Spoke out in 2013 about suffering from depression. Married (to former NUS president Mandy Telford), one daughter. Ed: Tapton Comprehensive Sch; Edinburgh.

CHALLENGERS
Simon Fell (C). Works in crime prevention. Mem, British Council

TN2020 network of future leaders. Patron, Fair Votes for All campaign. Married. Ed: Warwick (BA English). **Nigel Cecil** (Ukip) Shipyard worker. **Clive Peaple** (LD) Retired head teacher. Previously worked with British forces in Cyprus, adviser to Czech Republic after Velvet Revolution. Chaired, Rural Academy. Ed: Reading (BA history). **Robert O'Hara** (Green) Business owner and manager. Former teacher. Ed: St Peter's Coll, Oxford (BEd mathematics & computer science).

CONSTITUENCY PROFILE
Typically a Labour-leaning seat, the party has continued to hold the majority since about the time of the Second World War. The Conservatives won the seat in 1983, but Labour regained it in 1992. Barrow is an industrial town, a major deepwater port and shipbuilding town, capable of constructing nuclear submarines. Also an important area for electricity generation.

		Electorate	Turnout %	Change from 2010 %
		68,338	63.3	
J Woodcock	Lab Co-op	18,320	42.3	-5.8
S Fell	C	17,525	40.5	+4.2
N Cecil	Ukip	5,070	11.7	+9.8
C Peaple	LD	1,169	2.7	-7.3
R O'Hara	Green	1,061	2.5	+1.3
I Jackson	Ind	130	0.3	-0.3

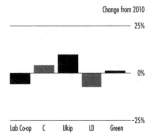

Change from 2010

Lab Co-op · C · Ukip · LD · Green

Basildon & Billericay

CONSERVATIVE HOLD

JOHN BARON
BORN Jun 21, 1959
MP 2001-

From the mainstream Tory right, campaigned against large travellers site in his constituency. Opp whip 2007-10; Shad min: health 2002-03, resigned in opposition to Iraq war, reappointed 2003-07. Mem, select cttees: foreign affairs 2010-15; education & skills 2001-02. Royal Regiment of Fusiliers (served in Berlin, Northern Ireland, Cyprus). Investment fund manager, director of Hendersons then Rothschild. Married, two daughters. Ed: Queen's Coll, Taunton; Jesus Coll, Cambridge (BA history and economics); RMA Sandhurst.

CHALLENGERS
Gavin Callaghan (Lab) Media adviser and speechwriter for Steve Rotheram. Cllr, Basildon, 2012-. Leader, Basildon Lab Group. Former: parly asst to Gloria De Piero MP; press officer to Dan

Jarvis; sports broadcaster, Betfred. Member of UCATT union. Writes for Sunderland football magazine *Seventy3*. Married. Ed: Newcastle (BA politics). **George Konstantinidis** (Ukip). Business consultant. Greek-born. Chairman, Ukip eastern region 2013-. Contested Central Bedfordshire 2011 council election. Married, four children. Ed: Pantios University of Athens (sociology); North Herts Coll (Dip business & finance). **Martin Thompson** (LD) Contested Basildon & East Thurrock 2005.

CONSTITUENCY PROFILE
The seat was created for the 2010 general election, at which the Conservatives gained the seat, despite prominent Labour support in each electoral ward. The seat merged most of the previous constituency of Billericay with parts of the former Basildon constituency. The latter is the commercial centre of southern Essex but the seat has pockets of severe deprivation.

		Electorate	Turnout %	Change from 2010 %
		68,459	62.9	
J Baron	C	22,668	52.7	-0.1
G Callaghan	Lab	10,186	23.7	+0.6
G Konstantinidis	Ukip	8,538	19.8	+16.0
M Thompson	LD	1,636	3.8	-11.9

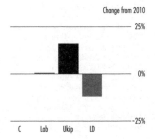

Change from 2010

C · Lab · Ukip · LD

Basildon South & Thurrock East

CONSERVATIVE HOLD

STEPHEN METCALFE
BORN Jan 9, 1966
MP 2010-

Lifelong Essex man and longtime Tory activist. PPS to Chris Grayling. Member, select cttee: science & technology, 2010-15. Cllr, Epping Forest DC 2002-07. Selected by open primary. Contested Ilford South 2005. Former dep chairman, Essex Conservative party. Creative director Metloc Printers, family-owned printing business. Trustee, Age Concern. Conservative Friends of Israel, Conservative Christian Fellowship. Amateur dramatics enthusiast. Married, one daughter, one son. Ed: Loughton School (head boy); Buckhurst Hill County HS Sixth Form.

CHALLENGERS

Ian Luder (Ukip) Tax accountant. Member, Bedford Council for 23 years. Contested Yeovil 1979 as Labour. Former Lord Mayor of London 2008-09. Appointed CBE,

2010. Married. Ed: Haberdashers' Aske's Boys' Sch; UCL (BA economics & economic history). **Mike Le-Surf** (Lab) Works at Mencap. Cllr, Brentwood BC 2007-. Leader of Brentwood BC Labour group. Contested Rayleigh & Wickford 2010. Married, two daughters. Ed: St Edwards Sch. **Geoff Williams** (LD) Mentor, Improvement & Devt Agency. Former FE lecturer. Cllr, Basildon BC 1981, 1986-; Essex CC 1993-97, 2004-05. Wife fellow cllr, Basildon BC. Contested South Basildon & East Thurrock, 2010. Ed: Kings Coll, London (BA German & French; MPhil German).

CONSTITUENCY PROFILE

The old Basildon seat was an iconic victory for the Conservatives in 1992, with David Amess's successful holding of the seat heralding their ultimate victory. Ukip asserted as prominent challenger at 2015 election, increasing their vote by 20.6 per cent, rising from fourth to second.

	Electorate	Turnout %	Change from 2010 %
	73,210	62.3	
S Metcalfe C	19,788	43.4	-0.5
I Luder Ukip	12,097	26.5	+20.6
M Le-Surf Lab	11,493	25.2	-5.8
G Williams LD	1,356	3.0	-10.4
K Smith Ind	401	0.9	
N O T A X ND	253	0.6	+0.3
S Hooper Ind	205	0.5	

Change from 2010

(bar chart: C, Ukip, Lab, LD, Ind; range 25% to -25%)

Basingstoke

CONSERVATIVE HOLD

MARIA MILLER
BORN Mar 26, 1964
MP 2005-

Quietly diligent, good on family policy. New breed Tory; hard-working mother who opposes all-women shortlists. Campaigned for the revenge pornography law. Min: women & equalities, 2012-14. SoS: CMS 2012-14. Resigned as cab min after expenses scandal and forced to apologise to the House. Parly under-sec: work & pensions 2010-12. Shad min: family 2007-10; family welfare 2006-07; education 2005-06. Mem, select cttees: children, schools & families 2007; trade & industry 2005-06. Advertising, marketing and PR career; Texaco, Grey Advertising, Saatchi Rowland. Married, three children. Ed: Brynteg Comprehensive, Bridgend; LSE (BSc economics).

CHALLENGERS

Paul Harvey (Lab) Associate

lecturer in social scienes, Southampton Solent. Deputy leader, Basingstoke Labour group. Cllr, Basingstoke & Dean 2003-. Leader, Basingstoke and Dean BC, 2005-06. Ed: Hull (BA politics; MA international politics); Reading (PhD international politics & defence). **Alan Stone** (Ukip) Self-employed antiques dealer, Squirrels Antiques. Chairman, Basingstoke Ukip group. **Janice Spalding** (LD) IT project planner, ATLAS. Has worked in the utility industry. Active player with Basingstoke Hockey Club. Ed: Gosforth HS; Huddersfield University (BA computing and business).

CONSTITUENCY PROFILE

The seat has returned a Conservative MP since the 1920s, although the 2001-05 parliament was briefly in the unusual position of being a mainland British seat represented by a Northern Irish political party: the MP Andrew Hunter having joined the Democratic Unionists.

	Electorate	Turnout %	Change from 2010 %
	79,662	66.6	
M Miller C	25,769	48.6	-2.0
P Harvey Lab	14,706	27.7	+7.3
A Stone Ukip	8,290	15.6	+11.5
J Spalding LD	3,919	7.4	-17.1
O Selim Ind	392	0.7	

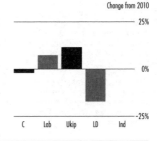

Change from 2010

(bar chart: C, Lab, Ukip, LD, Ind; range 25% to -25%)

Bassetlaw

LABOUR HOLD

JOHN MANN
BORN Jan 10, 1960
MP 2001-

Plain-speaking. PPS to: Tessa Jowell 2007-09; Richard Caborn 2005-07. Member, select cttees: Treasury 2009-10, 2003-05; unopposed bills 2004-10; information 2001-05. Cllr, Lambeth BC 1986-90. National training officer TUC 1990-95. Head of research & education AEEU. Company dir. Led detailed allegations against 12 former ministers regarding child abuse, 2014. Married, two daughters, one son. Ed: Bradford GS; University of Manchester (BA economics); ITD dip.

CHALLENGERS
Sarah Downes (C) Social care manager, Richmond Care Villages. Managing dir, Sarah Downes. Married to an armed forces veteran. Ed: Girton Coll, Cambridge (BA history). **David**

Scott (Ukip) Mechanic. Chairman Ukip Bassetlaw branch. Ed: Hartland Comprehensive; North Notts Coll. **Leon Duveen** (LD) Self-employed IT contractor. Served 18 months compulsory service, Israeli Army. Helped to set up Bassetlaw Against Fracking. Ed: Sheffield Hallam (mathematical sciences). **Kris Wragg** (Green) Software developer, Simcyp. Treasury officer, Bassetlaw Green party.

CONSTITUENCY PROFILE
In the northern part of Nottinghamshire, the seat consists of the towns of Worksop and Retford and several small villages. Like many former mining areas, it has suffered since the decline of the industry. Traditionally a safe Labour seat despite increasing levels of Conservative councillors on Bassetlaw Council. The party first won the seat in 1929. Major employers include Wilkinsons and Premier Foods, which produces Oxo in Worksop.

	Electorate	Turnout %	from 2010 %	Change
	77,480	63.6		
J Mann Lab	23,965	48.6	-1.8	
S Downes C	15,122	30.7	-3.2	
D Scott Ukip	7,865	16.0	+12.4	
L Duveen LD	1,331	2.7	-8.5	
K Wragg Green	1,006	2.0		

Change from 2010

25%

0%

-25%

Lab   C   Ukip   LD   Green

Bath

CONSERVATIVE GAIN

BEN HOWLETT
BORN Aug 21, 1986
MP 2015-

Managing healthcare consultant, Finegreen Associates. Said his party would not have a hope of winning the seat were it not for former LD MP Don Foster standing down. Cllr, Harwich TC 2007-11. Worked for the RUH and Min hospitals for six years. First Conservative Future chairman in five years to address party conference on the main stage. Leader, Conservative group, Harwich TC. Former chairman, Conservative Future 2010-13. Ed: Durham (BA history and politics); Sidney Sussex Coll, Cambridge (MPhil economic history).

CHALLENGERS
Steve Bradley (LD) Environmental consultant. Leading community campaigner. Originally from Ireland. Cllr, Lambeth BC, 2008-14 by-election. Former spokes,

Lambeth BC sustainability & climate change. Chairman, Green Lib Dems. Former marketing consultant, Procter & Gamble and Walt Disney. Involved in the Transition Towns movement. Hobbies include rugby and football. Ed: University of Bath (management, pres BUSU 1995-97.). **Ollie Middleton** (Lab) Student. Ed: Ralph Allen Sch; University of Westminster (currently reading politics & international relations). **Dominic Tristram** (Green) Former software architect. Ed: University of Wales, Aberystwyth (BSc; PhD computer science), The Open University (PgDip humanities).

CONSTITUENCY PROFILE
Compact seat comprising the ancient city of Bath, includes strong tourism and software and service industries as well as two universities, University of Bath and Bath Spa University. A former Conservative seat, but held by Don Foster for Lib Dems since 1992.

	Electorate	Turnout %	from 2010 %	Change
	60,869	77.5		
B Howlett C	17,833	37.8	+6.4	
S Bradley LD	14,000	29.7	-26.9	
O Middleton Lab	6,216	13.2	+6.3	
D Tristram Green	5,634	11.9	+9.6	
J Deverell Ukip	2,922	6.2	+4.3	
L Morgan-Brinkhurst Ind	499	1.1	+0.9	
J Knight Eng Dem	63	0.1		

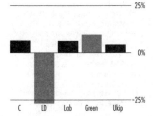

Change from 2010

25%

0%

-25%

C   LD   Lab   Green   Ukip

Batley & Spen

LABOUR HOLD

JO COX
BORN Aug 22, 1974
MP 2005-

Former head of policy at Oxfam. Also worked with Save the Children and NSPCC. National chairwoman, Labour Women's Network. Senior adviser, anti-slavery charity The Freedom Fund. Founder & CEO, UK Women. Nominated in 2009 by the Davos World Economic Forum as a young global leader. Enjoys climbing mountains. Married, two children. Ed: Heckmondwike GS; Pembroke Coll, Cambridge (BA social & political studies); LSE (Europe & the world).

CHALLENGERS
Imtiaz Ameen (C) Lawyer. Cllr, Kirklees BC 2003-07. Former spokesman, education. Contested Blackburn, 2005. Married, two children. **Aleksandar Lukic** (Ukip) IT Teacher, Heckmondwike GS. Third-generation British Serb.

Member: NUT; Computing At School. Ed: St John's Clifton & Heckmondwike GS; Edinburgh (computer science); Leeds Trinity University (PGCE secondary information & communications technology). **John Lawson** (LD) Dir, Medica Centre. Cllr, Kirklees Council 2010-. Member, Kirklees Theatre Trust. Ed: Byamshaw Sch of Art, London (fine art); University of Glamorgan (sociology).

CONSTITUENCY PROFILE
A former mill town with a large Asian population. The 'Spen' in the seat title refers to 'Spen Valley', a collection of former textile towns in semi-rural settings. A marginal seat between the Conservatives and Labour, with Batley voting predominantly Labour, and the remaining towns included in the 'Spen' leaning towards the Convervatives. The seat is ethnically mixed and the Conservatives have struggled recently. Lib Dem vote share decreased by 11.1 per cent.

	Electorate	Turnout %	Change from 2010 %
	78,373	64.4	
J Cox Lab	21,826	43.2	+1.0
I Ameen C	15,769	31.2	-2.3
A Lukic Ukip	9,080	18.0	
J Lawson LD	2,396	4.8	-11.1
I Bullock Green	1,232	2.4	+1.3
D Wheelhouse TUSC	123	0.2	
K Varley PSP	53	0.1	

Change from 2010

Lab   C   Ukip   LD   Green

Battersea

CONSERVATIVE HOLD

JANE ELLISON
BORN Aug 15, 1964
MP 2010-

Europhile on the Tory left, whose selection by open primary caused consternation with local party. Friend of Matthew Offord MP from Barnet BC (Cllr, 2006-08, 1991-94). Parly under-sec for public health, 2013-. Member, select cttees: backbench business 2013; WP 2012-13; business 2010-13. Contested Pendle 2005; Tottenham 2000; Barnsley 1997, 1996. John Lewis Partnership career: managed customer magazine, customer direct marketing. Bradford-born. Sings in choir, national trustee Sing for Pleasure. Spurs fan. Has partner. Ed: St Joseph's Coll; St Hilda's Coll, Oxford (BA PPE).

CHALLENGERS
Will Martindale (Lab) Research and policy manager, United Nations. Former finance worker, JP Morgan, BNP Paribas. Supported

Principles for Responsible Investment. Gov, John Burns Primary Sch. Member, Battersea Society. Married, one daughter. Ed: King's Coll (BSc mathematics); LSE (MSc comparative politics). **Luke Taylor** (LD) Transport planner. Member, Association of Liberal Democrat Engineers & Scientists. Married. Ed: Imperial College London (MEng aeronautical engineering). **Joe Stuart** (Green) Voluntary worker. Chairman: The Family Centre; North & South Leaseholders' Association. Vice-chairman: Doddington Business Centre.

CONSTITUENCY PROFILE
Once a reliably Labour area of south London, but gentrification brought young professionals from Chelsea and turned it Conservative in 2010. The north of the constituency contains Battersea Park, the power station and the new US embassy. To the south it includes half of Clapham Common and Balham.

	Electorate	Turnout %	Change from 2010 %
	76,106	67.1	
J Ellison C	26,730	52.4	+5.0
W Martindale Lab	18,792	36.8	+1.7
L Taylor LD	2,241	4.4	-10.3
J Stuart Green	1,682	3.3	+2.2
C Howe Ukip	1,586	3.1	+2.1

Change from 2010

C   Lab   LD   Green   Ukip

Beaconsfield

CONSERVATIVE HOLD

DOMINIC GRIEVE
BORN May 24, 1956
MP 1997-

One of few Tories to back Human Rights Act in maiden speech. Incisive and an accomplished Commons performer on legal issues but can look posh and out of touch on other topics. Attorney-general 2010-2014. Shad: SoS justice 2009-10; home secretary 2008-09; attorney-general 2003-09; min, home affairs 2001-03, Scotland 1999-2001. Opp spokes: constitutional affairs 1999-2001. Contested Norwood 1987. Made controversial comments about Britain's Pakistani community in 2013. Mem, select cttees: standards & privileges 2014-15; environmental audit, statutory instruments 1997-2001. Son of Percy Grieve MP. Married, two children, one deceased son. Ed: Westminster Sch, Magdalen Coll, Oxford (BA, MA modern history, OUCA president); London Polytechnic (PgDip law).

CHALLENGERS
Tim Scott (Ukip) Business development manager, Transact Investment Platform. Former army serviceman. Progressive rock fan. Married, two children. Ed: Royal GS, High Wycombe; Southampton (BA politics & international studies). **Tony Clements** (Lab) Co-editor, Brimingham University magazine *Red Brick* and housing associate. Chairman, Lab De Beauvoir Branch, Hackney. Exec-mem, LLHG. Former adviser to John Healey MP. Ed: Cambridge. **Peter Chapman** (LD) Voluntary worker. Cllr, Gerrards Cross PC 2003-11. Vice-chairman, Gerrards Cross PC. Contested Beaconsfield, 2005. Former magistrate.

CONSTITUENCY PROFILE
Close to Heathrow and M25 but retaining rural charm. Traditionally one of the safest Conservative seats in the country, achieving 63 per cent of vote in 2015, second highest in the country. Tony Blair contested unsuccessfully in 1982.

	Electorate	Turnout %	Change from 2010 %
	76,380	69.6	
D Grieve C	33,621	63.2	+2.2
T Scott Ukip	7,310	13.8	+8.8
T Clements Lab	6,074	11.4	-0.3
P Chapman LD	3,927	7.4	-12.2
D Hampton Green	2,231	4.2	+2.7

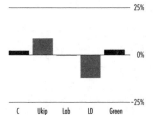

Change from 2010

| C | Ukip | Lab | LD | Green |

Beckenham

CONSERVATIVE HOLD

BOB STEWART
BORN Jul 7, 1949
MP 2010-

Decorated Army Colonel, nicknamed Bosnia Bob (after high media profile as British commander of UN forces in Bosnia). Has spoken out about possibly resigning as an MP because of anger over continuing squeeze on military spending. Freelance writer, broadcaster, lecturer. Political consultant. WorldSpace (MD); Hill & Knowlton (senior consultant). Member, selet cttees: defence, 2010-15; arms export controls 2011-14. Friend of Martin Bell. Campaigned with Adam Holloway 2005. Publications: *Broken Lives* 1993; *Leadership Under Pressure* 2009. Chief of policy, Supreme HQ Allied Powers of Europe. Raised in RAF family. Divorced, two children. Re-married, two children. Ed: RMA Sandhurst; Wales (international politics), Army Staff Coll; Joint Services Staff Coll.

CHALLENGERS
Marina Ahmad (Lab) Barrister. Founder member, Amnesty Bangladesh. Former worker, Crown Prosecution Department. Ed: Surrey (English & history); Bath (PgDip development studies); City (law). **Rob Bryant** (Ukip) Mem, Ukip Bromley. **Anuja Prashar** (LD) Lecturer in higher education. Worked at the Home Office as staff officer to the dir gen. Born in Kenya. Ed: Michigan (BA economics); Birkbeck (MSc race & ethnic relations); Open University (PhD multi-interdisciplinary studies).

CONSTITUENCY PROFILE
An affluent, middle-class seat sandwiched between Croydon and Bromley, south of London. Solidly Conservative since 1950. Became slightly vulnerable in 1997 by-election caused by the resignation of the MP Piers Merchant after an affair with a teenage girl, but the Conservatives still managed to hold on.

	Electorate	Turnout %	Change from 2010 %
	67,436	72.4	
B Stewart C	27,955	57.3	-0.6
M Ahmad Lab	9,484	19.4	+5.0
R Bryant Ukip	6,108	12.5	+9.3
A Prashar LD	3,378	6.9	-13.7
R Fabricant Green	1,878	3.9	+2.6

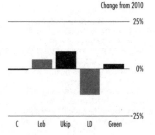

Change from 2010

| C | Lab | Ukip | LD | Green |

Bedford

CONSERVATIVE HOLD

RICHARD FULLER
BORN May 30, 1962
MP 2010-

Smooth, energetic local man and one-time student politican. Pursued international business career before returning to politics. Contested Bedford 2005. Mem, select cttee: regulatory reform 2012-15. Patron, Tory Reform Group. Small business ambassador. Enthusiastic to bring business experience to improving Bedford town centre. Partner, Investcorp (venture capital); LEK Consulting (management consultancy). Christian. Theatre enthusiast. Nat chairman, Young Conservatives 1985-87. Ed: Bedford Mod Sch; University Coll, Oxford (BA PPE, chairman, OUCA); Harvard Business Sch (MBA).

CHALLENGERS
Patrick Hall (Lab) Planning officer. MP for Bedford 1997-2010. Cllr, Bedfordshire Council 1989-97. Contested Bedford 2010;

Bedfordshire North 1992. Married; two stepsons. Ed: Bedford Modern Sch; University of Birmingham; Oxford Poly. **Charlie Smith** (Ukip) Consultant and property landlord. Ed: Pilgrim Upper Sch. **Mahmud Henry Rogers** (LD) Cllr, Beford BC 2006-2009. Former accountant. Ed: LSE (BSc economic history); Maastricht Graduate Sch Governance, Netherlands (MA public policy & human development). **Ben Foley** (Green) Senior research fellow, De Montfort University. Cttee member: Bedford Commuters' Association.

CONSTITUENCY PROFILE
A tight marginal between Labour and the Conservatives that previously had significant Liberal Democrat strength, particularly at a local level. In 2011 the Lib Dems had more councillors in the seat than the Conservatives, and also provided the elected mayor for the authority. There are sizeable Italian and Asian populations.

	Electorate	Turnout %	from 2010 % Change
	69,311	66.5	
R Fuller C	19,625	42.6	+3.7
P Hall Lab	18,528	40.2	+4.3
C Smith Ukip	4,434	9.6	+7.1
M Henry Rogers LD	1,958	4.3	-15.6
B Foley Green	1,412	3.1	+2.2
F Choudhury Ind	129	0.3	+0.0

Change from 2010

Bedfordshire Mid

CONSERVATIVE HOLD

NADINE DORRIES
BORN May 21, 1957
MP 2005-

Unpredictable, populist blogger. Self-proclaimed "Bridget Jones of Westminster". Social conservative, advocates reducing abortion limit. Some damage in expenses row, criticised for voicing fears of MP suicide. Suspended in 2012 for appearing on *I'm a Celebrity ... Get Me Out of Here!* Re-instated 2013. Mem, select cttees: panel of chairs 2011-15; health 2010-11; science & technology 2009-10; energy & climate change 2009-10; innovation, universities, science & skills 2007-08; science 2007; education & skills 2005-06. Adviser to Oliver Letwin 2002-05. Contested Hazel Grove 2001. Businesswoman, sold healthcare firm to Bupa and served as dir for them; nurse. Grew up on council estate. Divorced, three daughters. Ed: Halewood Grange; Warrington Dist Sch of Nursing.

CHALLENGERS
Charlynne Pullen (Lab) Research manager. Cllr, Islington 2010-14, chairwoman: education 2013-14, vice-chairwoman: policy & performance 2013-14; communities review 2011-13. Lab group sec 2010-13. Unite rep. Gov, Richard Reeves Foundation. Ed: Ousedale Sch; St Hugh's Coll, Oxford (modern history, vice-president OUSU); Open University (BSc economics & maths; MSc social research methods). **Nigel Wickens** (Ukip) Systems auditor & professional trainer. Contested East Midlands region 2014 European election. **Linda Jack** (LD) Finance consultant. Cllr, Bedford BC 2002-07. Contested Luton North 2005, Bedforshire Mid 2010. Bedfordshire Police Commissioner 2012. Ed: Sussex (BEd secondary education & teaching).

CONSTITUENCY PROFILE
A solidly Conservative seat, held by the Tories since 1931. Affluent settlements of rural Bedfordshire.

	Electorate	Turnout %	from 2010 % Change
	81,144	71.6	
N Dorries C	32,544	56.1	+3.6
C Pullen Lab	9,217	15.9	+1.1
N Wickens Ukip	8,966	15.4	+10.3
L Jack LD	4,193	7.2	-17.7
G Ellis Green	2,462	4.2	+2.8
T Ireland Ind	384	0.7	
A M Kelly Loony	294	0.5	

Change from 2010

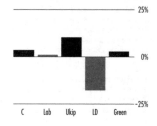

Bedfordshire North East

CONSERVATIVE HOLD

ALISTAIR BURT
BORN May 25, 1955
MP 2001-; 1983-1997

Mild-mannered, on the Tory Left. Minister of state for community and social care 2015-. Parly under-sec: FCO 2010-13; DSS 1992-95. Asst chief whip 2008-10. Dep party chair 2007-10. Shad minister, CLG 2005-08. Shad spokes, education 2001-02. Minister for the disabled 1995-97. MP, Bury North 1983-97. PPS to: Michael Howard 2003-05; Iain Duncan Smith 2002-03; Kenneth Baker 1985-90. Select cttees: ecclesiastical 2014-; admin 2009-10; selection 2008-10. Cllr, Haringey BC 1982-84. Patron, Habitat for Humanity GB. Solicitor, headhunter for Whitehead Mann GKR. Enjoys football, modern art. Married, one daughter, one son. Ed: Bury GS; St John's Coll, Oxford (BA jurisprudence.)

CHALLENGERS
Saqhib Ali (Lab) Customer

solution specialist, Lloyds Bank. Married, two sons, one daughter. Ed: Bedford Modern Sch; Leeds (BSc physiology & pharmacology); Stockholm Business Sch; Cranfield (executive MBA). **Adrianne Smyth** (Ukip) Property development business-owner. Worked in the aviation business. Breeds and trains horses and ponies, equine judge. Chairman, Ukip Hitchin & Harpenden Branch. Married. **Peter Morris** (LD) Photo journalist. Owns property valuation business. Former farmer. Married, one son. Ed: Bristol Polytechnic (valuation & estate management).

CONSTITUENCY PROFILE
A large, rural seat that borders Northamptonshire to the north, arcs to the southeast of Bedford, enclosing the city on three sides and extending south to the border of Hertfordshire. There is much arable farmland and the area is home to Jordans cereals. Historically a safe Conservative seat.

	Electorate	Turnout %	from 2010 % Change
	83,551	70.2	
A Burt C	34,891	59.5	+3.7
S Ali Lab	9,247	15.8	-0.4
A Smyth Ukip	8,579	14.6	+10.5
P Morris LD	3,418	5.8	-15.9
M Bowler Green	2,537	4.3	

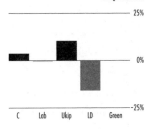

Change from 2010

Bedforshire South West

CONSERVATIVE HOLD

ANDREW SELOUS
BORN Apr 27, 1962
MP 2001-

Assistant whip, Treasury 2014-; Parly under-sec, minister for prisons, probation & rehabilitation 2014. Shad min: work & pensions 2006-10. Opp whip 2004-06. PPS: Iain Duncan Smith 2010-14; Michael Ancram 2004. Contested Sunderland N 1997. Member: W&P select cttee 2001-06. Bow Group 1982-. Chair, Con Christian Fellowship 2001-. Dir, CNS Electronics 1988-94. Underwriter, Great Lakes Re. TA officer, Hon Artillery Co, Royal Reg of Fusiliers 1981-94. Chartered insurer 1998. Enjoys tennis and bridge. Married, three daughters. Ed: Eton Coll; LSE (BSc economic industry & trade).

CHALLENGERS
Daniel Scott (Lab) Print & postal business-owner. Cllr, Watford BC 2002-06. Sch governor. Married, two children. Ed: University of

Liverpool. **John Van Weenen** (Ukip) Humanitarian & martial arts expert, helped introduce karate to UK. Honorary consul, Albanian Consulate in Northamptonshire as executive director of Task Force Albania charity. Appointed Order of Mother Teresa 1995. Featured on *This Is Your Life* 2000. MBE 1999. **Stephen Rutherford** (LD) Senior engineer, Cranfield Aerospace. Chair, local party branch. Former engineer in automotive and space industries. Married. Ed: Surrey (BEng engineering). **Emily Lawrence** (Green) Publisher, relationship manager, CourseSmart International. Ed: UCE, Birmingham (BA English language & literature).

CONSTITUENCY PROFILE
Conservative stronghold since its creation in 1983. Labour challeneged the seat in 1997, reducing the majority from 21,273 to a mere 132 votes. The seat incorporates Dunstable, Leighton Buzzard and the Houghton Regis development.

	Electorate	Turnout %	from 2010 % Change
	79,664	64.4	
A Selous C	28,212	55.0	+2.2
D Scott Lab	10,399	20.3	+0.7
J Van Weenen Ukip	7,941	15.5	+11.3
S Rutherford LD	2,646	5.2	-14.9
E Lawrence Green	2,106	4.1	

Change from 2010

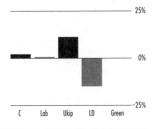

Belfast East

DUP GAIN

GAVIN ROBINSON
BORN Nov 22, 1984
MP 2015-

Barrister. Cllr, Belfast CC 2010-15, Lord Mayor, Belfast 2012-13. Won through a unionist pact with the UUP. Called a teflon man, but critised for failure to acknowledge defeated MP in acceptance speech after bitter 2015 campaign. First DUP representative to attend gay pride event. Unrelated to Peter Robinson, who held Belfast East until 2010. Married. Ed: Queen's University Belfast (LLB law; MA Irish politics).

CHALLENGERS
Naomi Long (Alliance) MP 2010-2015. Her unseating of Peter Robinson provided the biggest story of the Northern Ireland count in 2010 with a 26.1-point swing and the Alliance party's first election win in its history. Lord Mayor, Belfast 2009-10. Alliance deputy leader 2006-. Member, select cttees: NI affairs 2010-15; electoral

commision 2010-15. MLA for Belfast East 2003-10. Cllr, Belfast 2001-2010. Consultant engineer. A senior guider in the Girl Guides and active Presbyterian. Married. Ed: Bloomfield Collegiate Sch; Queen's University (MEng Civil Engineering). **Neil Wilson** (C) Marketing executive, Equiniti. Cllr, Newton Abbot TC 2011-3. Ed: LJM (BA history; MA European studies & politics). **Ross Brown** (Green) Former asst economist to the Treasury. Cllr, Belfast CC 2014-. Ed: Queen's, Belfast (BA economics). **Niall Ó Donnghaile** (SF) Press officer, SF in Stormont. Cllr, Belfast CC 2011-, mayor 2011-12, Belfast's youngest ever.

CONSTITUENCY PROFILE
Overwhelmingly unionist constituency, seeing nationalist parties struggling to achieve more that ten per cent of the vote combined, and with only 13 per cent identifying as Catholic. The seat contains Stormont, home of the Northern Ireland Assembly.

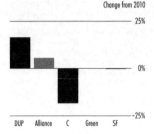

	Electorate	Turnout %	from 2010 % Change
	63,154	62.8	
G Robinson DUP	19,575	49.3	+16.6
N Long Alliance	16,978	42.8	+5.6
N Wilson C	1,121	2.8	-18.4
R Brown Green	1,058	2.7	
N Ó Donnghaile SF	823	2.1	-0.3
M Muldoon SDLP	127	0.3	-0.7

Change from 2010

Belfast North

DUP HOLD

NIGEL DODDS
BORN Sep 1, 1949
MP 2005-

Dour brains of the party who survived an IRA attack on himself and his wife in 1996 while visiting their son in hospital. Deputy leader, DUP 2008-. DUP Westminster spokesman: justice 2007-; FCO 2010-; business 2007-10; Treasury, work & pensions 2005-07. DUP chief whip 2001-08. Member, select cttees: statutory instruments 2009-10; members' allowances 2009. Secretary, Ulster DUP 1992-2008. Member, NI Assmebly 1998-2010. NI Forum for political dialogue 1996-98. Cllr, Belfast CC 1985-, lord mayor 1991-92, 1988-89. Vice-president, Association of NI Local Authorities. Privy cllr. Barrister. Formerly worked at European Parly Secretariat. OBE 1997. Married, one dauighter, two sons. Ed: Portora Royal Sch; St John's Coll, Cambridge (BA law); Queen's University. Belfast (cert PLS)

CHALLENGERS
Gerry Kelly (SF) MLA for Belfast North. Key proponent of Good Friday Agreement negotiations. Sinn Féin Policing spokes. Former Provisional IRA volunteer. Given prison life sentence, 1973 London bombings. Relocated to HMP Maze in Northern Ireland, later escaped. Extradited from Netherlands after three years on run, released in 1989. Married. Ed: St Peter's Secondary Sch. **Alban Maginness** (SDLP) Chair. SDLP 1985-91. Contested Belfast North 1992, 1997, 2001, 2005; European election 2009. Ed: St Malachy's; Ulster; Queen's University (NI law, MA human rights law). Jason O'Neill (Alliance) Ed: St Malachy's College; Queen's University, Belfast (law with politics).

CONSTITUENCY PROFILE
On the east of Belfast Lough, a socially mixed seat. Traditionally held by a unionist. Cecil Walker was the Ulster Unionist MP from 1983 until 2001.

	Electorate	Turnout %	from 2010 % Change
	68,552	59.2	
N Dodds DUP	19,096	47.0	+7.0
G Kelly SF	13,770	33.9	-0.1
A Maginness SDLP	3,338	8.2	-4.1
J O'Neill Alliance	2,941	7.3	+2.4
G Weir WP	919	2.3	
F Hughes Ind	529	1.3	+0.2

Change from 2010

Belfast South

SDLP HOLD

ALASDAIR McDONNELL
BORN Sep 1, 1949
MP 2005-

Leader of the SDLP 2011-. Faced criticism for saying he would leave the NI Assembly in 2016 and lead from Westminster. SDLP chief whip 2010-; Westminster spokes: BIS 2007-; CMS 2010-; health 2005-; Northern Ireland, Europe 2008-10; enterprise & regulatory reform, innovation & universities 2008-09 education 2005-08; employment & learning 2005-07; economic development 2005-07; Treasury 2005-07. SDLP chief whip 2010-. Member, NI affairs select cttee 2005-. Deputy leader, SDLP 2004-11. MLA for Belfast South 1998-2011. Cllr, Belfast CC: 1985-2011, deputy mayor 1995-96, 1977-81. Contested: Belfast South 2001, 1997, 92, 87, 83, 82 by-election, 79; Antrim N 1970. Doctor. Married, two daughters, two sons. Ed: St MacNissi's Coll; University Coll, Dublin (MC BCL BAO medicine).

CHALLENGERS
Jonathan Bell (DUP) MLA, Strangford 2010-, minister of enterprise, trade & investment 2015-. Cllr, Craigavon BC 1997-2005 (UUP 1997-2000), deputy mayor 2001-02, mayor 2002-03; Ards BC 2005 as DUP. NI select cttees: assemble & executive review 2010-11; employment & learning (dep chair) 2010-11; justice, environment 2010. Former NI Human Rights Commissioner. Ed: Queen's, Belfast (BSc psychology, MA PDip social work). **Paula Bradshaw** (Alliance) Dir, Greater Village Regeneration Trust. Cllr, Belfast CC 2014-. Ed: Belfast HS; Ulster (LLB law & government).

CONSTITUENCY PROFILE
Classic unionist seat, but a split in the unionist vote in 2005 broke this tradition, seeing the SDLP party gain the seat. Contains affluent areas and deprived estates. Home to city hall, Queen's University and the opera house, with an equal split between Catholics and Protestants.

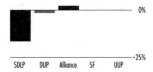

	Electorate	Turnout %	Change from 2010 %
	64,912	60.0	
A McDonnell SDLP	9,560	24.5	-16.5
J Bell DUP	8,654	22.2	-1.5
P Bradshaw Alliance	6,711	17.2	+2.3
M Ó Muilleoir SF	5,402	13.9	
R McCune UUP	3,549	9.1	
C Bailey Green	2,238	5.7	+2.7
B Stoker Ukip	1,900	4.9	
B Manton C	582	1.5	-15.8
L Kerr WP	361	0.9	

Change from 2010

SDLP DUP Alliance SF UUP

Belfast West

SF HOLD

PAUL MASKEY
BORN Jun 10, 1967
MP 2011-

MLA, Belfast West 2007-2012. NI Assembly cttees: deputy chair, ETI 2007-08; chair, public accounts 2008-12; Sinn Féin: deputy whip, spokesman, public accounts; governance 2011-12. Cllr, Belfast CC 2001-09, SF group leader until 2009. Enjoys five-a-side football. Married; two children. Ed: Edmund Rice Coll

CHALLENGERS
Gerry Carroll (PBP) People Before Profit's first elected councillor: Cllr, Belfast CC 2014-. Ed: St Mary's CBS; University of Ulster (BA politics, president Students' Union). **Alex Attwood** (SDLP) MLA for Belfast West 1998-. Minister for the environment 2011-13; social development 2010-11. NI Assembly cttees: executive review 2013-, 2007-10; office of first minister/ dep first minister 2013-, 2009-10;

employment & learning 2007-09. Solicitor. Cllr, Belfast CC 1985-. Appointed to Dublin Forum for Peace & Reconciliation 1997. Contested Belfast W 2011, 10, 05, 01. Married, children. Ed: St Malachy's Coll; Queen's University (LLB law, president Students' Union). **Frank McCoubrey** (DUP) Researcher. High Sheriff of Belfast 2009. Cllr, Belfast CC 1997-, deputy mayor 2000-01. Member of UDP, then leading member of UPRG, joining DUP in 2012. Involved in controversial appearance at loyalist rally in 2000.

CONSTITUENCY PROFILE
Since 1966, this seat has been held by nationalist MPs. Sinn Féin president Gerry Adams took the seat from the SDLP's Gerry Fitt in 1983. He lost it in 1992 to the SDLP's Joe Hendron, only to regain it five years later. After he resigned to become a member of the Republic of Ireland's parliament, Paul Maskey of Sinn Féin took the seat in 2011.

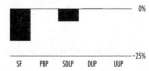

	Electorate	Turnout %	Change from 2010 %
	62,685	56.4	
P Maskey SF	19,163	54.2	-16.8
G Carroll PBP	6,798	19.2	
A Attwood SDLP	3,475	9.8	-6.5
F McCoubrey DUP	2,773	7.9	+0.3
B Manwaring UUP	1,088	3.1	
B Higginson Ukip	765	2.2	
G Catney Alliance	636	1.8	-0.1
J Lowry WP	597	1.7	
P Shea C	34	0.1	-3.0

Change from 2010

SF PBP SDLP DUP UUP

Bermondsey & Old Southwark

LABOUR GAIN

NEIL COYLE
BORN Dec 30, 1978
MP 2015-

Disability rights campaigner. Worked for shadow work & pensions min Kate Green. Former director of policy and campaigns at Disability Rights UK, and head of policy, National Centre for Independent Living. Cllr, Southwark BC 2010-, deputy mayor 2014-15. Deputy cabinet member 2011-13. Vice chairman, Walworth Comm C 2010-11. Previously PA to Ben Bradshaw. Lived in China. Married. Ed: Bedford Sch; University of Hull (British politics & legislative studies)

CHALLENGERS
Simon Hughes (LD) MP 1983-2015. Community politician, coalition rebel, his defeat was indicative of Lib Dems' collapse in 2015. LD deputy leader 2010-14. Min of state, justice 2013-15; LD shadow: SoS, ECC 2009; leader of HoC 2007-09; justice, London 2006-07;

attorney-gen 2005-07; spokes, home 1999-2003, health 1995-99, 88, efra 1992-94, 83-88 (Lib), education 1988-92. LD dep whip 1988-99. President, LD party 2004-08. Contested: LD leadership 2006, 1999; London mayor election 2004. Nat Young Liberals League. Liberal Lawyers Assoc. Barrister. Trainee EEC Brussels. Ed: Christ Coll, Brecon; Selwyn Coll, Cambridge (BA law); Coll of Europe, Bruges.
Jean-Paul Floru (C) Author on free market issues. Parliamentary liaison officer for Adam Smith Institute. Consultant to Freedom Alliance. Solicitor. Cllr, Westminster BC 2006-. Ed: Leuven University (LLM); Coll of Law (CPA & LPC).

CONSTITUENCY PROFILE
Central London, south of the river, facing the City across the Thames. Demographics would suggest safe Labour territory, but Simon Hughes held here for 32 years after the infamous 1983 by-election against Peter Tatchell, which registered a 44 per cent swing to Liberals.

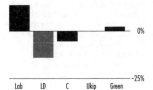

	Electorate	Turnout %	Change from 2010 %
	80,604	63.8	
N Coyle Lab	22,146	43.1	+13.8
S Hughes LD	17,657	34.3	-14.0
J Floru C	6,051	11.8	-5.3
A Beadle Ukip	3,254	6.3	
W Lavin Green	2,023	3.9	+2.3
K Abrams TUSC	142	0.3	
L Hall Ind	72	0.1	-0.2
D Cole AP	59	0.1	
S Freeman Rep Soc	20	0.0	

Change from 2010

Lab   LD   C   Ukip   Green

Berwickshire, Roxburgh & Selkirk

SNP GAIN

CALUM KERR
BORN Apr 5, 1972
MP 2015-

SNP group leader, environment & rural affairs 2015-. Worked in sales management at Avaya telecommunications. Director of a Citizens Advice Direct; chairman, Social Enterprise Direct. Chairman of Yes Scottish Borders in Scottish referendum. Enjoys rugby and whisky. Married, three children. Ed: University of St Andrew's (BA history).

CHALLENGERS
John Lamont (C) Solicitor. MSP for Ettrick, Roxburgh & Berwickshire/Roxburgh & Berwickshire 2007-. Chief whip for the Scottish Conservative parliamentary group. Contested Berwickshire, Roxburgh & Selkirk 2005, 2010. Ed: Kilwinning Academy; Glasgow (LLB law).
Michael Moore (LD) MP 1997-2015. Sec of state for Scotland

2010-13. LD shadow SoS: NI & Scotland 2008; int devt 2007-10; foreign affairs 2006-07; defence 2005-06. LD shadow minister: foreign affairs 2001-05. LD spokes: Scotland, transport 1997-2001. Select cttees: armed forces bill 2005-06; Scottish affairs 1997-99. Deputy leader Scottish Liberal Democrats 2003-10. MP Tweeddale, Ettrick & Lauderdale 1997-2005. EU business adviser to Nick Clegg 2014-15. Chartered accountant. Married, one daughter. Ed: Jedburgh GS; Edinburgh (MA politics & history).

CONSTITUENCY PROFILE
This large, rural Scottish seat reaches from the fishing town of Eyemouth, inland along the border with England and through the Cheviot Hills. The seat has a strong Liberal tradition - David Steel was MP of its predecessor - but its equivalent in the Scottish Parliament was taken by the Tories in 2007, making this a target seat for them in 2015 after the Lib Dems' vote collapse.

	Electorate	Turnout %	Change from 2010 %
	74,179	74.2	
C Kerr SNP	20,145	36.6	+27.4
J Lamont C	19,817	36.0	+2.2
M Moore LD	10,294	18.7	-26.7
K Lloyd-Jones Lab	2,700	4.9	-5.3
P Neilson Ukip	1,316	2.4	+1.2
P Stewart Green	631	1.2	
J Rae Ind	135	0.3	

Change from 2010

SNP   C   LD   Lab   Ukip

Berwick-upon-Tweed

CONSERVATIVE GAIN

ANNE-MARIE TREVELYAN
BORN Apr 6, 1969
MP 2015-

Chartered accountant. Founder, Dual the A1 campaign. Chairman, iNorthumberland advisory group. Contested Berwick-upon-Tweed 2010. Governor, Northumbria Healthcare Trust. Sch governor. Trustee, Oswin Trust. Married, two children. Ed: St Paul's Girls' Sch; Oxford Polytechnic (BA maths).

CHALLENGERS
Julie Pörksen (LD) Agricultural economist. Worked in business and charities. Lived in Peru for two years working to support fair trade and agricultural workers' rights. Trustee, Ashray charity. She enjoys playing sports with her two sons, watching wrestling and rugby. Married, two children. Ed: Ponteland HS; St Hugh's Coll, Oxford (BA biology); Wye College (MSc agricultural economics). **Scott Dickinson**

(Lab) Project director, Hadston House Youth and community projects. Cllr, Northumberland CC 2013-, business chairman, health and wellbeing scrutiny board chairman. Chairman, East Chevington PC. **Nigel Coghill-Marshall** (Ukip). Retired chartered insurance practitioner Contested City of Durham 2010. Married, two children.

CONSTITUENCY PROFILE
The most northerly constituency in England, covering the border town of Berwick-upon-Tweed and much of rural Northumberland, including Lindisfarne island and Alnwick, a market town known for its castle. Sparsely populated, dominated by agriculture, it is one of the smallest constituencies in England in terms of population, though it covers a large geographical area. Liberal for 40 years under Sir Alan Beith, secured in 1973 after tabloid revelations that Tory Lord Lambton used call girls.

	Electorate	Turnout %	Change from 2010 %
	58,098	69.6	
A Trevelyan C	16,603	41.1	+4.4
J Pörksen LD	11,689	28.9	-14.8
S Dickinson Lab	6,042	15.0	+1.8
N Coghill-Marshall Ukip	4,513	11.2	+7.9
R Roberts Green	1,488	3.7	
N Humphrey Eng Dem	88	0.2	

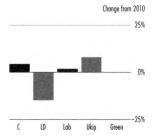

Change from 2010

Bethnal Green & Bow

LABOUR HOLD

RUSHANARA ALI
BORN Mar 14, 1975
MP 2010-

Vivacious and eloquent, Bangladeshi-born high-flyer. One of the first intake of female Muslim MPs in 2010. Spotted as a talent while still studying at university by Michael Young. Stepped down from the Labour front bench after refusing to support British military action in Iraq 2014. Shadow min: education 2013-14; international development 2010-13. Select cttee: Treasury 2014-. Associate dir, Young Foundation. Worked for Oona King, her Labour predecessor. Career: Institute for Public Policy Research; FCO; Home Office. Co-founder, Tower Hamlets Summer University. Helped develop Language Line. Commissioner, London Child Poverty Commission. Speaks Bengali. Moved to UK aged seven. Ed: Mulberry Sch; Tower Hamlets Coll; St John's Coll, Oxford (BA PPE)

CHALLENGERS
Matthew Smith (C) Solicitor, specialises in personal injury, clinical negligence and commercial litigation. Chairman, Bethnal Green & Bow Conservatives. Contested Cardiff C Welsh Ass election 2011. Worked with Policy Exchange and Conservative Research Group in the Welsh Ass. Ed: Mansfield Coll, Oxford (BA history); Oxford Brookes (PgDip law); City (LLM BVC) **Alistair Polson** (Green) Barrister, Garden Court Chambers specialises in murder and sex offences. Chairman, Tower Hamlets Green Party Ed: Glasgow (MA); City (Dip law)

CONSTITUENCY PROFILE
An east-end seat with a long history of immigrant communities — Huguenots, Jews and now Bangladeshi — and radical politics. Solidly Labour, although represented by Respect's George Galloway 2005-10. Tower Hamlets' disgraced mayor Lutfur Rahman has brought political focus to the area.

	Electorate	Turnout %	Change from 2010 %
	82,825	63.9	
R Ali Lab	32,387	61.2	+18.3
M Smith C	8,070	15.3	+1.3
A Polson Green	4,906	9.3	+7.6
P McQueen Ukip	3,219	6.1	
T Lashmore LD	2,395	4.5	-15.6
G Robbins TUSC	949	1.8	
M R Ali Community	356	0.7	
J Dewey CSA	303	0.6	
A Henderson Whig	203	0.4	
E Ball 30-50	78	0.2	
J Pavlou RFAC	58	0.1	

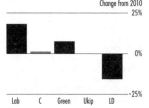

Change from 2010

Beverley & Holderness

CONSERVATIVE HOLD

GRAHAM STUART
BORN Mar 12, 1962
MP 2005-

Chairman, education select cttee 2010-, was unafraid to criticise Michael Gove on what he called "rushed and ill-thought-out changes" to policy. Member, select cttees: Liaison 2010-; CSF/ education & skills 2007-10; environmental audit 2006-10. Contested Cambridge 2001. Cllr, Cambridge CC 1998-2004. Chairman, Community Hospitals Acting Nationally Together 2005-10. Launched Rural Fair Share campaign 2012. Sole proprietor, Go Enterprises; MD, CSL Publishing; Director, Marine Publishing Co. Married, two daughters. Ed: Glenalmond Coll; Selwyn Coll, Cambridge (BA law & philosophy).

CHALLENGERS
Margaret Pinder (Lab) Legal consultant, writer and editor. Consultant editor, marine trade,

energy, aviation, and travel teams, Hill Dickinson. Cllr, Beverley TC 2011-, mayor 2012-13. Taught at Harvard on its Expository Writing Programme. Principal double bass of the Hull Philharmonic Orchestra. One daughter. Ed: King's Coll, Cambridge (MA English & modern languages); University of Nottingham (LLM public procurement law & policy). **Gary Shores** (Ukip) Science teacher. **Denis Healy** (LD) Business development manager, institution of mechanical engineers, Yorkshire & the North East. Worked as a marketing professional in the food industry. Contested Hull North 2010. Married, three children.

CONSTITUENCY PROFILE
The eastern part of the East Riding of Yorkshire, covering the rural hinterland of Hull, the traditional market town of Beverley to the north and then out to the east Yorkshire coast. Consistently Conservative since the 1920s, not always strongly, such as in 2001.

	Electorate	Turnout %	Change from 2010 %
	80,822	65.2	
G Stuart C	25,363	48.2	+1.0
M Pinder Lab	13,160	25.0	+3.9
G Shores Ukip	8,794	16.7	+13.2
D Healy LD	2,900	5.5	-17.2
R Howarth Green	1,802	3.4	+2.1
L Walton Yorks	658	1.3	

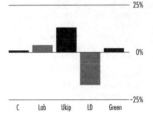

Change from 2010

C Lab Ukip LD Green

Bexhill & Battle

CONSERVATIVE HOLD

HUW MERRIMAN
BORN Jul 7, 1973
MP 2015-

MD & lawyer. Managed team of lawyers unwinding Lehman Brothers insolvency in London. Works in a hobby farming venture with his neighbour, a local butcher. Cllr, Wealden DC 2007-15. Chairman, Wealden Constituency Conservative Assoc. Contested Derbyshire NE 2010. Member of 'snow patrol' team in his village. Enjoys growing fruit, vegetables and flowers for his family and their bee hives. Married, three daughters. Ed: Buckingham County Secondary Modern; Aylesbury Coll; Durham University (LLB law).

CHALLENGERS
Geoffrey Bastin (Ukip) Worked in local government as principal building surveyor, a contracts manager in the construction industry, a design draughtsman with British Airports Authority.

Married, two daughters. **Michelle Thew** (Lab) Animal rights campaigner. CEO: Cruelty Free International (British Union for the Abolition of Vivisection); the European Coalition to End Animal Experiments. Frequent columnist on animal rights issues. Has worked in social justice and children's services. **Rachel Sadler** (LD) Personal adviser, AXA PPP healthcare. Chairwoman, Tunbridge Wells Lib Dems.

CONSTITUENCY PROFILE
Covers a large area; the largest settlement being the genteel seaside town of Bexhill, a popular retirement location with a large elderly population. Along the coast is the smaller seaside resort of Pevensey Bay; the rest of the seat is a swathe of rural territory. Battle Abbey commemorates William the Conqueror's victory at the Battle of Hastings. A safe Conservative seat, called Rye until 1983, when Rye itself was moved into the Hastings constituency.

	Electorate	Turnout %	Change from 2010 %
	78,796	70.1	
H Merriman C	30,245	54.8	+3.2
G Bastin Ukip	10,170	18.4	
M Thew Lab	7,797	14.1	+2.2
R Sadler LD	4,199	7.6	-20.4
J Kent Green	2,807	5.1	

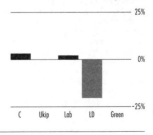

Change from 2010

C Ukip Lab LD Green

Bexleyheath & Crayford

CONSERVATIVE HOLD

DAVID EVENNETT
BORN Jun 3, 1949
MP 2005-; 1983-1997

Populist Essex Tory, won back seat in 2005 at second attempt. Lord Commissioner, Treasury & whip 2012-. PPS to Michael Gove 2010-2012. Shadow min, BIS 2009-10. Opposition whip 2005-09. Select cttees: administration 2013-; selection 2013-; education & skills 2005-06, 1986-92. PPS to: Gillian Shepherd 1996-7; Baroness Blatch, David Maclean 1995-6; John Redwood 1993-5; Baroness Blatch 1992-93. MP for Erith and Crayford 1983-97. Cllr, Redbridge BC 1974-78. Teacher, insurance broker, City director, lecturer. Married, two sons. Ed: Buckhurst Hill County HS for Boys, Ilford; LSE (BSc MSc economics & politics).

CHALLENGERS
Stef Borella (Lab) Pastry chef. Teaches at La Cucina Caldesi. Cllr, Bexley BC 2010-. Member, Academy of culinary arts. Worked at Savoy and Churchill hotels. School governor. Charlton Athletic fan. Ed: St Stephen's & Columba's Sch. **Chris Attard** (Ukip) Chairman, Ukip Bexley Branch. Former train driver. Married, five children. Ed: Parmiters GS; Erith College; University of Greenwich (BA philosophy & creative writing) **Richard Davis** (LD) Head of analytics, Lloyds. Worked as a biochemist & risk specialist. Ed: York (BSc MRes maths; PhD chemistry)

CONSTITUENCY PROFILE
This is the middle of three seats in the London Borough of Bexley – both geographically and politically – mostly a middle-class commuter area in the south, but becoming more industrial and Labour inclined as you head north east. A marginal seat, gained by Labour in 1997 and won back by David Evennett in 2005, one of the few Conservative MPs ousted in the 1997 landslide to win back the seat they lost

	Electorate	Turnout %	from 2010 % Change
	64,828	67.4	
D Evennett C	20,643	47.3	-3.2
S Borella Lab	11,451	26.2	-0.3
C Attard Ukip	9,182	21.0	+17.4
R Davis LD	1,308	3.0	-9.8
S Gardiner Green	950	2.2	+1.3
M Young Eng Dem	151	0.4	-0.7

Change from 2010

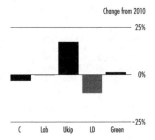

| C | Lab | Ukip | LD | Green |

Birkenhead

LABOUR HOLD

FRANK FIELD
BORN Jul 16, 1942
MP 1979-

Maverick champion of welfare reform, had unhappy year as minister for welfare reform 1997-98. Chaired Independent Review, Poverty & Life Chances 2010 as David Cameron's "poverty tsar", and the modern slavery bill 2014 select cttee. Could not make progress as Speaker candidate 2009 because of lack of support on his own side. Long courted by Tories. Select cttees: chair, social security/services 1987-97; member, ecclesiastical 2010-, 2002-05; public accounts 2002-05. Opposition spokesman: education 1980-81. Prominent Anglican; previously chairman, Churches Conservation Trust and King James Bible Trust. Former director, Poverty Action Group Low Pay Unit. Cllr, Hounslow BC 1964-68. Teacher. Ed: St Clement Danes GS; University of Hull (BSc economics).

CHALLENGERS
Clark Vasey (C) Works in corporate affairs, Fijitsu. Previously at Augmentiq and Bell Pottinger. Former research asst to Gerald Howarth. Founder, Blue Collar Conservatism. Ed: Hull (BA politics & legislative studies). **Wayne Harling** (Ukip) Leader, Young Independence 2007-08. Married. **Kenny Peers** (Green) Works for an environmental charity. Allotment holder.

CONSTITUENCY PROFILE
A gritty working class industrial seat facing Liverpool across the Mersey and connected to it through the Mersey tunnel. Faces unemployment and deprivation after decline in shipbuilding. A safe Labour stronghold, held by the party since its creation in 1950. Frank Field, the seat's longest serving MP, has attained towering majorities since the 1980s, the most impressive reaching 21,843 in the 1997 Labour landslide. He was not far off in 2015 with a 20,652 lead.

	Electorate	Turnout %	from 2010 % Change
	62,438	60.4	
F Field Lab	26,468	70.2	+7.7
C Vasey C	5,816	15.4	-3.5
W Harling Ukip	3,838	10.2	
K Peers Green	1,626	0.4	
A Brame LD	1,396	3.7	-14.9

Change from 2010

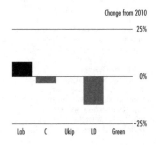

| Lab | C | Ukip | LD | Green |

Birmingham Edgbaston

LABOUR HOLD

GISELA STUART
BORN Nov 26, 1955
MP 1997-

Independent-minded, not afraid to take on her own party over Europe: a Eurosceptic after drafting EU constitution. Parly under-sec: health 1999-2001. PPS to Paul Boateng 1998-99. Member, select committees: defence 2010-; privacy & injunctions 2011-12; conventions 2006; foreign affairs 2001-10; social security 1997-98. Parly rep Convention on Future of Europe 2002-04. Amicus. Editor, *The House* magazine. Was Dep dir, London Book Fair. Lawyer. Lecturer, Worcester Coll of Tech & Birmingham Uni 1992-97. Divorced, widowed. Two sons. Ed: Staatliche Realschule, Bavaria; Manchester Poly (business studies); University of London International Programmes (LLB).

CHALLENGERS
Dr Luke Evans (C) GP. Teaches anatomy to medical students Associate Clinical Lead for CCG. Member, Birmingham & Edgbaston Debating Society. Played rugby for Harborne rugby club. School governor Ed: University of Birmingham (medicine). **Graham Short** (Ukip) Artist, engraver and craftsman. Makes the dies used to print the green portcullis on House of Commons headed paper. Made world's smallest engraving by etching "nothing is impossible" onto the edge of a razor blade. Calls himself the "hands of genius".

CONSTITUENCY PROFILE
A largely middle-class seat of leafy suburbs in the south west of Birmingham. Includes Edgbaston cricket ground and the main campus of Birmingham University. Held by the Conservatives for most of the 20th century, it fell to Labour in the 1997 landslide. The most vulnerable Labour-Tory marginal that Labour held on to in 2010 The seat has been represented by a female MP since 1953.

	Electorate	Turnout %	Change from 2010 %
	65,591	63.0	
G Stuart Lab	18,518	44.9	+4.2
L Evans C	15,812	38.3	+0.7
G Short Ukip	4,154	10.1	+8.3
P Simpson Green	1,371	3.3	+2.2
L Dargue LD	1,184	2.9	-12.5
G Ukandu Christian	163	0.4	
H Rai Ind	91	0.2	

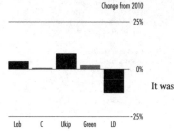

Change from 2010

It was

Birmingham Erdington

LABOUR HOLD

JACK DROMEY
BORN Apr 21, 1964
MP 2010-

Veteran union official who first emerged on public consciousness on Grunwick picket lines in 1970s. Select cttees: regulatory reform 2010-15; BIS 2010. Elected deputy general secretary of Unite/TGWU in 2003 after losing to Tony Woodley for general secretary. Seen as acceptable face of trade unions by Blairites but missed out on a seat in 1997. Shadow minister: policing 2013-15; CLG 2010-13. Distanced himself from Blair in cash for honours, secret loans row in 2006, as Labour party treasurer (2004-10). Shoehorned into a seat once Brown took over. Founder member, Greater London Enterprise Board. Former secretary, Brent Trades Council. Machine minder, Alperton Carton Company. Married to Harriet Harman, one daughter, two sons. Ed: Cardinal Vaughan GS, London.

CHALLENGERS
Robert Alden (C) Cllr Birmingham CC 2006-, leader Conservative group 2014-. Contested Birmingham Erdington 2010. School governor and director, Erdington Town Centre Business Improvement District. Ed: University of Birmingham (BA geography) **Andrew Garcarz** (Ukip) Senior projects manager, Health & Social Care Information Centre. Worked in health & social care. Married. Ed: Castle Vale Comp Sch; Matthew Boulton Tech Coll; North Birmingham Poly

CONSTITUENCY PROFILE
This largely residential seat is bounded by the M6 to the south east, dividing it from Birmingham city centre. It has significant areas of deprivation, although the Castle Vale estate in Tyburn improved with the replacement of tower blocks in the 1990s. Unemployment is high and the economy is more dependent on manufacturing than elsewhere. Labour since its creation in 1974.

	Electorate	Turnout %	Change from 2010 %
	65,128	53.3	
J Dromey Lab	15,824	45.6	+3.8
R Alden C	10,695	30.8	-1.8
A Garcarz Ukip	6,040	17.4	+15.1
A Holtom LD	965	2.8	-13.4
J Belcher Green	948	2.7	
T Woodley TUSC	212	0.6	

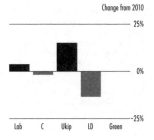

Change from 2010

Birmingham Hall Green

LABOUR HOLD

ROGER GODSIFF
BORN June 28, 1946
MP 1992-

Controversial, hard-edged ex-union official with a cockney accent. Spoke out against immigration. MP for: Birmingham, Sparkbrook & Small Heath 1997-2010; Small Heath 1992-97. Former cricket special adviser to Richard Caborn. Cllr, Lewisham BC 1979-90, mayor 1977. Member, Co-op party. Football fan, chairman Charlton Athletic Community Trust. GMB senior research officer. Political officer, APEX. Banker. Married, one daughter, one son. Ed: Catford Comp Sch, Lewisham.

CHALLENGERS
James Bird (C) Works in public affairs. Cllr, Birmingham CC 2010-14. Worked in IT and as a freelance journalist. Ed: Lancaster (BA politics & international relations); Birmingham City (PgDip broadcast journalism). **Jerry Evans**

(LD) Archaeologist: currently dir, Barbican Research Associates; previously Warwickshire Museum. Cllr, Birmingham CC 2003-. Contested Birmingham Hall Green 2010. Ed: Institute of Archaeology (BA archaeology); Bradford (PhD Roman pottery). **Elly Stanton** (Green) Local GP. Founder, GP Fair recruitment agency for NHS primary care. Married, one son, two daughters. Ed: Southampton Medical Sch.

CONSTITUENCY PROFILE
Despite retaining the same name and the Hall Green ward, Birmingham Hall Green has little in common with the seat that existed before 2010 and returned Conservative MPs up until 1997. It mostly consists of the old Sparkbrook & Small Heath seat, which had a far more solidly Labour past. Respect had a brief period of support, winning 25.1 per cent of the vote in 2010 and a seat on Birmingham CC in 2009. They received just 1.7 per cent in 2015.

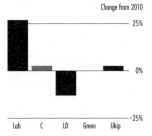

	Electorate	Turnout %	Change from 2010 %
	76,330	61.6	
R Godsiff Lab	28,147	59.8	+26.9
J Bird C	8,329	17.7	+2.7
J Evans LD	5,459	11.6	-13.0
E Stanton Green	2,200	4.7	
R Mondair Ukip	2,131	4.5	+2.6
S Peer Respect	780	1.7	-23.5

Change from 2010

— 25%

— 0%

— -25%

Lab   C   LD   Green   Ukip

Birmingham Hodge Hill

LABOUR HOLD

LIAM BYRNE
BORN Oct 2, 1970
MP 2004-

Left infamous "there's no money left" note during handover of chief sec to Treasury role (2009-10). Shadow min: BIS 2013-15; Cabinet Office 2010-11. Shadow SoS, work & pensions 2011-13. Min: Cabinet Office 2008-09; Treasury 2008; West Midlands 2007-08; home affairs 2006-08. Parly under sec, health 2005-06. Adviser, 1997 election campaign. Business liaison dir, office of Tony Blair 1996-97. Author of more than 20 books and pamphlets incl *Turning to Face the East*. Governor, Institute for Govt. Former: management consultant, Anderson Consulting; banker, NM Rothschild; co-founder EGS Group software. Married, one daughter, two sons. Ed: Burnt Mill Comp Sch; University of Manchester (BA politics & modern history; pres, Students' Union); Harvard University (MBA, Fulbright scholar).

CHALLENGERS
Dr Kieran Mullan (C) A&E doctor. Founder, ValueYou volunteer recognition scheme. Independent adviser on inquiry into NHS complaints procedures. Ed: KCL (MA healthcare law & medical ethics); Leeds (MBChB medicine). **Albert Duffen** (Ukip) Leads local Baptist church. Former: trade union rep; draughtsman, wheelchair production. **Phil Bennion** (LD) MEP, Midlands W 2012-. LD spokes, employment & transport. Arable farmer. Cllr: Staffordshire CC 2002-05; Lichfield DC 1999-2011. Member, LD fed policy cttee 2003-11. Ed: Aberdeen (BSc agricultural biology); Birmingham (BA history); Newcastle (PhD).

CONSTITUENCY PROFILE
In the hard fought 2004 by-election the Lib Dems narrowly missed out on this seat, managing a huge 27 per cent swing but ultimately falling short by 460 votes. It has since retained its status as safe Labour territory.

	Electorate	Turnout %	Change from 2010 %
	75,302	54.5	
L Byrne Lab	28,069	68.4	+16.4
K Mullan C	4,707	11.5	-0.2
A Duffen Ukip	4,651	11.3	+9.7
P Bennion LD	2,624	6.4	-21.3
C Nash Green	835	2.0	
A Chaffer Comm Brit	153	0.4	

Change from 2010

— 25%

— 0%

— -25%

Lab   C   Ukip   LD   Green

Birmingham Ladywood

LABOUR HOLD

SHABANA MAHMOOD
BORN Sep 17, 1980
MP 2010-

One of the first intake of female Muslim MPs in 2010. A passionate opponent of the Iraq war and 42-day detention, and an advocate of women's advancement and engagement in politics. Daughter of Birmingham Lab party chairman, made for controversial selection. Brummie born and raised. Shadow chief sec to Treasury 2015-. Shadow min: Treasury 2013-15; BIS 2011-13; home affairs 2010-11. Member, work & pensions select cttee 2010-11. Barrister specialising in professional indemnity litigation, Berrymans Lace Mawer. Pupillage at 12 Kings Bench Walk. Teaches as volunteer. GMB. Speaks Mirpuri, Urdu and Punjabi fluently. Enjoys creative writing. Ed: Small Heath Sch; King Edward VI Camp Hill Sch; Lincoln Coll, Oxford (BA law; JCR pres); Inns of Court Sch of Law (BVC).

CHALLENGERS
Isabel Sigmac (C) eCommerce professional; project director, Born Group commerce company. Cllr, Hertford TC 2011-15: chairwoman, development & leisure cttee. Ed: Barnet Coll (GNVQ); De Montfort (BA European & business studies); Middlesex (MA marketing management). **Clair Braund** (Ukip) Local businesswoman. Chairwoman, Ukip Central & South Birmingham. Married, one child. **Margaret Okole** (Green) Publishing career incl at Refugee Studies Centre. Sec, Birmingham Greens.

CONSTITUENCY PROFILE
Held by Labour since Second World War with the exception of year-long Liberal tenure after 1969 by-election. Until 2010 it was held by Clare Short, the left-wing cabinet minister who threatened to resign if Britain went to war in Iraq, but failed to do so until after the war had ended.

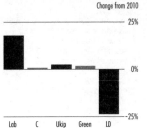

	Electorate	Turnout %	Change from 2010 %
	68,128	52.7	
S Mahmood Lab	26,444	73.6	+18.0
I Sigmac C	4,576	12.7	+0.8
C Braund Ukip	1,805	5.0	+2.5
M Okole Green	1,501	4.2	+1.8
S Iqbal LD	1,374	3.8	-23.7
T Burton Lib GB	216	0.6	

Change from 2010

Birmingham Northfield

LABOUR HOLD

RICHARD BURDEN
BORN Sept 1, 1954
MP 1992-

Outspoken supporter of Palestinians; chairman, Britain-Palestine APPG. Motor sports adviser to Richard Caborn 2002-07. PPS to Jeffrey Rooker 1997-2001. Shad min, transport 2013-15. Select cttees: chairman, West Midlands regional 2009-10; member, arms & export controls 2008-13; int devt 2005-13; trade & industry 2001-05. Chairman, Lab Campaign for Electoral Reform 1996-98. Founded Joint Action for Water Services 1985 to oppose water privatisation. Former trade union district officer. TGWU. Married, three stepchildren. Ed: Wallasey Tech GS; Bramhall Comp Sch; St John's FE Coll, Manchester; University of York (BA politics); University of Warwick (MA industrial relations).

CHALLENGERS
Rachel Maclean (C) Director,

Skilled and Ready employability program. Worked in banking. Married. Ed: St Hugh's Coll, Oxford (BA MA experimental psychology); Aston (MsC work & orginisational psychology); Stanford GSB (EPGC). **Keith Rowe** (Ukip) MD, Business Gift company. Contested Midlands West PCC 2014. Keen choral singer. Married, two children. Ed: North London Poly (HND business studies). **Steve Haynes** (LD) Performance consultant, Tomorrow People digital marketing agency. Ed: Birmingham (BA history & political science; MA interwar socio-political history).

CONSTITUENCY PROFILE
Lab-Con marginal, albeit one that leans to Labour and can normally be won by the Conservatives only in their very best years. It was held by the Tories through the 1980s (except for the 1982 by-election) but only by wafer-thin majorities. In 2010 the Labour majority here fell sharply, but not enough to put it into Conservative hands.

	Electorate	Turnout %	Change from 2010 %
	71,428	59.5	
R Burden Lab	17,673	41.6	+1.4
R Maclean C	15,164	35.7	+2.1
K Rowe Ukip	7,106	16.7	+13.5
S Haynes LD	1,349	3.2	-12.5
A Masters Green	1,169	2.8	+1.8

Change from 2010

Birmingham Perry Barr

LABOUR HOLD

KHALID MAHMOOD
BORN July 13, 1961
MP 2001-

Trade unionist and engineer. PPS to Tony McNulty 2004-06. Select cttees: home affairs 2009-10; broadcasting 2001-05. Attracted controversy by putting his name to "five myths Muslims must deny" article supporting Afghan war, ghost-written by Denis MacShane. Cllr, Birmingham CC 1990-93. Adviser, Danish International TU. Member, Lab finance & industry group, AEEU. Council member, Henry Jackson Society. Adviser, President of Olympic Council Asia. Twice divorced, child from first marriage, daughter from second. Ed: Golden Hillock Sch, Small Heath; University of Central England.

CHALLENGERS
Charlotte Hodivala (C) Deputy chairwoman of campaigning, Sutton Coldfield Conservative Association. Campaigner, Acocks

Green Focus Group. **Harjinder Singh** (Ukip) Financial adviser. Known locally as the "waving man" for campaigning 13 hours a day at a local junction. Married, one son. **Arjun Singh** (LD). **James Lovatt** (Green) Online marketing specialist, Rotary International in Great Britain & Ireland. Ed: Birmingham City (BA business studies); Coventry (HND project leadership & management); Buckingham (CIM integrated communications).

CONSTITUENCY PROFILE
Perry Barr is in northwest Birmingham. Until the 1970s it was a marginal seat, but the addition of non-white areas such as Handsworth in various rounds of boundary changes have made it into a Labour seat with solid majorities. Handsworth has suffered repeated outbreaks of rioting and racial tension, most notably in 1985 and 2005. A stronger manufacturing industry than any other Birmingham seat.

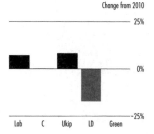

	Electorate	Turnout %	Change from 2010 %
	69,943	59.0	
K Mahmood Lab	23,697	57.4	+7.2
C Hodivala C	8,869	21.5	+0.2
H Singh Ukip	5,032	12.2	+8.2
A Singh LD	2,001	4.9	-17.1
J Lovatt Green	1,330	3.2	
R Punton TUSC	331	0.8	

Change from 2010

Birmingham Selly Oak

LABOUR HOLD

STEVE MCCABE
BORN Aug 4, 1955
MP 1997-

Old-style Commons operator. Shadow min, education 2013-15. Whip: opposition 2010; government 2007-10; assistant 2006-07. PPS to Charles Clarke 2003-05. Select cttees: home affairs 2010-13; HoL reform 2003-10; home affairs 2005-06; NI affairs 1998-2003; deregulation 1997-99. Cllr, Birmingham CC 1990-98. National & Local Govt Officers' Assoc shop steward. Former: social worker, lecturer, researcher. MSF, Unite. Divorced, one daughter, one son. Ed: Moray House Coll, Edinburgh (CQSW); University of Bradford (MA social work).

CHALLENGERS
Alex Boulter (C) Audit senior, CK Chartered Accountants. Contested West Midlands at 2014 European election. Father is a police officer in Stirchley. Ed: Bromsgove Sch;

Durham University (BA politics). **Steven Brookes** (Ukip) Solicitor. Chairman, Ukip Birmingham Central & South branch. Founder and director, Legisperitus commercial legal support. Has been trade union rep, lecturer and school governor. Ed: UCL (LLB law); Birmingham City (MA law); Coll of Law, Guildford (LSF); Wolverhampton (PgDip management). **Colin Green** (LD) Local campaigner. Software engineer, manufacturing sector. Married, one son. Ed: Staffordshire University (BSc engineering).

CONSTITUENCY PROFILE
The seat is towards the south of Birmingham and consists of the wards of Billesley, Bournville, Brandwood and Selly Oak. Once a marginal between Labour and Conservatives, Selly Oak has become increasingly solid for Labour, but the 2010 boundary changes made it more favourable for the Conservatives, with Labour's majority falling.

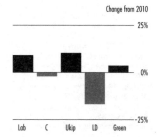

	Electorate	Turnout %	Change from 2010 %
	75,092	60.3	
S McCabe Lab	21,584	47.7	+9.1
A Boulter C	13,137	29.0	-2.1
S Brookes Ukip	5,755	12.7	+10.3
C Green LD	2,517	5.6	-16.7
C Thomas Green	2,301	5.1	+3.7

Change from 2010

Birmingham Yardley

LABOUR GAIN

JESS PHILLIPS
BORN Oct 9, 1981
MP 2015-

Equalities campaigner, has pledged to challenge sexism in Commons. Business devt manager, Sandwell Womens Aid, charity supporting domestic and sexual violence victims. Cllr, Birmingham CC 2012-; Victims' Champion for Birmingham 2012-. Was project manager, HealthLinks. Received Big Lunch community award 2013 for role in community cohesion. Married, two sons. Ed: University of Leeds (BA economic & social history & policy); University of Birmingham (PgDip public sector management).

CHALLENGERS
John Hemming (LD) MP 2005-15. Select cttes: backbench business 2010-15; procedure 2006-15; regulatory reform 2005-15. Contested: Yardley 2001, 1997, 1992; Birmingham Small Heath 1987;

Birmingham Hall Green 1983. Cllr, Birmingham CC 1990-2008, LD group leader 1998-2005. Entrepreneur, founded: JHC plc; e-commerce firm MarketNet; MMI Music Company. Married. Three daughters, one son. Ed: Magdalen Coll, Oxford (BA physics, MA). **Paul Clayton** (Ukip) Self-employed community tutor. Vice-chairman, Big Bang Prospects CIC, mentoring disadvantaged children. **Arun Photay** (C) Business devt manager, RBS. Cllr, Wolverhampton CC 2012-. Ed: University of Hertfordshire (BA economics).

CONSTITUENCY PROFILE
In the south-east of Birmingham. Once a Conservative-Labour marginal and for many years a bellwether seat. Tories were pushed into third place in 1997 and have been supplanted by Lib Dems as main opposition. When Labour's Estelle Morris retired, it was won by the Lib Dems in 2005 but regained by Labour in 2015 with an 11.7 point swing.

	Electorate	Turnout %	from 2010 %	Change
	72,146	57.0		
J Phillips Lab	17,129	41.6	+9.4	
J Hemming LD	10,534	25.6	-14.0	
P Clayton Ukip	6,637	16.1	+13.2	
A Photay C	5,760	14.0	-5.2	
G Bishop Green	698	1.7		
T Stephens Respect	187	0.5		
E Flynn TUSC	135	0.3		
P Johnson Soc Dem	71	0.2		

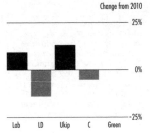

Change from 2010

Lab LD Ukip C Green

Bishop Auckland

LABOUR HOLD

HELEN GOODMAN
BORN Jan 2, 1958
MP 2005-

Popular, plain-speaking ally of Harriet Harman. Said immigrants working on construction sites should be able to speak English. Shadow min: work & pensions 2014-15; CMS 2011-14; justice 2010-11. Shadow SoS, work & pensions 2010. Parly under sec, work & pensions 2009-10. Asst govt whip 2008-09. Dep Commons leader 2007-08. Select cttes: ecclesiastical 2010-; procedure 2011-14. PPS to: Harriet Harman 2007. Former: head of strategy, the Children's Society; dir, Commission on the Future of Multi-Ethnic Britain; CEO, National Assoc of Toy & Leisure Libraries. GMB, Amnesty. Married, two children. Ed: Lady Manners Sch, Bakewell; Somerville Coll, Oxford (BA PPE).

CHALLENGERS
Christopher Adams (C) Dir, Hylia

computer services; operations dir, Undesk. Entrepreneur. Previously worked as a consultant. Played rugby for Durham and Darlington youth teams. Ed: Richmond Sch; Brasenose Coll, Oxford (BA Classics). **Rhys Burriss** (Ukip) Former Conservative supporter. Brought up on a council estate in Warwickshire. Previously: senior legal adviser, Int Criminal Tribunal for Rwanda; resident magistrate, Montserrat, Turks & Caicos Islands; dep chief clerk, Inner London Courts. Ed: Oxford (BA Brazilian & Portugese studies); Grey's Inn (bar).

CONSTITUENCY PROFILE
A seat in the southwest of County Durham, stretching westwards into farmland, open moorland and the Pennine hills with several small towns and villages. The rural part of the seat votes Conservative, but is easily outweighed by Labour voters in the old coal-mining towns in the eastern part of the seat, making this a reliable Labour seat. Held by the party since 1935.

	Electorate	Turnout %	from 2010 %	Change
	66,089	59.6		
H Goodman Lab	16,307	41.4	+2.5	
C Adams C	12,799	32.5	+6.2	
R Burriss Ukip	7,015	17.8	+15.1	
S White LD	1,723	4.4	-18.0	
T Robinson Green	1,545	3.9		

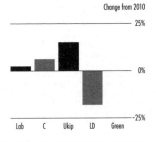

Change from 2010

Lab C Ukip LD Green

Blackburn

LABOUR HOLD

KATE HOLLERN
BORN Apr 12, 1955
MP 2015-

Originally from Dumbarton, Scotland. Cllr, Blackburn with Darwen BC 1995-2015, resigning when she became MP; leader of the Labour group 2004-15; and council leader 2004-07, 2010-15. Member, police & crime panel for Lancashire. Worked as study manager at a shoe factory; contracts manager at Blackburn College. Single parent, two daughters.

CHALLENGERS
Bob Eastwood (C) Semi-retired police officer, advanced to chief superintendent in 30-year career. National adviser on operations and security, Football League. Commissioned to support police development in Serbia. School governor. Board member, Health & Wellbeing Consortium. Married, four children. Ed: St Mary's RC

GS; Lancaster University (LLB law & politics). **Dayle Taylor** (Ukip) Studying politics & sociology at University of Chester, aged 21 at election. Works at McDonald's. Chairman, NW region Young Independence. **Gordon Lishman** (LD) Chairman, Gas Safe Charity. Pres, North West Lib Dems 2011-. Former DG, Age Concern. Awarded CBE in 2006 for services to older people. Contested: Pendle 1987, 1983; Bradford N Oct, Feb 1974. Ed: Manchester (economics & political science); UCLan (honorary fellow).

CONSTITUENCY PROFILE
Safe Labour seat since its re-creation in 1950. Until 2015 the seat had had only two MPs since then, both senior cabinet ministers: Barbara Castle and Jack Straw. The BNP and splinter group English First party have won seats on Blackburn & Darwen BC in the past, most recently the BNP retained their deposit in 2005.

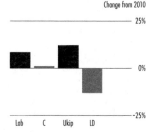

	Electorate	Turnout %	from 2010 % Change
	73,265	60.1	
K Hollern Lab	24,762	56.3	+8.5
B Eastwood C	12,002	27.3	+1.1
D Taylor Ukip	6,280	14.3	+12.2
G Lishman LD	955	2.2	-13.0

Change from 2010

25%

0%

-25%

Lab C Ukip LD

Blackley & Broughton

LABOUR HOLD

GRAHAM STRINGER
BORN Feb 17, 1950
MP 1997-

Successful, reforming council leader. Govt whip 2001-02. Parly sec, Cab Office 1999-2001. Select cttees: ECC 2013-; justice 2013-14; transport 2002-; science & technology 2009-; IUS 2007-09. Cllr, Manchester CC 1979-98, leader 1984-96. Amicus, Unite. Former: board chairman, Manchester Airport plc; analytical chemist; branch officer, MSF. Manchester United fan. Plays squash. Married, one son, one stepdaughter, one stepson. Ed: Moston Brook HS; University of Sheffield (BSc chemistry).

CHALLENGERS
Martin Power (Ukip) Grew up in Ireland, Blackley resident for 14 years. Social worker. Chairman, Ukip Blackley & Broughton. Former member of Irish govt statutory board overseeing fund

for survivors of Irish institutional abuse. Married, four children. **Michelle Tanfield-Johnson** (C) Owner and MD, It-green recycling company. Cllr, Wisbech TC 2013-; Fenland DC 2013-, cab member 2014-. Married, one child. Ed: University of Salford (BA media & music performance). **David Jones** (Green) Energy consultant and academic. Treasurer, NW Green party. Ed: Salford (BSc environmental & resource science; MSc energy technology for sustainable development); University of Bolton (PGCE); University of Nottingham (PhD).

CONSTITUENCY PROFILE
Cross-border seat in inner-city Manchester created in 2010, based on the old Manchester Blackley seat joined to two Salford wards. In the 1950s Blackley was regarded as a weathervane seat, but this is now solid Labour territory, as of 2013 one of the few seats to still have a solid slate of Labour councillors.

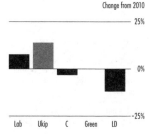

	Electorate	Turnout %	from 2010 % Change
	71,900	51.6	
G Stringer Lab	22,982	61.9	+7.7
M Power Ukip	6,108	16.5	+13.8
M Tanfield-Johnson C	5,581	15.0	-3.3
D Jones Green	1,567	4.2	
R Gadsden LD	874	2.4	-11.9

Change from 2010

25%

0%

-25%

Lab Ukip C Green LD

Blackpool North & Cleveleys

CONSERVATIVE HOLD

PAUL MAYNARD
BORN Dec 16, 1975
MP 1997-

Independent-minded, self-styled community champion. Long-standing special adviser and speechwriter to Liam Fox 1999-2007. PPS to Oliver Letwin 2012-15. Select cttees: work & pensions 2014-15; transport 2010-12. Worked at Reform think tank and as management consultant, Hodgart Temporal. Contested Twickenham 2005. Has mild cerebral palsy and epilepsy, accused Labour MPs of mocking him in 2011. Lay reader at local Catholic church. Member, Twentieth Century Society. Northwich Victoria FC supporter. Ed: St Ambrose Coll; University Coll, Oxford (BA modern history).

CHALLENGERS
Samuel Rushworth (Lab) Post-graduate researcher and associate tutor, UEA. Previously volunteer manager, British Red Cross. Married, four children. Ed: University of Manchester (BA economics & social studies, MA international development); Chambre de Commerce et d'industrie de Paris (advanced business French); UEA (MRes; PhD). **Simon Noble** (Ukip) Solicitor specialising in immigration, Pro Visas Immigration Solicitors. Defected from Conservatives in 2010. Cllr, Lancashire CC 1993-2001 for Conservatives. Contested Euro NW England 2014. Married, two sons. Ed: Uppingham Sch, Rutland; University of Manchester (BSc textile economics & management); Lancaster University (LLB law).

CONSTITUENCY PROFILE
Both the Blackpool seats are marginals between Labour and the Conservatives. Blackpool North was a Tory seat until the Labour landslide in 1997, and was won back by the Conservatives in 2010, helped somewhat by boundary changes that removed the Labour-voting town of Fleetwood.

	Electorate	Turnout %	Change from 2010 %
	62,469	63.1	
P Maynard C	17,508	44.4	+2.7
S Rushworth Lab	14,168	36.0	-0.5
S Noble Ukip	5,823	14.8	+10.7
S Close LD	948	2.4	-10.9
J Warnock Green	889	2.3	
J Walsh Northern	57	0.1	

Change from 2010

Blackpool South

LABOUR HOLD

GORDON MARSDEN
BORN Nov 28, 1953
MP 1997-

Earnest, constituency-focused loyalist. Shadow minister: transport 2013-15; BIS 2010-13. PPS to: John Denham 2009-10; Tessa Jowell 2003-05; Lord Irvine of Lairg 2001-03. Select cttees: ecclesiastical 2010-15, 2002-05; science & technology 2009-10; IUS 2007-09. Historian. Previously: editor, *History Today, New Socialist*; lecturer, Open University; public relations consultant; public affairs adviser, English Heritage. Contested Blackpool South 1992. Pres, British Resorts Assoc. GMB, Fabian. Ed: Stockport GS; New Coll, Oxford (BA history); Warburg Inst, London (PhD); Harvard (international relations, Kennedy Scholar).

CHALLENGERS
Peter Anthony (C) Entertainer for 30 years. Runs café bar in St Annes with partner, Paul. Owned a promenade hotel. Chairman, Queendeans Association. **Peter Wood** (Ukip) Worked in business and government overseas: Telefonica; Unisys global information technology compant. Cllr, Fylde BC 2010-12 for Conservatives. Volunteer at a primary sch. Married, two children. **Duncan Royle** (Green) Environmental consultant and qualified accountant. Worked for 18 years at BAE Systems in Warton. Married, two children. **Bill Greene** (LD) Retired IT professional and risk manager. Former Cllr, Fylde BC. Contested Blackpool North & Cleveleys 2010.

CONSTITUENCY PROFILE
Blackpool South was a Conservative seat until the Labour landslide in 1997 when it was won by Gordon Marden. The seat contains the bulk of Blackpool, including the three piers and the major attractions, but much of the town is severely deprived.

	Electorate	Turnout %	Change from 2010 %
	57,411	56.5	
G Marsden Lab	13,548	41.8	+0.7
P Anthony C	10,963	33.8	-2.0
P Wood Ukip	5,613	17.3	+13.5
D Royle Green	841	2.6	
B Greene LD	743	2.3	-12.2
A Higgins Ind	655	2.0	
L Chard Ind	73	0.2	

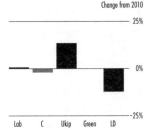

Change from 2010

Blaenau Gwent

NICK SMITH
BORN Jan 14, 1960
MP 2010-

From family with coal and steel background. Special interest in health issues. PPS to Douglas Alexander 2010-15. Member, public accounts select cttee 2010-15. Cllr, Camden BC 1998-2006. Policy & partnerships dir, Royal College of Speech & Language Therapists. Former: sec gen, European PLP; membership devt head, Lab; campaigns manager, NSPCC. AEEU, Community, Unite, GMB. Campaigner, 'Salt our streets' (to grit streets in snow) and 'turn on the lights' (street lights). Enjoys hiking. FRGS. Divorced, two daughters. Ed: Tredegar Comp Sch; Coventry University (BA history, politics & international relations); Birkbeck Coll, London (MSc economic & social change).

CHALLENGERS
Susan Boucher (Ukip) Worked in local govt for 31 years. Joined Ukip in 2015. Management adviser, Monmouthshire CC. Founding member, Young Communicants church group. Married, two children. **Tracey West** (C) Former cabin steward. Cttee member, Ebbw Vale Conservative Club. **Steffan Lewis** (PC) Cllr, Blackwood TC 2012-. Research & comms officer, National Assembly. PC press officer. Contested Islwyn 2010.

CONSTITUENCY PROFILE
Until recently one of the most solid Labour seats with opposition parties normally struggling to get more than 10 per cent. In 2005 it was won by Peter Law, standing as an independent. He was the Labour member for the Welsh assembly seat but was not selected by Labour owing to an all-woman shortlist. Law ran despite suffering from a brain tumour and died less than a year after his election. His agent, Dai Davies, defended the seat in the by-election, but it was reclaimed by Labour in 2010.

	Electorate	Turnout %	from 2010 %	Change
	51,332	61.7		
N Smith Lab	18,380	58.0	+5.6	
S Boucher Ukip	5,677	17.9	+16.4	
T West C	3,419	10.8	+3.8	
S Lewis PC	2,849	9.0	+4.9	
M Pond Green	738	2.3		
S Rees LD	620	2.0	-8.2	

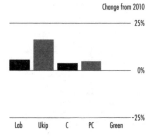

Change from 2010

Blaydon

DAVE ANDERSON
BORN Dec 2, 1953
MP 2005-

Trade union activist who cut his teeth in the miners' strike 1984-85: TUC general council 2000-05; Unison; NUM. PPS to: Bill Rammell 2006-10. Opp assistant whip 2010-11. Select cttees: backbench business 2012-15; NI affairs 2011-15, 2005-10; regulatory reform 2010-15. Previously: engineer, National Coal Board mines; care worker, Newcastle-upon-Tyne social services. Married. Ed: Maltby GS; Doncaster Technical Coll; Durham Technical Coll (mining & mechanical engineering); Moscow Higher Trade Union Sch; Durham University (DipSocSc).

CHALLENGERS
Mark Bell (Ukip). **Alison Griffiths** (C) Interim marketing and commercial director, Gisborne consultancy. Trustee, Meningitis Now. Fellow, British American Project. Enjoys equestrianism, competed to national championship level until 2001. Ed: University of Warwick (BA politics). **Jonathan Wallace** (LD) Cllr, Gateshead MBC 1987-, deputy leader of opposition 2011-. Self-employed horticulturalist and communications businessman. Blogger. Produces own food. Helped to set up local trading networks. Member, Marley Hill Community Assoc Management cttee.

CONSTITUENCY PROFILE
The former coal-mining territory contains a collection of small towns to the southwest of Newcastle. It takes in the fringes of Gateshead, the Metrocentre shopping centre and *The Angel of the North*. Blaydon is a safe Labour seat, held by the party since 1935. The Liberal Democrats have had successes at a local level and but dropped from second to fourth in 2010.

	Electorate	Turnout %	from 2010 %	Change
	67,706	66.4		
D Anderson Lab	22,090	49.2	-0.5	
M Bell Ukip	7,863	17.5		
A Griffiths C	7,838	17.4	+1.5	
J Wallace LD	5,497	12.2	-17.1	
P McNally Green	1,648	3.7		

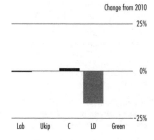

Change from 2010

Blyth Valley

LABOUR HOLD

RONNIE CAMPBELL
BORN Aug 14, 1943
MP 1987-

From old Labour left. Argued with Andrew Griffiths in the chamber after Esther McVey was targeted by Labour over her role in welfare cuts 2015. Select cttees: health 2005-07; catering 2001-10; public administration 1997-2001. Parly commissioner for administration 1987-97. Was chairman, Labour MPs northern regional group. Cllr: Blyth Valley BC 1974-88; Blyth BC 1969-74. NUM sponsored MP, former lodge chairman, Bates Colliery, Blyth. Miner for 28 years. Married, one daughter, five sons. Ed: Blyth Ridley County HS.

CHALLENGERS

Barry Elliott (Ukip) Property developer and runs local business. Was fireman. Cllr, Blyth TC. Contested Blyth Valley 2010. Involved in a row after Ronnie Campbell accused Ukip of scaremongering. Spoke out against allegations regarding election fraud in the 2013 local council elections. **Greg Munro** (C) Party Commons researcher. Dep chairman, Tooting Conservative Assoc 2014-. Has worked at Policy Exchange, and in parly offices of Anne Milton and Iain Duncan Smith. Ed: Leeds (BA political studies; MA British politics & parliamentary studies). **Philip Latham** (LD) Retired English teacher. Local and regional campaigner. Quaker. Cllr, Riding Mill PC for 11 years. Cllr, Tynedale DC until 2009.

CONSTITUENCY PROFILE

Blyth has been held by Labour since creation in 1950, with the brief exception between the two 1974 elections when it was won by its deselected Labour MP, Eddie Milne, standing as an independent. He was defeated by John Ryman, who also resigned the Labour whip and sat as an independent from 1986-87. His successor, Ronnie Campbell, has remained MP since.

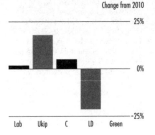

	Electorate	Turnout %	Change from 2010 %
	63,958	60.1	
R Campbell Lab	17,813	46.3	+1.8
B Elliott Ukip	8,584	22.3	+18.0
G Munro C	8,346	21.7	+5.1
P Latham LD	2,265	5.9	-21.3
D Furness Green	1,453	3.8	

Change from 2010

Lab   Ukip   C   LD   Green

Bognor Regis & Littlehampton

CONSERVATIVE HOLD

NICK GIBB
BORN Sep 3, 1960
MP 1997-

Quiet and industrious. Min of state for schools 2014-, 2010-12. Shadow min, schools 2005-10. Opposition spokes: trade & industry 1999-2001; Treasury 1998-99. Select cttees: draft voting eligibility bill 2013; education & skills 2003-05. Was chartered accountant for KPMG. Member, prime minister's policy board. Ed: Maidstone GS; Roundhay Sch, Leeds; Thornes House Sch, Wakefield; Durham University (BA law).

CHALLENGERS

Graham Jones (Ukip) Cllr, West Sussex CC 2013-. Draughtsman: Tesla Engineering; Royal Signals. Married. Ed: Merry Oak Boys Sch; Technical Coll (T1 mechanical engineering). **Alan Butcher** (Lab) Works for Cega, air ambulance and assistance company. Cllr, Littlehampton TC; Arun DC. Was a workplace rep, quality department, Body Shop. Founder, TGWU branch. Contested Worthing West 2001. Ed: UCL (BA linguistics; chair, UCL union council). **Francis Oppler** (LD) Runs office equipment firm. Cllr, Arun DC 1989-, leader of opp; West Sussex CC. Has served as mayor of Bognor Regis on two occasions. Worked as a chef. Ed: Nyewood & Bognor Comp Sch; Chichester Coll of Technology for City & Guilds (catering).

CONSTITUENCY PROFILE

A generally safe Conservative seat, held by the party since its creation in 1997. Ukip have a significant presence here, holding their deposit in 2005 and 2010 and winning the most votes in the area in the 2013 county council elections. The most westerly of the three coastal seats strung along the south of West Sussex. Seasonal tourism remains important to the economy and, like many south coast resorts, there is a high proportion of retired people, but some areas of deprivation.

	Electorate	Turnout %	Change from 2010 %
	73,095	64.5	
N Gibb C	24,185	51.3	-0.1
G Jones Ukip	10,241	21.7	+15.3
A Butcher Lab	6,508	13.8	-0.2
F Oppler LD	4,240	9.0	-14.5
S McDougall Green	1,942	4.1	

Change from 2010

C   Ukip   Lab   LD   Green

Bolsover

LABOUR HOLD

DENNIS SKINNER
BORN Feb 11, 1932
MP 1970-

Assiduous, volatile left-wing Tory-baiter, dubbed "Beast of Bolsover", who was almost turfed off his Commons bench by SNP in 2015. Continues to fight the class war. Excels at one-line put-down of opponents, most famously at state opening. Socialist Campaign Group. One of the MPs spied on by police during 1990s according to whistleblower Peter Francis. Chairman, Lab party 1988-89, vice-chairman 1987-88. Lab party NEC member 1999-, 1994-98, 1978-92. Cllr, Clay Cross UDC 1960-70; Derbyshire CC 1964-70. President Derbyshire Miners. Former miner. Widowed. Two daughters, one son. Ed: Tupton Hall GS; Ruskin Coll, Oxford.

CHALLENGERS
Peter Bedford (C) Chartered accountant. Works at Britvic.

Cllr, East Northamptonshire C 2007-11. Grew up in a single parent family. Enjoys horse-racing meetings. Ed: Ferrers Specialist Arts Coll; Leicester (law). **Ray Calladine** (Ukip) Sales and Marketing director, Nama Chemicals. Owns family business, Sensopolis. Fellow, Chartered Institute of Logistics & Transport. Chartered Chemist. Ed: Manchester (BSc chemical physics). **David Lomax** (LD) Former head of special needs at New Mills Sch. Runs Spire House Bed & Breakfast. Leader, High Peak DC 2003-07. Cllr: Derbyshire CC 2013-; High Peak DC 1991-, mayor 2011-12 & 1996-97. Contested Tatton 2010.

CONSTITUENCY PROFILE
A rural mining seat, used to have one of the biggest concentrations of coalmines in the country. Now the biggest employer is East Midlands Designer Outlet. So solidly Labour that Conservatives and Lib Dems do not always put up candidates at council elections.

	Electorate	Turnout %	from 2010 %	Change
	71,976	61.1		
D Skinner Lab	22,542	51.2	+1.2	
P Bedford C	10,764	24.5	-0.1	
R Calladine Ukip	9,228	21.0	+17.1	
D Lomax LD	1,464	3.3	-12.2	

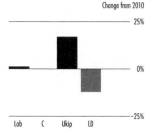

Change from 2010

Lab   C   Ukip   LD

Bolton North East

LABOUR HOLD

DAVID CRAUSBY
BORN Jun 17, 1946
MP 1997-

Member, cttees: panel of chairs 2010-; NW 2009-10; quadripartite, arms export controls 2006-10; defence 2001-10; social security 1999-2001; admin 1997-2001. Cllr, Bury C 1979-92. Contested: Bolton North East 1992; Bury North 1987. Chairman, Amicus trade union parly group. Sec, Unite 2010-. Member, UK delegation to Nato parly assembly 2014-. Voted against the Iraq war 2003. Shop steward works convenor, AEEU. Won Commons speech of the Year, *House Magazine* awards 2011. Engineer. Married, two sons. Ed: Derby GS, Bury; Bury Tech Coll.

CHALLENGERS
James Daly (C) Legal aid solicitor. Cllr, Bury North 2012-. Deputy leader, Bury Conservative group. Member, National Trust, Law Soc, Cons Councillors Assoc.

Board member, Bury CAB. School governor. Follows Huddersfield Giants rugby league club. Married, two sons. Ed: Moor End HS, Huddersfield; Greenhead Coll; Edge Hill Coll, Lancashire (BA history); Leeds Met University (PgDip law); Sheffield University (LPC). **Harry Lamb** (Ukip) Managing director, HiCharms, which imports chemicals from China to Europe. Contested Bolton West 2010. Two sons. Chess enthusiast. **Stephen Rock** (LD) Adult education teacher. Cllr: Horwich TC 2003-; Bolton BC 2004-. Worked for British Rail and in the aerospace industry. Married, three sons. Ed: Bolton Coll.

CONSTITUENCY PROFILE
Northwest of Manchester. Bolton has been the scene of significant regeneration in recent years. Beyond the centre are residential areas and some rural land at its northern extremities. A socially diverse seat in terms of income. Lower than average social housing.

	Electorate	Turnout %	from 2010 %	Change
	67,901	63.6		
D Crausby Lab	18,541	43.0	-3.0	
J Daly C	14,164	32.8	-3.7	
H Lamb Ukip	8,117	18.8	+14.6	
S Rock LD	1,236	2.9	-10.1	
L Diggle Green	1,103	2.6		

Change from 2010

Lab   C   Ukip   LD   Green

Bolton South East

LABOUR HOLD

YASMIN QURESHI
BORN Jul 5, 1963
MP 2010-

Personable and hard working. Opposed Iraq war, vocal about Muslim women's rights. Criminal law barrister and long-term Labour activist. Select cttees: high speed rail 2014-; home affairs 2013-15; privacy & injunctions 2011-12; political & constitutional reform 2011; justice 2010-. Contested Brent East 2005. Chairwoman, APPG on international justice. Secretary, APPG on legal and constitutional affairs. CPS prosecutor. Worked for UN Mission in Kosovo. Human rights adviser to Ken Livingstone as mayor of London. CAB. British Institute of Human Rights. Special interest in poverty, mental health and child abuse issues. USDAW, GMB. Pakistani-born, moved to Britain aged 9. Married to a prof cricketer. Ed: Westfield Comp, Watford; South Bank (BA law); Council of Legal Ed; UCL (LLM).

CHALLENGERS
Jeff Armstrong (Ukip) Worked in the rail industry. Never voted in a general election before 2005. Defended posting crude jokes on his Facebook page 2015. Married, four children. **Mudasir Dean** (C) Cllr, Bolton C 2012-. Deputy chairman, Bolton North East Conservative assoc. Chief whip, Conservative group, Bolton Council. Contested Rochdale 2010. Married, four children. Ed: Bolton (BA business administration). **Alan Johnson** (Green) Works in social care. Contested Bolton SE 2010. Worked in manufacturing industry. Bolton Green party's press officer and trade union link officer.

CONSTITUENCY PROFILE
The most industrial seat of Bolton's three constituencies. The traditionally industrial economy has diversified into service and public sector. The Royal Bolton Hospital NHS Foundation is a major employer here. Has a large Muslim community.

	Electorate	Turnout %	from 2010 %	Change
	69,692	58.5		
Y Qureshi Lab	20,555	50.5	+3.0	
J Armstrong Ukip	9,627	23.6	+19.7	
M Dean C	8,289	20.3	-5.3	
A Johnson Green	1,200	3.0	+1.4	
D Reynolds LD	1,072	2.6	-13.3	

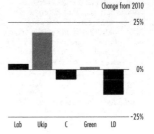

Change from 2010

Bolton West

CONSERVATIVE GAIN

CHRISTOPHER GREEN
BORN Aug 12, 1973
MP 2015-

Scientific instrumentation engineer. Contested Manchester Withington 2010. Engineering ambassador in schools. Taught English in Rwanda. Former member, Territorial Army. Has worked in pharmaceutical and manufacturing industries. Born in Northern Ireland and grew up in a deprived area of Liverpool. One of five children. Father worked as sergeant in the army's catering corp. Fitness enthusiast.

CHALLENGERS
Julie Hilling (Lab) MP for Bolton West 2010-15. PPS to Yvette Cooper's women and equalities team. Opposition whip 2013-15. Member, select cttees: standards & privileges 2011-12; transport 2010-12. Senior regional organiser, TSSA. NW learning organiser, NASUWT. Nat president, CYWU. Chairwoman, Socialist Education

Assoc. Amnesty, Howard League for Criminal Reform, Lab Friends of Palestine, Unite. Ed: University of Nottingham (BSc chemistry); Manchester Poly (Dip youth & community work). **Bob Horsefield** (Ukip) Lighting technician. Worked in the film and TV industry. Former member, Territorial Army. Member, Mensa 2011-. Married, five children. **Andrew Martin** (LD) Freelance fitness instructor. Cllr, Bolton C 2014-. Ed: University of Cambridge (law).

CONSTITUENCY PROFILE
On the outskirts of Greater Manchester. Includes very little of Bolton itself. It covers the suburban and rural land between Bolton and Wigan. Includes Green Belt land. Is home to commuters who work in Manchester. Home to Bolton Wanderers Football Club. The most affluent of the Bolton seats, with the largest proportion of home owners. A Conservative-Labour marginal.

	Electorate	Turnout %	from 2010 %	Change
	72,727	66.8		
C Green C	19,744	40.6	+2.3	
J Hilling Lab	18,943	39.0	+0.5	
B Horsefield Ukip	7,428	15.3	+11.3	
A Martin LD	1,947	4.0	-13.2	
A Smith Ind	321	0.7	+0.1	
J Vickers TUSC	209	0.4		

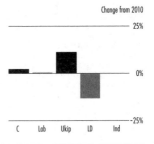

Change from 2010

Bootle

LABOUR HOLD

PETER DOWD
BORN Jun 20, 1957
MP 2015-

Head, care delivery framework, 5Boroughs NHS Partnership Trust. Cllr, Sefton C 1991-, leader 2008-15. Cllr, Merseyside CC 1981-86. Board member, Liverpool City Region Cabinet. Member, Liverpool City Region Combined Authority. Chairman, Merseyside Fire Authority 1990s. Chairman, Merseyside Fire and Rescue Service; South Sefton Primary Care Trust. Family has history of Labour activism. Worked in health and social care for 35 years in Merseyside. Qualified social worker with interest in education and mental health. Ed: University of Liverpool; Lancaster University.

CHALLENGERS
Paul Nuttall (Ukip) Deputy leader, Ukip 2010-. Chairman, Ukip 2008. MEP for North West England 2009-. Contested: Bootle 2010,

2005; Oldham East & Saddleworth 2011 by-election. Founder Ukip Sefton branch 2005-. Former lecturer. Survivor of Hillsborough disaster. Ed: Savio HS; Hugh Baird Coll; North Lincolnshire Coll (HND sports science); Edge Hill University (BA history); Liverpool Hope University (MA politics); UCLan (CertEd). **Jade Marsden** (C) Chairwoman, Liverpool Conservative Future. Cllr, Liverpool CC 2011-. Married, two children. **Lisa Tallis** (Green) Teacher. Has mobility problems as a result of a car accident in 2005.

CONSTITUENCY PROFILE
A working-class port to the north of Liverpool on the mouth of the River Mersey. The docks used to be the centre of its economy. Was the most bombed borough in the UK during Second World War. Undergoing extensive regeneration but unemployment is still high. More than a quarter of the population lives in social housing. A safe Labour seat.

	Electorate	Turnout %	Change from 2010 %
	70,137	64.4	
P Dowd Lab	33,619	74.5	+8.0
P Nuttall Ukip	4,915	10.9	+4.8
J Marsden C	3,639	8.1	-0.9
L Tallis Green	1,501	3.3	
D Newman LD	978	2.2	-13.0
P Glover TUSC	500	1.1	-0.0

Change from 2010

```
                                    25%

                                    0%

                                   -25%
Lab    Ukip    C    Green    LD
```

Boston & Skegness

CONSERVATIVE HOLD

MATT WARMAN
BORN Sep 1, 1981
MP 2015-

Former technology editor, *Daily Telegraph*. Used to being in the media, regularly appears on national TV and radio campaigning for better broadband across the country. Head, Conservative association, Hertfordshire. Former communications adviser to Conservative voluntary party. Member, Conservative Rural Action Group, NUJ. Married. Ed: Haberdashers' Aske's Boys Sch; Durham University (BA English).

CHALLENGERS
Robin Hunter-Clarke (Ukip) Cllr: Lincolnshire CC 2013-; Skegness TC 2011-15. Deputy leader, Ukip group, Lincolnshire CC 2013-. National exec member, Ukip 2014-15. Worked at Embassy Theatre, Skegness. Father, Dean Hunter-Clarke, Ukip Lincolnshire county councillor. Ed: Skegness GS;

University of Chester (law). **Paul Kenny** (Lab) Local community worker. Cllr, Lincolnshire 1993-. Former cllr, Boston BC; mayor 2013-14; deputy leader, Labour group. General Sec, GMB. Married. **David Watts** (LD) Trains in law and management. Cllr, Broxtowe BC 1999-. Contested Broxtowe 2010. Former solicitor. Married, two children. Methodist preacher. Ed: Huddersfield Poly (law); Coll of Law, London; Leicester (MSc criminal justice studies). **Victoria Percival** (Green) Runs business making baby carriers. Ed: Kitwood Girls Sch.

CONSTITUENCY PROFILE
A largely rural seat on the east coast of Lincolnshire. Largely dependent on tourism and agriculture. Home to Europe's biggest concentration of caravans. Boston houses a high number of European migrants. Held by the Conservatives since its creation in 1997.

	Electorate	Turnout %	Change from 2010 %
	67,834	63.9	
M Warman C	18,981	43.8	-5.7
R Hunter-Clarke Ukip	14,645	33.8	+24.3
P Kenny Lab	7,142	16.5	-4.2
D Watts LD	1,015	2.3	-12.4
V Percival Green	800	1.9	
C Pain IE	324	0.8	
P Johnson ND	170	0.4	
L Luxton Pilgrim	143	0.3	
R West BNP	119	0.3	-5.0

Change from 2010

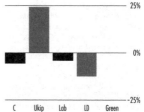

```
                                    25%

                                    0%

                                   -25%
C    Ukip    Lab    LD    Green
```

Bosworth

CONSERVATIVE HOLD

DAVID TREDINNICK
BORN Jan 19, 1950
MP 1987-

Suspended from Commons in first "cash for questions" scandal and forced to resign as PPS to Sir Wyn Roberts, 1991-94 but survived on backbenches. Select cttees: science & technology 2013-; health 2010-. Chairman, APPG for integrated healthcare 2002-. Contested Cardiff South & Penarth 1983. Former chairman, British Atlantic Group of Young Politicians, Future of Europe Trust. Career inc. manager, property co; marketing, comms; technology salesman; advertising account exec. Lietutenant Grenadier Guards 1968-71. Interested in alternative medicine. Divorced, one daughter, one son. Ed: Eton Coll; Cape Town (MBA); St John's Coll, Oxford (MLitt).

CHALLENGERS
Michael Mullaney (LD) Office manager. Cllr, Hinckley & Bosworth BC 2011-15. Contested Bosworth 2010. Former chairman, East Midlands Lib Dems. Member: Lib Dem English Council Exec. Worked as carer for elderly and disabled people. Ed: John Leas Sch; Northampton University (BA politics). **Chris Kealey** (Lab) Works for education charity. Previously worked at FCO. Appointed MBE in 2010 for his work in Afghanistan. Ed: Hastings HS; John Cleveland Coll. **David Sprason** (Ukip) Cllr, Leicestershire CC 2001-. Former deputy leader, Leicestershire CC. Former Conservative cllr who was sacked after he used his work laptop to watch pornography 2014.

CONSTITUENCY PROFILE
Rural seat to the west of Leicestershire. Bosworth was once home to a substantial mining industry. Closure of the Leicestershire pits led to significant unemployment but it is now at low level. History includes Battle of Bosworth.

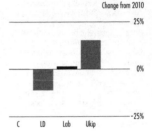

	Electorate	Turnout %	Change from 2010 %
	79,742	67.2	
D Tredinnick C	22,939	42.8	+0.2
M Mullaney LD	11,951	22.3	-11.1
C Kealey Lab	9,354	17.5	+1.5
D Sprason Ukip	9,338	17.4	+15.4

Change from 2010

Bournemouth East

CONSERVATIVE HOLD

TOBIAS ELLWOOD
BORN Aug 12, 1966
MP 2005-

Very eager, full of ideas, especially on specialist subjects such as Afghanistan. Parly under sec for FCO 2014-. PPS to: Jeremy Hunt 2013-14; David Lidlington 2011-13; Liam Fox 2010-11. Shadow minister, CMS 2007-10. Opposition whip 2005-07. Raised in the USA, Germany and Austria with UN-employed parents. Career: Army, including active service in Bosnia; researcher for Tom King MP; business manager London Stock Exchange. Treasurer, Bow Group. Ed: Vienna Int Sch; Loughborough University of Technology (design & tech); City University London (MBA).

CHALLENGERS
Peter Stokes (Lab) Works for an oil and gas company. Previous career: British Railways; the underground mining industry in Australia. Brother, David Stokes, contested Bournemouth West 2015. Supports AFC Bournemouth. Ed: Portchester Sch. **David Hughes** (Ukip) Retired. Ran an electrical retailing business. Contested Bournemouth East 2010. Served in the police service until 1970. Divorced, three children. **Jon Nicholas** (LD) Freelance consultant. Senior associate, Tim Parry Johnathan Ball Foundation for Peace; and Research in Practice for Adults. Worked as a facilitator for organisations inc the UN and Save the Children. Married, two boys. Ed: Glamorgan (BA psychology); Webber Douglas Academy.

CONSTITUENCY PROFILE
Small urban seat on south coast of England that includes most of the award-winning Bournemouth beach. Home to some of the UKs biggest free festivals. It is a fast-growing and prosperous town. Tourism is a key part of the local economy. Has been held by the Tories since its creation in 1974.

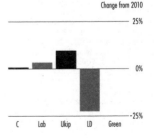

	Electorate	Turnout %	Change from 2010 %
	71,956	62.3	
T Ellwood C	22,060	49.2	+0.8
P Stokes Lab	7,448	16.6	+3.4
D Hughes Ukip	7,401	16.5	+9.6
J Nicholas LD	3,752	8.4	-22.5
A Keddie Green	3,263	7.3	
D Ross Bournemouth	903	2.0	

Change from 2010

Bournemouth West

CONSERVATIVE HOLD

CONOR BURNS
BORN Sep 24, 1972
MP 2010-

Right-wing Eurosceptic and ardent admirer of Margaret Thatcher. Belfast-born Catholic, pro-life. Member, Conservative Way Forward. Member, National cttee of Conservative Students. PPS to: Owen Paterson 2012; Hugo Swire 2010-12. Select cttees: administration 2014-; culture, media and sport 2012-; education 2010. Contested Eastleigh 2005, 2001. Cllr, Southampton CC 1999-2002. Communications, finance career: Associate dir, PLMR. Former head of business development, DeHavilland; Zurich Insurance. Board member, Spitfire Tribute Foundation. Lover of secondhand books. Ed: St Colomba's Coll, St Albans; University of Southampton (BA modern history & politics, Chairman, Conservative association.).

CHALLENGERS
Martin Houlden (Ukip) Runs a computer technology business. Cllr, Marlborough TC until 2011. Contested Devizes 2010 as an independent. Contributor, *Ukip Daily*. Married, two children. **David Stokes** (Lab) Works in construction. Member, Christians on the Left. Brother, Peter Stokes, contested Bournemouth East 2015. Married, three children. **Mike Plummer** (LD) Business & management studies lecturer, Bournemouth & Poole Coll. Contested New Forest West 2010. Married, two daughters.

CONSTITUENCY PROFILE
The town centre is included in this seat. The Bournemouth International Centre is used by all three major political parties to stage their annual conferences. Also includes Bournemouth Pavilion Theatre. Inland is the main campus of Bournemouth University. Has a high proportion of full-time students.

	Electorate	Turnout %	Change from 2010 %
	72,082	58.0	
C Burns C	20,155	48.3	+3.1
M Houlden Ukip	7,745	18.5	+11.3
D Stokes Lab	7,386	17.7	+2.9
M Plummer LD	3,281	7.9	-23.9
E McManus Green	3,107	7.4	
D Franklin Patria	99	0.2	

Change from 2010

(bar chart: C, Ukip, Lab, LD, Green — scale 25%, 0%, -25%)

Bracknell

CONSERVATIVE HOLD

PHILLIP LEE
BORN Sep 28, 1970
MP 2010-

Part-time GP and former local hospital doctor, vocal about the need for more mathematicians and scientists in the Commons. Contested Blaenau Gwent 2005, placed on A-list and beat Rory Stewart to selection. Select cttees: administration 2010-12; energy & climate change 2010-15. Member, Conservative Way Forward. Special interest in energy security. Enjoys sports and travelling. Keen waterskiier and alpine skiier. Ed: Sir William Borlase's GS, Marlow; King's Coll London, Keble Coll, Oxford (MSc human biology & biological anthropology); St Mary's Hospital Med Sch at Imperial Coll London (MBBS).

CHALLENGERS
James Walsh (Lab) Briefings Manager, NHS England. Parly asst & press officer to Andy Love 2013-.

Cllr, Slough BC 2008-14. Former journalist: Trinity Mirror Group. Ed: Royal Holloway, London. **Richard Thomas** (Ukip) Runs a pharmacy chain. Former Bracknell Forest cllr for the Conservatives, resigned in 2005 after 16 years. Non-exec dir, Wokingham PCT. Contested Leicester West 1997 for Conservatives. Married. Ed: Brakenhale Sch. **Patrick Smith** (LD) Engineer & acoustic consultant, SFL Group. Campaign spokesman, Bracknell Lib Dems. Married, one child. Ed: University of Southampton (BEng engineering).

CONSTITUENCY PROFILE
Home to several affluent villages and the Royal Military Academy at Sandhurst. Has attracted many high-tech industries such as Panasonic and Dell. Also home to Waitrose headquarters. Near the M4 and has good rail links to Heathrow Airport. Has been a safe Conservative seat since its creation in 1997.

	Electorate	Turnout %	Change from 2010 %
	78,131	67.9	
P Lee C	29,606	55.8	+3.4
J Walsh Lab	8,956	16.9	+0.1
R Thomas Ukip	8,339	15.7	+11.3
P Smith LD	3,983	7.5	-14.8
D Florey Green	2,202	4.2	+2.6

Change from 2010

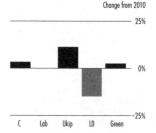

(bar chart: C, Lab, Ukip, LD, Green — scale 25%, 0%, -25%)

Bradford East

LABOUR GAIN

IMRAN HUSSAIN
BORN Jun 7, 1978
MP 2015-

Barrister. Born in Bradford. Cllr, City of Bradford MDC 2002-. Unsucessful contender, "Bradford Spring" by-election 2012 when George Galloway's Respect party won. Deputy leader, Bradford DC. Unite, Co-operative, Unison, GMB. Member, West Yorkshire Police and Crime Panel. LGA. Set up MAGIC, a youth programme that helps those at risk of slipping into crime. Married, two children. Ed: Honourable Society of Lincoln's Inn.

CHALLENGERS
David Ward (LD) MP for Bradford East 2010-15. Cllr, Bradford DC 1984-2010; dep leader, LD group. Contested Bradford North 2005, 2001, 1992, 1990 by-elections. Select cttees: education 2012-15; BIS 2010-12. Business development manager, Leeds Met Uni, seconded to

Bradford FC. NATFHE, Amnesty International, Liberal Friends of Palestine. Married, two sons. Ed: Boston GS; North Kesteven GS; Trent Poly (accountancy); Bradford (MBA, MPhil). **Iftikhar Ahmed** (C) Management consultant. Former president, Bradford Conservative Assoc. Married, three children. Ed: Buttershaw Upper Sch; Bradford (MBA business management). **Owais Rajput** (Ukip) Doctoral student, Leeds Metropolitan University. Defected to Ukip after 23 years in Labour party. Ed: Bradford (MA international politics; PhD).

CONSTITUENCY PROFILE
Created in the last election to replace Bradford North, it stretches from the edge of the city centre to Bolton and Undercliffe. According to 2011 census, almost a third of the population is Pakistani. It has the fifth highest proportion of Muslims in the country. There is a large manufacturing sector but much unemployment.

	Electorate	Turnout %	from 2010 Change %
	66,123	62.6	
I Hussain Lab	19,312	46.6	+13.8
D Ward LD	12,228	29.5	-4.2
I Ahmed C	4,682	11.3	-15.5
O Rajput Ukip	4,103	9.9	
D Stevens Green	871	2.1	
J Lewthwaite Brit Dem	210	0.5	

Change from 2010

(bar chart: Lab, LD, C, Ukip, Green — range -25% to 25%)

Bradford South

LABOUR HOLD

JUDITH CUMMINS
BORN Jun 26, 1967
MP 2015-

Cllr, Leeds City CC 2012-; Bradford MDC 2004-07. Member: West Yorkshire Fire and Rescue Authority; Aire Valley Regeneration Board; Halton Moor and Osmondthorpe project for the elderly; Civil and Public Service Assoc. Former agent for Chris Leslie who won Shipley Seat, 2010. Former benefits adviser. Worked across FE colleges in Yorkshire and the Humber. Labour party organiser. GMB. Unison. Enjoys running. Married, two children. Ed: University of Leeds (BA politics and parliamentary studies); Ruskin Coll, Oxford.

CHALLENGERS
Tanya Graham (C) Works in the public sector. Has worked in private sector and a not-for-profit organisation. Enjoys running and has completed the Bradford half

marathon. Married, two children. **Jason Smith** (Ukip) Sports hypnotist. Data subject matter expert, Univar. Dir, Trance-Form. Ukip Yorkshire & North Lincs regional secretary 2005-11. Bradford co-ordinator, NO2ID. Reached the final 100 of reality show *Big Brother* in 2008. Ed: Wyke Manor Upper Sch. **Andrew Robinson** (Green) Captain, Bradford Bulls. Played for Bradford Northern at scrum-half. Son has Crohn's disease. **Andrew Tear** (LD) Former soldier. Contested Leeds East 2010, 2005. Cllr, Leeds CC 2000-04.

CONSTITUENCY PROFILE
A diverse seat. Stretches from Queensbury in the west, to the village of Tong in the east. The seat is home to Muslims, Hindus, Buddhists and Sikhs. A working-class area. Unemployment is lower than the other Bradford seats. Owner-occupancy is high. A Labour seat since before the Second World War.

	Electorate	Turnout %	from 2010 Change %
	63,670	59.1	
J Cummins Lab	16,328	43.4	+2.2
T Graham C	9,878	26.3	-2.8
J Smith Ukip	9,057	24.1	+20.6
A Robinson Green	1,243	3.3	
A Tear LD	1,094	2.9	-15.4

Change from 2010

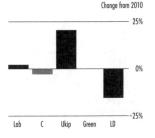

(bar chart: Lab, C, Ukip, Green, LD — range -25% to 25%)

Bradford West

LABOUR GAIN

NASEEM SHAH
BORN Nov 13, 1973
MP 2015-

Had a turbulent childhood, including her mother's imprisonment for murder and an arranged marriage at 15. Spent 12 years campaigning with the Southall Black Sisters for the release of her mother. Works as a carer for children with disabilities. Advocate for women with disabilities and their carers. Former chairwoman, Sharing Voices mental health charity. Volunteer, Samaritans. Former jobs inc: laundry services, crisp-packing factory. Mother of three.

CHALLENGERS
George Galloway (Respect) MP for Bradford West 2012-15. MP for Bethnal Green and Bow 2005-10, Glasgow Kelvin 1997-2005, Glasgow Hillhead 1987-97. Running for London mayor 2016. Contested Poplar and Limehouse

2010. Maverick, controversial, often lampooned. Opposed Iraq war and Gulf war. Travelled to Iraq several times, meeting both Saddam Hussein and Tariq Aziz. Expelled from Labour 2003, pulled off shock win in 2005. Presenter, Iran-backed Press TV. Pretended to be a cat on *Celebrity Big Brother*, 2006. Involved in founding Respect Party. Ed: Harris Academy. **George Grant** (C) Dir, business development company. Former journalist. Worked as a foreign policy and defence analyst in London, before moving to Libya in 2012. Married. Ed: Edinburgh (BA history); City (MA investigative journalism).

CONSTITUENCY PROFILE
According to the 2011 census, is home to the largest Asian/Asian British population: 43.3 per cent are of Pakistani origin, the highest proportion of all the constituencies in England and Wales. A history of racial tensions here, with riots breaking out in 1995 and 2001.

	Electorate	Turnout %	Change from 2010 %
	63,371	63.6	
N Shah Lab	19,977	49.6	+4.2
G Galloway Respect	8,557	21.2	+18.2
G Grant C	6,160	15.3	-15.9
H Boota Ukip	3,140	7.8	+5.8
A Griffiths LD	1,173	2.9	-8.8
C Hickson Green	1,085	2.7	+0.4
J Kirkcaldy Ind	100	0.3	
T Hirst Eng Dem	98	0.2	

Change from 2010

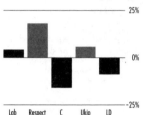

Lab Respect C Ukip LD

Braintree

CONSERVATIVE HOLD

JAMES CLEVERLY
BORN Sep 4, 1969
MP 2015-

GLA member for Bexley & Bromley, 2008-. Youth ambassador for Boris Johnson. Contested Lewisham East 2005. Chairman, London Fire & Emergency Planning Authority 2012-; Chairman, Partnership of Emergency Services. Officer, Territorial Army 1991-. Was called up by the TA during the Iraq war in 2004. Patron, Advocacy For All. Member, Met Police Authority 2008-12. Worked in magazine and digital publishing. Owns business that gives advice for small businesses. Awarded the Territorial Decoration 2003. Mother from Sierra Leone. Ed: Colfe's Sch; Thames Valley University (BA hospitality management).

CHALLENGERS
Richard Bingley (Ukip) Counter-terrorism expert and university

lecturer. Former Labour party press officer & cabinet visits co-ordinator during Tony Blair's time in office. Cllr, Thurrock 2006-10. Ed: University of Leeds (BA international relations). **Malcolm Fincken** (Lab) Retired teacher. Cllr, Braintree DC 1999-; Halstead TC for more than 30 years. Contested Saffron Walden 1997. Married, two children. **Matthew Klesel** (LD) Public affairs manager, Advertising Assoc. Parly researcher for Sir Alan Beith 2013-15. Former ward host, Broomfield Hospital NHS Trust. Ed: University of Kent (BA history).

CONSTITUENCY PROFILE
A rural seat at the northern edge of Essex. Relatively prosperous. Main population centre is Braintree. Close to Stansted Airport, many residents commute to London. Conservative Brooks Newmark held the seat from 2005. Stood down in 2015 after he was caught sending explicit texts and pictures to a single mother during a two-year affair.

	Electorate	Turnout %	Change from 2010 %
	73,557	68.4	
J Cleverly C	27,071	53.8	+1.2
R Bingley Ukip	9,461	18.8	+13.8
M Fincken Lab	9,296	18.5	-1.4
M Klesel LD	2,488	5.0	-13.9
P Jeater Green	1,564	3.1	+1.7
T Pereira Ind	295	0.6	
P Hooks BNP	108	0.2	-2.0

Change from 2010

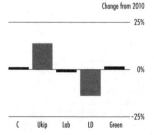

C Ukip Lab LD Green

Brecon & Radnorshire

CONSERVATIVE GAIN

CHRISTOPHER DAVIES
BORN Aug 18, 1967
MP 2015-

Former rural auctioneer. Cllr, Powys CC 2012-15. Ran Hay Veterinary Group 2009-15. Member, Brecon Beacons National Park Authority. Dir, Royal Welsh Show, Agricultural Society. Stood in the 2011 Welsh Assembly election for Brecon & Radnorshire. Married, two children. Ed: Morriston Comp Sch & Sixth Form.

CHALLENGERS
Roger Williams (LD) MP 2001-15 for Brecon & Radnorshire. LD opposition whip, Commons 2008-10; LD shad SoS, Wales 2007-10. LD whip 2008-15, 2004-07. LD rural affairs spokes 2002-15. Select ctees: Defra 2013-15; science & technology 2010-13; Defra 2005-10; Welsh affairs 2001-05. Cllr, Powys CC 1981-2002, Brecon Beacons National Park 1985-, chairman

1991-95. Farmer. Former chairman Brecon & Radnorshire NFU. Married, one daughter, one son. Ed: Christ Coll, Brecon; Selwyn Coll, Cambridge (BA land economy). **Matthew Dorrance** (Lab) Political assistant. Cllr, Powys CC 2012-. Contested Mid and West Wales 2011. Former mental health support worker. Ed: Brecon HS; Swansea University. **Darran Thomas** (Ukip) Forensic computer consultant. Ed: Llandrindod HS. **Freddy Greaves** (PC) Works for Powys CC. Former English teacher in Tokyo. Worked for home office. Married, two children.

CONSTITUENCY PROFILE
The largest seat geographically in Wales. Contains the towns of Brecon and Builth Wells, home to the annual Royal Welsh Show. Agriculture and tourism are key industries. An isolated rural seat made up largely of mountains and forest. Includes the Brecon Beacons National Park. A former Conservative-Lib Dem marginal.

	Electorate	Turnout %	from 2010 % Change
	54,311	73.8	
C Davies C	16,453	41.1	+4.6
R Williams LD	11,351	28.3	-17.8
M Dorrance Lab	5,904	14.7	+4.2
D Thomas Ukip	3,338	8.3	+6.1
F Greaves PC	1,767	4.4	+1.9
C Carmichael Green	1,261	3.2	+2.3

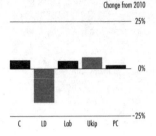

Change from 2010

C   LD   Lab   Ukip   PC

Brent Central

LABOUR GAIN

DAWN BUTLER
BORN 3 Nov, 1969
MP 2015-

Training consultant. MP for Brent South 2005-10. Third African-Caribbean woman to become a British MP. PPS to Jane Kennedy 2005-06. Government whip 2008-09. Minister for young citizens 2009-10. Contested Brent Central 2010. Officer, GMB. Trustee, Willesden Citizens Advice Bureau. Sits regularly as magistrate. Worked on a market stall, in a bakery and as a programmer / systems analyst. Launched "Bernie's List" in 2009. Named MP of the Year at the Women in Public Life Awards 2009. Jamaican immigrant parents and one of six children. Ed: Waltham Forest Coll of FE (Dip).

CHALLENGERS
Alan Mendoza (C) Co-founder & exec dir, the Henry Jackson Society. Cllr, Brent BC 2005-

10. Co-founder & co-president, Disraelian Union. Dir, Worldview Strategy Ltd. Often in the media. Ed: Gonville and Caius Coll, Cambridge (BA MPhil history; PhD Bosnian War). **Lauren Keith** (LD) PR Manager. Worked for John Pugh MP and Sarah Ludford MEP in comms and casework roles. Interested in medieval history. Ed: St Andrews (MA history). **Shahrar Ali** (Green) Deputy leader, Green party 2014-. The first BME deputy of a UK parliamentary party. Former researcher in the European Parliament. **Stephen Priestley** (Ukip) Locum mental health social worker. Married, two stepchildren.

CONSTITUENCY PROFILE
A diverse residential seat in northwest London, home to many migrant communities. Has the biggest Hindu temple outside India. According to the 2011 census, a quarter of the population is Afro-Caribbean. Contains Wembley Stadium and the huge Park Royal Industrial estate.

	Electorate	Turnout %	from 2010 % Change
	77,038	61.1	
D Butler Lab	29,216	62.1	+20.9
A Mendoza C	9,567	20.3	+9.2
L Keith LD	3,937	8.4	-35.8
S Ali Green	1,912	4.1	+2.6
S Priestley Ukip	1,850	3.9	
J Boyle TUSC	235	0.5	
K Malik Community	170	0.4	
N Coonan Ind	145	0.3	-0.1

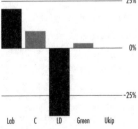

Change from 2010

Lab   C   LD   Green   Ukip

Brent North

LABOUR HOLD

BARRY GARDINER
BORN Mar 10, 1957
MP 1997-

Carefully spoken, well-groomed. Cheerleader for Tony Blair, became unlikely critic of Gordon Brown, leading to his premature departure as PM's special envoy for forestry (2007-08). PPS to Lord Mandelson 2009-10. Shadow min, Defra 2013-15. Parly under sec: Defra 2006-07; trade & industry 2005-06; Northern Ireland 2004-05. Member, select cttees: efra 2010-13; ECC 2010-13; Crossrail bill 2007; consolidation bills 2001-05; public accounts 1999-2002. PPS to Beverley Hughes 2002-04. General average adjuster. Chairman, Labour Friends of India. Cllr, Cambridge CC 1988-94, mayor 1992-93. MSF, GMB. Married, four children. Ed: Haileybury Coll; University of St Andrews (MA philosophy); Harvard (philosophy, Kennedy scholar); Corpus Christi, Cambridge (philosophy research).

CHALLENGERS
Luke Parker (C) Associate partner, IBM, previously at Logica, SAP. Grew up in a staunchly Labour household. Married, three children. Ed: Brighton (BA business studies); Said Business Sch, Oxford (PgDip advanced strategy). **Paul Lorber** (LD) Cllr, Brent BC 1982-2014, leader 2006-10. Contested Brent N 2001. Library volunteer. Born in Bratislava. **Alexander Craig** (Ukip) Leader, Christian People's Alliance 2004-13. Contested mayor of London 2008, came sixth in first preference. Works in office of Baroness Cox. Cllr, Newham BC 2004-10, opp leader 2006-10. Ed: Newcastle; Manchester Bus Sch.

CONSTITUENCY PROFILE
Diverse ethnic population may normally be associated with deprived inner-cities, but Brent North is mostly owner-occupied residential suburbs, a seat of prosperous Asians. Once safely Tory, it registered the biggest swing to Labour of the 1997 election.

		Electorate	Turnout %	Change from 2010 %
		82,196	63.6	
B Gardiner	Lab	28,351	54.3	+7.4
L Parker	C	17,517	33.5	+2.0
P Lorber	LD	2,607	5.0	-12.0
A Craig	Ukip	2,024	3.9	+3.2
S Bartle	Green	1,539	3.0	+1.6
E Jeffers	Ind	197	0.4	-1.0

Change from 2010

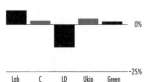

| Lab | C | LD | Ukip | Green |

Brentford & Isleworth

LABOUR GAIN

RUTH CADBURY
BORN May 14, 1959
MP 2015-

Local government officer. Cllr, Hounslow BC 1998-2015, deputy leader, 2010-12, cabinet member, 2010-13. Philanthropist, trustee, Barrow Cadbury Trust, endowed in 1920 by grandparents. Great-great-granddaughter of John Cadbury, founder of the chocolatier. Listed in *The Independent on Sunday's* Happy List in 2008. Quaker. Enjoys cycling. Married, two sons. Ed: The Mount Sch, York; Bournville FE Coll; University of Salford (BSc social science, geography & statistics).

CHALLENGERS
Mary Macleod (C) MP, Brentford & Isleworth 2010-15. Founded Westminster Women, forerunner of Women2Win. PPS to: Theresa Villiers 2014-15; Maria Miller 2012-14; Nick Herbert 2010-12. Member, home affairs select cttee 2010. Contested Ross, Skye & Inverness

W 1997. Small business ambassador for London. Chairwoman, APPG microfinance. Former ambassador for Actionaid. Chartered Institute of Marketing, Chartered Institute of Personnel & Devt. Ed: Dingwall Academy; Glasgow (MA literature & business). **Richard Hendron** (Ukip) Barrister. Former police inspector. Defected from Conservatives in 2012. **Joe Bourke** (LD) Chartered accountant. Lecturer at University of West London. Former chairman, Association of British Travel Agents' aviation cttee. Worked on Garret FitzGerald TD's election campaign 1981. Contested Dagenham & Rainham 2010. Honourary auditor, Brentford Chamber of Commerce.

CONSTITUENCY PROFILE
A mixed, marginal seat that changes as it follows the Thames westwards. From upmarket, reliably Conservative Chiswick, a mix of residential and office areas, to council estates around Brentford Towers and lower-quality housing in more varied areas of Brentford.

		Electorate	Turnout %	Change from 2010 %
		84,557	67.8	
R Cadbury	Lab	25,096	43.8	+10.2
M Macleod	C	24,631	42.9	+5.7
R Hendron	Ukip	3,203	5.6	+4.0
J Bourke	LD	2,305	4.0	-19.6
D Goldsmith	Green	2,120	3.7	+2.2

Change from 2010

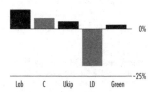

| Lab | C | Ukip | LD | Green |

Brentwood & Ongar

CONSERVATIVE HOLD

SIR ERIC PICKLES
BORN Apr 20, 1952
MP 1992-

The rotund face of municipal Conservatism. Likes to be seen as a plain-speaking Yorkshireman but is political operator. Secretary of state for communities & local government 2010-15. Minister, faith 2014-15. Chairman, Conservative party 2009-10; deputy 2005-07, 1993-97. Shadow: SoS, CLG 2007-09; min: local govt & regions 2002-03; transport 2001-02. Opp spokesman, social security 1998-2001. Cllr, Bradford CC 1979-91, leader 1988-90. Industrial trainer. Local government editor of *Conservative Newsline*. KBE 2015. Married. Ed: Greenhead GS; Leeds Poly.

CHALLENGERS
Michael McGough (Ukip) Semi-retired freelance writer and journalist. Member of Ukip national executive. Contested: Brentwood & O 2010; Chingford & WG 2005; East of England Euro election 2014, 09; London Assembly 2012, 08. Hon treasurer, Freedom Assoc. Married, two children. Ed: Queen Mary, London (BEng electrical engineering). **Liam Preston** (Lab) Parliamentary and policy officer, YMCA England. Chairman, British Youth Council 2010-12. Member, Advisory Council on Youth, Council of Europe 2014-. Ed: Canterbury Christ Church University (BA film, radio & TV studies); University of Kent (MA international security & politics). **David Kendall** (LD) Owns cleaning business. Cllr: Essex CC 2009-; Brentwood BC 1991-. Contested Brentwood & O 2010, 01. Ed: William Penn Sch; Havering Tech Coll.

CONSTITUENCY PROFILE
Affluent London commuter belt in Essex, suburban around Brentwood, Shenfield and Chipping Ongar, with the rest of the seat made up of more rural villages and woodland. A very safe Tory seat.

	Electorate	Turnout %	Change from 2010 %
	72,461	71.6	
E Pickles C	30,534	58.8	+1.9
M McGough Ukip	8,724	16.8	+12.8
L Preston Lab	6,492	12.5	+2.6
D Kendall LD	4,577	8.8	-14.7
R Hossain Green	1,397	2.7	+1.5
R Tilbrook Eng Dem	173	0.3	-0.6

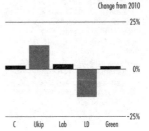

Change from 2010

C   Ukip   Lab   LD   Green

Bridgend

LABOUR HOLD

MADELEINE MOON
BORN Mar 27, 1950
MP 2005-

Maintained career in social work and mental health into parliament as chairwoman, APPG suicide prevention. Member, delegation to Nato parly assembly 2010. PPS to: Lord Hunt of Kings Heath 2009-10; Jim Knight 2007-08. Select cttees: defence 2009-; Welsh affairs 2005-06; efra 2005-07. Cllr, Bridgend 1991-2004. Mayor of Porthcawl 1995-96. Residential care home inspector, social worker. Widowed, one son. Ed: Whinney Hill Sch; Durham GS; Madeley Coll, Staffordshire (Cert Ed); Keele University (BEd); Cardiff University (CQSW DipSW social work).

CHALLENGERS
Meirion Jenkins (C) Director of a software company. Works for government advising on internet trade. Contested Birmingham Yardley, 2010. Four children. Ed: Aston Uni (BSc managerial studies, accounting & finance). **Caroline Jones** (Ukip) Café owner. Contested: Aberavon 2010 for Conservatives; South Wales PCC election 2012. **James Radcliffe** (PC) Researcher at Welsh Assembly. Worked as policy and research officer, Bevan Foundation. Volunteer, Dogs Trust. Married. Ed: Aberstwyth Uni (MA international politics). **Anita Davies** (LD) Registered blind. Chairwoman, Women Making a Difference. Cllr, Coity Higher Community. Champion in blind judo: world 1995, Europe 1998. Two children. Ed: University of Central England (rehabilitation studies).

CONSTITUENCY PROFILE
Dominated by Bridgend town, but reaches through rural land to the coast at Porthcawl. Relatively poor. A series of teenage suicides have brought unwanted attention to the area. The Ford engine plant is a notable local employer, and the seat has been Labour since 1987.

	Electorate	Turnout %	Change from 2010 %
	59,998	65.8	
M Moon Lab	14,624	37.1	+0.7
M Jenkins C	12,697	32.2	+1.8
C Jones Ukip	5,911	15.0	+12.9
J Radcliffe PC	2,784	7.1	+1.1
A Davies LD	1,648	4.2	-18.4
L Tallon-Morris Ind	763	1.9	
T White Green	736	1.9	
A David TUSC	118	0.3	
D Elston Pirate	106	0.3	
A Lloyd NF	66	0.2	

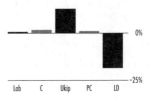

Change from 2010

Lab   C   Ukip   PC   LD

Bridgwater & Somerset West

CONSERVATIVE HOLD

IAN LIDDELL-GRAINGER
BORN Feb 23, 1959
MP 2001-

Third-great-grandson of Queen Victoria. Received an unofficial vote of no confidence from local party after allegations of back-stabbing in Jan 2015. Erased council leader from own official photograph because he was "narked" at him. Member, select cttees: works of art 2010-; statutory instruments 2010-; envionmental audit 2007-10; Crossrail bill 2005-07; constitutional affairs 2005-07; efra 2003-05; public admin 2001-10, Scottish affairs 2002-05. President, Tyne Bridge Conservative Association 1993-96. Cllr, Tynedale 1989-95. Former MD of own building and property company. Ran arable farm. Territorial Army, remains major in Army reserve. Married, two daughters, one son. Ed: Millfield Sch, Somerset; South of Scotland Agricultural Coll, (Nat Cert of agriculture).

CHALLENGERS
Stephen Fitzgerald (Ukip) Semi-retired management consultant. Ran a school charity in Zanzibar for seven years. Married, four children. **Mick Lerry** (Lab) Former teacher. Served on the national executive of NUT. Cllr, Sedgemoor DC 2011-, leader, Labour group. **Theo Butt Philip** (LD) Communications consultant. Cllr, Wells CC 2007-11, mayor 2013-14, deputy mayor 2012-13. Contested Bridgwater & SW 2010. Ed: Blue Sch, Wells; Lancaster University (BA politics with international relations).

CONSTITUENCY PROFILE
Safely Conservative. A dumbbell-shaped seat with Exmoor to the east and Bridgwater to the west. Coastal towns, popular retirement locations, give West Somerset the highest average age of any English local authority. Tourism is centred on Minehead's Butlins resort, with industry around Bridgwater and the Hinkley Point nuclear plants to the north.

	Electorate	Turnout %	Change from 2010 %
	80,491	67.6	
I Liddell-Grainger C	25,020	46.0	+0.7
S Fitzgerald Ukip	10,437	19.2	+14.4
M Lerry Lab	9,589	17.6	+0.5
T Butt Phillip LD	6,765	12.4	-15.9
J Harvey-Smith Green	2,636	4.8	+3.3

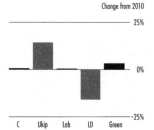

Change from 2010

Brigg & Goole

CONSERVATIVE HOLD

ANDREW PERCY
BORN Sep 18, 1977
MP 2010-

Eurosceptic rightwinger from humble background. Secondary school history teacher, advocates greater school discipline. Select cttees: NI affairs 2012-; health 2012-; regulatory reform 2010-; procedure 2010-11. Cllr, Hull CC 2000-10. Contested Normanton 2005. Vice-chairman, Hull & Goole Port Health Authority. Member, NASUWT, Countryside Alliance, Campaign against Political Correctness. East Yorkshire born and raised. Married, one son, one daughter. Ed: Wyke Sixth Form Coll; University of York (BA); Leeds University (PgDip law).

CHALLENGERS
Jacky Crawford (Lab) Qualified nurse and registered social worker. Dir, Crawford Social Care Consultancy. Sch governor. Member, Coll of Social Work,

British Association of Social Workers. Has identical twin. Ed: Goole GS; Lincoln (BA social work). **David Jeffreys** (Ukip) Maintenance engineer, Tesco, Goole. Served as telecommunications mechanic in the armed forces for ten years. Married. **Natalie Hurst** (Green) Partner, Just Grow sustainability social enterprise. Contested Scunthorpe, 2010. **Liz Leffman** (LD) Runs Clothesource quality control business. Cllr, West Oxfordshire DC 2012-. Vice chairwoman, West Oxfordshire CAB. Ed: Leeds (BA history of art & philosophy); Oxford Brookes (MA coaching & mentoring practice).

CONSTITUENCY PROFILE
A marginal seat between Labour and Conservatives, won by Labour when created in 1997, but falling to the Tories in 2010. The inland port of Goole is more working class than Lincolnshire's agricultural villages, with glass-making and distribution important employers.

	Electorate	Turnout %	Change from 2010 %
	68,486	63.2	
A Percy C	22,946	53.0	+8.2
J Crawford Lab	11,770	27.2	-5.9
D Jeffreys Ukip	6,694	15.5	+11.5
N Hurst Green	915	2.1	
L Leffman LD	764	1.8	-12.9
T Dixon Ind	153	0.4	
R Spalding IE	28	0.1	

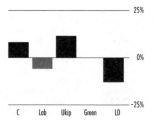

Change from 2010

Brighton Kemptown

CONSERVATIVE HOLD

SIMON KIRBY
BORN Dec 22, 1964
MP 2010-

Local entrepreneur. Asstistant whip 2015-. PPS to: Jeremy Hunt 2014-15; Hugh Robertson 2012-14. Select cttees: administration 2011-12; BIS 2010-12; environmental audit 2010-11. Co-founder, Surf 107 radio station, now Juice 107.2. Co-owner, C-Side pub & restaurant chain. Cllr: East Sussex CC, 2005-09, 1992-93; Brighton & Hove CC, 1996-99; Mid Sussex DC 1999-2001. Married, two daughters, five sons, one deceased. Ed: Hastings GS; Open University (BSc mathematical modelling); LSE (operational research).

CHALLENGERS
Nancy Platts (Lab) Campaigns and communications consultant. Contested Brighton Pavilion 2010. Dir: The Campaign Machine; Claremont, Maternity Alliance. Worked as PR and events officer, London Fire Brigade. Ed: Bexley Technical HS for Girls. London College of Printing (CAM Dip CIM Dip communications & marketing). **Ian Buchanan** (Ukip) Cllr: East Sussex CC 2013-; Peacehaven TC 2005-, mayor 2007-09. **Davy Jones** (Green) Yoga teacher. Previously council policy adviser; National Audit Commission official. **Paul Chandler** (LD) Former travel agent. Contested Worcester 2001, 1997. Former chairman, Association of Independent Travel Operators.

CONSTITUENCY PROFILE
Formerly the more Labour-leaning of the two Brighton seats, now the more Conservative. Kemptown is the eastern part of Brighton and the semi-rural suburbs and villages stretching out to the east of the city. At its western end it includes Queen's Park ward, the centre of Brighton's vibrant gay community. Farther inland are the council estates of Whitehawk and Moulsecoomb, the racecourse, and universities.

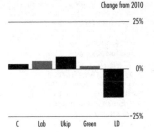

	Electorate	Turnout %	Change from 2010 %
	67,858	66.8	
S Kirby C	18,428	40.7	+2.7
N Platts Lab	17,738	39.2	+4.3
I Buchanan Ukip	4,446	9.8	+6.6
D Jones Green	3,187	7.0	+1.6
P Chandler LD	1,365	3.0	-15.0
J Shodeke SPGB	73	0.2	
M Taylor Ind	69	0.2	

Change from 2010

C   Lab   Ukip   Green   LD

Brighton Pavilion

GREEN HOLD

CAROLINE LUCAS
BORN Dec 9, 1960
MP 2010-

Articulate and intelligent, the UK's first Green MP. Credited with making Greens electable. Called for "progressive alliance" with the SNP. MP of the Year: *Pink News* 2014, *Total Politics* 2011, *Spectator* 2010 (newcomer). Leader, Green party 2008-12, principal speaker 2007-08, 2003-06. MEP, SE England 1999-2010. Select cttee: environmental audit 2010-. Contested Oxford East 1992. Cllr, Oxon CC 1993-97. Twice arrested during protests, latest in 2013. Member, Green party regional council 1997-99. Co-chairwoman, Green party council 1989-90. Green party nat press officer 1987-89. Author. RSPCA VP. CND national council, Green New Deal Group. Former Oxfam adviser, press officer. Married, two sons. Ed: Malvern Girls' Coll; University of Exeter (BA PhD English); University of Kansas, USA.

CHALLENGERS
Purna Sen (Lab) Deputy director of Institute of Public Affairs, LSE. Chairwoman, board of the Kaleidoscope Trust. Member, board of Rise. Adviser, Justice for Gay Africans. Served as head of human rights, Commonwealth Secretariat. Previously dir, Asia-Pacific programme, Amnesty International. Picked from an all-woman shortlist. Born in India, came to Britain at age of two. Two daughters. **Clarence Mitchell** (C) Media strategy adviser, spokesman for the McCann family. Former director of media monitoring at Central Office of Information and BBC journalist.

CONSTITUENCY PROFILE
Named after the Georgian seaside palace, this is affluent, touristy Brighton, full of students — a fifth of the population is aged 16-25 — from the deprived centre to inland Falmer. Once a Tory-Labour marginal, its quirky outlook made it the focus of Green campaigns.

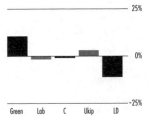

	Electorate	Turnout %	Change from 2010 %
	76,557	71.4	
C Lucas Green	22,871	41.8	+10.5
P Sen Lab	14,904	27.3	-1.7
C Mitchell C	12,448	22.8	-0.9
N Carter Ukip	2,724	5.0	+3.2
C Bowers LD	1,525	2.8	-11.0
N Yeomans Ind	116	0.2	
H Pilott SPGB	88	0.2	

Change from 2010

Green   Lab   C   Ukip   LD

Bristol East

LABOUR HOLD

KERRY MCCARTHY
BORN Mar 26, 1965
MP 2005-

First politician to deliver speech from an iPad. Shadow min: FCO 2011-; Treasury 2010-11; opposition asst whip 2010; work & pensions 2010; asst whip, Treasury 2009-10. PPS to: Douglas Alexander 2007-09; Rosie Winterton 2007. Select cttees: South West region 2009-10; Treasury 2005-07. Cllr, Luton BC 1995-2003. Director, Luton Airport 1999-2003. Solicitor. Ed: Denbigh HS; University of Liverpool (BA Russian & politics); City of London Polytechnic (law).

CHALLENGERS
Theodora Clarke (C) Founder & editor, *Russian Art & Culture* magazine. Vice-chairman, Cities of London & Westminster Conservatives 2013-. Conservative Women's Organisation dir of communications 2011-13. Art historian, lecturer and critic.

Worked at MoMA, New York. Political campaigner for Rory Stewart, 2010 election. Ed: Downe House Sch; Newcastle (BA combined studies); Courtauld Institute of Art (MA history of art). **James McMurray** (Ukip) Teacher. Defected from Tories in 2014. Cllr: Teignbridge DC 2011-15; Devon CC 2007-11; Teignmouth TC 2003-07; Portishead TC 2003-07. Ed: City of Bristol Coll; UWE (LLB; PGCE). **Lorraine Francis** (Green) Social worker and counsellor. **Abdul Malik** (LD) Owner, Pak Butchers. Chairman, Easton Jamia Masjid. Cllr, Bristol CC 2005-09, Bristol's first Asian Muslim cllr. Won *Bristol's Evening Post*'s social responsibility award 2011.

CONSTITUENCY PROFILE
The stronghold of Tony Benn 1950-83, it fell to the Tories until 1992, when Labour regained it. Predominantly residential and averagely well off, about 10 per cent of residents are ethnic minorities, concentrated in Eastville.

	Electorate	Turnout %	from 2010 %	Change
	71,965	64.2		
K McCarthy Lab	18,148	39.3	+2.7	
T Clarke C	14,168	30.7	+2.3	
J McMurray Ukip	7,152	15.5	+12.1	
L Francis Green	3,827	8.3	+6.5	
A Malik LD	2,689	5.8	-18.6	
M Gordon TUSC	229	0.5	+0.1	

Change from 2010

25%

0%

-25%

Lab   C   Ukip   Green   LD

Bristol North West

CONSERVATIVE HOLD

CHARLOTTE LESLIE
BORN Aug 11, 1978
MP 2010-

Local candidate, *Spectator*'s backbencher of the year 2013. At centre of political row after accepting donation from the hedge-fund boss Hugh Sloane, whose company was ordered to pay £13 million in unpaid tax. Heads Right Hook campaign to highlight social benefits of boxing. Special adviser to David Willetts as shadow education secretary. Select cttees: health 2013-; education 2010-13. Portland PR. Education associate, Young Foundation. Author, *More Good School Places* (Policy Exchange report). Bow Group, former editor, *Crossbow*. Worked in TV. Competitive swimmer and keen surfer. Ed: Badminton Sch; Millfield Sch; Balliol Coll, Oxford (BA Classics).

CHALLENGERS
Darren Jones (Lab) Solicitor, Bond

Dickinson. Grew up on Lawrence Weston council estate. Contested Torridge & WD 2010. Trustee, North Bristol Advice Centre. School governor. Worked in the NHS for nine years. Ed: Plymouth (BSc human bioscience); UWE (PgDip law). **Michael Frost** (Ukip) Salesman. Cllr, Bristol CC 2014-, Ukip's first in the city. Married. **Clare Campion-Smith** (LD) Former maths teacher. Cllr, Bristol CC 2006-; deputy leader, Lib Dem group; chairwoman, children's scrutiny commission.

CONSTITUENCY PROFILE
Geographically the largest of the four Bristol seats, stretching out to the Severn estuary (and technically including a large chunk of it). The seat contains affluent and Conservative parts of Bristol, such as Westbury and Stoke Bishop, balanced by council estates such as Southmead and Lockleaze and the heavy industry and manufacturing out at the Avonmouth Docks, making this a classic marginal.

	Electorate	Turnout %	from 2010 %	Change
	76,626	67.6		
C Leslie C	22,767	44.0	+6.0	
D Jones Lab	17,823	34.4	+8.5	
M Frost Ukip	4,889	9.4	+7.1	
C Campion-Smith LD	3,214	6.2	-25.3	
J Quinnell Green	2,952	5.7	+4.7	
A Lemon TUSC	160	0.3		

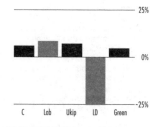

Change from 2010

25%

0%

-25%

C   Lab   Ukip   LD   Green

Bristol South

LABOUR HOLD

KARIN SMYTH
BORN Sep 8, 1964
MP 2015-

Career in healthcare, worked for the Bristol Clinical Commissioning Group. Locality manager, South Bristol Consortium. NHS manager. Previously trustee, Bristol Deaf Centre. Worked as a self-employed independent project and interim manager. Non-executive dir, Bristol North PCT. Political assistant, Valerie Davey MP 1997-2001. Unison. School governor. Married, three children. Irish immigrant parents. Ed: Uxbridge Technical Coll; UEA (BA economic & social studies); University of Bath (MBA).

CHALLENGERS
Isobel Grant (C) Chartered civil engineer. Structural engineer, Arup. Cllr, Ealing BC 2010-14. Married, four children. School governor. Ed: University of Manchester (MEng structural engineering). **Steve Wood** (Ukip).

Director, Able Investigations & Enforcements, specialist eviction team. Defended local council candidate John Langley's "unusual" porn career when revealed in national press. Ed: Hartcliffe Comp. **Tony Dyer** (Green) Works in IT after career in construction. Writes for *Bristol 24/7*. Married, one daughter. **Mark Wright** (LD) Computer programmer. Cllr, Bristol CC 2005-, cabinet member 2009-11. Contested Bristol S 2010. Married. Ed: University of Bristol (BSc chemistry; PhD astrophysics - Royal Astronomical Soc best PhD in the UK, 2002).

CONSTITUENCY PROFILE
A traditional white, working-class seat, stretching from the former industrial areas of Bristol south of the city centre, such as Bedminster, now prone to redevelopment, to more modern postwar council estates on the city's southern border where a high proportion of social housing remains. Labour since 1935, held by Dawn Primarolo 1987-2015.

	Electorate	Turnout %	from 2010 % Change
	81,996	62.0	
K Smyth Lab	19,505	38.4	-0.1
I Grant C	12,377	24.3	+1.4
S Wood Ukip	8,381	16.5	+13.9
T Dyer Green	5,861	11.5	+9.0
M Wright LD	4,416	8.7	-20.0
T Baldwin TUSC	302	0.6	+0.2

Change from 2010

Bristol West

LABOUR GAIN

THANGAM DEBBONAIRE
BORN Aug 3, 1966
MP 2015-

Research manager, Respect UK. Dir & lead independent practitioner, Domestic Violence Responses. Previously Women's Aid's first national children's officer. Former cellist. Ed: Bradford Girls' GS; Chetham's Sch of Music; St Johns City Coll of Technology; Oxford (mathematics, did not complete); University of Bristol (MSc management)

CHALLENGERS
Darren Hall (Green) Project manager. Editor, *Good Bristol* magazine. Worked for Home Office as crime and drugs regional manager. Engineer in RAF for 11 years. Runs Bristol Green Capital Partnership. Founding dir, The Pale Blue. Executive dir, The Big Green Week Community Interest Company. Board member, Bristol Community Land Trust.

Ed: Swansea (BEng mechanical engineering). **Stephen Williams** (LD) MP for Bristol West 2005-15. Abstained in vote on coalition plans to increase tuition fees. Parly under sec, CLG 2013-15. Shadow SoS, innovation, universities & skills 2007-10. Shadow min: CSF 2007; education 2006-07; health 2005-06. Select cttees: members' expenses 2011-15; political reform 2010-13; CSF 2007-08; public accounts 2005-06; education & skills 2005-07. Contested Bristol South 1997, Bristol West 2001. Ed: Bristol (BA history).

CONSTITUENCY PROFILE
Traditionally the Conservative seat in Bristol, with Victorian and Edwardian terraces of Clifton and leafy suburbs of Cotham. Growing diversity of St Pauls and large student population, together with the emerging 1990s left-field culture of Stokes Croft, pushed it towards the alternative politics of the Lib Dems (2005-15), and now the Greens.

	Electorate	Turnout %	from 2010 % Change
	89,198	72.0	
T Debbonaire Lab	22,900	35.7	+8.2
D Hall Green	17,227	26.8	+23.1
S Williams LD	12,103	18.9	-29.2
C Hiscott C	9,752	15.2	-3.2
P Turner Ukip	1,940	3.0	+1.8
D Parry Bristol	204	0.3	
S Weston LU	92	0.1	

Change from 2010

Broadland

CONSERVATIVE HOLD

KEITH SIMPSON
BORN Mar 29, 1949
MP 1997-

Military historian with parade-ground manner. Well-informed on foreign and defence issues. Appointed privy counsellor 2015. Shadow minister: FCO 2005-10; defence 2002-05. Opposition whip 1999-2001. Opp spokesman: efra 2001-02; defence 1998-99. Select cttees: intelligence & security 2015-; efra 2001-02. PPS to William Hague 2010-14. MP for Mid Norfolk 1997-2010. Member, Strategic Studies Internat Institute. Special adviser to defence secretaries 1988-90. Military historian, defence consultant, Sandhurst lecturer. Con research department. Ed: University of Hull (BA history); King's Coll, London (PGCE).

CHALLENGERS
Chris Jones (Lab) Consultant psychiatrist. NHS doctor for 30

years. Honorary senior lecturer, UEA. Keeps chickens and enjoys beekeeping. Married. Ed: Nottingham (medicine); UEA (PhD medical ethics). **Stuart Agnew** (Ukip) MEP for East of England 2009-. Farmer. NFU. Contested Broadland 2010; Norfolk North 2005; Norfolk Mid 2001. Ed: Gordonstoun; Royal Agricultural Coll. **Steve Riley** (LD) Runs his own manufacturing company. Cllr, Broadland DC 2013-. Was senior industrial relations negotiator. Married, two daughters, one son. **Andrew Boswell** (Green) Manages scientific computing facilities at UEA. Cllr, Norwich CC 2005-.

CONSTITUENCY PROFILE
Meanders through rural Norfolk with part of north Norfolk and the majority of Broadland DC, including market towns Wroxham, Acle and Aylsham. Created in 2010 with more of the old Norfolk Mid seat than the one that still bears the name and, like its predecessor, is comfortably Conservative.

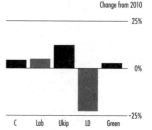

	Electorate	Turnout %	Change from 2010 %
	74,680	71.1	
K Simpson C	26,808	50.5	+4.3
C Jones Lab	9,970	18.8	+5.0
S Agnew Ukip	8,881	16.7	+12.2
S Riley LD	5,178	9.8	-22.6
A Boswell Green	2,252	4.2	+2.8

Change from 2010

Bromley & Chislehurst

CONSERVATIVE HOLD

ROBERT NEILL
BORN Jun 24, 1952
MP 2006-

Barrister, happiest in technical details of policy. Parly under sec: planning (CLG) 2010-12. Shadow min: CLG 2007-10; London 2007-08. Select cttees: political reform 2013-; justice 2012-13, 2007-10; constitutional affairs 2006-07. Vice-chairman, Conservative Party 2012-15, 2007-10. Member, London Assembly for Bexley & Bromley 2000-08, leader of Conservative group 2000-02. Contested Dagenham 1987, 1983. Served on former GLC and as Havering cllr 1974-90. Chairman, Greater London Conservatives 1996-99. Barrister. Married. Ed: Abbs Cross Technical HS; LSE (LLB).

CHALLENGERS
John Courtneidge (Lab) Writer and editor. Cllr, Hertford TC. Worked for Fair World Project. Research chemist, former

chemistry teacher. Quaker. Freeman of City of London. Ed: Bristol (BSc chemistry); UCL (PhD chemistry). **Emmett Jenner** (Ukip) Works in car maintenance, BMW. Contested Bromley & Chislehurst 2010. **Sam Webber** (LD) Communications consultant, Politics Home. Contested Bromley & Chislehurst 2010. Former intern to Simon Hughes. Engaged. Ed: Dulwich Coll; UEA (BA politics). **Roisin Robertson** (Green) Press officer, Bromley & Bexley Green party. Administrator. Runs edible wreaths company.

CONSTITUENCY PROFILE
Firmly in the Kentish part of London and, aside from a few housing estates in areas such as Mottingham, the seat consists of prosperous leafy suburbia. A safe Conservative seat, but only narrowly held in the 2006 by-election that followed the death of Eric Forth after an effective Lib Dem campaign. Normal large majority returned in 2010.

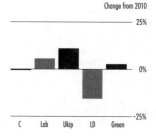

	Electorate	Turnout %	Change from 2010 %
	65,476	67.3	
R Neill C	23,343	53.0	-0.6
J Courtneidge Lab	9,779	22.2	+5.6
E Jenner Ukip	6,285	14.3	+11.0
S Webber LD	2,836	6.4	-15.5
R Robertson Green	1,823	4.1	+2.8

Change from 2010

Bromsgrove

CONSERVATIVE HOLD

SAJID JAVID
BORN Dec 5, 1969
MP 2010-

Supremely confident, highly successful business career. Youngest ever VP of Chase Manhattan Bank at age 24. Some say a future Con leader. Secretary of State: business, innovation & skills 2015-; culture, media & sport 2014-15. Min: equalities 2014. Treasury: financial secretary, 2013-14; economic secretary 2012-13. PPS to: George Osborne 2011-12; John Hayes 2010-11. Select cttees: public accounts 2012-13; work & pensions 2010. Reportedly left £3 million-a-year senior managing director role at Deutsche Bank to pursue politics. Long-standing Tory activist and charity fundraiser. Pakistani-Muslim heritage, the son of an immigrant bus driver. Married, three daughters, one son. Ed: Downend Sch, Bristol; University of Exeter (BA economics & politics).

CHALLENGERS
Tom Ebbutt (Lab) Operations director, Teaching Leaders. Cllr, Hackney BC 2010-. Worked for Deloitte Consulting. Fellow, On Purpose 2012-. Chairman of trustees, Education Partnership Africa 2008-. Ed: Waseley Hills HS; Trinity Hall, Cambridge (BA history). **Stuart Cross** (Ukip) Financial consultant, Lloyds TSB. Cllr, Worcester CC 2013-. **Bart Ricketts** (LD) Project coordinator, Kingston Eco-op. Cllr, Kingston upon Thames BC 2002-. Ed: Sacred Heart Coll; Kingston University (environmental science & business, president, Students' Union). **Spoz Esposito** (Green) Poet, singer, songwriter and playwright.

CONSTITUENCY PROFILE
Affluent commuter territory curling around the southern boundary of the West Midlands conurbation. While Bromsgrove itself has some reliable Labour areas in its council estates, on the whole this is a safe Tory seat.

	Electorate	Turnout %	from 2010 % Change
	73,329	71.3	
S Javid C	28,133	53.9	+10.2
T Ebbutt Lab	11,604	22.2	+0.4
S Cross Ukip	8,163	15.6	+9.9
B Ricketts LD	2,616	5.0	-14.6
S Esposito Green	1,729	3.3	

Change from 2010

25%

0%

-25%

C   Lab   Ukip   LD   Green

Broxbourne

CONSERVATIVE HOLD

CHARLES WALKER
BORN Sep 11, 1967
MP 2005-

Pugnacious backbencher. Aims to destigmatise mental health, admitted in Commons he suffers from OCD, declaring "I am a practising fruitcake". Chairman, procedure select cttee 2012-. Member, cttees: liaison 2012-; parliamentary standards authority 2010-; panel of chairs 2010-; marine bill 2008; public admin 2007-11; Scottish affairs 2005-10. Vice-chairman, 1922 committee 2010-. Contested Ealing N 2001. Cllr, Wandsworth BC 2002-06. Director, Debitwise, LSM processing & Blue Arrow recruitment company; Comms dir, CSQ. Married, one daughter, two sons. Ed: American Sch, London; University of Oregon (BSc politics).

CHALLENGERS
David Platt (Ukip) Web engineer. Owner Netpowersoft 2004-. Cllr,

Broxbourne BC 2014-. Contested Welwyn Hatfield 2010. Ed: Broxbourne Sch. **Edward Robinson** (Lab) Director, Culmer Raphael. Dir, EJC Robinson. Worked for Green Alliance and was journalist in Shanghai. Ed: Durham (BA politics & government); UCL (MA political economy). **Anthony Rowlands** (LD) Director of CentreForum liberal think tank. Contested: Hertsmere, 2010; St Albans, 1997. Cllr: St Albans DC 1990-; Hertfordshire CC 1993-97. Former teacher. Widowed, two children. Ed: Queen's Coll, Oxford (BA history, scholarship)

CONSTITUENCY PROFILE
A very affluent, safe Conservative commuter seat in Hertfordshire, north of London, mostly made up of leafy suburban dormitory towns. Tesco's national headquarters is here in Cheshunt. The only area with any significant Labour support is Waltham Cross, at the far south of the constituency by the London border.

	Electorate	Turnout %	from 2010 % Change
	72,944	63.1	
C Walker C	25,797	56.1	-2.7
D Platt Ukip	9,074	19.7	+15.6
E Robinson Lab	8,470	18.4	+0.8
A Rowlands LD	1,467	3.2	-10.2
R Secker Green	1,216	2.6	

Change from 2010

25%

0%

-25%

C   Ukip   Lab   LD   Green

Broxtowe

CONSERVATIVE HOLD

ANNA SOUBRY
BORN Dec 7, 1956
MP 2010-

Lawyer and former television journalist. Attracted controversy when footage cut from BBC documentary *Inside the Commons* allegedly showed her verbally abusing Ed Miliband. Min: small business 2015-; defence personnel, welfare and veterans 2014-15. Parly under sec: defence 2013-14; health 2012-13. PPS to Simon Burns 2010-12. Member, justice select cttee 2010. Contested Gedling 2005. Criminal barrister, KCH Chambers. Presenter, reporter, *Central News TV, This Morning, Grampian North Tonight.* Former NUJ shop steward. Tory Reform Group. First female Tory elected to NUS executive. Left Tories for SDP in 1980s, rejoined 2002. Elected Rector, University of Stirling. Divorced, two daughters. Ed: Hartland Comp Sch, Worksop; Uni of Birmingham (LLB law).

CHALLENGERS
Nick Palmer (Lab) Director, BUAV. MP for Broxtowe 1997-2010. PPS to Malcolm Wicks 2005-08. Former computer manager and head of computer services at Novartis. Contested Chelsea 1983. First ex-MP to sign on for unemployment benefit in 2010. Unite. Ed: Copenhagen (MSc); Birkbeck Coll (PhD maths). **Frank Dunne** (Ukip) MD, Upskill Assessment and Training. Married, two daughters. Ed: Oxford Brookes (CertEd HE). **Stan Heptinstall** (LD) Emeritus professor of thrombosis and haemostasis, University of Nottingham. Cllr: Nottinghamshire CC 1997-; Broxtowe BC 1991-15, mayor 2014-15; Stapleton TC 1999-. MBE 1997. Married, four children.

CONSTITUENCY PROFILE
A predominantly middle-class constituency. Boots is the main employer, with its headquarters close to the centre of Beeston. A high proportion of residents commute into Nottingham.

	Electorate	Turnout %	Change from 2010 %
	71,865	74.4	
A Soubry C	24,163	45.2	+6.2
N Palmer Lab	19,876	37.2	-1.1
F Dunne Ukip	5,674	10.6	+8.4
S Heptinstall LD	2,120	4.0	-12.9
D Kirwan Green	1,544	2.9	+2.1
R Barry JMB	63	0.1	

Change from 2010

25%

0%

-25%

C   Lab   Ukip   LD   Green

Buckingham

SPEAKER HOLD

JOHN BERCOW
BORN Jan 19, 1963
MP 1997-

A florid orator, the surprise choice of speaker (2009-) with backing of Labour MPs but few Conservatives. Remains unpopular with Tory leadership, but received backing of Commons in emotional debate at end of 2010-15 parliament. First Jewish speaker, and first not to wear traditional robes. Sharp, but sometimes struggles to assert his authority. Lost battle to secure first outsider as Commons clerk. Made unlikely journey from Thatcherite rightwinger to social liberal. Introduced Speaker's Lectures series in 2011. Speaker's cttees, chairman: independent parly standards authority 2009-; electoral commission 2009-; members estimate 2009-10. Shadow SoS, international development 2003-04. Quit as shad min for work & pensions in 2002 to defy whip and support unmarried couples' adoption rights. Shad chief Treasury sec 2001-02. Merchant banker, lobbyist, Saatchi & Saatchi, special adviser. Troubled marriage to Sally, Labour party member and unguarded tweeter, attracted attention. One daughter, two sons. Ed: University of Essex (BA government).

CHALLENGERS
David Fowler (Ukip) Local plumber. **Alan Francis** (Green) Transport Consultant. Chairman, Milton Keynes Transport Partnership. Previously research fellow, Open University. Former chairman, New Bradwell PC. Contested Milton Keynes North 2010.

CONSTITUENCY PROFILE
Solid Tory bulwark, with the market town of Buckingham and affluent villages covering most of the Vale of Aylesbury. Speaker unopposed by three main parties in 2015 and 2010. In 2010, Nigel Farage was injured in a plane crash on election day while contesting the seat.

	Electorate	Turnout %	Change from 2010 %
	77,572	69.2	
J Bercow Speaker	34,617	64.5	+17.2
D Fowler Ukip	11,675	21.7	+4.4
A Francis Green	7,400	13.8	

Change from 2010

25%

0%

-25%

Speaker   Ukip   Green

Burnley

LABOUR GAIN

JULIE COOPER
BORN Jun 20, 1960
MP 2015-

Oversaw Burnley's emergence as the UK's most enterprising town (department for BIS' Enterprising Britain Awards 2013) as council leader 2012-14. Cllr, Burnley BC 2005-. Introduced living wage to council operations. English teacher and previously director of Coopers Chemist, Burnley. Served on police and crime commissioner's panel and Lancashire Enterprise Partnership. Contested Burnley 2010. Burnley season ticket holder. Married, two children.

CHALLENGERS
Gordon Birtwistle (LD) MP, 2010-15. PPS to Danny Alexander 2010-12. Cllr, Burnley BC 1983-2010, leader 2006-10, mayor 2002-03. Labour Cllr, Great Harwood, 1974-76. Contested Burnley 1997, 1992, for SDP 1982. Ran engineering/machine trading firm. Married, two children. Ed: Accrington Coll. **Tom Commis** (Ukip) IT worker, Exertis Micro-P computer distribution. **Sarah Cockburn-Price** (C) PR for Virtalis robotics and virtual reality company. Cllr, Pendle BC 2014-. Married, one son. **Mike Hargreaves** (Green) Works with people with learning disabilities. Former engineer. Lead singer of punk rock band NotSensibles, famous for their song *I'm in Love with Margaret Thatcher*.

CONSTITUENCY PROFILE
Historically a safe Labour seat, but Liberal Democrats won in 2010 when former MP Kitty Ussher stood down after the expenses scandal. Covers former industrial towns, now dormitory towns for Manchester and Blackburn. The town has struggled economically, but there has been an upswing in recent years. Has a significant Asian population. Previous BNP strength here and a history of racial tension, with riots in 2001.

	Electorate	Turnout %	from 2010 % Change
	64,486	61.6	
J Cooper Lab	14,951	37.6	+6.3
G Birtwistle LD	11,707	29.5	-6.2
T Commis Ukip	6,864	17.3	+15.1
S Cockburn-Price C	5,374	13.5	-3.1
M Hargreaves Green	850	2.1	

Change from 2010

Lab   LD   Ukip   C   Green

Burton

CONSERVATIVE HOLD

ANDREW GRIFFITHS
BORN Oct 19, 1970
MP 2010-

Eurosceptic, farming and rural affairs specialist. Member, political & constitutional reform select cttee 2010-13. Chairman, Beer APPG. Shortlisted for Grassroot Diplomat Initiative Award. Contested: Dudley N 2001; West Midlands Euro election 2004. Chief of staff to: Eric Pickles 2007-10; Hugo Swire 2006-07; Theresa May 2004-06. Special adviser to West Midlands MEP team in Brussels 1999-2004. Manager, commercial lending, Leeds Building Society. Worked for family-run engineering business. Married. Ed: High Arcal Sch, Sedgley.

CHALLENGERS
Jon Wheale (Lab) Office manager to Dan Jarvis. Former army officer. Served as arms monitor with the United Nations mission in Nepal. Founded Labour Friends of the Forces. Was risk manager at DeVere and Christie's. Magistrate in adult & family court. Chairman, Trustees for East Staffordshire Family Support, Harvey Girls and Dads 4 Dads. Ed: Abbot Beyne Sch; Aberystwyth (BA international politics & strategic studies). **Mike Green** (Ukip) Runs training company, former police officer. **David MacDonald** (LD) Constituency manager and parly assist to Paul Burstow. Former PA exec, Working Links. Prev intern for Tim Farron and Willie Rennie. Ed: Hull (BA MA politics).

CONSTITUENCY PROFILE
Conservative since 1950 except 1997-2010. Burton-on-Trent itself is largely Labour, but the seat is balanced out by rural wards, making it marginal. Has strong associations with the brewing industry and is the home of Marmite. The seat stretches from Burton to the edge of the Peak District, including Uttoxeter, known for its racecourse. The nearby village of Rocester is the base of JCB, a big local employer.

	Electorate	Turnout %	from 2010 % Change
	75,300	65.5	
A Griffiths C	24,736	50.1	+5.6
J Wheale Lab	13,484	27.3	-4.6
M Green Ukip	8,658	17.6	+14.6
D MacDonald LD	1,232	2.5	-13.3
S Patrone Green	1,224	2.5	

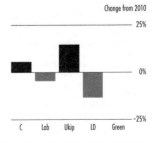

Change from 2010

C   Lab   Ukip   LD   Green

Bury North

CONSERVATIVE HOLD

DAVID NUTTALL
BORN Mar 25, 1962
MP 2010-

Anti-political correctness, anti-red tape Eurosceptic. Put forward the controversial plan to build an anaerobic digestion waste plant in Ramsbottom. Member, procedure select cttee 2010. Cllr, Rotherham MBC 2004-06, 1992-96. Contested: Bury North 2005; Morecambe & Lunesdale 2001; Sheffield Hillsborough 1997; Yorkshire & Humber Euro election 1999. Self-employed Notary Public, Nuttalls Notaries. Member, Notaries Society. Solicitor. Bury Rotary Club. CofE church warden. Married. Ed: Aston Comp Sch; London (LLB law, by correspondence).

CHALLENGERS
James Frith (Lab) Cllr, Bury MBC 2011-. Founder, All Together social enterprise. Board Member, WhatUni.com. Former MD, U-Explore E-learning. Campaigns & comms manager for Ruth Kelly 2004-05. Married, two children. **Ian Henderson** (Ukip) Managing consultant, Lorimer Black. Chairman, Ukip Greater Manchester. **John Southworth** (Green) Teacher, management. Married, two children. **Richard Baum** (LD) NHS planning manager. Cllr, Bury MBC 2007-11. Contested Bury North 2010. Ed: Birmingham (LLB law); Warwick (MA public management).

CONSTITUENCY PROFILE:
Lab-Con marginal. Currently one of two Conservative seats in Greater Manchester, after former Labour MP David Chaytor was caught up in expenses scandal in 2009 – he was later sentenced to 18 months' imprisonment. Covers former Lancashire mill towns on the edge of the West Pennine Moors, traditional towns that have remained comparatively affluent despite the decline of the textile industry and reinvented themselves as the Manchester commuter belt.

	Electorate	Turnout %	Change from 2010 %
	67,580	66.9	
D Nuttall C	18,970	41.9	+1.8
J Frith Lab	18,592	41.1	+5.9
I Henderson Ukip	5,595	12.4	+9.5
J Southworth Green	1,141	2.5	
R Baum LD	932	2.1	-14.9

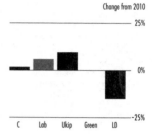

Change from 2010

Bury South

LABOUR HOLD

IVAN LEWIS
BORN Mar 4, 1967
MP 1997-

Labour loyalist who had key role in Labour adopting one nation stance. Shadow SoS for Northern Ireland 2013-, apologised to the families of Hyde Park victims for "catastrophic" errors in the Downey case. Shad SoS: int devt 2011-13; CMS 2010-11. Minister, FCO 2009-10. Parly under sec: int devt 2008-09; health 2006-08. Economic sec to Treasury 2005-06; education 2001-05. PPS to: Stephen Byers 1999-2001. Cllr, Bury MBC 1990-98. Lab Friends of Israel, vice-chairman 1997-2001. Unite. Charity executive chairman, Bury Mencap. Trustee, Holocaust Ed Trust. Divorced, two sons. Ed: William Julme GS; Bury FE Coll.

CHALLENGERS
Daniel Critchlow (C) CofE minister. Contested Wythenshawe & Sale East by-election 2014. Previously worked in a residential home. Married, one daughter. Ed: Bury CofE HS; Queen's, Belfast (BA MA theology); Sidney Sussex Coll, Cambridge (MPhil history); Ridley Hall, Cambridge (theology). **Séamus Martin** (Ukip) Former immigration officer. Author of martial arts guide. Ed: University of Salford (BA French & German). **Paul Ankers** (LD) Data analyst, British Gas and freelance copywriter. Cllr, Manchester CC 2007-11. Ed: Lincoln (BA media production).

CONSTITUENCY PROFILE
A Labour-leaning marginal, the seat was held by the Conservatives until 1997. Covers the southern part of the Metropolitan Borough of Bury (the town itself is almost wholly within Bury North) and former mill towns that have become residential suburbs since the decline of heavy industry. The seat has the highest proportion of Jewish residents outside London and the South East.

	Electorate	Turnout %	Change from 2010 %
	73,883	63.9	
I Lewis Lab	21,272	45.1	+4.6
D Critchlow C	16,350	34.6	+1.0
S Martin Ukip	6,299	13.3	+11.2
P Ankers LD	1,690	3.6	-14.6
G Heath Green	1,434	3.0	+2.0
V Morris Eng Dem	170	0.4	-0.7

Change from 2010

Bury St Edmunds

CONSERVATIVE HOLD

JO CHURCHILL
BORN Mar 18, 1964
MP 2015-

Health campaigner for improved cancer outcomes. Diagnosed with cancer when she was 31, was successfully treated but disease returned in her mid-40s, later given all-clear again. Director, SLS scaffolding contractor. Cllr, Lincolnshire CC 2013-. Was studying for a PhD in enterprises and social responsibility at Nottingham University but postponed owing to second bout of cancer. Married, four daughters. Ed: Dame Alice Harpur Sch, Bedford (BSc business; MSc occupational psychology).

CHALLENGERS
Bill Edwards (Lab) Principal, Bardfield food consultants. Previously worked for Food Research Association as research scientist. FRSC. Trustee, Braintree Community Assoc. Contested Braintree 2010. Member, Great Bardfield Historical Soc. Married. Ed: Romford County Tech HS; Bradford (BTech chemistry); Sheffield (research); York (DPhil). **John Howlett** (Ukip) Structural engineering consultant. Contested Bury StE 2010, 05, 01. **Helen Geake** (Green) Archaeologist, University of Cambridge. Former Channel 4 *Time Team* presenter. Married, three children. Ed: UCL (BA archaeology); York (DPhil). **David Chappell** (LD) Chartered surveyor, former banker. Worked in Saudi Arabia on King Solomon's mines project. Cllr, St Edmunsbury BC 2007-15.

CONSTITUENCY PROFILE
A safe Tory seat, returning Tory MPs since 1885, although David Ruffley held off Labour by just 368 votes in 1997 and kept the seat until 2015. The economy had been stagnating but the new Arc shopping centre has helped regeneration. Food manufacturing is a notable economic sector.

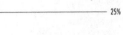

	Electorate	Turnout %	Change from 2010 %
	85,993	69.0	
J Churchill C	31,815	53.6	+6.1
B Edwards Lab	10,514	17.7	+1.1
J Howlett Ukip	8,739	14.7	+9.6
H Geake Green	4,692	7.9	+3.6
D Chappell LD	3,581	6.0	-20.4

Change from 2010

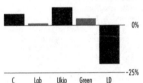

Caerphilly

LABOUR HOLD

WAYNE DAVID
BORN Jul 1, 1957
MP 2001-

Labour loyalist and former South Wales MEP (1989-99). Organiser of Ed Miliband's campaign for Lab leadership 2010. PPS to Ed Miliband 2013-15. Shadow minister: political & constitutional reform 2011-13; Europe 2010-11; Wales 2010. Leader, European parly Lab Party 1994-98, ex-officio Lab Party NEC. Parly under sec, Wales 2008-10. Asst govt whip 2007-08. PPS to MoD 2005. Select cttees: European scrutiny 2001-07; Welsh affairs 2007. Cllr, Cefn Cribwr 1985-91, chair 1986-87. VP Cardiff UN assoc. Pres Council for Wales of voluntary youth services. Teacher, organiser, youth policy adviser. Divorced. Ed: University Coll, Cardiff (BA history; PGCE); Univ Coll, Swansea (economic research).

CHALLENGERS
Sam Gould (Ukip) Businessman and former DJ. Founder of Student Lock-In shopping events. Was missionary in West Africa for two years. Married, two children. Ed: Cardiff (business management & marketing). **Leo Docherty** (C) Dir, Conservative Middle East Council. Cllr, South Oxfordshire DC 2011-. Ed: SOAS; RMA Sandhurst. **Beci Newton** (PC) Firefighter. Plays rugby. Married, two children. Ed: Cardinal Newman RC Sch. **Katy Beddoe** (Green) Youth worker, poet, left-wing activist and local campaigner.

CONSTITUENCY PROFILE
A former coal mining area, the seat is now a commuter town for Cardiff. Like most Valleys seats this is safe Labour territory, held by the party since 1918 with the brief exception of its MP's defection to the SDP in 1981. Its best-known MP is the former Welsh secretary Ron Davies, who fell from grace after being mugged on Clapham Common in "moment of madness". Davies later joined Plaid Cymru.

	Electorate	Turnout %	Change from 2010 %
	62,793	64.2	
W David Lab	17,864	44.4	-0.2
S Gould Ukip	7,791	19.3	+17.0
L Docherty C	6,683	16.6	-0.4
B Newton PC	5,895	14.6	-1.9
K Beddoe Green	937	2.3	
A Ayesh LD	935	2.3	-13.0
J Davies TUSC	178	0.4	

Change from 2010

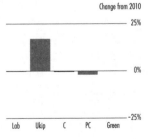

Caithness, Sutherland & Easter Ross

SNP GAIN

PAUL MONAGHAN
BORN Nov 11, 1966
MP 2015-

Housing support manger. Director: Highland Homeless Trust charity; Inverness MS Therapy Centre; Food for Families, Invergordon. Member, SSE Fairburn Windfarm Community Fund. Board member, UHI North Highland Coll and founding member, North Highland Coll Foundation. Married, one daughter. Ed: Inverness Royal Academy; University of Stirling (BSc psychology; PhD social policy).

CHALLENGERS
John Thurso (LD) MP 2001-15. First hereditary peer to sit in the Commons without renouncing his title, Viscount Thurso. Grandson of Sir Archibald Sinclair, Liberal leader 1935-45 and last Liberal to serve in Cabinet. Lib Dem shadow SoS: business 2008-10; Scotland 2003-06; transport 2003-05.

LD whip 2001-02. Member, HoL 1995-99. LD Lords spokesman 2001-03. Select cttees: chairman, finance and services 2010-15; member, Treasury 2006-; liason 2010-; banking standards 2012-13; HoL reform bill 2011-12; admin 2005-10; art works 2005-10. LD federal policy cttee 1999-2001. Ed: Eton Coll; Westminster Tech Coll. **John Erskine** (Lab) Chairman, Highlands & Islands Young Labour. Parly asst DWP. Ed: Dingwall Academy; Stirling (BA philosophy & politics).

CONSTITUENCY PROFILE
Covers the northernmost tip of the British mainland. Much of the electorate is concentrated in Easter Ross in the south, where there is a strong oil industry presence. Other industries are fishing, farming and tourism — especially in John o' Groats — and several distilleries. The seat's Labour MP, Robert Maclennan, defected to the SDP in 1981. The Lib Dems have a long history of winning this seat.

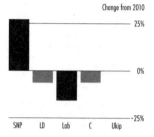

	Electorate	Turnout %	Change from 2010 %
	47,558	71.9	
P Monaghan SNP	15,831	46.3	+27.1
J Thurso LD	11,987	35.1	-6.3
J Erskine Lab	3,061	9.0	-15.7
A Graham C	2,326	6.8	-6.2
A T Murray Ukip	981	2.9	

Change from 2010

25%

0%

-25%

SNP · LD · Lab · C · Ukip

Calder Valley

CONSERVATIVE HOLD

CRAIG WHITTAKER
BORN Aug 30, 1962
MP 2010-

Australian-raised, son of a left-wing unionist. Self-assured, posits himself as a voice of common sense. Cllr, Calderdale MBC 2007-11, 2003-04. Cabinet member for children's services at time of highly critical serious case review. Cllr, Heptonstall PC 1998-2003. Election agent to Elizabeth Truss, 2005. Select cttees: education 2010-; able marine energy park development 2014-. Previously general manager, PC World. Retail Manager, Wilkinson. Began career at Pizza Hut, transferring to UK for a year. Member, One of two Mormon MPs. Divorced, two daughters, one son. Ed: Belmont HS; Tighes Hill Coll, NSW Australia.

CHALLENGERS
Josh Fenton-Glynn (Lab) Trade union officer, Leeds. Former pensions welfare officer, PCS

Union. Activist in Oxfam UK Poverty Programme and Child Poverty Action Group. Ed: Calder HS; Liverpool (BA political communication). **Paul Rogan** (Ukip) Self-employed textile broker. **Alisdair Calder McGregor** (LD) Senior service analyst, CDS communications. **Jenny Shepherd** (Green) Writer, lecturer and film-maker.

CONSTITUENCY PROFILE
Seen as a key Conservative-Labour marginal, even with Craig Whittaker's 6,000-strong majority in 2010. Its predecessor Sowerby was held by Labour from the war until the 1970s — the seat fell to the Tories in 1979 and remained Tory until won by Labour in the 1997 landslide. Covers former mill towns, now dormitory towns of Halifax, Huddersfield and Bradford. Hebden Bridge in the constituency has a reputation for being counter-cultural, and reportedly has the highest proportion of lesbian residents of any town in Britain.

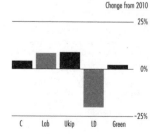

	Electorate	Turnout %	Change from 2010 %
	77,753	68.9	
C Whittaker C	23,354	43.6	+4.2
J Fenton-Glynn Lab	18,927	35.4	+8.4
P Rogan Ukip	5,950	11.1	+8.9
A Calder McGregor LD	2,666	5.0	-20.2
J Shepherd Green	2,090	3.9	+2.3
R Sutcliffe Yorks	389	0.7	
J Stead Song	165	0.3	

Change from 2010

25%

0%

-25%

C · Lab · Ukip · LD · Green

Camberwell & Peckham

LABOUR HOLD

HARRIET HARMAN
BORN Jul 30, 1950
MP 1982-

Long-standing member of Labour elite. Masterminded equalities bill. Shadow deputy PM 2010-15. Chair, Lab Party 2007-. Deputy leader, Lab Party 2007- (acting leader 2010 & 2015). Leader, House of Commons 2007-10. Shadow SoS: CMS 2011-; int devt 2010-11. Min: women & equality 2007-10, 1997-98; constitutional affairs 2005-07. Chair, modernisation of HoC cttee 2007-10. Solicitor gen 2001-05. Shad SoS: social security 1996-97; health 1996-96; employment 1994-95. Shad chief Treasury sec 1992-94. MP for Peckham 1982-1997. Lab Party NEC 1993-98. QC 2001. Chair, childcare comm. Legal officer, nat council for civil liberties. Solicitor. Married to Jack Dromey MP, one daughter, two sons. Niece (by marriage), Lord Longford. Ed: St Paul's Girls' Sch; University of York (BA politics).

CHALLENGERS
Naomi Newstead (C) Former housing professional. Contested London assembly election 2012. Married, three sons. Ed: Pimlico Sch. **Amelia Womack** (Green) Deputy leader Green Party 2014-. **Yahaya Kiyingi** (LD) "Whizkid" who Lib Dem Voice predicted as the future of the party in 2012. Approved as parly candidate before he could vote. Works in marketing. Born in Uganda, moved to Britain at age of five. Ed: Southampton (LLB law).

CONSTITUENCY PROFILE
One of the most poverty-stricken and deprived constituencies in the country, and the highest proportion of social housing, with about half in homes rented from the council or a housing association. The worst of the concrete estates have been demolished in regeneration projects, although gang crime remains a problem. Has highest proportion of Afro-Caribbeans of any seat.

	Electorate	Turnout %	Change from 2010 %
	80,507	64.1	
H Harman Lab	32,614	63.3	+4.1
N Newstead C	6,790	13.2	+0.1
A Womack Green	5,187	10.1	+7.1
Y Kiyingi LD	2,580	5.0	-17.4
D Kurten Ukip	2,413	4.7	
P Goyal AP	829	1.6	
R Fox NHAP	466	0.9	
N Wrack TUSC	292	0.6	
A Robertson CSA	197	0.4	
J Ogunleye WRP	107	0.2	-0.2
F Anscomb Whig	86	0.2	

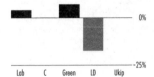

Change from 2010

Lab   C   Green   LD   Ukip

Camborne & Redruth

CONSERVATIVE HOLD

GEORGE EUSTICE
BORN Sep 28, 1971
MP 2010-

Self-effacing, straightforward, with quiet manner. Defra: min of state 2015-; under sec 2013-15. Select cttees: privacy and injunctions 2011-12; efra 2010-13. Press secretary to David Cameron 2005-07, squeezed out by arrival of Andy Coulson. Portland PR. Inspired to enter politics by James Goldsmith's Referendum party of 1997, contested Euro 1999 election for Ukip. Head of press to Michael Howard, 2005 election. Campaign dir, anti-Euro "No" Campaign. Worked in family business, Trevaskis Fruit Farm. Keen runner. Has partner. Ed: Truro Cathedral Sch; Truro Sch; Cornwall Coll.

CHALLENGERS
Michael Foster (Lab) Veteran media agent for Chris Evans and Sacha Baron Cohen. Runs Creative Access charity, fundraises

for UK community groups and Africa projects. Four daughters. Ed: BSc economics. **Bob Smith** (Ukip) Child and educational psychologist. Ukip founding member. **Julia Goldsworthy** (LD) MP for Falmouth & Camborne 2005-10. Former adviser to Danny Alexander. Contested Camborne & Redruth 2010. Runner-up on Channel 4 show *The Games*. Married. Ed: Fitzwilliam Coll, Cambridge (BA history); Birkbeck (PgCert economics).

CONSTITUENCY PROFILE
Has changed hands between Labour, Lib Dems and Tories since 1992, but three-way marginal ended in 2010. The seat forms a five-mile urban corridor parallel to Cornwall's west coast. Once prosperous from copper and tin mining, the area declined so much in 2000-06 that it became one of the poorest parts of the EU. Is undergoing major redevelopment with a new East-West road linking Camborne, Pool and Redruth.

	Electorate	Turnout %	Change from 2010 %
	66,944	68.5	
G Eustice C	18,452	40.2	+2.7
M Foster Lab	11,448	25.0	+8.6
B Smith Ukip	6,776	14.8	+9.7
J Goldsworthy LD	5,687	12.4	-25.0
G Garbett Green	2,608	5.7	+4.3
L Jenkin Meb Ker	897	2.0	+0.1

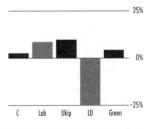

Change from 2010

C   Lab   Ukip   LD   Green

Cambridge

LABOUR GAIN

DANIEL ZEICHNER
BORN Sep 11, 1956
MP 2010-

Unison officer representing low-paid in public sector, campaigned to make Cambridge a living wage city. Worked in IT including for Phillips, Perkins Engines. Cllr, South Norfolk C 1995-2003. Parly researcher 1992-97. Interested in House of Lords reform; former co-ordinator, Campaign for a Democratic Upper House. Exec member of Labour's SERA group. Contested: Cambridge 2010; Norfolk Mid 2005, 01, 1997. Cambridge United season ticket holder. Enjoys music, cycling and walking. Partner. Ed: King's Coll, Cambridge (BA history).

CHALLENGERS
Julian Huppert (LD) MP, 2010-15. Research scientist, Cavendish Laboratory. Fellow, Clare Coll. Cllr, Cambridgeshire CC 2001-09, LD group leader. Contested Huntingdon 2005. MRSC,

MInstP. Son of geophysicist Herbert Huppert. Ed: Perse Sch; Trinity Coll, Cambridge (MSc natural sciences; PhD biological chemistry). **Chamali Fernando** (C) Barrister. Sought LD nomination for London mayor 2008, defected to Tories in 2009. Licensed attorney for New York State Bar. Ed: UCL (LLB law). **Rupert Read** (Green) Academic at UEA. Cllr, Norwich CC 2004-11. Ed: Balliol Coll, Oxford (PPE). **Patrick O'Flynn** (Ukip) MEP, East of England 2014-. Ukip dir of Comms, economics spokesman 2014-15. Chief poltical commentator, *Daily Express* 2006-14.

CONSTITUENCY PROFILE
Home not just to the university, but also hi-tech industry and a regional commercial centre. About one in five of the adult population are in full-time education. All three main parties are competitive here – it was held by the Conservatives until 1992, then was Labour for 13 years until swinging strongly to the Liberal Democrats in 2005.

	Electorate	Turnout %	from 2010 %	Change
	83,384	62.1		
D Zeichner Lab	18,646	36.0	+11.7	
J Huppert LD	18,047	34.9	-4.3	
C Fernando C	8,117	15.7	-9.9	
R Read Green	4,109	7.9	+0.4	
P O'Flynn Ukip	2,668	5.2	+2.8	
K Garrett RTP	187	0.4		

Change from 2010

Lab	LD	C	Green	Ukip

(25% / 0% / -25% scale)

Cambridgeshire North East

CONSERVATIVE HOLD

STEVE BARCLAY
BORN May 3, 1972
MP 2010-

Highly thought of in his party but down-to-earth and approachable. Solicitor specialising in financial crime prevention. Asst whip 2015-. Member, public accounts select cttee 2010-14. Contested: Lancaster & Wyre 2001 – lost by 481 votes; Manchester Blackley 1997. Adviser to Liam Fox as Conservative party chairman 2005. Chairman of organising cttee of Carlton political dinner 2007-. Selected by open primary. Head of anti-money laundering and sanctions for Barclays Bank. FSA, Guardian Royal Exchange, Axa Insurance. Served briefly in army, sponsored through university. Rugby player and keen skydiver. Married. Ed: Peterhouse, Cambridge (BA history); Coll of Law, Chester.

CHALLENGERS
Andrew Charalambous (Ukip)

Businessman. Founder of Britain's first eco-friendly nightclub. Eccentric Ukip housing and environmental spokesman. **Ken Rustidge** (Lab) Iraq veteran. NUT official. Former teacher, Robert Manning Technology Coll, Bourne Academy. **Lucy Nethsingha** (LD) Cllr, Cambridgeshire CC; Gloucester CC 2004-08; Truro CC 1999-2002. Deputy leader, LD group. Primary teacher. Married, three children. Ed: University of Southampton (BSc psychology); Cambridge (MPhil, MEd education & psychology).

CONSTITUENCY PROFILE
Stretches from the Lincolnshire and Norfolk borders, down to the edge of Ely and Peterborough. Rural and agricultural, the economy is built on farming, processing, storage, packaging and distribution. Clement Freud took a surprise by-election victory for the Liberals in 1973 (winning a 33-1 Ladbrokes bet), before it returned to Tory territory in 1987.

	Electorate	Turnout %	from 2010 %	Change
	82,990	62.4		
S Barclay C	28,524	55.1	+3.7	
A Charalambous Ukip	11,650	22.5	+16.8	
K Rustidge Lab	7,476	14.4	-3.3	
L Nethsingha LD	2,314	4.5	-15.5	
H Scott-Daniels Green	1,816	3.5		

Change from 2010

C	Ukip	Lab	LD	Green

(25% / 0% / -25% scale)

Cambridgeshire North West

CONSERVATIVE HOLD

SHAILESH VARA
BORN Sep 4, 1960
MP 2005-

Serious, but quietly effective. Parly under sec, min: MoJ 2013-. Assistant government whip 2010-12. Shadow deputy leader of the House 2006-10. Select cttes: finance & services 2011-13; administration 2010-11; efra 2005-06. Contested: Northampton South 2001; Birmingham Ladywood 1997. Vice-chair, Conservative Party 2001-05. Legal adviser and business consultant, London First. Solicitor, Richards Butler, CMS Cameron McKenna. VP, Small Business Bureau. Married, two sons. Ed: Aylesbury GS; Brunel University (LLB law).

CHALLENGERS
Peter Reeve (Ukip) Cllr: Cambridgeshire CC 2009-; Huntingdonshire DC 2009-, first Ukip cllr on both authorities. Local Government spokesman, national nominating officer and East of

England regional organiser. **Nick Thulbourn** (Lab) MD, NM Creations. Cllr, Peterborough CC 2012-. Cttees: audit; scrutiny and commissions; sustainable growth and environment, capital scrutiny. Deputy leader, Peterborough Labour group. Married, three children. Ed: University of Arts, London (BA print management). **Nick Sandford** (LD) Policy officer for woodland conservation. Cllr, Peterborough CC 1996-. Contested Peterborough; 2010, 05, 01. Board member: Peterborough Environment City Trust. Ed: Merton Coll, Oxford (BSc biochemisty).

CONSTITUENCY PROFILE
Contains a mix of suburban and rural land. Strongly Tory since its creation in 1997, there are still pockets of deprivation in Peterborough residential developments. Includes afffluent, rural villages in Huntingdonshire and parts of Peterborough to the south of the River Nene.

	Electorate	Turnout %	Change from 2010 %
	91,783	66.6	
S Vara C	32,070	52.5	+2.0
P Reeve Ukip	12,275	20.1	+11.8
N Thulbourn Lab	10,927	17.9	+0.9
N Sandford LD	3,479	5.7	-16.2
N Day Green	2,159	3.5	
F Belham CPA	190	0.3	

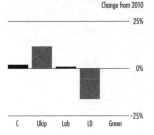

Change from 2010

C Ukip Lab LD Green

Cambridgeshire South

CONSERVATIVE HOLD

HEIDI ALLEN
BORN Jan 18, 1975
MP 2015-

Experienced Yorkshire-born businesswoman, one to watch according to some Tories. Inspired to enter politics after the 2011 Tottenham riots. Selected as candidate to replace Andrew Lansley in all-woman short list. Cllr, St Albans DC 2012-14, some controversy over not declaring her parliamentary ambitions earlier. MD of family business, RS Bike Paint, launched by parents in 1978. Formerly at ExxonMobil, Royal Mail. Married. Ed: UCL (BSc astrophysics).

CHALLENGERS
Dan Greef (Lab) History teacher. Former Norwich CC planning department administrator. Jesuit. Ed: University of Wales, Lampeter (BA archaeology). **Sebastian Kindersley** (LD) Runs market intelligence company.

Cllr: Cambridgeshire CC 2005-; South Cambs DC 1999-, leader 2005-06, opp leader 2008-14. Contested Cambridgeshire S 2010, coming second with more than 20,000 votes. Ed: St Columba's Coll, St Albans; Anglia Poly. **Marion Mason** (Ukip) Manager of a nursing home. Nurse for 40 years. Cllr, Stevenage BC 2010-14, defected from Conservatives in 2008. Contested: Stevenage 2010; Hertfordshire PCC 2012. **Simon Saggers** (Green) Runs Guilden Gate eco smallholding, Royston.

CONSTITUENCY PROFILE
A safe Tory seat, with various boundary changes since 1950. Mostly rural to the east of Cambridge, with much of the electorate scattered across small prosperous villages and one ward of Cambridge containing Addenbrooke's Hospital. Duxford is home to the Imperial War Museum's aviation branch. The village of Great Shelford is home of Barack Obama's ancestors.

	Electorate	Turnout %	Change from 2010 %
	84,132	73.2	
H Allen C	31,454	51.1	+3.7
D Greef Lab	10,860	17.7	+7.5
S Kindersley LD	9,368	15.2	-18.9
M Mason Ukip	6,010	9.8	+6.6
S Saggers Green	3,848	6.3	+4.5

Change from 2010

C Lab LD Ukip Green

Cambridgeshire South East

CONSERVATIVE HOLD

LUCY FRAZER
BORN May 17, 1972
MP 2015-

Barrister, retired to allow full focus on MP duties. Survived a troubled selection with allegations of miscounting against Heidi Allen (MP for Cambridgeshire South) — Conservative Home said it was a process that "would look iffy in a banana republic". QC 2013, called to the bar 1996, experienced in court litigation, arbitration and mediation. Acted in corporate insolvencies of Woolworths and Lehman Brothers. Represented Theresa May. Deputy chairman, Hampstead & Kilburn Conservative Association. Married, two children. Ed: Newnham Coll, Cambridge (LLM law, pres Cambridge Union).

CHALLENGERS
Jonathan Chatfield (LD) ATOC policy specialist. Former commercial manager, Network

Rail. Cllr, South Cambridgeshire DC 2002-15. Contested Cambridgeshire SE 2010, 05. Married, one son. Ed: Weymouth GS; Bradford (BA social sciences, president SU); Warwick (MBA). **Huw Jones** (Lab) Plant scientist, Nat Inst of Agricultural Botany, Cambridge. Unite. Two children. Ed: UEA (BSc chemistry & environmental science); Manchester (PhD life sciences). **Deborah Rennie** (Ukip) HR professional.

CONSTITUENCY PROFILE
Conservative since its creation in 1983, initially by the former foreign secretary Francis Pym, but for most of its existence by James Paice. Covers rural areas between Cambridge and Newmarket. The main population centres are the cathedral city of Ely, one of the smallest cities in England, and the town of Soham. The west of the seat includes Cambridge airport and the technology and biotech hub of Cambridge Science Village.

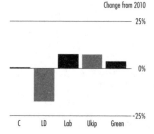

	Electorate	Turnout %	from 2010 %	Change
	84,570	70.4		
L Frazer C	28,845	48.5	+0.5	
J Chatfield LD	12,008	20.2	-17.5	
H Jones Lab	9,013	15.2	+7.5	
D Rennie Ukip	6,593	11.1	+7.4	
C Semmens Green	3,047	5.1	+3.8	

Change from 2010

C   LD   Lab   Ukip   Green

Cannock Chase

CONSERVATIVE HOLD

AMANDA MILLING
BORN Mar 12, 1975
MP 2015-

Market research director, Optimisa Research. Specialises in financial services. Cllr, Rossendale BC 2009-14, deputy Conservative leader. Released birth certificate in Apr 2015 to counter claims that she had no ties to Staffordshire. Former director, Quaestor 1999-09. Ed: UCL (BSc economics & statistics).

CHALLENGERS
Janos Toth (Lab) Area fundraising manager, Macmillan Cancer Support. Cllr: Cannock Chase DC 2011-15, 1992-2008; Staffs CC 2003-09, 1993-2001. Member: Stoke-on-Trent & Staffordshire fire & rescue authority 2005-09; Staffordshire police authority 1993-95. Former member on Bridgtown, Heath Hayes & Wimblebury, Norton Canes PC. Previously, waste control inspector for West Midlands Hazardous Waste Unit. Contested

Aldridge Brownhills 1997. Partner, two children. Ed: Wolverhampton Poly. **Grahame Wiggin** (Ukip) Distributor, Utility Warehouse distribution. Project management consultant. Ed: Wolverhampton Technical HS; Wolverhampton Tech Coll (HNC construction). **Ian Jackson** (LD) Retired management accountant. Cllr, Lichfield DC 2003-11, leader LD 2007-11. Contested Lichfield 2010. Married, four daughters.

CONSTITUENCY PROFILE
Cannock Chase was a surprise gain for the Conservatives in 2010. Aidan Burley won the seat with a swing of 14 per cent, one of the largest from Labour to the Tories in any contest in 2010. Burley stepped down after one term when criticised for organising a Nazi-themed stag do. His final remarks to Parliament were a criticism of MPs' pay. Before 2010 the seat had been relatively safely Labour, with a majority in excess of 20 per cent in the 2001 and 2005 elections.

	Electorate	Turnout %	from 2010 %	Change
	74,531	63.2		
A Milling C	20,811	44.2	+4.1	
J Toth Lab	15,888	33.7	+0.6	
G Wiggin Ukip	8,224	17.5	+14.0	
I Jackson LD	1,270	2.7	-14.3	
P Woodhead Green	906	1.9		

Change from 2010

C   Lab   Ukip   LD   Green

Canterbury

CONSERVATIVE HOLD

JULIAN BRAZIER
BORN Jul 24, 1953
MP 1987-

Exhibits excitable, slightly bombastic manner when debating favoured topics. Parly under-sec, defence, minister for reserves 2014-. Strong on defence issues: member, defence select cttee 2010-14, 1998-2001; decorated TA officer 1972-82; 1989-92; TD 1993. From military family. Shadow min: transport 2005-10; int affairs 2003-05; home affairs 2003, work & pensions 2002-03. Opp whip 2001-02. PPS to Gillian Shepherd 1990-93. 1922 executive cttee, 2010-. Former pres, Conservative Family Campaign 1995-2001. Chartered Consolidated and HB Maynard management consultant. Married, three sons. Ed: Brasenose Coll, Oxford (BA maths & philosophy, president OUCA); London Business Sch.

CHALLENGERS
Hugh Lanning (Lab) Former deputy general secretary, PCS union. Vice-chairman, Unite Against Fascism campaign 2012. Chairman, Palestine Solidarity Campaign. Columnist, *Morning Star*. **Jim Gascoyne** (Ukip) Works at specialist bank in City financing imports into Africa. Chairman, Ukip Canterbury 2013-. Contested Faversham & Kent Mid 2001. Married, children. **James Flanagan** (LD) Government affairs adviser, Internation Power energy firm. Cllr, Canterbury DC 2007-11. Married, three children. Ed: Bath (BSc economics). **Stuart Jeffery** (Green) NHS manager, nurse.

CONSTITUENCY PROFILE
Best known for its cathedral, it includes a number of surrounding villages and the seaside town of Whitstable, famous for its oysters. A solid Conservative seat, having been represented by the party continuously since the 19th century. The majority over Labour was reduced to less than 10,000 at the nadir of Tory fortunes in 1997 and 2001, but has grown since.

	Electorate	Turnout %	from 2010 %	Change
	83,481	64.0		
J Brazier C	22,918	42.9	-1.9	
H Lanning Lab	13,120	24.5	+8.4	
J Gascoyne Ukip	7,289	13.6	+9.8	
J Flanagan LD	6,227	11.7	-20.9	
S Jeffery Green	3,746	7.0	+4.7	
R Cox SPGB	165	0.3		

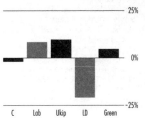

Change from 2010

C   Lab   Ukip   LD   Green

Cardiff Central

LABOUR GAIN

JO STEVENS
BORN Sep 6, 1966
MP 2015-

Trade union solicitor. People and organisation director, Thompsons Solicitors. Former resident in all four Cardiff constituencies. GMB, Unison, Fabians, Haldane, Co-operative Party. Key activist in NGO Justice for Colombia. Cardiff City FC season ticket holder, member Glamorgan CCC. Two sons. Ed: Elfed HS, Flintshire; Manchester (LLB law); Manchester Poly (solicitors' professional examination).

CHALLENGERS
Jenny Willott (LD) MP, 2005-15. Voted out before reaching high office. Cllr aged 24, MP at 30. Parly under-sec, employment, consumer & postal affairs 2012-14. Asst whip 2012-14. Lib Dem shad: sec, chancellor of duchy of Lancaster 2009-10, work & pensions 2008-09; min, justice 2008, youth affairs 2006-07. LD dep chief whip 2006-08. Select cttee, public administration 2005-10. Contested Cardiff Central 2001. Cllr, Merton BC 1998-2000. Area manager, Victim Support Wales 2003. Select cttes: selection 2014; work & pensions 2005-10. Head of advocacy, Unicef UK. Married, two sons. Ed: Wimbledon HS; Uppingham Sch; Durham (BA Classics); LSE (MSc economic devt studies). **Richard Hopkin** (C) Head of fixed income and managing director in securitisation division, AFME. Previously at JP Morgan, Deutsche Bank. Contested: European elections 2014; Welsh Assembly 2011. Speaks Welsh. Ed: Cambridge (LLB law).

CONSTITUENCY PROFILE
Takes in the centre of the Welsh capital and suburban areas in the north-east of the city. Home to Cardiff Castle, Millennium Stadium and a large student population. Historically a Conservative-Labour marginal in the 1980s.

	Electorate	Turnout %	from 2010 %	Change
	57,454	67.3		
J Stevens Lab	15,462	40.0	+11.2	
J Willott LD	10,481	27.1	-14.3	
R Hopkin C	5,674	14.7	-6.9	
A Raybould Ukip	2,499	6.5	+4.4	
C von Ruhland Green	2,461	6.4	+4.8	
M Pollard PC	1,925	5.0	+1.5	
S Williams TUSC	110	0.3	-0.2	
K Hubert Ind	34	0.1	-0.2	

Change from 2010

Lab   LD   C   Ukip   Green

Cardiff North

CONSERVATIVE HOLD

CRAIG WILLIAMS
BORN Jun 7, 1974
MP 2015-

Succeeds Jonathan Evans. Parly researcher to Byron Davies AM in Welsh Assembly. Cllr, Cardiff CC 2008-15. Serving member, Local Government Association General Assembly. Director, Tomorrow's Wales 2012-. Non-executive director, Cardiff Bus 2012-. Contested Cardiff West 2007, 11. Married, one son. Ed: Cardiff University.

CHALLENGERS
Mari Williams (Lab) Part-time teacher, former deputy head teacher. Took a year out from teaching to cycle around the world. Ed: Whitchurch HS; UCL. **Ethan Wilkinson** (Ukip) Student, languages. Interned at Terre des Hommes Italia. Trilingual. Mormon, former full-time missionary. Married, one son. Ed: Cardiff University (BA Italian & Spanish). **Elin Walker Jones** (PC) Part-time consultant clinical psychologist. Ed: Carmarthen Girls' Sch; Cardiff University. **Elizabeth Clark** (LD) Human resources manager and teacher. Cllr, Cardiff CC 2008-. Member, environmental scrutiny select cttee. Assoc for Public Service Excellence; Cardiff Business Technology (CBTC). Ed: Cardiff Met University, University of South Wales; University of Reading.

CONSTITUENCY PROFILE
Covers the affluent residential suburbs of northern Cardiff – Heath, Lisvane, Rhiwbina and Whitchurch. Home to Wales' biggest hospital, the University Hospital of Wales. High proportion of owner-occupied housing. This is a strongly middle-class area, largely Conservative at a local level, since 2007 at the Assembly level and at Westminster from 2010. Until the landslide of 1997 the seat was held by the Conservatives at every election except for 1966.

	Electorate	Turnout %	Change from 2010 %
	67,193	76.1	
C Williams C	21,709	42.4	+4.9
M Williams Lab	19,572	38.3	+1.2
E Wilkinson Ukip	3,953	7.7	+5.4
E Walker Jones PC	2,301	4.5	+1.2
E Clark LD	1,953	3.8	-14.5
R Osner Green	1,254	2.5	+1.7
J Green Ch P	331	0.7	+0.0
S Jenkins Change	78	0.2	

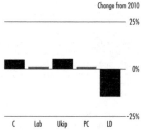

Change from 2010

Cardiff South & Penarth

LABOUR CO-OPERATIVE HOLD

STEPHEN DOUGHTY
BORN Apr 15, 1980
MP 2012-

Opp whip 2013-15. PPS to Rachel Reeves 2013-. Member, Welsh Affairs select cttee 2012-. Former policy adviser to Douglas Alexander. Previously head, Oxfam Cymru 2011. Won by-election in 2012 after Alun Michael's election as PCC for South Wales. Patron, LGBT Labour. Season ticket holder for Cardiff City FC. Ed: Llantwit Major Comp Sch; Corpus Christi Coll, Oxford (BA PPE); University of St Andrews (MLitt).

CHALLENGERS
Emma Warman (C) Compliance officer. Non-practising barrister. Deputy chair, LGBTory. Rugby fan. Ed: University of Reading (BA history); Coll of Law (PgDip), City University (BVC). **John Rees-Evans** (Ukip) UK-born, raised in Africa. Former serviceman in Territorial Army, parachute regiment. Played active role in anti-terrorist operations in Uganda. Climbed Kilimanjaro with his children, aged five, seven and nine at the time. Married. Ed: Jeppe Boys High, Johannesburg. **Ben Foday** (PC) Born and educated in Sierra Leone. Former Labour cllr, Cardiff CC 1993-99. **Nigel Howells** (LD) Communications officer for Eluned Parrott AM. Cllr, Cardiff CC 2012-. Cardiff council executive member, sport, culture & leisure 2010. School governor.

CONSTITUENCY PROFILE
Tory support is concentrated in the southern part of the seat, but overall this is a safe Labour constituency that has been represented by several senior Labour figures. First created in 1983 from the old Cardiff SE seat, initially represented by the former Labour prime minister Jim Callaghan. Stretches from Cardiff's eastern suburbs, through the old docklands and the redeveloped Cardiff Bay, southwards to Penarth.

	Electorate	Turnout %	Change from 2010 %
	75,714	61.6	
S Doughty Lab Co-op	19,966	42.8	+3.9
E Warman C	12,513	26.8	-1.5
J Rees-Evans Ukip	6,423	13.8	+11.2
B Foday PC	3,443	7.4	+3.2
N Howells LD	2,318	5.0	-17.3
A Slaughter Green	1,746	3.7	+2.5
R Saunders TUSC	258	0.6	

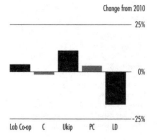

Change from 2010

Cardiff West

LABOUR HOLD

KEVIN BRENNAN
BORN Oct 16, 1959
MP 2001-

Shad minister for schools 2010-; further education, skills, apprenticeships & consumer affairs 2010. Min, FE 2009-10. Parly sec: Cab Office 2008-09. Parly under-sec: CSF 2007-08. Whip: govt 2006-07; asst govt 2005-06. PPS to Alan Milburn 2004-05. Member, public admin select cttee 2001-05. Socialist Health Assoc. Lab campaign electoral reform. Plays guitar in cross-party MP rock band, MP4 (with Greg Knight, Ian Cawsey and Pete Wishart). Cllr, Cardiff CC. Editor, organiser Cwmbran Community Press. Teacher. Research officer, special adviser to Rhodri Morgan as first min of Wales. Married, one daughter. Ed: St Alban's RC Comprehensive; Pembroke Coll, Oxford (BA PPE); Cardiff (PCGE history); Glamorgan (MSc education management).

CHALLENGERS
James Taghdissian (C) Barrister, Colleton Chambers. Chairman Polsloe, Heavitree and Newton Exeter Conservatives. Married, one son. Ed: Exeter (LLB law), Nottingham Trent (BVC). **Neil McEvoy** (PC) Cllr, Cardiff CC 2008-12, deputy leader. Member, Wales Council for Deaf People. **Brian Morris** (Ukip) Retired. Former accountant and long managerial experience in finance. **Cadan ap Tomos** (LD) Media officer, Welsh Lib Dem group at Welsh Assembly. Welsh translator. Ed: Ysgol Gyfun Penweddig; York (DipHE politics, chairman LD soc).

CONSTITUENCY PROFILE
Traditional solid Labour seat. Brief Conservative gain by Stefan Terlezki, 1983-1987. The urban part of the seat contains some upmarket housing around the cathedral, but is mostly made up of the large council estates of Ely and Caerau on the western edge of the city.

	Electorate	Turnout %	Change from 2010 %
	66,758	65.6	
K Brennan Lab	17,803	40.7	-0.6
J Taghdissian C	11,014	25.2	-4.5
N McEvoy PC	6,096	13.9	+6.9
B Morris Ukip	4,923	11.2	+8.5
C ap Tomos LD	2,069	4.7	-12.8
K Barker Green	1,704	3.9	+2.1
H Jones TUSC	183	0.4	

Change from 2010

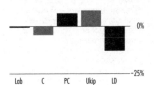

Lab C PC Ukip LD

Carlisle

CONSERVATIVE HOLD

JOHN STEVENSON
BORN Jul 4, 1963
MP 2010-

Amiable, softly-spoken Scot. Independent-minded with measured, low-profile approach. Cllr, Carlisle CC 1999-. Member, communities and local government select cttee 2012-. Chairman, APPG food & drink. Solicitor: Bendles, Carlisle; Dickinson Dees, Newcastle. Well-travelled. Keen golfer and marathon runner. Partner. Ed: Aberdeen GS; Dundee (BA history & politics); Coll of Law, Chester.

CHALLENGERS
Lee Sherriff (Lab) Support worker. Cllr, Carlisle CC 2012-. School gov. Campaigner for families and social care system. Sister of newly-elected Dewsbury MP Paula Sherriff. Three children. Ed: Morton Sch. **Fiona Mills** (Ukip) Accountant, North Cumbria University Hospital. Ukip branch sec. Suspended as

candidate due to allegations of financial irregularities within the party. Ed: Trinity HS. **Helen Davison** (Green) Mental health and well-being project convenor. **Loraine Birchall** (LD) Web developer and IT consultant. Vice-chair, Barrow & Furness LD. Former Amicus rep. Long-term campaigner for women in business.

CONSTITUENCY PROFILE
A marginal Labour-Conservative seat. It was narrowly retained by Labour throughout the 1980s, but fell to the Conservatives on more favourable boundaries in 2010. Carlisle is located in northwest England, near the Scottish border. The seat covers the surrounding rural areas to the south and west, including Dalston and the more affluent dormitory village of Wetheral. Since 2007 the city has been the home of the University of Cumbria, formed from the Cumbrian campuses of the University of Central Lancashire.

	Electorate	Turnout %	Change from 2010 %
	65,827	64.7	
J Stevenson C	18,873	44.3	+5.0
L Sherriff Lab	16,099	37.8	+0.5
F Mills Ukip	5,277	12.4	+10.1
H Davison Green	1,125	2.6	+1.2
L Birchall LD	1,087	2.6	-13.0
A Okam Ind	126	0.3	

Change from 2010

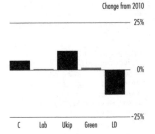

C Lab Ukip Green LD

Carmarthen East & Dinefwr

PLAID CYMRU HOLD

JONATHAN EDWARDS
BORN Apr 26, 1976
MP 2010-

Down to earth, son of working-class councillor and union man. PC shad spokes: Treasury 2010-; BIS 2010-; transport 2010-; communities and local government 2010-; CMS 2010-; Wales 2010-. Cllr, Carmarthen 2001-05; sheriff, Carmarthen 2002. Public affairs officer, Citizens Advice Cymru. Chief of staff to: Rhodri Glyn Thomas AM; Adam Price MP. Strategic adviser, PC National Campaigns Directorate. Member, Welsh affairs select cttee 2010-. Keen cricketer and Swansea City FC fan. Ed: Ysgol Gymraeg Rhydaman; Ysgol Gyfun Maes yr Yrfa; Aberystwyth (BSc history & politics, MSc economic international history).

CHALLENGERS
Calum Higgins (Lab) Barrister in training. Cllr, Carmarthenshire CC

2012-. Vice-chairman WLC group. Representative, mid & west fire and rescue authority 2012-. Local community activist. Choral singer and local rugby supporter. Ed: King's Coll, London (LLB law), Cardiff (MA governance & devolution). **Matthew Paul** (C) Barrister, Civitas Law. Married, two daughters. Ed: Clifton Coll; New Coll, Oxford (BA English); Glamorgan (PgDip law). **Norma Woodward** (Ukip) Nuclear reactor simulations worker, British Nuclear Design and Construction. Former computer programmer, systems analyst and lecturer. Married, two children.

CONSTITUENCY PROFILE
Created in 1997 mostly from the former seat of Carmarthen. Slight boundary changes at the 2010 general election, with the areas around Hermon and Llanpumsaint becoming part of the Carmarthen West and South Pembrokeshire constituency. Plaid Cymru since 2001.

	Electorate	Turnout %	from 2010 %	Change
	55,750	70.7		
J Edwards PC	15,140	38.4	+2.8	
C Higgins Lab	9,541	24.2	-2.3	
M Paul C	8,336	21.2	-1.2	
N Woodward Ukip	4,363	11.1	+7.7	
B Rice Green	1,091	2.8		
S Lloyd-Williams LD	928	2.4	-9.8	

Change from 2010

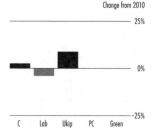

Carmarthen West & Pembrokeshire South

CONSERVATIVE HOLD

SIMON HART
BORN Aug 15, 1963
MP 2010-

Long-serving chief executive of Countryside Alliance before becoming an MP, formerly the director and press officer for the Campaign for Hunting. Member, select cttees: Welsh affairs 2012-; political and constitutional reform 2010-14. Chartered surveyor in Carmarthen and Haverfordwest. Served with Territorial Army for five years. Keen cricketer. Married, one son, one daughter. Ed: Radley Coll; Royal Agricultural Coll, Cirencester (Dip rural estate management).

CHALLENGERS
Delyth Evans (Lab) Management consultant, journalist and speechwriter. AM for Mid and West Wales 2000-03. Ed: Ysgol Gyfun Rhydfelen Sch; Aberystwyth (BA French); Cardiff (MA journalism). **John Atkinson** (Ukip)

Former officer in Royal Marines. Contested Carmarthen East & Dinefwr 2010. **Elwyn Williams** (PC) Cllr, Llangynwr CC 2012-. Mid & West Wales Fire Authority. School governor. **Gary Tapley** (Green) Tutor, Pembrokshire Coll. Ed: Milford Haven GS.

CONSTITUENCY PROFILE
Stretches from the town of Carmarthen in the east, to the southern tip of the Haven Waterway on the Pembrokeshire coast. Includes the traditional seaside resorts of Tenby and Saundersfoot. Laugharne was once home to the poet Dylan Thomas. Historically a marginal seat between the Labour Party and the Conservatives. Nicholas Ainger held the seat for the Labour party from 1997 until 2010, when the Conservative Simon Hart won it back and went on to hold it in 2015. The constituency was created in 1997 from parts of the former marginal seats of Pembroke and Carmarthen.

	Electorate	Turnout %	from 2010 %	Change
	57,755	69.9		
S Hart C	17,626	43.7	+2.6	
D Evans Lab	11,572	28.7	-4.0	
J Atkinson Ukip	4,698	11.6	+8.8	
E Williams PC	4,201	10.4	-0.0	
G Tapley Green	1,290	3.2		
S Runnett LD	963	2.4	-9.7	

Change from 2010

Carshalton & Wallington

LIBERAL DEMOCRAT HOLD

TOM BRAKE
BORN May 6, 1962
MP 2005-

The Liberal Democrats' sole representative left in London. LD shad min: home 2008-10; London & Olympics 2007-10; communities & local government 2006-07. LD shad SoS: transport 2005-06; international development 2003-05. LD whip 2000-04. LD spokes: transport 2002-03; environment, transport, regions, social justice 1997-2001. Member, select cttees: selection 2014-; home affairs 2008-10. Cllr: Sutton BC 1994-98; Hackney BC 1988-90. IT manager. Married, one daughter, one son. Ed: Lycee International, St Germain-en-Laye; Imperial Coll, London (BSc physics).

CHALLENGERS
Matthew Maxwell Scott (C) Corporate writer, BBC. Former speechwriter to CBI dir General. Cllr, Wandsworth BC 2010-14.

Chair, Conservative Group 2011-12. Dir, Wandle Park Regional Park Development Trust 2011-14. Sch governor. Married, two sons. Ed: Eton Coll; Edinburgh (MA politics). **Siobhan Tate** (Lab) Art and design teacher. Married, three children. Ed: Institute of Education (MA art & design). **Bill Main-Ian** (Ukip) Retired police officer. Former security guard to Princess Diana. Ed: Nairn Academy. **Ross Hemingway** (Green) Communications officer, Christian Aid. Ed: Nottingham (management).

CONSTITUENCY PROFILE
Consists of suburbs and housing estates. Many residents commute to London or Croydon. Socially diverse. Home to large Asian and Afro-Caribbean communities. Former solid Conservative seat, the Liberal Democrats gained it in 1997. The only Liberal Democrat seat in Greater London and one of only two in the south of England, the other being North Norfolk.

	Electorate	Turnout %	Change from 2010 %
	69,866	68.2	
T Brake LD	16,603	34.9	-13.4
M Maxwell Scott C	15,093	31.7	-5.2
S Tate Lab	7,150	15.0	+6.3
B Main-Ian Ukip	7,049	14.8	+11.9
R Hemingway Green	1,492	3.1	+2.4
A Dickenson CPA	177	0.4	
R Edmonds NF	49	0.1	

Change from 2010

| LD | C | Lab | Ukip | Green |

Castle Point

CONSERVATIVE HOLD

REBECCA HARRIS
BORN Dec 22, 1967
MP 2010-

A strong advocate of localism. A-lister who was special adviser and researcher to Tim Yeo MP. Special interest in protecting the Green Belt and concerned with chemical storage close to population centres. Cllr, Chichester DC 1999-2003. Member, select cttees: regulatory reform 2012-; BIS 2010-. Marketing dir at Phillimore & Co, publishers of British local history. Married, one son. Ed: The March Sch, Westhampnett; Bedales Sch; LSE (government).

CHALLENGERS
Jamie Huntman (Ukip) Small businessman, timber merchant. Cllr, Essex CC 2013-. **Joe Cooke** (Lab) Diversity & press officer. Carer and former systems analyst. Former Castle Point cllr. Chair, Ford & Associates. Unite TU. Gov, Southend University Hospital.

Trustee, Castle Point Citizens Advice Bureau. Active campaigner. Married, two daughters. Ed: Liverpool John Moores (BSc electrical engineering). **Dominic Ellis** (Green) Freelance videographer & editor. Taught film-making at University of Southampton. Ed: Westcliff HS; Southampton (BA film & English). **Sereena Davey** (LD) Marketing dir and freelance public affairs advisor. NSPCC parly advisor 2002-05. Vice-chairwoman, Elmbridge Community Link 2010-14. Ed: Essex (BA politics; MA international relations).

CONSTITUENCY PROFILE
Traditionally a comfortable Conservative seat falling to Labour in 1997 landslide; however, it was reclaimed by Bob Spink in 2001, a Tory who defected to Ukip in 2008, becoming their first MP. A south Essex seat on the Thames estuary, consisting of Canvey Island and the nearby towns of South Benfleet, Thundersley and Hadleigh.

	Electorate	Turnout %	Change from 2010 %
	68,170	66.7	
R Harris C	23,112	50.9	+6.9
J Huntman Ukip	14,178	31.2	
J Cooke Lab	6,283	13.8	-0.9
D Ellis Green	1,076	2.4	
S Davey LD	801	1.8	-7.6

Change from 2010

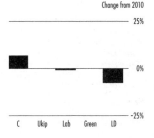

| C | Ukip | Lab | Green | LD |

Ceredigion

MARK WILLIAMS
BORN Mar 24, 1966
MP 2005-

Only Liberal Democrat MP in Wales. LD shad min: IUS 2007-10; Wales 2006-10; education 2005-06. Member, select cttee: Welsh affairs 2005-. Contested: Ceredigion 2001, 00 by-election; Monmouth 1997. Former pres, Ceredigion Liberal Democrats. Member, Welsh LD exec 1991-92. Teacher. NASUWT. Const asst to Geraint Howells MP. Married, three daughters, one son. Ed: Richard Hale Sch, Hertford; Aberystwyth (BSc politics & economics); Plymouth (PGCE primary education).

CHALLENGERS
Mike Parker (PC) Self-employed author and broadcaster. Former stand-up comedian, wrote article in 2001 where he said English racists relocate to Wales to get away from black people. English-born, moved to Ceredigion 2000. **Henrietta**

Hensher (C) Cakemaker. Contested Carmarthen E & Dinefwr Welsh Assembly elections 2011, 07. Ed: Stowe Sch, Royal Agricultural Coll. **Gethin James** (Ukip) Cllr, Ceredigion CC 2004-. Cab member, environmental services & housing 2008-14. Former lorry driver. Married, four children. **Huw Thomas** (Lab) Project manager, Sustrans. Cllr, Cardiff CC 2012-. Ed: Somerville Coll, Oxford (BA music); Aberystwyth (MSc international relations).

CONSTITUENCY PROFILE
Contains two traiditonal university towns: Aberystwyth and Lampeter. Has a long history of Liberal representation, though the main challengers have varied through the years. Was held by Labour from 1966 to 1974. A surprise win saw Cynog Dafis in 1992 gain the seat as a joint Plaid Cymru-Green candidate. The Liberal Democrats regained the seat however in 2005, and built up a substantial majority in 2010.

	Electorate	Turnout %	Change from 2010 %
	54,215	69.0	
M Williams LD	13,414	35.9	-14.2
M Parker PC	10,347	27.7	-0.6
H Hensher C	4,123	11.0	-0.5
G James Ukip	3,829	10.2	+7.7
H Thomas Lab	3,615	9.7	+3.9
D Thompson Green	2,088	5.6	+3.8

Change from 2010

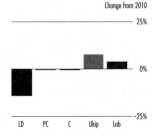

Charnwood

EDWARD ARGAR
BORN Dec 9, 1977
MP 2015-

Management consultant, head of public affairs for Serco. Cllr, Westminster CC 2006-15, cab mem: city management, transport & environment 2010-15; adult social care, health, sports & libraries 2008-10. Contested Oxford E 2010. Trustee to regeneration and environmental charity, Groundwork London. Enjoys walking, reading, films and cricket. Ed: Harvey GS; Oriel Coll, Oxford (BA history; MSt historical research).

CHALLENGERS
Sean Kelly-Walsh (Lab) Executive officer, Leicester Students' Union. Active charity volunteer, teaching English to underpriveledged children in India. Unite. Ed: King's Norton Boys Sch; University of Leicester (BA history & politics). **Lynton Yates** (Ukip) Cllr, Leicestershire CC 2013-, 1989-2001 for Conservatives. Suspended from 2015 election for

saying benefit claimants should be stripped of driving licenses. Ban lifted February 2015. **Simon Sansome** (LD) Adult social service worker. Cllr, Charnwood BC 2014-. Contested Birstall, Leicestershire 2010. Ed: Leicester (BA criminology). **Cathy Duffy** (BNP) Former llr, Charnwood. Contested Charnwood 2010. Lived in Spain.

CONSTITUENCY PROFILE
Charnwood takes parts of three different local authorities covering outer suburbs and the rural hinterland to the north of Leicester. Primarily affluent commuter villages. The large Charnwood Biomedical campus and Loughborough University are key employers in the area. Was created in boundary reforms 1997, when the Conservative Loughborough MP Stephen Dorrell jumped with his key rural voters to Charnwood: the largest part of it was previously in Loughborough. Has been a Tory stronghold with recent BNP strength: they kept their deposit here in 2010.

	Electorate	Turnout %	Change from 2010 %
	77,269	67.6	
E Argar C	28,384	54.3	+4.7
S Kelly-Walsh Lab	11,453	21.9	+2.2
L Yates Ukip	8,330	15.9	+12.6
S Sansome LD	3,605	6.9	-14.6
C Duffy BNP	489	0.9	-4.9

Change from 2010

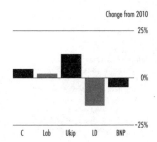

Chatham & Aylesford

CONSERVATIVE HOLD

TRACY CROUCH
BORN Jul 24, 1975
MP 2010-

Affable and well-connected with extensive Conservative party and lobbying experience. Epitome of new Tory, with east London accent. Parly under-sec, sport and tourism 2015-. Select cttees: speakers cttee on electoral commission 2013-; political & constitutional reform 2013-; CMS 2012-. Exec, 1922 cttee 2010-12. Head of public affairs, Aviva. Chief of Staff to: David Davis; Damian Green 2003. Political consultant: Westminster strategy; Harcourt. Researcher for various MPs including Michael Howard 1996-98. Member, Conservative Co-operative movement. Spurs fan. FA qualified coach. Lives with partner. Ed: Folkestone GS; University of Hull (BA law & politics).

CHALLENGERS
Tristan Osborne (Lab) Legal compliance consultant. Youngest Medway cllr 2011-. Member, CIPD, USDAW, Co-operative Party. Recorded criticising Miliband's party strategy. Ed: Kings Sch, Rochester; Durham University (BA natural sciences; MA business management). **Ian Wallace** (Ukip) Former Labour party donor and stalwart to Labour finance and industry group, defected to Ukip 2014. **Thomas Quinton** (LD) Chief operating officer, Hampshire Cultural Trust. Trustee, Pain UK 2014-. Ed: Inns of Court Sch of Law (law bar vocational course); LSE (BA law & social anthropology).

CONSTITUENCY PROFILE
In south east Kent. Chatham is historically associated with the Royal Navy and Chatham Dockyard. The docks have been regenerated for housing and tourism. A Con-Lab marginal, Chatham tending to vote Labour, Aylesford voting Tory. Held by Labour from 1997 but a Conservative gain in 2010.

	Electorate	Turnout %	from 2010 %	Change
	68,625	62.8		
T Crouch C	21,614	50.2	+4.0	
T Osborne Lab	10,159	23.6	-8.7	
I Wallace Ukip	8,581	19.9	+16.9	
T Quinton LD	1,360	3.2	-10.2	
L Balnave Green	1,101	2.6	+1.7	
J Gibson CPA	133	0.3		
I Riddell TUSC	125	0.3		

Change from 2010

[bar chart: C Lab Ukip LD Green, scale -25% to 25%]

Cheadle

CONSERVATIVE GAIN

MARY ROBINSON
BORN Jul 23, 1955
MP 2015-

Accountant. Cllr: South Ribble 2007-15; Penwortham TC 2007-13. Chairman, South Ribble Conservatives 2009-12, deputy 2006-09. Former school governor. Founded accountancy business with husband. Married, four children. Ed: Layton Hill Convent Sch; Preston Poly (accountancy foundation); Lancashire Polytechnic (LLB law)

CHALLENGERS
Mark Hunter (LD) MP, Cheadle 2005-15. Asst gov whip 2010-14. PPS to Nick Clegg 2007-10. LD shad min: transport 2008-10; foreign 2007; OPDM 2005-06. Select cttees: administration 2011-15; selection 2010-14; arms export controls 2008; business & enterprise 2008; business, enterprise regulatory reform 2007-08; trade & industry 2005-07.

Contested Stockport 2001. Cllr: Stockport MBC 1996-06, leader 2002-05; Tameside MBC 1980-89., chair, education 1997-01. Marketing executive, Guardian Media Group. Married, one daughter, one son. Ed: Audenshaw GS, Manchester. **Martin Miller** (Lab) Chief executive, Diocese of Manchester. Former cllr, Stockport MBC 1994-2002, 2003-04. Contested: Cheadle 2005, by-election, 2010; Hazel Grove 2001. **Shaun Hopkins** (Ukip) Former Royal Marines Commando. Telecomms consultant, MOD, ISAF, KFOR. Former milkman.

CONSTITUENCY PROFILE
An affluent commuter area that includes the exclusive suburbs of Cheadle Hulme and Bramhall. Home to several top-performing schools. Was briefly held by the Liberals between 1966 and 1970, then by the Conservatives until 2001 when it was won for the Lib Dems by 33 votes. It was Lib Dem until a 9-point swing sent it the Tories' way in 2015.

	Electorate	Turnout %	from 2010 %	Change
	73,239	72.5		
M Robinson C	22,889	43.1	+2.3	
M Hunter LD	16,436	31.0	-16.1	
M Miller Lab	8,673	16.3	+7.0	
S Hopkins Ukip	4,423	8.3	+5.6	
M Torbitt Ind	390	0.7		
D Carswell Above	208	0.4		
H Bashford IE	76	0.1		

Change from 2010

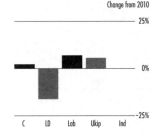

[bar chart: C LD Lab Ukip Ind, scale -25% to 25%]

Chelmsford

CONSERVATIVE HOLD

SIR SIMON BURNS
BORN Sep 6, 1952
MP 1987-

Urbane figure on the Tory left. Unusually for a Conservative, backs Hillary Clinton, owning a watch with her face on it. Used ministerial car while overseeing rail fares, claiming that he wasn't allowed to read ministerial documents on trains. Min: transport 2012-13, resigned to contest dep speaker election; health services 2010-12. Opposition whip 2005-10. Shadow min: health 2004-05; health & education 2001-04. Parly under-sec, health 1996-97. PPS to: Gillian Shepherd 1993-94; Timothy Eggar 1989-1993. Govt whip 1995-96; asst govt whip 1994-5. MP for Chelmsford West 1997-2010. Institute of Directors policy exec. Worked on George McGovern's pres campaign 1972. Divorced, one daughter, one son. Ed: Christ the King Sch, Ghana; Stamford Sch; Worcester Coll, Oxford (BA history).

CHALLENGERS
Chris Vince (Lab) Maths teacher. Cllr, Springfield PC 2012-. Ed: BEng engineering. **Mark Gough** (Ukip) Cllr, Harlow C 2008-12, 2000-04 for Conservatives. **Stephen Robinson** (LD) Comms consultant, Kids Inspire mental health care. Cllr: Essex CC 2012- 1993-2001; Chelmsford CC 2011-; Epping Forest DC 1990-98. Regional organiser, Yes to Fairer Votes. Former dir, RIBA. Contested: Chelmsford 2010; Chelmsford W 2005, 01. Ed: UCLan (BA law & politics).

CONSTITUENCY PROFILE
An affluent, middle-class city with a long association with hi-tech manufacturing since the world's first radio factory in 1899. Even with BAE and a2e, it is now more a commuter town, with many students. Regularly targeted by Lib Dems. The seat was recreated in 2010 after Chelmsford was divided 1997-2010 into rural Chelmsford West and a seat that paired east Chelmsford with rural Maldon.

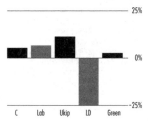

	Electorate	Turnout %	from 2010 %	Change %
	78,580	68.5		
S Burns C	27,732	51.5	+5.4	
C Vince Lab	9,482	17.6	+6.7	
M Gough Ukip	7,652	14.2	+11.4	
S Robinson LD	6,394	11.9	-24.9	
A Thomson Green	1,892	3.5	+2.6	
H Boyle Lib	665	1.2		

Change from 2010

Chelsea & Fulham

CONSERVATIVE HOLD

GREG HANDS
BORN Nov 14, 1965
MP 2005-

Chief secretary to the Treasury 2015-, understands the City. Combative, media-friendly attack dog against Labour. Deputy chief whip 2013-15, formerly asst whip 2011-12. PPS to George Osborne 2010-11. Banker and local campaigner. Shadow Treasury min 2009-10. MP, Hammersmith & Fulham 2005-10. Cllr, Hammersmith & Fulham BC 1998-2006, leader of Con group 1999-2003. Born in New York, has dual nationality, campaigned for Republicans. Married, one daughter, one son. Ed: Dr Challoner's GS, Bucks; Robinson Coll, Cambridge (BA history).

CHALLENGERS
Alexandra Sanderson (Lab) Operations and finance manager, The Money Charity. Previously office manager, Leathwiaite staffing. Former charity worker at Lourdes. Sch governor. Ed: Durham University (BA archaeology). **Simon Bailey** (LD) Management consultant at Deloitte. Previously at Detica. Debate co-ordinator at local school. Ed: Easingwold HS; Durham University (BSc physics). **Adrian Noble** (Ukip) Finance assistant at Royal Hospital for Neuro Disability. **Guy Rubin** (Green) Health researcher Cllr, Hammersmith & Fulham BC 1986-94.

CONSTITUENCY PROFILE
Newly created in 2010 from parts of Kensington & Chelsea and Hammersmith & Fulham, an unassailable Tory fortress of the fantastically wealthy Chelsea and the now expensively gentrified Fulham. High proportion of rented property and one of the highest levels of education: more than half of adults have a degree. Just over 50 per cent were born in the UK, with many European and US-born residents.

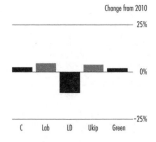

	Electorate	Turnout %	from 2010 %	Change %
	63,478	63.4		
G Hands C	25,322	62.9	+2.5	
A Sanderson Lab	9,300	23.1	+4.6	
S Bailey LD	2,091	5.2	-11.0	
A Noble Ukip	2,039	5.1	+3.9	
G Rubin Green	1,474	3.7	+2.0	

Change from 2010

Cheltenham

ALEX CHALK
BORN Aug 8, 1976
MP 2015-

Barrister at 6KBW College Hill, dealt with terrorism and homicide cases and advises journalists on Elveden and Weeting. Cllr, Hammersmith & Fulham BC 2006-2014, chair planning cttee. Involved in cutting council tax by 20 per cent. Married, two children. Ed: Winchester Coll; Magdalen Coll, Oxford (BA history); City University London (Dip law)

CHALLENGERS
Martin Horwood (LD) MP, Cheltenham 2005-15. Lib Dem Shadow minister, Defra 2006-10. Chair, APPG for tribal peoples. Select cttees: privacy 2011-12; environmental audit 2007-10; CLG 2006-07. Cllr, Vale of White Horse DC 1991-95. Active in Chris Huhne's two leadership campaigns. Contested: London & Westminster 2001; Oxford

East in 1992. Chairman, Union of Liberal Students 1981-82. Career as a marketing consultant. Former director of fundraising, Alzheimer's Soc. Worked for Oxfam. Member, World Development Movement. Married, one daughter and one son. Ed: Cheltenham Coll; Queen's College, Oxford (BA history, pres Oxford Liberal Soc). **Paul Gilbert** (Lab) CEO and founder LBC Wise Counsel. Solicitor. Vice Chairman, trustee to LawWorks. Married, two daughters. **Christina Simmonds** (Ukip) Business consultant.

CONSTITUENCY PROFILE
An affluent spa town, associated with racing and the Ladies' College, home to several light industrial and financial companies as well as GCHQ and Ucas. Held by the Conservatives until 1992 when Nigel Jones defeated the Tory lawyer John Taylor in a controversial election. Jones was attacked at his constituency surgery in 2000 by a man with a samurai sword, killing his assistant.

	Electorate	Turnout %	Change from 2010 %
	77,286	69.5	
A Chalk C	24,790	46.1	+5.0
M Horwood LD	18,274	34.0	-16.5
P Gilbert Lab	3,902	7.3	+2.1
C Simmonds Ukip	3,808	7.1	+4.8
A Van Coevorden Green	2,689	5.0	
R Lupson-Darnell Ind	272	0.5	

Change from 2010

25%

0%

-25%

C   LD   Lab   Ukip   Green

Chesham & Amersham

CHERYL GILLAN
BORN Apr 21, 1952
MP 1992-

Strong opponent of HS2, planned to run through constituency –admitted frustration at toeing the party line on it in govt. SoS for Wales 2010-12. Appointed to Council of Europe. Shadow SoS, Wales 2005-10. Shadow minister: home 2003-05; FCO 1998-01; trade & industry 1997-98. Opposition whip 2001-03. Parly under-sec, education & employment 1995-97. PPS to Lord Privy Seal 1994-95. Claimed dog food on expenses. Senior marketing consultant, Ernst & Young; marketing director, Kidsons Impey 1991-93. Married. Ed: Cheltenham Ladies Coll; Coll of Law.

CHALLENGERS
Alan Stevens (Ukip) Cllr, Bucks CC 2013-. Contituency chairman 2010-. Contested: Chesham & Amersham 2010; South East England Euro

election 2014. Former CEO, Central Railway project to develop UK-Europe line through Great Central route. Married, two children. Ed: Cambridge (BA history & law), INSEAD (MBA). **Ben Davies** (Lab) Comms adviser, IPPF, previously Amnesty International. Previously editor, newstatesman.com; BBC political journalist. Ed: London (BA history of art), Cardiff (PgDip journalism). **Kirsten Johnson** (LD) Classical pianist, has recorded 13 solo albums. US-born, moved to UK 1994. Married, three daughers. Ed: Hochschule für Musik, Vienna (piano); University of Missouri – Kansas City (PhD music)

CONSTITUENCY PROFILE
An affluent, safe Conservative seat, held by the party since its creation in 1974, normally with more than 50 per cent of the vote. Towns and villages set in the Chiltern hills, in the London commuter belt as the furthest outposts of the London Underground in zone 9. HS2 is a

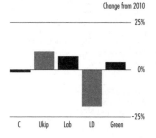

	Electorate	Turnout %	Change from 2010 %
	73,423	71.8	
C Gillan C	31,138	59.1	-1.3
A Stevens Ukip	7,218	13.7	+9.6
B Davies Lab	6,712	12.7	+7.1
K Johnson LD	4,761	9.0	-19.5
G Walker Green	2,902	5.5	+4.0

Change from 2010

25%

0%

-25%

C   Ukip   Lab   LD   Green

Chester, City of

LABOUR GAIN

CHRISTIAN MATHESON
BORN Jan 2, 1968
MP 2015-

Won with a majority of 93 after two recounts, the third-smallest in 2015. Unite HR manager and officer. Former manager in the electricity industry. Criticised in 2013 after it was revealed that he was Tom Blenkinsop's landlord for property he rented on expenses. Married, two daughters. Ed: Manchester GS; LSE (BSc economics & politics).

CHALLENGERS
Stephen Mosley (C) MP for City of Chester 2010-15. Member, science & technology select cttee 2010-15. Cllr: Cheshire CC 2005-09; Chester CC 2000-09, dep leader 2007-09. Member, Cheshire Fire & Rescue Authority. Dir: Severn Industrial Estates; Weblong IT consultancy. IBM. Has family and business links to Malawi. Married, one daughter, one son. Ed: King Edward's Sch,

Birmingham; Nottingham (BSc chemistry). **Steve Ingram** (Ukip) Runs own cleaning business. Former Labour supporter. Married, three children. **Bob Thompson** (LD) Retired HR director at INEOS ChlorVinyls. Director of Chester & District Housing. Trustee of Hoole Community Centre. Cllr, Cheshire West & Chester C 2002-15. Contested Eddisbury 2010. Partner, one son, one daughter. Ed: King's Sch, Chester; Nottingham (BSc industrial economics).

CONSTITUENCY PROFILE
Historic walled city, which became an upmarket residential area for upper classes fleeing the industrial sprawl of Manchester and Liverpool during the industrial revolution. Like much of Cheshire, remains relatively affluent; however, Labour support in housing estates makes it a marginal seat. Tory for most of the 20th century, Chester fell to Labour in the 1997 landslide, unseating Gyles Brandreth. Changed hands in 2010 and 2015.

		Electorate	Turnout %	from 2010 %	Change
		72,269	70.8		
C Matheson	Lab	22,118	43.2	+8.2	
S Mosley	C	22,025	43.1	+2.5	
S Ingram	Ukip	4,148	8.1	+5.5	
B Thompson	LD	2,870	5.6	-13.5	

Change from 2010

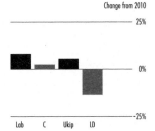

Lab   C   Ukip   LD

Chesterfield

LABOUR HOLD

TOBY PERKINS
BORN Aug 12, 1970
MP 2010-

Great-grandson of A. P. Herbert, the last MP for Oxford University. Shadow min: small businesses 2011-; children & families 2010-11. Select cttees: Statutory Instruments 2010-; Cllr, Chesterfield BC 2003-10. Founded rugby clothing company, Club Rugby. Goalkeeper for parly football team. Recruitment industry, IT sales, CCS Media. Youth Training Scheme, Sheffield computer firm. Founder and chair, Chesterfield flood victims appeal. Unite. Qualified rugby coach, former Chesterfield & Derbyshire rugby union player. Married, one daughter, one son. Ed: Trinity Sch, Leamington; Silverdale Sch, Sheffield.

CHALLENGERS
Mark Vivis (C) Lawyer. Intellectual property enforcement manager for Sony. Cllr, Chiltern DC 2011-.

Works with Prince's Trust. Former parly adviser to Cheryl Gillan. Ed: Chesham GS; Exeter (BA French & German); LSE (MSc EU govt); Coll of Law. **Stuart Yeowart** (Ukip) Driving instructor. Former police officer. Ed: Tupton Hall Sch. **Julia Cambridge** (LD) Parly spokesperson for Chesterfield LDs and freelance fashion designer. Lecturer for small businesses. Age UK care support volunteer. Chair, environmentalist preservation group. Born in Cyprus, where father was stationed with RAF. Married, one daughter. Ed: RCA (BA; MA design).

CONSTITUENCY PROFILE
A compact urban seat, mostly surrounded by the Derbyshire NE constituency. Historically a Labour seat, the Liberals built up strength here during the 1980s when the seat was represented by Tony Benn. When Benn retired in 2001 to "spend more time in politics" the Lib Dems won and Paul Holmes held the seat until 2010.

		Electorate	Turnout %	from 2010 %	Change
		72,078	63.2		
T Perkins	Lab	21,829	47.9	+8.9	
M Vivis	C	8,231	18.1	+2.3	
S Yeowart	Ukip	7,523	16.5	+13.4	
J Cambridge	LD	6,301	13.8	-24.0	
M Genn	Green	1,352	3.0	+1.7	
M Whale	TUSC	202	0.4		
T Holgate	Peace	129	0.3		

Change from 2010

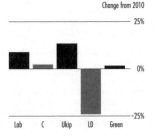

Lab   C   Ukip   LD   Green

Chichester

ANDREW TYRIE
BORN Jan 15, 1957
MP 1997-

Experienced politician from his days as special adviser to John Major and Nigel Lawson. Select cttees: chairman, Treasury 2010-, banking standards 2012-, tax law 2010; member: liason 2010-, reform of HoL 2009-10, justice 2007-10, const affairs 2005-07, conventions 2006. Shadow: paymaster gen 2004-05; financial sec 2003-04. Liberal Conservative interested in constitutional reform and human rights; campaigner against rendition, voted against Iraq war. Senior economist, European Bank for Reconstruction & Development. BP. Fellow Nuffield Coll, Oxford. Ed: Felstead Sch; Trinity Coll, Oxford (BA PPE); Coll of Europe (Dip economics); Wolfson Coll, Cambridge (MPhil int relations).

CHALLENGERS
Andrew Moncrieff (Ukip) Owns irrigation business. Works in Ukip's policy unit. Worked in City and lectured finance, MBA. **Mark Farwell** (Lab) Sociology lecturer, Southampton Solent University. Chairman, Southampton Solent UCU. Secretary of Portsmouth Supporters' Trust. Left school at 15 to train as engineer. Ed: South Downs Coll; Essex (BA government & sociology). **Andrew Smith** (LD) Computer programmer and analyst. Cllr: Chichester DC 1991-, leader 2005-06; West Sussex CC 2005-13. Elected representative on WSCC Pension Panel. Sussex Police Authority 2009-12.

CONSTITUENCY PROFILE
An ancient cathedral city, tourist centre, known for sailing and yachting – boat building is a major local industry. The rest of the seat takes in a large expanse of the rolling South Downs National Park, with the only other significant centre of population being the small market town of Midhurst. Conservative since 1924.

	Electorate	Turnout %	Change from 2010 %
	83,575	68.4	
A Tyrie C	32,953	57.7	+2.3
A Moncrieff Ukip	8,540	15.0	+8.1
M Farwell Lab	6,933	12.1	+1.7
A Smith LD	4,865	8.5	-18.9
J Richmond Green	3,742	6.6	
A Emerson Patria	106	0.2	

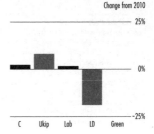

Change from 2010

Chingford & Woodford Green

IAIN DUNCAN SMITH
BORN Apr 9, 1954
MP 1992-

The quiet man who reinvented himself as "IDS", the voice of the Conservatives' social conscience, after a disastrous period as leader of the opposition 2001-03. Unclear whether his much-heralded Universal Credit reform has been a success. Had more influence after leadership than during; influenced party's thinking as chairman of Centre for Social Justice 2005-10. Rewarded with cabinet position (SoS work & pensions 2010-) also intended to placate Tory right. Shadow SoS: defence 1999-2001; W&P 1997-99. Novelist, received scathing critical reviews. Lieutenant in Scots Guards then career at GEC-Marconi, property and printing. Sent children to private schools, including Eton. Married, two daughters, two sons. Ed: RMA Sandhurst; Universita per Stranieri, Perugia; HMS Conway Cadet Sch.

CHALLENGERS
Bilal Mahmood (Lab) Corporate finance solicitor. Treasurer, Walthamstow CLP. Member, Co-op Party, GMB and Community Union. Regional director, Mosaic. Former trustee governor of English-Speaking Union. Immigrant parents. Ed: Nottingham (BA law & politics); Virginia Law Sch. **Freddy Vachha** (Ukip) Indian-born businessman, three-time Mensa chess champion. **Anne Crook** (LD) Primary school teacher. Volunteer adviser, Loughton CAB. Two children. Ed: City University London (LLB law).

CONSTITUENCY PROFILE
A northeast London seat straddling the boundary between Waltham Forest and Redbridge. This is white, owner-occupied Tory suburbia on the edge of Epping Forest and alongside the Chingford reservoirs in the Lee Valley. A safe Conservative seat associated with IDS and his Chingford predecessor Norman Tebbit.

	Electorate	Turnout %	Change from 2010 %
	66,691	65.7	
I Duncan Smith C	20,999	47.9	-4.8
B Mahmood Lab	12,613	28.8	+6.1
F Vachha Ukip	5,644	12.9	+10.3
A Crook LD	2,400	5.5	-11.3
R Tully Green	1,854	4.2	+2.7
L Hockey TUSC	241	0.6	
L McKenzie Class War	53	0.1	

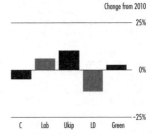

Change from 2010

Chippenham

CONSERVATIVE GAIN

MICHELLE DONELAN
BORN Apr 08, 1984
MP 2010-

Marketing professional, AETN UK, previously worked internationally. Made first speech at Conservative Party Conference aged 15, a year younger than William Hague. Trustee of local Help Victims of Domestic Violence charity. Volunteer, Bradford on Avon Emergency Community. Contested Wentworth & Dearne 2010. Ed: County HS, Leftwich; University of York (BA history & politics).

CHALLENGERS
Duncan Hames (LD) MP for Chippenham 2010-15. PPS to: Nick Clegg 2012-13; Sarah Teather 2010-12. Member, political & constitutional reform select cttee 2014-15. Contested: Westbury 2005, Watford 2001, Tottenham 2000. Cllr, West Wiltshire DC 2003-07. Owner and director, Chippenham Consultants financial advisers. Board member: Great Britain-China Centre; SW England Regional Development Agency. Management consultant, Deloitte. VP, Lib Dem Youth & Students 2000-02. Keen runner. Married to Jo Swinson, one son. Ed: Watford Boys GS; New Coll, Oxford (BA PPE). **Julia Reid** (Ukip) MEP for SW England 2014-. Research biochemist. Ed: Bath (BSc biochemistry; PhD pharmacology). **Andy Newman** (Lab) Telecoms engineer, Colston Engineering. Branch secretary, GMB. Married, two sons. Ed: King Edward's Sch, Bath; Bath Tech Coll; UWE (BEng engineering); Kellogg Coll, Oxford (MSc software & systems engineering).

CONSTITUENCY PROFILE
Compared with the sprawling, rural Conservative seats that dominate Wiltshire, Chippenham is tightly drawn around towns that recently voted Lib Dem. Created for the 2010 election, thanks to the growing electorate of Wiltshire.

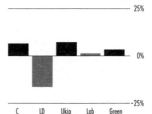

	Electorate	Turnout %	Change from 2010 %
	74,225	74.6	
M Donelan C	26,354	47.6	+6.5
D Hames LD	16,278	29.4	-16.4
J Reid Ukip	5,884	10.6	+7.2
A Newman Lab	4,561	8.2	+1.3
T Johnston Green	2,330	4.2	+3.4

Change from 2010

C LD Ukip Lab Green

Chipping Barnet

CONSERVATIVE HOLD

THERESA VILLIERS
BORN Mar 5, 1968
MP 2005-

After promotion in shadow cabinet, her position was given to Philip Hammond in the first coalition cabinet. Joined cabinet as SoS for Northern Ireland 2012-. Min, transport 2010-. Shadow SoS, transport 2007-10. Shadow chief sec to treasury 2005-07. Member, environmental audit select cttee 2005-06. Eurosceptic MEP, London 1999-2005. Former law lecturer, King's Coll London. Barrister, Lincoln's Inn. Divorced. Ed: Francis Holland Sch; University of Bristol (LLB); Jesus Coll, Oxford (BCL).

CHALLENGERS
Amy Trevethan (Lab) Sales assistant, Clark's. Cllr, Barnet BC 2014-. Unite, Unison, Co-op party, Fabians. Previously played for Queen's Park Rangers Ladies FC. Ed: Queen Elizabeth's Girls' Sch; Oxford (BA history, scholarship). **Victor Kaye** (Ukip) MD, Gadabouts Travel online travel agency. Former lecturer in travel & tourism, part of team that designed BTEC. FRSA. Contested Chipping Barnet 2005. Ed: BA politics, history & economics. **A M Poppy** (Green) Communications professional. Former peaceworker. **Marisha Ray** (LD) Specialist adviser at Whittington Hospital NHS Trust. Cllr, Islington BC 2002-10. Contested Croydon N 2012. Previously academic and industrial researcher. Ed: Trinity Coll, Cambridge (BSc; PhD physics).

CONSTITUENCY PROFILE
A north London seat — High Barnet is the last stop on the Northern Line. Has affluent residential streets of 1930s semi-detached houses, some deprived areas. The west and north of the seat give way to fields. Totteridge Lane has some of the highest house prices in the capital and Friern Village in the south is popular with minor celebrities. Tory since 1950.

	Electorate	Turnout %	Change from 2010 %
	77,853	68.1	
T Villiers C	25,759	48.6	-0.2
A Trevethan Lab	18,103	34.2	+8.9
V Kaye Ukip	4,151	7.8	+5.0
A M Poppy Green	2,501	4.7	+2.7
M Ray LD	2,381	4.5	-15.7
M Akhavan ND	118	0.2	

Change from 2010

C Lab Ukip Green LD

Chorley

LABOUR HOLD

LINDSAY HOYLE
BORN Jun 10, 1957
MP 1997-

Plain-speaking Lancastrian from party's traditional left, son of former Labour MP and peer Lord Hoyle. Chairman of ways and means and deputy speaker 2010-, won acclaim for "stealing the show" at 2013 budget. Parly asst to Beverley Hughes 2008-10. Select cttees: chair, panel of chairs 2010-; member, finance & services 2010-, BIS/ trade & industry 1998-2010, Euro scrutiny 2005-10, quadripartite 2006-07. Chair, APPG Gibraltar, British Virgin Islands. Cllr: Chorley BC 1980-98, deputy leader 1994-97, mayor 1997-98; Adlington TC 1980-98. Shop steward. Company director. Amicus. Wrote to BAA suggesting Heathrow be renamed Diana, Princess of Wales Airport after her death in 1997. Divorced, remarried, two daughters. Ed: Lords Coll, Bolton; Horwich Coll; Bolton TIC (City & Guilds construction).

CHALLENGERS
Rob Loughenbury (C) Senior communications consultant. Conservative Field Campaign Manager 2011-13. Co-ordinator of volunteers in Boris Johnson's mayoral campaign 2008. Actively involved in local charities: Derian House, Child Action North West. Chorley RUFC. Single parent, three children. Ed: Durham (BSc geography; MA research methods; PhD human geography). **Mark Smith** (Ukip) Runs electrical equipment manufacturing business. Married, four children.

CONSTITUENCY PROFILE
Divided between Chorley, a former cotton industry centre, and its more Conservative hinterland. A key marginal between Labour and the Tories, Chorley had been one of the more reliable indicators in the country, won by the party that went on to form the government in every election since 1964. Labours success at holding the seat in 2010 left Dartford as the best bellwether.

	Electorate	Turnout %	from 2010 % Change
	74,679	69.2	
L Hoyle Lab	23,322	45.1	+1.9
R Loughenbury C	18,792	36.3	-1.7
M Smith Ukip	6,995	13.5	+9.5
S Fenn LD	1,354	2.6	-11.4
A Straw Green	1,111	2.1	
A Maudsley Ind	138	0.3	-0.5

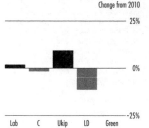

Change from 2010

Christchurch

CONSERVATIVE HOLD

CHRISTOPHER CHOPE
BORN: May 19, 1947
MP: 1997-; 1983-1992;

Abrasive right-winger, a Thatcherite survivor and keeper of her flame; honorary VP and former chairman of Thatcherite Conservative Way Forward group. Climate change sceptic. Referred to HoC staff as "servants" in debate. Outspoken critic of John Bercow as speaker. Shadow minister: Defra 2003-05, 1997-98; transport 2002-03; trade & industry 1998-99 . Parly under-sec: transport 1990-2; environment 1986-90. PPS to Peter Brooke 1986. MP for Southampton Itchen 1983-92. Barrister. Long-serving Cllr, Wandsworth BC, leader 1979-83. Consultant, Ernst & Young. Married, one daughter, one son. Ed: Marlborough Coll; University of St Andrews (LLB law).

CHALLENGERS
Robin Grey (Ukip) Runs own business. Former ground engineer, Qantas and social worker. Born in Lancashire, grew up in Australia. Married, three children. Ed: Southampton (social work). **Andrew Satherley** (Lab) Market access consultant, GfK market research. Ed: Highcliffe Comp; York (BSc health economics). **Andy Canning** (LD) Former economist for HSBC and Barclays. Cllr: Dorchester TC 1999-, mayor 2012-13; West Dorset DC 2003-. Chairman, West Dorset LDs. Contested: Dorset S 2001; Dorset PCC election 2012. Married, one son.

CONSTITUENCY PROFILE
An affluent retirement town between Bournemouth and the New Forest — with the highest proportion of over 60s of any seat in Great Britain. The seat is normally safely Conservative, but was briefly held by the Lib Dems after their 1993 by-election victory. Narrowly regained by the Tories in 1997, it has returned to form as a safe Tory seat.

	Electorate	Turnout %	from 2010 % Change
	69,302	71.7	
C Chope C	28,887	58.1	+1.7
R Grey Ukip	10,663	21.5	+13.0
A Satherley Lab	4,745	9.6	-0.3
A Canning LD	3,263	6.6	-18.7
S Dunn Green	2,149	4.3	

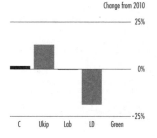

Change from 2010

Cities of London & Westminster

CONSERVATIVE HOLD

MARK FIELD
BORN Oct 6, 1964
MP 2001-

Cheerful rebel. Served as shadow culture minister (2005-06) but demoted after marriage-ending affair with Elizabeth Truss, now SoS at Defra. Shadow finance sec to the treasury 2005; Shadow minister for London 2003-05; opp whip 2003-04. Select cttees: intelligence 2010-15; procedure 2008-10; Crossrail 2007; const affairs 2003-04. Contested Enfield N 1997. Cllr, Kensington & Chelsea BC 1994-2002. Solicitor. Director, Kellyfield Consulting legal recruitment. Contributor to political panel shows, including *Westminster Hour*. Freeman, City of London. Divorced, remarried, one son, one daughter. Ed: Reading Sch; St Edmund Hall, Oxford, (BA law); Chester Coll of Law.

CHALLENGERS
Nik Slingsby (Lab) Lawyer, specialising in toy and product safety. Former chair, Westminster S CLP. Worked in Beijing. Ed: SOAS (BA Chinese). **Belinda Brooks-Gordon** (LD) University reader in psychology and social policy at Birkbeck, London. Former lecturer, Open University. Left school at 16, returned to education after having children. Cllr, Cambs CC 2009-13. Contested: Suffolk W 2010; E of England, Euro election 2014. Ed: Middlesex (BSc); Churchill Coll, Cambridge (MPhil; PhD psychology).

CONSTITUENCY PROFILE
The core of London, with many significant landmarks, parks, shopping areas, financial HQs and organs of state. Despite a weekday population of hundreds of thousands, the City of London has relatively few residents, mostly concentrated in the Barbican and Golden Lane estates. Instead the bulk live in Westminster, with some of the most expensive (and solidly Tory) residential real estate in the UK.

	Electorate	Turnout %	Change from 2010 %
	60,992	59.3	
M Field C	19,570	54.1	+1.9
N Slingsby Lab	9,899	27.4	+5.2
B Brooks-Gordon LD	2,521	7.0	-13.5
H Small Green	1,953	5.4	+3.3
R Stephenson Ukip	1,894	5.2	+3.4
E Desforges CSA	160	0.4	
J McLachlan CPA	129	0.4	
A Clifford Class War	59	0.2	

Change from 2010

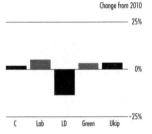

Clacton

UKIP HOLD

DOUGLAS CARSWELL
BORN Apr 3, 1971
MP 2005-

Anti-establishment maverick, defected from Conservative party 2014, easily winning 2014 by-election for Ukip. More moderate than his Ukip leader, unafraid to rebel. Refused to back Nigel Farage's return as party leader. Turned down £650,000 of public funding entitled to Ukip in parliament. Select cttees: public accounts 2009-10; CSF 2007-10; education 2006-07; human rights 2005-08. MP for Harwich 2005-10. Waged ultimately successful campaign to bring down Michael Martin as Speaker. Contested Sedgefield 2001. Blogger, author and media pundit. Commercial television then fund management (Invesco). Grew up in Africa. Son of Wilson Carswell, one of the first doctors to identify HIV in Africa. Married, one daughter. Ed: Charterhouse; UEA (BA history); King's Coll London (MA history).

CHALLENGERS
Giles Watling (C) Actor and theatre director, best known for playing vicar Oswald in *Bread*. Contested Clacton 2014 by-election. Cllr, Tendring DC 2007-. Active fund-raiser providing opportunity for disabled children to sail. Keen sailor himself, owns two yachts. Married, two daughters. **Tim Young** (Lab) Cllr, Colchester BC 1992-. Leader, Colchester Labour Group. Contested Clacton 2014. Ed: Clacton County HS. **Chris Southall** (Green) Engineer. Co-ordinator, Tendring Green party. Contested Clacton 2014, 10. Partner. Two children.

CONSTITUENCY PROFILE
A coastal seat, in which declining tourist destinations have turned into retirement ones. Some 30.2 per cent of locals are over 65. In 2014 Douglas Carswell defected to Ukip and resigned to cause a by-election, the first parliamentary defector to test his switch in a by-election since 1982. Previously held by Tories and allies since the 1930s.

	Electorate	Turnout %	Change from 2010 %
	68,936	64.1	
D Carswell Ukip	19,642	44.4	
G Watling C	16,205	36.7	-16.4
T Young Lab	6,364	14.4	-10.7
C Southall Green	1,184	2.7	+1.4
D Grace LD	812	1.8	-11.1

Change from 2010

Cleethorpes

CONSERVATIVE HOLD

MARTIN VICKERS
BORN Sep 13, 1950
MP 2010-

Cleethorpes-born long-serving councillor. Select cttees: transport 2013-; procedure 2012-. Contested Cleethorpes 2005. Cllr: NE Lincolnshire C 1999-2011; Great Grimsby BC 1980-94. Member, regional transport boards Yorkshire, Hull & Humber. Constituency agent to Edward Leigh MP. Printing industry, retail trade. Religion and railways buff. Lifelong Grimsby Town FC supporter. Went to university as mature part-time student, graduating in 2004. Church warden. Married, one daughter. Ed: Havelock Comp, Grimsby; University of Lincoln (BA politics).

CHALLENGERS
Peter Keith (Lab) Head of Sales at Asset International publisher. Former international 1,500m runner. Grew up in Belfast during the Troubles. Married to former MP Shona McIsaac. Ed: University of Newcastle (BA economics & politics). **Stephen Harness** (Ukip) Cllr, North East Lincolnshire C 2013-. Worked at Lindsey Oil Refinery. Contested Cleethorpes 2010. Married, two daughters. **Roy Horobin** (LD) History teacher. Trustee of Great Grimsby Ice Factory Trust. Chairman, Grimsby and Cleethorpes Lib Dems.

CONSTITUENCY PROFILE
A somewhat misleadingly named seat — it includes Cleethorpes, the seaside town south of Grimsby, but most of the seat is made up of territory north of Grimsby, curling round the southern bank of the Humber estuary to include the port of Barton-on-Humber and Immingham. The seat is home to two huge oil refineries just north of Immingham and Humberside airport. Cleethorpes was won by Labour on its creation in 1997 and taken by the Tories in 2010.

	Electorate	Turnout %	from 2010 % Change
	70,514	63.9	
M Vickers C	21,026	46.6	+4.5
P Keith Lab	13,133	29.1	-3.4
S Harness Ukip	8,356	18.5	+11.4
R Horobin LD	1,346	3.0	-15.2
C Thornton Green	1,013	2.3	
M Morland TUSC	215	0.5	

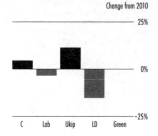

Change from 2010

C　Lab　Ukip　LD　Green

Clwyd South

LABOUR HOLD

SUSAN JONES
BORN Jun 1, 1968
MP 2010-

Seasoned charity fundraiser. Opposition whip 2011-15. PPS to Harriet Harman 2010-11. Member, Welsh affairs select cttee. Cllr, Southwark 2006-2009. Contested Surrey Heath 1997. Fundraiser, Housing Justice and medical research and church charities. Member of Institute of Fundraising. Labour Campaign for Electoral Reform. Christian Socialist. Unite. Speaks Welsh and Japanese; took parliamentary oath in Welsh and taught English in Japan for several years. Classical music enthusiast. Ed: Grango Comp; Ruabon Sch; University of Bristol (BA English, chair Labour club); Cardiff (MA English language).

CHALLENGERS
David Nicholls (C) Barrister, 11 Stone Buildings, specialises in insolvency and real estate. Cllr, Kensington & Chelsea BC 2014-. President, European Young Bar Association 2013-14. Board of dirs, American Counsel Assoc. Chairman, Young Barristers' Cttee 2012. Ed: Haberdashers' Aske's Boys' Sch; Keble Coll, Oxford (BA theology). **Mandy Jones** (Ukip) Small businesswoman. Teacher. Former shepherd, farm contractor. Ed: Llysfasi Coll. **Mabon ap Gwynfor** (PC) Former press officer to Simon Thomas AM and Elin Jones AM. Contested Brecon & Radnor 2005, Welsh Ass 2011 election. PC National Executive, 2010, 08, 05. Founder and chair NWHA. Married, one son. Ed: Bangor University (BA history, pres SU).

CONSTITUENCY PROFILE
A long rural seat, heading westwards into Wales from the English border. The west is remote and largely agricultural, the east an area once dominated by coal mining and steelworks. Mining heritage of the area to the south-west of Wrexham means the seat leans to Labour.

	Electorate	Turnout %	from 2010 % Change
	54,996	63.8	
S Jones Lab	13,051	37.2	-1.2
D Nicholls C	10,649	30.4	+0.2
M Jones Ukip	5,480	15.6	+13.3
M ap Gwynfor PC	3,620	10.3	+1.7
B Roberts LD	1,349	3.9	-13.4
D Rees Green	915	2.6	

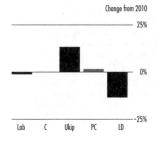

Change from 2010

Lab　C　Ukip　PC　LD

Clwyd West

CONSERVATIVE HOLD

DAVID JONES
BORN Mar 22, 1952
MP 2005-

Affable and ambitious. Secretary of State for Wales 2012-14, first Tory SoS for Wales representing a Welsh constituency since Nicholas Edwards in 1987. Parly under-sec, Wales 2010-12. Shadow min for Wales 2006-10. Select cttee: Welsh Affairs 2005-10. AM for North Wales 2002-03. Contested: Chester 2001, Conwy 1997; Welsh Assembly elections 1999. Chairman, Conwy Conservative Assoc 1998-99. Solicitor, senior partner David Jones & Co, Llandudno. Honorary life fellow, Cancer Research UK. Declared Freemason. Married, two sons. Ed: Ruabon GS; UCL (LLB Law); Coll of Law, Chester.

CHALLENGERS
Gareth Thomas (Lab) Barrister. MP for Clwyd West 1997-2005, prevented from standing in 2010 by an all-woman shortlist. PPS to Paul Murphy 2001-05. Member, Welsh affairs and human rights select cttees. Cllr, Flintshire CC 1995-1997. Ed: Rock Ferry HS; Aberystwyth (LLB law). **Warwick Nicholson** (Ukip) Former police inspector. Contested Clwyd West 2010, 05; Welsh Ass election, 2007; North Wales PCC 2012. Married, seven children. **Marc Jones** (PC) Former BBC, HTV journalist and producer; was editor of *Golwg*. Cllr, Wrexham BC 2008-12. Chairman, Caia Park Community Council. Trade unionist, treasurer of Undeb. Two children.

CONSTITUENCY PROFILE
A mixture of rural villages and coastal retirement towns, Clwyd West would be solid Tory territory in England. Even in Wales it is mostly Conservative, falling to Labour only in the 1997 and 2001 landslides. Contains the large seaside resort of Colwyn Bay, the second biggest town in north Wales and an important commercial hub in a rural hinterland.

	Electorate	Turnout %	Change from 2010 %
	58,657	64.8	
D Jones C	16,463	43.3	+1.8
G Thomas Lab	9,733	25.6	+0.9
W Nicholson Ukip	4,988	13.1	+10.9
M Jones PC	4,651	12.2	-3.2
S Lesiter-Burgess LD	1,387	3.7	-11.6
B English Soc Lab	612	1.6	
R Jepson Above	194	0.5	

Change from 2010

(bar chart with categories: C, Lab, Ukip, PC, LD)

Coatbridge, Chryston & Bellshill

SNP GAIN

PHIL BOSWELL
BORN Jul 23, 1963
MP 2015-

Knowledgeable about oil industry. Quantity surveyor and contracts engineer with Phillips 66, previously with Premier Oil, Shell, BP. Married, three children Ed: Glasgow Caledonian University (BSc quantity surveying); University of Reading (Dip arbitration)

CHALLENGERS
Tom Clarke (Lab) MP 1982-2015. Veteran backbencher who championed disabled rights. Minister: film & tourism 1997-98. Shadow: SoS for int devt 1993-4, Scotland 1992-3; Min for disabled rights 1995-97, personal social services 1987-92. Select cttees: standards & privileges 2010-; draft House of Lords reform bill 2011-13; administration 2008-10; health 1991-92; Scottish affairs 1982-87. MP Coatbridge & Chryston 1997-2005; Monklands West 1983-97; Coatbridge & Airdrie 1982-83. Cllr: Monklands DC 1974-82; Coatbridge TC 1964-74. JP 1972. GMB. President, Convention of Scottish Local Authorities 1978-80. Former asst director, Scottish Film Council. Entered Cannes Film Festival with amateur short film in 1973. CBE 1980. Ed: Columba HS, Coatbridge; Scottish Coll of Commerce. **Mhairi Fraser** (C) Scottish Affairs director, Con Future Women. Former parly asst and political researcher. Ed: Bangkok Patana Sch; Edinburgh (MA English).

CONSTITUENCY PROFILE
A gritty working-class seat to the east of Glasgow. Formerly the industrial heartland of Scotland, built on iron and coal and immigration. Went into decline after exhaustion of mines, but remains an industrial area. One of the country's safest Labour seats until 2015, when it registered a 36 percentage point swing to the SNP.

	Electorate	Turnout %	Change from 2010 %
	73,813	68.7	
P Boswell SNP	28,696	56.6	+39.8
T Clarke Lab	17,195	33.9	-32.7
M Fraser C	3,209	6.3	-1.8
S Cairns Ukip	1,049	2.1	
R Simpson LD	549	1.1	-7.4

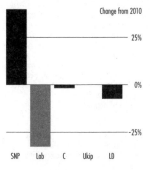

Change from 2010

(bar chart with categories: SNP, Lab, C, Ukip, LD)

Colchester

CONSERVATIVE GAIN

WILL QUINCE
BORN Dec 27, 1982
MP 2015-

Solicitor, Thompson Smith and Puxon. Cllr: Colchester BC 2011-, leader, Conservative group; East Herts DC 2007-09. Contested Colchester 2010. Grassroots Trustee, Colchester & Tendring 2011-. Married, one daughter. Ed: Aberystwyth University (LLB law), Bristol UWE (PgDip legal practice).

CHALLENGERS
Sir Bob Russell (LD) 1997-2015. Low-profile backbencher who prided himself on his attendance record in parliament. Lib Dem shadow minister: defence 2005-10. LD whip 2005-10, 1999-2002. LD spokesman: sport 1999-2005; home, legal affairs 1997-99. Select cttees: defence 2011-; Parly standards authority 2010-; administration 2010-11; armed forces bill 2011, 2005-06; regulatory reform 2005-06; home affairs 1998-10. Cllr,

Colchester BC 1971-2002, leader 1987-91, mayor 1986-87. Contested: Colchester 1979, Sudbury 1974. Journalist, publicity officer. Married, two daughters (one deceased), two sons. Ed: St Helena Boys Sch, Colchester; NE Tech Coll (NCTJ proficiency cert). **Jordan Newell** (Lab) Senior parly asst to Hazel Blears, previously Tony Wright, Ivan Henderson. Contested: Colchester 2010, Essex PCC election 2012. Drafted policy for NHS. Former regional organising asst for the East of England Labour Party. Ed: Colchester SF Coll.

CONSTITUENCY PROFILE
Colchester is an ancient town, a provincial capital in Roman Britain. It was military then and remains so, housing the 16th Air Assault Brigade and the Military Corrective Training Centre, the only military prison in Britain. Bob Russell lost almost 9,000 votes in 2015, handing a relatively safe Lib Dem seat to the Tories.

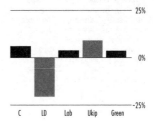

	Electorate	Turnout %	Change from 2010 %
	74,203	65.5	
W Quince C	18,919	38.9	+6.1
B Russell LD	13,344	27.5	-20.6
J Newell Lab	7,852	16.2	+3.9
J Pitts Ukip	5,870	12.1	+9.2
M Goacher Green	2,499	5.1	+3.6
K Scrimshaw CPA	109	0.2	

Change from 2010

Colne Valley

CONSERVATIVE HOLD

JASON McCARTNEY
BORN Jan 29, 1968
MP 2010-

RAF officer turned TV journalist. Member, transport select cttee 2013-. Member, 1922 exec cttee 2013-. Presenter, Calendar News & Sport, ITV Yorkshire, BBC local radio. Lecturer, Leeds Metropolitan University. RAF flight lieutenant, served in Turkey, Las Vegas and Iraq. Governor, SportsAid. Former father of chapel, NUJ at ITV. Huddersfield Town FC and Huddersfield Giants RLFC fan. Divorced, two daughters. Ed: Lancaster Royal GS; RAF Coll, Cranwell; Leeds Trinity Coll (PgDip broadcast journalism).

CHALLENGERS
Jane East (Lab) International development programme manager, previously international mobilisation coordinator, Amnesty International. Former social worker. Country manager,

Christian Aid 2011-14. VSO volunteer in Africa. Ed: Cardiff University (BA social policy) Queen's University Belfast (MA social work). **Melanie Roberts** (Ukip) Runs online bookshop and legal library. Mother of eight. Ed: Huddersfield (BA legal studies); Leeds (PgDip criminal justice studies). **Cahal Burke** (LD) Part-time teacher. Cllr, Kirklees C 2010-. Chair and founder, Lindley community group. Marathon runner, fundraiser. Father. Ed: Huddersfield (computing).

CONSTITUENCY PROFILE
Large sweeps of rural land between Greater Manchester and Huddersfield make up the main area of the seat, but the population is concentrated in the north. Includes west Huddersfield and its suburbs. Patches of deprivation here, but the seat is economically active, with many middle-class professionals. The BBC comedy series *Last of the Summer Wine* was filmed at Holmfirth.

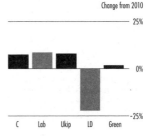

	Electorate	Turnout %	Change from 2010 %
	82,510	68.8	
J McCartney C	25,246	44.5	+7.5
J East Lab	19,868	35.0	+8.6
M Roberts Ukip	5,734	10.1	+8.0
C Burke LD	3,407	6.0	-22.2
C Ball Green	1,919	3.4	+1.8
P Salveson Yorks	572	1.0	
M Staniforth ND	54	0.1	

Change from 2010

Congleton

CONSERVATIVE HOLD

FIONA BRUCE
BORN Mar 26, 1957
MP 2010-

Long-term activist stalwart.
Passionate about social mobility,
proud of her northern mill-
town upbringing. Select cttes:
international development 2012-;
draft modern slavery bill 2014;
arms export controls 2013; Scottish
affairs 2010-13. Chairwoman,
APPG pro-life, said priority in
Westminster was "fighting for the
sanctity of human life". Contested
Warrington South 2005. Cllr
Warrington BC 2004-10. Award-
winning businesswoman, Women
in Business winner 2015. Solicitor,
Fiona Bruce & Co LLP and set up
free legal advice service. Co-author,
There is such a thing as society.
Ongoing work with school in
Tanzania. Kept a flock of sheep.
Evangelical christian. Married, two
sons. Ed: Burnley HS; Howell's
School, Llandaff; University of
Manchester (LLB law).

CHALLENGERS
Darren Price (Lab) Architect,
urban design consultant and
director. Cllr, Staffordshire
Moorlands DC 2013-. Sch
governor, chairman. Daughter has
Williams Syndrome. Ed: Sheffield
(PhD planning). **Lee Slaughter**
(Ukip) Investment consultant,
Allen Partnership. Cllr, Holmes
Chapel PC. Ed: Manchester
Metropolitan (MBA). **Peter Hirst**
(LD) Entrepreneur and market
coach. Cllr: Middlewich TC
1999-; Congleton BC 1999-2002.
Contested Congleton 2010
2005. Council member, Unlock
Democracy. Electoral Reform
Society. Married. Ed: Rydal Sch;
Manchester (MbChb physiology &
medicine).

CONSTITUENCY PROFILE
Safe Conservative seat since its
creation in 1983, coterminous with
the former Congleton council area,
now subsumed into the Cheshire
East unitary authority. Affluent
commuter area for Manchester.

	Electorate	Turnout %	Change from 2010 %
	72,398	70.4	
F Bruce C	27,164	53.3	+7.5
D Price Lab	10,391	20.4	+3.2
L Slaughter Ukip	6,922	13.6	+9.4
P Hirst LD	4,623	9.1	-22.8
A Heath Green	1,876	3.7	

Change from 2010

C	Lab	Ukip	LD	Green

Copeland

LABOUR HOLD

JAMIE REED
BORN Mar 14, 1973
MP 2005-

Strong supporter of nuclear power
industry. Shadow minister: health
2011-15; Defra 2010-11. Member,
select cttees: regulatory reform
2005-10; efra 2005-07. PPS to:
Harriet Harman 2008-10; Tony
McNulty 2006-08. Chairman,
APPG digital switchover. Public
affairs professional. Anti-racism
campaigner. GMB. Joked he was
a Jedi in maiden speech on in
parliament on religious freedom,
2005. Methodist. Married, three
sons. Ed: Whitehaven Sch;
Manchester Metropolitan (BA
English); Leicester (MA mass
communication).

CHALLENGERS
Stephen Haraldsen (C) Works
at Samuel Lindow Foundation.
Part-time student and lecturer in
international relations, UCLan.
Cllr, Copeland 2011-, youngest cllr.

Chairman, Copeland Conservative
Association 2014-. Ed: St Andrew's
(BSc sustainable development),
UCLan (PhD political geography).
Michael Pye (Ukip) Chartered
engineer in oil industry. Ed:
Cockermouth GS; Birmingham
(BEng chemical engineering).
Danny Gallagher (LD) Self-
employed business consultant. Cllr,
Preston CC 1994-2012. Contested
Wyre & Preston N 2010. Married,
one step-daughter. **Allan Todd**
(Green) Writes history textbooks
and revision guides. Former history
teacher. Previous Labour member.
Widowed, two daughters.

CONSTITUENCY PROFILE
A seat on the remote west coast
of Cumbria, a mixture of hill-
farming countryside, Lake District
wilderness, and some economically
depressed former mining or iron
works towns. Sellafield nuclear
power complex is the largest source
of local employment. Copeland and
its predecessor Whitehaven has
been Labour since 1935.

	Electorate	Turnout %	Change from 2010 %
	62,119	63.8	
J Reed Lab	16,750	42.3	-3.8
S Haraldsen C	14,186	35.8	-1.3
M Pye Ukip	6,148	15.5	+13.2
D Gallagher LD	1,368	3.5	-6.8
A Todd Green	1,179	3.0	+2.1

Change from 2010

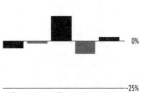

Lab	C	Ukip	LD	Green

Corby

CONSERVATIVE GAIN

TOM PURSGLOVE
BORN Nov 5, 1988
MP 2015-

Parly asst to Chris Heaton-Harris and Peter Bone. Cllr, Wellingborough BC 2007-, youngest cllr in the country at the time (18). Director 'Together Against the Wind' anti-wind farm campaign. Plays cricket locally, ECB umpire and former competitive swimmer. Ed: Sir Christopher Hatton Sch; Queen Mary, London (BA politics).

CHALLENGERS
Andy Sawford (Lab Co-op) MP 2012-15. Won 2012 by-election after chick-lit author Louise Mensch resigned, Labour's first by-election win since 1997. Son of former Kettering MP Phil Sawford. Shadow minister: communities & local government 2013-15. PPS to Stephen Twigg 2012-13. Member, CLG select cttee 2012-13. Previously: chief executive of Local

Government Information Unit; director of Connect Public Affairs. Cllr, Dartford BC 1999-2003. FRSA. Unite. Married, two children. Ed: Montsaye Comprehensive Sch, Rothwell; Durham University (BA history). **Margot Parker** (Ukip) MEP for the East Midlands 2014-. Former sales director for bespoke fragrance and lingerie companies. Board director of BPMA. Contested: Corby 2012; Sherwood 2010; East Midlands 2009 EU election for Libertas. Married, two sons. **Peter Harris** (LD) Executive President, American Freight Car. Cllr, Newark DC 2011-.

CONSTITUENCY PROFILE
Corby grew from a small village to become a medium-sized industrial town in the 1930s after the development of its steel industry. The economy has largely recovered from mass unemployment after 1980s industrial closures. Corby itself tends to vote Labour, but the solidly Tory rural areas make the constituency a close marginal.

	Electorate	Turnout %	from 2010 %	Change
	79,775	70.4		
T Pursglove C	24,023	42.8	+0.6	
A Sawford Lab Co-op	21,611	38.5	-0.2	
M Parker Ukip	7,708	13.7		
P Harris LD	1,458	2.6	-11.9	
J Hornett Green	1,374	2.5		

Change from 2010

C   Lab Co-op   Ukip   LD   Green

Cornwall North

CONSERVATIVE GAIN

SCOTT MANN
BORN Jun 24, 1977
MP 2005-

Former postman, "Poldark-look-a-like" according to local *Western Morning News*. Cllr: Cornwall CC 2009-, resigned as deputy leader 2012 after £16m of public money was proposed for a new Cornwall sports stadium; Cornwall North DC 2007-09. Honorary vice-president, Wadebridge Cricket Club. Married, one child. Ed: Wadebridge Sch.

CHALLENGERS
Dan Rogerson (LD) MP 2005-15. Constituency focused, from party's centre-left. Parly under-sec, Defra 2013-15. Lib Dem shadow minister: communities & local government 2006-10; arts, culture & heritage 2007; OPDM, 2006-07; efra 2005-06. LD whip 2007-10. Select cttees: environmental audit 2013-; efra 2005-13. Chairman, APPG Cheese. Contested Bedfordshire NE 2001. Cllr, Bedford BC 1999-

2002. Campaigns officer, Devon & Cornwall LDs 2002-04. Admin officer, De Montfort Uni, Research assistant, Bedford BC. Unison. Married, one daughter, two sons. Ed: St Mary's Sch, Bodmin; Bodmin Coll, Cornwall; University of Wales, Aberystwyth (BSc politics). **Julie Lingard** (Ukip) Self-employed letting agent. Former college lecturer. Married. Ed: Leicester Polytechnic (BA business studies); Kingston Business Sch (MA marketing). **John Whitby** (Lab) Artist and photographer. Retired business owner, World Leisure Marketing.

CONSTITUENCY PROFILE
A Liberal-Conservative battleground since the 1960s, a ten per cent swing gave the seat to the Tories in 2015 that the Lib Dems had held, albeit marginally, since 1992. A tourism hotspot with Padstow, Cornwall's northern beaches and Bodmin. Cornwall's economy has improved since it received EU funding in the early 2000s.

	Electorate	Turnout %	from 2010 %	Change
	67,192	71.8		
S Mann C	21,689	45.0	-8.1	
D Rogerson LD	15,068	31.2	-29.9	
J Lingard Ukip	6,121	12.7	+6.4	
J Whitby Lab	2,621	5.4	+0.1	
A Pennington Green	2,063	4.3		
J Jefferies Meb Ker	631	1.3	-0.1	
J Allman Restore	52	0.1		

Change from 2010

C   LD   Ukip   Lab   Green

Cornwall South East

CONSERVATIVE HOLD

SHERYLL MURRAY
BORN Feb 4, 1956
MP 2010-

Passionate fishing industry campaigner; wife of a trawler skipper who died in an accident in 2011. Member, select cttees: efra 2012-; environmental audit 2010-12. Cllr: Caradon DC 2003-09, leader Conservative group; Cornwall CC 2001-05. Member of the Objective One programme monitoring committee. Fishing industry representative: spokeswoman, Save Britain's Fish; director, the Fishermen's Association; Looe Fishermen's Protection Association; chairman of the South West Fish Producers' Organisation. Part-time doctor's receptionist for 20 years. Widowed, one daughter, one son. Ed: Torpoint Comprehensive.

CHALLENGERS
Phil Hutty (LD) Social work manager. Contested: Devon C 2010, Devon SW 2001. Devon CC

operations manager 2011-14. Key advocate for Cornish Language support and funding. Married, one son. Ed: University of Bristol. **Bradley Monk** (Ukip) 20-year old student of politics at University of Winchester. Photographed wearing Jimmy Savile mask at Halloween party. **Declan Lloyd** (Lab) A-Level student at election, at 18 the youngest Labour candidate. Ed: Truro Coll. **Martin Corney** (Green) Cllr, St Ives PC 2013-, VC 2014-. The Growing Project CIC, retired. Former computer programmer, Babcock International Group.

CONSTITUENCY PROFILE
A marginal between Conservatives and Liberals since the mid-19th century, although Sheryll Murray held with a 17,000 majority in 2015. Dependent on tourism, agriculture, fishing and commuting into Plymouth. The population centres are Saltash and Torpoint, two towns that face Plymouth across the river Tamar, but inland villages like Looe and Polperro attract tourists.

	Electorate	Turnout %	from 2010 % Change
	71,071	71.1	
S Murray C	25,516	50.5	+5.4
P Hutty LD	8,521	16.9	-21.8
B Monk Ukip	7,698	15.2	+9.0
D Lloyd Lab	4,692	9.3	+2.2
M Corney Green	2,718	5.4	+3.7
A Long Meb Ker	1,003	2.0	+0.7
G Trubody Ind	350	0.7	

Change from 2010

C LD Ukip Lab Green

Cotswolds, The

CONSERVATIVE HOLD

GEOFFREY CLIFTON-BROWN
BORN Mar 23, 1953
MP 1992-

Excitable, eccentric, bumbling shire Tory. Shadow SoS: international development 2007-10. Shadow min: FCO 2005-07. Opp deputy whip 2005; opp whip 1999-2001. Shadow spokes: CLG 2001-04; efra 2001. Select cttees: chairman, selection 2010-; member, selection 2005-; finance & services 2005-; liason 2010-; admin 2010-11, 2001; broadcasting 2000-01; public accounts 1997-99; environment 1992-97. PPS to: Douglas Hogg 1995-7. MP Cirencester & Tewkesbury 1992-7. Chartered surveyor and farmer. Freeman of City of London. Divorced, one daughter, one son. Ed: Eton Coll; Royal Agricultural College.

CHALLENGERS
Paul Hodgkinson (LD) Executive coaching consultant. Associate tutor, Roffey Park Institute.

Cllr: Gloustershire CC 2013-; Cotswold DC 2007-15, Lib Dem leader 2009-15. Civil partnership. Ed: Reading (BA French). **Chris Harlow** (Ukip) Semi-retired transport industry consultant. Teaches cycling proficiency to primary sch children. Married, children. Ed: Luton GS; Lancaster (BA history & politics). **Manjinder Singh Kang** (Lab) Solicitor at Vienna Kang Advocates, Birmingham, formerly Gurney Harden Solicitors. Ed: Sutton Coldfield Coll; Nottingham Trent (LLB, LPC law).

CONSTITUENCY PROFILE
Almost entirely within the Cotswolds Area of Outstanding Natural Beauty, this is an area of rolling hills, small picturesque market towns and villages of listed buildings built of Cotswold stone. Economically tourism and agriculture, particularly sheep and dairy farming, are important. Safely Conservative.

	Electorate	Turnout %	from 2010 % Change
	78,292	72.4	
G Clifton-Brown C	32,045	56.6	+3.5
P Hodgkinson LD	10,568	18.7	-10.9
C Harlow Ukip	6,188	10.9	+6.7
M Singh Kang Lab	5,240	9.3	-1.5
P Burgess Green	2,626	4.6	+2.9

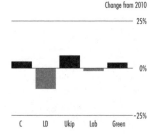

Change from 2010

C LD Ukip Lab Green

Coventry North East

LABOUR HOLD

COLLEEN FLETCHER
BORN Nov 23, 1954
MP 2015-

Customer services officer, Orbit Housing Group. Cllr, Coventry CC 2011-, 2002-04, 1992-2000. Recorded in hostile exchange on doorstep when canvassing in Coventry, 2015. National Policy Forum member. Labour Group Chair. West Midlands Regional Board Officer. Daughter of former cllr. Married, two sons. Ed: Lyng Hall Comprehensive Sch; Henley Coll, Coventry.

CHALLENGERS
Michelle Lowe (C) Cllr, Sevenoaks DC 2007-, vice-chairman. Former marketing communications specialist. Sch governor. Lives in Shoreham, Kent. Married, two children. Ed: Coventry University (BSc international & political studies). **Avtar Taggar** (Ukip) IT consultant and engineer. Worked overseas in Bahrain and UAE.

Second generation immigrant. Ed: University of Warwick (BSc business management). **Russell Field** (LD) Works for building society. Cllr, Coventry CC 2008-12, 2004-7, only Lib Dem on council 2008-12. Ed: Caludon Castle Sch; De Montfort University (BSc computer science). **Matthew Handley** (Green) Category buyer, TBS Building Supplies. Building renewables merchanting industry worker. Former logistics manager, Selfridges Birmingham. Married, one child. Ed: Sutton Coldfield Coll.

CONSTITUENCY PROFILE
The mainly working-class east of Coventry, and also the most ethnically mixed, with a significant Muslim and Sikh population. The seat includes University Hospital Coventry and the Ricoh Arena complex, home to Coventry City FC, as well as an exhibition centre and a casino. The safest of the three Coventry seats, which has been held by Labour since its creation in 1974.

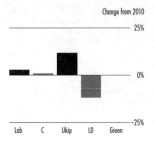

	Electorate	Turnout %	from 2010 % Change
	76,401	55.3	
C Fletcher Lab	22,025	52.2	+2.9
M Lowe C	9,751	23.1	+0.9
A Taggar Ukip	6,278	14.9	+11.9
R Field LD	2,007	4.8	-11.9
M Handley Green	1,245	3.0	
N Downes TUSC	633	1.5	
W Sidhu Ch M	292	0.7	-0.3

Change from 2010

25%

0%

-25%

Lab   C   Ukip   LD   Green

Coventry North West

LABOUR HOLD

GEOFFREY ROBINSON
BORN: May 25, 1938
MP 1976-

Stood for re-election in 2015 despite rumours that he was stepping down. Wealthy businessman at heart of 1990s New Labour project, previously close to Gordon Brown. Resigned after a tough period in government (Paymaster General 1997-98) when it was revealed that he had given Peter Mandelson an interest-free loan to buy a house. Opp spokes: trade & industry; regional affairs 1983-87; science 1982-83. Owner of *New Statesman* 1996-2008. Chairman of Coventry City FC 2005-2007. Founded TransTec car parts firm, faced questions over its collapse in 1999. Chairman, Jaguar Cars; MD, Leyland Innocenti. Joined Labour after meeting Harold Wilson at Yale. Married, one daughter, one son. Ed: Emmanuel Sch, London; Clare Coll, Cambridge; Yale (Wolf's Head Society).

CHALLENGERS
Parvez Akhtar (C) Engineer, Jaguar Land Rover. Contested Bedford mayoral by-election 2009. Former Conservative National Convention VP candidate. Founder, Westfield Cricket Club. Avid cricket player and fan. Father of five. Ed: Biddenham Upper Sch. **Harjinder Sehmi** (Ukip) Cllr, Coventry CC 2010-14 for Labour, defected to Ukip after losing seat in 2014. Born in India. **Laura Vesty** (Green) Waste Management Co-Ordinator, Coventry CC. Ed: Coventry University (BSc environmental science) **Andrew Furse** (LD) Cllr, Bath & Somerset NE C 1994-. Ed: UCL (BSc electronic engineering).

CONSTITUENCY PROFILE
The most rural of the three Coventry seats, this is the site of much of Coventry's industrial and manufacturing past: Coventry colliery, the Dunlop factory and Jaguar works. Safely Labour, with only two MPs — the first was Maurice Edelman — since the Second World War.

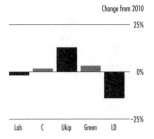

	Electorate	Turnout %	from 2010 % Change
	74,597	60.7	
G Robinson Lab	18,557	41.0	-1.8
P Akhtar C	14,048	31.1	+1.7
H Sehmi Ukip	7,101	15.7	+12.9
L Vesty Green	1,961	4.3	+3.3
A Furse LD	1,810	4.0	-13.9
D Nellist TUSC	1,769	3.9	

Change from 2010

25%

0%

-25%

Lab   C   Ukip   Green   LD

Coventry South

LABOUR HOLD

JIM CUNNINGHAM
BORN Feb 4, 1941
MP 1992-

Engineering background makes him one of old Labour generation with authentic links to shop floor. PPS to Mike O'Brien 2005-10. Member, select cttees: standards & privileges 2010; procedure 2005-06; ODPM 2005; const affairs 2003-05; panel of chairs 1998-2001; trade & industry 1997-2001; home affairs 1994-97. MP Coventry SE 1992-97. Cllr, Coventry 1972-92, leader 1988-92, deputy 1987-88. MSF shop steward. Engineer, Rolls Royce. Married, one daughter, one son, one stepdaughter, one stepson. Ed: Columba HS, Coatbridge; Tillicoultry Coll.

CHALLENGERS
Gary Ridley (C) PR and media executive, Swanswell drug and alcohol support services. Former press secretary to Philip Bradbourn MEP 2011-15. Cllr, Coventry CC 2002-12. Contested Coventry NW 2010. Ed: Coventry University.
Mark Taylor (Ukip) Defected to Conservatives two weeks after 2015 election, when he was chairman of the local party. National party had tried to parachute the pop preacher and former Christian Party leader George Hargreaves into seat before the election but . **Greg Judge** (LD) Campaigns support officer, Dignity in Dying. Political assistant, HoL. Former policy consultant to British Deaf Association. Exec member: Liberal Youth 2009-11; Lib Dem Disability Assoc 2010-12. Trustee, Spinal Injuries Association. Sch governor. Ed: Bristol (BSc deaf studies)

CONSTITUENCY PROFILE
The six southern wards of Coventry. Includes the most affluent and middle-class parts of the city, including the University of Warwick, but also the post-war council estates in Binley and Coventry city centre. Safely Labour, although predecessor seats have been Tory.

	Electorate	Turnout %	Change from 2010 %
	71,380	61.2	
J Cunningham Lab	18,472	42.3	+0.5
G Ridley C	15,284	35.0	+1.6
M Taylor Ukip	5,709	13.1	+9.2
G Judge LD	1,779	4.1	-14.0
B Gallaher Green	1,719	3.9	+2.5
J Griffiths TUSC	650	1.5	
C Rooney Mainstream	86	0.2	

Change from 2010

— 25%

— 0%

—-25%

Lab   C   Ukip   LD   Green

Crawley

CONSERVATIVE HOLD

HENRY SMITH
BORN May 14, 1969
MP 2010-

Eurosceptic and advocate for English votes for English laws. Member, European scrutiny select cttee 2010-. APPGs: chairman, the County; VC, transatlantic & international security. Cllr: West Sussex CC 1997-, leader 2003-10, youngest council leader in UK; Crawley BC 2002-04. Contested Crawley 2005, 01. Owns property investment company. Co-author of *Direct Democracy.* Keen vexillologist and skier. Married, one daughter, one son. Ed: Frensham Heights Sch, Farnham; UCL (BA philosophy).

CHALLENGERS
Chris Oxlade (Lab) Runs a radio production and event management business. Former radio presenter, Mercury FM. Cllr: Crawley BC 2011-; West Sussex CC 2009-. Director, Crawley Open House. Member, Progress. Contested Crawley 2010. Partner. Ed: Hazelwick Sch. **Chris Brown** (Ukip) Management consultant, BT Global Services. Married, two children. **Sarah Osborne** (LD) Psychotherapist, retrained after career in City of London. Cllr, Lewes DC 2011-, leader Lib Dem group 2014-, chairman Scrutiny cttee. Trustee, Homestart East Sussex. Partner, four daughters. **Guy Hudson** (Green) Founder, Village Water hygiene-sanitation charity

CONSTITUENCY PROFILE
Crawley is a new town, designated in 1946 which grew rapidly in the Fifties and Sixties to house overspill from London. Had a high proportion of council housing, but this was largely sold off through right to buy. Nearby Gatwick Airport dominates the local economy. Like many new towns tends to be a close Labour-Conservative marginal. Labour held it by 37 votes in 2005, losing the seat to the Tories in 2010.

	Electorate	Turnout %	Change from 2010 %
	73,940	65.7	
H Smith C	22,829	47.0	+2.3
C Oxlade Lab	16,303	33.6	+1.3
C Brown Ukip	6,979	14.4	+11.5
S Osborne LD	1,339	2.8	-11.7
G Hudson Green	1,100	2.3	+1.0

Change from 2010

— 25%

— 0%

—-25%

C   Lab   Ukip   LD   Green

Crewe & Nantwich

CONSERVATIVE HOLD

EDWARD TIMPSON
BORN Dec 26, 1973
MP 2008-

Wealthy son of Timpson shoe repair and key-cutting chain chief exec. Min of state for children and families 2015-. Parly under-sec for same brief 2012-15. PPS to Theresa May 2010-12. Member, select cttees: CSF 2008-10; human rights 2008-10. Former chairman, APPGs: adoption & fostering; looked-after children & care leavers. Family law barrister, specialising in vulnerable children cases. Marathon runner. Married, one son, two daughters. Ed: Uppingham Sch, Rutland; Durham University (BA politics); Coll of Law, London

CHALLENGERS
Adrian Heald (Lab) Consultant physician and researcher. International specialist in endocrinology and diabetes. Works at Leighton Hospital, Northwich Victoria Infirmary and Macclesfield

General Hospital. Research fellow, University of Manchester, visiting fellow University of Oxford. Contested Macclesfield 2010. Keen poet, tennis and piano player. Ed: Rossall Sch, Fleetwood; St Peter's Coll, Oxford (DM BM BCh MA chemistry & medicine). **Richard Lee** (Ukip) Company Director. Cllr, Minshull Vernon & D PC. Chairman: Cheshire; Crewe & Nantwich Ukip branches. Ed: Rainford HS. **Roy Wood** (LD) Maths teacher. Former systems analyst Contested Crewe & Nantwich 2010; Birkenhead 2001, 1997. Chair, sch governors Founding member of Wirral LA21 Environmental Forum. Ed: St Edwards Coll, Liverpool; University of Liverpool (BSc chemistry)

CONSTITUENCY PROFILE
Held by Labour from the seat's creation in 1983 until 2008, when it was the Tories' first by-election win in 26 years. Crewe's Labour-leaning electorate is balanced by Tory voters in Cheshire villages.

	Electorate	Turnout %	Change from 2010 %
	74,039	67.4	
E Timpson C	22,445	45.0	-0.9
A Heald Lab	18,825	37.7	+3.7
R Lee Ukip	7,252	14.5	+11.8
R Wood LD	1,374	2.8	-12.2

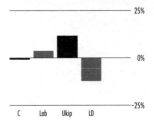

Change from 2010

Croydon Central

CONSERVATIVE HOLD

GAVIN BARWELL
BORN Jan 23, 1972
MP 2010-

Articulate political strategist, local Croydon man who served as Lord Ashcroft's right-hand man at CCHQ high command. Conservative party director of operations 2003-06. Whip (comptroller, HM household) 2015-. Lord commissioner, Treasury 2014-15. Asst whip 2013-14. PPS to: Michael Gove 2012 -13; Greg Clarke 2011-12. Select cttees: draft HoL reform bill 2011-12; science & technology 2010-12. 1922 executive committee, 2010-. Consultant, own business. Cllr, Croydon 1998-2010. Advised John Gummer as environment Sec. Married, three sons. Ed: Trinity Sch, Croydon; Trinity Coll, Cambridge (BSc natural sciences, president Cambridge Union).

CHALLENGERS
Sarah Jones (Lab) Communications

consultant, Gatwick airport. Housing association director. Former parly asst to Mo Mowlam and Geraint Davies. Previously head of campaigns, Shelter and chair of Croydon Central Labour party. Former communications officer for government Olympic executive and deputy director of communications for Olympic and Paralympic Games. Married, four children. **Peter Staveley** (Ukip) Transport planning consultant. Contested Lewisham West & Penge 2010. Sutton Ukip branch chairman. Ed: Central London Poly (MSc transport planning)

CONSTITUENCY PROFILE
Croydon Central may contain the commercial centre of Croydon, but it is the eastern part of the borough. Most of the seat is semi-detached, middle-of-the-road suburbia, although to the north of the constituency is more ethnically mixed. A marginal that was Labour 1997-2005, it returned Gavin Barwell by a wafer-thin majority in 2015.

	Electorate	Turnout %	Change from 2010 %
	78,171	67.7	
G Barwell C	22,753	43.0	+3.5
S Jones Lab	22,588	42.7	+9.1
P Staveley Ukip	4,810	9.1	+7.1
E Sutton Green	1,454	2.8	+1.6
J Fearnley LD	1,152	2.2	-11.0
A Ashley TUSC	127	0.2	
M Camden UKPDP	57	0.1	

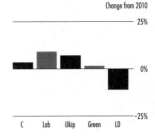

Change from 2010

Croydon North

LABOUR CO-OPERATIVE HOLD

STEVE REED
BORN Nov 12, 1963
MP 2012-

Won 2012 by-election after death of Malcolm Wicks. Shadow min: home 2013-15. Select cttees: public admin 2012-13. Cllr, Lambeth BC 1998-2012, opp leader 2002-06, leader 2006-12. Sought to make Lambeth Britain's first co-operative council where residents run services. Chairman: Central London Forward 2010-11; Vauxhall-Nine Elms regeneration strategy board. FRSA. GMB, Unite. OBE 2013. Appeared on *Independent on Sunday* Pink List 2010. Partner. Ed: University of Sheffield (BA English).

CHALLENGERS
Vidhi Mohan (C) Transport consultant, Mott MacDonald. Cllr: Croydon BC 2005-, shadow cabinet member for transport, environment. Sch governor. Born in India. **Winston McKenzie** (Ukip)

Perennial candidate for various parties. Joined Ukip in 2009 and stood for leadership in 2010. Fitness instructor, former boxer. Chairman, Lambeth & Croydon Ukip 2012-14, when he was suspended. Ukip spokes: Commonwealth 2012-15; CMS 2010-12. Contested: Croydon N 2012, Tottenham 2010; Croydon N for Veritas 2005; London Mayor 2008 and Brent E 2003 as independent. Born in Jamaica. **Shasha Khan** (Green) Business director and record label manager. Contested Croydon North 2012, 2010, 2005. Married, one daughter. **Joanna Corbin** (LD) Lawyer.

CONSTITUENCY PROFILE
The most urban and diverse of the three Croydon seats, with large areas of terrace housing and municipal tower blocks. Almost two thirds of the population are non-white: it has the second highest proportion of black residents of any constituency. Once reliably Conservative, demographic change has led to Labour support.

	Electorate	Turnout %	Change from 2010 %
	85,951	62.3	
S Reed Lab Co-op	33,513	62.6	+6.6
V Mohan C	12,149	22.7	-1.4
W McKenzie Ukip	2,899	5.4	+3.7
S Khan Green	2,515	4.7	+2.7
J Corbin LD	1,919	3.6	-10.4
G Hart TUSC	261	0.5	
L Berks Ind	141	0.3	+0.1
B Stevenson Comm	125	0.2	-0.1

Change from 2010

25%

0%

-25%

Lab Co-op   C   Ukip   Green   LD

Croydon South

CONSERVATIVE HOLD

CHRIS PHILP
BORN Jun 6, 1976
MP 2015-

Millionaire entrepreneur. Cllr: Camden BC 2006-10. Contested Hampstead & Kilburn 2010, lost by 42 votes to Glenda Jackson. Bow Group chairman 2004-05. Former adviser to Andrew Lansley. Founder of charity, Next Big Thing and co-founder to Pluto Capital. Author, *Work for the Dole: A Proposal to Fix Welfare Dependency.* Listed number 8 in startups.co.uk's Top 50 Entrepreneurs, one below Richard Branson. Married, two children. Ed: St Olave's GS, Orpington; University Coll, Oxford (BA physics; MA theoretical quantum mechanics).

CHALLENGERS
Emily Benn (Lab) Associate sales director, UBS. Cllr: Croydon BC 2014-. Contested East Worthing & Shoreham 2010, selected in 2007 when she was aged 17. Board of Fairfield, London Mozart Players,

London Youth Games. Royal Signals volunteer. Daughter of Stephen Benn (Viscount Stansgate), niece of Hilary, granddaughter of Tony. Ed: New Coll, Oxford (BA history & politics). **Kathleen Garner** (Ukip) Statistical worker, Office for National Statistics. Contested: Croydon South 2001; London Euro election 2004. Croydon branch secretary 1996-2014. Divorced, two children. Ed: Reading (BA German). **Gill Hickson** (LD) Community activist.

CONSTITUENCY PROFILE
A seat in the far south of London that has more in common with residential Surrey than the inner city. Apart from Waddon in the north of the seat, which contains a large council estate and tower blocks and sometimes returns Labour councillors, this seat consists of affluent, leafy dormitory suburbs for Croydon. This is a safe Conservative seat, held by the Tories since its creation in 1974.

	Electorate	Turnout %	Change from 2010 %
	82,010	70.4	
C Philp C	31,448	54.5	+3.6
E Benn Lab	14,308	24.8	+4.8
K Garner Ukip	6,068	10.5	+6.1
G Hickson LD	3,448	6.0	-16.9
P Underwood Green	2,154	3.7	+2.0
M Samuel Croydon	221	0.4	
J Bigger Class War	65	0.1	

Change from 2010

25%

0%

-25%

C   Lab   Ukip   LD   Green

Cumbernauld, Kilsyth & Kirkintilloch East

STUART McDONALD
BORN May 2, 1978
MP 2015-

Solicitor, Former Scottish parliamentary assistant to Shirley-Ann Somerville MSP and Jim Eadie MSP. SNP group leader, immigration, asylum and border control 2015-. Parly and public affairs officer for the Coalition for Racial Equality and Rights, Glasgow. Previously senior researcher for Yes campaign. Worked at Immigration Advisory Service as human rights lawyer. Member, Unite. Enjoys football, music and reading. Ed: Kilsyth Academy; University of Edinburgh (LLB law).

CHALLENGERS
Gregg McClymont (Lab) MP, 2010-15. Shadow min: work & pensions 2011-15; opp whip 2011. Select cttees: science & technology 2010-12; BIS 2010. Chair, PLP BIS departmental group 2010. History

fellow, St Hugh's Coll, Oxford, visiting fellow, Nuffield Coll, Oxford. Former speechwriter to Dr John Reid. Runs virtual think tank Ideas Scotland. . Unite, Community. Ed: Cumbernauld HS; University of Glasgow (MA history); UPenn (history, scholarship); St Jonh's Coll, University of Oxford (PhD history). **Malcolm Mackay** (C) Former chairman, Ukip Edinburgh & Lothians. Contested Scotland Euro 2014 election for Ukip. **John Duncan** (LD) Respiratory nurse specialist. Married, two children.

CONSTITUENCY PROFILE
The constituency with the longest name in Britain. To the west it has rural areas around Lennoxtown, Twechar and Milton of Campsie, but it is largely urban and has a high concentration of social housing. The working-class voters of Cumbernauld, 15 miles northeast of Glasgow, and Kilsyth, a former mining town, made it safe for Labour. The 2015 landslide meant the SNP eased to victory.

	Electorate	Turnout %	from 2010 %	Change %
	67,009	73.7		
S McDonald SNP	29,572	59.9	+36.1	
G McClymont Lab	14,820	30.0	-27.2	
M Mackay C	3,891	7.9	-0.4	
J Duncan LD	1,099	2.2	-7.3	

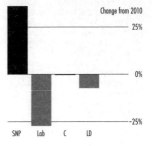

Change from 2010

SNP · Lab · C · LD

Cynon Valley

ANN CLWYD
BORN Mar 21, 1937
MP 1984-

Leftwinger tamed by Tony Blair with appointment as special envoy to PM on Iraq human rights 2003-10. Now mainly single issue campaigner on Iraq and NHS. Chair PLP 2005-06. Assistant to John Prescott 1994-95. Opp spokes foreign affairs 1994-95, employment 1993-94. Shadow sec: nat heritage 1992-3; Wales 1992; int devt 1989-92. Shad min: education, women's rights 1987-88. Select cttees: arms export 2011-; foreign affairs 2010-; int devt 1997-2005. Chairman: Inter-Parliamentary Union 2004-07; Tribune Group 1986-97. Lab Party NEC 1983-84. MEP Mid & West Wales 1979-84. Journalist, broadcaster. Contested Gloucester 1974, Denbigh 1970. *House* magazine health campaigner of the year 2014. Widowed. Ed: Holywell GS; Queen's Sch, Chester; University of Wales, Bangor.

CHALLENGERS
Cerith Griffiths (PC) Firefighter. Secretary to Fire Brigades' Union in Wales and FBU representative. Enjoys running and cycling. **Rebecca Rees-Evans** (Ukip) Married to fellow Ukip candidate, John Rees-Evans. Three children. **Keith Dewhurst** (C) Chairman, Diverse Cymru. MD, Keith Dewhurst business consultancy. Former justice of the peace, Manchester. Former engineer and manager, BBC, lead co-ordinator in Freeview set-up. Ed: Cheadle Hulme Sch; Salford (BSc pure and applied physics).

CONSTITUENCY PROFILE
The seat covers traditional former coal mining and iron working towns, typical of the Welsh valleys. Tower Colliery in Hirwaun was bought out and re-opened by its workers after its closure by British coal and was the last remaining deep coal mine in the Welsh valleys until it closed in 2008. Like most of the seats in the Welsh valleys, this is an utterly safe Labour seat.

	Electorate	Turnout %	from 2010 %	Change %
	51,421	59.3		
A Clwyd Lab	14,532	47.7	-4.8	
C Griffiths PC	5,126	16.8	-3.5	
R Rees-Evans Ukip	4,976	16.3	+13.0	
K Dewhurst C	3,676	12.1	+2.0	
A Jones LD	830	2.7	-11.1	
J Matthews Green	799	2.6		
C Beggs Soc Lab	533	1.8		

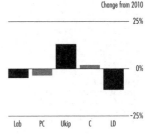

Change from 2010

Lab · PC · Ukip · C · LD

Dagenham & Rainham

LABOUR HOLD

JON CRUDDAS
BORN Apr 7, 1962
MP 2001-

Respected leftwinger who said of the aftermath of the 2015 election: "this could be the greatest crisis the Labour party has ever faced". Wrote 2015 party manifesto, Labour party policy review co-ordinator 2010-15. Contested deputy leadership 2007. Member, cttees: public accounts 2003-10. Dep political sec, PM's political office 1997-2001. Chief asst, General Sec Lab Party. Policy officer, Lab Party Policy Directorate 1989-94. TGWU. Taught Labour history at Oxford 2010-12. Married, one son. Ed: Oaklands RC Comp, Portsmouth; Warwick (BSc economics; MA industrial relations; PhD industrial & business studies); Wisconsin-Madison (visiting fellow).

CHALLENGERS
Peter Harris (Ukip) Owns Call Panda loyalty card consultancy

and Peter James Motor Group car repairs. Former president, Dagenham Chamber of Commerce. Sch governor. Ed: Paddington Green Coll. **Julie Marson** (C) Cllr: Thanet DC 2011-, deputy opp leader. Shadow cabinet member community services. Contested SE England Euro election 2014. Former corporate finance banker. Acting press officer, Channel Dash Association. Married, one son. Ed: Downing Coll, Cambridge (BA modern history). **Kate Simpson** (Green) Teacher.

CONSTITUENCY PROFILE
A solid, white, working-class Labour seat. Synonymous with the motor trade through the Ford Motor Works, although the downgrading of the factory in 2002 means the influence of Ford is waning. Like neighbouring Barking, the seat is undergoing large-scale redevelopment of brownfield land by the Thames. The BNP won 11 per cent of the vote here in 2010, making it a Ukip target seat.

	Electorate	Turnout %	Change from 2010 %
	69,049	62.4	
J Cruddas Lab	17,830	41.4	+1.2
P Harris Ukip	12,850	29.9	+26.3
J Marson C	10,492	24.4	-10.0
K Simpson Green	806	1.9	+1.2
D Capstick LD	717	1.7	-6.9
T Culnane BNP	151	0.4	-10.8
T London ND	133	0.3	
K Gandy Eng Dem	71	0.2	

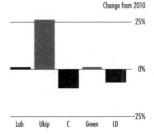

Change from 2010

Darlington

LABOUR HOLD

JENNY CHAPMAN
BORN Sep 25, 1973
MP 2010-

Strong local campaigner and Darlington's first female MP. Shadow minister for Justice 2011-15. Select cttee: consolidation, procedure 2010-15. Cllr, Darlington 2007-10. Vice-chairman, Progress 2012-. Researcher to Alan Milburn. Assistant prison psychologist, Durham, Dartmoor HMPs. Founder and chair, Newblood Live, youth music charity. Member, NE Strategic Partnership for Asylum & Refugee Support. Keen cyclist. Married, two sons. Ed: Hummersknott Sch, Darlington; Brunel University (BA psychology); Durham (MA medieval archaeology).

CHALLENGERS
Peter Cuthbertson (C) Account director, PB Political Consulting. Director, Centre for Crime Prevention. Cllr: Westminster CC

2014-. Previously researcher at: TaxPayers' Alliance; Margaret Thatcher Centre for Freedom. Former intern to Oliver Letwin and Nirj Deva MEP. Ed: Queen Elizabeth Sixth Form Coll; Essex (BA PPE); BPP Law Sch (Dip law). **Dave Hodgson** (Ukip) Engineering lecturer, Redcar & Cleveland Coll. Dir, Britannia Training. Ed: Teesside (BEng computer engineering & microelectronics); Huddersfield (PGCE). **Anne-Marie Curry** (LD) Cllr, Darlington BC 2008-. Former athlete and junior coach. **Michael Cherrington** (Green) Director, Red Pressures social care business.

CONSTITUENCY PROFILE
Unlike much of the rock-solid Labour areas surrounding it, Darlington was never a coal mining area — this was a prosperous railway and engineering town. A reliable Labour seat, but with solid Tory support in its western suburbs. Briefly held by Michael Fallon in 1983-87 before his relocation to the safer seat of Sevenoaks.

	Electorate	Turnout %	Change from 2010 %
	65,832	62.5	
J Chapman Lab	17,637	42.9	+3.5
P Cuthbertson C	14,479	35.2	+3.7
D Hodgson Ukip	5,392	13.1	+10.3
A Curry LD	1,966	4.8	-18.6
M Cherrington Green	1,444	3.5	
A Docherty TUSC	223	0.5	

Change from 2010

Dartford

CONSERVATIVE HOLD

GARETH JOHNSON
BORN Oct 12, 1969
MP 2010-

Campaigned against tolls on Dartford crossing. PPS to David Gauke 2014-15. Select cttees: human rights 2014-; justice 2013-14; science & technology 2012. Contested Dartford 2005, Lewisham West 2001. Cllr, Bexley 1998-2002. Defence solicitor, Thomas Boyd White. Keen cricketer. Married, one daughter, one son. Ed: Dartford GS; Coll of Law (LPC) UWE (PgDip law).

CHALLENGERS
Simon Thomson (Lab) Former BBC journalist. Contested Chatham & Aylesford 2013 local election. Gillingham FC football supporter and cricket fan. Married, two daughters. **Elizabeth Jones** (Ukip) Solicitor. Ukip Vice-chair Southwark. Criticised for screaming in heated radio debate against Socialist party

opponent in 2014. Contested Dulwich & West Norwood 2010; London Euro election 2014. Ed: Cardiff University. **Simon Beard** (LD) Researcher and tutor, LSE. Educational development adviser, Insight Education. Former parliamentary asst, Open Spaces Soc, ResPublica. Parly and policy officer, Dignity in Dying. Ed: Merton Coll, Oxford (BA PPE, exhibition); LSE (MSc PhD philosophy PgCert HE).

CONSTITUENCY PROFILE
The last Kent constituency before London. Following the 2010 election (and Labour holding onto Chorley and Luton South) Dartford is the country's strongest bellwether seat, having returned an MP from the party that went on to win each election since 1964. A commuter town with housing estates and Tory-leaning suburbs, large-scale housing projects around Bluewater shopping centre and a new town at Ebbsfleet could change future demographics of the seat.

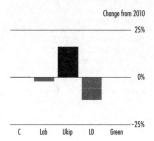

	Electorate	Turnout %	from 2010 %	Change
	76,686	68.4		
G Johnson C	25,670	49.0	+0.2	
S Thomson Lab	13,325	25.4	-2.1	
E Jones Ukip	10,434	19.9	+16.2	
S Beard LD	1,454	2.8	-11.9	
A Blatchford Green	1,324	2.5		
S Uncles Eng Dem	211	0.4	-4.0	

Change from 2010

Daventry

CONSERVATIVE HOLD

CHRIS HEATON-HARRIS
BORN Nov 28, 1967
MP 2010-

Combative, witty and Eurosceptic. Experienced, made name as East Midlands MEP (1999-2009), wrote about EU budget process, contested Tory MEP leadership, chief whip 2001-04. Select cttees: european scrutiny 2010-; public accounts 2010-. Contested Leicester South 2004, 1997. Founder member, Campaign for Parliamentary Reform. Management and public affairs consultant. What 4 Ltd, family fruit and veg wholesale business in New Covent Garden Market. Qualified football referee. Former chairman, EU Sports Platform. Married, two daughters. Ed: Tiffin GS for Boys; Wolverhampton Polytechnic (did not complete degree).

CHALLENGERS
Abigail Campbell (Lab) Freelance arts and literary consultant. External evaluator,

The Salmagundi. Programmer, Birmingham Literature Festival. Cllr, Daventry CC 2012-. Chairwoman, Children's Laureate cttee. Former officer at prisons, Arts Council. Married, two sons. Ed: Oxford (BA MPhil English). **Michael Gerard** (Ukip) Construction lawyer and adjudicator, former quantity surveyor Married, two daughters. Ed: Guildford Coll (HNC) Kingston (MSc); De Montfort (PgDip law). **Callum Delhoy** (LD) Student, Hills Road Sixth Form Coll.

CONSTITUENCY PROFILE
A largely rural, safe Conservative seat covering the northwestern part of Northamptonshire. Daventry's position on the M1 makes it a centre for warehousing and distribution, although most of the electorate are scattered across the small villages of western Northamptonshire. The seat contains Watford Gap, traditionally cited as the dividing point between the north and the south of England.

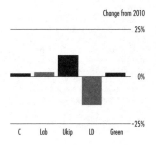

	Electorate	Turnout %	from 2010 %	Change
	72,753	72.2		
C Heaton-Harris C	30,550	58.2	+1.7	
A Campbell Lab	9,491	18.1	+2.3	
M Gerard Ukip	8,296	15.8	+11.3	
C Delhoy LD	2,352	4.5	-15.0	
S Whiffen Green	1,829	3.5	+2.0	

Change from 2010

Delyn

LABOUR HOLD

DAVID HANSON
BORN Jul 5, 1957
MP 1992-

Long-standing MP serving in middle-management positions under Labour leadership. Shadow: minister for immigration 2013-15; policing 2011-13; financial sec to Treasury 2010-11. Min: home 2009-10; justice 2007-09; NI office 2005-07; asst govt whip 1998-99. PPS to: Tony Blair as PM 2001-05; Alastair Darling 1997-98. Parly under-sec Wales 1999-2001, Member: Welsh Affairs select cttee 1992-95; leadership campaign team 1994-97. Cllr: Vale Royal BC 1983-91, leader 1989-91; Northwich TC 1987-91. Unite, USDAW. Director, Re-Solv. Manager, Plymouth Co-operative. Co-operative trainee. Married, two daughters, two sons. Ed: Verdin Comp, Winsford; Hull (BA drama, CertEd, VP Students' Union).

CHALLENGERS
Mark Isherwood (C) AM for

North Wales 2003-. Shadow Minister for Social Justice, Equality and Housing 2007-. Chairman, cross party groups: autism, disability, fuel poverty, funerals, hospices, neurological conditions. Cllr, Treuddyn CC 1999-2004. Ambassador, Clwyd Girl Guides. Founder, Chant Cymru hospitals foundation. Bank manager, Cheshire BS. Married, six children. Ed: Stockport GS; Newcastle (BA politics). **Nigel Williams** (Ukip) Runs photographic business. Former maths teacher and police officer, injured in miners' strike. Married, four children. Ed: Flint HS; Manchester Met. **Paul Rowlinson** (PC) Co-ordinator, Street Pastors. Translator.

CONSTITUENCY PROFILE
Once a close marginal seat, held by the Conservatives until 1992. Having been stripped of most of its north coast tourist towns in boundary changes, it now leans heavily to Labour, made up of industrial towns along the Dee estuary.

	Electorate	Turnout %	Change from 2010 %
	53,639	69.8	
D Hanson Lab	15,187	40.6	-0.2
M Isherwood C	12,257	32.7	-1.9
N Williams Ukip	6,150	16.4	+14.7
P Rowlinson PC	1,803	4.8	-0.2
T Rippeth LD	1,380	3.7	-11.9
K Roney Green	680	1.8	

Change from 2010

Denton & Reddish

LABOUR HOLD

ANDREW GWYNNE
BORN Jun 4, 1974
MP 2005-

Shadow minister: health 2011-15; transport 2010-11. Introduced successful private member's bill to restrict activities of 'vulture funds' trading debts of developing countries. PPS to: Ed Balls 2009-10; Jacqui Smith 2007-09; Baroness Scotland 2005-07. Select cttees: procedure 2005-10; Crossrail 2007. Cllr, Tameside MBC 1996-2008. European Co-ordinator Arlene McCarthy MEP. Researcher Andrew Bennet MP. National Computing Centre, Y2K team. ICL. Unite, Christian Socialists. Married, one daughter, two sons. Ed: Edgerton Park Community HS; Tameside Coll; NE Wales Inst (HND business & finance); Salford (BA politics & history).

CHALLENGERS
Lana Hempsall (C) Operation

director, Energy Market Analysis. Cllr, Broadland DC 2011-. Former teaching assistant. Qualified physiotherapist. Guide Dogs for the Blind Official Speaker. Charity worker. Married, children. Ed: University of Manchester (BA Physiotherapy). **Andrew Fairfoull** (Ukip) Chemistry teacher. North West region deputy chairman. Married. Ed: Westfield Coll, London (BSc chemistry); Chelsea Coll (MSc chemistry); City University London (MPhil chemistry). **Nick Koopman** (Green) Data manager.

CONSTITUENCY PROFILE
On the outskirts of Manchester. A Labour safe seat east of Manchester city centre, this area used to be industrial (cotton spinning and engineering) and retains more manual and skilled labourers than average. The M60 and M67 pass through the middle of the constituency and it has benefited from being part of the M60 investment corridor.

	Electorate	Turnout %	Change from 2010 %
	66,574	58.1	
A Gwynne Lab	19,661	50.8	-0.2
L Hempsall C	9,150	23.7	-1.2
A Fairfoull Ukip	7,225	18.7	+13.2
N Koopman Green	1,466	3.8	
M Jewell LD	957	2.5	-15.4
V Lofas Ind	222	0.6	-0.2

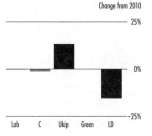

Change from 2010

Derby North

CONSERVATIVE GAIN

AMANDA SOLLOWAY
BORN Jun 6, 1961
MP 2015-

Described herself as "shocked" after winning by the smallest majority in England, 41 votes. Management consultant. Cllr, Ockbrook & Borrowash PC 2011-. Head of training and development, Baird Clothing. Counsellor. Mentor, Prince's Trust. Sch governor. Married, two children. Ed: Bramcote Hills GS.

CHALLENGERS
Chris Williamson (Lab) MP for Derby North 2010-15. Shadow min: CLG 2010-13. Social worker and welfare rights officer. Teetotal, vegan and vociferously against blood sports (trustee and former chairman, League Against Cruel Sports). Cllr, Derby CC 1991-2011, leader 2005-08, 2002-03. Vice-chairman, Derbyshire Fire & Rescue authority. Chairman, East Mids Empowerment Partnership.

Non-exec dir, Greater Derby NHS PCT. Former market trader, bricklayer. Twice divorced, once widowed. One daughter, one son. Ed: Castle Donnington HS; Thomas More RC Sch; Leicester Poly (CQSW). **Tilly Ward** (Ukip) Psychotherapy student, University of Derby. Former carer and horse-trainer. Married, two children. **Lucy Care** (LD) Chartered Engineer. Cllr, Derbyshire CC 1993, 1997-2010, cabinet member 2003-05, 2008-10. Former member to the Regional Assembly. Contested: Derby N 2010, Derby S 2005. Ed: Durham (engineering).

CONSTITUENCY PROFILE
The more leafy residential Derby seat, the only constituency in the East Midlands to change hands in 2015. Though Labour has held the seat for most of its history it has often been marginal, with the Tories holding 1983-97. A three-way marginal in 2010, fall in Lib Dem the vote made it a key gain over Labour in the 2015 election.

	Electorate	Turnout %	from 2010 % Change
	64,739	69.1	
A Solloway C	16,402	36.7	+5.0
C Williamson Lab	16,361	36.6	+3.5
T Ward Ukip	6,532	14.6	+12.8
L Care LD	3,832	8.6	-19.5
A Mason-Power Green	1,618	3.6	

Change from 2010

```
                          25%

  ████  ████  ████              0%
                    ████

                          -25%
  C    Lab   Ukip   LD   Green
```

Derby South

LABOUR HOLD

DAME MARGARET BECKETT
BORN Jan 15, 1943
MP 1983-; 1974-79

Veteran party loyalist, decided against stepping down in 2015. First female foreign sec 2006-07. Member: Labour NEC 2012-, 1980-81, cttee on standards in public life 2010-. President, No2AV 2011. Acting opp leader 1994. Dep leader opp 1992-94. Min: housing 2008-09. SoS: efra 2001-06; BIS 1997-98. Leader of HoC 1998-2001. Shadow: SoS, health 1994-95; president, board of trade 1995-97, leader HoC 1992-94; chief sec to treasury 1989-92; min: social security 1984-89. Parly under-sec, education, science 1976-79, asst whip 1975-76. Chair, select cttees: national security strategy 2010-; intelligence & security 2008; HoC modernisation 1998-2001. Contested Speaker election 2009. MP Lincoln 1974-79. Metallurgist. DBE 2013. Fabian, Unite, NUJ, Bectu. Married, two stepsons. Ed: Notre Dame HS; UMIST.

CHALLENGERS
Evonne Williams (C) Mentor, YMCA. Cllr, Derby CC 2000-. Sch governor. Ed: University of Derby (BA youth & community). **Victor Webb** (Ukip) Law costs draughtsman. Cllr, Tunbridge Wells BC 2011-15. Development director at SGM, Derby. Contested Tunbridge Wells 2010, 05, 01. **Joe Naitta** (LD) Head coach, Sporting Futures. Cllr, Derby CC 2008-, cabinet member 2008-10. Contested Derbyshire Dales.

CONSTITUENCY PROFILE
Held by Labour since its creation in 1950, but not always safely — when Margaret Beckett originally won in 1983 it was by 421 votes. Derby South contains the city centre and the more industrial south of the city, including the railworks and Rolls Royce factory as well as Pride Park. It is also the more ethnically diverse of the two Derby seats,with a significant Asian and Muslim population.

	Electorate	Turnout %	from 2010 % Change
	70,247	58.1	
M Beckett Lab	20,007	49.0	+5.7
E Williams C	11,179	27.4	-1.1
V Webb Ukip	6,341	15.5	+11.1
J Naitta LD	1,717	4.2	-16.3
D Foster Green	1,208	3.0	
C Fernandez TUSC	225	0.6	
D Gale Brit Ind	143	0.4	

Change from 2010

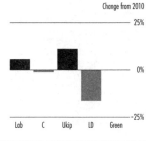

```
                          25%

  ████        ████             0%
        ████         ████

                          -25%
  Lab    C    Ukip   LD   Green
```

Derbyshire Dales

CONSERVATIVE HOLD

PATRICK MCLOUGHLIN
BORN Nov 30, 1957
MP 1986-

Plain-speaking working-class Tory, an ex-coal miner. Skilled in Commons procedures. Secretary of state for transport 2012-. Chief whip and parly sec to the Treasury 2010-12. Opposition whip: chief 2005-10; dep chief 1998-2005; pairing 1997-98. Govt whip: 1996-97; asst 1995-96. Parly under-sec: trade & industry 1993-94; employment 1992-93; transport 1989-92. PPS to: Lord Young of Graffham 1988-89, Angela Rumbold 1987-88. Contested 1983 Wolverhampton SE. Cllr: Staffordshire CC 1981-87; Cannock Chase DC 1980-87. Agriculture then Littleton Colliery; NUM/NCB member. Married, one daughter, one son. Ed: Cardinal Griffin Comp; Staffs Agriculture Coll.

CHALLENGERS
Andy Botham (Lab) Train Driver.

Cllr, Derbyshire CC 2013-, cabinet member, first Labour member for his ward since the 1950s. Aslef Union representative. Married, two daughters. **John Young** (Ukip) Regulatory consultant in agriculture, made the news for warning govt about horsemeat a year before it became a scandal. Former civil servant, worked at Defra and Food Standards Agency/Meat Hygiene Service. **Ben Fearn** (LD) Business services assistant, Derbyshire CC. Political blogger, *Views from Centre Left*. Methodist. Ed: Manchester (BA English language).

CONSTITUENCY PROFILE
A large rural seat largely made up of the Peak District and the picturesque villages within it; tourism is a mainstay of the local economy. A Conservatives stronghold, though there is some Labour support in Matlock. Held by the Tories since 1950, although the by-election that originally returned Patrick McLoughlin in 1986 was won by only 100 votes over the Liberals.

	Electorate	Turnout %	Change from 2010 %
	63,470	74.6	
P McLoughlin C	24,805	52.4	+0.3
A Botham Lab	10,761	22.7	+3.4
J Young Ukip	5,508	11.6	+7.8
B Fearn LD	3,965	8.4	-14.1
I Wood Green	2,173	4.6	+2.9
A Y'Mech Humanity	149	0.3	+0.2

Change from 2010

C Lab Ukip LD Green

Derbyshire Mid

CONSERVATIVE HOLD

PAULINE LATHAM
BORN Feb 4, 1948
MP 2010-

An experienced local government warhorse. Cut her political teeth fighting for grant-maintained status for local secondary school, as a cllr on the (then) Labour-controlled Derbyshire CC. Member, int devt select cttee. A grandmother, who became one of the oldest new female MPs in 2010. Cllr: Derby CC 1998-2010, 1992-96, mayor 2007-08; Derbyshire CC 1987-93. Contested Broxtowe 2001; Euro elections 2004, 1999 (East Midlands). OBE. 1995. Dir, Michael St Development. Proprieter, Humble Plc. Led social action projects to Uganda. Enjoys horse riding. Married, one daughter, two sons. Ed: Bramcote Hill Technical GS.

CHALLENGERS
Nicola Heaton (Lab) Cllr, Nottingham CC 2011-. Regional officer, Labour Party. Ed: Durham

University (BA economics). **Martin Fitzpatrick** (Ukip) Commercial manager, Lifting Gear Hire, Alfreton. Contested Sheffield Hallam 2010 as independent. Ed: St Thomas Moore Sch, Derby. Derby University (HND mechanical engineering). **Hilary Jones** (LD) Cllr, Derby CC 2000-, leader 2008-12, Lib Dem group leader. **Sue MacFarlane** (Green) Freelance singer-songwriter and voice coach.

CONSTITUENCY PROFILE
An unusually shaped seat, snaking around the north east of Derby, taking in suburbs and the huge new development of Oakwood and Allestree, which includes the University of Derby. The town of Belper was home to manufacturing and the base of Thorntons chocolates but, like most of this seat, is based more around retail, services and residential areas. Created for the 2010 election, the constituency was easily won by the Conservatives.

	Electorate	Turnout %	Change from 2010 %
	67,576	70.6	
P Latham C	24,908	52.2	+3.9
N Heaton Lab	12,134	25.4	+1.0
M Fitzpatrick Ukip	6,497	13.6	+11.0
H Jones LD	2,292	4.8	-15.7
S MacFarlane Green	1,898	4.0	

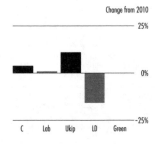

Change from 2010

C Lab Ukip LD Green

Derbyshire North East

LABOUR HOLD

NATASCHA ENGEL
BORN Apr 9, 1967
MP 2005-

Trade unionist and crusading backbencher as chair, backbench business select cttee 2010- . PPS to: John Denham 2009-10; Liam Byrne 2008-09; Peter Hain 2007-08. Member, cttees: liaison 2010-; reform of HoC 2009-; W&P 2005-07. *House* magazine Backbencher of the Year 2011. Trade union political fund ballot co-ordinator. Founder, Trade Union Co-ordinating Committee. Smith Institute. Subtitler for Teletext. GMB, UCATT Berlin-born and raised. Divorced, three sons. Ed: King's Sch, Canterbury; King's Coll, London (BA German & Portuguese); University of Westminster (MA technical & specialist translation).

CHALLENGERS
Lee Rowley (C) Senior manager, corporate change, Santander. Cllr,

Westminster CC 2006-14, cabinet member for transport who steered doomed parking charges in the West End, London, that led to council leader's resignation. Formerly at KPMG. Contested Bolsover 2010. Ed: St Mary's HS, Chesterfield; Lincoln Coll, Oxford (BA history); Manchester (MA history). **James Bush** (Ukip) Chemical engineer, senior process engineer, PM Group. Contested Derbyshire NE 2010. Married, two children. Ed: Bath (BEng chemical engineering). **David Batey** (LD) Engineer, Controls and Data Services. Cllr, Derby CC 2008-11, group chairman 2007-09. Contested Derby S 2010. Ed: Liverpool (BEng aero eng).

CONSTITUENCY PROFILE
Traditionally a coal mining area, a c-shaped seat that curls around the west of Chesterfield. Represented by Labour since 1935, but decline in mining and new private housing developments has weakened Labour and in 2015 their majority was reduced to less than 4%.

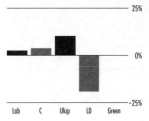

	Electorate	Turnout %	Change from 2010 %
	71,456	67.1	
N Engel Lab	19,488	40.6	+2.5
L Rowley C	17,605	36.7	+3.8
J Bush Ukip	7,631	15.9	+10.3
D Batey LD	2,004	4.2	-19.1
D Kesteven Green	1,059	2.2	
R Lane Ind	161	0.3	

Change from 2010

Lab C Ukip LD Green

Derbyshire South

CONSERVATIVE HOLD

HEATHER WHEELER
BORN May 14, 1959
MP 2010-

Long-serving councillor turned local govt representative in parliament. PPS to Jeremy Wright 2014-15. Select cttees: CLG 2010-; standards & reviews sub-cttee 2014-; standards & privileges 2010-14. VP, Local Govt Assoc 2011-. Exec member, 1922 cttee 2012-. Cllr, South Derbyshire DC 1995-2011, leader 2007-10, leader Con group 2002-10; Wandsworth BC 1982-86. Selected by open primary. Contested Coventry S 2005, 01. Dir, Brety Inns, manager, Rics Insurance, indemnity insurance broker, Lloyds. Assoc of the Chartered Insurance Institute. Married, one daughter. Ed: Grey Coat Hospital, London.

CHALLENGERS
Cheryl Pidgeon (Lab) Midlands regional secretary, UCATT. Former union official at TUC, GMB,

KFAT. Cllr: Erewash BC 2011-; Derbyshire CC 2011-13. Previously head of materials planning, Raleigh Industries bicycles. Contested Erewash 2010. Former MoD worker. Married, four children. Ed: Long Eaton GS; Nottingham Trent. **Alan Graves** (Ukip) IT company director. Cllr, Derbyshire CC 1995-2000, 2002-, defected from Labour 2009 to Ukip 2012. Contested Derby S 2010 as independent. Former kissogram in his teens. Married, three sons, **Lorraine Johnson** (LD) IT professional, BT.

CONSTITUENCY PROFILE
The seat has a long history of being a Lab-Conservative marginal (Labour 1997-2010). Covers the old pottery and mining town of Swadlincote and the more rural commuter towns and villages in Derby's southern hinterland. Colourful characters, including Edwina Currie and Labour DPM and foreign secretary George Brown have represented the constituency.

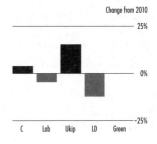

	Electorate	Turnout %	Change from 2010 %
	74,395	68.2	
H Wheeler C	25,066	49.4	+3.9
C Pidgeon Lab	13,595	26.8	-4.6
A Graves Ukip	8,998	17.7	+15.3
L Johnson LD	1,887	3.7	-12.2
M Bamkin Green	1,216	2.4	

Change from 2010

C Lab Ukip LD Green

Devizes

CONSERVATIVE HOLD

CLAIRE PERRY
BORN Apr 3, 1964
MP 2010-

Joined party in 2006 but quickly established herself within CCHQ as a policy adviser to George Osborne 2007-09 and early promotions in govt. Parly under-sec, transport 2014-. Asst whip, Treasury 2013-14. PPS to Philip Hammond 2011-13. Member, justice select cttee 2010-11. Adviser to PM on preventing sexualisation & commericalisation of childhood 2012-. Won first selection attempt, Women2Win member. First person in family to go to university. Career in City and US: Credit Suisse First Boston; McKinsey & Co; Bank of America. Homemaker 2000-07. Separated, two daughters, one son. Ed: Nailsea Comp; Brasenose Coll, Oxford (BA geography); Harvard Business Sch (MBA).

CHALLENGERS
David Pollitt (Ukip) Business

consultant. Cllr, Wiltshire CC 2013-. Married, two children. **Chris Watts** (Lab) IT consultant. President, Wiltshire and Swindon GMB. Married, three children. **Manda Rigby** (LD) Management consultant, former MD of Netgear UKI and head of enterprise marketing UK for Microsoft. Cllr, Bath & NE Somerset CC 2011-15. Former chairwoman, Bath City FC. Samaritan, writer. Voted *Bath Chronicle* Woman of the Year 2011. Ed: University of Bristol (BA politics, president Students' Union); Bath Spa (MA creative writing).

CONSTITUENCY PROFILE
Largely made up of rural country-side, dotted with historic market towns, including Marlborough and Devizes itself, home to Wadworth's brewery. The constituency has important military associations; to the south, the seat extends over part of Salisbury Plain and includes the Royal Sch of Artillery at Larkhill. A safe Conservative seat, held by the party since 1924.

	Electorate	Turnout %	Change from 2010 %
	69,211	70.8	
C Perry C	28,295	57.7	+2.7
D Pollitt Ukip	7,544	15.4	+10.9
C Watts Lab	6,360	13.0	+2.8
M Rigby LD	3,954	8.1	-18.9
E Dawnay Green	2,853	5.8	+4.1

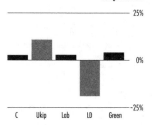

Change from 2010

Devon Central

CONSERVATIVE HOLD

MEL STRIDE
BORN Sep 30, 1961
MP 2010-

Compassionate Conservative with experience at Centre for Social Justice. Enthusiastic advocate of pavement politics, as modelled on Lib Dem grassroots activism. Whip, lord commissioner, Treasury 2015-. Asst whip 2014-15. PPS to John Hayes 2011-14. Member, NI affairs select cttee. Campaigned against post office and hospital closures (co-chairman, Crediton Hospital Campaign Group). Comm for Social Justice working group 2006-07. Launched "One Tonne Green Challenge" in UK. Founded Venture Marketing Group. History and culture buff; award-winning tourist guide. Qualified pilot. Married, three daughters. Ed: Portsmouth GS; St Edmund Hall, Oxford (BA PPE, president Oxford Union).

CHALLENGERS
John Conway (Ukip) Retired

tax inspector at Launceston Tax Office. Manages motorcycle training agency. Cllr, Launceton TC. Married, two sons. Ed: Torquay Boys GS. **Lynne Richards** (Lab) Business adviser. England director of a leading family charity. Ed: Exeter (Pg leadership & management). **Alex White** (LD) Management consultant, Accenture. Unicef volunteer, teaching assistant at Exeter Deaf Academy. LTA tennis coach. Ed: Warwick (LLB European law with German law).

CONSTITUENCY PROFILE
A large sprawling rural seat in the centre of Devon with no large towns. The south the constituency includes a large part of Dartmoor, including the Okehampton army camp and, at the far southern point of the constituency, the Benedictine Buckfast Abbey — the surprising source of the tonic wine infamously associated with binge drinking in Scotland. Created for the 2010 election.

	Electorate	Turnout %	Change from 2010 %
	72,737	74.9	
M Stride C	28,436	52.2	+0.7
J Conway Ukip	7,171	13.2	+7.8
L Richards Lab	6,985	12.8	+5.9
A White LD	6,643	12.2	-22.2
A Williamson Green	4,866	8.9	+7.0
A Price Ind	347	0.6	

Change from 2010

Devon East

CONSERVATIVE HOLD

HUGO SWIRE
BORN Nov 30, 1959
MP 2001-

Close friend of David Cameron.
Sacked as shadow SoS, culture
2005-07 after suggesting Tories
would scrap museum free entry in
govt, returned to roles in foreign
office. Min of state: FCO 2012-;
NI office 2010-12. Shad min: arts
2004-5; opp whip 2003-04. PPS to
Theresa May 2003. Member, select
cttee: NI 2002-05. Filmed cracking
jokes about people on benefits in
2015. Contested Greenock 1997.
Career: followed father's footsteps
in becoming dir, Sotheby's; non-
exec chairman, Photo-Me; head of
development, Nat Gallery; financial
consultant; Grenadier Guards.
Once dated Jerry Hall. Married,
two daughters. Ed: Eton Coll;
St Andrew's (left after one year
studying fine art); RMA, Sandhurst.

CHALLENGERS
Claire Wright (Independent)

Freelance in PR, formerly with
NHS and Devon CC. Cllr, Devon
CC 2013-, leader non-aligned
group, largest majority of any cllr
in south west; East Devon DC 2011-
15. Married, one daughter. **Andrew
Chapman** (Ukip) Retired tax agent.
Cllr, Surrey CC 1985-89 for Liberal/
Lib Dems. Chairman, Ukip Devon
East branch 2015-. Ed: Denstone
Coll, Uttoxeter; Goldsmiths.
Stephen Race (Lab) Account
director, Fleishman-Hillard.
Former senior parly researcher to
Ben Bradshaw 2007-11. VC, Fabian
Society 2013-; chairman, Young
Fabians 2012-13. Ed: Manchester
(BA literature & social sciences).

CONSTITUENCY PROFILE
Redrawn heavily in 2010, without
the eastern tip of Devon. In the
east lies Sidmouth and the historic
Ottery St Mary, with the western
boundary following the Exe to
Exmouth. Generally affluent and
ageing, with about one in three 65
or over. The seat and its predecessor
have been Tory since 1945.

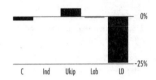

		Electorate	Turnout %	from 2010 % Change
		74,224	73.7	
H Swire	C	25,401	46.4	-1.9
C Wright	Ind	13,140	24.0	
A Chapman	Ukip	6,870	12.6	+4.4
S Race	Lab	5,591	10.2	-0.6
S Mole	LD	3,715	6.8	-24.4

Change from 2010

25%

0%

-25%

C   Ind   Ukip   Lab   LD

Devon North

CONSERVATIVE GAIN

**PETER HEATON-
JONES**
BORN Aug 2, 1963
MP 2015-

Former broadcaster, journalist,
BBC radio presenter and marketing
professional. Interviewed Tony
Blair as PM for BBC Swindon &
Wiltshire. Worked in Australia
as head of marketing for the
ABC's national radio stations Cllr:
Swindon BC 2010-14, retired after
criticism of holding council seat in
separate ward to where he lived;
Haydon Wick PC 2009-. Attracted
controversy in election period
after newspaper column "rant"
about farmers. Worked as a turkey
plucker as a student. Ed: University
of London.

CHALLENGERS
Sir Nick Harvey (LD) MP,
1992-2015. Prominent in Paddy
Ashdown's Lib-Lab project of 1990s.
From Lib Dems' centre-right. Min
for armed forces 2010-12. Spokesman
for Commons Commission during

expenses scandal. LD shadow SoS,
defence 2006-10. LD spokes: CMS
2001-03; health 1999-2001; const
1997-99; trade & industry 1994-97;
transport 1992-94. Select cttees:
standards & privileges 2012-15, 2005-
10; members estimate 2004-10; home
affairs 2005-06; Euro scrutiny
2004-05. VP, Fed of Economic
Devt Auths. Communications
and marketing consultant. Union
of Liberal Students. Married, one
daughter, one son. Ed: Queen's
Coll, Taunton; Middlesex Poly (BA
business studies). **Steve Crowther**
(Ukip) Writer and communications
consultant. Assistant to MEPs.
Contested Devon N 2010.

CONSTITUENCY PROFILE
A rural seat on the western edge
of Exmoor, with Barnstaple the
biggest town. Has been a Liberal-
Tory marginal since its creation
in 1950, previously represented
by the Liberal party leader
Jeremy Thorpe, who lost his seat
in 1979 while facing charges of
attempted murder.

		Electorate	Turnout %	from 2010 % Change
		74,737	70.0	
P Heaton-Jones	C	22,341	42.7	+6.7
N Harvey	LD	15,405	29.4	-17.9
S Crowther	Ukip	7,719	14.8	+7.5
M Cann	Lab	3,699	7.1	+1.9
R Knight	Green	3,018	5.8	+4.4
G Sables	Comm	138	0.3	

Change from 2010

25%

0%

-25%

C   LD   Ukip   Lab   Green

Devon South West

CONSERVATIVE HOLD

GARY STREETER
BORN Oct 2, 1955
MP 1992-

Evangelical Christian, interested in human rights and developing world. Contested deputy speaker election 2013. Shadow minister, foreign affairs 2003-04. Shad SoS, int devt 1998-2001. Parly sec, lord chancellor's department 1996-97. PPS to: Sir Nicholas Lyell 1994-95; Sir Derek Spencer 1993-5. Opp spokes, foreign affairs, Europe 1997-98. Asst govt whip 1995-96. Select cttees: ecclesiastical 2010-; panel of chairs 2009-; speaker's cttee on electoral reform 2006-; home affairs 2005-10. Vice-chairman, Conservative Party 2001-02. MP for Plymouth Sutton 1992-7. Cllr, Plymouth CC 1986-92. Solicitor, Foot & Bowden. Married, one daughter, one son. Ed: Tiverton GS; King's Coll, London (LLB law).

CHALLENGERS
Chaz Singh (Lab) Fundraising and training officer, Fata-He BME Development. Cllr, Plymouth CC 2011-, Plymouth's first Sikh cllr; deputy lord mayor 2012-13. Community champion, 2015 Meet the Mast South West awards. Married. **Robin Julian** (Ukip) MD, Torpedo Training HGV driving school. Cllr, Devon CC 2013-, leader Ukip group. **Tom Davies** (LD) Chartered accountant. Director, not-for-profit team at Grant Thornton LLP. Founding dir, Liberis NGO. Trustee, Plymouth Citizens Advice Bureau. Ed: Trinity Coll, Oxford (BA ancient & modern history). **Win Scutt** (Green) Assistant properties curator, English Heritage. Archaeological correspondent, BBC Radio.

CONSTITUENCY PROFILE
Has returned Tory MPs with sizeable majorities in recent decades. Largest settlements are generally affluent, on the outskirts of Plymouth. Home to third highest proportion of apprentices in England & Wales.

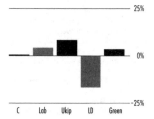

	Electorate	Turnout %	Change from 2010 %
	71,035	70.9	
G Streeter C	28,500	56.6	+0.6
C Singh Lab	8,391	16.7	+4.2
R Julian Ukip	7,306	14.5	+8.3
T Davies LD	3,767	7.5	-16.7
W Scutt Green	2,408	4.8	+3.5

Change from 2010

Devon West & Torridge

CONSERVATIVE HOLD

GEOFFREY COX
BORN Apr 30, 1960
MP 2005-

Attracted huge controversy for continuing extra-parliamentary work, earning £450,000 as a lawyer in 13 months up to November 2014. Said to be the country's highest earning MP. Invested in Phoenix Film Partners, under investigation by HMRC into its tax affairs. Select cttees: standards & privileges 2010-; efra 2006-10. Founded Thomas More Chambers, served as standing counsel to Mauritius. Appointed QC 2003. Contested Devon W 2001. Married, one daughter, two sons. Ed: King's Coll, Taunton; Downing Coll, Cambridge (BA English & law).

CHALLENGERS
Derek Sargent (Ukip) Benefit fraud consultant. Previously: benefit fraud investigator, North Devon DC; security consultant for Chevron Oil in Angola. Former Captain, Royal Marines, specialised in jungle warfare, served in Borneo, Singapore, Malaya, Australia and elsewhere. Married, two daughters. Ed: Swanage GS. **Paula Dolphin** (LD) Cllr: Cornwall CC/North Cornwall DC 2007-; Bude-Stratton TC 2004-12, mayor 2012-13. Born in Brazil, moved to UK 1995. Married. Ed: PUC-Campinas, Brazil (BA). **Mike Sparling** (Lab) Cllr, Plymouth CC 2014-. Projects support team officer, Plymouth Community Homes. Former parly researcher for Lord Foulkes, Baroness Adams, Lord McAvoy. Former flight attendant, Qantas. Regional organiser, Ed Miliband for Labour leader. Ed: Manchester (BA philosophy & politics).

CONSTITUENCY PROFILE
A large rural seat running down the western side of the border with Cornwall. Tourism is important on the northern coast, while the rest is rural and agricultural. Conservative 1924-1995, when Emma Nicholson defected to the Lib Dems, now returned to the Tories.

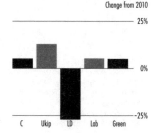

	Electorate	Turnout %	Change from 2010 %
	78,582	72.0	
G Cox C	28,774	50.9	+5.2
D Sargent Ukip	10,371	18.3	+12.9
P Dolphin LD	7,483	13.2	-27.1
M Sparling Lab	6,015	10.6	+5.4
C Simmons Green	3,941	7.0	+5.1

Change from 2010

Dewsbury

LABOUR GAIN

PAULA SHERRIFF
BORN Apr 16, 1975
MP 2015-

Service coordinator, dermatology care service manager in NHS with Virgin Care. Cllr, Wakefield C 2012-. Active in Save Dewsbury Hospital campaign. Chairwoman, Pontefract Business Forum. Worked in victim support for police. Unison. Sister, Lee Sherriff, contested Carlisle 2015. Ed: Morton Sch, Carlisle.

CHALLENGERS
Simon Reevell (C) MP, 2010-15. Criminal barrister specialising in defending service personnel at courts martial; re-trained in law after injury thwarted military career ambition (had army scholarship and cadetship). Member, Scottish affairs select cttee 2010-15. Born and brought up in West Yorkshire. Church warden. Married. Ed: Boston Spa Comp; Manchester Poly (BA economics); Poly of Central London (Dip law);

Sch of Law (BVC). **Mark Thackray** (Ukip) Founder, Tektronix textile machine manufacturer. Married, three daughters. Ed: Dewsbury & Batley Tech Coll. **Ednan Hussain** (LD) Team leader, PC World. Son of former Kirlees mayor. Married, two children. Ed: St John Fisher HS; Dewsbury Coll; University of Huddersfield (BA media & journalism). **Adrian Cruden** (Green) Personnel manager, VoiceAbility charity. Cllr, Kirkburton PC 2010-14. Married.

CONSTITUENCY PROFILE
An industrial former textile town in West Yorkshire. A diverse population, with a large Asian population in the textile areas with the Markazi mosque, one of the largest in Europe. Savile Town is overwhelmingly Muslim. Other areas are largely white and fertile ground previously for the BNP. A Labour seat since the 1920s with few exceptions, one of which was 2010-15, when the Conservatives held the seat.

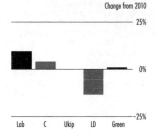

	Electorate	Turnout %	from 2010 %	Change
	79,765	67.2		
P Sherriff Lab	22,406	41.8	+9.6	
S Reevell C	20,955	39.1	+4.1	
M Thackray Ukip	6,649	12.4		
E Hussain LD	1,924	3.6	-13.4	
A Cruden Green	1,366	2.6	+1.0	
R Carter Yorks	236	0.4		
S Hakes CPA	94	0.2		

Change from 2010

Lab   C   Ukip   LD   Green

Don Valley

LABOUR HOLD

CAROLINE FLINT
BORN Aug 10, 1958
MP 1997-

Shadow SoS for energy & climate change 2011-; CLG 2010-11. Contesting deputy leadership election 2010. Quit as Europe minister (2008-09) after being denied promotion, launched attack on Brown's use of women as "window-dressing". Min: housing 2008; Yorks & Humber 2007-08; employment 2007-08; public health 2006-07. Parly under-sec: health 2005-07; home 2003-05. PPS to: John Reid 2002-03; Peter Hain 2001-02. Select cttees: modernisation HoC 2003; admin 2001-05; education & employment 1997-99. British American parly group 1997-. GMB researcher, pol officer. Shop steward, Nalgo. Fabians, Progress, Labour Friends of Israel. Divorced, re-married, one daughter, one son, one stepson. Ed: Twickenham Girls Sch; Richmond Coll; UEA (BA American history, literature & film).

CHALLENGERS
Carl Jackson (C) Management consultant, MSB Consultancy. Former policy adviser to David Davis. Co-edited, *Future of Conservatism*. Former columnist, *Yorkshire Post*. Manager, organisation supporting local microbreweries. Engaged. Sheffield Wednesday FC supporter. Family roots to local South Yorkshire miners. Ed: University Coll, Oxford (BA history); Oxford Brookes (Dip law). **Guy Aston** (Ukip) Business and behavioural training consultant. Defected from English Democrats. Married, one daughter.

CONSTITUENCY PROFILE
The rural hinterland around the south of Doncaster, mostly made up of traditional former colliery towns and villages. There are also a few more affluent towns like Tickhill and the upmarket Doncaster suburb of Bessacarr meaning Labour's position here is no longer as dominant as it once was.

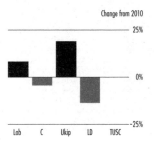

	Electorate	Turnout %	from 2010 %	Change
	71,299	59.6		
C Flint Lab	19,621	46.2	+8.3	
C Jackson C	10,736	25.3	-4.4	
G Aston Ukip	9,963	23.5	+19.1	
R Paterson LD	1,487	3.5	-13.6	
S Williams TUSC	437	1.0		
L Dutton Eng Dem	242	0.6	-3.5	

Change from 2010

Lab   C   Ukip   LD   TUSC

Doncaster Central

LABOUR HOLD

ROSIE WINTERTON
BORN Aug 10, 1958
MP 1997-

Hardened veteran. Opposition chief whip 2010-. Shadow: leader HoC 2010; min for women 2010. Min: local govt 2009-10; work & pensions 2008-09; Yorkshire & the Humber 2008-; transport 2007-08; health services 2003-07; parly sec, Lord Chancellor's dept 2001-03. Caught up in expenses scandal for claiming nearly £5,000 for "soundproofing" of walls. Select cttees: speaker's cttee for parly authority 2010-11; Speaker's electoral cttee 2009-10. Head of John Prescott's office as Labour deputy leader 1994-97. MD Connect Public Affairs. TGWU branch officer. Parly officer, Royal Coll of Nursing, Soutwark Council. Ed: Doncaster GS; Hull (BA history).

CHALLENGERS
Chris Hodgson (Ukip) MD, IT business. Former pit worker. Helps run domiciliary care agency with his wife. Ed: Colchester Royal GS, Sheffield City Poly (BSc engineering). **Zoe Metcalfe** (C) Works in primary school and runs family business. Cllr, Harrogate BC 2015-. Sch governor. Email administrator on Arkendale PC. **John Brown** (LD) Engineer, systems analyst, management consultant and part time FE lecturer teaching maths & IT. Contested Doncaster mayor election 2013. Ed: Amthorpe HS; Doncaster Coll; Loughborough (BTech); Lancaster (MA).

CONSTITUENCY PROFILE
Labour since 1964, although not as safely as other Doncaster seats. Made up of the large town of Doncaster itself, a successful regional retail, communications and transport centre, and the large former mining village of Armthorpe. Doncaster's local council has had an English Democrat mayor (2009-13), showcasing a populist sentiment in the city.

	Electorate	Turnout %	Change from 2010 %
	71,136	56.8	
R Winterton Lab	19,840	49.1	+9.4
C Hodgson Ukip	9,747	24.1	+20.7
Z Metcalfe C	8,386	20.8	-4.0
J Brown LD	1,717	4.3	-16.8
M Akram TUSC	421	1.0	
D Burnett Eng Dem	309	0.8	-3.6

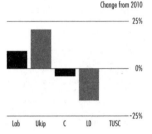

Change from 2010

Lab   Ukip   C   LD   TUSC

Doncaster North

LABOUR HOLD

ED MILIBAND
BORN Dec 24, 1969
MP 2005-

Leader of the opposition 2010-15. Brownite, unable to extricate Labour in voters' minds from his predecessor's role of financial crash. Once seen as more personable than elder brother David, contested against him to lead the party away from Blairism, leading many to say party picked the wrong brother. Labour united under him but, despite improvement in late TV appearances, few saw him as PM material. SoS, ECC 2008-10. Minister: cabinet office, Chancellor, Duchy of Lancaster, 2007-08. Parly sec, Cabinet Office 2006-07. Special adviser to Gordon Brown as chancellor 1997-2002. Chair, Council of Economic Advisers 2004-05. Govt fellow, lecturer, Harvard. TGWU/USDAW. First Jewish leader of Labour, son of Marxist academic Ralph. Married, two sons. Ed: Primrose Hill PS; Haverstock Comp Sch; Corpus Christi Coll, Oxford (BA PPE, JCR president); LSE (MSc economics).

CHALLENGERS
Kim Parkinson (Ukip) Self-employed business management consultant. Divorced, three children. Ed: University of Nottingham. **Mark Fletcher** (C) Chief of staff to Lord Popat. Ed: Danum Sixth Form; Jesus Coll, Cambridge (BA land economy, pres CUSU).

CONSTITUENCY PROFILE
The more rural northern part of Doncaster MBC, studded with former pit towns and villages. A traditional mining seat but industrial decline has brought the strains of deprivation and the slow transition from pit villages to commuter towns for Doncaster and Barnsley. Coal is still mined at Hatfield, one of the few remaining coal mines operating in Yorkshire, and a new carbon-capture coal fired power station is planned in the area.

	Electorate	Turnout %	Change from 2010 %
	70,898	55.7	
E Miliband Lab	20,708	52.4	+5.1
K Parkinson Ukip	8,928	22.6	+18.3
M Fletcher C	7,235	18.3	-2.7
P Baker LD	1,005	2.5	-12.3
P Kennedy Green	757	1.9	
D Allen Eng Dem	448	1.1	-4.0
M Jackson TUSC	258	0.7	+0.2
N The Flying Brick Loony	162	0.4	

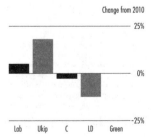

Change from 2010

Lab   Ukip   C   LD   Green

Dorset Mid & Poole North

CONSERVATIVE GAIN

MICHAEL TOMLINSON
BORN Oct 1, 1977
MP 2015-

Barrister on Western circuit. Chairman, Dorset area Conservative Association 2010-. Legal representation: min justice; DfT. Constituency campaign manager 2010. Participant in Project Umubano. Organiser of Christian Youth Camp with wife. Active member of Poole Hockey Club, Hamworthy Cricket Club. Married, three children. Ed: Hereford Cathedral Sch; London (BA Classics); Coll of Law (PgDip law).

CHALLENGERS
Vikki Slade (LD) Café and catering service owner. Attempted to succeed her mentor, Annette Brooke (MP 2001-15), for whom she was a personal asst. Cllr, Poole BC 2011-15. Chairwoman, Broadstone Chamber of Trade & Commerce. Young Enterprise volunteer. Former financial advisor and training recruitment manager. Married, four children. Ed: Tonbridge GS for Girls. **Richard Turner** (Ukip) Runs Willow Way Marina family business, Christchurch. Former motorcycle mechanic. Chair, Christchurch Ukip branch. Married, one son. Ed: Harlington Sch. **Patrick Canavan** (Lab) Former regional officer, Unite. Contested: Newton Abbot 2010; Torbay 2011 mayoral election. Sch & coll governor. Ed: Open University (BA); Leicester (MA LLM law).

CONSTITUENCY PROFILE
A largely rural area in the west, contrasts with more densely populated areas such as Broadstone, on the outskirts of Poole, in the east. This is generally a fairly affluent constituency that is economically active, with sizeable working and middle classes. Only about one in ten residents lives in social housing. The seat was taken from the Tories by the Lib Dems in 2001, and won back in 2015.

	Electorate	Turnout %	from 2010 %
	68,917	67.5	
M Tomlinson C	23,639	50.8	+6.3
V Slade LD	13,109	28.2	-16.9
R Turner Ukip	5,663	12.2	+7.7
P Canavan Lab	2,767	6.0	+0.1
M Chivers Green	1,321	2.8	

Change from 2010

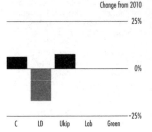

Dorset North

CONSERVATIVE HOLD

SIMON HOARE
BORN Jun 28, 1969
MP 2015-

MD in property development company. Business consultant. Cllr: Oxfordshire CC 2013-15; West Oxfordshire DC 2004-15. Contested: Cardiff South & Penarth 2010, criticised for calling himself "local" in campaign literature while cllr in Oxfordshire; Cardiff West 1997. Former chairman, Oxford Bow Group. Married, three daughters. Ed: Bishop Hannon HS; Greyfriars Hall, Oxford (BA modern history, VP OUSU).

CHALLENGERS
Steve Unwin (Ukip) Antiquarian and secondhand internet book seller. Former Conservative party election agent in 2001, 1997, 1992, 1987. Successful campaign agent to former incumbent MP, Bob Walter. Married, one daughter. Ed: Manor Secondary Modern, York; Nunthorpe GS; North Staffordshire Polytechnic (LLB law). **Hugo Miéville** (LD) Part-time teacher. Cllr, Blandford Forum TC 2011-. Former head of modern languages, Milton Abbey Sch. Member, Blanford-Mortain Twinning Association. Sch governor. Ed: Teignbridge GS; University of Warwick (BA; MA French studies). **Kim Fendley** (Lab) History teacher. Contested Dorset North 2009 CC elections. Ed: Swansea University (BA history); University of Bath (PGCE).

CONSTITUENCY PROFILE
Held by the Conservatives since 1950, if by small majorities when Lib Dems targeted the seat 2001-10. A rural seat centred upon the Blackmoor Vale and the chalk hills of Cranborne Chase and stretching from the outskirts of Poole up to the county borders with Somerset and Wiltshire. Mostly made up of small market towns, with livestock farming and the food industry still important parts of the local economy.

	Electorate	Turnout %	from 2010 %
	74,576	71.6	
S Hoare C	30,227	56.6	+5.6
S Unwin Ukip	9,109	17.1	+11.9
H Miéville LD	6,226	11.7	-25.3
K Fendley Lab	4,785	9.0	+3.6
R Barrington Green	3,038	5.7	+4.7

Change from 2010

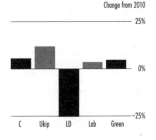

Dorset South

CONSERVATIVE HOLD

RICHARD DRAX
BORN Jan 29, 1958
MP 2010-

Privileged former soldier and journalist, early critic of coalition deal. Lives in 7,000-acre Charborough House estate; runs as farming business. Chooses not to use full name, Richard Grosvenor Plunkett-Ernle-Erle-Drax. Member, efra select cttee 2010-. Worked in family agricultural firm. Journalist: *BBC South Today; Radio Solent; Daily Telegraph; Daily Express; Tyne Tees TV; Yorkshire Evening Press.* Soldier, Coldstream Guards. Divorced, re-married, two daughters, two sons from first marriage. Ed: Harrow Sch; RMA Sandhurst; Royal Agricultural Coll (Dip rural land management); Westminster (Dip journalism).

CHALLENGERS
Simon Bowkett (Lab) Chief executive, Exeter CVS charity. Cllr: Exeter CC 2012-; Weymouth and Portland BC 2004-12. Unite. Children. **Malcolm Shakesby** (Ukip) Marine consultant. Former captain, Royal Merchant Navy. MBE 1987 for work as resue co-ordinator to Herald of Free Enterprise capsizing. As Conservative: cllr, Dorset CC 2001-09; contested Dorset S 1997. **Howard Legg** (LD) Property business manager and volunteer advisor. Cllr: Weymouth and Portland BC 1988-2012, twice mayor; Dorset CC 2009-13. Former teacher.

CONSTITUENCY PROFILE
Covers the south coast of Dorset: in the west is Weymouth and the tied island of Portland, to the east the Isle of Purbeck. A centre for tourism (resorts and Jurassic Coast), sailing (a 2012 Olympic venue) and quarrying. Historically a comfortable Conservative seat, but was one of two Labour gains in 2001 after Lib Dems voted tactically. Tories regained the seat in 2010.

	Electorate	Turnout %	Change from 2010 %
	71,974	67.5	
R Drax C	23,756	48.9	+3.8
S Bowkett Lab	11,762	24.2	-6.1
M Shakesby Ukip	7,304	15.0	+11.0
H Legg LD	2,901	6.0	-13.0
J Burnet Green	2,275	4.7	+3.5
M Stewkesbury Ind	435	0.9	
A Kirkwood Active Dem	164	0.3	

Change from 2010

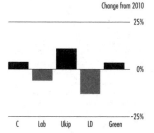

Dorset West

CONSERVATIVE HOLD

OLIVER LETWIN
BORN May 19, 1956
MP 1997-

Indefatigable intellectual with free-market instincts. Early Eurosceptic. Chancellor of the Duchy of Lancaster 2014-, in overall charge of cab office. Min: govt policy 2010-15; Cab Office 2010-14. Chairman, Policy Review and CRD/Policy Forum, 2005-. Shadow: chancellor 2003-05; SoS, Defra 2005, home 2001-03; chief sec to the Treasury 2000-01; financial sec to the Treasury 1999-2000; spokes, constl affairs, Scotland & Wales 1998-99. Member, deregulation select cttee 1998-99. Special adviser to Sir Keith Joseph. Contested: Hampstead & H 1992; Hackney N & SN 1987. MD, NM Rothschild & Son. Taught philosophy at Cambridge. FRSA. Married, one daughter, one son. Ed: Eton Coll; Trinity Coll, Cambridge (BA history; MA; PhD philosophy); London Business Sch; Princeton (Procter fellow).

CHALLENGERS
Ros Kayes (LD) Cognitive behavioural therapist and FE lecturer. Cllr: Dorset CC 2013-; West Dorset DC 2007-; Bridport TC 2006-. Contested South Dorset 2010. Former teacher and counsellor. Married, one daughter, one son. Ed: Christ Church, Oxford (BA English), Essex (MA sociology), UCL (PGCE), Plymouth (Advanced Dip counselling & psychotherapy). **David Glossop** (Ukip) Writing and editing professional. Former solider in army and Royal Marines. Volunteer watchkeeper, NCI.

CONSTITUENCY PROFILE
An affluent and consistently Conservative rural constituency, although was a close Tory-Lib Dem marginal in 1997. Like many seats on the south coast it is a popular retirement setting and has a high proportion of pensioners. The seat also contains Tolpuddle, the site of the TUC festival to commemorate the Tolpuddle Martyrs.

	Electorate	Turnout %	Change from 2010 %
	78,427	72.0	
O Letwin C	28,329	50.2	+2.6
R Kayes LD	12,199	21.6	-19.1
D Glossop Ukip	7,055	12.5	+8.7
R Rogers Lab	5,633	10.0	+3.3
P Barton Green	3,242	5.7	+4.6

Change from 2010

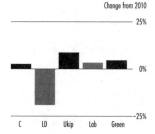

Dover

CONSERVATIVE HOLD

CHARLIE ELPHICKE
BORN Mar 14, 1971
MP 2010-

Campaigned heavily against privatisation of port of Dover, said it was the "best Christmas present the people of Dover could have" when it was rejected in 2012. Lord Commissioner, Treasury 2015-. PPS to: Iain Duncan Smith 2014-15; David Lidington 2013-14. 1922 exec committee, 2010-. Select cttees: consolidation 2010-; public admin 2010-13. Cllr, Lambeth BC 1994-98. Research fellow, Centre for Policy Studies. Tax lawyer: partner, Hunton & Williams. Founded E-Print, recycled paper printing specialist business. Research scientist for ICI Pharmaceuticals. Contested St Albans 2001. Married, one daughter, one son. Ed: Felsted Sch, Essex; University of Nottingham (LLB law); Inns of Court Sch of Law.

CHALLENGERS
Clair Hawkins (Lab) Local

employment charity worker. Former teacher. Cllr, Tower Hamlets 2006-10. Former career guidance adviser to young people. Campaigned for US Democrats 2004. GMB, Unison, Co-op. Ed: Deal Parochial & Castle Comm Sch; Queen Mary, London. **David Little** (Ukip) Businessman, owns graphic images company. Member, Dover Town Team. Publisher, *Dover Life* magazine. Mocked after paying Bulgarian to deliver anti-EU leaflets. Ed: Dover GS. **Sarah Smith** (LD) Cognitive psychologist. Former business director. In treatment for ovarian cancer. Married, two children.

CONSTITUENCY PROFILE
A diverse seat with a political tradition including coal mining, seaside resorts, picturesque countryside and the world's busiest passenger port. A Labour target before 1997, then kept thanks to the party's presence in Dover town centre, it fell to the Tories in their clean sweep of Kent in 2010.

	Electorate	Turnout %	from 2010 %	Change %
		72,929	68.9	
C Elphicke C		21,737	43.3	-0.7
C Hawkins Lab		15,443	30.8	-2.8
D Little Ukip		10,177	20.3	+16.8
S Smith LD		1,572	3.1	-12.7
J Trimingham Green		1,295	2.6	

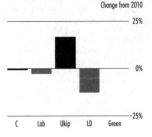

Change from 2010

Down North

INDEPENDENT HOLD

LADY SYLVIA HERMON
BORN Aug 11, 1955
MP 2001-

The UK's only independent MP. From mid-Ulster farming background. First elected as UUP, quit in 2010 over party's links with Conservatives. UUP spokesperson: home, trade & industry, youth and women 2001-05; CMS 2002-05. Select cttees: NI affairs 2005-; electoral commission 2003-10; works of art 2005-10. Cttee member addressing Patten Report Criminal Justice review 2000. Ulster Unionist exec 1999. Author, law lecturer, Queens University Belfast. Widow of former RUC chief constable Sir John Hermon, two sons. Ed: Dungannon HS; Aberystwyth (LLB law); Chester Coll of Law.

CHALLENGERS
Alex Easton (DUP) MLA for North Down 2003-. Assembly Private Secretary to the Department of health, social services and public

safety. Member, NI Assembly cttees: public accounts 2013-, 2011-12; regional development 2012-. Worked in healthcare. Cllr, North Down BC 2001-. Member, Orange Order. Married. Ed: Gransha Boys HS; Bangor Technical Coll. **Andrew Muir** (Alliance) President Alliance Party 2015-, chair 2013-15. Ticketing systems manager, Translink. Cllr, North Down BC 2010-, mayor 2013-14. Ed: Ulster (BA peace & conflict studies). **Steven Agnew** (Green) Leader, Green Party in Northern Ireland 2011-. MLA, North Down 2011-.

CONSTITUENCY PROFILE
Mostly middle-class protestant on the Ards peninsular, includes towns of Bangor and Rory McIlroy's home town of Holywood. Its history is predominantly Ulster Unionist, but in 1995 it was taken by the anti-Good Friday Agreement UK Unionist Party. Sylvia Hermon retook it for UUP in 2001, but after leaving in 2010 left the UUP with no seats in parliament for the first time.

	Electorate	Turnout %	from 2010 %	Change %
		64,207	56.0	
S Hermon Ind		17,689	49.2	-14.1
A Easton DUP		8,487	23.6	
A Muir Alliance		3,086	8.6	+3.0
S Agnew Green		1,958	5.5	+2.3
M Brotherston C		1,593	4.4	-15.9
J Lavery Ukip		1,482	4.1	
W Cudworth TUV		686	1.9	-3.0
T Woolley SDLP		355	1.0	-1.0
G Donnelly CSA		338	0.9	
T McCartney SF		273	0.8	+0.0

Change from 2010

Down South

SDLP HOLD

MARGARET RITCHIE
BORN Mar 25, 1958
MP 2010-

SDLP spokeswoman: environment, food and rural affairs 2010-; energy and climate change 2010-; regional development 2003-07. Member, environment, food and rural affairs select cttee 2012-. SDLP leader 2010-11. MLA for South Down 2003-12. Min, social development 2007-10. Cllr. Down DC 1985-2009. Parly asst and political researcher to Eddie McGrady MP. Launched the initiative programming scheme, *New Housing Agenda* 2008, aiming to tackle homelessness. Former social worker. Ed: St Mary's HS; Queen's University Belfast (BA geography & political science); Pg, administrative management.

CHALLENGERS
Chris Hazzard (SF) MLA for South Down 2012-. NI Assembly cttees: justice 2014-; education 2012-. Youngest MLA at selection.

Ed: Our Lady & St Patrick's Coll, Knock; Queens University Belfast (PhD international studies & political philosophy). **Harold McKee** (UUP) Farmer. Cllr, Newry & Mourne DC 2011-. Deputy chair, LGA governance. Married. Ed: Kilkeel HS. **Jim Wells** (DUP) Town planner. Cllr, Down DC 2001-. Contested Down S 2010, 05, 01. Said at hustings that children raised in homosexual parental backgrounds are more likely to be abused and bullied. Ed: Lurgan Coll; Queen's, Belfast.

CONSTITUENCY PROFILE
A rural seat in the coastal south east of Northern Ireland. Contains the burial place of St Patrick at Downpatrick. Agriculture and fishing are important industries. Mainly Catholic. Formerly a tight marginal seat between UUP and SDLP. Ex-Conservative minister Enoch Powell held the seat for 13 years from 1974 as UUP. SDLP have held the seat since 1987, Eddie McGrady holding it 1987-2010.

	Electorate	Turnout %	Change from 2010 %
	75,215	56.8	
M Ritchie SDLP	18,077	42.3	-6.1
C Hazzard SF	12,186	28.5	-0.2
H McKee UUP	3,964	9.3	
J Wells DUP	3,486	8.2	-0.4
H Reilly Ukip	3,044	7.1	
M Todd Alliance	1,622	3.8	+2.5
F Buchan C	318	0.7	-6.5

Change from 2010

SDLP	SF	UUP	DUP	Ukip

Dudley North

LABOUR HOLD

IAN AUSTIN
BORN Mar 6, 1965
MP 2005-

Shadow minister: work & pensions; CMS 2010-11; CLG 2010. Parly under-sec, CLG 2009-10. Asstistant government whip 2008-09. Minister for West Midlands 2008-10. PPS to Gordon Brown 2007-08. Special adviser to Gordon Brown 1999-2005. Dep dir, comms, Scottish Lab Party. Regional press officer, West Mids Labour. Married, one daughter, two sons. Ed: Dudley School; Essex (BA government).

CHALLENGERS
Les Jones (C) Replaced Afzal Amin after resignation over allegations in plotting with English Defence League. Cllr: Dudley MBC 1999-, leader 2011-12, deputy 2009-11, opp leader 2012-13. Contested Halesowen & Rowley Regis 2001, 2005; West Midlands PCC 2014 by-election. Member: West Midlands police & crime panel;

children services scrutiny 2014-. Trustee: Mary Stevens Hospice. Ed: Staffordshire (PgDip management studies, business administration & general management). **Bill Etheridge** (Ukip) MEP, West Midlands 2014-. Contested West Midlands PCC 2012 election. Former sales manager. Ed: Wolverhampton Poly, Parkfield HS. **Will Duckworth** (Green) Deputy leader, Green Party 2012-14. Cllr, Dudley TC 2012-. Former teacher. Contested Stourbridge 2012, West Midlands 2014 Euro election. Married.

CONSTITUENCY PROFILE
Covers the northern part of the of Dudley, the Black Country industrial town, including the town centre, zoo, castle as well as the Priory, Old Park Farm and Wrens Nest housing estates. To the north-west is the more affluent settlement Before the 1997 election, Dudley was divided into East and West constituencies, rather than the current North and South. Has been a consistent Labour seat.

	Electorate	Turnout %	Change from 2010 %
	60,718	62.6	
I Austin Lab	15,885	41.8	+3.2
L Jones C	11,704	30.8	-6.2
B Etheridge Ukip	9,113	24.0	+15.5
W Duckworth Green	517	1.4	
M Collins LD	478	1.3	-9.3
R Afzal Apni	156	0.4	
D Pitt TUSC	139	0.4	

Change from 2010

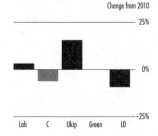

Lab	C	Ukip	Green	LD

Dudley South

CONSERVATIVE HOLD

MIKE WOOD
BORN Mar 17, 1976
MP 2015-

Parliamentary assistant and caseworker to Andrew Griffiths. Cllr: Dudley MBC 2014-, Conservative spokesman, finance; said he will donate cllr allowance to charity instead of by-election. Former policy adviser to European parliament in internal market legislation and environmental regulation. Asst to Earl of Stockton MEP 1999-2002. Vice-chairman, Wollaston & Stourbridge forum, 2014. Sch governor. Active campaigner, opposing council plans to close local children's centre. Married, one daughter, one son. Ed: University of Wales, Aberystwyth (BSc economics & law), Cardiff University (PgDip BVC).

CHALLENGERS
Natasha Millward (Lab) Trade union officer, Unison. Active campaigner, most prominently

local NHS and police employment cuts. Sch governor. **Paul Brothwood** (Ukip) Project manager. Cllr, Dudley MBC 2014-. Ed: Institute of Financial Services (Dip. financial services management). **Vicky Duckworth** (Green) Former primary school teacher. Contested West Midlands 2014 European parliament election. Ed: Newman University, Birmingham.

CONSTITUENCY PROFILE
A former Labour seat, the Conservatives have held the seat since Chris Kelly's election in 2010 that saw a 9.5 percentage point swing from Labour. Located in the West Midlands, the constituency is a prominent working-class residential region. The retail trade accounts for a high proportion of jobs here. The Dudley constituencies were formerly split into East and West, but these were replaced for the 1997 election by the current Dudley North and Dudley South.

	Electorate	Turnout %	from 2010 % Change
	60,363	63.3	
M Wood C	16,723	43.8	+0.7
N Millward Lab	12,453	32.6	-0.4
P Brothwood Ukip	7,236	18.9	+10.7
V Duckworth Green	970	2.5	
M Turner LD	828	2.2	-13.5

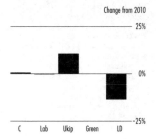

Change from 2010

C   Lab   Ukip   Green   LD

Dulwich & West Norwood

LABOUR HOLD

HELEN HAYES
BORN Aug 8, 1974
MP 2015-

Replaces Tessa Jowell, worked alongside her on council issues. Cllr: Southwark BC 2010-. Chartered town planner and managing dir, Allies & Morrison; Urban Practitioners (formerly Town Centres Ltd), company responsible for the London 2012 Olympic park masterplan. Launched online Sustainable Cities Project, but scrapped by Tory-Lib Dem coalition government 2010. Campaigner for health services, road safety, housing and education. Two daughters. Ed: Balliol Coll, Oxford (BA PPE); LSE (MSc social policy & administration).

CHALLENGERS
Resham Kotecha (C) Economic advisor and parly researcher. Chief operating officer, Women2Win 2012-. Former parly researcher to Baroness Jenkin 2012-13. Member: Women's India Assoc Youth Board

2013-. Volunteer: Tower Hamlets Coll 2011-12. Ed: Haberdashers' Aske's Girls' Sch, Emmanuel Coll, Cambridge (BA economics). **James Barber** (LD) Global category manager, Dentsu Aegis Network. Cllr: Southwark BC 2006-. "Online cllr of the year" 2011, Local Government Information Unit. Ed: Open University (Pg project management; Prof Dip management studies; PgCert. environmental decision making). **Rashid Nix** (Green) Education coach. Dir of political film *Why Don't Black People Vote?* Ed: South Bank University.

CONSTITUENCY PROFILE
A safe Labour seat, but not always: Dame Tessa Jowell, former Labour culture secretary, and minister for the Olympics took it from the Conservative Gerald Bowden in 1992. Diverse, the seat has both million pound houses and estates like Angell Town, and one in three live in social housing. One in four residents is Afro-Caribbean. Margaret Thatcher once lived here.

	Electorate	Turnout %	from 2010 % Change
	75,244	68.3	
H Hayes Lab	27,772	54.1	+7.5
R Kotecha C	11,650	22.7	+0.5
J Barber LD	5,055	9.8	-17.3
R Nix Green	4,844	9.4	+6.8
R Alagaratnam Ukip	1,606	3.1	+1.7
S Nally TUSC	248	0.5	
D Lambert Ind	125	0.2	
A Kanumansa AP	62	0.1	

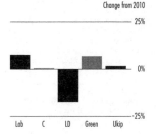

Change from 2010

Lab   C   LD   Green   Ukip

Dumfries & Galloway

SNP GAIN

RICHARD ARKLESS
BORN Jul, 7, 1975
MP 2015-

Businessman and solicitor, postponed legal career to run own online-based business, LED Warehouse UK. Spoke at more than 40 events during referendum campaing. Solicitor, ULL Solicitors. Stranraer-born, East-London raised. Married, two children. Ed: Stranraer Academy; Glasgow Caledonian University (BA financial services), Strathclyde Law Sch (LLB law); Glasgow Graduate Sch of Law (PgDip legal practice).

CHALLENGERS
Finlay Carson (C) IT consultant and business owner, CMS Broadband. Cllr, Dumfries & Galloway CC 2012-. Chair, stewartry area (business; community). Former farmer. Ed: Aberdeen (BSc agriculture). **Russell Brown** (Lab) MP 1997-2015. Shadow minister: Scotland

2013-15; defence 2010-11. PPS to: Gareth Thomas 2009-10; Jim Murphy 2008-10; Lord Drayson 2007; Douglas Alexander 2006-07; Alistair Darling 2005-06; Baroness Amos 2003-05, Lord Williams of Mostyn 2002-03. MP Dumfries 1997-2005. Cllr: Dumfries & Galloway 1995-97; Annandale & Eskdale DC 1988-96; Dumfries & Galloway Regional 1986-96. Chair, local community education project. ICI prod supervisor. TGWU branch sec chair. Married, two daughters. Ed: Annan Academy.

CONSTITUENCY PROFILE
Labour has held the seat since 2005. 2015 saw SNP gain the seat from third place in 2010. One of the UK's largest constituencies. Dumfries is the main town, nicknamed "Queen of the South", a nickname shared with its local football team. Employs the highest proportion of fishing, farming and forestry workers in Britain. Also includes Castle Douglas, Dalbeattie Kirkcudbright, and Newton Stewart.

	Electorate	Turnout %	Change from 2010 %
	75,249	75.2	
R Arkless SNP	23,440	41.4	+29.1
F Carson C	16,926	29.9	-1.7
R Brown Lab	13,982	24.7	-21.2
G Siddall Ukip	1,301	2.3	+1.0
A Metcalf LD	953	1.7	-7.2

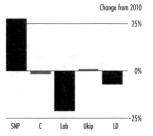

Change from 2010

SNP   C   Lab   Ukip   LD

Dumfriesshire, Clydesdale & Tweeddale

CONSERVATIVE HOLD

DAVID MUNDELL
BORN May 27, 1962
MP 2005-

Conscientious. Secretary of state for Scotland 2015-, as the country's only Tory MP. Burdened with unlikely appointment as shad SoS for Scotland 2005- as soon as entering office. Parly under-sec: Scotland 2010-15. MSP, south of Scotland, 1999-2005; transport, telecoms, IT spokes. Chairman, Scottish Conservatives 2011-14. Corporate lawyer, Biggart, Baillie & Gifford. BT Scotland – head of national affairs. Cllr: Dumfries & Galloway C 1986-87; Annandale & Eskdale DC 1984-86. Divorced, one daughter, two sons. Ed: Lockerbie Academy; University of Edinburgh (LLB law); Strathclyde University Business Sch (MBA).

CHALLENGERS
Emma Harper (SNP) Nurse and businesswoman. Runs B&B with husband. Member: Royal Coll of

Nursing; Assoc for Perioperative Practice; The Robert Burns World Federation; Dumfries Ladies Burns Club No. 1 (senior vice-president). Former private health worker, USA. Ed: Dumfries & Galloway Coll of Nursing & Midwifery (Nursing). **Archie Dryburgh** (Lab) Health & safety trainer and assessor, Magnox. Cllr: Dumfries & Galloway CC 2012-. Former territorial soldier 1979-85 and training officer. Chair, DG first management. Married, four children. Ed: Buckhaven HS.

CONSTITUENCY PROFILE
Marginal seat between Conservative and SNP during 2015 SNP surge. Only Tory seat in Scotland. Most renowned areas: Gretna Green, a favoured wedding venue; Lockerbie town, associatied with the terrorist bombing of Pan Am Flight 103 in 1988. Old industry trades such as opencast mining and knitwear manufacturing were formerly prominent in western regions. The Old Blacksmith's Shop and is a popular tourist attraction.

	Electorate	Turnout %	Change from 2010 %
	68,483	76.1	
D Mundell C	20,759	39.8	+1.8
E Harper SNP	19,961	38.3	+27.5
A Dryburgh Lab	7,711	14.8	-14.1
K Newton Ukip	1,472	2.8	+1.4
A Kubie LD	1,392	2.7	-17.1
J Jamieson Green	839	1.6	+0.5

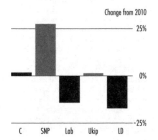

Change from 2010

C   SNP   Lab   Ukip   LD

Dunbartonshire East

JOHN NICOLSON
BORN Jun 23, 1961
MP 2015-

Journalist. Shadow SNP spokesman, culture, media and sport. Former speech writer to Senator Daniel P Moynihan. World Student Debating Champion, *Scotsman* Scottish universities' debating champion, *Observer* Mace British Isles Debating Champion. Former presenter: BBC *Breakfast*; *Newsnight*; *Panorama*; *Watchdog*; *ITV News*; *Public Eye*. Live anchor for BBC News 24 when Twin Towers struck, received Foreign Press Assoc award. Ed: Glasgow (MA English literature & politics); Kennedy Sch of Govt, Harvard University (Kennedy scholarship & Harkness Fellowship winner, American government).

CHALLENGERS
Jo Swinson (LD) MP 2005-15. Parly under-sec: employment relations & consumer affairs 2012 -; women & equalities 2012-.

PPS to: Nick Clegg 2012-14; Vince Cable 2010-2012. LD Shad Min: foreign 2008-10; women & equalities 2007. LD Shad SoS: Scotland 2006-07. LD whip and CMS spokes, 2005-06. Devt officer, UK Public Health Assoc Scotland. Marketing manager, Spaceandpeople Ltd. Marketing exec, Viking FM. Contested Hull East 2001, Scottish Parliament Strathkelvin & Bearsden 2003. Cllr, Milngavie CC. Ed: Glasgow; LSE (BSc management). **Amanjit Jhund** (Lab) Entrepreneur. Won: Ideas Competition 2008; RBS; Barclays BIDS competition 2008. Contested Windsor 2010. Ed: Edinburgh (MBChB BSc medicine, physiology), Harvard Medical Sch (gastroenterology & hepatology).

CONSTITUENCY PROFILE
To the northeast of Glasgow. A Liberal Democrat seat from 2005-15. SNP saw a 29.8 per cent increase in votes, 2015. Only seat, bar Ynys Môn, to be represented by all three main parties and the nationalists.

	Electorate	Turnout %	Change from 2010 %
	66,966	81.9	
J Nicolson SNP	22,093	40.3	+29.7
J Swinson LD	19,926	36.3	-2.4
A Jhund Lab	6,754	12.3	-21.8
A Polson C	4,727	8.6	-6.9
R Greer Green	804	1.5	
W Arasaratnam Ukip	567	1.0	-0.1

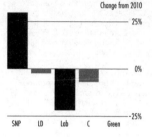

Change from 2010

Dunbartonshire West

MARTIN DOCHERTY
BORN Jan 21, 1971
MP 2015-

Policy adviser volunteer. Cllr: Glasgow CC 2012-.; Clydebank DC 1992-96 as youngest cllr at the time, beating incumbent Labour cllr of 25 years. Chair Clydebank SNP. Former liason secretary, West Dunbartonshire and secretary Clydebank SNP. Member: Volunteer Scotland. Lives with partner, John. Ed: Essex (BA politics); Glasgow Sch of Art (MPhil); GCFT (HND business administration).

CHALLENGERS
Gemma Doyle (Lab Co-op) MP Dunbartonshire W 2010-15. Part of self-proclaimed Facebook generation of new young Scottish intake in 2010. Contested European elections Scotland 2004. Political officer, parly Lab party. Conference development manager. Institute of Civil Engineers. Scottish Labour students, Chair Scottish Young

Labour. Researcher to Cathie Craigie MSP. Part-time case worker. Co-op; Unite. Ed: Our Lady & St Patrick's HS, Dumbarton; Glasgow (MA European civilisation). **Maurice Corry** (C) Businessman. Cllr: Argyll &Bute CC 2010. Armed Forces Veterans' Champion. Argyll & Bute Council. Former commissioned TA officer, Balkans 1990s; Afghanistan support role 2006. **Aileen Morton** (LD) Cllr: Argyll & Bute CC 2012-. Trustee: Helensburgh & District Access Trust. Ed: Notre Dame HS.

CONSTITUENCY PROFILE
Traditionally a Labour stronghold. SNP surge gained seat in 2015 with 34.5-point swing. Is entirely within the Dunbartonshire W council area. The Dunbarton Clydebank ward holds the Titan crane, an industrial landmark that draws poignant reminders of the region's shipbuilding history. Tourism is increasing in the area – many visit Loch Lomond and Trossachs, Scotland's first National Park.

	Electorate	Turnout %	Change from 2010 %
	69,193	73.9	
M Docherty SNP	30,198	59.1	+38.9
G Doyle Lab Co-op	16,027	31.3	-30.0
M Corry C	3,597	7.0	-0.6
A Morton LD	816	1.6	-6.5
C Muir Ind	503	1.0	

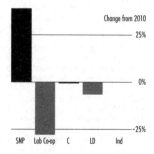

Change from 2010

Dundee East

SNP HOLD

STEWART HOSIE
BORN Jan 3, 1963
MP 2005-

Shadow SNP Westminster group leader, economy 2015-. SNP chief whip 2010-15. Deputy leader, parly group 2010-. SNP spokesman: treasury 2005-15; women 2005-07; home affairs 2005-07-. Member, Treasury select cttee 2010-. Contested Dundee East 2001, Kirkcaldy 1997, 1992; Scottish Parly election 1999. SNP youth convenor 1986-89. SNP nat sec 1999-03. Organisation convenor 2003-05. IT career. Football and rugby fan. Married, one daughter. Ed: Carnoustie HS; Bell Street Tech (HND computer studies); Dundee Coll of Tech.

CHALLENGERS
Lesley Brennan (Lab) Economist and business analyst. Cllr: Dundee CC 2012-. Contested MSP 2011 Scots Parly election. Former economic researcher. Volunteer,

ArtSocial Dundee cttee 2013. Married, three sons. Ed: Abertay University (BA economics); Edinburgh (MSc economics). **Bill Bowman** (C) Chartered Accountant. Former member of the board, UTI Group. Ed: George Watsons Coll; Edinburgh (BCom); Institute of Chartered Accountants of Scotland (CA). **Craig Duncan** (LD) Administrator. LD local party convenor. Volunteer: The Cinnamon Trust; Pet Fostering Service Scotland; Prince's Trust. Ed: Carnoustie HS; Heriot-Watt University (BA government & modern history).

CONSTITUENCY PROFILE
Takes in a series of mixed residential areas as far as the town of Carnoustie and Monifieth in the north-west. A former marginal seat between SNP and Labour, now considered an SNP stronghold as Stewart Hosie holds seat for third consecutive election with a 17.7-point swing in voting leading to a comfortable 19,162 majority.

	Electorate	Turnout %	Change from 2010 %
	66,960	72.0	
S Hosie SNP	28,765	59.7	+21.9
L Brennan Lab	9,603	19.9	-13.4
B Bowman C	7,206	15.0	-0.3
C Duncan LD	1,387	2.9	-7.7
H Grayshan Green	895	1.9	+0.5
L Parker-Hamilton CSA	225	0.5	
C Morelli TUSC	104	0.2	

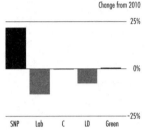

Change from 2010

Dundee West

SNP GAIN

CHRIS LAW
BORN Oct 21, 1969
MP 2015-

Said after election he "placed Labour in Dundee into retirement". Financial adviser. Branch treasurer and political engagement officer. Former business owner, 1950s motorcycle tours of the Himalayas. Founder, Spirit of Independence road tour of communities in a refurbished fire engine for Yes campaign. Ed: Madras Coll; University of St Andrews (MA cultural & social anthropology).

CHALLENGERS
Michael Marra (Lab) Deputy dir, Design in Action. Former senior political adviser to Leader of the oppostion in Scottish Parl 2010-12. Nephew of folk singer Michael Marra, brother of Jenny Marra MSP. Ed: University of Glasgow (MA history); LSE (MSc development economics & international development). **Nicola**

Ross (C) Former community learning & development worker, Edinburgh CC 2006-13. Ed: University of Dundee (MA politics; PgDip politics & policies in contemporary Europe; PgDip. community education; MSc professional studies). **Pauline Hinchion** (Green) Interim manager and consultant. Dundee & Angus Green Party convenor. Ed: Glasgow Caledonian University (social sciences & urban development).

CONSTITUENCY PROFILE
Marketed as a modern "City of Discovery" through high-tech gaming industry firms, multiple regeneration projects and the holding of two Dundee universities. Most famously represented by Winston Churchill from the 1908 by-election, although he was said to be very unpopular when defeated in 1922 by Edwin Scrymgeour, the UK's only elected prohibitionist MP. Chris Law registered a 28.9-point swing against a seat that had been safely Labour since 1945.

	Electorate	Turnout %	Change from 2010 %
	66,287	67.5	
C Law SNP	27,684	61.9	+33.1
M Marra Lab	10,592	23.7	-24.8
N Ross C	3,852	8.6	-0.7
P Hinchion Green	1,225	2.7	
D Coleman LD	1,057	2.4	-9.0
J McFarlane TUSC	304	0.7	-0.3

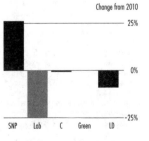

Change from 2010

Dunfermline & Fife West

SNP GAIN

DOUGLAS CHAPMAN
BORN Jan 5, 1955
MP 2015-

Personnel manager. Cllr: Fife CC 2007-. Previously in branch banking at TSB Scotland. Chairman, education cttee 2007-12. Spokes, COSLA education 2012. SNP: convenor; membership sec; education officer. Criticised for recommending disgraced MSP Bill Walker appeal against expulsion from SNP in 2012. Contested Kirkcaldy & Cowdenbeath 2010. Married, two children.

CHALLENGERS
Thomas Docherty (Lab) MP Dunfermline & Fife West 2010-15. Shadow deputy leader of the House of Commons 2014-15. Shadow minister, Defra 2013-14. Select cttees: parliamentary privilege 2012-15; procedure 2011-15; admin 2010-15; defence 2010-13; efra 2010-14; arms export controls 2010-13; armed forces 2011. Cumbrian-born

account dir, communications consultancy. Contested Tayside North 2001. Communications manager, Network Rail. Press & public affairs officer, BNFL. Labour Party research asst to Scott Barrie MSP. Dunfermline Athletic FC fan. Married, one son. Ed: St Benedict's RC Sch, Whitehaven; Open University (currently reading history). **James Reekie** (C) Customer consultant, entrepreneur & MA business student. Contested Dunfermline 2011 Scots Parly election. Ed: Edinburgh (LLB law). **Gillian Cole-Hamilton** (LD) Teacher. Contested North Ayrshire & Arran 2010. Married, one son. Ed: Aberdeen (French & German).

CONSTITUENCY PROFILE
The constituency formed in 2005 as an amalgamation of old Dunfermline West and parts of the old Dunfermline East seats. Traditionally Labour, seeing a variant elected party only twice, in the 2006 by-election with Lib Dem Willie Rennie and, now, in 2015.

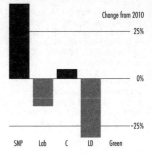

	Electorate	Turnout %	Change from 2010 %
	78,037	71.6	
D Chapman SNP	28,096	50.3	+39.6
T Docherty Lab	17,744	31.8	-14.5
J Reekie C	6,623	11.9	+5.1
G Cole-Hamilton LD	2,232	4.0	-31.1
L Campbell Green	1,195	2.1	

Change from 2010

25%

0%

-25%

SNP   Lab   C   LD   Green

Durham North

LABOUR HOLD

KEVAN JONES
BORN Apr 25, 1964
MP 2001-

Shadow minister: defence 2010-15; veterans 2010. Minister for veterans 2008-10, quoted as saying Joanna Lumley's campaign for Gurkha's rights was "irritating". Select cttees: admin 2010-13, 2005-09; armed forces bill 2011, 2005-06, defence 2001-09; civil contingencies bill 2003. Cllr, Newcastle CC 1990-2001, dep leader. GMB political officer, senior organiser. Parly asst NH Brown. Golf enthusiast. Ed: Newcastle Poly (BA government & public policy); University of Southern Maine.

CHALLENGERS
Laetitia Glossop (C) Recruitment professional, Crewdson & Partners. Previously at Korn Ferry, Egon Zehnder. Sch gov. Ed: Durham University. **Malcolm Bint** (Ukip) Semi-retired businessman. Director, The LED Studio.

Vice-chairman Ukip East Hants. Previously selected as Hampshire North West candidate 2015. Ed: Open University (BSc psychology; Cert social sciences). **Peter Maughan** (LD) Cllr, Whickham DC; Gateshead MBC 2012-. Contested Blaydon 1997, 2001, 2005. **Victoria Nolan** (Green) Runs clothes shop. Set up theatre company. Single mother of two.

CONSTITUENCY PROFILE
Along with its predecessor Chester-le-Street, has been represented by Labour since 1906. A seat made up of rugged moorland, former colliery towns and pit villages in the former Durham coalfield. The coal mines are long shut, and the seat has faced the economic problems associated with many former mining areas. The main town is the more affluent Chester-le-Street, known for its cricket ground and neighbouring the stately grounds of Lambton castle. Kevan Jones has held the seat with majorities over 10,000 each time.

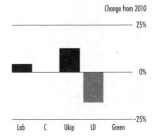

	Electorate	Turnout %	Change from 2010 %
	65,373	61.4	
K Jones Lab	22,047	54.9	+4.4
L Glossop C	8,403	20.9	-0.1
M Bint Ukip	6,404	16.0	+12.7
P Maughan LD	2,046	5.1	-15.9
V Nolan Green	1,246	3.1	

Change from 2010

25%

0%

-25%

Lab   C   Ukip   LD   Green

Durham North West

LABOUR HOLD

PAT GLASS
BORN Feb 14, 1956
MP 2010-

Education specialist, member education select ctteee 2010-15. Accused Conservative MPs of "barracking" Labour women with accents. PPS to Maria Eagle 2011-15. Government adviser on education 2006-10. Cllr, Lanchester PC 2007-. Acting assistant director of education, City of Sunderland. Fabian Soc; Unite; Amnesty Int; Co-operative Soc. FRSA. Married, one son, one stepson. Ed: St. Leonard's Sch, Durham; University of Sunderland (BEd); Northumbria University (MSc education & management);

CHALLENGERS
Charlotte Haitham-Taylor (C) Artist. Cllr: Wokingham BC 2010-. Controversy over residency 240 miles out of constituency. Married, one child. Ed: City & Guilds of London Art Sch

(BA fine art, painting). **Bruce Reid** (Ukip) Retired engineer. Contested Durham North 2010. **Owen Temple** (LD) Cllr, Durham CC 2008-. Contested: Durham 2010 North West halving Labour majority; Euro election 2014. Former financial advising dir. Ed: University of Nottingham (BA English literature).

CONSTITUENCY PROFILE
This seat, reliant upon its mining and steel town history, is a Labour stronghold; Pat Glass increased her majority to 10,056 in 2015. The constituency is largely rural and sparsley populated, covering Wear Valley and parts of the former Derwentside council area. Engineering, food production and processing are some of the newer industries supporting the local economy, following the decline in the coal and steel industries. Population is 98.9 per cent white, the third highest proportion in the country, and has a relatively high number of Christians.

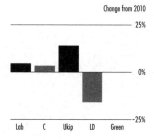

		Electorate	Turnout %	from 2010 %
		69,817	61.3	
P Glass	Lab	20,074	46.9	+4.6
C Haitham-Taylor	C	10,018	23.4	+3.4
B Reid	Ukip	7,265	17.0	+14.1
O Temple	LD	3,894	9.1	-15.8
M Shilcock	Green	1,567	3.7	

Change from 2010

Lab   C   Ukip   LD   Green

Durham, City of

LABOUR HOLD

ROBERTA BLACKMAN-WOODS
BORN Aug 16, 1957
MP 2005-

Shadow minister: housing 2015-; CLG 2011-; Cabinet Office 2010-11. PPS to: David Lammy 2008-10; Des Browne 2007-08; Hilary Armstrong 2006-07. Parly asst to Nick Brown as NE Min 2008-. Select cttees: science & technology/ IUS 2007-10; education & skills 2005-06; statutory instruments 2005-10. GMB, UCU. Professor, social policy and associate dean, Northumbria University, previously at Ruskin Coll, Oxford. Cllr, Oxford CC 1996-2000; Newcastle CC 1992-95. Married, one daughter. Ed: Methodist Coll, Belfast; Ulster University (BSc PhD social sciences).

CHALLENGERS
Rebecca Coulson (C) Self-employed, freelance musician and vocal coach. Contested Durham CC 2013 election. Carita Ensemble lead convenor. Columnist,

Conservative Home. Daughter of late philosopher EJ Lowe. Married. Ed: Magdalene Coll, Cambridge (BA music); Birkbeck, London (MA English & history). **Liam Clark** (Ukip) **Craig Martin** (LD) Science teacher. Leader, Scout Association Scout. Ed: York University (BSc physics) Durham University (PGCE). **Jonathan Elmer** (Green) MD, Democratise social enterprise. Former sustainable development manager Durham CC. Married, two children. Ed: Aberystwyth (BSc environmental biology).

CONSTITUENCY PROFILE
The small medieval city, dominated by its cathedral and ancient university, and the surrounding villages such as Waterhouses, Ludworth, Brandon, Coxhoe and Sherburn. The city itself has traditionally voted liberal (with a high student population) but former colliery villages on the outskirts make the seat safely Labour.

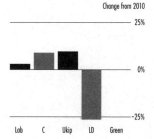

		Electorate	Turnout %	from 2010 %
		68,741	66.4	
R Blackman-Woods	Lab	21,596	47.3	+3.0
R Coulson	C	10,157	22.2	+9.0
L Clark	Ukip	5,232	11.5	+9.6
C Martin	LD	5,153	11.3	-26.4
J Elmer	Green	2,687	5.9	
J Marshall	Ind	649	1.4	
J Collings	Ind	195	0.4	

Change from 2010

Lab   C   Ukip   LD   Green

Dwyfor Meirionnydd

PLAID CYMRU HOLD

LIZ SAVILLE ROBERTS
BORN Dec 16, 1964
MP 2015-

Plaid Cymru's first female MP.
Rated Plaid Cymru's second-top
female politician, under Leanne
Wood. Cllr, Cyngor Gwynedd
CC, MorfaNefyn ward 2004-
15. Contested Welsh Assembly
elections 2003, 2007, 2011. Former
portfolio leader, education and
Welsh 2008-12. UCAC. Further
education lecturer and dir, Welsh
Medium. Former journalist,
Caernarfon & Denbigh Herald.
Married, two twin daughters. Ed:
Blackheath HS; Avery Hill Coll;
University of Wales, Aberystwyth
(BA Celtic studies).

CHALLENGERS
Neil Fairlamb (C) Clergyman,
Church in Wales. Chaplain to
mayor, RNLI, Royal Anglesey
Yacht Club. Contested Ynys
Môn 2013 Assembly by-election.
Former Classics teacher, taught

Nigel Farage at Dulwich Coll. Ed:
Bangor, Oxford and Aberystwyth
universities (history, English,
Theology); Cambridge (DipEd).
Mary Griffiths Clarke (Lab)
Filmmaker and photographer.
Co-chairwoman of support and
representation body Disability
Labour. Ed: National Film &
Television Sch; Central St Martins.
Christopher Gillibrand (Ukip)
Businessowner and translator.
Vice-chairman, Traditional Britain
Group. Former parly asst to Emma
Nicholson 1989-90. Ed: Exeter Coll,
Oxford (BSc chemistry); Greenwich
(MBA business administration).

CONSTITUENCY PROFILE
A mountainous and isolated area,
with tourism and agriculture as the
mainstays of the economy. Created
in 2010, replacing Meirionnydd
Nant Conwy. Plaid Cymru's safest
seat, the area was in 1974 the
first to return a Plaid MP at a
general election, and the seat has
the highest proportion of Welsh
speakers.

	Electorate	Turnout %	Change from 2010 %
	44,395	65.1	
L S Roberts PC	11,811	40.9	-3.5
N Fairlamb C	6,550	22.7	+0.4
M Griffiths Clarke Lab	3,904	13.5	-0.4
C Gillibrand Ukip	3,126	10.8	+8.1
L Hughes Ind	1,388	4.8	+0.3
S Churchman LD	1,153	4.0	-8.3
M Fothergill Green	981	3.4	

Change from 2010

PC C Lab Ukip Ind

Ealing Central & Acton

LABOUR GAIN

RUPA HUQ
BORN Apr 2, 1972
MP 2015-

Senior lecturer at Kingston
University, previously Manchester,
where she held Leverhulme
Trust Fellowship. Columnist and
newspaper contributor. Deputy
mayoress, Ealing BC 2010-11.
Contested North West region 2004
European elections; Chesham
& Amersham 2005. Featured in
BBC Schools series, *Look and Read*
aged 8. One son. Ed: Notting Hill
and Ealing HS; Cambridge (BA
political, social sciences and law);
UEL (PhD cultural studies, thesis
on youth culture).

CHALLENGERS
Angie Bray (C) MP Ealing C &
Acton 2010-15. PPS to Francis
Maude 2010-12, sacked after
rebelling on key Lords reform
vote. Select cttees: CMS 2012-15;
transport 2010. Contested East
Ham 1997. London Assembly

member, London West Central
2000-08. Leader, London Assembly
Con Group 2006-07. Media and
public affairs consultant, Ian Greer.
Press sec to Chris Patten as Con
Party Chair. Head of Broadcast
Unit, CCHQ press office. Radio
presenter and journalist, LBC radio,
BFBS Gibraltar. VP Conservative
Arab Network, Con Friends of
Poland. Ed: St Andrews (medieval
history); London Coll of Printing
(radio journalism). **Jon Ball** (LD)
MD, film and television production
company. Cllr, Ealing BC 2002-.
Council spokes, community
services & regeneration. Contested
Hayes & Harlington 2005; Ealing
C & Acton 2010. Ed: Merchant
Taylors Sch; Hatfield Poly.

CONSTITUENCY PROFILE
Covers Acton and the town centre
of Ealing. Mostly relatively affluent,
although there are more deprived
areas towards the industrial and
trading estates in the South Acton
estate. Diverse across ethnicity and
age groups. A Labour-Tory marginal.

	Electorate	Turnout %	Change from 2010 %
	71,238	71.4	
R Huq Lab	22,002	43.2	+13.1
A Bray C	21,728	42.7	+4.7
J Ball LD	3,106	6.1	-21.5
P Florence Ukip	1,926	3.8	+2.2
T Sharman Green	1,841	3.6	+2.1
J Notley Ind	125	0.3	
S Dore WRP	73	0.1	
T Rendle Above	54	0.1	
A Rygielski EP	39	0.1	

Change from 2010

Lab C LD Ukip Green

Ealing North

LABOUR HOLD

STEPHEN POUND
BORN Jul 3, 1948
MP 1997-

Shad min, NI 2010-. Opp whip 2010. PPS to: Sadiq Khan 2009-10; Stephen Timms 2007-09; Hazel Blears 2005-07. Member, select cttees: NI affairs 1999-10; standards & privileges 2003-05; broadcasting 1997-2001. Cllr, Ealing BC 1982-98. Mayor, Ealing 1995-96. T&GW branch officer. COHSE branch sec. Housing officer. Student. Hospital porter. Bus conductor. Seaman. Dir, Hanwell Community Centre. Married, one daughter, one son. Ed: LSE (BSc economics & industrial relations, President SU).

CHALLENGERS
Thomas O'Malley (C) Pensions manager. Cllr, Richmond BC 2010-. Vice-chair, audit. Lost out on Tory PPC nomination to battle Vince Cable in Twickenham 2015. Sch gov. Former staffer for party leaders John Major and William

Hague. Married, two children. Ed: New Coll, Oxford (BA history). **Afzal Akram** (Ukip) CEO, Smile group of businesses. Chairman, Ukip Ealing branch. Cllr, Waltham Forest BC, 2006-2014 as Labour and whip, disgraced after allegation he tried to influence planning vote outcome. Ed: Waltham Forest Coll. **Meena Hans** (Green) Adult education tutor. Ed: Southall Coll of Technology; Thames Valley (BA humanities: media studies and English); West Thames Coll (Cert ESOL); Hammersmith & West London Coll; Acton & West London Coll (Cert FE teaching).

CONSTITUENCY PROFILE
A north-west London seat near Heathrow, bisected by the A40. Conservative 1979-1997 under Harry Greenway, Stephen Pound has gradually increased the majority since 1997. A large ethnic minority community, with just over half the population non-white, and has the highest proportion of any seat (8.5 per cent) of people born in Poland.

	Electorate	Turnout %	Change from 2010 %
	73,836	65.7	
S Pound Lab	26,745	55.1	+4.8
T O'Malley C	14,419	29.7	-1.2
A Akram Ukip	3,922	8.1	+6.7
M Hans Green	1,635	3.4	+2.3
K McNamara LD	1,575	3.3	-9.9
D Hofman TUSC	214	0.4	

Change from 2010

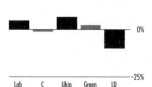

Ealing Southall

LABOUR HOLD

VIRENDRA SHARMA
BORN Apr 5, 1947
MP 2007-

Long-serving cllr, Ealing BC 1982-2010, elected as MP in by-election in 2007 aged 70. Indian-born (moved to UK in 1968), fluent in Punjabi, Hindi and Urdu. Select cttees: health 2010-; human rights 2007-; international development 2009-10; draft constitutional renewal bill 2008; justice 2007-10. PPS to Phil Woolas 2008-09. TGWU. Lab Party national ethnic minorities officer. Day services manager, learning disabilities. Bus conductor. Married, one daughter, one son. Ed: LSE (MA).

CHALLENGERS
James Symes (C) Chartered Accountant and Associate, KPMG. Founder, mountain bike manufacturers Drift-MTB. Former policy audit officer for Conservatives. Ed: University of Exeter (BA accounting & finance).

Jaspreet Mahal (Green) Politics & international relations student, SOAS. Ed: Villiers HS. **John Poynton** (Ukip) Self-employed, chartered management consultant. Former chartered accountant. Married, four children. Ed: Marlborough Coll; University of Edinburgh (BSc physics).

CONSTITUENCY PROFILE
A west London seat. Labour stronghold for over 50 years. Piara Khabra holds political history here as the first Sikh to become a British MP from 1992 until his death in 2007. Virendra Sharma increased Labour's vote shared by a relatively substatial 13.5 per cent in 2015. Ealing Southall is renowned for its large Asian community — more than two-thirds of the population is from an ethnic minority. There are significant Hindu and Muslim populations, but the seat has by far the highest proportion of Sikhs in any constituency in the UK and contains one of the largest Sikh gurdwaras outside of India.

	Electorate	Turnout %	Change from 2010 %
	65,495	66.1	
V Sharma Lab	28,147	65.0	+13.5
J Symes C	9,387	21.7	-8.1
J Mahal Green	2,007	4.6	+3.0
J Poynton Ukip	1,769	4.1	
K Kaushik LD	1,550	3.6	-11.4
J Singh Nat Lib	461	1.1	

Change from 2010

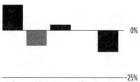

Easington

LABOUR HOLD

GRAHAME MORRIS
BORN Mar 13, 1961
MP 2010-

Easington-born and locally raised constituency worker to predecessor John Cummings. Best known for pioneering recognition of Palestine statehood as party policy. Member, health select cttee 2010-. Cllr, Easington DC 1987-2002. NHS medical laboratory scientific officer. ASTMS Health Service branch sec. First involved in politics through protesting with Anti-Nazi League. Sunderland FC fan. Son of a colliery electrician and British Coal canteen worker and Labour cllr. Married, two sons. Ed: Peterlee Howletch Comp; Newcastle Polytechnic (medical laboratory sciences; BTec higher national).

CHALLENGERS
Jonathan Arnott (Ukip) MEP, North East England 2014-. Retired maths teacher when selected. Recorded to have spoken more times in European parliament 2014 than any other British MEP. Former party gen sec, previously local elections coordinator. Contested: Sheffield South East 2010; Sheffield Attercliffe 2005. Chess candidate master. Married. Ed: Sheffield (MA mathematics). **Chris Hampsheir** (C) Pipelines engineer for Texas-based CB&I, oil & gas construction company. Born in Zambia. Former facilator at BBC. Contested London Ass 2012. Ed: Imperial Coll London (MEng mechanical engineering); Institution of Mechanical Engineers (CEng chartered engineering).

CONSTITUENCY PROFILE
A traditional coal mining seat on the Durham coast. The final mines closed in the early Nineties and the area suffers from the long term economic problems. Employment now circles retail and manufacturing. Said to be one of Labour's safest seats, its MPs including some of the most influential figures in Labour history: Sidney Webb, Ramsay MacDonald and Manny Shinwell

	Electorate	Turnout %	Change from 2010 %
	61,675	56.1	
G Morris Lab	21,132	61.0	+2.1
J Arnott Ukip	6,491	18.8	+14.1
C Hampsheir C	4,478	12.9	-0.8
L Armstrong LD	834	2.4	-13.6
S McDonnell NE Party	810	2.3	
M Warin Green	733	2.1	
S Colborn SPGB	146	0.4	

Change from 2010

Lab   Ukip   C   LD   NE Party

East Ham

LABOUR HOLD

STEPHEN TIMMS
BORN Jul 29, 1955
MP 1994-

Earnest technocrat. Survived stabbing at constituency event in May 2010. Shad min for employment 2010-15. Threatened to resign from frontbench if party did not grant free vote on same sex marriage act 2013. Parly under-sec: BIS 2009-10; DSS 1998-99. Treasury: financial sec 2008-10, 2004-05, 1999-2001. Min: work & pensions 2005-06; trade & industry 2002-04; education 2001-02; DSS 1999. PPS to: Mo Mowlam 1998; Andrew Smith 1997-98. MP, Newham North East 1994-1997. Cllr, Newham 1984-97, leader 1990-94. Computer/telecoms career. Married. Ed: Farnborough GS; Emmanuel Coll, Cambridge (MA maths, MPhil operational research).

CHALLENGERS
Samir Jassal (C) Cllr, Gravesham BC 2007-2011. Founding chair, East Ham Conservative Future group. Assisted Priti Maptel MP with PM's UK-India Diaspora Champion campaign and advises government on relations with Indian community. Ed: Dartford GS. **Daniel Oxley** (Ukip) Tour operator, Operas Abroad. Former teacher. Branch treasurer. Ed: Tower Collm, Rainhill; London Coll of Music. **Tamsin Omond** (Green) Environmental activist and journalist. Founder, Climate Rush. Named in *Most influential people under 30* list, *The Sunday Times*; *Daily Mail*. Contested Hampstead & Kilburn 2010 (Independent). Ed: Westminster Sch; Trinity Coll, Cambridge (BA English); Open University (MA environment).

CONSTITUENCY PROFILE
Highly multicultural east London seat, with the highest proportion of non-whites in the country. Also the second-largest electorate in the country. Much is deprived, densely packed inner-city terraced housing but there is rapid redevlopment. Safe Labour seat that Stephen Timms has held since its creation in 1997.

	Electorate	Turnout %	Change from 2010 %
	87,378	59.8	
S Timms Lab	40,563	77.6	+7.2
S Jassal C	6,311	12.1	-3.1
D Oxley Ukip	2,622	5.0	
T Omond Green	1,299	2.5	+1.3
D Thorpe LD	856	1.6	-10.0
M Aslam Community	409	0.8	
L Austin TUSC	230	0.4	

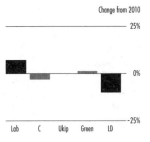

Change from 2010

Lab   C   Ukip   Green   LD

East Kilbride, Strathaven & Lesmahagow

SNP GAIN

DR LISA CAMERON
BORN Apr 8, 1972
MP 2015-

SNP spokeswoman, climate justice 2015-. NHS consultant for mental health and learning difficulties. Expert witness in court for domestic violence and child sexual abuse. Unite representative. Married, two daughters. Ed: University of Strathclyde (BA psychology); University of Stirling (MSc psychology & health); University of Glasgow (PhD clinical psychology).

CHALLENGERS
Michael McCann (Lab) MP, E Kilbride, Strathaven & Lesmahagow 2010-15. Researcher and election agent to predecessor Adam Ingram. Chairman, Scottish parly Lab party. Member, select cttes: int devt 2010-15. Cllr, S Lanarkshire CC 1999-2010. Deputy leader, S Lanarkshire CC 2007-2010. CPSA. Civil servant, Department for International Development (then ODA). Married,

one son, one daughter. Ed: St Bride's HS. **Graham Simpson** (C) Journalist. Sub-editor on *The Scottish Sun* newspaper. Cllr, East Kilbride West DC 2007 -. Chairman, Roads Safety Forum. Contested seat 2010. Ed: Royal HS. **Robert Sale** (Ukip) Heating and plumbing engineer. **Paul McGarry** (LD) Marketing manager, St Andrew's First Aid. Campaigner on human trafficking issues. Married, two chidren.

CONSTITUENCY PROFILE
Although not listed as one of Nicola Sturgeon's target seats for the 2015 election, Lisa Cameron stormed the poll with a 27.9-point swing from Labour to SNP. The seat and its predecessor had been comfortably Labour-held for decades. A sprawling seat, largely made up of moorland but with most of its electorate in the town of East Kilbride in the north. High employment, with a host of engineering, printing and textile companies surviving alongside new high-tech firms.

	Electorate	Turnout %	from 2010 %	Change
	83,071	72.9		
L Cameron SNP	33,678	55.6	+32.6	
M McCann Lab	17,151	28.3	-23.2	
G Simpson C	7,129	11.8	-1.2	
R Sale Ukip	1,221	2.0		
P McGarry LD	1,042	1.7	-8.2	
J Houston Ind	318	0.5	-0.1	

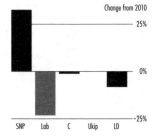

Change from 2010

East Lothian

SNP GAIN

GEORGE KEREVAN
BORN Sep 28, 1949
MP 2015-

Journalist and documentary filmmaker, chief executive of What If Productions. Associate editor of *The Scotsman* 2000-09. Formerly senior lecturer in economics at Edinburgh Napier University. Cllr, Edinburgh CC 1984-96. served on the board of the Edinburgh International Festival, Edinburgh Film Festival. Founded the Edinburgh Science Festival Contested Edinburgh East 2010. Member, International Marxist Group in younger years Ed: Kingsridge Secondary Sch; University of Glasgow (MA political economy).

CHALLENGERS
Fiona O'Donnell (Lab) MP 2010-15. Shadow minister, Defra 2011-12. Member, select cttees: international development 2012-15; standards & privileges 2013-15. Former debating partner of Charles Kennedy MP.

Campaign specialist, Labour party. Worked for: Douglas Alexander MP; Hugh Henry; Trish Godman; Johann Lamont MSPs; Catherine Stihler MEP. Career: Mental health and child behaviour specialist: Capability Scotland, NCH Scotland, Stonham Housing Assoc. GMB, Co-op. One daughter, three sons. Ed: Lochaber HS; Glasgow (English & history). **David Roach** (C) Communications consultant, Cardew Group. Ed: Kent (BA politics and international relations); LMH, Oxford (MSc Russian & eastern European studies).

CONSTITUENCY PROFILE
Another huge gain for the SNP. George Kerevan led the party from fourth place in 2010 to victory. A coastal seat running south and east of Edinburgh towards Dunbar. Home to Musselburgh race course and Musselburgh Links Old Golf Course, reputed to be oldest in the world. One of the MSPs of the respective Scottish Parliament seat is Iain Gray, former leader of Scottish Labour.

	Electorate	Turnout %	from 2010 %	Change
	79,481	74.3		
G Kerevan SNP	25,104	42.5	+26.5	
F O'Donnell Lab	18,301	31.0	-13.6	
D Roach C	11,511	19.5	-0.2	
E Spencer LD	1,517	2.6	-14.3	
J Rose Green	1,245	2.1	+0.4	
O Marshall Ukip	1,178	2.0	+0.9	
M Allan Ind	158	0.3		

Change from 2010

Eastbourne

CONSERVATIVE GAIN

CAROLINE ANSELL
BORN Jan 12, 1971
MP 2015-

Teacher, former director of studies, school inspector, Independent Schools Inspectorate. Cllr, Eastbourne BC 2012 -, chairwoman, scrutiny cttee, formerly opposition deputy leader. Sch governor. Married, three sons. Ed: Beresford House Sch.

CHALLENGERS
Stephen Lloyd (LD) MP, Eastbourne 2010-15. Famously quoted for saying party should have "died in a ditch" to defend position on tuition fees. PPS to Ed Davey 2014, resigned over DfT's road investment strategy, and unmet demands of local campaigners regarding the A27 road. Member, work & pensions select cttee 2010-14. Founded APPG on religious education in schs in 2010. Ousted sitting Tory MP in one of the Lib Dems' main election night triumphs in 2010. Unsuccessfully

sued by Nigel Waterson's over comments Lloyd made on his expenses. Contested: Eastbourne 2005; Beaconsfield 2001. Business development consultant: United Nations Environment Programme Finance Initiative, Federation of Small Businesses. Business devt director, Grass Roots. Born and raised in Mombasa, Kenya. Divorced, two stepchildren. Ed: St George's, Weybridge. **Nigel Jones** (Ukip) Historian, journalist and author. Contested SE England Euro election 2014. Partner, three children. **Jake Lambert** (Lab) Teacher. Led peace project in Israel and Palestine. Mem, Eastbourne trade council. Chair, Eastbourne Lab. NUT. Ed: Birmingham (BA history & philosophy).

CONSTITUENCY PROFILE
A Tory-Lib Dem marginal. One in four inhabitants of this Victorian seaside town is a pensioner. Tourism is important part of the economy, bolstered by language courses for overseas students and conferencing.

	Electorate	Turnout %	from 2010 %	Change %
	78,262	67.6		
C Ansell C	20,934	39.6	-1.2	
S Lloyd LD	20,201	38.2	-9.1	
N Jones Ukip	6,139	11.6	+9.1	
J Lambert Lab	4,143	7.8	+3.0	
A Durling Green	1,351	2.6		
P Howard Ind	139	0.3	+0.1	

Change from 2010

25%

0%

-25%

C   LD   Ukip   Lab   Green

Eastleigh

CONSERVATIVE GAIN

MIMS DAVIES
BORN Jun 2, 1975
MP 2015-

Former radio producer and journalist for West Sussex Today. and BBC. Cllr: Mid Sussex DC 2011-; Haywards Heath TC 2012-. Chairwoman, southern region CWO. Worked in road safety communications in the county. Married, two daughters. Ed: Royal Russell Sch; Collyer's; Swansea University (BA politics with international relations).

CHALLENGERS
Mike Thornton (LD) MP, Eastleigh 2013-15. Elected in by-election following charge of sitting MP Chris Huhne for perverting the course of justice. Member, select cttees: w&p, High Speed Rail 2014-15; European scrutiny 2013-14. Cllr: Eastleigh BC 2007 -; Bishopstoke PC 2008 -. Former business and development manager. Married, one daughter. Ed: Manchester Poly

(law). **Patricia Culligan** (Ukip) Former TV presenter, social worker and university lecturer. Previously worked in oil and energy sectors. Contested South East region 2014 for European election. Mother of three. Ed: Manchester (BA literature and history). **Mark Latham** (Lab) Business publisher. Spokes, Eastleigh Lab group. Campaigner on educational and NHS issues. Member, Moorgreen Hospital Stakeholders Group. Married, children. **Ron Meldrum** (Green) Cogntive therapist. Ed: Essex (BSc computer engineering).

CONSTITUENCY PROFILE
Affluent, owner-occupied suburbs of Southampton. The Lib Dems held Eastleigh since the 1994 by-election after Conservative MP Stephen Milligan's sudden death due to autoerotic asphyxiation. A loss in Lib Dem support in this constituency has proved catastrophic for the party's overall performance as this remained a key seat of defence.

	Electorate	Turnout %	from 2010 %	Change %
	79,609	69.7		
M Davies C	23,464	42.3	+2.9	
M Thornton LD	14,317	25.8	-20.7	
P Culligan Ukip	8,783	15.8	+12.2	
M Latham Lab	7,181	12.9	+3.3	
R Meldrum Green	1,513	2.7		
R Hall Beer BS	133	0.2		
D Clune TUSC	114	0.2		

Change from 2010

25%

0%

-25%

C   LD   Ukip   Lab   Green

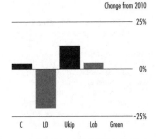

Eddisbury

CONSERVATIVE HOLD

ANTOINETTE SANDBACH
BORN Feb 15, 1969
MP 2015-

AM for North Wales 2011-15, resigned after election to English seat. Welsh Assembly: Shadow min, rural affairs. Member, select cttee: enviornment & sustainability. Former barrister at 9 Bedford Row chambers for ten years, serving two terms on the Bar Council. Taught English in Indonesia before landing a scholarship to Bar School Lincolns Inn. Now lives on family farm in Elwy valley. Contested Delyn 2010. Previously patron of Chrysalis charity. Married, one daughter, one deceased son. Ed: University of Nottingham (BA law; LLM international law).

CHALLENGERS
James Laing (Lab) Sports cameraman. Member and steward, Bectu. Contested Thanet North 2001. Lives with partner, two sons. Ed: Liverpool (BA political theory

& intitutions). **Rob Millington** (Ukip) Army veteran. Active campaigner against HS2 high speed rail link. **Ian Priestner** (LD) Non-exec dir, ASC Renewables. Former chief press officer, SDP. Ed: Keele (BA international relations); Westminster (LLB law); SOAS (MSc development studies). **Dr Andrew Garman** (Green) Semi-retired scientist, counsellor and psychotherapist. Ed: Chester (MA clinical counselling).

CONSTITUENCY PROFILE
A large rural seat in the south west of Cheshire made up of small, affluent villages and the salt-mining town of Winsford. Solidly Conservative since its formation in 1983. Antoinette Sandbach replaced Stephen O'Brien after he took a new humanitarian role with the UN. A once salt-mining and sand-quarrying community, the constituency has begun to shift its focus towards service and tourism, with Delamere Forest as one of the main picturesque attractions.

		Electorate	Turnout %	from 2010 % Change
		68,636	69.0	
A Sandbach C		24,167	51.0	-0.7
J Laing Lab		11,193	23.6	+2.1
R Millington Ukip		5,778	12.2	+8.0
I Priestner LD		4,289	9.1	-13.4
A Garman Green		1,624	3.4	
G Antar CSA		301	0.6	

Change from 2010

```
                                          25%


                                          0%



                                          -25%
  C      Lab     Ukip     LD     Green
```

Edinburgh East

SNP GAIN

TOMMY SHEPPARD
BORN Mar 6, 1959
MP 2015-

Founded and ran Edinburgh comedy club and fringe stalwart Stand. SNP spokesman, Cabinet Office 2015-. Cllr, Hackney BC 1986-93 as Labour. Former deputy general secretary of Scottish Labour Party. Deputy leader of local authortity for second term. Edinburgh South organiser of the Yes Scotland. Contested Bury St Edmunds 1992. Vice-president of NUS for two terms. Member, Scottish Comedy Agency. Joined SNP in Sep 2014. Ed: University of Aberdeen (BA politics & sociology).

CHALLENGERS
Sheila Gilmore (Lab) MP, 2010-15. Solicitor, specialising in women's rights and on legal aid cases. Cllr, Moredun 1991-2007. Convenor, housing 1999-2007. Select cttees: public admin 2013-15; w&p 2011-15; political & constitutional reform

2010-14. Contested Edinburgh Pentlands Scots Parly election 2007. Election agent to Nigel Griffiths. Co-founder, Edinburgh Women's Rape Crisis Centre. Married, three daughters, one son. Ed: George Watson's Coll; Kent (history & politics). **James McMordie** (C) Party office manager. Former fundraiser and operations manager, Better Together campaign. Taught in further education in Prague, prior to party roles. Ed: Glasgow (MA political science & govt); St Andrew's (MLitt Middle East & central Asian security studies). **Peter McColl** (Green) Writer and political campaigner. Former adviser to Mark Ballard MSP. Ed: Edinburgh (geography).

CONSTITUENCY PROFILE
A former Labour seat that was held by veteran Labour MP, Gavin Strang for over 40 years. Home to Scotland's most notable tourist sites such as Edinburgh Castle, Holyrood Palace, the Royal Mile & the Scottish Parliament building.

		Electorate	Turnout %	from 2010 % Change
		66,178	71.2	
T Sheppard SNP		23,188	49.2	+28.8
S Gilmore Lab		14,082	29.9	-13.5
J McMordie C		4,670	9.9	-1.0
P McColl Green		2,809	6.0	+0.9
K Utting LD		1,325	2.8	-16.6
O Corbishley Ukip		898	1.9	
A Saleem TUSC		117	0.3	-0.4

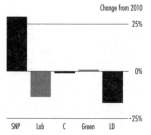

Change from 2010

```
                                          25%



                                          0%



                                          -25%
  SNP    Lab    C    Green    LD
```

Edinburgh North & Leith

SNP GAIN

DEIDRE BROCK
BORN Dec 8, 1961
MP 2015-

Deputy lord provost of Edinburgh. Raised in Perth, Australia, moved to Scotland in 1996. Previously ran parly office of Rob Gibson MSP. Board member: Edinburgh International Festival Council; the Centre for the Moving Image (Edinburgh International Film Festival/Filmhouse); and Creative Edinburgh. Cllr, Edinburgh CC 2007-. Two daughters. Ed: John Curtin University (BA English); West Australian Academy of Performing Arts.

CHALLENGERS
Mark Lazarowicz (Lab Co-op) MP, Edinburgh North & Leith 2001-15. Shadow minister, international development, 2010-11. Select cttees include: environmental audit 2007-15; modernisation HoC 2005-10 efra 2002-05; Scottish affairs 2001-03.

PM's special representative on carbon trading 2008-10. PPS to: David Cairns 2007-08. SERA; Co-operative party; Chair Scottish Labour party 1989-90. TGWU. Gen sec, British Youth Council Scotland. Organiser, Scottish ed and action for devt. Married, one daughter, three sons. Ed: St Andrew's (MA moral philosophy & medieval history); Edinburgh (LLB law). **Iain McGill** (C) Dir, Harmony Employment Agency. Cllr, New Town & Broughton CC. Contested: Edinburgh C 2011; Edinburgh N & Leith 2010; Midlothian 2005; Airdrie & Shotts 2007; Forth byelection 2008. Ed: Drummond Community HS.

CONSTITUENCY PROFILE
Labour held the seat since and predecessor since 1945, including by Malcolm Chisholm who became MSP and Scottish minister. A close Lib Dem-Labour marginal in 2005 and 2010. Includes the Georgian new town, running to the substantially redeveloped port of Leith.

	Electorate	Turnout %	from 2010 %	Change
	80,978	71.6		
D Brock SNP	23,742	40.9	+31.3	
M Lazarowicz Lab Co-op	18,145	31.3	-6.2	
I McGill C	9,378	16.2	+1.2	
S Beattie-Smith Green	3,140	5.4	+3.2	
M Veart LD	2,634	4.5	-29.3	
A Melville Ukip	847	1.5		
B Whitehead TUSC	122	0.2	-0.3	

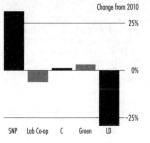

Change from 2010

SNP   Lab Co-op   C   Green   LD

Edinburgh South

LABOUR HOLD

IAN MURRAY
BORN Aug 10, 1976
MP 2010-

Labour's only Scottish MP. Shadow secretary of state for Scotland 2015-. Minister, trade & investment 2011-15. PPS to Ivan Lewis 2010-15. Select cttees: environmental audit 2010-11; arms export controls 2010-11. Came through recount in 2010 to hold off Lib Dem challenge and admitted he didn't expect to win. Cllr, Edinburgh CC 2003-10. Spokesman: finance; social inclusion. Partner, Aspen Bar & Grill. Campaign manager, Edinburgh Pentlands 2001, 1997. USDAW. Supporter, Care for the Wild. Edinburgh-born and raised local businessman. Has partner. Ed: Wester Hailes Ed Centre; Edinburgh (social policy & law).

CHALLENGERS
Neil Hay (SNP) Self-employed business developer. Former

SNP organiser: Edinburgh South; City Assoc. Leader, Yes campaign, Edinburgh S. Involved in internet troll calling elderly voters (Alzheimer Scotland union members) 'quislings'. Volunteer, Bethany Night Shelter. Married, two children. **Miles Briggs** (C) Political adviser. Previously lived in Canada, working for Executive Council of Prince Edward Island. Contested NE Fife 2010. Ed: Perth GS; Robert Gordon University (BA politics & management). **Phyl Meyer** (Green) Development worker assiting disabled people and driving instructor. Ed: Strathclyde (BEng electrical & mechanical engineering; BSc physics & applied physics).

CONSTITUENCY PROFILE
Historically held by the Conservative Sir William Darling (great uncle of former chancellor Alistair Darling) 1945-57. A prosperous constituency to the south of the city, but taking in several council estates, it has been Labour since 1987 and is now the only Labour seat in Scotland.

	Electorate	Turnout %	from 2010 %	Change
	65,846	74.9		
I Murray Lab	19,293	39.1	+4.4	
N Hay SNP	16,656	33.8	+26.1	
M Briggs C	8,626	17.5	-4.1	
P Meyer Green	2,090	4.2	+2.2	
P Subbaraman LD	1,823	3.7	-30.3	
P Marshall Ukip	601	1.2		
C Fox SSP	197	0.4		

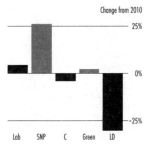

Change from 2010

Lab   SNP   C   Green   LD

Edinburgh South West

SNP GAIN

JOANNA CHERRY
BORN Mar 18, 1966
MP 2015-

Legal advocate for 20 years (1995-); took silk in 2009. SNP group leader, justice and home affairs 2015-. Co-founder and leader of 'Lawyers for Yes' during independence referendum campaign. Convenor, Faculty of Advocates Law Reform cttee 2013-15. Chair, Clark Foundation Legal Education Advisory. Previously Standing Junior Counsel to Scottish government 2003-08. Author of *Mental Health and Scots Law in Practice*. Former tutor, University of Edinburgh. Member, Scottish Women's Rights Centre Advisory Group. Ed: University of Edinburgh (LLB law; LLM, Vans Dunlop Scholar; Dip LP).

CHALLENGERS
Ricky Henderson (Lab) Convenor, health, social care & housing. Cllr, Edinburgh CC 1999-, member,

cttees: sport, culture & tourism 1999-2007; transport in the council administration 1999-2007. Holder of finance portfolio. Deputy leader, Lab council group. Married, two children. Ed: Linlithgow Academy. **Gordon Lindhurst** (C) Legal advocate. Contested: Linlithgow 1999; 2003 Scottish election; Linlithgow & Falkirk E 2001; Livingston by-election 2005; Edinburgh Western 2011. Ed: Edinburgh (LLB Scots law); Glasgow (PgDip Scots law); Heidelberg (LLM European & German law).

CONSTITUENCY PROFILE
Previously held by former Labour chancellor, Alistair Darling 2005-15, after the change in boundaries for his Edinburgh Central seat. The SNP took this from fourth place in 2010. Takes in old tenement areas such as Dalry and Fountainbridge as well as the more affluent suburbs of Colinton and Craiglockart and Conservative-leaning villages.

	Electorate	Turnout %	Change from 2010 %
	72,178	71.5	
J Cherry SNP	22,168	43.0	+30.8
R Henderson Lab	14,033	27.2	-15.6
G Lindhurst C	10,444	20.2	-4.0
R Doherty Green	1,965	3.8	+1.9
D Farthing-Sykes LD	1,920	3.7	-14.3
R Lucas Ukip	1,072	2.1	

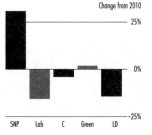

Change from 2010

Edinburgh West

SNP GAIN

MICHELLE THOMSON
BORN Mar 11, 1965
MP 2015-

Property management executive. SNP group leader, business, innovation & skills 2015-. Previously MD of pro-independence network and economic think tank, Business for Scotland. Former financial services industry worker and professional pianist. Ed: Royal Scottish Academy of Music & Drama; MSc in IT.

CHALLENGERS
Michael Crockart (LD) MP, Edinburgh W 2010-15. Systems developer and IT project manager, Standard Life. Born and raised in Perth. Former police officer with Lothian & Borders police. Longstanding Lib Dem activist. PPS to Michael Moore in 2010 but resigned to rebel on tuition fees vote. Contested: Edinburgh N & Leith 2005; Scottish Parliament elections 2007. Enjoys photography

and listening to classical music. Married, two sons. Ed: Perth HS; Edinburgh (BSc social sciences). **Lindsay Paterson** (C) Policy manager, Royal Coll of Physicians of Edinburgh. Cllr, Edinburgh CC 2012-. Former researcher in Holyrood. Contested: Livingston 2003; Coatbridge, Chryston & Bellshill 2005; Kirkcaldy & Cowdenbeath 2010. Ed: St Andrews (MA history & international relations). **Cammy Day** (Lab) Cllr, Edinburgh CC 2008-. Contested Edinburgh West 2010. Scottish Youth Parliament supporter.

CONSTITUENCY PROFILE
Lies to the west and northwest of Edinburgh city centre. safe in recent times for the Liberal Democrats (1977-2015). Formerly held by the Conservatives (1966-1977). It takes in working-class areas such as Stenhouse as well as the affluent Murrayfield area. Covers leafy suburbs, reaching along the Firth of Forth to South Queensferry and Edinburgh airport.

	Electorate	Turnout %	Change from 2010 %
	71,749	76.5	
M Thomson SNP	21,378	39.0	+25.8
M Crockart LD	18,168	33.1	-2.8
L Paterson C	6,732	12.3	-10.9
C Day Lab	6,425	11.7	-16.0
P Black Green	1,140	2.1	
O Inglis Ukip	1,015	1.9	

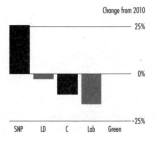

Change from 2010

Edmonton

LABOUR CO-OPERATIVE HOLD

KATE OSAMOR
BORN Aug 15, 1968
MP 2015-

Enfield NHS GP practice manager. Unite activist. Nigerian born. NEC 2014-. Previously worked in voluntary sector as advice and support worker for hard to reach communities. Daughter of Martha Osamor, former Haringey cllr and community leader, Broadwater Farm estate, Tottenham. One son. Ed: UEL (BA third world studies).

CHALLENGERS
Gönül Daniels (C) Senior Systems Engineer. Works on network infrastucture for GLA, previously in the Houses of Parliament. Runs internet café and dry-cleaning businesses. Chairwoman of governors for an academy. Former technical engineer: Enfield BC; Bank of England. Married, four children. Ed: Minchenden Sch; Waltham Forest Coll (HND, IT). **Neville Watson** (Ukip) CEO,

Life Youth Resource Centre and Christian life coach. Former management and sales trainer: British Gas; American Express. Contested Tottenham 2010. Ed: Edith Cavell Secondary Sch. **Douglas Coker** (Green) Taught community politics at Hackney Coll. Former chair of local party branch and member of Enfield Alliance Against the Cuts.

CONSTITUENCY PROFILE
An outer London seat, but inner city in character. Mutlicultural, with large afro-carribean and Cypriot communities, an area of tower blocks and social housing. Apart from the Lee Valley Leisure Complex, the east of the seat is dominated by industrial parks Generally a safe Labour seat since the Second World War, though narrowly gained by Conservatives in 1983. Labour's Andy Love regained the seat in 1997. All wards concerned in local elections are also predominantly Labour bar one — Bush Hill Park, with two Tories.

	Electorate	Turnout %	from 2010 % Change
	66,015	62.6	
K Osamor Lab Co-op	25,388	61.4	+7.8
G Daniels C	9,969	24.1	-5.7
N Watson Ukip	3,366	8.1	+5.6
D Coker Green	1,358	3.3	+2.0
D Schmitz LD	897	2.2	-8.4
L Peacock TUSC	360	0.9	

Change from 2010

Ellesmere Port & Neston

LABOUR HOLD

JUSTIN MADDERS
BORN Nov 22, 1972
MP 2015-

Employment solicitor. Cllr: Cheshire West & Chester BC 2008-15; Ellesmere Port and Neston BC 1998-2009. Leader, Ellesmere Port & Neston BC 2007-09. Opp and Labour leader, Cheshire W and Cheshire BC 2011-14. Legally represented high-profile sports personalities, Ian Sibbit and Andrew Henderson. Contested Tatton 2005. Married, three sons. First in family to attend university. Ed: University of Sheffield (LLB law).

CHALLENGERS
Katherine Fletcher (C) Businesswoman. Owner of antique and vintage furniture company BritishOriginals. Former small business transformation dir, then head of stratergy, for Lloyds Bank. Previously managing consultant with global consultancy firm Capgemini before moving to

South Africa as safari ranger in unfenced tented camp. Ed: Altrincham GS; Nottingham (BSc biological anthropology). **Jonathan Starkey** (Ukip) Musician. Supplies music to broadcast industries in 55 countries. Cllr, Ellesmere Port and Neston BC. Contested Ellesmere Port & Neston 2010 as an independent. Married, two daughters, one son. Ed: Royal Northern Coll of Music; Chichester (MA popular music). **Trish Derraugh** (LD) Cllr, Neston TC 2011 -. Previously worked in financial, construction and manufacturing industries. Ed: Helsby GS; Aigburth Vale HS.

CONSTITUENCY PROFILE
Straddles the base of the Wirral peninsula to include Ellesmere Port on the Mersey estuary and the town of Neston. Major employers include the Vauxhall car plant, which makes the Astra, and the Stanlow oil refinery. Justin Madders replaces Andrew Miller, who held the seat since 1992. Strongly Labour.

	Electorate	Turnout %	from 2010 % Change
	68,134	68.6	
J Madders Lab	22,316	47.8	+3.1
K Fletcher C	16,041	34.3	-0.5
J Starkey Ukip	5,594	12.0	+8.3
T Derraugh LD	1,563	3.3	-11.7
M Palmer Green	990	2.1	
F Dowling TUSC	192	0.4	
J Dyer ND	31	0.1	

Change from 2010

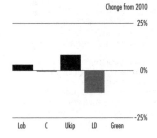

Elmet & Rothwell

CONSERVATIVE HOLD

ALEC SHELBROOKE
BORN Jan 10, 1976
MP 2010-

Independent-minded. Interested in Middle Eastern politics. PPS to: Hugo Swire 2014-15; Mike Penning 2012-14; Theresa Villiers 2010-12. Member, select cttees: CLG 2014-15; backbench business 2013-14. Rebel MP, Eurosceptic. Contested Wakefield 2005. Cllr, Leeds CC 2004-10. Campaign manager, Elmet 2001. Project manager for nanofactory at Leeds University; became researcher and assistant to pro vice-chancellor. Mechanical engineer, Lucas Heavy Duty Engineering. Ed: St George's CofE Sch, Gravesend; Brunel University (BSc mechanical engineering).

CHALLENGERS
Veronica King (Lab) Stakeholder relations manager, Alzheimer's Society, previously external affairs manager. Deputy head of press for Ken Livingston's London mayor campaign 2012. Research officer for Islington BC; communities coordinator, GLA. Former Vice-president, welfare, in NUS. Ed: Cardinal Heenan; University of Liverpool (BA politics & communication studies; welfare & equal opportunities officer). **Paul Spivey** (Ukip) Pre-delivery inspection manager, Audi UK. Cllr, Kippax PC. Chair of Leeds Ukip party branch. Former apprentice mechanic. **Stewart Golton** (LD) Cllr, Leeds CC 1998-, LD leader. Ed: Newcastle University (BA politics)

CONSTITUENCY PROFILE
A rural hinterland to the east of Leeds, including the traditional market town of Wetherby and former coal mining towns and villages. According to the 2011 census, a quarter of the population works in retail and manufacturing. Conservative since its creation in 2010. Formed by combining the seats of Elmet and Morley & Rothwell, both of which returned Labour MPs from 1997.

	Electorate	Turnout %	from 2010 %	Change %
	79,143	73.0		
A Shelbrooke C	27,978	48.4	+5.8	
V King Lab	19,488	33.7	-0.8	
P Spivey Ukip	6,430	11.1	+8.3	
S Golton LD	2,640	4.6	-11.8	
D Brooks Green	1,261	2.2		

Change from 2010

25%

0%

-25%

C   Lab   Ukip   LD   Green

Eltham

LABOUR HOLD

CLIVE EFFORD
BORN Jul 10, 1958
MP 1997-

An energetic and effective constituency campaigner. Brownite. Shadow min, sport 2011-15. PPS to: John Healey 2009-10; Margaret Beckett 2008-09. Member, select cttees: CLG 2010-11; transport 2002-09; standing orders 1999-2000; procedure 1997-2001. Vice-chair, London Group of Lab MPs. Member, Lab Friends of India. Cllr, Greenwich BC 1986-98. TGWU. Partner, family-owned jewellery and watch repair business. Ex-cabbie. Millwall FC supporter. Married, three daughters. Ed: Walworth CS; Southwark FE Coll.

CHALLENGERS
Spencer Drury (C) Teacher and Sixth Form director. Trustee, Eltham United Charities. Cllr, Greenwich BC 2002-, Conservative leader on council. Contested: Greenwich & Woolwich 2010; Eltham 2005; Lewisham East 1997 for Referendum Party. Worked at the Office of Fair Trading. Married, two children. Ed: Keele University (BA politics & economics); Brunel University (MA Britain in the European Union). **Peter Whittle** (Ukip) Writer and broadcaster. Ukip culture spokesperson 2014-. Founder and dir, New Culture Forum. Ed: University of Kent (chairman, Conservative assoc). **Alex Cunliffe** (LD) Barrister, 4KBW, Chambers of Lawrence Power. Contested Erith & Thamesmead 2010. Ed: Swansea (BA French, Italian & legal studies).

CONSTITUENCY PROFILE
A southeast London seat in the borough of Greenwich, popular with commuters. There is a large amount of green space including Avery Hill park, now a campus for the University of Greenwich. According to the 2011 census, over a quarter of the population lives in social housing. Has changed hands between Labour and the Tories a number of times, last in 1997.

	Electorate	Turnout %	from 2010 %	Change %
	63,998	67.4		
C Efford Lab	18,393	42.6	+1.1	
S Drury C	15,700	36.4	-1.2	
P Whittle Ukip	6,481	15.0	+12.6	
A Cunliffe LD	1,308	3.0	-9.6	
J Parker Green	1,275	3.0	+2.0	

Change from 2010

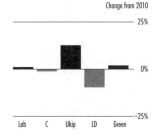

25%

0%

-25%

Lab   C   Ukip   LD   Green

Enfield North

LABOUR GAIN

JOAN RYAN
BORN Sep 8, 1955.
MP 2015-

MP for Enfield N 1997-2010, one of five former MPs to return in 2015. Figured in expenses scandal, claimed most of any MP in 2006-2007 tax year (£173,691), caught in second-homes controversy and asked to repay £5,121 mortgage expenses. Special rep to Cyprus 2007-08, later fired for backing leadership change. Parly under-sec, home office 2006-07. Whip, Treasury 2003-06, asst 2002-03. Vice chairwoman, Labour party 2007-08. Select cttees: CSF 2007; selection 2001-06. Former teacher. Cllr, Barnet BC 1990-1998. Ed: City of Liverpool Coll (BA history & sociology); Polytechnic of the South Bank (MSc sociology).

CHALLENGERS
Nick de Bois (C) MP 2010-15. Secretary, 1922 backbench cttee 2012-15. Select cttees: justice 2011-

15; public admin 2010-11. Contested: Enfield N 2005, 2001; Stalybridge & Hyde in 1997. MD, Rapiergroup marketing agency. PR assistant, Advertising Standards Authority. Rugby fan. Speaks French and German. Divorced, remarried. Three daughters, one son from first marriage. Ed: Culford Sch; Cambridge Coll of Arts & Tech (HND business studies). **Deborah Cairns** (Ukip) Learning support assistant. Vice-chairman, Enfield & Haringey Ukip branch. Area campaign manager, European parly elections 2014. **David Flint** (Green) Retired management consultant and post office worker.

CONSTITUENCY PROFILE
The northernmost constituency in London. A varied seat, with very affluent, village-like areas in the west and industrial areas to the east. It includes large Turkish, Afro-Caribbean, Indian, Bangladeshi, Cypriot and Italian communities. A significant amount of social housing. A Labour-Conservative marginal.

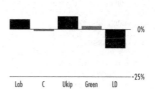

	Electorate	Turnout %	from 2010 % Change
	68,119	67.7	
J Ryan Lab	20,172	43.7	+5.2
N de Bois C	19,086	41.4	-0.9
D Cairns Ukip	4,133	9.0	+6.9
D Flint Green	1,303	2.8	+1.7
C Jenkinson LD	1,059	2.3	-9.9
Y Awolola CPA	207	0.5	
J Simpson TUSC	177	0.4	

Change from 2010

Enfield Southgate

CONSERVATIVE HOLD

DAVID BURROWES
BORN Jun 12, 1969
MP 2005-

Social conservative. Shadow justice minister 2007-10. Select cttees: public accounts 2014-15; draft human tissue & embryos bill 2007; draft legal services bill 2006; armed forces bill 2005-06. PPS to: Owen Paterson 2012-14; Oliver Letwin 2010-12; Francis Maude 2010. Faced embarrassment after campaigners accidentally canvassed in neighbouring consitutency, Edmonton. Solicitor and consultant. Chair, Conservative Christian Fellowship. Officer, Conservative Friends of Israel group. Contested Edmonton 2001. Arsenal FC fan and keen cricketer. School governor. Married, six children. Ed: Highgate Sch; University of Exeter (LLB law).

CHALLENGERS
Bambos Charalambous (Lab) Housing lawyer for Hackney BC. Cllr, Enfield BC 1994-, cabinet

member for leisure, culture, sport, young people and localism. Contested: Enfield Southgate 2010; Epping Forest 2005. Member, Amnesty International, Positive Women, Unison, GMB. Married, two children. Ed: Liverpool Polytechnic (LLB law); University of North London (LPC law). **David Schofield** (Ukip) Cllr, LB Enfield C 2002-06 for the Conservatives. Called Nick de Bois a "c***" and a female councillor a "lap dancer" in leaked texts, 2014. **Jean Robertson-Molloy** (Green) Retired social worker.

CONSTITUENCY PROFILE
A prosperous part of Enfield borough. Home to sizeable Jewish, Indian and Cypriot populations. The north is semi-rural as it takes in Trent Park and the Middlesex University campus. Famous for the 1997 Labour landslide, when Michael Portillo lost to Labour's Stephen Twigg. Tory David Burrowes retook the seat in 2005 and has held on to it ever since.

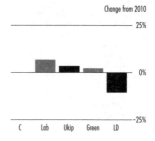

	Electorate	Turnout %	from 2010 % Change
	64,938	70.6	
D Burrowes C	22,624	49.4	-0.1
B Charalambous Lab	17,871	39.0	+6.8
D Schofield Ukip	2,109	4.6	+3.5
J Robertson-Molloy Green	1,690	3.7	+2.3
P Smith LD	1,518	3.3	-10.5

Change from 2010

Epping Forest

CONSERVATIVE HOLD

ELEANOR LAING
BORN Feb 1, 1958
MP 1997-

Deputy Commons speaker 2013-. Shadow min: justice 2007-10; women & equality 2005-07. Shadow SoS, Scotland 2005. Shadow min: women 2004-05; children 2003. Opposition whip 1999-2000. Member, select cttees: panel of chairs 2013-15; Scottish affairs 2013-14; human rights 2010-11; political & constitutional reform 2010-13. Opposition spokes 2000-01. Special adviser to John MacGregor 1989-94. Solicitor. Contested Paisley North 1987. Divorced, one son. Ed: St Columba's Sch; University of Edinburgh (BA; LLB; first female president, Students' Union).

CHALLENGERS
Andrew Smith (Ukip) Chartered accountant. Founder and chair, Epping Forest Ukip branch 2001-13. Treasurer, Ukip national party

2004-06. Contested: Epping Forest 2010, 2005, 2001; Essex PCC 2012; Ukip MEP Eastern Counties 2009. Founded Young Conservatives, Cambridgeshire 1965-. Member, FCS at University. Ed: University of Exeter (BA economics & statistics). **Gareth Barrett** (Lab) Public affairs manager, British Soft Drinks Association. Cllr, Brentwood BC, 2014-. Chairman, licensing cttee 2014-. Former public affairs manager, British Beer & Pub Assoc. Ed: Essex (BSc economics), Birkbeck, London (MSc public policy & management).

CONSTITUENCY PROFILE
In the southeastern corner of Essex, lying next to the boundary with Greater London. Includes affluent residential areas like Chigwell and Loughton, as well as the northern part of the eponymous Epping Forest. Home to a sizeable Jewish community. Popular with commuters due to good transport links. Safely Conservative since 1974.

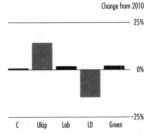

	Electorate	Turnout %	Change from 2010 %
	73,545	67.1	
E Laing C	27,027	54.8	+0.8
A Smith Ukip	9,049	18.3	+14.4
G Barrett Lab	7,962	16.1	+1.9
J Whitehouse LD	3,448	7.0	-14.5
A Widdup Green	1,782	3.6	+2.2
M Wadsworth Young	80	0.2	

Change from 2010

C   Ukip   Lab   LD   Green

Epsom & Ewell

CONSERVATIVE HOLD

CHRISTOPHER GRAYLING
BORN Apr 1, 1962
MP 2001-

Leader of the HoC 2015-. Secretary of state, justice and lord chancellor 2012-15. Suffered predictable but humiliating demotion to min, work & pensions 2010-, after stint as shadow home secretary 2009-10. Shadow: SoS, work & pensions 2007-09, transport 2005-07; leader of the HoC 2005; minister: health 2005, higher education 2004-05, public services, health & education 2003-04. Opposition whip 2002. Cllr, Merton BC 1998-2002. Media career. Change consultant and European marketing dir, Burson Marsteller. Contested Warrington 1997. Married, one daughter, one son. Ed: Sidney Sussex Coll, Cambridge (BA history).

CHALLENGERS
Sheila Carlson (Lab) GMB union member and regional officer.

Building industry worker. Cllr, Epsom & Ewell BC 1997-15, borough mayoress 2011-12. Trained as special needs teacher. Worked in an animal laboratory, Imperial Cancer Research. Married, three children. **Robert Leach** (Ukip) Self employed tax accountant, author and lecturer. Served on the General Synod 1995-2005. Chair, *The Church of England Newspaper*. Musician. Married, three children. **Stephen Gee** (LD) Managing partner and co-founder, John Rowan & Partners construction consultancy. Contested Wimbledon 2005. Married, one son, one daughter. Ed: University of Reading (BSc quantity surveying).

CONSTITUENCY PROFILE
Within the London commuter belt, runs from Worcester Park in the north, to Ashtead in the south. An affluent and desirable area. Home to the Derby horse race. A solid Conservative seat, has returned a Tory MP since its creation as Epsom in 1885.

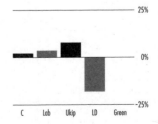

	Electorate	Turnout %	Change from 2010 %
	78,633	72.7	
C Grayling C	33,309	58.3	+2.1
S Carlson Lab	8,866	15.5	+3.6
R Leach Ukip	7,117	12.5	+7.8
S Gee LD	5,002	8.8	-18.1
S McGrath Green	2,116	3.7	
L Blackman Ind	612	1.1	
G Harfoot ND	121	0.2	

Change from 2010

C   Lab   Ukip   LD   Green

The 2015 House of Commons

Seats by party

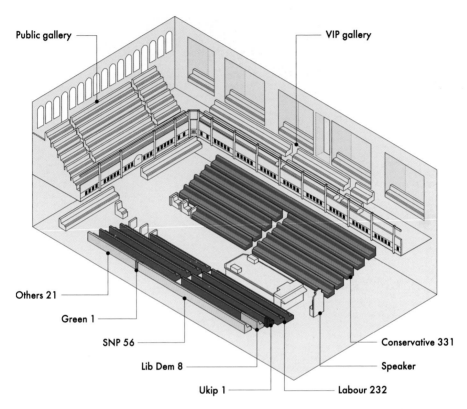

Public gallery

VIP gallery

Others 21

Green 1

SNP 56

Lib Dem 8

Ukip 1

Conservative 331

Speaker

Labour 232

Vote share, %

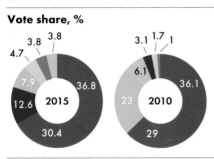

2015: 3.8, 3.8, 4.7, 7.9, 12.6, 30.4, 36.8

2010: 3.1, 1.7, 1, 6.1, 23, 29, 36.1

Key to party colours

- Conservative
- DUP
- Green
- Labour
- Lib Dem
- Plaid Cymru
- SDLP
- Sinn Fein
- SNP
- Ukip
- UUP
- Other

Number of votes per MP elected

Source: Electoral Reform Society

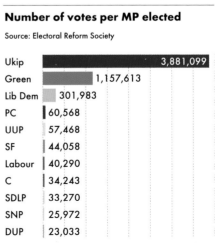

Ukip	3,881,099
Green	1,157,613
Lib Dem	301,983
PC	60,568
UUP	57,468
SF	44,058
Labour	40,290
C	34,243
SDLP	33,270
SNP	25,972
DUP	23,033

The political map of Britain 2015

2010 results

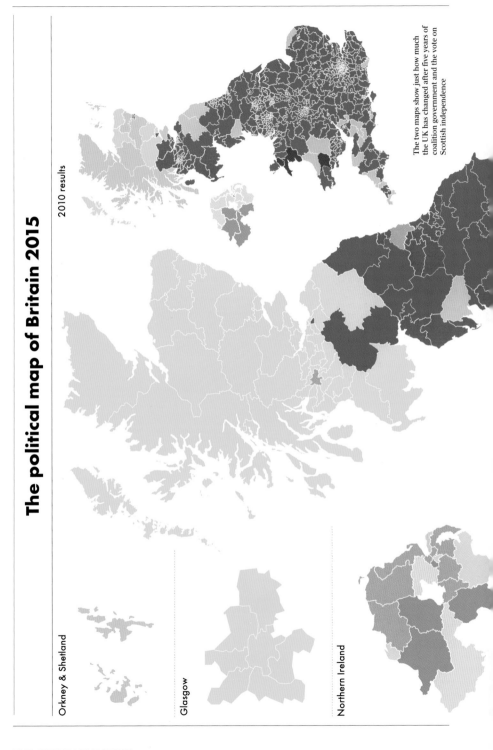

The two maps show just how much the UK has changed after five years of coalition government and the vote on Scottish independence

Orkney & Shetland

Glasgow

Northern Ireland

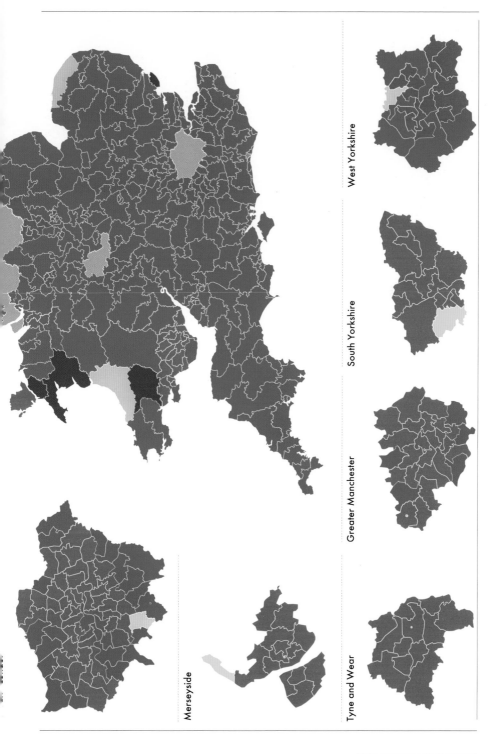

West Yorkshire

South Yorkshire

Greater Manchester

Merseyside

Tyne and Wear

The road to N° 10

How the parties fared in the opinion polls

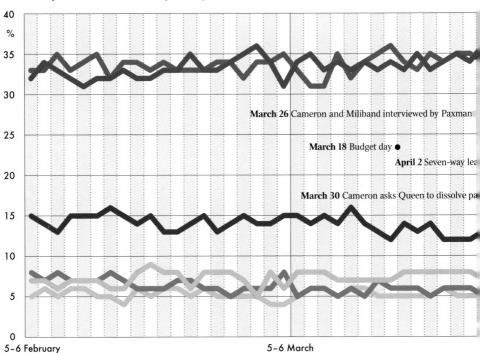

40
%
35
30
25
20
15
10
5
0

March 26 Cameron and Miliband interviewed by Paxman

March 18 Budget day ●

April 2 Seven-way lea

March 30 Cameron asks Queen to dissolve pa

5–6 February   5–6 March

What mattered to the voters before the election

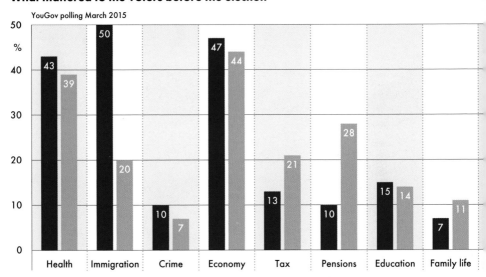

YouGov polling March 2015

50
%
40
30
20
10
0

| Health | Immigration | Crime | Economy | Tax | Pensions | Education | Family life |

Health: 43, 39
Immigration: 50, 20
Crime: 10, 7
Economy: 47, 44
Tax: 13, 21
Pensions: 10, 28
Education: 15, 14
Family life: 7, 11

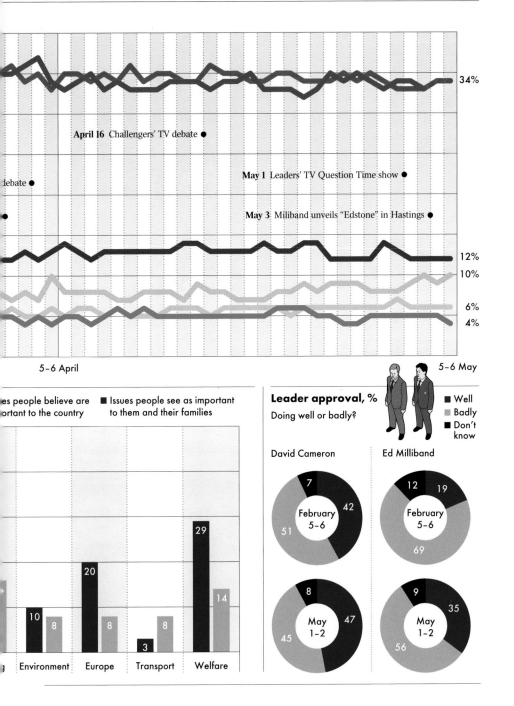

34%

April 16 Challengers' TV debate ●

debate ●

May 1 Leaders' TV Question Time show ●

May 3 Miliband unveils "Edstone" in Hastings ●

12%
10%

6%
4%

5–6 April   5–6 May

...es people believe are ...ortant to the country   ■ Issues people see as important to them and their families

Leader approval, %
Doing well or badly?

■ Well
■ Badly
■ Don't know

Environment   Europe   Transport   Welfare
10 | 8   20 | 8   3 | 8   29 | 14

David Cameron

February 5–6
7
42
51

May 1–2
8
47
45

Ed Milliband

February 5–6
12   19
69

May 1–2
9   35
56

The electorate 2015

Ethnicity

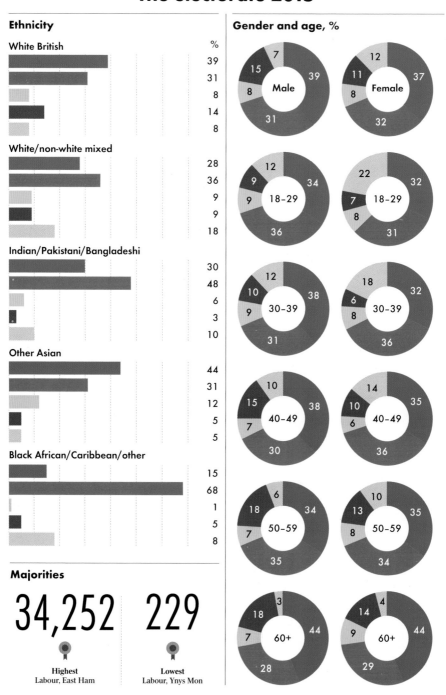

White British

	%
	39
	31
	8
	14
	8

White/non-white mixed

	28
	36
	9
	9
	18

Indian/Pakistani/Bangladeshi

	30
	48
	6
	3
	10

Other Asian

	44
	31
	12
	5
	5

Black African/Caribbean/other

	15
	68
	1
	5
	8

Majorities

34,252   229

Highest
Labour, East Ham

Lowest
Labour, Ynys Mon

Gender and age, %

Male: 7, 15, 8, 31, 39
Female: 12, 11, 8, 32, 37

18–29 Male: 12, 9, 9, 36, 34
18–29 Female: 22, 7, 8, 31, 32

30–39 Male: 12, 10, 9, 31, 38
30–39 Female: 18, 6, 8, 36, 32

40–49 Male: 10, 15, 7, 30, 38
40–49 Female: 14, 10, 6, 36, 35

50–59 Male: 6, 18, 7, 35, 34
50–59 Female: 10, 13, 8, 34, 35

60+ Male: 3, 18, 7, 28, 44
60+ Female: 4, 14, 9, 29, 44

Employment status

Full-time

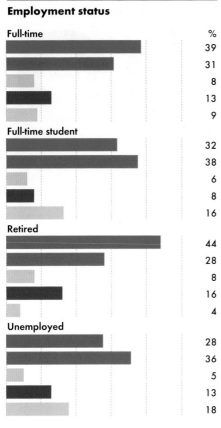

	%
	39
	31
	8
	13
	9

Full-time student

	32
	38
	6
	8
	16

Retired

	44
	28
	8
	16
	4

Unemployed

	28
	36
	5
	13
	18

Annual household income

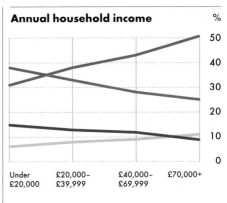

%
50
40
30
20
10
0

Under £20,000	£20,000– £39,999	£40,000– £69,999	£70,000+

Housing status

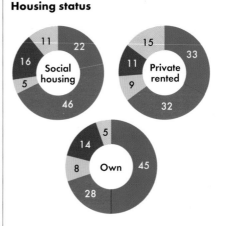

Social housing — 11, 22, 16, 5, 46

Private rented — 15, 33, 11, 9, 32

Own — 5, 14, 8, 28, 45

Work sector, %

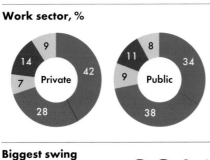

Private — 9, 14, 7, 28, 42

Public — 8, 11, 9, 38, 34

Biggest swing

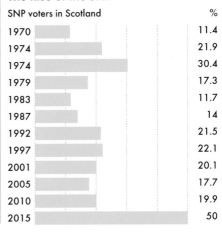

39%

Labour-SNP, Glasgow North East
(Biggest swing in UK general election history)

The Rise of the SNP

SNP voters in Scotland

	%
1970	11.4
1974	21.9
1974	30.4
1979	17.3
1983	11.7
1987	14
1992	21.5
1997	22.1
2001	20.1
2005	17.7
2010	19.9
2015	50

MPs' backgrounds 2015

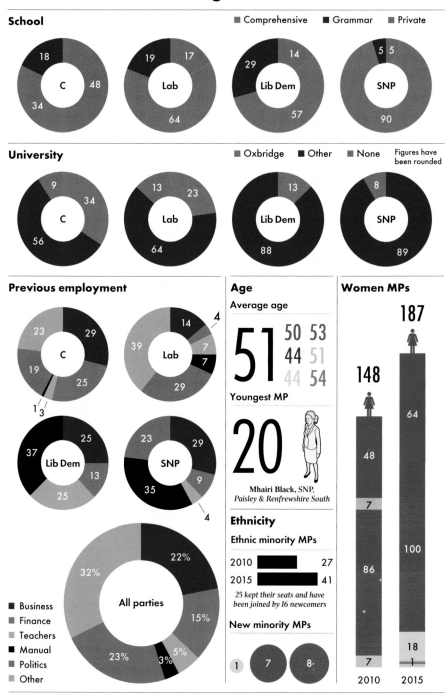

School

■ Comprehensive   ■ Grammar   ■ Private

C — 48, 18, 34
Lab — 64, 19, 17
Lib Dem — 57, 29, 14
SNP — 90, 5, 5

University

■ Oxbridge   ■ Other   ■ None   Figures have been rounded

C — 56, 9, 34
Lab — 64, 13, 23
Lib Dem — 88, 13
SNP — 89, 8

Previous employment

C — 29, 25, 19, 23, 1, 3
Lab — 14, 7, 7, 29, 39, 4
Lib Dem — 25, 13, 25, 37
SNP — 29, 9, 35, 23, 4

All parties
22% | 15% | 5% | 3% | 23% | 32%

■ Business
■ Finance
■ Teachers
■ Manual
■ Politics
■ Other

Age

Average age

51
50 53
44 51
44 54

Youngest MP

20

Mhairi Black, SNP,
Paisley & Renfrewshire South

Ethnicity

Ethnic minority MPs

2010 — 27
2015 — 41

25 kept their seats and have been joined by 16 newcomers

New minority MPs

1   7   8

Women MPs

187

148

2010 — 7, 48, 86, 7
2015 — 1, 18, 100, 64

2010   2015

Erewash

CONSERVATIVE HOLD

MAGGIE THROUP
BORN Jan 27, 1957
MP 2015-

Businesswoman. Independent marketing consultant, Maggie Throup Marketing. Former biomedical scientist, Calderdale Health Authority. Sales exec. Dir, pharmaceuticals, In-Vitro Diagnostic Div. Contested: Colne Valley 2005; Solihull 2010, lost out by fewer than 200 votes. Trustee, Carers Centre. Trustee & chair, Drug Rehabilitation CIC. Ed: Bradford Girls' GS; University of Manchester (BSc biology).

CHALLENGERS
Catherine Atkinson (Lab) Barrister. Cllr, Kensington & Chelsea BC 2006-10. Contested Kensington & Chelsea 2005. Sec, Society of Labour Lawyers. Awarded the Lincoln's Inn Gluckstein prize. Enjoys dancing. Married. Ed: Sacred Heart HS; University of Edinburgh (MDiv

divinity); City University London (law conversion). **Philip Rose** (Ukip) Self-employed sales agent. Previously: president, Placerville & Sacramento Valley Railroad; director, Folsom Historical Society. Cllr, Erewash BC 2007-09. Ed: Sheffield Hallam (BA public administration); Derby (MA marketing); Chartered Institute of Marketing. **Martin Garnett** (LD) Associate pharmacy professor, University of Nottingham. Formerly on strategy team, Engineering & Physical Sciences Research Council. Cllr, Draycott PC 1995-99. Contested Erewash 2010, 05, 01, 1997.

CONSTITUENCY PROFILE
A suburban seat in the south eastern corner of Derbyshire. Traditionally the local economy was industrial with iron working, coal mining and lace making dominant industries. Manufacturing continues, employing one in six people. Tory leaning Con-Lab marginal.

	Electorate	Turnout %	Change from 2010 %
	71,937	67.2	
M Throup C	20,636	42.7	+3.2
C Atkinson Lab	17,052	35.3	+1.1
P Rose Ukip	7,792	16.1	+14.3
M Garnett LD	1,658	3.4	-14.1
R Hierons Green	1,184	2.5	+1.3

Change from 2010

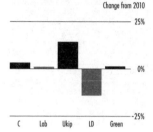

Erith & Thamesmead

LABOUR HOLD

TERESA PEARCE
BORN Feb 1, 1955
MP 2010-

Left-winger and long-term constituency activist. Lancashire-born but London-raised, became single mother aged 18, relied on council housing. Member, select cttees: Treasury 2011-; work & pensions 2010-; unopposed bills 2013-. Backed in 2010 selection as candidate by predecessor MP John Austin in face of national party support for Georgia Gould, the daughter of Blair's pollster Lord (Philip) Gould. Cllr: Erith BC 1998-2002; Bexley BC 1998-2002. Campaigned against incinerator in constituency. Senior manager, PwC's tax investigations team. Inland Revenue. GMB. Two daughters. Ed: St Thomas More Sch.

CHALLENGERS
Anna Firth (C) Barrister. Cllr, Sevenaoks DC 2011 -. "Mothers

at home matter" campaigner. Lost out to Kelly Tolhurst for Rochester & Strood by-election nomination following defection of Mark Reckless to Ukip. School governor. Previously investment banker. Married, three children. Ed: Durham University (LLB law). **Ronie Johnson** (Ukip) CEO, regional charity working with young offenders. Former Labour party member. Married, three children. Ed: South Bank University (BA European social policy). **Simon Waddington** (LD) Works in international communications. Married.

CONSTITUENCY PROFILE
Southeast of London. Straddles the boroughs of Greenwich and Bexley. HMP Belmarsh is here. A significant proportion of the workforce are in transport, storage and support services jobs as well as manufacturing, including one end of Crossrail, being constructed here. A safe Labour seat since its creation in 1995.

	Electorate	Turnout %	Change from 2010 %
	69,787	61.1	
T Pearce Lab	21,209	49.8	+4.9
A Firth C	11,684	27.4	-4.1
R Johnson Ukip	7,368	17.3	+14.6
S Waddington LD	972	2.3	-9.8
A Garrett Green	941	2.2	+1.5
S Cordle CPA	255	0.6	-0.3
G Moore Eng Dem	188	0.4	-0.7

Change from 2010

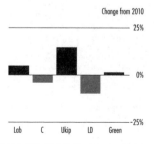

Esher & Walton

CONSERVATIVE HOLD

DOMINIC RAAB
BORN Feb 25, 1974
MP 2010-

Ex-FCO adviser and lawyer. Parly under-sec at MoJ; minister for human rights 2015-. Member, select cttees: education 2013-15; human rights 2010-13. Author, *The Assault on Liberty*. Selected by open primary. Chief of staff to: David Davis as shadow home sec; Dominic Grieve as shadow justice sec. FCO posting to The Hague. Linklaters career, secondment to Liberty. Black belt, third dan karate – former member, British squad. Son of Czech refugee. Married. Ed: Dr Challoners GS, Amersham; LMH, Oxford (BA law); Jesus Coll, Cambridge (LLM international law).

CHALLENGERS
Francis Eldergill (Lab) Head of fixed income technology, LCH. Clearnet. Career includes Pension Corporation, Bank of America and JP Morgan. Contested Esher & Walton 2010. Married, two sons. Ed: Stamford Sch. **Nicholas Wood** (Ukip) Chemistry lecturer, Kingston University. Works as an NHS locum pharmacist. Previously worked in the pharmaceutical industry. Ed: Bristol (PhD antibiotics). **Andrew Davis** (LD) Founded cycle-insurance and car breakdown cover firm ETA. Cllr, Elmbridge BC 2012-. Ed: Kent (urban studies). **Olivia Palmer** (Green) Works for community housing group. Finance administrator. Ed: BA philosophy & human rights; MA human rights & int relations.

CONSTITUENCY PROFILE
Stockbroker commuter territory for the capital. Much of the constituency is designated as green belt land and includes Sandown Park racecourse. Low unemployment and high property prices. A safe Conservative seat. At a local level Elmbridge council is largely contested between the Tories and various local residents' associations.

	Electorate	Turnout %	Change from 2010 %
	79,894	71.3	
D Raab C	35,845	62.9	+4.0
F Eldergill Lab	7,229	12.7	+2.0
N Wood Ukip	5,551	9.7	+6.5
A Davis LD	5,372	9.4	-15.4
O Palmer Green	2,355	4.1	
M Heenan CSA	396	0.7	
D Reynolds Ind	228	0.4	-0.3

Change from 2010

Exeter

LABOUR HOLD

BEN BRADSHAW
BORN Aug 30, 1960
MP 1997-

Contender for Labour deputy leadership 2015. Member, select cttees: CMS 2012-; ecclesiastical 2010-; privacy and injunctions 2011-12; European scrutiny 1998-2001. SoS, CMS 2009-10. Min: south west 2007-09; health 2007-09; Defra 2006-07. Parly under-sec: Defra 2003-06; privy council office 2002-03; FCO 2001-02. PPS to John Denham 2000-01. Member: Lab Campaign for Electoral Reform; Lab Movement for Europe. BBC Radio 4 reporter (Sony News Reporter Award 1993). Journalist - BBC correspondent at fall of Berlin Wall. Civil partnership. Ed: Thorpe St Andrew Sch, Norwich; Sussex (BA German); Freiburg University, Baden-Württemberg.

CHALLENGERS
Dom Morris (C) FCO Adviser. Works in conflict zones on behalf of British government in Pakistan and Afghanistan. Syria Conflict Pool Programme manager. Previously RAF flying trainer, before accident put a halt to career and moved to deliver Prince's Trust programmes for underprivileged young people. Ed: University of Birmingham (MA international political economy of conflict, security and development). **Keith Crawford** (Ukip) Property developer and former soldier. Contested: South West region European election 2014; Exeter 2010. **Diana Moore** (Green) Business advisor. Has worked with social enterprises and charities.

CONSTITUENCY PROFILE
Situated in South West England. Home to the University of Exeter, the Met Office's weather forecasting headquarters and the county council offices — the three largest employers in the city. Has a high proportion of students. Largely white although there is a significant Chinese community.

	Electorate	Turnout %	Change from 2010 %
	76,964	70.2	
B Bradshaw Lab	25,062	46.4	+8.2
D Morris C	17,879	33.1	+0.1
K Crawford Ukip	5,075	9.4	+5.7
D Moore Green	3,491	6.5	+5.0
J Mason LD	2,321	4.3	-16.0
E Potts TUSC	190	0.4	

Change from 2010

Falkirk

SNP GAIN

JOHN MCNALLY
BORN Feb 1, 1951
MP 2015-

A trusted and respected local councillor, Falkirk C 2005-. Owner of a long-running barber. Described by former Falkirk West Labour MP, Dennis Canavan, as a "man of the people". Contested Falkirk in 2010. Came second, securing the biggest swing from Labour (8.9 points) in any Scottish seat. Member: Denny Bowling Club; Denny & Dunipace Heritage Society. Married, two children. Ed: St Patricks PS; St Modans Secondary Sch.

CHALLENGERS
Karen Whitefield (Lab) MSP for Airdrie & Shotts 1999-2011; chair, education ctee. Shadow min: children. Convenor, Cross-Party Group on Diabetes. Former PA to Rachel Squire. Replaced Eric Joyce's as candidate for the Falkirk constituency after his conviction

for assault. **Alison Harris** (C) Chartered accountant, runs own accountancy practice. Married, two children. **David Coburn** (Ukip) MEP for Scotland 2014-. Businessman. Worked as an art dealer, City trader and owned a freight company. Contested Old Bexley & Sidcup 2010. His office was banned from Wikipedia for editing his own page, 2015.

CONSTITUENCY PROFILE
Seat of the 2013 Labour selection scandal which saw the party and Unite clash. Falkirk and its predecessor Falkirk West have both been consistently Labour, but both of its most recent MPs have ended up leaving the party and sitting as independents. While Labour have historically had a decent majority here, there has always been SNP support and they held a comfortable second place since the 1990s until taking the seat in 2015. Originally a heavy industrial town, but is now more dominated by retail and administration.

	Electorate	Turnout %	from 2010 %	Change %
	83,380	72.4		
J McNally SNP	34,831	57.7	+27.5	
K Whitefield Lab	15,130	25.1	-20.6	
A Harris C	7,325	12.1	+0.9	
D Coburn Ukip	1,829	3.0	+0.5	
G Milne LD	1,225	2.0	-8.3	

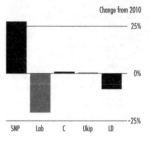

Change from 2010

SNP   Lab   C   Ukip   LD

Fareham

CONSERVATIVE HOLD

SUELLA FERNANDES
BORN Apr 3, 1980
MP 2015-

Committed and vigilant volunteer for Conservatives since age 16. Political family background; mother served 16 years as local cllr, contested Brent East by-election 2003, attempted to rival mother in selection for Brent East's Conservative candidate. Contested Leicester East 2005. Served as Ward chairman of Westminster Conservatives. Barrister, No 5 Chambers, specialising in planning, local government and public law. Awarded Pegasus scholar, 2010. Called to bar at Middle Temple. Founder and trustee, Africa Justice Foundation. Ed: Queens' Coll, Cambridge (MA law; chair, CUCA); Université de Paris Pantheon-Sorbonne (LLM); New York Bar.

CHALLENGERS
Malcolm Jones (Ukip) Self employed property repair

contractor. Previously tutor and apprentice printer. Former president and vice-president of GPMU Wessex region. Ed: Southampton City Coll; University of Southampton (BA social science perspectives, social & cultural anthropology). **Stuart Rose** (Lab) Works as a print manager. Former cllr, Fareham BC; vice chairman, environmental cttee. **Matthew Winnington** (LD) Cllr, Portsmouth CC 2012-. Executive officer for DWP, 2002-2014. Atum Creations' Community consultant. Ed: University of Liverpool (BA Egyptology).

CONSTITUENCY PROFILE
Safely Conservative, held by the party since its creation in 1974, and prior to that the Fareham & Gosport seat was similarly Tory. This is an affluent residential seat situated between Southampton and Portsmouth. The economy is largely white collar, based around the offices, call centres and retail parks strung along the motorway.

	Electorate	Turnout %	from 2010 %	Change %
	77,233	70.8		
S Fernandes C	30,689	56.1	+0.8	
M Jones Ukip	8,427	15.4	+11.3	
S Rose Lab	7,800	14.3	+0.1	
M Winnington LD	4,814	8.8	-15.0	
M Grindey Green	2,129	3.9	+2.4	
N Gregory Ind	705	1.3		
H Hines Ind	136	0.3		

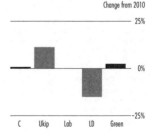

Change from 2010

C   Ukip   Lab   LD   Green

Faversham & Kent Mid

CONSERVATIVE HOLD

HELEN WHATELY
BORN Jun 23, 1976
MP 2015-

Well-supported campaigner and activist for quality care in the NHS. Previously policy advisor to Hugo Swire. Contested Kingston & Surbiton 2010. Management consultant: McKinsey & Co healthcare firm; PricewaterhouseCoopers; AOL Time Warner. Active volunteer within a homeless organisation. Taught English in Kathmandu, Nepal. Avid horse rider, representing Surrey in national competitions, achieving sixth place in British Junior Eventing Championships, and captain of Oxford University's riding team. Married, one son, two daughters. Ed: Woldingham Sch; Westminster Sch; LMH, Oxford (BA PPE).

CHALLENGERS
Peter Edwards-Daem (Ukip) Cllr, Medway C 1997-2003 for Labour.

Founded swimming pool business. Formerly: self-employed European researcher incl for Peter Skinner MEP; lifeguard and swimming instructor; police officer; farmer. Married, three children. **Michael Desmond** (Lab) Cllr, Hackney BC 2001-, 1990-1998. Speaker (civic mayor) 2013-14. Chair, Labour Edgware branch 1977-82. MD, On The House estate agents. GMB, Co-op party. Ed: Orange Hill GS; Bedford Coll, London University (BA social science & administration).

CONSTITUENCY PROFILE
A safe Conservative seat, held by the party since its creation in 1997. The constituency includes the town of Faversham in the Swale council area, then stretches south across the North Downs and through little country roads to take in the rural villages around Maidstone, the villages along the M20 and the suburbs of Maidstone itself, such as Shepway and Bearsted.

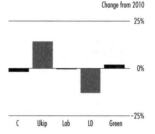

	Electorate	Turnout %	Change from 2010 %
	69,523	65.9	
H Whately C	24,895	54.4	-1.8
P Edwards-Daem Ukip	8,243	18.0	+14.3
M Desmond Lab	7,403	16.2	-0.4
D Naghi LD	3,039	6.6	-13.0
T Valentine Green	1,768	3.9	+2.0
H K Davidson Loony	297	0.7	-0.2
G Butler Eng Dem	158	0.3	

Change from 2010

Feltham & Heston

LABOUR CO-OPERATIVE HOLD

SEEMA MALHOTRA
BORN Aug 7, 1972
MP 2011-

Elected in December 2011 by-election following the death of Alan Keen. Shadow min for preventing violence against women & girls 2014-. Contested London assembly SW London 2004. Opposition whip 2013-15. PPS to Yvette Cooper 2012-14. Member, Justice select cttee 2012-13. Chairwoman, Parliamentary Labour Party Business Interest Group 2012-2014. Was freelance business and public service adviser. Former chairwoman, Fabian Society. Ed: University of Warwick (BA politics & philosophy); Aston University (MSc business IT).

CHALLENGERS
Simon Nayyar (C) PR guru and managing partner, Newgate Communications. "One of the best-known figures in the UK lobbying industry" according to

Public Affairs News. Previously held senior roles at Edelman and Citigate Dewe Rogerson. Contested Hackney South & Shoreditch 2010. Assisted in Conservative Friends of India launch. Ed: York (BA history). **Peter Dul** (Ukip) Retired international marine insurance worker. Said that people are not responsible for climate change. Contested Richmond Park 2010, 05.

CONSTITUENCY PROFILE
Feltham and Heston are to the south and east of Heathrow airport respectively, and the airport is a major source of local employment and, thanks to its possible expansion, a major political issue locally. The seat was Conservative between 1983-92, but in 1997 and 2001 Labour secured majorities nearing 60 per cent of the vote. The Tories enjoyed an 8.4-point swing in 2005 and have had success at local elections, but the Labour majority is still substantial and was further bolstered by the 2010 boundary changes.

	Electorate	Turnout %	Change from 2010 %
	82,328	60.0	
S Malhotra Lab Co-op	25,845	52.3	+8.7
S Nayyar C	14,382	29.1	-4.9
P Dul Ukip	6,209	12.6	+10.5
R Crouch LD	1,579	3.2	-10.6
T Firkins Green	1,390	2.8	+1.7

Change from 2010

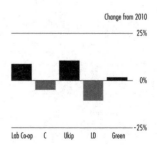

Fermanagh & South Tyrone

UUP GAIN

TOM ELLIOTT
BORN Dec 11, 1963
MP 2015-

Leader of UUP 2010-12, resigned after hostility he faced as leader. MLA for Fermanagh & South Tyrone 2003-; UUP spokesperson for justice; member, agriculture & rural development cttee 2014-. Past County Grand Master of the Orange Order within Fermanagh; assistant secretary to the Grand Lodge of Ireland. Cllr, Fermanagh DC 2001-10. Contested Fermanagh & South Tyrone 2005. Spent 18 years as a part-time member of the Ulster Defence Regiment and the Royal Irish Regiment. Married, one daughter, one son. Ed: Duke of Westminster HS, Ballinamallard & Kesh; Enniskillen Coll of Agriculture (Cert in agriculture).

CHALLENGERS
Michelle Gildernew (SF) MP for Fermanagh & South Tyrone 2001-15. MLA for Fermanagh & South

Tyrone 1998-2012; agriculture and rural development min 2007-11. SF press officer 1997-. Married, two sons, one daughter. Ed: University of Ulster. **John Coyle** (SDLP) Cllr, Fermanagh and Omagh DC 2014-. Farmer and retail worker. Chair: Mulleek Community Association; SDLP Fermangh Executive. **Tanya Jones** (Green) Self-employed writer, publisher, fair trade supplier and bookseller. Former teacher and solicitor. Ed: King's Coll, Cambridge (MA English); York (MA medieval studies); Coll of Law, York.

CONSTITUENCY PROFILE
Generally, a UUP-Sinn Féin marginal, often with very small majorities. The MP since the 2001 election had been Michelle Gildernew of Sinn Fein, but in 2010 she won by just 4 votes over an independent candidate, Rodney Connor, and was beaten by the UUP in 2015. There is an almost 60/40 split in religious affiliation in this seat in southwest NI, the majority being Catholic.

	Electorate	Turnout %	from 2010 % Change
	70,106	72.6	
T Elliott UUP	23,608	46.4	
M Gildernew SF	23,078	45.4	-0.2
J Coyle SDLP	2,732	5.4	-2.3
T Jones Green	788	1.6	
H Su Alliance	658	1.3	+0.4

Change from 2010

— 25%

— 0%

—-25%

UUP   SF   SDLP   Green   Alliance

Fife North East

SNP GAIN

STEPHEN GETHINS
BORN Mar 28, 1976
MP 2015-

SNP spokesman, Europe 2015-, former special adviser to FM of Scotland on European and international affairs, energy and climate change. Consultant on international development and worked on democratisation projects in Africa. Formerly: NGO Links, based in Tbilisi; Saferworld in arms control and peace-building in the former Soviet Union and Balkans. Contested Scotland region in European elections 2014. Worked at Scotland Europa, helping Scottish organisations gain influence and funding in the EU; political adviser, committee of the regions in the EU. Worked in office of MSP Andrew Wilson. Married, one daughter. Ed: Perth Academy; University of Dundee (LLB law); University of Kent (research MA role of devolved assemblies in resolving inter-ethnic conflict).

CHALLENGERS
Tim Brett (LD) Cllr, Fife C 2003-; leader of Lib Dem group 2012-; chair, social work ctte, 2007-2012. Formerly senior manager, NHS Tayside; director, Health Protection Scotland; managed mission hospital in Sierra Leone. Married, three children. Ed: Gravesend GS; University of Bristol. **Huw Bell** (C) Business consultant for economic and market growth. Former RAF intelligence officer. Ed: University of Reading (BSc agriculture).

CONSTITUENCY PROFILE
This seat and its predecessor, East Fife, have a long Liberal tradition, and was once represented by the Liberal prime minister, Herbert Asquith. A National Liberal MP held the seat from 1929-61 and the Unionists took hold after. The seat remained in Tory hands until 1987 when it was won by the Lib Dem Sir Menzies Campbell, who built a substantial majority, but on his resignation in 2015 it fell to the SNP.

	Electorate	Turnout %	from 2010 % Change
	62,003	73.0	
S Gethins SNP	18,523	40.9	+26.7
T Brett LD	14,179	31.3	-13.0
H Bell C	7,373	16.3	-5.5
B Thomson Lab	3,476	7.7	-9.5
A Collins Green	1,387	3.1	
M Scott-Hayward Ind	325	0.7	

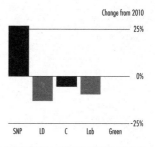

Change from 2010

— 25%

— 0%

—-25%

SNP   LD   C   Lab   Green

Filton & Bradley Stoke

CONSERVATIVE HOLD

JACK LOPRESTI
BORN Aug 23, 1969
MP 2010-

Strong voice for the TA; served five month tour in Afghanistan as a gunner. Passionate about social mobility having left school at 15. Diagnosed with bowel cancer in 2013. PPS to Desmond Swayne 2014-15. Select cttees: armed forces bill 2011; NI affairs 2010-. Cllr, Bristol CC 1999-2007. Contested Bristol E 2001; South West England Euro election 2004. Member, Freedom Association, Conservative Way Forward. Financial services and residential property consultant. Worked in family ice cream business. Interested in military history (member, the Churchill Centre, General George Patton Historical Society). Married, one daughter, two sons. Ed: Brislington Comp.

CHALLENGERS
Ian Boulton (Lab) Dir, Flexible

Training Partners. Cllr, South Gloucestershire C 2011-, chairman 2013-14. Worked at RBS and NatWest banks. **Ben Walker** (Ukip) Cllr, South Gloucestershire 2011-15, Conservative. Mayor of Bradley Stoke 2010-12. Formerly served in the Royal Navy. FA coach. **Pete Bruce** (LD) Works in social development and for Silvertree Solutions, company helping to build relationships between organisations. Ed: Queens' Coll, Cambridge (BA engineering; MEng manufacturing technology & management); Exeter (Postgrad cert sustainable development). **Dr Diana Warner** (Green) GP at Stoke Gifford & Conygre Medical Centre. Two children.

CONSTITUENCY PROFILE
Created for the 2010 election, when this seat north of Bristol was expected to be a three-way marginal but the Conservatives came top with a comfortable 41 per cent of the vote. Filton is a centre for the aviation industry.

	Electorate	Turnout %	Change from 2010 %
	70,722	69.4	
J Lopresti C	22,920	46.7	+5.9
I Boulton Lab	13,082	26.6	+0.2
B Walker Ukip	7,261	14.8	+11.7
P Bruce LD	3,581	7.3	-18.0
D Warner Green	2,257	4.6	+3.7

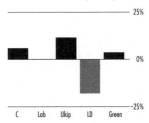

Change from 2010

Finchley & Golders Green

CONSERVATIVE HOLD

MIKE FREER
BORN May 29, 1960
MP 2010-

Energetic Thatcherite. Pioneer of "easyCouncil" local govt model as cllr, Barnet 2001-10 (leader 2006-09) and 1990-94. Criticised over council's deposits in Icelandic banks. PPS to: Eric Pickles 2013-14; Nick Boles 2014, resigned to vote against recognition of Palestinian state. Select cttees: w&p 2013; Scottish affairs 2010-13; CLG 2010-11. Contested Harrow W 2005. Self-employed consultant on regeneration and local govt. Banking career, incl Barclays; Bradford & Bingley. Management consultant, Deloitte Touche Tohmatsu. Prev retail catering career: KFC, Pizza Hut. Married. Ed: Chadderton GS; St Aidan's, Carlisle; University of Stirling (BA accountancy & business law – did not take finals).

CHALLENGERS
Sarah Sackman (Lab) Barrister, public and environmental law.

Guest lecturer, LSE. Volunteer, Toynbee Hall. Ed: Queens' Coll, Cambridge (BA history); City (CPE); Harvard Law School (LLM). **Richard King** (Ukip) Former IT investment banker. Married, one adopted daughter. Runs local martial arts club. Ed: Nottingham (BEng civil engineering). **Jonathan Davies** (LD) Retired solicitor. Treasurer, Golders Green Synagogue. Contested Finchley 1997. Vice-chairman, Lib Dem Friends of Israel. Cllr, Barnet Council 1994-98. **Adele Ward** (Green) Publisher, author and freelance, Ward Wood Publishing. Ed: Newlands Sch; Royal Holloway, London (MA creative writing).

CONSTITUENCY PROFILE
A well-to-do residential seat with a large Jewish population. Politically it is closely associated with Margaret Thatcher, its MP for 33 years. Labour unexpectedly won in 1997, on new boundaries, but the seat was finally regained by the Conservatives in 2010.

	Electorate	Turnout %	Change from 2010 %
	72,049	70.5	
M Freer C	25,835	50.9	+4.9
S Sackman Lab	20,173	39.7	+6.1
R King Ukip	1,732	3.4	+1.7
J Davies LD	1,662	3.3	-13.8
A Ward Green	1,357	2.7	+1.1

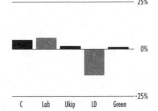

Change from 2010

Folkestone & Hythe

CONSERVATIVE HOLD

DAMIAN COLLINS
BORN Feb 4, 1974
MP 2010-

Former chief of staff to Michael Howard, whose seat he inherited. Heads New Fifa Now, which lobbies for reform of Fifa. PPS to: Philip Hammond 2014-15; Theresa Villiers 2012-14. Select cttees: consolidation bills 2010-; culture, media and sport 2010-12. Political officer, Bow Group (2003-04). Contested Northampton North, 2005. PR and advertising career: Lexington Communications; Influence Communications; M&C Saatchi. Conservative research department and press office. Founding director, Conservative Arts and Creative Industries Network. Supports Manchester Utd, cricket fan. Married, one daughter, one son. Ed: St Mary's HS; Belmont Abbey Sch, Herefordshire; St Benet's Hall, Oxford (BA modern history; OUCA president).

CHALLENGERS
Harriet Yeo (Ukip) Cllr, Ashford BC 2011-15 (Labour); 2015- (ind). Member, Labour's national executive committee, 2005-13, chairwoman 2012-13. President, TSSA 2011-13. Replaced Janice Atkinson MEP, expelled over expenses after asking a restaurant to bill her £3,150 for a £950 meal. **Claire Jeffrey** (Lab) Youth and community worker. Unite. Vice-chairman, Folkestone and Hythe Labour party. Ed: Canterbury Christ Church (BA history). **Lynne Beaumont** (LD) Cllr, Shepway DC 2012-. Dir, Why Not Campaign, marketing and lobbying company. Ed: Shrewsbury HS for Girls.

CONSTITUENCY PROFILE
The seat includes the southernmost Kent coastline, the cinque ports of Hythe and New Romney, and the town of Folkestone. It has been held by the Conservatives since its creation in 1950, although Shepway DC has twice been controlled by the Lib Dems since 1991.

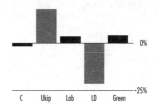

	Electorate	Turnout %	from 2010 %
	83,612	65.8	
D Collins C	26,323	47.9	-1.6
H Yeo Ukip	12,526	22.8	+18.2
C Jeffrey Lab	7,939	14.4	+3.6
L Beaumont LD	4,882	8.9	-21.4
M Whybrow Green	2,956	5.4	+4.2
S Cruse TUSC	244	0.4	
R Kapur Young	72	0.1	
A Thomas SPGB	68	0.1	

Change from 2010

Forest of Dean

CONSERVATIVE HOLD

MARK HARPER
BORN Feb 26, 1970
MP 2005-

Eurosceptic and strong supporter of Israel. Resigned as immigration minister (2012-14) as cleaner did not have visa. Chief whip, parly sec to Treasury 2015-. Minister: work & pensions 2014-. Parly sec, Cabinet Office 2010-12. Shad min: w&p 2007-10; defence 2005-07. Select cttees: administration 2014, 2005-06; w&p 2009. Auditor, KPMG; analyst and manager, Intel; established own accountancy practice. Member, the Freedom Association. Enjoys travel. Married. Ed: Headlands Sch, Swindon; Brasenose Coll, Oxford (BA PPE).

CHALLENGERS
Steve Parry-Hearn (Lab) Employment trainer, Shaw Trust. Former police officer, S Wales Police 1997-2000. Contested Somerset N 2010. Ed: Sandfields Comp Sch, Port Talbot. **Steve**

Stanbury (Ukip) Owner and Commercial Dir, Wellbeing Solutions Management. Ed: City University London (politics). **James Greenwood** (Green) Runs a property business. Contested Forest of Dean 2010. Former banker and international charity fundraiser. Ed: University of Edinburgh (MA business & economics). **Chris Coleman** (LD) Solicitor advocate. Cllr, Gloucestershire CC 2013-; Cheltenham BC 2002-. Contested Forest of Dean 2010, 2005. Married, one son. Ed: University of Northampton (LLB law); Staffordshire (LPC).

CONSTITUENCY PROFILE
Despite being a rural southern seat, Forest of Dean has historically been Labour (1918-79) because of its coal mining heritage. With the closure of the mines it drifted from Labour, and was won by the Conservatives in 1979. After returning to Labour in 1997 and 2001, it was won back by the Conservatives in 2005.

	Electorate	Turnout %	from 2010 %
	69,882	70.9	
M Harper C	23,191	46.8	-0.0
S Parry-Hearn Lab	12,204	24.6	+0.5
S Stanbury Ukip	8,792	17.8	+12.6
J Greenwood Green	2,703	5.5	+3.6
C Coleman LD	2,630	5.3	-16.6

Change from 2010

Foyle

SDLP HOLD

MARK DURKAN
BORN Jun 26, 1960
MP 2005-

SDLP leader 2001-10, chairman 1990-95. MLA for Foyle 1998-2010. Deputy first minister 2001-02. Minister of finance and personnel 1999-2001. SDLP spokes: w&p, int devt 2011-; FCO, Justice, home affairs, treasury 2010-. Select cttee: political & constitutional reform 2013-. Cllr, Derry CC 1993-2000. Member, SDLP talks team 1996-98, 1991-92. Asst to John Hume MP 1984-98. Married, one daughter. Ed: St Columb's Coll, Derry; Queen's University Belfast (BA politics, VP, Students' Union); Ulster University (PgDip public policy management).

CHALLENGERS
Gearóid Ó hEára (SF) Mayor, Derry 2004-05. Member, NI Police Board. Irish language activist. Cllr, Derry CC 1989-2005. Former board member, Arts Council NI. Ed: BA Irish studies; diploma in further

and higher education; MBA. **Gary Middleton** (DUP) MLA Foyle 2015-. Cllr, Derry CC 2011-15, dep mayor 2013-15. Ed: Ulster University (BSc computer science; Advanced Dip civic leadership & community planning.) **Julia Kee** (UUP) Worked in the community development and peace building initiatives. **David Hawthorne** (Alliance) Organic farmer, environmental consultant. Former adviser, National Trust NI. Ed: MA environmental management.

CONSTITUENCY PROFILE
One of the most nationalist constituencies in Northern Ireland, it has been an SDLP stronghold since it was created in 1983. Foyle encompasses NI's second city, Londonderry, which suffers relatively high levels of deprivation because of the decline of its manufacturing base. After being awarded UK City of Culture 2013, there has been massive investment in new museums, theatres, hotels and shopping facilities.

	Electorate	Turnout %	from 2010 %	Change
	70,035	52.8		
M Durkan SDLP	17,725	47.9	+3.2	
G Ó hEára SF	11,679	31.6	-0.4	
G Middleton DUP	4,573	12.4	+0.5	
J Kee UUP	1,226	3.3		
D Hawthorne Alliance	835	2.3	+1.7	
K Thompson Ukip	832	2.3		
H Badenoch C	132	0.4	-2.9	

Change from 2010

25%

0%

-25%

SDLP   SF   DUP   UUP   Alliance

Fylde

CONSERVATIVE HOLD

MARK MENZIES
BORN May 18, 1971
MP 2010-

Interested in energy security and planning system. PPS to: Alan Duncan 2013-14, resigned over allegations made by a Brazilian male escort that Menzies paid him for sex and drugs; Mark Prisk 2012-13; Charles Hendry 2010-12. Select cttees: Draft protection of charities bill 2014-; Scottish affairs 2014-. Contested: Selby 2005; Glasgow Govan 2001. Marketing career: ASDA, Morrisons. Won IGD/Unilever Social Innovation Marketing award in 2007. Marks & Spencer graduate trainee. Brought up in Ayrshire by widowed mother. Ed: Keil Sch (assisted place); University of Glasgow (MA economic & social history).

CHALLENGERS
Jed Sullivan (Lab) Youth and community worker. Unite convenor, Blackpool council. Anti-

fracking campaigner. Temporarily removed his Twitter account after inappropriate tweets. **Paul White** (Ukip) Hotel manager, Kings Hotel, Blackpool. Ed: Barr Beacon Sch. **Mike Hill** (Independent) Chartered electrical engineer. Standing on an anti-fracking ticket. Married, twin sons. Ed: Loughborough (electrical and electronic engineering). **Fred van Mierlo** (LD) Consultant, Harwood Levitt Consulting. Former writer at European Student Think Tank. Ed: Bristol (BA geography); Leiden (MA European union studies).

CONSTITUENCY PROFILE
The Fylde is the flat peninsula between the River Ribble and Morecambe Bay. Has been Conservative since the First World War. Affluent area with a high level of owner-occupation. The largest town is the resort of Lytham St Annes. Major industries include nuclear fuels and aerospace. Tests for shale gas extraction took place here: fracking is a major local issue.

	Electorate	Turnout %	from 2010 %	Change
	65,679	66.3		
M Menzies C	21,406	49.1	-3.1	
J Sullivan Lab	8,182	18.8	-1.0	
P White Ukip	5,569	12.8	+8.3	
M Hill Ind	5,166	11.9		
F van Mierlo LD	1,623	3.7	-18.3	
B Dennett Green	1,381	3.2	+1.7	
E Clarkson Northern	230	0.5		

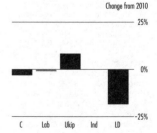

Change from 2010

25%

0%

-25%

C   Lab   Ukip   Ind   LD

Gainsborough

CONSERVATIVE HOLD

SIR EDWARD LEIGH
BORN Jul 20, 1950
MP 1983-

Suggested Ofsted be put in special measures following its criticism of faith schools in 2015. Select cttees include: chairman, public accounts commission 2011-, public accounts committee 2001-10; member, members' expenses 2011-, panel of chairs 2010-; chairman, liaison 2001-10. Parly under-sec, DTI 1990-93. PPS to John Patten 1990. Cllr: GLC 1974-81; Richmond BC 1974-78. Member, Conservative research Dept, private secretary to Margaret Thatcher. Barrister, arbitrator. Married, three daughters, three sons. Ed: Oratory Sch, London; French Lycée, London; Durham University (BA history).

CHALLENGERS
David Prescott (Lab) Dir, Commucan, corporate communications consultancy. Former journalist: BBC News,

GMTV. Father is Lord Prescott. Ed: Stradbroke Coll, Sheffield (journalism). **John Saxon** (Ukip) Former electronics engineer, RAF; established business to run Barnsley Enterprise Agency. Lived in France for several years. **Lesley Rollings** (LD) Teacher and community development & liaison manager, Gainsborough Academy. Cllr: Lincolnshire CC 2013-; West Lindsey DC 2000-. Former Gainsborough mayor. **Geoffrey Barnes** (Green) Public health consultant in North East Lincs.

CONSTITUENCY PROFILE
Agricultural area in northwest Lincolnshire, stretching from Gainsborough in the west to the Lincolnshire Wolds in the east, and the villages around Lincoln in the south. The seat includes RAF Scampton, the home of the Red Arrows. Although majorities have sometimes fallen below 10,000, this has remained a solidly Conservative seat since well before the Second World War.

		Electorate	Turnout %	Change from 2010 %
		73,212	67.3	
E Leigh	C	25,949	52.7	+3.4
D Prescott	Lab	10,500	21.3	+5.7
J Saxon	Ukip	7,727	15.7	+11.5
L Rollings	LD	3,290	6.7	-21.2
G Barnes	Green	1,290	2.6	
C Darcel	Lincs Ind	505	1.0	

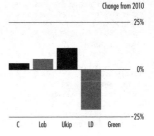

Change from 2010

Garston & Halewood

LABOUR HOLD

MARIA EAGLE
BORN Feb 17, 1961
MP 1997-

Shadow secretary of state for environment, food and rural affairs 2013-; transport 2010-13. Shadow minister, equalities office 2010. Shadow solicitor-general 2010. Minister, justice, government equalities office 2009-10. Parly under-sec: justice 2007-09; GEO 2008-09; NI Office 2006-07; education 2005-06; DWP (disabled people) 2001-05. PPS to John Hutton 1999-2001. Member, public accounts select cttee 1997-99. Press officer and political education officer, Labour party. Solicitor. Ed: Formby HS; Pembroke Coll, Oxford (BA PPE); Coll of Law, London.

CHALLENGERS
Dr Martin Williams (C) A doctor specialising in patients with severe mental illness. Special constable for 13 years. Five generations

of his family from Merseyside. Ed: Magdalene Coll, Cambridge (medicine; chairman, CUCA); University of Bristol. **Carl Schears** (Ukip) Electrician and business dir, Scented Spring. **Anna Martin** (LD) Runs Big You Little You, pregnancy & childbirth retail service. Contesting Liverpool CC 2015. Two children. **Will Ward** (Green) Varied career in industry, farming, education, and youth work.

CONSTITUENCY PROFILE
The southern tip of Liverpool and its neighbouring towns combine affluent, middle-class residential areas with some of the most troubled slums in Liverpool. This once made it a marginal seat with the Conservatives and Labour vying for power, but Liverpool's antipathy towards the Conservatives and the decline of the old working class Protestant vote have turned this into a safe Labour seat since 1983. More recently the Lib Dems have become the challenger here.

		Electorate	Turnout %	Change from 2010 %
		74,063	66.1	
M Eagle	Lab	33,839	69.1	+9.6
M Williams	C	6,693	13.7	-2.5
C Schears	Ukip	4,482	9.2	+5.6
A Martin	LD	2,279	4.7	-15.5
W Ward	Green	1,690	3.5	

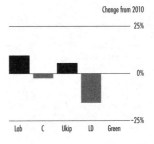

Change from 2010

Gateshead

LABOUR HOLD

IAN MEARNS
BORN Apr 21, 1957
MP 2010-

Very experienced in local government. Interested in regional development, energy and the environment. Select cttees: backbench business 2014-; high speed rail bill 2014-; BB business 2010-14; education 2010-. Cllr, Gateshead 1983-2010 (dep leader 2002-10). Led campaign for North East Assembly prior to 2004 referendum. Chairman, Council of Local Education Authorities. LGA representative, held several board roles. Member, Unison and Unite. Has partner. Two children from previous marriage. Ed: St Mary's Technical Sch, Newcastle.

CHALLENGERS
John Tennant (Ukip) MEP assistant. Contested Gateshead 2010. **Tom Smith** (C) Works for Prudential in pensions and insurance. Previously worked in events and publishing. Ed: Oxford (BA history & politics). **Frank Hindle** (LD) Cllr, Gateshead 1991-; leader, Lib Dem group 2011-. Chairman, Northern Region Lib Dems 2009-11. Former lecturer in Computing, Northumbria University. Member, university governing body 2008-10. Married, one daughter. Ed: University of Sheffield (BSc maths); Newcastle (MSc computer systems & software design).

CONSTITUENCY PROFILE
The Gateshead seat was created in 2010, having previously been split into two, both with a solid history of Labour representation. Gateshead has suffered with the decline of its manufacturing industry but has recently seen substantial redevelopment, particularly in the old quayside areas where a cultural quarter has been created. Beyond the quayside, Gateshead remains largely white, working class, with social housing comprising a quarter of its homes.

	Electorate	Turnout %	from 2010 %	Change %
	63,910	59.5		
I Mearns Lab	21,549	56.7	+2.6	
J Tennant Ukip	6,765	17.8	+14.9	
T Smith C	5,502	14.6	-0.3	
F Hindle LD	2,585	6.8	-14.5	
A Redfern Green	1,548	4.1	+3.1	

Change from 2010

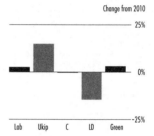

Lab   Ukip   C   LD   Green

Gedling

LABOUR HOLD

VERNON COAKER
BORN Jun 17, 1953
MP 1997-

Manager for Ed Balls's leadership campaign in 2010. Shadow SoS: defence 2013-; NI 2011-13. Shadow min: home affairs 2010-11; schools 2010. Min: children, schools & families 2009-10; Home Office 2008-09. Parly under-sec, Home Office 2006-08. Whip: govt 2005-06; asst govt 2003-05. PPS to: Tessa Jowell 2002-03; Estelle Morris 2002; Stephen Timms 1999-2002. Cllr, Rushcliffe BC 1983-97. Member social sec select cttee 1998-99. Hon fellow, Unicef. Teacher, NUT member. Married, one daughter, one son. Ed: Drayton Manor GS; University of Warwick (BA politics); Trent Poly (PGCE).

CHALLENGERS
Carolyn Abbott (C) Director, family ironworking business. Contested: Chesterfield 2010; Barnsley East and Mexborough 2005; Sheffield Heeley 2001. Ed: Lancaster University (BA PPE). **Lee Waters** (Ukip) Chairman, Ukip Gedling branch. Ed: Hertfordshire University **Robert Swift** (LD) Telecoms marketing, including time in UAE. Ed: Keele University (BA politics & philosophy; SU president; MA business administration).

CONSTITUENCY PROFILE
A comparatively affluent and middle-class residential area in the suburbs of Nottingham, Gedling, and its predecessor Carlton, used to be regarded as safe Conservative seats, with a majority of almost 19 per cent in 1992. It fell to Labour in the 1997 landslide, and, unlike many other suburban seats that returned to the Tory fold in 2010, it has remained in Labour's hands. The former Conservative international development secretary Andrew Mitchell did not seek re-election here and instead ended up as MP for the genuinely safe Tory berth of Sutton Coldfield.

	Electorate	Turnout %	from 2010 %	Change %
	70,046	68.5		
V Coaker Lab	20,307	42.3	+1.2	
C Abbott C	17,321	36.1	-1.2	
L Waters Ukip	6,930	14.4	+11.4	
R Swift LD	1,906	4.0	-11.3	
J Norris Green	1,534	3.2		

Change from 2010

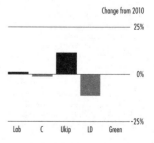

Lab   C   Ukip   LD   Green

Gillingham & Rainham

CONSERVATIVE HOLD

REHMAN CHISHTI
BORN Oct 4, 1978
MP 2010-

Former adviser to Benazir Bhutto. Contested Horsham 2005 for Labour against Francis Maude; defected and became special adviser to Maude when he was chairman of Conservative party. PPS to Nick Gibb 2014-15. Select cttees: justice 2012-; human rights 2011-14. Tory Cllr, Medway 2006-. Labour Cllr, Medway 2003-06. Pakistani-born. Barrister, Lincoln's Inn. Keen cricketer and runner. Ed: Fort Luton HS; Sixth Form Rainham Mark GS, Chatham GS; Aberystwyth University (LLB law).

CHALLENGERS
Paul Clark (Lab) Political strategist and former trade union officer. MP Gillingham 1997-2010. Asst govt whip 2003-05. PPS to: Ed Balls 2007-08; John Prescott 2005-07. Parly under-sec, transport 2008-10. Cllr, Gillingham BC 1982-1990. Hon

Doc at University of Greenwich. Ed: Keele (BA economics & politics); Derby (Dip management studies). **Mark Hanson** (Ukip) Long-serving obstetrician at Medway hospital. Stepped aside as parliamentary candidate for Mark Reckless in Rochester and Strood. **Paul Chaplin** (LD) Auditor to medical profession. Sits on the clinical commissioning groups urgent care management panel. Treasurer, Medway Lib Dem party. Governor, SE Coast Ambulance Service. **Neil Williams** (Green) Business architect, Lloyd's of London.

CONSTITUENCY PROFILE
A densely populated urban seat encompassing two contrasting towns: Rainham is affluent while Gillingham has pockets of deprivation. A boundary change prior to 2010 cut out a less affluent area, to the disadvantage of Labour, which subsequently lost the seat, have taken it in 1997 after decades of Tory representation.

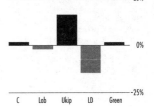

	Electorate	Turnout %	Change from 2010 %
	72,609	64.8	
R Chishti C	22,590	48.0	+1.8
P Clark Lab	12,060	25.6	-2.1
M Hanson Ukip	9,199	19.5	+16.3
P Chaplin LD	1,707	3.6	-14.5
N Williams Green	1,133	2.4	+1.7
J Berry TUSC	273	0.6	
R Peacock ND	72	0.2	
M Walters ND	44	0.1	

Change from 2010

Glasgow Central

SNP GAIN

ALISON THEWLISS
BORN Sep 13, 1982
MP 2015-

SNP shadow spokeswoman, cities 2015-. Cllr, Glasgow CC 2007-15; spokeswoman, land and environmental services. Interested in local govt and democracy. Married, one son, one daughter.

CHALLENGERS
Anas Sarwar (Lab) Glasgow born and bred, and son of his predecessor, Mohammed Sarwar, the first UK Muslim MP. Resigned as deputy leader, Scottish Labour party 2014. Shadow min, int devt 2014-. Select cttees: int devt 2010-12, arms export controls 2010-12. Contested Scottish parliament 2007 (top of regional list for Glasgow). Unite. Founder, Y-Vote youth political engagement programme. Dentist. Married, one son. Ed: Hutchesons' GS; University of Glasgow (BDS dentistry). **Simon Bone** (C) Senior consultant, Net

Consulting. Chairman, Babbage Institute 2014-. Dir, Propertas 2012-. Ed: Cambridge (MA computer science); Oxford (Dip creative writing); Harvard (MC-MPA politics). **Cass MacGregor** (Green) Physiotherapy clinical specialist. Ed: Blairgowrie HS; Queen Margaret University Coll, Edinburgh (BSc physiotherapy); Keele (MSc pain science and management).

CONSTITUENCY PROFILE
Covers the main commercial and shopping areas of Glasgow, and the city centre's two university campuses. Glasgow's economic renewal since the 1990s has led to rapidly rising property prices and some gentrification, especially in the areas closest to the city centre, making the seat the most educated and affluent in Glasgow. There are pockets of poverty, such as the Gorbals and the Calton area, in parts of which life expectancy is in the low 50s. Like most of the Glasgow seats, this has historically been a safe Labour seat.

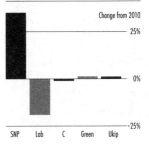

	Electorate	Turnout %	Change from 2010 %
	70,945	55.4	
A Thewliss SNP	20,658	52.5	+35.0
A Sarwar Lab	12,996	33.1	-19.0
S Bone C	2,359	6.0	-1.1
C MacGregor Green	1,559	4.0	+1.4
S Maskell Ukip	786	2.0	+1.2
C Young LD	612	1.6	-14.8
J Marris CSA	171	0.4	
A Elliott TUSC	119	0.3	
K Rhodes SEP	58	0.2	

Change from 2010

Glasgow East

SNP GAIN

NATALIE McGARRY
BORN Sep 7, 1981
MP 2015-

SNP spokeswoman, disabilities 2015-. Works in charity sector. Convenor, Glasgow SNP. Co-founder, Women for Independence. Contested Cowdenbeath Scots Parly by-election 2014. Republican, courted controversy after tweet appearing to disown parliamentary oath to monarch. Media commentator, written for *The Scotsman*, *The Herald*. Partner is Tory cllr who campaigned against Scottish independence. Ed: University of Aberdeen (LLB law).

CHALLENGERS
Margaret Curran (Lab) MP 2010-15. Shad SoS: Scotland 2011-. Shad min: W&P 2010-11. Member W&P select cttee 2010. Contested Glasgow East by-election 2008. MSP for Glasgow Baillieston 1999-2011. Scottish executive: Min 2003 -07; Shadow cabinet sec:

justice 2007; health and well-being 2007-08; without portfolio 2008-09. Community education lecturer. Member, TGWU. Married, two sons. Ed: University of Glasgow (MA history & economic history); Dundee Coll (PgCert community education). **Andrew Morrison** (C) Associate, TaxAssist Falkirk. Contested Glasgow Pollok Scottish Parliament 2011. Ed: Oxford Brookes (BSc applied accountancy); Glasgow Caledonian (ACCA). **Arthur Thackeray** (Ukip) Scottish party chairman of Ukip. Joined Scottish Defence League protest in 2012 and an EDL protest in 2011.

CONSTITUENCY PROFILE
This seat is in the eastern part of Glasgow and comprises mainly postwar tenements and terraces. Historically it is a safe Labour constituency but the 2008 by-election that followed the death of David Marshall was won by the SNP with a swing of 22 per cent. However, Labour regained the seat with ease in the 2010 election.

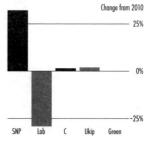

		Electorate	Turnout %	Change from 2010 %
		70,378	60.3	
N McGarry	SNP	24,116	56.9	+32.1
M Curran	Lab	13,729	32.4	-29.2
A Morrison	C	2,544	6.0	+1.5
A Thackeray	Ukip	1,105	2.6	+2.0
K Long	Green	381	0.9	
G McLelland	LD	318	0.8	-4.3
L McLaughlan	SSP	224	0.5	-0.9

Glasgow North

SNP GAIN

PATRICK GRADY
BORN Feb 2, 1980
MP 2015-

SNP spokesman, international development 2015-. Charity worker, lived in Africa. Policy officer, Scottish parliament. National Secretary, SNP 2012-. Convenor, Glasgow Kelvin SNP; led Yes campaign, Glasgow Kelvin. Contested Glasgow North 2010. Former national secretary, SNP students. Ed: University of Strathclyde (MA history).

CHALLENGERS
Ann McKechin (Lab) MP 2001-15. Shadow SoS: Scotland 2010-11. Shadow min: Scotland 2010. Parly under-sec, Scotland 2008-10. PPS to Jacqui Smith 2005. Member, select cttees: arms export controls 2011-; BIS 2011-; int devt 2005-10; standing orders 2001-05; Scottish Affairs 2001-05. MP for Glasgow Maryhill 2001-05. Solicitor. Council member, world development movement. TGWU, Unite. Ed:

Sacred Heart HS, Paisley; Paisley GS; University of Strathclyde (LLB Scots law). **Lauren Hankinson** (C) Parly adviser, David Mundell 2014-. Stakeholder engagement officer, Better Together 2014. Lawyer, comms professional and researcher. Ed: Durham (BA social sciences); College of Law (LLB law). **Dr Martin Bartos** (Green) Cllr, Glasgow CC 2012-. Ed: Edinburgh (neuroscience, medicine, computer science) **Jade O'Neil** (LD) Web developer, Helphound. com. Convenor, Scottish Lib Dem Women. Ed: Bridgewater College; Xabia International Coll, Spain.

CONSTITUENCY PROFILE
One of the less safe Labour seats in Glasgow as the Liberal Democrats have significant strength. It had, nevertheless, been Labour-held from 1987 until 2015. The University of Glasgow falls in its boundaries as does the Summerston council estate and the handsome sandstone tenements and Victorian houses popular with the middle classes.

		Electorate	Turnout %	Change from 2010 %
		58,875	62.7	
P Grady	SNP	19,610	53.1	+41.2
A McKechin	Lab	10,315	27.9	-16.6
L Hankinson	C	2,901	7.9	+0.8
M Bartos	Green	2,284	6.2	+3.0
J O'Neil	LD	1,012	2.7	-28.6
J Robertson	Ukip	486	1.3	
A McCormick	TUSC	160	0.4	-0.5
R Benson	CSA	154	0.4	

Glasgow North East

SNP GAIN

ANNE McLAUGHLIN
BORN Mar 8, 1966
MP 2015-

Worked in fundraising and communications. SNP spokes, civil liberties 2015-. MSP for Glasgow 2009-11. Contested: Glasgow Provan in Scottish Parliament 2011; Inverclyde by-election 2011. Convener, Provan SNP. Ed: Royal Scottish Academy of Music and Drama; University of Glasgow (BA dramatic studies).

CHALLENGERS
Willie Bain (Lab) MP 2009-15. Fought off tough challenge from SNP to take 2009 by-election. PPS to Sadiq Khan 2010-. Shadow Min: Scotland 2011-13; env, food & rural affairs 2010-11; transport 2010. Select cttees: BIS 2013-; tax law rewrite bills 2009-10. Election agent to Michael Martin. Lecturer, researcher: University of Strathclyde Law School; London Southbank University. Member,

Unite; Progress; Fabian Society; Amnesty International. Ed: St Roch's Sch, Glasgow; University of Strathclyde (LLB law, LLM). **Annie Wells** (C) Retail manager, Marks & Spencer. **Zara Kitson** (Green) Executive assistant, LGBT Youth Scotland. Contested Dunfermline for Scottish parliament 2013. Ed: Glasgow (MA public policy). **Eileen Baxendale** (LD) Former social worker. Cllr, South Lanarkshire C 2007-. Married, five children. Ed: London; Columbia University, NY (philosophy & economics).

CONSTITUENCY PROFILE
Registered the largest swing of the election, and one of the biggest in British political history: 39.3 percentage points from Labour to SNP. Traditionally a Labour bastion where the party won 68.3 per cent of the vote in 2010. Contains innermost Dennistoun, which has seen a little gentrification, but elsewhere are some of the UK's the most deprived estates.

	Electorate	Turnout %	from 2010 %	Change %
	66,678	56.8		
A McLaughlin SNP	21,976	58.1	+43.9	
W Bain Lab	12,754	33.7	-34.7	
A Wells C	1,769	4.7	-0.7	
Z Kitson Green	615	1.6		
E Baxendale LD	300	0.8	-6.9	
G Johnson CSA	225	0.6		
J Cocozza TUSC	218	0.6	-0.1	

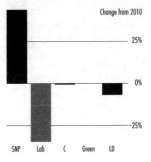

Change from 2010

Glasgow North West

SNP GAIN

CAROL MONAGHAN
BORN Aug 2, 1972
MP 2015-

Physics teacher. SNP spokeswoman, public services and education 2015-. Former head of science at Hyndland Secondary, Glasgow. SQA consultant. Former university lecturer training teachers. SSTA. Was planning a career move into stonemasonry, her passion. Married, one son, two daughters. Ed: St Thomas Aquinas Secondary, Glasgow; University of Strathclyde (BSc laser physics and optoelectronics); St Andrew's Coll, Bearsden (PGCE).

CHALLENGERS
John Robertson (Lab) MP 2000-15. PPS to: Yvette Cooper 2009-10; Kim Howells 2005-08. Select cttees: panel of chairs 2010-; energy and climate change 2009-; European scrutiny 2003-10; Scottish affairs 2001-05. Chairman, all-party group on nuclear energy. MP for Glasgow

Anniesland 2000-05. Amicus. CWU and NCU political, education officer. GPO, Post Office, BT. Election agent for Donald Dewar MP, and MSP. Married, three daughters. Ed: Shawlands Acad; Langside Coll (ONC electrical engineering); Stow Coll (HNC electrical engineering). **Roger Lewis** (C) Associate dir, Coutts. Analyst, HSBC. Former chairman, Kennington Ward, Vauxhall Conservative Assocation. Ed: LSE (BSc government & history). **James Harrison** (LD) Development officer, QAA Scotland. Ed: Glasgow (MA social sciences, president, Lib Dem soc 2009-10).

CONSTITUENCY PROFILE
This former Labour seat lies on the River Clyde's north bank and includes upwardly mobile areas such as Scotstoun as well as more deprived areas such as the Drumchapel housing estate. Previously Glasgow Garscadden, the core of this seat was held by Donald Dewar, and Labour retained the seat after his death in 2000.

	Electorate	Turnout %	from 2010 %	Change %
	68,418	64.1		
C Monaghan SNP	23,908	54.5	+39.3	
J Robertson Lab	13,544	30.9	-23.2	
R Lewis C	3,692	8.4	-1.5	
J Harrison LD	1,194	2.7	-13.1	
M Crawford Green	1,167	2.7	+0.2	
C MacKenzie CSA	213	0.5		
Z Streatfield Scottish CP	136	0.3		

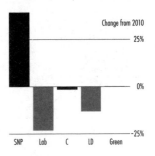

Change from 2010

Glasgow South

SNP GAIN

STEWART MCDONALD
BORN Aug 24, 1986
MP 2015-

Caseworker, James Dornan
MSP. Party organiser, Cathcart
constituency. Formerly: campaign
manager, 2011 Holyrood election for
Cathcart campaign; parliamentary
case worker for Anne McLaughlin
MSP. Was retail manager and
holiday rep in Tenerife. Originally
from Castlemilk. Ed: Govan HS.

CHALLENGERS
Tom Harris (Lab) MP 2001-15.
Shadow min: Defra 2012-13. Parly
under-sec: transport 2006-08. PPS
to: Patricia Hewitt 2005-06; John
Spellar 2003-05. Select cttees:
transport 2014-15; administration
2013-15; science & technology
2001-04. MP, Glasgow South
2005-15; Glasgow Cathcart
2001-05 Lab Friends of Israel.
Reporter, *East Kilbride News*. Press
officer, PR career: Strathclyde
Passenger Transport Exec; East

Ayrshire council; Glasgow CC;
Strathclyde RC; Scottish Lab party.
NUJ, Amicus, Unison. Divorced,
remarried, three sons, one from
first marriage. Ed: Napier Coll
(HND journalism). **Kyle Thornton**
(C) Student at University of
Glasgow (politics & European
studies). VC (finance), British Youth
Council 2013-. Chairman, Scottish
Youth Parliament 2013-14. **Alastair
Whitelaw** (Green) Retired, career
in university administration.
Member, UCU. Married, two
children.

CONSTITUENCY PROFILE
Once the most Conservative part
of Glasgow, it covers the most
affluent parts of the city. That all
changed with the growth of the
Castlemilk estate and the decline
of the Tories in Scotland. The old
Glasgow Cathcart seat was held by
the Tories until 1979. Since then it
had become the sort of safe Labour
seat that typifies Glasgow until
falling to the SNP in 2015 with a
23.9-point swing.

	Electorate	Turnout %	Change from 2010 %
	74,051	65.9	
S McDonald SNP	26,773	54.9	+34.7
T Harris Lab	14,504	29.7	-22.0
K Thornton C	4,752	9.7	-1.7
A Whitelaw Green	1,431	2.9	+0.5
E Hoyle LD	1,019	2.1	-9.7
B Smith TUSC	299	0.6	-0.3

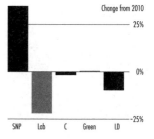

Change from 2010

SNP   Lab   C   Green   LD

Glasgow South West

SNP GAIN

**CHRISTOPHER
STEPHENS**
BORN March 20, 1973
MP 2015-

Passionate union campaigner and
senior Unison activist. SNP group
leader, justice & home affairs 2015-.
Local government officer, Glasgow
CC. Member, SNP National
Executive cttee. Convenor, Glasgow
Pollok Constituency Assoc.
Sec, SNP Trade Union Group.
Contested: European Scotland
region 2014; Glasgow Pollock 2011
Scots parly, 2007; Glasgow South
West 2010. Son of shipyard welder.
Partick Thistle supporter. Married.
Ed: Trinity HS, Renfrew

CHALLENGERS
Ian Davidson (Lab Co-op) MP
1992-2015. Passionately Eurosceptic
and anti-Euro: founder, Labour
against the Euro. Select cttees:
liaison 2010-15; public accounts
1997-2010; Scottish affairs 2005-15,
chair 2010-15. Co-operative party.
Cllr, Strathclyde RC 1978-92.

Member, new Europe advisory
council. Secretary, Labour MPs
trade union group. Glasgow SW
2005-2015; Glasgow Pollok 1997-
2005; Glasgow Govan 1992-97.
Project manager. Married, one
daughter, one son. Ed: Jedburgh
GS; University of Edinburgh (MA
politics & geography); Jordanhill
Coll. **Gordon McCaskill** (C)
Retired police officer. Cllr, East
Renfrewshire C 2007-, leader
Conservative group. Contested
Paisley and Renfrewshire South
2010. **Sarah Hemy** (Ukip) Retail
manager. Treasurer, Ukip Glasgow
& District Branch 2012-. Partner,
one daughter. **Sean Templeton**
(Green) Advocate specialising in
criminal law and children's cases.

CONSTITUENCY PROFILE:
Made up of parts of the former
seats of Glasgow Pollok and Govan.
It contains areas of deprivation,
high crime and poor health. It was
considered safe Labour territory,
generally being won by majorities
of around 40 per cent, but fell to
the SNP in 2015.

	Electorate	Turnout %	Change from 2010 %
	66,209	61.8	
C Stephens SNP	23,388	57.2	+40.8
I Davidson Lab Co-op	13,438	32.8	-29.7
G McCaskill C	2,036	5.0	-1.6
S Hemy Ukip	970	2.4	
S Templeton Green	507	1.2	
I Nelson LD	406	1.0	-8.0
B Bonnar SSP	176	0.4	

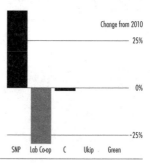

Change from 2010

SNP   Lab Co-op   C   Ukip   Green

Glenrothes

SNP GAIN

PETER GRANT
BORN Oct 12, 1960
MP 2015-

Accountant, public sector until 2007. Cllr, Fife C 1992-15, council leader 2007-12, SNP group leader. Contested Glenrothes by-election 2008. Former public sector auditor. Amateur musician. Member of Leslie Bowling Club. Brought up in Lanarkshire in a working class Labour household. Amateur musician. Married.

CHALLENGERS
Melanie Ward (Lab Co-op) Anti-poverty campaigner. Was at the forefront of campaigns against corporate tax dodging. Head of Advocacy, ActionAid UK. Senior parly researcher, David Blunkett 2006-08. Previously worked as: human rights observer, Ecumenical Accompaniment Programme in Palestine and Israel; political adviser, Christian Aid. President, NUS Scotland 2004-06. Ed: Stirling

(BA human resource management); SOAS (MA international studies, relations & diplomacy). **Alex Stewart-Clark** (C) Managing trustee, Passion Trust, supports biblical drama performances. Former works manager, Nehemiah Project, alcohol and drug rehabilitation centre. Trustee, Philo Trust & Orphans International. Ed: London Business Sch. **Jane Ann Liston** (LD) Cllr, Fife C 1995-2007. Appeared on *Brain of Britain*, *Mastermind, A Question of Genius*. Secretary, Railfuture Scotland.

CONSTITUENCY PROFILE
Glenrothes and its predecessor seat, Central Fife, have both been safely held by Labour historically. However, even before 2015 there was significant SNP support winning the Central Fife seat for the Scottish parliament in 2007. Glenrothes is the administrative centre of Fife, and it is a typical new town, characterised by modern, low-rise housing.

	Electorate	Turnout %	from 2010 % Change
	69,781	68.2	
P Grant SNP	28,459	59.8	+38.1
M Ward Lab Co-op	14,562	30.6	-31.7
A Stewart-Clark C	3,685	7.7	+0.5
J A Liston LD	892	1.9	-5.8

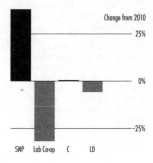

Change from 2010

SNP   Lab Co-op   C   LD

Gloucester

CONSERVATIVE HOLD

RICHARD GRAHAM
BORN Apr 4, 1958
MP 2010-

Former investment banker, diplomat and airline manager. PPS to: Hugo Swire 2012-14; Lord Howell 2010-12. PM's trade envoy to Indonesia 2012-. Member w&p select cttee 2010. Chairman, APPG: occupational pensions; Indonesia; China. Cllr, Cotswold DC 2003-07. Contested SW England European elections 2004. Director and head of int business, Baring Asset Management. Founder chairman, British Chamber of Commerce Shanghai. FCO diplomacy: First Sec of British High Commission in Kenya, Peking; British Trade Commissioner China. General manager, Cathay Pacific. Keen cricketer. Married, one daughter, two sons. Ed: Eton Coll; Christ Church, Oxford (BA history).

CHALLENGERS
Sophy Gardner (Lab) Director,

comms business. President, Royal British Legion Gloucester City Branch. Unite. Former RAF officer. Ed: Newnham Coll, Cambridge (MA geography; MPhil). **Richard Ford** (Ukip) Former millionaire businessman, founded Travelscope. Forced to declare bankruptcy after it went bust in 2007. Divorced, two children. Ed: Durham University (LLB law). **Jeremy Hilton** (LD) Local govt consultant. Cllr, Gloucestershire CC 2001-13, leader LD group 2005-13. Chair, LGA's fire services management cttee 2014-. Contested Gloucester 2010, 20, 1987.

CONSTITUENCY PROFILE
Traditional manufacturing dependence has diversified with tourism becoming important, and the financial sector thriving. Yet this is the most deprived district in Gloucestershire since boundary changes led to the loss of the more affluent Longlevens ward. The seat was Tory from 1970-97 but Labour reclaimed it from 1997 to 2010.

	Electorate	Turnout %	from 2010 % Change
	82,949	63.4	
R Graham C	23,837	45.3	+5.4
S Gardner Lab	16,586	31.6	-3.6
R Ford Ukip	7,497	14.3	+10.7
J Hilton LD	2,828	5.4	-13.9
J Ingleby Green	1,485	2.8	+1.8
G Ridgeon Loony	227	0.4	
S Powell TUSC	115	0.2	

Change from 2010

C   Lab   Ukip   LD   Green

Gordon

SNP GAIN

ALEX SALMOND
BORN Dec 31, 1954
MP 2015-; 1987-2010

Said a "Scottish lion has roared" after the SNP's landslide. Led the 2014 campaign for Scottish independence, stepped down as first minister (2007-14) after Scotland voted No. Leader, SNP 2004-2014, 1990-2000; deputy leader 1987-1990, took his party into the mainstream of British politics. MP for Banff & Buchan 1987-2010. MSP for: Aberdeenshire East 2011-; Gordon 2007-2011; Banff & Buchan 1999-2001. Previously economist at RBS. Married. Ed: Linlithgow Academy; Edinburgh Coll of Commerce (HNC business studies); University of St Andrews (MA economics & history; VP Students' Union).

CHALLENGERS
Christine Jardine (LD) Media consultant, Scottish Lib Dems 2012-. Scotland media adviser to

the government 2011-12. Contested: Aberdeen Donside 2013 by-election; Euro election Scotland 2014. Journalist, lecturer, writer: *Deeside Piper*; BBC Scotland. Married, daughter. Ed: Braidfield HS; University of Glasgow (MA modern history & politics). **Colin Clark** (C) Farmer. Married, one son. Ed: Heriot Watt University. **Braden Davy** (Lab) Parliamentary assistant, Dame Anne Begg. Member, Aberdeen City youth council, Fabians, Electoral Reform Society. Former assistant manager, McDonalds. Ed: Durham University (Cert economics).

CONSTITUENCY PROFILE
The area is dominated by farming and forestry and there are several whisky distilleries around its picturesque hills and rivers. It includes the market towns of Huntly, Keith and Inverurie. A Liberal Democrat seat under Malcolm Bruce from its creation in 1983 to the SNP upheaval of 2015.

	Electorate	Turnout %	Change from 2010 %
	79,393	73.3	
A Salmond SNP	27,717	47.7	+25.5
C Jardine LD	19,030	32.7	-3.3
C Clark C	6,807	11.7	-7.0
B Davy Lab	3,441	5.9	-14.2
E Santos Ukip	1,166	2.0	

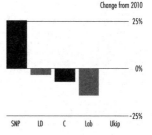

Change from 2010

Gosport

CONSERVATIVE HOLD

CAROLINE DINENAGE
BORN Oct 28, 1971
MP 2010-

Daughter of TV presenter Fred Dinenage. Parly under-sec for women, equalities and family justice 2015-. PPS to Nicky Morgan 2014-15. Select cttees: BIS 2012-; science & technology 2012-13. Small Business Ambassador for the South 2013-. Co-chairwoman, APPG for maths and numeracy; vice-chairwoman APPG armed forces (navy). Contested Portsmouth South 2005. Cllr, Winchester DC 1998-2003. Director of Recognition Express, manufacturer of corporate identity products, 1997-2013. Divorced, re-married Mark Lancaster. Two children. Ed: Oaklands RC Comp Sch, Waterlooville; Swansea University (BA English & politics).

CHALLENGERS
Christopher Wood (Ukip) Cllr, Fareham BC 2014-; Hampshire CC 2013-. Worked in wardrooms

of HMS *Collingwood* and HMS *Sultan*, trained to be submarine warfare officer at Britannia Royal Naval College. Ed: Bay House SF Coll; Cardiff (BA economic & social studies in politics). **Alan Durrant** (Lab) Semi-retired teacher. Labour spokes for Gosport. Formerly worked with Portsmouth Water and SE Regional Assembly. **Rob Hylands** (LD) Pub landlord. Cllr, Gosport BC 2009-. Contested Gosport 2010. Previously computer games programmer. Married, six children. Ed: Brune Park Secondary Sch.

CONSTITUENCY PROFILE
A safe Conservative seat, held since creation in 1974. The MP until 2010, Sir Peter Viggers, was forced to retire after being responsible for one of the most iconic claims in the MPs expenses scandal: a £1,600 floating duck house. Gosport has traditionally been associated with the military and the Royal Navy, although many of these facilities have been closed.

	Electorate	Turnout %	Change from 2010 %
	73,271	65.1	
C Dinenage C	26,364	55.3	+3.5
C Wood Ukip	9,266	19.4	+16.3
A Durrant Lab	6,926	14.5	-2.4
R Hylands LD	3,298	6.9	-14.1
M Cassidy Green	1,707	3.6	+2.4
J Roberts Ind	104	0.2	

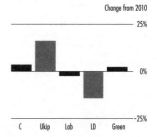

Change from 2010

Gower

CONSERVATIVE GAIN

BYRON DAVIES
BORN Sept 4, 1952
MP 2015-

Retired police officer at the Metropolitan police, ended his career as a senior detective. AM for South Wales West 2011-15; shadow min for transport; whip. Contested Gower Welsh Assembly 2007. Dir, Blue Line Solutions Europe, security and investigations company. Married, one son. Ed: Gowerton Boys' GS; University of West London (LLB law).

CHALLENGERS
Liz Evans (Lab) National officer, PCS. Women's officer, Swansea East Labour party. Previously worked for the Land Registry, Welsh Assembly, Job Centre, Swansea University and as a full time carer. Branch secretary, Landore Ward. Enthusiastic musician. Partner. Ed: University of York (BA philosophy). **Colin Beckett** (Ukip) Osteomyologist.

Joined the army at 15; chief inspector, Royal Oman Police; medical sales. Ed: Oxford Brookes University. **Darren Thomas** (PC) Cllr, Gorseinon TC: deputy mayor 2012. Worked in retail services. Ed: Penyrheol CS; Trinity College, Carmarthen. **Mike Sheehan** (LD) Professor of International Relations, Swansea University. Cllr, Aberdeen CC 1984-92. Former sch governor. Married.

CONSTITUENCY PROFILE
Gower is a Labour-Conservative marginal, which had, until 2015, been Labour since 1910, remaining tantalisingly out of Conservative reach, sometimes by only small majorities (1,205 in 1983). The result in 2015 was much closer – the closest of the election – with the Tories winning by just 27 votes. The Gower peninsula with its seaside resorts and residential villages is Conservative but the industrial former mining and tin-making towns north of Swansea vote Labour.

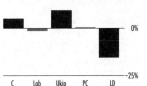

	Electorate	Turnout %	Change from 2010 %
	61,820	69.2	
B Davies C	15,862	37.1	+5.1
L Evans Lab	15,835	37.0	-1.4
C Beckett Ukip	4,773	11.2	+9.6
D Thomas PC	3,051	7.1	+0.5
M Sheehan LD	1,552	3.6	-15.4
J Marshall Green	1,161	2.7	
D B B Von Claptrap Loony	253	0.6	
S Roberts Ind	168	0.4	
M Evans TUSC	103	0.2	

Change from 2010

25%

0%

-25%

C   Lab   Ukip   PC   LD

Grantham & Stamford

CONSERVATIVE HOLD

NICK BOLES
BORN Nov 2, 1965
MP 2010-

Min of state for skills 2014-; equalities 2014-15. Parly under-sec: DECC, planning 2012-14. PPS to Nick Gibb 2010-12. CCHQ staffer responsible for planning policy implementation. Contested: Hove 2005; London mayoral primary 2007 but withdrew after diagnosis of Hodgkin's Lymphoma. Cllr, Westminster CC 1998-2002. Founded Policy Exchange think tank. Ran own paint and decorating supply company. Ed: Winchester Coll; Magdalen Coll, Oxford (BA PPE); Harvard (Kennedy scholarship).

CHALLENGERS
Marietta King (Ukip) MD, furniture manufacturing and retailing firm; chairman, Rosebrook UK management firm. Chairwoman, Ukip Rutland, Melton & Harborough branch

2006-13. Contested Harborough 2010. Widowed, two daughters. **Barrie Fairbairn** (Lab) Solicitor; director, Barrie Fairbairn Solicitors. Was lay director, Midlands Co-operative Society. Civil partnership. Ed: University of Manchester (BSc chemistry). **Harrish Bisnauthsing** (LD) Retired computer engineer. Cllr: South Kesteven DC 2003-; Stamford TC 1987-, mayor 2002-03. Contested Grantham & Stamford 2010.

CONSTITUENCY PROFILE
Politically Grantham is most widely associated with Margaret Thatcher, who grew up in the town and whose father owned a grocer's shop and served as mayor in 1945-46. However, Grantham itself is probably the most Labour-leaning section of the seat. Its sentiments are outweighed by the rural areas and the seat is normally safely Conservative, apart from a brief interruption between 2007-10 when the sitting MP, Quentin Davies, defected to the Labour party.

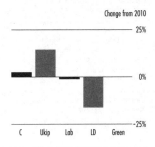

	Electorate	Turnout %	Change from 2010 %
	81,151	66.2	
N Boles C	28,399	52.8	+2.5
M King Ukip	9,410	17.5	+14.5
B Fairbairn Lab	9,070	16.9	-1.1
H Bisnauthsing LD	3,263	6.1	-16.1
A Campbell Green	1,872	3.5	
I Selby Ind	1,017	1.9	
J Hansen Lincs Lnin	724	1.4	-0.4

Change from 2010

25%

0%

-25%

C   Ukip   Lab   LD   Green

Gravesham

CONSERVATIVE HOLD

ADAM HOLLOWAY
BORN Jul 29, 1965
MP 2005-

PPS to David Lidington 2010-11.
Select cttees: public admin
2014-; defence 2012-14, 2006-10;
arms export controls 2009-10.
Commissioned Grenadier Guards.
Media career: presented *World
In Action*, Granada TV, ITN
reporter. Ed: Cranleigh Sch, Surrey;
Magdalene Coll, Cambridge
(BA social & political science);
Imperial Coll London (MBA);
RMA Sandhurst.

___

CHALLENGERS
Tanmanjeet Singh Dhesi
(Lab) Project director in family
construction business. Cllr,
Gravesham BC 2007-, mayor 2011-
12. Chairman, Gravesham CLP.
Ed: UCL (BA mathematics with
management studies); Keble Coll,
Oxford (MSc applied statistics);
Fitzwilliam Coll, Cambridge
(MPhil history & politics). **Sean

Marriott (Ukip) Energy lawyer.
Former engineer. founder and
CEO, Harmarney International
telecommunications management
firm. Married, two children. Ed:
University of Sheffield (BEng
electronic engineering); De
Montfort University (PgDip law;
LPC). **Mark Lindop** (Green)
Futures trader. **Anne-Marie
Bunting** (LD) Senior parly
researcher, Sir Menzies Campbell.
Charity development: Young
Epilepsy; Prison Reform Trust;
Catch22. Ed: Leicester (BA history);
LSE (MA history).

___

CONSTITUENCY PROFILE
This seat in northwest Kent is a
classic marginal. Until 2005, when
it fell to the Tories, it was the pre-
eminent bellwether seat — won
by the party that went on to form
the government at every election
since the First World War, with the
exceptions of 1929 and 1951 — and
in both those cases Gravesend
was won by the party that got the
largest national share of the vote.

	Electorate	Turnout %	from 2010 %	Change
	74,307	67.5		
A Holloway C	23,484	46.9	-1.7	
T S Dhesi Lab	15,114	30.1	+1.3	
S Marriott Ukip	9,306	18.6	+13.8	
M Lindop Green	1,124	2.2	+0.8	
A Bunting LD	1,111	2.2	-11.1	

Change from 2010

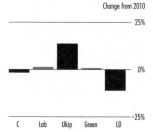

Great Grimsby

LABOUR HOLD

MELANIE ONN
BORN June 19, 1979
MP 2015-

Grew up on the Nunsthorpe and
Grange estates. Family background
in fishing and docking industry.
Regional organiser, Unison
Yorkshire and Humberside. Head
of compliance unit, Labour party
2001-10. Contested European
parliament for Yorkshire &
Humberside 2009. One son. Ed:
Healing CS; Middlesex University
(BA politics, philosophy &
international studies).

___

CHALLENGERS
Marc Jones (C) Has been the
owner of various property and
letting companies. Director,
Lincoln Business Improvement
Grp. Cllr: Lincolnshire CC 2013-;
Lincoln CC 2007-12. Chairman,
Lincoln Cons Assoc. **Victoria
Ayling** (Ukip) Runs music and
property businesses. Former
barrister. Cllr: Lincolnshire

CC 2013-; East Lindsey DC.
Contested Great Grimsby 2010
for Conservatives. **Steve Beasant**
(LD) Former maintenance fitter.
Cllr, NE Lincolnshire C 2003-.
Chairman: local authority pupil
referral unit; Safer and stronger
communities scrutiny panel. Ed:
University of York (BA politics &
sociology); PgCert public sector
modernisation. **Vicky Dunn**
(Green) Project director, advising
SMEs on renewables. Ed: York
(MChem chemistry); Leeds (PhD
environmental chemistry).

___

CONSTITUENCY PROFILE
Great Grimsby has been Labour
since 1945, although it was
only narrowly held in the 1977
by-election that followed Tony
Crosland's death. It is a major
North Sea port and industrial
centre at the mouth of the Humber
estuary and has a long association
with the fishing industry. Frozen
food is a major industry in the
town of Grimsby, along with
pharmaceuticals and chemicals.

	Electorate	Turnout %	from 2010 %	Change
	58,484	57.7		
M Onn Lab	13,414	39.8	+7.1	
M Jones C	8,874	26.3	-4.2	
V Ayling Ukip	8,417	25.0	+18.8	
S Beasant LD	1,680	5.0	-17.4	
V Dunn Green	783	2.3		
G Calder Ind	390	1.2	-1.4	
V O'Flynn TUSC	173	0.5		

Change from 2010

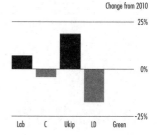

Great Yarmouth

CONSERVATIVE HOLD

BRANDON LEWIS
BORN Jun 20, 1971
MP 2010-

Min of state: housing and planning 2014-. Parly under-sec: CLG 2012-14. Select cttees: electoral commission 2013-; w&p 2010-12; regulatory reform 2010-12. Campaign manager for Eric Pickles in 2005. Contested Sherwood 2001. Cllr, Brentwood BC 1998-2009, leader 2004-09. Former director, Woodlands Schools, runs private primary schools. Former barrister. Marathon runner. Married, one daughter, one son. Ed: Forest Sch, Epping; University of Buckingham (BSc economics; LLB law); King's College London (LLM commercial law).

CHALLENGERS
Lara Norris (Lab) Charity worker. Former office manager, Gavin Shuker. Lived for a time in a women's refuge with her two children. Worked at HomeStart.

Re-married. Ed: Hertfordshire University (BA psychology); (MA). **Alan Grey** (Ukip) Professional musician. Used to own a musical instrument retailer. Cllr, Norfolk CC 2013-. Married, four children. **James Joyce** (LD) Sub-postmaster. Cllr: Norfolk CC 2005-; Broadland DC 2004-. Member, Norfolk Police Authority 2005-2012. Contested Norfolk PCC election 2012. **Harry Webb** (Green) Student. Care worker. Cllr, Caister-on-Sea PC. Great Yarmouth Green party co-ordinator.

CONSTITUENCY PROFILE
Great Yarmouth is a Conservative leaning Con-Lab marginal seat which has been keenly contested between Labour and the Tories, but is usually only winnable for Labour in their better victories, such as the Blair landslides and in 1966. It has also been a key target for Ukip. The seat consists of Great Yarmouth, a seaside resort and ferry port, as well as the rural hinterland and the surrounding villages.

	Electorate	Turnout %	from 2010 %	Change
	69,793	63.7		
B Lewis C	19,089	42.9	-0.2	
L Norris Lab	12,935	29.1	-4.1	
A Grey Ukip	10,270	23.1	+18.3	
J Joyce LD	1,030	2.3	-12.1	
H Webb Green	978	2.2	+1.2	
S Townley CSA	167	0.4		

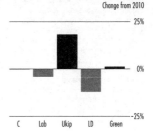

Change from 2010

C   Lab   Ukip   LD   Green

Greenwich & Woolwich

LABOUR HOLD

MATTHEW PENNYCOOK
BORN Oct 29, 1982
MP 2015-

Grew up in single-parent family. First person in family to go to university. Worked for: Child Poverty Action Group; the Fair Pay Network; Resolution Foundation; Institute of Public Policy Research. Cllr, Greenwich BC 2010-15. Trustee, Greenwich Housing Rights. Partner. Ed: LSE (BA history & international relations); Balliol Coll, Oxford (MPhil international relations).

CHALLENGERS
Matt Hartley (C) Media and communications manager, Money Advice Trust. Cllr, Greenwich BC 2014-, deputy leader of opposition. Volunteer board member, Greenwich & Bexley Credit Union. Ed: Warwick (MEng computer science); Leeds Metropolitan (MSc corporate communications). **Ryan Acty** (Ukip) IT support consultant.

Formerly: corporal, British Army serving in Kosovo and Iraq; elderly care assistant. Member of Parochial Church Council. **Abbey Akinoshun** (Green) Employment law consultant. Former clinical service manager, NHS. Member of the Nursing & Midwifery Council 2006-08. **Tom Holder** (LD) Founder, Speaking of Research, organisation explaining animal research. Former maths and economics teacher. Ed: Pembroke Coll, Oxford (BA PPE); Canterbury Christ Church (PGCE).

CONSTITUENCY PROFILE
Despite being safely Labour now, the predecessor seat was held by the SDP. The seat returned to Labour in 1992 after the SDP merger with the Liberals. This is mostly an inner city, working class seat, with a quarter of people in council housing and a significant ethnic minority population. However, there are some pockets of affluence, particularly around Blackheath Standard and Greenwich Common.

	Electorate	Turnout %	from 2010 %	Change
	73,315	63.7		
M Pennycook Lab	24,384	52.2	+3.0	
M Hartley C	12,438	26.6	+2.1	
R Acty Ukip	3,888	8.3		
A Akinoshun Green	2,991	6.4	+3.8	
T Holder LD	2,645	5.7	-12.5	
L Chamberlain TUSC	370	0.8	+0.1	

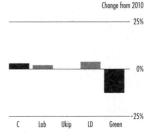

Change from 2010

C   Lab   Ukip   LD   Green

Guildford

CONSERVATIVE HOLD

ANNE MILTON
BORN Nov 3, 1955
MP 2005-

Former nurse who worked in the NHS for 25 years. Treasurer of HM household, dep chief whip 2015-; vice chamberlain 2014-15; lord comissioner, Treasury 2012-14. Parly under-sec, health 2010-12. Shad min: health 2007-10; culture & tourism 2006-07. Select cttees: selection 2013-14; health 2005-06. Former vice-chairwoman, Conservative Medical Society. Cllr, Reigate BC 1999-2004. RCN union steward. Married, one daughter, three sons. Ed: Haywards Heath GS; St Bartholomew's Hospital (RGN); Polytechnic of the South Bank (Dip district nursing).

CHALLENGERS
Kelly-Marie Blundell (LD) Runs own fundraising consultancy. Blogger: Huffington Post; *The Guardian*. Member, LD Federal Policy cttee 2012-. Vice-

chairwoman, Lib Dem Disability Assoc. Worked in employment law. Ed: University of Kent (LLB law). **Richard Wilson** (Lab) Pilot, British Airaways. Member, BALPA. Ed: University of Strathclyde (BA electronic & electrical engineering). **Harry Aldridge** (Ukip) Founder and director of a shipping company. Contested: Horsham 2010; European SE England 2009. Former chairman Young Independence. **John Pletts** (Green) Retired architect worked in Africa and the Middle East. Contested Guildford 2005.

CONSTITUENCY PROFILE
The Conservative party had a firm hold of this seat from 1906 until it was broken in 2001 after an anti-incinerator campaign by the Lib Dems. Four years later Guildford returned to the Tories and it has remained in their hands since. The eponymous town is in the north of the seat and to the south is Cranleigh, which claims to be the largest village in England.

	Electorate	Turnout %	from 2010 Change %
	76,554	70.5	
A Milton C	30,802	57.1	+3.8
K Blundell LD	8,354	15.5	-23.8
R Wilson Lab	6,534	12.1	+7.0
H Aldridge Ukip	4,774	8.8	+7.0
J Pletts Green	2,558	4.7	
S Parker Guildford	538	1.0	
J Morris Peace	230	0.4	
G Smyth CSA	196	0.4	

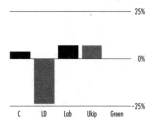

Change from 2010

Hackney North & Stoke Newington

LABOUR HOLD

DIANE ABBOTT
BORN Sept 27, 1953
MP 1987-

Candidate for Labour London mayoral selection. Left-wing firebrand turned television pundit; now a veteran MP. Surprise last-minute candidate for Labour leadership in 2010. Britain's first black female MP. Shadow min, public health 2010-13. Select cttees: foreign affairs 1997-2001; Treasury 1995-97; Treasury & civil service 1989-95. Lab party NEC 1994-97. Member of Socialist Campaign Group. Cllr, Westminster CC 1982-86. Member, GLA Advisory Cabinet for women & equality 2000-08. Equality officer, ACTT. Researcher, Thames TV; reporter, TV-am; PR and press officer, GLC. Divorced, one son. Ed: Harrow County Girls' GS; Newnham Coll, Cambridge (BA history).

CHALLENGERS
Amy Gray (C) Government

relations manager, Tesco. Former teacher. School governor. Married. Ed: Rugby Sch; Magdalen Coll, Oxford (BA English). **Heather Finlay** (Green) Representative on the City & Hackney patient and public involvement subcommittee. Was a midwife in the NHS. **Simon de Deney** (LD) Teacher trainer, actor and writer. Ran Hackney's Yes to AV campaign, gaining the highest percentage in the country (60 per cent). **Keith Fraser** (Ukip) Chartered surveyor. Married, one child. Ed: University of Westminster (BSc urban estate management).

CONSTITUENCY PROFILE
A cosmopolitan and multi-ethnic seat: it has one of the ten highest proportions of black residents in the UK, and a significant Muslim and Jewish population. It is a solid Labour seat held by Diane Abbott since 1987 in spite of the pockets of Conservative strength in the Stamford Hill area. Despite some gentrification, this is mostly a seat of council and social housing.

	Electorate	Turnout %	from 2010 Change %
	83,195	60.0	
D Abbott Lab	31,357	62.9	+7.9
A Gray C	7,349	14.7	+0.2
H Finlay Green	7,281	14.6	+10.0
S de Deney LD	2,492	5.0	-18.9
K Fraser Ukip	1,085	2.2	
J Homan AWP	221	0.4	
J Silberman Comm Lge	102	0.2	

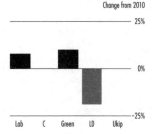

Change from 2010

Hackney South & Shoreditch

LABOUR CO-OPERATIVE HOLD

MEG HILLIER
BORN Feb 14, 1969
MP 2005-

Shadow Secretary of State, ECC 2010-11. Shadow min, home office 2010. Parly under-sec, home office 2007-10. PPS to Ruth Kelly 2006-07. Select cttee: public accounts 2011-; NI affairs 2005-06. Cllr, Islington BC 1994-2002, mayor 1998-99. Member of London Assembly, NE London 2000-04. Journalist. Merchant Navy service. Member, TGWU, Fabians, Labour Co-operative. Married, two daughters, one son. Ed: Portsmouth HS; St Hilda's Coll, Oxford (BA PPE); City University London (Dip newspaper journalism).

CHALLENGERS
Jack Tinley (C) Corporate banker. Associate director of utilities, Lloyds Banking Group. Arsenal season ticket holder. Ed: Nottingham HS; University of Leeds (BA management

studies). **Charlotte George** (Green) Film director and writer. Previously: theatre administrator; comms officer, Australian Drug Foundation; journalist at govt relations firm. Co-ordinator, Hackney Green Party. Ed: University of Melbourne (BA political science & cinema studies); RMIT, Melbourne (BComm). **Ben Mathis** (LD) Works for London Overground. LGBT Lib Dems. **Angus Small** (Ukip) Specialist in forensic accounting. Ed: Durham (BA economic history & sociology).

CONSTITUENCY PROFILE
Labour would surely have won this safe seat in every election since 1935, but for the coincidence of two MPs defecting in a row; Ron Brown (MP 1974-83) to the SDP, and Brian Sedgemore (MP 1983-2005) to the Lib Dems. Given the close proximity to the city, the central Hackney area is being gentrified. However, the proportion of social housing remains one of the highest in London.

	Electorate	*Turnout %*	*Change from 2010 %*
	79,962	59.5	
M Hillier Lab Co-op	30,663	64.4	+8.7
J Tinley C	6,420	13.5	-0.1
C George Green	5,519	11.6	+8.1
B Mathis LD	2,186	4.6	-17.8
A Small Ukip	1,818	3.8	+2.3
B Debus TUSC	302	0.6	
P Birch CSA	297	0.6	
T Adewuyi CPA	236	0.5	
R Higgs Ind	78	0.2	-0.1
B Rogers WRP	63	0.1	
G Shrigley Campaign	28	0.1	

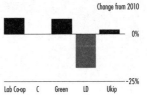

Change from 2010

Halesowen & Rowley Regis

CONSERVATIVE HOLD

JAMES MORRIS
BORN Feb 4, 1967
MP 2010-

Passionate advocate of localism agenda. PPS to Esther McVey 2014-15. Member, CLG select cttee 2010-14. CEO, Localis local government think tank. Director, London Policy Institute. Set up small computer software businesses. Founder, Mind the Gap, campaign to promote civic engagement. Cricketer. Married, one daughter, one son. Ed: Nottingham HS; University of Birmingham (BA English); Oxford (Postgrad research); Cranfield Management Sch (MBA business administration).

CHALLENGERS
Stephanie Peacock (Lab) Works for GMB Union, Halesowen. Former teacher. Recently wrote and presented a Channel 4 broadcast on low paid workers. Ed: Queen Mary, London (BA history); Institute of Education, London

(PGCE). **Dean Perks** (Ukip) Self-employed builder. Cllr, Dudley BC 2014-. **Peter Tyzack** (LD) Freelance property and planning adviser. Former teacher. Cllr, South Gloucestershire C 2007-11. Contested: Filton 2010; Bristol NW 2001; Bristol East 1997. **John Payne** (Green) Former further education and sixth-form college lecturer. Former member of Labour party and the Respect Coalition.

CONSTITUENCY PROFILE
In the south of the sprawling West Midlands conurbation, this constituency takes in Halesowen, a middle-class, dormitory suburb, and Rowley Regis, a more traditional black country manufacturing area dominated by terraced housing and council estates. The seat is very much a marginal — Halesowen tends to the Conservatives while Rowley Regis tends to vote Labour. It was won by Labour on its creation in 1997, but returned to the Conservatives in 2010.

	Electorate	*Turnout %*	*Change from 2010 %*
	74,203	59.1	
J Morris C	18,933	43.2	+2.0
S Peacock Lab	15,851	36.2	-0.4
D Perks Ukip	7,280	16.6	+10.2
P Tyzack LD	905	2.1	-12.8
J Payne Green	849	1.9	

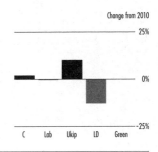

Change from 2010

Halifax

LABOUR HOLD

HOLLY LYNCH
BORN Oct 8, 1986
MP 2015-

Born and grew up in Halifax. Communications officer and assistant to Yorkshire and Humber MEP Linda McAvan. Local candidate who won controversial selection process, from all-woman shortlist, after the local Labour party disqualified 130 new members from voting. Former marketing adviser. Takes over from Linda Riordan (MP 2005-10), stepping down from ill health. Married. Ed: Brighouse HS; Lancaster University (BA history & politics).

CHALLENGERS
Philip Allott (C) MD, PR and marketing agency Allott & Associates. Local campaigner; started campaign to save local post offices. Contested: Halifax 2010; Bolton West 2005; Brent North 2001. Author of *The Donkeyman*,

based on the life of his father. Married, one daughter, one son. Ed: Harrogate Coll; Leeds Metropolitan University (LLB law). **Liz Phillips** (Ukip) One of the earliest members to the Referendum party. **Mohammad Ilyas** (LD) Driving instructor. Cllr, Calderdale C 2008-12. Born in Pakistan, moved to UK in 1973. Married, four children. **Gary Scott** (Green) Account manager, Suma Wholefoods. Former marketing manager, YHA. Worked abroad with UN. Married, three children.

CONSTITUENCY PROFILE
Halifax gave its name to the bank whose current incarnation, HBOS, is the biggest private employer in this West Yorkshire seat. Once a wool town, it retains a large working class and significant manufacturing presence. Labour has held the seat since 1987 but margins of victory have often been narrow. The seat briefly turned blue during the Thatcher years, and the BNP has had some success.

	Electorate	Turnout %	Change from 2010 %
	70,461	62.1	
H Lynch Lab	17,506	40.0	+2.6
P Allott C	17,078	39.0	+5.0
L Phillips Ukip	5,621	12.9	+11.4
M Ilyas LD	1,629	3.7	-15.4
G Scott Green	1,142	2.6	
A Javed Respect	465	1.1	
T Bendrien Ch P	312	0.7	

Change from 2010

Haltemprice & Howden

CONSERVATIVE HOLD

DAVID DAVIS
BORN Dec 23, 1948
MP 1987-

Champion of civil liberties who has retreated from frontline since 2010 and was critical of coalition. Resigned as MP and shadow home secretary (2003-08) in June 2008 in protest at 42-day detention powers, re-elected July 2008. Contested Tory leadership in 2005, 01. Shad Lord Chancellor 2002-03. Select cttees (1997-2001): chairman, public accounts, member, liason. Minister of state, FCO 1994-97. MP Boothferry 1987-97. Career, Tate & Lyle. Territorial SAS. Married, two daughters, one son. Ed: University of Warwick (BSc molecular & computing science); London Business Sch (MSc business); Harvard Business Sch (AMP).

CHALLENGERS
Edward Hart (Lab) Community care and adult social worker. Former steward, Unison North Lincolnshire.

Contested Haltemprice & Howden 2005. Ed: Cottingham HS; University of Hull (BA politics & social policy; MA social work). **John Kitchener** (Ukip) Contesting Hull CC election 2015. Contested Gateshead Metropolitan BC 2014. **Carl Minns** (LD) Trainee maths teacher. Former comms consultant. Amateur photographer. Cllr, Hull CC 2002-11, leader 2006-11. Ed: Lincoln (BA politics & regional studies); Huddersfield (PgCert public sector modernisation). **Tim Greene** (Green) Statistician, Hull CC.

CONSTITUENCY PROFILE
Mainly consists of the middle-class suburbs of Hull that lie outside the city boundaries, Normally a safe Tory seat, it was heavily targeted by the Lib Dems in 2005, albeit unsuccessfully. In the 2008 by-election, Labour, the Lib Dems and Ukip declined to put up a candidate leaving Davis against the Greens, National Front and 23 other fringe and independent candidates.

	Electorate	Turnout %	Change from 2010 %
	71,205	68.5	
D Davis C	26,414	54.2	+3.9
E Hart Lab	10,219	21.0	+5.3
J Kitchener Ukip	6,781	13.9	
C Minns LD	3,055	6.3	-20.2
T Greene Green	1,809	3.7	+2.3
D Wallis Yorks	479	1.0	

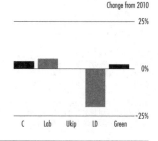

Change from 2010

Halton

LABOUR HOLD

DEREK TWIGG
BORN July 9, 1959
MP 1997-

Shadow minister, health 2010-11. Parly under-sec: defence 2006-08; transport 2005-06; education & skills 2004-05. Gov whip 2003-04; asst gov whip 2002-03. PPS to: Stephen Byers 2001-02; Helen Liddell 1999-2001. Member, select cttees: defence 2013-; arms export controls 2013-14; draft voting eligibility, prisoners 2013; children, schools & families 2009-10; public accounts 1998-99. Cllr, Halton BC 1983-97; Cheshire CC 1981-85. GMB. Political consultant. Civil servant, dept for education & employment. Interested in military history. Married, one daughter, one son. Ed: Bankfield HS, Widnes; Halton Coll of FE.

CHALLENGERS
Matthew Lloyd (C) CEO, Omniplex E-learning software company. Cllr, Alderley Edge

PC 2010-15. Married. Ed: Cardiff University (BSc computer systems); University of Warwick (MBA knowledge management). **Glyn Redican** (Ukip) Former Labour cllr, Halton BC; mayor 2002-03. Landlord at The Wine Bar in Runcorn. Defected in 2013. **Ryan Bate** (LD) Geography teacher. Cllr, Grappenhall & Thelwall PC 2012-. Former finance analyst, BP. Ed: Lancaster (BA geography); Manchester Metropolitan (PGCE); Institute of Education, London (MA geography education). **David Melvin** (Green) Employment lawyer. Former Unite official. Defected from Labour in 2014.

CONSTITUENCY PROFILE
A safe Labour seat since its creation in 1983. Consists of the towns of Runcorn and Widnes, facing each other across the Mersey. Both are industrial towns dominated by the chemicals industry. The port of Runcorn has expanded since it was designated a new town since the 1960s.

	Electorate	Turnout %	from 2010 %	Change
	72,818	61.8		
D Twigg Lab	28,292	62.8	+5.2	
M Lloyd C	8,007	17.8	-2.4	
G Redican Ukip	6,333	14.1	+11.1	
R Bate LD	1,097	2.4	-11.4	
D Melvin Green	1,017	2.3	+0.7	
V Turton Ind	277	0.6		

Change from 2010

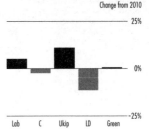

| Lab | C | Ukip | LD | Green |

Hammersmith

LABOUR HOLD

ANDY SLAUGHTER
BORN Sept 29, 1960
MP 2005-

Effective local campaigner. Brought into Miliband's front bench as shadow justice minister 2010-15. PPS to: Lord Malloch-Brown 2007-09; Lord Jones 2007-08; Stephen Ladyman 2005-07. Select cttees: human rights 2010; London regional; CLG 2009-10; CSF 2007-09; regulatory reform 2005-07. MP for Ealing Acton & Shepherds Bush 2005-10. Contested Uxbridge 1997. Cllr, Hammersmith & Fulham BC 1986-2005, leader 1996-2005, dep leader 1991-96. Former barrister, specialising in criminal, housing and personal injury law. Former researcher, Michael Meacher. Co-op party, GMB, Unite. Ed: Latymer Upper Sch; University of Exeter (BA English).

CHALLENGERS
Charlie Dewhirst (C) Works for UK sport. Former sports journalist.

Cllr, Hammersmith & Fulham BC 2010-. Ed: University of Edinburgh (MA business studies). **Millicent Scott** (LD) Former democratic engagement officer, European Parliament; development manager, Association for Citizenship Teaching. Ed: St Paul's GS; LSE (BA European studies with German); University of Edinburgh (MSc nationalism & citizenship). **David Akan** (Green) Planning manager, construction company. Co-chairman and elections officer, West Central London Green Party. Married. Ed: BA politics & history.

CONSTITUENCY PROFILE
This west London seat was created in 2010, having been paired with affluent Fulham for the previous three elections. Hammersmith & Fulham was a tight marginal seat, won by the Conservatives in 2005. The return to a Hammersmith seat, as had existed before 1997, makes the seat a more comfortable Labour one.

	Electorate	Turnout %	from 2010 %	Change
	72,254	66.4		
A Slaughter Lab	23,981	50.0	+6.2	
C Dewhirst C	17,463	36.4	+0.0	
M Scott LD	2,224	4.6	-11.3	
D Akan Green	2,105	4.4	+2.9	
R Wood Ukip	2,105	4.4	+3.2	
S Brennan ND	82	0.2		

Change from 2010

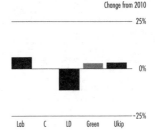

| Lab | C | LD | Green | Ukip |

Hampshire East

CONSERVATIVE HOLD

DAMIAN HINDS
BORN Nov 27, 1969
MP 2010-

Treasury: exchequer secretary 2015-; assistant whip, 2014-15. PPS to Mark Francois 2012-14. Member, select cttee: education 2010-12. Contested Stretford & Urmston 2005. Previously: chairman, Bow Group; freelance consultant; strategy director, Greene King brewery; InterContinental Hotels; Holiday Inn Worldwide; management consultant, Mercer Management. Career in pubs, brewing and hotel industries as strategist and marketer. Married, one daughter. Ed: St Ambrose GS, Altrincham; Trinity Coll, Oxford (BA PPE; president, student union).

CHALLENGERS
Peter Baillie (Ukip) Retired director of corporate communications, GKN automotive and aerospace group; Barclays Group. Former *Daily Express* journalist. Writer at *Ukip Daily.* Enjoys yachting. Widowed, one son. **Richard Robinson** (LD) Chartered accountant for AGI media, previously British Council. Cllr, Buriton PC 2002-04. Married, three children. Ed: Imperial Coll London (BSc chemistry with management science). **Alex Wilks** (Lab) Sales adviser, Debenhams. Previously a care worker. Ed: University of Surrey (BA politics with policy studies).

CONSTITUENCY PROFILE
A safe Conservative seat, the area has been represented by the party since the late 19th century. Michael Mates held the seat from 1974 until his retirement in 2010. A mostly rural constituency to the north of Portsmouth; the South Downs National Park takes up a large proportion of the seat. Settlements are mostly affluent villages set in the Hampshire countryside and prosperous market towns that originally grew up along the route from London to Portsmouth.

	Electorate	Turnout %	from 2010 %
	72,600	71.1	
D Hinds C	31,334	60.7	+3.9
P Baillie Ukip	6,187	12.0	+9.1
R Robinson LD	5,732	11.1	-19.4
A Wilks Lab	5,220	10.1	+2.2
P Bisset Green	3,176	6.2	

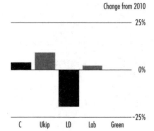

Change from 2010

C   Ukip   LD   Lab   Green

Hampshire North East

CONSERVATIVE HOLD

RANIL JAYAWARDENA
BORN Sept 3, 1986
MP 2015-

Won open primary to take over James Arbuthnot's seat. Background in financial services, including: government relations manger, Lloyds Banking Group; lobbying MEPs in Brussels on European financial regulation. Cllr, Basingstoke & Deane BC 2008-15, deputy leader 2012-15, cab member 2011-15. Freeman, City of London. FRSA. Member, Carlton Club. Interested in local history. Married, one daughter. Ed: Robert May's Sch; Alton Coll; LSE (BSc government).

CHALLENGERS
Graham Cockarill (LD) Insurance broker, Willis Group Holdings. Former telemarketing executive. Cllr: Hart DC 2002-; Yateley TC. Ed: Essex (BA history & politics). **Dr Amran Hussain** (Lab) National delivery officer, NHS England. Healthcare consultant. Adviser: CQC; WHO. Special adviser on health to House of Lords. Lecturer in healthcare management. Olympics volunteer: London 2012; Sochi 2014. Ed: Ilford County High GS (20 GCSEs); Oxford and Durham (medical clinical sciences/graduate medical studies); Birkbeck, London (MA government, policy & politics). **Robert Blay** (Ukip) Suspended for threatening to shoot Tory rival. Former accountant. Previously chairman, local Conservative association.

CONSTITUENCY PROFILE
A very safe Conservative seat created in 1997, and even in that Labour landslide election Tories won over 50 per cent of the vote. The Monster Raving Loony party was based at a pub in Yateley until 2011. An affluent and desirable residential area, home to London commuters and significant comms and defence industries, including Virgin Media and Serco.

	Electorate	Turnout %	from 2010 %
	74,025	73.0	
R Jayawardena C	35,573	65.9	+5.3
G Cockarill LD	5,657	10.5	-15.0
A Hussain Lab	5,290	9.8	+0.0
R Blay Ukip	4,732	8.8	+4.6
A Johnston Green	2,364	4.4	
M M Bobetsky Loony	384	0.7	

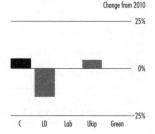

Change from 2010

C   LD   Lab   Ukip   Green

Hampshire North West

CONSERVATIVE HOLD

KIT MALTHOUSE
BORN Oct 27, 1966
MP 2015-

Chosen from a wide field to succeed Sir George Young. London Assembly member for West Central; dep London mayor: business & enterprise 2012-15; policing 2008-12, seen as successful in reducing crime. Cllr, Westminster CC 1998-2006; dep leader 2000-06. Vice-chairman, London Enterprise Partnership 2012-15. Contested Liverpool Wavertree 1997. Chairman, County Finance Group. Finance director, Alpha Strategic. Former accountant, Deloitte. Married, three children. Ed: Liverpool Coll; Newcastle University (BA economics & politics).

CHALLENGERS
Sue Perkins (Ukip) Director, ThinkInfinity, support for dyslexic learners. Examiner. Former mathematics and economics teacher. Captain, Royal Army Educational Corps. Married, two sons. Ed: St Bernard's GS, Slough; Lancaster University (BA economics & marketing); Open University (BA mathematics & statistics); PGCE. **Andrew Adams** (Lab) Born in Northern Ireland. Operations manager, First Great Western. Cllr, Micheldever PC. Civil partnership. Ed: University of Reading (BA English). **Alexander Payton** (LD) Barrister, civil law. Cllr: Newbury TC 2013-; West Berkshire 2003-07. Former Thatcham cllr, mayor of Thatcham 2006-07. Contested Havant 2010. Ed: Eton Coll, Oxford (BA Classics).

CONSTITUENCY PROFILE
A large, rural constituency spanning an area from the western outskirts of Basingstoke to the border with Wiltshire. This is an affluent seat with a large middle class. Manufacturing and agriculture are traditionally important. It has been a safe Tory seat for decades.

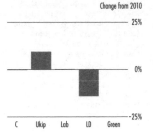

	Electorate	Turnout %	Change from 2010 %
	79,223	69.7	
K Malthouse C	32,052	58.1	-0.2
S Perkins Ukip	8,109	14.7	+9.5
A Adams Lab	7,342	13.3	+0.2
A Payton LD	5,151	9.3	-14.1
D Hill Green	2,541	4.6	

Change from 2010

Hampstead & Kilburn

LABOUR HOLD

TULIP SIDDIQ
BORN Sep 16, 1982
MP 2015-

Grandfather was one of the founders of Bangladesh, and aunt is the current prime minister of Bangladesh. Cllr, Camden BC 2010-14; chair, Camden library network; oversaw Camden's engagement with 2012 Olympics. Former policy adviser to Tessa Jowell; dep field director for Ed Miliband's leadership campaign. Previously worked: Brunswick Group LLP; corporate social responsibility; Unite, Co-operative party. FRSA. Married. Ed: UCL (BA English); King's Coll, London (MA politics, policy & government).

CHALLENGERS
Simon Marcus (C) Co-founder, Boxing Academy educational charity. Cllr, Camden BC 2012-. Education consultant. Worked for British Chamber of Commerce, Brussels. Contested Barking 2010. Ed: Sussex (BA politics); King's Coll, London (MA war studies). **Maajid Nawaz** (LD) Co-founder and chairman, Quilliam, anti-extremism think-tank. Ed: SOAS (BA Arabic & law); LSE (MSc political theory). **Rebecca Johnson** (Green) Nuclear disarmament expert. Works on international security with the UN. Vice-pres, CND. FRSA. Ed: Bristol (BA philosophy & politics); SOAS (MA int relations of far east); LSE (PhD int relations).

CONSTITUENCY PROFILE
Hampstead is portrayed as the home of the liberal intelligensia, although high house prices mean it is increasingly the home to city financiers and celebrities. Kilburn is more socially deprived with a large proportion of social housing and large Irish and Caribbean communities. The retiring MP Glenda Jackson had a majority of just 42 in 2010 but her successor Tulip Siddiq was more than 1,000 votes clear.

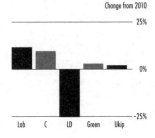

	Electorate	Turnout %	Change from 2010 %
	80,241	67.3	
T Siddiq Lab	23,977	44.4	+11.6
S Marcus C	22,839	42.3	+9.6
M Nawaz LD	3,039	5.6	-25.6
R Johnson Green	2,387	4.4	+3.0
M Nielsen Ukip	1,532	2.8	+2.1
T E Carroll Ind	113	0.2	+0.0
R Ellison U Party	77	0.1	

Change from 2010

Harborough

CONSERVATIVE HOLD

SIR EDWARD GARNIER
BORN Oct 26, 1952
MP 1992-

From the social liberal wing of Tories, and a former lawyer for *The Guardian*. Solicitor-general 2010-12. Shadow attorney-general 2009-10, 1999-2001. Shadow min: justice 2007-10; home affairs 2005-07; Lord Chancellor's dept 1997-99. PPS to: Roger Freeman 1996-97; Sir Nicholas Lyell, Sir Derek Spencer 1995-97; Alastair Goodlad, David Davis 1994-95. Select cttees: human rights 2014-; home affairs 1992-95; statutory instruments 1992. Advisory board, Samaritans. Barrister; QC 1995. Knighted in 2012. Married, one daughter, two sons. Ed: Wellington Coll; Jesus Coll, Oxford (BA history); Coll of Law, London.

CHALLENGERS
Sundip Meghani (Lab) Solicitor. Lead investigator, Independent Police Complaints Commission.

Parents expelled from Uganda in 1970s. Cllr, Leicester CC 2011-15. Former TV news presenter. VC, Co-op Party Leicester West. Ed: Brunel University (BSc politics & history); De Montfort University (GDip law; PgDip legal practice). **Mark Hunt** (Ukip) Former police officer. Parachute Regiment Falklands veteran. Married, two children. **Zuffar Haq** (LD) Businessman. Founder, international aid charity. Contested: Leicester South by-election 2011; Harborough 2010; Leicester W 2005. Married, three sons, one daughter (deceased). Ed: De Montfort Univeristy (BA).

CONSTITUENCY PROFILE
The seat includes the town of Market Harborough, the relatively affluent and ethnically diverse suburbs of Leicester and a swathe of countryside and small villages in between. Harborough has been held by the Conservatives since 1950 and used to be a target for the Liberal Democrats, in particular the area of Oadby and Wigston.

	Electorate	Turnout %	from 2010 %	Change
	77,760	67.5		
E Garnier C	27,675	52.7	+3.8	
S Meghani Lab	8,043	15.3	+2.6	
M Hunt Ukip	7,539	14.4	+11.7	
Z Haq LD	7,037	13.4	-17.7	
D Woodiwiss Green	2,177	4.2		

Change from 2010

(bar chart: C, Lab, Ukip, LD, Green; scale 25%, 0%, -25%)

Harlow

CONSERVATIVE HOLD

ROBERT HALFON
BORN March 22, 1969
MP 2010-

Strong campaigner, published pamphlet urging more Conservatives to join trade unions. Minister without portfolio, cabinet office 2015-. Member, Prospect. Organised a petition to make St George's day a public holiday. Deputy chairman, Conservative Party 2015-. PPS to George Osborne 2014-15. Contested Harlow 2005, 2001. 1922 executive committee, 2010-. Member, select cttee: public administration 2010-14. Member, Conservative Way Forward. Political consultant, Conservative Friends of Israel. Former chief of staff to Oliver Letwin. Board member, Centre for Social Justice. Policy analyst and public affairs consultant. Lives with partner. Ed: Highgate Sch; University of Exeter (BA politics; MA Russian & eastern European politics).

CHALLENGERS
Suzy Stride (Lab) Youth and community worker in East London. Director, Burnt Mill Academy Trust Sch, Harlow. Selected from all-women shortlist. Policy adviser, Baroness Jan Royall, on engaging youth in politics. Ed: Girton Coll, Cambridge (BA geography). **Sam Stopplecamp** (Ukip) General manager, Harlow community transport. Former HGV driver. Four daughters.

CONSTITUENCY PROFILE
An Essex new town built in 1947. A working class Conservative seat, characterised as the home of "white van man". It has a comparatively high proportion of social housing and is dominated by the skilled working and lower middle class. Harlow has historically been a marginal seat contested between Labour and the Conservatives. In 2005 it was one of the most marginal in the country, with a Labour majority of 97, and the last to declare.

	Electorate	Turnout %	from 2010 %	Change
	67,994	65.1		
R Halfon C	21,623	48.9	+4.0	
S Stride Lab	13,273	30.0	-3.7	
S Stopplecamp Ukip	7,208	16.3	+12.7	
M Sackwild Green	954	2.2		
G Seeff LD	904	2.0	-11.6	
D Brown TUSC	174	0.4		
E Butler Eng Dem	115	0.3		

Change from 2010

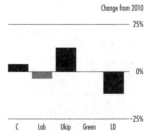

(bar chart: C, Lab, Ukip, Green, LD; scale 25%, 0%, -25%)

Harrogate & Knaresborough

CONSERVATIVE HOLD

ANDREW JONES
BORN Nov 28, 1963
MP 2010-

Proud Yorkshireman. Parly under-sec for transport 2015-. PPS to: Jeremy Hunt 2013-15; Andrew Mitchell 2012-13; Justine Greening 2011-12; Mark Prisk 2010- 11. Member, select cttee: regulatory reform 2010-. Cllr, Harrogate BC 2003-11. VC, APPG: Green Belt. Former chair of Bow Group. Interested in renewable energy and recycling. Sales and marketing: Bettys & Taylors of Harrogate; M&C Saatchi; Going Places; Kingfisher; Superdrug; B&Q). Contested Harrogate & Knaresborough 2001. Enjoys cricket and squash; member of Yorkshire CCC. Ed: Bradford GS; University of Leeds (BA English).

CHALLENGERS
Helen Flynn (LD) Cllr, Harrogate BC 2012-. Member, Federal Policy cttee. Vice Chair Lib Dem Education Association. Member, North Yorkshire Police and Crime Panel. Worked in creative positions in publishing. Contested Skipton & Ripon 2010. Married, two sons. Ed: Sidney Sussex, Cambridge (MA Classics). **David Simister** (Ukip) Owns and runs a public relations firm. Cllr, North Yorkshire CC 2013-. Partner, two daughters. **Jan Williams** (Lab) English teacher in comprehensive school. Retired solicitor and family law specialist, previously volunteered at Oxfam. Two sons. Ed: Leeds (MA education).

CONSTITUENCY PROFILE
A genteel North Yorkshire town that became a thriving spa town for the English elite in the 19th century, historically Harrogate was the safe Conservative seat, but in 1997 it was lost to the Liberal Democrats. Phil Willis comfortably held the seat for 13 years, but failed to pass on his substantial majority to his casework assistant Claire Kelley in 2010.

	Electorate	Turnout %	Change from 2010 %
	77,379	69.0	
A Jones C	28,153	52.7	+7.0
H Flynn LD	11,782	22.1	-21.7
D Simister Ukip	5,681	10.6	+8.7
J Williams Lab	5,409	10.1	+3.7
S Oakes Green	2,351	4.4	

Change from 2010

Harrow East

CONSERVATIVE HOLD

BOB BLACKMAN
BORN April 26, 1956
MP 2010-

A highly divisive but successful political operator, eventually elected in 2010. Mainstream Tory right. Voted against equal marriage "on principle". Select cttees: backbench business 2012-; CLG 2010-. Cllr, Brent BC 1986-2010; dep leader 2006-10; leader 1991-96; leader, Conservative group 1990-96. Contested: Brent North 2005; Bedford & Kempston 1997; Brent South 1992. Greater London Assembly member 2004-08. Career at BT, rose to regulatory compliance manager. Worked in sales for Unisys. Spurs fan. Enjoys bridge and chess. Married. Christian, United Reform. Ed: Preston Manor HS; University of Liverpool (BSc physics & maths; president, Students' Union).

CHALLENGERS
Uma Kumaran (Lab) Poltical adviser, Islington Council. Labour party group officer, Islington. School governor at a local infant and nursery. Ed: Queen Mary, London (BA politics; MSc public policy). **Aidan Powlesland** (Ukip) Invented war computer game. Worked in Hong Kong. Director, Cleanbrite, provides cleaning services. Ed: Cambridge (BA history). **Ross Barlow** (LD) Office manager, Diamond Family Group. Ed: Exeter (BA politics; MA critical global politics). **Emma Wallace** (Green) 'Creativity consultant'; founder, House on the Hill, retreat in the Pyrenees.

CONSTITUENCY PROFILE
A suburban seat on the edge of London, Harrow East is traditionally marginal between Labour and the Conservatives, and has remained so despite the growing numbers of ethnic minority voters, therefore one of the few seats that has a majority of ethnic minority voters with a Conservative MP.

	Electorate	Turnout %	Change from 2010 %
	70,980	69.0	
B Blackman C	24,668	50.3	+5.7
U Kumaran Lab	19,911	40.6	+3.1
A Powlesland Ukip	2,333	4.8	+2.9
R Barlow LD	1,037	2.1	-12.2
E Wallace Green	846	1.7	+0.1
N Asante TUSC	205	0.4	

Change from 2010

Harrow West

GARETH THOMAS
BORN July 15, 1967
MP 1997-

Shad minister: FCO 2013-15; cabinet office 2011-13; BIS 2010-11. Min: int devt 2008-10; BERR 2008-09. Parly under-sec DfID 2003-08. PPS to Charles Clarke 1999-2003. Member, select cttee: environmental audit 1997-99. Chairman, Co-operative party 2000-10. Cllr, Harrow BC 1990-97. Amicus. Teacher. Ed: Hatch End HS; Aberystwyth University (BSc economics & politics); King's Coll London (MA imperial & commonwealth studies); Thames Polytechnic (PGCE).

CHALLENGERS
Hannah David (C) Owner of Borehamwood-based Let's Meat restaurant. Non-practising solicitor. Cllr, Hertsmere BC 2004-13. Chair, Hendon Ward Conservatives. Three children. Studying for MA at UCL. **Mohammad Ali**

Bhatti (Ukip) Barrister. President, Honorable Society of Lincoln's Inn Student Union. **Christopher Noyce** (LD) Solicitor. Partner, Lovell Son & Pitfield. Cllr Harrow C 2006-, 1986-2002. Contested: Harrow West 2010, 2005, 2001, 1992; Bedford 1997. Ed: Pembroke Coll, Oxford (LLB law); College of Law, Guildford. **Rowan Langley** (Green) Electronics engineer. Co-founder, Harrow Green party. Contested: Harrow West 2010; Brent South 2005.

CONSTITUENCY PROFILE
A suburban seat on the edge of London, Harrow West was regarded as a safe Conservative seat until 1997 when it fell to Labour with a 17 per cent swing. Since then the growing ethnic minority population, and boundary changes in 2010 which removed the Conservative voting area of Pinner, yielded Labour gains. One of only about 25 seats where a minority of the population is white.

	Electorate	Turnout %	from 2010	Change %
	69,643	66.9		
G Thomas Lab Co-op	21,885	47.0	+3.4	
H David C	19,677	42.2	+5.4	
M A Bhatti Ukip	2,047	4.4	+2.3	
C Noyce LD	1,567	3.4	-12.8	
R Langley Green	1,310	2.8	+1.5	
K Trivedi Ind	117	0.3		

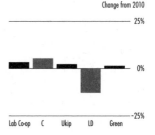

Change from 2010

Lab Co-op   C   Ukip   LD   Green

Hartlepool

IAIN WRIGHT
BORN May 9, 1972
MP 2004-

Elected as successor to Peter Mandelson after he became European commissioner in 2004. Shad min: BIS 2011-15; education 2010-11; apprenticeships 2010. Parly under-sec: children 2009-10; CLG 2007-09. PPS to Rosie Winterton 2005-06. Select cttees: finance & services 2010-; public accounts 2007; modernisation of HoC 2006-08; public admin 2005. Cllr, Hartlepool BC 2002-05. GMB. Former chairman, Lab Friends of Israel. Chartered accountant: One NorthEast. Hartlepool United fan. Married, one daughter, three sons. Ed: Manor CS, Hartlepool; Hartlepool Sixth Form Coll; UCL (BA history; MA history).

CHALLENGERS
Phillip Broughton (Ukip) Supervisor at Tesco. Cllr, Stockton-on-Tees BC 2007-11 for

Conservatives. Semi-professional wrestler. Runs a small business promoting the sport. Contested NE England Euro election 2014. **Richard Royal** (C) Senior corporate affairs manager, Britvic. MD, Lionheart Public Affairs. Founder, Westminster Russia Forum (originally Conservative Friends of Russia). Former trustee, Mind. Ed: Lancaster University (BA history & politics; MA defence & security analysis). **Stephen Picton** (Independent) Taxi driver. Former army chef. Ed: English Martyrs Sch.

CONSTITUENCY PROFILE:
Hartlepool is a reliable Labour seat, politically most associated with its former MP Peter Mandelson, 1992-2004. The seat consists of the north eastern port of Hartlepool, an industrial town, and the rural villages surrounding it. The port, the steel and chemical industries, ship breaking and Hartlepool nuclear power station are all important local employers.

	Electorate	Turnout %	from 2010	Change %
	69,516	56.8		
I Wright Lab	14,076	35.6	-6.9	
P Broughton Ukip	11,052	28.0	+21.0	
R Royal C	8,256	20.9	-7.2	
S Picton Ind	2,954	7.5		
M Holt Green	1,341	3.4		
S Allison Hospital	849	2.2		
H Allen LD	761	1.9	-15.2	
J Hobbs Ind	201	0.5		

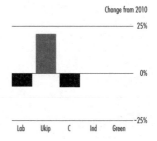

Change from 2010

Lab   Ukip   C   Ind   Green

Harwich & Essex North

CONSERVATIVE HOLD

BERNARD JENKIN
BORN April 9, 1959
MP 1992-

Veteran, Eurosceptic rightwinger. Close to Iain Duncan Smith as leader. Tasked with boosting diversity as deputy party chairman 2005-06. Select cttees: parly privilege 2012-; public admin, chairman 2010-; defence 2006-10; social security 1993-97. 1922 executive cttee, 2010-. Shad min: trade & industry 2005; transport 1998-2001. Shad SoS: regions 2003-05; defence 2001-03. PPS to Michael Forsyth 1995-97. MP Essex N 1997-2010; Colchester N 1992-97. Var opp spokes roles. Pol adviser to Leon Brittan 1986-88. Venture capital manager. Married, two sons. Ed: William Ellis Sch; Corpus Christi Coll, Cambridge (BA English).

CHALLENGERS
Edward Carlsson Browne (Lab) Historian. Worked as librarian and careworker. Ed: Corpus Christi Coll, Cambridge (BA Anglo-Saxon, Norse & Celtic); UCL (MA language, culture & history); Aberdeen (PhD Scandinavian studies). **Mark Hughes** (Ukip) Cllr, Royston TC 2014-. Owner, Mark Hughes & Associates, financial advisory. Former senior consultant, Lloyds Banking Group. Contested East England Euro election 2014. **Dominic Graham** (LD) Cllr, Colchester BC 2014-. Solicitor specialising in personal injury. Married with children. Ed: UCLan (LLB law); College of Law, York.

CONSTITUENCY PROFILE
A safe Conservative seat. Along with predecessors North Essex and Colchester North, has been held by the Tories since its creation in 1983. It mostly consists of rural hinterland around Colchester; many of the towns used to rely on fishing or shipmaking, but are now dormitories for Colchester commuters or coastal retirement destinations.

	Electorate	Turnout %	from 2010 % Change
	69,289	69.9	
B Jenkin C	24,722	51.0	+4.1
E Carlsson Browne Lab	9,548	19.7	-0.2
M Hughes Ukip	8,464	17.5	+12.3
D Graham LD	3,576	7.4	-16.2
C Flossman Green	2,122	4.4	+2.5

Change from 2010

Hastings & Rye

CONSERVATIVE HOLD

AMBER RUDD
BORN Aug 1, 1963
MP 2010-

Well-connected former banker. Was "aristocracy adviser" to *Four Weddings and a Funeral*. Secretary of state for energy & climate change 2015-. Parly under-sec, DECC 2014-15. Assistant whip, Treasury 2013-14. PPS to George Osborne 2012-13. Member, select cttee: environment 2010-12. Contested Liverpool Garston 2005. Recruitment consultant. Financial journalist, *Corporate Finance*. Chairman, Travel Intelligence. Venture capital, Lawnstone. Banker, JP Morgan. Chairwoman, Hastings Local Traders Group. Divorced (from journalist AA Gill), one daughter, one son. Ed: University of Edinburgh (MA history); UPenn (history).

CHALLENGERS
Sarah Owen (Lab Co-op) Political adviser to Lord Sugar in the House of Lords. Previously worked in emergency planning dept, London Fire Brigade. Ed: Sussex (BA int relations & human rights). **Andrew Michael** (Ukip) Parachuted in after being on Channel 4's *Gogglebox*, from which he had to resign. Controversial selection: allegedly kicked out Ralph Atkinson in "toffs at the top" Ukip policy. **Jake Bowers** (Green) Blacksmith and freelance journalist: BBC, ITV, Sky TV, *Guardian*, *Big Issue* and *Ecologist*. Worked with environmental action group Earth First! globally, which led to him being imprisoned in Malaysia and Scotland. Married, three daughters.

CONSTITUENCY PROFILE
Located on the coast at the eastern end of Sussex, features the resort of Hastings and the tourist town of Rye. Was created in 1983 by the merger of the Hastings and Rye seats. An unusual Labour gain in 1997 as the Lib Dems had been in second place in 1992. The seat was regained by the Tories in 2010.

	Electorate	Turnout %	from 2010 % Change
	75,095	67.8	
A Rudd C	22,686	44.6	+3.5
S Owen Lab Co-op	17,890	35.1	-2.0
A Michael Ukip	6,786	13.3	+10.5
J Bowers Green	1,951	3.8	
N Perry LD	1,614	3.2	-12.5

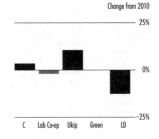

Change from 2010

Havant

CONSERVATIVE HOLD

ALAN MAK
BORN Nov 19, 1983
MP 2015-

Corporate lawyer, Clifford Chance. Elected through open primary, attacked for exaggerating his CV. From humble background, family ran small business in York, campaigned for Tories from sixth form. Founder and chairman, British Legion's Young Professionals' network. Non-executive director and investor in a range of businesses, incl StreetHub.com, retail start-up. Former president, Magic Breakfast. Member, Conservative Christian Fellowship. Ed: St Peter's Sch, York (assisted place scholarship); Peterhouse, Cambridge (BA law; won ECS Wade Prize); Oxford Institute of Legal Practice (PgDip law & business).

CHALLENGERS
John Perry (Ukip) Career in Finance. Chair, Ukip Havant

branch. Cllr, Hayling East. Ed: Southampton (BSc electronics). **Graham Giles** (Lab) Founded int devt charity, Europe to Europe. Developed probabtion schemes across Europe. Former justice consultant, World Bank. Assisted dissidents in Eastern-bloc nations, at one stage banned from Romania. Ed: Exeter (BPhil social work & criminal justice; MPhil probation studies); Bucharest (DSoc). **Steve Sollitt** (LD) Management accountant working for the NHS in Southampton. Cllr: Eastleigh BC 2010-; Southampton CC 1994-2011. Contested: South East England Euro election 2014; Southampton Test 2005; Basingstoke 2001; Portsmouth North 1997.

CONSTITUENCY PROFILE
A safe Tory seat since it was formed in 1983, David Willetts has held it since 1992-2015. The seat is located between Portsmouth and Chichester with good links to London, Portsmouth and Brighton.

	Electorate	Turnout %	from 2010	Change %
	70,573	63.5		
A Mak C	23,159	51.7	+0.6	
J Perry Ukip	9,239	20.6	+14.7	
G Giles Lab	7,149	16.0	-1.8	
S Sollitt LD	2,929	6.5	-16.9	
T Dawes Green	2,352	5.3		

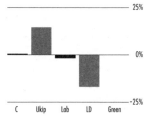

Change from 2010

Hayes & Harlington

LABOUR HOLD

JOHN McDONNELL
BORN Sep 8, 1951
MP 1997-

Left-wing rebel, received marginal support in 2007 bid for Labour leadership; candidate again in 2010, withdrew to allow Diane Abbott through. Consistent but little-noticed champion of socialism. Select cttees: justice 2013-; unopposed bills 2001-02; regulatory reform 1999-2002. Cllr, GLC 1981-86. Chair, Britain & Ireland Human Rights Centre. Shop steward. Unison. Researcher, NUM, TUC. Chief exec, Assoc of London Authorities 1987-95. Editor, *Labour Herald*. Divorced, remarried. Two daughters from first marriage, one son from second. Ed: Brunel University London (BSc government & politics); Birkbeck, London (MSc politics & sociology).

CHALLENGERS
Pearl Lewis (C) Quality assurance manager and secretary of the

University Learning and Teaching cttee, University of Buckingham. Cllr, Luffield Abbey Distrcit 2010-. Ed: Essex (BA politics & international relations). **Cliff Dixon** (Ukip) Communications and consumer electronics professional. Chairman, Ukip Hillingdon. Resigned from the English Democrats in 2011. **Satnam Kaur Khalsa** (LD) Auditor and accountant. Contested: H&H 2010; Feltham 2005. Ed: Woodfield GS.

CONSTITUENCY PROFILE
Traditionally a Labour seat, it was won by the Tories in 1983 after the defection of the previous Labour MP, Neville Sanderson, to the SDP and held by them until 1997. Since then it has returned to a safe Labour seat represented by John McDonnell. A west London, historically industrial, seat including Heathrow, which is both the major source of employment and a huge political issue because of third runway plans. Has a large Muslim and Sikh population.

	Electorate	Turnout %	from 2010	Change %
	74,875	60.2		
J McDonnell Lab	26,843	59.6	+4.8	
P Lewis C	11,143	24.7	-4.7	
C Dixon Ukip	5,388	12.0		
S K Khalsa LD	888	2.0	-6.8	
A Munro Green	794	1.8	+1.0	

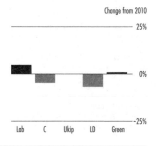

Change from 2010

Hazel Grove

WILLIAM WRAGG
BORN Dec 11, 1987
MP 2015-

Graduate of Teach First – primary school teacher who mentored children with special educational needs. Caseworker for David Nuttall. Cllr, Stockport MBC 2011-15. Former chair, Hazel Grove Conservative Association. Ed: Poynton HS; University of Manchester (BA history).

CHALLENGERS
Lisa Smart (LD) Background in international finance. Director, Stockport Credit Union, provides an alternative to loan sharks. Trustee, New Horizons canal boat, charity to help disabled people and their carers. Director, Mustard Seed Relief Mission Christian international development charity; ran Girls to Zambia charity. School governor. Member, Canal & Riverboat Trust; Marple and District Women's Institute. Ed:

Cardinal Newman Coll, Preston; Durham (BSc mathematics); London Business School (MBA business & administration). **Michael Taylor** (Lab) Founder, Think More Networks content marketing. Founder of Manchester debating salon Discuss; chairman of Downtown in Business, Manchester. Former editorial director of business journal *Insider*. Married, five children. Ed: Lancaster Royal GS; Manchester (BSocSc sociology)

CONSTITUENCY PROFILE
A suburban seat that makes up the south eastern corner of Greater Manchester. Leads up to the Pennine hills at its eastern end. Commuter area with a high proportion of owner-occupiers. Has a long history as a Liberal-Tory battleground. It was created in Feb 1974, carved out of the old Cheadle seat. Conservative Tom Arnold was MP for 23 years, but for much of it his majority over the Liberals was only wafer thin, and the seat finally fell to the Liberal Democrats convincingly in 1997.

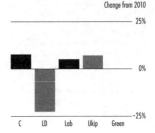

	Electorate	Turnout %	from 2010 %	Change
	63,098	68.5		
W Wragg C	17,882	41.4	+7.8	
L Smart LD	11,330	26.2	-22.6	
M Taylor Lab	7,584	17.6	+5.1	
D Palmer Ukip	5,283	12.2	+7.1	
G Reid Green	1,140	2.6		

Change from 2010

Hemel Hempstead

MIKE PENNING
BORN Sep 29, 1957
MP 2005-

A burly ex-fireman with an estuary accent. Effective working class patriot; a populist right-winger. Minister: policing, crime, criminal justice & victims 2014-; disabled people 2013-14; NI 2012-13. Parly under-sec: transport 2010-. Shad min, health 2007-10. Member, health select cttee 2005-07. Contested Thurrock 2001. Was deputy head of media, Conservative Central Office 2000-04. Adviser to William Hague's shad cabinet. Political journalist, *Express* and freelance. Lecturer. Served in Army with Grenadier Guards, then became fireman. Married, two daughters. Ed: Appleton Comp; King Edmund Comp, Essex.

CHALLENGERS
Tony Breslin (Lab) Director: Orwell Youth Prize; Breslin Public Policy. Chair, Industry

Qualifications exam board. Trustee, Adoption UK. Married, two sons. Ed: Manchester (BSc management sciences), Leicester (PGCE); Institute of Education (EdD). **Howard Koch** (Ukip) General practice dentist. NHS IT supplier. Lecturer. Ukip chairman for Hemel Hempstead. Ed: Royal Dental Hospital (dentistry); Open University (BSc computer science; Dip IT). **Rabi Martins** (LD) Cllr, Watford BC 1994-99, 2000-. Retired business management consultant. Human rights campaigner. Contested: Luton North 2010; Regents Park & Kensington North 2005; Luton South 2001; Hornchurch 1997.

CONSTITUENCY PROFILE
Often a marginal between Labour and the Conservatives; in 2010 it saw the biggest swing in the country from Labour to Conservative — more than 14 points — pushing Conservative support over 50 per cent and Labour into third place.

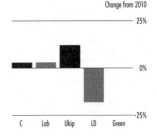

	Electorate	Turnout %	from 2010 %	Change
	74,616	66.5		
M Penning C	26,245	52.9	+2.9	
T Breslin Lab	11,825	23.8	+3.0	
H Koch Ukip	7,249	14.6	+12.1	
R Martins LD	2,402	4.8	-18.0	
A Borgars Green	1,660	3.3		
B Hall Ind	252	0.5	-0.0	

Change from 2010

Hemsworth

LABOUR HOLD

JON TRICKETT
BORN Jul 2, 1950
MP 1996-

Leading figure in grassroots left organisation Compass. Among first to call for Blair's resignation. PPS to: Gordon Brown 2008-10; Peter Mandelson 1997-98. Deputy party chair 2013-. Shadow min: without portfolio 2013-; cabinet office 2010-13. Member, select cttees: public administration 2010; unopposed bills 2001-10; public accounts 2001-06; education & employment 2001. Cllr, Leeds CC 1984-96, leader 1989-96. GMB. Worked as plumber and builder. Married, two daughters, one son. Ed: Roundhay GS, Leeds; University of Hull (BA politics); University of Leeds (MA political sociology).

CHALLENGERS
Christopher Pearson (C) Complex disabilities specialist provider, CJP Outreach Services. Cllr, Calderdale C 2015-. Enjoys motorsports. **Steve**

Ashton (Ukip) Chairman, Ukip Wakefield Branch. Worked for Yorkshire Water. Married with children. Ed: Leeds Metropolitan (BA civil engineering & business information management). **Mary Macqueen** (LD) Career in conservation; conservation and collections officer, Wakefield Council. Ed: UEL (BSc archaelogy); Leicester (Dip museum studies). **Martin Roberts** (YF) Operations manager. Supporter of Leeds United FC.

CONSTITUENCY PROFILE
Traditionally one of Labour's safest seats. Much of this West Yorkshire constituency, southeast of Wakefield, is green belt land untouched by motorways, with the population concentrated in the towns of Hemsworth and South Kirkby. Its economy was dependent on coal mining and was devastated by pit closures. Associated problems of poor health persist and large numbers of people work in routine occupations.

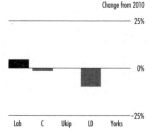

	Electorate	Turnout %	from 2010 %	Change
	72,714	58.3		
J Trickett Lab	21,772	51.3	+4.6	
C Pearson C	9,694	22.9	-1.5	
S Ashton Ukip	8,565	20.2		
M Macqueen LD	1,357	3.2	-9.7	
M Roberts Yorks	1,018	2.4		

Change from 2010

Lab   C   Ukip   LD   Yorks

Hendon

CONSERVATIVE HOLD

MATTHEW OFFORD
BORN Sep 3, 1969
MP 2010-

Athletic adventurer who explored the Libyan desert and sailed the Fastnet Race. Member, environmental audit select cttee 2012-. Political advisor: Local Govt Assoc; Conservative Central Office. Friend of Jane Ellison from Barnet Council days - cllr, Barnet BC 2002-. Contested Barnsley East & Mexborough 2001. Media analyst: BBC; MediaLink. Keen scuba diver, sailer and wild swimmer. FRGS. Christian, described same-sex marriage as "an attack on religion". Married. Ed: Amery Hill Sch, Alton; Nottingham Trent University (BA photography); Lancaster University (MA environment, culture & society) King's Coll, London (PhD).

CHALLENGERS
Andrew Dismore (Lab) Solicitor. MP Hendon 1997-2010, lost seat by

106 votes. AM, London Assembly for Barnet & Camden 2012-. Cllr, Westminster CC, 1982-, Labour group leader, 1990-. Chairman, joint committee on human rights, 2005-2010. Ed: Warwick (LLB law); LSE (LLM); Coll of Law. **Raymond Shamash** (Ukip) Semi-retired dentist. Was medical officer in Israeli army during Yom Kippur War. Replaced candidate Jeremy Zeid who stood down after saying Israel should kidnap Obama. Ed: Leeds (dentistry). **Alasdair Hill** (LD) Biology teacher. Worked on malaria research projects in West Africa. Ed: Aberdeen (BSc tropical environmental science); London Sch of Hygiene & Tropical Medicine (MSc medical parasitology); Goldsmiths (PGCE).

CONSTITUENCY PROFILE
North west London ethnically diverse seat. Held by Labour from 1997-2010 but the predecessor seat, Hendon North, was safely Conservative. The result in 2010 was one of the closest in the country.

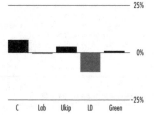

	Electorate	Turnout %	from 2010 %	Change
	74,658	66.5		
M Offord C	24,328	49.0	+6.7	
A Dismore Lab	20,604	41.5	-0.6	
R Shamash Ukip	2,595	5.2	+3.2	
A Hill LD	1,088	2.2	-10.2	
B Samuel Green	1,015	2.1	+0.9	

Change from 2010

C   Lab   Ukip   LD   Green

Henley

CONSERVATIVE HOLD

JOHN HOWELL
BORN Jul 27, 1955
MP 2008-

Won by-election after Boris Johnson's election to mayor of London; lives in the shadow of his predecessor. PPS to: Andrew Lansley 2012-14; Sir George Young 2010-12; Greg Clark 2010-11. Select cttees: justice 2014-; w&p 2008-10. VP, local government assoc 2010-11. Business career: partner, Ernst & Young; led British business delegations to G7 meetings; board member, Know How Fund. Business journalist, BBC World Service. Cllr, Oxford CC 2004-09. Amateur dramatist. Married, two daughters, one son. Ed: Battersea GS; University of Edinburgh (MA archaeology); St John's Coll, Oxford (DPhil prehistoric archaeology).

CHALLENGERS
Sam Juthani (Lab) Economist, Wrap, formerly Home Office. Sch governor. Ed: St Edmund's

Hall, Oxford (BA PPE); Barcelona Graduate Sch of Economics (MSc specialised economic analysis). **Sue Cooper** (LD) Systems analyst, Institute of Hydrology. Cllr, South Oxfordshire DC 1991-2011, chair 1996-97. Operational researcher: ICI paints division, ABM. Has been: student adviser; statistics tutor; sch governor; Benson parish clerk. Strong interest in waste management, chaired Oxfordshire Waste Management Partnership. Married, six children. **Christopher Jones** (Ukip) Medical writer. **Mark Stevenson** (Green) Former maths teacher. Leads group to create hydro-electric generator in Thames.

CONSTITUENCY PROFILE
Like other rural seats in Oxfordshire, it is an affluent middle class area and strongly Tory, but at a local level the Lib Dems have some support, particularly closer to Oxford itself. John Howell was preceded by Boris Johnson, and former deputy prime minister Michael Heseltine.

	Electorate	Turnout %	Change from 2010 %
	78,243	70.6	
J Howell C	32,292	58.5	+2.3
S Juthani Lab	6,917	12.5	+1.6
S Cooper LD	6,205	11.2	-13.9
C Jones Ukip	6,007	10.9	+7.5
M Stevenson Green	3,815	6.9	+4.4

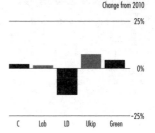

Change from 2010

C Lab LD Ukip Green

Hereford & Herefordshire South

CONSERVATIVE HOLD

JESSE NORMAN
BORN June 23, 1962
MP 2010-

Thoughtful, friend and Eton contemporary of Boris Johnson. Sacked as govt adviser for abstaining from Syrian intervention vote. Compassionate conservatism but departed from leadership policy with *Churchill's Legacy: The Conservative case for the Human Rights Act*. Policy adviser to Boris Johnson during mayoral campaign and George Osborne as shadow chancellor. Select cttees: commons governance 2014-; consolidation 2010-; treasury 2000-. Shortlisted for Samuel Johnson Prize in 2013 for biography of Edmund Burke. Philosophy researcher and teacher, UCL. Worked at Barclays. Worked for and ran educational project giving away textbooks in eastern Europe. Married, three children. Ed: Eton Coll; Merton Coll, Oxford (MA Classics); UCL (MPhil; PhD philosophy).

CHALLENGERS
Nigel Ely (Ukip) Works in the security industry. Ex-SAS soldier. **Anna Coda** (Lab) Science teacher. Chair, Hereford & Herefordshire S CLP. Voluntary worker, Oxfam; representative, NUT, NASUWT. Ed: Leicester (BSc chemistry; PGCE). **Lucy Hurds** (LD) Self-employed small business consultant. Contested Herefordshire N 2010. Sec, West Midlands Lib Dem regional exec cttee, chairman, fundraising. Runs graduate enterprise programme for local unemployed graduates.

CONSTITUENCY PROFILE
A rural seat on the border with Wales, it includes the historic city of Hereford and most of agricultural south Herefordshire. The former Hereford seat had been a Liberal target for many years before it was won on the back of Paul Keetch's local credentials in 1997. Keetch retired in 2010 and the seat was won back by the Conservatives.

	Electorate	Turnout %	Change from 2010 %
	70,711	66.8	
J Norman C	24,844	52.6	+6.3
N Ely Ukip	7,954	16.8	+13.5
A Coda Lab	6,042	12.8	+5.5
L Hurds LD	5,002	10.6	-30.5
D Toynbee Green	3,415	7.2	

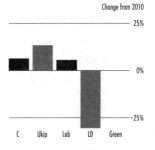

Change from 2010

C Ukip Lab LD Green

Herefordshire North

CONSERVATIVE HOLD

BILL WIGGIN
BORN June 4, 1966
MP 2001-

Schoolmate of David Cameron. Asst govt whip, Treasury 2010-12; opp whip 2009-10. Shad min: agriculture, fisheries 2005-09; Defra 2005, 2003. Shad sec: Wales 2003-05. MP, Leominster 2001-2010. Contested Burnley 1997. Banker. Manager of foreign exchange dept, Commerzbank. City of London Freeman. Was officer, Territorial Army. Owns smallholding with Hereford cattle, Ryeland sheep. Countryside Alliance. Enjoys shooting and fishing. Married, one daughter, two sons. Ed: Eton Coll; University of Wales, Bangor (BA economics).

CHALLENGERS
Jonathan Oakton (Ukip) Sales director. Contested: West Bromwich West by-election 2000; West Midlands European 1999; Birmingham Edgbaston 1997 for Referendum Party. **Jeanie Falconer** (LD) Runs Frome Valley Wines. Previously: director, European Public Policy Advisers 1986-1999; journalist in Turkey. Married. Ed: Edinburgh (MA history). **Sally Prentice** (Lab) Partnerships manager. Cllr, Lambeth 2002-, 1993-98. Defector from Lib Dems. Worked for Age Concern, HM Treasury. Ed: King Alfred's Sch, Wantage; Somerville Coll, Oxford (BA PPE). **Daisy Blench** (Green) Policy manager, British Beer & Pub Assn. Daughter of campaigner, Felicity Norman. Ed: Essex (BA politics & international relations).

CONSTITUENCY PROFILE
A largely agricultural seat covering the upper half of Herefordshire county, this is solid Conservative territory. This seat and its predecessor, Leominster, have only had a break in Conservative representation since 1910 between 1998 and 2001, when the Tory MP Peter Temple-Morris defected to the Labour party.

	Electorate	Turnout %	from 2010 % Change
	66,683	72.0	
B Wiggin C	26,716	55.6	+3.9
J Oakton Ukip	6,720	14.0	+8.3
J Falconer LD	5,768	12.0	-19.0
S Prentice Lab	5,478	11.4	+4.3
D Blench Green	3,341	7.0	+3.7

Change from 2010

[bar chart: C, Ukip, LD, Lab, Green; axis 25%, 0%, -25%]

Hertford & Stortford

CONSERVATIVE HOLD

MARK PRISK
BORN June 12, 1962
MP 2001-

Tweeted that he had been asked to make way for a younger generation when sacked as housing minister 2012-13. Failed to alleviate housebuilding woes for coalition. Minister, BIS 2010-12. Shad min: business 2005-10. Opp whip 2004-05. Shadow: paymaster general 2003-04; financial sec 2002-03. Select cttees: electoral commission 2012-13; regulatory reform: 2008-09; Welsh affairs 2001-05. Founder, East Hertfordshire Business Forum. Member, Prince's Trust. Founding chair, Youth for Peace through Nato. Chartered surveyor, then formed marketing consultancy. Married. Ed: Truro Sch; University of Reading (BSc land management).

CHALLENGERS
Katherine Chibah (Lab) Music teacher, accomplished viola player. Cllr Enfield BC 2014-. Member, Musicians Union, Unite, Co-operative party. History graduate **Adrian Baker** (Ukip) Physics teacher. Secretary, Ukip Hertford & Storford branch. **Michael Green** (LD) Works for European Bank for Reconstruction & Development. Former dep head, NatWest Moscow office. Cllr, St Albans DC 2006-14. Contested: Clacton 2010; St Albans 2005. Ed: Leeds (BA Russian); INSEAD (MBA). **Sophie Christophy** (Green) Columnist, *Herts & Essex Observer*. Works part-time at Waitrose. Charity worker.

CONSTITUENCY PROFILE
South east Hertfordshire seat containing a group of affluent residential towns popular for commuters and the green belt countryside between them. Until 1983 Hertford was part of the Hitchin seat, and was represented by Labour MP, Shirley Williams 1964-74. Excluding those ten years period, the seat and its predecessor have been strongly Conservative.

	Electorate	Turnout %	from 2010 % Change
	78,906	71.3	
M Prisk C	31,593	56.1	+2.3
K Chibah Lab	10,084	17.9	+4.2
A Baker Ukip	7,534	13.4	+10.3
M Green LD	4,385	7.8	-18.2
S Christophy Green	2,681	4.8	

Change from 2010

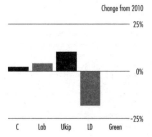

[bar chart: C, Lab, Ukip, LD, Green; axis 25%, 0%, -25%]

Hertfordshire North East

CONSERVATIVE HOLD

SIR OLIVER HEALD
BORN Dec 15, 1954
MP 1992-

Genial figure, returned to frontline in coalition cabinet, knighted when replaced in 2014. Solicitor general, attorney general's office 2012-14. Shadow: SoS, justice 2004-07; chancellor of the Duchy of Lancaster 2005-07; leader of the House 2003-05. minister: work & pensions; 2002-03. spokesman, health 2001-02, home affairs 2000-01; whip 1997-2000. Parly under-sec, social security 1995-97. PPS to: William Waldegrave 1994-95; Sir Peter Lloyd 1994. Select cttees include: House of Lords governance 2014-; draft House of Lords reform 2011-12; ecclesiastical, standards & privileges 2010-12; W&P 2007-12; selection 2009-10; HoC modernisation 2003-05. Contested Southwark & Bermondsey 1987. Barrister, QC. Married, two daughters, one son. Ed: Reading Sch; Pembroke Coll, Cambridge (MA law).

CHALLENGERS
Chris York (Lab) NHS CPFT dep lead governor. Cllr, Farcet PC 2012-. Unite, Co-op party. Chairman, local neighbourhood police panel; Stanground Youth Project group. Labour regional board member. Contested Cambs NW 2010. **William Compton** (Ukip) Microbrewery owner. Chairman, Much Hadam PC. Defected from Conservatives in 2010. **Joe Jordan** (LD) Scientist and software engineer, Solarflare Comms. Ed: Sidney Sussex Coll, Cambridge (BSc natural sciences); Imperial Coll, London (PhD physics).

CONSTITUENCY PROFILE
A safe Tory seat, narrowly withstood Labour's 1997 onslaught. Much of the land in this seat is given to agriculture, primarily arable. It reaches from Baldock on the border with Bedfordshire, clockwise to Royston on the Cambridgeshire border, running through the area between Stevenage and Hertford.

	Electorate	Turnout %	from 2010 % Change
	73,944	70.7	
O Heald C	28,949	55.4	+1.8
C York Lab	9,869	18.9	+2.4
W Compton Ukip	6,728	12.9	+8.8
J Jordan LD	3,952	7.6	-15.8
M May Green	2,789	5.3	+3.6

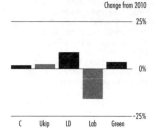

Change from 2010

Hertfordshire South West

CONSERVATIVE HOLD

DAVID GAUKE
BORN Oct 8, 1971
MP 2005-

Thoughtful Eurosceptic from Tory right. Knowledgable on economics. At Treasury: financial secretary 2014-; exchequer secretary 2010-14. Shadow minister: Treasury 2007-10. Contested Brent East 2001. Select cttees: tax law rewrite bills 2009; Treasury 2006-07; procedure 2005-06. Completed Parliamentary Police Scheme in 2006-07, spending 22 days with Hertfordshire Constabulary. Centre for Policy Studies member. Con Friends of Israel. Solicitor, Macfarlanes. Patron: Hospice of St Francis; Three Rivers Museum. Ipswich Town FC supporter. Married, three sons. Ed: Northgate HS, Ipswich; St Edmund Hall, Oxford (BA law); Chester Coll of Law.

CHALLENGERS
Simon Diggins (Lab) Strategic planner to Joint Forces Command,

after 35-year career in army. Was military advisor to UN. OBE 2000. Career almost derailed by affair revealed in 2009. Partner. Two children. Ed: Solihull Sch Durham (BA history); Cambridge (MPhil international relations & affairs). **Mark Anderson** (Ukip) Works in logistics. Married, two children Ed: Hull (BA history & archaeology). **Nigel Quinton** (LD) Head of petroleum exploration, Tower Resources. Freelance energy consultant. Contested Hitchin & Harpenden 2010. Cllr, Welwyn Hatfield BC 2006-08. Chair, Welwyn Hatfield Liberal Democrats. Ed: Emmanuel Coll, Cambridge (BA geological sciences).

CONSTITUENCY PROFILE
A safe Conservative seat up the western side of Hertfordshire, the southern part of the seat around Rickmansworth and Chorleywood is solid London suburbia, with more rural areas in the Chilterns area of outstanding natural beauty around Tring.

	Electorate	Turnout %	from 2010 % Change
	79,666	71.9	
D Gauke C	32,608	56.9	+2.7
S Diggins Lab	9,345	16.3	+4.8
M Anderson Ukip	6,603	11.5	+9.0
N Quinton LD	5,872	10.3	-17.7
C Pardy Green	2,583	4.5	
G Cartmell CSP	256	0.5	

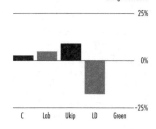

Change from 2010

Hertsmere

CONSERVATIVE HOLD

OLIVER DOWDEN
BORN Aug 1, 1978
MP 2015-

David Cameron's former deputy chief of staff. Regarded as a rising star, was seen as one of the government's most accomplished advisers – despite mismanaging an interview in the US when he said he was often "surprised" by government behavior and was frequently on "crisis management". Prior to 2010, was head of political section of Conservative Research Department. Trained as a lawyer. Previously: management consultant, Hill & Knowlton lobbying firm; account director, LLM comms agencies. Was teacher in Japan. Nicknamed "Olive". Married, two children. Ed: Parmiters' Sch, Watford; Trinity Hall, Cambridge (BA law).

CHALLENGERS
Richard Butler (Lab) Electrician. Cllr, Hertsmere BC 2011-; Elstree & Borehamwood TC 2007-, deputy mayor 2014-. Member, Unite. Joined Labour party at 15. **Frank Ward** (Ukip) Defected to Ukip after 45 years of Labour Party membership. Labour cllr, Hertsmere BC 1983-2007. Retired chartered builder and chartered manager. Chair, Ukip Hertsmere branch 2013-. Married. **Sophie Bowler** (LD) Works in anti-money laundering for BDO accountancy firm. Previously assistant to Bill Newton Dunn MEP. Worked in Sydney State Parliament and for New South Wales govt. Ed: Leeds (BA international relations).

CONSTITUENCY PROFILE
A safe Conservative seat, held by the party since its creation in 1983, most famously by Cecil Parkinson. Houses a collection of middle-class commuter towns just outside the boundary of Greater London such as Potters Bar, Radlett, Elstree and Borehamwood. The seat has the third highest Jewish population in the country.

	Electorate	Turnout %	from 2010 %	Change
	73,753	67.9		
O Dowden C	29,696	59.3	+3.3	
R Butler Lab	11,235	22.4	+3.7	
F Ward Ukip	6,383	12.7	+9.1	
S Bowler LD	2,777	5.5	-11.8	

Change from 2010

(bar chart: C, Lab, Ukip, LD; scale 25% / 0% / -25%)

Hexham

CONSERVATIVE HOLD

GUY OPPERMAN
BORN May 18, 1965
MP 2010-

Describes himself as "rather on the left" of Tory party, supporter of living wage, mansion tax and industrial activism. Survived emergency surgery on a brain tumor in 2011 and now champions NHS in Parliament. Blogger. Asst whip 2015-. PPS to: James Brokenshire 2014-15; Mark Harper 2012-14. Barrister, won 2007 Bar Pro Bono Award for Free Representation Unit work, judicial review challenge and campaign against local hospital closures. Contested: Caernarfon 2005; North Swindon 1997. Adviser to Michael Ancram as shad foreign sec. Cllr, Wiltshire 1995-99. Amateur steeplechase jockey, survived serious accident 2006. Marathon-runner. Long-term partner. Ed: Harrow Sch; University of Buckingham (LLB law); University of Lille, France (Diploma).

CHALLENGERS
Liam Carr (Lab) Biology lecturer, Newcastle Coll. Blogger RMT, UCU. Married, two daughters. **David Nicholson** (Ukip) Former Merchant Navy seaman, farm worker and shopkeeper. Previously Conservative cllr. Three children. **Jeff Reid** (LD) Runs company selling stationery. Cllr, Northumberland CC 2008-, leader of Lib Dems 2013-. Contested Blyth Valley 2010, 2005, 2001. Ed: Newcastle Coll (photography). **Lee Williscroft-Ferris** (Green) Language teacher. Former editor, *So So Gay*. Ed: Northumberland (BA French & German); Durham (PGCE).

CONSTITUENCY PROFILE
A sparsely populated large seat stretching into desolate moorland, and right to the Scottish border. One of only two Conservative seats in the Tory desert that is northeast England. In 1997 it almost fell: the Tory majority over Labour was cut to only 222 votes, but Labour have since fallen back.

	Electorate	Turnout %	from 2010 %	Change
	60,614	71.5		
G Opperman C	22,834	52.7	+9.5	
L Carr Lab	10,803	24.9	+5.9	
D Nicholson Ukip	4,302	9.9		
J Reid LD	2,961	6.8	-23.1	
L Williscroft-Ferris Green	2,445	5.6		

Change from 2010

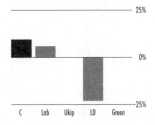

(bar chart: C, Lab, Ukip, LD, Green; scale 25% / 0% / -25%)

Heywood & Middleton

LABOUR HOLD

LIZ MCINNES
BORN Jan 1, 1957
MP 2014-

Won by-election after death of Jim Dobbin, closely fought against Ukip. Cllr, Rossendale BC 2010-. Worked as clinical scientist NHS from 1981 until becoming an MP. Senior biochemist, Pennine Acute Hospitals NHS Trust. Cllr, Rossendale BC 2000-14. Secretary, Unite Pennine Acute Branch. Partner, one son. Ed: Hatershaw CS; Oxford (BSc biochemistry); University of Surrey (MA).

CHALLENGERS
John Bickley (Ukip) Rocked Labour heartland by losing 2014 by-election by just 614 votes. Ran technology business using EU cash that went bust. Worked for Sony. Wrote controversial "it's time for Ukip" tweet after *Charlie Hebdo* attack. Raised on a council estate. Married, two children. **Iain Gartside** (C) Credit analyst, RBS.

Cllr, Bury MBC 2004-. Leader, Bury Conservatives. Contested 2014 by-election. Sch governor. Ed: Moorside HS; University of Salford (BA politics & history). **Anthony Smith** (LD) Businessman. Secretary, local Lib Dems. Joined Ryalux Carpets with YTS after school. Four children. Ed: Salford (BSc business information systems). **Abi Jackson** (Green) Account exec, Softcat IT infrastructure. Ed: Huddersfield (BSc psychology; MA human & health sciences).

CONSTITUENCY PROFILE
The seat covers some of the more affluent suburbs of Rochdale and the two neighbouring towns of Heywood & Middleton, both former mill towns that are now largely residential, with mixtures of more affluent private developments and overspill council estates. The seat has been held by the Labour party since its creation in 1983. The BNP performed relatively strongly here in 2010, and Ukip almost pipped Labour to the post in 2014.

	Electorate	Turnout %	Change from 2010 %
	79,989	60.7	
L McInnes Lab	20,926	43.1	+3.0
J Bickley Ukip	15,627	32.2	+29.6
I Gartside C	9,268	19.1	-8.1
A Smith LD	1,607	3.3	-19.4
A Jackson Green	1,110	2.3	

Change from 2010

Lab Ukip C LD Green

High Peak

CONSERVATIVE HOLD

ANDREW BINGHAM
BORN June 23, 1962
MP 2010-

Not afraid to defy whips. Proud of his credentials as a life-long resident, keen to develop area's tourism trade. Strong local campaigner on pensions system for employees. PPS to: Mark Francois 2014-15. Select cttees: European scrutiny 2013-; work & pensions 2010-12. Cllr, High Peak BC 1999-2011. Contested High Peak BC 2005. Dir, family firm distributing engineering equipment. Buxton FC supporter. Married. Ed: Long Lane CS, Chapel-en-Frith; High Peak FE Coll (catering).

CHALLENGERS
Caitlin Bisknell (Lab) Cllr, High Peak BC 1999-15, leader 2011-15, leader of Labour group 2003-15. Chair, sch governors. Contested High Peak 2010. Married, two children. Former journalist, *Shropshire Star*. Ed: University of

Keele (BA politics & philosophy). **Ian Guiver** (Ukip) Sales and marketing career. Ed: York (BA history & politics). **Stephen Worall** (LD) Currently studying for a PhD in Nanoscience at University of Manchester. Cllr, Charlesworth PC 2011-. Worked as sales assistant at Woolworths, Card Factory. Ed: Manchester (MChem chemistry). **Charlotte Farrell** (Green) Works with partner making orthopaedic footwear. Trained and worked as a nurse for 15 years. Requalified as a solicitor.

CONSTITUENCY PROFILE
High Peak largely consists of mostly uninhabited areas of the Peak District at the northern end of Derbyshire. The majority of the electorate live in towns in the west of the seat that look towards Greater Manchester. Despite being largely rural, the Tory voting villages are balanced out by Labour support in the towns, making this a key marginal seat between Labour and the Conservatives.

	Electorate	Turnout %	Change from 2010 %
	73,336	69.3	
A Bingham C	22,836	45.0	+4.1
C Bisknell Lab	17,942	35.3	+3.7
I Guiver Ukip	5,811	11.4	+8.1
S Worrall LD	2,389	4.7	-17.1
C Farrell Green	1,811	3.6	+1.7

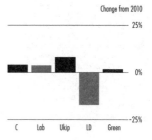

Change from 2010

C Lab Ukip LD Green

Hitchin & Harpenden

PETER LILLEY
BORN Aug 23, 1943
MP 1983-

Survivor from Tory cabinets of Thatcher and Major eras. Stood for leadership in 1997, helping to split Tory right. Controvesial member of ECC select cttee (2012-) as he is non-exec director of Tethys Petroleum. Dep opp leader 1998-99; shad chancellor 1997-98. SoS: social security 1992-97; trade 1990-92. Treasury: financial sec 1989-90; economic sec 1987-89. PPS to: Nigel Lawson 1984-87; Lord Bellwin/William Waldegrave 1984. MP St Albans 1983-97. Economic consultant, financial analyst specialising oil and energy. Chairman, Bow Group 1973-75. Married. Ed: Dulwich Coll; Clare Coll, Cambridge (MA natural sciences & economics).

CHALLENGERS
Rachel Burgin (Lab) Transaction support manager, Trinity

International. Paralegal. Member, exec cttee, Labour finance & industry group. Cllr, Parton PC 2007-10. Married. Ed: Birmingham (BA history); Keele (CPE law); University of the West of England (LPC legal practice). **John Stocker** (Ukip) Founded telecomms construction business. Former marine engineering officer. **Pauline Pearce** (LD) Nicknamed "Hackney heroine" for shouting down yobs during London riots. Co-founder, Good Love Caribbean Food selling products from local community in Hackney.

CONSTITUENCY PROFILE
The towns of both Harpenden and Hitchin have excellent transport connections, making them popular commercial and industrial hubs, as well as attractive to commuters. Mostly rural but contains several industrial estates. Many affluent residents, particularly professional and managerial. Has been a safe Conservative seat since its creation in 1997.

	Electorate	Turnout %	from 2010 %
	74,839	74.0	
P Lilley C	31,488	56.9	+2.3
R Burgin Lab	11,433	20.7	+7.1
J Stocker Ukip	4,917	8.9	+5.8
P Pearce LD	4,484	8.1	-18.6
R Wise Green	3,053	5.5	+4.0

Change from 2010

[bar chart: C, Lab, Ukip, LD, Green; scale 25% to -25%]

Holborn & St Pancras

SIR KEIR STARMER
BORN Sep 20, 1962
MP 2015-

One of Labour's star new candidates, intellectually minded and forthright. Pushed to run for Labour leadership days after becoming MP, he quickly ruled himself out. Director of Public Prosecutions 2008-13, responsible for cases incl: assisted suicide; retrial of Stephen Lawrence case; MPs' expenses. Human rights barrister. Appointed QC 2002. KCB 2014. Previously joint head, Doughty Street Chambers. QC of the Year 2007, Chambers & Partners. Author of law textbooks. Named after socialist Keir Hardie. Arsenal fan. Had violin lessons with Norman Cook (Fat Boy Slim). Married, one son, one daughter. Ed: Reigate GS; University of Leeds (LLB law); St Edmund Hall, Oxford (BCL).

CHALLENGERS
Will Blair (C) Associate director, Fishburn PR firm; previously in

comms: Bell Pottinger, Weber Shandwick. Former assistant to Damian Green. RAF reservist. Ed: Oxford (BA history). **Natalie Bennett** (Green) Leader, Green party 2012-. Founding chairwoman, Green Party Women. Journalist: former sub-editor The Times; editor, Guardian Weekly. Contested Holborn 2010. Ed: Sydney (BScAgr agricultural science); New England (BA Asian studies); Leicester (MA mass communication). **Jill Fraser** (LD) First Lib Dem mayor of Camden (2006-07). Cllr Camden BC 2003-14. Contested Holborn 2005. Tenants' rights campaigner. Chip-shop worker.

CONSTITUENCY PROFILE
The Lib Dems' inroads into this traditionally safe Labour seat were wiped out in 2015. The Greens though continued to progress, increasing their vote from 3 to 13 per cent. Social housing accounts for half of homes, and there is a significant Bangladeshi Muslim population.

	Electorate	Turnout %	from 2010 %
	86,864	63.2	
K Starmer Lab	29,062	52.9	+6.8
W Blair C	12,014	21.9	+1.5
N Bennett Green	7,013	12.8	+10.1
J Fraser LD	3,555	6.5	-21.4
M Spencer Ukip	2,740	5.0	+3.9
S O'Donnell CSA	252	0.5	
V Hudson AWP	173	0.3	
D O'Sullivan SEP	108	0.2	

Change from 2010

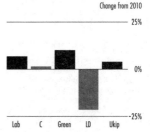

[bar chart: Lab, C, Green, LD, Ukip; scale 25% to -25%]

Hornchurch & Upminster

CONSERVATIVE HOLD

DAME ANGELA WATKINSON
BORN Nov 18, 1941
MP 2001-

Right-wing populist of the old Monday Club sort. Govt whip 2010-12; opp whip 2005-10, 2002-04. Shad min: CLG 2005; education 2004-05. Member, Con Way Forward. Select cttees: work & pensions 2013-14; selection 2010-13; European scrutiny 2002-3; home affairs 2001-2. Cllr: Essex CC 1997-2001; Havering BC 1994-98. Local government officer. Cttee manager, Basildon DC. Worked in special school. Early career, banking. Divorced, two daughters, one son. Ed: Wanstead County HS; Anglia Poly (HNC public admin).

CHALLENGERS
Lawrence Webb (Ukip) Contested London mayoral election for Ukip. First Ukip councillor elected in London, Havering BC 2013-. Political assistant to Gerard Batten MEP 2004-. Former

member of TA. Ran nightclub in Tokyo. Ed: Open University (BSc environmental science). **Paul McGeary** (Lab) Project Manager, NE London NHS Trust. Cllr, Havering BC 2010-14. Ed: University of East London (HNC construction management). **Jonathan Mitchell** (LD) Criminal barrister, 25 Bedford Row. Cllr, Southwark BC 2006-14. Contested Dulwich & Norwood W 2010, 05. Ed: Trinity Coll, Dublin (BA PPE).

CONSTITUENCY PROFILE
Created in 2010 from the merger of the old Hornchurch and Upminster seats, pitting two Tory MPs, Angela Watkinson and James Brokeshire, against one another for selection. Both Hornchurch and Upminster were won by Labour in its 1997 landslide, but were regained by the Conservatives in relatively short order and the combined seat is solidly Tory. The easternmost seat in Greater London, it is mostly an affluent, middle-class residential area of owner-occupied housing.

	Electorate	Turnout %	from 2010 %	Change
	79,331	69.6		
A Watkinson C	27,051	49.0	-2.5	
L Webb Ukip	13,977	25.3	+20.0	
P McGeary Lab	11,103	20.1	-0.7	
J Mitchell LD	1,501	2.7	-11.2	
M Collins Green	1,411	2.6	+1.5	
P Borg BNP	193	0.4	-6.1	

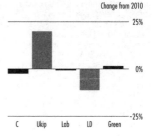

Change from 2010

Hornsey & Wood Green

LABOUR GAIN

CATHERINE WEST
BORN Sep 14, 1966
MP 2015-

Cllr, Islington C, 2002-14; leader 2010-13. Chairwoman of London councils' transport and environment committee. Awarded title of local authority leader of the year 2013 for work leading Islington Fairness Commission. Member, LGA finance panel. Previously worked in welfare and housing with immigrants. Speaks five languages. Former case worker for David Lamy MP. Married, two children. Ed: SOAS (BA social science & languages; MA Chinese studies).

CHALLENGERS
Lynne Featherstone (LD) MP, Hornsey & Wood Green 2005-10. Previously rising star in Lib Dems. Active in Chris Huhne's leadership campaigns of 2006 & 2007. Min of state, Home Office 2014-15. Parly under-sec: int devt

2012-14; equalities 2010-12. LD shad min: youth & equalities 2008-10; shad SoS: int devt 2006-07. Member, GLA 2000-05. Cllr, Haringey BC 1998-2006. Strategic design consultant. Divorced, two daughters. Ed: S Hampstead HS; Oxford Poly (Dip communication & design). **Suhail Rahuja** (C) Fund manager, Trafalgar Asset Managers. Cllr, Westminster CC 2006-. Contested Manchester Central 2010. Ed: Stanford Graduate Sch of Business (MBA). **Gordon Peters** (Green) Former director of social services in Hackney; health and social development consultant in Bangladesh, Latvia, and Georgia.

CONSTITUENCY PROFILE
The western half of Haringey Borough, the seat was Tory until 1992 but by 1997 appeared to be rock solid Labour, with Barbara Roche enjoying a majority of over 20,000. The Lib Dems supplanted Labour in 2005 but Labour took it back in 2015.

	Electorate	Turnout %	from 2010 %	Change
	79,241	72.9		
C West Lab	29,417	50.9	+16.9	
L Featherstone LD	18,359	31.8	-14.7	
S Rahuja C	5,347	9.3	-7.4	
G Peters Green	3,146	5.4	+3.2	
C Morrison Ukip	1,271	2.2		
H Spiby-Vann CPA	118	0.2		
F Sweeney WRP	82	0.1		
G Moseley Hoi	45	0.1		

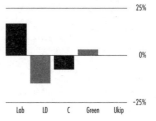

Change from 2010

Horsham

CONSERVATIVE HOLD

JEREMY QUIN
BORN Sep 24, 1968
MP 2015-

Selected from 100 applicants after Francis Maude stood down. From university joined NatWest Securities which later became part of Deutsche Bank, currently managing director. Served on secondment at the Treasury as senior corporate finance adviser during financial crisis. Contested Meirionnydd Nant Conwy 1997. Chairman, Buckingham Con Assoc 2010-13. Voluntary: director, local credit union; helped establish free school for autistic children; ambassador, Debate Mate charity. Member, Countryside Alliance. Married. Ed: St Albans Sch; Hertford Coll, Oxford (BA history; pres, Oxford Union).

CHALLENGERS
Roger Arthur (Ukip) Cllr Horsham DC 2007-15; former Conservative deputy leader, defected in 2013.

Retired chartered engineer. Married. Ed: NW Kent and Medway colleges of technology (Dip EE) then chartered engineer, electrical power system design. **Morwen Millson** (LD) Cllr, West Sussex CC 1989-. Director, 4TheYouth charity providing youth services. Former teacher. Married, two sons. Ed: University of Newcastle (BSc botany). **Martyn Davis** (Lab) Education consultant. Former cllr. Member, GMB. **Darrin Green** (Green) Social worker and care manager, West Sussex CC.

CONSTITUENCY PROFILE
A very safe Conservative seat in the north eastern part of West Sussex, held by the party under various boundary permutations since 1880. The Labour candidate in 2005 was Rehman Chishti, who defected to the Conservatives shortly afterwards and was elected as the Tory MP for Gillingham at the 2010 election. Said to be the birthplace of poet Shelley.

	Electorate	Turnout %	from 2010 %	Change
	78,181	72.8		
J Quin C	32,627	57.3	+4.6	
R Arthur Ukip	7,969	14.0	+8.9	
M Millson LD	6,647	11.7	-20.5	
M Davis Lab	6,499	11.4	+3.9	
D Green Green	2,198	3.9	+2.8	
J Smith S New	375	0.7		
J Duggan Peace	307	0.5		
J Rae Ind	303	0.5	+0.4	

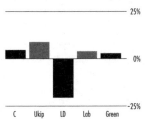

Change from 2010

C Ukip LD Lab Green

Houghton & Sunderland South

LABOUR HOLD

BRIDGET PHILLIPSON
BORN Dec 19, 1983
MP 2010-

Interested in housing, transport, family and Armed Forces. Opp whip 2013-. Select cttees: electoral commission 2010-; home affairs 2010-13. Member, Labour party national policy forum. Formerly women's refuge manager, Wearside Women in Need. Worked on regeneration projects for Sunderland CC. Member, GMB, Co-operative party. Married. Ed: St Robert of Newminster Sch, Washington; Hertford Coll, Oxford (BA history; chairwoman, OULC).

CHALLENGERS
Richard Elvin (Ukip) Runs own travel business, former teacher. Chairman, Ukip Wearside branch. Second place in both Middlesborough 2012 and South Shields 2013 by-elections. Ed: Northern Counties Coll, Newcastle. **Stewart Hay** (C)

Solicitor and former detective inspector. Contested Northumbria PCC election. Ed: Northumbria University. Father of one. **Alan Robinson** (Green) Teacher. Married, two children. **Jim Murray** (LD) Senior partner, James Murray Solicitors. Cllr, Sefton MBC 2004-08. Contested Bootle 2010. Former social worker. Two sons. Ed: Leeds (BSc maths & chemistry); Nottingham (LLM law).

CONSTITUENCY PROFILE
The seat underwent substantial changes in the 2010 boundary review, swapping the eastern part of Washington for part of the dismembered Sunderland South seat. On old and new boundaries it is solidly Labour and, with various other boundaries, the Houghton seat has been held by Labour since 1935. Has undergone significant social and economic changes over the past 20 years, with the rise of the service sector. Home to the 125-acre Doxford International Business park.

	Electorate	Turnout %	from 2010 %	Change
	68,316	56.3		
B Phillipson Lab	21,218	55.1	+4.8	
R Elvin Ukip	8,280	21.5	+18.8	
S Hay C	7,105	18.5	-3.0	
A Robinson Green	1,095	2.8		
J Murray LD	791	2.1	-11.9	

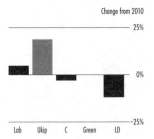

Change from 2010

Lab Ukip C Green LD

Hove

LABOUR GAIN

PETER KYLE
BORN Sep 9, 1970
MP 2015-

Chief executive of Working for Youth, a charity aiming to tackle youth unemployment. Regained this marginal seat for Labour after the sitting Tory MP Michael Weatherley stepped down. Member, LGBT Labour. Former trustee, Pride. Former adviser to Cabinet Office on social exclusion. Aid worker in 1990s. Ed: Sussex (BA human geography & international development; DPhil community economic development).

CHALLENGERS
Graham Cox (C) Former detective chief superintendent, Sussex CID. Cllr, Brighton & Hove CC 2011-15. Interest in transport (opp spokes on council), anti-social behaviour, local infrastructure. Member, Sussex CCC. Former sales assistant: BHS, Co-Op, Debenhams. Enjoys

cycling. Ed: St Andrew's Secondary Modern, Worthing. **Christopher Hawtree** (Green) Freelance writer. Cllr, Brighton & Hove CC 2011-2015. Campaigned successfully to keep open Hove library. **Kevin Smith** (Ukip) Retired partner in car dealership. Former motor mechanic, salesman and sales and marketing dir for a BMW dealership. Born in India. Married, three children. **Peter Lambell** (LD) Self-employed business analyst. Cllr, Surrey CC 2009-13. Married.

CONSTITUENCY PROFILE
With its reputation as a genteel retirement town, Hove was one of the more surprising Labour gains in its 1997 landslide.In the Seventies and Eighties the seat had been a Tory stronghold. Nick Boles narrowly failed to win it back for the Conservatives it in 2005. It finally returned to Tory control in 2010 only to revert to Labour in 2015. It is the weakest of the three Brighton & Hove seats for the Green party.

	Electorate	Turnout %	from 2010 %	Change
	73,505	71.0		
P Kyle Lab	22,082	42.3	+9.3	
G Cox C	20,846	39.9	+3.2	
C Hawtree Green	3,569	6.8	+1.7	
K Smith Ukip	3,265	6.3	+3.8	
P Lambell LD	1,861	3.6	-19.0	
J Barnard-Langston Ind	322	0.6	+0.5	
D Hill TUSC	144	0.3		
D Dixon Loony	125	0.2		

Change from 2010

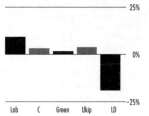

Huddersfield

LABOUR CO-OPERATIVE HOLD

BARRY SHEERMAN
BORN Aug 17, 1940
MP 1979-

Blairite, unlikely leader of attempts to overthrow Gordon Brown in 2009. Knowledgeable on education policy, well-connected charity entrepreneur. Leads Labour's Schools to Work Commission. Chairman, select cttees: children, schools & families 2007-10, education & skills 2001-07. Opp spokes: disabled people's rights 1992-94; home affairs 1988-92; education & employment 1983-88. MP Huddersfield East 1979-83. Former lecturer. AUT, Amicus. Married, three daughters, one son. Ed: Hampton GS; Kingston Tech College; LSE (BSc economics); University of London (MSc political sociology).

CHALLENGERS
Itrat Ali (C) Background in pharmaceutical industry, now working with local clinical

commissioning groups and hospitals in protocol setting. Member, Yorkshire Con Policy Forum. Chair, Yorkshire & Humber Con Muslim Forum. Contested Makerfield 2010. Married, two daughters. Ed: Loughborough (BSc medicinal & pharmaceutical chemistry). **Rob Butler** (Ukip) Head of science, Manchester comprehensive. Involved in national curriculum science review. Ed: Huddersfield (PgDip teaching & learning). **Andrew Cooper** (Green) Develops sustainable energy projects. Cllr, Kirklees BC 1999-. **Zulfiqar Ali** (LD) Businessman.Mayor of Rochdale, 2010. Cllr, Rochdale BC 1998-12.

CONSTITUENCY PROFILE
The town of Huddersfield was built around the wool industry and retains its working-class roots. There is a high proportion of social housing and unemployment, but there is a strong education sector. Labour has held the seat since its creation in 1950.

	Electorate	Turnout %	from 2010 %	Change
	65,265	62.0		
B Sheerman Lab Co-op	18,186	44.9	+6.1	
I Ali C	10,841	26.8	-1.0	
R Butler Ukip	5,948	14.7		
A Cooper Green	2,798	6.9	+2.9	
Z Ali LD	2,365	5.8	-18.9	
M Forster TUSC	340	0.8	+0.1	

Change from 2010

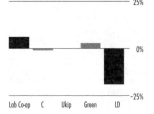

Hull East

LABOUR HOLD

KARL TURNER
BORN April 15, 1971
MP 2010-

Took over the seat from the former deputy prime minister John Prescott, a friend of his father, a councillor, and beat Prescott's own son in the selection process. Involved with John Prescott "East Hull pride" campaign. Shad solicitor-general 2014-. Opp assistant whip 2013-. Select cttees: home affairs 2012-13; justice 2010-13. Barrister: Wilberforce Chambers; Max Gold Solicitors. Took A levels and degree as mature student having been self-employed antiques seller on leaving school. Rugby player. Ed: Biggin Hill Junior HS; Bransholme HS; Hull Coll; University of Hull (LLB law).

CHALLENGERS
Richard Barrett (Ukip) Cllr, Hull CC 2014-, ousting long-serving Labour councillor and former Lord

Mayor David Gemmell. **Christine Mackay** (C) Medical & scientific liaison manager for pharmaceutical company. Chairwoman, Burundi orphanage charity. Two children. Ed: Hull (BSc health studies; MEd education; LDP systems thinking; MBA.) **David Nolan** (LD) Runs own market research business. Cllr, Hessle TC 2013-; Former cllr, East Riding C.

CONSTITUENCY PROFILE
At a parliamentary level Hull East is solidly Labour and has returned a Labour MP since 1935. At a local level Labour's long dominance was briefly broken between 2000 and 2011 with a period of no overall control before the Lib Dems took control from 2007 until 2011, when Labour won it back. The seat includes Hull's vast working docks on the Humber estuary and the redeveloped residential Victoria Docks. Away from the dockside developments the seat is largely working class with a high proportion of council housing.

	Electorate	Turnout %	Change from 2010 %
	65,606	53.6	
K Turner Lab	18,180	51.7	+3.8
R Barrett Ukip	7,861	22.4	+14.3
C Mackay C	5,593	15.9	-0.7
D Nolan LD	2,294	6.5	-16.3
S Walpole Green	806	2.3	
M Clayton Yorks	270	0.8	
M Cooper NF	86	0.2	-2.3
V Hoodless Soc Dem	54	0.2	

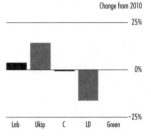

Change from 2010

Lab   Ukip   C   LD   Green

Hull North

LABOUR HOLD

DIANA JOHNSON
BORN Jul 25, 1966
MP 2005-

Shad min, Home Office 2010-; health 2010. Parly under-sec: children, schools & families 2009-10. Assistant gov whip 2007-09. PPS to Stephen Timms 2005-07. Cllr, Tower Hamlets BC 1994-2002. Member, London Assembly, GLA, 2003-04. Former barrister specialising in employment, immigration and education. Legal member, Mental Health Act Commission. Previously volunteer/locum lawyer, Tower Hamlets Law Centre and other community law centres. National officer FDA trade union. TGWU, Unison. Ed: Northwich County GS; Sir John Deans Coll, Cheshire; Queen Mary, London (LLB law).

CHALLENGERS
Sergi Singh (Ukip) Shopkeeper. Vice-chairman, Ukip Yorkshire and North Lincolnshire branch.

Dehenna Davison (C) Student, British politics & legislative studies, University of Hull. Former president Hull University Conservative Future. Member, North Hull Conservatives Exec. **Mike Ross** (LD) Cllr, Hull CC 2002-. Contested Hull West & Hessle 2010. Leader, Lib Dem group on the Council. Married, one child. Ed: Hull (BA politics). **Martin Deane** (Green) Teacher. Chairman, Hull & East Riding Green party. Director, City of Hull & Humber environment forum. Contested Hull North 2010, 2005. Ed: Hull (MSc psychology).

CONSTITUENCY PROFILE
While Labour won Hull North by only a whisker in 2010, it has historically been a safe Labour seat, held since 1964 (between 1974 and 1983 it was called Hull Central). Mostly a working-class area. The seat covers the northern part of Hull, which has huge deprived council estates, and the University of Hull campus.

	Electorate	Turnout %	Change from 2010 %
	63,650	55.5	
D Johnson Lab	18,661	52.8	+13.6
S Singh Ukip	5,762	16.3	+12.2
D Davison C	5,306	15.0	+1.9
M Ross LD	3,175	9.0	-28.3
M Deane Green	2,066	5.9	+4.4
V Butler Yorks	366	1.0	

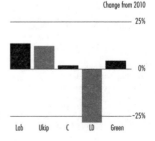

Change from 2010

Lab   Ukip   C   LD   Green

Hull West & Hessle

LABOUR HOLD

ALAN JOHNSON
BORN May 17, 1950
MP 1997-

Genial ex-postman once mooted as a replacement for Ed Miliband as Labour leader. Author of popular memoirs. Shad chancellor 2010-11, stood down on personal grounds. Home sec 2009-10. SoS: health 2007-09; education & skills 2006-07; trade & industry 2005-06; work & pensions 2004-05. Min: education & skills 2003-04; trade & industry 2001-03. Parly under-sec: trade & industry 1999-2001. PPS to Dawn Primarolo 1997-99. Labour party NEC member 1995-97. Postman. TUC general council member. General sec, CWU. Divorced twice, two daughters, two sons. Ed: Sloane GS, Chelsea.

CHALLENGERS
Paul Salvidge (Ukip) Commercial manager. Former cllr (Lab), Hull CC. Chairman, Ukip Hull & Hessle branch. Ed: Hull GS;

Central London Poly (law); Hull (MA European Union, policies & politics; MBA). **Jo Barker** (C) Last-minute candidate as previous Tory PPC defected to Ukip. Managing director, commercial property firm. Contested Birmingham Hall Green 2010. Ed: Liverpool (BSc geography). **Claire Thomas** (LD) Previously worked in manufacturing company, and as university lecturer. Cllr, Hull CC 2008-. Ed: Sheffield (BA English language with linguistics); Exeter (MA international relations); Hull (PhD international politics).

CONSTITUENCY PROFILE
As with the other Hull seats, this is safely Labour. The seat covers the city centre of Hull itself, much of the docks and the working class neighbourhoods of western Hull. Hessle lies to the west of the city and is a former shipbuilding town. The Yorkshire end of the Humber Bridge sits in this seat. The main employer is the KCOM Group. KC Stadium is also based here.

	Electorate	Turnout %	Change from 2010 %
	59,008	53.9	
A Johnson Lab	15,646	49.2	+6.7
P Salvidge Ukip	6,313	19.9	+14.5
J Barker C	5,561	17.5	-2.7
C Thomas LD	3,169	10.0	-14.3
A Needham Green	943	3.0	
P Spooner TUSC	171	0.5	+0.1

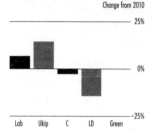

Change from 2010

Lab Ukip C LD Green

Huntingdon

CONSERVATIVE GAIN

JONATHAN DJANOGLY
BORN Jun 3, 1965
MP 2001-

Wealthy son of multimillionaire textile magnate and philanthropist, Sir Harry. Parly under-sec, justice 2010-12. Shadow solicitor-general 2005-10. Shad min: business 2005-10; home affairs 2004-05. Select cttees: trade and industry 2001-05; statutory instruments 2001-02. Cllr, Westminster CC 1994-2001. Solicitor, partner SJ Berwin LLP. Ran mail order retail business with wife. Married, one daughter, one son. Ed: University Coll Sch; Oxford Poly (BA law and politics); Coll of Law, Guildford.

CHALLENGERS
Dr Nik Johnson (Lab) Consultant paediatrician, Hinchingbrooke Hospital. Ed: Dame Allan's, Newcastle. **Paul Bullen** (Ukip) Managing director of boating company. Former RAF officer; aeronautical engineer, pilot and

marine surveyor. Contested Cambridgeshire PCC election 2012. Cllr, Cambridgeshire CC 2013-; Ukip group leader. **Rod Cantrill** (LD) Financial adviser. Managing director, Millington Advisory Partners. Cllr, Cambridge CC 2004-. Married, two children. Ed: St Catharine's Coll, Cambridge (BA architecture). **Tom MacLennan** (Green) Teacher. Former clinical scientist, Barts & London NHS Trust. Married, two children. Ed: University of Kent (BSc molecular & cellular biology).

CONSTITUENCY PROFILE
A solid Conservative seat. Under its previous MP, the former prime minister John Major, it was sometimes the safest Tory seat in the country. It is made up of four historic market towns and the surrounding villages in the west of Cambridgeshire, all affluent, economically successful and growing. The seat contains RAF Brampton and the US Air Force base at RAF Alconbury.

	Electorate	Turnout %	Change from 2010 %
	82,404	67.9	
J Djanogly C	29,652	53.0	+4.2
N Johnson Lab	10,248	18.3	+7.3
P Bullen Ukip	9,473	16.9	+10.9
R Cantrill LD	4,375	7.8	-21.1
T MacLennan Green	2,178	3.9	+2.7

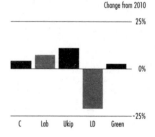

Change from 2010

C Lab Ukip LD Green

Hyndburn

LABOUR HOLD

GRAHAM JONES
BORN Mar 3, 1966
MP 2010-

Opp asst whip 2010-. Cllr: Hyndburn BC 2002-10, Labour leader 2006-10; Lancashire CC 2009-10. Former: graphic designer, specialising in prepress; lecturer in prepress. Worked for Blackburn and Darwen C on refuse collection, and Lancashire CC as a carer home assist. Partner, one son, one daughter. Ed: St Christopher's CofE HS, Accrington; Accrington and Rossendale Coll; UCLan (BA applied social studies).

CHALLENGERS
Kevin Horkin (C) Businessman - opticians and country-wear stores. Cllr: Ribble Valley BC 2011-15; Clitheroe TC 2011-; Hyndburn BC 1985-89. Mayor of Clitheroe 2013-14. Chairman, Ribble Valley Community Safety Partnership. Ed: Holy Family Catholic Coll, Accrington. **Janet Brown** (Ukip)

Manager, Slimming World. **Kerry Gormley** (Green) Creative Director at crafts organisation. Former art director at national newspapers. District leader of local SGI-UK. Contested Hyndburn 2010. Three children. **Alison Firth** (LD) Development officer, University of Manchester, focusing on engaging with schools. Cllr, Manchester CC 1984-2011. Lord Mayor of Manchester 2009-10. Former teacher. Contested: Wythenshawe & Sale East 2005; Sheffield Brightside 2001.

CONSTITUENCY PROFILE
A collection of small former textile towns, with much owner-occupied terraced housing. Historically this has been a Labour-leaning marginal between the Tories and Labour. Its predecessor Accrington was held continuously by Labour from 1945 to 1983. In 1983 Hyndburn was won by the Tories by just 21 votes and it was retained until Labour took it back in the 1992 election.

	Electorate	Turnout %	Change from 2010 %
	68,341	62.8	
G Jones Lab	18,076	42.2	+1.1
K Horkin C	13,676	31.9	-2.0
J Brown Ukip	9,154	21.3	+17.9
K Gormley Green	1,122	2.6	+1.5
A Firth LD	859	2.0	-9.8

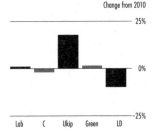

Change from 2010

Ilford North

LABOUR GAIN

WES STREETING
BORN Jan 21, 1983
MP 2015-

Ousted Lee Scott MP by 589 votes overturning a majority of 5,400 in 2010. Long standing Labour and LGBT campaigner. National pres of NUS 2008-10, photographed in 2010 with multiple Lib Dem MPs pledging no rise to tuition fees. Cllr, Redbridge BC 2010-, dep leader 2014-. Former head of education, Stonewall (led Education for All campaign to tackle homophobia in schools). Head of policy and strategic comms, Oona King's bid for 2012 London mayor. Previously public sector consultant, PwC. Ed: Westminster Sch; Selwyn Coll, Cambridge (BA history; pres, SU).

CHALLENGERS
Lee Scott (C) MP 2005-15. Chairman, regulatory reform select cttee 2014-. PPS to Chris Grayling 2012-14. Cllr, Redbridge BC 1998-. Formerly: dir, Scott & Fishell; sales

executive for companies including Toshiba. Married, three daughters, two sons. Ed: Clarke's Coll, Ilford; London Coll of Distributive Trades. **Philip Hyde** (Ukip) Runs own horticulture company; former City trader. Cllr, Havering LB 2014-. **Richard Clare** (LD) Environmental health officer, Festival Republic. Former chairman, Yorkshire & Humber Lib youth. Former intern to MP Norman Baker. Ed: Sheffield Hallam (BSc biology).

CONSTITUENCY PROFILE
Ilford North is mostly made up of semi-detached, lower middle class suburban housing, popular with London commuters. Typically Conservative territory, Labour's strength drawn most notably from the Hainault council estate. Won by Labour in 1997, having been heavily adjusted in the boundary changes, but fell to the Tories again in 2005. Having been one of the most ethnically diverse seats to return a Conservative MP, it returned to Labour in 2015.

	Electorate	Turnout %	Change from 2010 %
	78,162	62.6	
W Streeting Lab	21,463	43.9	+9.6
L Scott C	20,874	42.7	-3.1
P Hyde Ukip	4,355	8.9	+7.1
R Clare LD	1,130	2.3	-10.4
D Reynolds Green	1,023	2.1	+0.9
D Osen Ind	87	0.2	

Change from 2010

Ilford South

LABOUR CO-OPERATIVE HOLD

MIKE GAPES
BORN Sep 4, 1952
MP 1992-

Select cttees: foreign affairs (chairman) 2005-; arms export controls 2008-; national security strategy 2010; liaison 2005-10; defence 2003-05. PPS to: Lord Rooker 2001-02; Paul Murphy 1997-99. Member, Labour party national policy forum 1996-2005. Chairman, Co-op party parly group 2000-01. Member, Nato parlimentary assembly 2002-05. Worked at Labour party HQ for 15 years, international sec 1989-92. Contested Ilford North 1983. Union official. TGWU member. Divorced, one daughter, two stepdaughters. Ed: Buckhurst County HS; Fitzwilliam Coll, Cambridge (MA economics; sec, SU); Middlesex Poly (Dip industrial relations).

CHALLENGERS
Christopher Chapman (C)
Content development manager at

Marketing Week and Econsultancy. Cllr: Tower Hamlets BC 2014-; Runnymede BC 2008-12. Ed: Royal Holloway (BA politics & international relations). **Amjad Khan** (Ukip) Commodity trader. **RoseMary Warrington** (Green) Former business analyst and IT consultant. Community volunteer. Sec, London Green party. Ed: Queen Mary Coll, University of London (BSc mathematics). **Ashburn Holder** (LD) Runs own electronics business. Former financial consultant. Co-opted member, Redbridge council's external scrutiny panel.

CONSTITUENCY PROFILE
Ilford South was used to be a marginal and a good bellwether seat. From 1951 to 2005 it was won by the party that formed the government in every election except 1992, when it was narrowly gained by Labour. Demographic changes and the Tories' difficulties in appealing to ethnic minorities have made it a safe Labour seat.

	Electorate	Turnout %	Change from 2010 %
	95,023	54.6	
M Gapes Lab Co-op	33,232	64.0	+14.6
C Chapman C	13,455	25.9	-1.5
A Khan Ukip	2,705	5.2	+3.0
R Warrington Green	1,506	2.9	+0.3
A Holder LD	1,014	2.0	-15.0

Change from 2010

25%

0%

-25%

Lab Co-op   C   Ukip   Green   LD

Inverclyde

SNP GAIN

RONNIE COWAN
BORN Sep 6, 1959
MP 2015-

IT consultant, ran his own IT company. Founded Yes Inverclyde independence organisation. Supported SNP since age of 16. Member, Greenock Wanderers. Morton fan. Father was James "Jimmy" Clews Cowan, a Scottish footballer. Three children.

CHALLENGERS
Iain McKenzie (Lab) MP 2011-15, elected in by-election after death of David Cairns. Sacked as PPS to shadow defence secretary Vernon Coaker after voting against airstrikes in Iraq. Select cttees: Scottish affairs 2015-, 2011-13; efra 2012-. Cllr, Inverclyde C 2003-2011, leader 2011. Career as technician and large enterprise procurement officer at IBM and Wise Group. Married, two sons. Ed: Greenock HS; James Watt Coll. **George Jabbour** (C) Raised

in Syria before heading to Imperial College on scholarship. Named as one of the 40 under-40 rising stars by Financial News; worked as investment banker, Goldman Sachs. Ed: Damascus University (civil engineering); Imperial Coll London (MSc finance); The Lebanese University (law). **John Watson** (LD) Retired planner and urban regeneration consultant. Married.

CONSTITUENCY PROFILE
Until 2015 considered an extremely safe Labour seat. It had been represented by the party since 1936, with a brief break in 1981 when Dickson Mabon defected to the SDP. David Cairns, a former Catholic priest, was MP from 2001 until his death in 2011. His selection as Labour candidate required a change in the law to allow him to stand, as at the time the House of Commons Clergy Disqualification Act and Catholic Relief Act still barred former priests from sitting in the Commons.

	Electorate	Turnout %	Change from 2010 %
	59,350	75.2	
R Cowan SNP	24,585	55.1	+37.6
I McKenzie Lab	13,522	30.3	-25.7
G Jabbour C	4,446	10.0	-2.0
J Watson LD	1,106	2.5	-10.9
M Burrows Ukip	715	1.6	+0.5
C Hamilton CSA	233	0.5	

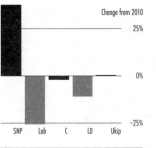

Change from 2010

25%

0%

-25%

SNP   Lab   C   LD   Ukip

Inverness, Nairn, Badenoch & Strathspey

SNP GAIN

DREW HENDRY
BORN May 31, 1964
MP 2015-

SNP group leader, transport 2015-. Background in retail, manufacturing and new technology. Cllr, Highland C 2007-, leader 2012-, leader SNP group 2011-, SNP group spokes for development & enterprise. SNP Cosla leader. Founded Inverness-based digital marketing company, Teclan Ltd, first private sector company in Inverness to commit to paying living wage. Former director with a multinational appliance manufacturer. Honorary consul to Romania in Inverness. Married, four children. Ed: Grove Academy, Dundee; Dundee and Angus Coll.

CHALLENGERS
Danny Alexander (LD) Key Lib Dem strategist, chief of staff to Nick Clegg 2007-10 and his right-hand man in coalition. MP, INBS 2005-15. SoS Scotland 2010; Chief sec to Treasury 2010-15.

LD shad SoS: W&P 2007-08; whip 2006-07. LD spokes work & pensions 2005-07. Head of comms: Cairngorms Nat Park; Britain in Europe. Dep dir, European Movement. Press officer, Scottish Lib Dems. Married, two daughters. Ed: Lochaber HS; Fort William; St Anne's Coll, Oxford (BA PPE). **Mike Robb** (Lab) IT consultancy owner. Contested INBS 2010. Married, two sons. Ed: Edinburgh (BSc physics). **Edward Mountain** (C) Farmer, surveyor and businessman. Chairman, Highland Conservatives. Contested Caithness Sutherland & Ross SP 2011. Ed: Royal Agricultural University (BSc rural land management); Sparsholt Coll (Dip farm management).

CONSTITUENCY PROFILE
Held by Danny Alexander since its creation in 2005; unseated in 2015 by SNP with 10,000 majority. One of the largest constituencies in the UK. Tourism is a key industry, employing a third of the workforce in hotels and restaurants.

	Electorate	Turnout %	from 2010 %	Change
	77,268	74.6		
D Hendry SNP	28,838	50.1	+31.4	
D Alexander LD	18,029	31.3	-9.4	
M Robb Lab	4,311	7.5	-14.6	
E Mountain C	3,410	5.9	-7.4	
I O'Reilly Green	1,367	2.4	+0.7	
L Durance Ukip	1,236	2.2	+0.9	
D Boyd SCP	422	0.7		

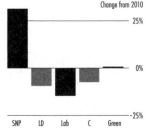

Change from 2010

SNP LD Lab C Green

Ipswich

CONSERVATIVE HOLD

BEN GUMMER
BORN Feb 19, 1978
MP 2010-

Steady riser in party. Parly under-sec for care quality 2015-. Entered parliament as his father, John Gummer, former Cabinet minister, left. Campaigned on services at Ipswich hospital. PPS to: Nicky Morgan 2014-; Michael Gove 2013-14; Alan Duncan 2012-13; Andrew Feldman 2012. Select cttees: justice 2010-12; regulatory reform 2010-12. Worked for Sancroft, his father's corporate responsibility consultancy. Ran small engineering firm. Author of book about the black death, *The Scourging Angel.* Married, one son. Ed: Peterhouse Coll, Cambridge (BA history).

CHALLENGERS
David Ellesmere (Lab) Cllr, Ipswich BC 1995-, leader 2011-. Software developer specialising in marketing automation services, HTK Ltd. Partner. Ed: Sussex

(BSc artificial intelligence). **Maria Vigneau** (Ukip) Former PR director, Roche pharmaceuticals. Ed: Nottingham (BA archaeology & ancient history). **Barry Broom** (Green) Self-employed software developer. **Chika Akinwale** (LD) Motivational writer and speaker. Founder and director, Cambridge Leadership Academy. Two children. Ed: Sheffield Hallam (BSc pharmaceutical sciences).

CONSTITUENCY PROFILE
The seat is drawn tightly around urban Ipswich, a working port which has seen significant redevelopment in recent decades. Big employers include the Environment Agency and insurance firm AXA, which has a call centre here. A marginal that has changed hands many times. The most Labour inclined seat in Suffolk, it has been mainly held by the party since 1945, with periods of Conservative representation in 1970-1974, 1987-1992 and then again since 2010.

	Electorate	Turnout %	from 2010 %	Change
	74,498	65.4		
B Gummer C	21,794	44.8	+5.6	
D Ellesmere Lab	18,061	37.1	+2.4	
M Vigneau Ukip	5,703	11.7	+8.8	
B Broom Green	1,736	3.6	+1.9	
C Akinwale LD	1,400	2.9	-15.4	

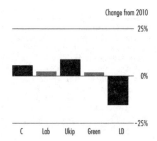

Change from 2010

C Lab Ukip Green LD

Isle of Wight

CONSERVATIVE HOLD

ANDREW TURNER
BORN Oct 24, 1953
MP 2001-

Right-winger. Select cttees: public admin 2013-; political & constitutional reform 2010-; panel of chairs 2010-; justice 2008-10; education & skills 2001-05. 1922 executive cttee, 2006-12, 2001-03. Vice-chairman, Con party 2003-05. Shad min, Cabinet Office 2005-06. Cllr, Oxford CC 1979-96. Sheriff of Oxford 1994-95. Contested: Isle of Wight 1997; Hackney South & Shoreditch 1992. Formerly: education consultant; dir, Grant-Maintained Schs Foundation; special adviser, SoS for Social Services; Con researcher; teacher. Ed: Rugby Sch; Keble Coll, Oxford (BA geography; MA geography); University of Birmingham (PGCE); Henley Management Coll.

CHALLENGERS
Iain Mckie (Ukip) Portfolio manger, BH funds. Former head of emissions trading, Bank of America Merill Lynch. **Vix Lowthion** (Green) Geology lecturer. Studying BSc Geology, Energy & Sustainability at Open University. Ed: York (BA history). **Stewart Blackmore** (Lab) MD, Ventnor Gold Club. Hospitality and tourism professional. **David Goodall** (LD) Project manager for intl research and devt company. Cllr: West End PC 2011-; Eastleigh BC 2002-15. Ed: Portsmouth Poly (BSc electrical engineering).

CONSTITUENCY PROFILE
By far the largest electorate of any seat in the UK, just short of the default size where an extra seat has to be added under the fifth boundary review. The economy is largely based on tourism and, with a large number of seaside resorts, a quarter of the population are pensioners. The Cowes Week regatta is popular. Traditionally a battleground between the Tories and Lib Dems, but has been a Tory hold since 2001.

	Electorate	Turnout %	Change from 2010 %
	108,804	64.6	
A Turner C	28,591	40.7	-6.0
I McKie Ukip	14,888	21.2	+17.7
V Lowthion Green	9,404	13.4	+12.1
S Blackmore Lab	8,984	12.8	+1.2
D Goodall LD	5,235	7.5	-24.3
I Stephens Ind	3,198	4.6	+4.5

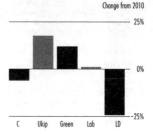

Change from 2010

Islington North

LABOUR HOLD

JEREMY CORBYN
BORN May 26, 1949
MP 1983-

Archetypal bearded 1980s left-wing rebel. Refusal to send son to grammar school contributed to marriage breakdown. Socialist Campaign group member. Threw hat into ring of Labour leadership race, 2015. Select cttees: justice 2011-; London regional 2009-10; social security 1991-97. APPG: on a raft of groups including Chagos Islands (chairman); Mexico (chairman); Bolivia; Britain-Palestine. Cllr, Haringey BC 1974-84. Former: NUPE full-time organiser. Member, Unison. Married, separated. Three sons. Ed: Adams GS, Newport.

CHALLENGERS
Alex Burghart (C) Policy dir, Centre for Social Justice. Former: policy adviser, DfE; adviser, Tim Loughton MP; researcher and lecturer, King's College London. Ed: Christ Church, Oxford (BA MSt history); King's Coll, London (PhD modern history). **Caroline Russell** (Green) Transport campaigner. Green spokes, local transport. Cllr, Islington BC 2014-. Former lecturer. Married, three children. Ed: Goldsmiths, London (MA fine art); City University, London (BEng civil engineering). **Julian Gregory** (LD) Barrister at Monckton Chambers. Married. Ed: Clare Coll, Cambridge (LLB law); Brasenose Coll, New Coll, Oxford (BCL law; MPhil comparative government & political science).

CONSTITUENCY PROFILE
A compact, densely-populated seat in North London, the smallest in the country by area. Includes areas of gentrification but also deprived and crime-ridden parts of Islington. Safely Labour since the 1930s, though the sitting MP, Michael O'Halloran, defected to the SDP in 1981 and fought the seat as an independent in 1983, having lost the SDP selection.

	Electorate	Turnout %	Change from 2010 %
	73,325	67.1	
J Corbyn Lab	29,659	60.2	+5.8
A Burghart C	8,465	17.2	+3.0
C Russell Green	5,043	10.2	+7.2
J Gregory LD	3,984	8.1	-18.6
G Clough Ukip	1,971	4.0	+2.4
B Martin SPGB	112	0.2	

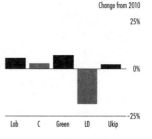

Change from 2010

Islington South & Finsbury

LABOUR HOLD

LABOUR HOLD

EMILY THORNBERRY
BORN Jul 27, 1960
MP 2005-

Respected rags-to-riches MP who resigned as shadow attorney-general (2011-2014) after "white van" tweet in Rochester & Strood campaign. Shad min: health 2010-11; energy and climate change 2010. PPS to Joan Ruddock 2009-10. Select cttees: environmental audit 2005-07; CLG 2006-09. Barrister, Michael Mansfield's Chambers; Tooks Court. Unite. Married, one daughter, two sons. Ed: CofE Secondary Modern, Guildford; Burlington Danes, Shepherd's Bush; University of Kent (BA law).

CHALLENGERS
Mark Lim (C) Doctor. NHS career: currently programme dir, urgent care; speciality registrar; senior house officer. Chairman, Islington Cons 2012-14. Ed: Cambridge (MB BCh medicine & surgery; MPhil public health). **Terry Stacy** (LD)

Cllr: Islington BC 2002-14, leader of opp 2010-13, leader 2008-10; Tower Hamlets BC 1998-2002. Dir, Housing Ombudsman Service. Tenant inspection adviser to Audit Commission. Lives in social housing. **Pete Muswell** (Ukip) IT consultant. Former telecoms engineer. Ed: Dame Alice Owen. **Charlie Kiss** (Green) Order compliance officer, Camden BC. Former printer. Ed: South Bank (BA business studies); Middlesex (MA international relations); Birkbeck, London (PgCert economics).

CONSTITUENCY PROFILE
A fashionable residential area lived in by Tony Blair before he became PM, and closely associated, for a time, with New Labour. Historically a safe Labour seat where Chris Smith (1983-2005) built a strong majority but after he retired it came under threat from the Lib Dems. However, in 2015, the Lib Dems lost 23.2 per cent of their vote share, putting them into third place.

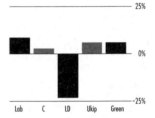

	Electorate	Turnout %	Change from 2010 %
	68,127	65.0	
E Thornberry Lab	22,547	50.9	+8.7
M Lim C	9,839	22.2	+2.8
T Stacy LD	4,829	10.9	-23.2
P Muswell Ukip	3,375	7.6	+6.0
C Kiss Green	3,371	7.6	+6.0
J Kirton CSA	309	0.7	

Change from 2010

Lab C LD Ukip Green

Islwyn

LABOUR CO-OPERATIVE HOLD

CHRIS EVANS
BORN Jul 7, 1976
MP 2010-

Parly researcher to previous MP Don Touhig before being selected for this safe seat to fight the 2010 election. PPS to: Chris Leslie 2013-15; Mary Creagh 2012-13. Select cttees: environmental audit 2012-14; justice 2010-12. Contested Cheltenham 2005. Official, Union of Finance Staff. Marketing exec, University of Glamorgan. Personal account manager, Lloyds TSB. Bookmaker. Unite, Fabian Society, Co-op party. Ed: Porth County CS; Pontypridd Coll; Trinity Coll, Carmarthen (BA history).

CHALLENGERS
Joe Smyth (Ukip) At present works in transport and logistics. Served in Royal Engineers: joined at 16 as Army apprentice; attached to 3 Para during Falklands dispute. Campaign manager, 2014 Euro elections Wales region. Chairman,

Ukip Swansea branch 2013-14. Partner, one daughter, two sons. **Laura Jones** (C) Welsh Assem mem for SE Wales 2003-07, as baby of the house. Cllr, Llanbadoc CC 2012-. Former owner of cleaning business. Married, one son. Ed: Plymouth (BA politics). **Lyn Ackerman** (PC) Cllr, Caerphilly CBC 1999-, chair, health social care & well-beings scrutiny cttee. **Brendan D'Cruz** (LD) Visiting lecturer, University of South Wales. Educational consultant. Ed: Plymouth (BSc computing & informatics; PhD); Northampton (PgDip teaching & learning; PgCert).

CONSTITUENCY PROFILE
A traditional former coal-mining seat in the Welsh valleys. Has a strong ruby tradition. Along with its predecessor Bedwellty, Islwyn has been continuously held by Labour since creation in 1918, most notably by former Labour leader Neil Kinnock, who represented it from 1970 to 1995.

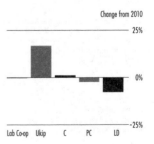

	Electorate	Turnout %	Change from 2010 %
	55,075	64.3	
C Evans Lab Co-op	17,336	49.0	-0.2
J Smyth Ukip	6,932	19.6	+16.9
L Jones C	5,366	15.2	+1.2
L Ackerman PC	3,794	10.7	-2.3
B D'Cruz LD	950	2.7	-7.7
P Varley Green	659	1.9	
B Von Magpie Loony	213	0.6	
J Rawcliffe TUSC	151	0.4	

Change from 2010

Lab Co-op Ukip C PC LD

Jarrow

LABOUR HOLD

STEPHEN HEPBURN
BORN Dec 6, 1959
MP 1997-

Football-loving Geordie, a loyal Labour footsoldier. Select cttees: administration 2009-10; Northern Ireland 2004-10; accommodation & works 2003-05; defence 1999-2001; administration 1997-2001. Cllr, South Tyneside MBC 1985-97, deputy leader 1990-97. APPG on shipbuilding (vice-chairman). President, Jarrow FC. Member, UCATT. Research asst to Don Dixon MP. Ed: Springfield CS, Jarrow; Newcastle University (BA politics).

CHALLENGERS
Steve Harrison (Ukip) Labour party member until 2003. Cllr, South Tyneside MBC 2013-14 Ukip; 2006-13 as independent. **Nick Mason** (C) Head of fundraising strategy, Royal National Institute for Blind People. Former banker. Cllr, North Dorset DC 2007-11.

Fellow, RSA. Ed: Marlborough Coll; Pembroke Coll, Oxford (BA PPE; pres, Oxford Union); Cass Business Sch (PgDip fundraising & strategic marketing); London Business Sch (MBA). **David Herbert** (Green) Retired health & safety adviser, construction industries. Former miner. Married, two daughters. **Stan Collins** (LD) IT and business systems consultant. Vice-pres, Lib Dems 2004-06. Member, Lake District National Park Authority. Cllr: Cumbria CC 2005-; South Lakeland DC 1979-. Member, Lib Dem Federal Policy cttee 2000-; Federal Executive 2001-13. Contested Westmorland 1997, 1992.

CONSTITUENCY PROFILE
The Jarrow hunger march of 1936, a protest over crushing unemployment in the town after the closure of the shipyard, was a landmark in the history of the Labour movement, and this has since been a safe Labour seat, often gaining majorities more than 40 per cent of the vote.

	Electorate	Turnout %	Change from 2010 %
	63,882	60.4	
S Hepburn Lab	21,464	55.7	+1.7
S Harrison Ukip	7,583	19.7	
N Mason C	6,584	17.1	-3.6
D Herbert Green	1,310	3.4	
S Collins LD	1,238	3.2	-15.3
N Hall TUSC	385	1.0	

Change from 2010

[bar chart: Lab, Ukip, C, Green, LD; axis 25%, 0%, -25%]

Keighley

CONSERVATIVE HOLD

KRIS HOPKINS
BORN Jun 8, 1963
MP 2010-

Vice-chamberlain (whip) 2015-; Parly under-sec: CLG 2013-. PPS to Andrew Robathan 2012-13. Member, NI Affairs select cttee 2011-12. Cllr, Bradford MDC 1998-2010, leader 2006-10, dep leader 2004-06. Contested: Halifax 2005, Leeds West 2001. Tory Reform group. Lecturer in media theory, communications and digital media. Former army private, Duke of Wellington's Regiment. Married, one daughter. Enjoys photography. Ed: Oakbank Sch, Keighley; University of Leeds (BA communications & cultural studies).

CHALLENGERS
John Grogan (Lab) MP for Selby 1997-2010. Chairman, Labour Yorkshire & Humber Devt Board. Contested: Selby 1992, 1987; York 1989. Former Lab party press

officer. Ed: St Michael's RC Coll, Leeds; St John's Coll, Oxford (BA history & economics; pres, OUSU). **Paul Latham** (Ukip) Management consultancy and business devt background. Organiser, Ukip West Yorkshire region. Ed: University of Leeds (MBA). **Ros Brown** (Green) Teacher. Completing doctorate at Cambridge. **Gareth Epps** (LD) Community relations policy manager. Cllr: Reading BC 2007-2011; Oxfordshire W DC 2000-2006. LD Fed Conference cttee. Ed: Manchester (BA modern languages; MA European politics & policy).

CONSTITUENCY PROFILE
A seat that covers the former textile town of Keighley and the prosperous Victorian spa town of Ilkley. To the south it includes villages such as Haworth, famed for its links to the Brontes. Keighley, which provides the bulk of Labour support, has had problems with racial tension and the seat was a BNP target in 2005.

	Electorate	Turnout %	Change from 2010 %
	68,865	71.3	
K Hopkins C	21,766	44.3	+2.4
J Grogan Lab	18,713	38.1	+2.3
P Latham Ukip	5,662	11.5	+8.4
R Brown Green	1,661	3.4	
G Epps LD	1,321	2.7	-12.1

Change from 2010

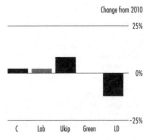

[bar chart: C, Lab, Ukip, Green, LD; axis 25%, 0%, -25%]

Kenilworth & Southam

CONSERVATIVE HOLD

JEREMY WRIGHT
BORN Oct 24, 1972
MP 2005-

Risen through ranks during Cameron premiership. Attorney-general 2014-; Parly under-sec: justice 2012-14. Govt whip 2010-12; opposition whip 2007-10. Member, constitutional affairs select cttee 2005-07. Chair, Warwick and Leamington Con Assoc 2002-03. MP for Rugby & Kenilworth 2005-10. Criminal law QC. Married, one son, one daughter. Enjoys golf. Ed: Taunton Sch, Somerset; Trinity Sch, New York; University of Exeter (LLB law); Inns of Court Sch (BVC).

CHALLENGERS
Bally Singh (Lab) Leadership and organisation specialist, NFU Mutual. Cllr, Coventry CC 2010-. Campaigned for Obama 2012. Married, one daughter. Ed: Coventry University (BA international relations & politics).

Harry Cottam (Ukip) Solicitor, own practice. Contested Stratford upon Avon 2005. **Richard Dickson** (LD) Director, Bucks Community Foundation. Previously development director, Cord peacebuilding charity. Married, three daughters. Ed: Aston (BSc managerial & administrative studies). **Rob Ballantyne** (Green) Runs bookkeeping and financial management practice. Married, two children. Ed: Newcastle (BA philosopy & politics).

CONSTITUENCY PROFILE
Kenilworth & Southam is a large seat taking in the rural commuter villages that lie between Rugby, Warwick and Coventry. Mostly rural. The largest town is Kenilworth, best known for its castle but now largely a suburban dormitory town for commuters to Coventry and Brimingham. The seat was created for 2010 and was easily won by the Conservatives, who confimed their dominance in 2015 with 58 per cent of the vote.

	Electorate	Turnout %	from 2010 %	Change
	65,245	74.8		
J Wright C	28,474	58.4	+4.8	
B Singh Lab	7,472	15.3	+1.0	
H Cottam Ukip	5,467	11.2	+8.7	
R Dickson LD	4,913	10.1	-17.6	
R Ballantyne Green	1,956	4.0	+2.8	
N Green Loony	370	0.8		
J Foster-Smith Digital	139	0.3		

Change from 2010

Kensington

CONSERVATIVE HOLD

VICTORIA BORWICK
BORN April 26, 1956
MP 2015-

Replaced Sir Malcolm Rifkind after he resigned in March 2015 in wake of cash-for-access allegations. Deputy mayor of London 2012-15; member, GLA 2008-. Cllr, Kensington & Chelsea BC 2002-, member, family & children's services scrutiny cttee 2009-. Failed to win Conservative nomination for mayor in 2004 and 2008. Member of advisory council, Open Europe. Governor, Royal Brompton & Harefield hospitals. Events management: director of events, P&O; director, Olympia Fine Art & Antiques Fair; DMG World Media. Married, three sons, one daughter. Ed: Wispers Sch, Midhurst.

CHALLENGERS
Rod Abouharb (Lab) Senior lecturer in International Relations, UCL. Married. Ed: Brunel (BSc

politics & modern history); Buffalo University (MA political science); Binghamton (PhD international relations). **Robin McGhee** (LD) Freelance journalist incl *Prospect*. Ed: St Anne's Coll, Oxford (BA history; captained team on *University Challenge*). **Robina Rose** (Green) Independent filmmaker; BBC Community Programme Unit. Former chairwoman, London branch CPRE.

CONSTITUENCY PROFILE
A well-to-do west London seat. Includes Earl's Court, South Kensington and Notting Hill. Solidly Conservative. Was originally created for the 1974 election but was abolished in 1997, and replaced by two seats: Regent's Park and Kensington North, which was won by Labour, and Kensington & Chelsea. The latter was held by a series of high profile Tory MPs: Alan Clark, Michael Portillo and Malcolm Rifkind, who took over the recreated Kensington seat at the 2010 general election.

	Electorate	Turnout %	from 2010 %	Change
	61,333	56.8		
V Borwick C	18,199	52.3	+2.2	
R Abouharb Lab	10,838	31.1	+5.6	
R McGhee LD	1,962	5.6	-13.9	
R Rose Green	1,765	5.1	+2.9	
J Bovill Ukip	1,557	4.5	+2.3	
T Auguste CSA	211	0.6		
A Knight AWP	158	0.5		
T Abse Green Soc	115	0.3	-0.2	
R Courtenay New IC	23	0.1		

Change from 2010

Kettering

CONSERVATIVE HOLD

PHILIP HOLLOBONE
BORN Nov 7, 1964
MP 2005-

Covets high rankings in theyworkforyou.com, based on number of speeches and questions. Right-wing, and supporter of backbench populist schemes. Proud of how little he claims in parliamentary expenses. Select cttees: panel of chairs 2010-; backbench business 2010-12; transport 2006-10. Cllr: Kettering BC 2003-; Bromley BC 1990-94. Deputy chairman, Kettering Con Assn 2002-11. Investment bank analyst. Served in TA. Divorced, one daughter, one son. Ed: Dulwich Coll; LMH, Oxford (BA history & economics).

CHALLENGERS
Rhea Keehn (Lab) Project manager, governance and communications, Volkswagen. Trustee, Care & Repair, charity that helps elderly stay in their homes.

Ed: University of Birmingham (BA social policy; pres, SU); BPP Law Sch (GDL). **Jonathan Bullock** (Ukip) Defected from Tories, 2012. Cllr, Kettering BC 2007-15, cabinet member 2007-12. Contested: EU East Midlands 2014, 2004; Gedling 2001; Manchester Gorton 1992. Former director of policy, Chartered Institute of Logistics & Transport. Ed: Portsmouth (BA politics). **Rob Reeves** (Green) Self-employed tutor. **Chris McGlynn** (LD) Facilities officer, Environment Agency. Contested Daventry 2010. Ed: Open University (BSc environmental sciences).

CONSTITUENCY PROFILE
A semi-rural seat in Northamptonshire with a thriving economy and low unemployment. Its location and transport links mean the town has branched from the shoe industry into service and distribution. Historically, a Tory-Labour marginal, but the Tories have held the seat since 2005 and their majority grew in 2015.

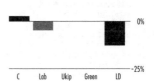

	Electorate	Turnout %	Change from 2010 %
	70,155	67.3	
P Hollobone C	24,467	51.8	+2.7
R Keehn Lab	11,877	25.2	-4.8
J Bullock Ukip	7,600	16.1	
R Reeves Green	1,633	3.5	
C McGlynn LD	1,490	3.2	-12.7
D Hilling Eng Dem	151	0.3	-1.7

Change from 2010

C   Lab   Ukip   Green   LD

Kilmarnock & Loudoun

SNP GAIN

ALAN BROWN
BORN Jun 21, 1970
MP 2015-

Principal engineer, Grontmij engineering consultancy. Cllr, East Ayrshire C 2007-; cabinet member; chairman, grants committee; spokes, housing and strategic planning. Trustee and director roles: Kilmarnock Leisure Centre; Irvine Valley Regeneration Partnership. Married, two sons. Enjoys camping. Ed: Loudoun Academy; University of Glasgow (BEng: civil engineering).

CHALLENGERS
Cathy Jamieson (Lab Co-op) MP, Kilmarnock & Loudoun 2010-15. Shad min: Treasury 2011-15. Hard-working and ultra-loyal reputation. MSP 1999-2011 (min: justice; education & young people; dep leader, Labour, Scottish parliament). Social worker. Principal officer, Who Cares? Scotland, advocacy

organisation for young people in residential care. Married, one son. Ed: Glasgow School of Art (BA fine art); Goldsmiths Coll (Dip art therapy); Glasgow (Dip social work); Glasgow Caledonian (Cert management). **Brian Whittle** (C) Athlete. Won gold medal in 4 x 400 metres relay at European athletics championships in 1994 and 1986, when he ran with one shoe after the other came off. Married, three daughters. **Rod Ackland** (LD) Retired IT specialist. Contested: Scottish parly Coatbridge & Chryston 2011; Cumbernauld, Kilsyth & Kirkintilloch East 2010.

CONSTITUENCY PROFILE
Former home to Johnnie Walker whisky until closed in 2012. Home to Scotland's first privately-run prison, HMP Kilmarnock. Labour had seen this as a safe seat since its creation in 1983, although the SNP had definitely been in second place for the past 20 years. To take the seat in 2015 the SNP achieved a 29.7 per cent increase in its vote.

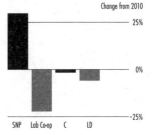

	Electorate	Turnout %	Change from 2010 %
	75,233	71.7	
A Brown SNP	30,000	55.7	+29.7
C Jamieson Lab Co-op	16,362	30.4	-22.2
B Whittle C	6,752	12.5	-1.6
R Ackland LD	789	1.5	-5.9

Change from 2010

SNP   Lab Co-op   C   LD

Kingston & Surbiton

CONSERVATIVE GAIN

CONSERVATIVE GAIN

JAMES BERRY
BORN Apr 8, 1983
MP 2015-

Barrister, Serjeants' Inn, specialising in healthcare and police issues. Acted for Surrey police in Leveson inquiry. Interested in education. Enjoys cooking. Married. Ed: UCL (LLB law); Harvard Law Sch (LLM law).

CHALLENGERS
Edward Davey (LD) MP, Kingston & Surbiton 1997-2015. SoS, energy and climate change 2012-15. Parly under-sec, BIS 2010-12. Chairman of LD's 2010 election campaign. LD shad SoS: foreign affairs 2007-10; trade & industry 2006; education & skills 2005-06; chief sec to treasury 2001-02. Chief of staff to Sir Menzies Campbell 2006-07. LD Whip 1997-2000. LD spokes: ODPM 2002-05; London 2000-03; economy 1999-2001; treasury 1997-99. Member, federal policy cttee. Management consultant. Married,

one son. Ed: Jesus Coll, Oxford (BA PPE); Birkbeck Coll, London (MSc economics). **Lee Godfrey** (Lab) Business director, energy consultancy. Served in the Royal Navy. Chairman, Surrey Libraries Action Movement. Ed: University of Lancaster (BSc operational research and operations management). **Ben Roberts** (Ukip) Works for recruitment firm specialising in education sector. Former teacher.

CONSTITUENCY PROFILE
An affluent seat in south-west London. Also covers Chessington, home to the World of Adventures theme park. Kingston is a major retail hub for the seat. Kingston University is a big local employer. The residential seat was created in 1997 and at the time was one of the most marginal in the country. Ed Davey went on to build up a robust majority for the Lib Dems but the nationwide backlash in 2015 saw him unseated by newcomer James Berry.

	Electorate	Turnout %	from 2010 % Change
	81,277	72.9	
J Berry C	23,249	39.2	+2.7
E Davey LD	20,415	34.5	-15.3
L Godfrey Lab	8,574	14.5	+5.1
B Roberts Ukip	4,321	7.3	+4.8
C Keogh Green	2,322	3.9	+3.0
D Gill CPA	198	0.3	-0.1
L Fogarty TUSC	174	0.3	

Change from 2010

25%

0%

-25%

C   LD   Lab   Ukip   Green

Kingswood

CONSERVATIVE HOLD

CONSERVATIVE HOLD

CHRIS SKIDMORE
BORN May 17, 1981
MP 2010-

Historian and author. Select cttees: education 2012-14; health 2010-13. APPG: green belt (chairman); history and archives (vice-chairman); disability. Former: chairman, Bow Group 2007-08; dir, Con public service improvement group (2007). Previously education adviser to Michael Gove and David Willetts. Honorary research fellow Bristol University. Achieved one of the highest swings of the 2010 election. Ed: Bristol GS; Christ Church Coll, Oxford (BA history; St Cyres and Dixon Scholar).

CHALLENGERS
Jo McCarron (Lab) Artist and community activist. Labour party southwest regional board 2013-.Led Response2route campaign against Bus Rapid Transit scheme through Newbridge, Bath. Campaigner of the Year in Pride in Bath awards.

Received £10,000 donation from Lord Oakshott. Married, two sons. Ed: Hanham High Comp Sch. University of Hertfordshire (BA fine art). **Duncan Odgers** (Ukip) Electrical engineer specialising in water projects. Dir, Cornwall-based MEICA Engineering. Ed: Nantwich Agricultural Coll; Bristol Polytechnic (HNC electrical & electronic engineering). **Adam Boyden** (LD) Environmental consultant. Cllr: Frome TC 2013-; Mendip DC 2011-. Ed: UEA (BSc environmental sciences); Oxford Brookes (MSc environmental assessment & management).

CONSTITUENCY PROFILE
A key Labour-Conservative marginal, covering the eastern suburbs of Bristol, which has regularly changed hands. It was won by Labour upon its creation in 1974, was Conservative in the years 1979-92, and was held by Labour throughout its period in government from 1997. It returned to the Conservatives in 2010.

	Electorate	Turnout %	from 2010 % Change
	67,992	70.8	
C Skidmore C	23,252	48.3	+7.9
J McCarron Lab	14,246	29.6	-5.7
D Odgers Ukip	7,133	14.8	+11.6
A Boyden LD	1,827	3.8	-13.1
C Nanu Green	1,370	2.9	+2.1
J Lake BNP	164	0.3	-2.4
R Worth TUSC	84	0.2	
L Bryan Vapers	49	0.1	

Change from 2010

25%

0%

-25%

C   Lab   Ukip   LD   Green

Kirkcaldy & Cowdenbeath

SNP GAIN

ROGER MULLIN
BORN Mar 12, 1948
MP 2015-

SNP spokesman, Treasury 2015-. Educational consultant. Previously owned social research company Inter-Ed, conducting organisation culture study assignments for UN; dir, Momentous Change educational services. Social sciences tutor: honorary professor, University of Stirling; Open University; University of Edinburgh. Columnist, *TES Scotland*. Former vice-convener and NEC member, SNP. Contested: Ayr 1999 Scottish parliament; Paisley North 1992, 1990 by-election; Kirkcaldy 1987; South Ayrshire Oct 1974, Feb 1974. Married, three daughters. Ed: Stow Coll, Glasgow (HNC electrical engineering); University of Edinburgh (MA sociology).

CHALLENGERS
Kenny Selbie (Lab Co-op) Equalities officer, West Lothian

council. Selected to replace retiring MP Gordon Brown, the former prime minister. Cllr, Fife C 2012-, portfolio holder for community safety. Former HR officer, Scottish prison service. Ed: Northumbria (BA politics & media relations); Fife Coll (CIPD PgCert HR management; CIPD Masters prof devt scheme). **Dave Dempsey** (C) Former software engineer. Cllr, Fife C 2007-, leader of Conservative group. Contested Cowdenbeath 2014 Scottish parliament by-election. Ed: Edinburgh (BSc mathematics). **Jack Neill** (Ukip) Studying criminal justice at the University of the West of Scotland. Ed: Inverkeithing HS.

CONSTITUENCY PROFILE
Kirkcaldy & Cowdenbeath, and its predecessor Dunfermline East, had traditionally been solidly Labour. The prime minister, Gordon Brown, had 65 per cent of the vote in 2010 compared with the SNP's 14 per cent; it was a primary seat Labour hoped to hold in 2015.

	Electorate	Turnout %	Change from 2010 %
	75,941	69.7	
R Mullin SNP	27,628	52.2	+37.9
K Selbie Lab Co-op	17,654	33.4	-31.2
D Dempsey C	5,223	9.9	+0.6
J Neill Ukip	1,237	2.3	+0.7
C Leslie LD	1,150	2.2	-7.2

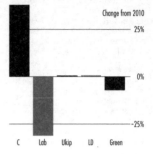

Change from 2010

C Lab Ukip LD Green

Knowsley

LABOUR HOLD

GEORGE HOWARTH
BORN June 29, 1949
MP 1986-

From Lab right. Parly under-sec: NI 1999-2001; home 1997-99. Opp spokes: home 1994-97; environment 1989-94. Select cttees: finance & services 2012-; panel of chairs 2009-; modernisation of HoC 2005-10; public accounts 2002-03. Cllr: Knowsley BC 1975-86 (dep leader 1982-83); Huyton DC 1971-75. MP for: Knowsley N 1986-97; Knowsley N & Sefton E 1997-2010. Teacher. Engineer. Chief exec Wales TUC sponsored co-op centre, Cardiff 1984-86. Married, one daughter, two sons. Ed: Huyton Secondary Sch; Kirkby Coll; Liverpool Poly (BA social sciences).

CHALLENGERS
Louise Bours (Ukip) MEP, NW region 2014-. Cllr (Con): Congleton BC 2004-09; Congleton TC 2003-15. Congleton town mayor

2006-07. National exec cttee, Ukip 2011-. Actress: TV shows and adverts; worked with D'Oyly Carte Opera Company. Ed: Mountview Conservatoire for the Performing Arts; Lancaster University (BA social science). **Alice Bramall** (C) Account manager, PPS group. Cllr, Milton Keynes C 2012-. Parly researcher to MP Mark Lancaster 2010-13. Ed: Durham (BA politics). **Carl Cashman** (LD) Studying philosophy & politics at University of Liverpool. Cllr, Prescot TC 2013-14. **Vikki Gregorich** (Green) Accountant for housing association.

CONSTITUENCY PROFILE
An area of run down council estates that is an extremely safe Labour seat. The local authority is uniformly Labour, and in Kirkby the party regularly has councillors returned unopposed, a rarity in metropolitan councils. In the 2000s some Lib Dem councillors were returned in Prescot but, by 2012, Labour held every council seat in the borough.

	Electorate	Turnout %	Change from 2010 %
	79,109	64.1	
G Howarth Lab	39,628	78.1	+7.3
L Bours Ukip	4,973	9.8	+7.2
A Bramall C	3,367	6.6	-2.3
C Cashman LD	1,490	2.9	-10.4
V Gregorich Green	1,270	2.5	

Change from 2010

Lab Ukip C LD Green

Lagan Valley

DUP HOLD

JEFFREY DONALDSON
BORN Dec 7, 1962
MP 1997-

Was member of UUP, known for his opposition to leader David Trimble, causing him to defect in 2003. He won the seat for the DUP in 2005 after a re-alignment of unionist politics in the area. DUP spokesman roles include: equality, ECC 2010-; defence 2007-; efra 2011-12; transport 2009-10, 2005-07; home 2007-10; int devt 2005-10; education 2004-05. MLA for Lagan Valley 2003-10. VP, Ulster Unionist Council 2000-03. Elected to NI Assembly at 22, serving 1985-86. Asst to James Molyneaux MP. Enoch Powell's constituency agent 1982-84. His cousin Samuel Donaldson was the first policeman to be murdered by the IRA in the Troubles. Former assistant grand master, Orange Order. Ulster Defence Regiment. Partner, financial services. Married, two daughters. Ed: Castlereagh Coll.

CHALLENGERS
Alexander Redpath (UUP) Solicitor, Herbert Smith Freehills. Cllr, Lisburn & Castlereagh CC 2014-, dep mayor 2015-. Chair, Young Unionists. Ed: Queen's University Belfast (LLB law). **Trevor Lunn** (Alliance) MLA for Lagan Valley 2007-. NI Assembly cttees: chair, equality requirements; member, agriculture 2013-14; education 2012-, 2007-11; regional devt 2010-11; public accounts 2007-11. **Pat Catney** (SDLP) Cllr, Lisburn & Castlereagh CC 2011- (initially Lisburn CC), member, environmental services and planning cttee. Was bar owner.

CONSTITUENCY PROFILE
One of five seats that form the suburban ring around Belfast. It contains Lisburn which was recently granted city status and parts of strongly republican West Belfast. The city was held for decades by James Molyneaux, the former UUP leader, succeeded in 1997 by Donaldson.

		Electorate	Turnout %	Change from 2010 %
		71,140	55.9	
J Donaldson	DUP	19,055	47.9	-1.9
A Redpath	UUP	6,055	15.2	
T Lunn	Alliance	5,544	13.9	+2.5
P Catney	SDLP	2,500	6.3	+1.3
A Love	Ukip	2,200	5.5	
S Morrison	TUV	1,887	4.7	-3.9
J McGeough	SF	1,144	2.9	-1.1
J Orr	Ind	756	1.9	
H Osborne	C	654	1.6	-19.5

Change from 2010

[bar chart: DUP, UUP, Alliance, SDLP, Ukip — showing 25%, 0%, -25% scale]

Lanark & Hamilton East

SNP GAIN

ANGELA CRAWLEY
BORN June 3, 1987
MP 2015-

SNP spokeswoman, equalities, women & children 2015-. Cllr, South Lanarkshire C 2012-, member, executive and community services cttee. Former Parly asst to: Bruce Crawford MSP; Clare Adamson MSP. Interned as a legal asst, Aamer Anwar & Co Solicitors. Convenor: Young Scots for Independence. NEC member. Volunteer for Royal Princess Trust for Young Carers. Holiday tour operator for Education Travel Group. Ed: John Ogilvie HS; University of Stirling (BA politics); University of Glasgow (law LLB, Student at time of election).

CHALLENGERS
Jimmy Hood (Lab) MP for Lanark & Hamilton East 1987-2015. Select cttees: chair, european scrutiny 1998-2006; member, panel of chairs 2001-. Member, Co-op Party. Cllr,

Newark & Sherwood DC 1979-97. NUM official. Leader Notts striking miners in 1984-85 national miners' strike. Ed: Nottingham (BA politics, industrial relations & economics). **Alex Allison** (C) Farmer. Cllr, South Lanarkshire C 2007-11. Chair, Young Farmers Club. Former regional chairman, NFU. Married, two children. **Donald MacKay** (Ukip) Financial director, Mortgage Information Centre. Treasurer, Ukip Scotland 2007-14. Business development manager, Scottish Amicable. Ed: Glasgow (MA political science & govt).

CONSTITUENCY PROFILE
This seat consists of a compact urban area towards Glasgow, tied to a huge larger rural area to the south. It contains the large service and administrative town of Hamilton, and the former industrial town of Larkhall. Created in 2005 after extensive boundary changes in the local area, this was considered a safe Labour seat until the SNP upheaval in 2015.

		Electorate	Turnout %	Change from 2010 %
		78,846	70.1	
A Crawley	SNP	26,976	48.8	+27.8
J Hood	Lab	16,876	30.5	-19.4
A Allison	C	8,772	15.9	+0.9
D MacKay	Ukip	1,431	2.6	+1.3
G Cullen	LD	1,203	2.2	-9.1

Change from 2010

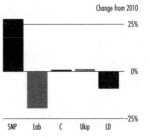

[bar chart: SNP, Lab, C, Ukip, LD — showing 25%, 0%, -25% scale]

Lancashire West

LABOUR HOLD

ROSIE COOPER
BORN Sep 5, 1950
MP 2005-

Defected from Lib Dems in 1999 having been a prominent local councillor in Liverpool. PPS to: Ben Bradshaw 2007-10; Lord Rooker 2006-07. Select cttees: health 2010-; administration 2010-12; justice 2010; NI 2005-10; northwest 2009-10. Contested: Euro election NW England 2004; and, for Lib Dems, Liverpool Broadgreen 1992; Knowsley N 1987, 1986 by-election. Cllr, Liverpool CC 1973-2000. Lord mayor of Liverpool 1992-93. PR and communications professional. USDAW. Former: director, Merseyside Centre for Deaf People; vice-chairwoman, Liverpool Health Authority. Ed: Bellerive Convent GS, Liverpool; University of Liverpool.

CHALLENGERS
Paul Greenall (C) NHS criminal psychologist and lecturer at University of Liverpool. Cllr, West Lancashire BC 2001-, deputy leader 2014-. Mayor of West Lancashire 2012-13. Contested St Helens N 2010. Married, two children. Ed: Liverpool JMU (BSc psychology); Manchester Metropolitan (MSc forensic psychology; PhD psychology). **Jack Sen** (Ukip) Worked in land management. Married. Ed: Syracuse University, New York (BA colonial history). **Ben Basson** (Green) Countryside ranger for West Lancs BC; union rep, GMB Union. Married, one daughter. Ed: Liverpool JMU (BSc wildlife conservation).

CONSTITUENCY PROFILE
A classic marginal where the rural areas tend to vote Conservative but are outweighed by the Labour-voting towns. While the seat was Tory in the 1980s, Labour held it with a 9 per cent majority in 2010, rising to 17 per cent in 2015, suggesting that the seat is now one the Tories could only challenge for in a very good year.

	Electorate	Turnout %	Change from 2010 %
	70,945	70.0	
R Cooper Lab	24,474	49.3	+4.1
P Greenall C	16,114	32.4	-3.8
J Sen Ukip	6,058	12.2	+8.5
B Basson Green	1,582	3.2	+2.2
D Lewis LD	1,298	2.6	-11.0
D Braid WVPTFP	150	0.3	

Change from 2010

25%

0%

-25%

Lab   C   Ukip   Green   LD

Lancaster & Fleetwood

LABOUR GAIN

CATHERINE SMITH
BORN June 16, 1985
MP 2015-

Campaigns and policy officer, British Association of Social Workers. Contested Wyre & Preston N 2010. Trustee, local charity Empowerment. Led NHS campaigns defending the Royal Lancaster Infirmary and the Fleetwood Hospital. NW regional role on NUS National Executive Committe. Engaged. Enjoys cycling. Ed: Barrow Sixth Form Coll; Lancaster University (BA sociology and gender studies).

CHALLENGERS
Eric Ollerenshaw (C) MP for Lancaster & Fleetwood 2010-15. PPS to Baroness Warsi 2012-15. Member, standards & privileges select cttee 2010. Previously leader of the Con group on GLA (2002-04; member, 2000-04). Cllr, Hackney BC 1990-2007, leader 2000-01. Former member London Development Agency board. Contested Heywood & Middleton 1992. Former teacher. Ed: LSE (BSc economics). **Matthew Atkins** (Ukip) Studying for PhD in law at Lancaster Uni. Seminar tutor to undergraduates and part-time member of legal/admin staff at NW Inshore Fisheries & Conservation Authority. Ed: Oxford (BA law); Lancaster (LLM law). **Chris Coates** (Green) Freelance project manager. Lancaster City C 2003-15. Contested Morecambe & Lunesdale 2010.

CONSTITUENCY PROFILE
Created for 2010 election; previously Lancaster had been paired with Wyre, making it a marginal. The new seat was much more of a challenge for the Conservatives, Fleetwood is Labour voting and there is a strong Labour and Green presence in Lancaster. The Tories managed to win the seat in 2010 by just 333 votes, but it was narrowly won back by Labour in 2015.

	Electorate	Turnout %	Change from 2010 %
	60,883	68.6	
C Smith Lab	17,643	42.3	+7.0
E Ollerenshaw C	16,378	39.2	+3.2
M Atkins Ukip	4,060	9.7	+7.3
C Coates Green	2,093	5.0	+0.6
R Long LD	1,390	3.3	-15.8
H Elletson Northern	174	0.4	

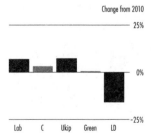

Change from 2010

25%

0%

-25%

Lab   C   Ukip   Green   LD

Leeds Central

LABOUR HOLD

HILARY BENN
BORN Nov 26, 1953
MP 1999-

Intellectual with communitarian instincts, not known to take controversial stand. Son of Tony Benn. Shad foreign SoS 2015-; shad SoS for CLG 2011-15. Shad leader, HoC 2010-11. SoS: environment, food and rural affairs 2007-10; int devt 2003-07. Min: DfID 2003. Parly under-sec: home 2002-03; DfID 2001-02. Special adviser to David Blunkett 1997-99. Cllr, Ealing BC 1979-99, dep leader 1986-90. Contested Ealing North 1987, 1983. Chairman, Assoc of London Authorities Education cttee. MSF: research officer; head of policy and communications. Unite. Widowed, remarried. One daughter, three sons. Ed: Holland Park CS; University of Sussex (BA Russian & east European studies).

CHALLENGERS
Nicola Wilson (C) Co-founder, Yorkshire steel business. Married, two children. **Luke Senior** (Ukip) Mortgage broker. Former surveyor. Ed: Morley HS; Leeds Metropolitan. **Michael Hayton** (Green) Runs security and event management company. Helped run kitchen during Occupy London 2011.

CONSTITUENCY PROFILE
The centre of Leeds, including the city's retail and commercial heart and its two universities, are part of this seat. A deprived area made up of mostly rented and often low quality housing. A significant Asian minority and a large student population. Two major employers are Leeds General Infirmary and St Jamse's University Hospital. Home to Leeds United FC's ground. A safe Labour seat, held by the party since its recreation in 1983. The 1999 by-election, in which Hilary Benn was elected, had a turnout of only 19.6 per cent, the second lowest on record since the Second World War.

	Electorate	Turnout %	from 2010 %	Change %
	81,799	55.1		
H Benn Lab	24,758	55.0	+5.7	
N Wilson C	7,791	17.3	-2.9	
L Senior Ukip	7,082	15.7		
M Hayton Green	3,558	7.9		
E Spriggs LD	1,529	3.4	-17.4	
L Kitching TUSC	330	0.7		

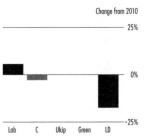

Change from 2010

Leeds East

LABOUR HOLD

RICHARD BURGON
BORN Sep 19, 1980
MP 2015-

Stands to the populist left of the party, describing himself as a socialist. Seen as a union candidate, with links to Communist party, nephew of former MP Colin Burgon. Trade union lawyer and activist. Next Generation Labour, steering cttee. He replaces the retiring George Mudie who held the seat since 1992. Ed: Cardinal Heenan RC HS; St John's Coll, Cambridge (BA law; chairman, Labour Club.)

CHALLENGERS
Ryan Stephenson (C) Chief of staff, Alec Shelbrooke MP. Contested 2014 Euro election. Deputy campaign manager, Elmet & Rothwell seat 2010. **Mark Maniatt** (Ukip) Gas and solid fuel engineer, owns small family business. Trained as a plasterer and has worked in construction industry for 39 years. **Ed Sanderson** (LD) Solicitor, Jones Myers LLP. Contested Doncaster North 2010. Formerly vice-president, Liberal Youth. Ed: Cardinal Heenan RC HS; University of Warwick (BA politics). **Kate Bisson** (Green) Member of sustainability team, Leeds Beckett University. Previously helpline officer, Bat Conservation Trust. Ed: Nottingham (BA English); University of East London (MSc environment and energy studies).

CONSTITUENCY PROFILE
Much of this seat is made up of a sprawl of council estates to the east of Leeds. It also stretches into the inner-city and the Harehills area which has densely packed terraced housing populated by Asian and black communities. To the south is Temple Newsam country park, with its more middle class surroundings. A safe Labour seat since its creation in 1950, most famously associated with Denis Healey, MP 1950 to 1992.

	Electorate	Turnout %	from 2010 %	Change %
	64,754	59.0		
R Burgon Lab	20,530	53.8	+3.4	
R Stephenson C	7,997	20.9	-2.2	
M Maniatt Ukip	7,256	19.0		
E Sanderson LD	1,296	3.4	-14.1	
K Bisson Green	1,117	2.9		

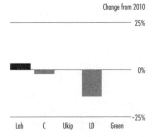

Change from 2010

Leeds North East

LABOUR HOLD

FABIAN HAMILTON
BORN April 12, 1955
MP 1997-

Survivor from left. Took party to court to halt all-women shortlists before 1997 election. Select cttees: int devt 2013-; arms export controls 2013-, 2008-10; political reform 2010-; national security 2010-; foreign affairs 2001-10; administration 1997-2001. VC, Lab Friends of Israel. Member, Co-op party, Fabian Soc. Cllr, Leeds CC 1987-98. Unite. Formerly: computer systems consultant, Apple Macintosh; graphic designer. Married, two daughters, one son. Ed: Brentwood Sch, Essex; University of York (BA social sciences).

CHALLENGERS
Simon Wilson (C) Specialist finance supplier, road transport sector. Cllr, Wakefield MDC 2008-12. Chairman, Morley & Outwood Conservative Assoc. Contested

Rotherham by-election 2012. Children's sports coach. Married, two children. Ed: Queen Elizabeth GS, Wakefield. **Warren Hendon** (Ukip) Chartered electrical engineer. Treasurer for Ukip Leeds branch. **Aqila Choudhry** (LD) Executive director, People in Action, a learning disabilities charity. Community volunteer. Contested Leeds NE 2010. Two children.

CONSTITUENCY PROFILE
Leeds NE was traditionally a Tory stronghold, represented by Sir Keith Joseph for 30 years. Social change has made the seat more sympathetic to Labour as large Victorian houses have been converted into flats and homes of multiple occupancy. It was first won by Labour in 1997, when the candidate originally selected, Liz Davies, was blocked by the NEC and replaced by Fabian Hamilton. It has become increasingly safe since, Labour holding with a majority of 7,000 in 2015.

	Electorate	Turnout %	from 2010 %	Change
	69,097	69.9		
F Hamilton Lab	23,137	47.9	+5.2	
S Wilson C	15,887	32.9	-0.2	
W Hendon Ukip	3,706	7.7	+5.9	
A Choudhry LD	2,569	5.3	-14.3	
E Carter Green	2,541	5.3		
C Foote Green Soc	451	0.9	-0.3	

Change from 2010

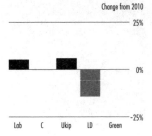

Leeds North West

LIBERAL DEMOCRAT HOLD

GREG MULHOLLAND
BORN Aug 31, 1970
MP 2005-

LD shad min: health 2007-10; schools 2006-07; int devt 2005-06. Select cttees: public admin 2010-; work & pensions 2005-10. Cllr, Leeds CC 2003-05. Member of a raft of APPGs, and chairman of the Save the Pub group. Member: Camra; Trade injustice and debt action Leeds. Co-founder, Campaign for an English National Anthem. Campaigner, Cafod. Formerly account dir for marketing agencies. Married, one daughter. Ed: St Ambrose Coll, Altrincham; University of York (BA politics; MA public admin & public policy).

CHALLENGERS
Alex Sobel (Lab) General manager, Social Enterprise Yorkshire & Humber. Cllr, Leeds CC 2012-. Operations manager, Labour Yes to Fairer Votes 2012. Regional manager, Ed Miliband

for Leader, 2010. Married, two sons. Ed: Leeds (BSc information systems). **Alex Story** (C) Works in news production: founded Story Productions; financial reporter, Dow Jones; asst producer, CNBC. Contested: Yorkshire EU 2014; Wakefield 2010; Denton & Reddish 2005. Rowed for GB in 1996 Olympics. In winning Cambridge boat race team 1997 and 1998. Married, three children. Ed: St Edmund's Coll, Cambridge (BA modern & medieval languages). **Tim Goodall** (Green) Professional development officer, University of Leeds.

CONSTITUENCY PROFILE
Prior to falling to Labour in its 1997 landslide, Leeds North West was a reliable Tory seat. Like many with a high student population, the 2005 election saw a large shift to the Lib Dems on the back of Iraq and student fees, and the party won the seat from third place. It held it in 2010 and, despite losing 11 per cent of its vote, again in 2015.

	Electorate	Turnout %	from 2010 %	Change
	61,974	70.0		
G Mulholland LD	15,948	36.8	-10.7	
A Sobel Lab	13,041	30.1	+9.1	
A Story C	8,083	18.6	-7.9	
T Goodall Green	3,042	7.0	+5.9	
J Metcalfe Ukip	2,997	6.9	+5.5	
B Buxton Yorks	143	0.3		
M Davies Green Soc	79	0.2	-0.1	
M Flanagan Above	24	0.1		

Change from 2010

Leeds West

LABOUR HOLD

RACHEL REEVES
BORN Feb 13, 1979
MP 2010-

Highly thought of within party and seen as potential future chancellor. Caught up in furore after *Newsnight* editor dubbed her "boring snoring". Shadow SoS work & pensions 2013-. Shad chief sec, treasury 2011-13. Shad min, work and pensions 2010-2011. Author, *Why Vote Labour?*. Contested Bromley & Chislehurst 2006 by-election, 2005. Economist: HBOS; Bank of England inc stint at Brit Embassy in Washington. Amicus, Fawcett Society, Amnesty, Fabian Society, Co-op party. Married, one daughter. Ed: Cator Park Sch, Bromley; New Coll, Oxford (BA PPE); LSE (MSc economics).

CHALLENGERS
Alex Pierre-Traves (C) Freelance marketing consultant. Previously worked for Gyro, KPMG. Ed:

Loyola University, Chicago (BA international studies & politics); London Metropolitan (MA British & EU politics); Coll of Law, London (LLB). **Anne Murgatroyd** (Ukip) Voluntary worker. Retired district nurse. Co-founder, Leeds & Pudsey Ukip branch; sec 2014-; vice-chairman 2013-14. Ed: Open University (BSc social science). **Andrew Pointon** (Green) Local government officer.

CONSTITUENCY PROFILE
A largely working class seat held by Labour for the post-war period, except the four years from 1983 when, after years of nursing the seat, it was won by the Liberal MP Michael Meadowcroft. Labour regained it in 1987 and Meadowcroft went on to lead those Liberals who rejected the merger with the SDP that founded the Lib Dems. The Greens and BNP have had some success here locally. Home to Leeds prison which opened in 1847 and is known as Armley jail.

	Electorate	Turnout %	from 2010 %	Change
		64,950	59.2	
R Reeves Lab		18,456	48.0	+5.7
A Pierre-Traves C		7,729	20.1	+0.4
A Murgatroyd Ukip		7,104	18.5	+15.6
A Pointon Green		3,217	8.4	+3.7
L Coyle LD		1,495	3.9	-20.3
M West CSA		217	0.6	
B Mayor TUSC		205	0.5	

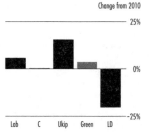

Change from 2010

Lab   C   Ukip   Green   LD

Leicester East

LABOUR HOLD

KEITH VAZ
BORN Nov 26, 1956
MP 1987-

Prominent figure in British-Indian community; in 1987, first MP of Asian origin since 1922. His sister, Valerie Vaz, is MP for Walsall South. Chair, home affairs select cttee 2007-15. Member, cttees: admin 2012-; national security 2010-; liaison 2007-; 1987-92. Min: FCO 1999-2001. Parly under-sec, Lord Chancellor's dept 1999. PPS to: Ross Cranston 1998-99; Lord Falconer 1997-98; John Morris 1997-99. Opp spokes: envt, food and rural affairs 1992-97. Contested Richmond & Barnes 1983. Unison. Lab party national exec 2007-10. British Council board member. Barrister. Married, one daughter, one son. Ed: Latymer Upper Sch; Gonville & Caius Coll, Cambridge (BA law; MA; MCFI); Coll of Law.

CHALLENGERS
Kishan Devani (C) Consultant

for wealth management company. Deputy chairman, London Region Conservatives. Won Asian Achievers Award in Community Service 2012. Former teacher. Ed: (law). **Susanna Steptoe** (Ukip) Marketing director. Former English teacher; broadcasting asst, BBC Radio Leicester. Ed: Warwick (BA English). **Nimit Jethwa** (Green) IT specialist: deployment engineer, ticketing company; web developer, Curve Theatre. **Dave Raval** (LD) Entrepreneur focusing on new technology. Contested: Hackney South & Shoreditch 2010; Bexleyheath & Crayford 2005.

CONSTITUENCY PROFILE
An urban seat in the commercial and engineering centre of Leicester, with a large Asian population. Leicester East is generally Labour territory; it was briefly held by the trenchant Conservative MP Peter Bruinvels at the height of Tory popularity in 1983 but was regained by Labour in 1987 and has become increasingly safe since then.

	Electorate	Turnout %	from 2010 %	Change
		75,430	63.7	
K Vaz Lab		29,386	61.1	+7.4
K Devani C		11,034	23.0	-1.5
S Steptoe Ukip		4,290	8.9	+7.4
N Jethwa Green		1,468	3.1	+1.5
D Raval LD		1,233	2.6	-11.6
M Barker TUSC		540	1.1	
T Darwood ND		117	0.2	

Change from 2010

Lab   C   Ukip   Green   LD

Leicester South

LABOUR CO-OPERATIVE HOLD

JONATHAN ASHWORTH
BORN Oct 14, 1978
MP 2011-

Entered parliament in by-election after Sir Peter Soulsby resigned to run (successfully) to be mayor of Leicester. Shadow min, Cabinet Office 2013-15; opp whip 2011-13. Led parliamentary discussion on interning Richard III in Leicester. Adviser to Gordon Brown while PM, head of party relations for Ed Miliband 2010-11. National sec, Labour Students 2000. Married, one daughter. Ed: Philips HS, Whitefield; Bury Coll; University of Durham (BA politics & philosophy).

CHALLENGERS
Leon Hadji-Nikolaou (C) Heart surgeon at Glenfield Hospital, Leicester. Chairman, Charnwood Conservative Association. Married, two daughters. **Peter Stone** (Ukip) Businessman and engineer.

Claimed he had never voted until 2014 Euro elections. **Gabby Garcia** (Green) Project management consultant, retail brands. Press and comms officer, Leicestershire Green party. **Anita Prabhakar** (LD) Solicitor specialising in constitutional and corporate law. Ed: Nottingham Trent (MA law)

CONSTITUENCY PROFILE
Both socially and ethnically diverse. Home to the two Leicester Universities and the King Power football stadium. Once a Conservative-Labour marginal, it moved strongly towards Labour through the 1990s and was considered safely Labour until Jim Marshall's death in 2004. The subsequent by-election was fought under the shadow of Iraq and won by the Lib Dems from third place. They held the seat for a year before being defeated in the 2005 election by Sir Peter Soulsby, the Labour candidate they had beaten in the by-election. The seat has since remained strongly Labour.

	Electorate	Turnout %	Change from 2010 %
	73,518	62.5	
J Ashworth Lab Co-op	27,473	59.8	+14.2
L Hadji-Nikolaou C	9,628	21.0	-0.4
P Stone Ukip	3,832	8.3	+6.8
G Garcia Green	2,533	5.5	+3.9
A Prabhakar LD	2,127	4.6	-22.3
A Walton TUSC	349	0.8	

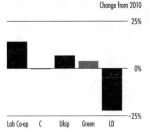

Change from 2010

Lab Co-op   C   Ukip   Green   LD

Leicester West

LABOUR HOLD

LIZ KENDALL
BORN June 11, 1971
MP 2010-

Candidate for Labour leadership, Blairite and pro-business. Shadow minister: care & older people 2011-; health 2010-11. Member, education select cttee 2010. Formerly director: Ambulance Services Network; Maternity Alliance. Assoc director, health and social care, Institute for Public Policy Research; public health researcher, King's Fund. Former special adviser to Patricia Hewitt and Harriet Harman. Member: Unite; Fabian Soc; Co-op party. Ed: Watford Girls GS; Queens' Coll, Cambridge (BA history).

CHALLENGERS
Paul Bessant (C) MD, Retail Knowledge, which tackles retail crime. Cllr, Hinckley & Bosworth BC 2007-. Married, two sons Ed: Countesthorpe Coll, Leicestershire. **Stuart Young** (Ukip) Bookmaker.

Ed: Newparks Sch and Gateways Coll, Leicester. **Peter Hague** (Green) Has just completed PhD in computational astrophysics at University of Leicester. Previously a web developer. Married, one son. **Ian Bradwell** (LD) Former member, Braunstone Community Disability awareness campaigner. Organisation. Blind, inspired by David Blunkett.

CONSTITUENCY PROFILE
This seat has the highest proportion of social housing in Leicester, at about 30 per cent, and the highest percentage of white residents. The centre of the seat, the Westcote area, is popular with young professionals and students. Safely Labour and the only Leicester seat to remain in Labour hands in the 1983 Conservative landslide. Past MPs for Leicester West include the diarist Harold Nicolson, Barnett Janner, his son Greville Janner and Patricia Hewitt, the former health secretary.

	Electorate	Turnout %	Change from 2010 %
	63,204	54.6	
L Kendall Lab	16,051	46.5	+8.1
P Bessant C	8,848	25.6	-1.5
S Young Ukip	5,950	17.2	+14.8
P Hague Green	1,878	5.4	+3.7
I Bradwell LD	1,507	4.4	-18.3
H Rawling TUSC	288	0.8	+0.4

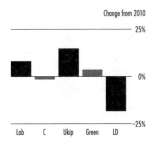

Change from 2010

Lab   C   Ukip   Green   LD

Leicestershire North West

CONSERVATIVE HOLD

ANDREW BRIDGEN
BORN Oct 28, 1964
MP 2010-

Eurosceptic: active in Business for Sterling campaign to save the pound. Select cttees: regulatory reform 2010-; draft deregulation bill 2013. Founded AB Produce, vegetable suppliers. Former East Midlands chairman, Institute of Directors. Military history buff. Separated, two sons. Ed: The Pingle Sch, Swadlincote; University of Nottingham (BSc biological science).

CHALLENGERS
Jamie McMahon (Lab Co-op) Regional director, National Deaf Children's Society. Member, East Mids Labour Regional Board. Contested Gainsborough 2010. Vice-chairman, Young Labour 2009-11. Ed: University of Nottingham (BA politics; chairman of Labour students). **Andy McWilliam** (Ukip) Retired dentist.

Co-author, *Working with your Dentist*. Married, two daughters. Ed: University of Newcastle (BDS dentistry). **Mark Argent** (LD) IT consultant and web designer. Secretary, East of England Faiths Council 2001-2006. Writes on music and spirituality: former editor, *Early Music News*. Ed: Cambridge (BA natural sciences & theology). **Benjamin Gravestock** (Green) Part-time delivery driver. Police constable, 2009-14. Married, two sons.

CONSTITUENCY PROFILE
Historically a key marginal between the Conservatives and Labour. It was held by the Tories from its creation in 1983 until it fell to Labour 1997 as part of the party's landslide. The seat returned to the Tories in 2010, and in 2015 the party took nearly half of the vote, indicating that this is no longer a marginal. Includes former coal-mining villages like Coalville and more rural and Tory voting areas around Ashby-de-la-Zouch.

	Electorate	Turnout %	from 2010 %	Change
	72,194	71.4		
A Bridgen C	25,505	49.5	+4.9	
J McMahon Lab Co-op	14,132	27.4	-2.7	
A McWilliam Ukip	8,704	16.9	+14.7	
M Argent LD	2,033	3.9	-12.7	
B Gravestock Green	1,174	2.3		

Change from 2010

25%

0%

-25%

C   Lab Co-op   Ukip   LD   Green

Leicestershire South

CONSERVATIVE HOLD

ALBERTO COSTA
BORN Nov 13, 1972
MP 2015-

Lawyer who has worked in Whitehall for Treasury Solicitor's Department representing the home secretary and minister for justice. Principal solicitor at Costa Carlisle Solicitors. Contested Angus 2010. Grew up in Scotland. Associate member, Chartered Institute of Arbitrators. Member, Institute of Directors. Replaced Andrew Robathan MP (1992-2015) who stood down. Married, one son, one daughter. Ed: University of Glasgow (MA LLB Law; president, students' representative council); University of Strathclyde (PgDip legal practice).

CHALLENGERS
Amanda Hack (Lab) Head of economic development, Asra Housing Group, property and regeneration provider. Cllr, Braunstone TC 2011-;

Braunstone mayor 2013-14. Married, one son, one daughter. Ed: De Montford (BA business studies). **Barry Mahoney** (Ukip) Chartered accountant. Contested: Northamptonshire South 2010; Daventry 2005; Kettering 2001; Euro East Midlands 2014, 1999. Ed: UEA. **Geoffrey Welsh** (LD) Product director, software company. Cllr: Leicestershire CC 2013-; Blaby DC 1992-, leader of Lib Dem group. Married, three children.

CONSTITUENCY PROFILE
A slice of middle England in the middle of England. A largely rural constituency. South Leicestershire consists of commuter towns and villages clustered close to Leicester itself, and more rural areas farther south. The seat, as with its predecessor Blaby, is a Conservative stronghold. The best known MP to represent the constituency (when it was Blaby) is the former chancellor Nigel Lawson.

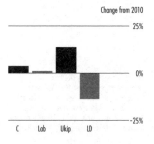

	Electorate	Turnout %	from 2010 %	Change
	76,877	70.2		
A Costa C	28,700	53.2	+3.8	
A Hack Lab	11,876	22.0	+1.2	
B Mahoney Ukip	9,363	17.4	+13.7	
G Welsh LD	3,987	7.4	-13.6	

Change from 2010

25%

0%

-25%

C   Lab   Ukip   LD

Leigh

LABOUR HOLD

ANDY BURNHAM
BORN Jan 7, 1970
MP 2001-

Key member of Ed Miliband's team and candidate for Labour leadership in 2015, supported by unions, Rachel Reeves and Dan Jarvis. Also stood for leader in 2010. Shadow SoS: health 2011-; education 2010-11. SoS: health 2009-10; CMS 2008-09. Chief sec to Treasury 2007-08. Min: health 2006-07. Parly under-sec: home 2005-06. PPS to: Ruth Kelly 2004-05; David Blunkett 2003-04. Special advivser to Chris Smith, researcher to Tessa Jowell. Member, health select cttee 2001-03. Co-op party, TGWU, Unison. Former: chairman, Supporters Direct; administrator, Football Task Force; Parly officer, NHS confederation. Everton fan. Married, two daughters, one son. Ed: St Aelred's RC HS, Newton-le-Willows, Merseyside; Fitzwilliam Coll, Cambridge (BA English).

CHALLENGERS
Louisa Townson (C) Final year PhD student at UCL (neuropharmacology of osteoarthritis pain); associate, Deallus Consulting. Dep-chairwoman, London Conservative Future. Ed: UCL (BSc pharmacology; president, UCLU Con Soc). **Les Leggett** (Ukip) Former police sergeant. Community volunteer. Cllr, (Con) Stockport MBC 2002-07. **Bill Winlow** (LD) Emeritus professor of Neuroscience, UCLan. Cllr: Lancashire CC 2009-; Leeds CC 1986-99. Ed: Newcastle (BSc zoology); St Andrews (PhD neuroscience).

CONSTITUENCY PROFILE
A working class seat on the SE edge of Greater Manchester, consisting of three former mill and coal mining towns, Leigh, Tyldesley and Golborne. A safe Labour constituency, having been held by the party since before the Second World War.

		Electorate	Turnout %	Change from 2010 %
		75,974	59.4	
A Burnham	Lab	24,312	53.9	+5.8
L Townson	C	10,216	22.6	+1.7
L Leggett	Ukip	8,903	19.7	+16.3
B Winlow	LD	1,150	2.6	-15.6
S Hall	TUSC	542	1.2	

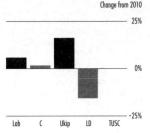

Change from 2010

Lab   C   Ukip   LD   TUSC

Lewes

CONSERVATIVE GAIN

MARIA CAULFIELD
BORN Aug 6, 1973
MP 2015-

Nurse and research sister leading a team in the field of breast cancer research at the Royal Marsden hospital, London. Ousted Norman Baker who had been Lib Dem MP here since 1997. Cllr, Brighton & Hove CC 2007-11. Sussex No2AV co-ordinator. Non-exec director of local housing charity BHT Sussex. Volunteers as an Urban Shepherd.

CHALLENGERS
Norman Baker (LD) MP for Lewes 1997-2015. Resigned as Home Office minister saying working there like "walking through mud". Min: home office 2013-14. Parly under-sec: transport 2010-13. LD shadow SoS, transport 2007-10; shad min, Cabinet Office, Chancellor of Duchy of Lancaster 2007; shad SoS, environment 2005-06; LD spokes: home 2001-02; CMS 1997-2001; environment,

food and rural affairs 1997-99. Cllr: Lewes DC 1987-99 (leader 1991-97); East Sussex CC 1989-97. Teacher, lecturer, company dir. Ed: Royal Holloway London (BA German). **Ray Finch** (Ukip) MEP for SE England 2014-. Cllr, Hampshire CC 2013-, leader Ukip group 2013-14. Assistant to Nigel Farage 2011-. Contested Eastleigh 2010. Former engineer at Virgin Media. **Lloyd Russell-Moyle** (Lab) Consultant, UN. Vice-president, European Youth Forum 2013-14. Fellow, RSA. Ed: Bradford (BA peace studies; Dip international practice).

CONSTITUENCY PROFILE
A large, sprawling rural seat covering much of the countryside to the north of Brighton, the South Downs and the valley of the river Ouse. Its bonfire night celebrations are among the biggest in the country. The seat returned Tory MPs for over a century until it was won by Norman Baker in 1997, and until his defeat in 2015 was a Lib Dem stronghold.

		Electorate	Turnout %	Change from 2010 %
		69,481	72.7	
M Caulfield	C	19,206	38.0	+1.3
N Baker	LD	18,123	35.9	-16.2
R Finch	Ukip	5,427	10.7	+7.3
L Russell-Moyle	Lab	5,000	9.9	+4.9
A Stirling	Green	2,784	5.5	+4.1

Change from 2010

C   LD   Ukip   Lab   Green

Lewisham Deptford

LABOUR HOLD

VICKY FOXCROFT
BORN March 3, 1977
MP 2015-

Her detractors complain that she has never had a "proper" job as she has worked only for unions but Labour regards her highly since she spearheaded the successful Save Lewisham Hospital campaign as chairwoman of the Labour group on Lewisham council. She replaces the retiring Dame Joan Ruddock, MP since 1987, and took 60 per cent of the vote. Finance sector officer, Unite, 2002-. Previous: political officer, Amicus; research officer, AEEU. Cllr, Lewisham BC 2010-14. Chairwoman, Labour Students 2001. Ed: De Montford University (BA business studies).

CHALLENGERS
Bim Afolami (C) Corporate lawyer, Simpson Thacher & Bartlett. Former treasurer, Bow Group. Fellow, RSA. Married, one son. Ed: Eton Coll; University Coll, Oxford

(BA history; vice-president, Oxford Union); BPP Law Sch, London (Grad Dip law). **John Coughlin** (Green) Freelance translator. Cllr, Lewisham BC 2014-, the sole non-Labour councillor. Ed: Sch of Slavonic and East European Studies, University of London (BA German & Russian). **Michael Bukola** (LD) Former tax specialist with Deloitte & Touche. Cllr, Southwark BC 2010-14. Adviser to Brian Paddick's 2012 mayoral campaign. Ed: Northumbria (BA business administration).

CONSTITUENCY PROFILE
Unlike the other two Lewisham seats, Deptford has been held by Labour since 1935, often with big majorities. Some support for the Greens who had 10 per cent of the vote in 2005, and in 2006 increased their number of councillors to six. Despite disappointment in the 2010 local elections, when they lost all but one councillor, they increased their vote share twofold in the 2015 general election.

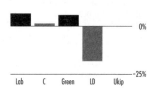

	Electorate	Turnout %	Change from 2010 %
	73,426	64.6	
V Foxcroft Lab	28,572	60.3	+6.6
B Afolami C	7,056	14.9	+1.4
J Coughlin Green	5,932	12.5	+5.8
M Bukola LD	2,497	5.3	-18.1
M Dimambro Ukip	2,013	4.2	
H Mercer PBP	666	1.4	
M Malcolm CPA	300	0.6	-0.6
C Flood TUSC	286	0.6	
P Badger Dem Ref	74	0.2	
D Harvey Ind	30	0.1	

Change from 2010

Lab C Green LD Ukip

Lewisham East

LABOUR HOLD

HEIDI ALEXANDER
BORN April 17, 1975
MP 2010-

Capable former councillor. Lewisham BC 2004-10; deputy mayor of Lewisham, cabinet member for regeneration 2006-10. Opposition whip 2013-. Select cttees: selection 2013-; regulatory reform 2010-12. Forker: chairwoman, Greater London Enterprise; dir, Lewisham's local education partnership; campaign manager, Clothes Aid. Researcher to Joan Ruddock MP 1999-2005. Unite. Married. Ed: Churchfields SS, Swindon; Durham University (BA geography; MA European urban & regional change).

CHALLENGERS
Peter Fortune (C) Training and development manager, Newsquest. Cllr, Bromley BC 2014-, portfolio holder for education. Married, two children. Ed: Bishop Thomas Grant Sch, Lambeth. **Anne**

Marie Waters (Ukip) Founder, Sharia Watch UK. Defected from Labour in 2013. **Julia Fletcher** (LD) Librarian for law firm. Cllr, Lewisham BC 2002-14; deputy leader, LD group. Ed: Exeter (BA history); Goldsmiths (MA English local and regional history); UCL (MA library & information studies). **Störm Poorun** (Green) Ecologist and national campaigner on environmental protection. Dir, Brickhurst Trust. Chief exec, Olan Trust.

CONSTITUENCY PROFILE
A suburban seat on the cusp of inner-city London, Lewisham East was historically a marginal. It was held by the Conservatives from 1983-1992 having been won in 1983 mostly because Labour lost support to the SDP candidate Polly Toynbee. It has since become solidly Labour and the Tories are no longer competitive at a parliamentary level. Locally they are struggling too and in 2014 lost the last of their councillors on Lewisham BC.

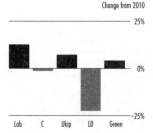

	Electorate	Turnout %	Change from 2010 %
	73,428	58.5	
H Alexander Lab	23,907	55.7	+12.6
P Fortune C	9,574	22.3	-1.3
A M Waters Ukip	3,886	9.1	+7.2
J Fletcher LD	2,455	5.7	-22.5
S Poorun Green	2,429	5.7	+4.2
N Long PBP	390	0.9	
M Martin CPA	282	0.7	

Change from 2010

Lab C Ukip LD Green

Lewisham West & Penge

JIM DOWD
BORN Mar 5, 1951
MP 1992-

Interested in animal welfare, member, League Against Cruel Sports; WWF; IFAW; RSPB. Select cttees: science & technology 2012-; health 2001-10. Whip: government 1997-2001; opposition 1993-95. Cllr, Lewisham BC 1974-94, mayor of Lewisham 1992. MP, Lewisham West 1992-10. Former electronics engineer, Plessey. Member: Co-op party; Labour Friends of Palestine & Middle East; Unite; GMB. Partner of Janet Anderson, former MP for Rossendale & Darwen. Ed: Sedgehill CS, Lewisham; London Nautical Sch.

CHALLENGERS
Russell Jackson (C) Senior manager, financial regulation, BoE. Previously manager of Int Banking Policy, FSA. Cllr: Bromley BC 2010-14; Croydon BC 2006-10, dep mayor of Croydon 2009-10.

Married. Ed: Kingston University (BA politics). **Tom Chance** (Green) Local government officer, GLA. Green spokes, and national housing team co-ordinator. Ed: Reading (MA philosophy). **Gary Harding** (Ukip) Graphic designer, M&S, 1979-2009. Deaf. Chairman, Silent World Sans Frontieres. Ed: Southwark Coll (BEC). **Alex Feakes** (LD) Science teacher. Cllr, Lewisham BC 2006-14. Former chartered accountant, tax consultant. Ed: Imperial Coll London (BSc physics); Birkbeck Coll (MSc bioinformatics).

CONSTITUENCY PROFILE
Once a Conservative-held marginal, the seat has become increasingly safe for Labour because of an increase in the ethnic minority population and transformation of suburban family homes into flats and houses of multiple occupancy. The 2010 boundary changes helped the Tories slightly, but not enough to move the seat on to the target list.

	Electorate	Turnout %	Change from 2010 %
	72,289	66.6	
J Dowd Lab	24,347	50.6	+9.5
R Jackson C	11,633	24.2	-1.3
T Chance Green	4,077	8.5	+6.4
G Harding Ukip	3,764	7.8	+5.3
A Feakes LD	3,709	7.7	-20.4
M Powell-Davies TUSC	391	0.8	
D Hansom Ind	160	0.3	
G Whale Lib GB	44	0.1	

Change from 2010

Lab · C · Green · Ukip · LD

Leyton & Wanstead

JOHN CRYER
BORN April 11, 1964
MP 2010-

Hard-left union official, MP for Hornchurch 1997-2005. Defeated in 2005 but returned to his old place in the Commons, on the rebels' front bench in 2010. Eurosceptic. Son of left-wing MPs Ann Cryer and the late Bob Cryer. Select cttees: justice 2014-; treasury 2010-11; deregulation & reform 1997-2002. Member, Bennite Socialist Campaign Group. Political officer: Unite, Aslef. Journalist: *Tribune; Morning Star; Labour briefing; Guardian*. Amnesty International. Married, two sons, one daughter, sister-in-law is Rachel Reeves. Ed: Oakbank Sch, Keighley; Hatfield Poly; London Coll of Printing.

CHALLENGERS
Matthew Scott (C) Snior research and parly asst, David Evennett MP 2005-. Cllr, Bexley BC 2006-10. Deputy chairman, Bexleyheath

and Crayford Cons. Ed: Beths GS; The University of Birmingham (BA public policy, government & management). **Ashley Gunstock** (Green) Teacher, theatrical director, actor. Former original cast member, *The Bill*. Spokes, Redbridge Green party. Enjoys football and art. Married, one son. **Rosamund Beattie** (Ukip) Diamond appraiser. Volunteer dog walker. Ed: Cardiff (BSc institutional management).

CONSTITUENCY PROFILE
Created as a cross-borough seat in 1997, combining somewhat ill-matched wards from Waltham Forest and Redbridge. Despite recent redevelopment of old estates in the Waltham Forest area, crime and deprivation problems remain. Wanstead is more suburban and middle-class, whereas Leyton is an inner-city, multicultural working class area. Safely Labour and had 58 per cent of the vote in 2015 due to former Lib Dem voters switching to Labour.

	Electorate	Turnout %	Change from 2010 %
	64,746	62.9	
J Cryer Lab	23,858	58.6	+15.0
M Scott C	8,939	22.0	-0.3
A Gunstock Green	2,974	7.3	+5.9
R Beattie Ukip	2,341	5.8	+3.1
C Quilliam LD	2,304	5.7	-22.0
M Aziz Ind	289	0.7	

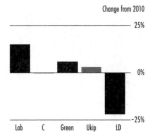

Change from 2010

Lab · C · Green · Ukip · LD

Lichfield

CONSERVATIVE HOLD

MICHAEL FABRICANT
BORN Jun 12, 1950
MP 1992-

Whip: govt 2010-12; opposition 2005-10. Vice-chairman, Conservative party 2012-14. Shad min: economic affairs 2003-05. PPS to: Michael Jack 1996-97. Select cttees: administration 2014-, 2009-10; selection 2010-13; CMS 2001-05; finance & services 2001-04. MP for Mid-Staffordshire 1992-97. Contested South Shields 1987. Senior director and co-founder, International Broadcasting Electronics & Investment Group. Broadcaster, current affairs, BBC Radio. Economist. Ed: Brighton, Hove & Sussex GS; Loughborough University (BSc economics & law); University of Sussex (MSc systems & econometrics).

CHALLENGERS
Chris Worsey (Lab) Co-founder, training and employment company. Chairman, Black Country Youth Unemployment Commission. Cllr, Sandwell MBC 2012-. Ed: Keele (BA English & international politics); Warwick (MA public policy). **John Rackham** (Ukip) Pub licensee for nearly 50 years. Fellow, British Institute of Innkeeping. Panel member, Pubs Independent Conciliation and Arbitration Service. Married. **Paul Ray** (LD) Solicitor, banking and finance partner, Browne Jacobson. Married, three children. Ed: Aston (BSc managerial & administrative studies).

CONSTITUENCY PROFILE
The rural villages and suburban areas in Lichfield tend to lean towards the Conservatives, cancelling out Labour strength in the former mining town of Burntwood. An ultra-marginal on its creation in 1997, with Labour coming within 238 votes of winning. Since then Labour's support has faded and in 2015 Michael Fabricant enjoyed a towering majority of 18,000.

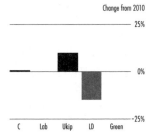

	Electorate	Turnout %	from 2010 %	Change %
	83,339	61.8		
M Fabricant C	28,389	55.2	+0.8	
C Worsey Lab	10,200	19.8	-0.0	
J Rackham Ukip	8,082	15.7	+10.0	
P Ray LD	2,700	5.3	-14.9	
R Pass Green	1,976	3.8		
A Bennetts Class War	120	0.2		

Change from 2010

Lincoln

CONSERVATIVE HOLD

KARL MCCARTNEY
BORN Oct 25, 1969
MP 2010-

Traditionalist interested in the Commonwealth, education and transport. Select cttee, transport 2012-. Member, 1922 exec cttee 2012-. Cllr, Wrothan PC 1997-2003. Contested Lincoln 2005. Magistrate. Dir, corporate strategy and communications consultancy, clients incl TFL, Strategic Rail Authority. Former: PR manager for Norton Rose; Conservative party researcher and agent, including for the MP Dame Angela Rumbold. Keen rugby and football fan. Married, two sons. Ed: Birkenhead Sch; Neston HS; Willink Sch, Burghfield; St David's University Coll (BA geography; SU president); Kingston University Business Sch (MBA).

CHALLENGERS
Lucy Rigby (Lab) Lawyer, Office of Fair Trading. Previously solicitor specialising in competition law, Slaughter & May. One of the Labour candidates to receive £10,000 from Lord Oakeshott. Cllr, Islington BC 2010-12. Worked on UN Criminal Tribunal for the former Yugoslavia. Married, one son, one daughter. Ed: Durham University (BA politics & history). **Nick Smith** (Ukip) Ex-army. Chairman, Lincoln Ukip branch. Contested Lincoln 2010, 2005. **Ross Pepper** (LD) Optical assistant, Specsavers. Local election agent. Ed: Lincoln (BA international relations).

CONSTITUENCY PROFILE
The oldest constituency in Britain, having been in continuous existence since 1265. In 1972 the sitting Labour MP Dick Taverne resigned to re-contest his seat as an Independent Democratic Labour candidate. He won and, narrowly held the seat again in February 1974, but lost it in the second election that year. It has been a bellwether seat since October 1974.

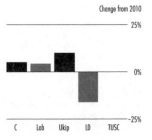

	Electorate	Turnout %	from 2010 %	Change %
	74,121	63.2		
K McCartney C	19,976	42.6	+5.1	
L Rigby Lab	18,533	39.6	+4.3	
N Smith Ukip	5,721	12.2	+10.0	
R Pepper LD	1,992	4.3	-16.0	
E Smith TUSC	344	0.7		
H Powell Lincs Ind	286	0.6		

Change from 2010

Linlithgow & Falkirk East

SNP GAIN

MARTYN DAY
BORN Mar 26, 1971
MP 2015-

Born in Falkirk, raised and educated in Linlithgow. Took the seat from Labour's Michael Connarty who had held it in its various incarnations since 1992. Cllr, West Lothian CC 1999-; SNP spokes, development & transport. Member of a raft of local committees. Election agent: Falkirk East 2011; Linlithgow & Falkirk East 2010; Linlithgow 1999. Community campaigner. Former bank worker. Member, Chartered Institute of Bankers in Scotland.. Married. Ed: Linlithgow Academy.

CHALLENGERS
Michael Connarty (Lab) MP: Linlithgow & Falkirk E 2005-15; Falkirk E 1992-2005. Left-wing but thoughtful champion of mining communities. PPS to Tom Clarke 1997-98. Select cttees: European scrutiny 1998-2015, chairman 2006-10; liaison 2006-10. Cllr, Stirling DC 1977-90, leader 1980-90. Former teacher. Contested Stirling 1987, 1983. Married, one daughter, one son. Ed: Stirling (BA economics); Glasgow & Jordanhill Coll of Ed (Dip coll ed). **Sandy Batho** (C) HR specialist. Previously HR consultant: Royal Zoological Society of Scotland; Northern Rock; National Trust for Scotland; Royal Mail. Ed: Aberdeen (MA economics & politics). **Alistair Forrest** (Ukip) HGV driver. Contested Livingston 2010. Served in RAF.

CONSTITUENCY PROFILE
Created from two contrasting seats: the working-class Falkirk and the Edinburgh commuter town of Linlithgow, once home to Scottish monarchs. Includes birthplace of Alex Salmond. The mixed feel of this seat is completed by the industrial area around Bathgate and Bo'ness. Traditionally, strongly Labour but SNP reclaimed the seat in 2015 with a 23 per cent swing.

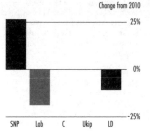

	Electorate	Turnout %	from 2010 %	Change
	86,955	70.8		
M Day SNP	32,055	52.0	+26.6	
M Connarty Lab	19,121	31.0	-18.8	
S Batho C	7,384	12.0	+0.0	
A Forrest Ukip	1,682	2.7		
E Farthing-Sykes LD	1,252	2.0	-10.8	
N McIvor NF	103	0.2		

Change from 2010

Liverpool Riverside

LABOUR CO-OPERATIVE HOLD

LOUISE ELLMAN
BORN Nov 14, 1945
MP 1997-

Fiercely pro-Israel. APPG: chairwoman, Britain-Israel; vice-president, against anti-Semitism. Vice-chairwoman, Labour Friends of Israel. Select cttees: national policy statements 2010-; liaison 2008-; transport 2002-, chairwoman 2008-. Cllr, W Lancs DC 1974-87; Lancs CC 1970-97 (leader 1981-97). A vice-president of LGA 2011-. Founder chairwoman, NW Regional Assocn. Open University lecturer in FE. Co-op party. TGWU. Married, one daughter, one son. Ed: Manchester HS for Girls; University of Hull (BA sociology & history); University of York (MPhil social admin).

CHALLENGERS
Martin Dobson (Green) Self-employed business dir developing web applications for people unable to read or write. Green party spokes, culture, media and sport. Left Labour in 2003 over Iraq war. Previously campaigns manager, Oxfam. Ed: University of Bradford. **Jackson Ng** (C) Partner, Chan Neill Solicitors. Adviser to Lord Wei of Shoreditch. Director, Conservative Friends of the Chinese. Director, Diaspora Group social enterprise. Ed: SOAS (LLB law); LSE (law); Coll of Law, London (LPC). **Joe Chiffers** (Ukip) Solicitor advocate, MSB Solicitors. Enjoys power-lifting. Married.

CONSTITUENCY PROFILE
Includes the city centre and the banks of Mersey. Liverpool is dominated by Labour, which has easily won all the seats since the abolition of Lib Dem-held Liverpool Mossley Hill in 1997. The old Liverpool Scotland seat was once the heart of the Irish immigrant community and was the only example of an Irish Nationalist MP being returned on the mainland, being represented by TP O'Connor for 44 years.

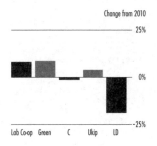

	Electorate	Turnout %	from 2010 %	Change
	70,950	62.4		
L Ellman Lab Co-op	29,835	67.4	+8.1	
M Dobson Green	5,372	12.1	+8.6	
J Ng C	4,245	9.6	-1.3	
J Chiffers Ukip	2,510	5.7	+3.9	
P Childs LD	1,719	3.9	-18.9	
T Mulhearn TUSC	582	1.3		

Change from 2010

Liverpool Walton

LABOUR HOLD

STEVE ROTHERAM
BORN Nov 4, 1961
MP 2010-

Leading figure in parliament fighting for transparency over Hillsborough disaster; arranged Justice Collective charity single that was 2013 Christmas No 1. Select cttees: CMS 2011-; CLG 2011. Cllr, Liverpool CC 2002-10. Lord mayor of Liverpool 2008-09; dep lord mayor 2007-08. Formerly senior business manager, Learning Skills Council. A bricklayer by trade, he went on to found his own construction company. Married, three children. Ed: Ruffwood CS; Kirkby FE Coll; Liverpool John Moores University (MA urban renaissance).

CHALLENGERS
Steve Flatman (Ukip) 6.4 per cent increase in vote since 2010. Contested Breightmet PC 2015 election. **Norsheen Bhatti** (C) Solicitor, International Maritime Organisation. Contested: Stoke Central 2010 (Con); Battersea 2005, Brent East 2001 (Lib Dems). Former assistant to Paddy Ashdown. Ed: Keele University (BA international relations & law; president, Lib Dem soc). **Jonathan Clatworthy** (Green) Retired priest, university chaplain and author. Ed: Wales (BA Latin); The University of Manchester (Dip social administration); Salisbury Theological Coll; Southampton (Cert theology); Manchester (MPhil theology).

CONSTITUENCY PROFILE
Walton covers the northern part of Liverpool, and includes both of the city's major football stadiums (Anfield and Goodison Park). Held by the Conservatives until 1964, but now an utterly safe Labour seat: it had the largest percentage majority of any UK seat in 2010 and in 2015, when Mr Rotheram polled 81 per cent of the votes, nearly 28,000 ahead of his nearest rival.

		Electorate	Turnout %	Change from 2010 %
		62,868	61.1	
S Rotheram	Lab	31,222	81.3	+9.3
S Flatman	Ukip	3,445	9.0	+6.4
N Bhatti	C	1,802	4.7	-1.8
J Clatworthy	Green	956	2.5	
P Moloney	LD	899	2.3	-11.9
A Karran	Ind	56	0.2	
J Bishop	Plural	23	0.1	

Change from 2010

25%

0%

-25%

Lab   Ukip   C   Green   LD

Liverpool Wavertree

LABOUR CO-OPERATIVE HOLD

LUCIANA BERGER
BORN May 13, 1981
MP 2010-

Shadow minister: public health 2013-; ECC 2010-13. Select cttees: finance and services 2010; business, innovation and skills 2010. Formerly: Govt strategy unit, Accenture; government & parly manager, NHS Confederation. Member and former dir, Lab Friends of Israel. Shot to prominence in 2005 due to friendship with Euan Blair and resignation from NEC of NUS in anti-Semitism dispute. Member: Unite; Co-op party; Fabian Society; Progress. Likes Bollywood films and weight training. Ed: Haberdashers' Aske's Sch; University of Birmingham (BCom commerce & Spanish); Birkbeck Coll, London (MSc government, politics & policy).

CHALLENGERS
James Pearson (C) Project manager, defence industry. Cllr, Trafford MBC 2004-10; chairman, Greater Manchester Fire & Rescue Authority 2009-10. Officer, Army Reserves, served in Afghanistan and Cyprus. Married, one son. **Adam Heatherington** (Ukip) Works in IT: system support and training. Active campaigner. Contested: mayor of Liverpool 2012; Liverpool West Derby 2010. Ed: (BA IT and history); (PGCE); (MSc computing). **Leo Evans** (LD) Politics student at University of Liverpool; re-established university's Liberal Youth Society. As sixth former, won NI Schools Debating Competition.

CONSTITUENCY PROFILE
The last Liverpool seat held by the Tories, lost in 1983. In the 2000s it became one of the more successful Lib Dem targets. However, their fall from a strong second to fourth in 2015 and the collapse of support in local elections since the coalition was formed suggests it is no longer a viable target for them.

		Electorate	Turnout %	Change from 2010 %
		61,731	66.4	
L Berger	Lab Co-op	28,401	69.3	+16.2
J Pearson	C	4,098	10.0	+2.5
A Heatherington	Ukip	3,375	8.2	+5.9
L Evans	LD	2,454	6.0	-28.2
P Cranie	Green	2,140	5.2	+3.7
D Walsh	TUSC	362	0.9	
N McCarthy	Ind	144	0.4	-0.0

Change from 2010

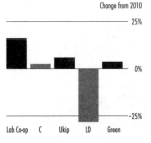

25%

0%

-25%

Lab Co-op   C   Ukip   LD   Green

Liverpool West Derby

LABOUR CO-OPERATIVE HOLD

STEPHEN TWIGG
BORN Dec 25, 1966
MP 2010-

The face of the Labour 1997 election landslide when he unseated Michael Portillo in Enfield Southgate, a seat he then lost to the Tories in 2005. Once seen as über-Blairite but later repositioned himself. Chairman, Progress; dir, Foreign Policy Centre. First openly gay MP when elected. Several posts in education: shad SoS 2011-13; min, schools 2004-05; parly under-sec 2002-04. Shad min: political & constitutional reform 2013-15; foreign & commonwealth affairs 2010-11. Dep leader of HoC 2001-02. Cllr, Islington BC 1992-97. Previously: pol consultant, Rowland Sallingbury Casey; research asst, Margaret Hodge MP; parly officer, Amnesty Int; pres, NUS. Amicus, Co-op, Fabian Soc. Ed: Southgate CS; Balliol Coll, Oxford (BA politics & economics).

CHALLENGERS
Neil Miney (Ukip) Critical care practitioner at NHS trust. Chairman, Ukip Liverpool, Wavertree 2009-. Contested Liverpool Wavertree 2010. Married, one son. **Ed McRandal** (C) Account director, Insight Consulting Group. Former aide to Andrew Lansley. Ed: Bristol University (MSc international relations). **Stephen Radford** (Lib) President of the Liberal party, representing those who rejected the merger with the SDP in 1989. Non-exec advisor, trustees of Liverpool Pride. Cllr, Liverpool CC 1984-.

CONSTITUENCY PROFILE
A residential ultra safe Labour seat covering an area of econmic deprivation. One of the last holdouts of old Liberal party. Liberal strength is concentrated in the ward represented by the party's president, Steve Radford, who has contested the last five elections and came second in 1997 and 2001.

	Electorate	Turnout %	Change from 2010 %
	63,875	64.2	
S Twigg Lab Co-op	30,842	75.2	+11.0
N Miney Ukip	3,475	8.5	+5.4
E McRandal C	2,710	6.6	-2.7
S Radford Lib	2,049	5.0	-4.3
R Lawson Green	996	2.4	
P Twigger LD	959	2.3	-10.2

Change from 2010

25%

0%

-25%

Lab Co-op   Ukip   C   Lib   Green

Livingston

SNP GAIN

HANNAH BARDELL
BORN June 01, 1983
MP 2015-

SNP group leader, fair work & employment 2015-. Persuaded by Alex Salmond to work on the SNP's 2007 Holyrood election campaign producing SNPtv online. At the time she was an asst producer at GMTV. Later became his office manager, 2007-10. Subsequently: worked for U.S. State Dept in Edinburgh Consulate managing protocol and press; head of comms and marketing, Stork oil and gas service; comms manager, Subsea 7, engineering and construction contractors. Previously member policy cttee, Grampian Chamber of Commerce. Won Pushkin Prize as teenager. Ed: Broxburn Academy; University of Stirling (MA film & media, politics & English).

CHALLENGERS
Graeme Morrice (Lab) MP Livingston 2010-15. Cllr, West Lothian DC 1987-2012, council leader 1995-2007. Member, select cttee: Scottish Affairs 2013-15, 2011-12. PPS to: Harriet Harman 2013-15; Margaret Curran 2011-13. Wholesale and retail career. Unite. Partner. Ed: Broxburn Academy; Edinburgh Napier (SHND business studies). **Chris Donnelly** (C) Self-employed policy consultant: Windsor & Maidenhead BC; Slough BC. Ed: University of Newcastle (LLB law); Girton Coll, Cambridge (MPhil criminology). **Nathan Somerville** (Ukip) Sales assistant, Tesco.

CONSTITUENCY PROFILE
Labour comfortably held Livingston until the SNP's 2015 victories. A new town built in the sixties to ease pressure on Glasgow, Livingston's largest private employer is BSkyB's call centre. Jim Devine, MP 2005-10, was banned from standing for Labour in 2010 and later jailed for fraudulent expenses claims. Its best known MP was foreign secretary Robin Cook.

	Electorate	Turnout %	Change from 2010 %
	82,373	69.9	
H Bardell SNP	32,736	56.9	+31.0
G Morrice Lab	15,893	27.6	-20.8
C Donnelly C	5,929	10.3	-0.5
N Somerville Ukip	1,757	3.1	+2.1
C Dundas LD	1,232	2.1	-9.0

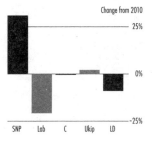

Change from 2010

25%

0%

-25%

SNP   Lab   C   Ukip   LD

Llanelli

LABOUR HOLD

NIA GRIFFITH
BORN Dec 4, 1956
MP 2005-

Left-winger from South Wales valleys. Shad min: Wales 2011-; BIS 2010-11. PPS to: Harriet Harman 2008-10; Hilary Benn 2007-08. Select cttees: Welsh affairs 2005-; European scrutiny 2005-07, 2010-; human rights 2006-07. Deputy mayor of Carmarthen 1998-1999; Sheriff of Carmarthen 1997-1998; cllr, Carmarthen TC 1987-99. Former language teacher; adviser for LEA; schools inspector; author sch textbooks. Divorced. Ed: Somerville Coll, Oxford (BA modern languages); UCNW, Bangor (PGCE).

CHALLENGERS
Vaughan Williams (PC) Welsh teacher. Formerly: cleaner; dockside worker; shop assistant. Ed: Bangor University; Aberystwyth University (PGCE). **Kenneth Denver Rees** (Ukip) Defected

from Lib Dems in 2014. Retired, having spent 42 years as engineer in steel industry. Former cllr: Llanelli TC, mayor, 2001-02; Dyfed CC; Carmarthenshire CC 2008-12. Board mem, National Examination Board in Supervisory Management. **Selaine Saxby** (C) Dir, LessBounce. com sports bra retailer. Founder, Pink Aerobics, raising funds for breast cancer charities. Campaign manager to Wilfred Emmanuel-Jones, Chippenham 2010. Ed: Cambridge (BSc mathematics & management studies).

CONSTITUENCY PROFILE
A South Wales seat that was once focused on the coal and steel industries, but now has a more diverse manufacturing base. It remains working class, with a large population living in social housing, and severe deprivation near the seafront. The coast is home to many pensioners. Long Labour tradition, but Plaid Cymru is a serious challenger here in elections to the Welsh Assembly.

	Electorate	Turnout %	from 2010 %	Change
	59,314	65.0		
N Griffith Lab	15,948	41.3	-1.1	
V Williams PC	8,853	23.0	-7.0	
K D Rees Ukip	6,269	16.3	+13.5	
S Saxby C	5,534	14.4	-0.0	
C Phillips LD	751	2.0	-8.5	
G Smith Green	689	1.8		
S Caiach PF	407	1.1		
S Jones TUSC	123	0.3		

Change from 2010

Lab · PC · Ukip · C · LD

Londonderry East

DUP HOLD

GREGORY CAMPBELL
BORN Feb 15, 1953
MP 2001-

DUP shad min: international development 2010-13; work & pensions 2007-10; transport 2009-11; defence 2005-07; CMS 2005-07. Select cttees: NI affairs 2004-08; transport 2001-04. Member Legislative Assembly, Northern Ireland, for East Londonderry 1998-. Barred for two days from speaking in NI Assembly after yawning when Sinn Féin member spoke Irish. NI Assembly min: culture, arts & leisure 2008-09; reg development 2000-01. Member, NI Forum for Political Dialogue 1996-98. Contested: Londonderry East 1997; Foyle 1992, 1987, 1983. Cllr, Derry CC 1981-2011. Former civil servant, ran a publishing company. Dir, Causeway Press. Married, one son, three daughters. Ed: Londonderry Tech Coll; Magree Coll (Extra-Mural Cert political studies).

CHALLENGERS
Caoimhe Archibald (SF) Research officer, Teagasc Irish agriculture and food development authority. Member, Conradh na Gaeilge, which promotes Irish language. Ed: Queen's Belfast (BSc biology; PhD molecular mycology). **William McCandless** (UUP) Retired businessman. Cllr, Coleraine BC 2011-, defected from DUP in 2012. **Gerry Mullan** (SDLP) Cllr: Limavady BC 2001-; mayor 2013-14; mem: Roe Valley enterprise agency; policing and community safety partnership.

CONSTITUENCY PROFILE
Located in northwest Northern Ireland and mainly rural. The largest town is Coleraine, the home of the main campus of the University of Ulster. A history of DUP and UUP presence. Has been held by DUP Gregory Campbell, since 2001. His predecessor UUP Willie Ross was a strong opponent of the Belfast Agreement and was MP from the seat's creation in 1974.

	Electorate	Turnout %	from 2010 %	Change
	66,925	51.9		
G Campbell DUP	14,663	42.2	+7.6	
C Archibald SF	6,859	19.8	+0.5	
W McCandless UUP	5,333	15.4		
G Mullan SDLP	4,268	12.3	-3.2	
Y Boyle Alliance	2,642	7.6	+2.1	
N Paine CSA	527	1.5		
L St Clair-Legge C	422	1.2	-16.6	

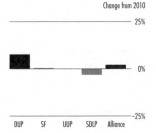

Change from 2010

DUP · SF · UUP · SDLP · Alliance

Loughborough

CONSERVATIVE HOLD

NICKY MORGAN
BORN Oct 10, 1972
MP 2010-

Took over Michael Gove's brief as education sec in sweeping 2014 reshuffle, hoped to be more appeasing to teachers' unions. SoS: education; min: women & equalities 2014-; financial sec to treasury 2014; economic sec to treasury 2013-14. Asst whip 2012-13. PPS to David Willetts 2010-12. Contested: Loughborough 2005; Islington South & Finsbury 2001. Previously corporate solicitor specialising in M&A: Travers Smith; Allen & Overy; Theodore Goddard. Married, one son. Ed: Surbiton HS; St Hugh's Coll, Oxford (BA law, MA law); Coll of Law, Guildford (LPC).

CHALLENGERS
Matthew O'Callaghan (Lab) Freelance international business consultant. Cllr: Melton BC 2007-15; Leics CC 1997-2009.

Multilingual. Former researcher and professor at universities around the world. Partner. Ed: Birmingham (BSc chemistry; PhD chemistry); London Business Sch (MBA). **Bill Piper** (Ukip) Financial services consultant. Cllr (independent), Lutterworth TC, mayor 2009-10. Trained as marine engineer. Worked in optic sales. **Steve Coltman** (LD) Self-employed chemist. Retired project manager, Fisher Scientific. Former chairman, Assn of LD Engineers & Scientists. Ed: University of Southampton (BSc chemistry); UEA (MSc organic chemistry).

CONSTITUENCY PROFILE
A key marginal and bellwether seat, having been won by the party that received the most seats at every general election since February 1974. Before that the seat included part of the Leicestershire coalfield and was safely Labour. Ethnically diverse, has large Bangladeshi and Chinese populations.

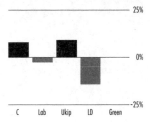

	Electorate	Turnout %	from 2010 %	Change
	72,644	71.6		
N Morgan C	25,762	49.5	+7.9	
M O'Callaghan Lab	16,579	31.9	-2.6	
B Piper Ukip	5,704	11.0	+9.2	
S Coltman LD	2,130	4.1	-14.2	
M Sisson Green	1,845	3.6		

Change from 2010

Louth & Horncastle

CONSERVATIVE GAIN

VICTORIA ATKINS
BORN March 22, 1976
MP 2015-

Selected as Tory candidate to replace the retiring veteran MP Sir Peter Tapsell. Criminal barrister, fraud and criminal regulatory specialist at Red Lion Chambers. Appointed to attorney-general's list and Serious Fraud Office's list of specialist fraud prosecutors. Fought Gloucestershire PCC 2012. Father is MP and MEP Sir Robert Atkins. Enjoys horseriding. Married, one son. Ed: Cambridge (BA law).

CHALLENGERS
Colin Mair (Ukip) Process engineering consultant. Cllr, Lincolnshire CC 2013-, Ukip group leader. Former soldier, Royal Signals. Ed: University of Leeds (BSc biochemistry & physiology). **Matthew Brown** (Lab) Cllr, North East Lincs C 2010-. Former steward, Grimsby Town FC. Ed: University of Hull

(BA business & management; MA globalisation & governance, vice-president, student union). **Lisa Gabriel** (LD) Freelance writer and musican. Former guitar teacher. Contested: Lincoln 2005, 2001, 1997; East Midlands Euro 2004, 1999. Ed: Bishop Grosseteste Coll (BEd music, drama, education & psychology). **Romy Rayner** (Green) Owns a company selling cloth nappies. Studying for evolutionary biology and environmental science degree.

CONSTITUENCY PROFILE
A rural, solidly Conservative seat, covering much of the Lincolnshire Wolds and the county's North Sea coast. Was created out of the East Lindsey constituency 1983-87. Settlements are mostly villages and hamlets, and market and seaside towns. Louth & Horncastle and its predecessors have been held by the Tories since before the war. Sir Peter Tapsell held the seat from 1966 to 2015, making him the longest serving MP.

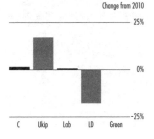

	Electorate	Turnout %	from 2010 %	Change
	74,280	67.8		
V Atkins C	25,755	51.2	+1.5	
C Mair Ukip	10,778	21.4	+17.1	
M Brown Lab	9,077	18.0	+0.7	
L Gabriel LD	2,255	4.5	-17.7	
R Rayner Green	1,549	3.1		
D Simpson Lincs Ind	659	1.3	+0.2	
P Hill Loony	263	0.5		

Change from 2010

Ludlow

CONSERVATIVE HOLD

PHILIP DUNNE
BORN Aug 14, 1958
MP 2005-

Businessman who co-founded the Ottakar's book chain, now part of Waterstones. Min of state for defence procurement 2015-. Parly under-sec, defence 2012-15. Asst govt whip 2010-12. Opp whip 2008-10. Select cttees: Treasury 2007-08; public accounts 2006-09; work & pensions 2005-06. Deputy chairman, Conservative party's international office 2008-10. Cllr, South Shropshire DC 2001-07. Former merchant & investment banker in New York, Hong Kong and London. NFU member; responsible for family farm. Former director, Juvenile Diabetes Research Foundation. Married, two daughters, two sons. Ed: Eton Coll; Keble Coll, Oxford (BA PPE).

CHALLENGERS
David Kelly (Ukip) Retired headmaster. Married, three sons. Ed: Sussex (BA American studies); Keele (MA American literature); Bolton Coll Education (PGCE); Crewe & Alsager Coll (Dip. education management). **Charlotte Barnes** (LD) Owns electrical contracting business with husband. Cllr, Shropshire CC 2011-. Two sons. **Simon Slater** (Lab) Cllr, Solihull MBC 2006-14, defected from Lib Dems. Parly asst, Roger Godsiff MP. Former lecturer, University of Liverpool. Contested Meriden 2010 for Lib Dems.

CONSTITUENCY PROFILE
Normally a safe Conservative seat, but held by the Liberal Democrats from 2001-05. A large, rolling rural seat, dotted with small market towns and villages, the biggest settlement is Ludlow, an historic market town and an administrative centre for the south of Shropshire. The seat also includes Much Wenlock, renowned for the 19th century Wenlock Olympian Games, which were a forerunner of the modern Olympic movement.

	Electorate	Turnout %	Change from 2010 %
	66,423	72.4	
P Dunne C	26,093	54.3	+1.5
D Kelly Ukip	7,164	14.9	+10.5
C Barnes LD	6,469	13.5	-19.3
S Slater Lab	5,902	12.3	+5.6
J Phillips Green	2,435	5.1	+4.2

Change from 2010

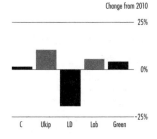

Luton North

LABOUR HOLD

KELVIN HOPKINS
BORN Aug 22, 1941
MP 1997-

Left-winger and member of Socialist Campaign Group. Adviser on yachting to Richard Caborn 2002-07. Select cttees: public admin 2011-, 2002-10; draft deregulation bill 2013; transport 2010-11; European scrutiny 2007-; Crossrail bill 2005-07. Vice-chairman central region Lab party. Cllr, Luton BC 1972-76. Delegate, Luton TUC. Unison/Nalgo policy and research officer. TUC economics department. Married, one daughter, one son. Ed: Queen Elizabeth's GS, High Barnet; University of Nottingham (BA politics, economics & maths).

CHALLENGERS
Dean Russell (C) Creative strategy director, Lewis PR. Cllr, St Albans DC 2010-13. Adviser: APPG *Women in Parliament* report; Armed Forces charity, Give Us Time. Former columnist, *Third Sector*. Ed: De Montford University (BSc physics & business studies; MPhil physics & material science). **Allan White** (Ukip) Previously worked in healthcare. **Aroosa Ulzaman** (LD) Works in a legal aid law firm. Former student cttee member, Human Rights Lawyers' Assoc. Contested Luton BC 2011. Ed: University of Westminster (LLB law). **Sofiya Ahmed** (Green) Co-chairwoman, London Young Greens. NUS London women's officer.

CONSTITUENCY PROFILE
Conservative until 1997, the seat has been safely Labour since. The constituency is wholly urban and primarily residential, with a high proportion of ethnic minorities. A commuter seat with good transport links. In the 2011 census almost half the population was non-white and one in five were Muslim. Luton reportedly has the highest proportion of taxi drivers per head in the UK.

	Electorate	Turnout %	Change from 2010 %
	66,533	64.0	
K Hopkins Lab	22,243	52.3	+3.0
D Russell C	12,739	29.9	-1.9
A White Ukip	5,318	12.5	+8.9
A Ulzaman LD	1,299	3.1	-8.1
S Ahmed Green	972	2.3	+1.1

Change from 2010

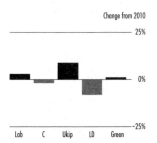

Luton South

LABOUR CO-OPERATIVE HOLD

GAVIN SHUKER
BORN Oct 10, 1981
MP 2010-

Pastor of the City Life Church, Luton, determined to improve the town's reputation. Shadow min: int devt 2013-; environment 2011-13. PPS to Sadiq Khan 2010-11. Member, transport select cttee 2010-11. Received strong support for campaign in 2010 from the Christian Socialist Movement. Chair: Co-op party parly group. Formerly associate pastor, City Life Church Cambridge. Worked for: Fusion UK charity; Endis, web development company. Member, Unite. Married, one daughter. Ed: Icknield HS; Luton Sixth Form Coll; Girton Coll, Cambridge (BA social & political science).

CHALLENGERS
Katie Redmond (C) Systems engineer, Lockheed Martin. Ambassador for Stemnet. Member, political cttee of Carlton Club.

Ed: Chelmsford County HS; Southampton (BEng aerospace engineering). **Yasin Rehman** (Ukip) Dir, international education business. Defected from Labour. Married, four children. Ed: Leeds (BEng); Queens Coll, Oxford (DPhil). **Ashuk Ahmed** (LD) Community development coordinator for local housing association. Ed: De Montfort (BA applied social & community studies).

CONSTITUENCY PROFILE
Until it was retained by Labour in 2010 this had been one of the most reliable bellwether seats in the country, won by the party that went on to form the government in every election since 1951. There is a high proportion of people who have never worked in what was historically a manufacturing town. Luton Airport has become an increasingly key part of the economy since the Vauxhall car plant closed in 2002. Has large Pakistani and Bangladeshi communities.

	Electorate	Turnout %	Change from 2010 %
	67,234	62.8	
G Shuker Lab Co-op	18,660	44.2	+9.3
K Redmond C	12,949	30.7	+1.3
Y Rehman Ukip	5,129	12.2	+9.8
A Ahmed LD	3,183	7.5	-15.1
S Hall Green	1,237	2.9	+2.1
A Malik Ind	900	2.1	
P Weston Lib GB	158	0.4	

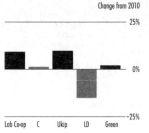

Change from 2010

Macclesfield

CONSERVATIVE HOLD

DAVID RUTLEY
BORN Mar 7, 1961
MP 2010-

Career as a senior executive, he campaigns on issues relating to business and the economy. PPS to: David Lidington 2014-; Damian Green 2010-14. Min: immigration 2010-12. Member, treasury select cttee 2010. Special adviser to Cabinet Office, MAFF, Treasury 1994-96. Former marketing dir: Barclays Bank; Halifax General Insurance; Asda Stores; Safeway Stores; PepsiCo. Mountaineer (chair, APPG on Mountaineering), rock climber, ornithologist. Member, Bow Group. Contested St Albans, 1997. One of two practising Mormons in Commons. Married, two daughters, two sons. Ed: Priory Sch, Lewes; LSE (BSc economics); Harvard (MBA).

CHALLENGERS
Tim Roca (Lab) University administrator. Officer, Unison.

Ed: University of Lancaster (BA history, president, Student Union). **Adrian Howard** (Ukip) Works for a manufacturing business. **Neil Christian** (LD) Barrister working in family, chancery and personal injury. Contested 2014 Euro election, North West England. Ed: University of St Andrews (MA medieval history); Coll of Law (PGDL BVC law). **Joan Plimmer** (Green) Accountant. Married, three children. Ed: University of Manchester (BA history).

CONSTITUENCY PROFILE
The town of Macclesfield lies at the centre of the seat, surrounded by Cheshire countryside. The constituency includes the Jodrell Bank observatory. An affluent area, popular as a base for commuters into Manchester, it has been held by the Conservative since 1918. Among its MPs were Sir Nicholas Winterton, who represented the seat for 39 years, and Garfield Weston, the founder of Associated British Foods.

	Electorate	Turnout %	Change from 2010 %
	71,580	69.3	
D Rutley C	26,063	52.6	+5.6
T Roca Lab	11,252	22.7	+2.4
A Howard Ukip	6,037	12.2	+9.3
N Christian LD	3,842	7.8	-15.3
J Plimmer Green	2,404	4.9	+3.2

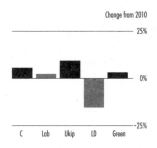

Change from 2010

Maidenhead

THERESA MAY
BORN Oct 1, 1956
MP 1997-

Clergyman's daughter, moderniser with penchant for fashion. Home secretary 2010-. Min for women & equalities 2010-12. Eurosceptic, with contempt for the Human Rights Act. Coined "nasty party" term as chairwoman of Conservative party 2002-03. Shadow SoS: w&p 2009-10; CMS 2005; family 2004-05; env & transport 2001-04; education 1999-2001. Shadow minister: women 2007-10. Shadow Leader of HoC 2005-09. Cllr, Merton BC 1986-1994. Payment clearing services career, international affairs adviser. Received freedom of the City of London. Married. Ed: Wheatley Park Comp; St Hugh's Coll, Oxford (BA geography).

CHALLENGERS
Charles Smith (Lab) Lawyer. Volunteer, CAB. Campaign co-ordinator, 2012 GLA elections. Ed: University of Warwick (French & History). **Tony Hill** (LD) Retired head teacher, trustee and governor. Former chairman, Maidenhead CAB. Contested Maidenhead 2010. Ed: Christ's Coll, Cambridge. **Herbie Crossman** (Ukip) Security consultant. Cllr, Harrow 1994-98, left Lib Dems mid-way through term. Contested 2009 Euro election for Libertas. **Emily Blyth** (Green) Musician and songwriting teacher. Local Green party support officer and membership secretary. Ed: University of Sunderland.

CONSTITUENCY PROFILE
Affluent and middle class, Maidenhead has been Conservative since the Windsor & Maidenhead seat was split in 1997. Consists of the town of Maidenhead itself, with its strong high-tech and pharmaceutical industries, and includes a swathe of countryside up to the suburbs of Reading. House prices are among the highest outside London and is set to rise with the development of Crossrail.

	Electorate	Turnout %	from 2010 %	Change %
	74,963	71.8		
T May C	35,453	65.8	+6.4	
C Smith Lab	6,394	11.9	+4.8	
T Hill LD	5,337	9.9	-18.3	
H Crossman Ukip	4,539	8.4	+6.1	
E Blyth Green	1,915	3.6	+2.7	
I Taplin Ind	162	0.3		
J Wilcox Class War	55	0.1		

Change from 2010

C	Lab	LD	Ukip	Green

Maidstone & The Weald

CONSERVATIVE HOLD

HELEN GRANT
BORN Sep 28, 1961
MP 2010-

The Conservative's first black woman MP. Solicitor, founded own firm. Specialist in family law and sat on reform commission for Centre for Social Justice. Parly under-sec: sport & tourism 2013-; women & equalities; justice 2012-13. Select cttee: justice 2010-11. Special adviser to Oliver Letwin, chairman of party policy review 2006-10. Con social mobility task force; Con social justice policy group. Joined Tories 2006; Labour 2004-05. Formerly non-exec dir, Croydon PCT. Married, two sons. Ed: St Aidans Comp, Carlisle; University of Hull (LLB law); Coll of Law.

CHALLENGERS
Jasper Gerard (LD) Journalist, former chief interviewer, *The Sunday Times*. Columnist, *The Times*, *Observer*, *Telegraph*. Author. Married, two children. Ed: Durham University (BA philosophy). **Eddie Powell** (Ukip) Semi-retired advertising and marketing businessman. Cllr, Maidstone BC 2014-. **Allen Simpson** (Lab) Head of public policy, Corporate banking, Barclays. Ed: University of York (BA politics & sociology). **Hannah Patton** (Green) Youth worker. Former member, Youth Parliament for Maidstone.

CONSTITUENCY PROFILE
Maidstone is relatively affluent with only small patches of deprivation, helping to explain decades of Conservative representation. The seat was held most famously by Ann Widdecombe, MP 1987-2010. Maidstone's economy is dominated by retail and administration, and the area is home to many London commuters. The seat covers most of Maidstone itself and a chunk of Kentish countryside. The seat contains only a small portion of the Weald, a much larger area of historically wooded countryside.

	Electorate	Turnout %	from 2010 %	Change %
	73,181	68.3		
H Grant C	22,745	45.5	-2.5	
J Gerard LD	12,036	24.1	-11.9	
E Powell Ukip	7,930	15.9	+12.5	
A Simpson Lab	5,268	10.5	+0.8	
H Patton Green	1,396	2.8	+1.5	
P Hobday NHAP	583	1.2		
R Kinrade Ind	52	0.1		

Change from 2010

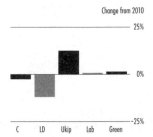

C	LD	Ukip	Lab	Green

264 | THE NEW PARLIAMENT

Makerfield

LABOUR HOLD

YVONNE FOVARGUE
BORN Nov 29, 1956
MP 2010-

Inherited the seat in 2010 from Ian McCartney, for whom her husband, Paul Kenny, was a press officer. Shadow min: education 2014-; defence 2013-14; transport 2013; Opp Whip 2011-13. Select cttees: procedure 2014-; consolidation bills 2010-; health 2010-11. Cllr, Warrington BC 2004-10. Chief Exec, St Helens CAB. Former: housing officer, Moss Side; estate manager, Manchester CC. Member. Co-op party, Unite. Mensa member. Named Citizen's Advice Parliamentarian of the Year 2011. Married, one daughter. Ed: Sale GS; University of Leeds (BA English).

CHALLENGERS
Andrew Collinson (Ukip) IT consultant. Former policeman. **Zehra Zaidi** (C) Lawyer working in international development.

Adviser to Andrew Mitchell 2010-12. Worked with Unicef & the UN Development Programme. Dir, DiverCity is Right. Contested SW England European election 2009. Ed: University of Warwick (LLB European law); LSE (LLM); Coll of Law. **John Skipworth** (LD) Educational consultant. Cllr, Harrow C 1985-98. Ed: Marple Hall GS, Stockport. **Philip Mitchell** (Green) Carer. Chairman, Blackpool Green party. Anti-fracking campaigner.

CONSTITUENCY PROFILE
A constituency of small, traditional former mill and coal mining towns deep in the south Lancashire coalfield. The main population centres are Ashton-in-Makerfield, Winstanley, Hindley and Orrell. With the decline of coal mining, new industries such as engineering have developed here. Along with predecessor seats, Makerfield has been held by Labour for more than a century, with a majority of 13,000 in 2015.

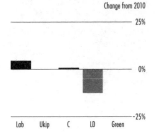

	Electorate	Turnout %	from 2010 %
	74,370	60.2	
Y Fovargue Lab	23,208	51.8	+4.5
A Collinson Ukip	10,053	22.5	
Z Zaidi C	8,752	19.5	+0.8
J Skipworth LD	1,639	3.7	-12.5
P Mitchell Green	1,136	2.5	

Change from 2010

- Lab
- Ukip
- C
- LD
- Green

Maldon

CONSERVATIVE HOLD

JOHN WHITTINGDALE
BORN Oct 16, 1959
MP 1992-

Secretary of state, culture, media & sport, following tenure as chairman, CMS select cttee 2005-15; led role in cttee's phone hacking investigation. Compelled Murdochs to attend session. *Spectator* magazine's inquisitor of the year, 2011. Previously described BBC licence fee as regressive. Close to Baroness Thatcher after serving as her pol sec (1988-92). Vice-chairman, 1922 cttee 2010-15. Shadow SoS: CMS 2004-05, 2002-03; efra 2003-04; trade & industry 2001-02. PPS to: William Hague 1999-2001; Eric Forth 1994-96. Opp Treasury spokes 1998-99. Opp whip 1997-98. Manager, NM Rothschild & Sons. OBE 1990. Divorced, one daughter, one son. Ed: Winchester Coll; UCL (BSc economics).

CHALLENGERS
Beverley Acevedo (Ukip) Runs

local family business. **Peter Edwards** (Lab) Researcher for Chris Leslie MP. Former journalist, *City AM, Yorkshire Post, Evening Star*, Ipswich. Board member, the Simon Community homeless charity. Ed: York (BA English); Edinburgh (MA Eng lit). **Ken Martin** (Ind) Stood to highlight waste in current party system. **Zoe O'Connell** (LD) IT engineer. Secretary of the LGBT+ Lib Dems. Transgender activist. Mem, Lib Dem Federal Conference cttee. Served in the Army Reserve. Three children. Ed: Brunel (BSc comp sci).

CONSTITUENCY PROFILE
Has a history of solid Conservative representation. A rural seat in the east of Essex, it is made up mostly of small villages with the yachting town of Burnham-on-Crouch in the south and the ancient town of Maldon to the north. Bradwell, on the Dengie peninsula, is the site of a decommissioned nuclear power station, and is expected to be the site of a new plant.

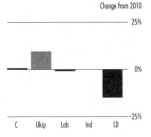

	Electorate	Turnout %	from 2010 %
	69,455	69.2	
J Whittingdale C	29,112	60.6	+0.8
B Acevedo Ukip	7,042	14.7	+9.6
P Edwards Lab	5,690	11.8	-0.8
K Martin Ind	2,424	5.1	
Z O'Connell LD	2,157	4.5	-14.8
R Graves Green	1,504	3.1	
J Marett TSPP	116	0.2	

Change from 2010

- C
- Ukip
- Lab
- Ind
- LD

Manchester Central

LABOUR CO-OPERATIVE HOLD

LUCY POWELL
BORN Oct 10, 1974
MP 2012-

Vice-chairman of Labour's 2015 election campaign. Manager of Ed Miliband's campaign to lead Labour; his chief of staff 2010-12. Elected in 2012 after what is believed to be the lowest voter turnout since the Second World War (18.2 per cent). Shadow min: Cabinet Office 2014-; education 2013-14. Member, select cttee: transport 2012-13. Contested Manchester Withington 2010. Ed: Parrs Wood HS; Xaverian Coll, Manchester; Somerville Coll, Oxford (BSc chemistry), King's Coll London (MSc).

CHALLENGERS
Xingang Wang (C) Senior manager, Scotiabank. Magistrate. Born and raised in mainland China. Lives in Surrey. Married, three daughters. Ed: Beijing Jiaotong University (BEng transportation management engineering); Imperial Coll (MSc transport); Oxford (MSc mathematical finance); Surrey (PhD accounting & finance). **Myles Power** (Ukip) Works for property developers in legal department. Ukip vice-chairman & secretary, Manchester 2014-. Ed: Belmont Abbey, Hereford. **Kieran Turner-Dave** (Green) Former domestic abuse administrator, Manchester Probation Service. TEFL tutor. Ed: Manchester (BA philosophy). **John Reid** (LD) Founder of CDR technology company providing data recovery services.

CONSTITUENCY PROFILE
Safe Labour seat with one of the largest electorates in the country. Levels of owner-occupation remain low, with most residents in private rented or social housing. The seat covers the University of Manchester with its large student population. It also has the highest proportion of people of Chinese ethnic background in the country.

	Electorate	Turnout %	from 2010 %	Change
	98,435	46.1		
L Powell Lab Co-op	27,772	61.3	+8.5	
X Wang C	6,133	13.5	+1.8	
M Power Ukip	5,033	11.1	+9.6	
K Turner-Dave Green	3,838	8.5	+6.2	
J Reid LD	1,867	4.1	-22.5	
L Kaye Pirate	346	0.8		
A Davidson TUSC	270	0.6		
J Davies Comm Lge	72	0.2		

Change from 2010

Lab Co-op   C   Ukip   Green   LD

Manchester Gorton

LABOUR HOLD

GERALD KAUFMAN
BORN Jun 21, 1930
MP 1970-

Veteran MP, Father of the House 2015-. Ex-journalist with a gift for an eye-catching turn of phrase. Shadow SoS: foreign 1987-92; home 1983-87; environment 1980-83. Minister: industry 1975. Parly under-sec: industry 1975; environment 1974-75. Opp spokesman, environment 1979-80. Chairman, CMS select cttee 1997-2005. Member, select cttees: Speaker's committee on electoral commission 2003-; liaison 1992-2005. MP Ardwick 1970-83. Lab party press liaison officer 1965-70. Journalist, *Mirror, New Statesman*. Writer, *That Was The Week That Was*. Booker Prize judges chairman, 1999. Ed: Leeds GS; Queen's Coll, Oxford (BA PPE).

CHALLENGERS
Laura Bannister (Green) Allotment and gardening co-ordinator, Mind. Previously project co-ordinator at Co-op financial services. Ed: Dover GS for Girls; Manchester (BSocSc social policy & criminology, MA political economy). **Mohammed Afzal** (C) Member, deputy chairman and chairman, Manchester Conservative Federation. **Phil Eckersley** (Ukip) Managing dir, Bridgewater Home Care. Ed: Manchester (BSc commercial management & quantity surveying). **Dave Page** (LD) Operations manager. Chairman, LGBT+ Lib Dems Ed: UMIST (BEng software engineering).

CONSTITUENCY PROFILE
A tough inner-city seat to the south of Manchester city centre, has suffered from gang violence in recent years. Home to many of Manchester's students and a large Asian and Muslim population. A safe Labour seat since 1935. There was a significant shift to the Lib Dems after the Iraq war, but this has vanished.

	Electorate	Turnout %	from 2010 %	Change
	72,959	57.6		
G Kaufman Lab	28,187	67.1	+17.0	
L Bannister Green	4,108	9.8	+7.0	
M Afzal C	4,063	9.7	-1.4	
P Eckersley Ukip	3,434	8.2		
D Page LD	1,782	4.2	-28.4	
S Hickman TUSC	264	0.6	-0.7	
C Chesha Pirate	181	0.4	-0.2	

Change from 2010

Lab   Green   C   Ukip   LD

Manchester Withington

LABOUR GAIN

JEFF SMITH
BORN Jan 26, 1963
MP 2015-

Events manager. Cllr, Manchester CC 1997-15, executive member for housing (formerly finance, children's services). DJ. School governor. Board member, Southway Housing Trust. Member: Co-operative party, Unite, Socialist Education Association, Friends of the Earth, Withington Civic Soc. Ed: Old Moat Primary Sch; University of Manchester.

CHALLENGERS
John Leech (LD) MP for Manchester Withington 2005-15. Surprise winner of seat in 2005 after campaign to try to save Christie hospital, Manchester. Took a leading role in the campaign to pardon Alan Turing. LD shadow min: transport 2006-10. Select cttees: CMS 2013-; transport 2005-10. Cllr, Manchester CC 1998-2008, dep leader, Manchester Lib Dems

group. Customer relations, RAC. Trainee manager, McDonald's. Ed: Manchester GS; Loretto Coll, Hulme; Brunel University (BA history & politics). **Rob Manning** (C) Senior consultant, EY, with specialism in local public services. Ed: Manchester (LLB law; LLM corporate governance). **Lucy Bannister** (Green). Student activist. Ed: Manchester (BSc chemistry). **Mark Davies** (Ukip) Works in sales for IT companies, recently returned from USA. Former sales executive, Electronic Data Systems. Ed: Leeds University.

CONSTITUENCY PROFILE
Withington, in south Manchester, was once a desirable middle-class area and a safe Conservative seat. As the middle classes moved out into Cheshire, many family homes were converted into rental flats for students. Is now attracting young professionals. Switched from Tory to Labour under Thatcher before a surprise win for the Lib Dems in 2005. Labour won it back in 2015.

	Electorate	Turnout %	Change from 2010 %
	80,590	62.0	
J Smith Lab	26,843	53.7	+13.3
J Leech LD	11,970	24.0	-20.7
R Manning C	4,872	9.8	-1.4
L Bannister Green	4,048	8.1	+6.3
M Davies Ukip	2,172	4.4	+2.8
M Farmer Ind	61	0.1	0.0

Change from 2010

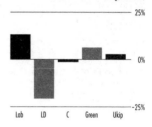

Mansfield

LABOUR HOLD

SIR ALAN MEALE
BORN Jul 31, 1949
MP 1987-

Backbencher formerly close to John Prescott. Speaker's panel HoC 2010. Council of Europe: mem 2000-; chief whip, Lab delegation 2010-: leader, Lab delegation 2012-. Parly under-sec: environment, transport & regions 1998-99. PPS to John Prescott 1994-98. Select cttees include: panel of chairs 2011-; draft voting eligibility (prisoners) bill 2013; Crossrail bill 2005-07; draft gambling bill 2003-04; court of referees 1999-2002; home affairs 1989-92. Opposition whip 1992-94. Member: Co-op party; Commonwealth War Graves Commission 2002-10. Adviser to Richard Caborn 2002-05. Aslef gen sec asst. Nacro officer. Honorary senator of Louisiana. Married, one daughter, one son. Ed: St Joseph's RC Sch, Bishop Auckland; Durham University; Ruskin Coll, Oxford; Sheffield Hallam (MA).

CHALLENGERS
Andrea Clarke (C) Criminal defence solicitor. Cllr, North Kesteven DC. Married, two sons. Ed: Brock University, Ontario (BSc chemistry), University of Birmingham (LLB law, MBA). **Sid Pepper** (Ukip) Started his own business aged 16. Separated, three daughters, one from second partner. Ed: Mansfield GS.

CONSTITUENCY PROFILE
A traditional former mining town on the western edge of Nottinghamshire. The coal mines closed long ago and unemployment problems have been exacerbated by the closures of other industries, such as the Mansfield Brewery and the AG Barr factory. It has been held by the Labour party since the 1920s, although not always entirely safely (in 1987 it was an ultra-marginal). The local Mansfield Independent Forum is extremely strong at a local level and this has translated into significant independent challenges.

	Electorate	Turnout %	Change from 2010 %
	77,534	60.9	
A Meale Lab	18,603	39.4	+0.7
A Clarke C	13,288	28.2	+1.8
S Pepper Ukip	11,850	25.1	+18.9
T Rogers LD	1,642	3.5	-12.0
P Frost Green	1,486	3.2	
K Seymour TUSC	324	0.7	

Change from 2010

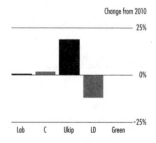

Meon Valley

CONSERVATIVE HOLD

GEORGE HOLLINGBERY
BORN Oct 12, 1963
MP 2010-

Interested in countryside issues, entrepreneurship. Whip (lord commissioner, Treasury) 2015-. PPS to Theresa May 2012-. Select cttees: speaker's advisory cttee on works of art 2010-; communities 2010-12. Contested Winchester 2005, campaign manager for Andrew Hayes 2001. Cllr, Winchester CC 1999-2010; Alresford TC 1999-2003. Start-up specialist. Business career: Thompson Sowerbutts (property investment); chairman, Companion Care veterinary chain; chairman & founder, Pet Depot; Companion Care Veterinary Group. Venture capitalist. Stockbroker, Robert Fleming & Co. Keen fly fisherman. Enjoys field sports. Chairman, APPG angling. Married, three children. Ed: Radley Coll; LMH, Oxford (BSc human sciences); UPenn (MBA).

CHALLENGERS
Dave Alexander (Ukip) Automotive engineer, Navigant Research. Cllr, Horndean PC 2014-. Ed: Brunel University (BSc mech eng). **Gemma McKenna** (Lab) Public affairs and policy officer, Fixers, young person's charity. Former parly researcher, Paul Goggins MP. Ed: Portsmouth (BA international business); Manchester (MA development economics); Middlesex (PhD social policy). **Chris Carrigan** (LD) Principle architect, business strategy & transformation, Marks & Spencer. Council member, Electoral Reform Society. Ed: Exeter (BSc computer science, operational research).

CONSTITUENCY PROFILE
Meon Valley, to the north of Portsmouth, was created in 2010 as an extra seat for Hampshire. With the exception of parts of Waterlooville, it is affluent and middle class. Home ownership is among the highest for the region, according to the 2011 census.

	Electorate	Turnout %	from 2010 % Change
	72,738	71.1	
G Hollingbery C	31,578	61.1	+4.8
D Alexander Ukip	7,665	14.8	+11.9
G McKenna Lab	5,656	10.9	+4.6
C Carrigan LD	4,987	9.6	-22.9
D Korchien Green	1,831	3.5	

Change from 2010

C Ukip Lab LD Green

Meriden

CONSERVATIVE HOLD

CAROLINE SPELMAN
BORN May 4, 1958
MP 1997-

Steadily rose through Tory ranks in opposition, unceremoniously sacked as SoS, environment, food & rural affairs (2010-12) prompting ageism row. Conservative party chairwoman 2007-09. Shadow SoS: CLG 2009-10, 2004-05; efra 2003-04; int devt 2001-03. Shadow min: without portfolio 2007-09; ODPM 2005-07; women 2001-04 Select cttees: ecclesiastical 2014-; modern slavery bill 2014; environmental audit 2013-. Shadow spokeswoman, health 1999-2001. Whip 1998-99. Research fellow, University of Kent, business consultant. Married, one daughter, two sons. Ed: Herts & Essex HS for Girls; Queen Mary Coll, London (BA European studies).

CHALLENGERS
Thomas McNeil (Lab) Charity and social enterprise lawyer. Special constable, Metropolitan Police. Volunteer, Barnardo's. Ed: Durham University (BA philosophy, politics & psychology); Coll of Law (PDip law), BPP Law School (LPC); Hughes Hall, Cambridge (MPhil planning, growth & regeneration). **Mick Gee** (Ukip) Former soldier now working for Jaguar Land Rover.**Ade Adeyemo** (LD) Chairman, Solihull & Meriden LD. Chartered civil engineer. Adviser, the Warwickshire Society.

CONSTITUENCY PROFILE
A slim rural green belt that divides the Birmingham conurbation from Coventry known as the "Meriden Gap", which traditionally claims to be the centre point of England. The seat was a Labour-Tory marginal before the Conservative victory of 1979. It is now a generally safe Conservative seat. Labour is strong in Castle Bromwich and Chelmsley Wood, although in recent years the Green party have made inroads here.

	Electorate	Turnout %	from 2010 % Change
	81,079	64.9	
C Spelman C	28,791	54.7	+3.1
T McNeil Lab	9,996	19.0	-1.5
M Gee Ukip	8,908	16.9	+14.3
A Adeyemo LD	2,638	5.0	-12.8
A Gavin Green	2,170	4.1	+2.8
C Booth IE	100	0.2	

Change from 2010

C Lab Ukip LD Green

Merthyr Tydfil & Rhymney

LABOUR HOLD

GERALD JONES
BORN Aug 21, 1970
MP 2015-

Development officer, Gwent Association of Voluntary Organisations. Cllr, Caerphilly CBC 1995-15, deputy leader 2004-08, 2014-15, cabinet member, housing. Chair, Merthyr Tydfil and Rhymney constituency Lab party 2008-12. Election agent: Dai Harvard 2005 & 10; Huw Lewis AM 2003, 07 & 11. Member, GMB, Co-op. Trustee, Phillipstown Residents and Community Association. Volunteer dir, White Rose Resource Centre, set up as part of regeneration for New Tredegar. Secretary, New Tredegar Communities Partnership. Chairman, White Rose Primary Sch. Vice-chairman, Phillipstown PS. Ed: Bedwelty Comp Sch; Ystrad Mynach Coll.

CHALLENGERS
David Rowlands (Ukip). Self-

employed. Chairman, Ukip Wales 2000-05. Ed: Pontllanfraith GS; Newport Coll (HND business studies). **Bill Rees** (C) Head of commercial, energy construction services, British Gas. Ed: University of Warwick (BSc economics); Selwyn Coll, Cambridge (MPhil economics). **Rhayna Mann** (PC) Researcher and caseworker for Jocelyn Davies AM. Married, stepmother of four. **Elspeth Parris** (Green) Social worker. Former church minister. Ed: Glasgow (MSc maths – did not complete); De Montfort (DipSW); Cardiff (CertHE theology)

CONSTITUENCY PROFILE
A Welsh valley seat, Merthyr was once an industrial boom town but its iron and coal industries went into early decline. Rhymney is also a former coal mining town and suffered a similar, if later, fate. The area continues to struggle and has some of the worst health problems in Britain. Created for the 1983 general election.

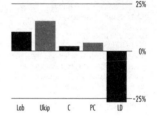

	Electorate	Turnout %	Change from 2010 %
	61,719	53.0	
G Jones Lab	17,619	53.9	+10.2
D Rowlands Ukip	6,106	18.7	+16.0
B Rees C	3,292	10.1	+2.5
R Mann PC	3,099	9.5	+4.4
B Griffin LD	1,351	4.1	-26.9
E Parris Green	603	1.8	
E Blanche Ind	459	1.4	-4.4
R Griffiths Communist	186	0.6	

Change from 2010

Middlesbrough

LABOUR HOLD

ANDY MCDONALD
BORN Mar 8, 1958
MP 2012-

Elected in 2012 after the death of Sir Stuart Bell. PPS to: Chuka Umunna 2013-; Emily Thornberry 2013. Member, justice select cttee 2012-. Lawyer, specialist in serious injuries and advised HoC defence select cttee on armed forces compensation (2003). Cllr, Middlesbrough BC 1995-99. Married, two sons, two daughters. Ed: St George's Secondary Sch, St Mary's Sixth Form Coll, Leeds Polytechnic (BA law).

CHALLENGERS
Nigel Baker (Ukip) Former learning mentor and teacher, Blakeston Sch, Stockton-on-Tees. Previously member, Labour party; joined Ukip 2014. **Simon Clarke** (C) Senior policy adviser to parly chairman of education select cttee. Former solicitor, Slaughter & May. Married. Ed: University

Coll, Oxford (BA history, president OUCA). **Hannah Graham** (Green) Member, NEC, NUS. Ed: Teeside University (BSc computing). **Richard Kilpatrick** (LD) Chairman of Middlesbrough and East Cleveland Liberal Democrats. Works in campaigns and public affairs. Ed: Acklam Grange Sch; Northumbria University (BA politics).

CONSTITUENCY PROFILE
Labour stronghold represented for almost 30 years by Sir Stuart Bell. Middlesbrough is a large industrial town on the south bank of the Tees and this seat includes much of the town itself, after the east and west of the town were united into one constituency in 1974. The area is overwhelmingly working class and includes deprived and poverty-stricken areas such as the Thorntree estate. To the north it contains the large industrial areas along the Tees. Ukip came second here in 2012, and repeated its success in 2015.

	Electorate	Turnout %	Change from 2010 %
	61,868	52.9	
A McDonald Lab	18,584	56.8	+10.9
N Baker Ukip	6,107	18.7	+15.0
S Clarke C	5,388	16.5	-2.3
H Graham Green	1,407	4.3	
R Kilpatrick LD	1,220	3.7	-16.2

Change from 2010

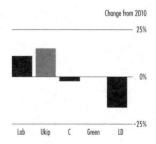

Middlesbrough South & Cleveland East

LABOUR HOLD

TOM BLENKINSOP
BORN Aug 14, 1980
MP 2010-

Opposition whip 2011-15. Select cttees: selection 2013-; environment, food and rural affairs committee 2010-12; Treasury 2011; standards & privileges 2010-11. Regional officer for Community Trade Union. Constituency researcher to former MP Ashok Kumar, who died March 2010. Member, Honorary president, Guisborough Town FC. Married. Ed: St Mary's Sixth Form Coll, Saltersgill; Teeside University (BSc PPE); University of Warwick (MA continental philosophy).

CHALLENGERS
Will Goodhand (C) UK board director, TNS market research. Former dir, Ipsos ASI. DJ, Core Digital Radio 2006-07. Speaks French. Ed: Christ Church, Oxford (BA law). **Steve Turner** (Ukip) Small-business owner. Cllr, Redcar

and Cleveland BC 2015-. Married, three sons. **Ben Gibson** (LD) Broadcast journalism student at University of Bedfordshire. Presents community radio show, CVFM. Previously worked on the Middlesbrough Youth Empowerment Project. **Martin Brampton** (Green) Software engineer, international database company. Married: Ed: West Hartlepool GS.

CONSTITUENCY PROFILE
The seat is a mix of coastal, rural and suburban areas with an economy mainly reliant on the farming and chemical industries. In 2011 this area had one of the highest proportion of miners of any seat, thanks to the Boulby potash and salt mine, which is among the deepest in Europe. Was created in 1997 to replace the Langbaurgh seat. Middlesbrough South and Cleveland East has been Labour since it was created in 1997 to replace the Tory marginal Langbaurgh seat.

	Electorate	Turnout %	from 2010 % Change
	71,153	64.2	
T Blenkinsop Lab	19,193	42.0	+2.8
W Goodhand C	16,925	37.1	+1.4
S Turner Ukip	6,935	15.2	+11.1
B Gibson LD	1,564	3.4	-12.5
M Brampton Green	1,060	2.3	

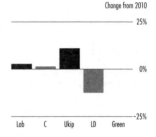

Change from 2010

Midlothian

SNP GAIN

OWEN THOMPSON
BORN Mar 17, 1978
MP 2015-

Moved to Loanhead, in the constituency, at the age of 7 and delivered his first political leaflets the following year. Became the youngest councillor in Scotland when he was elected to Midlothian Council in 2005. Cllr, Midlothian C 2005-, leader 2013-15. Assistant to: Clare Adamson MSP; Rob Gibson MSP. Secretary, SNP COSLA Group. Honorary VP, SNP Students. Ed: Beeslack Community HS; Edinburgh Napier (BA accounting & finance).

CHALLENGERS
Kenny Young (Lab) Cllr, Midlothian BC 2014-. Press manager for Ed Milliband 2010-12; Press officer, GB on the road, Gordon Brown's tour of the UK 2010. Previously press manager, Scottish Opera. Ed: Edinburgh (MA history). **Michelle Ballantyne** (C) Runs charity

dealing with substance abuse. Director of her husband's figurine manufacturing company. Cllr, Scottish Borders C 2012-. Con leader 2012-. Former operational manager, NHS Lothian. Ed: Heriot-Watt (BSc quality management). **Ian Baxter** (Green) Self-employed bookkeeper. Cllr, Midlothian C 2012-. Treasurer, Scottish Green party. Ed: Edinburgh (BSc physics). **Gordon Norrie** (Ukip) Married, three children. **Aisha Mir** (LD) Runs family business. Ed: University of the West of Scotland (BA business & marketing).

CONSTITUENCY PROFILE
Spreading southwards from the Edinburgh commuter belt, this former mining county was traditional Labour heartland until the SNP surge pushed it out in 2015. Its most famous MP was William Gladstone, whose victorious 1880 Midlothian campaign is sometimes cited as the first modern political campaign.

	Electorate	Turnout %	from 2010 % Change
	67,875	71.2	
O Thompson SNP	24,453	50.6	+30.0
K Young Lab	14,594	30.2	-16.8
M Ballantyne C	5,760	11.9	+0.0
I Baxter Green	1,219	2.5	+1.0
G Norrie Ukip	1,173	2.4	+1.5
A Mir LD	1,132	2.3	-14.8

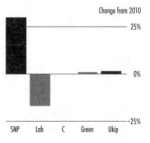

Change from 2010

Milton Keynes North

CONSERVATIVE HOLD

MARK LANCASTER
BORN May 12, 1970
MP 2005-

One of the few soldiers in the House of Commons; Army officer then major with TA (Territorial Decoration, VRSM). Served in Afghanistan during 2006 summer recess. Minister for defence personnel, welfare and veterans 2015-. Lord commissioner, Treasury 2012-. PPS to Andrew Mitchell 2010-12. Shadow min: int devt 2007-10. Opposition whip 2006-07. Select cttees: armed forces bill 2011; int devt 2009-10; CLG 2008-09; defence 2006; office of the deputy prime minister 2005-06. Dir, Kimbolton Fireworks 1993-2005. Cllr, Huntingdon DC, 1995-99. Plays for Commons cricket team. Married to Caroline Dinenage MP, one daughter from previous relationship. Ed: RMA Sandhurst; University of Buckingham (BSc business studies), honourary PhD; Exeter (MBA).

CHALLENGERS
Emily Darlington (Lab) Head of policy and corporate affairs, New Philanthropy Capital. Previously Treasury special adviser for Alistair Darling; head of communications, GMB union. Ed: Concordia University, Montreal (BA political science). **David Reilly** (Ukip) Worked in sales, pizza delivery and care. **Paul Graham** (LD) Senior lecturer in politics, University of Buckingham. Contested Glasgow North West 2005. Ed: Exeter (BA politics); LSE (MSc PhD political theory).

CONSTITUENCY PROFILE
Milton Keynes, the biggest planned new town in Britain, is built on a grid of roundabouts with a central shopping and leisure district. The town has mainly been constructed since the 1960s and has a younger population than most of the southeast. Created in 1992 when the existing Milton Keynes seat was split into two. Historically a Tory-Labour marginal.

	Electorate	Turnout %	from 2010 %	Change
	84,892	68.0		
M Lancaster C	27,244	47.2	+3.8	
E Darlington Lab	17,491	30.3	+3.5	
D Reilly Ukip	6,852	11.9	+8.6	
P Graham LD	3,575	6.2	-15.9	
J Marklew Green	2,255	3.9	+2.6	
K Simpson TUSC	163	0.3		
D Mortimer Ind	112	0.2	+0.0	

Change from 2010

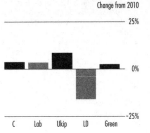

Milton Keynes South

CONSERVATIVE HOLD

IAIN STEWART
BORN Sep 18, 1972
MP 2010-

Scottish-raised headhunter who worked for Virginia Bottomley at Odgers, Ray & Berndtson. PPS to Patrick McLoughlin 2013-. Member, transport select cttee 2010-13. Contested: Milton Keynes South West 2005, 2001; Glasgow Rutherglen, Scottish Parliament 1999. Ran research unit in Westminster analysing legislation for clients, including Conservatives. Accountant, Coopers & Lybrand. Deputy chairman LGBTory, 2009-11. Enjoys opera, good wine and whisky, and running marathons. Ed: Hutchesons' GS, Glasgow; University of Exeter (BA politics).

CHALLENGERS
Andrew Pakes (Lab Co-op) Special adviser to Mary Creagh, previously to Nicky Gavron, when deputy mayor of London. Cllr, Southwark 2006-10. NUS president

1998-2000. Member, Co-op. Contested Milton Keynes N 2010. Ed: University of Hull (BA politics; MA environmental management). **Vince Peddle** (Ukip) Senior design engineer. Chairman, Ukip Milton Keynes & Buckinghamshire. **Lisa Smith** (LD) Cllr, Aylesbury Vale DC 2011-. Member, Aylesbury Homeless Action Group. Trustee, Vale of Aylesbury Housing Trust.

CONSTITUENCY PROFILE
Slightly more densely populated than its northern neighbour, this seat contains old railway lines, many modern estates and the Second Word War code-breaking centre of Bletchley Park. It also includes Woodhill prison and the Open University headquarters. Amazon distribution centre is based here. Has a larger than average number of people employed in the retail sector. As with Milton Keynes in general, the seat has a notably young population. Labour took it from the Tories in 1997 but lost it in 2010.

	Electorate	Turnout %	from 2010 %	Change
	87,968	67.1		
I Stewart C	27,601	46.9	+5.3	
A Pakes Lab Co-op	18,929	32.1	-0.2	
V Peddle Ukip	7,803	13.2	+9.5	
L Smith LD	2,309	3.9	-13.8	
S Pancheri Green	1,936	3.3	+1.9	
S Fulton Ind	255	0.4		
M Gibson Real	116	0.2		

Change from 2010

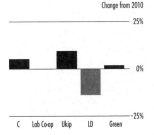

Mitcham & Morden

LABOUR HOLD

SIOBHAIN McDONAGH
BORN Feb 20, 1960
MP 1997-

Assistant govt whip 2007-08. PPS to John Reid 2005-07. Declined communities brief in 2001 to remain a backbencher. Select cttees: education 2012-; London regional 2009-10; unopposed bills 2002-10; health 2000-05; social security 1997. Cllr, Merton BC 1982-97. Contested Mitcham & Morden 1992, 87. GMB. Development co-ordinator, Battersea Churches Housing Trust; housing adviser; Wandsworth homeless persons unit; housing benefits assistant; clerical officer, DHSS. Her sister, Baroness McDonagh, used to be general secretary of Labour party. Ed: Holy Cross Convent, New Malden; University of Essex (BA politics).

CHALLENGERS
Paul Holmes (C) Senior parliamentary adviser to Stephen Hammond 2011-. Cllr, Southampton CC 2008-12. Chairman, Southampton University Conservatives. Ed: University of Southampton (politics & international relations). **Richard Hilton** (Ukip) Former Cllr, Merton C. Under investigation over a tweet suggesting Jihadi John should have killed himself 2015. **Mason Redding** (Green) **Diana Coman** (LD) Chairman, Grenfell housing and training social enterprise. Contested Mitcham & Morden 2010, Christchurch 2005.

CONSTITUENCY PROFILE
One of the most densely populated constituencies in the country. Mainly made up of interwar suburban housing developments and large council estates. The area is increasingly multi-ethnic, with large black, Asian and Polish communities. Retail and social work are the two largest employers in the area. A safe Labour seat, but was held by the Conservatives for much of the 1980s.

	Electorate	Turnout %	from 2010 % Change
	68,474	65.9	
S McDonagh Lab	27,380	60.7	+4.2
P Holmes C	10,458	23.2	-2.1
R Hilton Ukip	4,287	9.5	+7.5
M Redding Green	1,422	3.2	+2.3
D Coman LD	1,378	3.1	-8.8
D Coke CPA	217	0.5	

Change from 2010

25%

0%

-25%

Lab   C   Ukip   Green   LD

Mole Valley

CONSERVATIVE HOLD

SIR PAUL BERESFORD
BORN Apr 6, 1946
MP 1992-

New Zealand-born dentist with a low profile. Select cttees: standards & privileges 2010-; finance & services 2010-; communities 2006-10. Parly under-sec: environment 1994-97. MP Croydon Central 1992-97. Knighted in 1990 for work on inner-city rehabilitation; long-serving Wandsworth cllr 1978-94 and leader 1983-92. Married, one daughter, three sons. Ed: Waimea Coll, New Zealand; University of Otago, NZ (dentistry).

CHALLENGERS
Paul Kennedy (LD) Lawyer and actuary. Worked at HM Treasury and supported review of actuarial profession. Member, Green Liberal Democrats. Two children. Ed: Trinity Coll, Cambridge (BSc natural sciences). **Paul Oakley** (Ukip) Barrister. Chairman, Ukip, Greenwich & Lewisham 2012-. Chairman, Greater London Young Conservatives 1996-1997. Contested St Helens North for Conservatives, 2005. Ed: Ainsdale HS and King George V Sixth Form, Merseyside. University of Bristol. **Leonard Amos** (Lab) Works for national property management company. Member, Disability Labour executive committee 2013-. Left school at 16. Ed: Buckinghamshire Chilterns University Coll.

CONSTITUENCY PROFILE
A rural seat stretching across the North Downs southwest of London, Mole Valley is an affluent slice of commuter belt. The two main towns are Dorking, the administrative centre for Mole Valley Council, and Leatherhead, home to Unilever's UK headquarters and to many of Exxon's UK offices and a cluster of high-tech and research businesses. A safe Tory seat previously held by the former home secretary and education secretary Kenneth Baker.

	Electorate	Turnout %	from 2010 % Change
	74,317	74.2	
P Beresford C	33,434	60.6	+3.1
P Kennedy LD	7,981	14.5	-14.3
P Oakley Ukip	6,181	11.2	+6.1
L Amos Lab	4,565	8.3	+1.3
J Fewster Green	2,979	5.4	+3.8

Change from 2010

25%

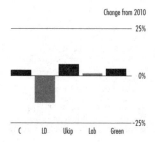

0%

-25%

C   LD   Ukip   Lab   Green

Monmouth

CONSERVATIVE HOLD

DAVID DAVIES
BORN Jul 27, 1970
MP 2005-

Deeply right-wing, global-warming sceptic and Welsh-speaker. Elected unopposed as chairman, Welsh affairs select cttee 2010-. Former special constable for Brit Transport Police. Select cttees: national policy statements 2010-; liason 2010-; Welsh affairs 2005-; home 2007-10. Assembly Member for Monmouth 1999-2007, argued against extension of Assembly powers. Contested Bridgend 1997. Brief stint at British Steel and in TA. Lorry driver, took over family haulage business. Amateur boxer ("Tory Tornado"). Married, two daughters, one son. Ed: Bassaleg Comp, Newport.

CHALLENGERS
Ruth Jones (Lab) Selected on all-women list. Physiotherapist. Trade union rep; president, Wales TUC, 2006. Two children. **Gareth Dunn** (Ukip) Physics teacher. Contested: European elections, 2014; Welsh Assembly, 2011; general election, 2010; Scottish Parliament, 2003. **Veronica German** (LD) Executive director, Dolen Cymru Wales Lesotho Link. AM South Wales East 2010-11. Cllr: Torfaen 2008-12; Newport 2004-2010. Former teacher. Ed: Aston (BSc chemical engineering); Birmingham (MSc biochemical engineering).

CONSTITUENCY PROFILE
The seat is on the border with England and, in many ways, has more in common with its English neighbours than with the Welsh valleys to the west. It has one of the lowest proportions of Welsh speakers of any seat, a third of the population in the 2011 census were born in England and there is little support for Plaid Cymru. The seat is mostly countryside, and a Tory-leaning marginal that has been won by Labour only in its very best years.

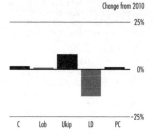

	Electorate	Turnout %	Change from 2010 %
	65,706	72.2	
D Davies C	23,701	49.9	+1.6
R Jones Lab	12,719	26.8	+0.9
G Dunn Ukip	4,942	10.4	+8.0
V German LD	2,496	5.3	-14.1
J Clark PC	1,875	4.0	+1.2
C Were Green	1,629	3.4	+2.2
S Morris Eng Dem	100	0.2	

Change from 2010

Montgomeryshire

CONSERVATIVE HOLD

GLYN DAVIES
BORN Feb 16, 1944
MP 2010-

Ousted Lembit Öpik in 2010. Interested in health issues after treatment for colon cancer. Member, Welsh affairs select cttee 2012-, 2010. PPS to Cheryl Gillan 2010-12. AM for Mid & West Wales 1999-2007. Cllr, Montgomeryshire DC 1979-89 (chairman 1985-89). Contested Montgomeryshire 1997. Former farmer. Chairman, Development Board for Rural Wales. Member: Wales Tourism Board, Welsh Development Agency. President, Campaign for Protection of Rural Wales. Recently learnt Welsh to fluency. Blogger. Keen golfer. Married, four children. Ed: Llanfair Caereinion HS; Aberystwyth University (Dip international law & politics).

CHALLENGERS
Jane Dodds (LD) Child protection social worker. Former cllr, Richmond BC 2006-10. Previously worked for Refugee Council. Brought up in Welsh-speaking home. **Des Parkinson** (Ukip) Welsh-born retired policeman. Married, with two adult children. **Martyn Singleton** (Lab) Student, journalism. Contested Welsh Parliament election 2011. Ed: Bangor (BA history & politics); Staffordshire (MA journalism).

CONSTITUENCY PROFILE
A rural and sparsely populated seat including the towns of Welshpool and Newtown, mostly mountainous in the west but turning to fertile, rolling farmland towards the English border in the east. The west is home to more Welsh-speakers than the east. Agriculture is important, employing about a tenth of the population. There is a strong Liberal tradition and until 2010 the seat had been held by the Liberals and Liberal Democrats almost continuously since 1880, most notably by the former party leader Clement Davies.

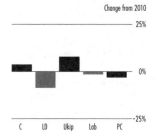

	Electorate	Turnout %	Change from 2010 %
	48,491	69.6	
G Davies C	15,204	45.0	+3.7
J Dodds LD	9,879	29.3	-8.6
D Parkinson Ukip	3,769	11.2	+7.8
M Singleton Lab	1,900	5.6	-1.5
A Griffith PC	1,745	5.2	-3.1
R Chaloner Green	1,260	3.7	

Change from 2010

Moray

SNP HOLD

ANGUS ROBERTSON
BORN Sep 28, 1969
MP 2001-

Leader, SNP Westminster group 2007-, group leader, constitution 2015-. Westminster dep leader 2005-07. Campaign director, 2015 general election. SNP spokesman: foreign affairs and defence 2001-; Europe and for Office of the deputy prime minister 2005-07. Member, European scrutiny select cttee 2001-10. National organiser, Student Nationalists Federation. Member: Nat Exec, Young Scottish Nationalists, SNP international bureau. European policy adviser, SNP group Scottish Parliament. Communication consultant. Journalist. Speaks German. Ed: Broughton HS, Edinburgh; Aberdeen (MA politics & international relations).

CHALLENGERS
Douglas Ross (C) Cllr, Moray C 2012-. PPS to Mary Scanlon MSP.

Contested Moray 2010. Chairman, Sport Moray executive cttee. Ed: Forres Academy; Scottish Agricultural Coll. **Sean Morton** (Lab) Cllr Moray 2012-. Researcher, Scottish Parliament. Parliamentary officer, Labour Friends of Israel 2007. Former health recruitment consultant. University of Stirling (MA international politics); the University of Aberdeen (MA history). **Robert Scorer** (Ukip) Army service 1983-97. Single parent.

CONSTITUENCY PROFILE
Moray has long been one of the SNP's safest seats. The large rural constituency in northeast Scotland stretches down into the Cairngorms National Park. The River Spey runs through the seat and its valley forms a premier area for the distilling of malt whisky, including Glenfiddich and Glenlivet. The main centres of population are Forres and Elgin. The RAF Lossiemouth base is an important employer.

	Electorate	Turnout %	from 2010 % Change
	71,685	68.8	
A Robertson SNP	24,384	49.5	+9.8
D Ross C	15,319	31.1	+5.0
S Morton Lab	4,898	9.9	-7.2
R Scorer Ukip	1,939	3.9	+1.3
J Paterson LD	1,395	2.8	-11.7
J MacKessack-Leitch Green	1,345	2.7	

Change from 2010

SNP	C	Lab	Ukip	LD

Morecambe & Lunesdale

CONSERVATIVE HOLD

DAVID MORRIS
BORN Jan 3, 1966
MP 2010-

Former hairdresser who ran his own salon. Commercial property investor. Interested in tourism and business. PPS to Stephen Crabb 2014-15. Select cttees: political reform 2014-; science & technology 2010-14; admin 2012-14. Contested: Carmarthen West & South Pembrokeshire 2005; Blackpool South 2001. Member, Institute of Directors; National Hairdressing Council. Adviser to Greenwich University on study into effects of minimum wage. Former musician and songwriter, used to be in band with Rick Astley. Divorced, two sons. Ed: St Andrews Nassau, Bahamas.

CHALLENGERS
Amina Lone (Lab) Co-director of Social Action & Research Foundation, a community interest company. Cllr Manchester CC

2010-. former chairwoman of the NW Women's Solidarity Forum. Single mother of four. **Steve Ogden** (Ukip) Owns a bicycle shop. Cllr, Morecambe TC 2014-. Chairman, Ukip Lancaster & Morecambe 2013-. **Matthew Severn** (LD) Insurance broker. Cllr South Lakeland DC 2014-. Methodist Church. Married. **Phil Chandler** (Green) IT manager, Lancaster University. Member, Unite. Married, two daughters.

CONSTITUENCY PROFILE
At the very northern edge of Lancashire. The urban southwestern part along the coast includes the industrial ferry port of Heysham, along with its nuclear power station, and the holiday resort of Morecambe. To the east it stretches into the rural Pennines. Once a reliable Conservative seat, this, like many others, fell to Labour in the 1997 landslide. After being narrowly regained by the Tories in 2010, it was held comfortably in 2015.

	Electorate	Turnout %	from 2010 % Change
	66,476	65.1	
D Morris C	19,691	45.5	+4.2
A Lone Lab	15,101	34.9	-4.4
S Ogden Ukip	5,358	12.4	+8.2
M Severn LD	1,612	3.7	-10.0
P Chandler Green	1,395	3.2	+1.9
M Dawson ND	85	0.2	

Change from 2010

C	Lab	Ukip	LD	Green

Morley & Outwood

CONSERVATIVE GAIN

ANDREA JENKYNS
BORN 16 Jun 16, 1974
MP 2015-

Pulled off the coup of the 2015 election by ousting Ed Balls. Cllr, Lincolnshire CC 2009-13. International business development manager. Previously: retail manager; school music tutor. Trustee, MRSA Action UK after father died of superbug in 2011. Ed: University of Lincoln (BA international relations & politics). Open University (Dip economics).

CHALLENGERS
Ed Balls (Lab Co-op) A divisive figure who rose to prominence under Gordon Brown's leadership and took this seat in 2010. Shadow chancellor, 2010-15. Candidate for Lab leadership 2010. SoS: children, schools and families 2007-10. Econ sec to the Treasury 2006-07. MP Normanton 2005-10. Chairman, Fabian Soc 2007-08. Chief econ adviser to Treasury 1999-2004, economic adviser to Gordon Brown 1994-99. Econ leader writer and columnist, *Financial Times*. Teaching fellow, Harvard. TGWU/Unison. Married to Yvette Cooper MP, two daughters, one son. Ed: Nottingham HS; Keble Coll, Oxford (BA PPE); JFK Sch of Govt, Harvard (MPA, Kennedy Scholar). **David Dews** (Ukip) Civil engineer. Cllr, Wakefield DC, 2014-. Contested Pudsey 2010. Ed: Imperial Coll, London. **Rebecca Taylor** (LD) MEP, Yorkshire & the Humber 2012-14. Ed: Leeds (Japanese & management)

CONSTITUENCY PROFILE
Created in 2010 from the old Morley & Rothwell seat and part of the abolished Normanton seat previously held by Ed Balls. Morley, once a textile and coal-mining town, and Outwood, a former pit village, have both experienced a huge expansion of house building over a few decades. About a sixth of the population lives in social or council housing. Predecessor seats were Labour-held.

	Electorate	Turnout %	from 2010 %	Change %
	76,179	63.3		
A Jenkyns C	18,776	38.9	+3.6	
E Balls Lab Co-op	18,354	38.0	+0.5	
D Dews Ukip	7,951	16.5	+13.4	
R Taylor LD	1,426	3.0	-13.8	
M Hemingway Green	1,264	2.6		
A Craven Yorks	479	1.0		

Change from 2010

C · Lab Co-op · Ukip · LD · Green

Motherwell & Wishaw

SNP GAIN

MARION FELLOWS
BORN May 5, 1949
MP 2015-

SNP whip 2015-. Business studies teacher for 19 years at West Lothian Coll. Cllr, North Lanarkshire, 2012-15. Active member, EIS trade union. Senior campaigner for local Yes campaign, which won majority locally. Also contested: general election, 2010; Scottish Parliament, 2007. Married, three children. Ed: Heriot-Watt (accountancy & finance); Strathclyde (MA further education).

CHALLENGERS
Frank Roy (Lab) MP 1997-2015. Lifelong Motherwell and Labour man, held key organising role in recent Scottish by-election campaigns. Whip: govt 2006-10; asst govt 2005-06. PPS to: Helen Liddell 2001, 1997-99; John Reid 1999-2001. Member, select cttees: foreign affairs 2010-; selection 2008-10; defence 2001-05; social security 1997-98. GMB. Shop steward, ISTC. PA to Helen Liddell. Steelworker, Ravenscraig works. Married, one daughter, one son. Ed: Our Lady HS, Motherwell; Motherwell Coll (HNC marketing); Glasgow Caledonian (BA consumer and management studies). **Meghan Gallacher** (C) Works in call centre. Ed: West of Scotland (BA politics).

CONSTITUENCY PROFILE
Embodies the post-industrial character of much of central-belt Scotland. The area once thrived on heavy industry, based around Ravenscraig, the largest steel mill in western Europe. The closure of the steelworks dealt a major blow to the economy. The former site of the steelworks became the largest brownfield site in the country and is being transformed under a £1.2bn redevelopment programme. The seat has been solidy Labour since the 1940s. It has a role in history as the first seat ever won by the SNP, during the political truce at the end of the Second World War.

	Electorate	Turnout %	from 2010 %	Change %
	70,269	68.7		
M Fellows SNP	27,275	56.5	+38.4	
F Roy Lab	15,377	31.9	-29.2	
M Gallacher C	3,695	7.7	-1.7	
N Wilson Ukip	1,289	2.7		
R Laird LD	601	1.3	-8.6	

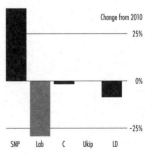

Change from 2010

SNP · Lab · C · Ukip · LD

Na h-Eileanan an Iar (Western Isles)

ANGUS MacNEIL
BORN Jul 21, 1970
MP 2005-

Gained overnight fame as MP who brought "cash for honours" claims to attention of Scotland Yard. SNP spokesman: Scotland 2008-; transport 2010-; constitutional reform 2010-; environment 2005-10; work & pensions 2007-08. Scottish affairs select cttee member, 2005-08. Contested Inverness E 2001. Convener, Lochaber SNP. Education lecturer, Inverness Coll. Worked for BBC Scotland. Primary sch teacher. Started Gaelic Medium Unit, Isle of Mull. Active crofter. Married, three daughters. Ed: Castlebay Sch, Barra; Nicolson Inst, Stornoway; University of Strathclyde (BEng civil engineering); Jordanhill Coll (PGCE).

CHALLENGERS
Alasdair Morrison (Lab) MSP, Northern Isles 1999-2007. Led local Better Together campaign. Journalist and former editor, *An Gaidheal Ur* newspaper. Worked for the BBC in Inverness. Ed: Paible Sch, North Uist; Nicolson Institute, Isle of Lewis. **Mark Brown** (C) Financial services client manager. Ed: Portobello HS. **John Cormack** (SCP) Chairman, Scottish Christian Party. **Ruaraidh Ferguson** (LD) Trainee lawyer. Contested Scots parliament election 2007.

CONSTITUENCY PROFILE
Formerly known as the Western Isles, it took its Gaelic name in 2005 to reflect the importance of the language in the Outer Hebrides. It has the smallest electorate – about one fifth of the Isle of Wight at just more than 20,000 – but is one of the largest seats geographically. The only town is the fishing port of Stornoway on the Isle of Lewis, from where ferries sail to the mainland. Sunday observance is widely held. It has been an SNP-Labour marginal since the war.

	Electorate	Turnout %	Change from 2010 %
	21,744	73.3	
A MacNeil SNP	8,662	54.4	+8.7
A Morrison Lab	4,560	28.6	-4.3
M Brown C	1,215	7.6	+3.2
J Cormack SCP	1,045	6.6	
R Ferguson LD	456	2.9	-4.6

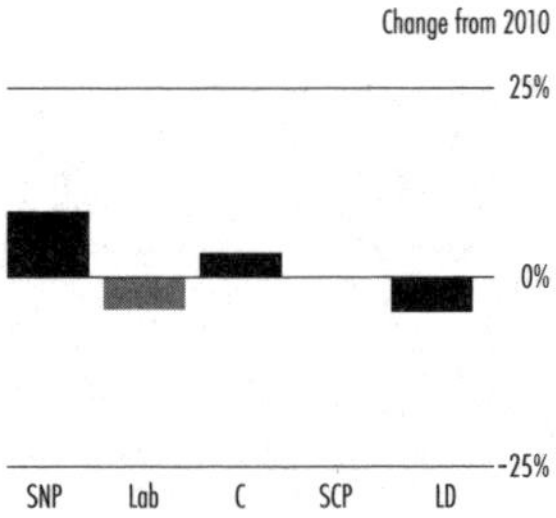

Change from 2010

[bar chart showing: SNP, Lab, C, SCP, LD with scale 25%, 0%, -25%]

Neath

CHRISTINA REES
BORN Feb 21, 1954
MP 2015-

Took the seat over from Peter Hain, its MP since 1991, after being selected from all-woman shortlist beating much-fancied Mabel McKeown, formerly on Harriet Harman's staff. MEP candidate. Cllr: Bridgend BC 2012-; Porthcawl TC 2012-; Mid-Glamorgan CC 1988-95. Squash professional. Development officer national coach, Wales Squash and Racketball 2004-. Justice of the Peace 1990-. Unite; GMB. Former barrister. Divorced from former cab min Ron Davies, who resigned from Blair government after his "moment of madness" with a male stranger on Clapham Common. Ed: Cynffig Comp Sch; Ystrad Mynach Coll; University of Wales (LLB law); Bar of England and Wales.

CHALLENGERS
Daniel Thomas (PC) Cllr, Blaenhonddan CC 2013-. Case worker, National Assembly for Wales 2013-2014. Former electrical engineer. Ed: Birchgrove Comp Sch. **Richard Pritchard** (Ukip) Former royal marine for nine years. Civil servant for 25 years. **Edmund Hastie** (C) Financial adviser. Cllr, Tunbridge Wells BC 2011-. Former army officer. Ed: Gorseinon Coll.

CONSTITUENCY PROFILE
A former coal-mining area in the South Wales valleys, Neath is a mixture of industrial and rural areas, running up to the foothills of the Brecon Beacons. A working-class seat and Labour stronghold. About a quarter of the population are Welsh-speaking, and Neath and Port Talbot had the highest proportion in favour of devolution in the 1997 referendum. Many commute to Swansea. The Welsh Rugby Union was born here. Plaid Cymru has come second in the last two elections, albeit a considerable way behind Labour.

	Electorate	Turnout %	Change from 2010 %
	56,099	66.2	
C Rees Lab	16,270	43.8	-2.5
D Thomas PC	6,722	18.1	-1.8
R Pritchard Ukip	6,094	16.4	+14.2
E Hastie C	5,691	15.3	+2.3
C Brock Green	1,185	3.2	
C Bentley LD	1,173	3.2	-11.8

Change from 2010

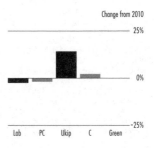

[bar chart showing: Lab, PC, Ukip, C, Green with scale 25%, 0%, -25%]

New Forest East

CONSERVATIVE HOLD

JULIAN LEWIS
BORN Sep 26, 1951
MP 1997-

Passionate champion of nuclear defence and leading Conservative supporter of John Bercow. Visiting senior research fellow of the Centre for Defence Studies, King's Coll, London. Select cttees: defence 2014-, 2000-01; arms export controls 2014-; intelligence 2010-. Shadow min: defence 2005-10, and 2002-05; Cabinet Office 2004-05. Opposition whip 2001-02. Author. Former deputy director, Conservative research department. Defence consultant, political researcher. Royal Naval Reserve. Ed: Dynevor GS, Swansea; Balliol Coll, Oxford (MA philosophy & politics); St Antony's Coll, Oxford (DPhil strategic studies).

CHALLENGERS
Roy Swales (Ukip) Lecturer, learning & development specialist. Formerly served in British Army, 1973-2014. Ed: Surrey University (Dip archaeology & landscape studies), Winchester University (MA education). **Andrew Pope** (Lab) Computer engineer. Cllr, Southampton CC 2011-. Chairman, Hampshire Co-operative party. **Bruce Tennent** (LD) Cllr, Hampshire CC 2009-; Eastleigh BC 2006-. Ed: Eastney Modern, Portsmouth; Portsmouth Poly (electrical & electronic engineering); London South Bank (PG Cert local governance for councillors); Portsmouth (MPA public administration).

CONSTITUENCY PROFILE
Much of the New Forest national park lies within this seat but most of the electorate live in the towns along Southampton Water and in Totton. Esso's Fawley refinery, near the village of the same name, is the largest oil refinery in the country. Socioeconomically diverse, the New Forest has returned Conservative MPs since 1910.

	Electorate	Turnout %	from 2010 %	Change %
	72,720	68.0		
J Lewis C	27,819	56.3	+3.4	
R Swales Ukip	8,657	17.5	+12.5	
A Pope Lab	6,018	12.2	+2.4	
B Tennent LD	4,626	9.4	-20.9	
S May Green	2,327	4.7	+2.7	

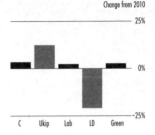

Change from 2010

C Ukip Lab LD Green

New Forest West

CONSERVATIVE HOLD

DESMOND SWAYNE
BORN Aug 20, 1956
MP 1997-

Close to David Cameron, with whom he runs. Rightwinger who opposed Britain's EEC membership in 1975 referendum. TA officer, served in Iraq July-Dec 2003. Min, int dev 2014-, taking over from Alan Duncan. Govt whip 2012-14. Privy Counsellor. PPS to: David Cameron 2005-12; Michael Howard 2004-05. Shadow min: int. affairs 2003-04; Northern Ireland 2004. Opposition whip 2002-03. Opposition spokesman: defence 2001-02; health 2001. Member, select cttees: admin 2012-13; defence 2005-06; ecclesiastical 2005; procedure 2002-05; Scottish affairs 1997-2001; social security 1999-2001. Dir, property development firm. Former manager, risk management systems, RBS. Married, two daughters, one son. Ed: Bedford Sch; University of St Andrews (MA theology).

CHALLENGERS
Paul Bailey (Ukip) Businessman involved in manufacture of printing equipment. **Lena Samuels** (Lab) Marketing and communications professional. Comms manager, the Hampton Trust. Former vice-chairwoman of Hampshire Police Authority. Non-executive director of University Hospital Southampton. Broadcaster, BBC Radio Solent. Ed: Queen Mary, London (MA English). **Imogen Shepherd-DuBey** (LD) IT consultant. Cllr, Winnersh PC. Ed: University of West London.

CONSTITUENCY PROFILE
A long thin seat running down the western edge of the New Forest National park. It includes the western fringes of the park itself, the market towns of Ringwood, Fordingbridge and New Milton that border it and, in the south, the port of Lymington and the coastal villages of Milford-on-Sea and Barton-on-Sea. Popular tourist destination. A safe Tory seat.

	Electorate	Turnout %	from 2010 %	Change %
	68,465	69.3		
D Swayne C	28,420	60.0	+1.1	
P Bailey Ukip	7,816	16.5	+10.6	
L Samuels Lab	5,133	10.8	+1.0	
I Shepherd-DuBey LD	3,293	7.0	-16.4	
J Richards Green	2,748	5.8	+3.6	

Change from 2010

C Ukip Lab LD Green

Newark

CONSERVATIVE HOLD

ROBERT JENRICK
BORN Jan 9, 1982
MP 2014-

Elected in 2014 after Patrick Mercer's resignation in wake of "cash for questions" furore. A leading proponent of flood defences. Sent 40,000 Christmas cards to constituents. Member, health select ctttee 2014-. PPS to: Esther McVey 2015; Amber Rudd 2014-15. Contested Newcastle-under-Lyme in 2010. Former: solicitor; international MD, Christie's. Married, two daughters. Ed: Wolverhampton GS; St John's Coll, Cambridge (BA history); UPenn (Thouron Fellow). Coll of Law (Grad Dip law 2005); BPP Law Sch (LPC 2006).

CHALLENGERS
Michael Payne (Lab) Deputy leader and cllr, Gedling BC 2011-. Cllr, Nottinghamshire CC 2013-. Ed: University of Lancaster (LLB law, Student union president). **Brian**

Mapletoft (Ukip) Accountant. Cllr, Hazlemere PC 2011-15, chairman, 2013-15. Chairman, Wycombe District Assoc of Local Councils. Ed: Magnus GS; Manchester (BA history, economics & politics. Chairman, Conservative assoc). **David Dobbie** (LD) Security officer. Cllr: West Lindsey DC 2011-15; Gainsborough TC 2012-; 2005-11. Chairman, Gainsborough Lib Dems 2012-14; 2006-10. Married. Ed: Bishop Vesey's GS; University of Sunderland (BSc materials science); Sheffield Hallam (PGCE).

CONSTITUENCY PROFILE
A long, mostly rural seat that stretches down the eastern side of Nottinghamshire, with the river Trent and the Great North Road both running through its middle. The main population centres are the cathedral town of Southwell and the market town of Newark. Former prime minister William Gladstone was MP here 1832-45. A safe Tory seat since the Labour MP Fiona Jones was defeated in 2001.

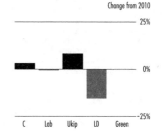

	Electorate	Turnout %	from 2010 % Change
	73,724	70.9	
R Jenrick C	29,834	57.0	+3.2
M Payne Lab	11,360	21.7	-0.6
B Mapletoft Ukip	6,294	12.0	+8.2
D Dobbie LD	2,385	4.6	-15.4
E Forster Green	1,792	3.4	
H Tyrer Consensus	637	1.2	

Change from 2010

Newbury

CONSERVATIVE HOLD

RICHARD BENYON
BORN Sep 4, 1960
MP 2005-

Archetypal rural, ex-military man. Son of the former MP Bill Benyon and great-great-grandson of the prime minister Lord Salisbury. Wealth estimated at £100 million, making him one of richest MPs. Parly under-sec: Defra 2010-2013. Shadow min: environment, food and rural affairs 2009-10, Opposition whip 2007-09. Select cttees: defence 2014-; arms export 2014-; environmental audit 2010-13; home affairs 2005-07. Cllr, Newbury DC 1991-95, led Conservative group, contested Newbury 2001, 1997. Former army officer, Royal Green Jackets, farmer and chartered surveyor. Trustee, Help for Heroes. Vice Chair, CAB 1994-. Remarried, three sons from first marriage, two from second. Ed: Bradfield Coll; Royal Agricultural Coll (Dip real estate management, land economy).

CHALLENGERS
Judith Bunting (LD) Television producer. Exec at a deaf-run production house, Remark. Former director and producer on *Tomorrow's World, Horizon*. Married, two children. Ed: Peterborogh County Girls; Fitzwilliam Coll, Cambridge (MSc natural sciences). **Catherine Anderson** (Ukip) Charity project manager. Defected from Tories. Ed: King's Coll London (BA languages & philosophy). **Jonny Roberts** (Lab) Associate editor, Westminster Forum Projects. Married.

CONSTITUENCY PROFILE
Geographically the largest seat in Berkshire, and a mostly rural constituency made up of the towns along the River Kennett and the villages to the north. Newbury is the biggest town and the administrative centre of West Berkshire. Long held by the Tories, a 1993 by-election gave Lib Dem David Rendel a shock victory. The Tories won back the seat in 2005.

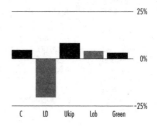

	Electorate	Turnout %	from 2010 % Change
	79,058	72.5	
R Benyon C	34,973	61.0	+4.6
J Bunting LD	8,605	15.0	-20.5
C Anderson Ukip	6,195	10.8	+8.3
J Roberts Lab	4,837	8.4	+4.2
P Field Green	2,324	4.1	+3.2
P Norman AD	228	0.4	+0.2
B Singleton Ind	85	0.2	-0.1
A Stott PSP	53	0.1	

Change from 2010

Newcastle upon Tyne Central

LABOUR HOLD

CHI ONWURAH
BORN April 12, 1965
MP 2010-

Chartered engineer who worked to bring wireless comms to Africa. Shadow min: cabinet office 2013-; BIS 2010-13. Formerly: head of international tech strategy, Ofcom; partner, Hammatan Ventures tech consultancy; director, market devt, Telegent; dir, product strategy, Global Telesystems. Nat exec, Anti Apartheid Movement. Member: Fabians, Co-op Society, Institute of Engineering and Technology. Advisory Board, OU Business Sch. Lived in Nigeria but foced back by Biafran Civil War. Ed: Kenton Comp; Imperial Coll, London (BEng electrical engineering); Manchester Business Sch (MBA).

CHALLENGERS
Simon Kitchen (C) Executive lead, Dementia Action Alliance, working with 2,000 organisations for the Alzheimer's Society. Previously senior advisor at Sustainable Development Commission. Ed: York (BA history). **Daniel Thompson** (Ukip) Semi-retired antique dealer. Chairman of local campaign against road scheme, STURR. **Nick Cott** (LD) Distance learning lecturer, Open University. Cllr, Newcastle CC 2000-. Chairman, Newcastle Lib Dems. Member, ministerial advisory group on education 2010-12.

CONSTITUENCY PROFILE
The central part of the city of Newcastle upon Tyne, once a driver of heavy industry, shipbuilding and coal mining, now is a hub for service industry and retail. Includes Newcastle's lively East Quayside area, Newcastle United football club and the city's Chinatown. There are high numbers of professionals but also areas of severe deprivation. The seat is ethnically diverse. Labour since 1945, with the exception of 1983-87, Lib Dems challenged in 2005 but have since faded.

	Electorate	Turnout %	from 2010 % Change
	61,061	57.5	
C Onwurah Lab	19,301	55.0	+9.1
S Kitchen C	6,628	18.9	-0.5
D Thompson Ukip	5,214	14.9	+12.7
N Cott LD	2,218	6.3	-17.8
A Johnson Green	1,724	4.9	+3.3

Change from 2010

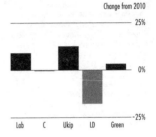

| Lab | C | Ukip | LD | Green |

Newcastle upon Tyne East

LABOUR HOLD

NICHOLAS BROWN
BORN Jun 13, 1950
MP 1983-

Tough enforcer. Before the 2015 election, claimed George Osborne was treating the northeast as "his northern outhouse". Shadow parly sec and chief whip 2010; shad dep whip 1995-97. Parly sec and chief whip 2008-2010, 1997-98; deputy whip 2007-08. Min: regional affairs 2007-10; DWP 2001-03; MAFF 1998-2001. Opp whip: deputy 1995-97. Select cttees: independent parly standards authority 2010-15; administration 2007-08; selection 2007-08. Various opp spokes 1985-95. Cllr, Newcastle upon Tyne CC 1980-84. Formerly: Legal adviser GMBATU. Proctor & Gamble advertising dept. Ed: Tunbridge Wells Tech HS; Manchester (BA).

CHALLENGERS
Duncan Crute (C) Runs tailoring company Crutes la Mar. Worked in marketing consultancy. Ed: University of Buckingham; University of Strathclyde. **David Robinson-Young** (Ukip) Barrister, Dere Street Barristers. Former police officer. Ed: Northumbria University (LLB law). **Wendy Taylor** (LD) Consultant clinical oncologist. Cllr, Newcastle CC 1988-. Contested Newcastle East 2010. **Andrew Gray** (Green) Archivist, Durham University; Cornwall CC. Ed: Winchester Coll; Cambridge (BA Classics)

CONSTITUENCY PROFILE
Socioeconomically, the constituency has contrasting halves. The universities dominate the north, where many students and young professionals live. The south has large council estates and severely deprived areas, including Byker Wall estate, the setting for the TV series *Byker Grove*. The great shipbuilding industry of the Tyne has declined from its glory days. The service and retail sectors are now important for jobs. The seat is traditionally a safe Labour one.

	Electorate	Turnout %	from 2010 % Change
	74,112	52.9	
N Brown Lab	19,378	49.4	+4.4
D Crute C	6,884	17.6	+1.5
D Robinson-Young Ukip	4,910	12.5	
W Taylor LD	4,332	11.0	-22.2
A Gray Green	3,426	8.7	+7.1
P Phillips TUSC	170	0.4	
M Stevenson Comm Brit	122	0.3	

Change from 2010

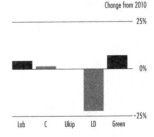

| Lab | C | Ukip | LD | Green |

Newcastle upon Tyne North

LABOUR HOLD

CATHERINE MCKINNELL
BORN Jun 8, 1976
MP 2010-

Newcastle born and raised, one of eight children. Shadow: minister, Treasury 2013-15, education 2011-13; solicitor general 2010-11. Member, political & constitutional reform select cttee 2010. Chairman: international anti-corruption APPG; member: diabetes; multiple sclerosis; HIV/Aids. Assists husband in café events business. Formerly: solicitor (employment specialist), Dickinson Dees. Member, Unite. Married, three children. Ed: Sacred Heart Comp; University of Edinburgh (politics & history, finance officer, Edinburgh students' association); University of Northumbria (CPE; LPC).

CHALLENGERS
Stephen Bates (C) Head of European Insight team, ARYZTA baking manufacturer. Previously at Brakes. Ed: Nottingham (BA history); Newcastle (MSc, international food marketing); Imperial Coll London (PhD economics). **Tim Marron** (Ukip) Former shopkeeper, training as a teachers' assistant at Newcastle Coll. Married, two sons. Ed: St Cuthberts GS. **Anita Lower** (LD) Cllr, Newcastle CC 1994-; leader, Lib Dem opposition 2013-; deputy council leader 2010-2013. Married, two children. Ed: La Sagesse Sch.

CONSTITUENCY PROFILE
Geographically the largest constituency within the city. It covers a diverse mixture of urban and rural areas north of Newcastle. Home to major employers including Nestlé, Newcastle Airport, Sage Group and Warbutons. Residents are comfortably well off but although the area is increasingly middle-class, it is shaped politically by the legacy of old Tyneside industries and has a long Labour history.

	Electorate	Turnout %	from 2010 %	Change
	67,267	66.7		
C McKinnell Lab	20,689	46.1	+5.2	
S Bates C	10,536	23.5	+5.3	
T Marron Ukip	7,447	16.6	+13.7	
A Lower LD	4,366	9.7	-23.4	
A Whalley Green	1,515	3.4	+2.7	
V Rook NE Party	338	0.8		

Change from 2010

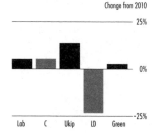

| Lab | C | Ukip | LD | Green |

Newcastle-under-Lyme

LABOUR HOLD

PAUL FARRELLY
BORN Mar 2, 1962
MP 2001-

Left of party, playing leading role in opposing higher university tuition fees as new MP in 2005. Abstained after heavy pressure. Select cttees: privacy & injunctions 2011-12; consolidation bills 2001-; CMS 2005-10; unopposed bills 2002-10; sci/tech 2003-05. Member, Socialist Education Assoc. Formerly: journalist, *The Observer, Independent on Sunday, Reuters;* corporate financier, Barclays de Zoete Wedd. Married. three children. Ed: Wolstanton County GS; Marshlands Comp; St Edmund Hall, Oxford (BA PPE).

CHALLENGERS
Tony Cox (C) Maintenance engineer, automotive sector. Four year apprenticeship in engineering industry. Cllr, Wirral BC 2008-14. Married. **Phil Wood** (Ukip) Chartered accountant. MD, Barringtons chartered accountants. Member, Staffs Chamber of Commerce 1985- (dep president); Shropshire chamber of commerce 2008-. Ed: Wolstanton GS; North Staffs Polytechnic. Ed: Durham Business sch (AVN Mastery business development). **Ian Wilkes** (LD) Runs local post office. Cllr, Newcastle BC 2005-. Cllr, Betley PC 1975-1986 (chairman twice). Dir, Hitmix Radio.

CONSTITUENCY PROFILE
Consists of the large market town of Newcastle-under-Lyme and extends westwards to include rural towns and villages. With a potteries and coal-mining history the seat is traditionally Labour-leaning but is turning into a Lab-Con marginal. A number of distribution companies have based themselves at Lymedale Business Park. Has been held by Labour since Josiah Wedgewood joined the party from the Liberals in 1919. Paul Farrelly held the seat in 2015 by a slim majority of 650 over his Tory opponent.

	Electorate	Turnout %	from 2010 %	Change
	66,752	64.4		
P Farrelly Lab	16,520	38.4	+0.5	
T Cox C	15,870	36.9	+2.6	
P Wood Ukip	7,252	16.9	+8.8	
I Wilkes LD	1,826	4.3	-15.4	
S Gibbons Green	1,246	2.9		
D Nixon Ind	283	0.7		

Change from 2010

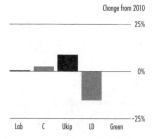

| Lab | C | Ukip | LD | Green |

Newport East

LABOUR HOLD

JESSICA MORDEN
BORN May 29, 1968
MP 2005-

Brought in to run the Labour party's operations in Wales, where politics has traditionally been male-dominated. PPS to: Peter Hain 2009-10, 2007-08; Paul Murphy 2008-09. Select cttees: Welsh affairs 2010-; 2005-07; modernisation of HoC 2005-06; constitutional affairs, 2005-07; justice 2007-10. Vice-chairman, steel and other metal-related industries APPG. Formerly: Welsh Labour party, gen sec; SE Wales organiser; worked for GMB; researcher, MPs Llew Smith and Huw Edwards. Partner, one daughter, one son. Ed: Croesyceiliog Comp; University of Birmingham (BA history).

CHALLENGERS
Natasha Asghar (C) TV presenter, Zee Entertainment Enterprise. Contested: Welsh Assembly 2011, 07; Euro 2009. Former radio DJ, Buzz Asia Radio. Worked in retail banking, Barclays. Ed: Rougemont Sch, Newport; University of London (MA contemporary British politics & media). **David Stock** (Ukip) Material handling instructor; 27 years in steel industry. Two children. Ed: Hartridge Comp. **Paul Halliday** (LD) Retail development manager, ethical handicrafts company. Minister. Ed: Lipscomb University, Nashville (BA theology). **Tony Salkeld** (PC) Office manager, Jocelyn Davies AM. Ex-Army.

CONSTITUENCY PROFILE
Runs along the River Severn, from Caldicot to the River Usk. The eastern half of Newport is home to many of Newport's prefabs, which are being replaced. The now-closed Llanwern steelworks used to be a major employer. Has become a home for the hi-tech industry. The seat remains working class and has historically been represented by Labour.

	Electorate	Turnout %	Change from 2010 %
	56,018	62.7	
J Morden Lab	14,290	40.7	+3.7
N Asghar C	9,585	27.3	+4.3
D Stock Ukip	6,466	18.4	+16.5
P Halliday LD	2,251	6.4	-25.8
T Salkeld PC	1,231	3.5	+1.4
D Mclean Green	887	2.5	
S Singh Bhatoe Soc Lab	398	1.1	+0.8

Change from 2010

Lab   C   Ukip   LD   PC

Newport West

LABOUR HOLD

PAUL FLYNN
BORN Feb 9, 1935
MP 1997-

Veteran left-winger and outspoken anti-war campaigner. Opp spokes, health 1988-89. Select cttees: home affairs 2013-; political & constitutional reform 2011; public administration 2005-; environmental audit 2005-; Welsh affairs 1997-98. Former sec, Welsh group of Lab MPs. Cllr, Gwent 1974-83; Newport BC 1972-81. Chemist in steel industry 1955-1984; radio broadcaster; Labour MEP research officer. Remarried, two stepchildren; one son, one daughter (deceased) from first marriage. Ed: St Illtyd's Coll; University Coll of Wales, Cardiff.

CHALLENGERS
Nick Webb (C) PR consultant; dir, MPC Cymru. Former executive officer, HMRC. Contested Newport East Welsh Assembly 2011 and Gwent PCC election 2012. Ed: Glamorgan (BA history). **Gordon Norrie** (Ukip) Retired police officer. Conservative cllr, Bromley BC 2006-14; deputy mayor 2009-10. Married. **Simon Coopey** (PC) Works for a local freight company. Member, Electoral Reform Society. Ed: Bettws HS; University of Wales, Newport (BA business marketing). **Ed Townsend** (LD) PR consultant. Station manager, Bay TV Swansea. Cllr, Newport CC 2004-, dep council leader 2008-11. Contested general election 2010, 2005. Former journalist, *Daily Post*.

CONSTITUENCY PROFILE
On the northern banks of the Severn and the western banks of the River Usk. The Office for National Statistics is one of the largest employers here. Created in 1983, the seat was initially won by the Tories in their 1983 landslide but Paul Flynn took it for Labour in 1987 and has held it since. Although there is substantial Tory support, it is unlikely to be sufficient to win the seat soon.

	Electorate	Turnout %	Change from 2010 %
	62,145	64.9	
P Flynn Lab	16,633	41.2	-0.0
N Webb C	13,123	32.5	+0.2
G Norrie Ukip	6,134	15.2	+12.3
S Coopey PC	1,604	4.0	+1.2
E Townsend LD	1,581	3.9	-12.7
P Bartolotti Green	1,272	3.2	+2.0

Change from 2010

Lab   C   Ukip   PC   LD

Newry & Armagh

SINN FEIN HOLD

MICKEY BRADY
BORN Oct 7, 1950
MP 2015-

Former welfare rights officer. MLA, Newry & Armagh 2007-; SF spokes, welfare and older people; deputy chairman, social development committee; member, health, social services & public safety cttee. APGs: trade unions 2013- (vice-chairman); mental health 2012-; football 2012-. Enjoys hurling.

CHALLENGERS
Danny Kennedy (UUP) MLA 1998-; dep leader, UUP 2007-11. NI minister: regional development 2011-; employment and learning 2010-11. UUP assembly spokes, education 1998-2002. Cllr, Newry & Mourne DC 1985-. Former British Telecom employee. Contested Newry & Armagh general election 1997. Ed: Newry HS. **Justin McNulty** (SDLP) Sports performance consultant. Former Irish Gaelic football manager

and player for Armagh. Part of Armagh team that won All-Ireland championship in 2002. Qualified civil engineer. **Kate Nicholl** (Alliance) Researcher for Anna Lo MLA. Lived in Zimbabwe until she was a teenager. Ed: UCL (BSc anthropology). **Robert Rigby** (C) Business development manager. Chairman, Catholic Union of Great Britain. Cllr, Westminster CC 2010-.

CONSTITUENCY PROFILE
A seat bordering the Republic of Ireland. Towns to the south, such as Crossmaglen, are 99 per cent Catholic and have suffered deprivation while farther north the seat is staunchly protestant. Armagh is home to the heads of the Catholic Church and the Anglican Church of Ireland. Created in boundary changes in 1983, as part of an expansion of NI constituencies from 12 to 17. Newry attained city status in 2002 as part of the Queen's golden jubilee celebrations. The SDLP held the seat until 2005.

	Electorate	Turnout %	Change from 2010 %
	77,622	64.3	
M Brady SF	20,488	41.1	-0.9
D Kennedy UUP	16,312	32.7	
J McNulty SDLP	12,026	24.1	+0.7
K Nicholl Alliance	841	1.7	+0.5
R Rigby C	210	0.4	-18.6

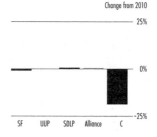

Change from 2010

SF   UUP   SDLP   Alliance   C

Newton Abbot

CONSERVATIVE HOLD

ANNE MARIE MORRIS
BORN Jul 5, 1957
MP 2010-

Former business mentor, marketing consultant, corporate lawyer. Member, work & pensions select cttee 2012-. Co-chairwoman, micro businesses APPG. Cllr, West Sussex CC 2005-07. Worked for Ernst and Young. Federation of Small Businesses. Enjoys hourse riding Singing and amateur dramatics enthusiast. Partner, stepchildren. Ed: Bryanston Sch; Hertford Coll, Oxford (BA law); Coll of Law, London; Open Uni (MBA); Harvard (leadership programme); Strathclyde Uni Sch of Coaching (Dip executive coaching).

CHALLENGERS
Richard Younger-Ross (LD) CEO YRD, architectural and planning services. MP for Teignbridge 2001-10, defeated after boundary changes in which constituency was renamed Newton Abbott.

Cllr Devon CC 2013-. Contested Teignbridge 1997, 1992. Former vice-chairman, National Young Liberals. Married. Ed: Oxford Poly. **Rod Peers** (Ukip) Previously school chair of governors. Two children. **Roy Freer** (Lab) Pub landlord. Married. Ed: University of Wales, Bangor (BA sociology and criminology).

CONSTITUENCY PROFILE
The old Teignbridge constituency was replaced by a much smaller seat in 2010 with 20,000 fewer electors. It takes in the coast between Exmouth and Torbay, including the town of Newton Abbot and the strip of coast between the estuaries of the Teign and the Exe. The 22 miles of coast are the focus of a growing tourism industry. The old seat was safely Tory until taken by Lib Dem Richard Younger-Ross in 2001. Anne Marie Morris won it back for the Tories 2010 by just 523 votes but increased her majority to 11,300 in 2015.

	Electorate	Turnout %	Change from 2010 %
	69,743	69.1	
A M Morris C	22,794	47.3	+4.3
R Younger-Ross LD	11,506	23.9	-18.1
R Peers Ukip	6,726	14.0	+7.6
R Freer Lab	4,736	9.8	+2.8
S Smyth-Bonfield Green	2,216	4.6	+3.2
S Brogan TUSC	221	0.5	

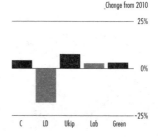

Change from 2010

C   LD   Ukip   Lab   Green

Norfolk Mid

CONSERVATIVE HOLD

GEORGE FREEMAN
BORN Jul 12, 1967
MP 2010-

A former NFU parliamentary officer, who grew up on a farm and enjoys country pursuits. Led movember campaign in parliament. Minister for life sciences 2014-. Member, CLG select cttee, 2010. Government adviser on life sciences to Rt Hon David Willetts 2011-13; PPS to Greg Barker 2010-12. Co-founder, 2020 group of Con MPs. Venture capitalist: founded 4D-Biomedical consultancy, MD 2003-10. Adviser, Norwich Research Park. Founder and former chairman, the Norfolk Way, to promote the county. Contested Stevenage 2005. Spitfire fan. Enjoys sailing and cycling. Married, one son, one daughter. Ed: Radley Coll; Girton Coll, Cambridge (BA geography).

CHALLENGERS
Anna Coke (Ukip) Involved

in family farming and forestry business with her husband, including extreme adventure high rope course. Ran her own sheep station in Australia after career in financial consultancy. Widowed, remarried, two children from first marriage. **Harry Clarke** (Lab) Former NHS director, health campaigner, hospital inspector. Associate member, Institute of Health Management. Ed: Hull (MSc health administration). **Paul Speed** (LD) Insurance broker, Marsh UK. Conductor, brass bands. Football referee.

CONSTITUENCY PROFILE
There has been a seat called Norfolk Mid since 1983 but the present one was recreated for the 2010 election, taking in parts of the old Mid Norfolk, Norfolk South and Norfolk South West. It mostly covers Breckland district, and the council is a major employer in the town of Dereham. Historically Tory and held by George Freeman in 2015 by 17,276 votes.

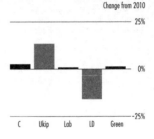

	Electorate	Turnout %	from 2010 % Change
	76,975	67.8	
G Freeman C	27,206	52.1	+2.6
A Coke Ukip	9,930	19.0	+13.5
H Clarke Lab	9,585	18.4	+0.9
P Speed LD	3,300	6.3	-15.9
S Jackson Green	2,191	4.2	+1.3

Change from 2010

C Ukip Lab LD Green

Norfolk North

LIBERAL DEMOCRAT HOLD

NORMAN LAMB
BORN Sep 16, 1957
MP 2001-

Contender to replace Nick Clegg as Liberal Democrat leader. Architect of plan for part-privatisation of Royal Mail. Minister of state: community & social care 2012-15. Parly under-sec, employment relations & consumer affairs 2012. Asst govt whip and chief political adviser to Nick Clegg 2010-12. LD shadow SoS: health 2006-10; trade and industry 2005-06. Chief of staff to Sir Menzies Campbell 2006. PPS to Charles Kennedy 2003-05. LD spokes: Treasury 2002-05; int devt 2001-02. Select cttees: Treasury 2003-05. Cllr, Norwich CC 1987-91. Former solicitor, employment specialist. Married, two sons. Ed: Wymondham Coll, Norfolk; University of Leicester (LLB law).

CHALLENGERS
Ann Steward (C) Manages tourism businesses. Cllr, Breckland C 2003-

15, Norfolk CC 2009-13. Married, one daughter. **Michael Baker** (Ukip) Businessman with retail interests. Cllr, Norfolk CC 2013-; Former cllr North Norfolk DC. Married, one daughter, three stepsons. Ed: Gresham's Sch; Surrey (BEng chemical engineering). **Denise Burke** (Lab) Runs Good Care Guide website. Worked with mayor of London on childcare and youth strategy. Chairwoman North Norfolk Labour party 2012-. Former tax inspector. Married.

CONSTITUENCY PROFILE
A rural seat, stretching along the north coast of Norfolk from Wells-next-the-Sea to the Norfolk Broads and taking in much of the Norfolk coast area of natural beauty. Made up of small villages, towns and fishing villages, it has one of the highest proportions of elderly people of any constituency in UK. In 2001 Norman Lamb became the first Liberal to represent the seat since 1918. It had previously been Conservative for 31 years.

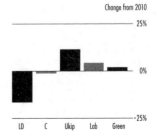

	Electorate	Turnout %	from 2010 % Change
	68,958	71.7	
N Lamb LD	19,299	39.1	-16.4
A Steward C	15,256	30.9	-1.2
M Baker Ukip	8,328	16.9	+11.5
D Burke Lab	5,043	10.2	+4.4
M Macartney-Filgate Green	1,488	3.0	+2.0

Change from 2010

LD C Ukip Lab Green

Norfolk North West

CONSERVATIVE HOLD

HENRY BELLINGHAM
BORN Mar 29, 1955
MP 2001-; 1983-97

Enjoys country sports and is passionate about rural issues. Enthusiastic member of Lords and Commons cricket team. Distant ancestor shot dead PM Spencer Perceval in 1812. Parly under-sec, FCO 2010-12. Shadow min: justice 2006-10; BIS 2002-05; trade & industry 2002-03. Opposition whip 2005-06. Select cttees: high speed rail 2014-; trade & industry 2002-03; NI affairs 2001-02; environment 1987-91. MP Norfolk North West 1983-97. Ran consultancy firm 1997-2001 after defeat. Previous roles include PPS to Malcolm Rifkind 1991-97. Barrister. Member, Cambridge University Liberal Club. Married, one son. Ed: Eton Coll; Magdalene Coll, Cambridge (BA law).

CHALLENGERS
Joanne Rust (Lab) Shop steward.

Early years and child development officer, Norfolk CC, seconded to be Norfolk campaigns organiser for Unison. **Richard Coke** (Ukip) Farmer and businessman. Runs high rope adventure company with wife. Cllr, Norfolk CC 2013-, Ukip group leader. Contested Mid-Norfolk 2010. Married. Ed: Radley Coll; Sandhurst. **Michael de Whalley** (Green) Self-employed IT consultant. Iraq service, Royal Auxiliary Air Force 2003. Ed: King Edward VII Sch, King's Lynn; Open University. **Hugh Lanham** (LD) Chartered accountant. Cllr, North Norfolk DC 2007-11.

CONSTITUENCY PROFILE
Covers the rural coast around the Wash and includes Kings Lynn and Hunstanton. A popular tourist and retirement area. According to the 2011 census, it has the highest proportion of people living in caravan parks of any area in England and Wales. Although held by Labour 1997-2001, it is now safely Conservative.

	Electorate	Turnout %	from 2010 %	Change
	72,400	65.4		
H Bellingham C	24,727	52.2	-2.0	
J Rust Lab	10,779	22.8	+9.5	
R Coke Ukip	8,412	17.8	+13.9	
M de Whalley Green	1,780	3.8	+2.2	
H Lanham LD	1,673	3.5	-19.7	

Change from 2010

[bar chart: C, Lab, Ukip, Green, LD with scale 25%, 0%, -25%]

Norfolk South

CONSERVATIVE HOLD

RICHARD BACON
BORN Dec 3, 1962
MP 2001-

Works forensically on the select committe for public accounts 2001-; european scrutiny 2003-07. Very critical of financial mismanagement and fraud in the EU. Contested Vauxhall 1997. Formerly: investment banker; financial journalist; PR consultant. Co-author of *Conundrum: Why every government gets things wrong and what we can do about it.* Married, two children. Ed: King's Sch, Worcester; LSE (BSc politics & economics).

CHALLENGERS
Deborah Sacks (Lab) Waste management consultant. Chartered surveyor. Cllr, Tasburgh PC 2007-, Camden 1992-98. Former regional planner, East of England regional assembly. Ed: UEA (BSc physics); UWE (MA town planning). **Barry Cameron** (Ukip) Owner, Senator

Business Consultants. Ed: Hull (BA politics). **Jacky Howe** (LD) Contested 2010. Cllr, Norfolk CC 2005-09, deputy leader Lib Dem group. Lobbyist Green Energy Bill. Widow, two children. **Catherine Rowett** (Green) Professor of philosophy, UEA. Ed: King's Coll, Cambridge (BA MA PhD Classics).

CONSTITUENCY PROFILE
A triangle of rural Norfolk between Norwich and the Suffolk border. This is a picturesque wedge of the Norfolk Broads, made up of small market towns and villages and running up to commuter villages just outside Norwich itself. The seat also includes the Lotus Cars base in the former RAF base at Hethel. Famous for its Dad's Army connections. This is one of the most affluent seats in Norfolk and has been safely Tory since 1950. The Lib Dems advanced at a local level for a time in the 1990s but it never translated into a real challenge at Westminster level.

	Electorate	Turnout %	from 2010 %	Change
	78,885	72.4		
R Bacon C	30,995	54.3	+4.9	
D Sacks Lab	10,502	18.4	+5.2	
B Cameron Ukip	7,847	13.7	+9.5	
J Howe LD	4,689	8.2	-21.2	
C Rowett Green	3,090	5.4	+3.6	

Change from 2010

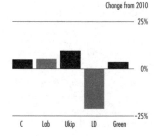

[bar chart: C, Lab, Ukip, LD, Green with scale 25%, 0%, -25%]

Norfolk South West

CONSERVATIVE HOLD

ELIZABETH TRUSS
BORN Jul 26, 1975
MP 2010-

Avid campaigner for retention of RAF bases in her constituency. Founded the Free Enterprise Group of Conservative MPs, which supports a more entrepeneurial culture in Britain. Secretary of state, Defra 2014-; parly under-sec: education 2012-14. Select cttee, justice 2010-12. Dir, Reform think tank 2008-09. Cllr, Greenwich BC 2006-2010. Contested Calder Valley 2005; Hemsworth 2001. Formerly: regulatory economics dir, Cable & Wireless; commercial analyst, Shell. Member, Chartered Institute of Management Accountants. Co-author *After the Coalition* and *Britannia Unchained*. Married, two daughters. Ed: Roundhay Sch, Leeds; Merton Coll, Oxford (BA PPE).

CHALLENGERS
Paul Smyth (Ukip) Cllr, Norfolk

CC 2013-. Runs own business consultancy. Officer RAF for 26 years. Ed: KCL (MA defence studies). **Peter Smith** (Lab) Trade unionist. Playwright. Former teacher and community worker. Union rep. Contested Norfolk SW 2010. Ed: Durham (BA English; Dip social administration); Cambridge Institute of Education (PGCE). **Rupert Moss-Eccardt** (LD) Security consultant. Cllr, Cambridgeshire CC 2005-11. Contested Norfolk SW 2010. Ed: Nottingham (BSc chemical engineering); Open University (BSc IT).

CONSTITUENCY PROFILE
A largely rural seat in Norfolk, stretching from rich agricultural fenland in the west to the pine forests around Thetford in the east. The electorate is scattered across small villages, the market towns of Downham and Swaffham and the much larger town of Thetford. Thetford has a large Portuguese community. Safe Tory seat.

	Electorate	Turnout %	Change from 2010 %
	76,970	65.1	
E Truss C	25,515	50.9	+2.6
P Smyth Ukip	11,654	23.3	+17.0
P Smith Lab	8,649	17.3	-1.3
R Moss-Eccardt LD	2,217	4.4	-17.2
S Walmsley Green	2,075	4.1	+2.5

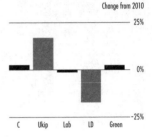

Change from 2010

Normanton, Pontefract & Castleford

LABOUR HOLD

YVETTE COOPER
BORN Mar 20, 1969
MP 1997-

Fierce intellect and steely determination. Candidate for Labour leadership 2015. Shadow: home secretary 2011-; foreign secretary 2010-11; minister: women & equalities 2010-13. SoS, work & pensions 2009-10. Chief secretary to Treasury 2008-09. Min: DCLG 2006-08; ODPM 2005-06. Parly under-sec: ODPM 2003-05; health 1999-2002. Parly sec, lord chancellor's dept 2002-03; Leader writer: *The Independent; The Economist*. Policy adviser to Lab treasury teams 1992-95. Domestic policy specialist, Bill Clinton 1992 pres campaign. Economic researcher to John Smith 1991-92. TGWU, GMB. Married to Ed Balls, his 2015 defeat cleared the obstacles for her leadership campaign. Two daughters, one son. Ed: Balliol Coll, Oxford (BA PPE); LSE (MSc economics); Harvard (Kennedy Scholar).

CHALLENGERS
Nathan Garbutt (Ukip) Management officer. Chairman, Wakefield Ukip branch 2010-. Co-founder, LGBT Ukip group. Vice-chairman, Yorkshire & North Lincolnshire Ukip branch. Ed: Knottingley HS; Pontefract New Coll. **Beth Prescott** (C) Caseworker for Matthew Hancock. Youth leader and church minister. Former apprentice. Ed: Heckmondwike GS. **Edward McMillan-Scott** (LD) Vice-president, European parliament 2004-14. MEP: York 1984-94; North Yorkshire 1994-99; Yorkshire & Humber 1999-2014.

CONSTITUENCY PROFILE
A staunch Labour seat on the eastern edge of West Yorkshire. Once a big coal mining area, the only deep mine left is across the North Yorks border at Kellingley. Ferrybridge does however have a series of coal-fired power stations. The seat is a mix of commuter areas for Leeds and Wakefield and some manufacturing at Castleford.

	Electorate	Turnout %	Change from 2010 %
	82,592	55.6	
Y Cooper Lab	25,213	54.9	+6.7
N Garbutt Ukip	9,785	21.3	
B Prescott C	9,569	20.9	-3.6
E McMillan-Scott LD	1,330	2.9	-13.5

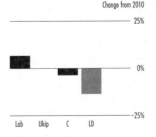

Change from 2010

Northampton North

CONSERVATIVE HOLD

MICHAEL ELLIS
BORN Oct 13, 1967
MP 2010-

Lifelong Northampton man, selected by open primary. Criminal barrister, worked on legal aid cases. Select cttees: home affairs 2011-; statutory instruments 2010-. Cllr, Northampton CC 1997-2001. Chairman, APPG for Queen's Diamond Jubilee 2010-13. Campaigned for extra funds to reduce potholes, granted in the 2014 Budget. Society of Conservative Lawyers. Enjoys gym and theatre. Ed: Wellingborough Sch; University of Buckingham (LLB law); Inns of Court School of Law, City University (BVC).

CHALLENGERS
Sally Keeble (Lab) MP for Northampton North 1997-2010. Leader of Southwark council 1990-93. Hon Fellow, South Bank University. Parly under-sec: international development

2002-03; DfT 2001-02. PPS to Hilary Armstrong 1999-2001. Member, transport select cttee 2005-10. Former journalist and communications dir. Married, one son, one daughter. Ed: Cheltenham Ladies' Coll; St Hugh's Coll, Oxford (BA theology). **Tom Rubython** (Ukip) Journalist and author. **Tony Clarke** (Green) National party spokesman, foreign affairs; Lab MP, Northampton South, 1997-2005. **Angela Paterson** (LD) Former secondary school teacher. Computer industry.

CONSTITUENCY PROFILE
North of the town centre, this is a compact urban seat, mostly consisting of suburbs built after Northampton's designation as a new town in the 1960s. Industry includes distribution and financial services. The constituency includes Northampton University, which was established in 2005. Labour held this traditionally Tory seat 1997-2010.

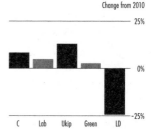

	Electorate	Turnout %	from 2010 % Change
	59,147	66.6	
M Ellis C	16,699	42.4	+8.3
S Keeble Lab	13,454	34.1	+4.8
T Rubython Ukip	6,354	16.1	+13.1
T Clarke Green	1,503	3.8	+2.7
A Paterson LD	1,401	3.6	-24.4

Change from 2010

Northampton South

CONSERVATIVE HOLD

DAVID MACKINTOSH
BORN Apr 2, 1979
MP 2015-

Selected in open primary after Brian Binley announced 2015 retirement. Family has lived in Northampton for more than 100 years. Cllr, Northamptonshire CC 2009-. Youngest leader, Northampton BC 2011-15. Overseeing regeneration of Northampton, including new rail and bus stations, and establishment of UK's biggest Enterprise Zone. Board mem: Royal & Derngate Theatre; Northampton Enterprise Partnership. Chairman, KidsAid Foundation. Patron: The Hope Centre, Northampton; the Caring and Sharing Trust. Ed: Roade Sch; Durham University (BA politics).

CHALLENGERS
Kevin McKeever (Lab) PR consultant. Partner at Portland. Policy adviser. Called to Bar 2013. Contested Harborough 2010.

Ed: Durham University (LLB law); BPP Law School; Harvard, Kennedy Sch of Gov, leadership and organisation. **Rose Gibbins** (Ukip) Has worked for the foreign office, the NHS and the Probation Service. Married, three children. Ed: The Open University (BA social science). **Sadik Chaudhury** (LD) Small business owner and trustee of local mosque. Cllr, Northampton BC 2007-11.

CONSTITUENCY PROFILE
A compact urban seat that, as a result of the 2010 boundary changes, lost an affluent, rural area to the south and the prosperous outskirts of the town. In return it has gained a small industrial area in the west of the town, with the net effect of losing about 20,000 electors. With the exception of Duston and Weston, most of this seat is relatively deprived. Under different boundaries, it turned Labour in 1997 but was won back by the Tories in 2005.

	Electorate	Turnout %	from 2010 % Change
	61,284	63.5	
D Mackintosh C	16,163	41.6	+0.7
K McKeever Lab	12,370	31.8	+6.4
R Gibbins Ukip	7,114	18.3	+13.4
S Chaudhury LD	1,673	4.3	-15.1
J Hawkins Green	1,403	3.6	+2.7
K Willsher Ind	161	0.4	-5.3

Change from 2010

Northamptonshire South

CONSERVATIVE HOLD

ANDREA LEADSOM
BORN May 13, 1963
MP 2010-

Interested in early years mental health, and in banking reform and regulation. Praised in her straight-to-the-point handling of the Libor affair. Advocate of localism. Minister, DECC 2015-. Economic secretary, Treasury 2014-15. Select cttees: public accounts 2014-; Treasury 2010-14. Contested Knowsley South 2005. Cllr, S Oxon DC 2003-07 . Head of corporate governance, Invesco Perpetual. Financial institutions director, Barclays Bank. Married, two sons and one daughter. Ed: Tonbridge Girls' Grammar; University of Warwick (BA political science).

CHALLENGERS
Lucy Mills (Lab) Research and marketing consultant. Cllr, Silverstone PC. Foundation governor, Silverstone Schools Federation. Married, three

daughters. Ed: UCL (BA economics). **Roger Clark** (Ukip). **Tom Snowdon** (LD) Chartered engineer. Contested: Amber Valley 2010; Derbyshire North East 2005. Ed: Brinkburn GS; University of Wolverhampton (BSc applied sciences); University of Leicester (MBA). **Damon Boughen** (Green) Charity sector. Ed: University of Northampton (BA business studies); University of Warwick (MA international relations & affairs).

CONSTITUENCY PROFILE
A rural and sparsely populated seat. The largest towns are Brackley and Towcester, both traditional market towns. Towcester, the administrative centre for South Northamptonshire council, covers part of Silverstone motor racing circuit, which provides a centre for high-tech industry. Sretches to the outskirts of Milton Keynes and is an affluent area but the working class is also well represented. Has a Conservative tradition stretching back decades.

	Electorate	Turnout %	from 2010 %	Change
	85,092	71.5		
A Leadsom C	36,607	60.2	+4.9	
L Mills Lab	10,191	16.7	-0.6	
R Clark Ukip	8,204	13.5	+9.5	
T Snowdon LD	3,613	5.9	-15.1	
D Boughen Green	2,247	3.7	+2.6	

Change from 2010

Norwich North

CONSERVATIVE HOLD

CHLOE SMITH
BORN May 17, 1982
MP 2009-

Surprise appointment as government assistant whip (2010-11) ruffled feathers among more experienced Conservative MPs. Resigned from the Cabinet Office (parly secretary 2012-13) to focus on her const role as MP. Economic secretary, Treasury 2011-12. Select cttees: work & pensions 2009-10; public accounts 2011-12; transport 2013-. Management consultant, Deloitte. seconded to Conservatives' implementation unit (assistant to James Clappison as shad work & pensions minister). Ed: Methwold HS, Norfolk; Swaffham Sixth Form Coll; York (BA Eng lit).

CHALLENGERS
Jessica Asato (Lab) Policy adviser and researcher. Works part-time as political adviser to Tessa Jowell. Former acting dir, Progress. Dir,

Labour Yes to AV campaign. "Social media lead" on David Miliband's leadership campaign. Chairwoman, Fabian Society. Cllr, Islington BC 2011-13. Married, one daughter. Ed: Trinity Hall, Cambridge (BA law). **Glenn Tingle** (Ukip). **Adrian Holmes** (Green) Geophysicist born and bred in Norfolk. **James Wright** (LD) IT consultant. Cllr, Norwich CC 2010-, leader of Lib Dems 2011-. Former DJ at Norwich Waterfront. Married. Ed: Anglia Ruskin (BSc business information systems).

CONSTITUENCY PROFILE
Includes the outer suburbs of Norwich such as Thorpe St Andrew and Sprowston. While the areas towards central Norwich have a substantial amount of social housing, the constituency is largely made up of private housing developments, but not always affluent ones. Contains Norwich airport. Chloe Smith took the seat in a by-election in 2009 after Labour MP Ian Gibson resigned.

	Electorate	Turnout %	from 2010 %	Change
	65,136	66.9		
C Smith C	19,052	43.7	+3.1	
J Asato Lab	14,589	33.5	+2.0	
G Tingle Ukip	5,986	13.7	+9.3	
A Holmes Green	1,939	4.5	+1.5	
J Wright LD	1,894	4.3	-13.9	
M Hardy Ind	132	0.3	-0.0	

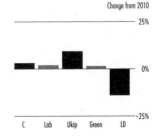

Change from 2010

Norwich South

LABOUR GAIN

CLIVE LEWIS
BORN Sep 11, 1971
MP 2015-

Former BBC eastern region's chief political reporter. Former army reservist, toured Afghanistan in 2009. School governor. Norwich City FC season ticket holder. First in family to go to university. Ed: University of Bradford (BA economics, SU president).

CHALLENGERS
Lisa Townsend (C) Parly assistant to James Morris. Account manager. Ed: Sheffield Hallam University (LLB law); UCL (LLM law). **Lesley Grahame** (Green) Nurse. Married, two children, one deceased. Ed: UEA (BA development studies). **Simon Wright** (LD) Former maths teacher who ousted Charles Clarke, a Labour big beast, to take one of the biggest scalps of the 2010 election. PPS to: Nick Clegg 2013-; David Laws 2012-13. Cllr, North Norfolk DC 2003-07. Memberm

environmental audit select cttee 2010-. Constituency agent to Norman Lamb MP. Married. Ed: Dereham Neatherd HS, Norfolk; Imperial Coll, London (BSc mathematics); Kings Coll London (PGCE). **Steve Emmens** (Ukip) Fundraiser for a charity. Enjoys martial arts and motorcycling. Married.

CONSTITUENCY PROFILE
Norwich South covers most of the city centre and the suburb of New Costessey. The seat includes the "Golden Triangle" near the University of East Anglia, where Victorian properties attract students and young professionals. Historically Labour's strongest seat in Norfolk, because of the high proportion of council tenants, it surprisingly fell to the Lib Dems in 2010 but reverted to Labour in 2015. Norwich Union is the largest employer. The majority of the city's historical features, including its Norman castle and cathedral, lie within the constituency.

	Electorate	Turnout %	from 2010 %
	74,875	64.7	
C Lewis Lab	19,033	39.3	+10.6
L Townsend C	11,379	23.5	+0.6
L Grahame Green	6,749	13.9	-1.0
S Wright LD	6,607	13.6	-15.7
S Emmens Ukip	4,539	9.4	+7.0
D Peel Class War	96	0.2	
C Ceker Ind	60	0.1	

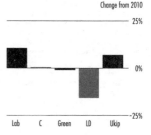

Change from 2010

Nottingham East

LABOUR CO-OP HOLD

CHRIS LESLIE
BORN Jun 28, 1972
MP 2010-; 1997-2005

The "baby of the house" of the 1997 intake when he took the solid Tory seat of Shipley. After losing it in 2005 set up think-tank, New Local Government Network. Ran Gordon Brown's leadership campaign and became embroiled in Labour donations row. Supported Ed Balls in 2010 Labour leadership election. Shadow chancellor 2015-. Shadow chief sec, Treasury 2013-. Shadow min, Treasury 2010-13. Parly under-sec: const affairs 2003-05; ODPM 2002-03. Parly sec, Cabinet office 2001-02. PPS to Lord Falconer of Thoroton 1998-2001. Married, one daughter. Ed: Bingley GS; Leeds (BA politics & parly studies; MA ind & lab studies).

CHALLENGERS
Garry Hickton (C) Team manager, Co-op group. Cllr, Erewash BC 2007-. Contested Ashfield 2010.

Married, one son. **Fran Loi** (Ukip) Part-time business consultant and volunteer martial arts instructor. Nottinghamshire county representative for Ukip. **Antonia Zenkevitch** (Green) MA human security. **Tad Jones** (LD) Medical researcher, Health Research Authority. Ed: Liverpool (BSc pharmacology); St Andrews (PhD biochemistry); Nottingham Trent (MA international relations).

CONSTITUENCY PROFILE
In the eastern part of Nottingham, but very much an inner-city seat. The St Anns and Arboretum areas are largely made up of social housing and are some of the most ethnically diverse areas of Nottingham, while Sneinton has a reputation for crime and violence, although this has declined in recent years. Nottingham Trent University's City campus lies within the seat as does Nottingham racecourse and HMP Nottingham. Safe Labour seat since the Tories were voted out in 1992.

	Electorate	Turnout %	from 2010 %
	60,464	58.2	
C Leslie Lab Co-op	19,208	54.6	+9.2
G Hickton C	7,314	20.8	-2.9
F Loi Ukip	3,501	9.9	+6.5
A Zenkevitch Green	3,473	9.9	+7.1
T Jones LD	1,475	4.2	-20.1
S Soar Ind	141	0.4	
J Stephenson Ind	97	0.3	

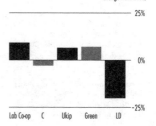

Change from 2010

Nottingham North

LABOUR HOLD

GRAHAM ALLEN
BORN Jan 11, 1953
MP 1987-

Obsessive about constitutional reform, and interested in pre-school intervention for poor children. Select cttees: liason 2010-; speaker's cttee on electoral commission 2010-; chair political and constitutional reform 2010-; reform of HoC 2009-10. Govt whip 1997-2001. Shad min: environment 1996-97; transport 1995-96; culture 1994-95; constitutional affairs 1992-94; soc security 1991-92. Warehouseman, Nottingham. Labour party officer: research 1978-83; local govt in GLC 1983-84. Political fund ballots campaign nat co-ordinator 1984-86. GMBATU research and education officer 1986-87. Married, one daughter. Ed: Forest Fields GS, Nottingham; City of London Poly (BA politics & economics); University of Leeds (MA political sociology).
CHALLENGERS

Louise Burfitt-Dons (C) Writer, social commentator, anti-bullying campaigner. Founded Act Against Bullying. Dir, Boosting Britain. Founder, UK Kindness movement. Married, two daughters. **Stephen Crosby** (Ukip) Manufacturing engineer. **Kat Boettge** (Green) East Midlands regional co-ordinator for Green party. Contested European elections 2014. **Tony Sutton** (LD) Retired technical manager, Boots. Cllr, Nottingham CC 2005-11. Contested Nottingham S 2010, 05. Ed: National Coll of Food Technology (BSc food technology).

CONSTITUENCY PROFILE
A largely residential seat curling around the north of Nottingham and dominated by large local authority housing developments such as Aspley. Private ownership has increased through right-to-buy but it remains a constituency with one of the highest proportions of local authority housing in the country. A safe Labour seat.

	Electorate	Turnout %	Change from 2010 %
	65,918	53.6	
G Allen Lab	19,283	54.6	+6.0
L Burfitt-Dons C	7,423	21.0	-3.8
S Crosby Ukip	6,542	18.5	+14.6
K Boettge Green	1,088	3.1	
T Sutton LD	847	2.4	-14.7
C Meadows TUSC	160	0.5	

Change from 2010

Lab	C	Ukip	Green	LD

Nottingham South

LABOUR HOLD

LILIAN GREENWOOD
BORN Mar 26, 1966
MP 2010-

Shadow min: transport 2011-. Opposition assistant whip 2010-11. Select cttees: regulatory reform 2010-; transport 2010. Research officer, Civil & Public Services Association, local authority conditions of service advisory board. Union official (Unison regional organiser, manager, officer). Member, Co-operative party, Compass, the Fabian Society, Fawcett Society. Keen runner and hill-walker. Married, three daughters. Ed: Canon Slade Sch, Bolton; St Catharine's Coll, Cambridge (BA economics & social & political sciences); Southbank Polytechnic (MSc sociology & social policy).

CHALLENGERS
Jane Hunt (C) Caseworker for Nicky Morgan. Cllr, Charnwood BC. Contested Leicester East 2005,

2010. Married, two children. **David Hollas** (Ukip) Retired army officer. Ed: Bramcote Hills GS; Sandhurst. **Adam McGregor** (Green). **Deborah Newton-Cook** (LD) EU policy adviser. Ambassador for Nottingham in Brussels. Former dir, Nottingham Brussels Office. Secretary, Lib Dems in Europe. Contested Euro elections 2014, 2009, 2004.

CONSTITUENCY PROFILE
The most varied and politically competitive of the three Nottingham seats. Nottingham South contains the city centre of Nottingham and some deprived areas nearby, such as the Meadows estate, as well as the leafier, more desirable Wollaton area. The seat includes the main campuses of Nottingham University and the Clifton campus of Nottingham Trent University and as a result has one of the highest proportions of students of any seat in the country. A Labour seat since 1992.

	Electorate	Turnout %	Change from 2010 %
	68,987	63.0	
L Greenwood Lab	20,697	47.6	+10.3
J Hunt C	13,761	31.7	-1.3
D Hollas Ukip	4,900	11.3	+8.9
A McGregor Green	2,345	5.4	+3.9
D Newton-Cook LD	1,532	3.5	-19.5
A Clayworth TUSC	230	0.5	

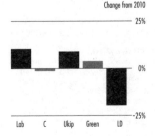

Change from 2010

Lab	C	Ukip	Green	LD

Nuneaton

CONSERVATIVE HOLD

MARCUS JONES
BORN Apr 5, 1974
MP 2010-

Forthright, mainstream Tory. Interested in local government and the housing market. Minister, DCLG 2015-. PPS to: Sajid Javid 2013-. Select cttees: administration 2012-; backbench 2012-13. Chairman, APPG for town centres 2010-. Cllr, Nuneaton & Bedworth BC 2005-, leader 2008-09, leader Con group 2006-09. Member, backbench business cttee & the administration cttee in the HoC. Small business ambassador for the Midlands. Conveyancing manager for Tustain Jones & Company Solicitors. Coventry City supporter. Keen angler. Married, one son and one daughter. CofE. Ed: St Thomas More RC School, Nuneaton; King Edward IV Sixth Form Coll.

CHALLENGERS
Vicky Fowler (Lab) Personal tutor. Outreach ambassador.

Cllr, Nuneaton BC 2011-14. Ed: University of Warwick (BA politics). **Alwyn Waine** (Ukip) Council official, education. Previously IT technician in a school and a nurse. **Keith Kondakor** (Green) Born and brought up in Nuneaton. Cllr: Nuneaton & Bedworth BC 2012-; Warwickshire CC 2013-. Ed: University of Birmingham (BEng electronic engineering). **Christina Jebb** (LD) Retired teacher. Stress management consultant. Cllr: Staffordshire CC 1989-2013; Staffs Moorlands DC; Endon PC. FRSA.

CONSTITUENCY PROFILE
Nuneaton is within easy reach of the West Midlands conurbation and is increasingly popular with commuting professionals. The town was built on industry, however, and there is still a strong working class and some areas of deprivation. Includes the small semi-rural area west of Hartshill. Under old boundaries the Tories held it from 1983 to 1992 before Labour won it back until 2010.

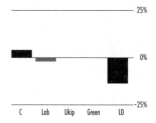

	Electorate	Turnout %	from 2010 %	Change
	68,032	67.3		
M Jones C	20,827	45.5	+4.0	
V Fowler Lab	15,945	34.9	-2.0	
A Waine Ukip	6,582	14.4		
K Kondakor Green	1,281	2.8		
C Jebb LD	816	1.8	-13.6	
P Reilly TUSC	194	0.4		
S Paxton Eng Dem	104	0.2		

Change from 2010

C   Lab   Ukip   Green   LD

Ochil & South Perthshire

SNP GAIN

TASMINA AHMED-SHEIKH
BORN Oct 5, 1970
MP 2015-

Solicitor appointed OBE in 2014 for services to business and the Asian community. SNP group leader, trade & investment 2015-. Member, SNP national executive cttee. SNP Women's officer. Advisory board member, Yes Scotland. Partner, Hamilton Burns WS Solicitors. Formerly actress, star of Asian televsion serials. Winner, Scottish Asian Businesswoman of the Year Award 2010. Ed: University of Strathclyde (Dip legal practice, LLB law); University of Edinburgh (MA economics, int law and French).

CHALLENGERS
Gordon Banks (Lab) MP, 2005-15. Shadow minister: Scotland 2013-15; BIS 2010-11. PPS to James Purnell 2006-09. Select cttees: regulatory reform 2005-10; unopposed bills 2005-10; Scottish affairs 2005-06; NI affairs 2005-06. Contested

Mid Scotland & Fife regional list 2003 Scottish Parl. Unite. Worked in construction industry for 31 years. Member of Coeliac Society. Married, one daughter, one son. Ed: Glasgow Coll of Building (City & Guilds construction tech & concrete practice); University of Stirling (BA history & politics). **Luke Graham** (C) Accountant, Marks & Spencer. Moved to area to work on Better Together campaign. Ed: University of Sheffield (BA economics & social policy, finance officer in SU).

CONSTITUENCY PROFILE
Takes in most towns and villages between two big hubs of Perth and Stirling. To the north are the small towns of Crieff and Auchterarder, home of the Gleneagles hotel. In the south is the more industrial area of Clackmannanshire, with brewing and glassmaking. Created in 2005, had been expected to be a marginal seat between Labour and SNP. Was held by Labour until 2015.

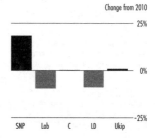

	Electorate	Turnout %	from 2010 %	Change
	77,370	74.8		
T Ahmed-Sheikh SNP	26,620	46.0	+18.4	
G Banks Lab	16,452	28.4	-9.5	
L Graham C	11,987	20.7	+0.2	
I Stefanov LD	1,481	2.6	-8.8	
M Gray Ukip	1,331	2.3	+0.9	

Change from 2010

SNP   Lab   C   LD   Ukip

Ogmore

LABOUR HOLD

HUW IRRANCA-DAVIES
BORN Jan 22, 1963
MP 2002-

Mildly rebellious instincts curbed by appointment to government, but stood down from front bench after 2015 election "to play a full and constructive role in the rebuilding of the Labour party". Shadow minister: Defra 2011-15; energy & climate change 2010-11; marine & natural environment 2010. Parly under-sec: environment, food & rural affairs 2008-10; Wales office 2007-08. Asst gov whip 2006-07. PPS to: Tessa Jowell 2005-06; Jane Kennedy 2003-05. Select cttees: statutory instruments 2002-04; procedure 2002-. Leisure facility management. Swansea Institute of Higher Education senior lecturer and course director. Married, three sons. Ed: Gowerton Comp; Crewe and Alsager Coll (BA combined studies); Swansea Institute of Higher Education (MSc European leisure resort management).

CHALLENGERS
Jane March (C) Cllr, Tunbridge Wells BC 2011-. Farmer. Admin & marketing, fruit growers co-operative. Cllr, Horsmonden PC, chairwoman. **Glenda Davies** (Ukip) Dementia care nurse for private healthcare company. Former science teacher. Ed: Mid Glamorgan Sch of Nursing (RGN); UEA (BSc; PhD chemistry); UWIC (PGCE). **Tim Thomas** (PC) Local government statistian & research officer. Contested Bridgend, Welsh Assembly 2011. Ed: Swansea University. **Gerald Francis** (LD) Heating and plumbing engineer. Cllr, East Hertfordshire DC 1997-2001.

CONSTITUENCY PROFILE
A traditional, working-class mining and ironworking seat in the Welsh valleys, based around the Garw Valley and Ogmore Vale. Former mining communities such as Blaengarw have suffered deprivation and the area was in the spotlight after several youth suicides in recent years. An utterly safe Labour seat.

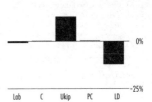

	Electorate	Turnout %	Change from 2010 %
	55,320	63.7	
H Irranca-Davies Lab	18,663	52.9	-0.9
J March C	5,620	15.9	+0.4
G Davies Ukip	5,420	15.4	+13.1
T Thomas PC	3,556	10.1	+0.5
G Francis LD	1,072	3.0	-12.1
L Brophy Green	754	2.1	
E Saunders TUSC	165	0.5	

Change from 2010

Old Bexley & Sidcup

CONSERVATIVE HOLD

JAMES BROKENSHIRE
BORN Jan 8, 1968
MP 2005-

Minister: immigration 2015-; security and immigration 2014-15. Parly under-sec, Home Office 2010-14. Shadow min, home affairs 2006-10. Member, select cttee: constitutional affairs 2005-06. MP, Hornchurch 2005-10 (seat abolished). Corporate lawyer; partner at Jones Day Gouldens. Former national vice-chairman Young Conservatives. Strong supporter of doing more to tackle the war on drugs. Interested in community radio and cricket. Involved with Cancer Research UK. Married, two daughters, one son. Ed: Davenant Foundation GS; Cambridge Centre for Sixth Form Studies; Exeter (LLB law).

CHALLENGERS
Ibby Mehmet (Lab) Democracy and governance manager, Goldsmiths SU. Political adviser,

Qatar Embassy. Ed: University of Essex (LLB law). **Catherine Reilly** (Ukip) Former senior manager, local goverment. Contested Bexley BC 2014. **Jennifer Keen** (LD) Senior public affairs officer, Guide Dogs for the Blind Association. Taught English to immigrants in Brixton. Built houses for an NGO in Argentina. Ed: St Catherine's Coll, Oxford (BA modern history). **Derek Moran** (Green). Vet and partner in veterinary practice. Two children.

CONSTITUENCY PROFILE
Conservative-voting suburbia in southeast London, largely comprising private housing, dating from the 1930s. The titular "Old Bexley" refers to the smaller village-like part of Bexley, close to the border with Dartford. The constituency and its predecessor returned Sir Edward Heath from 1950 until he retired in 2001. In 1997 Labour cut Heath's majority to 6.9 per cent but the Conservatives have since built up a towering majority.

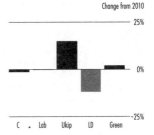

	Electorate	Turnout %	Change from 2010 %
	66,035	70.8	
J Brokenshire C	24,682	52.8	-1.3
I Mehmet Lab	8,879	19.0	-0.3
C Reilly Ukip	8,528	18.2	+14.9
J Keen LD	1,644	3.5	-11.9
D Moran Green	1,336	2.9	+2.0
B Gill NHAP	1,216	2.6	
L Williams Ch P	245	0.5	
N Finch BNP	218	0.5	-4.2

Change from 2010

Oldham East & Saddleworth

LABOUR HOLD

DEBBIE ABRAHAMS
BORN Sep 15, 1960
MP 2011-

Elected in 2011 after sensational voiding of 2010 result because the sitting MP, Phil Woolas, was found to have made false statements about his Lib Dem rival. PPS to Andy Burham. Chairwoman, Labour party health cttee. Member, National Policy Forum. Vice-chairwoman, APPG: on dementia; on Kashmir. Chairwoman, APPG on health in all policies. Select cttee, work & pensions 2011-. Chairwoman of Rochdale Primary Care Trust. Contested Colne Valley 2010. Married, two daughters. Ed: University of Salford (BSc biochemistry and physiology); University of Liverpool (MSc health education & public health).

CHALLENGERS
Sajjad Hussain (C) Chief executive of a housing association. Married, children. Ed: University of Birmingham. **Peter Klonowski** (Ukip) Media officer, Ukip Oldham. Cllr, Oldham BC 2014. **Richard Marbrow** (LD) Former communications officer for Chris Davies MEP. Cllr Liverpool CC 1998-2007. Ed: University of Liverpool (BSc molecular biology). **Miranda Meadowcroft** (Green) Supports deaf and hearing-impaired children at a local school.

CONSTITUENCY PROFILE
At the eastern side of Greater Manchester, reaching from central Oldham up into the Pennines. It covers an area of deprived terraces in Oldham, the prosperous and unusually named town of Shaw and Crompton, and the middle-class villages and hamlets of Saddleworth. There are racial tensions here in some areas and Oldham has a large Muslim population. In 2001 there were race riots in the town and the BNP performed strongly, with 10 per cent of the vote. A former marginal between Labour and Lib Dems.

	Electorate	Turnout %	from 2010 % Change
	72,005	61.8	
D Abrahams Lab	17,529	39.4	+7.5
S Hussain C	11,527	25.9	-0.5
P Klonowski Ukip	8,557	19.2	+15.4
R Marbrow LD	5,718	12.9	-18.8
M Meadowcroft Green	1,152	2.6	

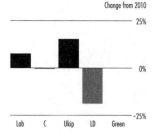

Change from 2010

Oldham West & Royton

LABOUR HOLD

MICHAEL MEACHER
BORN Nov 4, 1939
MP 1970-

Leftwinger. Interested in environmental issues. Contested party leadership in 2007. Min environment, and privy counsellor 1997-2003. Shadow Cabinet 1983-97, principal opp spokesman for: environmental protection; education & employment; transport; citizen's charter & science; overseas devt & co-operation; social security; employment; health & social security. Parly under-sec: trade 1976-79; health & social security 1975-76; industry 1974-75. Lab NEC 1983-89. University lecturer. Appeared briefly as himself in the 1985 BBC drama *Edge of Darkness*. Divorced, remarried. Two daughters, two sons, all from first marriage. Ed: Berkhamstead Sch; New Coll, Oxford (BA Classics); LSE (Dip social administration).

CHALLENGERS
Francis Arbour (Ukip) Health and social care consultant. Ed: University of Manchester. Army reservist. **Kamran Ghafoor** (C) Owns portfolio of petrol stations and properties. Former Labour cllr, Oldham BC. Contested Oldham W 2010. Ed: University of Salford (BA IT; MA information systems). **Garth Harkness** (LD) SEN support worker. Maths teacher. Cllr: Oldham BC 2012-; Saddleworth PC 2011-.

CONSTITUENCY PROFILE
Oldham is a former centre for the textile industry, a town of red brick mills and dense terraced housing. There is a large Asian population and the town has a history of racial tension that culminated in the Oldham riots in 2001. These were blamed on self-segregation between communities. The BNP polled more than 16 per cent in 2001, after the riots, but the seat has been Labour since its creation in 1950.

	Electorate	Turnout %	from 2010 % Change
	72,341	59.6	
M Meacher Lab	23,630	54.8	+9.3
F Arbour Ukip	8,892	20.6	+17.4
K Ghafoor C	8,187	19.0	-4.7
G Harkness LD	1,589	3.7	-15.4
S Hart Green	839	1.9	

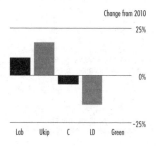

Change from 2010

Orkney & Shetland

LIB DEM HOLD

ALISTAIR CARMICHAEL
BORN Jul 15, 1965
MP 2001-

From the Lib Dems' centre-left. Quit LD front bench to vote for EU referendum in 2008. SoS for Scotland, 2013-15. Deputy chief whip 2010-13. LD shadow SoS: Scotland, 2008-10, NI 2007-08; transport 2006-07. LD shadow spokes: home affairs 2004-05; energy 2001-05. Scottish LD spokes, energy review 2001-02. Select cttees: members' allowances 2009-10; public accounts 2005-06; Scottish affairs 2001-05, 2008-10; international development 2001-02. Member, LD federal policy cttee 2004-. Solicitor. Procurator fiscal depute. Married, two sons. Ed: Islay HS; Aberdeen (LLB Scots law, Dip LP).

CHALLENGERS
Danus Skene (SNP) Retired teacher and former chairman, Shetland Arts. Previously education

official at Tayside regional council. Board, Scottish qualification authority. Contested Tayside North for Lib Dems 1983, 87. Married, three children. Ed: Eton; University of Sussex (BA politics & African studies); University of Chicago (MA public administration); Aberdeen University (MEd). **Donald Cameron** (C) Lawyer. Contested Highlands 2010. Ed: University of Oxford; City University. **Gerry McGarvey** (Lab) Parly assistant to Dame Anne McGuire MP. Freelance writer and researcher. Ed: University of Kent; University of Edinburgh.

CONSTITUENCY PROFILE
Britain's most northerly constituency, which also has the most disparate population in the UK. Orkney is a group of 70 islands; Shetland has 100. The two largest oil depots in Europe are situated here. The only town is Lerwick. A Lib Dem stronghold, it became the party's only seat in Scotland after the 2015 election.

	Electorate	Turnout %	from 2010 %	Change
	34,551	65.8		
A Carmichael LD	9,407	41.4	-20.6	
D Skene SNP	8,590	37.8	+27.2	
D Cameron C	2,025	8.9	-1.6	
G McGarvey Lab	1,624	7.2	-3.5	
R Smith Ukip	1,082	4.8	-1.6	

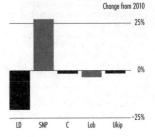

Change from 2010

LD SNP C Lab Ukip

Orpington

CONSERVATIVE HOLD

JOSEPH JOHNSON
BORN Dec 23, 1971
MP 2010-

Respected financial journalist, and brother of Boris, with whom he struggles to avoid endless comparisons. Minister: universities and science, 2015-; Cabinet Office, 2014-15. Parly sec: Cabinet Office, 2013-14. Asst whip, Treasury 2012-14. PPS to Mark Prisk, minister for business and enterprise, 2012. Select cttee: public accounts, 2010-12. Head of Lex column and associate editor of the *Financial Times*, previously South Asia bureau chief. Corporate financier, investment banking division of Deutsche Bank. Married, two children. Ed: Balliol Coll, Oxford (BA modern history); Institut d'Etudes Européennes, Université Libre de Bruxelles; Insead (MBA).

CHALLENGERS
Idham Ramadi (Ukip) Local government officer. Ed: St Mary's

Church of England HS, Hendon; University of Westminster (BA); LSE (MSc). **Nigel de Gruchy** (Lab) Sec, Orpington Labour party. Retired general sec, NASUWT. Ed: University of Reading (BA economics & philosophy), University of London, external programme (PGCE). **Peter Brooks** (LD) Financial systems officer, Tunbridge Wells BC. Former scientist. Management accountant. Contested Bromley 2005. Ed: University of Sheffield (BSc MSc chemistry); Swansea University (PhD chemistry).

CONSTITUENCY PROFILE
An affluent area with a high owner-occupier rate and little social housing. Geographically the largest seat in London, it covers the southeastern corner of the capital and a substantial part of open Kent countryside between Farnborough and Biggin Hill aerodrome. The electorate, however, lives mostly in leafy suburbia. The seat has been Tory since 1970.

	Electorate	Turnout %	from 2010 %	Change
	68,129	72.0		
J Johnson C	28,152	57.4	-2.3	
I Ramadi Ukip	8,173	16.7	+13.9	
N de Gruchy Lab	7,645	15.6	+6.6	
P Brooks LD	3,330	6.8	-17.7	
T Galloway Green	1,732	3.5	+2.5	

Change from 2010

C Ukip Lab LD Green

Oxford East

LABOUR HOLD

ANDREW SMITH
BORN Feb 1, 1951
MP 1987-

In opposition, attacked Tory plans to privatise Britain's air traffic control service, declaring "our air is not for sale", before implementing the sell-off when in government. SoS, work & pensions 2002-04. Chief sec to Treasury 1999-2002. Min, education & employment 1997-99. Shadow SoS, transport 1996-97. Shadow chief sec to the Treasury 1994-96. Opp spokes: Treasury & econ affairs 1992-96; education 1988-92. Select cttees: southeast regional, 2009-10; social service, 1988-89. Cllr, Oxford CC 1976-87. Mem, executive of TU group, Lab MPs. Keen gardener. Married, one son. Ed: Reading Sch; St John's Coll, Oxford (BA PPE).

CHALLENGERS
Melanie Magee (C) HR manager, Oxford & Cherwell Valley Coll. Cllr, Cherwell DC 2011-, vice-chairman of council 2014-. Mayor of Bicester 2013. Married. Ed: Oxford Brookes University. **Ann Duncan** (Green) Former World Bank economist. Also worked for Dept for Int Devt. Ed: Newnham Coll, Cambridge; Oxford (PgD). **Alasdair Murray** (LD) Former journalist. Ed: Oxford (BA history); Central European University (Dip European studies); City University London (PgCert journalism). **Ian Macdonald** (Ukip) Software developer. Contested Oxford CC 2014, 2011.

CONSTITUENCY PROFILE
An urban seat covering most of Oxford. It includes the centre of the city and 29 university colleges. According to the 2011 census it is ethnically diverse, with a big private rental sector and a significant amount of social housing. Its workforce is highly qualified. Andrew Smith beat the Lib Dems in 2010 by 4,581 votes and greatly increased his majority in 2015.

	Electorate	Turnout %	from 2010 % Change
	78,974	64.2	
A Smith Lab	25,356	50.0	+7.6
M Magee C	10,076	19.9	+1.1
A Duncan Green	5,890	11.6	+9.2
A Murray LD	5,453	10.8	-22.9
I Macdonald Ukip	3,451	6.8	+4.5
C Artwell Ind	160	0.3	
M Hatter Loony	145	0.3	
J Morbin TUSC	108	0.2	
K Parkin SPGB	50	0.1	

Change from 2010

Lab   C   Green   LD   Ukip

Oxford West & Abingdon

CONSERVATIVE HOLD

NICOLA BLACKWOOD
BORN Oct 16, 1979
MP 2010-

Civil libertarian, classically trained musician. PPS to Matthew Hancock 2013-14. Select cttee, home affairs 2010-. APPGs: Co-chairwoman, women, peace & security; secretary, overseas development 2010-. Researcher to Andrew Mitchell MP 2007. Works with Conservative party human rights group. Co-founder, Conservative party social action project. Vice-chairwoman, Conservative party 2010-13. Adviser to Conservative international development team. Announced in March 2015 that she has Ehlers-Danlos syndrome. Ed: Trinity Coll of Music (classical singing from age 14); St Anne's Coll, Oxford (BA music); Emmanuel Coll, Cambridge (MPhil musicology).

CHALLENGERS
Layla Moran (LD) Physics teacher. Contested Battersea 2010. Ed: Imperial Coll London (BSc physics); Brunel University (PGCE); Institute of Education, UCL (MA comparative education). **Sally Copley** (Lab) Campaigns director, Oxfam. Previously worked at Save the Children, Shelter and Stonewall. Co-chaired End Child Poverty Coalition. Partner, two sons. **Alan Harris** (Ukip) Chairman, Oxford West and Abingdon Ukip.

CONSTITUENCY PROFILE
The larger and much more rural of the two Oxford seats and tenth most marginal seat of the 2010 election. Oxford West contains some of the northern suburbs of the city and a few colleges on the outskirts of the city centre. Includes the large village of Kidlington and the town of Abingdon. It was Tory until 1997 but tactical voting helped the Lib Dems to retain it until 2010. Nicola Blackwood increased her 2010 majority of 176 to 9,582 in 2015.

	Electorate	Turnout %	from 2010 % Change
	79,767	71.8	
N Blackwood C	26,153	45.7	+3.4
L Moran LD	16,571	29.0	-13.1
S Copley Lab	7,274	12.7	+2.1
A Harris Ukip	3,963	6.9	+4.2
L Sanders Green	2,497	4.4	+2.3
H Salisbury NHAP	723	1.3	
M Foster SPGB	66	0.1	

Change from 2010

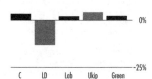

C   LD   Lab   Ukip   Green

Paisley & Renfrewshire North

SNP GAIN

GAVIN NEWLANDS
BORN Feb 2, 1980
MP 2015-

Business manager of restaurant chain; business analyst. Fundraiser for SNP Renfrew and Gallowhill branch. Cllr, Renfrewshire C 2011-. Former treasurer, St James' Pre-5 Centre. Rugby fan. Played for Paisley rugby club for 17 years; captain for three years. Married, two daughters. Ed: Trinity HS; James Watt Coll.

CHALLENGERS
Jim Sheridan (Lab) MP 2001-2015. PPS, MoD team 2005-06, resigned over Lebanon conflict. Member, select cttees: CM&S 2010-15; panel of chairmen 2009-15; int devt 2007-09; public accounts 2003-05; broadcasting 2003-05; information 2001-04. MP for West Renfrewshire 2001-05. Cllr, Renfrewshire 1999-2001. TGWU convener. Married, one daughter, one son. Ed: St Pius Secondary Sch, Drumchapel. **John**

Anderson (C) Works for a trade organisation. Previously worked for a Conservative Association. Ed: University of Glasgow (LLB law). **James Speirs** (LD) Works for a disability chairty. Ed: Royal Agricultural Coll (Dip rural estate management). **Ryan Morrison** (Green) Law student. Member, Scottish Youth Parliament for Paisley 2010-12.

CONSTITUENCY PROFILE
Occupying an area of the south bank of the river Clyde. Although based on the town of Paisley, this seat takes in a large part of West Renfrewshire. It is a mixed constituency, ranging from Glasgow airport through former industrial areas to the more leafy and affluent edges of Glasgow. Paisley is the area's main town, while the biggset local employers include the Braehead shopping centre and business park. The working-class centre of Paisley still provides the bulk of the electorate, giving Labour its base of support.

	Electorate	Turnout %	from 2010 %	Change %
	66,206	76.2		
G Newlands SNP	25,601	50.7	+31.7	
J Sheridan Lab	16,525	32.8	-21.3	
J Anderson C	6,183	12.3	-2.4	
J Speirs LD	1,055	2.1	-8.4	
R Morrison Green	703	1.4		
A Doyle CSA	202	0.4		
J Halfpenny TUSC	193	0.4		

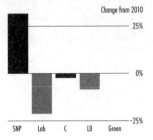

Change from 2010

Paisley & Renfrewshire South

SNP GAIN

MHAIRI BLACK
BORN Sep 12, 1994
MP 2015-

The UK's youngest MP since at least the Reform Act of 1832. Student at the University of Glasgow at election. Speeches raised eyebrows during independence campaign. Said "No" voters were gullible and selfish and that she fantasised about "putting the nut" on Labour cllrs. Season ticket holder for Partick Thistle. Ed: University of Glasgow (BA politics & public policy).

CHALLENGERS
Douglas Alexander (Lab) MP 1997-2015. Acolyte of Gordon Brown. Sister is Wendy Alexander (MSP, Scottish Lab leader 2007-08). Shadow foreign sec 2011-15. Shadow SoS: work & pensions 2010-11; int'l dev 2007-10; transport & Scotland 2006-07. Min: Europe 2005-06; FCO & DTI 2004-05; Cabinet Office & Duchy of Lancaster 2003-04; Cabinet Office 2002-

03; DTI 2001-02. GE campaign co-ordinator 2007-15, 1999-2001. Speechwriter and researcher for Gordon Brown. Solicitor, Brodies WS, Digby Brown. Married, one daughter, one son. Ed: Edinburgh (MA politics & modern history; LLB law). **Fraser Galloway** (C) Solicitor. Associate, Hogan Lovells. Parly researcher, HoC 2012. Ed: Stewart's Melville Coll, Edinburgh; National University of Singapore (LLB law); University of Glasgow (LLB law); BPP Law Sch (Dip law).

CONSTITUENCY PROFILE
Modelled on the old Paisley South seat. It is based on the southern part of Paisley, including Paisley University and most of the town centre, but spreads west to Elderslie then beyond to the rural towns and villages around Kilbarchan and Lochwinnoch. The southern part of the seat is less prosperous than the north. It has a mixed electorate and until 2015 the Labour vote from the urban areas dominated.

	Electorate	Turnout %	from 2010 %	Change %
	61,281	75.4		
M Black SNP	23,548	50.9	+32.9	
D Alexander Lab	17,864	38.6	-21.0	
F Galloway C	3,526	7.6	-2.3	
E McCartin LD	1,010	2.2	-7.4	
S Webster SSP	278	0.6	-0.3	

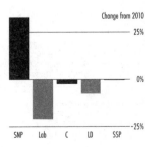

Change from 2010

Pendle

CONSERVATIVE HOLD

ANDREW STEPHENSON
BORN Feb 17, 1981
MP 2010-

Campaigned against hospital and healthcare cuts. Vice-chairman, Conservative party with responsibility for youth, 2010-13. Chairman, Tatton Conservative Assoc 2006. Cllr, Macclesfield BC 2003-07. Self-employed insurance broker, Stephenson & Threader. Member, Selrap (railway campaign group). National deputy chairman, Conservative Future 2001-02. President, Nelson Brass Band 2010-13. Methodist. Supporter of homeopathy. Ed: Poynton County HS; Royal Holloway, London (BSc business management).

CHALLENGERS
Azhar Ali (Lab) Director: Rumi consultants; East Lancashire Regeneration Ltd. Cllr, Lancashire CC 2013-. Govt adviser 2005-10. Member, Unite. Ambassador, White Ribbon Campaign. Trustee,

F.E.W. Ed: Leeds University (MA business administration). **Michael Waddington** (Ukip) Former retained fireman. **Graham Roach** (LD) Automation and instrument engineer. Mayor of Pendle 2014-15. Cllr: Pendle BC 2007-; Colne TC 2007-. Left school after O levels.

CONSTITUENCY PROFILE
A Pennine seat, named after a prominent hill and the Forest of Pendle. Mostly consists of former mill towns that grew up along the Leeds-Liverpool canal. The textile industry is long gone, leaving small towns of terraced Victorian housing, attractive to commuters and tourists. At Barnoldswick, in the north, the Rolls-Royce factory is a major employer. About 30 per cent of the seat's population works in manufacturing. There are pockets of severe deprivation although rural areas towards the Ribble Valley are more affluent. Labour took the seat from the Conservatives in 1992, but it swung back in 2010.

	Electorate	Turnout %	Change from 2010 %
	64,657	68.7	
A Stephenson C	20,978	47.2	+8.3
A Ali Lab	15,525	34.9	+4.0
M Waddington Ukip	5,415	12.2	+8.9
G Roach LD	1,487	3.4	-16.9
L Fisk Green	1,043	2.4	

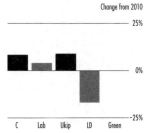

Change from 2010

Penistone & Stocksbridge

LABOUR HOLD

ANGELA SMITH
BORN Aug 16, 1961
MP 2005-

Came to brink of resignation over abolition of 10p tax. Shadow min: env, food & rural affairs 2014-; shadow deputy leader of Commons 2011-14. Opposition assistant whip 2010-11. PPS to Yvette Cooper 2005-08. Select cttees: administration 2010-12; procedure 2010-11; transport 2009-10; regulatory reform 2005-07. MP, Sheffield Hillsborough 2005-2010. Cllr, Sheffield CC (cabinet member for education). Unison. Sheffield First for Learning & Work. Married, one stepdaughter, one stepson. Supports Sheffield Wednesday football club. Ed: Toll Bar Sch; Nottingham (BA English).

CHALLENGERS
Steve Jackson (C) Works in construction and engineering to regenerate brownfield land. DITA. Cllr, Harrogate BC 2011-.

Representative, Jennyfield Styan Community Centre. **Graeme Waddicar** (Ukip) Self-employed manufacturer for aromatherapy products. Married, three children from first marriage. Ed: Bradford University (BA business studies). **Rosalyn Gordon** (LD) Chairwoman, Liberal Democrat Women.

CONSTITUENCY PROFILE
Covers the northwest suburbs of Sheffield and the steel town of Stocksbridge. The northern part of the seat covers the rural villages in the foothills of the Pennines around the market town of Penistone. To the east is the former mining village of Dodworth. Traditional industrial areas dominate, creating a strong Labour base, although with the decline of coal and steel some of the old allegiances went with it. By the standards of South Yorkshire, this counts as a marginal and it is only a divided opposition that keeps it in Labour hands.

	Electorate	Turnout %	Change from 2010 %
	71,048	66.0	
A Smith Lab	19,691	42.0	+4.3
S Jackson C	12,968	27.7	-3.5
G Waddicar Ukip	10,738	22.9	+18.8
R Gordon LD	2,957	6.3	-14.8
C Porter Eng Dem	500	1.1	+0.0

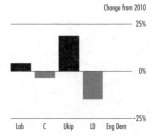

Change from 2010

Penrith & The Border

CONSERVATIVE HOLD

RORY STEWART
BORN Jan 3, 1973
MP 2010-

Former soldier, diplomat, author and Harvard professor. Former Labour supporter. Campaigned for mobile phone companies to provide wider coverage. Parly under-sec Defra 2015-. Select cttees: national security strategy 2014-; liaison 2014-; defence 2014-; foreign affairs 2010-14. Chairman, APPG for mountain rescue. Officer, Black Watch. Diplomat, Indonesia and Montenegro. Coalition deputy governor of two Iraqi provinces. Founded Turquoise Mountain (NGO in Afghanistan). Professor and director of Carr Center for Human Rights, Harvard University. Episcopalian. Tutor to Princes William and Harry. Married, one son. Ed: Eton; Balliol Coll, Oxford (BA history & philosophy).

CHALLENGERS
Lee Rushworth (Lab) Admin

officer, DWP. Union rep. Married, two children. Ed: Wirral Metropolitan Coll (C&G plumbing). **John Stanyer** (Ukip) Semi-retired businessman. Northwest chairman, Ukip. Married, three children. Left school at 16 for electrical and mechanical apprenticeship. **Neil Hughes** (LD) Former teacher. Cllr, Eden DC 2003-. Has worked for a housing association and Defra. Member, Eden's NHS commissioning body. **Bryan Burrow** (Green) Drama therapist and outreach worker.

CONSTITUENCY PROFILE
A geographically huge constituency stretching from Gretna Green to the Solway Firth and Yorkshire Dales. It is sparsely populated and dependent on agriculture and tourism in the Lake District. According to the 2011 census, more than 50 per cent of the population is aged over 45. The 2001 foot-and-mouth epidemic resulted in a large swing to the Conservatives, which they still maintain.

	Electorate	Turnout %	Change from 2010 %
	65,209	67.4	
R Stewart C	26,202	59.7	+6.3
L Rushworth Lab	6,308	14.4	+1.4
J Stanyer Ukip	5,353	12.2	+9.4
N Hughes LD	3,745	8.5	-19.9
B Burrow Green	2,313	5.3	

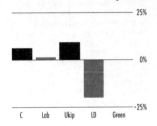

Change from 2010

Perth & Perthshire North

SNP HOLD

PETE WISHART
BORN Mar 9, 1962
MP 2001-

Plays keyboard in MPs' rock band, MP4. SNP chief whip 2001-07. SNP spokesman: CMS 2001-; constitution 2010-; home affairs, justice 2007-10; international development 2005-10; transport, env, food & rural affairs 2001-05. MP, North Tayside 2001-05. Select cttees: works of art 2008-12; Scottish affairs 2008-10; admin 2005-08. Vice-chairman, APPG on intellectual property. Member, national council, NEC. Executive vice-convener fundraising SNP. Musician, former member of the band Runrig. Musicians' Union. Separated, one son. Ed: Queen Anne HS, Dunfermline; Moray House Coll of Education (Dip CommEd).

CHALLENGERS
Alexander Stewart (C) Support worker, Ark Housing Assoc. Cllr,

Perth & Kinross C 1999-. Deputy leader, Scottish Conservative group of councillors. Management cttee, Boweswell House. Worked in hotel management & fashion retail. Married. **Scott Nicholson** (Lab) PhD student, University of West of Scotland. Member, policy committee, Society for General Microbiology. **Peter Barrett** (LD) Former manager, builders' merchant. Cllr, Perth and Kinross C 2003-, LD group leader 2012-.

CONSTITUENCY PROFILE
Covers a huge swathe of remote mountains, forest and moorlands as well as the lowland area around Perth itself, where most of the electorate lives. Perth, made a city in 2012 as part of the Queen's diamond jubilee celebrations, is the retail and financial centre. Nearby Scone Abbey was the traditional coronation site for Scottish monarchs. The Tories and the SNP have historically vied for control in these areas but the SNP has held the seat since 1995.

	Electorate	Turnout %	Change from 2010 %
	72,447	74.8	
P Wishart SNP	27,379	50.5	+10.9
A Stewart C	17,738	32.7	+2.2
S Nicholson Lab	4,413	8.1	-8.3
P Barrett LD	2,059	3.8	-8.5
L Ramsay Green	1,146	2.1	
J Myles Ukip	1,110	2.1	
X McDade Ind	355	0.7	

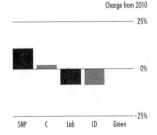

Change from 2010

Peterborough

CONSERVATIVE HOLD

STEWART JACKSON
BORN Jan 31, 1965
MP 2005-

Overlooked in the coalition government. PPS to Owen Paterson 2010-11. Shadow min, communities & local government 2008-10. Opposition whip 2007-08. Select cttees: public accounts 2012-; health 2006-07; regulatory reform 2005-07. Chairman APPG, Pakistan 2007-10. Contested Peterborough 2001; Brent South 1997. Cllr, Ealing CC 1990-98. Helped to set up Conservative Voice. Vice-president, Local Government Association. Bank manager, Lloyds TSB. Married, one daughter. Ed: London Nautical School; Chatham House GS; Royal Holloway Coll, London (BA economics & public administration); Thames Valley University (MA human resources management).

CHALLENGERS
Lisa Forbes (Lab) Cllr,

Peterborough CC 2012-. Former flight consultant, Thomas Cook. Married, four children. **Mary Herdman** (Ukip) Runs property business. Previously Cllr, Thorney PC. Contested: Peterborough CC 2014; Peterborough at 2005 general election. **Darren Fower** (LD) Cllr, Peterborough CC 2004-, 2000-01. Media development officer at Shine charity. Business analyst. Ed: De Montfort University (BA mass media & contemporary politics).

CONSTITUENCY PROFILE
Peterborough, once a Victorian industrial town, has grown massively since the 1970s after being designated as a new town in 1967. It is an economically successful city with strong service and distribution industries on the back of good transport links. There is a significant Asian Muslim population, but also many Italian immigrants and more recent eastern European immigration. A key marginal between the Conservatives and Labour.

	Electorate	Turnout %	from 2010 %	Change %
	72,521	64.9		
S Jackson C	18,684	39.7	-0.7	
L Forbes Lab	16,759	35.6	+6.1	
M Herdman Ukip	7,485	15.9	+9.2	
D Fower LD	1,774	3.8	-15.9	
D Bisby-Boyd Green	1,218	2.6	+1.4	
C Ash Lib	639	1.4		
J Fox Ind	516	1.1	+0.2	

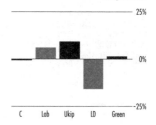

Change from 2010

Plymouth Moor View

CONSERVATIVE GAIN

JOHNNY MERCER
BORN Aug 17, 1981
MP 2015-

Former army captain and Afghanistan veteran. Said two main missions this parliament were increased mental health provision and government funding to veterans in passionate early speech in Jun 2015. Married, two daughters. Ed: RMA Sandhurst.

CHALLENGERS
Alison Seabeck (Lab) MP, Plymouth Moor View 2010-15; Devonport 2005-10. Shad min: defence 2011-15; CLG 2010-11. PPS to Geoff Hoon 2008-09, 2006-07. Labour Women's Network. Parliamentary adviser to Nick Raynsford MP 1992-2005. Parly assistant to Roy Hattersley as shad home sec. Select cttees: defence 2010; backbench business 2010; SW regional 2009-10; regulatory reform 2005-07; assist government whip 2007-08. Member and official

Amicus-MSF. Fawcett Society. Unite. Divorced, remarried Nick Raynsford MP, two daughters from first marriage. Ed: Harold Hill GS; NE London Poly (gen studies). **Penny Mills** (Ukip) Former chairman, CPRE Torridge. Critic of renewable energy. **Stuart Bonar** (LD) Public affairs adviser, Royal College of Midwives. Former assistant to Sarah Ludford MEP and Norman Baker. Contested Plymouth MV 2010. Ed: Devonport HS; Royal Holloway, London (BA history & politics); Birkbeck, London (MA American politics).

CONSTITUENCY PROFILE
A maritime seat in Devon. The Moor View seat is the northern part of the city and the more working class, containing council housing developments. Maritime industries remain important with electronics, engineering and boat building having primary roles. Before 2015 it had been Labour-held since 1992, when former SDP leader David Owen stood down.

	Electorate	Turnout %	from 2010 %	Change %
	69,146	61.6		
J Mercer C	16,020	37.6	+4.3	
A Seabeck Lab	14,994	35.2	-2.0	
P Mills Ukip	9,152	21.5	+13.8	
S Bonar LD	1,265	3.0	-13.9	
B Osborn Green	1,023	2.4	+1.4	
L Parker TUSC	152	0.4		

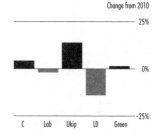

Change from 2010

Plymouth Sutton & Devonport

CONSERVATIVE HOLD

OLIVER COLVILE
BORN Aug 26, 1959
MP 2010-

Communications consultant from a naval family. Took the seat at his third attempt in 2010 (also contested 2005, 2001). In a minority of Conservative MPs not to vote against the government in any big rebellions. Select cttees: backbench business 2013-; NI affairs 2010-. APPG: chairman, Excellence in built env 2012 (vice-chairman 2010-12); pharmacy 2010-; for Zambia and Malawi 2011-. Dir, Polity Communications. Proprietor, Oliver Colvile & Associates. National Society of Conservative Agents 1981-93. Account dir of a division, Saatchi & Saatchi. Member: Addis Army; Plymouth Cricket Club; Plymouth Albion Rugby Club. Ed: Stowe Sch, Buckingham.

CHALLENGERS
Luke Pollard (Lab Co-op) Former head of public affairs, ABTA travel association. Previously worked for Labour HQ. Contested SW Devon 2010. Ed: Christleton HS; Exeter (BA politics, SU president). **Roy Kettle** (Ukip) Ran his own transport cafe business. **Libby Brown (**Green) Occupational therapy student, Plymouth University. **Graham Reed** (LD) Renewable energy consultant and glassblower. Cllr, Stirling C 2007-12. Former chair, British Society of Scientific Glassblowers. Contested Stirling 2010. Married. Ed: Stirling (BA history and politics).

CONSTITUENCY PROFILE
The seat takes in Plymouth's modern centre and touristy waterfront to the south. The city was largely destroyed during the Second World War and had to be rebuilt. Historically one of the most important naval bases in Britain, Devonport is still the largest in western Europe. Under varying boundaries, the seat was Tory before Labour took it in 1997.

	Electorate	Turnout %	from 2010 %	Change
	69,146	69.4		
O Colvile C	18,120	37.8	+3.5	
L Pollard Lab Co-op	17,597	36.7	+5.0	
R Kettle Ukip	6,731	14.0	+7.5	
L Brown Green	3,401	7.1	+5.0	
G Reed LD	2,008	4.2	-20.5	
L Rossington Communist	106	0.2		

Change from 2010

C   Lab Co-op   Ukip   Green   LD

Pontypridd

LABOUR HOLD

OWEN SMITH
BORN May 2, 1970
MP 2010-

Interested in urban regeneration and welfare reform. Shad SoS, Wales 2012-. Shad min, Wales 2010-11. Select cttee, Welsh affairs 2010-11. BBC producer with Radio 4 *Today* programme. Special adviser to Paul Murphy as SoS for Wales and NI. Director, Amgen (world's largest biotech company). Member, Unite. Contested Blaenau Gwent by-election 2006. Cites Jean Jaures among political heroes. Local man, Pontypridd RFC fan. Enjoys fishing. Married, two sons, one daughter. Ed: Coed-y-Lan Comp, Pontypridd; Sussex Uni (BA history & French).

CHALLENGERS
Ann-Marie Mason (C) Works in the art department of University of South Wales. Life model. Former Labour Cllr, Bristol CC, then early member of SDP, before joining Tories. Volunteer media co-ordinator & researcher for Alzheimer's Society. Ed: University of Glamorgan (BA creative art; MA TV and film scriptwriting). **Andrew Tomkinson** (Ukip). **Mike Powell** (LD) Plumbing and heating engineer. Cllr, Rhondda Cynon Taff CBC 1999-. Contested Pontypridd 2010. **Osian Lewis** (PC) Researcher, Welsh Assembly 2011-. Founding member, United Nations Assoc. Former dir, Tomorrow's Wales 2012-14. Ed: SAE Institute, Oxford (BA audio production); Cardiff University (MA economics).

CONSTITUENCY PROFILE
Covers the lower Taf and Ely valleys and is home to a large middle-class population, a strong service sector and the University of South Wales. This seat is the transition point between the struggling, post-industrial towns of the Welsh valleys and the commuter villages that lie in the orbit of Cardiff. Held by Labour since the 1920s.

	Electorate	Turnout %	from 2010 %	Change
	58,929	64.3		
O Smith Lab	15,554	41.1	+2.3	
A Mason C	6,569	17.3	+1.2	
A Tomkinson Ukip	5,085	13.4	+10.1	
M Powell LD	4,904	13.0	-18.2	
O Lewis PC	4,348	11.5	+4.2	
K Clay Green	992	2.6	+1.6	
D Biggs Soc Lab	332	0.9	-0.4	
E Pearson TUSC	98	0.3		

Change from 2010

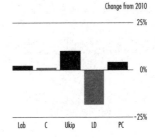

Lab   C   Ukip   LD   PC

Poole

CONSERVATIVE HOLD

ROBERT SYMS
BORN Aug 15, 1956
MP 1997-

Active constituency MP on the Tory right. Asst whip 2012-13. Shadow min: communities and local govt 2005-07; ODP 2003-05. Opposition whip 2003. Vice-chairman Conservative party 2001-03. Opposition spokesman on environment, food and rural affairs 1999-2001. Select cttees: high speed rail bill 2014-15; finance & services 2013-15; administration 2013-14; draft detention of terrorist suspects bills 2011-15; liaison 2010-12; regulatory reform 2010-12; health 2007-10, 1997-2000. PPS to Michael Ancram 1999-2000. Cllr: N Wilts DC 1983-87; Wilts CC 1985-87. Contested Walsall North 1992. Ran family haulage and plant hire business. Fellow, Chartered Institute of Building. Divorced, remarried but separated. One daughter, one son. Ed: Colston's Sch, Bristol.

CHALLENGERS
David Young (Ukip) Business consultant. Ed: Oxford (Balliol Coll, BA philosophy and theology; PhD political philosophy). **Helen Rosser** (Lab) Contested Bournemouth BC 2011. Ed: Lancaster University. **Philip Eades** (LD) Former publican. Mayor of Poole 2013-14. Cllr, Poole BC 2003-. Contested Poole 2010. Married, one son, one daughter. Ed: Dorset Institute of Higher Education.

CONSTITUENCY PROFILE
An affluent town on the south coast, just west of Bournemouth. Poole has an extremely diverse economy: it is an important cargo and ferry port, a tourist destination in its own right, a manufacturing centre and a service and commercial centre. The Sandbanks peninsula to the south of the town has some of the most expensive housing in the country and is home to "millionaire's row". A solid Conservative seat, held by the party since its re-creation in 1950.

	Electorate	Turnout %	from 2010 %
	72,557	65.3	
R Syms C	23,745	50.1	+2.6
D Young Ukip	7,956	16.8	+11.5
H Rosser Lab	6,102	12.9	+0.1
P Eades LD	5,572	11.8	-19.9
A Oliver Green	2,198	4.6	
M Howell Poole	1,766	3.7	
I Northover ND	54	0.1	

Change from 2010

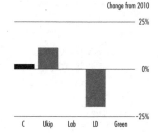

Poplar & Limehouse

LABOUR HOLD

JIM FITZPATRICK
BORN Apr 4, 1952
MP 1997-

Shad min: transport 2010-13; env, food & rural affairs 2010. Min: env, food & rural affairs 2009-10. Parly under-sec: transport 2007-09; T&I 2006-07; ODPM 2005-06. PPS to Alan Milburn 1999-2001. Vice-chamberlain 2003-05. Gov whip 2002-05; asst govt whip 2001-02. Select cttees: transport 2013-; env, food & rural affairs 2013-; selection 2003-05. Vice-chairman: APPG Bangladesh; Animal Welfare; Housing. MP Canning Town 1997-2010. London Lab Exec, chairman Greater London Lab party 1991-2000. Hon treas London Lab MPs reg group. Received Freedom of the City of London. Firefighter, driver, trainee; fire brigade long service and good conduct medal. Fire Brigades Union NEC. GPMU. Remarried. Two children from first marriage. Ed: Holyrood R.C. Senior Sch.

CHALLENGERS
Chris Wilford (C) Head of policy and public affairs, Chartered Institute of Arbitration. Parliamentary researcher House of Lords 2011-12. Contested Tower Hamlets mayor 2014. Ed: King's Coll, London (BA film & American studies); LSE (MSc media & communications). **Nicholas McQueen** (Ukip) Florist and cousin of fashion designer Alexander McQueen. **Maureen Childs** (Green) Chairwoman Green Seniors. **Elaine Bagshaw** (LD) Business manager, Financial Conduct Authority. Ed: University of Birmingham.

CONSTITUENCY PROFILE
An east London seat. To the north it covers Bromley-by-Bow and Mile End, once home to the Jewish community, now dominated by Bangladeshi Muslims. A seat of extremes, from severe deprivation to the gleaming skyscrapers of Canary Wharf. Long a strong Labour seat.

	Electorate	Turnout %	from 2010 %
	82,076	62.2	
J Fitzpatrick Lab	29,886	58.6	+18.6
C Wilford C	12,962	25.4	-1.7
N McQueen Ukip	3,128	6.1	+4.9
M Childs Green	2,463	4.8	+3.9
E Bagshaw LD	2,149	4.2	-6.9
H Pierre TUSC	367	0.7	
R Mugenzi RFAC	89	0.2	

Change from 2010

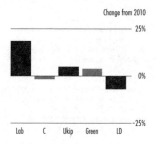

Portsmouth North

CONSERVATIVE HOLD

PENNY MORDAUNT
BORN Mar 4, 1973
MP 2010-

Min, armed forces 2015-. First female military veteran elected to HoC. Contested Portsmouth North 2005. PPS to Philip Hammond 2013-14. Parly under-sec, CLG 2014-. Select cttees: privacy & injunctions 2011-12; defence 2010-13; European scrutiny 2010-13; arms export controls 2010-13. Chairwoman APPG: life sciences 2010-; ageing and older people 2010-. Conservative party head of youth (under Major), head of broadcasting (under Hague). Chief of staff to David Willets 2005. Named *Spectator* Parliamentarian of the Year 2014. Dir, Diabetes UK. Comms dir, National Lottery. Royal Navy reservist. Fellow, RSA. Ed: Oaklands RC Comp; Reading University (BA philosophy).

CHALLENGERS
John Ferrett (Lab) Official,

Prospect Union. Cllr, Portsmouth CC 2012-. Leader of Labour group. Contested Portsmouth South 2010. Married, three children. Ed: City of Portsmouth Boys Sch; Open University (politics & economics). **Mike Fitzgerald** (Ukip) Works in the hi-tec industry. Contested Portsmouth North 2010. **Darren Sanders** (LD) Account manager, Indigo lobbying company. Cllr, Portsmouth CC 2012-. Former Cllr, Lambeth BC. Contested: Portsmouth North 2001, 2010; Streatham 2005.

CONSTITUENCY PROFILE
Portsmouth is a densely populated city on the south coast, technically situated on an island although the numerous causeways mean it is effectively a peninsula. The city has a strong naval history with defence the main local employer. IBM has its UK HQ here. Formerly a key Conservative-Labour marginal and bellwether seat, won by the party that gained most seats ever since its creation in 1974.

	Electorate	Turnout %	from 2010 %	Change
	73,105	62.1		
P Mordaunt C	21,343	47.0	+2.8	
J Ferrett Lab	10,806	23.8	-4.0	
M Fitzgerald Ukip	8,660	19.1	+15.0	
D Sanders LD	2,828	6.2	-13.9	
G Ellis Green	1,450	3.2	+2.2	
J Woods TUSC	231	0.5	+0.2	
S George JACP	72	0.2		

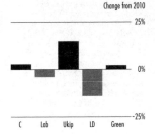

Change from 2010

Portsmouth South

CONSERVATIVE GAIN

FLICK DRUMMOND
BORN June 16, 1962
MP 2015-

Former insurance broker, Ofsted inspector, TA intelligence officer. Former board member, Healthwatch. Previously Director of corporate affairs, Conservative Middle East Council. Contested Portsmouth South 2010. Governor, Milton Park Primary School. Trustee, Portsmouth CAB. Married, four children. Ed: Hull University (BA SE Asian studies); University of Southampton (MA global politics).

CHALLENGERS
Gerald Vernon-Jackson (LD) Leader of Portsmouth CC 2004-14. Stepped down as leader when Ukip gained six seats in local elections, 2014. Leader of Liberal Democrats in Local Government in England and Wales. Vice-chairman, Local Government Association. Dir: Solent Local Economic

Partnership. Member, Lib Dem National Executive. Adviser to David Rendel MP. Ed: University of Liverpool (BA history); University of Southampton (MSc social work). **Sue Castillon** (Lab) Director of own community support social enterprise. Ed: Brunel University (MA youth & community studies). **Steve Harris** (Ukip) Retired US Navy officer. Ed: Valley Forge Military Academy. **Ian McCulloch** (Green) Part-time librarian and archivist.

CONSTITUENCY PROFILE
The southern half of Portsea Island includes Portsmouth city centre and the historic dockyard, home to the Royal Navy — a huge employer — and the Mary Rose. Portsmouth is the UK's most densely populated city outside inner London. The area near Portsmouth Harbour and docks is significantly more deprived than elsewhere. Home to University of Portsmouth. Historically Conservative, but held by Lib Dems from 1997 to 2015.

	Electorate	Turnout %	from 2010 %	Change
	71,639	58.5		
F Drummond C	14,585	34.8	+1.6	
G Vernon-Jackson LD	9,344	22.3	-23.6	
S Castillon Lab	8,184	19.5	+5.9	
S Harris Ukip	5,595	13.4	+11.2	
I McCulloch Green	3,145	7.5	+5.8	
M Hancock Ind	716	1.7		
S Hoyle TUSC	235	0.6		
D Jerrard JACP	99	0.2		

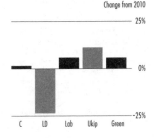

Change from 2010

Preseli Pembrokeshire

CONSERVATIVE HOLD

STEPHEN CRABB
BORN Jan 20, 1973
MP 2005-

Quiet, solid, local man. Raised by single mother in council housing. SoS, Wales 2014-. Whip and parly under-sec Wales 2012-14. Asst govt whip 2010-12. Opposition whip 2009-10. Member, select cttees: Treasury 2008-09; international devt 2007-09; Welsh affairs 2005-07. Leader of Project Umubano, Conservative's social action scheme in Rwanda and Sierra Leone. Election observer, OSCE Bosnia-Herzegovina 1998. Chair, North Southwark & Bermondsey Conservative assoc (1998-2000). Policy and campaigns manager, London Chamber of Commerce. Patron of Pembrokeshire Mencap. Marketing consultant. Marathon runner. Married, one daughter, one son. Ed: Tasker Milward Sch, Haverfordwest; Bristol (BSc politics); London Business Sch (MBA); Open University (French).

CHALLENGERS
Paul Miller (Lab) Delivery manager, V4 Services. Cllr, Pembrokeshire CC 2012-, opposition leader. Ed: University of Southampton (BA economics). **Howard Lillyman** (Ukip) Retired. Founding member, Preseli Pembrokeshire Ukip. Worked for: Oxford University's chemistry dept; the British Motor Corporation. Enjoys scuba diving. Lives with partner. Ed: City & Guild (UEI Quals). **Chris Overton** (Independent) Consultant obstetrician and gynaecologist. Ed: University of Liverpool (MBChB medicine).

CONSTITUENCY PROFILE
Predominantly rural. Made up of parts of English-speaking south Pembrokeshire and a large Welsh-speaking population in the north of the country. Pembrokeshire Coast National Part and tourism is a key employer. Conservative MP Stephen Crabb retook the seat in 2015 by 4,969 votes.

		Electorate	Turnout %	from 2010 %	Change
		57,291	70.8		
S Crabb	C	16,383	40.4	-2.4	
P Miller	Lab	11,414	28.1	-3.0	
H Lillyman	Ukip	4,257	10.5	+8.2	
C Overton	ISWSL	3,729	9.2		
J Osmond	PC	2,518	6.2	-3.0	
F Bryant	Green	1,452	3.6		
N Tregoning	LD	780	1.9	-12.6	
R Maile	Worth	23	0.1		

Change from 2010

25%

0%

-25%

C   Lab   Ukip   ISWSL   PC

Preston

LABOUR CO-OPERATIVE HOLD

MARK HENDRICK
BORN Nov 2, 1958
MP 2000-

Engineering background, started out in the European Parliament before becoming an MP in 2000 Preston by-election. Opp assistant whip 2010-13. PPS to: Ivan Lewis 2009-10; Jack Straw 2007-08; Margaret Beckett 2003-07. Member, select cttees: foreign affairs 2012-; international devt 2009-10; European scrutiny 2001-04. Chair APPGs: China 2010-12; Brazil 2008-10; Romania 2007-. VC APPG: Thailand 2010-; Singapore 2009-. MEP Lancs Central 1994-99. Cllr, Salford CC 1987-95. Chair, Eccles Labour party 1990-94. Member, Co-operative party, GMB. Engineer and lecturer. Married. Ed: Salford GS; Liverpool Poly (BSc electrical & electronic engineering); University of Manchester (MSc computer science, Cert Ed); Volkshochschule, Hanau, Germany (ZDF German).

CHALLENGERS
Richard Holden (C) Deputy head of press for the Conservative party until Jan 2015. Ed: QEGS, Blackburn; LSE (BSc government & history). **James Barker** (Ukip) Businessman. Chairman, Preston and Wyre Ukip. Enjoys chess and hiking. Two children. Ed: technical apprenticeship in HM Forces. **Gemma Christie** (Green) Voice and performance tutor. Associate coach, Performing Arts Nework and Development Agency. Health campaigner. **Jo Barton** (LD) Cllr, Sefton BC 2014-. Cllr, Barnstable TC 2007-11.

CONSTITUENCY PROFILE
Preston is the administrative centre for Lancashire. The UCLan is based here with 32,000 students. 19 per cent of the population gave their ethnicity as Asian in the 2011 census. A Labour seat since 1983. Labour's Mark Hendrick held the seat in 2015 with a majority of 12,067 votes. Lib Dems dropped from second to fifth in 2015.

		Electorate	Turnout %	from 2010 %	Change
		59,981	55.8		
M Hendrick	Lab Co-op	18,755	56.0	+7.8	
R Holden	C	6,688	20.0	-1.7	
J Barker	Ukip	5,139	15.4	+10.9	
G Christie	Green	1,643	4.9		
J Barton	LD	1,244	3.7	-20.7	

Change from 2010

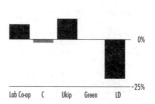

25%

0%

-25%

Lab Co-op   C   Ukip   Green   LD

Pudsey

STUART ANDREW
BORN Nov 25, 1971
MP 2005-

Experienced charity fundraiser. PPS to Francis Maude 2012-. Member, select cttee: Welsh affairs 2010-12. Cllr, Leeds CC 2003-10. Contested Wrexham 1997. Spent early years in Llanfairpwllgwyngyllgogerychwyrndrobwllllantysiliogogogoch. Fundraising manager, Martin House Children's Hospice. Member, Institute of Fundraisers. Patron of LGBTory. Headbutted by Falkirk MP, Eric Joyce, in a HoC bar 2012. Previously: East Lancashire Hospice; Hope House Children's Hospice; British Heart Foundation. Has long-term partner. Ed: Ysgol David Hughes, Menai Bridge, Anglesey.

CHALLENGERS
Jamie Hanley (Lab) Lawyer. Represented Labour internationally, accompanied US President Carter to oversee the Palestinian Presidential elections.

Cllr, Horsforth TC 2011-15, leader of the Labour Group. Contested Pudsey 2010. School governor. Married, two sons. Ed: University of Hull (BA law). **Roger Tattersall** (Ukip) Digital content manager, Faculty of Education Social Sciences and Law, University of Leeds. Ed: Leeds Metropolitan University (HNC mechanical & production engineering); University of Leeds (BA history & philosophy of science). **Ryk Downes** (LD) Cllr, Leeds CC 2004. Former chair, West Yorkshire Integrated Transport Authority.

CONSTITUENCY PROFILE
Covers many towns and villages between the cities of Leeds and Bradford. Engineering and textiles are among local industries while Leeds Bradford Airport also provides jobs. Mostly an affluent residential area for commuters to both cities, Pudsey has long been held by the Tories but often with narrow majorities and has subsequently never been a safe seat.

		Electorate	Turnout %	from 2010 % Change
		70,533	72.2	
S Andrew	C	23,637	46.4	+8.0
J Hanley	Lab	19,136	37.6	+2.5
R Tattersall	Ukip	4,689	9.2	+6.7
R Downes	LD	1,926	3.8	-17.1
C Allen	Green	1,539	3.0	

Change from 2010

C	Lab	Ukip	LD	Green

Putney

JUSTINE GREENING
BORN April 30, 1969
MP 2005-

Has worked hard to develop her skills on the front bench as a combative performer. Was the youngest female Conservative MP in the HoC until 2009. SoS: int devt 2012-; transport 2011-12. Economic secretary to the Treasury 2010-11. Shadow min: CLG 2009-10; Treasury 2007-09. Conservative vice-chairwoman 2005-10. Member, select cttees: public accounts 2010-11; work and pensions 2005-07. Bow Group member, former officer. Sales, business, finance manager, Centrica, GSK, SmithKline Beecham. Auditor PwC. Ed: Oakwood Comp, Rotherham; University of Southampton (BA business economics & accounting); London Business Sch (MBA).

CHALLENGERS
Sheila Boswell (Lab) Cllr,

Wandsworth BC until 2014. Trustee, HomeStart. Worked at Oxfam and Save the Children. Mother of singer of rock band The Kooks. One son. **Andy Hallett** (LD) Policy manager, Citizens Advice Bureau. Former policy manager, Consumer Futures. Ed: LSE (BSc government & economics). **Chris Poole** (Green) Audit exec, Grant Thornton. Former teacher. Trustee, the Wandsworth Citizen's Advice Bureaux. Ed: University of Bristol (BSc politics; PgCert education); Open University (Cert business studies).

CONSTITUENCY PROFILE
On the south bank of the Thames covering Putney itself, Southfields and Roehampton. A largely affluent leafy, owner-occupied suburbia. There is also a substantial amount of social housing and a large number of tower blocks in the council estate in Roehampton. Won by Labour in 1997, but retaken by the Justine Greening for the Tories in 2005.

		Electorate	Turnout %	from 2010 % Change
		63,918	67.0	
J Greening	C	23,018	53.8	+1.7
S Boswell	Lab	12,838	30.0	+2.6
A Hallett	LD	2,717	6.4	-10.6
C Poole	Green	2,067	4.8	+3.4
T Ward	Ukip	1,989	4.7	+3.6
G Dessoy	AWP	184	0.4	

Change from 2010

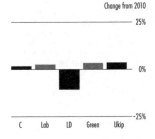

C	Lab	LD	Green	Ukip

Rayleigh & Wickford

CONSERVATIVE HOLD

MARK FRANCOIS
BORN Aug 14, 1965
MP 2001-

Quiet and unassuming. Staunchly Eurosceptic, lost out on preferred brief in coalition deal. Min: communities and resilience 2015-; Portsmouth 2015-; armed forces 2013-15. Govt whip, vice-chamberlain of HM Household 2010-12. Shadow min: Europe 2007-10. Shadow: paymaster general 2005-07, economic secretary to the treasury 2004-05; opposition whip 2002-04. Member, select cttees: armed forces bill 2011; administration 2010-12; selection 2010-13; environmental audit 2001-05. PC. Infantry officer in TA. Public affairs consultant. Hill-walking enthusiast. Divorced. Ed: St. Nicholas Comp, Basildon; Bristol University; King's Coll, London (MA war studies).

CHALLENGERS
John Hayter (Ukip) Higher courts

solicitor-advocate. Cllr, Rochford DC 2014-. Contested Rayleigh & Wickford 2010 for English Democrats. Married, two sons. Ed: High Wycome Royal GS; Queen Mary, London (law). **David Hough** (Lab) Primary school teacher. Blogger. Former lorry driver. Ed: Colchester University. **Linda Kendall** (Independent) Worked for Ford Motor Company. Widowed. Three daughters. Ed: Anglia Ruskin University. **Mike Pitt** (LD) Maths teacher. Cllr, Cambridge CC 2012-, 2007-11. Contested Bedfordshire NE 2010.

CONSTITUENCY PROFILE
The Crouch and Roach rivers frame the east of this seat, from which the old Rayleigh seat extended to the southern boundaries of Chelmsford. Wickford is undergoing regeneration through the Thames Gateway project. Most of this seat is fairly affluent. A safe Tory seat, Mark Francois held it in 2015 with a majority of 17,230 votes.

	Electorate	Turnout %	from 2010 %	Change
	77,870	68.3		
M Francois C	29,088	54.7	-3.2	
J Hayter Ukip	11,858	22.3	+18.1	
D Hough Lab	6,705	12.6	-1.9	
L Kendall Ind	2,418	4.5		
M Pitt LD	1,622	3.1	-12.1	
S Yapp Green	1,529	2.9		

Change from 2010

25%

0%

-25%

C   Ukip   Lab   Ind   LD

Reading East

CONSERVATIVE HOLD

ROBERT WILSON
BORN Jan 2, 1965
MP 2005-

The first MP selected by an open primary, keen advocate of consultative politics that reaches beyond his party. Min, civil society 2014-. PPS to: George Osborne 2013-14; Jeremy Hunt 2010-12. Parly sec to Cabinet office 2014-. Opp whip 2009-10. Shadow min, higher ed 2007-09. Cllr, Reading BC 1992-96, 2003-06. Contested: Carmarthen West & Pembrokeshire South 2001; Bolton NE 1997. Conservative campaign manager Reading East 1992. Entrepreneur health, comms. Published two books within the last government about the coalition and ministerial scandals. Adviser to David Davis MP. Married, four children. Ed: Wallingford Sch; University of Reading (BA history).

CHALLENGERS
Matt Rodda (Lab) Charity

project manager. Former civil servant, DfE. Cllr, Reading BC 2011-. Survived Ladbroke Grove rail crash. Member, The Assoc of Labour Councillors, Co-op party, NUJ, FDA, GMB. Married, two children. **Jenny Woods** (LD) Scientist. Astrophysics research, University of Oxford. Renewable energy and environment research, Rutherford Appleton Labratory. Academic Management, University of Bath. Vice chair, Assoc of Lib Dem Engineers and Scientists. Won the 2014 'Patsy Calton Award'. Ed: Oxford (MA physics; DPhil astrophysics).

CONSTITUENCY PROFILE
A commercial centre and commuter town in the Thames Valley in Berkshire. An affluent town, home to light, hi tech and service industry. Contains University of Reading and the majority of its students. Labour overturned decades of Tory representation in 1997 but lost in 2005. Rob Wilson retook the seat in 2015 by 6,520 votes.

	Electorate	Turnout %	from 2010 %	Change
	74,651	67.6		
R Wilson C	23,217	46.0	+3.4	
M Rodda Lab	16,697	33.1	+7.6	
J Woods LD	3,719	7.4	-20.0	
C Forrester Ukip	3,647	7.2	+5.1	
R White Green	3,214	6.4	+4.2	

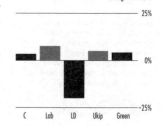

Change from 2010

25%

0%

-25%

C   Lab   LD   Ukip   Green

Reading West

CONSERVATIVE HOLD

ALOK SHARMA
BORN Sep 7, 1967
MP 2010-

Became a member of the Conservative party aged 11. PPS to Mark Hoban 2010-12. Conservative VC for BME communities. Co-chair, Conservative Friends for India. Member, select cttees: Treasury 2014-; science & technology 2010-11. Former chair, Bow Group's economic affairs committee. FRSA. Worked as chartered accountant, company auditor, consultant and tutor. Ran own business. School governor. Enjoys cycling and walking. Married, two daughters. Ed: Reading Blue Coat Sch; University of Salford (BSc applied physics with electronics).

CHALLENGERS
Victoria Groulef (Lab) Charity projects manager. Runs fair trade lingerie business. Former BBC producer. Sch governor. Married, two children. **Malik Azam** (Ukip) Grew up on a council estate in Sheffield. Partner. **Meri O'Connell** (LD) Youth justice worker. Gum and candy taster, Mondelez International. Cllr, Reading BC 2012-. Lead cllr for Adult & Children's Social Care. School governor. **Miriam Kennet** (Green) Founder and dir, The Green Economics Institute. **Suzanne Ferguson** (Independent) Principle process engineer. Ed: Surrey (MEng chemical engineering).

CONSTITUENCY PROFILE
From just beyond the town centre, this Berkshire seat stretches west through the suburbs. Reading has areas of deprivation and relatively high numbers of working classes but the middle classes predominate. Ethnically diverse with a significant number of black and Asian residents. A classic marginal, held by the Tories from its creation in 1983 until the Labour landslide of 1997, it remained Labour until 2010, before falling to Alok Sharma.

	Electorate	Turnout %	from 2010 %	Change
	72,302	67.0		
A Sharma C	23,082	47.7	+4.5	
V Groulef Lab	16,432	34.0	+3.4	
M Azam Ukip	4,826	10.0	+6.8	
M O'Connell LD	2,355	4.9	-15.2	
M Kennet Green	1,406	2.9	+1.7	
S Ferguson Ind	156	0.3		
N Adams TUSC	83	0.2		
P West Roman	64	0.1		

Change from 2010

C   Lab   Ukip   LD   Green

Redcar

LABOUR CO-OPERATIVE GAIN

ANNA TURLEY
BORN Oct 9, 1978
MP 2015-

Policy adviser on local government. Deputy dir, New Local Government Network. Former special adviser to David Blunkett and Hilary Armstrong on child poverty and social exclusion. Coordinates the Co-operative Councils Network. Writes for the *Guardian*. Editor of Progressive Localism blog. Former civil servant. Dir, local community centre. Trustee, Sure Start children's centre. School governor.

CHALLENGERS
Josh Mason (LD) Press and campaigns officer for Ian Swales MP. Cllr, Redcar & Cleveland BC 2011-, deputy leader 2015. Dir, Coast and Country Housing. Worked in the theatre. Involved with an improvised comedy group. School governor. Enjoys classical music. Ed: Prior Pursglove Coll; Durham University (BA history & Classics). **Chris Gallacher** (Ukip) Owner, CCAD business. Major, British Army 1995-2011. Worked at ICI. Ed: St Thomas RC. **Jacob Young** (C) Process operator in the chemical industry, SABIC. Deputy chairman, Yorkshire & the Humber Conservative Future. Ed: University of Teeside (HNC chemical engineering). **Peter Pickney** (Green) President, RMT Union 2012-.

CONSTITUENCY PROFILE
An industrial seat on the southern bank of the Tees estuary. Redcar itself is a Victorian seaside town, but this seat is mostly heavy industry. The bulk of the population is English and 98.4% is white. Was previously a safe Labour seat, held by the party since its creation in 1974. The closure of the steelworks in 2009 hit the town hard and was the foundation of an immense swing at the 2010 election, when the Lib Dems took the seat. Labour won it back in 2015 by a 18.9-point swing.

	Electorate	Turnout %	from 2010 %	Change
	64,825	63.1		
A Turley Lab Co-op	17,946	43.9	+11.1	
J Mason LD	7,558	18.5	-26.7	
C Gallacher Ukip	7,516	18.4	+13.9	
J Young C	6,630	16.2	+2.4	
P Pinkney Green	880	2.2		
P Lockey NE Party	389	1.0		

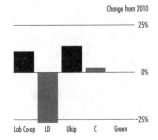

Change from 2010

Lab Co-op   LD   Ukip   C   Green

Redditch

CONSERVATIVE HOLD

KAREN LUMLEY
BORN Mar 28, 1964
MP 2010-

A TV regular from the outset of Jacqui Smith's expenses trauma. Interested in education. Cllr: Redditch BC 2001-03; Clwyd CC 1993-96; Wrexham BC 1991-96. Deputy chair, Welsh Young Conservative Party 1986-87. Member: transport 2012-; Welsh affairs select cttee 2010-. Company secretary, RKL Geological Services. Assistant at John Bull Group. Trainee accountant, Ford Motor Company. Trainer, Westminster Foundation for Democracy. Contested: Redditch 2005, 2001; Delyn 1997. Enjoys knitting. Married, one daughter, one son. Ed: Rugby HS for Girls; East Warwickshire Coll.

CHALLENGERS
Rebecca Blake (Lab) Teacher in adult learning. Cllr, Redditch BC 2003-07, 2011-15. Co-founder

& vice chair, Redditch Mental Health Action Group. Seasonal tutor. Married. **Peter Jewell** (Ukip) Businessman. Former dir, Lexicon UK. Played cricket and rugby in southern Africa for twenty years. Chair, British and Commonwealth Cricket Trust. Dir, WCCC. Former chair, Bromsgrove and Redditch Magistrates Court. Member, English Cricket Board Discipline Commission. **Hilary Myers** (LD) CEO, Rochdale Boroughwide User Forum mental health charity. Former Cllr, Todmorden TC 2007-11. Contested Calder Valley 2010. Ed: University of Reading (BA English & history).

CONSTITUENCY PROFILE
Redditch expanded after becoming a new town in the 1960s, which saw large new housing developments spring up to home the overspill population of Birmingham. Was won on its creation in 1997 by Jacqui Smith, whose expenses and troubled stint as home secretary led to defeat in 2010.

	Electorate	Turnout %	from 2010 %	Change
	65,529	67.3		
K Lumley C	20,771	47.1	+3.6	
R Blake Lab	13,717	31.1	+0.9	
P Jewell Ukip	7,133	16.2	+12.8	
H Myers LD	1,349	3.1	-14.6	
K White Green	960	2.2	+1.3	
S Colton Ind	168	0.4	+0.2	

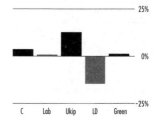

Change from 2010

Reigate

CONSERVATIVE HOLD

CRISPIN BLUNT
BORN Jul 15, 1960
MP 1997-

One Nation Tory from a military background, served in the army 1979-1990, rising to captain. Miscalculated by quitting as shadow trade & industry minister in first, unsuccessful, attempt to topple Iain Duncan Smith. Parly under-sec, justice 2010-12. Shadow min, national security 2009-10. Opposition whip 2004-09. Member, select cttees: draft voting eligibility bill 2013; finance & services 2005-09; defence 2003-04, 1998-2000. Contested West Bromwich East 1992. Forum of private business representative, special adviser to Malcolm Rifkind 1993-97. Passionate about protecting the greenbelt. Separated, one daughter, one son. Ed: Wellington Coll; RMA Sandhurst; Durham University (BA politics); Cranfield Institute of Technology (MBA).

CHALLENGERS
Joe Fox (Ukip) Works in the care sector. Ukip's treasurer in Reigate. Worked in plastics and magnetic recording tape. Four children. **Ali Akhlakul** (Lab) Family emigrated from Bangladesh to the UK in 1960. Has previously worked in restaurants and management. Ed: Denbigh HS. **Anna Tarrant** (LD) Cllr, Reigate and Banstead BC 2008-12. Has worked as a probation officer with the Youth Offending Team. Trained as a teacher in further education. Ed: Reading (BA social work).

CONSTITUENCY PROFILE
Has good transport links to London, Brighton and the south coast so is popular with commuters. Bisected by a designated area of outstanding natural beauty and the M25. About 70 percent is greenbelt which, combined with population growth well above the national average, makes demand for housing a key issue. Conservative-held since 1945.

	Electorate	Turnout %	from 2010 %	Change
	73,429	69.9		
C Blunt C	29,151	56.8	+3.4	
J Fox Ukip	6,817	13.3	+9.1	
A Akhlakul Lab	6,578	12.8	+1.5	
A Tarrant LD	5,369	10.5	-15.8	
J Essex Green	3,434	6.7	+4.5	

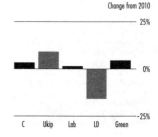

Change from 2010

Renfrewshire East

SNP GAIN

KIRSTEN OSWALD
BORN Dec 21, 1972
MP 2015-

SNP spokesperson, armed forces & veterans 2015-. Head of human resources, South Lanarkshire Coll. Active Yes campaigner. Worked in human resources for Motherwell Coll. Husband, Davinder Bedi, joined the Labour party in 2015 in opposition to independence. Married, two sons. Ed: Carnoustie HS; University of Glasgow (BA history).

CHALLENGERS
Jim Murphy (Lab) MP for Renfrewshire E 2005-15. Leader, Scottish Labour Party 2014-. SoS, Scotland 2008-10. Shadow SoS: int devt 2013-14; defence 2010-13; Scotland 2010. Min: FCO 2007-08; DWP 2006-07. Parly sec, Cabinet Office 2005-06. Whip: govt 2003-05, asst govt 2002-03. PPS to Helen Liddell 2001-02. MP, Eastwood 1997-2005. Pres NUS

& NUS Scotland. Married, one daughter, two sons. Ed: Bellarmine SS; Milnerton HS, Cape Town; Strathclyde (politics & European law, did not graduate). **David Montgomery** (C) Medical director, oncology for Pfizer UK. Doctor. Collects wine. Ed: University of Glasgow (BSc MSc MBChB medicine, surgical oncology). **Graeme Cowie** (LD) Studying for a PhD in public law, Glasgow University. President, Glasgow University Lib Dems. Ed: Glasgow (LLB law & politics). **Robert Malyn** (Ukip) Assistant researcher to MEP David Coburn. Ed: Eastwood HS; University of Paisley (BA business economics with finance).

CONSTITUENCY PROFILE
An affluent, middle-class commuter area with a high proportion of owner-occupiers and professionals. Has the largest Jewish population of any seat in Scotland, with almost half of Scotland's Jewish population living here. Oswald ousted SLP leader.

	Electorate	Turnout %	Change from 2010 %
	69,982	81.1	
K Oswald SNP	23,013	40.6	+31.7
J Murphy Lab	19,295	34.0	-16.8
D Montgomery C	12,465	22.0	-8.4
G Cowie LD	1,069	1.9	-7.3
R Malyn Ukip	888	1.6	+0.8

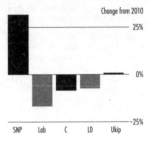

Change from 2010

Rhondda

LABOUR HOLD

CHRIS BRYANT
BORN Jan 11, 1962
MP 2001-

Likeable, excitable and funny, but not taken seriously since posing on a gay website in underpants. Former clergyman, first MP to hold civil partnership at Commons. Shad SoS CMS 2015-. Shad min: CMS 2014-15; DWP 2013-14; home affairs 2011-13; justice 2010-11; Europe 2010. Parly under-sec, FCO 2009-10. Dep leader HoC 2008-09. PPS to: Harriet Harman 2007-08; Lord Falconer 2005-06. Member, select cttees: modernisation of Hoc 2007-10; HoL reform 2002-05. Const affairs team 2005-. Contested Wycombe 1997. Cllr, Hackney LBC 1993-98. BBC European affairs head. Lab party local govt devt officer, agent. Chair: Lab Movement for Europe; Christian Socialist Movement. Ordained priest. Ed: Cheltenham Coll; Mansfield Coll, Oxford (BA English); Ripon Coll, Cuddesdon (MA Cert theology).

CHALLENGERS
Shelley Rees-Owen (PC) Welsh television actress. Dir, Theatr Ieuenctid, which mentors young people. Cllr, Rhondda Cynon Taf CBC 2012-. School governor. Member: Rhondda Listening Friends; Pentwyn Allotment Society; Rhondda Civic Scoiety. Police crime panel. Husband, one daughter. **Ron Hughes** (Ukip) Travel agent and tour operator. Worked in special needs care for young people. Adopted. **Lyn Hudson** (C) Cllr, Cardiff CC 2008-. Member, Cardiff and Vale of Glamorgan Community Health Council.

CONSTITUENCY PROFILE
In the south of Wales valleys to the north west of Cardiff. A coal mining territory. While the mines have gone it retains the character of a mining community, along with the economic deprivation that the departure of the mines left behind. Labour is entrenched in the culture of the Rhondda.

	Electorate	Turnout %	Change from 2010 %
	51,809	60.9	
C Bryant Lab	15,976	50.7	-4.6
S Rees-Owen PC	8,521	27.0	+8.9
R Hughes Ukip	3,998	12.7	+11.5
L Hudson C	2,116	6.7	+0.3
G Summers LD	474	1.5	-9.2
L Rapado Green	453	1.4	

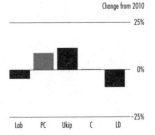

Change from 2010

Ribble Valley

CONSERVATIVE HOLD

NIGEL EVANS
BORN Nov 10, 1957
MP 1992-

Voluble, excitable, combative
Thatcherite who speaks out
frequently. Career dented due to
arrest on suspicion of rape and
sexual assault, but later acquitted
of all charges. Chair of ways &
means 2010-13. Shadow SoS, Wales
2001-03. Conservative vice-chair
1999-2001. PPS to: William Hague
1996-97; Tony Baldry 1995-96;
David Hunt 1993-95. Member,
select cttees: administration 2014-;
backbench business 2014-; public
administration 2014-; panel of
chairs 2009-13; CMS 2005-09;
trade & industry 2003-05; Welsh
affairs 2003-05; environment
1997. Contested: Ribble Valley
by-election 1991; Pontypridd by-
election 1989; Swansea West 1987.
Owned longstanding family-run
Swansea newsagents. Ed: Dynevor
Sch; University Coll, Swansea
(BA politics).

CHALLENGERS
David Hinder (Lab) Businessman.
Contested Altrincham & Sale
1987. Two children. Ed: Blessed
Edward Jones RC HS; University
of Leeds; Manchester Business
Sch (MBA). **Shirley Parkinson**
(Ukip) Cllr, Little Hoole PC.
Married, one daughter. Ed: Wye
Coll, University of London (plant
tisse culture biotechnology &
biochemistry). **Jackie Pearcey**
(LD) Activist. Analyst programmer,
BCP Software. Cllr, Manchester CC
1991-. Contested Davyhulme 1992;
Manchester Gorton 1997, 2001;
Bolton West 2010.

CONSTITUENCY PROFILE
One of the most affluent areas in
Lancashire. A predominantly rural
seat thought to be the inspiration
for much of JRR Tolkein's Middle
Earth. The area around Bamber
Bridge is more socially mixed and
industrial. Manufacturing is a key
employer. Safe Conservative seat
but won by Lib Dems on a huge
swing in 1991.

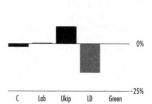

	Electorate	Turnout %	Change from 2010 %
	77,873	67.1	
N Evans C	25,404	48.6	-1.7
D Hinder Lab	11,798	22.6	+0.5
S Parkinson Ukip	8,250	15.8	+9.1
J Pearcey LD	2,756	5.3	-15.3
G Sowter Green	2,193	4.2	
D Brass Ind	1,498	2.9	
G Astley Ind	288	0.6	
T Johnson IPAP	56	0.1	

Change from 2010

Richmond (Yorks)

CONSERVATIVE HOLD

RISHI SUNAK
BORN May 12, 1980
MP 2015-

Head of Policy Exchange's BME
research unit. Dir, Catamaran
Ventures investment firm.
Previously worked for charity
hedge fund The Children's
Investment. Co-founded an
investment firm. Member, Boys &
Girls Club, Santa Monica. School
governor. Hindu. Son-in-law of
billionaire Infosys boss Narayana
Murthy. Married, two daughters.
Ed: Winchester Coll, Lincoln
Coll, Oxford (BA PPE); Stanford
University (MBA, Fulbright
Scholar).

CHALLENGERS
Matthew Cooke (Ukip)
Entrepreneur. Member, Chartered
Assoc of Certified Accountants.
Grew up on a council estate.
Married, two children. Ed: Stirling
University (BAcc accountancy).
Mike Hill (Lab) Unison regional

organiser & political officer.
Member, Co-operative party. **John
Harris** (LD) Former mayor and
husband to Baroness Angela Harris
of Richmond, HoL deputy speaker.
Ex-teacher. Cllr: Richmond TC
1995-; Richmondshire DC 1999-
2011. Former member, Yorkshire &
Humber Assembly, scrutiny board.
Former CAB member & teacher.
Married, two sons. **John Blackie**
(Ind) Cllr, Richmondshire District
Council.

CONSTITUENCY PROFILE
A geographically huge seat that
covers a vast swathe of rural North
Yorkshire, including much of the
Yorkshire Dales National Park,
Swaledale and Wensleydale. The
seat of William Hague from 1989
to 2015. Most of the constituency
is small villages and hamlets.
The local economy relies upon
agriculture and tourism, though
the constituency also includes the
army base at Catterick Garrison.
One of the safest Tory seats in the
country.

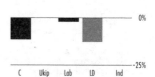

	Electorate	Turnout %	Change from 2010 %
	83,451	64.7	
R Sunak C	27,744	51.4	-11.4
M Cooke Ukip	8,194	15.2	
M Hill Lab	7,124	13.2	-2.1
J Harris LD	3,465	6.4	-12.7
J Blackie Ind	3,348	6.2	
L Rowe Green	2,313	4.3	+1.5
R Scott Ind	1,811	3.4	

Change from 2010

Richmond Park

CONSERVATIVE HOLD

ZAC GOLDSMITH
BORN Jan 20, 1975
MP 2010-

Multi-millionaire environmentalist and former green adviser to David Cameron. Known for prettyboy looks and charming manner. Faced scrutiny over claiming large amounts for signs and jackets for his election campaign. Dep chair, Tory Quality of Life policy group. Member, select cttee: environmental audit 2010-. Received Mikhail Gorbachev's Global Green Award for International Environmental Leadership in 2004. Edited *the Ecologist*. Published *The Constant Economy*. Poker enthusiast. Son of Sir James Goldsmith. Divorced. Remarried, two daughters and one son from first marriage, one daughter from second marriage. Ed: King's House Sch; The Mall Sch; Hawtreys Sch; Eton Coll (expelled after drugs found in his room); Cambridge Centre for Sixth-Form Studies.

CHALLENGERS
Robin Meltzer (LD) Tutor in English. Campaigner. Former senior producer, BBC. Ed: Shenfield HS; Selwyn Coll, University of Cambridge (BA English). **Sachin Patel** (Lab) Trainee manager at high street supermarket. Member: National Young Labour committee; Usdaw. Ed: Orleans Park SS; Richmond Coll, Twickenham. **Andrée Frieze** (Green) Freelance journalist and editor. School governor. Founder, Latchmere House Action Group. Ed: University of Kent, Canterbury (BA history).

CONSTITUENCY PROFILE
Richmond Park is a large royal park in southwest London, home to a herd of over 600 deer. Seat consists of the residential areas bordering it: Richmond itself, Kew and, to the south of the park, Kingston upon Thames. An affluent, middle-class suburban seat. Contains Kew Gardens. Zac Goldsmith retook the seat in 2015 by 23,015 votes.

	Electorate	Turnout %	from 2010 %	Change %
	77,297	76.5		
Z Goldsmith C	34,404	58.2	+8.5	
R Meltzer LD	11,389	19.3	-23.5	
S Patel Lab	7,296	12.3	+7.3	
A Frieze Green	3,548	6.0	+5.0	
S Naz Ukip	2,464	4.2	+3.0	

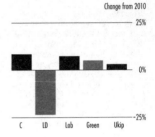

Change from 2010

Rochdale

LABOUR HOLD

SIMON DANCZUK
BORN Oct 24, 1966
MP 2010-

One of the main players calling for a child abuse inquiry. Unseated Lib Dems in 2010 despite Gillian Duffy's "bigoted woman" incident in Rochdale. Cllr, Blackburn with Darwen BC 1993-2001. Mem, select cttee: CLG 2012-. Co-founder and director, Vision 21 social research agency. Researcher: *The Big Issue*; Opinion Research Corporation; Bolton TEC. Founder member, Labour Friends of Palestine, AEU, GMB. Raised in Burnley. Started work in factory aged 16, retrained and went to university as mature student. Won Political Campaigner of the Year award 2014. Divorced & remarried, one daughter, one son from first marriage. Ed: Gawthorpe Comp; Lancaster (BA economics & sociology).

CHALLENGERS
Mohammed Masud (Ukip)

Housing officer. Cllr, Rochdale BC 2001-12 for Labour & Lib Dems. Three children. **Azi Ahmed** (C) Management consultant, internet practice. Ed: University of the Arts London (MA media technology). **Andy Kelly** (LD) Project consultant in the public sector, runs own business. Teacher, public speaking. Cllr, Rochdale BC 2010-14, lost seat as LD group leader. Am dram director. Ed: Salford Coll of Performing Arts.

CONSTITUENCY PROFILE
In the north of Greater Manchester, this seat extends from Rochdale across the South Pennine Moors. It has not yet recovered from the decline of the textile industry. Has a strong tradition of Liberal support. For twenty years it was represented by Cyril Smith. Labour's Simon Danczuk won the seat in 2010 just 899 votes ahead of the Lib Dems, most likely a narrow margin due to Gordon Brown's controversial remarks. In 2015 he retook the seat, the Lib Dems coming fourth.

	Electorate	Turnout %	from 2010 %	Change %
	79,170	57.4		
S Danczuk Lab	20,961	46.1	+9.8	
M Masud Ukip	8,519	18.8	+14.4	
A Ahmed C	7,742	17.0	-1.1	
A Kelly LD	4,667	10.3	-24.2	
F Ahmed Rochdale	1,535	3.4		
M Hollinrake Green	1,382	3.0		
K Bryan NF	433	1.0	-3.9	
M Salim IZB	191	0.4	-0.8	

Change from 2010

Rochester & Strood

CONSERVATIVE GAIN

KELLY TOLHURST
BORN Aug 23, 1978
MP 2015-

Supervisor, SFS, Northfleet. Dir, marine surveyors & consultants Tolhurst Associates. Cllr, Medway BC 2011-. Contested 2014 by-election but lost out to Mark Reckless. Dir, Skipper UK. Trustee: Chatham Maritime Trust; Action for Borstal Community Project. Vocal critic of Israel. Father ran a boatbuilding business. Ed: Old Chapter HS.

CHALLENGERS
Mark Reckless (Ukip) MP 2014-15 for Ukip, 2010-14 for Conservatives, defected to Ukip in sensational move during autumn conference season of 2014. Missed a vote in the HoC due to having too much to drink in 2010. Member, select cttee: home affairs 2010-14. Cllr, Medway 2007-11. Contested Medway 2005, 2001. Solicitor, Herbert Smith. UK economist, Warburgs investment

bank. Barings. Conservative party policy unit. Married, two sons. Ed: Marlborough Coll; Christ's Church, Oxford (BA PPE); Columbia (MBA); Coll of Law (LLB).
Naushabah Khan (Lab) Works in public affairs, Curtin & Co. Former policy advisor for department of education. Sch gov. Former advisor, Peter Skinner MEP. Keen kickboxer. Ed: Birmingham (BA history, vice-president of student union); BPP Law School (Grad Dip law). **Clive Gregory** (Green) Freelance musician and sound engineer. Runs PA hire business, Clive Sound.

CONSTITUENCY PROFILE
A largely industrial seat in the conurbation of Medway in Kent. Rochester & Strood is geographically the largest of the Medway seats. The peninsula and Isle of Grain are largely marshland with heavy industry in the south. A mixed demographic of middle & working classes. Part of the London commuter belt.

	Electorate	Turnout %	from 2010 % Change
	79,000	66.5	
K Tolhurst C	23,142	44.1	-5.1
M Reckless Ukip	16,009	30.5	
N Khan Lab	10,396	19.8	-8.7
C Gregory Green	1,516	2.9	+1.4
P Bray LD	1,251	2.4	-13.9
D Burn TUSC	202	0.4	

Change from 2010

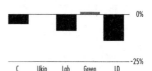

Rochford & Southend East

CONSERVATIVE HOLD

JAMES DUDDRIDGE
BORN Aug 26, 1971
MP 2005-

Has a slightly intense manner but a mischevious sense of humour. Hardline Eurosceptic. Was under scrutiny during the expenses scandal. Parly under-sec FCO 2014-. Govt whip 2010-12. Opposition whip 2008-10. Select cttees: draft deregulation bill 2013; liaison 2012-14; regulatory reform 2012-14. Banker, Barclays, ran operations in Botswana. Founder member, YouGov. Research assistant to Bernard Jenkin, campaign manager Stephen Shakespeare, Exec cttee Conservative Way Forward. Contested Rother Valley 2001. Member: MCC; Carlton Club. Enjoys DIY and real ale. Married, two sons, one daughter. Ed: Huddersfield New Coll; Wells Blue Sch; Essex (BA government).

CHALLENGERS
Ian Gilbert (Lab) Deputy leader,

Southend BC 2014-. Leader of Labour group. Technical director, Nicholas Hall IT services. Cllr, Southend BC 2008-. Cricket and chess fan. Ed: University of Birmingham (BSocSc economics & political science). **Floyd Waterworth** (Ukip) Cllr, Southend on sea BC 2014-. Disowned by Ukip after allegedly warned a fellow councillor that he would interfere with his chances of getting re-elected. Acting chairman, Ukip South Essex. Was suspended but allowed to carry on as group council leader with the suspension later revoked.

CONSTITUENCY PROFILE
Mainly consists of the central and eastern part of the Georgian seaside resort of Southend. As with most British seaside towns it has declined since its heyday, but tourism remains a major part of the economy. The London, Tilbury & Southend railway line finishes here. Originally held by arch-Eurosceptic Sir Teddy Taylor 1980-1997.

	Electorate	Turnout %	from 2010 % Change
	71,935	60.6	
J Duddridge C	20,241	46.4	-0.5
I Gilbert Lab	10,765	24.7	+4.4
F Waterworth Ukip	8,948	20.5	+14.7
S Cross Green	2,195	5.0	+3.3
P Gwizdala LD	1,459	3.4	-16.1

Change from 2010

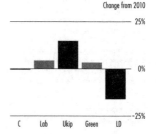

Romford

CONSERVATIVE HOLD

ANDREW ROSINDELL
BORN Mar 17, 1966
MP 2001-

Epitome of Essex Tory with robust right-wing outlook and attack-dog instincts. Supports re-introducing the death penalty. Controversially claimed that a pregnant cabinet minister would be unable to give the job her full attention. Chair, APPG: British Overseas Territories; Central America; Polar Regions. Chair, Young Conservatives 1993-94. Shad min, home affairs 2007-10. Opposition whip 2005-07. Select cttees: foreign affairs 2010-; panel of chairs 2010-; regulatory reform 2001-05. VC, Conservative party 2004-05. Member, national union executive cttee Conservative party 1986-88, 1992-94. Cllr, Havering BC 1990-2002. Contested: Thurrock 1997; Glasgow, Provan 1992. Freelance journalist. Parliamentary researcher to Vivian Bendall MP. Ed: Marshalls Park Comp, Romford.

CHALLENGERS
Gerard Batten (Ukip) MEP for London 2004-. Contested: Barking by-election 1994; Harlow 1997; West Ham 2001; Dagenham 2005; London mayor 2008-. **Samuel Gould** (Lab) Previously worked for Dagenham & Rainham MP, Jon Cruddas. Ed: University of Essex (BA politics). **Ian Sanderson** (LD) Retired chartered engineer. Open University tutor. Chair of a local Scout group. Member, Harold Wood focus team. School governor. Married, one daughter, deceased son. Ed: Queen's University, Belfast; Open University.

CONSTITUENCY PROFILE
Part of Greater London and home to Havering council but has historic links to Essex. Overwhelmingly white and largely well off, with above-average numbers of owner-occupiers and self-employed. A major office and retail centre for northeast London. Historically a Tory and Labour marginal.

	Electorate	Turnout %	from 2010 % Change
	72,594	67.7	
A Rosindell C	25,067	51.0	-5.0
G Batten Ukip	11,208	22.8	+18.4
S Gould Lab	10,268	20.9	+1.4
I Sanderson LD	1,413	2.9	-9.1
L Tooley Green	1,222	2.5	+1.5

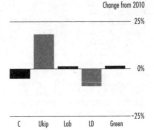

Change from 2010

C   Ukip   Lab   LD   Green

Romsey & Southampton North

CONSERVATIVE HOLD

CAROLINE NOKES
BORN Jun 26, 1972
MP 2010-

The daughter of Roy Perry, a pro-European former Tory MEP. Dubbed "Cameron cutie" when she was elected. Interested in farming and food issues. Recieved harrassment from Fathers4Justice after the Conservatives failed to carry out promised legislation on family law. PPS to Mark Harper 2014-15. Select cttees: education 2014-; environmental audit 2010-. Member, Parly beer group. Chair, APPG on body image. Contested: Romsey 2005; Southampton Itchen 2001. Cllr, Test Valley BC 1999-. CEO, National Pony Society. Divorced, one daughter. Ed: La Sagesse Convent, Romsey; Peter Symonds Coll, Winchester; University of Sussex (BA government & politics).

CHALLENGERS
Ben Nicholls (LD) Reasearch

fellow, University of Buckingham Centre for Education and Employment Research. Founder, RicNic youth theatre company. School governor. Former policy advisor, DfE. Ed: Winchester Coll; Selwyn Coll, Cambridge (BA music). **Darren Paffey** (Lab) Lecturer in Spanish and linguistics at University of Southampton. Cllr, Southampton CC 2011-. School governor. Married, two children. Ed: University of Southampton (BA French & Spanish linguistics; PhD sociolinguistics). **Sandra James** (Ukip) Cllr, West Sussex CC 2013-. Has worked in the aerospace, finance and IT industries.

CONSTITUENCY PROFILE
A large Hampshire seat. Mostly consists of the affluent towns and villages of the Test Valley, stretching northwards from Southampton. Romsey is a medieval town whose abbey and stately home attract tourists. Home to a large student population. Unemployment is low.

	Electorate	Turnout %	from 2010 % Change
	66,519	72.8	
C Nokes C	26,285	54.3	+4.6
B Nicholls LD	8,573	17.7	-23.5
D Paffey Lab	5,749	11.9	+5.5
S James Ukip	5,511	11.4	+8.8
I Callaghan Green	2,280	4.7	

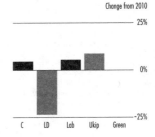

Change from 2010

C   LD   Lab   Ukip   Green

Ross, Skye & Lochaber

SNP GAIN

IAN BLACKFORD
BORN May 14, 1961
MP 2015-

SNP spokesman, pensions 2015-. Runs consultancy business with his wife. Ran against Douglas Alexander in 1997 Paisley by-election. Was sacked as treasurer for SNP through a vote of no confidence, 2000. Former MD of Deutsche Bank in Scotland and the Netherlands. Married, three children, three stepchildren. Ed: Royal HS, Edinburgh.

CHALLENGERS
Charles Kennedy (LD) MP 1983-2015. Died suddenly Jun 2015, aged 55. Leader of the Liberal Democrats 1999-2006, taking party to highest number of seats since 1923. Resigned after admitting to a drink problem. Opposed coalition, abstained when MPs voted on the agreement. Parly Assembly of the Council of Europe 2010-. Select cttee: works of art 2010-15. Part of

Better Together. Vice-pres, Liberal International 2006-. President, European Movement 2008-. Alliance, SDP, LD spokes, various roles, 1987-99. LD party pres 1990-94. Member LD federal exec cttee, policy cttee. Rector, University of Glasgow 2008-14. PC. Journalist, broadcaster. Divorced, one son. Ed: Lochaber HS, Fort William; Glasgow (MA PPE); Indiana University; University of Glasgow (honorary doctorate). **Lindsay McCallum** (C) Chief of staff to Ruth Davidson MSP. Ed: University of Glasgow (English & Scottish literature).

CONSTITUENCY PROFILE
Geographically the largest seat in the UK, but one of the smallest in terms of electorate. Most of the seat is extremely remote and sparsely populated. Takes in the UK's tallest peak, Ben Nevis, as well as Glencoe. This was a safe seat for the Liberal Democrats, or at least for Charlie Kennedy, who held it for 32 years.

	Electorate	Turnout %	Change from 2010 %
	54,169	77.2	
I Blackford SNP	20,119	48.1	+33.0
C Kennedy LD	14,995	35.9	-16.8
L McCallum C	2,598	6.2	-6.0
C Conniff Lab	2,043	4.9	-10.2
A Thomas Green	1,051	2.5	+0.3
P Anderson Ukip	814	2.0	+0.1
R Campbell Ind	191	0.5	-0.3

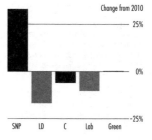

Change from 2010

Rossendale & Darwen

CONSERVATIVE HOLD

JAKE BERRY
BORN Dec 29, 1978
MP 2010-

Smart, unpretentious and approachable Liverpudlian lawyer. Interested in social housing and supporting manufacturing. Member of No 10 policy unit, advising PM on housing regional growth and local government 2013. PPS to Grant Shapps 2010-. Agent to Amber Rudd 2005. Solicitor, commerical property specialist: City Law Partnership; DWF; Halliwells. Shareholder, Tung Sing Housing Association. Enjoys walking and water-skiing. Married. Ed: Liverpool Coll; Sheffield (LLB law); Coll of Law, Chester.

CHALLENGERS
Will Straw (Lab) Son of Jack Straw looking to follow in his father's footsteps. Founder, Left Foot Forward blog. Associate dir, strategic development, IPPR. Victim of tabloid sting after trying

to sell cannabis when father was home secretary. Married, one son. Ed: New Coll, Oxford (PPE, SU president); Columbia University (Masters, public administration, Fulbright Scholar).**Clive Balchin** (Ukip) Owner, James Trickett & Son. Chairman, Rossendale and Darwen Con assoc. President, Rawtenstall Chamber of Commerce. Married, two sons. Ed: Ewell Coll. **Karen Pollard-Rylance** (Green) Dyslexia assessor and tutor, Salford City Coll. Married.

CONSTITUENCY PROFILE
A long hilly constituency stretching along Lancashire's boundary with Greater Manchester and consisting of the Darwen and Rossendale valleys in the West Pennine Moors. The main towns, Rawtenstall, Bacup and Darwen are all traditional former Lancashire textile towns. A Conservative-Labour marginal seat. It was won by the Conservatives in 1983, gained by Labour in 1992 and regained by the Tories in 2005.

	Electorate	Turnout %	Change from 2010 %
	84,011	58.4	
J Berry C	22,847	46.6	+4.8
W Straw Lab	17,193	35.1	+2.8
C Balchin Ukip	6,862	14.0	+10.6
K Pollard-Rylance Green	1,046	2.1	
A Anwar LD	806	1.6	-16.5
K Scranage Ind	122	0.3	+0.0
S Thomas TUSC	103	0.2	
S Hargreaves Northern	45	0.1	

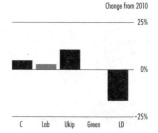

Change from 2010

Rother Valley

LABOUR HOLD

SIR KEVIN BARRON
BORN Oct 26, 1946
MP 1983-

Solid reputation as a hard-working backbencher; quietly influential. Select cttees: chair, standards 2013-; privileges 2013-15, 2010-13; health 2005-10. Member, standards 2013-15; privileges 2013-15; independent standards authority 2010-15; standards & privileges 2005-13; health 2005-10. PPS to Neil Kinnock 1985-88. National Coal Board. Amicus. Knighthood. Supporter of Rotherham United Football Club. Widowed & remarried, two daughters & one son from first marriage, step-father to two sons, one daughter. Ed: Maltby Hall; Sheffield (day release, social sciences); Ruskin Coll, Oxford (Dip labour studies).

CHALLENGERS
Allen Cowles (Ukip) Former IT programme manager. Cllr, Rotherham MBC 2014-. Ukip

Rotherham branch secretary. **Gareth Streeter** (C) PR officer, Oasis trust. Son of Gary Streeter MP. Lives in Croydon. Christian blogger. Long-term partner. Ed: London Sch of Theology (BA theology). **Robert Teal** (LD) Small busines owner. Dir, Rotherham Enterprise Agency. Contested PCC election South Yorkshire 2012. Magistrate. Ed: Sheffield Poly; Huddersfield; Open University (BA business studies).

CONSTITUENCY PROFILE
The southernmost seat in South Yorkshire, to the south of Rotherham itself. Situated in the South Yorkshire coalfield and is mostly made up of small former pit towns and villages that grew up with the expansion of coal mining, and which have fallen into decline. Further east in places like Maltby, deprivation is evident in both the old housing and the new council estates. Safe Labour seat, held since it was created in 1918.

	Electorate	Turnout %	from 2010 %	Change
	74,275	63.3		
K Barron Lab	20,501	43.6	+2.7	
A Cowles Ukip	13,204	28.1	+22.5	
G Streeter C	10,945	23.3	-5.1	
R Teal LD	1,992	4.2	-13.1	
S Pilling Eng Dem	377	0.8		

Change from 2010

Lab Ukip C LD Eng Dem

Rotherham

LABOUR HOLD

SARAH CHAMPION
BORN Jul 10, 1969
MP 2012-

Took over after disgraced Denis McShane's resignation, but controversy over selection when no local candidate was shortlisted. First woman MP for Rotherham, nicknamed "Mother Teresa". Seen to have learned the ropes of parliament quickly after only short membership of Labour party. PPS to Tristram Hunt 2013-. Member, select cttee: transport 2012-. Chair, APPG for victims & witnesses 2014-. Member, Labour parliamentary women's group. CEO, Bluebell Wood Children's Hospice 2008-12. CEO, Chinese Arts Centre, Manchester 1996-2008. Ed: Prince William Comp, Oundle; University of Sheffield (BA psychology).

CHALLENGERS
Jane Collins (Ukip) MEP for Yorkshire 2014-. Contested:

Scunthorpe 2010; Barnsley Central 2011 by-election; Rotherham 2012 by-election. **Sebastian Lowe** (C) Practice leader for construction, Holtby Turner recruitment agency. Chairman, Vauxhall Conservatives. Ed: King's Coll, Cambridge (BA English). **Janice Middleton** (LD) Retired headteacher. Party secretary, Rotherham. Lib Dem representative, Yorkshire & Humberside Executive. Worked on the board of 'Film Club' charity.

CONSTITUENCY PROFILE
A working class industrial town to the northeast of Sheffield. Historically it was a steel-making town and it remains a key part of the economy. The decline of hevy industry has led to high unemployment. The Labour council was taken over by government commissioners after a child sex abuse scandal in the borough. Its ethnic minority community is mostly in the north with tensions reflected in BNP success. Labour held since 1933.

	Electorate	Turnout %	from 2010 %	Change
	63,698	59.4		
S Champion Lab	19,860	52.5	+7.9	
J Collins Ukip	11,414	30.2	+24.3	
S Lowe C	4,656	12.3	-4.4	
J Middleton LD	1,093	2.9	-13.1	
P McLaughlin TUSC	409	1.1		
A Walker BNP	225	0.6	-9.8	
D Walker Eng Dem	166	0.4		

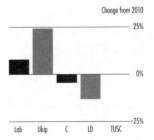

Change from 2010

Lab Ukip C LD TUSC

Rugby

CONSERVATIVE HOLD

MARK PAWSEY
BORN Jan 16, 1957
MP 2010-

Interested in land use and planning issues. Member, select cttee: CLG 2010-. Member, APPG: small business; manufacturing; micro-business. PPS to Anna Soubry 2014-15. Contested Nuneaton 2005. Cllr, Rugby BC 2002-07. Son of James Pawsey, MP Rugby 1979-97. Successful businessman, founded catering trade supply firm with brother; firm acquired by FTSE100 company. Enjoys rugby and wine appreciation. Plays for Lords & Commons rugby team. Married, two daughters, two sons. Ed: Lawrence Sheriff Sch, Rugby; Reading (BSc estate management).

CHALLENGERS
Claire Edwards (Lab) Cllr, Rugby BC 2002-15. Leader of Labour group. Office manager & company secretary, Warwickshire Race Equality Partnership. Former

press officer and researcher to MP and MEP. Member, Unite. Trustee, Hill Street Youth & Community Centre. Ran research centre at Warwick Business School. **Gordon Davies** (Ukip) Works for Cemex, specialising in purchasing and supply chain management. Chairman, Ukip Rugby branch. Enjoys salsa dancing. **Ed Goncalves** (LD) Dir, Climate Group environmental organisation. Dir, 'Kidney Kids', a kidney disease charity. Former campaigns manager, WWF. Former investigative journalist. Donated a kidney to son in 2013. Married, two sons. Ed: Leeds (BA politics & parliamentary studies).

CONSTITUENCY PROFILE
Most famous for its public school and as the birthplace of the sport of rugby. The town itself is far more industrial and working class than its public history may suggest. An engineering and industrial town, producing turbines and cement. Has a large Indian community.

	Electorate	Turnout %	from 2010 %
	79,557	61.6	
M Pawsey C	24,040	49.1	+5.0
C Edwards Lab	13,695	28.0	-3.5
G Davies Ukip	6,855	14.0	+13.1
E Goncalves LD	2,776	5.7	-14.2
T White Green	1,415	2.9	+1.9
P McLaren TUSC	225	0.5	

Change from 2010

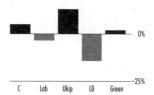

Ruislip, Northwood & Pinner

CONSERVATIVE HOLD

NICK HURD
BORN May 13, 1962
MP 2005-

Urbane son of former foreign secretary Douglas Hurd, making him the fourth successive generation in his family to become an MP. Quietly impressive and well-liked. Parly under-sec: Cabinet Office 2010-14. Shadow min: charities 2008-10. Opp whip 2007-08. Select cttees: draft protection of charities bill 2014-; environmental audit 2005-10. Kensington & Chelsea borough champion for Steve Norris 2003. Member, Vote No to the EU Constitution campaign. Business consultant, banker, represented British bank in Brazil. Chief of staff to Tim Yeo MP. Freeman of the City of London. Divorced and remarried, two daughters and two sons from first marriage, one son and one daughter from second marriage. Ed: Eton; Exeter Coll, Oxford University (BA Classics).

CHALLENGERS
Michael Borio (Lab) Public affairs officer, Independent Age. Cllr, Harrow C 2014-. Chair, Harrow East CLP. Member, Co-op party; Unite; Fabian Society. Ed: Middlesex (BA American studies & political studies), Brunel (MSc public affairs & lobbying). **Gerard Barry** (Ukip) Commercial property surveyor. Special Constable, Metropolitan Police 2005-15. **Joshua Dixon** (LD) Office Assistant, T101 IT consultancy. Chair, Hillingdon Liberal Democrats 2013-14. Lib Dem federal executive member. Ed: Brunel (BA politics).

CONSTITUENCY PROFILE
The most northwesterly seat in London, made up of wealthy, middle-class suburbia. It is residential in character, an affluent commuter area. The western part of the seat is semi-rural taking in Ruislip Common, the village of Harefield & the farms surrounding it. This is a solid Conservative seat.

	Electorate	Turnout %	from 2010 %
	73,219	70.0	
N Hurd C	30,521	59.6	+2.1
M Borio Lab	10,297	20.1	+0.6
G Barry Ukip	5,598	10.9	+8.2
J Dixon LD	2,537	5.0	-11.7
K Pillai Green	1,801	3.5	+2.0
W Kennedy TUSC	302	0.6	
S Yogalingam Nat Lib	166	0.3	

Change from 2010

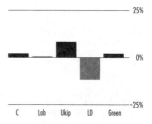

Runnymede & Weybridge

CONSERVATIVE HOLD

PHILIP HAMMOND
BORN Dec 4, 1955
MP 1997-

Mild-mannered choice for foreign secretary 2014-. Millionaire with the air of a provincial bank manager, an archetypal old-fashioned Tory. Respected as a solid performer in previous role as Tories' public spending supremo. SoS: transport 2010-14. Shadow chief sec to the Treasury 2007-10, 2005. Shadow sec: work and pensions 2005-07. Shadow min: local govt 2002-05; T&I, small business 2001-02; health 1998-2001. Business career, director roles inc property, oil & gas. Malawi govt consultant. Married, two daughters, one son. Ed: Shenfield Sch, Brentwood; University Coll, Oxford (MA PPE).

CHALLENGERS
Arran Neathey (Lab) Marketing manager, British Gas. Ed: University of Kent (BA business adminstration). **Joe Branco** (Ukip) Independent foreign exchange trader. Married, three children **John Vincent** (LD) Head of safety analysis, EASA. Cllr, Surrey CC 1993-97. Contested Crawley 2010. Contested European elections, South East England 2009, 2004. Ed: Coventry University (BSc electrical & electronic engineering); Gloucestershire Coll (DMS management studies); Henley Business Sch (CAA management). **Rustam Majainah** (Green) Pricing administrator, Total Gas & Power.

CONSTITUENCY PROFILE
Made up of several extremely affluent towns and villages in the London commuter belt. The M25 runs through the middle. With good train links into London it provides a home to major company headquarters. A safe Conservative seat. Has been represented by the Conservatives continuously since the mid-nineteenth century, with the exception of a single term after the Liberal landslide of 1906.

	Electorate	Turnout %	Change from 2010 %
	73,744	67.9	
P Hammond C	29,901	59.7	+3.8
A Neathey Lab	7,767	15.5	+2.1
J Branco Ukip	6,951	13.9	+7.4
J Vincent LD	3,362	6.7	-14.9
R Majainah Green	2,071	4.1	+2.7

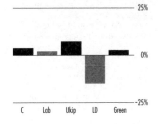

Change from 2010

Rushcliffe

CONSERVATIVE HOLD

KENNETH CLARKE
BORN Jul 2, 1940
MP 1970-

Pugnacious, with unrivalled ministerial experience including tenure as chancellor 1993-97. Can be off-message. A traditionalist about parliament. Europhile views thrice thwarted party leadership bids: came second in 1997 and 2001; eliminated first round 2005. Returned to frontline politics in 2009 but left in 2014. Min without portfolio 2012-14. Lord Chancellor, SoS for justice 2010-12. Shadow SoS: business 2009-10; home 1992-93; ed, sci 1990-2. Shadow min: health 1988-90. Pres, Tory Reform Group 1997-. Pres, Conservative Europe Group. Barrister. Cigar-smoking former non-exec dir of BAT. Motor-racing enthusiast. Married, one daughter, one son. Ed: Gonville & Caius Coll, Cambridge (BA LLB).

CHALLENGERS
David Mellen (Lab) Childrens worker. Cllr, Nottingham CC 2007-. Former primary school headteacher. Ed: Trent Polytechnic. **Matthew Faithfull** (Ukip) Software engineering contractor. Contested Rushcliffe 2010. **Richard Mallender** (Green) Chairman, Nottingham Green party. WPL planning officer, Nottingham CC. Cllr, Rushcliffe BC 2007-. Married, two step-daughters. **Bob Johnston** (LD) Retired academic and biology lecturer. Previously interviewer, Office for National Statistics. Cllr: Oxfordshire CC 2013-, 1993-2009; Vale of White Horse DC 1982-, leader 1997-2001. Widower, one son.

CONSTITUENCY PROFILE
Includes middle-class suburb of West Bridgford and the rural south of Nottinghamshire, mostly made up of villages of affluent commuters. Nottingham airport and the headquarters of Nottinghamshire county council are based here. A safe Conservative seat.

	Electorate	Turnout %	Change from 2010 %
	73,294	75.3	
K Clarke C	28,354	51.4	+0.2
D Mellen Lab	14,525	26.3	+5.6
M Faithfull Ukip	5,943	10.8	+6.7
R Mallender Green	3,559	6.5	+4.1
B Johnston LD	2,783	5.0	-16.7

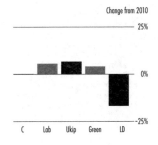

Change from 2010

Rutherglen & Hamilton West

SNP GAIN

MARGARET FERRIER
BORN Sep 10, 1960
MP 2015-

SNP spokeswoman, Scotland office 2015-. Manager in blue-chip manufacturing construction company in Motherwell. Studying teacher training at Glasgow University. Community Cllr for Halfway. Member, Amnesty International. Previously a volunteer for Citizens Advice Bureau.

CHALLENGERS
Tom Greatrex (Lab Co-op) MP 2010-15. Shad min: energy 2011-; Scotland 2010-11. Special adviser to SoS for Scotland: Jim Murphy, Des Browne; Douglas Alexander 2007-10. Member, select cttees: procedure 2010-; EEC 2010. Chair, APPG for Malawi 2011-. Member, Co-operative party, GMB. Dir, corporate affairs, NHS 24. Head of policy & public affairs, East Dunbartonshire

Council. Industrial organiser, GMB. Special adviser to Nick Brown 1997-99. Researcher, Lab party whips office. Avid Fulham FC fan. Married, twin daughters. Ed: The Judd Sch, Tonbridge; LSE (BSc economics, government & law). **Taylor Muir** (C) Student at University of Strathclyde (LLB law). Part-time Sales Advisor for Sky. **Janice MacKay** (Ukip) Minute secretary, Scottish cttee. Contested Rutherglen and Hamilton West 2010, 05; Hamilton South 2001 **Tony Hughes** (LD) Retired chartered engineer. Convenor, North Glasgow Lib Dems. Married.

CONSTITUENCY PROFILE
Scotland's oldest burgh. A suburban constituency on the southeastern edge of Glasgow. Much of it used to be in Glasgow Rutherglen but these were combined with parts of Hamilton South to form a new seat before 2005. An area that still carries echoes of heavy industry and is dominated by high-density housing.

	Electorate	Turnout %	Change from 2010 %
	82,701	69.7	
M Ferrier SNP	30,279	52.6	+36.5
T Greatrex Lab Co-op	20,304	35.2	-25.6
T Muir C	4,350	7.6	-2.1
J MacKay Ukip	1,301	2.3	+0.8
T Hughes LD	1,045	1.8	-10.2
Y Maclean CSA	336	0.6	

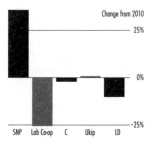

Change from 2010

Rutland & Melton

CONSERVATIVE HOLD

SIR ALAN DUNCAN
BORN Mar 31, 1957
MP 1992-

Flirtatious, dapper Thatcherite-turned-moderniser, nicknamed "Hunky Dunky". Failed leadership bid in 2005. Min: international dev 2010-14. Shadow min: prisons 2009-10. Shadow leader of House 2009. Demoted from shadow cabinet for comments over MPs expenses "rations". Shadow sec: trade & industry, business 2005-09; trans 2005; int dev 2004-05; constitutional affairs 2003-04. Con party vice-chair 1997-98. Opp spokes roles and PPS to: William Hague 1997-98; Dr Brian Mawhinney 1993-94. Contested Barnsley West & Penistone 1987. Oil trader with Shell. KCMG. PC. Knighted in 2014. First openly gay Tory MP, came out in 2002. Ed: Merchant Taylors' Sch, Northwood; St John's Coll, Oxford (BA politics & economics, pres, Oxford Union); Harvard.

CHALLENGERS
Richard Billington (Ukip) Runs a business in the financial services industry. Former teacher. Married, four children. **James Moore** (Lab) History lecturer, University of Leicester. Contested Bosworth 2005 for Lib Dems. Ed: Christ Church Coll, Oxford (BA PPE); University of Manchester (PhD political culture). **Ed Reynolds** (LD) Works in renewable energy sector for Navitron. Married, one son. Ed: Uppingham; UWE (BA politics).

CONSTITUENCY PROFILE
This huge rural seat in the East Midlands encompasses the borough of Melton, which has Melton Mowbray at its centre, and the district of Rutland, with the main towns of Oakham and Uppingham. Rutland was the second least deprived local authority in the country in 2007. Retail and manufacturing are big employers. It has been Conservative since 1945.

	Electorate	Turnout %	Change from 2010 %
	79,789	68.4	
A Duncan C	30,383	55.6	+4.5
R Billington Ukip	8,678	15.9	+11.3
J Moore Lab	8,383	15.4	+1.1
E Reynolds LD	4,407	8.1	-17.7
A McQuillan Green	2,325	4.3	
M Gordon Ind	427	0.8	-0.3

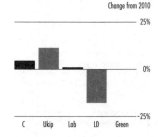

Change from 2010

Saffron Walden

CONSERVATIVE HOLD

SIR ALAN HASELHURST
BORN Jun 23, 1937
MP 1970-74; 1977-

Courteous old-style Tory, was prominent as a pro-European Tory wet but since 1997 has been a mainstay of the Commons establishment. Passionate about commonwealth. Deputy speaker 2010. Chairman, ways and means 1997-2010. PPS: Mark Carlisle 1979-81; Robert Carr 1973-74. MP, Middleton & Prestwich 1970-74. Select cttee: administration 2010-. Commonwealth Parliamentary Association 2010-. Member, select cttees: ecclesiastical 2010-; liaison 2010-; finance & services 2008-; European legislation 1982-97. Public affairs consultant. Knighted 1995. PC. Passionate about cricket, published several books on the topic. Married, three children. Ed: Cheltenham; Oriel Coll, Oxford.

CHALLENGERS
Peter Day (Ukip) Former Elvis impersonator. Former Conservative Cllr, Cambridge CC. Married. **Jane Berney** (Lab) Chartered accountant, auditor in the City. School governor. Married, two children. Ed: University of Manchester (BA history); Chinese University of Hong Kong (MA public & comparative history); Open University (PhD history). **Mike Hibbs** (LD) Architect. Partner, Hibbs and Walsh Associates. Mayor of Saffron Walden 1993-4, 2008-9. Cllr, Saffron Walden TC 1988-. Married, four children.

CONSTITUENCY PROFILE
The largest and most rural seat in Essex, covering 360 square miles. It takes in the northwest of the county along the M11 and includes the rural hinterland of Bishops Stortford and Chelmsford. The main population centres are Saffron Walden itself and Great Dunmow. Stanstead airport is the constituencys biggest employer. An affluent area. Safe Tory seat.

	Electorate	Turnout %	from 2010 %	Change
	80,615	71.4		
A Haselhurst C	32,926	57.2	+1.7	
P Day Ukip	7,935	13.8	+9.7	
J Berney Lab	6,791	11.8	+2.1	
M Hibbs LD	6,079	10.6	-16.9	
K Stannard Green	2,174	3.8	+2.4	
H Asker Uttlesford	1,658	2.9		

Change from 2010

C Ukip Lab LD Green

Salford & Eccles

LABOUR HOLD

REBECCA LONG-BAILEY
BORN Sept 22, 1979
MP 2015-

Controversial all-women shortlist selected high-flying lawyer over local cllr, although she grew up in the constituency. Daughter of dockworker, who worked in call centres and factories before training to be a solicitor. Specialises in NHS contracts. Solicitor: Hill Dickinson 2007-; Halliwells 2003-07. Married, one son. Ed: Catholic High, Chester; Manchester Metropolitan University (BA politics & sociology).

CHALLENGERS
Greg Downes (C) Vicar at King's Church, High Wycombe. Former teacher, prison chaplain and college lecturer. Married, two daughters. Ed: Oxford University. **Paul Doyle** (Ukip) Runs a logistic company. Former serviceman. **Emma Van Dyke** (Green) Chairwoman, Salford Green party. Volunteer, mental health charity. Suffers from an "invisible illness" and gets disability benefits. Married. **Charlie Briggs** (LD) Cllr and council leader, Burnley BC 2011-. Former Cllr, Lancashire CC. Ex-wife, Lynne Briggs, former Burnley Cllr, died in 2014 from cancer.

CONSTITUENCY PROFILE
This Greater Manchester seat combines most of the old Salford seat with the northern part of Eccles, once known for the number of Coronation Street stars among its residents. Sandwiched between the River Irwell and the Manchester Ship Canal and pushing right up towards Manchester City Centre itself. This is a constituency of decline and redevelopment. Salford Quays have undergone regeneration with MediaCity and the Lowry arts centre based there. The area has more people living alone than many other parts of England and Wales and ranks 10th for this in the 2011 census. The seat has been Labour for decades.

	Electorate	Turnout %	from 2010 %	Change
	74,290	58.2		
R Long-Bailey Lab	21,364	49.4	+9.3	
G Downes C	8,823	20.4	-0.1	
P Doyle Ukip	7,806	18.0	+15.4	
E Van Dyke Green	2,251	5.2		
C Briggs LD	1,614	3.7	-22.6	
B Berry Reality	703	1.6		
N Bailey TUSC	517	1.2	-0.6	
S Clark Pirate	183	0.4		

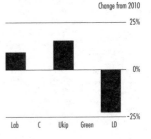

Change from 2010

Lab C Ukip Green LD

Salisbury

CONSERVATIVE HOLD

JOHN GLEN
BORN Apr 1, 1974
MP 2010-

PPS to Eric Pickles 2012-15. Select cttees: defence 2010-12; arms export controls 2010-12. Sits on Downing Street policy board with responsibility for constitutional affairs. Chairman, APPG on global uncertainties 2013-. Contested Plymouth Devonport 2001. Management consultancy career, Accenture. Stints at Conservative research department; seconded to head of political section during William Hague's leadership, returned as deputy dir, then dir 2004-06. Parly researcher to Michael Bates and Gary Streeter 1996-97. Board, Centre for Policy Studies, 2009-. Chippenham Constitutional Club. Married, one stepdaughter, one stepson. Ed: King Edward's Sch, Bath; Mansfield Coll, Oxford (BA history; JCR President); Judge Institute, Cambridge (MBA).

CHALLENGERS
Thomas Corbin (Lab) Train driver for South West Trains. Cllr, Salisbury CC 2013-. Treasurer, Salisbury & District TUC. Union rep, Aslef. Married. **Paul Martin** (Ukip) Financial adviser. Contested Isle of Wight 2010 for Middle England party. **Reetendra Nath Banerji** (LD) Management consultant specialising in change management. Former teacher. Contested Tower Hamlets mayoral election 2014.

CONSTITUENCY PROFILE
A large rural seat covering the southeastern part of Wiltshire. The main settlement is the cathedral city of Salisbury. The southern part of the seat includes the prehistoric monument Stonehenge. The Ministry of Defence is a key employer here. According to the 2011 census, the population is 96 per cent white. A reliable Conservative seat held in 2015 by John Glen, who increased his share of the vote to 55 per cent.

	Electorate	Turnout %	from 2010 %	Change
	69,590	72.9		
J Glen C	28,192	55.6	+6.4	
T Corbin Lab	7,771	15.3	+7.7	
P Martin Ukip	6,152	12.1	+9.3	
R N Banerji LD	5,099	10.1	-26.9	
A Craig Green	2,762	5.5	+4.4	
K A Pendragon Ind	729	1.4	+0.9	

Change from 2010

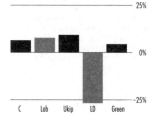

Scarborough & Whitby

CONSERVATIVE HOLD

ROBERT GOODWILL
BORN Dec 31, 1956
MP 2005-

Farmer. Staunch Eurosceptic. Parly under-sec, transport 2013-. Lord Commissioner, whip 2012-13. assist govt whip 2010-12. Shad min: transport 2007-10. Opp whip 2006-07. MEP for Yorkshire and the Humber, 1999-2004, spokesman for environment 2001-04. Contested: general elections Redcar 1992 and NW Leicestershire 1997; two Euro parly elections. NFU member, runs 250-acre family farm. Steam traction engine fan. Speaks French, German and some Russian. Married, one daughter, two sons. Ed: Bootham Sch, York; Newcastle (BSc agriculture).

CHALLENGERS
Ian McInnes (Lab) Youth worker. Provider-support lead, National Citizen Service, Cabinet Office 2013. Trustee, Council for Learning Outside the Classroom. Speaks

French. Ed: Whitby Community Coll. **Sam Cross** (Ukip) Property landlord. Cllr, N Yorkshire CC 2013-, Scarborough BC 2007-. Separated, four children. **David Malone** (Green) Documentary film maker, I-330 and financial blogger. Author of *The Debt Generation*. Married, three children. **Michael Beckett** (LD) Trust administrator, Mennonite Trust. Cllr, Malton TC 2006-. Chairman, Ryedale & District Mencap. Married. Ed: Goldsmiths, University of London (BA politics & economics); Leeds Met (Dip).

CONSTITUENCY PROFILE
Much of this seat is rural but most of the electorate live in the two coastal towns that give the seat its name. Many people work in hotels and catering: the area has the fourth highest proportion employed in such occupations in the UK, according to the 2011 census. Between 1918 and 1997, Scarborough was Tory, then Labour until 2005 when Robert Goodwill took the seat.

	Electorate	Turnout %	from 2010 %	Change
	73,511	64.9		
R Goodwill C	20,613	43.2	+0.4	
I McInnes Lab	14,413	30.2	+3.9	
S Cross Ukip	8,162	17.1	+14.1	
D Malone Green	2,185	4.6	+3.1	
M Beckett LD	2,159	4.5	-18.0	
J Boddington Green Soc	207	0.4	+0.2	

Change from 2010

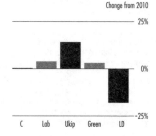

Scunthorpe

LABOUR HOLD

NIC DAKIN
BORN Jul 10, 1955
MP 2010-

Former council leader who had long career in teaching. Opp whip 2011-. Cllr, N Lincs C 1995-2007, leader 1997-2003. Select cttees: procedure 2011-; education 2010-11. Member to over 20 APPGs. Former principal of John Leggott Sixth Form Coll, Scunthorpe. English teacher. Member, NUT, Friends of the Earth, Child Poverty Action Group, Lincolnshire Wildlife Trust. Member, Yorkshire Forward 2003-07. Keen squash player and avid Scunthorpe Utd fan. Married, two daughters, one son. Ed: Longslade Upper Sch, Birstall, Leicestershire; Hull (BA history); King's Coll, London (PGCE).

CHALLENGERS
Jo Gideon (C) CEO, the Knowledge Hive. Cllr, Thanet DC 2003-. Co-founder, Futures for Heroes. Member, Conservative Women's Organisation. Dir of fundraising, the ELLA Foundation 2009-11. Ed: Birmingham (BA German). **Stephen Howd** (Ukip) Barrister specialising in business law at Howd Law. Contested Cleethorpes 2001 for Conservatives. Hispanophile. Ed: Christ Church Coll, Oxford (BSc physics); Jesus Coll, Cambridge (LLM law). **Des Comerford** (Independent) Fashion retailer. Former judo competitor, lifetime member, British Judo Assoc.

CONSTITUENCY PROFILE
Consists of Scunthorpe, a gritty industrial town and small villages to the south of the M180. Dominated by the steel industry. Tata Steel is by far the biggest local employer. According to the 2011 census, the seat has the highest rank in England and Wales for the proportion of people working in manufacturing. Held by Labour's Elliot Morley from 1987 to 2010, when the baton passed to Nic Dakin.

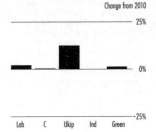

	Electorate	Turnout %	from 2010 %	Change
	64,010	57.7		
N Dakin Lab	15,393	41.7	+2.1	
J Gideon C	12,259	33.2	+0.5	
S Howd Ukip	6,329	17.1	+12.6	
D Comerford Ind	1,097	3.0		
M Dwyer Green	887	2.4	+1.3	
S Dodd LD	770	2.1	-16.2	
P Elsom Ind	206	0.6		

Change from 2010

25%

0%

-25%

Lab C Ukip Ind Green

Sedgefield

LABOUR HOLD

PHIL WILSON
BORN May 31, 1959
MP 2007-

Friend and former aide to Tony Blair, whom he helped to win the selection as Labour's candidate for Sedgefield in 1983. Local miner's son with a world-weary manner. Opp asst whip 2010-. PPS to: Andy Burnham 2009-10; Vernon Coaker 2008-09. Member, select cttees: public accounts 2007-10; regulatory reform 2007-10; NE region 2009-10. Board, progress 2012-. Usdaw, CSPA, TGWU, GMB. Former: PR consultant; civil servant, National Savings; adviser, Gala Coral. Has partner, two children, three stepchildren. Ed: Trimdon Secondary Modern; Sedgefield Comp Sch.

CHALLENGERS
Scott Wood (C) Businessman and project manager. Former Army tank commander. Ed: Newton Aycliffe ITEC (BTEC computer studies). **John Leathley** (Ukip) Regional sec, NE Ukip 2015-. Easington branch treasurer. Regional chairman, Young Independence NE 2014-. Ed: City of Sunderland Coll; Durham University (BA primary education). **Stephen Glenn** (LD) Youth worker. Former parly assistant to Alistair Carmichael. Organiser, Northern Ireland Yes to Fairer Votes. Contested Linlithgow and East Falkirk 2005, 2010. Member executive, LGBT+ Lib Dems. Ed: Kingston University (BA economics).

CONSTITUENCY PROFILE
A former mining seat in county Durham that returned Tony Blair from to 1983 to 2007. Sedgefield itself is a small town of 5,000, from where the Tories draw what little strength they have in the constituency. The rest of the seat is made up of former coalfields and mining villages, now diversifying into light engineering. A Safe Labour seat.

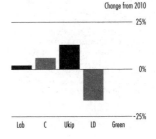

	Electorate	Turnout %	from 2010 %	Change
	62,860	61.6		
P Wilson Lab	18,275	47.2	+2.1	
S Wood C	11,432	29.5	+6.1	
J Leathley Ukip	6,426	16.6	+12.9	
S Glenn LD	1,370	3.5	-16.4	
G Robinson Green	1,213	3.1		

Change from 2010

25%

0%

-25%

Lab C Ukip LD Green

Sefton Central

LABOUR HOLD

BILL ESTERSON
BORN Oct 27, 1966
MP 2010-

Long-serving Medway councillor, 1995-2010, passionate about education and children's services. Cites Dennis Skinner as his political hero for his constituency dedication and party loyalty. Member, select cttees: CLG 2011-13; draft Lords reform 2011-12; education 2010-; environment, food and rural affairs 2010-11. PPS to Stephen Twigg 2011-13. Director, Leaps & Bounds training consultancy. Manages a hockey team. Enjoys cricket. Married, one daughter, one son. Ed: Rochester Mathematical Sch; University of Leeds (BSc maths & philosophy).

CHALLENGERS
Valerie Allen (C) Commercial director, General Welding Supplies. Local magistrate. Deputy lieutenant for Cheshire. Contested St Helens South & Whiston 2010.

Married, two children. Ed: Bishop Rawstorne Secondary Modern. **Tim Power** (Ukip) IT consultant for NHS. MD tech consultancy firm, Power IT Solutions. Former project manager, Pennine Acute Hospitals NHS Trust. Two sons. Ed: University of Essex (BA business administration and management). **Paula Keaveney** (LD) Lecturer in PR, Edge Hill University. Former journalist and PR exec. Cllr, Liverpool CC 2002-12, lost her seat as leader of opposition. Appeared on *Mastermind*.

CONSTITUENCY PROFILE
A suburban seat stretching along the Irish sea coast between Southport and Liverpool. It is a relatively affluent location with some of the most desirable areas of housing in Merseyside. Has the highest proportion of owner-occupation of any seat in the UK according to the 2011 census. Home to the Aintree racecourse and Grand National.

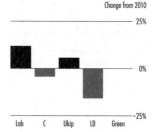

	Electorate	Turnout %	from 2010 %	Change %
	67,746	72.4		
B Esterson Lab	26,359	53.8	+11.9	
V Allen C	14,513	29.6	-4.3	
T Power Ukip	4,879	10.0	+5.7	
P Keaveney LD	2,086	4.3	-15.7	
L Melia Green	1,184	2.4		

Change from 2010

25%

0%

-25%

Lab / C / Ukip / LD / Green

Selby & Ainsty

CONSERVATIVE HOLD

NIGEL ADAMS
BORN Nov 30, 1966
MP 2010-

Successful businessman from humble background; son of a school cleaner and caretaker. His constituency party snubbed A-listers including Anne McIntosh MP, whose seat was abolished, to select him. PPS to: Lord Hill 2013-14; Lord Strathclyde 2010-13. Devised Selby Means Business cheque book. No 10 policy board with responsibility for economic affairs. Select cttee: environment, food and rural affairs 2010. Contested Rossendale & Darwen 2005. Dir, NGC Networks. Founded Advanced Digital Telecom, having left school at 17. Early career selling advertising for newspapers, Yellow Pages. Keen cricketer. Married, one son, three daughters. Ed: Selby High Sch.

CHALLENGERS
Dr Mark Hayes (Lab) GP. Chief

clinical officer for Vale of York NHS CCG. Former partner, Tadcaster medical centre. Wildlife photographer and beekeeper. Married, two daughters, one son. Ed: Cheadle Hulme Sch; University of Sheffield (MB ChB medicine). **Colin Heath** (Ukip) Energy surveyor. Royal Navy veteran. Adviser to party MEPs on wind turbines and energy policy. Former Cllr, Cawood PC. **Nicola Turner** (LD) MD, CCTV manufacturing company. Cllr, Kirklees BC 2006-, LD group leader.

CONSTITUENCY PROFILE
A largely rural North Yorkshire seat between York, Harrogate and Pontefract. Selby was traditionally a shipbuilding town on the tidal Ouse but with the decline of that industry its economy is now largely based on agriculture, tourism to Selby Abbey and as a commuter town for York and Leeds. Unemployment is below the national average. Gained by the Tories at the 2010 election.

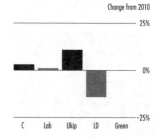

	Electorate	Turnout %	from 2010 %	Change %
	76,082	69.4		
N Adams C	27,725	52.5	+3.1	
M Hayes Lab	14,168	26.8	+1.1	
C Heath Ukip	7,389	14.0	+10.8	
N Turner LD	1,920	3.6	-14.1	
I Richards Green	1,465	2.8		
I Wilson TUSC	137	0.3		

Change from 2010

25%

0%

-25%

C / Lab / Ukip / LD / Green

Sevenoaks

CONSERVATIVE HOLD

MICHAEL FALLON
BORN May 14, 1952
MP 1997-; 1983-92

Thatcherite with good inquisitor instincts on financial matters. Secretary of state for defence 2014-. Min: DECC 2013-14; BIS 2012-14. Member, treasury select cttee 1999-2012. Parly under-sec: schools 1990-1992; govt whip 1988-1990; PPS to Cecil Parkinson 1987-88. MP, Darlington 1983-92. Research assistant. Former company director of Quality Care Homes (nursing homes) and Just Learning (nurseries). Member, advisory council, Social Market Foundation 1994-2000. President, Royal London Society for the Blind 2010-. Married, two sons. Ed: Epsom Coll, Surrey; Univeristy of St Andrews (MA Classics & ancient history).

CHALLENGERS
Steve Lindsay (Ukip) Dir, Effective FX. Cllr, Sevenoaks DC 2013-. Collects antiques. Married, five children. **Christopher Clark** (Lab) Communications business partner, for TfL. Founding exec member, Labour transport group. Exec, Labour humanists. Cllr, Ashford BC 2011-.Contested: SE England, Euro parly election 2014; Ashford, general election 2010. Ed: King's Coll, London (BA English), York (MA literatures of conflict). **Alan Bullion** (LD) Principal analyst and special reports publisher, Informa Agra. Contested SE England, Euro parly election 2014; Sevenoaks 2010, Hammersmith & Fulham 2005.

CONSTITUENCY PROFILE
A popular commuting zone for London, with rolling countryside and traditional villages. Unemployment is low. According to the 2011 census, almost three-quarters of homes are owner-occupied. Has been Conservative since its creation, apart from 1923-24, when it was Liberal. Held by Michael Fallon in 2015 with an increased majority of 19,561.

	Electorate	Turnout %	Change from 2010 %
	70,741	70.9	
M Fallon C	28,531	56.9	+0.1
S Lindsay Ukip	8,970	17.9	+14.3
C Clark Lab	6,448	12.9	-0.4
A Bullion LD	3,937	7.9	-13.5
A Boleyn Green	2,238	4.5	

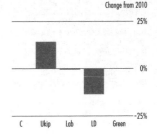

Change from 2010

C   Ukip   Lab   LD   Green

Sheffield Brightside & Hillsborough

LABOUR HOLD

HARRY HARPHAM
BORN Feb 21 1954
MP 2015-

Left replacement for moderate David Blunkett. NUM rep during 1984-85 miners' strike. Celebrated the death of Baroness Thatcher with a toast and tweet. Agent, David Blunkett 1993-2015. Cllr, Sheffield CC 2000-15, deputy leader 2012-2015. Chairman, South Yorkshire police and crime panel 2012. Member: city region housing board; Sheffield health and wellbeing board. Supports Manchester United. Ed: Eastbourne Comp; Nothern Coll; University of Sheffield (BA politics).

CHALLENGERS
John Booker (Ukip) Domestic appliance retailer and engineer, Ace Domestics. Cllr, Sheffield CC 2014-. Worked for MoD in naval ordnance, apprentice gauge maker 1980-85. Ed: Yewlands Comp Sch; Stannington Coll. **Elise Dünweber** (C) Dir, Nordic Securities, institutional brokerage services. Cllr, Elmbridge BC 2011-. Trustee, Queen Elizabeth's training coll for the disabled. **Jonathan Harston** (LD) IT Consultant. Cllr, Sheffield CC 1999-2010. Contested Sheffield B&H 2010. Ed: Stirling University (BSc computing science). **Christine Gilligan Kubo** (Green) Lecturer, Sheffield Business Sch. Non exec dir, Sheffield Renewables.

CONSTITUENCY PROFILE
Mainly a residential area to the north, made up of mostly inter-war and post-war housing estates. The seat includes Hillsborough stadium, associated with the 1989 disaster. The population is young and ethnically diverse. Nearly four in ten homes are social housing, and unemployment is generally high. Renowned for its steel and cutlery industry. Manufacturing also remains important. Strong Labour seat. David Blunkett held Sheffield Brightside from 1987-2010 when this new seat was formed.

	Electorate	Turnout %	Change from 2010 %
	73,090	54.8	
H Harpham Lab	22,663	56.6	+1.6
J Booker Ukip	8,856	22.1	+18.0
E Dünweber C	4,407	11.0	-0.5
J Harston LD	1,802	4.5	-15.5
C Gilligan Kubo Green	1,712	4.3	
M Bowler TUSC	442	1.1	-0.6
J Saxton Eng Dem	171	0.4	

Change from 2010

Lab   Ukip   C   LD   Green

Sheffield Central

LABOUR HOLD

PAUL BLOMFIELD
BORN Aug 25, 1953
MP 2010-

Advocate of electoral and constitutional reform. Voted 2015's most inspiring leader in higher education in the *Guardian* University Awards 2015, set up APPG on students. Sec, APPG, universities 2013-. PPS to Hilary Benn 2010-. Member, select cttee: BIS 2010-. General manager, Sheffield University students' union 2003-10. Former governor, Sheffield City Polytechnic. Chairman, Sheffield City Trust 1997-2008. Anti-apartheid campaigner. Member: Unison, Unite, GMB, Co-op party. Married to MEP Linda McAvan, one son. Ed: Abbeydale Boys GS; Tadcaster GS; St John's Coll, York (BA theology; pres Student Union).

CHALLENGERS
Dr Jillian Creasy (Green) GP. National spokeswoman, Green

party, on health and social care. Cllr, Sheffield CC 2004-15. Leader of the Green group, Sheffield CC 2006-15. Contested Sheffield Central 2010. **Stephanie Roe** (C) Solicitor. Ed: University of Leeds (BSc biochemistry); Coll of Law (BVC, GDL). **Joe Otten** (LD) Self-employed IT consultant. Cllr, Sheffield CC 2011-. Member, Electoral Reform Society. Married. Ed: University of Sheffield (BSc maths). **Dominic Cook** (Ukip) Chartered water and environmental manager. Network planning engineer, Yorkshire Water Services.

CONSTITUENCY PROFILE
Ranked first in England and Wales for the highest proportion of students in full time education according to the 2011 census. Includes Sheffield University and both campuses of Sheffield Hallam University. A third of the constituency is in the Peak District. It is one of the greenest in Britain, with a reported 2 million trees.

	Electorate	Turnout %	from 2010 %	Change
	77,014	57.4		
P Blomfield Lab	24,308	55.0	+13.7	
J Creasy Green	6,999	15.8	+12.1	
S Roe C	4,917	11.1	+1.0	
J Otten LD	4,278	9.7	-31.3	
D Cook Ukip	3,296	7.5	+5.9	
S Andrew Communist	119	0.3		
A Halsall Pirate	113	0.3		
E Breed Eng Dem	68	0.2		
T Brown Above	42	0.1		
M Driver WRP	33	0.1		

Change from 2010

Lab Green C LD Ukip

Sheffield Hallam

LIBERAL DEMOCRAT HOLD

NICK CLEGG
BORN Jan 7, 1967
MP 2005-

Resigned as leader (2007-15) of the Lib Dems after party's agonising defeat in the 2015 election. One of just eight Lib Dem MPs elected compared with 57 in 2010. Deputy prime minister 2010-15, held party together in relatively stable coalition. LD shadow SoS, home 2006-07, led Lib Dem's campaign against ID cards. LD spokesman, foreign 2005-06. MEP East Midlands 1999-2004. Member, Maghreb & Arab Maghreb Union delegation 2002-04. European Commission official, led negotiations with Russia, China. Lobbyist, GPlus. Former journalist, *Financial Times*. Lectured at Sheffield and Cambridge universities. Married, three sons. Ed: Westminster Sch; Robinson Coll, Cambridge (BA social anthropology), Minnesota Fellowship Award; Coll of Europe, Bruges (Dip European affairs).

CHALLENGERS
Oliver Coppard (Lab) Manager of South Yorkshire local enterprise scheme, Dearne Valley Eco Vision, developing low carbon economy in former coal-mining communities. Previously parly asst to Meg Munn MP. Volunteer on Barack Obama's 2012 campaign. Developed 2012 Olympic legacy project in Barnsley. Ed: High Storrs Sch; Leeds (BA politics). **Ian Walker** (C) Engineer, MD, Rotary Electrical UK. Former chairman, audit sub-committee, NHS North of England. Dir, South Yorkshire strategic health authority 2000-13. Ed: Leeds (BA politics).

CONSTITUENCY PROFILE
A largely rural seat covering the southwest corner of Sheffield. An affluent seat, ranked second in England and Wales for the proportion of people in professional occupations. Unemployment is low. Conservative until 1997, tactical Tory voters appeared to keep Clegg in office over Labour, his majority slashed from 15,284 to 2,353.

	Electorate	Turnout %	from 2010 %	Change
	73,658	75.3		
N Clegg LD	22,215	40.0	-13.4	
O Coppard Lab	19,862	35.8	+19.7	
I Walker C	7,544	13.6	-10.0	
J Jenkins Ukip	3,575	6.4	+4.1	
P Garbutt Green	1,772	3.2	+1.4	
C Reeve Ind	249	0.5		
S Clegg Eng Dem	167	0.3	-0.8	
J Stop the Fiasco Wild Ind	97	0.2		

Change from 2010

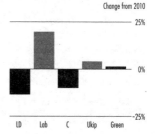

LD Lab C Ukip Green

Sheffield Heeley

LOUISE HAIGH
BORN July 22, 1987
MP 2015-

Replaced Meg Munn who stood down after 14 years as MP. Working for digital start-up company. The new MP's family has strong connections to Sheffield's industrial heart including an uncle who took part in miners' strike 1984-85. Political researcher for Lisa Nandy MP. Co-ordinator, APPG international corporate responsibility. Worked in corporate governance for Aviva. Call centre worker. Unite shop steward. Ed: Sheffield HS; University of Nottingham (BA politics).

CHALLENGERS
Howard Denby (Ukip) Electrical engineer. Trained as apprentice with Holset engineering. Widower. **Stephen Castens** (C) Marketing consultant. MD, the Innovation People. Managing partner, Ogilvy RED. Contested Euro election,

East Midlands 2014. Married, three children. Ed: Malvern Coll; University of York (BA economics). **Simon Clement-Jones** (LD) IT consultant. Cllr, Sheffield CC 2004-15. Member, South Neighbourhood Action Group. Contested Sheffield Heeley 2010. Assoc of Lib Dem Engineers & Scientists. Ed: Sheffield Hallam University (BEng mechanical engineering). **Rita Wilcock** (Green) Community health worker and disability rights campaigner.

CONSTITUENCY PROFILE
A seat in southwest Sheffield running from middle-class outskirts through large post-war council estates. It is bordered on its western side by the River Sheaf, from which Sheffield takes its name. According to the 2011 census nearly 30 per cent of adults have no qualifications and a similar proportion live in social housing. Held by Labour since 1974. In 2015 Louise Haigh increased the party's majority to 12,054.

	Electorate	Turnout %	from 2010 %	Change
	69,265	60.7		
L Haigh Lab	20,269	48.2	+5.6	
H Denby Ukip	7,315	17.4	+13.7	
S Castens C	6,792	16.2	-1.2	
S Clement-Jones LD	4,746	11.3	-17.1	
R Wilcock Green	2,566	6.1	+3.7	
A Munro TUSC	238	0.6		
D Haslett Eng Dem	122	0.3		

Change from 2010

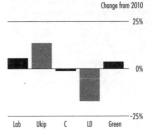

| Lab | Ukip | C | LD | Green |

Sheffield South East

CLIVE BETTS
BORN Jan 13, 1950
MP 1992-

Criticised Ofsted over Rotherham sexual abuse. Select cttees: CLG chairman 2010-, member 2006-; national policy statements 2010-; liaison 2010-; panel of chairs 2009-; finance & services 2005-; ODPM 2002-06; urban affairs 2002-05. Whip: govt 1998-2001; asst govt 1997-98; opp 1996-7. Member, Labour leader campaign team 1995-96, Labour housing group. Contested: Louth 1979; Sheffield, Hallam 1974. Cllr, Sheffield CC 1976-92; leader 1987-82. Economist: TUC, Derbyshire CC, S Yorks CC, Rotherham BC. Chairman S Yorks Pension Authority. President, South East CAB 1998-. Captain, parliament football club. Sheffield Weds fan. Enjoys scuba diving. Lives with partner. Ed: King Edward VII Sch, Sheffield; Pembroke Coll, Cambridge (BA economics & politics).

CHALLENGERS
Steven Winstone (Ukip) Scrap metal merchant and accountant, MD and owner of Advanced Metal Innovation. Previously worked for Walker Thompson Accountants. Married, two children. Ed: Bablake Sch, Coventry; City Coll Coventry (AAT accounting). **Matt Sleat** (C) Senior lecturer, politics, University of Sheffield. Author of realist political theory research texts. Co-editor, the *European Journal of Political Theory*. Ed: Leicester (BA politics); York (MA, PhD). **Gail Smith** (LD) Chiropodist. Cllr, Sheffield CC 2008-12. Contested Sheffield SE 2010, 05, 01.

CONSTITUENCY PROFILE
The post-industrial eastern part of the city. Key industries – wholesale, manufacturing and health and social care. According to the 2011 census unemployment is above the UK average and 31 per cent of adults have no qualifications. Renamed after the 2010 election. Held by Labour since 1935.

	Electorate	Turnout %	from 2010 %	Change
	70,422	59.2		
C Betts Lab	21,439	51.4	+2.7	
S Winstone Ukip	9,128	21.9	+17.3	
M Sleat C	7,242	17.4	0.0	
G Smith LD	2,226	5.3	-18.0	
L Duckenfield Green	1,117	2.7		
J Battersby CSA	207	0.5		
I Whitehouse TUSC	185	0.4		
M Roberts Eng Dem	141	0.3		

Change from 2010

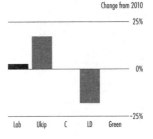

| Lab | Ukip | C | LD | Green |

Sherwood

CONSERVATIVE HOLD

MARK SPENCER
BORN Jan 20, 1970
MP 2010-

Farmer and businessman. On the liberal wing of the Conservative party, advocates localism and environmental issues. Criticised after saying jobseekers should learn "discipline of timekeeping". PPS to Baroness Stowell 2014-15. Member, select cttees: efra 2013-; environmental audit 2010-. APPG, sustainable resource (co-chairman); coalfield communities. Cllr: Gedling BC 2003-11; Notts CC 2005-13. Member, East Midlands regional assembly 2009-10. Runs Spring Lane farm shop. Chair, National Federation of Young Farmers' Clubs 2000, Royal Agricultural Society. Married, two children. Ed: Colonel Frank Seeley Sch, Calverton; Shuttleworth Agricultural Coll.

CHALLENGERS
Léonie Mathers (Lab) Senior

parly assistant, Yvette Cooper MP 2011-13. Campaigns and constituency manager, Ed Balls MP 2009-11. Trustee, Cahn Memorial Homes 2005-10. Ed: Holgate Sch; University of Leeds. **Sally Chadd** (Ukip) Director, non-profit heritage conservation organisation, St George's Trust. Former head of continuing education, University of London. Contested: 1984 EU election for Con; Rushcliffe 1997 for the Referendum party. Ed: Newark Lilley and Stone Girls' HS; Cambridge; University of London (MSc); Yale Law Sch (PgD research).

CONSTITUENCY PROFILE
North of Nottingham city centre, the Sherwood constituency includes Sherwood Forest, famed in the legend of Robin Hood. This is a traditional coal mining area, based on the Dukeries coalfield that opened in the 1920s. A Lab-Con marginal that has been held by both parties since it was created in 1983.

	Electorate	Turnout %	Change from 2010 %
	73,334	69.1	
M Spencer C	22,833	45.0	+5.8
L Mathers Lab	18,186	35.9	-2.9
S Chadd Ukip	7,399	14.6	+11.6
L Davies-Bright Green	1,108	2.2	
D Mosley LD	1,094	2.2	-12.7
D Perkins Class War	78	0.2	

Change from 2010

25%

0%

-25%

C   Lab   Ukip   Green   LD

Shipley

CONSERVATIVE HOLD

PHILIP DAVIES
BORN Jan 5, 1972
MP 2005-

A rebellious Tory MP, voting against the whip regularly. Opposes sex education in schools. Controversially suggested that vulnerable jobseekers, including disabled workers, should be able to work below the minimum wage. Had a shouting match with Jon Snow in the Channel 4 newsroom 2014. Member: Better off out; Campaign against political correctness. Member, select ctees: privacy & injunctions 2011-12; backbench business 2010-12; panel of chairs 2010-; modernisation of the house 2007-10; CMS 2006-. Contested Colne Valley 2001. Marketing manager, Asda. Race horse owner and breeder. Readers' Representative of the Year, *Spectator* awards 2011. Divorced, two sons. Ed: Old Swinford Hospital Sch; Huddersfield (BA historical & political studies).

CHALLENGERS
Steve Clapcote (Lab) Medical scientist and lecturer, University of Leeds, previously lecturer in Pharmacology, University of Sheffield. University & coll union rep and caseworker. Ed: Wales (BSc animal science); Edinburgh (MSc animal genetics); Liverpool (PhD genetics of disease resistance). **Waqas Ali Khan** (Ukip) Worked at JD Sports, Royal Mail. Voluntary youth worker. Ed: Bingley GS; Bradford Coll; Bradford (BSc accounting & finance, MSc finance).

CONSTITUENCY PROFILE
North and west of Bradford and takes in small towns and rural areas. Primarily a residential seat, it is home to large numbers of middle-class professionals. Was held by Sir Marcus Fox for the Conservatives for 27 years until 1997, when it went to Labour. Philip Davies won it for the tories in 2005 and held it in 2015. A safe Conservative seat.

	Electorate	Turnout %	Change from 2010 %
	70,466	71.7	
P Davies C	25,269	50.0	+1.4
S Clapcote Lab	15,645	31.0	+2.5
W A Khan Ukip	4,479	8.9	
K Warnes Green	2,657	5.3	+2.3
A Martin LD	1,949	3.9	-16.2
D Hill Yorks	543	1.1	

Change from 2010

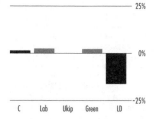

25%

0%

-25%

C   Lab   Ukip   Green   LD

Shrewsbury & Atcham

CONSERVATIVE HOLD

DANIEL KAWCZYNSKI
BORN Jan 24, 1972
MP 2005-

Distinctive as one of the tallest MPs. Criticised for not regularly attending meetings when he was a member of select cttees. PPS to: David Jones 2012-; James Paice and Richard Benyon 2010-2012. Special adviser to PM on central & eastern Europe 2014-. Select cttees: international devt 2008-10; justice 2007-09; environment, food and rural affairs 2005-07. Chairman, APPG: Saudi Arabia; Libya; Poland. Contested Ealing Southall 2001. Former international account manager, telecommunications. Chairman Sterling Uni Con Assoc. Divorced & living with partner, one daughter. Ed: St George's Coll; Stirling University (BA business studies with French & Spanish).

CHALLENGERS
Dr Laura Davies (Lab) Served for ten years in the Royal

Army Medical Corps. Tutor at Birmingham's Queen Elizabeth Hospital. Member, Royal Coll of Surgeons. Married, one son. Ed: Leicester (BSc biochemistry); Warwick (medicine). **Suzanne Evans** (Ukip) Deputy chairman, Ukip, nominated as Nigel Farage's interim replacement after his non-resignation. Ukip head of policy 2014-15. Creative dir, Suzanne Evans Comms. Cllr (Con), Merton LB 2010-14. Former broadcaster and journalist. Founder, Lipoedema UK. Ed: The Corbet Sch; Shrewsbury Sixth Form Coll; Lancaster (BA religious studies). **Christine Tinker** (LD) Tennis coach. Former army officer. Ed: Warwick (BA politics).

CONSTITUENCY PROFILE
Consists of the town of Shrewsbury itself and the small villages in the surrounding countryside. Despite having a lower than average unemployment rate, there are some very deprived areas such as Ditherington. Won by Labour in 1997 but returned to Tories in 2005.

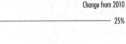

		Electorate	Turnout %	Change from 2010 %
		76,460	70.8	
D Kawczynski	C	24,628	45.5	+1.6
L Davies	Lab	15,063	27.8	+7.3
S Evans	Ukip	7,813	14.4	+11.4
C Tinker	LD	4,268	7.9	-21.1
E Bullard	Green	2,247	4.2	+3.1
S McNeillie	Atom	83	0.2	

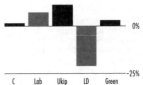

Change from 2010

Shropshire North

CONSERVATIVE HOLD

OWEN PATERSON
BORN Jan 24, 1956
MP 1997-

Close to Iain Duncan Smith. SoS: Defra 2012-14; NI 2010-12. Shadow SoS: NI 2007-10. Chairman, UK 2020 think tank. Shadow min: transport 2005-07; agriculture 2005-06; PPS to: Iain Duncan Smith 2001-03. Opposition whip 2000-01. Select cttees: agriculture 2000-01; European scrutiny 1999-2000; Welsh affairs 1997-01. Contested Wrexham 1992. Member: 92 and No Turning Back groups; Con Way Forward. Tanner, president COTANCE. British Leather Co Ltd. Interested in architecture. Member, Shropshire Cricket Club. Married, one daughter, two sons. Ed: Radley Coll; Corpus Christi Coll, Cambridge (MA history).

CHALLENGERS
Graeme Currie (Lab) Social care inspector for Court of Protection

and regulator for Health & Care Professions Council. Dir, Complete Social Work. Formerly social services manager for Shropshire NHS Primary Care Trust. Cllr, Oldham BC 1994-2003. Married, one daughter, one son. Ed: University of Leeds. **Andrea Allen** (Ukip) Retired modern langauges teacher. Cllr, Whitchurch Rural PC 2013-. Chairwoman, Whitchurch town twinning assoc. Rides dressage. **Tom Thornhill** (LD) Birmingham University student. Chairman, University of Birmingham Lib Dems.

CONSTITUENCY PROFILE
A mainly rural seat on the England-Wales border. Dotted with small towns, villages, castles and other ancient landmarks. The biggest town is Oswestry. About one in ten people here were born in Wales and 70 per cent are Christian. A solid rural Conservative seat. John Biffen, the former Conservative cabinet minister, was MP from 1961-1997.

		Electorate	Turnout %	Change from 2010 %
		78,910	66.6	
O Paterson	C	27,041	51.4	0.0
G Currie	Lab	10,547	20.1	+1.9
A Allen	Ukip	9,262	17.6	+12.9
T Thornhill	LD	3,148	6.0	-15.0
D Kerr	Green	2,575	4.9	+3.3

Change from 2010

Sittingbourne & Sheppey

CONSERVATIVE HOLD

GORDON HENDERSON
BORN Jan 27, 1948
MP 2010-

Staunch Eurosceptic. Member, regulatory reform select cttee 2010-. Contested: Sittingbourne & S 2005; Luton S 2001. Cllr: Swale BC 1986-95, dep leader of Tory group; Kent CC 1989-93. Former constituency agent to Roger Gale. Dir, Swale Community Action Project. Formerly: self-employed management consultant; operations manager, Beams UK; dir, Unwins Wine Group; manager, Woolworths. Married, two daughters, one son. Ed: Fort Luton HS, Chatham.

CHALLENGERS
Richard Palmer (Ukip) Runs a small training company. Served in the Army and ambulance service. Cllr, Newington PC. Contested Dartford 2010. Married, three children. **Guy Nicholson** (Lab) Group chairman, Greater London Enterprises. Cllr, Hackney BC 1998-. Local gov rep, London EU investment programmes management committee. Board, Barbican Centre. Regional Council member, Arts Council England. Former theatre designer. Ed: Central Sch of Art & Design (BA theatre design). **Keith Nevols** (LD) Works for Local Government Ombudsman. Contested Sittingbourne 2010. Married. Ed: Aberystwyth (BA history).

CONSTITUENCY PROFILE
A north Kent seat. Sheppey is divided from the mainland by the Swale. It is largely marshland and nature reserves for birdlife. Industry includes construction, manufacturing and the Isle of Sheppey's three prisons. About 60 companies are based at the Kent Science Park. Labour held this seat from 1997 to 2010, when it lost it to Gordon Henderson by 12,000 votes. In 2015 his majority was again about 12,000, but this time Ukip took the runners-up spot.

	Electorate	Turnout %	from 2010 %	Change
	76,018	65.0		
G Henderson C	24,425	49.5	-0.6	
R Palmer Ukip	12,257	24.8	+19.5	
G Nicholson Lab	9,673	19.6	-5.0	
K Nevols LD	1,563	3.2	-13.2	
G Miller Green	1,185	2.4		
M M Young Loony	275	0.6	-0.1	

Change from 2010

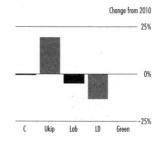

Skipton & Ripon

CONSERVATIVE HOLD

JULIAN SMITH
BORN Aug 30, 1971
MP 2010-

Asst whip 2015-. PPS to: Justine Greening 2012-15; Alan Duncan 2010-12. Member, select cttee: Scottish affairs 2010. Founder and former MD, Arq International, executive recruitment business. Former deputy chairman Bethnal Green & Bow Conservatives. Founded Hoxton Apprentice, training scheme. Co-authored Arculus Report on regulation with Kenneth Clarke. Married. Ed: Balfron HS; Millfield Sch (sixth form bursary); University of Birmingham (BA English & history).

CHALLENGERS
Malcolm Birks (Lab) Chartered architect. Former cricketer for MCC and Cambridge. Married. Ed: South Craven Sch, Cross Hills; Jesus Coll, Cambridge (BA architecture; Dip architecture; MPhil environmental design in architecture). **Alan Henderson** (Ukip) Works in business management. Chairman, Ukip Harrogate. Married, two children. **Jacqueline Bell** (LD) Social worker. Cllr, East Lothian C 2007-12. Contested: Stockton S 2010; Richmond 2005; Midlothian 2001; Yorshire 2014 Euro. Ed: University Coll of North Wales (BA social theory & institutions); Edinburgh University.

CONSTITUENCY PROFILE
A large seat taking in the western part of the Yorkshire Dales and two of the Yorkshire "three peaks", stretching across the Pennines to Ribblesdale. Most residents are in small agricultural market towns and the cathedral city of Ripon. The main industries are agriculture and tourism. Created in 1983 from parts of the former seats of Skipton and Ripon. One of the safest seats in England, formed in an area with a long history of Conservative representation.

	Electorate	Turnout %	from 2010 %	Change
	76,243	71.6		
J Smith C	30,248	55.4	+4.9	
M Birks Lab	9,487	17.4	+7.3	
A Henderson Ukip	7,651	14.0	+10.5	
J Bell LD	4,057	7.4	-25.0	
A Brown Green	3,116	5.7		

Change from 2010

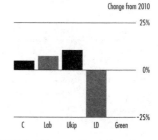

Sleaford & North Hykeham

CONSERVATIVE HOLD

STEPHEN PHILLIPS
BORN Mar 9, 1970
MP 2010-

Practising barrister who was much criticised for missing meetings and select cttees to attend trials. He claimed that the attacks were motivated by envy of his earnings, some £1 million in two years. Member, select cttees: public accounts 2014-; European scrutiny 2010-. Became one of the youngest QCs in 2009; Crown Court Recorder. Specialises in insurance law. Short Army career. Divorced, two daughters, one son. Ed: Canford, Dorset; Oriel Coll, Oxford (BA; BCL law).

CHALLENGERS
Jason Pandya-Wood (Lab) Head of sociology, School of Social Sciences, Nottingham Trent University. Former youth worker and community activist. FRSA. Married, one daughter. Ed: De Montford University (BA youth & community development; PhD social policy). **Steven Hopkins** (Ukip) Doctor - forensic medical examiner. Ed: Dundee (medicine); King's Coll London (MSc physiology). **Matthew Holden** (LD) Works in public sector. Previously worked in financial services. Cllr, Colwick PC 2013-. Partner, two sons. Ed: Lincoln (BA psychology).

CONSTITUENCY PROFILE
A large rural seat in the east of Lincolnshire, stretching from the edge of Grantham, the birthplace of Margaret Thatcher, to the outskirts of Lincoln. People are older than average and likely to be self-employed. Farming has declined but is still an important industry. Held by the Tories since 1997. Previously represented by Douglas Hogg, who stood down after infamously claiming on expenses the cost of having his moat cleaned. In 2015 Ukip nearly took second place from Labour, increasing its vote share from 4 per cent to 16 per cent.

	Electorate	Turnout %	Change from 2010 %
	88,188	70.2	
S Phillips C	34,805	56.2	+4.6
J Pandya-Wood Lab	10,690	17.3	+0.4
S Hopkins Ukip	9,716	15.7	+12.1
M Holden LD	3,500	5.7	-12.5
M Overton Lincs Ind	3,233	5.2	-1.2

Change from 2010

C   Lab   Ukip   LD   Lincs Ind

Slough

LABOUR HOLD

FIONA MACTAGGART
BORN Sep 12, 1953
MP 1997-

Opera-loving heiress from Labour's centre-left. Donated £14,268 to Comic Relief in 2013 after posting a Twitter message and pledging £1 for every retweet. Shad min: equalities 2010-11. Parly under-sec, home 2003-06. PPS to Chris Smith 1997-2001. Select cttees include: intelligence & security 2014-; public accounts 2011-14; children, school and families 2007-10. Secretary & founder, APPG: prostitution & global sex trade. Cllr, Wandsworth BC 1986-90. Former: dir, joint council for welfare of immigrants; vice-president, NUS; chairwoman, Liberty; teacher and lecturer. Ed: Cheltenham Ladies' Coll; King's Coll, London (BA English); Goldsmith's Coll, London (PGCE); Inst of Education (MA).

CHALLENGERS
Gurcharan Singh (C) Housing professional. Cllr, Ealing BC 1982-, deputy leader 2000-02, mayor 2003-04. Defected from Labour, 2007. Fabian. Adviser, Pakistan Sikh Gurdwara Prabandhak cttee. Former adviser, David Cameron. Married, three children. Ed: Meerut University (BSc physics, chemistry & maths); Vardhman Coll, Bijnor (MSc maths). **Diana Coad** (Ukip) Former: patisserie owner; timber broker. Cllr, Slough BC (Con, now Ukip) 2007-. Contested as Con: Slough 2010, 2001; Stourbridge 2005. **Tom McCann** (LD) Cllr, Wokingham BC 2012-. Contested Hampshire NW 2010; Slough 2005.

CONSTITUENCY PROFILE
A major business centre to the west of London that is home to many household names such as Mars, Nintendo and ICI. Ethnically diverse, with large Muslim and Sikh communities. Conservative until 1997, it is now one of Labour's most reliable seats in the southeast, and one of only four the party held in the region in 2015.

	Electorate	Turnout %	Change from 2010 %
	86,366	55.9	
F Mactaggart Lab	23,421	48.5	+2.7
G Singh C	16,085	33.3	-1.0
D Coad Ukip	6,274	13.0	+9.8
T McCann LD	1,275	2.6	-11.9
J Edmonds Green	1,220	2.5	+1.4

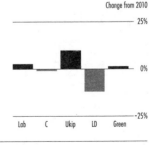

Change from 2010

Lab   C   Ukip   LD   Green

Solihull

CONSERVATIVE GAIN

JULIAN KNIGHT
BORN Jan 5, 1972
MP 2015-

Writer and journalist. He beat a field of 38 candidates to become the Conservative parliamentary candidate. Money & property editor, *The Independent on Sunday*. Former personal finance and consumer affairs reporter, BBC News. Author of books in the *"for Dummies"* series on British politics, euro-zone crisis, tax law, wills and how to play cricket. Married. Ed: Chester Catholic HS; Hull University (BA history).

CHALLENGERS
Lorely Burt (LD) MP 2005-15. First woman to chair Lib Dems' parliamentary party, 2007-12. Asst whip 2014-15. LD shad min: BIS 2006-10; NI 2005-06. Opp whip 2005-06. PPS to: Danny Alexander 2012-15. Select cttees: regulatory reform 2006-10; Treasury 2005-06. Contested Dudley South 2001. Cllr,

Dudley MBC 1998-2003. Former: dir, marketing consultancy company. Married, one daughter, one stepson. Ed: University Coll of Wales, Swansea (BSc economics); Open University (MBA). **Philip Henrick** (Ukip) Chairman, Ukip Solihull and Meriden. International sales manager, Tetronics capital goods manufacturer. Spent 16 years as a manager in the motor industry. Ed: Sheffield (BA Spanish & business studies).

CONSTITUENCY PROFILE
One of the most affluent and sought-after areas in the region, and popular with commuters. Mainly suburban. It has among the highest rates of owner-occupiership in the UK. Solihull was in the past a solid Tory seat, held from 1983 until 2005 when the Lib Dems made a surprise gain, which they held in 2010 by the slimmest of margins. In 2015 the Conservatives regained the seat with a majority of nearly 13,000.

	Electorate	Turnout %	Change from 2010 %
	77,251	70.9	
J Knight C	26,956	49.2	+6.7
L Burt LD	14,054	25.7	-17.2
P Henrick Ukip	6,361	11.6	+9.4
N Knowles Lab	5,693	10.4	+1.5
H Allen Green	1,632	3.0	
M Nattrass IE	50	0.1	
M Ward DP	33	0.1	

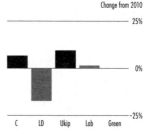

Change from 2010

C LD Ukip Lab Green

Somerset North

CONSERVATIVE HOLD

LIAM FOX
BORN Sep 22, 1961
MP 1992-

Neoconservative. Stepped down as sec of state for defence (2010-11) after revelations that he had taken a friend with him on several official trips. Shad SoS: defence 2005-10; foreign 2005; health 1999-2003. Ran Michael Howard's 2003 leadership campaign. Co-chairman, Con party 2003-05. Parly under-sec, FCO 1996-7. MP for Woodspring 1992-2010. Govt whip 1995-96; asst govt whip 1994-95. Chairman Con health, social services policy cttee 2001. Contested Roxburgh & Berwickshire 1987. Patron, Mencap. Founded charity, Give Us Times. Former GP. Married, one daughter, one son. Ed: St. Bride's HS; University of Glasgow (MB medicine; MRCGP).

CHALLENGERS
Greg Chambers (Lab) Junior

doctor. Previously worked in IT. Partner, one daughter. Ed: Leeds (BSc maths & philosophy); Plymouth (BMBS medicine); Exeter (MBBS medicine). **Ian Kealey** (Ukip) Runs his holiday lets business. Former maths teacher and nuclear physicist. Ed: Bristol (BSc engineering). **Marcus Kravis** (LD) Works in tourism business. Director of a renewable energy company. Former Cllr, Minehead TC. Married, three children. **David Derbyshire** (Green) Interim chief exec of a children's charity. Married, two children.

CONSTITUENCY PROFILE
This is primarily a commuter area to the south of Bristol, it includes the town of Portishead and the Victorian seaside resort of Clevedon as well as Bristol airport. Ranked tenth lowest in the UK for the proportion of claimants of job seekers' allowance in Dec 2014, unemployment is low. Firmly Conservative since it was created in 1983 under the name Woodspring.

	Electorate	Turnout %	Change from 2010 %
	80,115	73.6	
L Fox C	31,540	53.5	+4.2
G Chambers Lab	8,441	14.3	+3.2
I Kealey Ukip	7,669	13.0	+9.1
M Kravis LD	7,486	12.7	-23.0
D Derbyshire Green	3,806	6.5	

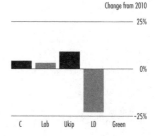

Change from 2010

C Lab Ukip LD Green

Somerset North East

CONSERVATIVE HOLD

JACOB REES-MOGG
BORN May 24, 1969
MP 2010-

Eurosceptic son of the late *Times* editor William Rees-Mogg. Select cttees: HoC governance 2014-; procedure 2010-; European scrutiny 2010-. Contested: The Wrekin 2001, Central Fife 1997, famed for campaigning with his nanny. Investment banker, pension fund manager. Founder, Somerset Capital Management. Former: dir, Lloyd George Management, including spell in Hong Kong; analyst, J Rothschild Investment Management. Married, three sons, one daughter. Ed: Eton Coll; Trinity Coll, Oxford (BA history; president OUCA).

CHALLENGERS
Todd Foreman (Lab) Lawyer specialising in banking regulation. Cllr, Kensington & Chelsea BC 2010-14. Board member, Kensington & Chelsea CAB.

Married. Ed: Grinnell Coll (BA political science & French), UPenn (JD); King's Coll, London (LLB banking & finance). **Ernie Blaber** (Ukip) Served as a Royal Marines Commando for 22 years. Held senior management positions. Married, two children. **Wera Hobhouse** (LD) Former modern languages teacher. Cllr, Rochdale BC 2006-14; leader, Lib Dem group 2011-14. Contested Heywood & Middleton 2010. Four children. Ed: University of Manchester (BA history). **Katy Boyce** (Green) Final year student in French and politics at the University of Bath.

CONSTITUENCY PROFILE
Borders Bristol to the west and circles Bath. It includes affluent Keynsham, and more rural Radstock and Midsomer Norton. Called Wansdyke until 2010, it was held by Labour from 1997 until 2010 when Rees-Mogg won the seat by just under 5,000 votes. He more than doubled his majority in 2015.

	Electorate	Turnout %	from 2010 % Change
	69,380	73.7	
J Rees-Mogg C	25,439	49.8	+8.5
T Foreman Lab	12,690	24.8	-6.8
E Blaber Ukip	6,150	12.0	+8.6
W Hobhouse LD	4,029	7.9	-14.5
K Boyce Green	2,802	5.5	+4.2

Change from 2010

| C | Lab | Ukip | LD | Green |

Somerton & Frome

CONSERVATIVE GAIN

DAVID WARBURTON
BORN Oct 28, 1965
MP 2015-

Entrepreneur, composer and pianist. Managing partner and founder, Oflang Partners, a property restoration company; co-founder and dir, MyHigh online retailer; founder and chairman, The Pulse youth orchestra; founder and former CEO, Pitch Entertainment Group, a mobile entertainment software firm. Former teacher, Royal Coll of Music junior dept. Studied with the celebrated composer Sir Peter Maxwell Davies. Dep chairman, Wells Conservative Assoc. Adviser, the Shakespeare Globe trust. FRSA. Married, one son, one daughter. Ed: Reading Sch; Waingels Coll; Royal Coll of Music (DipRCM; MMus); King's Coll London.

CHALLENGERS
David Rendel (LD) Selected as parliamentary to replace David

Heath who stepped down. MP for Newbury 1993-2005. Candidate for LD leadership, 1999. LD federal exec cttee, only member to vote against LD joining coalition with Conservatives. Cllr: West Berkshire C 2011-15; Newbury C 1987-1995. Married, three sons. Ed: Eton Coll; Magdalen Coll, St Cross Coll, Oxford (BA physics & philosophy; won boat race 1974). **Alan Dimmick** (Ukip) Retired engineer. Cllr, Somerset CC 2013-, Ukip group leader 2013-.

CONSTITUENCY PROFILE
A large constituency, covering almost 900 square miles bordering Wiltshire, Bath, northeast Somerset and Dorset. Largely rural and agricultural especially around Blackmoor Vale. Home ownership is high, unemployment low. Some 26 per cent of the population are in "skilled trades". Having been a Lib Dem-Conservative battleground for years, David Warburton took 53 per cent of the vote in 2015 to the Lib Dems' 19 per cent.

	Electorate	Turnout %	from 2010 % Change
	83,527	72.2	
D Warburton C	31,960	53.0	+8.5
D Rendel LD	11,692	19.4	-28.1
A Dimmick Ukip	6,439	10.7	+7.5
T Simon Green	5,434	9.0	
D Oakensen Lab	4,419	7.3	+2.9
I Angell Ind	365	0.6	

Change from 2010

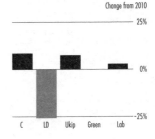

| C | LD | Ukip | Green | Lab |

South Holland & The Deepings

CONSERVATIVE HOLD

JOHN HAYES
BORN Jun 23, 1958
MP 1997-

A leading figure of the "faith, flag and family" Tory right. Min of state: security 2015-; transport 2014-15; without portfolio, Cabinet Office; DECC 2012-13; futher education 2010-12. Shadow min: BIS 2009-10; higher ed 2009; vocational ed 2005-09; transport 2005; local govt 2003-05; agriculture 2002-03. Opposition whip 2001-02. Contested NW Derbyshire 1992, 1987. Member, 1922 cttee. Cllr, Notts CC 1985-88. IT company director, The Data Base. PC. Married, two sons. Ed: Colfe's GS; University of Nottingham (BA politics; PGCE history & English; chair, UCA).

CHALLENGERS
David Parsons (Ukip) Dir, Cor Nobile consultancy. Cllr, Blaby DC 2011-. Resigned as Leicestershire CC leader in 2012 after expenses scandal and promptly thrown out of Conservatives. Defected in 2014. Appointed CBE in 2009 for services to local and regional govt. Former science teacher. Worked on campaigns of Roger Helmer MEP and Mark Reckless MP. Former chair, East Midlands Regional Assembly. Married, three children. Ed: St John's Coll, Oxford (BSc chemistry, president SU). **Matthew Mahabadi** (Lab) Marketing consultant. Engaged. Ed: University of Manchester (BA philosophy & politics). **Dan Wilshire** (Green) 19-year-old student at election, University of Birmingham (BSc economics).

CONSTITUENCY PROFILE
One of the UK's most rural seats, the area is characterised by old market towns and villages in the Fens, with agriculture, food processing and bulb growing the major industries. Has one of the highest number of eastern Europe residents in England and Wales. Tory since it was created in 1997.

	Electorate	Turnout %	Change from 2010 %
	77,015	63.9	
J Hayes C	29,303	59.6	+0.5
D Parsons Ukip	10,736	21.8	+15.4
M Mahabadi Lab	6,122	12.4	-1.6
D Wilshire Green	1,580	3.2	+1.8
G Smid LD	1,466	3.0	-12.5

Change from 2010

25%

0%

-25%

C   Ukip   Lab   Green   LD

South Ribble

CONSERVATIVE HOLD

SEEMA KENNEDY
BORN Oct 6, 1974
MP 2015-

Property lawyer. Controversially selected for a constituency 200 miles away from her home in St Albans, 40 days after she became local cllr there. Moved to Iran as baby, but forced to flee due to Islamic revolution. Resigned as constituency chairman for St Albans in 2009 after unsuccesful deselection campaign against Anne Main. Cllr, St Albans DC 2014-15. Contested Ashton-under-Lyne 2010. Board director, Tustin Developments. Formerly: solicitor, Slaughter and May; Bevan Brittan. Speaks French and Farsi. Married, three sons. Ed: Westholme Sch, Blackburn; Pembroke Coll, Cambridge (BA Oriental studies); Coll of Law.

CHALLENGERS
Veronica Bennett (Lab) Senior political caseworker, Bill Esterson.
Cllr, Sefton BC 2012-. Ed: Sacred Heart Coll; Kings Coll, Cambridge (BA theology). **David Gallagher** (Ukip) Senior editor and translator, Unbabel translation service. Vice chairman, Ukip West Lancashire. Cllr, Aughton PC 2011-, former Conservative. Author on European literature. Ed: Nottingham (LLB law); Cambridge (MA German & Spanish); Oxford (MSt European literature); Royal Holloway, London (PhD); Chartered Institute of Insurance.

CONSTITUENCY PROFILE
A rural constituency, home to truck manufacturer Leyland who employ 1,000 people. Contains many smaller villages between Preston and Southport. Has been growing economically with a new Waitrose distribution centre and business parks. According to the 2011 census 76 per cent of the seat's population are Christians, one of the highest percentages in England and Wales. Unemployment is low. A Labour-Conservative marginal.

	Electorate	Turnout %	Change from 2010 %
	76,489	68.5	
S Kennedy C	24,313	46.4	+1.0
V Bennett Lab	18,368	35.1	+0.4
D Gallagher Ukip	7,377	14.1	+10.4
S McGuire LD	2,312	4.4	-9.7

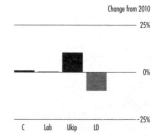

Change from 2010

25%

0%

-25%

C   Lab   Ukip   LD

South Shields

LABOUR HOLD

EMMA LEWELL-BUCK
BORN Nov 8, 1978
MP 2013-

Social worker, specialised in child protection. Selected after David Miliband's move to New York. Select cttees: draft protection of charities bill 2014-; Defra 2013-. PPS to Ivan Lewis 2013-. Member, APPG for hunger & food poverty. Cllr, South Tyneside BC 2004-13. Co-op party. From a family of shipyard workers, descendant of William Wouldhave, the inventor of the lifeboat. Married. Ed: Northumbria University (BA politics & media studies); Durham University (MA social work).

CHALLENGERS
Norman Dennis (Ukip) Pastor. Cllr, South Tyneside C 2014-. Formerly: bandsman, Royal Green Jackets; music teacher; prison counsellor; apprentice, Tyne Dock Engineering Company. Was in the army. Two children.

Ed: Westoe Boys' Sch; Mortimer Road Sch. **Robert Oliver** (C) Head of government & politics, Dame Allan's Sch. Cllr, Sunderland CC 2004-14, leader Conservative group 2011-14. Former member, Adult Partnership Board; Standing Advisory Council on Religious Education. Contested Houghton & Sunderland South 2010. **Shirley Ford** (Green) Chair, South Tyneside Green party. Administrator in primary school Contested South Shields 2010. Married, one daughter. Ed: Trinity Coll, Cambridge (BA social anthropology).

CONSTITUENCY PROFILE
The only seat since 1832 to have never elected a Conservative MP. Labour-held since 1935. Suffers from high unemployment following decline of its shipbuilding and coal mining industries, although the Port of Tyne is a large employer and catalyst for regeneration. A largely white seat however it has a significant Yemeni population.

	Electorate	*Turnout %*	*from 2010 %* *Change*
	62,730	57.8	
E Lewell-Buck Lab	18,589	51.3	-0.8
N Dennis Ukip	7,975	22.0	
R Oliver C	6,021	16.6	-5.0
S Ford Green	1,614	4.5	+2.4
L Nightingale Ind	1,427	3.9	+1.9
G Gordon LD	639	1.8	-12.5

Change from 2010

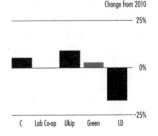

Southampton Itchen

CONSERVATIVE GAIN

ROYSTON SMITH
BORN May 13, 1964
MP 2015-

Relationship management and political communications consultant. Cllr: Southampton CC 2000-, opposition leader; council leader 2010-12. Chairman, Hampshire Fire & Rescue Authority. Awarded George Medal for bravery after he tackled murderer Seaman Ryan Donovan on board HMS *Astute* in 2011. Former maintenance engineer, BA at Heathrow. Served in RAF for 10 years as a ground engineer with Nimrod maritime reconnaissance fleet. Contested Southampton Itchen 2010, losing by 192 votes. Enjoys cooking and hill walking. Ed: Bitterne Park Sch.

CHALLENGERS
Rowenna Davis (Lab Co-op) Journalist and author. Appeared as political pundit, Sunday Politics and others. Freelance journalist for *Guardian, Independent, New*

Statesman. Wrote *Tangled up in Blue* about Blue Labour movement. Involved with charity Headliners, training journalists from deprived areas. Cllr, Southwark BC 2011-14. Unite; NUJ; Make Justice Work. Ed: Balliol Coll, Oxford (BA PPE; won Oxford Leadership Prize); City University (MA journalism). **Kim Rose** (Ukip) Jeweller, Scarletts. Quoted Mein Kampf at hustings, then repeated phrase in appearance on *The Daily Show with Jon Stewart*. Accused of bribing voters by giving out sausage rolls at campaign event. Contested: Itchen 2005, 2001 Ukip; 1997 Socialist Labour.

CONSTITUENCY PROFILE
A large container and cruise port on the south coast including most of the city centre and docks. There are a lot of full-time students. A Con-Lab marginal: remained in Labour from 1992 to 2015 with Labour gaining strong majorities in the 1997, 2001 and 2005 elections, but that stronghold reduced significantly in 2010 and fell in 2015.

	Electorate	*Turnout %*	*from 2010 %* *Change*
	72,309	61.8	
R Smith C	18,656	41.7	+5.4
R Davis Lab Co-op	16,340	36.6	-0.2
K Rose Ukip	6,010	13.4	+9.1
J Spottiswoode Green	1,876	4.2	+2.8
E Bell LD	1,595	3.6	-17.3
S Atkins TUSC	233	0.5	+0.1

Change from 2010

Southampton Test

LABOUR HOLD

ALAN WHITEHEAD
BORN Sep 15, 1950
MP 1997-

Expert on local government. Parly under-sec: transport 2001-02. PPS to: Baroness Blackstone 1999-2001; David Blunkett 1999-2000. Select cttees: standards & privileges 2005-13; environmental audit 2010-; DECC 2009-; constitutional affairs 2003-07. Lab Party Nat Policy Forum. Cllr, Southampton CC 1980-92, leader 1984-92. Chairman, PRASEG. Contested: Southampton Test 1992, 1987, 1983; New Forest 1979. Prof of Public Policy, Southampton Institute. Dir: Outset, BIIT, Southampton Environment Centre. Divorced & remarried, one daughter, one son, both from remarriage. Ed: Southampton (BA politics & philosophy; PhD political science).

CHALLENGERS
Jeremy Moulton (C) Pensions manager, Friends Life financial services. Cllr, Southampton CC 2002-; deputy leader, Conservative group. School governor. Contested Southampton Test 2010. Ed: Exeter (BA politics); Southampton (MSc international banking & finance). **Pearline Hingston** (Ukip) Lecturer and teacher. Jamaican born, came to the UK by ship aged 11. Former Labour member. Contested Test 2010. Ed: Leeds (MEd). **Angela Mawle** (Green) Former nurse and health visitor. Was CEO, UK Public Health Association. Ed: Southampton (BSc environmental science); Imperial Coll London (MSc environmental sciences).

CONSTITUENCY PROFILE
Named for Southampton's largest river. Major employers include Southampton University and the NHS. According to the 2011 census, it has a large private rental sector and a large number of 16-24 year olds. 20 per cent of residents were born abroad. Historically a Con-Lab marginal but Whitehead has held the seat since 1997.

	Electorate	Turnout %	from 2010 %	Change
	70,285	62.1		
A Whitehead Lab	18,017	41.3	+2.8	
J Moulton C	14,207	32.6	-0.5	
P Hingston Ukip	5,566	12.8	+8.8	
A Mawle Green	2,568	5.9	+3.9	
A Ford LD	2,121	4.9	-17.5	
C Davis Ind	770	1.8	+1.5	
N Chaffey TUSC	403	0.9		

Change from 2010

Lab C Ukip Green LD

Southend West

CONSERVATIVE HOLD

SIR DAVID AMESS
BORN Mar 26, 1952
MP 1983-

Active in conservative social policy areas. 1922 exec cttee, 2010-. PPS to: Michael Portillo 1988-97; Lord Skelmersdale 1988; Edwina Currie 1987-88. Select cttees: backbench business 2012-; panel of chairs 2001-; health 1998-2007. Cllr, Redbridge BC 1982-86. MP for Basildon 1983-97. Contested Newnham NW 1979. Junior school teacher, underwriter. Pro-life. Asked a question in Parliament of "cake", the "made-up drug" after *Brass Eye* sting in 1997. Received 2012 "Outstanding Achievement Award" at the Charity Champion parliamentary reception. Knighted in 2015. Married, four daughters, one son. Ed: St Bonaventure's GS; Bournemouth Coll of Technology (BSc economics).

CHALLENGERS
Julian Ware-Lane (Lab) IT consultant specialising in software testing, Cognitran. Previously at Vodafone, UBS, Lloyds. Former civil servant. Cllr, Southend BC 2012-. Married, six children. Ed: Fairfax HS for Boys. **Brian Otridge** (Ukip) Works in the IT industry, including on defence contracts. Editor, *Ukip Daily*. Former aircraft engineer, RAF. Divorced, three children. **Paul Collins** (LD) Works for Lloyds Insurance in the City. Cllr, Southend BC 2010-14. School governor. Married, three children.

CONSTITUENCY PROFILE
A compact seat, covering some of the more affluent residential and seafront areas to the west. Home to the longest pleasure pier in the world. Tourism is still an important industry but Southend is also home to London commuters. According to the 2011 census, it has one of the smallest social housing sectors in England and Wales. Unemployment is relatively low. Conservative held since the seat was created in 1950.

	Electorate	Turnout %	from 2010 %	Change
	66,876	66.6		
D Amess C	22,175	49.8	+3.8	
J Ware-Lane Lab	8,154	18.3	+4.9	
B Otridge Ukip	7,803	17.5	+13.6	
P Collins LD	4,129	9.3	-20.1	
J Fuller Green	2,083	4.7	+3.2	
J Moss Eng Dem	165	0.4	-0.9	

Change from 2010

C Lab Ukip LD Green

Southport

LIBERAL DEMOCRAT HOLD

JOHN PUGH
BORN Jun 28, 1948
MP 2001-

Lost 8,000 votes but held on to seat. Producing report on social and economic issues facing the north. Co-chairman, LD parly cttee for health & social care 2010-13.Shad min: health 2009-10, 2006-07; Treasury 2008-10; transport 2005-06. LD spokes: education 2002-05. Select cttee: public accounts 2014-; CLG 2013-15; CLG 2013-; 2006-10. Cllr, Sefton MBC 1987-2001. Co-founder, Beveridge Group. Former member, Merseyside Police Authority. North West Arts Board, Merseyside Partnership. Teacher, philosophy head, Merchant Taylors Boys Sch. Married, three daughters, one son. Ed: Maidstone GS; University of Durham (BA philosophy); University of Liverpool (MA logic, MEd); University of Nottingham (MPhil theology); University of Manchester (PhD logic).

CHALLENGERS
Damien Moore (C) Manager, Asda. Cllr, Preston CC 2012-. Office, Lancashire Area exec. Former chair, Preston Conservative Assoc. Ed: UCLan (BA history). **Liz Savage** (Lab) Teacher. Cllr, West Lancashire BC 2011-. Gave speech on education at 2014 Labour conference. Ed: Bradford (BA international relations). **Terry Durrance** (Ukip) Retired ambulance control superintendent. Chair, Ukip Southport. Married. **Laurence Rankin** (Green) Planning & corporate services manager, Environment Agency. Co-ordinator, Sefton Green party.

CONSTITUENCY PROFILE
The northern part of Sefton borough council, following the coast up west of South Ribble. Known for its beaches, the main focus for this seaside town is tourism. More than one in five of the population are pensioners. A Conservative-Liberal marginal, in Lib Dem hands since 1997.

	Electorate	Turnout %	from 2010 %	Change
	67,328	65.5		
J Pugh LD	13,652	31.0	-18.7	
D Moore C	12,330	28.0	-7.9	
L Savage Lab	8,468	19.2	+9.8	
T Durrance Ukip	7,429	16.9	+11.7	
L Rankin Green	1,230	2.8		
J Barlow Southport	992	2.3		

Change from 2010

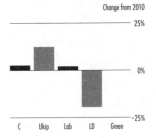

LD   C   Lab   Ukip   Green

Spelthorne

CONSERVATIVE HOLD

KWASI KWARTENG
BORN May 26, 1975
MP 2010-

Articulate with calm demeanour. Select cttees: work & pensions 2013-; transport 2010-13. Former chair, Bow Group. Contested: Brent East 2005; London Assembly List 2008. Financial analyst: WestLB, JP Morgan Cazenove and Odey Asset Management. Journalist and author. Born in UK to Ghanaian parents. Ed: Eton Coll (King's scholar; Newcastle scholar); Trinity Coll, Cambridge (BA Classics & history; PhD economic history; member of winning University Challenge team 1995); Harvard (Kennedy Scholar).

CHALLENGERS
Redvers Cunningham (Ukip) Barrister and businessman. Worked in insurance in the City of London for 20 years. Chair, Ukip Runnymede, Weybridge & Spelthorne. Married, two

children. **Rebecca Geach** (Lab) Asst media planner, Sky. Married, one daughter. Ed: Guildford HS; Farnborough Hill; Liverpool (BA social & economic history); NoSweat Journalism (print journalism); Open University (BSC mathematics). **Rosie Shimell** (LD) Account manager, MHP Communications. Associate, FCA. Cllr, Southwark BC 2010-. Was senior account exec, Portcullis Public Affairs. Member, Dulwich Area Housing Forum; Assoc of LD Cllrs. Ed: Homerton Coll, Cambridge (BA SPS).

CONSTITUENCY PROFILE
A suburban seat on the northern edge of Surrey, although it has some open green belt areas and reservoirs. It is just south of Heathrow airport which is a major factor in the local economy. In 2011, 15 per cent of its workforce is in "transport and storage" jobs. Homes are mostly privately owned and unemployment low. Safe Conservative seat.

	Electorate	Turnout %	from 2010 %	Change
	71,592	68.6		
K Kwarteng C	24,386	49.7	+2.6	
R Cunningham Ukip	10,234	20.9	+12.4	
R Geach Lab	9,114	18.6	+2.1	
R Shimell LD	3,163	6.4	-19.4	
P Jacobs Green	1,724	3.5		
J Griffith ND	230	0.5		
P Couchman TUSC	228	0.5	+0.1	

Change from 2010

C   Ukip   Lab   LD   Green

St Albans

CONSERVATIVE HOLD

ANNE MAIN
BORN May 17, 1957
MP 2005-

Dogged Commons performer. Bruised by expenses controversy, ordered to repay £7,100 on second home claims in 2010. Chairwoman, APPG: Bangladesh 2013-. Member, select committees: panel of chairs 2010-15; ECC 2009-10; CLG 2006-10. Cllr, South Bucks DC 2001-05; Beaconsfield PC 1999-2002. English and drama teacher. Carer for terminally ill husband, who died in 1991, then single parent, since remarried. Two daughters, one son from first marriage, one son from second. Ed: Bishop of Llandaff Sch; University Coll of Wales, Swansea (BA English); University of Sheffield (PGCE).

CHALLENGERS
Kerry Pollard (Lab) PR consultant. MP, St Albans 1997-2005. Former housing association director. Cllr: St Albans DC 1982-97; Hertforshire CC 1989-97. Sch governor. Married, five sons, two daughters. Ed: Open University (BA industrial relations). **Sandy Walkington** (LD) Party policy adviser. Ran Lib Dems' 2005 election comms. Previously director of public affairs for TfL and BT. Contested St Albans 1987, 83. Ed: Trinity Hall, Cambridge (BA economics & law). **Chris Wright** (Ukip) Business adviser. Previously owned IT software business. Retired lieutenant-colonel in Royal Signals. Coaches cricket to children.

CONSTITUENCY PROFILE
An affluent commuter town north of London — a fifth of the population commute there every day — and a string of villages along M25. Tory since 1906, except 1945-50, it was represented by a string of Conservative MPs, including the Thatcher-era cabinet minister Peter Lilley, until 1997, but following boundary changes was re-captured by Labour. It fell again to the Tories in 2005.

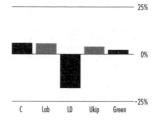

	Electorate	Turnout %	from 2010 %
	72,507	75.1	
A Main C	25,392	46.7	+5.9
K Pollard Lab	12,660	23.3	+5.7
S Walkington LD	10,076	18.5	-17.9
C Wright Ukip	4,271	7.9	+4.0
J Easton Green	2,034	3.7	+2.3

Change from 2010

St Austell & Newquay

CONSERVATIVE GAIN

STEPHEN DOUBLE
BORN Dec 19, 1966
MP 2015-

Director: Phoenix Corporate events company; Bay Direct Media marketing org. Charity worker and church leader. Cllr: St Austell TC 2009-, Cornwall Council 2009-13. Mayor, St Austell 2013-14. Married, three sons. Ed: Poltair Sch; Cornwall Coll (BTEC business studies).

CHALLENGERS
Stephen Gilbert (LD) MP 2010-15. PPS to Ed Davey 2012-. LD spokesman, defence 2011-12. Asst whip 2010-12. Member, select cttees: European scrutiny 2013-15; CLG 2010-13. Former chairman, APPG: housing. Cllr: Haringey BC 2002-05; Restormel BC 1998-2002. Business consultant in Cornwall. Public affairs manager, Fidelity International fund management house. Adviser to Investment Management Association. Researcher to Lembit Öpik MP and Robin Teverson MEP. Ed: Fowey Community Sch; St Austell Coll; Aberystwyth (BSc international politics); LSE (MScEcon international relations). **David Mathews** (Ukip) Teacher. Married, two children. **Deborah Hopkins** (Lab) Suspended, later reinstated, as party's PPC after calling coalition "murdering bastards" and DWP "evil" on Twitter. **Steve Slade** (Green) Cllr, Newquay TC 2013-. Founder: Ecological Garden Design. Ed: Central London Poly (BSc ecology).

CONSTITUENCY PROFILE
St Austell, inland near the southern coast of Cornwall, is grouped with the tourist resort and surfing centre of Newquay on the north coast. The seat includes a Georgian harbour at Charlestown, which frequently appears on film and television. More than 20 per cent of residents are pensioners. The previous seat returned Liberal MPs since 1974, but became a LD-Conservative marginal in 2010.

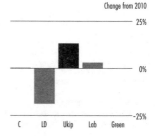

	Electorate	Turnout %	from 2010 %
	76,607	65.7	
S Double C	20,250	40.2	+0.3
S Gilbert LD	12,077	24.0	-18.8
D Mathews Ukip	8,503	16.9	+13.2
D Hopkins Lab	5,150	10.2	+3.1
S Slade Green	2,318	4.6	
D Cole Meb Ker	2,063	4.1	-0.2

Change from 2010

St Helens North

LABOUR HOLD

CONOR MCGINN
BORN Jul 31, 1984
MP 2015-

Northern Ireland-born special adviser to shadow defence secrtary Vernon Coaker. Socialist Societies rep on Labour NEC. Chairman, Labour Party Irish Society 2010-12. Vice-chairman: Fabians 2011-12; Young Labour 2007, resigned citing disagreeing with Human Fertilisation and Embryology Bill. Member, Windle Labour Club. Winner, Churchill Fellowship, 2002. Worked for London-based Irish mental health charity Immigrant Counselling and Psychotherapy. Son of former Sinn Fein cllr. Roman Catholic. Married, one son. Ed: St Pauls HS, Bessbrook; London Metropolitan University (BA history & politics).

CHALLENGERS
Paul Richardson (C) Works in financial services. Former RAF officer of 16 years. Previously chairman: London Chamber of Commerce; London Regional Forum of the Chartered Management Institute. Married, one son, one daughter. Ed: Edge Hill University. **Ian Smith** (Ukip) Semi-retired company chairman. Engineer. Son of coal miner. Ed: St Helens Technical Coll. Married, children. **Denise Aspinall** (LD) Programme lead and lecturer in mental health nursing, Bangor University; mental health nurse. Previously at Liverpool John Moores University. Contested Ellesmere Port & Neston 2010.

CONSTITUENCY PROFILE
St Helens is a white, working-class industrial town. Its coal mines are gone, the last ones having closed in the early 1990s, but glass industry remains in the form of Pilkington glass factory. The seat includes the villages of Rainford and Billinge, Haydock and Newton-le-Willows. It has long been staunchly Labour, often reliably producing Labour majorities in excess of 20 per cent.

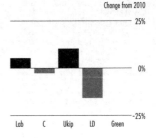

	Electorate	Turnout %	from 2010 %	Change
		75,262	61.5	
C McGinn Lab		26,378	57.0	+5.3
P Richardson C		9,087	19.7	-2.7
I Smith Ukip		6,983	15.1	+10.4
D Aspinall LD		2,046	4.4	-15.8
E Ward Green		1,762	3.8	

Change from 2010

Lab C Ukip LD Green

St Helens South & Whiston

LABOUR HOLD

MARIE RIMMER
BORN Apr 27, 1947
MP 2015-

Overlooked in 2001 when Labour parachuted Shaun Woodward in as candidate after previous MP retired with little notice. Cllr, St Helens MBC 1978, leader 2010-13. Awarded CBE in 2005 for services to local government. Arrested and charged for assault while campaiging against Scottish independence at a Glasgow polling station. She denies the allegation and trial was delayed until August 2015. Formerly Pilkingtons glass factory worker, rising up the ranks from work in accounts, to procurement. Trustee of food bank and support services organisation St Helens Hope Centre. Member: Unite. Divorced. Ed: Lowe House Girls Sch.

CHALLENGERS
Gillian Keegan (C) Venture capital investor. Former vice-president of travel services group Travelport. Apprentice at Delco Electonics. Married, two stepsons. Ed: Liverpool John Moores University (BA business); London Business Sch (MSc leadership & stratergy). **John Beirne** (Ukip) Owner of Avanti hairdressers. Former Lib Dem Cllr, St Helens MBC 1990-2012. Mayor, 2008-09. **Brian Spencer** (LD) Former electrician. Cllr, St Helens MBC 1980-82, 1983-96, 1990-2012, leader 2006-10. Fined for assaulting Labour candidate after losing seat. Contested St Helens S & W 2010.

CONSTITUENCY PROFILE
Comprising southern St Helens and the former mining town of Whiston, this is a very safe Labour seat, with the party normally managing to muster in excess of 50 per cent of the vote and majorities of more than 20 points. The outgoing MP, Shaun Woodward, previously served as the Conservative MP for Witney, David Cameron's seat, until defecting to Labour in 1999.

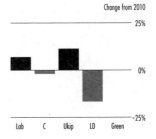

	Electorate	Turnout %	from 2010 %	Change
		77,720	62.3	
M Rimmer Lab		28,950	59.8	+7.0
G Keegan C		7,707	15.9	-1.9
J Beirne Ukip		6,766	14.0	+11.3
B Spencer LD		2,737	5.7	-16.6
J Chan Green		2,237	4.6	

Change from 2010

Lab C Ukip LD Green

St Ives

CONSERVATIVE GAIN

DEREK THOMAS
BORN Jul 20, 1972
MP 2015-

Construction company owner and stonemason. Sole trader of DG Thomas Building Service. Cllr: St Buryan PC 2012-; Penwith DC 2005-08. Community worker, church volunteer. Sch governor. Board member of YMCA Penzance. Trained as Cornish mason apprentice. Contested St Ives 2010, came second by 1,700 votes. Married, two sons.

CHALLENGERS
Andrew George (LD) MP 1997-2015. LD shad SoS, int devt 2005-06. LD shad min: rural affairs 2002-05; disabilities 2000-01; fisheries 1997-2001. PPS to Charles Kennedy 2001-02. Member, select cttees: health 2010-15; CLG 2007-10; agriculture 1997-2000. Contested St Ives 1992. Married, one daughter, one son. Ed: Helston GS; Helston Sch; University of Sussex (BA cultural and community studies); University Coll, Oxford (MSc agricultural economics). **Graham Calderwood** (Ukip) Lawyer, duty solicitor, solicitor advocate, specialist in criminal and children's law. Semi-retired. Two children. Ed: Bishop Wordsworth's Sch, Salisbury. **Cornelius Olivier** (Lab) Former CAB worker. Won unfair dismissal case against Job Centre after being sacked for standing in local election. Cllr, Penzance TC. Partner, one daughter.

CONSTITUENCY PROFILE
The southwestern tip of England, including Lands End and the Lizard. Local economy used to be based on tin mining and fishing, but with the decline of both industries it is now more reliant on tourism. The seat also contains the Isles of Scilly, which are home to about 2,000 people. Held by Liberal Democrats 1997-2015 after a 34-year Conservative stint. Nearly half of constituents are aged 45 or over.

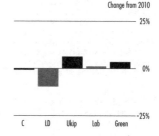

	Electorate	Turnout %	Change from 2010 %
	65,570	73.7	
D Thomas C	18,491	38.3	-0.7
A George LD	16,022	33.2	-9.6
G Calderwood Ukip	5,720	11.8	+6.3
C Olivier Lab	4,510	9.3	+1.2
T Andrewes Green	3,051	6.3	+3.5
R Simmons Meb Ker	518	1.1	+0.2

Change from 2010

Stafford

CONSERVATIVE HOLD

JEREMY LEFROY
BORN May 30, 1959
MP 2010-

Coffee and cocoa trader with extensive business and charitable experience in Tanzania. Self-described One Nation Conservative. Contested: Newcastle-under-Lyme 2005; European parliament (West Mids) 2004. Cllr, Newcastle-under-Lyme BC 2003-07. Member, select cttee: international devt 2010-15. MD, African Speciality Products. Worked in Tanzania for 11 years with Schluter Group. Co-founder, Equity for Africa charity. Chartered accountant, Arthur Andersen. Grad trainee, Ford Motor Co. Member: Amnesty, Countryside Alliance. Keen musician and sportsman. Christian. Married, two children. Ed: Highgate Sch; King's Coll, Cambridge (BA Classics).

CHALLENGERS
Kate Godfrey (Lab) Author. Consultant on infrastructure financial management, led field research in Iraq, Yemen and Libya. Previously UN development worker. Ed: Christ Church, Oxford (BA history; LLM private international law). **Edward Whitfield** (Ukip) Accountant. Former general commissioner for income tax, previously ceramic materials seller for family firm, Whitfields' Minerals. Ed: Yalet Hall Sch.

CONSTITUENCY PROFILE
North of West Midlands conurbation. Consists of the town of Stafford and its rural hinterland. Formerly a shoemaking town, now it is a centre for heavy engineering and the construction of turbines and engines. The seat is bisected by the M6, which runs northwards through its middle. For most of the past century it has been a Tory seat (exceptions being the 1945 Labour landslide and 1997-2010). The losing Conservative candidate in 1997 was David Cameron.

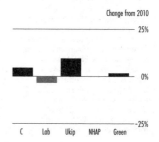

	Electorate	Turnout %	Change from 2010 %
	68,705	71.0	
J Lefroy C	23,606	48.4	+4.5
K Godfrey Lab	14,429	29.6	-3.4
E Whitfield Ukip	6,293	12.9	+9.5
K Howell NHAP	1,701	3.5	
M Shone Green	1,390	2.9	+1.7
K Miller LD	1,348	2.8	-13.6

Change from 2010

Staffordshire Moorlands

CONSERVATIVE HOLD

KAREN BRADLEY
BORN Mar 12, 1970
MP 2010-

Chartered accountant who entered politics when seconded to Michael Howard's shadow Treasury team by KPMG. Sure-footed. Parly under-sec: home office 2014-. Lord commissioner, whip 2013-14; asst whip 2012-13. Member, select cttees: administration 2012-14; work & pensions 2010-12. Contested, Manchester Withington 2005. Accounting career with KPMG, Tory Policy Unit, Policy Exchange and Deloitte. Associate member, Institute of Chartered Accountants (ACA) and Chartered Institute of Taxation (CTA). Detective fiction enthusiast. Married, two sons. CofE. Ed: Buxton Girls Sch; Imperial Coll, London (BSc mathematics).

CHALLENGERS
Trudie McGuinness (Lab)
Strategic director of marketing, PR, recruitment at South Staffordshire Coll. Ed: Biddulph HS; Jesus Coll, Oxford University (BA PPE). **George Langley-Poole** (Ukip) Farmer. **John Redfern** (LD) Retail supervisor, Stoke-on-Trent College. Cllr, Staffordshire Moorlands DC 1998-. Contested Stoke-on-Trent Central 2010, 05. Ed: Sandbach GS; University of Warwick (MA industrial relations). **Brian Smith** (Green) Former railway district manager. RMT unionist.

CONSTITUENCY PROFILE
The electorate of this seat is mostly in the commuter towns and villages to the west of the seat. The Peak District location and Alton Towers amusement park at the southern end of the constituency make tourism and leisure important factors in the local economy. The seat was created from Leek in 1983 and won by the Conservatives. It was held by Labour between 1997 and 2010, but this coincided with a period of more favourable boundaries for the party.

	Electorate	Turnout %	Change from 2010 %
	63,104	67.5	
K Bradley C	21,770	51.1	+5.9
T McGuinness Lab	11,596	27.2	-2.7
G Langley-Poole Ukip	6,236	14.6	+6.5
J Redfern LD	1,759	4.1	-12.6
B Smith Green	1,226	2.9	

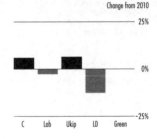

Change from 2010

Staffordshire South

CONSERVATIVE HOLD

GAVIN WILLIAMSON
BORN June 25, 1976.
MP 2010-

PPS to: David Cameron 2013-; Patrick McLoughlin 2012-13; Owen Paterson 2012; Hugo Swire 2011-12. Interested in manufacturing, involved in Staffordshire pottery industry: helped to turn around one company; brought another out of administration. Member, select cttee: NI affairs 2010-11. Chairman, APPG: motor neurone disease. Contested Blackpool North & Fleetwood 2005. Cllr, North Yorks 2001-05. Managing director, architectural design practice. Former chairman, Stoke on Trent Conservative Association. Previously trustee of local CAB. Well travelled. Married, two daughters. Ed: Raincliffe Sch; Scarborough Sixth Form Coll; Uni of Bradford (BA social sciences).

CHALLENGERS
Kevin McElduff (Lab) Owner and director of TMS Insight Group. Former local politican with Sandwell MBC. Contested Staffordshire South 2010. Ed: University of Sheffield (BA political theory & institutions). **Lyndon Jones** (Ukip) Tory defector. Former chairman, Staffordshire S Conservative Association. Contested EU election West Midlands 2014. Married. **Robert Woodthorpe Browne** (LD) Multilingual reinsurance industry professional. Leads party's delegations to the European Liberal Democrat party. Married, one son. Ed: Birkbeck Coll, London (BA Spanish).

CONSTITUENCY PROFILE
This is a long thin seat, curling around the west of the Metropolitan West Midlands and covering the rural hinterland of Wolverhampton and Dudley. It has no substantial towns, and is made up of commuter villages. Previously South West Staffordshire, this is a safe Conservative seat.

	Electorate	Turnout %	Change from 2010 %
	84,243	58.9	
G Williamson C	29,478	59.4	+6.2
K McElduff Lab	9,107	18.4	-2.0
L Jones Ukip	8,267	16.7	+11.2
R Woodthorpe Browne LD	1,448	2.9	-13.8
C McIlvenna Green	1,298	2.6	

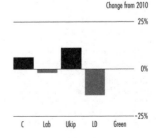

Change from 2010

Stalybridge & Hyde

LABOUR CO-OPERATIVE HOLD

JONATHAN REYNOLDS
BORN Aug 28, 1980
MP 2010-

Selected amid huge row over Peter Mandelson's involvement after failing to make initial shortlist for the seat. Shad min: energy and climate change 2013-. PPS to Labour party leader Ed Miliband (2011-13). Opp asst whip 2010-11. Member, select cttees: finance & services 2010-12; science & technology 2010-12. Cllr, Tameside MBC 2007-11. Deputy chairman, Longdendale & Hattersley District Assembly. Trainee solicitor, Addleshaw Goddard. Labour party NEC 2003-05. Member: Co-operative party; Unite. Enjoys gardening. Married, one daughter, one son, one son from previous partner. Ed: Houghton Kepier Comp; Sunderland City Coll; Manchester (BA politics & modern history); BPP Law School, Manchester (GDL; LPC).

CHALLENGERS
Martin Riley (C) Former chief marketing officer, Pernod Ricard. Previously president of the World Federation of Advertisers. Married, four children. Ed: Queen's Coll, Oxford (BA modern languages). **Angela McManus** (Ukip) Nurse at Tameside Hospital. Contested Ashton-under-Lyne 2010.

CONSTITUENCY PROFILE
A collection of traditional working-class mill towns on the eastern edge of Greater Manchester, stretching up into the Pennines. Since the Second World War several large council estates have been built, including the Hattersley estate (now part-demolished and redeveloped), changing the seat from a Labour-Conservative marginal to safe Labour. Until 2010 it was held by the Labour frontbencher James Purnell, who resigned from the cabinet inprotest at Gordon Brown's continuing leadership.

	Electorate	Turnout %	Change from 2010 %
	69,081	59.4	
J Reynolds Lab Co-op	18,447	45.0	+5.4
M Riley C	11,761	28.7	-4.2
A McManus Ukip	7,720	18.8	+15.5
J Ross Green	1,850	4.5	+2.9
P Flynn LD	1,256	3.1	-14.0

Change from 2010

Lab Co-op, C, Ukip, Green, LD

Stevenage

CONSERVATIVE HOLD

STEPHEN MCPARTLAND
BORN Aug 9, 1976
MP 2010-

Former Tory party local agent (NE Herts), called on the party to create a dedicated urban campaigning unit. PPS to: Lord Livingston 2014-. Member, select cttee: science & technology 2011-12. Chairman, APPG: respiratory health; literacy; child and youth crime. Membership director, British American Business. Campaign manager for local council, parliamentary and European election campaigns. Trustee, The Living Room charity. Avid reader. Stevenage FC fan. Married. Ed: Liverpool Coll; University of Liverpool (BA history); Liverpool John Moores (MSc technology management).

CHALLENGERS
Sharon Taylor (Lab Co-op) Senior civilian management postholder at Hertfordshire Constabulary. Cllr, Stevenage BC 1997- (leader

2006-); Hertfordshire CC 2006-. Worked for British Aerospace. Ed: Stevenage Girls' GS; University of Hertfordshire (BA English). **David Collins** (Ukip) Born into farming background. Started own business aged 22. **Susan van de Ven** (LD) Cllr, Cambridgeshire CC 2009-; South Cambridgeshire DC 2013-10. Former teacher and copy editor. Born in Lebanon. Ed: Oberlin College, Ohio (BA) Harvard University (MA Middle Eastern studies; EdD).

CONSTITUENCY PROFILE
The first of the postwar new towns, Stevenage boomed in the 1950s and 1960s. The seat as it exists today was formed from parts of Hertford and Stevenage, Hitchin, and East Hertfordshire after boundary changes in 1983. It has since mirrored the national mood, being held by the Conservatives during Margaret Thatcher's premiership, falling to Labour in 1997, before returning once more to the Tories in 2010.

	Electorate	Turnout %	Change from 2010 %
	70,597	67.7	
S McPartland C	21,291	44.5	+3.1
S Taylor Lab Co-op	16,336	34.2	+0.8
D Collins Ukip	6,864	14.4	+9.9
S van de Ven LD	1,582	3.3	-13.3
G White Green	1,369	2.9	
T Palmer TUSC	175	0.4	
C Vickers Eng Dem	115	0.2	-0.6
D Cox Ind	67	0.1	-0.0

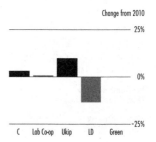

Change from 2010

C, Lab Co-op, Ukip, LD, Green

Stirling

SNP GAIN

STEVEN PATERSON
BORN Apr 25, 1975
MP 2015-

Parly asst to Bruce Crawford MSP. Worked for national tourist board Visit Scotland. Author and guide. Cllr, Stirling C. Ed: Cambusbarron PS; Stirling HS; Robert Gordon University (publishing); University of Stirling (BA history and politics).

CHALLENGERS
Johanna Boyd (Lab) Considered a rising star in the Labour party. Especially passionate about improving services for families and children. Scotland's youngest woman council leader. Cllr, Stirling BC 2012-, leader 2013-. Barrister specialising in local government and planning law, housing and human rights at Cornerstone Barristers. Featured in Legal 500. French speaker. Married, two sons, one daughter. Ed: Dollar Academy; King's Coll, London (LLB European studies). **Stephen Kerr** (C)

Regional sales leader for American personal care corporation Kimberley-Clark. Married, four children. Ed: Forfar Academy; University of Stirling (BA business). **Mark Ruskell** (Green) First ever Green party representative to be elected to Stirling Council. MSP for Mid-Scotland & Fife 2003-07.

CONSTITUENCY PROFILE
Consists of the small city of Stirling, the neighbouring towns and villages, the fertile agricultural land around it and a wide expanse of desolate mountains stretching to the northwest. An affluent area and a popular commuter area, it also contains the University of Stirling and the towns of Bannockburn and Dunblane. This was once a Conservative seat, held narrowly in 1987 and 1992 by Michael Forsyth, later to become Scottish secretary. He was one of the Conservative cabinet ministers who lost their seats on election night 1997 to Labour and the Conservatives are even further behind now than they were then.

	Electorate	Turnout %	Change from 2010 %
	67,236	77.5	
S Paterson SNP	23,783	45.6	+28.3
J Boyd Lab	13,303	25.5	-16.3
S Kerr C	12,051	23.1	-0.8
M Ruskell Green	1,606	3.1	+1.5
E Wilson LD	1,392	2.7	-11.9

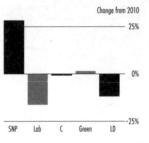

Change from 2010

Stockport

LABOUR HOLD

ANN COFFEY
BORN Aug 31, 1946
MP 1992-

Low-key establishment figure with a penchant for dangling earrings. Member, select cttees: draft HoL reform bill 2011-12; issue of privilege (police searches on parliamentary estate) 2009-10; modernisation of the HoC 2000-10. Joint PPS to: Alistair Darling 1998-2009; Tony Blair as PM 1997-98. Opp health spokesperson 1996-97. Opp whip 1995-96. Cllr, Stockport MBC 1984-92. USDAW. Divorced, one daughter. Remarried. Ed: Bodmin & Bushey GS; South Bank Poly (BSc sociology); Walsall College of Education (PgCert education); Manchester (MSc psychiatric social work).

CHALLENGERS
Daniel Hamilton (C) Partner at Bell Pottinger, leads engagement with Tory policy commissions. Former director, Big Brother

Watch. Cllr, Runnymede BC 2007-11. Former adviser to Nirj Deva MEP. Freeman of the City of London. Author. Ed: Royal Holloway, London (BA politics & international relations). **Steven Woolfe** (Ukip) MEP for North West England 2014-. Ukip spokesman, migration and financial affairs. Ed: Aberstwyth University. **Daniel Hawthorne** (LD) Works for New Chartered Housing Trust. Cllr, Stockport MBC 2010-. Ed: University of Liverpool.

CONSTITUENCY PROFILE
Situated to the southeast of Manchester, Stockport sits astride the M60. The sandstone market town was traditionally industrial, with a specialist millinery heritage, but is now a busy urban centre. It has fairly average socioeconomic class distribution but the highest percentage of economically active residents in Greater Manchester, further bolstered by recent regeneration work. It switched from Tory to Labour in 1992.

	Electorate	Turnout %	Change from 2010 %
	63,931	62.0	
A Coffey Lab	19,771	49.9	+7.2
D Hamilton C	9,710	24.5	-0.8
S Woolfe Ukip	5,206	13.1	+10.9
D Hawthorne LD	3,034	7.7	-17.3
G Lawson Green	1,753	4.4	+2.7
J Pearson LU	175	0.4	

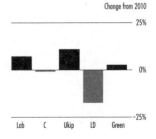

Change from 2010

Stockton North

LABOUR HOLD

ALEX CUNNINGHAM
BORN May 1, 1955
MP 2010-

Humble community figure. Has led campaign supporting a ban on smoking in cars. Select cttees: education 2011-15; armed forces Bill 2011; work and pensions 2010-11. Cllr: Stockton-on-Tees BC 1999-2010; Cleveland CC 1984-97. Runs own PR/web design consultancy having worked in PR for the gas industry (head of comms, Transco). Trained journalist, previously worked in newspapers and radio. Christian. Member, Socialist Education Association. Cites Michael Foot and Tony Benn among political heroes. Married, two sons. Ed: Branksome Comp; Queen Elizabeth Sixth Form Coll; Coll of Technology, Darlington.

CHALLENGERS
Chris Daniels (C) Director of a corporate finance business, works for Standard Chartered. Ed: Trinity Hall, Cambridge (BA, chairman of CUCA); College of Law, York (legal practice). **Mandy Boylett** (Ukip) Managing dir, marketing and advertising firm, Shopping Trolley Ltd. Ed: University of Bath (statistics, mathematics). **Anthony Sycamore** (LD) Classical and jazz pianist. Former music lecturer at Durham University. Previously investment banker. Ed: Oxford (BA music); Royal Northern College of Music.

CONSTITUENCY PROFILE
Includes northern Stockton, Billingham and western parts of Stockton-on-Tees. Created from split of Stockton in 1983, when the sitting MP was Bill Rodgers, one of the four SDP founders. Rodgers contested Stokton North at its first election, but finished third. Since then it has been a safe Labour seat. In 2010 the sitting MP Frank Cook was de-selected, stood as an independent and came fifth, the least successful of four sitting MPs who stood as independents.

	Electorate	Turnout %	from 2010 %	Change
	66,126	59.8		
A Cunningham Lab	19,436	49.1	+6.3	
C Daniels C	11,069	28.0	+2.0	
M Boylett Ukip	7,581	19.2	+15.2	
A Sycamore LD	884	2.2	-13.8	
J Tait NE Party	601	1.5		

Change from 2010

Lab   C   Ukip   LD   NE Party

Stockton South

CONSERVATIVE HOLD

JAMES WHARTON
BORN Feb 16, 1984
MP 2010-

Fresh-faced centrist, local Stockton-on-Tees man. Second youngest MP in the Commons during 2010-15 parliament. Self-proclaimed Eurosceptic. Parly under-sec DCLG 2015-. Member, select cttee: public accounts 2010-12. One of 53 Tory MPs to rebel against whip to vote to call for real-terms cut in EU budget in coalition's first defeat on EU spending in 2012. Chairman of Stockton Conservative Assocation 2002-07. Company law solicitor at northeast legal firm BHP Law, Darlington. Member, Conservative Friends of Israel; officers training corps at university. Christian. Ed: Yarm Sch; University of Durham (LLB law); Coll of Law, York (LPC).

CHALLENGERS
Louise Baldock (Lab Co-op) Marketing consultant. Set up pressure-group Labour Against the Bedroom Tax. Given £10,000 by former Lib Dem Lord Oakeshott to fight seat. Former civil servant. Cllr, Liverpool CC 2006-14. Blogger. Fiancé died of carbon monoxide posining in 1999. Ed: Conyers Sch, Yarm; Teesside Poly (BA humanities). **Ted Strike** (Ukip) Runs own business. former firefighter. **Drew Durning** (LD) Runs online organic products business. Ed: University of Reading (BA economics and psychology); University of Brunel (MA international marketing).

CONSTITUENCY PROFILE
Straddling the traditional boundary between Yorkshire and Co Durham, Stockton South is a relatively affluent and middle-class seat compared with most seats in the northeast. Contains the southern part of Stockton itself and the towns of Thornaby, Yarm, Ingleby Barwick and Eaglescliffe. Regarded as a marginal seat between Labour and the Conservatives.

	Electorate	Turnout %	from 2010 %	Change
	75,109	69.0		
J Wharton C	24,221	46.8	+7.8	
L Baldock Lab Co-op	19,175	37.0	-1.3	
T Strike Ukip	5,480	10.6	+7.7	
D Durning LD	1,366	2.6	-12.5	
J Lovell Green	952	1.8		
S Walmsley IASI	603	1.2		

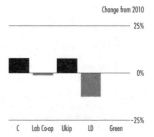

Change from 2010

C   Lab Co-op   Ukip   LD   Green

Stoke-on-Trent Central

LABOUR HOLD

TRISTRAM HUNT
BORN May 31, 1974
MP 2010-

Urbane, smooth Blairite TV historian and friend of Peter Mandelson, controversially seen to have helped him into the seat, prompting locals to stand against him. Son of Labour peer. Named "hottest MP" by *Attitude* magazine 2015. Shadow SoS: education 2013-. Shadow min: education 2013. Member, select cttees: parliamentary privilege 2012-15; works of art 2011-13; draft House of Lords reform bill (joint) 2011-12; political and constitutional reform 2010-13. BBC/Channel 4 documentaries. Lecturer in British history at Queen Mary, Uni of London. Associate fellow, Centre for History & Economics, King's Coll Cambridge. Research Fellow, IPPE. Ed: University Coll Sch; Trinity Coll, Cambridge (history); Chicago (postgrad fellowship); King's Coll, Cambridge (PhD history).

CHALLENGERS
Mick Harold (Ukip) Self-employed businessman, property development manager. Chairman, Stoke-on-Trent Ukip. Married. Ed: Thistley Hough HS. **Liam Marshall-Ascough** (C) Cabin crew, Virgin Atlantic. Cllr, Crawley BC 2012-. Ed: Southampton Uni (BA archeology and history). **Mark Breeze** (Ind) Son of the late city cllr Paul Breeze. **Zulfiqar Ali** (LD) Consultant physician, Stepping Hill Hospital. Contested Stoke-on-Trent South 2010.

CONSTITUENCY PROFILE
Stoke-on-Trent Central covers the middle two towns, Stoke and Hanley, of the six that form the city centre and main retail centre for Stoke. Tristram Hunt's selection as Labour candidate here was controversial, as the seat's PPC shortlist did not feature any local candidates and was imposed by the national party. The local party banch secretary, Gary Elsby, resigned in protest.

		Electorate	Turnout %	Change from 2010 %
		62,250	49.9	
T Hunt	Lab	12,220	39.3	+0.5
M Harold	Ukip	7,041	22.7	+18.3
L Ascough	C	7,008	22.6	+1.5
M Breeze	Ind	2,120	6.8	
Z Ali	LD	1,296	4.2	-17.5
J Zablocki	Green	1,123	3.6	
A Majid	CSA	244	0.8	
P Toussaint	Ubuntu	32	0.1	

Change from 2010

Stoke-on-Trent North

LABOUR HOLD

RUTH SMEETH
BORN Jun 29, 1979
MP 2015-

Edinburgh-born lifelong trade unionist and Labour campaigner who claims she has leafleted for the party since the age of 8. Name came to attention of press when mentioned as a source on US communiqués about a potential 2009 snap election in UK with a recommendation to "strictly protect" her identity. Deputy director of anti-extremist activist group Hope not Hate. Mother is a former trade union official. Father was a blacklisted trade union rep. Former director of national campaigns for the British-Israel Communication Centre. Previously headed government relations team for London-based multinational catering company Sodexo. Ex-PR worker for Nestlé. Contested Burton 2010. Married. Ed: University of Birmingham (politics & international relations).

CHALLENGERS
Ben Adams (C) IT consultant, runs own company, Request Systems. Cllr, Staffordshire CC 2009-. Married, two children. Ed: Open University (BSc). **Geoff Locke** (Ukip) Contested Stoke-on-Trent North 2010. **Paul Roberts** (LD) Retired accountant. Worked for Kimberley-Clark for 20 years. Taught management at Open University. Former Cllr, Chester CC 1996-2009. Contested Crewe and Nantwich 2005. Married, two children.

CONSTITUENCY PROFILE
Stoke-on-Trent is an amalgamation of six towns, heavily associated with the industrial pottery industry. This is also a former coal-mining area, but the last coal mine in Stoke closed in the 1990s. This seat covers the northernmost two of the six towns, Burslem and Tunstall, as well as Kidsgrove. The wider city is solidly Labour, this seat having been held by the party since its creation in 1950.

		Electorate	Turnout %	Change from 2010 %
		72,689	53.2	
R Smeeth	Lab	15,429	39.9	-4.4
B Adams	C	10,593	27.4	+3.6
G Locke	Ukip	9,542	24.7	+18.5
P Roberts	LD	1,137	2.9	-14.8
S Adam	Green	1,091	2.8	
J Millward	Ind	508	1.3	
C Pond	Ind	354	0.9	

Change from 2010

Stoke-on-Trent South

LABOUR HOLD

ROB FLELLO
BORN Jan 14, 1966
MP 2005-

Shadow min: justice 2010-13, resigned to focus on other parly interests. Member, select cttees: finance & services 2010-; science & technology 2005-07. Chairman: APPG freight transport. PPS to: Hazel Blears 2007-09; Lord Falconer of Thoroton 2006-07. Member, Parliamentary Friends of Colombia. Cllr, Birmingham CC 2002-04. Former party regional organiser, previously CEO of Malachi Community Trust. Worked for Inland Revenue and PwC as personal tax adviser. Unite, Unity, USDAW. Ancient history enthusiast. Divorced, one daughter, one stepson. Ed: Kings Norton Boys' Sch; University of Wales, Bangor (BSc chemistry).

CHALLENGERS
Joe Rich (C) Barrister in consumer law at Five Papers chambers,

London. Cllr: Uttelsford DC 2011-; Ugely 2007-11. Married, three daughters. Ed: Eton Coll; Magdalene Coll, Cambridge (BA law, chairman CUCA). **Tariq Mahmood** (Ukip). Barrister, Cornwall St Chambers. Fluent in Urdu, Punjabi, Hindi and Pothwari, Married, four children. Ed: Manchester (LLB; MA healthcare law & ethics). **Peter Andras** (LD) Professor in computer science at Keele University. Cllr, Newcastle CC 2011-14. Contested Washington & Sunderland W 2010. Former director of Civitas Foundation for the Civil Society.

CONSTITUENCY PROFILE
Stoke-on-Trent South covers Longton and Fenton, the two most southerly of the six original pottery towns in Staffs, as well as the Mier Park estate and Trentham, the most middle-class suburb of Stoke. Historically it is the least safe for Labour of all Stoke seats, but the constituency has still been Labour since its creation in 1950.

	Electorate	Turnout %	from 2010 %	Change
	68,788	56.9		
R Flello Lab	15,319	39.2	+0.4	
J Rich C	12,780	32.7	+4.3	
T Mahmood Ukip	8,298	21.2	+17.8	
P Andras LD	1,309	3.4	-12.5	
L Bellamy Green	1,029	2.6		
M Wright TUSC	372	1.0		

Change from 2010

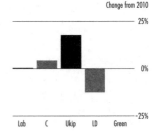

Stone

CONSERVATIVE HOLD

SIR WILLIAM (BILL) CASH
BORN May 10, 1940
MP 1984-

Obsessive opponent of European Union (led Maastricht rebels), chairman, European scrutiny select cttee but professed "undying loyalty" to David Cameron after 2015 election. Shadow SoS, constitutional affairs 2003. Shadow attorney-general 2001-03. Member, select cttees: parly privilege 2012-15; liaison 2010-15; consolidation bills 2005-10; European scrutiny 1998-15. KBE 2014. Embattled after expenses scandal revealed that he claimed £15,000 to pay his daughter's rent. He later repaid the money. Wrote biogrpahy of Victorian liberal John Bright, 2012. Solicitor with own practice. Has "disassociated" himself from his son William, who unsuccessfully contested Warwickshire N for Ukip. Married, one daughter, two sons. Ed: Stoneyhurst Coll; Lincoln College, Oxford (BA history).

CHALLENGERS
Sam Hale (Lab) Director of printer parts and consumables company. Member, North Staffs, UK Youth Parliament 2009. Ed: Moorlands Sixth Form Coll; Lancaster University (BA PPE). **Andrew Illsley** (Ukip) Marketing consultant. Chairman, Ukip Stone branch. Married, two children. **Martin Lewis** (LD) Retired civil servant for HMC&E, now HMRC, for 37 years. Taught English as a foreign language in Hamburg. Member, PCS. Two stepsons. Ed: King Edward VI GS.

CONSTITUENCY PROFILE
A sprawling rural seat in Staffordshire, including much of the countryside between Stoke and Stafford. In the top decile of English constituencies by geographical size, Stone was recreated in 1997, having been abolished in 1950, from parts of the neighbouring seats of Stafford, Staffordshire Moorlands and Mid Staffordshire.

	Electorate	Turnout %	from 2010 %	Change
	67,339	69.8		
B Cash C	25,733	54.7	+4.1	
S Hale Lab	9,483	20.2	-0.5	
A Illsley Ukip	7,620	16.2	+11.0	
M Lewis LD	2,473	5.3	-17.2	
W Naylon Green	1,191	2.5	+1.5	
J Coutouvidis Ind	531	1.1		

Change from 2010

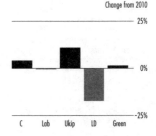

Stourbridge

CONSERVATIVE HOLD

MARGOT JAMES
BORN Aug 28, 1957
MP 2010-

Independent-minded Thatcherite whose business acumen has generated respect among peers. Asst whip 2015-. PPS to: William Hague 2013-15; Lord Green of Hurstpierpoint 2011-13. Member, select cttees: arms export controls 2010-12; BIS 2010-12. Chairwoman, APPG trade & investment. Pro-Israel. Contested Holborn & St Pancras 2005. Cllr, Kensington & Chelsea BC 2006-08. Vice-chairwoman Conservative party (for women's issues). Head of European healthcare, Ogilvy & Mather advertising agency. Founder and CEO, Shire Health Group. Worked for Maurice James Industries, father's business. Partner. Ed: Millfield Sch; LSE (BSc economics & government).

CHALLENGERS
Pete Lowe (Lab) Nurse. National officer, Managers in Partnership. Former regional officer, Unison. Cllr, Dudley MBC 2003-04, 2006-, leader 2014-. Married, two daughters. Ed: Thorns Secondary Sch; Halesowen Coll. **Jim Carver** (Ukip) MEP, West Midlands 2014-. Runs family umbrella business. Served with Royal Marines. Contested: Preseli P 2010; Cheltenham 2005; Orpington 1999. Widowed, remarried. Ed: Orpington Coll. **Chris Bramall** (LD) Retired solicitor. Cllr, Dudley MBC 1995-2004. Son of former Labour MP Sir Ashley Bramall. Ed: Christ's Coll, Cambridge (BA economics & politics).

CONSTITUENCY PROFILE
A Black Country constituency covering the southwest of the borough of Dudley and towns of Stourbridge, Amblecote and Cradley. It is largely white and lower middle-class. The seat was created in 1997 and held by Labour until 2010. Stourbridge is a rare seat that has had three female MPs in a row.

	Electorate	Turnout %	Change from 2010 %
	69,077	66.6	
M James C	21,195	46.1	+3.4
P Lowe Lab	14,501	31.5	-0.2
J Carver Ukip	7,774	16.9	+12.4
C Bramall LD	1,538	3.3	-13.0
C Kiever Green	1,021	2.2	+1.4

Change from 2010

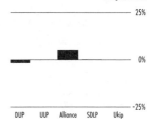

Strangford

DUP HOLD

JIM SHANNON
BORN Apr 21, 1964
MP 2010-

Countryside pursuits enthusiast who describes himself in Dod's as a self-employed pork retailer. Had the highest expenses claim of any MP in 2013: £229,262. DUP spokesman: human rights 2012-; health & transport 2010-. Served in: Ulster Defence Regiment 1974-77; Royal Artillery 1977-88. MLA For Strangford 1998-2010. Forum for Political Dialogue 1996-98. Cllr, Ards BC, 1985-2010, mayor 1991-92. Laughed off least sexiest MP rating, 2011. Married, three sons. Ed: Coleraine Academical Inst.

CHALLENGERS
Robert Burgess (UUP) Farmer. Cllr: Newry, Mourne & Down DC 2015-; Down DC 1999-15, former chairman. **Kellie Armstrong** (Alliance) Vice-chairwoman, Alliance party, convenor of Political Organisation group. NI director, Community Transport Association. Cllr: Ards & North Down BC 2014-; Ards BC 2013-14. Previously ran Pact, providing local access for people in Ards Peninsula. Married, one daughter. Ed: Assumption GS, Ballynahinch. **Joe Boyle** (SDLP) Works for PwC. Cllr: Ards & North Down BC 2014-; Ards BC 2005-14. Contested NI Assembly election 2011, 07, 03, each time finishing one place below cut-off. Ed: St Colman's Coll, Newry. **Joe Jordan** (Ukip) Works in property management. Cllr, Newtownabbey BC 2005-, defected from DUP in 2014. Former president of Belfast Chamber of Commerce during 2012 flag-flying protests. Ed: Grosvenor GS; University of Ulster (BSc business studies).

CONSTITUENCY PROFILE
Surrounds Strangford Lough and covers much of the Ards Peninsula. Main industries are farming, fishing and tourism. Dominantly Protestant. Represented by Ulster Unionists until 2001, when the DUP took over.

	Electorate	Turnout %	Change from 2010 %
	64,286	52.8	
J Shannon DUP	15,053	44.4	-1.6
R Burgess UUP	4,868	14.4	
K Armstrong Alliance	4,687	13.8	+5.1
J Boyle SDLP	2,335	6.9	+0.2
J Jordan Ukip	2,237	6.6	
J Andrews C	2,167	6.4	-21.5
S Cooper TUV	1,701	5.0	-0.6
S Bailie SF	876	2.6	-1.0

Change from 2010

Stratford-on-Avon

CONSERVATIVE HOLD

NADHIM ZAHAWI
BORN Jun 2, 1967
MP 2010-

Well-spoken co-founder and former CEO of YouGov. Had to apologise for claiming parliamentary expenses relating to second home. Select cttees: foreign affairs 2014-; arms export controls 2010-15; BIS 2010-15; privacy & injunctions 2011-12. Founder member, 2020 group free enterprise. Interested in immigration and business. Cllr, Wandsworth BC 1994-2006. European marketing dir, Smith & Brooks, children's merchandise company. Contested Erith & Thamesmead 1997. Enjoys horseriding and showjumping. CofE. Married, three children. Ed: King's Sch, Wimbledon; UCL (BSc chemical engineering).

CHALLENGERS
Edward Fila (Ukip) Director, Edward Fila Associates motor trade recruitment specialists. Chairman, Stratford Ukip branch. Former publican. Married, three children. Ed: Holy Cross Academy, Edinburgh; Napier Coll of Science & Tech (building). **Jeff Kenner** (Lab) Professor of European law, University of Nottingham. Cllr, Stratford DC 2012-. Ed: King's Coll, London (LLB law); UCL (LLM law). **Elizabeth Adams** (LD) Pharmacist and domestic violence campaigner. Two daughters.

CONSTITUENCY PROFILE
A large, affluent, rural seat, making up the western part of Warwickshire and stretching from the edge of the Cotswolds up to the outskirts of Redditch and urban West Midlands. Settlements are mostly historic market towns and villages, the most famous being Stratford-upon-Avon, birthplace of William Shakespeare. A safe Tory seat, held by the Conservatives since its creation in 1950 with the brief exception of 1995-1997 when Alan Howard defected to Labour.

	Electorate	Turnout %	Change from 2010 %
	70,914	72.6	
N Zahawi C	29,674	57.7	+6.1
E Fila Ukip	6,798	13.2	+9.6
J Kenner Lab	6,677	13.0	+3.5
E Adams LD	6,182	12.0	-17.1
D Giles Green	2,128	4.1	+3.1

Change from 2010

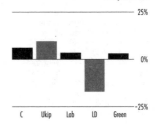

Streatham

LABOUR HOLD

CHUKA UMUNNA
BORN Apr 21, 1964
MP 2010-

Charismatic, always seen as future party leader but stepped away from 2015 Labour leadership election. Darling of the soft left, seen as Blairite, mentored by Jon Cruddas. *Question Time* regular. Shadow SoS, BIS 2011-. Shadow min, BIS 2011. Member, Treasury select cttee 2010-11. Management cttee, Compass pressure group. Inevitably nicknamed the British Obama. Strong on youth engagement issues. Specialist employment law solicitor: Rochman Landau; Herbert Smith. Board member, Generation Next. GMB, Unite. Nigerian/Irish/ English descent, Streatham-raised. Son of Bennett, Crystal Palace FC director and tribal leader who died in car crash after standing for Nigerian state governor on anti-bribery ticket. Ed: University of Manchester (LLB English & French law); Nottingham Law Sch (LPC).

CHALLENGERS
Kim Caddy (C) Chartered accountant. Cllr, Wansdworth BC 2012-. Ed: Christ Church, Oxford (BSc biology). **Amna Ahmad** (LD) Comms & healthcare policy consultant, Open Road. Ed: James Allen's Girls' Sch; St Hugh's Coll, Oxford (BA history & politics). **Jonathan Bartley** (Green) Green Party spokesman, work & pensions. Director, Ekklesia religious think tank. Chairman, CSIE. Author. Challenged David Cameron in 2010 about inclusion of disabled children in mainstream schools. Ed: LSE.

CONSTITUENCY PROFILE
Covers Streatham and parts of Clapham and Brixton. When the seat used to be a solidly middle-class suburb it was continously held by the Tories from its creation in 1918 until 1992 when it fell to Labour. As it has become increasingly inner-city in character and diverse make-up it has moved further into Labour's column and by 2001 it was a safe Labour seat.

	Electorate	Turnout %	Change from 2010 %
	78,673	63.5	
C Umunna Lab	26,474	53.0	+10.2
K Caddy C	12,540	25.1	+6.8
A Ahmad LD	4,491	9.0	-26.8
J Bartley Green	4,421	8.9	+7.0
B Machan Ukip	1,602	3.2	
A Beast CSA	192	0.4	
U Mirza TUSC	164	0.3	
D Gayle WRP	49	0.1	-0.2

Change from 2010

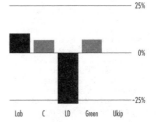

Stretford & Urmston

LABOUR HOLD

KATE GREEN
BORN May 2, 1960
MP 2010-

Well-regarded, Scottish-born poverty and families campaigner. Pledged to make 2015 election memorable by taking action to support the 850,000 people living with dementia across the UK. Shad min: work & pensions 2013-15; equalities 2011-13. Chief exec, Child Poverty Action Group; dir, National Council for One Parent Families. Unafraid to criticise Labour. Select cttee: work & pensions 2010-11. Contested Cities of London & Westminster 1997. GLA candidate West London 2000. Member: Fawcett Society, Fabians, Amicus. Chairwoman, London Child Poverty Commission; member, Nat Employment Panel. Trustee, IFS. Whitehall & Industry Group secondee to Home Office. Magistrate. Former career, Barclays Bank. OBE. Divorced. Ed: Currie HS; Edinburgh (LLB law).

CHALLENGERS
Lisa Cooke (C) Dir, Lisa Cooke Associates. HR consultant, Royal Mail. Cllr, Trafford MBC 2011-. Member of the Chartered Institute of Personnel and Development. Married, two children. **Kalvin Chapman** (Ukip) Solicitor, Berg. Ed: King's Coll London (LLB law); Northumbria (LPC). **Geraldine Coggins** (Green) Counsellor. Worked as lecturer in philosophy at Keele, York and Aberdeen universities. Ed: Trinity Coll, Dublin (BA philosophy); St Andrews (MLitt philosophy); Durham (PhD philosophy).

CONSTITUENCY PROFILE
Covers the inner-city area of Stretford, Salford city centre, Urmston and Carrington. Stretford is more ethnically mixed; Urmston middle class and Conservative. The balance of this seat, created in 1997, is heavily in Labour's favour, despite a solid rump of Conservative support, but it is unlikely to become a marginal.

	Electorate	Turnout %	from 2010 %
	69,490	66.8	
K Green Lab	24,601	53.0	+4.5
L Cooke C	12,916	27.8	-0.9
K Chapman Ukip	5,068	10.9	+7.6
G Coggins Green	2,187	4.7	+2.7
L Ankers LD	1,362	2.9	-14.0
P Bradley-Law Whig	169	0.4	
P Carson PP UK	83	0.2	

Change from 2010

Stroud

CONSERVATIVE HOLD

NEIL CARMICHAEL
BORN Apr 15, 1961
MP 2010-

Former cow and sheep farmer turned PR consultant. Steered private member's bill on Antarctica through the Commons to the statute book, visited the continent with the British Antarctic Survey in 2013. Select cttee, environmental audit, education 2010-. Contested: Stroud 2001; Leeds East 1992. Chief exec, Strategic Impact public affairs, 1998-2000. Consultant, JBP, Bristol, 2001-05. Non-exec dir, Artloan. Proprietor, TLB Carmichael, woodland developer. NFU. Former chairman of Northumbria Daybreak charity. Visiting lecturer in British political history and rural economics at Sunderland and De Montfort universities. Renovating a Massey-Ferguson 135 tractor. Married, two daughters, one son. Ed: St Peter's Sch, York; University of Nottingham (BA politics).

CHALLENGERS
David Drew (Lab Co-op) MP for Stroud 1997-2010. Backbench rebel in Blair/Brown years. Cllr: Stevenage BC 1981; Stroud DC 1987-1995; Stonehouse TC 1987-. Former sernior lecturer in education at UWE. Natfhe. Married, two daughters, two sons. Ed: Nottingham (BA economics); UWE (MA history). **Caroline Stephens** (Ukip). Maths teacher. Leading campaigner in bringing financial education into national curriculum, 2013. Worked at CAB. Stroud Ukip chairman. Two children. Ed: UWE (BSc maths).

CONSTITUENCY PROFILE
Consists of Stroud and the small market towns and villages in the Severn valley. For most of the post-war period the seat has been Tory, falling to Labour only in 1945 and 1997-2010. The Green party have significant representation on the local council and this has sometimes translated into parliamentary support.

	Electorate	Turnout %	from 2010 %
	80,522	75.5	
N Carmichael C	27,813	45.7	+4.9
D Drew Lab Co-op	22,947	37.7	-0.9
C Stephens Ukip	4,848	8.0	+5.7
S Lunnon Green	2,779	4.6	+1.9
A Walker-Smith LD	2,086	3.4	-12.0
R Wilson Ind	246	0.4	+0.2
D Michael FPT	100	0.2	

Change from 2010

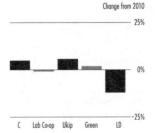

Suffolk Central & Ipswich North

CONSERVATIVE HOLD

DANIEL POULTER
BORN Oct 30, 1978
MP 2010-

Healthcare specialist, worked as NHS obstetrician and gynaecologist. Ran medical and lifestyle advice clinics for the homeless and people with alcohol or substance misuse problems. Parly under-secretary: health 2012-15. Member, select cttees: health 2011-12; draft House of Lords reform bill 2011-12. Worked on Preston Home Energy and Water Conservation Project as deputy leader, Reigate & Banstead BC 2008-10. Cllr, Hastings BC 2006-07. Won open primary. Married. Keen cricketer and rugby player. Ed: Battle Abbey Sch; University of Bristol (LLB law); Guys, Kings and St Thomas' Sch of Medicine (medicine).

CHALLENGERS
Jack Abbott (Lab) Renewable-energy worker. Cllr, Debenham

PC 2013-. Ed: Debenham HS; University of Sheffield. **Mark Cole** (Ukip). Runs driving school. Served in Bosnia and Germany with TA. Married, one son. **Jon Neal** (LD) Associate dir, Kendalls Communications. Former head of communications at research and training charity IGD. Married, two children. Ed: University of Hull (BA British politics & legislative studies).

CONSTITUENCY PROFILE
The North Ipswich part of the seat is relatively small (if well populated): the village-turned-housing estate of Whitton and the middle-class residential area of Castle Hill. The majority of the seat is a much larger chunk of rural Suffolk. Historically, this tended to be a Liberal seat but with the decline of the party in the 1950s it fell to the Conservatives and has stayed with them ever since. The estates of Ipswich provide Labour with some support but on the whole this is a safe Tory seat.

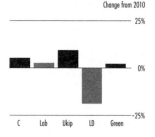

	Electorate	Turnout %	from 2010 %	Change
	78,782	68.7		
D Poulter C	30,317	56.1	+5.3	
J Abbott Lab	10,173	18.8	+2.6	
M Cole Ukip	7,459	13.8	+9.4	
J Neal LD	3,314	6.1	-18.8	
R Griffiths Green	2,664	4.9	+2.2	
T Holyoak Eng Dem	162	0.3		

Change from 2010

Suffolk Coastal

CONSERVATIVE HOLD

THERESE COFFEY
BORN Nov 18, 1971
MP 2010-

Scientist and businesswoman. Was appointed Beer Parliamentarian of the Year after visiting all 118 pubs in her constituency in 2014. Deputy leader of HoC 2015-. Assistant whip: Treasury 2014-15. PPS to Michael Fallon 2012-14. Member, select cttee: CMS 2010-12. Contested: Wrexham 2005; SE England Euro elections 2009, 04. Ex-BBC property finance manager, following career at Mars Drinks as finance director. Chartered management accountant. Football and live music fan, Camra member. Ed: St Mary's Coll, Crosby; St Edward's Coll, Liverpool; Somerville Coll, Oxford (BSc chemistry); UCL (PhD chemistry).

CHALLENGERS
Russell Whiting (Lab) Works for an NGO in London. Cllr, Stapleford TC 2011-13. Apologised

after critising the "pseudo-worship" of the army. Conservative member until 2010. Married. Ed: Orwell HS; Nottingham (BA politics). **Daryll Pitcher** (Ukip) Manager, Esprit de Corps armed forces support. Cllr, Isle of Wight C 2013-. Ed: Portsmouth (BA politics). **James Sandbach** (LD) Campaigns and research manager to Low Commission. Barrister. Former social policiy officer at CAB. Contested: Putney 2010; Castlepoint 2005. Married. Ed: St Andrew's (MTheol theology); UCL (MA history); KCL (MA international politics); Westminster (PhD conflict resolution).

CONSTITUENCY PROFILE
A long thin seat, covering most of Suffolk's coast with the exception of Lowestoft in the north. Held comfortably by the Conservatives since its creation in 1983, although their majorities dropped below 5,000 in 1997 and 2001. Until 1832 part of the seat was one of the most notorious rotten boroughs.

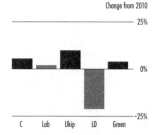

	Electorate	Turnout %	from 2010 %	Change
	78,782	70.6		
T Coffey C	28,855	51.9	+5.5	
R Whiting Lab	10,013	18.0	+2.0	
D Pitcher Ukip	8,655	15.6	+9.8	
J Sandbach LD	4,777	8.6	-21.2	
R Smith-Lyte Green	3,294	5.9	+3.9	

Change from 2010

Suffolk South

CONSERVATIVE HOLD

JAMES CARTLIDGE
BORN April 30, 1974
MP 2015-

Chosen by local association after MP Tim Yeo's deselection in 2014. Entrepreneur, charity "dragon" and Conservative political campaigner. Cllr, Babergh DC 2013-. Director of Share to Buy. Political researcher for Conservatives, who helped IDS to prepare for PMQs while leader. Volunteer small business adviser, St Mungo's Broadway. Former leader writer, *Daily Telegraph*, also freelance, the *Guardian*, *The Spectator*. Contested Lewisham Deptford 2005. Plays drums for Assington pub band Tequila Mockingbird. Married, one daughter, three sons. Ed: University of Manchester (BA economics); Middlesex University (MSc interactive computing).

CHALLENGERS
Jane Basham (Lab) Human resources worker. Former chief exec, Ipswich and Suffolk Council

for Racial Equality. Fought Suffolk PCC election 2012, narrowly defeated after coming top of first preference. Former dir, EqualTwo. Ed: Gravesend GS for Girls; Suffolk Coll. **Steven Whalley** (Ukip) Career in IT and telecoms. Married, two children. Ed: Stamford Sch; Essex (BSc physics; MSc computer science). **Grace Weaver** (LD) Senior account executive, MHP Communications. Former political researcher for DeHavilland and youth leader for Stonewall. Young ambassador for Diana Award, 2005. Ed: Corpus Christi, Oxford (BA PPE).

CONSTITUENCY PROFILE
A long rural seat, stretching along Suffolk's border with Essex, from Shotley penisula, through the Dedham Vale and westwards to Sudbury. The main population centres are the historic market towns of Sudbury and Hadleigh, and the villages clustered around the fringes of Ipswich. A safe Conservative seat, represented by deselected Tim Yeo 1983-2015.

	Electorate	Turnout %	from 2010 %	Change %
	73,220	70.9		
J Cartlidge C	27,546	53.1	+5.3	
J Basham Lab	10,001	19.3	+4.9	
S Whalley Ukip	7,897	15.2	+8.1	
G Weaver LD	4,044	7.8	-23.1	
R Lindsay Green	2,253	4.3		
S Todd CPA	166	0.3		

Change from 2010

Suffolk West

CONSERVATIVE HOLD

MATTHEW HANCOCK
BORN Oct 2, 1978
MP 2010-

Economic adviser (chief of staff to George Osborne 2005-10) who sacrificed career in No 11 to forge his own path. Worked in family computer software firm then at Bank of England before joining Tory high command. Longstanding activist. Was made to repay £1,674 after being found to have misused HoC facilities in 2014. Min: Cabinet Office and paymaster-general 2015-; Portsmouth 2014-15; business, enterprise & energy 2014-15; skills & enterprise 2013-14. Parly under-sec: skills 2012-13. Member, select cttees: standards & privileges 2010-12; public accounts 2010-12. Married, three children. Ed: King's Sch Chester; Exeter Coll, Oxford (BA PPE); Christ's Coll, Cambridge (MA economics).

CHALLENGERS
Julian Flood (Ukip) Cllr, Suffolk

CC 2013-. Ran plant nursery. Former RAF pilot. Two children. **Michael Jefferys** (Lab) Former teacher. Previously assistant principal at Newmarket College. Cllr: Forest Heath DC 2011-15; Newmarket TC. **Elfreda Tealby-Watson** (LD) Project co-ordinator, Domestic Building Work. Volunteer, Great Chesterford Primary Academy. Cllr, Uttlesford DC 2000-07. Ed: Queens' Coll, Cambridge (BA history); Keele University (MA American politics & institutions).

CONSTITUENCY PROFILE
Until 1997 this seat was called Bury St Edmunds, but at the previous set of boundary changes the town was moved into a new constituency, leaving this as the rural west of the countryside surrounding the town itself. It is a comfortably safe Conservative seat, with the only real Labour strength around Haverhill. The seat and its predecessor have been represented by the Conservative party since the 19th century.

	Electorate	Turnout %	from 2010 %	Change %
	76,197	64.6		
M Hancock C	25,684	52.2	+1.6	
J Flood Ukip	10,700	21.7	+15.3	
M Jefferys Lab	8,604	17.5	+2.7	
E Tealby-Watson LD	2,465	5.0	-18.4	
N Pettitt Green	1,779	3.6		

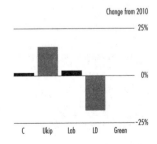

Change from 2010

Sunderland Central

LABOUR HOLD

JULIE ELLIOTT
BORN Jul 29, 1963
MP 2010-

Sunderland born and raised, from a working-class family. Shadow min: energy and climate change 2013-15. Member, select cttees: BIS 2011-13; European scrutiny 2010-. PPS to Caroline Flint 2010-13. APPG: Co-chairwoman, primary care and public health. Political, policy, media and research officer, GMB. Regional organiser, National Asthma Campaign. Regional organiser, Labour Party, agent Tynemouth 1997. Four children. Ed: Seaham Northlea Comp; Newcastle Poly (government & public policy).

CHALLENGERS
Jeffrey Townsend (C) Consultant, Aspect Consulting. Political dir, Mining Industry Group. Former international affairs adviser to Pauline Latham MP and chief of staff to Mark Lancaster MP. Enjoys jujitsu. Ed: Bedford Sch;

University of Birmingham (BA; MA international relations). **Bryan Foster** (Ukip) Businessman. Founder member of Sunderland City Centre Traders Association. Married. Ed: Bede GS. **Rachel Featherstone** (Green) Senior lecturer in research methods, Teeside University. Ed: Sunderland (BA sociology & politics); Durham (MA politics). **Adrian Page** (LD) Photographer and fine art student. Served in army as private, later dog handler. Ed: Blackburn Coll (fine art).

CONSTITUENCY PROFILE
The centre of Sunderland and the coastal village of Ryhope to the south. It also includes Roker (the site of Sunderland AFC's former stadium), Monkwearmouth and the affluent suburb of Fulwell. The Tories managed to return cllrs in five out of the nine Sunderland Central wards in the last parliament, but the seat is still unlikely to ever be a marginal. Large-scale inward investment and regeneration is under way.

	Electorate	Turnout %	from 2010 % Change
	72,933	57.3	
J Elliott Lab	20,959	50.2	+4.3
J Townsend C	9,780	23.4	-6.7
B Foster Ukip	7,997	19.2	+16.6
R Featherstone Green	1,706	4.1	
A Page LD	1,105	2.7	-14.3
J Young ND	215	0.5	

Change from 2010

Lab   C   Ukip   Green   LD

Surrey East

CONSERVATIVE HOLD

SAM GYIMAH
BORN Aug 10, 1976
MP 2010-

British-born but spent childhood in Ghana. Lauded as successful businessman but faced questions over liquidation of business ClearStone, which he founded. Parly under-sec, education 2014-. Parliamentary secretary, cabinet office 2014-15. Lord commissioner: Treasury 2013-14. PPS to David Cameron 2012-13. Select cttees: international development 2011-12; electoral commission 2010-12. Investment banker, Goldman Sachs. Former chairman, Bow Group. Arsenal fan. Married, one son. Ed: Achimota Sch, Accra; Freman Coll, Herts; Somerville Coll, Oxford (BA PPE, president Oxford Union).

CHALLENGERS
Helena Windsor (Ukip) Runs Mycoplasma Experience research company. Former Wellcome researcher. Cllr, Surrey CC 2013-.

Married, three children, two stepchildren. Ed: Bromley Coll of Tech; North East London Poly (BSc applied biology). **Matt Wilson** (Lab) Chief exec, Safe Families for Children. Married, two sons. Ed: Manchester Met (interactive arts, design and applied arts); Salford (MSc management); KCL (MA theology & politics). **David Lee** (LD) Customer service trainer. Cllr, Whyteleafe VC 2015, 2010-12. Contested Surrey East 2010. Ed: Reigate Sixth Form; Porstmouth (BA German).

CONSTITUENCY PROFILE
The easternmost part of Surrey county, a collection of affluent commuter towns and villages in the London greenbelt. Gatwick airport is a major employer. A safe Conservative seat, represented by chancellor and foreign secretary Geoffrey Howe, 1974-92. He was replaced by Peter Ainsworth, who served in the shadow cabinets of Hague, Duncan Smith and Cameron but retired in 2010.

	Electorate	Turnout %	from 2010 % Change
	79,654	70.4	
S Gyimah C	32,211	57.4	+0.7
H Windsor Ukip	9,553	17.0	+10.1
M Wilson Lab	6,627	11.8	+2.8
D Lee LD	5,189	9.3	-16.6
N Dodgson Green	2,159	3.9	
S Pratt Ind	364	0.7	-0.1

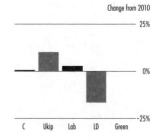

Change from 2010

C   Ukip   Lab   LD   Green

Surrey Heath

CONSERVATIVE HOLD

MICHAEL GOVE
BORN Aug 26, 1967
MP 2005-

Arch moderniser, bête noire of the teaching establishment during turbulent period as secretary of state for education 2010-14. Demoted to chief whip, 2014-15, after Lynton Crosby warned Cameron that he was toxic to the party. Promoted again to justice secretary (2015-) after election, despite lack of legal training. Skilled debater, excitable and loves a media fight. Failed in attempt to sack John Bercow as chief whip. Embarrassed when his smartwatch played Beyoncé during cabinet meeting, 2015. Shadow SoS: CSF 2007-10. Shadow minister: housing 2005-07. Former journalist: *The Times*, BBC News, Scottish Television, *Aberdeen Press and Journal*. Former chairman, Policy Exchange. Married to columnist Sarah Vine, one daughter, one son. Ed: Robert Gordon's Coll, Aberdeen; LMH, Oxford (BA English).

CHALLENGERS
Paul Chapman (Ukip) Chartered engineer and consultant. Fellow, Inst of Chemical Engineers. Married, one daughter. **Laween Atroshi** (Lab) Chief research officer, Mid-Essex NHS Trust. Ed: Oxford (CPD nanomedicine); St George's (BSc biomedical informatics); KCL (post-grad primary care). **Ann-Marie Barker** (LD) Research consultant, Accelerator Solutions management consultancy. Cllr, Woking BC 2004-08, 2010-14, LD group leader 2013-14. Married, two daughters. Ed: Brunel (BSc history & politics).

CONSTITUENCY PROFILE
Mostly made up of merged towns and villages in the Aldershot urban area: Camberley, Frimley and Ash, all middle-class commuter areas. It also includes Deepcut Barracks, headquarters of Royal Logistical Corps. Very safe Tory seat, represented by Gove after his predecessor Nick Hawkins was deselected by the local association.

	Electorate	Turnout %	Change from 2010 %
	79,515	68.5	
M Gove C	32,582	59.9	+2.2
P Chapman Ukip	7,778	14.3	+8.0
L Atroshi Lab	6,100	11.2	+1.0
A Barker LD	4,937	9.1	-16.8
K Lawson Green	2,400	4.4	
J Brimicombe Christian	361	0.7	
B Smith Ind	273	0.5	

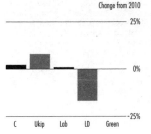

Change from 2010

Surrey South West

CONSERVATIVE HOLD

JEREMY HUNT
BORN Nov 1, 1966
MP 2005-

Amiable yet ambitious, from the soft Tory left. Secretary of state for health 2012-, appointment criticised for his support of homeopathy and desire to reduce abortion time limit. Smooth, not one to want to raise eyebrows. Still seen as future leader. Issued apology after revealed to have misled Commons over who would foot compensation bill for victims of Jimmy Savile. SoS, culture, olympics, media & sport 2010-12. Plucked from shadow culture brief to be one of the five "faces" of the Tory campaign in 2010. Shadow SoS, CMS 2007-10. Shad min, disabled people 2005-07. Member, int devt select cttee 2005-06. Management consultant, Outram Cullinan & Co. Founder and MD, Hotcourses. Taught English in Japan. Ed: Charterhouse; Magdalen Coll, Oxford (BA PPE).

CHALLENGERS
Mark Webber (Ukip) IT consultant for City and Canary Wharf firms specialising in banking and capital markets technology. Tower Hamlets Ukip branch chairman. Ed: Farnborough SF Coll; London. **Howard Kaye** (Lab) Train driver, Virgin/East Coast. Aslef rep. Married, three children, one stepson. **Louise Irvine** (NHAP) GP in Lewisham, chairwoman of successful Save Lewisham Hospital campaign. Member, BMA council. Married, two children. Ed: Aberdeen (MBChB medicine).

CONSTITUENCY PROFILE
Much of Waverley borough is included in a constituency that borders Sussex and Hampshire. The seat and its predecessors have been represented by the Conservative party since 1910 by three cabinet ministers in a row: the former SoS for employment, Maurice MacMillan, former SoS health, Virginia Bottomley, and now health secretary Jeremy Hunt.

	Electorate	Turnout %	Change from 2010 %
	77,050	74.1	
J Hunt C	34,199	59.9	+1.2
M Webber Ukip	5,643	9.9	+7.3
H Kaye Lab	5,415	9.5	+3.5
L Irvine NHAP	4,851	8.5	
P Haveron LD	3,586	6.3	-23.9
S Ryland Green	3,105	5.4	+4.2
P Robinson S New	320	0.6	

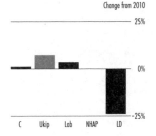

Change from 2010

Sussex Mid

CONSERVATIVE HOLD

SIR NICHOLAS SOAMES
BORN Jan 14, 1966
MP 1983-

Bombastic, anachronistic. Brightens the chamber. Grandson of Sir Winston Churchill. One Nation Tory with close interest in the military. Shadow SoS: defence 2003-05. Min: armed forces 1994-97. Joint parly sec MAFF 1992-94. PPS to: Nicholas Ridley 1987-89, John Gummer 1984-86. Member, select cttees: administration 2013-14; standards & privileges 2006-10; consolidation bills 2001-05; public administration 1999-2000; European legislation 1984-85. 1922 executive committee, 2010-12. MP, Crawley 1983-97. Commissioned into 11th Hussars. Equerry to Prince of Wales. Stockbroker then PA to Sir James Goldsmith. Asst dir, Sedgwick Group. Divorced. Remarried. One son from first marriage. Two children from second marriage. Ed: Eton Coll; Mons Officer Cadet Sch.

CHALLENGERS
Greg Mountain (Lab) Benefits manager, HMRC. Former policy manager, DWP. Ed: University of London (BSc economics).
Toby Brothers (Ukip) Solicitor at Edward Hayes LLP. Practised law in Australia. Married. Ed: St Edward's Sch, Oxford; Kingston (LLB law). **Daisy Cooper** (LD) Operations and projects manager for Hacked Off campaign group. Contested Suffolk Coastal 2010. Dir, Commonwealth Advisory Bureau. Ed: University of Leeds (LLB law); University of Nottingham (LLM international law).

CONSTITUENCY PROFILE
Consists of three towns, East Grinstead, Haywards Heath and Burgess Hill, and a rural area to the west around the village of Cuckfield. Has been Tory since its creation in 1974. Although in the 70s and 80s it was a solid Tory fortress, there has since been considerable Lib Dem strength.

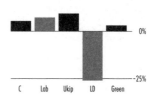

	Electorate	Turnout %	from 2010 %
	79,520	72.3	
N Soames C	32,268	56.1	+5.4
G Mountain Lab	7,982	13.9	+7.3
T Brothers Ukip	6,898	12.0	+9.5
D Cooper LD	6,604	11.5	-26.0
M Diboll Green	2,453	4.3	+3.1
B Adam Ind	958	1.7	
B Von Thunderclap Loony	329	0.6	+0.1

Change from 2010

C   Lab   Ukip   LD   Green

Sutton & Cheam

CONSERVATIVE GAIN

PAUL SCULLY
BORN Apr 29, 1968
MP 2015-

Partner, Nudge Factory PR. Former head of office for Alok Sharma MP. Cllr, Sutton BC 2006-10, leader of opposition 2007-10. Married, two children. Ed: Bedford School; University of Reading (failed to complete BSc chemistry & food science).

CHALLENGERS
Paul Burstow (LD) MP 1997-2015. Minister, health 2010-12. Chief whip 2006-10. LD shadow SoS health 2003-05. LD spokesman: London 2005-06; older people 1999-2003; local govt 1997-99; disabled people 1997-98. Chairman, LD parliamentary party 2012-13. Member, select cttees: public accounts 2008-10; modernisation of HoC 2006-07; finance and services 2006-10; draft mental incapacity bill 2003; health 2003-06. Former member SDP/Liberal

Alliance, London regional LD exec, federal policy cttee. Political sec, LD Cllrs Assoc 1996-97. Cllr, Sutton 1986-, deputy leader 1994-99. Married, two daughters, one son. Ed: Carshalton FE College; South Bank Poly (BA business studies). **Emily Brothers** (Lab) Labour's first transgender candidate. Blind since childhood. Disability campaigner. Former programme head, Equality & Human Rights Commission. Divorced, one son, one daughter. Ed: Teeside University (BA humanities). **Angus Dalgleish** (Ukip) Ed: Harrow County GS; University Coll Hospital (medicine).

CONSTITUENCY PROFILE
Solidly middle-class suburban seat on southwestern fringe of London, it is predominantly white, with no major ethnic groups, little social housing and generally affluent. It was won by the Liberal Democrats in 1997 when a swathe of well-off voters swung heavily towards the party. They narrowly retained the seat in 2010.

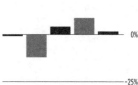

	Electorate	Turnout %	from 2010 %
	69,160	72.2	
P Scully C	20,732	41.5	-0.8
P Burstow LD	16,811	33.7	-12.0
E Brothers Lab	5,546	11.1	+4.2
A Dalgleish Ukip	5,341	10.7	+8.7
M Tomlinson Green	1,051	2.1	+1.6
D Ash NHAP	345	0.7	
P Gorman TUSC	79	0.2	

Change from 2010

C   LD   Lab   Ukip   Green

Sutton Coldfield

CONSERVATIVE HOLD

ANDREW MITCHELL
BORN Mar 23, 1956
MP 2001-; 1987-97

Embrolied in 'Plebgate' fiasco, lost legal suit for libel. Close ally of David Davis and Lord Ashcroft. Lost his original Gedling seat in 1997. Committed to international development, especially in Africa. Son of a Tory MP, wealthy descendant of El Vino wine merchant founders. Parly sec to the Treasury and chief whip 2012. SoS, int devt 2010-12. Shadow SoS, int dev't 2005-10. Vice-chairman, Conservative party 1992-93. Organiser, Tories' Project Umubano in Rwanda. Shadow minister: home affairs 2004-05; Treasury 2003-04. Parly under-sec, DSS 1995-97. Whip: ass't gov't 1992-93, gov't 1993-95. PPS to: John Wakeham 1990-92; William Waldegrave 1988-90. Served in Army, UN Cyprus. Married, two daughters. Ed: Jesus Coll, Cambridge (BA history, chairman CUCA).

CHALLENGERS
Robert Pocock (Lab) CEO, MEL research and consultancy company. Cllr, Birmingham CC 2012-. Member, council overview and scrutiny cttee for devolution & public engagement. Contested Sutton Coldfield 2001, 2010. Ed: Royal Holloway, UoL (BSc physics); Aston University (PhD enironmental science). **Marcus Brown** (Ukip) Teacher. Married, two children. Ed: Bishop Vesey's GS. **Dr Richard Brighton-Knight** (LD) Doctor. Contested Sutton Coldfield 2010, 2001. Ed: University of Birmingham (MB ChB, medicine; MPH).

CONSTITUENCY PROFILE
A solidly middle class seat to the north of Birmingham. Prestigious, leafly and affluent, it covers the most desirable residential areas in the city. A very safe Conservative seat, it has been held continuously by the party since its creation in 1945. Formerly held by Sir Norman Fowler, the party chairman.

	Electorate	Turnout %	Change from 2010 %
	74,956	67.9	
A Mitchell C	27,782	54.6	+0.7
R Pocock Lab	11,365	22.4	+2.0
M Brown Ukip	7,489	14.7	+11.6
R Brighton-Knight LD	2,627	5.2	-12.9
D Ratcliff Green	1,426	2.8	+1.8
M Sleigh Ubuntu	165	0.3	

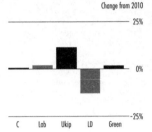

Change from 2010

Swansea East

LABOUR HOLD

CAROLYN HARRIS
BORN Sep 18, 1960
MP 2015-

Selected from all-woman shortlist, senior parly asst and constituency office manager for retiring MP Sian James. Former regional manager for a children's cancer charity. Wales regional dir, Community Logistics. Former project manager, Guilding Hands Charity. Married, three sons, one deceased after road accident. Ed: Llwyn y bryn GS; Brynhyfrd JS; Swansea University (BSc economics).

CHALLENGERS
Clifford Johnson (Ukip). **Dr Altaf Hussain** (C) Retired orthoepaedic surgeon and doctor of 25 years for NHS. School governor. Chairman, Wales Conservative Muslim Forum. Executive member, CMF. Cllr, Newcastle HC 2012-. Ed: Jammu and Kashmir University, India (MBBS); Kasmir University (MS); University of Liverpool

(MChOrth). **Dic Jones** (PC) Full time engineering trainer. Deputy chairman, board of governors, Ysgol Gynradd Gymraeg Tirdeunaw. Has worked for the Land Registry, BT. Married. Ed: Dynevor Sch. **Amina Jamal** (LD) Therapist, previously practitioner for Public Health Wales. Former project manager in Macedonia for Tipping The Balance for Health. Widowed, three daughters. Ed: Swansea University (history & economics); Cardiff University (MSc health education).

CONSTITUENCY PROFILE
The more working class and industrial of the two Swansea seats, covering the large council estates, the docks and the industrial estates along the river Tawe. Big local employers include the Driver and Vehicle Licensing Agency and Morriston Hospital. It remains a very safe Labour seat, having been held by the party since 1922, and returned one of their strongest majorities in the 1997 landslide.

	Electorate	Turnout %	Change from 2010 %
	58,011	58.0	
C Harris Lab	17,807	53.0	+1.5
C Johnson Ukip	5,779	17.2	+14.6
A Hussain C	5,142	15.3	+0.5
D Jones PC	3,498	10.4	+3.7
A Jamal LD	1,392	4.1	-14.2

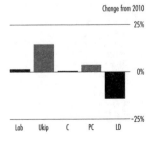

Change from 2010

Swansea West

LABOUR CO-OPERATIVE HOLD

GERAINT DAVIES
BORN May 3, 1960
MP 2010-; 1997-2005

Became the first newly elected MP in last parliament to present a private bill: the Credit Card Regulation (Child Pornography) Bill 2010. Backbencher as MP Croydon Central (1997-2005). Member, Parly Assembly of the Council of Europe 2010-15. PPS to: justice team 2003-05. Member, select cttees: European scrutiny 2013-15; Welsh affairs 2010-15; public accounts 1997-2003. Cllr, Croydon LBC 1986-97. GMB, Co-op. After 2005 defeat worked for Environment Agency Wales. Chairman, Lab Finance & Industry Group Wales. Company director. Parly ambassador, NSPCC. School governor. Marketing manager, Colgate Palmolive. Group product manager, Unilever. Member, MSF. Married, three daughters. Ed: Llanishen Comprehensive, Cardiff; Jesus College, Oxford (BA PPE).

CHALLENGERS
Emma Lane (C) Relationship director, Lloyds. Cllr, Ellingham, Harbridge and Ibsley PC 2007-. Married, three children. Ed: Royal Holloway, UoL (BA Classics). **Martyn Ford** (Ukip) Ed: Swansea University (MA history). **Chris Holley** (LD) Cllr, Swansea 1985-, leader 20014-12. Worked for TIMET, trained as apprentice mechanical fitter machinist. Widowed, two daughters. **Harri Roberts** (PC) Area manager, Burroughs Machines.

CONSTITUENCY PROFILE
Swansea West includes the city centre and its neighbourhoods, rebuilt after the old town centre was razed in the blitz, Swansea University and some of the more affluent outlying suburbs of the city. A reliable Labour seat (Alan Williams represented the area continuously for 46 years) but traditionally the less secure of the two Swansea seats. Conservatives ran Labour a close second in 2010.

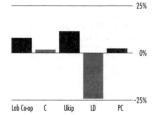

	Electorate	Turnout %	from 2010 % Change
	58,776	59.8	
G Davies Lab Co-op	14,967	42.6	+7.9
E Lane C	7,931	22.6	+1.8
M Ford Ukip	4,744	13.5	+11.5
C Holley LD	3,178	9.0	-24.2
H Roberts PC	2,266	6.5	+2.4
A Wakeling Green	1,784	5.1	+3.9
R Job TUSC	159	0.5	-0.1
M Rosser Ind	78	0.2	-0.8
B Johnson SPGB	49	0.1	

Change from 2010

Swindon North

CONSERVATIVE HOLD

JUSTIN TOMLINSON
BORN Nov 5, 1976
MP 2010-

Runs TB Marketing, major print supplier for local Conservative branches. Parly under-sec for disabled people 2015-. PPS to Ed Vaizey 2014-15. Member, select cttees: public accounts 2012-14; consolidation bills 2010-15. Cllr, Swindon BC 2000-10. Reported fellow MP Sadiq Kahn to police for allegedly using a phone while driving. Contested Swindon North 2005. Marketing executive, Point to Point. Sales & marketing manager, First Leisure. Student politician, became national chairman of Conservative Future. Married. Ed: Harry Cheshire HS, Kidderminster; Oxford Brookes (BA business & marketing).

CHALLENGERS
Mark Dempsey (Lab)
Environmental policy adviser, HP. Cllr, Swindon BC 2010-.

Contested The Cotswolds 2010. Ed: University of Gloucestershire (BA physical geography; MA environmental policy). **James Faulkner** (Ukip) Telecoms and IT systems engineer. Married, one son. **Poppy Hebden-Leeder** (Green) Ed: Keele University (BA business administration and environmental management); Bangor University (BSc bimolecular sciences). **Janet Ellard** (LD) Volunteer coordinator, Gloucestershire Nightstop. Modern languages teacher. Parly asst to Veronica German AM, previously Michael German AM.

CONSTITUENCY PROFILE
Both Swindon seats are marginals, gained by Labour in 1997 but won by the Tories in 2010. Swindon North is the marginally more Conservative seat, with a lower proportion of social housing and a slightly less ethnically diverse electorate. It includes the town of Highworth to the northeast, a traditional market town and base for tourists visiting the Cotswolds.

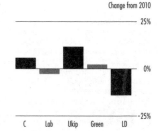

	Electorate	Turnout %	from 2010 % Change
	81,005	64.5	
J Tomlinson C	26,295	50.3	+5.8
M Dempsey Lab	14,509	27.8	-2.7
J Faulkner Ukip	8,011	15.3	+11.7
P Hebden-Leeder Green	1,723	3.3	+2.3
J Ellard LD	1,704	3.3	-14.0

Change from 2010

Swindon South

CONSERVATIVE HOLD

ROBERT BUCKLAND
BORN Sep 22, 1968
MP 2010-

Barrister, QC, interested in the detail of criminal justice policy, and in local planning and development issues. Has denied attempting to avoid tax after being named as an investor in Invicta Film Partnerhip No 25, which is being investigated by HMRC. Solicitor-general 2014-. Member: Conservative Group for Europe; Tory Reform Group. Member, select cttees: justice 2014; standards 2014-15; human rights 2013-15; standards and privileges 2012-14; justice 2010-13. Contested Swindon South 2005; Preseli Pembrokeshire 1997; Islwyn 1995. Cllr, Dyfed CC 1993-96. Crown Court recorder. Society of Conservative Lawyers. Co-ordinator, Swindon SEN Network. Anglican. Enjoys rugby and cricket. Married, two children. Ed: St Michael's School, Bryn; Hatfield Coll, Durham (BA law).

CHALLENGERS
Anne Snelgrove (Lab) MP for Swindon South 2005-10. PPS to Gordon Brown 2009-10. Former drama teacher and LEA adviser. Cllr: Berkshire CC 1993-8; Bracknell TC 1995-99. Contested Bracknell 1997. Married. Ed: City University. **John Short** (Ukip) Former deputy CEO, Swindon BC. **Damon Hooton** (LD) Retired from army, works for Sainsbury's. Cllr: Frome TC 2007-; mayor of Frome 2009-10; Mendip DC 2003-. Married, three sons.

CONSTITUENCY PROFILE
With economic expansion has come population growth, Swindon being split into two seats in 1997. Swindon South also includes some more rural areas to the south of the town, including several villages and the town of Wroughton, whose former RAF base is now home of the Science Museum's storage depot. It is the marginally more Labour seat, with more social housing and ethnic diversity.

	Electorate	Turnout %	from 2010 %	Change
	73,956	66.6		
R Buckland C	22,777	46.2	+4.5	
A Snelgrove Lab	16,992	34.5	+0.2	
J Short Ukip	5,920	12.0	+7.7	
D Hooton LD	1,817	3.7	-13.9	
T Kimberley-Fairbourn Green	1,757	3.6	+2.3	

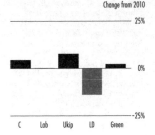

Change from 2010

Tamworth

CONSERVATIVE HOLD

CHRISTOPHER PINCHER
BORN Sep 24, 1969
MP 2010-

IT consultant and history buff; cites Duff Cooper and William Pitt among political heroes. Midlander, born in Walsall and raised in Wombourne. Member, select cttees: ECC 2010-; standing order 2011-; armed forces bill 2011. Member, 1922 committee. Treasurer, Conservative Friends of Azerbaijan. Contested: Tamworth 2005; Warley 1997. Conservative Way Forward. Member: Tamworth's Hodge Lane Nature Reserve; the Peel Society. Patron, Canwell Show. Consultancy career as manager at Dublin-based Accenture. Former deputy dir, Conservative Collegiate Forum. Grand Prix and horse-racing enthusiast. Ed: Ounsdale Sch, Wolverhampton; LSE (BSc government & history).

CHALLENGERS
Carol Dean (Lab) Office manager

for Richard Burden MP. Cllr, Staffordshire CC 2013-, 2001-09. School governor. Married, three children. **Jan Higgins** (Ukip) Former manager, family support charity. **Jenny Pinkett** (LD) Retired teacher. Contested: Tamworth 2010, 2001, 1997; Cannock Chase 2005. Married, two children. Ed: Cartrefle Coll, Wrexham; Open University (BA; Adv Dip education).

CONSTITUENCY PROFILE
Consists of the compact Tamworth council area itself and some rural wards of Lichfield to the west and north. Historically the seat is most associated with Sir Robert Peel, whose 1834 Tamworth manifesto was the foundation of the modern Conservative party. It is a Conservative-Labour marginal, held by the Tory whip and former regimental sergeant-major David Lightbown until his death in 1996, after which it was won by Labour on a 22 per cent swing. The seat won back by the Conservatives in 2010.

	Electorate	Turnout %	from 2010 %	Change
	71,912	65.6		
C Pincher C	23,606	50.0	+4.3	
C Dean Lab	12,304	26.1	-6.6	
J Higgins Ukip	8,727	18.5	+13.6	
J Pinkett LD	1,427	3.0	-13.2	
N Holmes Green	1,110	2.4		

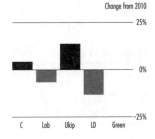

Change from 2010

Tatton

CONSERVATIVE HOLD

GEORGE OSBORNE
BORN May 23, 1971
MP 2001-

Shrewd political operator, feared rather than loved within his own party and beyond. Chancellor of the exchequer 2010-; first secretary of state 2015-. Inextricably linked to David Cameron. Masterminded 2010 election campaign. Politically courageous but seen as arrogant by many Tory MPs. Cut his hair and went on 5:2 diet in effort to appeal more to voters. Was caught up in so-called yachtgate affair in 2008. Shad chancellor 2005-10. Shad chief sec, Treasury 2004-05. Shad min, econ affairs 2003-04. Opp whip 2003. Head of CRD political section 1994-5. Downing St pol office 1997, shad cab sec. William Hague's political sec and speechwriter 1997-2001. Freelance journalist. Married, one daughter, one son. Ed: St Paul's Sch; Magdalen Coll, Oxford (BA history).

CHALLENGERS
David Pinto-Duschinsky (Lab) Managing dir, Africa regional office for Standard Chartered Bank. Former SPAD to Charles Clarke and Alistair Darling. Ed: Oxford University (BA PPE); Harvard University (MA public policy). **Stuart Hutton** (Ukip) Chartered engineer. **Gareth Wilson** (LD) IT software designer. Married, two children. Ed: Altrincham GS.

CONSTITUENCY PROFILE
A semi-rural seat in Cheshire, Tatton lies to the immediate southwest of Greater Manchester, and largely consists of affluent villages. In 1997 this traditionally Tory seat was lost to the news reporter Martin Bell, who stood as an independent candidate against the incumbent Neil Hamilton, who had become embroiled in the cash-for-questions scandal. Labour and the Liberal Democrats stood aside for Bell and he successfully won the seat.

	Electorate	Turnout %	from 2010 %	Change
	64,512	70.2		
G Osborne C	26,552	58.6	+4.0	
D Pinto-Duschinsky Lab	8,311	18.4	+1.1	
S Hutton Ukip	4,871	10.8		
G Wilson LD	3,850	8.5	-14.1	
T L Rothery Green	1,714	3.8		

Change from 2010

25%

0%

-25%

C   Lab   Ukip   LD   Green

Taunton Deane

CONSERVATIVE GAIN

REBECCA POW
BORN Oct 10, 1960
MP 2015-

Broadcaster, journalist and gardener, has lived in constituency for 27 years. Selected in open primary. Former BBC, ITV and C4 reporter. Worked for NFU. Set up own public relations and communications business. Former cllr, Stoke St Mary. Married, three children. Ed: Imperial Coll London (BSc rural environment studies).

CHALLENGERS
Rachel Gilmour (LD) Dir, Rachel Gilmour Associates management consultancy. British Red Cross fundraiser. Previously head of strategy, planning and resources, UK Environment Agency, and director of communications at NFU (first woman on its board). Former media adviser to Sir Nick Harvey MP. Lectured at Somerset College of Arts and Technology. Cllr, Mid Devon DC

1995-. Contested: Nottingham North 1997; Totnes 2001. French speaker. Married, four children. Ed: Cheltenham Ladies Coll; SOAS (law); King's Coll, London (BA English). **Laura Bailhache** (Ukip) Solicitor. Ed: University of Oxford (history), UWE (BA law studies). **Neil Guild** (Lab) Local government officer and former soldier. Married, two children. Ed: Kings Coll, Taunton; University of Swansea (BA history).

CONSTITUENCY PROFILE
Set in the vale between Quantocks and Blackdown Hills, Taunton is the county town of Somerset. The seat includes the industrial town of Wellington to the west. It was traditionally a Tory seat, but was won with a 3,000 vote majority by the Lib Dems in 1997 and has changed hands between the two parties since then. There was a name change and relatively minor boundary changes in 2010, which brought the seat into line with the local council boundaries.

	Electorate	Turnout %	from 2010 %	Change
	81,830	70.7		
R Pow C	27,849	48.1	+5.9	
R Gilmour LD	12,358	21.4	-27.7	
L Bailhache Ukip	6,921	12.0	+8.3	
N Guild Lab	5,347	9.2	+4.1	
C Martin Green	2,630	4.5		
M Rigby Ind	2,568	4.4		
S German TUSC	118	0.2		
B Gauld Ind	96	0.2		

Change from 2010

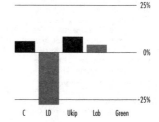

25%

0%

-25%

C   LD   Ukip   Lab   Green

Telford

CONSERVATIVE GAIN

LUCY ALLAN
BORN Oct 2, 1964
MP 2015-

Chartered accountant. Non-exec dir, Wandsworth NHS. Founder, Family First child protection campaign. Cllr, Wandsworth BC 2006-12. School governor. Married, one son. Ed: University of Durham (BA anthropology); Kingston Law School (LLM law).

CHALLENGERS
David Wright (Lab) MP 2001-15. Known as "demolition Dave" for his record in levelling tower blocks. Opp whip 2010-12. Asst govt whip 2009-10. Member, select cttees: administration 2013-15; armed forces bill 2011; selection 2010-13; CLG 2009, 2007; draft civil continencies bill 2003; procedure 2001-05; environmental audit 2001-05. PPS to: Jane Kennedy 2007-08; John Hutton 2006; David Miliband 2005-6; Rosie Winterton 2004-05. Cllr: Oakengates TC

1989-2000; Wrekin DC 1989-97. Local govt officer. Housing strategy manager Sandwell MBC. Married. Ed: Wrockwardine Wood Comp, Shropshire; New Coll, Telford; Wolverhampton Poly (BA humanities). **Denis Allen** (Ukip) Former RAF officer and KwikFit management trainer. Cllr, Telford and Wrekin Council 2013-. Former North Shrophire and Telford and Wrekin cllr for Conservatives. Conteted North Shropshire 1997 for Referendum Party; Telford 2010 for Ukip. Ed: Bedford Modern.

CONSTITUENCY PROFILE
Telford is a rapidly growing new town development. There is significant high tech and computer industry here, and HMRC is a major local employer. It is a marginal seat and until 1997 it was part of The Wrekin, a Tory-Labour marginal. In 1997 the expanding population lead to the creation of a new Telford seat, which was held by Labour up until the 2015 election.

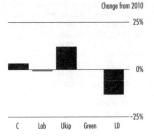

	Electorate	Turnout %	Change from 2010 %
	66,166	61.4	
L Allan C	16,094	39.6	+3.3
D Wright Lab	15,364	37.8	-0.9
D Allen Ukip	7,330	18.0	+12.2
P Hawkins Green	930	2.3	
I Croll LD	927	2.3	-13.2

Change from 2010

C   Lab   Ukip   Green   LD

Tewkesbury

CONSERVATIVE HOLD

LAURENCE ROBERTSON
BORN Mar 29, 1958
MP 1997-

The Nicholas Winterton of his day. Rightwinger whose comments on immigration have caused controversy. His assistant Mark Calway, referred to the Prophet Muhammad as a child abuser in a tweet. Shadow min: NI 2005-10; Treasury 2003-05; trade and industry 2003. Opposition whip 2001-03. Elected unopposed as chairman, select cttee: NI 2010-15. Member: liaison 2010-15; education & skills 2001; social security 1999-2001. Consultant in industrial management, charity fundraising and PR. Factory owner. Divorced, remarried. Ed: St James' CofE Secondary Sch; Farnworth GS; Bolton Higher Ed Inst (management service Dip).

CHALLENGERS
Ed Buxton (Lab) Governor, 2gether NHS Trust. Cllr, Brockworth

PC 2010-. Aid worker in former Yugolavia in the 1990s. Married. **Alistair Cameron** (LD) English teacher and clerk to three school governing bodies. Cllr: Cheltenham BC 1986-98; Gloucestershire CC 2000-05. Contested: Tewkesbury 2010, 2005; Gloucestershire PCC 2012. Ed: Bristol University (BA history). **Stuart Adair** (Ukip) Project programmer, DX Group. Gloucestershire county chairman, Ukip 2014-. Contested: Gloucestershire CC 2013; Tewkesbury BC 2015.

CONSTITUENCY PROFILE
The rural north of Gloucestershire, Tewkesbury and countryside between Cheltenham and Gloucester. It includes outskirts of Cheltenham (villages of Prestbury and Swindon Village) and Gloucester (Longford and Churchdown) and the north of the Cotswolds Area of Outstanding Natural Beauty. A reliable Tory seat, held in various forms since the late nineteenth century.

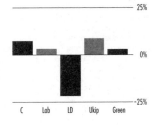

	Electorate	Turnout %	Change from 2010 %
	78,500	70.5	
L Robertson C	30,176	54.5	+7.3
E Buxton Lab	8,204	14.8	+3.2
A Cameron LD	7,629	13.8	-21.7
S Adair Ukip	7,128	12.9	+8.8
J Clarke Green	2,207	4.0	+3.0

Change from 2010

C   Lab   LD   Ukip   Green

Thanet North

CONSERVATIVE HOLD

SIR ROGER GALE
BORN Aug 20, 1943
MP 1983-

Belligerent backbencher. Vice-chairman, Conservative party 2001-03. Member, parly assembly of Council of Europe 2012-15. Member, select cttees: procedure 2007-15; panel of chairs 1997-15; televising of proceedings of the House 1987-89; home affairs 1987-92. PPS to: Jeremy Hanley 1993-94; Archibald Hamilton 1992-93. Television producer, director and broadcaster; rose to BBC director of children's television. Belonged to NUJ and acting unions. Contested Birmingham Northfield 1982. Divorced twice, remarried. One daughter from second marriage, two sons from third marriage. Ed: Hardye's Sch; Guildhall Sch of Music and Drama (LGSM&D).

CHALLENGERS
Piers Wauchope (Ukip) Barrister. Former Conservative cllr in Camden. Cllr, Tunbridge Wells 2012-. Contested Hampstead & Highgate 2005 for Conservatives. Contested Kent PCC 2012 for Ukip. Chairman, Society of Ukip Lawyers. Member, Ukip NEC. **Frances Rehal** (Lab) PhD student. Early years consultant. Children's centre locality coordinator, Kent CC. Awarded MBE for services to children and families. School governor. Married, one daughter, one son. Ed: University of Greenwich (BSc health visiting); Canterbury Christ Church University (PhD, completing).

CONSTITUENCY PROFILE
Consists of the northeastern coast of Kent, made up of the seaside towns of Margate, Westgate-on-Sea, Birchington and Herne Bay with their rural hinterlands. Despite the comparative poverty in Thanet, this is a solid, safe Conservative seat. Thanet North has been held by Sir Roger Gale since its creation in 1983, when Cherie Blair stood for Labour.

	Electorate	Turnout %	Change from 2010 %
	70,504	66.7	
R Gale C	23,045	49.0	-3.7
P Wauchope Ukip	12,097	25.7	+19.2
F Rehal Lab	8,411	17.9	-3.6
E Targett Green	1,719	3.7	
G Cunningham LD	1,645	3.5	-15.9
C Mckenzie Thanet	136	0.3	

Change from 2010

(bar chart: C Ukip Lab Green LD, range -25% to 25%)

Thanet South

CONSERVATIVE HOLD

CRAIG MACKINLAY
BORN Oct 7, 1966
MP 2015-

Former leader of Ukip, rightwinger with an especially checkered political history. Party leader 1997, deputy leader 1997-2000 but defected to Tories in 2005. Chartered accountant, specialist in tax affairs. Partner at Beak Kemmenoe accountants. Cllr, Medway BC 2007-. Contested: Gillingham 2005, 1997, 1992; Totnes 2001; Kent PCC election 2012; EU elections London 1999, SE England 2004. Previously member of Anti-Federalist League. Married. Ed: Rainham Mark GS; University of Birmingham (BSc zoology & comparative physiology). Member, Institute of Chartered Accountants, Chartered Institute of Taxation.

CHALLENGERS
Nigel Farage (Ukip) Pint-swigging Ukip co-founder and leader 2010-, 2006-09. Resignation rejected. Chairman, EFD in Euro parl. MEP, South East England 1999-. Contested Buckingham 2010. Suffered non-life threatening injuries after plane he was travelling in flying pro-Ukip banner crashed on polling day 2010. Commodities trader. Divorced, remarried. Two sons from first marriage, two daughters from second. Ed: Dulwich Coll. **Will Scobie** (Lab) Cllr: Kent CC 2013-; Thanet DC 2011-. Mayor of Margate 2012-13. Former parly asst to Mary Honeyball MEP. Married, two children. Ed: Dane Court GS; University of York (history and politics); University of Kent (MA European governance).

CONSTITUENCY PROFILE
A coastal seat, snaking around the eastern coast of the Isle of Thanet, south into Dover to include historic port of Sandwich and rural villages inland from it. The seat was held by the Conservatives during the Thatcher years but fell to Labour in 1997, before being recpatured by the Tories in 2010.

	Electorate	Turnout %	Change from 2010 %
	70,182	70.4	
C Mackinlay C	18,838	38.1	-9.9
N Farage Ukip	16,026	32.4	+26.9
W Scobie Lab	11,740	23.8	-7.6
I Driver Green	1,076	2.2	
R Timpson LD	932	1.9	-13.2
A Murray ND	318	0.6	
R Bailey Manston	191	0.4	
N Askew Reality	126	0.3	
G Birchall Thanet	63	0.1	
D McCastree Ind	61	0.1	
Z Abu-Obadiah Zeb	30	0.1	

Change from 2010

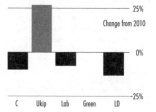

(bar chart: C Ukip Lab Green LD, range -25% to 25%)

Thirsk & Malton

CONSERVATIVE HOLD

KEVIN HOLLINRAKE
BORN Sep 28, 1963
MP 2015-

Local man, suceeds Anne McIntosh who was deselected. MD and co-founder of Hunters estate agents. Co-owner of Vizzihome, later bought by online-property market giants, Zoopla. Previously branch manager of international financial services company, Prudential. Tory PPC for Dewsbury 2010, but stepped aside owing to business committments. Married, four children. Ed: Easingwold School; Sheffield Hallam University (BSc physics, did not complete).

CHALLENGERS
Alan Avery (Lab) Runs Blackthorn Press publishers. Retired army officer and English teacher. Cllr, Pickering TC 1986-90. School governor. Married, three sons. Ed: UoW (BA history); KCL (MA war studies). **Toby Horton** (Ukip) Dir, television production

company. Former chairman of the Richmond Tory Association and aide to William Hague MP, then Conservative party leader. Contested: Sedgefield 1983; Rother Valley 1992 for Conservatives; Sedgefield 2007, Thirsk & Malton 2010 for Ukip. **Di Keal** (LD) Media and communications manager at Alzheimer's Society. Former comms worker at Defra. Cllr, Rydale DC 2012-, 2003-11. Married, three daughters. Ed: Beverley HS; University of Warwick (BA sociology & social administration).

CONSTITUENCY PROFILE
An affluent rural seat in North Yorkshire, with a high rate of owner-occupiers and low unemployment. The economy is largely based on tourism and agriculture, but many residents commute into York. The seat was created in 2010, but it and its predecessors have returned Conservative MPs since the 19th century, apart from a brief Lib Dem period after a by-election in 1986.

	Electorate	Turnout %	Change from 2010 %
	77,451	67.6	
K Hollinrake C	27,545	52.6	-0.3
A Avery Lab	8,089	15.5	+1.9
T Horton Ukip	7,805	14.9	+8.4
D Keal LD	4,703	9.0	-14.3
C Newsam Green	2,404	4.6	
J Clark Lib	1,127	2.2	-1.6
P Tate Ind	692	1.3	

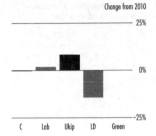

Change from 2010

Thornbury & Yate

CONSERVATIVE GAIN

LUKE HALL
BORN Jul 8, 1986
MP 2015-

Southwest area manager, Farmfoods. Former district manager for Lidl. Constituency chairman, south Gloucestershire Conservatives and deputy chairman, Bristol and South Gloucestershire Conservatives. Nominated for 2013 National Conservative Excellence Awards for his campaigning in South Gloucestershire. Ed: John Cabot Academy.

CHALLENGERS
Steve Webb (LD) MP 1997-2015. Softly spoken, left-leaning economist with detailed knowledge of the benefits system. Min: work & pensions 2010-15. Shad sec: work & pensions 2009-10; energy & climate change 2008-09. Shad min: countryside 2008. Shad sec: efra 2007-08. Chairman, LD manifesto team 2006-07. Shad sec: health

2005-; work & pensions 2001-05. Member, select cttee, ecclesiastical 2002-05. Spokes, social security and welfare 1997-2001. Institute for Fiscal Studies. Social policy professor, University of Bath. Ed: Hertford Coll, Oxford Uni (BA PPE). **Russ Martin** (Ukip) Former Chairman of South Gloucestershire Federation of Small Business. Wiorks in security management and training. **Hadleigh Roberts** (Lab) Account executive, Remarkable Group marketing agency. Ed: University of Bath (BA French & Spanish; MA interpreting & translation, president Labour society).

CONSTITUENCY PROFILE
A swathe of market towns and villages to the north of Bristol, mostly affluent commuter towns and villages. High economic growth; low unemployment. The seat's predecessor, Northavon, was narrowly won from the Conservatives by Steve Webb in 1997.

	Electorate	Turnout %	Change from 2010 %
	65,884	73.7	
L Hall C	19,924	41.0	+3.9
S Webb LD	18,429	37.9	-14.0
R Martin Ukip	5,126	10.6	+7.0
H Roberts Lab	3,775	7.8	+0.8
I Hamilton Green	1,316	2.7	

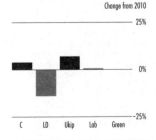

Change from 2010

Thurrock

CONSERVATIVE HOLD

JACKIE DOYLE-PRICE
BORN Aug 5, 1969
MP 2010-

Asst whip 2015-. Having first been elected in 2010 with UK's 5th smallest majority - 95 - she held the seat in 2015, increasing her margin to 536. Interest in financial services and the economy: previously an associate for the Financial Services Authority. Member, select cttee: public accounts 2010-14. Chairwoman, APPG Gurkha welfare. Former: assistant private sec, lord mayor of City of London 2000-05; parliamentary officer, City of London. Contested Sheffield Hillsborough 2005. Ed: Notre Dame RC Sch, Sheffield; Durham (BA economics & politics).

CHALLENGERS
Polly Billington (Lab) Head of comms and campaigns, Citizens' Advice. Special adviser: Ed Miliband 2007-10; Labour

party 2010-2013. Previously BBC reporter and producer. Ed: University of Sussex (BA history & French); UCLan (PgDip broadcast journalism). **Tim Aker** (Ukip) MEP, East of England. 2014-. Cllr, Thurrock BC 2014-. Former head of Ukip policy unit. Previously worked for Taxpayers' Alliance and Get Britain Out. Ed: University of Nottingham (BA history & politics). **Rhodri Jamieson-Ball** (LD) Education consultant. Former transport planner. Cllr, Islington LB 2006-14.

CONSTITUENCY PROFILE
An industrial and largely white working class seat on the Thames Estuary, including the major container port of Tilbury. Also covers more affluent areas such as the Chafford Hundred development, near the Lakeside shopping centre. A fierce three-way battle in 2015 ended with the Tories taking 34 per cent of the vote, Labour 33 per cent and Ukip 32 per cent.

	Electorate	Turnout %	Change from 2010 %
	77,569	63.9	
J Doyle-Price C	16,692	33.7	-3.1
P Billington Lab	16,156	32.6	-4.0
T Aker Ukip	15,718	31.7	+24.3
R Jamieson-Ball LD	644	1.3	-9.4
J Barnes CSA	244	0.5	
D Munyambu ND	79	0.2	
A Kristilolu AP	31	0.1	

Change from 2010

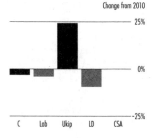

Tiverton & Honiton

CONERVATIVE HOLD

NEIL PARISH
BORN May 26, 1956
MP 2010-

A farmer committed to rural interests. PPS to John Hayes 2014-15. Member, select cttee: environment, foot and rural affairs 2010-. Member APPGs: beef & lamb; eggs, pig and poultry; dairy. MEP, South West 1999-2009. Euro parly agriculture spokes, deputy Con chief whip. Chairman: Australia and New Zealand delegation 2004-07; agriculture and rural development, 2007-09. Contested Pontypool 1997. Cllr: Sedgemoor DC 1983-96; Somerset CC 1989-93. Election monitor for Zimbabwe presidential election 2000. Animal welfare campaigner; previously managed family farm. Married, one daughter, one son. Ed: Brymore Agricultural Sch; Taunton Coll.

CHALLENGERS
Graham Smith (Ukip) Handyman.

Former cabinetmaker. Chairman, Tiverton and Honiton Ukip branch. Married, three children. **Caroline Kolek** (Lab) Teacher. Cllr, Honiton TC 2014-, mayor 2015-. Member, Assoc of Teachers and Lecturers. Council member, General Teaching Council for England 2008-12. Married, four children, two step-children. Ed: Open University (BA) Exeter (MA). **Stephen Kearney** (LD) Businessman. CEO of charity Regenerate. Visiting lecturer, University of Brighton. Founding dir, UK Youth Parliament. **Paul Edwards** (Green) Casual administrative assistant.

CONSTITUENCY PROFILE
An ultra-safe Conservative seat covering the eastern part of Devon along the borders with Somerset and Dorset. It includes two areas of outstanding natural beauty. Tiverton, once at the heart of the lace-making industry, is now a dormitory town for Exeter. Other main centres are Honiton, Axminster and Seaton.

	Electorate	Turnout %	Change from 2010 %
	76,270	70.5	
N Parish C	29,030	54.0	+3.7
G Smith Ukip	8,857	16.5	+10.5
C Kolek Lab	6,835	12.7	+3.8
S Kearney LD	5,626	10.5	-22.9
P Edwards Green	3,415	6.4	+4.9

Change from 2010

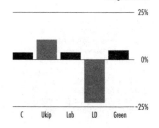

Tonbridge & Malling

CONSERVATIVE HOLD

THOMAS TUGENDHAT
BORN Jun 27, 1973
MP 2015-

Strategy expert. Dir, strategy consultancy, Lashkar & Co. Army officer, TA; when Iraq war broke out in 2003 he, as an Arabic speaker, was mobilised. Helped to establish the National Security Council of Afghanistan. Adviser to governor, Helmand Province 2006-07. MBE for operations in Afghanistan 2010. Military assistant to chief of defence staff 2010-13. Strategic advisory panel, Arthur John Capital 2013-15. Former energy analyst. Established Armed Forces Muslim Assoc. Speaks five languages including Pashto and Arabic. Married, one son. Ed: University of Bristol (BA theology) Gonville & Caius Coll, Cambridge (MPhil Islamic studies).

CHALLENGERS
Robert Izzard (Ukip) Retired IT sales manager, Adobe Software.

Claire Leigh (Lab) Head of international partnerships, Overseas Development Institute think-tank. Chairwoman, Labour campaign for international development. Former senior policy adviser, Cabinet Office. Member, Fabian Society Women's Network. Ed: Cambridge (BA history), Oxford (MPhil politics & international relations). **Mary Varrall** (LD) Garden designer and consultant. Former chairwoman, Etchingham PC. Contested Bexhill and Battle 2010, 2005.

CONSTITUENCY PROFILE
A rural seat with the market town of Tonbridge at its heart. Covers a wide expanse of west Kent, from Edenbridge to East Peckham. An affluent and attractive swathe of the London commuter belt, and as solidly Conservative as would be expected. Held by Sir John Stanley from its creation in 1974 until his retirement in 2015 with no serious threat to the long-term Tory dominance.

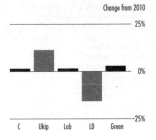

	Electorate	Turnout %	Change from 2010 %
	74,877	71.7	
T Tugendhat C	31,887	59.4	+1.5
R Izzard Ukip	8,153	15.2	+11.5
C Leigh Lab	7,604	14.2	+1.6
M Varrall LD	3,660	6.8	-15.7
H Porter Green	2,366	4.4	+2.9

Change from 2010

Tooting

LABOUR HOLD

SADIQ KHAN
BORN Aug 18, 1970
MP 2005-

Running for London mayor 2016. Opposed 90-day detention for terror suspects. First Muslim to attend Cabinet. Shadow lord chancellor 2010-15. Shad SoS: justice 2010-15; transport 2010. Shad min for London 2013-15. Min, transport 2009-10. Parly under-sec, CLG 2008-09. Asst govt whip 2007-08. Member, public accounts select cttee 2005-07. PPS to Jack Straw 2007. Cllr, Wandsworth BC 1994-2006, dep leader Lab group 1996-2001. Former human rights lawyer. GMB, Unison, CWU. Chairman, Muslim Council of Britain's legal affairs cttee. Married, two daughters. Ed: University of North London (LLB law); Coll of Law, Guildford (Law Soc finals).

CHALLENGERS
Dan Watkins (C) Business development dir, Energy Alert risk agency. Founder, Contact

Law 2006-. Volunteer, Careers Development Group 2011-. Married. Ed: Tiffin GS; Cambridge University (BA economics). **Esther Obiri-Darko** (Green) Chemistry teacher. Member: UN Women UK; Women Worldwide Advancing Freedom and Equality. Ed: University of British Columbia (chemistry, earth science). **Philip Ling** (LD) Strategic pricing manager, Thomson Reuters. Treasurer, Chinese Lib Dems. **Przemek De Skuba Skwirczynski** (Ukip) Investment banker. Ed: Wellington Coll, LSE (BSc economics).

CONSTITUENCY PROFILE
A densley populated and traditionally working-class area. There is a large Asian population, particularly Indian and Pakistani residents, and a large black community. Attractive housing and good transport links have drawn in middle-class professionals. Labour is still managing to fight off a strong Tory challenge here.

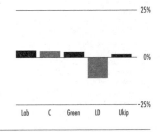

	Electorate	Turnout %	Change from 2010 %
	76,778	69.7	
S Khan Lab	25,263	47.2	+3.7
D Watkins C	22,421	41.9	+3.4
E Obiri-Darko Green	2,201	4.1	+2.9
P Ling LD	2,107	3.9	-10.9
P D S Skwirczynski Ukip	1,537	2.9	+1.6

Change from 2010

Torbay

CONSERVATIVE GAIN

KEVIN FOSTER
BORN Dec 31, 1978
MP 2015-

Cllr, Coventry CC 2002-14, opposition leader 2011-13. Member, Torquay town centre community partnership steering group. Worked for Philip Bradbourn, MEP for the West Midlands; company secretary, AW CompuTech 2005-11; Paralegel, Howell & Co 2003-04; Contested Coventry South 2010. Trustee, Coventry Law Centre 2004-08. Interests include military history. Ed: Hele's Sch, Plymouth; University of Warwick (LLM, international economic law); BVC.

CHALLENGERS
Adrian Sanders (LD) MP 1997-2015. Opposition deputy chief whip 2006-10. Shad spokes: CLG 1997-2002; Defra 1999-2001. Oppositon whip, commons 1997-2001. Select cttees: panel of chairs 2013-2015; transport 2013-15; CMS 2005-13; modernisation of the HoC 2006-

08; selection 2006-10; office of the deputy PM: housing, planning, local govt and regions 2003-05. Cllr, Torbay BC 1984-86. Previously in insurance. Married. Ed: Torquay Boys' GS. **Tony McIntyre** (Ukip) Retired teacher. Dir, Devon Wheels to Work. Chairman, Ukip SW 2013-. Contested Taunton Deane 2010. Married, one child. Ed: Oswestry Sch; Bede Coll (Cert Ed); Open University (BA). **Su Maddock** (Lab) Fellow, Manchester Business Sch. Dir, Whitehall Innovation Hub 2007-10. Ed: Leeds (BSc psychology).

CONSTITUENCY PROFILE
Torbay is a natural bay on the south coast and is a popular tourist destination, making the industry an important employer. It is also a powerful magnet for retired people. The seat is a marginal between the Liberal Democrats and the Conservatives, and the former MP Adrian Sanders had a majority of only 12 when he was elected in 1997.

	Electorate	Turnout %	Change from 2010 %
	76,259	63.1	
K Foster C	19,551	40.7	+2.0
A Sanders LD	16,265	33.8	-13.2
T McIntyre Ukip	6,540	13.6	+8.3
S Maddock Lab	4,166	8.7	+2.1
P Hermes Green	1,557	3.2	+2.3

Change from 2010

[bar chart: C, LD, Ukip, Lab, Green with scale 25% / 0% / -25%]

Torfaen

LABOUR HOLD

NICK THOMAS-SYMONDS
BORN May 26, 1980
MP 2015-

Barrister, Civitas Law, specialising in chancery and commercial law. Secretary, Torfaen Constituency Labour party 2009-15. Replaces former Welsh secretary Paul Murphy who stepped down. Previously lecturer in politics, St Edmund Hall, Oxford. Fellow, Royal Historical Society. Author of biographies of Clement Attlee and Aneurin Bevan. Member, Unite. Married, two daughters. Ed: St Alban's RC HS, Pontypool; St Edmund Hall, Oxford (BA PPE); University of Glamorgan (PDip law); Cardiff University (BVC).

CHALLENGERS
Graham Smith (C) Railway engineer. Adviser and campaign manager to parly and local govt candidates. Cllr, Torfaen CBC 2008-. Ed: Caerleon Comp Sch; Brunel University (BEng

mechanical engineering). **Ken Beswick** (Ukip) Businessman, office supplies and printing. Previously management accountant. Former: officer, Royal Naval Reserve; cllr, Torfaen BC. Ed: Monkton House Sch, Cardiff. **Boydd Hackley-Green** (PC) Farmer. Previously worked in the financial sector. Helped set up Varteg and Garndiffaith Voice. **Alison Willott** (LD) Chairwoman, Monmouth and Torfaen Lib Dems. Cllr, Merton BC 1994-98. Former teacher. Contested several elections.

CONSTITUENCY PROFILE
A safe Labour seat to the north of Newport held, along with its predecessor, since 1918, although the size of the majority is steadily declining. It was 24,536 in 1997. Once famed for its coal and iron industries, these have been replaced by manufacturing. Leo Abse, the pioneer of divorce and gay rights legislation in the Sixties, was MP here from 1958 to 1987.

	Electorate	Turnout %	Change from 2010 %
	61,896	61.3	
N Thomas-Symonds Lab	16,938	44.7	-0.1
G Smith C	8,769	23.1	+3.1
K Beswick Ukip	7,203	19.0	+16.7
B Hackley-Green PC	2,169	5.7	+0.4
A Willott LD	1,271	3.4	-13.3
M Cooke Green	746	2.0	+0.8
J Cox Soc Lab	697	1.8	
M Griffiths Communist	144	0.4	

Change from 2010

[bar chart: Lab, C, Ukip, PC, LD with scale 25% / 0% / -25%]

Totnes

SARAH WOLLASTON
BORN Feb 27, 1962
MP 2010-

A popular local MP whose majority has soared from 4,927 on her election in 2010 to 18,285 in 2015. Select cttees: health 2010- (chairwoman 2014-); liaison 2014-; Previously NHS doctor for 24 years including 11 as GP in South Devon; examiner for the Royal College of GPs. Former police forensic examiner. Member: BMA; RCGP. Married, two daughters, one son. Ed: Tal-Handaq Service Children's Sch, Malta; Watford GS; Guy's Hospital Medical Sch (BSc pathology); KCL (UMDS medicine).

CHALLENGERS
Justin Haque (Ukip) Stockbroker. Recently launched software company with his wife. Ed: Wandsworth Comp; Newcastle (history & politics). **Nicky Williams** (Lab) Fundraiser, RSPB and Woodland Trust. Cllr,

Plymouth CC 2010-14. Contested PCC election Devon 2012. Partner, two children. Ed: Open University (BA social sciences). **Gill Coombs** (Green) Self-employed learning and development practitioner. Ed: Trowbridge Coll (Ad Cert therapeutic counselling); Schumacher Coll, Plymouth Uni (MSc hollistic science). **Julian Brazil** (LD) Bookkeeper. Cllr: Devon CC 2005-; South Hams DC 2003-.

CONSTITUENCY PROFILE
One of the largest coastal constituencies in England so tourism, farming and fishing are key local industries. There are many service sector jobs and unemployment is low. Home ownership is high and the proportion of people over sixty is among the biggest in the UK. An affluent and picturesque area that been represented by the Conservatives since 1924, although until 2015 the Lib Dems were always contenders.

	Electorate	Turnout %	from 2010 %	Change
		68,630	68.6	
S Wollaston C		24,941	53.0	+7.1
J Haque Ukip		6,656	14.1	+8.1
N Williams Lab		5,988	12.7	+5.3
G Coombs Green		4,845	10.3	+7.8
J Brazil LD		4,667	9.9	-25.7

Change from 2010

Tottenham

DAVID LAMMY
BORN Jul 19, 1972
MP 2000-

Seeking Labour nomination for London mayor in 2016. Shadow min, higher education & intellectual property 2010. Min: higher education & intellectual property 2008-10. Parly under-sec, DIUS 2007-08, Min: culture 2005-07; constitutional affairs 2003-05; health 2002-03. Select cttees include: works of art 2010-15; ecclesiastical 2010-15. PPS to Estelle Morris 2001-02. Member: GLA 2000; Archbishops' Council 1999-2002. Member: Fabian Soc; Christian Socialist Movement. Barrister at Lincoln's Inn. Author of *Out of the Ashes: Britain After the Riots,* 2011. Married, three children. Ed: The King's Sch, Peterborough; SOAS (LLB law); Harvard Law Sch, (LLM).

CHALLENGERS
Stefan Mrozinski (C) Corporate

lawyer, associate at White & Case. Volunteered in Sierra Leone 2012. School governor. Married. Ed: LSE (LLB law); St John's Coll, Cambridge (MPhil international relations); Coll of Law (legal practice). **Dee Searle** (Green) Dir, Barleycomm Communication. Advisor, If Project 2014-, Wolfstar 2014-. Former dir of comms and external affairs, University of the Arts London. Ed: Stanford University Sch of Business; Queen Mary, London (BSc chemistry, biochemistry).

CONSTITUENCY PROFILE
An inner-city seat in north London with a multicultural population. A fifth of residents are black, there is a significant Asian presence and there are large Cypriot, Turkish, Irish, eastern European and Jewish communities. Blighted by crime, guns and drugs. Notorious for riots in 1985, when PC Keith Blakelock was killed, and in 2011. Has returned Labour MPs since 1935 and still a very safe seat.

	Electorate	Turnout %	from 2010 %	Change
		70,809	60.1	
D Lammy Lab		28,654	67.3	+8.0
S Mrozinski C		5,090	12.0	-2.9
D Searle Green		3,931	9.2	+6.8
T Ozen LD		1,756	4.1	-13.6
T Saeed Ukip		1,512	3.6	+2.4
J Sutton TUSC		1,324	3.1	+0.5
T Mahmood Peace		291	0.7	

Change from 2010

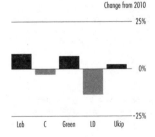

Truro & Falmouth

CONSERVATIVE HOLD

SARAH NEWTON
BORN Jul 19, 1961
MP 2010-

On entering parliament took her oath of allegiance in Cornish. She increased her majority from 435 to 14,000 in 2015. Asst whip 2015-. Select cttees: ecclesiastical 2014-; science & technology 2012-; administration 2010-12. Parliamentary ambassador for carers 2013-. APPGs: vice-chairwoman, social care; co-chairwoman, sepsis; arts and health. Cllr, Merton LBC. Former dir: International Longevity Centre. Dir, Age Concern England. Marketing career: Citibank, American Express. FRSA. Member, Falmouth Tall Ships Assoc. Married, two daughters, one son. Ed: Falmouth Sch; King's Coll London (BA history).

CHALLENGERS
Simon Rix (LD) Head of programmes, Good Growth. Cllr,

Cornwall C 2013-. Policy adviser to Simon Hughes MP 1994-95. Health and environmental campaigner. Married, two children. Ed: UCL (BSc phsyics & astronomy), University of Exeter (PgCert energy policy). **Stuart Roden** (Lab) Unison regional organiser. Cllr, Truro CC, mayor 2005-06. Former NHS worker. **John Hyslop** (Ukip) Consultant radiologist. Founding trustee, Heart Race Cornwall.

CONSTITUENCY PROFILE
Stretching from Perranporth on the north coast to the Roseland Peninsula in the south, the area is one of Cornwall's top leisure destinations. Based around the River Fal. The commercial port of Falmouth is an important employer and boasts one of the deepest natural harbours in the world. Low unemployment. Previously a strong Liberal Democrat seat, the Conservatives just pipped the party in 2010 after boundary changes and apear to be consolidating their hold.

	Electorate	Turnout %	from 2010 % Change
	73,601	70.0	
S Newton C	22,681	44.0	+2.3
S Rix LD	8,681	16.8	-24.0
S Roden Lab	7,814	15.2	+5.5
J Hyslop Ukip	5,967	11.6	+7.7
K Westbrook Green	4,483	8.7	+6.9
L Rich Ind	792	1.5	
S Richardson Meb Ker	563	1.1	-1.0
R Evans NHAP	526	1.0	
S Guffogg PPP	37	0.1	

Change from 2010

```
                                    25%

                                    0%

                                    -25%
   C      LD     Lab    Ukip   Green
```

Tunbridge Wells

CONSERVATIVE HOLD

GREG CLARK
BORN Aug 28, 1967
MP 2005-

Erudite moderniser from party's soft left. SoS: CLG 2015-. Min: universities, science & cities 2014-15; Cabinet Office 2013-15; decentralisation & cities 2010-12; Financial sec, Treasury 2012-13. Shadow SoS: energy and climate change 2008-10. Shad min: Cabinet Office 2007-08; charities, voluntary bodies & social enterprise 2006-07. Member, select cttee: public accounts 2005-07. Cllr, Westminster CC 2002-05. Director of policy, Conservative party 2001-05; special adviser to Ian Lang MP 1996-97. Former: BBC director of commercial policy; consultant, Boston Consulting Group; teaching and research assistant, LSE and Open University 1991-94. Married, two daughters, one son. Ed: St Peter's Comp, Middlesbrough; Magdalene Coll, Cambridge (BA economics); LSE (PhD).

CHALLENGERS
Kevin Kerrigan (Lab) Systems engineer, Cisco. Cllr, Horsmonden PC 2003-09. Married, four children. Ed: University Coll Cork (BEng electrical & electronics engineering). **Colin Nicholson** (Ukip) Runs window cleaning business. Vice-chairman, Ukip Tunbridge Wells. **James MacCleary** (LD) National literature and messaging manager, Lib Dems 2014-. SE campaigns officer, Lib Dems 2011-14. Lives with partner. **Marie Jones** (Green) Dir of office services business. Married, two sons, two step-sons.

CONSTITUENCY PROFILE
The spa town of Tunbridge Wells is surrounded by the agricultural land of the Weald and villages such as Lamberhurst, Goudhurst and Sandhurst. Popular tourist destination. A big retail centre. Affluent, popular with commuters, low unemployment. A very safe Conservative seat since its creation in 1974.

	Electorate	Turnout %	from 2010 % Change
	73,429	70.0	
G Clark C	30,181	58.7	+2.4
K Kerrigan Lab	7,307	14.2	+3.4
C Nicholson Ukip	6,481	12.6	+8.5
J MacCleary LD	4,342	8.4	-16.9
M Jones Green	2,659	5.2	+3.4
G Naismith Ind	458	0.9	+0.6

Change from 2010

```
                                    25%

                                    0%

                                    -25%
   C    Lab    Ukip    LD    Green
```

Twickenham

CONSERVATIVE GAIN

TANIA MATHIAS
BORN Jun 21, 1964
MP 2015-

Overturned Vince Cable's 12,000 majority to win the seat by 2,000 votes, making the former business secretary one of the election's most high profile casualties. Cllr, Richmond BC 2010-15. Doctor. Previously refugee worker for the United Nations. Member: BMA; British Assoc for Counselling and Psychotherapy; Wildfowl and Wetlands Trust; Amnesty International; Conservative Councillors' Assoc. Married. Ed: St Paul's Girls' School; Christ Church Coll, St Catherine's Coll, Oxford (medicine, JCR president).

CHALLENGERS
Vince Cable (LD) MP, Twickenham 1997-2015. SoS, BIS 2010-15. LD shad chancellor 2003-10. LD spokes 1997-2003. Acting leader, Lib Dems 2007. Cllr, Glasgow CC 1971-74,

Labour. Special adviser to: World Environ & Devt Commission; Commonwealth gen sec; John Smith. Chief economist, Shell. Former lecturer. Widowed, one daughter, two sons. Remarried. Ed: Fitzwilliam Coll, Cambridge (MA natural science; president Cambridge Union); Glasgow (PhD economics). **Nick Grant** (Lab) Barrister, head of legal services, Sainsbury's. Vice-chairman, Labour finance & industry group. Two children. Ed: York (BA English); Birkbeck, London (MSc politics); City University (Dip law); BVC.

CONSTITUENCY PROFILE
An affluent, residential constituency on the banks of the Thames best known as the home of English rugby. Good rail links to central London and low unemployment. Vince Cable took the seat for the Lib Dems from the long-serving MP Toby Jessel in 1997, and had steadily increased his majority until being unseated in 2015.

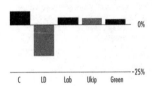

	Electorate	Turnout %	from 2010 %	Change
	80,242	77.3		
T Mathias C	25,580	41.3	+7.2	
V Cable LD	23,563	38.0	-16.4	
N Grant Lab	7,129	11.5	+3.8	
B Edwards Ukip	3,069	5.0	+3.5	
T Williams Green	2,463	4.0	+2.8	
D Stockford Christian	174	0.3		
D Wedgwood Magna Carta	26	0.0	-0.0	

Change from 2010

25%

0%

-25%

C   LD   Lab   Ukip   Green

Tynemouth

LABOUR HOLD

ALAN CAMPBELL
BORN Jul 8, 1957
MP 1997-

Opposition deputy chief whip 2010-15. Shadow min: home affairs 2010. Parly under-sec, home office 2008-10. Whip 2006-08; asst whip 2005-06. PPS to: Adam Ingram 2003-05; Lord Macdonald of Tradeston 2001-03. Select cttees: selection 2006-08, 2010-; public accounts 1997-2001. Treasurer, Northern group of Labour MPs 1999-2005. Campaign coordinator, Tynemouth Labour. Former teacher. Married, one daughter, one son. Ed: Blackfyne SS, Consett; Lancaster (BA politics); Leeds (PGCE); Newcastle Poly (MA history).

CHALLENGERS
Glenn Hall (C) Corporate lawyer. Cllr, Tunbridge Wells BC 2007-15. Campaigns for the National Autistic Society. Married, two children. Ed: Whickham Comp,

Gateshead; Durham University (BA history); Georgetown University (Fulbright Fellow). **Gary Legg** (Ukip) Technical and safety trainer and assessor, Northern Rail. Chairman, Ukip North Tyneside 2013-. RAF 1982-2010. Unite. Member, British Mountaineering Council. Married, two daughters. Ed: Preston HS; Glenrothes Coll (HNC computer support). **Julia Erskine** (Green) Former administrator. Contested Tynemouth 2010. **John Paton-Day** (LD) Artist. Cllr, Scottish Borders C 2007-. Married, two children. Ed: Coventry University.

CONSTITUENCY PROFILE
A coastal seat on the northern bank of the Tyne. Regeneration projects are under way in areas once dominated by coal mining and ship building. Coastal towns to the north are more middle class, with residents commuting to Newcastle. The seat returned Tory MPs from 1950 to 1997 but has been safely Labour ever since.

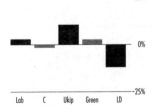

	Electorate	Turnout %	from 2010 %	Change
	77,523	69.0		
A Campbell Lab	25,791	48.2	+2.9	
G Hall C	17,551	32.8	-1.6	
G Legg Ukip	6,541	12.2	+10.5	
J Erskine Green	2,017	3.8	+2.8	
J Paton-Day LD	1,595	3.0	-11.9	

Change from 2010

25%

0%

-25%

Lab   C   Ukip   Green   LD

Tyneside North

LABOUR HOLD

MARY GLINDON
BORN Jan 13, 1957
MP 2010-

Interested in renewable energies, health and older people. Select cttees: CLG 2013-; environment, food and rural affairs 2010-. PPS to Mary Creagh MP. Cllr, North Tyneside 1995-2010, mayor 1999-2000. Administration officer, DWP and child maintenance and enforcement commission 2008-10. Worked in call centres, hospital, and as sales assistant. Voluntary sector work who ran North Shields People's Centre. GMB. Member, North Tyneside Trades Union Council. Founder, Battle Hill Community Development project. Married, one daughter, two step-children. Ed: Sacred Heart GS, Newcastle; Newcastle Poly (BSc sociology).

CHALLENGERS
Martin McGann (C) Advocacy manager, LPC Law. Worked as

a paralegal at HMRC 2007-10. Ed: University of Reading (LLB law); Manchester Metropolitan University (BVC law). **Scott Hartley** (Ukip) Served in the RAF for 13 years providing healthcare to military personnel. Married. **John Appleby** (LD) Head of School of mechanical and systems engineering, University of Newcastle. Cllr, Newcastle CC 2004-07. Contested Tynemouth 2010. Contested North Tyneside mayoral election 2013. Married, three children.

CONSTITUENCY PROFILE
Stretching along the Tyne from North Shields to Wallsend up to the former mining communities of Seaton Burn and Burradon. Mining and ship-building industries have seen decline. Famous residents include Sting, dozens of professional footballers and railway engineer Robert Stephenson. A large amount of social housing and high unemployment. Has been held by Labour for decades.

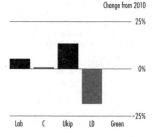

	Electorate	Turnout %	Change from 2010 %
	79,286	59.1	
M Glindon Lab	26,191	55.9	+5.3
M McGann C	8,997	19.2	+0.9
S Hartley Ukip	7,618	16.3	+13.5
J Appleby LD	2,075	4.4	-18.5
M Collins Green	1,442	3.1	
T Wall TUSC	304	0.7	
B Batten NF	191	0.4	-0.9

Change from 2010

Tyrone West

SINN FEIN HOLD

PAT DOHERTY
BORN Jul 18, 1945
MP 2001-

Named by the UUP MP David Burnside under parliamentary privilege in 2002 as a member of the Provisional IRA's ruling council, his brother was a member of the gang involved in the 1975 Balcombe Street siege. Vice-president, Sinn Fein 1988-2009. MLA for West Tyrone 1998-2012; chairman, agriculture & rural development 1999-2003. Leader of Sinn Fein delegation to Dublin Forum for Peace and Reconciliation. Member, talks team 1997-98. Site engineer. Married, three daughters, two sons. Ed: St Joseph's Coll, Lochwinnoch.

CHALLENGERS
Thomas Buchanan (DUP) MLA for West Tyrone 2003-. NI Assembly cttees: standards and privileges 2015-; agriculture and rural development 2011-; chair,

employment and learning 2011-; justice 2010-11; environment 2010-11. Cllr, Omagh DC 1993-. Member, Omagh 2010 Task Force. Contested Tyrone W (Westminster) 2010. **Daniel McCrossan** (SDLP) SDLP constituency representative and member of governing party executive. Former finance administrator. Ed: Liverpool John Moores University (LLB). **Ross Hussey** (UUP) MLA for West Tyrone 2011-. Cllr, Omagh DC 2005-. Former reservist (for 26 years) in the Royal Ulster Constabulary. Ed: Open University (BA history; Cert law).

CONSTITUENCY PROFILE
A rural seat, midway between Belfast and Londonderry. Omagh was the scene of the 1998 IRA car bomb that killed 29 people. Agriculture and manufacturing are important employers in the constituency. Has one of the largest Catholic populations in Northern Ireland and is overwhelmingly nationalist.

	Electorate	Turnout %	Change from 2010 %
	63,854	60.5	
P Doherty SF	16,807	43.5	-4.9
T Buchanan DUP	6,747	17.5	-2.3
D McCrossan SDLP	6,444	16.7	+2.7
R Hussey UUP	6,144	15.9	
S Donnelly Alliance	869	2.3	-0.1
C McClean Green	780	2.0	
B Brown CSA	528	1.4	
C Leyland C	169	0.4	-13.7
S White Ind	166	0.4	-0.9

Change from 2010

Ulster Mid

SINN FEIN HOLD

FRANCIE MOLLOY
BORN Dec 16, 1950
MP 2013-

Sinn Fein veteran. MLA for Mid Ulster 1998-2013. NI Assembly: deputy speaker 2006-13, principal speaker 2011-13; cttees include, standards and privileges 2012-13, office of the first minister 2011-12, environment 2011-13. Director of elections for Bobby Sands in 1981. Cllr, Dungannon BC 1993-2015, 1985-89, mayor 2001. Member, NI forum for political dialogue, Sinn Féin talks team. Contested NI European parly election 1994. Married, four children. Ed: St Patrick's, Dungannon; Felden govt training centre (Engineering); University of Ulster; Newry Further Education Coll (foundation studies humanities).

CHALLENGERS
Sandra Overend (UUP) MLA for Mid Ulster 2011-. Assembly Private Sec (APS) to Danny

Kennedy MLA 2014-. Former: UUP women's development officer; office manager for her father Billy Armstrong MLA. Previously an accountant. Married, three children. Ed: University of Ulster (BSc accountancy). **Ian McCrea** (DUP) MLA for Mid Ulster 2007-. APS Arlene Foster MLA. NI Assembly: finance & personnel 2013-; environment 2013-, 2007-10; standards & privileges 2010-14; regional devt 2009-13. Cllr, Cookstown DC 2001-. **Malachy Quinn** (SDLP) Health worker. Former member of SDLP youth executive. Cllr Mid-Ulster DC.

CONSTITUENCY PROFILE
A rural seat comprising mainly villages but which includes Cookstown. According to the 2011 census, has one of the lowest recorded crime rates in NI. The local economy is largely agricultural. Tourism centres on Lough Neagh, the largest fresh water lake in UK and Ireland. A safe Sinn Féin seat.

	Electorate	Turnout %	Change from 2010 %
	67,831	60.3	
F Molloy SF	19,935	48.7	-3.3
S Overend UUP	6,318	15.4	
I McCrea DUP	5,465	13.4	-1.0
M Quinn SDLP	5,055	12.4	-1.9
G Ferguson TUV	1,892	4.6	-2.7
A Day Ukip	863	2.1	
E Bullick Alliance	778	1.9	+0.9
H Scullion WP	496	1.2	
L Nicholson C	120	0.3	-10.8

Change from 2010

Upper Bann

DEMOCRATIC UNIONIST PARTY HOLD

DAVID SIMPSON
BORN Feb 16, 1959
MP 2005-

MLA for Upper Bann 2003-2010. Former vice-president, DUP. DUP Westminster spokesman: communities & local government 2010-; BIS 2009-; education, international development 2007-10; transport 2007-09; trade & industry 2005-07. Select cttees: NI affairs 2008-; transport 2007-08; statutory instruments 2005-09. Cllr, Craigavon BC 2001-10, mayor 2004-05. Contested Upper Bann 2001. Worked in food manufacturing industry. Married, two daughters, one son. Ed: Killicomaine HS, Portadown; Coll of Business Studies, Belfast.

CHALLENGERS
Jo-Anne Dobson (UUP) MLA for Upper Bann 2011-. NI Assembly: member, cttees: health, social services & public safety 2014-; agriculture & rural development

2011-; education 2011-14. Cllr, Craigavon BC 2010-12. Married, two sons. Ed: Banbridge Academy. **Catherine Seeley** (SF) Teacher. Cllr, Armagh City, Banbridge and Craigavon BC 2014-. Ed: Queen's University Belfast (BA history & politics). **Dolores Kelly** (SDLP) MLA for Upper Bann 2003-. Deputy leader, SDLP. Cllr, Craigavon BC 1993-2010, mayor 1999-2000. Former occupational therapist. Ed: St Michael's GS, Lurgan; University of Ulster. Married, four children.

CONSTITUENCY PROFILE
A largely urban seat covering the towns of Lurgan and Portadown. Areas of severe deprivation on the Brownlow estates. Strong manufacturing sector. This was the seat of David Trimble, then Ulster Unionist leader, who was defeated by the current MP in 2005 after a bitter contest. Has one of the highest populations in a NI constituency and saw some of the worst violence of the Troubles.

	Electorate	Turnout %	Change from 2010 %
	80,052	59.0	
D Simpson DUP	15,430	32.7	-1.2
J Dobson UUP	13,166	27.9	
C Seeley SF	11,593	24.6	-0.2
D Kelly SDLP	4,238	9.0	-3.8
P Lavery Alliance	1,780	3.8	+0.8
M Kelly CSA	460	1.0	
D Harte WP	351	0.7	
A S Bhogal C	201	0.4	-25.3

Change from 2010

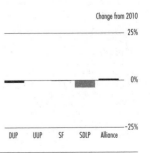

Uxbridge & Ruislip South

CONSERVATIVE HOLD

BORIS JOHNSON
BORN Jun 19, 1964
MP 2015-; 2001-08

Instantly recognisable. Mayor of London 2008-, double-jobbing to 2016. Thinly disguised leadership ambitions. One nation Tory, but Eurosceptic. Member of David Cameron's political cabinet 2015-. Oversaw 2012 London Olympics. *Telegraph* columnist, former editor of *The Spectator*. Fired from *The Times* after falsifying a quote. Author of 2014 Churchill biography. MP for Henley 2001-08. Shadow min: higher education 2005-07; arts 2004, sacked from front bench by Michael Howard after lying about an affair. Bullingdon Club at Oxford. Brother of Jo Johnson MP and journalist Rachel Johnson; son of Stanley Johnson MEP; grandson of president of ECHR James Fawcett. Divorced, remarried, five children. Ed: Ashdown House; Eton Coll; Balliol Coll, Oxford (BA Classics, pres Oxford Union).

CHALLENGERS
Chris Summers (Lab) Journalist, specialising in crime for the BBC. Cllr, Ealing borough 2010-; vice-chairman, planning cttee 2012-14. Member: Heathrow Airport Consultative Cttee; Local Authorities' Aircraft Noise Council; London Road Safety Council; RAF Northolt Advisory cttee. Ed: Corfe Hills Sch, Dorset. **Jack Duffin** (Ukip) Press officer, Ukip 2014-. National chairman, Young Independence 2014-. Former chef. Ed: Stratton Upper Sch, Biggleswade.

CONSTITUENCY PROFILE
A relatively affluent, commuter-belt constituency with a big student population. Both Buckinghamshire New University and Brunel University have a campus here. Ethnically diverse. Owing to its proximity to Heathrow airport the percentage of people working in the transport industry is among the highest in the country. Safe Conservative seat.

	Electorate	Turnout %	Change from 2010 %
	70,634	63.4	
B Johnson C	22,511	50.2	+2.0
C Summers Lab	11,816	26.4	+3.0
J Duffin Ukip	6,346	14.2	+11.4
M Cox LD	2,215	4.9	-15.0
G Lee Green	1,414	3.2	+2.1
G Harbord TUSC	180	0.4	
J Thompson Ind	84	0.2	
H L Hope Loony	72	0.2	
S Moosun Community	52	0.1	
L T Jug Eccentric	50	0.1	
M Doherty Ind	39	0.1	
J Lawrence Realist	18	0.0	
J Jackson ND	14	0.0	

Change from 2010

C   Lab   Ukip   LD   Green

Vale of Clwyd

CONSERVATIVE GAIN

DR JAMES DAVIES
BORN Feb 27, 1980
MP 2015-

GP; resigning post after unseating Labour MP in 2015 election with a majority of 237. Cllr: Denbighshire CC 2004-; Prestatyn TC 2008-. Previously worked at Glan Clwyd hospital. Member, BMA. Trustee, local environment assoc. Clinical champion for dementia. Enjoys walking. Married, one son. Ed: King's Sch, Chester; Christ's Coll, Cambridge (MA, MB BChir medicine).

CHALLENGERS
Chris Ruane (Lab) MP, Vale of Clwyd 1997-2015. Opposition whip, Commons 2011-13. PPS to: David Miliband 2009-10; Caroline Flint 2007-08; Peter Hain 2002-07. Cllr, Rhyl TC 1988-99. Founder member Rhyl anti-apartheid, environmental association. NUT. Former primary sch deputy head. Married, two daughters.

Ed: Blessed Edward Jones RC HS, Rhyl; Wales (BSc economics, history, politics); Liverpool (PGCE). **Paul Davies-Cooke** (Ukip) Teacher, Coleg Cambria Northop. Detachment commander, Army Cadet Froce, Mold. Married, three children. **Mair Rowlands** (PC) Trainee sustainable development practitioner, Welsh Institute for Natural Resources, Bangor University. Cllr, Bangor CC 2012-. Ed: Ysgol Gyfun Gymraeg Glantaf; University of Wales, Bangor (BA Welsh & theology, president, Students' Union 2010-12).

CONSTITUENCY PROFILE
Covers the valley of the river Clywd, stretching inland from the north Wales coast. At its seaward end are the coastal resorts of Kinmel Bay, Rhyl and Prestatyn. Employment along the coast is mainly seasonal. The western half of Rhyl is one of the most deprived areas in Wales. Held by Labour since its creation in 1997 but won at the 2015 election by James Davies.

	Electorate	Turnout %	Change from 2010 %
	56,505	62.4	
J Davies C	13,760	39.0	+3.8
C Ruane Lab	13,523	38.4	-3.9
P Davies-Cooke Ukip	4,577	13.0	+11.5
M Rowlands PC	2,486	7.1	+1.2
G Williams LD	915	2.6	-10.0

Change from 2010

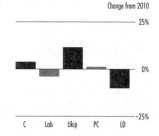

C   Lab   Ukip   PC   LD

Vale of Glamorgan

ALUN CAIRNS
BORN Jul 30, 1970
MP 2010-

Interested in special educational needs. Parly under-sec, Wales 2014-. Lord commissioner, Treasury (whip) 2014-15. Select cttees: public administration 2011-14; Welsh affairs 2010-11. Contested Vale of Glamorgan 2005, Gower 1997. AM for South Wales West region 1999-2011 (shadow min: education and lifelong learning 2007-08; local govt 2008-09; heritage 2009-10). Welsh Con spokesman: econ devt 1999-2000; econ devt & Europe 2000-03. Financial service compliance, Lloyds TSB. Enjoys shooting and skiing. Married, one son. Ed: Ysgol Gyfun Ysalyfera; University of Wales (MBA).

CHALLENGERS
Chris Elmore (Lab) Cllr, Vale of Glamorgan C 2008-; Cabinet member, children's services. Member: Barry Communities

First; Barry YMCA Hub. Independent member, Cardiff and Vale University Health Board. Worked in further education, at the National Assembly and Westminster. Ed: Cardiff Met University (BA history & culture). **Kevin Mahoney** (Ukip) Former gas engineering supervisor. Cllr, Vale of Glamorgan C 2012-. Contested: Vale of Glamorgan 2007 Welsh Assembly; 2010 general election. Ed: Stanwell Sch, Penarth. **Ian Johnson** (PC) Head of policy, Plaid Cymru. Cllr, Vale of Glamorgan 2012-. Contested Vale of Glamorgan 2010. President, Adoxton Barry FC.

CONSTITUENCY PROFILE
The seat covers the rolling countryside along the south Wales coast, to the southwest of Cardiff. The main population centre is the large resort and industrial port of Barry. A diverse constituency with many residents commuting to Cardiff. Cardiff airport is a major employer.

	Electorate	Turnout %	from 2010 %	Change
	72,187	71.1		
A Cairns C	23,607	46.0	+4.2	
C Elmore Lab	16,727	32.6	-0.3	
K Mahoney Ukip	5,489	10.7	+7.6	
I Johnson PC	2,869	5.6	+0.1	
D Morgan LD	1,309	2.6	-12.7	
A Armstrong Green	1,054	2.1	+1.1	
S Reed CSA	238	0.5		

Change from 2010

Vauxhall

KATE HOEY
BORN Jun 21, 1946
MP Jun 1989-

Against Iraq war, pro-fox hunting. Chairwoman, Countryside Alliance 2005-14. Parly under-sec: CMS 1999-2001; home 1998-99. PPS to Frank Field 1997-98. Select cttees: NI Affairs 2007-; science & technology 2004-05; social security 1994-97; broadcasting 1991-97. Cllr: Hackney BC 1978-92; Southwark BC 1988-89. Contested Dulwich 1987, 1983. Senior lecturer. Educational adviser, Arsenal FC. Member, GMB. Vice-pres: British Wheelchair Basketball Assoc; Surrey County Cricket Club. Ed: Belfast Royal Academy; Ulster Coll of Phys Ed (Dip teaching); City of London Coll (BSc economics).

CHALLENGERS
James Bellis (C) Economist. Director, Frontier Economics. Former consultant: IBM; PwC. Ed: University of Liverpool (BA

economics). **Gulnar Hasnain** (Green) Co-founder: T15B 2014-, CoinSummit 2013-. Former head of environment strategy for mayor of London's economic development agency. Ed: Imperial Coll London (MEng chemical engineering); Birkbeck (MSc development studies); University of Chicago (MBA). **Adrian Hyyryläinen-Trett** (LD) Recruitment consultant, translation services. Former chairman, LGBT+ Lib Dems. Campaigner for same-sex marriage. Married. Ed: Eaton Comp Sch, Norwich; University of Kent (BA European studies).

CONSTITUENCY PROFILE
An inner-city seat in Lambeth that faces Westminster across the River Thames. Landmarks include the London Eye, and the National Theatre. Ethnically diverse with large Jamaican and Ghanaian communities. Densely populated with a high percentage of social housing. Won by Labour MPs since it was created in 1983.

	Electorate	Turnout %	from 2010 %	Change
	81,698	58.7		
K Hoey Lab	25,778	53.8	+4.0	
J Bellis C	13,070	27.3	+5.7	
G Hasnain Green	3,658	7.6	+6.0	
A Hyyryläinen-Trett LD	3,312	6.9	-18.2	
A Nnorom Ukip	1,385	2.9		
M Chapman Pirate	201	0.4		
S Hardy LU	188	0.4		
L Jensen CSA	164	0.3		
W S Ghani Whig	103	0.2		
D Lambert SPGB	82	0.2		

Change from 2010

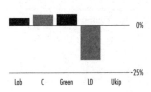

Wakefield

LABOUR HOLD

MARY CREAGH
BORN Dec 2, 1967
MP 2005-

Put herself forward as candidate for Labour leadership, 2015. Shadow SoS: international devt 2014-; transport 2013-14; efra 2010-13. Opposition asst whip 2010. Shadow min: health 2010. Asst govt whip 2009-10. PPS to: Andy Burnham 2006-09; Lord Warner 2006. Select cttees: Yorkshire and the Humber regional 2009; finance & services 2007-10; human rights 2005-07. Cllr, Islington BC 1998-2005, leader Lab group 2000-04. Lecturer in entrepreneurship, Cranfield Sch of Management 1997-. Married, one daughter, one son. Ed: Bishop Ullathorne RC CS, Coventry; Pembroke Coll, Oxford (BA modern languages); LSE (MSC European studies).

CHALLENGERS
Antony Calvert (C) PR consultant. Dir, HardHat communications

consultancy. Cllr, Wakefield 2004-07. Contested Morley & Outwood 2010. Ed: Outwood Grange Sch. **Alan Hazelhurst** (Ukip) MD, AutoSLM, IT solutions. **Finbarr Cronin** (LD) Dir, Ingredients Recruitment Ltd. Cllr, Sitlington PC 2013-. Worked in the logistics sector. Married, one daughter. Ed: De Montfort University (BA business studies, human resources); University of Leeds (MA politics).

CONSTITUENCY PROFILE
A former mining area, it covers the city of Wakefield and a number of smaller and more rural villages. The National Coal Mining Museum is situated in the small village of Overton. Has been developing its cultural sector. Largely white with a significant Pakistani community. Manufacturing is an important industry. Unemployment is higher than average and the social sector is relatively large. Mary Creagh held the seat at the 2015 election by 2,613 votes.

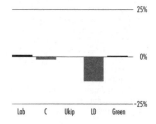

	Electorate	Turnout %	from 2010 %	Change
	70,521	60.9		
M Creagh Lab	17,301	40.3	+1.0	
A Calvert C	14,688	34.2	-1.5	
A Hazelhurst Ukip	7,862	18.3		
F Cronin LD	1,483	3.5	-12.9	
R Thackray Green	1,069	2.5	+0.5	
M Griffiths TUSC	287	0.7		
E Barr CSA	283	0.7		

Change from 2010

Wallasey

LABOUR HOLD

ANGELA EAGLE
BORN Feb 17, 1961
MP 1992-

Determined campaigner on equality issues. Shadow leader, HoC 2011-. Shadow chief sec, treasury 2010. Shadow min, treasury 2010. Min: DWP 2009-10. Exchequer sec, Treasury 2007-09. Parly sec, home 2001-02. Parly und-sec: social security 1998-2001; environment 1997-98. Opp whip 1996-97. Member, Labour NEC 2005-10. Select cttees: independent parly standards 2011-15; public accounts 2007-09; Treasury 2003-07; public accounts 2002-03, 1995-96. Twin sister, Maria Eagle MP. COHSE parly liaison officer, press officer, researcher. Civil partnership. Enjoys cricket. Ed: Formby HS; Pembroke Coll, Oxford (BA PPE); Coll of Law, London (law).

CHALLENGERS
Chris Clarkson (C) Corporate

development manager, Virgin. Cllr, Salford CC 2011-; member, licensing & regulatory panel. Ed: University of Dundee (LLB law). **Geoff Caton** (Ukip). Denied being homophobic after caught saying being an "a** bandit" was nothing to be proud of. **Julian Pratt** (Green) Worked as a GP in Sheffield and in other NHS roles. **Kris Brown** (LD) Formerly Labour. Enjoys motorsport. Partner, one daughter.

CONSTITUENCY PROFILE
A compact seat on the northeastern tip of the Wirral Peninsula. Covers residential areas, docklands and council estates. A diverse seat, there is severe deprivation in Seacombe, by the docks, and Moreton, to the west, while a £70m regeneration is under way in the seaside town of New Brighton. Wallasey has high unemployment with significant levels of poor health. Angela Eagle took the seat from the Tories in 1992 and it has since become Labour bastion.

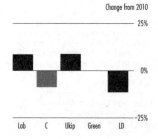

	Electorate	Turnout %	from 2010 %	Change
	65,495	66.2		
A Eagle Lab	26,176	60.4	+8.6	
C Clarkson C	9,828	22.7	-8.7	
G Caton Ukip	5,063	11.7	+8.8	
J Pratt Green	1,288	3.0		
K Brown LD	1,011	2.3	-11.3	

Change from 2010

Walsall North

LABOUR HOLD

DAVID WINNICK
BORN Jun 26, 1933
MP 1979-; 1966-70

Long-serving centrist with instinct for popular mood. Select cttees: home 1997-; Treasury and civil service 1989-92; procedure 1989-97. MP, Croydon S 1966-70. Cllr: Willesden BC 1959-64; Brent BC 1964-66. Contested: Walsall North by-election 1976; Croydon Central 1974; Croydon South 1970; Harwich 1964. Chairman, UK Immigrants advisory service. Served in the army 1951-53. Member, British-Irish Inter-Parly Body 1990-2005, British co-chairman 1997-2005. Vice-pres, Association of Professional, Executive, Clerical & Computer Staff. Divorced. One son. Ed: LSE (Dip social admin).

CHALLENGERS
Douglas Hansen-Luke (C) Investment consultant. Managing partner, HLD Partners and CEO, Bfinance financial services.

Fundraising adviser for Oxford University. Chairman and founder of Gulf Tories. Ed: Stowe Sch; Jesus Coll, Oxford (BA PPE). **Elizabeth Hazell** (Ukip) Trainee electrician. Cllr, Walsall C 2014-. Ukip Walsall branch treasurer 2008-. Contested Walsall N 2010. Ed: Brownhills Community Sch; Walsall Coll. **Nigel Jones** (LD) Former teacher. Methodist preacher. Cllr, Newcastle-under-Lyme BC 2002-15; Lib Dem group leader. Married, one son.

CONSTITUENCY PROFILE
Once the "leather capital of the world" Walsall has long been dependent on traditional manufacturing industries. The seat has areas of severe deprivation and unemployment has been high. It has the second highest percentage of people with no qualifications in England and Wales. Held by Labour MP David Winnick since 1979. In the 2015 election he increased his majority from 990 to 1,937.

	Electorate	Turnout %	Change from 2010 %
	67,080	55.0	
D Winnick Lab	14,392	39.0	+2.0
D Hansen-Luke C	12,455	33.8	-0.5
E Hazell Ukip	8,122	22.0	+17.2
N Jones LD	840	2.3	-10.9
P Smith TUSC	545	1.5	
M Harrison Green	529	1.4	

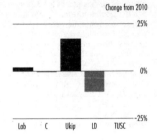

Change from 2010

Lab C Ukip LD TUSC

Walsall South

LABOUR HOLD

VALERIE VAZ
BORN Dec 7, 1954
MP 2010-

Select cttees: HoC governance 2014-; regulatory 2010-; health 2010-. Contested Twickenham 1987. Cllr, Ealing 1986-90. Former TV presenter on Network East. Deputy district judge. Solicitor, government legal service; deputy district judge. Set up community law firm Townsend Vaz. Member: Lay Advisory Panel of the Coll of Optometrists; Law Society. Sister of Keith Vaz MP. Married, one daughter. Ed: Twickenham County GS, Bedford Coll, University of London (BSc biochemistry); Sidney Sussex Coll, Cambridge (research animal nutrition); Coll of Law, London (CPE; French).

CHALLENGERS
Sue Arnold (C) PR consultant, Haselour House Media. Deputy PCC, Staffordshire 2012-. Cllr, Lichfield DC 2011-. Co-founded

free weekly *Walsall Advertiser* in 1981, becoming company director at 23. Ambassador, Institute of Recruiters. Married, one son. **Derek Bennett** (Ukip) Retired, former stonemason and manager for family business. Contested: Walsall South 2010, 2005, 2001 for Ukip; Walsall North 1997 for Referendum Party. **Charlotte Fletcher** (Green) Freelance makeup artist. Instructor ACF. **Joel Kenrick** (LD) Junior consultant, the Boston Consulting Group. Interim head of public affairs, WWF-UK 2012-13. Special adviser DECC 2010-12. Parly researcher to Chris Huhne 2007-08.

CONSTITUENCY PROFILE
Including parts of Walsall, Moxley and Darlston, the area's economy was hit by the decline in mining. According to the 2011 census, 25 per cent of households are in social housing. About a third of residents are of Asian origin with significant Hindu, Muslim and Sikh communities. A solid Labout seat.

	Electorate	Turnout %	Change from 2010 %
	67,743	61.8	
V Vaz Lab	19,740	47.2	+7.5
S Arnold C	13,733	32.8	-2.5
D Bennett Ukip	6,540	15.6	+7.2
C Fletcher Green	1,149	2.8	
J Kenrick LD	676	1.6	-12.8

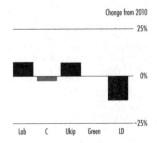

Change from 2010

Lab C Ukip Green LD

Walthamstow

STELLA CREASY
BORN Apr 5, 1977
MP 2010-

Won "Best Constituency Tweeter" award at the 2015 Political Twitter Awards. Shadow min: BIS 2013-15; home afairs 2011-13. Select cttees: public accounts commission 2011-15; public accounts 2010-11. PPS, Andy Burnham 2011. Cllr, Waltham Forest 2002-06, mayor 2003, dep mayor 2002-03. Speechwriter and researcher to Douglas Alexander, Charles Clarke, Ross Cranston. Head of campaigns and PR at the Scout Association. Dep dir, Involve. Trustee for voluntary action group. Member: Unite, Fabians, Socialist Environment & Research Association, Labour Women's Network. Ed: Colchester HS; Magdalene Coll, Cambridge (BA psychology); LSE (PhD psychology, won Richard Titmuss prize).

CHALLENGERS
Molly Samuel-Leport (C) Former

world and European karate champion. Karate coach. Skills tutor, Crisis, homeless charity. Member, Karate England board. 1989 *Sunday Times* International Sportswoman of the Year. Married, two daughters. Ed: Sarah Bonnell Girls Sch; Havering Coll (CertEd, further ed). **Michael Gold** (Green) Works in the travel industry. Occupy London activist. Former member of the Labour party. **Paul Hillman** (Ukip) Self-employed IT consultant. Married, two children.

CONSTITUENCY PROFILE
A multicultural, working-class suburb in northeast London. Said to have the longest outdoor street market in Europe. Unemployment is above average. There is a large black and Asian community and, according to the 2011 census, Walthamstow has relatively high numbers of people living alone. Very safe Labour seat: Stella Creasy held her seat in 2015 with a majority of 23,195 votes. The Conservatives came second.

	Electorate	Turnout %	from 2010 % Change
	67,289	62.1	
S Creasy Lab Co-op	28,779	68.9	+17.0
M Samuel-Leport C	5,584	13.4	-0.6
M Gold Green	2,661	6.4	+4.5
P Hillman Ukip	2,507	6.0	+4.0
S Cheung LD	1,661	4.0	-24.8
N Taaffe TUSC	394	0.9	+0.3
E Merton ND	129	0.3	
J Leff WRP	81	0.2	

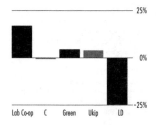

Change from 2010

Wansbeck

IAN LAVERY
BORN Jan 6, 1963
MP 2010-

Successor to Arthur Scargill as NUM leader 2002-10; on the front line of the 1984-85 miners' strike. Branded New Labour an "abject failure". Declared he had no respect for the police after conviction for public order offence at a football match in 1985. Select cttees: draft regulation bill 2013; energy and climate change 2010-; regulatory reform 2010-; NI affairs 2010-11. Cllr, Wansbeck DC 1995-2003. Gen sec, NUM Northumberland branch. NCB miner, Ellington, Lynemouth collieries. Chairman: Ashington FC; Hirst Welfare Centre. Married, two sons. Ed: Ashington Community HS; New Coll, Durham (HNC mining).

CHALLENGERS
Chris Galley (C) Global distribution scheduling manager,

Shell. Sheep farmer. Member: Board Park rugby club; NFU; National Sheep Assoc; Chatham House. Ed: LSE (BA economics). **Melanie Hurst** (Ukip) Assistant to Jonathan Arnott MEP. Former civil servant. Daughter of miner. Married, she and her husband have eight children between them. **Tom Hancock** (LD) Involved in the Yes to Fairer Votes campaign. Self-published musician and recording artist. Ed: Prudhoe Community HS; University of York (BA politics).

CONSTITUENCY PROFILE
A former mining area on the coast of Northumberland. Main centres are the old colliery towns of Ashington and Bedlington. The area was hit hard by the decline of coal mining, and unemployment is high, particularly among 16 to 24-year-olds. There is however still some work in mining and quarrying. A largely white population. The seat has been held by the Labour party since 1945. Ian Lavery held the seat in 2015 with a

	Electorate	Turnout %	from 2010 % Change
	63,273	60.9	
I Lavery Lab	19,267	50.0	+4.2
C Galley C	8,386	21.8	+4.2
M Hurst Ukip	7,014	18.2	+15.7
T Hancock LD	2,407	6.3	-21.2
C Hedley Green	1,454	3.8	+2.2

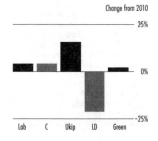

Change from 2010

Wantage

CONSERVATIVE HOLD

EDWARD VAIZEY
BORN Jun 5, 1968
MP 2005-

Tory moderniser, close to David Cameron. Min of state: culture & the digital economy 2014-. Parly under-sec: culture, 2010-14; BIS 2010. Shadow min: arts 2006-10. Select cttees: environmental audit 2006-07; modernisation of HoC 2005-07. Speechwriter for Michael Howard as leader; election aide to Iain Duncan Smith, 2001 GE. Contested Bristol East 1997. Barrister, family law & childcare. Editor, Blue Books politcal series. Dir, Consolidated Comms. Trustee, the Trident Trust. Married, one daughter, one son. Ed: St Paul's Sch; Merton Coll, Oxford (BA history); City (Dip law).

CHALLENGERS
Stephen Webb (Lab) Scientist, Rutherford Appleton Laboratory. Cllr, East Hendred PC. Ed: Imperial Coll, London (PhD

biomedical optics). **Alex Meredith** (LD) Solicitor, RWE Npower Renewables. Cllr, Faringdon TC 2014-. Married, one daughter. Ed: UCL (LLB law). **Lee Upcraft** (Ukip) Physicist within the defence industry. Chairman, Ukip Oxfordshire. Served in the Territorial Army. Married, two daughters. **Kate Prendergast** (Green) Communications consultant. Ed: Oxford (DPhil archaeology).

CONSTITUENCY PROFILE
A rural seat in the northeast of Oxfordshire. An affluent area where employment levels are some of the highest in the country. Major employers include agriculture, racing stables and high-tech companies. According to the 2011 census, more than a third of the workforce is highly qualified. A Conservative seat since 1983 but briefly Labour in 2005 when Tory MP Robert Jackson defected. Returned to the Tories in that year's general election.

	Electorate	Turnout %	Change from 2010 %
	83,516	69.8	
E Vaizey C	31,092	53.3	+1.3
S Webb Lab	9,343	16.0	+2.1
A Meredith LD	7,611	13.1	-14.9
L Upcraft Ukip	7,288	12.5	+8.2
K Prendergast Green	2,986	5.1	+3.3

Change from 2010

C   Lab   LD   Ukip   Green

Warley

LABOUR HOLD

JOHN SPELLAR
BORN Aug 5, 1947
MP 1992-; 1982-83

Leading figure on Labour right and opponent of elected Lords. Shadow min, foreign and commonwealth affairs 2010-15. Govt whip 2008-10. Min: NI 2003-05; transport 2001-03; armed forces 1999-2001. Parly under-sec: defence 1997-99. Shadow spokes: defence 1995-97; NI 1994-95. Opp whip 1992-94. Select cttees: administration 2010-13; selection 2010; finance & services 2009-10; conventions 2006; defence 1983-87; energy 1983. MP: Warley West 1992-97; Birmingham Northfield 1982-83. Nat officer, Electrical, Telecommunication and Plumbing Union. Widowed. One daughter. Ed: Dulwich Coll; St Edmund's Hall, Oxford (BA PPE).

CHALLENGERS
Tom Williams (C) Management consultant for engineering company. Barrister. Former Royal

Naval reserve. Ed: Somerville Coll, Oxford (BSc physics); Newcastle University (MSc environmental engineering). **Pete Durnell** (Ukip) Technical consultant. Enjoys cricket. Widower, three strep children. Ed: King Charles First Sch, Kidderminster; Coventry Polytechnic (BSc computer science). **Rob Buckman** (Green) Self-employed chartered management accountant. Runs a small business.

CONSTITUENCY PROFILE
Centred on the town of Smethwick, this seat has a large amount of social housing and high unemployment. A third of adults do not have any qualifications. Ethnically diverse, has large Asian populations and a sizeable black community. Has the highest percentage of Sikhs of any constituency in England and Wales. Solidly Labour apart from a short-lived Tory hold in the 1964 general election, a campaign dominated by race issues.

	Electorate	Turnout %	Change from 2010 %
	63,740	59.4	
J Spellar Lab	22,012	58.2	+5.3
T Williams C	7,310	19.3	-5.5
P Durnell Ukip	6,237	16.5	+9.7
R Buckman Green	1,465	3.9	
C Smith LD	805	2.1	-13.4

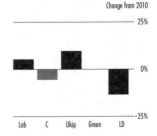

Change from 2010

Lab   C   Ukip   Green   LD

Warrington North

LABOUR HOLD

HELEN JONES
BORN Dec 24, 1954
MP 1997-

Shadow min: home affairs 2013-15; CLG 2011-13. Shadow dep leader, HoC 2010-11. Opposition whip: Commons 2010. Shadow min: justice 2010. Vice-chamberlain, whip 2009-10. Asst whip, Treasury 2008-09. PPS to: Dawn Primarolo 2007-08. Select cttees: selection 2009-10; administration 2005-07; education & skills 2003-07; standing orders 2001-10; unopposed bills 2001-10; education & employment 1999-2001; standing orders 1999-2000; public administration 1998-2000. Cllr, Chester CC 1984-91. MSF Lab party liaison officer. Solicitor. Eng teacher. Justice & peace officer, Liverpool Archdiocese. MIND devt officer. Member: Unite, USDAW. Married, one son. Ed: UCL (BA English); Chester Coll; Liverpool (MEd); Manchester Metropolitan University.

CHALLENGERS
Richard Short (C) Council Environmental health practitioner. Chairman, Wigan Conservative Federation. Northwest co-ordinator, Conservative policy forum. Farm labourer. Black belt in jujitsu. Married, two daughters, one son. Ed: Kings GS; Bedford HS; Salford University (BSc environmental sciences). **Trevor Nicholls** (Ukip) Businessman. Former Labour activist. Ed: Dallam Sch; Bewsey Secondary Modern Sch. **Stefan Krizanac** (LD) Works for Royal Mail. Cllr, Warrington BC 2014-. **Sarah Hayes** (Green) Full-time cryptic crossword setter for national newspapers.

CONSTITUENCY PROFILE
A former industrial town on the Mersey. Designated as a new town in the 1960s, it has grown massively with huge new housing developments. Ikea opened its first store here in 1987. Unemployment is higher than average. Safely held by Labour for decades.

	Electorate	Turnout %	from 2010 % Change
	72,632	62.5	
H Jones Lab	21,720	47.8	+2.3
R Short C	12,797	28.2	-2.1
T Nicholls Ukip	7,757	17.1	
S Krizanac LD	1,881	4.1	-16.7
S Hayes Green	1,264	2.8	

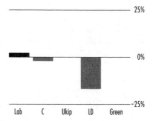

Change from 2010

Warrington South

CONSERVATIVE HOLD

DAVID MOWAT
BORN Feb 20, 1957
MP 2010-

Experienced businessman. PPS to: Anna Soubry 2014-15; Greg Clark 2012-14. Select cttees: draft financial services bill 2011; Scottish affairs 2010-12. Cllr, Macclesfield BC 2007-08. Accountant. Partner, Arthur Andersen; global managing partner, Accenture. Chairman, Fairbridge. Member: ACA, Institute of Petroleum, Parliamentary Office of Science and Technology. Dir, Warrington FC. Cadet pilot, RAFVR. Keen chess and golf player. Married, three daughters, one son. Ed: Lawrence Sheriff GS, Rugby; Imperial Coll (BSc civil engineering).

CHALLENGERS
Nick Bent (Lab) Businessman. Consultant on energy and environmental issues. Director and co-founder of education charity Tutor Trust. Special adviser, Tessa Jowell 2003-07. Contested Warrington S 2010. Ed: Manchester GS; Magdalen Coll, Oxford (LLB law); Harvard School of Govt (MPP). **Malcolm Lingley** (Ukip) Works in traffic management. Former factory and warehouse worker. **Bob Barr** (LD) Visiting professor to University of Liverpool school of environmental sciences. Cllr, Warrington BC 2006-. Honorary Fellow, University of Manchester, former lecturer in geography. Ed: Durham (BA geography); Manchester (PhD social information systems).

CONSTITUENCY PROFILE
The more affluent of the two seats covering Warrington, a former industrial town on the Mersey between Liverpool and Manchester. According to the 2011 census, 75 per cent of households in the constituency are owner-occupied and more than a third of houses have two or more cars. David Mowat won a second term in the 2015 general election.

	Electorate	Turnout %	from 2010 % Change
	85,566	69.4	
D Mowat C	25,928	43.7	+7.9
N Bent Lab	23,178	39.1	+6.1
M Lingley Ukip	4,909	8.3	+5.3
B Barr LD	3,335	5.6	-21.9
S Davies Green	1,765	3.0	+2.2
K Bennett TUSC	238	0.4	

Change from 2010

Warwick & Leamington

CONSERVATIVE HOLD

CHRIS WHITE
BORN Apr 28, 1967
MP 2010-

Named as "Social Value Ambassador" by the govt for his Public Services Social Enterprise & Social Value Bill 2010. Select cttees: international development 2010-15; arms export controls 2010-15. Cllr, Warwick DC 2008-10. Contested: Warwick & Leamington 2005; Birmingham Hall Green 2001. Freelance PR consultant, formerly of Century Public Relations. Former engineer. Worked in supply and development engineering at MG Rover in Longbridge. Trustee: Victim Support; Policy Connect. Patron, Cord charity. Divorced. Ed: St Gregory's Comp Sch, Tunbridge Wells; University of Manchester (BEng engineering); Bath (MBA).

CHALLENGERS
Lynette Kelly (Lab) Cllr, Coventry CC 2004-. Former research fellow, University of Warwick. Previously Bosnian refugee resettlement oficer, Coventry CC. Married, four children. Ed: Coventry University (BSc applied social science); University of Warwick (PhD ethnic relations). **Alastair MacBrayne** (Ukip) Wine merchant, MD of MacBrayne Wines. Married, two stepsons. Ed: Cheltenham Coll (WSET Dip wine). **Haseeb Arif** (LD) Works in medicine. Ed: North Leamington Sch; Royal Holloway, London (BSc biological science).

CONSTITUENCY PROFILE
A prosperous constituency that includes the towns of Warwick and Leamington Spa. Warwick's castle and historic buildings makes it a tourist destination. Generally a prosperous constituency. The National Grid's gas control centre is based here. Unemployment is below average. Historically a safe seat for the Conservative party, most famously represented by Anthony Eden 1923-1957. Chris White held the seat in 2015 by 6,606 votes.

	Electorate	Turnout %	from 2010 %	Change
	71,570	70.7		
C White C	24,249	47.9	+5.4	
L Kelly Lab	17,643	34.9	-0.5	
A MacBrayne Ukip	4,183	8.3	+6.4	
H Arif LD	2,512	5.0	-13.3	
A Minott Green	1,994	3.9	+2.5	

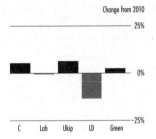

Change from 2010

Warwickshire North

CONSERVATIVE HOLD

CRAIG TRACEY
BORN Aug 21, 1974
MP 2015-

Eurosceptic. Senior partner, Dunelm Insurance Brokers 1996-. Director of Politically Correct, political consultancy 2014-. Board member, Southern Staffordshire employment and skills board 2014-. West Midlands co-ordinator, Conservative Voice 2012-. Trustee, Lichfield Garrick Theatre 2012-. Chairman, North Warwickshire Conservative Assoc 2012-14. Treasurer, Tamworth Conservative Assoc. Family comes from a mining background near Durham. Married. Ed: Framwellgate Moor Comp Sch, Durham.

CHALLENGERS
Mike O'Brien (Lab) MP, Warwickshire N 1992-2010. Min: health services 2009-10; energy 2008-09; pensions 2007-08; trade and industry 2001-05; immigration 1997-2001. Solicitor General 2005-07. QC and public law barrister, No5 chambers. Former business law lecturer. Ed: North Staffordshire Polytechnic (BA history & politics); PGCE. **William Cash** (Ukip) Spear's Magazine founder & editor. Ukip heritage & tourism spokesman. Former journalist: The Times; Daily Telegraph; Daily Mail. Son of veteran Tory MP Bill Cash, who said he "completely disassociates" himself from his son. Married. Ed: Westminster Sch; Magdalene Coll, Cambridge.

CONSTITUENCY PROFILE
Historically a coal mining area covering semi-rural commuterland between Birmingham, Coventry, Nuneaton and Tamworth. Local economy is now based on manufacturing. Thousands of Olympic torches were manufactured in Exhall. Lower than average unemployment and a high number of home owners. Held by Labour from 1992 but was narrowly won in 2010 by the Conservatives.

	Electorate	Turnout %	from 2010 %	Change
	70,152	67.5		
C Tracey C	20,042	42.3	+2.1	
M O'Brien Lab	17,069	36.0	-4.0	
W Cash Ukip	8,256	17.4	+14.6	
A Beddow LD	978	2.1	-9.5	
I Bonner Green	894	1.9		
E Hunter TUSC	138	0.3		

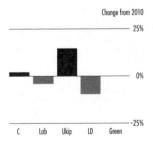

Change from 2010

Washington & Sunderland West

LABOUR HOLD

SHARON HODGSON
BORN Apr 1, 1966
MP 2005-

Was involved in Labour's Woman to Woman campaign 2015. Shadow min: equalities 2013-15; education 2010-13. Opposition whip: commons 2010. Asst whip Treasury 2009-10. PPS to: Dawn Primarolo 2008-09; Bob Ainsworth 2007-08; Liam Byrne 2006-07. Select cttees: ecclesiastical 2010-15; north east 2009-10; children schools & families 2007-10; court of referees 2007-; European scrutiny 2006; regulatory reform 2005-10. Constituency sec, Mitcham and Morden CLP 2002-05. Women's officer, Tyne Bridge CLP 1998-2000. Payroll and accounting clerk. Member, Fabian Society 2004-. Married, one daughter, one son. Ed: Heathfield Senior HS, Gateshead; Newcastle Coll (HEFC English); National Education Centre (TUC Dip Lab party organising).

CHALLENGERS
Aileen Casey (Ukip) Youth worker for local special needs group, Pit Stop and Deaf Club. Former computer systems trainer for Brian Mills, Liverpool. Two children. **Bob Dhillon** (C) Finance dir. Cllr, Warwick DC 2007-. Mayor, Warwick 2013-14. Saved council chairman's life after performing CPR at a speech. Suspended for six months from Conservative party for derogatory remarks towards colleague. Forced to pay back travel expenses in 2013. Youth team coach. Cttee member, Rotary International. Married. Ed: University of Bath (BA IT).

CONSTITUENCY PROFILE
Created in 2010. Mostly made up of the 1960s new town of Washington and the western suburbs of the city of Sunderland. Historically associated with the coal industry, many communities grew up around the pits. Home to the ancestors of the first US president. A safe Labour seat.

	Electorate	Turnout %	from 2010 Change %
	68,188	54.6	
S Hodgson Lab	20,478	55.0	+2.4
A Casey Ukip	7,321	19.7	+16.3
B Dhillon C	7,033	18.9	-3.0
A Murphy Green	1,091	2.9	
D Haney LD	993	2.7	-14.4
G Duncan TUSC	341	0.9	

Change from 2010

25%

0%

-25%

Lab   Ukip   C   Green   LD

Watford

CONSERVATIVE HOLD

RICHARD HARRINGTON
BORN Nov 4, 1957
MP 2010-

Wealthy businessman and former property developer. Select cttee: international development 2010-12. Member: Tory Reform Group; Conservative Friends of Israel. Conservative party treasurer 2008-. Chair and trustee, Variety Club Children's Society 1998-2001. Shareholder and non-exec dir, Eden Financial. Founded Harvington Properties. Was responsible for re-development of One Devonshire Gardens hotel in Glasgow. Began career at John Lewis. Jewish. Married, two sons. Ed: Leeds GS; Keble Coll, Oxford (law).

CHALLENGERS
Matt Turmaine (Lab) Development manager, health & social care board. Cllr, Watford BC 2012-. Previously head of client services and fulfilment, BBC

Worldwide. **Dorothy Thornhill** (LD) Mayor of Watford 2002-. Cllr, Watford BC 2002-. Former teacher and assistant head teacher. Hon vice-president, Watford FC. MBE 2012 for services to local government. Married, two children. **Nick Lincoln** (Ukip) Business owner and independent financial adviser. Ed: Kings Langley Comp Sch; Wolverhampton (BA American studies & politics); Chartered Insurance Institute (DipPFS).

CONSTITUENCY PROFILE
Covers the borough of Watford and some of the commuter villages around it, including Abbots Langley and Langleybury. Part of the London commuter belt, but is also an economic centre in its own right. The area was once known for engineering and brewing, but printing is the only traditional industry that remains a big employer in the area. Trinity Mirror Printing is based here. Ethnically diverse.

	Electorate	Turnout %	from 2010 Change %
	84,270	66.6	
R Harrington C	24,400	43.5	+8.5
M Turmaine Lab	14,606	26.0	-0.7
D Thornhill LD	10,152	18.1	-14.3
N Lincoln Ukip	5,481	9.8	+7.6
A Cottrell-Boyce Green	1,332	2.4	+0.8
M O'Connor TUSC	178	0.3	

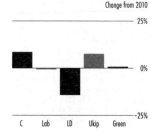

Change from 2010

25%

0%

-25%

C   Lab   LD   Ukip   Green

Waveney

CONSERVATIVE HOLD

PETER ALDOUS
BORN Aug 26, 1961
MP 2010-

Local man from farming background, involved in family pig and arable farm. Select cttee, environmental audit 2010-15. Member, Countryside Alliance. Contested Waveney 2005. Cllr: Waveney DC 1999-2002; Suffolk CC, dep leader Con group 2002-05. Member: Royal Institue of Chartered Surveyors; Farmers' club. Chartered surveyor. CofE. Sports enthusiast, season ticket holder Ipswich Town FC. Ed: Harrow; Reading (BSc land management).

CHALLENGERS
Bob Blizzard (Lab) MP, Waveney 1997-2010. Lord commissioner, Treasury 2008-10. Assistant government whip, 2007-08. Energy sector consultant. PPS to Nick Brown in 2001-03 but resigned over Iraq. Chairman, APPG for

British offshire oil & gas 1997-2007; renewable transport fuels 2007; British-Brazilian 1997-2007; British-Chilean 2005-07; British-Latin America 2004-07. Leader, Waveney DC 1992-97. Former teacher. School governor. Ed: Birmingham (BA). **Simon Tobin** (Ukip) Former foreman on diamond mines in Botswana and South Africa. Previously engineer in Royal Engineers, military apprentice. Mayor of Southwold in 2014. Cllr, Waveney DC 2006-11. **Graham Elliott** (Green) Smallholder. Cllr, Waveney DC 2007-.

CONSTITUENCY PROFILE
The northeastern corner of Suffolk, close to the Norfolk border. Lowestoft was once a fishing port, but this industry has declined over the years. Waveney has suffered from the depletion of its fishing fleet and from poor transport links. Unemployment is high. It is a centre for the offshore oil and gas industry and jobs are being created in the renewable energy industry.

	Electorate	Turnout %	from 2010 % Change
	80,171	65.1	
P Aldous C	22,104	42.4	+2.1
B Blizzard Lab	19,696	37.7	-1.0
S Tobin Ukip	7,580	14.5	+9.3
G Elliott Green	1,761	3.4	+1.1
S Gordon LD	1,055	2.0	-11.3

Change from 2010

C Lab Ukip Green LD

Wealden

CONSERVATIVE HOLD

NUS GHANI
BORN Sep 1, 1972
MP 2015-

Selected in open primary of 400 members of the public. Contested Birmingham Ladywood 2010. Worked as a health policy campaigner for Age Concern and Breakthrough Breast Cancer. Has worked in the City. Headed communications and fundraising for BBC World Service. Parents are Kashmiri immigrants. Married, one son Ed: Bordesley Green Girls' Sch; University of Central England; Leeds University (MA international relations).

CHALLENGERS
Peter Griffiths (Ukip) Shop owner, Uckfield. Retired from career in aviation. Former chairman of Withyam Conservative association. **Solomon Curtis** (Lab) University of Sussex politics student. Former member of UK Youth Parliament 2012-13. Aged 18, was youngest

candidate in the 2015 election. Ed: Robertsbridge Community Coll; Skinners Sch, Tunbridge Wells. **Giles Goodall** (LD) Assistant to director general for justice, European commission. Former press and media manager for the European commission. Journalist, GOPA-Cartermill Communication 2004-06. Ed: Royal Holloway, London (BA European studies); Coll of Europe (MA European public administration).

CONSTITUENCY PROFILE
A rural seat, mostly situated in the High Weald area of outstanding natural beauty and including the Ashdown Forest. The population is divided between the three main towns and many small villages and hamlets. Small businesses are key. Has a high percentage of self-employed people. Unemployment is low. Agriculture and tourism are important industries here. Lots of families and homeowners. Has been held by the Conservatives since the seat's creation in 1983.

	Electorate	Turnout %	from 2010 % Change
	80,252	71.1	
N Ghani C	32,508	57.0	+0.5
P Griffiths Ukip	9,541	16.7	+10.7
S Curtis Lab	6,165	10.8	+1.2
G Goodall LD	5,180	9.1	-16.2
M Smith Green	3,623	6.4	+3.8

Change from 2010

C Ukip Lab LD Green

Weaver Vale

CONSERVATIVE HOLD

GRAHAM EVANS
BORN Nov 10, 1963
MP 2010-

Campaigned on Northwich Vision regeneration, and against the closure of Northwich Victoria infirmary. PPS to: Michael Fallon 2014-15; Greg Barker 2014-. Select cttees: work & pensions 2012-15; administration 2011-13. Cllr, Macclesfield BC 2000-09. Contested Worsley 2005. Sales and marketing management, roles with Hewlett Packard and BAE Systems. Worked as a special constable for the Cheshire Constabulary. Regularly donates blood. Married, three children. Ed: Poynton County HS; Manchester Met Uni Business School (Business, Dip marketing management).

CHALLENGERS
Julia Tickridge (Lab) Cllr, Cheshire West and Chester 2011-15. Careers adviser and lecturer. Previously worked for

ICI Chemicals in Germany and London. Sch governor. Volunteer, Samaritans listening. Member, Helsby Running Club. Married, one son. Ed: Bangor University (BA German & Italian). **Amos Wright** (Ukip) Cllr, Rudheath PC. **Mary Di Mauro** (LD) Senior campaign activist for Lisa Smart 2014-. Caseworker, office of Sir Andrew Stunell MP. Deputy leader of the opposition, Manchester CC 2010-14. Former teacher. **Chris Copeman** (Green) Veterinary surgeon and low energy housing designer.

CONSTITUENCY PROFILE
Covers the lower valley of the river Weaver. Salt mining has historically been the major industry here and has led to the establishment of a huge chemical works at Winnington. Winsford has the largest rock salt mine in the UK. A lot of families. 70 per cent describe themselves as Christian. Labour held the seat from 1997, but lost it in 2010 to the Conservatives.

	Electorate	Turnout %	from 2010 %	Change
	68,407	68.5		
G Evans C	20,227	43.2	+4.6	
J Tickridge Lab	19,421	41.4	+5.2	
A Wright Ukip	4,547	9.7	+7.4	
M Di Mauro LD	1,395	3.0	-15.7	
C Copeman Green	1,183	2.5	+1.8	
J Whyte TUSC	94	0.2		

Change from 2010

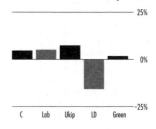

Wellingborough

CONSERVATIVE HOLD

PETER BONE
BORN Oct 19, 1952
MP 2005-

Self-proclaimed founding member of Hots: Harriet Harman's Official Tory Supporters. Select cttees: backbench business 2010-12; panel of chairs 2010-15; health 2007-10; trade & industry 2005-07; statutory instruments 2005-10; 1922 executive committee, 2010-. Right-winger, member of Cornerstone Group. Chartered accountant, ran PLC and family business, electronics and travel companies; dubbed Britain's meanest boss in 1995 for paying trainee 87p an hour. Cllr, Southend-on-Sea 1977-86. Married, one daughter, two sons. Ed: Stewards Comp, Harlow; Westcliff-on-Sea GS, Essex.

CHALLENGERS
Jonathan Munday (Ukip) NHS GP. Forced to apologise after accusing German Twitter user of contributing nothing

to the NHS except "piles and STDs". Chairman, Victoria GP Commissioning Consortium. Cllr, Kensington & Chelsea BC 1986-2002, mayor 1998-99. Magistrate. School governor. Married. Ed: Brentwood Sch; Lincoln Coll, Oxford University; Emmanuel Coll, Cambridge University. **Richard Garvie** (Lab) Suspended from the party after fraud conviction in April 2015, but name still appeared on ballot papers. Broadcaster and sports programme presenter. Managerial positions in supermarkets. Ed: Our Lady and Pope John Sch, Corby. **Chris Nelson** (LD) Science teacher.

CONSTITUENCY PROFILE
Including Rushden, Hingham and Ferrers. Transport links allow many of its residents to commute to work. According to the 2011 census, 20 per cent of its workforce are in wholesale and retail jobs. A £115m employment park is planned for Wellingborough. Held by Labour from 1997 to 2005.

	Electorate	Turnout %	from 2010 %	Change
	77,127	65.4		
P Bone C	26,265	52.1	+3.9	
J Munday Ukip	9,868	19.6	+16.4	
R Garvie Lab	9,839	19.5	-5.9	
C Nelson LD	2,240	4.4	-12.7	
M Turner-Hawes Green	2,218	4.4	+3.5	

Change from 2010

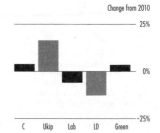

Wells

CONSERVATIVE GAIN

JAMES HEAPPEY
BORN Jan 30, 1981
MP 2015-

Management consultant. Former army major, executive officer to the chief of the general staff, Ministry of Defence. Former parly researcher to Liam Fox MP. Married, one son, one daughter. Ed: Queen Elizabeth Hospital, Bristol; University of Birmingham (BA politics); RMA, Sandhurst.

CHALLENGERS
Tessa Munt (LD) MP, Wells 2010-15. Contested: Wells 2005; Ipswich 2001 by-election; Suffolk South 2001. Trainer, marketing, and sales roles in hotel and leisure industry. FE lecturer. Teacher. Social services manager. Cllr for Childline. Married, three children. Ed: St Joseph's Priory, Dorking; Reigate County Sch; Sutton HS for Girls. **Helen Hims** (Ukip) Runs a family business in Shipham. Local party chairman and

regional representative. Married, four children. **Chris Inchley** (Lab) Gardener, Kilver Court designer village. Cllr: Mendip DC 2011-; Shepton Mallet TC 1995-. Management committee member, CAB. **Jon Cousins** (Green) Cllr, Glastonbury TC. Co-founding member, Glastonbury Harvest Show. Trustee, Glastonbury and Sharpham Burial Board.

CONSTITUENCY PROFILE
A largely rural Somerset seat that includes the Mendip Hills and part of the Somerset levels to the south. Wells is England's smallest city with a population of about 10,000. Also includes Glastonbury, home of the famous festival. Somerset relies on its small and micro businesses related to tourism and agriculture. Shepton Mallet is known for its traditional cider-making. Low unemployment, a high proportion of homeowners and a largely white population. A traditionally Conservative seat, held by the Lib Dems in 2010-15.

	Electorate	Turnout %	from 2010 Change %
	79,405	71.7	
J Heappey C	26,247	46.1	+3.6
T Munt LD	18,662	32.8	-11.2
H Hims Ukip	5,644	9.9	+6.9
C Inchley Lab	3,780	6.6	-0.9
J Cousins Green	2,331	4.1	+3.0
P Arnold ND	83	0.2	
D Dobbs Birthday	81	0.1	
G Watkins Ind	76	0.1	

Change from 2010

Welwyn Hatfield

CONSERVATIVE HOLD

GRANT SHAPPS
BORN Sep 14, 1968
MP 2005-

Self-made early Cameron supporter. Came under criticism when a recording revealed he had a second job as a "multi million-dollar web marketer" under pseudonym Michael Green when he became an MP. Min of state: DfID 2015-. Min without portfolio, Cabinet Office 2012-15. Min of state, CLG 2010-12. Shad min: housing 2007-10. Vice-chairman, campaigning, Con party 2005-10. Select cttees: Speaker's cttee on the electoral commission 2010-12; public administration 2005-07. Contested: Welwyn Hatfield 2001; N Southwark & Bermondsey 1997. Founded PrintHouse Corporation, design print & web devt co. Married, three children. Ed: Watford Boys GS; Cassio Coll, Watford (OND business & finance); Manchester Polytechnic (HND business & finance).

CHALLENGERS
Anawar Miah (Lab) Barrister, Great James Street Chamber. President, British Bangladeshi Practicing Barristers Association. Married, four children. Ed: Lincoln's Inn. **Arthur Stevens** (Ukip) Runs a property management business. Grew up on a council estate in Edmonton. Worked in the financial services industry. Married, four children. **Hugh Annand** (LD) Campaigner. Contested: South Shields by-election 2012; Hertfordshire NE 2010; East of England Euro election 2014.

CONSTITUENCY PROFILE
Consists of the town of Hatfield and the garden city of Welwyn Garden City, built as a new town in 1920. A mixture of urban, suburban and rural areas. Welwyn Garden City includes the headquarters for Tesco. Home to the University of Hertfordshire. Low unemployment. Grant Shapps first won the seat in 2005 with one of the largest Tory swings in the country.

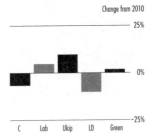

	Electorate	Turnout %	from 2010 Change %
	73,264	68.5	
G Shapps C	25,281	50.4	-6.6
A Miah Lab	13,128	26.2	+4.8
A Stevens Ukip	6,556	13.1	+9.7
H Annand LD	3,140	6.3	-10.1
M Scheimann Green	1,742	3.5	+1.8
M Green Ind	216	0.4	+0.1
R Shattock TUSC	142	0.3	

Change from 2010

Wentworth & Dearne

LABOUR HOLD

JOHN HEALEY
BORN Feb 13, 1960
MP 1997-

Shadow SoS for health 2010-11. Shadow min, housing & planning 2010. Min of state: CLG, housing 2009-10; CLG 2007-09. SoS: Treasury, financial 2005-07; economic 2002-05. Parly under-sec: education & skills 2001-02. Select cttees: electoral commission 2007-09; public accounts 2005-07; tax law rewrite bills 2004-09. PPS to Gordon Brown 1999-2001. Member, GMB. Head of communications: TUC, MSF. Tutor, campaigns manager. Disability charity campaigner. Journalist and editor, *The House* magazine. Married, one son. Ed: Lady Lumley's Comp, Pickering; St Peter's Sch, York; Christ's Coll, Cambridge (scholar, BA).

CHALLENGERS
Mike Hookem (Ukip) MEP for Yorkshire 2014-. Chair, Ukip

Yorkshire & North Lincolnshire cttee 2012-14. Contested Hull East 2010. Former RAF serviceman, commando engineer, Royal Engineers, carpenter and businessman. Married, two children. Ed: Francis Askew HS for Boys, Hull. **Michael Naughton** (C) Policy adviser to conservative group in European parliament. Contested Euro election Yorkshire & the Humber 2014. **Edwin Simpson** (LD) Cllr, Doncaster MBC 1980-88, 1996-2010. Leader, Lib Dem opposition group.

CONSTITUENCY PROFILE
Consists of small mining communities in the South Yorkshire valleys. Comprises of satellite settlements to two large Yorkshire towns, separated by green buffers, in a band north of Rotherham and southeast Barnsley. Traditionally an industrial area, it was hit by pit closures from the 1980s. Unemployment remains high, and many jobs are in manufacturing.

		Electorate	Turnout %	Change from 2010 %
		74,283	58.1	
J Healey	Lab	24,571	56.9	+6.3
M Hookem	Ukip	10,733	24.9	+16.7
M Naughton	C	6,441	14.9	-2.7
E Simpson	LD	1,135	2.6	-13.5
A England	Eng Dem	309	0.7	

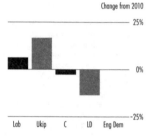

Change from 2010

Lab Ukip C LD Eng Dem

West Bromwich East

LABOUR HOLD

TOM WATSON
BORN Jan 8, 1967
MP 2001-

Led failed coup against Tony Blair in 2006 prompting resignation as junior defence minister. His investigations into phone hacking led to the setting up of the Leveson Inquiry. Deputy leadership contender 2015. Labour party dep chairman, campaign co-ordinator 2011-13. Parly sec, Cab Office 2008-09. Asst govt whip 2007-08. Parly under-sec, defence 2006. Whip: govt 2005-06; asst govt 2004-05. Member, Labour party national exec 2005-10. PPS to Dawn Primarolo 2003-04. Select cttees: CMS 2009-12; home 2001-03. Nat coordinator Lab FPTP campaign. Lab party nat devt officer. Dir: Tribune; Policy Network. AEEU nat political officer. Advertising account exec. Marketing officer, Save the City of Wells. Married, one daughter, one son. Ed: King Charles I Sch, Kidderminster.

CHALLENGERS
Olivia Seccombe (C) Public affairs manager, Dairy Crest. Political researcher: Countryside Alliance 2010-12, Theresa May MP 2008-10. Speaks Spanish. Ed: Uni of York (BA English). **Steve Latham** (Ukip) Works for National Express. Worked for Hiatt, Patent Shaft, Bailey & Mackey. Was in care from age 13-18. Had a heart bypass 2012. Married, two children. **Flo Clucas** (LD) Cllr: Cheltenham BC 2014-; Liverpool CC 1986-12. Adviser to the mayor of Liverpool EU funding 2012-. President, ALDE Gender Equality Network.

CONSTITUENCY PROFILE
Small, urban seat. A working-class area with high unemployment. More than a third of its potential workforce have no qualifications. One in five of the population is Asian in origin and the area is home to one of the largest Sikh communities in the country. The seat is undergoing regeneration. Held by Labour since 1974.

		Electorate	Turnout %	Change from 2010 %
		63,641	58.9	
T Watson	Lab	18,817	50.2	+3.7
O Seccombe	C	9,347	24.9	-4.0
S Latham	Ukip	7,949	21.2	+18.6
F Clucas	LD	751	2.0	-11.2
B Lim	Green	628	1.7	

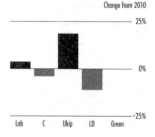

Change from 2010

Lab C Ukip LD Green

West Bromwich West

LABOUR CO-OPERATIVE HOLD

ADRIAN BAILEY
BORN Dec 11, 1945
MP 2000-

Caught up in a minor scandal in 2012 after claiming expenses for attending a remembrance service and for apparently trivial food and drink items. Select cttees: national security strategy 2010-15; liaison, Commons 2010-15. Chairman, select cttee: BIS 2010-15; West Midlands regional 2009-10; business & enterprise 2008-09; European scrutiny 2007-10. PPS to: Bob Ainsworth 2007; Adam Ingram 2006-07; Hilary Armstrong 2006; John Hutton 2005-06. Co-operative party political organiser 1982-2000. Cllr, Sandwell BC 1991-2000, deputy leader 1997-2000. Librarian Cheshire CC 1971-82. GMBATU member 1982-. Married, one stepson. Ed: Cheltenham GS; Exeter University (BA economic history); Loughborough Coll of Librarianship (PdDip).

CHALLENGERS
Graham Eardley (Ukip) Associate of the Chartered Institute of Credit Management. Bruges Group events officer. Deanery synod representative. Member, Lichfield diocesan board of patronage. **Paul Ratner** (C) Dir, Ratner Capital Pension Consultancy, set up business at 25. Ed: Merchant Taylors' Sch; University of Warwick (BA economics, politics & international Studies). **Mark Redding** (Green) Runs a sporting goods company.

CONSTITUENCY PROFILE
In the heart of the Black Country, made up of industrial towns like Tipton and Wednesbury. The decline of engineering and manufacturing has left high unemployment here. Ethnically diverse, 15 per cent of residents are Asian and the BNP have had a presence here. Was former Commons speaker Betty Boothroyd's seat from 1974-2000. Solid Labour seat.

	Electorate	Turnout %	Change from 2010 %
	65,533	53.5	
A Bailey Lab Co-op	16,578	47.3	+2.4
G Eardley Ukip	8,836	25.2	+20.9
P Ratner C	8,365	23.9	-5.5
M Redding Green	697	2.0	
K Trench LD	550	1.6	-10.4

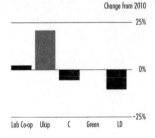

Change from 2010

Lab Co-op   Ukip   C   Green   LD

West Ham

LABOUR HOLD

LYN BROWN
BORN Apr 13, 1960
MP 2005-

Shadow min: CLG 2013-15. Opposition whip, Commons 2010-13. Assistant whip, Treasury 2009-10. PPS to: John Denham 2007-09; Phil Woolas 2006-07. Select cttees: crossrail bill 2007; CLG 2005-06; ODPM 2005-06. Unison. Member, Co-op party, Fabian Society. Contested Wanstead & Woodford 1992. Founder, London Library Development Board. Member: London Region Sports Board; London Arts Board; Museums, Libraries & Archives Council, London. Married. Ed: Plashet Comp; Whitelands Coll, Roehampton (BA English & religious studies).

CHALLENGERS
Festus Akinbusoye (C) Senior parly assist to Mark Lancaster MP and Iain Stewart MP 2013-. Managing director, Ikan Facilities

Management. Deputy chairman, Milton Keynes Conservative Assoc 2011-13. Adviser and partner, Milton Keynes Equality Council 2011-12. School governor. Speaks Yoruba. Three children. Ed: St Paul's Way Sch; London Institute (BA business & corporate communications); SOAS (MA international studies & diplomacy); PR Academy (PgDip public relations & image management). **Jamie McKenzie** (Ukip) Interior designer. Chair, Young Independence, London. **Rachael Collinson** (Green) Freelance digital fundraising and campaigning consultant.

CONSTITUENCY PROFILE
A deprived seat in the London Borough of Newham. Has one of the highest proportions of ethnic minorities of any seat in the country. In the 2011 census only 35 per cent gave their ethnicity as white. Has high child poverty rates. More than a quarter of the population is Muslim.

	Electorate	Turnout %	Change from 2010 %
	90,634	58.3	
L Brown Lab	36,132	68.4	+5.8
F Akinbusoye C	8,146	15.4	+0.8
J McKenzie Ukip	3,950	7.5	+5.9
R Collinson Green	2,651	5.0	+3.7
P Reynolds LD	1,430	2.7	-8.8
A Uzoka CPA	369	0.7	-2.1
C Bogie Community	115	0.2	

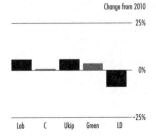

Change from 2010

Lab   C   Ukip   Green   LD

Westminster North

LABOUR HOLD

KAREN BUCK
BORN Aug 30, 1958
MP 2010-

PPS to Ed Miliband 2013-. Son posted videos on his YouTube channel smoking "joints" on gangsta rap videos in 2015. Shadow min: education 2011-13; work & pensions 2010-11. Parly assist to Tony McNulty 2008-10. Parly under-sec, transport 2005-06. Select cttees: work & pensions 2010; London regional, chair 2009-10; children, schools & families 2009-10; home 2006-09; work & pensions 2001-05; selection 1999-2001; social security 1997-2001. Cllr, Westminster 1990-97. Disabled people's services. Employment charity worker. Hackney Borough specialist officer. Named Child Poverty Action Group's MP of the Year. Married, one son. Ed: Chelmsford HS; LSE (BSc economics, MSc economics, MA social policy & administration).

CHALLENGERS
Lindsey Hall (C) Runs art and antiques business with husband. Cllr, Westminster CC 2007-. Known as "anti-fraudstar" on council for taking down benefit fraudsters. Former reporter. School governor. Married, three daughters. **Nigel Sussman** (Ukip) Managing dir, High Court Collections. Former commercial director at JBW Group. Former member of CIPS Congress. **Kirsty Allan** (LD) Caseworker for Lynne Featherstone MP. Ed: Royal Holloway, London (BA history; MA public history). **Jennifer Nadel** (Green) Barrister.

CONSTITUENCY PROFILE
One of the smallest and most densely populated seats in the UK. Includes highly expensive residential areas such as Mayfair, Knightsbridge and Belgravia, but also deprived areas in the north of the borough. Includes Lord's cricket ground. Racially diverse. Has the highest percentage of Arab residents in the country.

	Electorate	Turnout %	from 2010 % Change
	62,346	63.4	
K Buck Lab	18,504	46.8	+3.0
L Hall C	16,527	41.8	+3.3
N Sussman Ukip	1,489	3.8	+3.0
K Allan LD	1,457	3.7	-10.2
J Nadel Green	1,322	3.4	+2.1
G Fajardo Ch P	152	0.4	+0.1
N Ward Ind	63	0.2	-0.1

Change from 2010

Change from 2010

Lab   C   Ukip   LD   Green

Westmorland & Lonsdale

LIBERAL DEMOCRAT HOLD

TIM FARRON
BORN May 27, 1970
MP 2005-

MP From the Lib Dems' centre-left. Candidate for Lib Dem dep leader 2015, 2010. Quit LD front bench to vote for EU referendum in 2008. LD shad sec: Defra 2008-10. LD shad min: countryside 2007-08; home 2007. PPS to Sir Menzies Campbell 2006-07. LD spokes: youth affairs 2005-06. Select cttees: European scrutiny 2010-13; environmental audit 2006-07; education & skills 2005-06. Contested: Westmorland & Lonsdale 2001; South Ribble 1997. Cllr: South Lakeland DC 2004-08; Lancashire CC 1993-2000; South Ribble BC 1995-99. Head of faculty admin, St Martin's Coll. Married, four children. Ed: Lostock Hall HS, Preston; Runshaw Tertiary Coll; Newcastle (BA politics).

CHALLENGERS
Ann Myatt (C) Consultant

dermatologist, South Cumbria NHS. Married, two children. Ed: University of Leeds (MBChB medicine). **Alan Piper** (Ukip) Owner, Sun Hotel, Coniston 2000. Project management consultant, UBS Investment Bank 1997-99, Bank of Scotland 1996. **John Bateson** (Lab) Hospitality manager. Cllr, Kendal BC 2006-10. Mayor of Kendal, 2009-10. Contested W&L 2001. Teacher and examiner. Ed: Kendal GS. **Chris Loynes** (Green) Lecturer and researcher in outdoor education, University of Cumbria.

CONSTITUENCY PROFILE
A large, sparsely populated constituency in Cumbria. In the heart of the Lake District, it includes the towns of Kendal and Windermere and parts of the Lake District National Park and the Yorkshire Dales National Park. Tourism is its main industry. Agriculture is important. According to the 2011 census, it has the lowest rate of unemployment in England and Wales.

	Electorate	Turnout %	from 2010 % Change
	65,857	74.3	
T Farron LD	25,194	51.5	-8.5
A Myatt C	16,245	33.2	-3.0
A Piper Ukip	3,031	6.2	+4.6
J Bateson Lab	2,661	5.4	+3.2
C Loynes Green	1,798	3.7	

Change from 2010

LD   C   Ukip   Lab   Green

Weston-Super-Mare

CONSERVATIVE HOLD

JOHN PENROSE
BORN Jun 22, 1964
MP 2005-

Min, constitutional reform 2015-. Lord commissioner Treasury, whip 2014-15; asst whip Treasury 2013-14. Parly under-sec: CMS 2010-. Shadow min: business 2009-10. PPS to Oliver Letwin as chair, Con policy review 2006-09. Select cttees: selection 2014-15; administration 2012-13; regulatory reform 2009-10; work & pensions 2005-09. Contested: Weston-Super-Mare 2001; Ealing Southall 1997. Publishing career: chair Logotron, educational software; MD, Longman, Thomson. Management consultant, McKinsey. Banking, JP Morgan. Head of research, Bow Group. Married, two daughters Ed: Ipswich Sch; Downing Coll, Cambridge (BA law); Columbia (MBA).

CHALLENGERS
Tim Taylor (Lab) HR manager,

performance & reward, Lloyds Banking Group. Cllr, Weston-Super-Mare TC 2011-, Labour group leader. Married, two daughters. Ed: Warwick (BA history); Nottingham Trent (CIPD). **Ernie Warrender** (Ukip) Former stockbroker, gardener, assembly line worker at Ford and salesman. Contested Bath 2010. One child. **John Munro** (LD) External affairs adviser, British Retail Consortium. Previously campaigns manager, National Campaign for the Arts. Constituency manager, Bath 2005-08. Ed: Wyvern Sch; Keele (BA politics).

CONSTITUENCY PROFILE
Victorian seaside resort on the west coast of England. Tourism is the mainstay of the local economy, with agriculture also important in north Somerset. Some deprivation: the area reportedly had 11 per cent of all UK drug rehabilitation places in 2009. Once a safe Conservative seat, it fell to the Lib Dems in 1997 before the Tories returned in 2005.

	Electorate	Turnout %	Change from 2010 %
	79,493	66.1	
J Penrose C	25,203	48.0	+3.7
T Taylor Lab	9,594	18.3	+7.3
E Warrender Ukip	9,366	17.8	+15.2
J Munro LD	5,486	10.4	-28.8
R Lawson Green	2,592	4.9	
R Lavelle Eng Dem	311	0.6	+0.1

Change from 2010

Wigan

LABOUR HOLD

LISA NANDY
BORN Aug 9, 1979
MP 2010-

Respected campaigner on children and housing, unafraid to take on party establishment. From Labour's pragmatic "soft left". Cites J.S. Mill among political heroes. Shadow min: Cabinet Office 2013-15; education 2013. Select cttee, education 2010-12. Cllr, shad Cab member for housing & regeneration, Hammersmith & Fulham BC 2006-10. Senior policy adviser, the Children's Society. Parly researcher to Neil Gerrard MP. Member: Unite, Communication Workers Union, Co-operative Party, Amnesty International. Local theatre director. Ed: Parrs Wood Comp, Manchester; Newcastle Upon Tyne (BA politics); Birkbeck Coll, London (MSc politics & govt).

CHALLENGERS
Caroline Kerswell (C) Legal assist

& development, Ali Almihdar Outer Temple Chambers. Solicitor consultant, LV Priestley & Son solicitors. Member, Arab British Chamber of Commerce 2011-. Ed: University Coll, London (LLB); Coll of Law (BVC; LLM international law); BPP Law Sch; SOAS (Dip Arab language). **Mark Bradley** (Ukip) Project manager in health & social care. Served in Royal Navy 1990-2012. **Will Patterson** (Green) IT administrator and environmental campaigner. **Mark Clayton** (LD) Contested Wigan 2010. Cllr, Manchester CC 2006-14.

CONSTITUENCY PROFILE
Mainly urban, the seat covers the town of Wigan but also countryside around former pit villages such as Crooke and Standish. The decline of the coal and cotton industries hit the area's economy hard. Centre for food manufacturing. Includes Europe's biggest canned food production site. High unemployment. Has been solidly Labour since 1918.

	Electorate	Turnout %	Change from 2010 %
	76,068	59.5	
L Nandy Lab	23,625	52.2	+3.7
C Kerswell C	9,389	20.7	-4.0
M Bradley Ukip	8,818	19.5	+13.8
W Patterson Green	1,273	2.8	
M Clayton LD	1,255	2.8	-12.6
G Fairhurst Wigan	768	1.7	
B Parr Ind	165	0.4	

Change from 2010

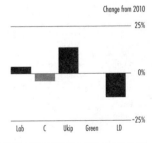

Wiltshire North

CONSERVATIVE HOLD

JAMES GRAY
BORN Nov 7, 1954
MP 1997-

Survived two de-selection attempts after he had an affair while his wife had cancer. Shadow sec: Scotland, 2005. Shadow min: countryside 2002-05; defence 2001. Opposition whip 2000-01. Select cttees: arms export controls 2013-15; defence 2013-15; procedure 2010-15; finance & services 2010-13; panel of chairs 2010-15; efra 2007-10; regulatory reform 2005-10. Special adviser to John Gummer, Michael Howard 1991-95. Dir, Baltic Futures Exchange 1989-91. Territorial Army 1977-84. Divorced, remarried. One daughter, two sons from previous marriage. Ed: Glasgow HS; University of Glasgow (MA history), Christ Church, Oxford (history thesis).

CHALLENGERS
Brian Mathew (LD) Aid worker, water, sanitation and hygiene

adviser. Postings include East Timor, Zimbabwe and Sudan with WaterAid, World Vision, DfID. Contested: North Somerset 2010; South West Euro election, 2014. Ed: Millfield Sch; UEA (BA development studies); Reading (MA rural social development); Cranfield (PhD water & sanitation). **Pat Bryant** (Ukip) MD of risk management consulting company. Member: Countryside Alliance, British Horse Society. Contested Devizes 2010. Widowed, one daughter, one son.

CONSTITUENCY PROFILE
Rural seat on the edge of the Cotswolds. Has one of the highest percentages of family households in the country. Manufacturing is important. Defence is also a big employer. Includes former RAF base at Lyneham. Between 2007 and 2011 the bodies of British servicemen killed in Afghanistan were repatriated via Lyneham and then driven through Royal Wootton Bassett. Safe Conservative seat.

	Electorate	Turnout %	Change from 2010 %
	67,858	74.5	
J Gray C	28,938	57.2	+5.7
B Mathew LD	7,892	15.6	-20.6
P Bryant Ukip	5,813	11.5	+7.6
P Baldrey Lab	4,930	9.8	+3.1
P Chamberlain Green	2,350	4.7	+3.4
S Killane Ind	390	0.8	
G Wareham Ind	243	0.5	

Change from 2010

Wiltshire South West

CONSERVATIVE HOLD

ANDREW MURRISON
BORN Apr 24, 1961
MP 2001-

Former medical officer in Royal Navy, recalled in 2003 for Iraq war. Parly under sec: NI office 2014-15. Shadow min: defence 2007-10; health 2004-07; public services, education 2003-04. MP for Westbury 2001-10. PPS to Andrew Lansley 2010-12. Appointed special representative for the centenary commemoration of the First World War 2011. Research assist to Lord Freeman. *PH7* magazine editorial advisory board. Surgeon Commander, Royal Navy, 1981-2000. Locum consultant occupational physician and GP. Married, five daughters. Ed: The Harwich Sch; Bristol (MBChB MD medicine); Hughes Hall, Cambridge (DPH).

CHALLENGERS
Matthew Brown (Ukip) Small business corporate and financial

strategy adviser. Previously investment banker and management consultant in Madrid. Member: Camra. Drummer. Two stepchildren. Ed: City University (BA business); Manchester Business School (MBA). **George Aylett** (Lab) 19-year-old with 230,000 Twitter followers. Deputy member UK Youth parliament. Ed: Ralph Allen Sch. **Trevor Carbin** (LD) Driving instructor and archaeologist. Cllr: Wiltshire C 2009-; West Wiltshire DC 1995-2009; Wiltshire CC 2001-05.

CONSTITUENCY PROFILE
Formerly Westbury, which had returned a Tory MP at every general election since 1924, renamed in 2010 after boundary changes. A large constituency in a predominantly rural county covering part of Salisbury Plain and the towns around its western fringe. Predominantly white population. Unemployment is low. Local government and defence are big employers.

	Electorate	Turnout %	Change from 2010 %
	73,030	70.7	
A Murrison C	27,198	52.7	+1.0
M Brown Ukip	9,030	17.5	+12.0
G Aylett Lab	6,948	13.5	+2.0
T Carbin LD	5,482	10.6	-19.9
P Randle Green	2,985	5.8	

Change from 2010

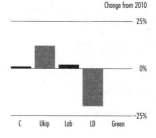

Wimbledon

CONSERVATIVE HOLD

STEPHEN HAMMOND
BORN Feb 4, 1962
MP 2005-

Took an £800-an-hour job at Inmarsat months after he lost his job as SoS for transport in the cabinet reshuffle 2014. Parly under sec: transport 2012-14. PPS to Eric Pickles 2010-2012. Shadow min, transport 2005-10. Select cttees: public accounts 2014-15; crossrail bill 2007; regulatory reform 2005-08. Former Merton Cllr and long-term Tory activist. Stockbroker, UBS Philips and Drew. Directorial roles: Dresdner Kleinwort Benson Securities and Commerzbank Securities. Played hockey for a National League team and county. Married, one daughter. Ed: King Edward VI Sch, Southampton; Richard Hale Sch, Hertford; Queen Mary, London (BSc economics).

CHALLENGERS
Andrew Judge (Lab) Barrister, Westgate Chambers. Cllr, Merton

BC 1995-, leader 2001-06. Contested Wimbledon 2010. Married. Ed: University of Kent (LLB law); Birkbeck Coll (MSc politics & administration); UCL (LLM environmental law). **Shas Sheehan** (LD) Chair of the Wimbledon Cancer Friendship Group. Former head of office to Susan Kramer. Cllr, Richmond BC 2006-10. Contested Wimbledon 2010. Teacher. Board of trustees at Merton and Lambeth CAB. Married, three children. Ed: UCL (BSc chemistry). **Peter Bucklitsch** (Ukip) Accountant. Former property developer. Contested Thanet South 2010 for Lib Dems.

CONSTITUENCY PROFILE
Best known for the tennis tournament. Suburban, and housing is expensive. Nearly 40 per cent of residents are aged 25-44. Has the lowest rate of unemployed 16 to 24-year-olds in the country. Ethnically diverse and home to Buddhapadipa Temple, the first Buddhist temple in the UK.

	Electorate	Turnout %	Change from 2010 %
	65,853	73.5	
S Hammond C	25,225	52.1	+3.0
A Judge Lab	12,606	26.0	+3.8
S Sheehan LD	6,129	12.7	-12.3
P Bucklitsch Ukip	2,476	5.1	+3.2
C Barraball Green	1,986	4.1	+2.9

Change from 2010

Winchester

CONSERVATIVE HOLD

STEVE BRINE
BORN Jan 28, 1974
MP 2010-

Former journalist, interested in health and the media. MoS: DWP, disabled people 2013-14; policing, HO & MoJ 2014-. Select cttees: draft voting eligibility, (prisoners) bill 2013; justice 2011-15. PPS to Mike Penning 2013-. Member, Conservative Way Forward. Worked with specialist golf marketing agency, the Azalea Group. Reporter and producer, BBC Radio Surrey, Southern Counties Radio. Consultant Conservative Research Department. Keen golfer and skier. Married, one daughter, one son. Ed: Bohunt Comp, Liphook; Liverpool Hope University (BA history, student union pres).

CHALLENGERS
Jackie Porter (LD) Teacher. Cllr, Hampshire CC 2005-. Chairman, Street Reach youth

charity. Contested Winchester 2005. Married, two children. Ed: University of Manchester (BSc textile sciences & engineering). **Mark Chaloner** (Lab) Family law barrister. Cllr, Southampton CC 2012-. Member: British Association of Adoption and Fostering; Unison; Unite; GMB. Married, two daughters. Ed: University of Cambridge (LLM law). **Martin Lyon** (Ukip) Quantity surveyor and health & safety practitioner. Qualified abritator. Cllr, Bishopstoke PC 2012-. Cllr, Hampshire CC 2013-.

CONSTITUENCY PROFILE
On the edge of the South Downs, the cathedral city of Winchester is England's ancient capital and former seat of King Alfred. Home to Winchester College. A key Hampshire tourist destination. Low unemployment. Large employers include IBM, which has its headquarters in the area. Includes the University of Winchester. Historically a Conservative seat.

	Electorate	Turnout %	Change from 2010 %
	74,119	74.6	
S Brine C	30,425	55.0	+6.5
J Porter LD	13,511	24.4	-18.7
M Chaloner Lab	4,613	8.3	+2.9
M Lyon Ukip	4,122	7.5	+5.4
M Wilks Green	2,645	4.8	

Change from 2010

Windsor

CONSERVATIVE HOLD

ADAM AFRIYIE
BORN Aug 4, 1965
MP 2005-

Wealthy entrepreneur, the first black Tory MP. Shadow min, innovation & science 2007-10. Anti- MPs' expenses, chairman: members' expenses select cttee 2011-. Select cttees: CSF 2007-08; innovation, universities & skills 2007. Founder of IT company Connect Support Services. Chairman, Adfero. Wealth estimated at £50m. London chairman, Business for Sterling, campaigned against Euro. Anti-immigration. Born in Wimbledon to Ghanaian father. Divorced, remarried, one daughter, two sons, one stepson. Ed: Imperial Coll (BSc agricultural economics).

CHALLENGERS
Fiona Dent (Lab) Self-employed consultant and fine artist. Background includes nursing, social work, probation, charity management, community regeneration. Governer of Frimley Health NHS Trust. Ed: University of West London (LLB law, PgDip socio-legal studies). **Tariq Malik** (Ukip) Accountant. Financial controller for UK business. **George Fussey** (LD) Professional biologist and curator of Eton Coll natural history museum. Head of career education, Eton. Cllr, Windsor & Maidenhead 2011-15. Fellow, Soc of Biology, Linnean Soc, Royal Soc of Medicine. **Derek Wall** (Green) Principal speaker, Green party 2006-08. Head of economics, Duff Miller Coll; tutor, Goldsmiths, London.

CONSTITUENCY PROFILE
One of the wealthiest constituencies in the country. Home to Windsor Castle, Eton College, the Household Cavalry Regiment and Royal Ascot. Has among the highest employment rates in England and Wales. There are also large Hindu and Sikh communities. Held by the Conservatives since 1874.

	Electorate	Turnout %	from 2010 %	Change
	74,119	67.7		
A Afriyie C	31,797	63.4	+2.6	
F Dent Lab	6,714	13.4	+3.5	
T Malik Ukip	4,992	10.0	+6.7	
G Fussey LD	4,323	8.6	-13.8	
D Wall Green	1,834	3.7	+2.4	
W Da Costa Ind	500	1.0	+0.6	

Change from 2010

C   Lab   Ukip   LD   Green

Wirral South

LABOUR HOLD

ALISON McGOVERN
BORN Dec 30, 1980
MP 2010-

Mainstream Labour, locally-raised candidate. Shadow min: education 2014-15; international development 2013-14. Oppositon whip, Commons 2013. Select cttees: Speaker's advisory cttee on works of art 2010-15; international development 2010-13. Cllr, Southwark BC 2006-10, deputy leader Labour group. Researcher, HoC 2002-06. Vice-chair, Progress 2012-. Public affairs manager for Network Rail, The Art Fund and Creativity Culture & Education. Member, Unite. Trustee, South London Gallery 2006-10. Grew up in Bromborough. Liverpool FC fan. Married, one daughter. Ed: Wirral GS for Girls; UCL (BA philosophy); Birkbeck Coll (PgCert economics).

CHALLENGERS
John Bell (C) Retired teacher and lecturer. Contested: Alyn and Deeside 2007; Delyn 2005; Clwyd South 2011 Welsh Assembly elections. Ed: University of Keele (BA economics & politics; PGCE). **David Scott** (Ukip) Lecturer in psychology, University of Chester. Contested Wirral South 2005. Ed: Quarry Bank HS; University of Aberdeen (BSc psychology); Open University (BA, MSc advanced educational & social research methods); University of Liverpool (PhD). **Elizabeth Jewkes** (LD) Vice chair, Lib Dem Christian Forum. Contested: Chester 2010; Vale of Clwyd 2005; Ellesmere Port & Neston 1992.

CONSTITUENCY PROFILE
A middle-class suburban seat with good links to Liverpool. Has a largely white, Christian population with few ethnic minority residents. Held by the Tories from its creation in 1982 until Labour took it in a 1997 by-election. Alison McGovern took the seat in 2010 by a margin of 521 votes, increasing her majority to 4,599 in 2015.

	Electorate	Turnout %	from 2010 %	Change
	56,956	73.5		
A McGovern Lab	20,165	48.2	+7.4	
J Bell C	15,566	37.2	-2.3	
D Scott Ukip	3,737	8.9	+5.7	
E Jewkes LD	1,474	3.5	-13.0	
P Cartlidge Green	895	2.1		

Change from 2010

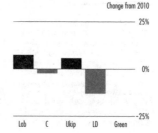

Lab   C   Ukip   LD   Green

Wirral West

LABOUR GAIN

MARGARET GREENWOOD
BORN Mar 14, 1959
MP 2015-

Web consultant. Former English teacher and travel writer. Committed campaigner for the NHS and environmental issues. Launched The Save Hilbre and Dee Estuary campaign. Enjoys hill walking and theatre.

CHALLENGERS
Esther McVey (C) MP 2010-15. Min of state: employment, work & pensions 2014-15;. Parly under sec: disabled people 2012-13. PPS to Chris Grayling 2010-2012. Contested Wirral West (old boundaries) 2005. MD, Making It. Founder, 'Winning Women' Dir, JG McVey and Co. Patron, Wirral Holistic Therapeutic Cancer Care. Ed: Belvedere Sch; Queen Mary & Westfield University (LLB law); City University (MA radio journalism); Liverpool John Moores (MSc corporate

governance; studying for PhD in leadership & entrepreneurship).
Hilary Jones (Ukip) Funeral Director. Joined the WRAC in 1974 before joining Merseyside Police in 1977. **Peter Reisdorf** (LD) IT analyst at Crowder water industry consultancy. Cllr, Wirral BC 2000-2011. Contested: Wirral W 2010; Wallasey 2001, 1997.

CONSTITUENCY PROFILE
The most affluent and most rural of the four constituencies on the Wirral peninsula in northwest England. Popular with commuters. According to the 2011 census, 56.2 per cent of the population is female. A largely white, Christian population. Has a high percentage of homeowners and a small social rented sector. The bulk of residents work in wholesale or retail trade, health, social work and education. Traditionally a Conservative seat but fell to Labour between 1997 and 2010. Retaken by Labour in the 2015 election by a slim margin of 417 votes.

	Electorate	Turnout %	Change from 2010 %
	55,377	75.6	
M Greenwood Lab	18,898	45.2	+8.9
E McVey C	18,481	44.2	+1.7
H Jones Ukip	2,772	6.6	+4.3
P Reisdorf LD	1,433	3.4	-13.4
D James ND	274	0.7	

Change from 2010

Witham

CONSERVATIVE HOLD

PRITI PATEL
BORN Mar 29, 1972
MP 2010-

First female Asian Tory MP. Left the Conservative party to work on the Referendum party's 1997 election campaign before rejoining under William Hague. Min, employment 2015-. Exchequer sec: Treasury 2014-15. Select cttees: draft deregulation bill 2013; public administration 2011-14; members' expenses 2011-15. 1922 executive committee, 2010-. Conservative party policy board 2013-. First UK Indian diaspora champion 2013-. Contested Nottingham North 2005. Dir, Weber Shandwick Corporate Communications. Deputy press sec to William Hague as leader of opposition. Enjoys racing, cricket and rock music. Hindu. Married, one son. Ed: Westfield Girls Sch, Watford; Keele University (BA economics); University of Essex (MSc British government).

CHALLENGER
Gary Cockrill (Ukip) Foster carer. Passenger transport driver. Cllr, Hatfield Peverel PC 2013-15. Chair, South Essex Ukip 2013-14. Deputy chair, South Essex Ukip 2011-12. Contested Southend West 2010. Previously motorcycle courier, domestic appliance service engineer. Church pastor 2002-08. Member, National Autistic Society. Married, two children. Ed: Beths GS; Woolwich Coll. **John Clarke** (Lab) Senior lecturer, UEL. Chair, Black Notley PC. Ed: UMIST (BSc mathematics & management sciences; PGCE); Leeds University (MSc mathematical education).

CONSTITUENCY PROFILE
A largely rural constituency created in 2010 in recognition of Essex's growing population. Largely prosperous, with affluent commuter villages and farming communities. According to the 2011 census, most residents are owner-occupiers and there are few council homes.

	Electorate	Turnout %	Change from 2010 %
	67,090	70.3	
P Patel C	27,123	57.5	+5.3
G Cockrill Ukip	7,569	16.1	+9.5
J Clarke Lab	7,467	15.8	-2.7
J Hayes LD	2,891	6.1	-13.6
J Abbott Green	2,038	4.3	+1.3
D Scrimshaw CPA	80	0.2	

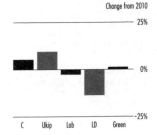

Change from 2010

Witney

DAVID CAMERON
BORN Oct 9, 1966
MP 2001-

Led Conservatives into widely unexpected majority, first prime minister since Lord Salisbury in 1900 to increase party's share of the vote after being in No 10 more than 18 months. Compassionate Conservative, legalised same-sex marriage. Govt administered health and welfare reforms, austerity measures, and committed to an EU referendum. Leader of the opposition 2005-10. Conservative leader 2005-. Shadow SoS: education 2005. Shadow minister: local government 2004; privy council office 2003. Head, political section, Conservative research department 1988-92; member, John Major's PMQs briefing team. Special adviser to: Norman Lamont; Michael Howard. Carlton Communications. Married, one daughter, two sons, one deceased: Ivan, who had cerebral palsy and epilepsy, died 2009.

Ed: Heatherdown Sch; Eton Coll; Brasenose Coll, Oxford (BA PPE. Member, Bullingdon Club).

CHALLENGERS
Duncan Enright (Lab) MD, Evidence-based Networks 2013-. Dir and head of health care and publishing, LeaderShape 2013-. Senior associate, Maverick Publishing Specialists 2013-. Cllr: West Oxfordshire DC 2012-; Witney TC 2011-. Contested Witney 1997. Ed: Wadham Coll, Oxford (BA physics; PGCE). **Simon Strutt** (Ukip) Managing partner, The Marketing Works Married, two sons. Ed: Oxford (BA PPE)

CONSTITUENCY PROFILE
A large rural seat in the west of Oxfordshire. Economy relies on agriculture, high-tech motorsport, the large RAF base at Brize Norton and tourism from the Cotswolds and Blenheim Palace. Affluent with high employment. Home to various Formula One teams. Has been won by Conservative MPs since 1974.

	Electorate	Turnout %	from 2010 %
	79,767	73.3	
D Cameron C	35,201	60.2	+1.4
D Enright Lab	10,046	17.2	+4.2
S Strutt Ukip	5,352	9.2	+5.7
A Graham LD	3,953	6.8	-12.7
S Macdonald Green	2,970	5.1	+1.0
C Peedell NHAP	616	1.1	
C Bex Wessex Reg	110	0.2	+0.1
C Tompson Ind	94	0.2	+0.1
V Saunders VAT	56	0.1	
B Smith Elmo	37	0.1	
D Jackson LP	35	0.1	
N Handley ND	12	0.0	

Change from 2010

Woking

JONATHAN LORD
BORN Sep 17, 1962
MP 2010-

Marketing consultant who won open primary selection. Former chairman of Guildford Conservative Association and campaign manager for Anne Milton in 2005 campaign. Cllr: Surrey 2009-; Westminster 1994-2002; deputy leader. Deputy chair, Surrey Area Conservatives 2007-09. Oldham-born, cut his teeth contesting Oldham West & Royton 1997. Former dir, Saatchi & Saatchi. Keen cricketer. Married, one daughter, one son. Ed: Shrewsbury Sch; Kent Sch, Connecticut; Merton Coll, Oxford (BA modern history, OUCA president).

CHALLENGERS
Jill Rawling (Lab) Business development manager, Relate relationship charity. Women's officer, CLP 2012. Former buyer for Holland & Barrett; spent ten

years running an art gallery. One daughter. **Chris Took** (LD) Sales director, PageSuite digital publishing. Cllr, Ashford BC 2003-07. Contested Ashford 2010, 05. Leading figure in campaign to retain wardens in sheltered accommodation. Married. Ed: University of Kent (BA European politics). **Rob Burberry** (Ukip) Constituency manager for Nigel Farage MEP, Janice Atkinson MEP, Diane James MEP, Ray Finch MEP. Ukip national co-ordinator, police & crime commissioner elections 2012. Ed: University for the Creative Arts (HND journalism).

CONSTITUENCY PROFILE
The largest town in Surrey. Has high employment and a large Pakistani community. Home to many commuters. It has the first purpose-built mosque in Britain, the Shah Jahan Mosque. Famous former residents include Paul Weller and H. G. Wells. Conservative since the seat was created in 1950.

	Electorate	Turnout %	from 2010 %
	74,287	70.0	
J Lord C	29,199	56.2	+5.9
J Rawling Lab	8,389	16.1	+8.1
C Took LD	6,047	11.6	-25.8
R Burberry Ukip	5,873	11.3	+7.5
M Robson Green	2,109	4.1	
D Wade CSA	229	0.4	
R Temple Magna Carta	77	0.2	+0.1
A Woolford TEP	41	0.1	

Change from 2010

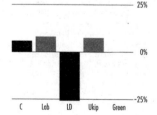

Wokingham

CONSERVATIVE HOLD

JOHN REDWOOD
BORN Jun 15, 1951
MP 1987-

Challenged John Major's leadership in 1995 and contested again in 1997. Chair, Conservative Economics competitiveness policy group 2005-. Shadow SoS: deregulation 2004-05; environment, transport & regions 1999-2000; T&I 1997-99. SoS: Wales 1993-95. Min: environment 1992-93; 1990-2. Parly under-sec, DT&I 1989-90. Cllr, Oxon. Chief policy adviser to Thatcher in the 1990s. Fellow, All Souls, Oxford. Visiting Professor, Middlesex University Business Sch. Investment analyst, NM Rothschild; chair, Concentric plc. Divorced, one daughter, one son. Ed: Kent Coll; Magdalen Coll, Oxford (MA modern history); St Antony's Coll (DPhil modern history).

CHALLENGERS
Andy Croy (Lab) Accountant and former teacher. Ed: Forest Sch; SOAS. **Clive Jones** (LD) Managing Director of toy company for more than ten years, set up his own business in 2009. President, British Toy & Hobby Association trade organisation. Vice-chair, Early Lib Dems. Married, two daughters. Ed: Bulmershe Sch. **Phil Cunnington** (Ukip) General manager, NHS Mental Health in Hampshire. Two daughters. Ed: Langley GS. **Adrian Windisch** (Green) Engineer. Contested Reading West 2010, 05.

CONSTITUENCY PROFILE
An affluent, middle-class constituency. Contains the historic market town of Wokingham and a wide area south of Reading. Home to London commuters, company headquarters and high-tech industry. Includes the Thames Valley Police Training College, the Atomic Weapons Establishment at Burghfield and part of the University of Reading. Held by the Conservatives since 1950, and by John Redwood since 1987.

	Electorate	Turnout %	from 2010 %	Change
	77,881	71.9		
J Redwood C	32,329	57.7	+5.0	
A Croy Lab	8,132	14.5	+4.4	
C Jones LD	7,572	13.5	-14.5	
P Cunnington Ukip	5,516	9.9	+6.8	
A Windisch Green	2,092	3.7	+2.7	
K Lokuciewski Ind	358	0.6	-3.7	

Change from 2010

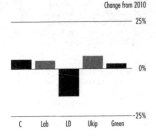

C   Lab   LD   Ukip   Green

Wolverhampton North East

LABOUR HOLD

EMMA REYNOLDS
BORN Nov 2, 1977
MP 2010-

Centrist, lobbyist. Established the APPG on aerospace in Wolverhampton. Shadow SoS, CLG 2015-. Shadow min: CLG, housing 2013-15; FCO 2010-13. Select cttee, foreign affairs 2010. Was special adviser to Geoff Hoon MP as minister for Europe, chief whip. Political adviser to Robin Cook as president, Party of European Socialists in Brussels. Small Business Europe. Sec: APPG for British Sikhs; human trafficking. Multi-lingual. GMB. Locally-raised, Wolverhampton Wanderers fan. Ed: Perton Middle Sch; Codsall HS; Wulfren Coll; Wadham Coll, Oxford (BA PPE).

CHALLENGERS
Darren Henry (C) General manager, Harvest Fine Foods. Served in RAF 1987-2013, Squadron Leader. Mentor to veterans with Help for Heroes. RFU referee. School governor. Married, two daughters. Ed: Bedford Modern. **Star Etheridge** (Ukip) Cllr, Dudley MBC 2014-. Ukip disability spokesman 2012-. Member, CAPC, TFA. Separated, three children. Ed: University of Bolton (BA business studies & law, PGCE); Manchester Metropolitan University (PGDL law); Liverpool John Moores University (LPC law). **Ian Jenkins** (LD) Worked in the glass industry. Married, two daughters. **Becky Cooper** (Green) Teacher. Ed: Wolverhampton (BA design).

CONSTITUENCY PROFILE
At the northwestern corner of the West Midlands urban area. Was an industrial city and, while the service sector now dominates, engineering is still an important part of the local economy, particularly aerospace. UTC Aerospace Systems is based here. Unemployment is high. Has three times the national average of council homes.

	Electorate	Turnout %	from 2010 %	Change
	61,073	55.7		
E Reynolds Lab	15,669	46.1	+4.7	
D Henry C	10,174	29.9	-4.4	
S Etheridge Ukip	6,524	19.2	+15.9	
I Jenkins LD	935	2.8	-10.8	
B Cooper Green	701	2.1		

Change from 2010

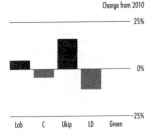

Lab   C   Ukip   LD   Green

Wolverhampton South East

PAT MCFADDEN
BORN Mar 26, 1965
MP 2005-

Party fixer turned politician. Shrewd, good union links. Disciple of Donald Dewar. Political secretary, PM's office 2002-05. Shadow min: FCO 2014-15. Shadow SoS, BIS 2009-10. Min: employment relations & postal affairs, Dep BERR & BIS 2007-09. Parly sec, Cabinet Office 2006-07. TGWU. Member, Labour party national executive cttee 2007-10. Select cttees: parliamentary commission on banking standards 2012-13; Treasury 2011-14. Passionate Celtic fan. Ed: Holyrood Sch; Edinburgh (MA politics).

CHALLENGERS
Suria Photay (C) Adjudicator, Financial Ombudsman Service. Paralegal, Gladstone & Kent Law 2011-. Former employment law legal adviser, Bradical. Speaks French and Punjabi. Ed:

Wolverhampton GS; Aberystwyth University (LLB law); Coll of Law, Birmingham (Bar). **Barry Hodgson** (Ukip) Freelance management consultant. Treasurer and nominating officer, Pensioners party 2004-12. Founder & chairman, Wolverhampton branch, Ukip 2010-. Member, College & University Lecturer's Union. Vice-chair, Wolverhampton Civic & Historical Society. Contested South West region 2009 Euro elections for the Pensioners party. Married, two daughters. Ed: Bilston Boys' GS; Wolverhampton Poly. **Ian Griffiths** (LD) Has cerebral palsy. Gay, married. Ed: Bilston Community Coll.

CONSTITUENCY PROFILE
Situated around the market town of Bilston. Has lots of car manufacturing factory jobs and the highest percentage of long-term unemployed people in England and Wales. Unemployment is nearly twice the national average. Held by Labour since its creation in 1974.

	Electorate	Turnout %	Change from 2010 %
	62,561	55.6	
P McFadden Lab	18,539	53.3	+5.8
S Photay C	7,761	22.3	-6.2
B Hodgson Ukip	7,061	20.3	+12.6
I Griffiths LD	798	2.3	-12.9
G Kauldhar Green	605	1.7	

Change from 2010

25%

0%

-25%

Lab   C   Ukip   LD   Green

Wolverhampton South West

ROB MARRIS
BORN Apr 8, 1955
MP 2015-

MP for Wolverhampton SW 2001-10. Solicitor. Trade unionist. Member, select cttee: trade & industry 2005-10. PPS to Shaun Woodward 2007-10. *The House's* Backbencher of the Year 2008. Chair, Whitmore Reans Welfare Centre. Trustee, Believe to Achieve. Cautioned for damaging a van when climbing over car bonnet to catch a bus. Early Greenpeace member. Wolves season ticket holder. Spent nine years in Canada, worked for the British Columbia Forest Service. Ed: St Edward's Sch, Oxford; University of British Columbia (BA sociology & history); Birmingham Poly (law).

CHALLENGERS
Paul Uppal (C) MP for Wolverhampton SW 2010-15. PPS to David Willetts 2012-14. Select cttee, environmental audit 2011-13.

Contested Birmingham Yardley 2005. Self-employed businessman and commercial property manager. Cites Gorbachev, Reagan and Lincoln as political heroes. Sikh of East African descent, trustee of a Sikh temple. Married, three children. Ed: Harborne Hill School, Birmingham; Warwick (BA politics & sociology). **Dave Everett** (Ukip) Businessman. Lived on Warstones Estate for 25 years. Ed: Highfields Comp Sch. **Andrea Cantrill** (Green). **Neale Upstone** (LD) Technical director and IT consultant. Cllr, Cambridge CC 2006-14. Partner, one daughter.

CONSTITUENCY PROFILE
In the northwest of the West Midlands. Its Sikh population is among the largest in England and Wales. Includes the main Wolverhampton University campus and Molineux stadium. Was once regarded as safe Tory territory, held by Enoch Powell from 1950-1974, and remained Conservative until Labours 1997 landslide.

	Electorate	Turnout %	Change from 2010 %
	60,375	66.6	
R Marris Lab	17,374	43.2	+4.2
P Uppal C	16,573	41.2	+0.5
D Everett Ukip	4,310	10.7	+7.0
A Cantrill Green	1,058	2.6	
N Upstone LD	845	2.1	-13.9
B Booth Ind	49	0.1	

Change from 2010

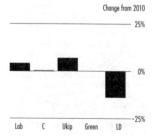

25%

0%

-25%

Lab   C   Ukip   Green   LD

Worcester

ROBIN WALKER
BORN Apr 12, 1978
MP 2010-

Son of long-serving former Worcester MP Lord Walker. PPS to Nicky Morgan 2015-; Liz Truss 2014-15; Andrew Robathan 2013-14. Select cttees: arms export controls 2012-13; BIS 2012-15; Welsh affairs 2011-12. Press officer to Oliver Letwin, 2005. Assistant to Richard Adams PPC for Worcester 2001. PA and driver to Stephen Dorrell 1997. Partner of Finsbury Ltd, advising industry on press and financial communications. Member: Armed Forces Parly Scheme; Conservative Middle East Council, Tory Reform Group; TRG; Commonwealth Parly Assoc. Formerly worked in recruitment. Enjoys watching cricket and rugby. Married. Ed: St Paul's Sch; Balliol Coll, Oxford (BA history).

CHALLENGERS
Joy Squires (Lab) Consultant in regeneration. Politics and European studies lecturer, University of Wolverhampton. Cllr, Worcester CC 2012-. Grew up on council estate. Married, two sons. **James Goad** (Ukip) Heritage consultant, CH2M Hill 2005-. Member, Chartered Institute for Archaeologists. Ed: Birkenhead Boys' Sch; University of Birmingham (BA ancient history & archaeology). **Louis Stephen** (Green) Previously worked as an engineering manager at Bosch. Married, two children.

CONSTITUENCY PROFILE
A cathedral city and county town built around the River Severn and flanked by the M5 to its east. Has a largely white population, many of whom commute to Birmingham. Low unemployment. Home to the vast porcelain collection at the Museum of Royal Worcester. Historically a Conservative seat, it fell to Labour during its 1997 landslide. Was regained by the Conservatives in 2010.

	Electorate	Turnout %	from 2010 %	Change
	71,003	70.0		
R Walker C		22,534	45.3	+5.8
J Squires Lab		16,888	34.0	+0.5
J Goad Ukip		6,378	12.8	+10.1
L Stephen Green		2,024	4.1	+2.6
F Smith LD		1,677	3.4	-16.1
P McNally TUSC		153	0.3	
M Shuker Ind		69	0.1	-0.1

Change from 2010

Worcestershire Mid

NIGEL HUDDLESTON
BORN Oct 13, 1970
MP 2015-

Selected in open primary. Industry head of travel, Google 2011-. Cllr, St Albans DC 2011-14. Contested Luton South 2010. Member, Tory Reform Group. Dir, Deloitte 2002-10. Senior manager, Arthur Andersen Business Consulting 1993-02. Freeman of the City of Lincoln. Enjoys travelling. Married, one son, one daughter. Ed: Robert Pattinson Comp; Oxford (BA PPE, sabb officer); UCLA (MBA entertainment management).

CHALLENGERS
Richard Keel (Ukip) Runs a construction business. Imports tractors and collectables from the USA. Contested Worcestershire CC election 2013. Married. **Robin Lunn** (Lab) Business partnerships manager, AXA Wealth. Cllr, Worcestershire CC 2009-. Contested Worcestershire Mid 2010. Member, CAB, local admissions forum. **Margaret Rowley** (LD) Head of knowledge management, Worcestershire Acute Hospitals NHS Trust. Cllr, Wychavon DC 1995-. Author of canal guides. Contested Worcestershire Mid 2010, 05. Ed: Nottingham University (BSc zoology); Loughborough University (MA librarianship). **Neil Franks** (Green) Runs a sustainability consultancy company. Married, two children.

CONSTITUENCY PROFILE
A rural seat that covers the stretch of countryside inbetween Worcester and Redditch, south of Birmingham. The local economy is largely made up of fruit growing, farming, distribution as well as tourism. The Vale of Evesham is sometimes called the fruit basket of England. A high number of people describe themselves as gypsies or Irish travellers here. Safe Tory seat. Peter Luff won the seat for the Tories in 2010.

	Electorate	Turnout %	from 2010 %	Change
	73,069	71.5		
N Huddleston C		29,763	57.0	+2.5
R Keel Ukip		9,231	17.7	+11.7
R Lunn Lab		7,548	14.5	-0.5
M Rowley LD		3,750	7.2	-16.2
N Franks Green		1,933	3.7	+2.5

Change from 2010

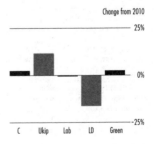

Worcestershire West

CONSERVATIVE HOLD

HARRIETT BALDWIN
BORN May 2, 1960
MP 2010-

Smart, enthusiastic and straightforward. Economic secretary to the Treasury, City minister 2015-. Govt whip 2014-15; assist whip 2014. PPS to: Esther McVey 2013-14; Mark Hoban 2012-13. Select cttees: administration 2014; work & pensions 2010-12. Contested Stockton North 2005. Investment manager, JP Morgan. Campaigned with Business for Sterling. Centre for Policy Studies. Centre for Social Justice supporter and fundraiser, helped to write social enterprise policy. Married, one son, two step-daughters. Ed: Quaker Friends' Sch; Marlborough Coll; Lady Margaret Hall, Oxford (BA French & Russian); McGill University, Toronto (MBA).

CHALLENGERS
Richard Chamings (Ukip) Principal, White House Vets.

Chair: Ukip West Midlands 2001-04; Ukip Worcester & District 1995-05. Contested Worcester 2005, 01. Member, British Veterinary Assoc. Married, four daughters. Ed: Kelly Coll, Devon; Edinburgh (BVM&S, MRCVS veterinary). **Daniel Walton** (Lab) Managing dir, OLPRO camping and caravanning equipment. Previously sales director of leisure companies. Married, three children. Ed: Sheffield Coll; University of Wales, Bangor (BA criminology). **Dennis Wharton** (LD) Former headteacher, now self-employed. Community worker.

CONSTITUENCY PROFILE
A large rural constituency bordering Gloucestershire in the south and reaching to the Birmingham commuter belt in the north. The largest population centre is the Victorian spa town of Great Malvern, which is the home of Malvern Coll and Malvern Girl's Coll. Fruit growing and agriculture are important here.

	Electorate	Turnout %	from 2010 % Change
	73,415	73.7	
H Baldwin C	30,342	56.1	+5.8
R Chamings Ukip	7,764	14.4	+10.4
D Walton Lab	7,244	13.4	+6.6
D Wharton LD	5,245	9.7	-28.1
J Roskams Green	3,505	6.5	+5.3

Change from 2010

C · Ukip · Lab · LD · Green

Workington

LABOUR HOLD

SUE HAYMAN
BORN Jul 28, 1962
MP 2015-

The first female MP to be elected in the Border region. Public affairs consultant. Cllr, Cumbria CC 2013-. Contested Halesowen & Rowley Regis 2010; Preseli Pembrokeshire 2005. Trustee, Asha Women's Centre 2008-2011. Member: Labour Women's Network; RSPB; GMB; Labour Animal Welfare Society. Head of public affairs, Copper Consultancy. Sings in local choir. Keeps hens. Married, two children. Ed: Anglia Ruskin University (BA English literature).

CHALLENGERS
Rozila Kana (C) Project manager, Association of Chief Police Officers. Has worked for police since 1999, now in counter-terrorism. Previously worked as an administrative officer for the Employment Service; NHS PTC in Hyndburn & Ribble Valley. Born

and raised in Kenya. Married, two children. **Mark Jenkinson** (Ukip) Small businessman. Founding chairman, Ukip West Cumbria 2012-14. Married, four children. Ed: St Josephs RC SS; West Cumbria Coll. **Phill Roberts** (LD) Retired social worker. Served in the SAS. Community politics advocate. Married, three children. **Jill Perry** (Green) Jam maker and former language teacher. Contested North West region 2014.

CONSTITUENCY PROFILE
Much of the seat is made up of the Lake District National Park and surrounding countryside which brings in millions of visitors every year. According to the 2011 census, it has the highest percentage of white residents in England and Wales. The main industries used to be coal and steelworks. New businesses have sprung up in footware, plastics and cardboard. Low unemployment. Has been held by Labour since 1918 except after a Tory by-election win in 1976.

	Electorate	Turnout %	from 2010 % Change
	58,672	65.6	
S Hayman Lab	16,282	42.3	-3.2
R Kana C	11,596	30.2	-3.7
M Jenkinson Ukip	7,538	19.6	+17.4
P Roberts LD	1,708	4.4	-9.1
J Perry Green	1,149	3.0	
R Ivinson ND	190	0.5	

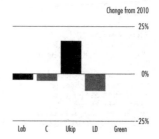

Change from 2010

Lab · C · Ukip · LD · Green

Worsley & Eccles South

LABOUR HOLD

BARBARA KEELEY
BORN Mar 26, 1952
MP 2005-

Close interest in improving support services for support carers. Dep leader HoC 2009-10. Asst govt whip 2007-08. PPS to: Harriet Harman 2006-07; Jim Murphy 2006-07. MP, Worsley 2005-10. Shadow dep leader of the HoC 2010. Shadow min for health 2010; CLG 2010-11. Cllr, Trafford BC 1995-2004. Worked as a systems programmer at IBM UK. Consultant, Princess Royal Trust for Carers 2001-05. Member, Amnesty International. Voluntary sector consultant. Married. Ed: Mount St Mary's RC Coll, Leeds; Salford (BSc politics & contemporary history).

CHALLENGERS
Iain Lindley (C) Marketing and publicity officer, Rochdale Boroughwide Housing assoc. Cllr, Salford CC 2004-. Contested

Worsley & Eccles S 2010. Member: Conservative Councillors' Assoc; Co-op group; Friends of Walkden Station. Former commons caseworker. Ed: Eccles Coll; University of York (BA politics). **Owen Hammond** (Ukip) Retired RAF pilot and airline captain. Started a business selling air freight 2004-. Adopted. Married, two sons. Ed: Buckhurst Hill County HS. **Christopher Bertenshaw** (Green) From a socialist background, joined Greens in 2014.

CONSTITUENCY PROFILE
Includes some of the most sought-after residential areas in Greater Manchester. There are pockets of deprivation and as a whole the seat is mostly working class, made up of former mining towns such as Walkden. There are higher than average numbers of single parent families and jobless households here, according to the 2011 census. Barbara Keeley won the seat when it was created in 2010 and retook it in 2015.

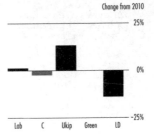

	Electorate	Turnout %	Change from 2010 %
	72,174	58.3	
B Keeley Lab	18,600	44.2	+1.3
I Lindley C	12,654	30.1	-2.4
O Hammond Ukip	7,688	18.3	+13.4
C Bertenshaw Green	1,242	3.0	
K Clarkson LD	1,100	2.6	-13.9
S North TUSC	380	0.9	
M McNally Reality	200	0.5	
G Berg Ind	184	0.4	

Change from 2010

Worthing East & Shoreham

CONSERVATIVE HOLD

TIM LOUGHTON
BORN May 30, 1962
MP 1997-

Often seen wearing jeans at Westminster. Has a laconic sense of humour and performed an excruciating rap dance on TV reality show. Parly under-sec: education 2010-12. Shadow min: children 2003-10; health & education 2003. Opposition spokes, various 2000-03. Select cttees: home affairs 2014-15; draft mental health bill 2004-05; environmental audit 1997-2001. General election PA to Tim Eggar 1987. Fund manager, Flemings. Non-exec dir, Netlink. Married, two daughters, one son. Ed: the Priory Sch; Warwick (BA classical civilisation); Clare Coll, Cambridge (Research, Mesopotamian archaeology).

CHALLENGERS
Tim Macpherson (Lab) Dir, Angling Trust 2014-. Owner: Sussex Angling Media 2011;

Sussex Angling TV 2014-. Media consultant, Blue Sea Media 2003-. Former global asset manager relationship consultant, IPE. Married, three children. Ed: Bexhill Coll; Bangor University (BSc biology). **Mike Glennon** (Ukip) Retired. Worked in advertising and marketing. Cllr, West Sussex CC 2013-, Opposition leader 2013-. Married. Ed: Priory Comp Sch, Lewes; University of Greenwich (BA international marketing & German). **Bob Smytherman** (LD) Town crier. Cllr: Worthing BC 2014-; West Sussex CC 2009-.

CONSTITUENCY PROFILE
Takes in the residential parts of East Worthing, industrial Shoreham-by-Sea and smaller outlying communities. Local govt, tourism and the service sector are big employers here. Much of the seafront area is relatively poor, with tourism providing seasonal employment. Further inland there are more affluent patches. It has returned a Tory MP since 1997.

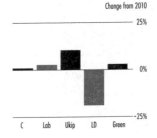

	Electorate	Turnout %	Change from 2010 %
	74,272	67.2	
T Loughton C	24,686	49.5	+1.0
T Macpherson Lab	9,737	19.5	+2.8
M Glennon Ukip	8,267	16.6	+10.4
B Smytherman LD	3,360	6.7	-18.8
J Doyle Green	2,605	5.2	+2.9
C Walker NHAP	1,243	2.5	

Change from 2010

Worthing West

CONSERVATIVE HOLD

SIR PETER BOTTOMLEY
BORN Jul 20, 1944
MP 1975-

Husband of Baroness Bottomley, health SoS in Major's Cabinet. Issued a public denial of any involvement in child sex abuse in a bid to counter false claims circulating on the internet 2014. Parly under-sec: NI 1989-90; transport 1986-89; employment 1984-86. Select cttees: high speed rail bill 2014-15; draft defamation bill 2011; ecclesiastical 2010-15; constitutional affairs 2003-05. MP: Eltham 1983-97; Greenwich, Woolwich West 1975-83. President, Conservative Trade Unionists 1978-80, former TWGU member. Knighted for public service 2011. Married, two daughters, one son. Ed: Westminster Sch; Trinity Coll, Cambridge University (BA economics).

CHALLENGERS
Tim Cross (Ukip) Qualified rugby coach and referee. Lived and worked in Australia for 10 years. Contested: Worthing W 2005, 01, 1997; Euro election for SE region 2004. Ed: Oundle Sch; Royal Agricultural Coll, Cirencester (Dip agriculture). **Jim Deen** (Lab) Retired, conservation volunteer, Steyning Downland Scheme. Contested Worthing 1992. Former journalist and research scientist at the Glasshouse Crops Research Institute in Rustington. **Hazel Thorpe** (LD) Cllr, Worthing BC 2000-. Former teacher, head of SEN department. Previously draftswoman.

CONSTITUENCY PROFILE
Includes most of the seaside town of Worthing and coastal villages. Most jobs are in the service sector, tourism and retail. Local government and manufacturing is important. According to the 2011 census, 26.5 per cent of residents are over 65, one of the highest percentages in the country. Tory held since it was created in 1997.

	Electorate	Turnout %	Change from 2010 %
	75,617	67.1	
P Bottomley C	26,124	51.5	-0.3
T Cross Ukip	9,269	18.3	+12.3
J Deen Lab	7,955	15.7	+3.9
H Thorpe LD	4,477	8.8	-19.0
D Aherne Green	2,938	5.8	+3.8

Change from 2010

Wrekin, The

CONSERVATIVE HOLD

MARK PRITCHARD
BORN Nov 22, 1966
MP 2005-

Animal welfare campaigner. Called for a review of laws that grant anonymity in sexual assault cases after an investigation into a rape allegation against him was dropped in 2014. Panel of chairs 2012-15. Sec, 1922 committee, 2010-. Member, select cttees: international devt 2012-13; national security strategy 2010-15; transport 2008-10; Welsh affairs 2007-10; work & pensions 2006-08; environmental audit 2005-07. Contested Warley 2001. Cllr, Harrow, Woking. CCO press officer 1997. Career in marketing. Married. Ed: Aylestone Sch, Hereford; London Guildhall University (MA marketing management; PgDip marketing); University of Buckingham (MA international diplomacy).

CHALLENGERS
Katrina Gilman (Lab) Works in the criminal justice system. Grew up on a council estate, single-parent family. Speaks French. **Jill Seymour** (Ukip) Ukip MEP for West Midlands 2014-. Company sec 1990-2014. Previously sat on the Ukip National Exec board and has been a Ukip branch chairman. Farmer's daughter. **Rod Keyes** (LD) Retired chartered insurer. School governor. Enjoys his narrow boat. Married, one son. **Cath Edwards** (Green) Sustainability consultant at 3 Green Rs. Chair, Telford and Wrekin Green party.

CONSTITUENCY PROFILE
A rural seat, curving around the town of Telford, taking in market and old mining towns. Has a significant agricultural sector and is home to Harper Agricultural University College. There is also a substantial military presence in the area, with RAF Cosford here. Named after its towering volcanic hill. It has a history of switching hands between Labour and the Tories.

	Electorate	Turnout %	Change from 2010 %
	65,942	68.9	
M Pritchard C	22,579	49.7	+2.0
K Gilman Lab	11,836	26.1	-1.1
J Seymour Ukip	7,620	16.8	+12.3
R Keyes LD	1,959	4.3	-13.1
C Edwards Green	1,443	3.2	

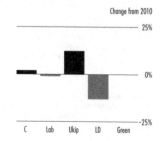

Change from 2010

Wrexham

LABOUR HOLD

IAN LUCAS
BORN Sep 18, 1960
MP 2001-

Was solicitor to Trevor Rees-Jones, the sole survivor of the crash that killed Diana, Princess of Wales. Shadow min: defence 2014-15; FCO 2011-14; BIS 2010-11; business and regulatory reform 2010. Parly under-sec: BIS 2009-10. Asst govt whip 2008-09. PPS to: Liam Byrne 2007-08; Bill Rammell 2005-06. Select cttees: draft constitutional renewal bill 2008; public accounts 2007; transport 2003-05; environmental audit 2001-03; procedure 2001-02. Member: Gresford Community Council, Wrexham 1987-91; Fabian Society. Amicus, MSF. Married, two children. Ed: Greenwell Comp Sch, Gateshead; RGS, Newcastle; New Coll, Oxford (BA jurisprudence); Coll of Law, Christleton.

CHALLENGERS
Andrew Atkinson (C) Owner, AA Cleaning Services. Cllr: Herefordshire CC 2011-; Ross-on-Wye TC 2011-15. Former caseworker to Jesse Norman MP. Left school at 16 and became window cleaner. Married, two sons. Ed: University of Worcester (Dip leadership & management). **Niall Plevin-Kelly** (Ukip) Regional inspector, OFTEC. Served in the Royal Marines. Former teacher. Married. Ed: Ratcliffe Coll for Boys, Leicestershire; University of Plymouth (BSc microbial & cellular biology). **Carrie Harper** (PC) Cllr: Caia Park CC 2012-. NE Wales representative of the campaign group Cymuned.

CONSTITUENCY PROFILE
North east of Wales. Borders England. The majority of the seat is made up of the town of Wrexham itself, the biggest town in north Wales. A former industrial town once dominated by mining. Has one of the UK's largest industrial parks, which provides jobs for many people in the area.

	Electorate	Turnout %	Change from 2010 %
	50,992	64.2	
I Lucas Lab	12,181	37.2	+0.4
A Atkinson C	10,350	31.6	+6.2
N Plevin-Kelly Ukip	5,072	15.5	+13.2
C Harper PC	2,501	7.6	+1.5
R Walsh LD	1,735	5.3	-20.5
D Munnerley Green	669	2.0	
B Edwards Ind	211	0.6	

Change from 2010

(bar chart: Lab, C, Ukip, PC, LD; scale 25% to -25%)

Wycombe

CONSERVATIVE HOLD

STEVEN BAKER
BORN Jun 6, 1971
MP 2010-

Won the first seat he was interviewed for. Claims to offset his carbon footprint from sky-diving and other high-octane hobbies. Select cttees: Treasury 2014-15; transport 2010-13. RAF engineer officer, chartered engineer. Technology consultant for various companies including Lehman Brothers. Dir, the Cobden Centre. Former associate consultant, Centre for Social Justice. Cornwall-born. Married. Ed: Poltair Comp Sch, Cornwall; St Austell Sixth Form Coll; Southampton (BEng aerospace systems engineering); St Cross Coll, Oxford (MSc computer science).

CHALLENGERS
David Williams (Lab) Barrister. Appointed QC 2013. Chair, Society of Labour Lawyers 1990-. ASTMS, MSF 1986-98. Nominated for International Family Lawyer of the Year. Ed: Cedars Upper Sch; Leicester (LLB law); Inns of Court Sch of Law. **David Meacock** (Ukip) Cllr, Chiltern DC 1999-14. Faced criticism after sending a group email accusing a child of taking his son's toy. Married, two children. Ed: Dr Challoner's GS; Royal Coll of Music; University of Reading. **Steve Guy** (LD) Telecoms consultant. Transmission planner, Ericsson. Cllr, Wycombe DC 2009-11. Contested Wycombe 2010. School governor. Married, Ed: Queen Mary's GS, Walsall. **Jem Bailey** (Green) Contested Beaconsfield 2010. Married.

CONSTITUENCY PROFILE
Dominated by the town of High Wycombe and affluent villages around the Chiltern Hills. Is one of the few areas to retain grammar schools. According to the 2011 census, 13.4 per cent of residents are Muslim. About one in four residents is from an ethnic minority.

	Electorate	Turnout %	Change from 2010 %
	76,371	67.4	
S Baker C	26,444	51.4	+2.8
D Williams Lab	11,588	22.5	+5.2
D Meacock Ukip	5,198	10.1	+5.7
S Guy LD	4,546	8.8	-20.0
J Bailey Green	3,086	6.0	
D Fitton Ind	577	1.1	+0.7

Change from 2010

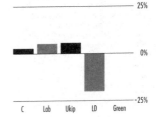

(bar chart: C, Lab, Ukip, LD, Green; scale 25% to -25%)

Wyre & Preston North

CONSERVATIVE HOLD

BEN WALLACE
BORN May 15, 1970
MP 2005-

Parly under-sec, Northern Ireland 2015-. Assistant whip, Treasury 2014-15. Shadow min, Scotland 2007-10. MP for Lancaster & Wyre 2005-10. PPS to Ken Clarke 2010-14. Select cttees: administration 2014-15; Scottish affairs 2005-10. MSP North East Scotland 1999-2003. Contested West Aberdeenshire and Kincardine 1999 Scottish parl election. EU, overseas dir, Qinetiq 2003-05. Army officer, Scots Guards. Member, Queen's Bodyguard of Scotland, Royal Archers 2007-. Former ski instructor, Austrian National Ski school. Married, one daughter, two sons. Ed: Millfield Sch; Sandhurst.

CHALLENGERS
Ben Whittingham (Lab) Teacher. Labour party's young people champion in the Wyre. Tweeted that Churchill was a "racist and white supremacist" 2014. Ed: University of Edinburgh (MA modern languages). **Kate Walsh** (Ukip) Owns a traditional toy shop. Part-time teacher. Member, local business group. Enjoys climbing. **John Potter** (LD) Video producer, head of AV production, Express Gifts. Cllr, Preston CC 2010-. Ed: UCLan (BA audio visual media with journalism). **Anne Power** (Green) Retired teacher. Anti-fracking protester. Won the Local Hero Award at the *Observer* Ethical Awards 2014.

CONSTITUENCY PROFILE
A fairly rural constituency, its largest towns are Poulton-le-Fylde, Thornton and Garstang. Major employers include BAE Systems. Manufacturing is important employer. Has one of the lowest unemployment rates in England and Wales. It has the lowest percentage of people in social housing in the country. Created in 2010.

	Electorate	Turnout %	from 2010 %	Change %
	70,697	70.6		
B Wallace C	26,528	53.2	+0.8	
B Whittingham Lab	12,377	24.8	+3.5	
K Walsh Ukip	6,577	13.2	+8.4	
J Potter LD	2,712	5.4	-16.1	
A Power Green	1,699	3.4		

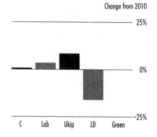

Change from 2010

C   Lab   Ukip   LD   Green

Wyre Forest

CONSERVATIVE HOLD

MARK GARNIER
BORN Feb 26, 1963
MP 2010-

Investment banker and hedge fund adviser, cousin of Edward Garnier MP. Secretly recorded dismissing "dog-end voters" in the "outlying regions" 2014. Select cttees: parliamentary commission on banking standards 2012-13; Treasury 2010-15. Contested Wyre Forest 2005. Cllr, Forest of Dean DC 2003-07. Partner, AugMentor. Management consultant, Strategic Planning Solutions. Severn Capital LLP; CGR Capital; Bear Stearns; Edmond de Rothschild Securities; Daiwa Securities Europe; South China Securities; Swiss Bank Corp Int; WI Carr. Freeman, City of London. Enjoys shooting and fishing. Married, one daughter, two sons. Ed: Charterhouse.

CHALLENGERS
Matthew Lamb (Lab) Director of sixth form, Sandwell Coll, West Bromwich. Cllr, Worcester CC 2010-. Partner, one daughter. Ed: King Charles I HS; University of Birmingham (PhD political science). **Michael Wrench** (Ukip)Runs his own business. Former soldier. Cllr, Wyre Forest DC. Contested Wyre Forest 2010. **Richard Taylor** (Independent Community and Health Concern) MP for Wyre Forest 2001-10. Retired physician and surgeon. Ed: Clare Coll, Cambridge (BA); Westminster Medical Sch (MBBChir).

CONSTITUENCY PROFILE
Covers the three towns of Kidderminster, Stourport and Bewdley and the surrounding rural villages. Kidderminster is an industrial town and a centre for the carpet industry. According to the 2011 census, four times the national average describe themselves as gypsies or Irish travellers. From 2001 to 2010 the seat was held by Dr Richard Taylor, an independent. The Conservatives retook the seat in 2010.

	Electorate	Turnout %	from 2010 %	Change %
	77,451	63.8		
M Garnier C	22,394	45.3	+8.4	
M Lamb Lab	9,523	19.3	+4.9	
M Wrench Ukip	7,967	16.1	+13.2	
R Taylor Ind CHC	7,211	14.6	-17.1	
A Crick LD	1,228	2.5	-9.4	
N McVey Green	1,117	2.3		

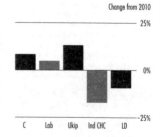

Change from 2010

C   Lab   Ukip   Ind CHC   LD

Wythenshawe & Sale East

LABOUR HOLD

MICHAEL KANE
BORN Jan 9, 1969
MP 2014-

Elected in by-election after the death of Paul Goggins. Backed David Miliband in the 2010 leadership election. Select cttees: Treasury 2014-; environmental audit 2014-. Cllr, Manchester CC 1991-2008. Former: office manager to Jonathan Reynolds; parly assist to James Purnell; Tameside Council, senior exec assist in council leader's office; teacher. Former chief exec, Movement for Change. Flautist. Married. Ed: St Paul's RC HS; Loreto Coll, Hulme.

CHALLENGERS
Fiona Green (C) Mediator, Green Doors Mediation. Solicitor. Director of a social enterprise. Married, children. Enjoys playing chess. Ed: University of Manchester (LLB law). **Lee Clayton** (Ukip) Security consultant

and auditor. Former paratrooper. Cllr, Wistaston PC. Former healthcare assistant. Married, two children. Ed: Poundswick HS. **Victor Chamberlain** (LD) Campaigns and communications, Association of Liberal Democrat Councillors. Cllr, Manchester CC 2010-14. Ed: LSE (BA geography). **Jessica Mayo** (Green) Works for Mind. Anti-fracking campaigner. Ed: Manchester Metropolitan University.

CONSTITUENCY PROFILE
Mostly made up of the huge interwar council estate of Wythenshawe, built to house the overspill population of Manchester and one of the largest council estates in the country. Significant employers include Manchester airport and Wythenshawe hospital. According to the 2011 census, 33 per cent of the population live in social housing, nearly double the national average. The seat has been held by Labour since its creation in 1997.

	Electorate	Turnout %	from 2010 %	Change %
	75,980	56.9		
M Kane Lab	21,693	50.1	+6.0	
F Green C	11,124	25.7	+0.2	
L Clayton Ukip	6,354	14.7	+11.2	
V Chamberlain LD	1,927	4.5	-17.9	
J Mayo Green	1,658	3.8		
J Disco Loony	292	0.7		
L Worthington TUSC	215	0.5	-0.2	

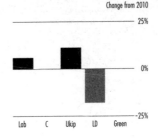

Change from 2010

Yeovil

CONSERVATIVE GAIN

MARCUS FYSH
BORN Nov 8, 1970
MP 2015-

Owns and runs a consultancy firm, Isys Biomed Limited. Selected in open primary. Cllr, Somerset CC 2013-. Cllr, South Somerset DC 2011-15. Worked for Mercury Asset Management. Born in Australia, moved to UK aged 3. Married, one daughter. Ed: Oxford University (literature).

CHALLENGERS
David Laws (LD) MP for Yeovil 2001-15. Min: education & Cabinet Office 2012-15; Cabinet Office & education 2012-15. Chief sec to Treasury May 2010, resigned pending inquiry into Commons allowances for second home rent to male lover. LD shad sec: children, schools & families 2007-10; work & pensions 2005-07; chief sec to Treasury 2002-05. Select cttees: draft financial services bill 2011; tax law rewrite bill

2002-05. LD spokesman, defence 2001-02. Investment banker. Ed: St George Coll, Surrey; King's Coll, Cambridge University (BA economics). **Simon Smedley** (Ukip) Runs a commercial property company. Churchwarden. Worked as a ski guide and holiday rep in Europe. Ed: King's Coll Sch, Wimbledon. **Sheena King** (Lab) Works in air traffic control. Gamesmaker at London 2012 Olympic Games. One son. Ed: Maidstone GS. **Emily McIvor** (Green) Policy adviser. Contested: South West Region European election 2014; Tiverton & Honiton 1997.

CONSTITUENCY PROFILE
The southernmost seat in Somerset, bordering Dorset and Devon. A centre of the aircraft and defence industries, Yeovil has various aerospace businesses. Helicopter manufacturer AgustaWestland is among its biggest employers. Held by the Liberal Democrats from 1983 to 2015.

	Electorate	Turnout %	from 2010 %	Change %
	82,446	69.1		
M Fysh C	24,178	42.5	+9.6	
D Laws LD	18,865	33.1	-22.6	
S Smedley Ukip	7,646	13.4	+9.3	
S King Lab	4,053	7.1	+1.9	
E McIvor Green	2,191	3.9		

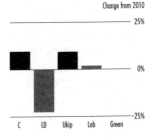

Change from 2010

Ynys Môn

LABOUR HOLD

ALBERT OWEN
BORN Aug 10, 1959
MP 2001-

Select cttees: panel of chairs 2010-15; DECC 2010-15; Welsh affairs 2006-10, 2001-05; accommodation & works 2001-05. Press officer, const Lab party 1996-2000. Cllr, 1997-99. RMT, NUS official. Worked as a welfare rights & employment adviser, CAB and Anglesey CC. Isle of Anglesey CC centre manager. Member, WEA North Wales management cttee. Chair, Anglesey regeneration partnership. Joined the Merchant Navy in 1976. Married, two daughters. Ed: Holyhead County Comp, Anglesey; Coleg Harlech (Dip industrial relations); University of York (BA politics).

CHALLENGERS
John Rowlands (PC) Worked in communications at Environment Agency Wales and the Rivers Authority. Previously teacher

and BBC Wales radio producer. Married, three daughters. Ed: Ysgol Glan Clwyd; University of Wales, Aberystwyth (BA geography; PGCE). **Michelle Willis** (C) Managing Director, Carelink Homecare Services. Former A&E nurse. Children. Ed: The Royal Free Hospital (RGN nursing); Bangor University (MBA). **Nathan Gill** (Ukip) MEP for Wales 2014-. Leader of Ukip in Wales 2014-. Worked as an assistant to John Bufton MEP. **Mark Rosenthal** (LD) Runs eco holiday property business. Worked in civil engineering.

CONSTITUENCY PROFILE
An island constituency off the northwest coast of Wales. Apart from industrial Holyhead it is largely rural, agricultural and Welsh speaking. Wales's only nuclear power station is located here and is a significant employer. Tourism also provides many jobs. A ferry port on Holy Island provides a transport link to Ireland.

	Electorate	Turnout %	from 2010 % Change
	49,944	69.9	
A Owen Lab	10,871	31.1	-2.2
J Rowlands PC	10,642	30.5	+4.3
M Willis C	7,393	21.2	-1.3
N Gill Ukip	5,121	14.7	+11.2
M Rosenthal LD	751	2.2	-5.4
L Screen Soc Lab	148	0.4	

Change from 2010

```
                              25%


                                    0%


                              -25%
 Lab    PC    C    Ukip    LD
```

York Central

LABOUR CO-OPERATIVE HOLD

RACHAEL MASKELL
BORN Jul 5, 1972
MP 2015-

NHS senior physiotherapist. Head of Health, Unite. National campaigner defending the NHS. Member, Labour's National Executive cttee 2011-15. Organiser and trade union official, TUC. GMB. Unite. Enjoys cycling. Ed: UEA (BSc physiotherapy).

CHALLENGERS
Robert McIlveen (C) European affairs specialist, Network Rail 2014-, public affairs manager 2010-. Former research fellow, Policy Exchange. Ed: University of Warwick (BA history & politics); University of Sheffield (PhD politics). **Ken Guest** (Ukip) Works in international oil and gas industry. Married, two children. Ed: Aston University (BSc geology, physics & mathematics); University of Leeds (MSc geophysics). **Jonathan Tyler**

(Green) Railwayman. Founding member of the Green party in 1976. Married, two children. Ed: Trinity Coll, Cambridge (BA history & economics). **Nick Love** (LD) Works for Socius24 software company. Contested Wentworth & Deane 2010. Ed: York St John University.

CONSTITUENCY PROFILE
Takes in most of the heart of the city. Popular tourist destination – York Minster, one of the largest Gothic cathedrals in Europe is here. This coupled with the museums attract a million visitors each year. Service industries provide the bulk of jobs, with education and health work. Rowntree was based here when it developed the Kit Kat, Smarties and Aero brands in the 1930s. Some brands, inluding Yorkie are still produced at the York factory. Has a largely white population with people of Chinese descent making up the largest minority ethnic group. Was created for the 2010 election.

	Electorate	Turnout %	from 2010 % Change
	75,351	63.3	
R Maskell Lab Co-op	20,212	42.4	+2.4
R McIlveen C	13,496	28.3	+2.2
K Guest Ukip	4,795	10.1	+7.7
J Tyler Green	4,791	10.1	+6.5
N Love LD	3,804	8.0	-17.2
C Whitwood Yorks	291	0.6	
M Ollerhead TUSC	288	0.6	

Change from 2010

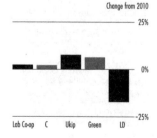

```
                              25%


                                    0%


                              -25%
 Lab Co-op  C   Ukip  Green  LD
```

York Outer

CONSERVATIVE HOLD

JULIAN STURDY
BORN Jun 3, 1971
MP 2010-

Plain-speaking Yorkshire farmer, supplies McCain with potatoes. Succeeded in changing law on abandoned and neglected horses. PPS to: Brandon Lewis 2014-15; Patrick McLoughlin 2013-14; Simon Burns 2012-13. Select cttee, transport 2010-12. Cllr, Harrogate BC 2002-07. Contested Scunthorpe 2005. Son of Robert Sturdy MEP. Runs farming and property business. Keen cricketer and Leeds Utd fan. Married, one daughter, one son, Ed: Ashville Coll, Harrogate; Harper Adams University (agriculture).

CHALLENGERS
Joe Riches (Lab) Works at York Station. Worked in adult social care services, Avalon. Cllr, York CC 2011-15. Member, TSSA, RMT. **James Blanchard** (LD) Cllr, Kirklees C 2011-15; Islington 2002-06. Previously account manager, PPS Group public policy consultancy. Former head of youth and student office for Lib Dems. Ed: Leeds University (BSc computer science); Leeds Metropolitan University (Adv Cert public relations). **Paul Abbott** (Ukip) Runs Post Office branch. **Ginnie Shaw** (Green) Trustee, management cttee of York Racial Equality Network 2002-. Chairs housing association.

CONSTITUENCY PROFILE
A doughnut-shaped constituency, which encircles the York Central seat and links up the city's outer suburbs. It was created for the 2010 election from parts of four old constituencies. The University of York, based in Heslington, employs thousands of people locally, many working in its state of the art bioscience research facility. It is one of the top research universities in the country. The largest ethnic minority population is of Chinese origin.

	Electorate	Turnout %	from 2010 % Change
	78,561	68.6	
J Sturdy C	26,477	49.1	+6.1
J Riches Lab	13,348	24.8	+7.7
J Blanchard LD	6,269	11.6	-24.4
P Abbott Ukip	5,251	9.7	+7.7
G Shaw Green	2,558	4.8	

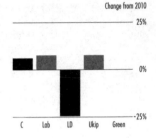

Change from 2010

C Lab LD Ukip Green

Yorkshire East

CONSERVATIVE HOLD

GREG KNIGHT
BORN Apr 4, 1949
MP 2001-; 1983-97

Plays drums in MP rock band, MP4. Chair, select cttee: procedure 2010-12. Vice-chamberlain of the Royal Household 2012-13. Shadow min: transport 2005; environment & transport 2003-05; CMS 2003. Dep shad leader of the House 2002-03. Min: DTI 1996-7. Whip, 1989-96. Select cttees: finance & services 2013-15; draft detention of terrorist suspects bills 2011-15; reform of the HoC 2009-10. PPS to David Mellor, 1987-89. Chair, cttee ODPM 1993-2002. Vice-chairman Conservative parly candidates assoc 1997-2001. MP for Derby North 1983-97. Solicitor. Knighted for political service 2013. Ed: Alderman Newton's Grammar; London & Guildford Law Colls.

CHALLENGERS
Kevin Hickson (Lab) Senior lecturer, politics, University of Liverpool. Cllr: Cheshire East 2012-; Crewe TC 2013-. Member, University & College Union. Ed: University of Warwick (BA politics); University of Southampton (PhD). **Steph Todd** (Ukip) Former Tory, defected to Ukip in 2013. Cllr, Richmondshire DC 2009-. School governor. Worked for Gulf Air Bahrain. **Robert Adamson** (LD) Retired fire service officer trainer. Author. Has MS. Trustee of MS Society. Contested Yorkshire E 2010; Darlington 2005, 01.

CONSTITUENCY PROFILE
Covers the northern part of the East Riding of Yorkshire. Takes in the countryside and coast and is traditionally dependent on farming, fishing and tourism. The main centre of population is the seaside resort and fishing port of Bridlington. The rest of the seat is made up of countryside of the East Yorkshire Wolds. Has been Conservative since the seat was created in 1997.

	Electorate	Turnout %	from 2010 % Change
	81,030	61.7	
G Knight C	25,276	50.6	+3.1
K Hickson Lab	10,343	20.7	+0.4
S Todd Ukip	8,955	17.9	+13.7
R Adamson LD	2,966	5.9	-15.2
M Maloney Green	1,731	3.5	+2.0
S Arnold Yorks	720	1.4	

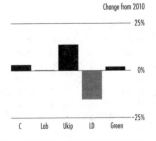

Change from 2010

C Lab Ukip LD Green

Lavery, I	370	Lillyman, H	302	Lucas, R	188	Maile, R	302
Lavery, J	173	Lim, B	378	Luder, I	89	**Main, A**	334
Lavery, P	365	Lim, M	240	Lukic, A	91	Main-Ian, B	139
Lavin, W	97	Lincoln, N	374	**Lumley, K**	306	Mair, C	261
Law, C	178	Lindhurst, G	188	Lunn, R	389	Majainah, R	315
Lawrence, E	94	Lindley, I	391	Lunn, T	246	Majid, A	341
Lawrence, J	366	Lindop, M	210	Lunnon, S	345	**Mak, A**	222
Laws, D	395	Lindsay, R	347	Lupson-Darnell, R	143	Malcolm M	254
Lawson, G	339	Lindsay, S	321	Luxton, L	112	**Malhotra, S**	196
Lawson, J	91	Ling, P	359	**Lynch, H**	214	Malik, A	122
Lawson, K	349	Lingard, J	153	Lynch, R	80	Malik, A	263
Lawson, R	259	Lingley, M	372	Lyon, M	383	Malik, K	117
Lawson, R	381	Lishman, G	106	Lyons, D	83	Malik, T	384
Lazarowicz, M	187	Liston, J A	207	Lyons, L	84	Mallender, R	315
Leach, R	192	Little, D	173			Malone, D	318
Leadsom, A	287	Lloyd, A	119	**M**		Maloney, M	397
Leathley, J	319	Lloyd, D	154	Macartney-Filgate, M	283	**Malthouse, K**	217
Lee, D	348	Lloyd, M	215	MacBrayne, A	373	Malyn, R	307
Lee, G	366	Lloyd, S	185	MacCleary, J	362	Mambuliya, J	86
Lee, P	114	Lloyd-Jones, K	97	MacDonald, D	127	Maniatt, M	248
Lee, R	157	Lloyd-Williams, S	138	Macdonald, I	294	**Mann, J**	90
Leech, J	267	Locke, G	341	Macdonald, S	386	Mann, R	269
Leff, J	370	Lockey, P	305	MacFarlane, S	164	**Mann, S**	153
Leffman, L	120	Lofas, V	162	MacGregor, C	203	Manning, R	267
Lefroy, J	336	Loi, F	288	Machan, B	344	Manton, B	96
Legg, G	363	Lokuciewski, K	387	Mackay, C	234	Manwaring, B	96
Legg, H	172	Lomax, D	110	MacKay, D	246	Mapletoft, B	278
Leggett, L	253	London, T	160	MacKay, J	316	Marbrow, R	292
Leigh, C	359	Lone, A	274	Mackay, M	159	March, J	291
Leigh, E	201	Long, A	154	MacKenzie, C	205	Marcus, S	217
Lemon, A	122	Long, K	204	MacKessack-Leitch, J	274	Marett, J	265
Lerry, M	120	Long, N	95	**Mackinlay, C**	356	Marklew, J	271
Lesiter-Burgess, S	150	Long, N	254	**Mackintosh, D**	286	Marra, M	178
Leslie, C	122	Long, R	247	Maclean, R	103	Marriott, S	210
Leslie, C	245	**Long-Bailey, R**	317	Maclean, Y	316	Marris, J	203
Leslie, C	288	**Lopresti, J**	198	MacLennan, T	235	**Marris, R**	388
Le-Surf, M	89	Lorber, P	118	Macleod, M	118	Marron, T	280
Letwin, O	172	**Lord, J**	386	**MacNeil, A**	276	Marsden, B	87
Lewell-Buck, E	331	Loughenbury, R	147	Macpherson, T	391	**Marsden, G**	107
Lewis, B	211	**Loughton, T**	391	Macqueen, M	224	Marsden, J	112
Lewis, C	288	Lovatt, J	104	**Mactaggart, F**	327	Marshall, J	180
Lewis, D	247	Love, A	246	**Madders, J**	189	Marshall, J	209
Lewis, I	128	Love, J	75	Maddock, S	360	Marshall, O	184
Lewis, J	277	Love, N	396	Magee, M	294	Marshall, P	187
Lewis, M	342	Lovell, J	340	Maginness, A	95	Marson, J	160
Lewis, O	299	Lowe, M	155	Mahabadi, M	330	Martin, A	111
Lewis, P	222	Lowe, P	343	Mahal, J	182	Martin, A	201
Lewis, R	205	Lowe, S	313	Mahmood, B	145	Martin, A	324
Lewis, S	108	Lower, A	280	**Mahmood, K**	104	Martin, B	239
Lewthwaite, J	115	Lowry, J	96	**Mahmood, S**	103	Martin, C	180
Leyland, C	364	Lowthion, V	239	Mahmood, T	342	Martin, C	354
Liddell-Grainger, I	120	Loynes, C	380	Mahmood, T	361	Martin, K	265
Lidington, D	83	**Lucas, C**	121	Mahoney, B	252	Martin, M	254
Lilley, P	230	**Lucas, I**	393	Mahoney, K	367	Martin, P	318